W9-BSX-054

The Selected Letters of
Ralph Ellison

730 iversi
ew York,
December 2

Dear Mr. Porter,

ard for allowing
essay. Thanks al
er of those ti
total bust.

y friend Cal gli
apacities. Inde
of which we're i
lk-lubricating p
reminded him tha
your old colleg
ions of that pei
n throwing me to
se of instructio
two.

had that oppor
ed that, despit
e. I suspected
tudents were go
of the initial
ssentially diff
at Tuskegee.
students had be
nd one which pr
discipline.
I could resp
appeared to be
cation than th
eat sacrifice.
fact that th
now to convert
reative actio
has been our
ng to do so, a
ssentially di
ogans, an untl
ngless self-in
ssay it strik
because it
al. Even yo
oviding channe
pes and aspil
ys my mother
was so entra
without food
kitchen. I was getting drunk on ide
faith helped to keep my feet down there on that re
But then, even for a doubter, faith is a gamble on
a compass against chaos and, as you discovered, be

The Selected Letters of

RALPH ELLISON

EDITED BY

JOHN F. CALLAHAN
and **MARC C. CONNER**

With Introductory Essays by
John F. Callahan

RANDOM HOUSE | NEW YORK

Published in the United States by Random House,
an imprint and division of Penguin Random House LLC, New York.

RANDOM HOUSE and colophon are registered trademarks
of Penguin Random House LLC.

Hardback ISBN 978-0-8129-9852-8
Ebook ISBN 978-0-8129-9853-5

Printed in the United States of America on acid-free paper

randomhousebooks.com

246897531

First Edition

Book design by Barbara M. Bachman

THIS BOOK

IS DEDICATED TO THE

LIVING MEMORY OF

RALPH ELLISON

Contents

—

General Introduction · 3

Letters from the Thirties · 17

Letters from the Forties · 111

Letters from the Fifties · 265

Letters from the Sixties · 567

Letters from the Seventies · 657

*Letters from the
Eighties and Nineties* · 749

Acknowledgments · 983

Chronology · 985

Photograph Credits · 1003

Index · 1005

The Selected Letters of
Ralph Ellison

General Introduction

RALPH ELLISON'S LIFE COMES CLOSE TO SPANNING the twentieth century, though as the years go by he casts a glance back to the Civil War and Reconstruction of the nineteenth century and ahead to the fast-approaching digital age of the twenty-first. Born in 1913, about five and a half years after Oklahoma was admitted to the Union, he lost his father, a protective companion, at the age of three. Raised by his mother, Ida, with rigorous love, Ellison grew up in the mostly nurturing, close black community of the vibrant Deep Deuce section of Oklahoma City during the Jim Crow era. His story is an African American variation of the American dream. Long after leaving Oklahoma City, this young man from the provinces, who became a sophisticated man of the world, remembers "when I lay on a pallet in the moon-drenched kitchen door and listened and dreamed of the time when I would leave and see the world" (letter to Albert Murray, July 24, 1953).

Written over six decades, Ellison's letters range from boyhood notes to his mother to detailed exchanges—and sometimes trenchant sparring matches over ideas—with some of the most distinguished figures of American intellectual and literary life: Richard Wright, Kenneth Burke, Stanley Edgar Hyman, Albert Murray, Saul Bellow, Romare Bearden, Robert Penn Warren, Richard Wilbur,

Harold Bloom, Hugh Kenner. Equally important, and perhaps sometimes more so for what they reveal about his private self and boyhood experience, are letters to old friends and relations from Oklahoma City, that frontier dream world of his childhood to which Ellison returned with increasing frequency: Virgil Branam, Jimmy Stewart, Camille and Mamie Rhone, Charles Etta Tucker, Hester Holloway, H.B.O. "Hoolie" Davis. Perhaps sensing that he might not live to write a formal autobiography, in the last years of his life Ellison wrote more and more letters that record memories of the people, places, and events of his early years in Oklahoma and what that experience continued to mean in his life and work.

Between March 1933 and June 1993, Ellison wrote letters to an expanding and expansive company of individuals. Even in the parochial "Dear Mama" letters he writes from Tuskegee, we see glimmers of the defiant, lyrical mind whose observations discern fluid changes in American life, society, and personality over the next sixty years. In fact, personality fascinated Ellison so completely that he dared assume the stance of bystander as well as participant—a dual perspective that infuses some of the letters with a feel of both biography and autobiography.

Consider two letters, each from the rich trove of the 1950s, that stake out Ellison's quest as a person, citizen, and writer. After hearing a radio bulletin announce the 1954 *Brown v. Board of Education* decision, Ellison is "wet-eyed" as he reflects on what is ahead now that integration is the law of the land: "Well, so now the judges have found and Negroes must be individuals." He ends this remarkable letter, "Anyway, here's to integration, the only integration that counts: that of the personality"—a profound toast hailing individual personal integration (letter to Morteza Sprague, May 19, 1954). For Ellison, the Supreme Court's ruling goes hand in hand with the challenge faced by each citizen, each person, to create an integrated self—an arduous task that, decade by decade, threads its way through his letters.

In another letter written not long after publication of *Invisible Man,* he regrets that he has "lost the delight of corresponding," a harrowing condition "since there was a time when I was more myself when writing a letter than at any other time" (letter to Richard Wright, January 21, 1953). Rather than accept "loss of delight" as a chronic affliction, Ellison gives his correspondence an even more central place in his thinking, feeling, and writing life than was the case in the lead-up to and immediate aftermath of *Invisible Man.*

Considered as a whole, Ellison's letters tell his story on several levels. Biographically, the correspondence tells of his metamorphosis from an impressionable, ambitious outsider into an articulate, accomplished denizen of Harlem who, while making a mark in New York, nevertheless sustains fierce allegiance to his Oklahoma roots. Artistically, the letters follow his changes from a down-and-out, former aspiring symphonic composer into a writer, then a first-rate contemporary novelist, and finally a man of letters whose embrace of American complexity leads to a defiant patriotism bred of his need "to affirm while resisting" (letter to John Callahan, August 12, 1983). "Personally," he wrote *Time* on November 27, 1958, more than a year after his return to the United States from Rome, to correct its mischaracterization of him as a Negro writer in exile, "I am too vindictively American, too full of hate for the hateful aspects of this country, and too possessed by the things I love here to be too long away." Undoubtedly read by millions of Americans, his letter expresses the double delight of someone able to both master and express "the only integration that counts: that of the personality."

THE LETTERS OF RALPH ELLISON testify to the fluidity and change he sees in American life and society, as well as in himself and his relationships. Perhaps the first things to strike a reader coming for the first time to Ellison's correspondence are its remarkable longevity and the fascinating variety of people he wrote to over those sixty years in the intimate form of the letter. Decade by decade, year by year, Ellison unfolds his lifelong ambition and anxiety, confidence and uncertainty, anger and serenity— and most of all, perhaps, a quality of intensity that became vivid in his painterly observations of the natural and social terrain around him during his daily comings and goings.

Three weeks after his twentieth birthday, Ellison writes the first letter in this volume to his mother from the State Training School for Negro Boys in Boley, an all-black town founded before Oklahoma became a state. A fetching self-deprecation presages the humor peppered through the letters: "I'm Mr. Ellison out here and I forget to answer sometimes."

The 1930s produce a series of letters, many deeply personal, that mark young Ellison's growth from a dependent young man to a fiercely independent writer-to-be. From June 1933 to May 1936 his letters are written by hand at Tuskegee Institute in rural Alabama. Almost all are to his mother, Ida; a few others are to his younger brother, Herbert, and his stepfather, John Bell; and an ambiguous one is to Vivian Steveson, his old flame from Oklahoma City. The impoverished young man writing "Dear

Mama" from Tuskegee is sometimes a lonesome college student viscerally aware of his mother's sacrifices, at other times a self-absorbed trumpet player whose secret wish is to write a symphony by the age of twenty-six, like Richard Wagner. In July 1936, after his junior year, he goes to New York to earn money for his senior year while shaking free of a manipulative, abusive dean at Tuskegee.

There, encouraged by Langston Hughes, whom he meets outside the Harlem YMCA his first morning in New York, he studies sculpture with Richmond Barthé and lives in a room in the studio. Soon Ellison meets Richard Wright, and the two quickly become good friends; their bull sessions at the Harlem branch office of the *Daily Worker* give Ellison access to a typewriter, which he uses to respond to Wright's urging that he try his hand at writing. Under Wright's inciting influence, young Ellison first writes a book review for Wright's (and Dorothy West's) quarterly, *New Challenge,* then his first short story, "Hymie's Bull." Before he realizes what's happened, Ellison puts away his trumpet in favor of the writer's pen.

Just when Ellison feels the true surge of a writer inside and is beginning to be noticed in the radical world that Wright dominates in Harlem, catastrophe strikes out in Dayton, Ohio, where his mother moved in the summer of 1936. Informed by a relative in mid-October 1937 that his mother is critically ill, he catches a train and arrives at her Cincinnati hospital to find her so racked with pain she does not recognize him. The next morning she dies with him at her bedside. A day later, October 17, 1937, he writes the first of several signal letters from Dayton, this one handwritten and addressed simply to "Dear Folks." Two others he types to Dick Wright on "this very old Typewriter" telling of "wild pears" in the woods, "antagonism" between his brother, Herbert, and himself, and "no *Daily* nor *Masses* to be had here" (letter to Richard Wright, October 27, 1937).

By April 1938 Ellison is back in New York, newly hired by the Works Progress Administration (WPA), researching and writing primarily about African American urban folklore in Harlem, when he is not pursuing the fiction begun in Dayton. He marries Rose Poindexter, a strong-willed theatrical artist with ambitions of her own; they grow apart and by 1942 the marriage exists only in name. During this period Ellison expands his circle of acquaintances, and his letters, with their sensuous impressions of New York City and Harlem in particular, show the writer in him taking charge of his personality.

Throughout the 1940s Ellison furiously writes fiction, book reviews, essays, and not least letters. His letters are written mostly in New York City; a few are penned in Waitsfield, Vermont, a writing hideaway; one or two are from Quogue, on eastern Long Island; and in 1945 several are written at sea. During World War II he rejects the segregated U.S. Army in favor of the merchant marine, and during his last voyage on the wild Atlantic, he writes letters that mingle elemental and personal realities, intimate and cosmic sensibilities. In the forties his letters show signs of the self-conscious, self-critical, maturing artist who inches from apprentice to journeyman until the summer of 1945, when, sitting at his typewriter in the open door of a barn in Vermont, his fingers tap out the first sentence of *Invisible Man*. He perseveres through successive drafts in the late forties to the decisive, bold revisions in 1951 that raise his first novel to the level of the classic it became and still remains.

The letters show how intellectually, aesthetically, and personally rich the decade is for Ellison. His frequent correspondents include Fanny McConnell Ellison, whom he meets and immediately falls in love with in June 1944 and marries in August 1946; Richard Wright, who evokes extraordinary intensity and filial loyalty; literary critic Stanley Edgar Hyman and his counterpoint, literary philosopher Kenneth Burke; and Ida Guggenheimer, his patron, to whom he dedicates *Invisible Man*. Some of these letters track his gradual, sometimes painfully slow composition of *Invisible Man* and his artistic courage in digging down to the root of his material and revising Chapter 1 for publication in a late 1947 issue of *Horizon*, Cyril Connolly's important London magazine.

EXCEPT FOR SOME SEVEN LETTERS to his close friend Albert Murray, there is a gap in Ellison's correspondence between his August 13, 1948, letter to Stanley Edgar Hyman and a March 26, 1952, letter to Ellen Wright. This was an intense period of composition and revision on *Invisible Man*. Yet when he resumed writing letters after the novel's publication, the 1950s turned out to be his most prolific decade for correspondence. Like those of the forties, his fifties letters are rich and multifaceted, written to a widening circle of old Oklahoma family and friends such as the Rhone family and boyhood friend Virgil Branam, whose caustic note condemning the 1956 Southern Manifesto spurred Ellison to write "Tell It Like It Is, Baby"; literary friends including Saul Bellow, John Cheever, Richard Stern, Paul Engle, Horace Cayton, and Harry Ford; Tuskegee folk of lesser and greater note including Morteza Sprague and William L. Dawson; and black and white young people he did not know whose letters about *Invisible Man* touched him.

Of special interest are many letters Ellison wrote from Rome in which his perceptions of America seem sharper, closer, and more vividly and presciently imagined for his being in another country while the civil rights movement back home was shaking America to its foundation. Ellison's Rome correspondence also broods, rejoices, questions, exults, and wavers over his progress (and lack thereof) on the second novel with its newly created characters, Reverend Hickman and orphan Bliss, and its tangled theme of fathers and sons. These letters include all but one written in the 1950s, to his close friend Albert Murray, collected separately in *Trading Twelves* along with Murray's letters to Ellison.

Other letters tell of urgent private matters, most notably the passion, guilt, grief, and complex ownership he expresses surrounding his affair in Rome in 1956–57 and the fissures it opened in his marriage to Fanny. Unsurprisingly, these are among the most intense, tautly self-controlled yet gut-wrenching letters he writes to her. Always present in Ellison's letters to Fanny are his observations on the day-to-day ups and downs of the life they are living. Ellison is also compelled to write from Rome, and later New York City during his stopover there in October 1956, of how the civil rights movement seems to be changing. Inquiring what the movement's development portends for America and the lives of black Americans, he throws into relief those unreconstructed elements of American society and culture still fiercely arrayed against the canny tactics and moral high ground displayed by acts of various contemporary civil rights campaigns, with special focus on the roles of the black church and its ministers and the brave young people who integrated southern public schools in the face of vicious white mobs.

Such passages exist side by side with idiosyncratic exchanges with childhood friends from Oklahoma, where Ellison indulges his obsession with jazz, technology, and photography. In addition, one finds sustained investigations of literature and the craft of writing. Almost against his will, Ellison breaks his silence and begins to write revealingly—sometimes guardedly, sometimes openly—about his second novel, particularly during his remarkable decade-long correspondence with Albert Murray. From these excursions it becomes clear that his earliest picaresque episodes, driven by the actions and voices of wild vernacular characters, subsequently led him to characters, plots, and themes that take center stage in his rapidly changing conception of the epic unfinished novel on his hands.

For almost forty years after the triumph of *Invisible Man,* the letters are snapshots of Ellison battling with his second novel: How long would the game go on? Would the novelist come to bat down two runs with the bases loaded and two outs in the bottom of the ninth? Would he still be in the batter's box, digging his spikes into the dirt at home plate, when an umpire, dressed in black, appeared to call the game on account of darkness? If the lights had stayed on, would he have smashed home the winning runs? The official scorecard is lost. The record left is *Juneteenth, Three Days Before the Shooting . . . ,* and all the notes now in the Library of Congress.

The letters of the turbulent 1960s began auspiciously, with Ellison's excitement over the imminent publication of "And Hickman Arrives," a long, carefully edited excerpt of the novel-in-progress—the prologue from Book I, leading to episodes from Book II. Saul Bellow called these pages "every bit as good as *Invisible Man*" and hastened to feature Ellison's work as the lead piece in his new journal, *The Noble Savage.* That said, a number of Ellison's letters from the sixties reflect preoccupation and frustration over his slow progress. As the decade winds on and his essay collection *Shadow and Act** (1964) appears while the second novel does not, his letters wane. They all but cease from late 1964 until December 1967, nine days after a mysterious fire ravages the Ellisons' newly purchased summer home in the woods outside the Berkshire town of Plainfield, Massachusetts.

The embers are still warm on December 8 when Ellison writes Charles Valentine to explain why he must pass up writing the foreword to his book: "The loss was particularly severe for me, as a section of my work-in-progress was destroyed." The taut facts of understatement neither exaggerate nor make light of the damage. Having taken Fate's punch, Ellison leans in to resume fighting: "Fortunately, much of my summer's work on the new novel is still in mind and if my imagination can feed it I'll be all

---

* Praised upon publication, as Arnold Rampersad wrote forty years later, "for a rising generation of black writers, *Shadow and Act* would become a Bible as they sought to reconcile their love of literature and art with a nation that too often tried to excuse or exclude Negroes from the ranks of humanity." (Rampersad, p. 410)

right, but I must work quickly." His spare account of what was lost and where he is inside himself make this letter the most suggestive take we have of the actual loss and its impact, as well as the task ahead.

RALPH ELLISON'S ABIDING CONCERN with craft and citizenship finds another outlet in the letters of the 1960s and 1970s, the period when he composes some of his most luminous essays on American culture and also does some of his most sustained and successful writing on the second novel. By the 1980s, after his retirement from the Albert Schweitzer Chair in the Humanities at New York University (NYU), the letters become less about the second novel and more focused on essays he is writing. Too, as more and more relatives and old friends pass away in Oklahoma, he produces vivid letters about the old days and the old life in what he still called the Territory. Many of these letters, like those written to Richard Wright in the 1940s, have friendship as their theme; notably in the long letter-cum-essay written to poet and longtime friend Richard Wilbur in 1987, Ellison seems to carry on the meditation on friendship in Cicero's "De Amicitia."

Across the decades Ellison's letters chart his gradual emergence as a preeminent American essayist. Essays written during his struggles with the second novel—"Society, Morality and the Novel" (1957), "Tell It Like It Is, Baby" (1956/1965), "The World and the Jug" (1963–64), "The Little Man at Chehaw Station" (1977–78), "Going to the Territory" (1980), and "An Extravagance of Laughter" (1986)—articulate his view of American artistic and cultural life and language. Against this backdrop the letters are an invaluable window on both his essays and his fiction and on Ellison's uniquely American destiny in its abiding vicissitude during his years as a citizen in what he calls, always with a chuckle, this "crazy country."

IN THE FIRST YEAR of the 1970s Ellison, whose public support for President Lyndon Johnson complemented his deep skepticism about and opposition to black separatism and much in the Black Power movement, basked in the glow of his essay "What America Would Be Like Without Blacks," written for *Time* magazine's "Race in America" special issue of April 6, 1970. His presence in the sun grew even stronger when *The Atlantic Monthly* put him on its December cover to show off the brilliant, extraordinary essay/interview "Indivisible Man," by James Alan McPherson in close collaboration with Ellison. This long, fascinating piece featured excerpts from conversations between Ellison and McPherson and indicated clearly that the unfinished novel was alive and well. (Coincidentally, the interviews for "Indivisible Man" were conducted and the essay written close to the time Fanny Ellison was retyping and labeling the manuscripts of the completed Book I and nearly complete Book II.)

Yet his correspondence from the seventies hints at the distractions occasioned by his nearly decade-long professorship at NYU as well as his proud membership on the board of the Colonial Williamsburg Foundation. Letters tell of other honors equally important to him, such as the dedication of the Ralph Ellison Library in Oklahoma City in 1976, an occasion in his life superbly observed and reflected upon in Jervis Anderson's 1976 *New Yorker* profile of Ellison. In the late 1970s and into the 1980s Ellison writes to younger writers and scholars besides McPherson, such as Michel Fabre, Horace Porter, Robert O'Meally, Michael Harper, Alan Nadel, and Henry Louis Gates Jr., as well as old friends Jim Randolph and Jimmy Stewart, the latter now a celebrated citizen of Oklahoma City.

IN 1979 HIS RETIREMENT FROM NYU signals a new phase of Ellison's life. In several letters he vows to devote the decade to finishing the long-awaited second novel. And indeed, the 1980s are a prolific period for Ellison the writer—but Ellison the letter writer, not Ellison the novelist. The quantity of letters he writes eclipses his output in fiction and essays, though he does produce several splendid short essays as well as write from start to finish the long and canonical autobiographical essay "An Extravagance of Laughter," published in *Going to the Territory* in 1986.

By any measure it's the letters that show us Ralph Ellison over these last years of his quest for "the integration of personality." As he grows older, he writes more and more letters—often long ones—to those he knew growing up in Oklahoma. These seem juxtaposed naturally with those he writes to newer friends; all give off an intensity that perhaps he could not so easily summon when he turned his hand, as he often did, to the unfinished novel. Increasingly, reminiscence becomes the watermark of his letters, even those he writes to friends whom he also sees in person. It is intriguing if mysterious to calculate the interrelationship between these letters of remembrance and the backward feel of lengthy sequences he writes and revises for the second novel, often from drafts he typed on thin blue or yellow paper and corrected in pencil in the margins in the 1950s and early 1960s and which now rest silently alongside the computer on his desk.

Eight letters are here from the 1990s, each one vitally concerned with the past. Perhaps the most important is to Lowry Ware, the South Carolina native and author of *Old Abbeville*. Ware's chapter on Ellison's grandfather "Big Alfred" Ellison, the sheriff of Abbeville in the late 1870s before the franchise was taken away from black men, earned Ellison's strong appreciation and gratitude. His "vivid but spotty memories" of visiting his grandfather as a suddenly fatherless three-and-a-half-year-old mingle with Ware's account of the place and stir up a vision of what the little boy experienced nearly eighty years before: "Abbeville's huge moths, its butterflies, and the swarms of fireflies that an older neighborhood boy taught me to catch and store in a bottle, and the fun of watching them twinkle and glow through the glass at nightfall . . . the tall pecan trees, which were said to have been planted by my father, and with the fruit of which I was distantly familiar thanks to Christmas holidays when my Aunt Lucretia was sure to receive a gunny sack filled with that delicious share of her old home's bounty."

Ellison's surmise of his grandfather's approval—dim to the three-year-old, brightly haloed for the old man writing—comes because Big Alfred "was said to have been quite proud of my father so I think he found me acceptable." Now older than his grandfather was at meeting him, Ellison imagines the little boy he was sensing the possibility the man is only now able to express: "We got along fairly well, perhaps because we were united in our mutual grief." Writing three-quarters of a century later, the man composing at the computer turns the disturbing memory of "a violent night-time storm" the little boy experienced once upon a time in Abbeville into a creative fable of belonging to the universe's different cycles of history and nature: "The next morning the air was quite clear and as I accompanied my Uncle Jim on a walk to assess the storm's damage we came upon a nest of fledging birds that had been blown from their home in a tree.

> So around and about I had come
> Upon that which I had started from."

After Ellison's death in 1994, that letter of September 7, 1990, has had the unforeseen, restorative consequence of filling in a hole in his biography. It also tips the scales regarding his true date of birth in favor of March 1, 1913, by showing him act his age as a boy of three instead of a mind-boggling prodigy of two.

*

Ida Milsap Ellison and Fanny McConnell Ellison were, respectively, the original keepers of Ellison's flame. His mother saved his letters, notes, and cards to her, and he kept hers to him, so after she passed away in an inhospitable Cincinnati hospital, he was able to put the precious correspondence together and in order. From the time he moved to New York in the summer of 1936 and snagged a typewriter, he made carbons of his letters. The habit continued during his five months in Dayton. From then on, back in New York or wherever life took him, he made copies of his letters. He kept them around, if haphazardly, until he and Fanny were married in 1946 and she started careful files of the couple's correspondence.

In accord with her husband's wishes, shortly after his death Fanny deeded his books, manuscripts, drafts, letters, and papers of all kinds to the Library of Congress. During negotiations she allowed Alice Birney, the gifted specialist in the Manuscript Division assigned charge of the Ellison Papers, into what she called "the little room" in the Ellison apartment at 730 Riverside Drive. Dr. Birney saw at once the rare quality and value of the correspondence. Back at the Library of Congress Donna Ellis did too. As senior archivist of the Manuscript Division, Ellis directed a dedicated group of archivists who arranged the enormous piles of letters, manuscripts, notes, and memorabilia in good order and prepared a finding aid to guide scholars and readers through the labyrinth of the collection.

The Ellison Papers are in two parts: the bulk of the material arranged and described as Part I in 1997, the remainder processed as Part II in 2010 after Fanny Ellison's death. In "Part I: General Correspondence, 1930–1996," Boxes 35 through 79 house Ralph Ellison's individual correspondence. There are alphabetically arranged folders for individual correspondents and a miscellaneous folder or folders for every letter in the alphabet (e.g., " 'A' Miscellaneous, 1939–1993").

In almost every case the Library of Congress collection is the source and repository of letters in this volume. Exceptions are Ellison's three letters to Sanora Babb, one of which exists in partial form at the Library of Congress but is one of the three complete Ellison letters in the Harry Ransom Center at the University of Texas, Austin; six letters to Saul Bellow from the Special Collections Research Center of the Regenstein Library at the University of Chicago; and the originals of several Ellison letters to Richard Wright (not in the Ellison Papers) belonging to the Wright Archive in the Beinecke Rare Book and Manuscript Library at Yale University.

The Selected Letters of Ralph Ellison is organized chronologically by decade, with an introduction preceding the letters of each decade. Footnotes are included to identify persons, places, events, titles, and other matters germane to the particular letter referred to, or to provide context for an important idea, issue, or relationship mentioned in the letter. On the few occasions when Ellison has something wrong, a footnote attempts to provide more accurate information.

Silent corrections were made to correct typos, misspellings (except words Ellison seems to have chosen deliberately for effect as in "Mamma" in a December 23, 1934, letter), and confusing punctuation, such as in a run-on sentence. Dialect is untouched. Brackets within letters signify missing or illegible words or phrases; they also indicate where a likely word is inserted in a letter's text. When Ellison has clearly finished but not signed a letter, "[Ralph]" is inserted. On the rare occasions where Ellison's paragraphs go on at extraordinary length and shift suddenly from one topic to another, mostly in a letter or two to Albert Murray previously published in *Trading Twelves*,* these paragraphs have been divided into two to avoid confusion.

A last thing I would note is that Ralph Ellison did not change his composing habits much from hand to typewriter to computer. He had a palpable tendency to be as careful to "tell it like it is" in a letter as he was in his most ambitious fiction or essays, out of self-respect and respect for the person he was writing to, even if that person was a stranger who had written him about *Invisible Man*. He put more than a few of his letters through multiple drafts and revisions, sometimes as many as four or five, each one mining extra nuance out of a sentence, an observation, an idea, or a memory. It's as if his narrator's famous question looms over each letter: "Who knows but that, on the lower frequencies, I speak for you?" If we listen carefully, we may hear Ellison answer, "Who knows? I know." And we'll sense that he's speaking to us.

John F. Callahan

---

* Previously published letters of Ellison's include the following published with permission of the Estate in the March 1, 1999, issue of the *New Republic:* Ida Bell, April 20 and August 30, 1937; Richard Wright, October 27, 1937; Kenneth Burke, August 25, 1947; Mrs. Henry Dickinson Turner (excerpt), March 31, 1953; M. D. Sprague (excerpt), May 19, 1954; The Editor of *Time*, November 27, 1958; Sydney Spiegel, December 13, 1959; Bela Zampleny, May 18, 1964 (excerpt); Stanley Edgar Hyman, May 29, 1970; Hank Wilson, May 18, 1971; Horace Porter, December 22, 1976; G. A. Smith, March 20, 1977; Alberta and Thomas Brown, August 13, 1978; John Taggart, February 27, 1979; James Randolph, May 2, 1982; Professor James L. Roark, November 23, 1982; John Roche, November 6, 1984; Robert O'Meally (excerpt), April 17, 1989; Lowry Ware, September 7, 1990.

Letters from the Thirties

RALPH ELLISON'S LETTERS FROM THE 1930S TELL an affecting story of his journey from boy to man. He writes from Tuskegee, Alabama; from New York City; and, in between, from Dayton, Ohio, where, after his mother's unexpected death, he enters the months of his young man's moratorium, writing Richard Wright that boyhood is over.

"Geography is fate," Ellison often said in later life, sometimes swiveling a formidable cigar between his thumb and fingers. Certainly the thirties letters show these three places shaping the emotional and psychological geography he was fated to bring to his life. Tuskegee, home to the flourishing, first-among-equals national black college in the black belt of the fiercely Jim Crow Deep South; Dayton, epitome of small-town middle America, surrounded by woods teeming with game and wild pears; New York, the country's greatest city, with the "black metropolis" of Harlem within its borders—in different ways each place sharpened the edges of a personality that Ellison associated with the territory in which he was born and bred: the southwestern part of Oklahoma, in particular Oklahoma City.

The young Ralph Ellison who arrived at Tuskegee was a homeboy just leaving home. Still a kid, he was savvy and street-smart about some things, naive about others, especially the false masks and true faces of power. Of the more than fifty letters he wrote from Tuskegee, all but six were to his mother, Ida Bell. (Four were to his younger brother, Herbert, whom Ralph affectionately calls "Huck," and instructs to "watch your tenses and endings, don't write fool when you mean fooling or fooled"; one was to his stepfather, John Bell, referred to as "Mister John" or "Mr. Bell," whom he praises as a generous, much "above the average stepfather"; and a long letter was to Vivian Steveson, his old flame from Oklahoma City.)

"Dear Mama," he writes his first day at Tuskegee, a salutation that for the next three years alternates only with "Dearest Mama." His sign-offs on the numerous letters to his mother are not so uniform. They seem to vary according to his shifting sense of self at the moment he is writing. "Your Hobo Son, Ralph W. Ellison," he wittily signs that first letter. Other sign-offs over the years include "Your son" (multiple times), "Till next time," "Ralph," "Your son Ralph," "Your son Ralph W. Ellison," "As ever," "Yours as ever," more and more often "With love" or "Love," and, on one occasion, "Be good."

His first letter contains a list of fourteen items he needs ASAP and unpaid bills he wants his mother to pay in Oklahoma City. There is plenty of rushed chatter, but he does not mention the deep gash he received just above his eye fleeing railroad bulls in Decatur, Alabama, on the last leg of his journey to Tuskegee. That omission belies the frankness that usually marks Ellison's letters to his mother. For three years at Tuskegee he writes her about his mundane activities; his joys and sorrows, intense and fleeting; his adventures and needs, financial and emotional; and his gradual awareness, in the process of becoming a young man, of the unforgiving nature of the world. He writes with enviable ease about all facets of his life, holding back little, as if writing his mama was a way of keeping faith with himself, especially his feelings.

Not far beneath the conventions of Ralph's mother-son relationship there is often the strong feel of a steady, abiding friendship. Always his mother, Mama is also a friend-in-trust with whom young Ellison is comfortable—or, if not always comfortable, at least determined to share the flow of his life.

Ralph's lot at Tuskegee was a difficult one. "You know I travel with the richer gang here and this clothes problem is a pain," he writes with a larger dash of self-pity than perhaps he realizes. At the same time that he sympathizes with the on-and-off employment and hand-to-mouth existence of his mother and stepfather in the Oklahoma City of the Depression, his letters home are full of appeals for money. He asks for as much as "Mama" and "Mister John" can spare for his band uniform, black drill shoes, winter coat, and other incidental needs and small pleasures: "I have no razor blades, no soap, no haircut, no toothpaste, no anything. I wish you would send as many of these as possible as soon as possible. You could send a box, and you could cook a cake? and send a few sardines etc."

Reminders of the amount and due date of Tuskegee's numerous fees and charges usually accompany Ralph's list of personal needs. Yet, sensing his sacrificing mother's "Ellison pride," he also includes details of his activities, accomplishments, and musical performances, especially his occasional solos, ready-made for her to share with family and friends back in Oklahoma City—those he calls "dear folks" in letters and knows are rooting for him to succeed as their native son.

However, what stands out more than eighty years later is Ellison's candor with his mother about the deeper currents merging with the flow of his ordinary life. Writing to her, he shares his personality along with the point of view he is developing toward the world around him.

Consider his chilling, yet not sensationalized account of brazen, repeated efforts by the Tuskegee registrar and dean of men to compel him to trade sexual favors in exchange for official permission to be away from campus for a week in the summer. "This is just some more of the mess I've mentioned before," he writes his mother in August 1934. "The person trying to study should not be worried and nagged at because he does not consent to prostitute himself."

Though Ida Bell's response to her son is not explicit, Ralph's comments imply she has understood him and he has been comforted by her quiet support for his refusal to accept the abusive conditions imposed on him, even if the consequences are forfeiting privileges that are his due as a Tuskegee student and free person. Other accounts of how power works in the world, written to his mother from Tuskegee and later from New York, foreshadow his "On Being the Target of Discrimination." Written and published in 1989, this memoir/essay is a riveting, witty account of how in the years after his father's death, when he was three and his brother Herbert a mere six or seven weeks old, their mother fought Jim Crow by schooling her boys in the power of little conspiracies to resist segregation by pretending to accept its values and conditions.

His letters to his mother also display a disarming honesty and directness about how Ellison sees the young women at Tuskegee. Though not graphic, his observations leave no doubt that, for him, sexual activity is necessary, normal, and healthy. His nonchalance makes clear he feels no need to conceal or evade his experience for fear of his mother's disapproval.

In the last letter he wrote from Tuskegee in June 1936, he refuses to fudge his diminishing romantic interest in his former Oklahoma City girlfriend, Vivian Steveson, whom his mother continues to regard with favor. "You seem to feel that I miss her. This is a nice romantic way to have things happen: but in this case it's hardly true to life. There are two or three others who have come my way since she did and I must confess that I miss either of them much more than I ever did miss Vivian, and I would much rather see anyone of them any day than that little lady. You must understand Mama that I don't feel just as you do about things."

Other letters are memorable for touching, sometimes amusing, expressions of Ellison's love for his mother. He closes an upbeat, chatty Christmas letter of 1934 with a play on the nickname he bristled at hearing white men use to her face as a small boy. "Be a good Brownie," he tells her, tongue in cheek, "and write soon." And in March 1935, he brags of showing close friends Walter Williams and Hazel Harrison a charming photograph just received from Ida. "The picture," he writes her, "is the most appreciated thing you have sent since I've been here . . . and when you looked up at me from the frame—well I felt very strange, it was the next best thing to seeing you."

AS PIECED TOGETHER FROM the letters, 1936 gradually becomes a year of drastic change for Ralph and his mother. On the Fourth of July, Ida and Ralph are passengers on trains traveling from Oklahoma City and Tuskegee, respectively, toward different destinations. Ida journeys to Ohio, Herbert in tow—first to Cincinnati, where she has a sister, then to Dayton, where thirty or so of her relations are clustered; and, finally, to check out Cleveland, home of an old friend. Weeks later she returns to Dayton permanently.

For his part, Ralph has grown dubious that "Tuskegee's new program will suit people interested in things I am." Months earlier he has written his mother of wanting "to go to New York and work on the boats," a more lucrative and stimulating venue for summer employment, he believes, than the odd jobs up for grabs in Tuskegee. In late June, receiving a belated check from the state of Oklahoma large enough to cover much of the expenses for the coming year at Tuskegee, he, too, boards a train on July 4.

This time he travels coach, a paying passenger rather than what he briefly seemed to be three years before—a hobo hiding in a boxcar.

ONCE IN NEW YORK the Tuskegee schoolboy learns how to use charm and mother wit to make his way. "I'm following your formula with success," young Ellison writes Langston Hughes, whom he encountered in the lobby of the Harlem YMCA his first morning in the city: "you know, 'be nice to people and let them pay for meals.' It helps so very much. Thus far I've paid for just two dinners and the others check out so late I don't need breakfast leaving only my lunch to be paid for."* Ellison's tones of amusing, ingratiating fraternity are not lost on the generous Hughes. He soon prevails on a friend, the sculptor Richmond Barthé, to accept Ralph as a student. Impressed with the young man and his talent for sculpture, Barthé invites Ralph to live in a room in his Greenwich Village studio, and sets him up with a job as assistant to noted psychiatrist Harry Stack Sullivan.

From that point on, young Ellison gives no sign of preferring the backwoods of Alabama to the cosmopolitan streets of New York.

On September 3, 1936, in a casual and vehement letter, he tells his mother, "I don't think it is likely that I return to Tuskegee this year as I don't have the money necessary and I am yet in their debt up to $60.00, and I feel a year away will do me good," adding for good measure, "I hate the people down there anyway." By October his self-confidence is such that he challenges the brilliant pianist Hazel Harrison, his former Tuskegee teacher and mentor, on a point of aesthetics, declaring that, no matter what his artistic medium, an artist "reveals himself in the amount of meaning he reveals in his work."

As the year comes to a close, he has moved uptown to Harlem from Barthé's studio in the Village. When Ralph's job with Sullivan ends on mutual good terms, a patient's father hires him for a higher salary as a laboratory assistant at the A. C. Horn Paint factory across the East River on Long Island.

Life goes on. Letters cease until the end of April 1937, when he writes his mother that seeing the usually welcome change of season intensifies his feelings of painful estrangement from the world. Spring is likely to be "the hellish season," for he is "closed up in [a] factory nine hours out of

---

* Ellison had previously met Hughes briefly at one of Hughes's readings at Tuskegee.

twenty-four," marked by fate "to stand inside and look at the ships sail-ing up the East River as it sparkles in the sunlight." Yet by letter's end we imagine him winking as he tells his mother to "watch out for the spring fever."

Months later, in early August, seemingly out of nowhere, Ralph writes his younger brother. He's just received desperate news from Herbert that their mother has suffered a painful fall, crippling enough to stop her from working. Unfortunately, we don't have Herbert's words to put beside Ralph's response. Nonetheless, clearly Herbert expects his older brother to drop everything and come to Dayton to take command. Ralph's swift reply is one of frustration at his younger brother's inability to be specific about their mother's condition, let alone comprehend his situation in New York City. In helpless, flailing, tough tones, Ralph pleads for specif-ics: "Please take time and tell me just what is wrong with mama. You said she needs an operation, for what? What are the relatives there doing to help? You must remember that such things as these happen and we have to face them, you should have realized that when you undertook to leave Oklahoma City. Where is John Bell? Have you written him?"

Gradually realizing that, perhaps through no fault of his own, Herbert lacks the capacity to handle these questions, Ralph strikes through the carapace of angry self-control to his own feelings of vulnerability and grief: "Tell mama to write me herself and tell me what has happened. I feel bad as hell because there is nothing I can do to help just now but it's a fact."

No letters follow until the end of August, when Ralph writes his mother several pages full of rich details about the vitality and poverty of the lives he observes in Harlem, alongside revelation of his joblessness and the need to establish residence in New York "to go on relief in order to get a job on the W.P.A." Though grateful for the dollar bill his mother has sent him, he tells her, "You must not try to send me anything as long as you yourself are unable to work." From there he takes off at length about the human condition highlighted by the Great Depression: "I am very disgusted with things as they are and the whole system in which we live." He salts his comments with striking evocations of lives stubbornly lived around him. "It makes me very angry to think of the causes behind all the misery in the world, and the way it's all concentrated here in Harlem. I hope something happens to change it all."

Then the letter takes an abrupt personal turn: "Please let me hear from you soon, and you must remember not to worry about me. Tell me how your hip is doing and if you are able to walk."

Abruptly again, he changes the subject to the excitement buzzing in the air of Harlem over that night's fight between Joe Louis and Tommy Farr.* Only in a postscript does he say he's "heard from Herbert this morning and he told me where you are, and about the policy [her expired life insurance]. So to save it I have put my horn in pawn. I hope it reaches you in time."

A month later, on the last day of September, Ellison writes his next— and, it turns out, last—letter to his mother. It is more a note than a letter. In it Ralph tamps down whatever urgency he may feel coming from Dayton. With taut nonchalance he mentions Herbert's news that he is "planning to take a job," segues uncomfortably to his mother, then, somewhat tunelessly, goes back to Herbert: "I do hope he gets something worthwhile. He told me you were still having a lot of trouble with your hip. I hope it has stopped by now. He still talks about your relatives, whom he doesn't like. He thinks that relatives should be nice generous people. Too bad he had to find them different." After trivial details about his laundry, Ralph signs off from a distance as painful as it is palpable: "Please let me know how you are feeling and write me of any new developments. Love, Ralph."

Ida Bell's condition worsens with a swiftness that catches everyone by surprise. After receiving an urgent message from his mother's sister, Ralph rushes to Cincinnati by train. When he arrives at the hospital, his mother is too delirious to recognize him. The next morning she passes away, apparently unaware that Ralph is at her bedside. Afterward, listening to her doctor's fumbling, incoherent explanation of his misdiagnosis of his mother's condition as arthritis, Ralph feels an alarming, infuriating sense of the doctor's incompetence. When he is finally shown the death certificate, the cause of his mother's death reads "tuberculosis of the hip."

Until Ellison's own death almost sixty years later, a sense of aching pain came into his face and voice whenever he spoke about the needless, premature end of his mother's life. The few letters that survive from his time in Dayton belong to a precarious young man coming back to life as a surer, stronger person. Writing Richard Wright ten days after his mother's

---

* Farr, the British heavyweight champion, challenged Joe Louis for the world title. They fought on August 30, 1937, before a raucous crowd of seventy thousand in Yankee Stadium. Farr lasted the full fifteen rounds, and Louis won a narrow decision on points.

death, he acknowledges starkly the "end of childhood." Immediately from those depths he summons a lyrical appreciation for "pears growing wild in the woods . . . and fine full flavored butter nuts, which are new to me, and which I find very tasty."

From that letter on, sensations from the world around him temper his grief, brighten the flow of life, and accelerate his ambition to become a writer. In early November he signs off another letter to Wright with a comic exhortation: "Writers of the World Must Write!!!!" And he heeds his own charge, writing passionately and nonstop through months of freezing days and nights, until March 1938, when, bundle of manuscripts in hand, he returns to New York and is hired by the WPA's Federal Writers' Project.

MORE THAN A YEAR PASSES between Ellison's letter to Marie Toynet Howard, his friend and perhaps lover at Tuskegee, for whom he expresses lingering feelings, and a letter to Langston Hughes, when Ralph is married and settled back in New York. The riffing in the second letter is characteristic of the repartee between him and Hughes. One cannot miss the growing influence of Harlem on his imagination as he tells Hughes that "it takes some little optimism to any longer expect the mountain to come to Mohammad; so I, Mohammad Ras De Terror, come to the mountain." From the streets of Harlem the spectral presence of Ras De Terror stalks Ellison's mind and eventually takes up restless residence in the pages of *Invisible Man* as Ras the Exhorter, Ras the Destroyer.

Of the small cache of Ralph's letters from 1939, the tour de force is a long epistle to Joe Lazenberry. Beginning with his discovery that Lazenberry is alive and well, emphatically not dead, as he'd heard more than once, Ralph writes his old pal from Tuskegee one of his longest and best letters. The prose brims with intense pleasure as he discovers and animates a connection thought defunct. Quite apart from passages reliving college hijinks, Ralph writes page after page recounting his life's twists and turns in the three years since he left Tuskegee for New York, including the fullest account we have of life with his new wife, Rose Poindexter.

Having justified his own life with verve, he returns to the immediate present of the letter, urging Joe to abandon the trip he's planning to the Soviet Union and head for Mexico instead. Seized with boldness, Ralph sketches out a work he imagines his friend writing. It would be a book "considered from the point of view that the cultural and economic condition of the two peoples [Mexicans and black Americans] are so very similar."

The letter to Lazenberry is precious on the merits and because it is the fullest autobiographical account we have from the thirties. In it, Ellison bursts with excitement at the light that suddenly appears from the past to cast both present and future in high relief. During the spell he falls under, Ellison, however briefly, sees his fate as a writer—not as a lone soldier so much as a founding member of a brigade including Richard Wright, Theodore "Ted" Ward, and now, he hopes, his former main man, Joe Lazenberry, whom he has brought back from the dead to agitate and inspire his own heart.

As happens from time to time with Ellison the letter writer, silence follows. In this case it is fitting that the letter to Lazenberry is the last to come from him in the decade of the 1930s. In it he converses so freely with past and present that he foreshadows some of the meditative letters from the 1940s that accelerate his progress toward *Invisible Man*.

John F. Callahan

TUSKEGEE NORMAL AND INDUSTRIAL INSTITUTE

FOUNDED BY BOOKER T. WASHINGTON

FOR THE TRAINING OF COLORED YOUNG MEN AND WOMEN

SCHOOL OF MUSIC
WILLIAM L. DAWSON, DIRECTOR

TUSKEGEE INSTITUTE, ALABAMA

June 26, 1933

Dear Mama,

I arrived here Saturday Night at twelve o'clock safely and well. I have been told I could stay, but unless something happens I will just make enough to pay for my food for the summer. Send me that money by Money Order, and make it thirty dollars if possible. Mama please send my horn right away I need it. You can send it Parcel Post for about fifty cents and I will write Malcome and have him to have it wrapped for shipping. See Leo Whitby about that trunk and send all the things I have listed here.

(over)

TUSKEGEE NORMAL AND INDUSTRIAL INSTITUTE

FOUNDED BY BOOKER T. WASHINGTON

FOR THE TRAINING OF COLORED YOUNG MEN AND WOMEN

SCHOOL OF MUSIC
WILLIAM L. DAWSON, DIRECTOR

TUSKEGEE INSTITUTE, ALABAMA

1. hats
2. rain coats
3. Wash rags & towles
4. shoes
5. shirts and ties
6. all the book on music and all the music paper ect.
7. Suits
8. The little box which stays on my dresser
9. Some hair grease. (if you have it)
10. Tooth brush.
11. Place the Music and Vivians Pictures and letters in my bag and send the picture of you her and my self.
12. under ware and sox
13. Comb and brush
14. handkerchiefs

And every other thing that you think I'll need. Pay on my trunk, Pay May Brothers and see that there Plenty of water kept at the building. I am working now for the band director Captain, Drye but I dont think its permanant. This is a beautiful place and its looks like a small town, the food is good enough and I'll like it here. I am going to work hard to stay but I wont you to see just what you can do to help doing the school term. You wont regret it the least bit. See its raining

TUSKEGEE NORMAL AND INDUSTRIAL INSTITUTE

FOUNDED BY BOOKER T. WASHINGTON

FOR THE TRAINING OF COLORED YOUNG MEN AND WOMEN

SCHOOL OF MUSIC
WILLIAM L. DAWSON, DIRECTOR

TUSKEGEE INSTITUTE, ALABAMA

here again and be shure to send my coat, dont send the over coat until late this Fall. How have you been? and how is Herberts, and Mr. Bell tell them hello. I came from Indiana by myself. Charlie got sick at the stomach so I come through Kintucky, Tenn. and Alabama alone. I would have arrived sooner but missed two connections and was put off the train at Decature Ala. Friday night. Some times I rode tops, sometimes coal cars but most of the time I was inside, its a good experience for me. I'm sorry I didnt see you before I left but you didnt come and I almost missed the train at that. I've got to close Mama but send those things right away and I'll tell you all about it next time. Tell Herbert to tell the drug Store gang I said hello. Well I've got to clean a horn, be good and tell me whats going on I'll write. Malcome

your Hobo Son,
Ralph W. Ellison

To Ida Bell
STATE TRAINING SCHOOL FOR NEGRO BOYS
BOLEY, OKLAHOMA

―――――――

J. H. LILLEY, SUPERINTENDENT
MARCH 23, 1933

Dear Mama,*

I am just writing because I thought I would be home by now. Guess I'll be there Sunday. How are you and the rest of the gang? I'm hoping you are all well. I've had a cold since I've been here but otherwise I'm all right.

I'm not on pay out here but am helping with the band and I don't know just what Mr. Lilly intends doing but I shall stay a while and find out. The food out here is good. My washing and pressing is done free and I have nothing to do but teach some of the dumb guys music—they act pretty nice though and some are good musicians. I'm <u>Mr.</u> Ellison out here and I forget to answer sometimes. There are twenty boys here from Oklahoma City, and as far as I can see they are better off than they were at home, they get good food, fresh air, and not too much work, and good treatment all around. I'm lonesome out here on this hill. Have you seen Vivian? I'm not as I said on pay here and I've got to get back to see about that weekly payment on my horn. I just owe twenty-three dollars but it has to be paid. This [is] a good chance for me to find out how much I know and so far I have found that [I] know as much and more than the fellows here about some parts of the work. So far he has been pretty good to me and it was more than I expected. <u>Please</u> have me some clean shirts and underwear when I get home. Well be good and tell the others hello. I'll see you Sunday if possible and now to bed it's near nine o'clock.

Your son,

Ralph W. Ellison

My address is at top of page.

―――――――

* Several months before Ellison left Oklahoma City for Tuskegee in June 1933, he writes his mother from the State Training School for Negro Boys in Boley, Oklahoma, where he appears to be auditioning for a job. Boley was established as an all-black town in 1905.

To Ida Bell
JUNE 26, 1933

Dear Mama,[*]

I arrived here Saturday Night at twelve o'clock safely and well. I have been told I could stay but unless something happens I will just make enough to pay for my food for the summer. Send me that money by money order and make it thirty dollars if possible. Mama, please send my horn right away. I need it. You can send it parcel post for about fifty cents and I will write Malcolm and have him have it wrapped for shipping. See Leo Whitby about that trunk and send all the things I have listed here.

1. hats
2. rain coat
3. Wash rags & towels
4. Shoes
5. Shirts and ties
6. All the books on Music and all the music paper, etc.
7. Suits
8. The little box which stays on my dresser
9. Some hair grease (if you have it)
10. Tooth brush
11. Place the Music, and Vivian's Picture, and letter in my bag and send the picture of you, her and myself.
12. Under wear and socks
13. Comb and brush
14. Handkerchiefs

And every other thing that you think I'll need. Pay on my horn, pay May Brothers and see that there's plenty of water kept at the building. I am working now for the band director Captain Drye but I don't think it's permanent. This is a beautiful place and it looks like a small town, the food is good enough and I'll like it here. I am going to work hard to stay but I want you to see just what you can do to help during the school term. You won't regret it the least bit. Gee it's raining here again and be sure to

---

[*] Ellison's first letter from Tuskegee, in which he downplays his harrowing journey hoboing on freights in favor of urgent requests for things he needs for his new life at college.

send my coats. Don't send the overcoat until late this fall. How have you been? And how is Herbert, and Mr. Bell? Tell them hello. I came from Indiana by myself. Charlie got sick at the stomach so I came through Kentucky, Tenn. and Alabama alone. I would have arrived sooner but missed two connections and was put off the train at Decatur, Ala. Friday night. Some times I rode tops, sometimes coal cars but most of the time I was inside. It's a good experience for me.* I'm sorry I didn't see you before I left but you didn't come and I almost missed the train at that. I've got to close, Mama but send those things right away and I'll tell you all about it next time. Tell Herbert to tell the Drug Store gang I said hello. Well I've got to clean a horn. Be good and tell me what's going on. I'll write Malcolm.

Your Hobo Son,
Ralph W. Ellison

To John Bell

JULY 4, 1933

Dear Mr. Bell,†

I was surprised when I received your letter because I thought I knew the writing on the envelope but couldn't guess just whose it was. I was very glad to hear from you and you don't know how much I appreciate what you are doing for me and I thank you very much.

My bag and horn arrived in good condition and was I glad to receive the suits and shoes. I was one of the worst looking guys on the campus and now some people don't recognize me. Ask Mama to write and tell me where my class ring is. I didn't receive it and I left it in the box with the rest of my stuff. She sent a razor and no blades and I'm <u>broke</u>. Don't fail to send my robe and all the <u>shoes</u> I have and all the white pants. I think I'll work in the bakery shop a while and I'll have to dress in white. I don't want to ask you all for too much and if you can't get what I ask for without getting in a strain just let it go. You might ask Mama to keep the credit good at May Bros. and to send two pairs of pajamas as soon as possible because I am full of cold from sleeping undressed. I need soap,

---

* Ellison does not mention the gash on the forehead he received while railroad detectives chased him as he changed freights in Decatur, Alabama. This happened two years after the nine Scottsboro Boys were hauled off a freight and charged with rape by two young white women who had been riding in the same car as the men.

† John Bell was Ralph's stepfather, whom Ida married in 1929.

toothpaste, <u>stamps</u>, <u>ties</u>, socks. Please send the trunk as soon as possible. I wondered if you all missed me around home. I miss you all and I get kinda lonesome sometimes but it has to be. I don't fit in well just yet with these southern people but I will because they are friendly and easy to get along with; in fact, they are too friendly. Here the boys just take my room but we get along. Write and tell me what's going on there and is it true that people don't know where I am? How is Huck?* and tell him to be good. Tell mama to write next time and pray that I am admitted to the school of Music. Tell her not to worry about me worrying about Vivian. I'm very much all right and there are a number of swell girls here. Thank her for having the shoes fixed and to see if there are any other there as good. Send both overcoats. I can have the black one fixed free. I am playing in the band and doing fine but I have a bad cold to overcome and a lot of weight to regain. Love to Mama and Herbert and thanking you again I am as ever

> Your
> Ralph W. Ellison

PS Tell mama not to forget my ring.

To Ida Bell
TUSKEGEE INSTITUTE, ALABAMA
SUNDAY, JULY 16, 1933

Dear Mama,

I received the trunk and everything in good condition. I was just waiting for a stamp to mail a letter asking why you didn't write but yours beat me to it. I am still working in the bakery and everything but I am just earning my board. I put that money in the postal savings and [talked] to Capt. Neely about it and he told me to get as much more as possible. The fees are about $57.00 and I [need] to get as near that as possible. And he told me to tell you to start thinking about my uniform that will cost $17.00 though I might be able to get a second hand one for about $10.00. There're so many [chores] here that I don't have much spare time. I get up at 4:30 am and work until (one) 1:00 and then I eat and practice, go to

---

* Huck, as in *The Adventures of Huckleberry Finn,* was Ellison's mischievous, affectionate nickname for his younger brother, Herbert, who was seventeen at the time.

dinner, practice again then to bed. I am getting used to the people now and I find them dull. They don't know what to talk about or how to talk but I guess they are all right. I hope you are well and happy. Don't work too hard. Write sooner next time. It's lonesome here and I get homesick. I have to get back to work now so be good and tell Huck hello and I bet he has my ties (ha ha).

> Until next time
> I remain as ever
> Ralph W. Ellison

To Ida Bell

JULY 23, 1933

Dear Mama,

I received your letter, and it found me well and without the cold. I have wanted to come home pretty badly and maybe that is why you felt my presence.

I am glad you are well and working and I hope you stay well. I wrote a letter before you sent your last one, telling you about the trunk and everything. If you received it let me know in your next letter. I am still working in the bakery and hoping for the best. It was too bad about "May's" fire and I hope you don't have any trouble paying them.

While you are getting the socks, I wish you would send me that yellow sweater I wrote about. It won't cost much without sleeves.

Just how much do you owe on the cornet? Do you ever see Tom or Maybelle? There's a boy here from Tulsa who said he wrote telling me he was coming here and that you answered. He came through all right yesterday morning.

Tell Herbert to write and tell me some news. Tell Mr. Bell hello and that the key to the trunk was fine, only it took me half an hour to discover how it worked (ha!/ho!)

There isn't much happening here just now, work and etc. is all. I hope I'll have more to say next time. Be good, and try to send that music.

> Till next time,
> Ralph

PS Don't forget the uniform, it's important.

To Ida Bell

Tuskegee Inst Ala.

AUGUST 4, 1933

Dear Mama,

I received both your letters and I am glad to know you are well and everything. I am still working and I like Tuskegee more each day. I have met a chum of Maxine's and she is doing everything to make things pleasant for me. Her name is Julia Moore and she is good looking, from one of the best families and her father is a doctor at the Government's hospital and he has money. I was lucky enough to get in with the best here and so you see I have plenty to do. I have met Rev. Bethel and his two daughters but I don't know Miss Delaney. Don't tell everyone the solo I am to play, it isn't important. However you can send my march as soon as possible because Capt. and I are going to try to fix it up for the football season. You might also send the "Carnival of Venice" solo.

Tell Jamie that I'll write soon, I've started five times but something always happened I stay so busy. I am trying not to worry but I don't have any intentions of coming home soon I'm better off here and as for that dream, you're the only person I'd come there to see now. As for the other, I evened up the score with her and I'm glad that I left to come here. There are too many girls that I haven't seen and strange to say they seem to like me. I sorry Mr. Bell got another cut and tell him I hope he is able to get a better job soon.

I write Mr. Barnes and the others as soon as I get some time. I am still studying with Captain Drye and some day I think I'll be able to play like an artist. How is Herbert? Tell him to tell Malcolm I'll write soon that I have a little news. I don't think much of anything Mrs. Slaughter has to say about me. Please do what you can about the uniform. I can't do without it. It is important! Any little thing you send will be a great help, you don't know how far a dollar will go down here. I still need socks etc. Be good Mama and don't worry about me. I'll make it all right. Pray that I keep my mind on my studies and everything else will come to me. Thank for the stamps. I was out and write often I don't hear from anyone else there. This is all till next time.

> With Love,
> Ralph

To Ida Bell
Tuskegee Institute
AUGUST 20, 1933

Dear Mama,

I was glad to hear from you and I wish you wouldn't wait so long next time. I received the music and thanks a lot. I'm well and I weigh 160 lbs. now so you see I'm quite all right. I haven't received any cards from anyone yet, ask Dillon did he send them to Tuskegee Inst. or just "Tuskegee"? Your son is cleaning up <u>and</u> cooking. I made the corn bread for the teachers' tables and I use a dozen and a half eggs in it along with three lbs. mush and three lbs. flour! The bread for the students is made in a trough about five feet long and three feet wide and we mix it with our hands, arms, and sometimes elbows (ha ha). I don't know how to make light bread yet but I help make it into loaves. We serve rolls every morning except Sunday and Mon. and I know how to roll them too. At dinner and supper we serve sliced bread and I slice it and I also have charge of the "slide" where the bread is given the waiters. We made from five to fifteen gallons of ice cream a day and all the deserts used by the school. Today we gave them cookies and apple float. If I have time I'll be a real baker soon but when school starts I think I'll have to find a new job. The school furnishes the sheets and pillowcases so don't send any, they also have a regular laundry here operated by students and they do fair work. I don't intend writing Son [and] them! No Mama, I haven't decided just what I'm going to take if I don't get in the Music school, but I'll know just as soon as Mr. Dawson gets here. Have you done anything about the money for the uniforms? They will send me home if I don't have it and they don't give one much time after school starts. I have just thirty dollars ($30.00) and I don't know what they will tell me but I can still trust that the Lord will let me get by. <u>Don't</u> forget the uniform. If you send any money for the school, send it to me. If you don't I won't know it and I might not be given credit for it. I am told there are crooks in the office. I don't believe it but it's best to play safe. Send all my stiff collars and handkerchiefs. I'll need a pair of shoes if I go to Chicago but that will wait. Vivian said you all talked together, what was it about? Yes, I still write her*

---

* Vivian Steveson was Ralph's steady girl for several years in Oklahoma City. Only one of his letters to her, dated June 1, 1935, was in his papers (and is included here), but most of hers survive, including several addressed to "Waldo Ellison."

and she's all right. I don't know myself just how I feel about her. It's funny.

Tell Herbert hello and Mr. Bell too. I've got to eat and tonight I play that solo. Wish me luck. I'll tell you more next time.

Don't forget the uniform!

Your Son
Ralph W. Ellison

To Ida Bell
TUSKEGEE INSTITUTE
AUGUST 25, 1933

Dear Mama,

I have just talked with the secretary of the music school about entering and to enter I will need to have $30.00 more and $26.25 every three months which is about $8.25 a month. This pays for two lessons a week on the cornet and one on the piano along with harmony and English and physical education.

Now I have $30.00 and it will take all of it and then some. Captain Drye tells me it is best to enroll now and then I might be able to owe the school later on. I am also depending on a job working at night to pay my board that is $20.50 a month.

This <u>does not include the uniform</u>. Mama I know this is stiff but if you can start me, please do. It is just the first time is bad. I think you can pay the $8.25 a month.

This is what it is going to cost in full and you can see

$20.00 - - - - books, library fee, etc.
15.75 - - - - Cornet lesson
10.50 - - - - piano
20.00 - - - - board
<u>17.50</u> - - - - uniform
83.75 - - - - first three months
-$30.00
53.75
- <u>20.50</u> - - - - board I think I'll get for working at night
$33.25

Please tell me what you can do as soon as possible school starts in two weeks and I've got to know. Things are rushing me. I hope you're well and good luck to you and Mr. John and Huck. This is in a hurry so excuse it please.

Your Son

Ralph

To Herbert Ellison

TUSKEGEE INSTITUTE ALA,

SEPT. 4, 1933

Dear Herb:

Boy but I was glad to hear from you and surprised too. How's the gang? Tell Old Raymond I wish he was here to take care of the pretty ones. Are you working any? How does Tycine look? Tell about her and why doesn't Hettie like her? Tell Dr. Nelson that I've seen the Veterans Hospital and I think it's one of the most beautiful places I've ever seen. Tell him the Moores are good friends of mine, especially Miss Moore. Tell Dr. Youngblood that if he came here he would be married in a month. Tell him they are beautiful and brown-skinned. Hello to Bowen, Lloyd, and all the fellows I know. How's Frank Mead? I believe you would like it here. You can learn to do so many useful things you could learn to be a real baker here or, you could learn to be an electrician, a carpenter, a plumber, a machine worker, a mechanic or any number of useful trades. We have a high school department and a grade school right here on the grounds and you could attend either of these. Try to pass as much as possible and when I've been here a while I'll try to get you a pull so you can have a job. Boy but I miss you a lot and I wish you were here. Try and be good and don't give mama any trouble. Have you any new girls? Write and give me the low down on things, and tell Malcolm that Ben Townsend made the trip safely and is in school. This is a busy week, Huck, and I must close. I'm playing for an operetta the school is having tonight.

Your Brother

Answer soon.

Ralph W Ellison

To Ida Bell
TUSKEGEE INSTITUTE
SEPT. 4, 1933

Dear Mama,

You don't know how glad I was to hear from you and Herbert. I'm quite busy just now trying to learn just what course I will be able to take. I'm still waiting for an answer to my last letter and I am trying to get in the music school. Thanks a lot for the five spots and I'm so sorry I had to ask for more. If I don't get in the Music S. you will have to pay for my lessons on the cornet. Thanks, that little book will be the <u>best</u> thing in my scrapbook and thanks again to you and Mr. John for paying it out. New students are arriving every day and the place looks like an ant bed. All the good-looking girls avoid this place, it seems all who are arriving are not so hot. I was in Columbus, Georgia two weeks ago. I went with Chubbie and Gordon to visit a Dr. Brewer. Write me the address where you used to live in Atlanta I might go there some day soon. Vivian is all right I guess. It will work out as the Lord intends it should. Though Chubbie and I like each other we don't pretend we love, I respect her and she me, we don't kiss [and] we get along fine. I'm writing Herbert soon and if I make a good reputation here in about two years I might be able, with your help, to get him in school. Good luck to all and be good till next time.

Ralph W. Ellison

To Ida Bell
TUSKEGEE INST.
SEPT 22, 1933

Dear Mama

I am sorry that I didn't make myself clear about the money. I had enrolled in the school of music and thought the money I had paid would take care of the fees but I was told I would have to pay $30.50 tuition in the music department 15.75 for cornet and 10.50 for piano. Along with this I was to get harmony, English and solfeggio (in training). I was working in the bakery from five until nine forty five in the morning and then I went to my first class at ten. This job paid board or enough of it to get me by.

Well I had started and I like the course fine, in fact so well that I don't want any other, but now I find it will cost $30.00 more cash, and $8.00 a month starting three months after the payment of the $30.00. This may be paid in a lump sum or may be sent as I say in monthly payments.

They required us to pay $40.00 tuition when we enter school, work students and all. I decided that since I couldn't keep up with the music it was best to come home, there's nothing else left here for me and I was told to drop the course until I paid the money.

I was hoping that you would be able to pay the fees but since you aren't I'll try to stay here a year and study education though I don't know what subjects I'll major in. If you can pay fifteen dollars every month please let me know, Mama. I wouldn't like to drop my cornet work. It's just five dollars and twenty five cents a month. It's quite a disappointment but I'll make the best of it. Now I was unable to find a second hand uniform, they were all too small [or] too large. Most of them were sold before I got here. The new uniform went up from $17.00 to $24.00 since the N.L.A. has been going and I paid all the money you sent on it and now I need $15.00 more to get it when it arrives. I can't do without it because we are sent home if we don't have one. Ask Malcolm. It's a hard go down here and when you don't have money you have to endure <u>too</u> much because the officials and department head make you do just as they want you to. I worked harder this summer than I have ever before and just made $20.00 a month and when the books were checked at the end of the summer I owed them $5.00. So Mama I hope you can understand why I don't want to stay here and take a lot of studies I don't like and while the books in the music school only cost about $4.00 those in the School of Education will cost about seven or eight since all the old books are sold. But you do the best you can and I'll stay till they run me away whether I like the course or not. Thanks for the things. I was more than glad to get them but don't you pay much for things. Cheap ones will do just so they are of a good color. If we get to Chicago next month I'll need an overcoat so don't forget.

Pray that things turn for the best and some miracle will happen by which I will be able to take music. Hello to Herbert and Mr. John tell them I thank them for what they've done and don't you worry about me and I'm waiting your next letter. The thirty dollars will have to be paid all at once, Mr. Bradley says. I hope you stay well. Be good.

Your Son
Ralph W Ellison

To Ida Bell

Tuskegee Inst Ala

OCT 1, 1933

Dear Mama;

When I opened your letter and money order fell out you could have pushed me over with a feather. I haven't [written] since I had no idea that you all would send me that much money and I don't know how to thank you and Mr. John.

I hope you aren't putting yourselves in too great strain for me. I am going to reenter the school of music because I feel that is what you intended since you sent enough to pay for my uniform and the music fees too. I had almost given it up and had entered the School of Education but now I can do something worthwhile. I had prayed to go on in music but when the change came I just said the Lord intended me to wait a year so I am repaid for not losing faith. Now I won't have to spend $12.00 for books and laboratory fees.

Now about going to Chicago. We are to go <u>if</u> they get the $2,000 and I think we will. We shall leave on the 18th of this month. Please send my overcoat and if you can my little black sweater and two music books, the black one by Oscar Coon, and the big green one belonging to Mrs. Breaux* called "Harmonia Natural and its Uses." I need the books though if the green one isn't there don't bother about it. My uniform hasn't come yet but it is supposed to get here soon. We are working hard to get the band in shape and it keeps me on the go, however it is something I like to do and I am well enough to stand it.

Tell Mr. John that there aren't many like him to be found and that I thank him again and again. Tell Herbert that I'll answer as soon as I get money to buy paper and to be a good boy. Tell the Randolphs hello and that I intend to stay here as long as I can. Send the address but don't worry about money to spend in Chicago. I am learning to do without and I don't even get my hair cut often (smile).

Pray that I won't lose any more time and don't worry about me. I'll find some way to get by 'cause you see there's nothing to pay for but two

---

* Zelia Breaux had been superintendent of music for the Oklahoma City Negro schools and Ralph's music teacher at Douglass School. Ralph credited her with revealing to him "the basic discipline required of the artist." He learned of her death when he arrived in Oklahoma for his cousin May Belle's funeral.

books and hair cuts and sometimes a suit to be pressed. Gee I've got to study before it's time to turn out the lights. Thanks so much Mama and may God bless you.

> Your Son
> Ralph

PS Tell Huck to tell Mrs. Breaux she almost had me back in the band again but things turned out better and that I'll write her soon.

> Ralph

To Herbert Ellison
TUSKEGEE INSTITUTE
OCT. 11, 1933

Dear Herbert;

I know you wonder what's wrong that I don't answer your letter and the truth is that I've been too busy to do anything for myself.

Boy the fact that you're out of the P.V. class was sure a pleasant surprise. You will have to work hard on your music and show them that you can learn it. It's worthwhile and will help you get advantages that others don't get. Who are the new teachers, and who teaches you music? That was too bad about Brown and you might tell him I wish him a speedy recovery. When are you going out for football? I read where the team beat Boley. Go out and make that team if it takes the next two years, it will help you. All you want to do is to keep in the eye of the public and be able to do something. Make a reputation and live up to it! I had charge of the Campus Dance Orchestra a while but I have stopped now.

The young lady was Miss Julia (Chubby) Moore a classmate of Maxine, and my girl this summer. She helped me quite a bit this summer. I received the money and boy was I glad! You could've knocked me down with a feather. I hope you are well and that you are studying hard. Study now and when examination comes around you won't have to worry. Tell the gang, Jim and Doctor Whiley hello. Tell Raymond I wish him good luck and I hope he goes to Denver. He deserves the break. Well, old boy, be good and work hard. I'll try to answer sooner next time.

> Ralph

PS. Ask Lydia Branam's address and send it. Tell her hello for me.

To Ida Bell

TUSKEGEE INST

NOV 5, 1933

Dear Mama,

I was very glad to receive your letter and the stationary.

I had a good time in Chicago although I didn't have but two dollars to spend, and this was part of my uniform money. I had a hard time finding uncle Will but I did and I recognized him right away. He is the same, only smaller and he drinks a lot. I met his wife and aunt Minnie. A person wouldn't believe that you were related to them you are so different. They treated me fine and he gave me a shirt and three ties. He hasn't worked in three years and they are supported by the little work his wife can get and they are on the charity list of the city of Chicago.

Will lives in one of the poorer districts but aunt Minnie lives in a much better one. She is a big yellow woman about the size of Mrs. Tolliver or larger with bobbed hair and seems to be pretty nice. You might think you are having it hard but thank the Lord because of the three you are doing the best. Will's address is 3250 La Salle. We stayed at the Y.M.C.A. and took our meals there. We were kept busy playing out at the fair four times and there were two parades. The fair is worth seeing and I wish you all could see it next year. We played football in the rain and tied 0–0 but we have won two games since, yesterday we beat Morehouse of Atlanta 26–6. Armistead Perrio was quarterback for them, his people live on seventh street. I am glad Herbert is doing so well in school. Tell him to keep it up it won't take long to get through and here there are some fellows older than me in the Jr. high depts.

Tell Jammie hello for me and to be good. Be sure and send the picture!

Yes Mama I do need more covering. It gets quite cold here and I've been sleeping under my coat. I had to spend $1.50 of the money you sent for a music book and $2.00 for an English book. I'm sorry but I have to have the books, and my uniform hadn't arrived and now they are on me about it. I thought I would be making a little cash playing but there's nothing to do right now. Tell Herbert I'll right write soon and tell Mr. John hello. I'm glad you were able to pay all the bills so soon and that you are buying some new clothes. I am quite well except two teeth that will have to be filled soon. Be good and I'll try to tell more about the fair next time.

Ralph

To Ida Bell
Tuskegee Institute Ala
Nov 11, 1933

Dear Mama,

I received your letter today and as you asked me to I am answering by return mail. I am altogether again though I do have a slight cold. I expected you to answer my letter in Cinn. but you didn't. I have been very busy since I've been back. I had to make up some examinations and that took my time. However I passed in my exams making one A and one B. I have been able to stay in school all quarter and I think I will be in next if Mr. Williams finds it possible to see me through. The only trouble just now is to keep clean. Last week my old suit was so dirty that one of my fellow students asked me what on earth was wrong. Next month I will need $5.00 to make out. I am working but I don't make all of my board. How are things and people there in Oklahoma City? I am glad to hear you are well and I hope you are happy. I had a nice trip but did not care for Cinn. It is too dirty and hilly. I am doing well in all of my subjects but one and I have started to work upon it. Please get word to Malcolm and tell him that Mr. Dawson's Symphony is to be broadcast on the 16th, next Friday at 1:00 p.m. by the Philadelphia Philharmonic Orchestra. Please see that he gets this information. Yesterday I spent in Montgomery viewing the S. H. Kress Art Collection of Paintings. I had a wonderful time of it and came back feeling a lot better afterward. I don't think you should strain to try to get me home Christmas, you need the money for other things I'm sure. I would like to come but I understand. Please tell Mr. & Mrs. Randolph that I said hello and that I think of them often, which is a lot more than I could say of most of the other people there. How is Mr. Herbert and his school work? Give him my love. I'm writing Mr. Bell so don't worry about me and write again.

With Love
Ralph

To Ida Bell
TUSKEGEE INSTITUTE
NOV. 26 1933

Dearest Mama,

I had just about given up hearing from you again. I had mailed that letter a long time before it reached you and just why it took so long I don't know because I am prompt about answering your letters. I am sorry this happened and I will see to it that it doesn't happen again. I am still busy as ever trying to work and get my lessons. That isn't so easy because they keep me going all the time. I am not making enough to pay my board but they haven't said any thing about it. I owe the school $34.00 up to date and that means I'll have to work all of next summer to pay it off.

You know I hope that the quarter is about to change and that means I will have to pay $26.50 for my music. The quarter starts next month. You asked about the $65.00 lasting the year. No it doesn't, the tuition is $17.00 a quarter. Maybe I'll have to pay it and maybe I won't but I'll let you know. Well, Mama I've worn holes in my black shoes and I can't do without them and I've worn holes in two teeth and I can't do without them (smile). I don't have any underwear and I need a haircut. You know, Mama I hate to have to ask for something every time I write home but I hope you understand next year things won't be so bad. I am sending a program from the "Green Pastures" which played here on the twenty-fifth. It was swell and if it comes to Oklahoma City don't miss it. (Let Malcolm see the program.)

We played our home coming game that day against Fisk and of course we won. It was a big day, the band formed the word "FISK" and the girls pulled off some stunts and that night after the game we saw the "Green Pastures."* There were [3,000] people in our gym, and a large number were white. People came from miles around. Allen Bethel was down from Talladega to the game and I met Bill Harvey who is manager of the Fisk team. Tell Doctor Randolph that Jessie O. Thomas looked me up when he was here and that he will see me when he comes back in a few days. Thank him because this man has much influence here being president of

---

* *Green Pastures* was a Pulitzer Prize–winning 1930 Marc Connolly play featuring African American actors and actresses in roles dramatizing Old Testament stories with some relevance to African American folklore.

the alumni association. Mama, I hope you are all well and that things are running smooth. I haven't got the uniform yet.

Tell Mr. Bell and Herbert hello and be good.

Ralph

To Ida Bell
Tuskegee Institute ALA
DEC 4, 1933

Dearest Mama,

I was glad to receive a letter so soon from you and the money order is more than appreciated because I sure needed the money. I got my uniform and had my shoes fixed and bought socks and underwear. The teeth will cost $6.00. I have four cavities instead of two and they cost $1.50 a piece. I will have to wait until later to have them fixed. Mama, when I get ahead I will need just a dollar along to get a suit pressed or to have my hair cut. I had my shoes fixed because I didn't have enough to buy new ones. I have just finished my quarter examinations and now it's time to register for the second quarter and I will when the fees arrive.

I will write those people all cards. Christmas, I stay too busy to write anyone but a select few. Vivian writes but I don't have time to think of her any more. She can't understand that my mind is on my studies now and I can't think of anything but it, if I want to get ahead. I don't have anything against her but now I can't afford to think of her.

This music requires all of a person's time and Mr. Dawson won't allow any other people to work and take it so you see I'm lucky. It's warm here and just gets cold by spells. Be good and tell Mr. Bell I hope he is well.

I shall answer Herbert. I'll try to say more next time.

Thanks for what you are doing, and by the way I am trying to get a new job that pays more but it is doubtful that I'll get [it].

Be good till next time.

Your Son
Ralph

To Ida Bell
TUSKEGEE INSTITUTE
DEC 14, 1933

Dear Mama,

I had just planned to mail you a letter when yours arrived. Things look bad for me just now because the dean has ordered all who haven't registered to leave the school Monday. A number have left already and others are leaving soon. The fees for the Music alone are $28.25 and the tuition is $17.50 that makes a total of $45.75. This doesn't include my board. I really don't see how I am going to make it because I didn't understand it would cost that much when I started. Won't you answer right back and tell me what you can do? I made good grades this quarter and I would like to go on. They are hard to deal with here and insist that they have all of the money at once. Mama, if I had known I wouldn't have spent the $10.00 for other things. This is more important and I thought you had all of the other money.

There isn't any news here. We had a fire in another of the girls' buildings and that is all. I tried to talk to the dean about registering but he won't allow me until I pay my fees, so you see I'm out of school. However, I am still working, and when some of these fellows go home I hope to find a better job. Tell Mr. John and Herbert to hold things down. Be good yourself and answer right Back!

Your Son,
Ralph W. Ellison

To Ida Bell
TUSKEGEE INSTITUTE ALA.
JAN 10, 1934

Dearest Mama;

I had almost forgotten this to be a new year, and started to write 1933 instead of 34. I hope this will find you well and as happy as possible. I am all right now but my stomach still bothers me sometimes. I am still out of school but I haven't got a full time job just yet, and there is no prospect of getting one soon. However I shall stay until asked to leave and then I shall go—somewhere. I haven't spent but $2.00 of the thirty you sent and I have the other, and I intend to keep it. That was just half of what I need every quarter to pay my entrance fees and I hope next quarter Ill have all of this even if I cant pay the thirty dollars I owe on my board. I would liked to have been there Christmas but it was impossible. It didn't seem like Xmas here but I had a fair time. I am still invited everywhere and went somewhere every day though we only have a week of idleness. That white woman was almost right about my coming home because they sent home a big gang and they haven't stopped yet.

Be sure and send me one of your new pictures and my last quarter's grades I don't know what I made. How did you like the "Green Pastures"?

Tonight Vady Shaw Kar, a world famous dancer and his company will be here. I'll tell you about it next time. How is Mr. Bell and Herbert? Tell Herbert he is the only one who thought to send me an Xmas card and I thank him and appreciated it and will write him when I get stamps. Love to you all and tell Huck to tell Malcolm he owes me a letter. Be good.

Ralph W. Ellison

To Ida Bell
I need stamps!!
TUSKEGEE INSTITUTE
FEB. 1, 1934

Dear Mama;

I received your box of stationary and was glad to get the picture. You look well, even better than when I saw you last. I am glad and I hope your good health will continue. I like the coat and hat. I myself am in fair health I weigh 167–8 lbs. Still working in the "Bakery" but I am tired of it all. I don't feel right out of school. Mr. Dawson asked me to stop attending classes, because it might get him into trouble. He told me he received your letter and told me if I got in school he could help me with my music fees, but there was nothing he could do until I registered. He advised me to pay the money I had and try to find an extra job. I paid the money and I now owe $36.00 on this quarter's fees. I don't have a job yet. I have found a new friend here in the person of Walter Bowie Williams, the Librarian. He is about twenty-eight years of age and hails from New York. He has been here five or six years and is quite a fellow when away from his office. He has any number of rarer books, and allows me to come to his room to read them. He is about the size of Laurence Thomas, and likes to curl up in his big chair and talk to me about the problems of the world, religion, arts, music or anything that might arise. Sometimes we talk and drink coffee until early morning not often however. He is, or seems to be a fine fellow. Several fellows go to drink his coffee and to talk and we all like him.

He promised out of his own free will to give me a job this summer as one of the sub-librarians. I hope I am able to stay and get the job. I went to classes until this week and thought you would send something so I could get credits for the work.

Tell Herbert I am proud to know him and he might pass again in May.

How is Mr. Bell, tell him I hope he is well. Write soon won't you—? I shall look for one soon.

> Be Good,
> Ralph W. Ellison

To Ida Bell
TUSKEGEE INSTITUTE ALA
FEB. 14, 1934

Dear Mama;

I received your letter a day or two ago, and was glad to hear from you. I have stopped worrying, and I just hope to attend class this next quarter. I feel that next year won't be so bad and I intend to work this summer on some job where I can make some of my fees for next year. I am very anxious to know just what it is you plan to send me. I always get a kick out of receiving packages, and by the way, my black shoes have worn out on the tops as well as the bottom. I work in the gray ones and the brown ones need half soleing. I will have to have black ones right away because they are a part of the uniform.

I am very glad that Herbert has improved so much, and I hope he will continue to do so. How are the Randolphs these days? How is work coming on the new school? I see by the Black Dispatch* that quite a few young people have gotten married. Some of the same who said that I would last year. Well I didn't and I don't intend for a long-long-time. I don't know how I will feel when I get back there my friends are so different and older. Tell Jamie hello if you see her. I will write the Branams, and I am glad you sent the clipping. I am sorry to hear about the illness. Tell Mr. John hello

---

* The respected Oklahoma City African American community newspaper, started by Roscoe Dunjee in 1914–15.

and that I wish him good health and luck. I shall close Mamma so be good and answer soon.

> Your Son,
> Ralph W. Ellison

To John Bell
TUSKEGEE INST. ALA.
MARCH 2, 1934

Dear Mr. John;

I was surprised and glad to hear from you. I am glad to know you are all well and I am glad to say I am well. I received your package with the quilts in it and I thought it was swell and too good for my room. I am sorry to write this; I got a pair of shoes on credit from a man I need to play for this summer, Mr. Forts and I was to pay him as soon as my money came to buy shoes. My black ones were worn out and I needed a pair to drill and podium. These only cost $4.90 and they are pretty good shoes. I am very sorry because these you sent me are swell but they are a little large. I shall consider these as a gift from you and I hope you are able to get the money back. The socks are always welcome. I wear them out too fast. You don't realize just how much I appreciate what you and Mama are doing for me. I feel ashamed that I have to take so much of your money and not return any at all. I don't feel at anytime that you aren't doing the best you can for me and I am sure you would send me straight through school. I consider myself lucky because you are above the average stepfather; I hope you are able to get a nice house at a cheap price. How is work at the store? If you see Mr. Clauber tell him I asked about him.

Is Mama still doing church work? (smile) I want to start school as soon as possible so tell Mama not to make it too long because I can't lose any more time. Thanks for the shoes, money, blanket and everything, be good and tell Mama and Herbert hello. Please write again soon and thanks again for the shoes, and I think I can hold off until you can change the other shoes into cash. If not, I will pay him out of the $28.00 because it isn't enough without the other. I shall mail these right back as soon as possible.

> Wishing you well,
> Your stepson
> Ralph W. Ellison

To Ida Bell
TUSKEGEE INST ALA.
MARCH 21 1934

Dear Mama;

I received your package, or at least I received a package from some of you and I want to thank the sender for it. The shirts and socks were needed badly and they came just in time. Things are quiet here and the weather is changeable, sometimes its warm the next it's cold. They are sending folks away again and two of the best band men are leaving soon because they can't pay.

The school has a new policy and next year most of the students will be paying students. I have been admitted to the College depts. but I am $10.00 short on my music fees. Won't you please send this by return mail. I am using valuable time on my instruments especially the piano.

They are making changes in the dining division and a number of us have been laid off. This means that I won't make anything at all this month. I might have to pay $10.00 on that at the end of the month. April first I go to work at the library. This is a better job and its pay all but four dollars of the months board each month. They have said that all students who wished to stay this summer would have to pay the first quarter's tuition for next year and all of this year's debts. I hope you will write soon as possible I want to get started.

Thank Mr. John for the presents he sent and tell Herbert that I think of him and will write soon. I'm busy trying to find a job until the first of the month. I am well and I hope you all are also. Take good care of your self and answer <u>this</u> letter. You didn't answer the last.

Ralph W Ellison

To Ida Bell
TUSKEGEE INST.
APRIL 17, 1934

Dear Mama;

I am sorry you waited so long to write me because I wasn't in school and I will have to repeat part of this quarters' work next year. I haven't had a chance to see about the bill yet but I do know that I didn't have any teeth fixed though I do need some work done on my mouth.

There must be another mistake because I wasn't in school last quarter and this quarter I was registered through the help the Government is giving students so you see I shouldn't have to pay for this quarter just now anyway. I have the job in the Library now and it pays from sixteen to eighteen dollars a month and I hope to stay ahead of my board bill if I can make two more dollars a month in some other job.

I hate you had to move where you did but I hope you like it too. I am well and I hope all of you are as well. Love to Herbert and Mr. John and have Malcolm write me

When did you get the little broken picture? I don't hear from V anymore or at least she quit writing. Be good. Pray.

Ralph W. Ellison

To Ida Bell

Tuskegee Institute

MAY 2, 1934

Dear Mama;

I was glad to hear from [you] after such a long time. I feel like I've been away a long time, and I have, almost a year. I hope I'm not so changed that you won't know me when I do return. School is out on the 26th of this month, and examinations will start sooner. I missed so much time out that I don't know how much I will pass in, but I do know that a lot of my course will have to be made up next year. Things are dull here, the campus is pretty but that's about all.

I am waiting until the end of the month to clear up my bill because a lot of it will be charged off since I wasn't in school the second quarter. No I don't think I will have to pay the Government but I will have to make good grades. I am in awful bad shape, one of my roommates has graduated and the other was in an accident and is in the hospital. I have no razor blades, no soap, no haircut, no toothpaste, no anything. I wish you would send as many of these as possible as soon as possible. You could send a box, and you could cook a cake? and send a few sardines etc. The food here isn't the best in the world and a chance to eat anything else is welcomed. I got a letter from Vivian.

If the book about Booker T. Washington is still there, hold on to it. It will be worth a lot some day. Let me know if you still have the account at Mays or Strains, I will need a pair of shoes (white) soon. What did

Maybelle have to say of interest? Sorry about Tete, hello to her. I'm out of stamps again. Be good and pray I need it to keep going please Love to Mr. John and Mr. Herbert. How is his schoolwork, and singing?

I hear from Virgil sometimes now. I hope you are as well as V said you looked.

Time for bed!

Love
Ralph

To Ida Bell
CARNEGIE LIBRARY
TUSKEGEE INSTITUTE, ALABAMA
MAY 27, 1934

Dear Mama,

I had to wait until now to write you because of my being busy the last week. School has been like a nightmare. I had to appear four or five times on the various programs. The school of music gave its annual recital and I had to play a solo that night while the other times I had the brass quartet that is composed of two trumpets and two trombones. Every night this week has been some kind of a program that we were all forced to attend. Graduation Thursday at which events seventy-four college and fifty-five or six high school [students] received diplomas; I am sending programs so you may see just what happened down here in the south. I wanted to come home very badly the other night after seeing some of the students leaving for home. The campus is almost deserted of students. Only a few are allowed to remain for the summer and those who aren't are fast leaving. The Youngbloods came by on their way to South Carolina, and spent the night. Tell Jim his young man will be picking the college he wants to attend in a few years. I don't think I will come home though so don't expect me. I will write Mrs. Cook as soon as I think she is at home. I was very sorry to hear [*missing passage*]

Now about school, I am sending a statement showing how much I made and how much it costs me to attend school and I want you to know that I was supposed to be home now because I owe the school $72.00. However, I don't have to leave because Mr. Williams, the librarian, told the office that he would take care of my account. I hope that you will be able to repay some of it anyway. But he is demanding it just now, and I am sure he won't help; just the same he will need it sometime during the year.

The money I received from the government was just a little over $6.00 and I thought it was about forty dollars (smile). I have been bothered with my stomach again but I'm all right now. I am glad you are well and the same is [for] Huck and Mr. Bell.

Answer soon.

P.S. I played my solo in a tuxedo.

To Ida Bell
TUSKEGEE INST
JUNE 15, 1934

Dear Mama;

I suppose that by now you have received my card from Pensacola. And I might add that I hope it was as much a surprise to you as it was to me. I went down with my boss and some friends, young teachers from Atlanta. We spent the three days at the home of Mrs. Taylor, the mother of one of my friends who graduated this year

They have a swell place in a quiet neighborhood not far from the bay. There are two daughters in the family, one works in an insurance office and the other teaches in the system there. They have two cats and a dog and they are swell people and animals to know, Mrs. Taylor especially.

We spent each day in the Gulf swimming and laying in the sun. You should see me Now I am so black you wouldn't know me. I eat plenty of good fish drank some beer swam had a good time and hated to leave. The trip was expensive but it didn't cost me anything thanks to my good friends. I drove most of the way back 250 mi. I am sorry to know that you have lost your job, and about such an affair it makes you lose faith in people. But maybe it was good. You might have gotten sick again. I am very glad to hear about your new home and I glad you are pleased with it. I still have my key so don't be surprised if I walk in on you some night (smile). I shall have to write someone soon because I am getting ragged. My grey suit is worn out and the pants of my brown one are very thin in the seat. They did well though one is almost four years old and the other is three. I have one pair of shoes and they are not enough because most of my work is walking back and forth from the desk to the stacks of books. I guess you can understand now why I wanted the shoes. It's so hot here that I do need a white suit of some kind but I could make it with a couple of good linen pants and a sweater. I was supposed to go to Nashville to the Fisk graduation with the Moores but I had to back out. I don't know whether we will go to Chicago this year or not, but we are supposed to go in Oct.

I am sending my receipt from the music school and there you can see where the other money went. The school of music is separate and the fees are not included in the bill and my uniform cost $24.00 remember? I am not in the best of health anymore, the food is making my stomach bad again. I would like to come home Christmas it won't cost much. The fare to Cinn. was only $9.00 in May and that's cheap. I am sending a coupon please mail it promptly. I need those magazines. And Mama I need a razor. Mine can't be found. Give my love to Herbert and Mr. Bell and write soon.

Love
Ralph

To Ida Bell
TUSKEGEE INSTITUTE ALA
JULY 1, 1934

Dear Mama,

I was very glad to hear from you in spite of the sad news. I had read about it in the paper and wondered why you hadn't written me about it. Have you decided to allow Herbert to go to Detroit? How long is he to stay?

You can't tell it might be a good trip for him. I wouldn't mind taking the trip myself. I am glad to know you feel better because job or no job that's the thing that counts. I feel somewhat better myself in spite of the heat and bad food. Please ask Herbert to find which one of the shoes Dr. Nelson wants. Thanks for the dollar.

Tell Mr. Bell that I received my magazines and thanks How about the razor though? It hasn't shown up And about shoes don't wait too long because I am walking with one foot on the ground now, ha ha. It was funny in which the way my grey suit wore out. You know I expected the seat to give way first, but they wore out on the thighs. How I did it I don't know. You know it is so hot here that the sweat will wear a piece of heavy cloth out in no time and all I have is heavy. I might get a chance to drive my boss to his home in Albany New York in August. He wants me to spend some two weeks at his mother's home there but I don't know if I can make it. However if I write for your permission to leave the campus don't be surprised. There's nothing going on around here now and I spend most of my time working and studying. Tell Herbert and Mr. John that I hope they are still

well and good luck to them both. Be good Mama and stay well. I'll write
more next time.

Ralph W Ellison

To Ida Bell
~~Walter B. Williams~~ THIS HAPPENS TO BE MY
~~Tuskegee Institute~~ FRIEND'S STATIONERY
ALABAMA
2 JULY 1934

Dear Mama;

I received your letter a day or two ago and was surprised that you hadn't
heard from me. I answered your letter and thanked you for the shoes and
razor, and I also sent my pants measurements. I have been bothered quite
a lot with my stomach lately because of the food but haven't had to go to
bed yet. If you have the letter now please let me know. I don't think I will
get to go to New York yet awhile but I might go to Florida again for a week
or ten days. I hope you are well and sorry that I caused you worry. There
is nothing here just now of interest so I don't have much to say. Try to
send the pants. I need them badly. You know I travel with the richer gang
here and this clothes problem is a pain. I need new ties shirts socks black
shoes & a suit. If you can send me $23.00 I can get a suit made and save
the discount rate. My club brother is a tailor. I have been told to apply for
government aid again this year and I'll get what we are supposed to get. I
should have it somewhat easy this year. I hope to make enough to pay two
quarters expenses at least, but I will still owe the fees for my Music. How
is Mr. Bell and my fine brother? Tell them I hope the heat is too much for
them, and that there are plenty watermelons to be eaten. I hope you do
come to Chicago and I will want to come Christmas so don't forget it. I
get lonesome sometimes—I would like to see you. I still go around with
Chubby, the girl I wrote about last year we have a good time dancing reading hiking on Sunday mornings or just talking. I think she is a fine young
woman and am sure you would like her.

I shall write for that excuse soon, and when you write you might say
that I am going to see if my stomach wont improve. Give my love to all
interested.

Ralph W. Ellison

To Ida Bell
TUSKEGEE INSTITUTE
JULY 18, 1934

Dear Mama,

I received your letter a few days after receiving the shoes. I like the shoes just fine, and as luck would have it they arrived just in time. I had a party to attend and was wondering just what I was going to wear upon my feet.

There is naught here but heat and discomfort. I have been well lately in spite of the food. I don't know whether I shall get to New York or not, but I'm praying that I shall. I intend to study there as soon as I get a chance. I am not at all satisfied with this place because I am not getting all I might. I want to attend the Juilliard School of Music in N.Y. However I will have to make the best of this until I am able to leave. I hope I am able to come home Christmas. I want to see you. I don't want to live there anymore. I hope you understand that and the family and a few friends are all I want to see and as bad and hard as it might seem I don't want to see V, and I hope she feels the same way about me.

That is the truth and I can't help but say it.

I am glad Herbert isn't giving any trouble, and I hope he doesn't. I think Detroit might be just the place for him since he is sure to get the best instruction there. Gee you must think my feet have become very large (smile) but the shoes were just the right size and I liked them fine. Please thank Mr. John and tell him the razor came today. I hope you are able to come to Chicago this fall. I am sure you will like it, and if we have a few dollars we will be able to see the town. I must say, however, that I hope Minnie has a better place this year than she did last. It was good that you didn't come here, the Negroes still try to get so much money out of me as possible and that would have been an excuse to get more. I made fifty dollars last month and they sent the payroll back saying it was too much. They cut it down, but I don't know how much.

I will write Maybelle and the others as soon as I get a chance. I don't like to write and lately you are the only one to receive a letter from me. These (enclosed) are my measurements and it might be a good idea to keep them. Please remember that my hair needs cutting and my clothes cleaning once in a while (smile). I will try to write more next time and sooner. Say hello to the Randolphs and Walt and Saretta Love to you all,

Ralph

To Ida Bell
WALTER B. WILLIAMS
TUSKEGEE INSTITUTE
ALABAMA
AUGUST 13, 1934

Dear Mama,

I hoped to write this letter from Pensacola but I was not allowed to go. I sent all the wires because I thought you hadn't answered my letter but I found that Neely had your letter and had failed to tell me about it. He waited until Sat, the day I was to leave to tell me that if I left he wouldn't give me work when school starts. He also said if I was sick I should be in the hospital. I am not that sick and I do know the cause of his acting in this manner. This is just some more of the mess I've mentioned before. I see nothing I can do about it. He is the biggest man here so far as the student is concerned and if I kick up a racket now I would never get a job when I graduated, this dump is too powerful. You must understand that the reputation that this place has and what it really is, are two different things. I made one big mistake by coming here to take music. A music student should have the opportunity to hear good music all the time—I've heard no worthwhile music since I've been here. The person trying to study should not be worried and nagged at because he does not consent to prostitute[*] himself. Nor should one have to listen to the ravings of a bunch of small-minded niggers who won't be satisfied unless they show how important they are. On top of it all I have to go without haircuts and shaves, without shoes, and with holes in my pants and constantly worrying if I will have money to get in school or if I will have enough to stay. It is all true and I feel that I might as well give it all up and try to get a job as a waiter or a bell boy some where in New York. I asked you to write and tell me what you would be able to do when school starts and you didn't even take time to answer my letter. I don't ask for much but there are some

---

[*]   Ellison uses "prostitute" advisedly. The dean of students expected special favors in exchange for granting him permission to be away from Tuskegee.

things I have to have. There is no way to make any money here at least honestly. If some change doesn't take place I shall have to leave—in fact I want to leave. I feel I am wasting my time staying here. I started to leave Sat. but I was completely broke. If I get away from here I am through with Negro schools. I want to go to the Juilliard School in New York and am going to try to do it. I don't feel well, the food keeps my stomach upset and lately my eyes have been bothering.

If I enter the hospital it will take what little money I have made this summer to pay the bill. If there is any work there let me know I will gladly come home as much as I dislike it. Please don't repeat what I've said to any one but Mrs. Breaux. People move high around here for knowing too much. Ask her what I should do about the whole matter and please do me the honor to answer.

Ralph

To Ida Bell
WALTER S. WILLIAMS
TUSKEGEE INSTITUTE
ALABAMA
[21 AUG. 1934]*

Dear Mama,

I am writing this time to ask that you send by return mail, an excuse permitting me to go back to Florida. I have been invited to spend that much time with Mrs. Taylor. In writing the Dean, please state that you desire me to go there for the change and that you think it will help my stomach. This is all truth and will save a lot of time and questioning. I want to leave in a week so please hurry. I can't ask you to be too sure that the money for my first quarter's work be here on time. Please tell me how much money you will be able to send because since the school has been put on a cash basis I want to be allowed to stay without my fees and if late they will cost four dollars each day they are so. I have made $40.00 to the good this summer, it isn't much but will it will help. It is at least my first month's board and tuition, however there remains my Music fee, to make that much. They even started to close school this summer so at that I'm lucky. Please write

---

* Ralph's handwritten original has "21 Aug. 1933" in brackets. The handwriting is not his; perhaps one of the staff at the Library of Congress inserted it. In any case it clearly seems to have been written between his two letters to his mother of August 13 and 28, 1934.

Neely a special for my excuse and be good. Pray for me—I need it—and tell your other two boys I said hello and luck to them.

Ralph

PS Any change you could send is welcome (smile).

To Ida Bell
WALTER BE. WILLIAMS
TUSKEGEE INSTITUTE
ALABAMA
AUGUST 28, 1934

Dear Mama,

I received both your letters, but I have been waiting, trying to decide just what I am going to do. I think that since I have worked all summer and made a little credit I might well as use it, at least as long as I can. I have enough to make it for one quarter I think, but I am not sure weather they will except credit on my music for they have might demand cash. Please try to get about thirty ($30.00) if possible because with that and the assistance that Mr. Williams can give me on my work I will be able to make it a while, providing that this (N)egro who has caused me all the trouble will leave me alone. I got the address of the fellow in Conn. but I think it's too much a chance to take considering the climate and the possibility that I won't get the job after I get there. It going to be very hard this year because my clothes are just about gone and I don't get along with the people at all. They don't understand me and—you understand I don't like people anyway and I try to leave them alone but they insist that I look at them and remember that they have a few jobs a little money etc. But I know they are dumb and shallow and think that money is all there is in the world, never realizing that the finer things can't be bought and that a few people in the world, yes even Negroes, love books, music, art, beauty nature and the other things which are good and great. I hope you understand what I am trying to say because it's what is on my mind. I spend most of my time reading and listening to what good music I can hear. I talk to Walter and discuss the different aspects of Art and ethics, morals, and sometimes, God. I don't believe about him as I used to but I still believe in his greatness, that he exists and I know he answers prayers. As for Church I don't know what to think man has made it so rotten. I doubt Mama, if I'll ever be rich but I will be as big a man as possible and if I don't become a great composer I hope that I will be respected because of the way I shall try to live. I'll try to do what's right and like you I have learned not to allow talk keep me from it and I shall try to understand people and can give them their faults even though they condemn me because of mine. You know I got in an argument with a girl I sent from the Library for talking, and she said she doubted that I was a man (ha! ha!). I don't know whether that is the general opinion but it's funny. You wouldn't believe it. Most of these people don't understand anything but planning and that type of mind and when a person doesn't think as they do they think there's something wrong with them and too I don't go with any of the campus girls and even the officials don't like the campus fellows to go around with the Hospital people. The fools want every one to think alike to accept their master slave attitude and if you don't you are a stuck up Nigger and a sissy. Well, the knowledge that I am a one here did cost me, and all ways will, much unhappiness. I do know that I am.

How is Viv and who does she go around with. I don't know just how I feel about her. You see, mama, to do what I want to will take years and years of hardship and work and it would be unfair for me to even think to ask her to wait for me because I might be very hard to live with and I don't think any woman will understand my love for music and could stand my giving so much time to it. I don't know but maybe we were wrong about each other and even now she has found some one she likes even better than me. I haven't any girl, they take too much time and I don't have the money, but I do go around with Julia and Gordon and I have a fair time at it. I hope things are running smooth there in spite of the scarcity of money. I am going to stay here a while and fight it. Answer this soon and you can tell Mr. Bell & Herbert hello, and you must forgive me for writing such a long letter. Be good.

With Love,
Your son Ralph

To Ida Bell
Tuskegee Inst
OCT 2, 1934

Dear Mama,

I suppose you have thought some mean things of me for not writing, but I have the same old excuse. I have been busy since the first day of school with no let-ups whatever. I scrambled around and got in school and the

Music dept. I made enough to pay all but $2.75 and you sent the $5.00 for which, thanks too much. I am in school for one quarter sure but after Christmas the Lord only knows what will happen. These parties are still making it difficult for me to get along but they cant get me down. Mr. Williams sends his regards, he has helped me a whole lot, and for which I am very thankful. Gee, the box was swell and was quite a surprise. I needed something on that order for my crazy stomach that has been acting up again. Thanks for it all; it was well appreciated. Please don't hold Mrs. Cook to blame, it is my fault, because I forgot to write. I need the money and I am sorry I didn't write. Don't say a thing to Mrs. Breaux either I can fight my own battles. I haven't written her in a year anyway. I hope she is in good health.

Dr. Haywood's daughter is here along with a boy and girl from there. The enrollment is smaller this year than last, and the students are better appearing and seem more intelligent. The band is smaller this year but we hope to make it into a good musical organization. I don't know how long it will last, but I am the soloist and conducted one half of last Sunday's concert. Capt. Drye might change it but I hope he won't. You see I like it. O yes, I took the money I had left and had my black shoes soled. They needed it badly. You mentioned Elwood being ragged, well you should [see] your son. He has only one pair of pants and they haven't been pressed in months. If you can send me a pair of slacks and some underwear.

Not sure of Chicago trip this year but I can only hope. Gordon is Chubbie's brother, and she is not married. That is a false report. Who does Maxine teach? Say hello to Herbert and Mr. Bell and tell him I will answer his nice little letter soon. Tell the Randolphs hello for me. Be good and keep well and don't worry about me it will work out some way.

With Love,
Ralph

To Ida Bell
Cinn. Ohio
Oct. 24, 1934

Dear Mama,

I am taking time out to write tonight and I am sorry I haven't had time to do so before. We were told just the night before we were to leave that we were going, so I had no time to write. We are traveling by bus this time, but

I think the fellows like it just as well as they did the last time. We came up through Tenn. and Ky. arriving in Chicago about twenty-four hours after departing. We stayed at the Y.M.C.A. as we did before. I didn't go to many dances this trip but to the opera and museum. I met a number of people I liked and had a good time in general. We were in Chicago five days, playing one concert at Gary. We played at the high school there, but I was unable to get around to where we lived. However, the night I attended the opera I met the assistant principal of the school, an interesting person who was very kind to me when we got to Gary. We play Ky. State here Sat. and then we go back to school, to books and to work (smile). Won't you send me your sister's address, I would like to look her up while I'm here. I didn't get to see Uncle Will this time, too busy. I hope you and the others are well and getting the most of life. I am sick today with a cold and had to spend the day in bed. Yes, and while in bed, I fell in love with a picture on the cover of *Opportunity,* the Negro magazine (Smile). You know I'm really quite a fool. I don't know how I like this place, it's big and everything but as I said, I spent the day in bed. We expect to visit Wilberforce one day this week, but I don't know just when. Give my love to Herbert and Mr. Bell and tell them I will write when I get back. Send your ans. special to me at the Y.M.C.A. (Colored) Cinn. Ohio. And if you have spare dollar send it, I, as usual am broke.

Ralph

To Ida Bell
TUSKEGEE INST. ALA.
NOV 16, 1934

Dear Mama,

I was very surprised to hear from you again so soon after I had answered your previous letter. However, it was very welcome. I have intended to tell you before that it isn't necessary to send the letters special delivery because we get our mail at meal time and the post office is just facing the dining hall. Please don't get the idea that I think you have lost interest in me. I realize more each day the struggle you had to put up to keep Herbert and myself going. I just couldn't understand why you hadn't written. I am sorry that Herbert isn't in school any longer. Just what [does] he intend to do for himself, he will be grown before he realizes it. I shall write Miss Harris but you must tell her I didn't get her letter until this week. We have been busy here because of homecoming week. It was a big day but we lost the football fame to Wilby* College. Caterina Jaboro gave a recital afterwards that I enjoyed very much. After that we had a dance to round up the day. Don't work too hard, and give my love to Mr. Bell and Herbert. I'll try to write more next time.

As ever,
Ralph

To Ida Bell
TUSKEGEE INST ALA.
DEC. 9, 1934

Dear Mama,

I am sorry I had to wait so long before writing but I have been very busy and just now I am having my final quarter examinations. I received the box and enjoyed the contents very much. I spent Thanksgiving with the band in Montgomery where we only had dry sandwiches to eat. My health is sometimes a little off due to the food but most of the time it is good. I am hoping to get in school this next quarter and I will let you know as soon as possible. The weather is getting bad down here and my shoes are gone again. The bucks are the only ones left and I wonder if you will have the same man repair them who repaired the black ones should I send them (please answer). Maybe next Christmas I will be able to visit you but from your letter I don't see that it is possible this year. How are Mr. Bell and Herbert? This time give them my love. I hope this will find you well and that you will answer as soon as possible. I still have other exams to prepare so I must cut this one short. Be good and pray.

With love
Ralph

To Ida Bell
TUSKEGEE INST ALA.
DEC 23, 1934

Dear Mamma,

I received your letter day before yesterday and was surprised to hear that you had failed to receive any of my letters. You see I have written thanking you both for the money you have sent. I have gotten in school this quarter

---

*   Short for Wilberforce College.

and I see my way clear for three months at least. Mr. Williams is seeing to that. My marks will be there shortly I think and hope you will be pleased with them. They are all I can offer just now. All the kids are gone home for the holidays and Mr. Williams went to New York yesterday making this a lonesome place for me. There will be a few dances but I can't make them. No not with these patched pants and no shoes. I will be glad when school starts. I can forget when I start my lessons. I am getting so that the only time I feel safe is when I am with music. I am sorry about the job. It seems bad and unfair that you have such a time in spite of your trying to live right. It makes me wonder if it is worthwhile. Tell Mr. Bell that I received the shirts and that I think it's a swell present. I'm sorry I can't come home but maybe before I finish my work here I will. I sent Miss Harris a card and you can ask her if she received it and the letter I sent.

Tell Herbert hello for me and to be a good fellow. How are the Browns, the Randolphs, Slaughters, Stevesons?* Please let me know what has happened to Malcolm.

I don't know just who Annie Mae married, she didn't say why she was back in Montgomery and I didn't question after she said she wasn't working.

I guess Ill spend these ten days practicing the piano, and reading. I hope you will have a very pleasant Christmas and New Year's. I will write

---

* Here Ralph calls the roll of Christmastime greetings to Oklahoma City families whose members were crucial to him as a boy and remained so for the rest of his life. They are among his "dear folks." References and letters to them abound in his correspondence: Lucretia Ellison Brown, his aunt, became an even greater presence in his life after the sudden death of her brother, Ralph's father, in 1916, as did her children, especially her older son, Tom, who presented a freewheeling, irreverent model of a man.

The Randolphs, too, opened worlds to Ralph, especially patriarch Jefferson Davis (J. D.) Randolph, and his wife, Saretta. Their eldest child, Edna Randolph Slaughter, was for years Ida Bell Ellison's best friend, and Edna's children, Wyatt junior and Saretta, were family to Ralph. Edna's younger sisters, Camille and Iphigenia ("Cute"), were like big sisters to Ralph and Herbert. Her brothers, dentist Dr. Thomas Jefferson ("Bud") Randolph and pharmacist Dr. James ("Jim") Randolph, employed Ralph in jobs that taught him the responsibilities of the big world. The Randolphs and the Slaughters had leading roles in the black community of Oklahoma City.

Vivian Steveson was a sophisticated young lady and her family prosperous, due apparently to her father's success as a gambler. Though he lost touch with his friend Malcolm Whitby, Ralph never forgot Malcolm pushing him to go to Tuskegee to study with William Dawson, or discovering Guy de Maupassant's fiction and the prefaces of George Bernard Shaw in the library of Malcolm's father, Dr. A. Baxter Whitby, a prominent dentist and NAACP leader in Oklahoma City.

sooner next time. I wasn't sure if I was to be in school this year quarter. But I am in. I guess that's as fine a Christmas present I could have. Be a good Brownie and write soon.

Your son
Ralph

To John Bell
TUSKEGEE INST ALA
[UNDATED]*

Dear Mr. Bell

Sorry I have to answer your letter in this manner, but I don't have another stamp and I've owed you a letter for along time.

I am glad you were able to get a job with the chance to learn something useful and I wish you all of the success possible. What happened to Harry Katz? Did he go out of business or did he lose everything? You know I feel as if I had been away about five years and I think that when I do return I will have to learn how to act all over again. Do Negroes still wait tables there at the O.C. club and the Shriner? I haven't had a tray in my hands in years and I guess I've forgotten how to serve. If you see Tom Brown tell him I said he'd better keep his wife off of Mr. Frisco's cars (ha ha). I am glad you like the grades, and I will try to send some just as good the next time and you might tell Mrs. Abby that I do take Education—it is the psychology of education. I made the highest mark in three sections in this subject and like it very much.

Thanks for the news. I'll try to send you some soon for there's nothing going on just now.

Yours as ever,
Ralph
Oklahoma City, OKla.

---

* This undated letter from Ralph was perhaps written in response to John Bell's of February 5, 1934. In it Bell tells Ralph that he started a job on January 28, 1934, "working for Mr. Boland in the Oklahoma Club. I give rubdowns both massage and hycloric. When I learn it thoroughly it will be a real trade, you know there is a demand for anyone that knows the trade. Dr. Boland said he was going to teach it all to me. . . . I really have a heart. I'm in sympathy with you." John Bell then signs off, "Let me hear from you, your step Dad and friend, John Bell." For a sense of Bell's affection, admiration, and generosity toward Ralph, see the November 3, 1934, letter that follows from Bell.

Oklahoma City, Okla.

11 – 3 1934

Mr. Ralph Waldo Ellison.—

Dear Ralph,

I rec'd your postal you wrote from Chicago. Very glad to hear from you. Am sure you enjoyed your trip while there. So sorry you are not able to do the thing you desire, in fact the things your talent beckons you to do. I really know you have the talent for music, being an instructor for some big hit to Broadway. I know you could be it if you had the Finance to be it with, and I only wish I was able to put you through for I know you have the Vim and Courage. A person takes the chance, as you did when you left home without anything to go upon, sure needs a helping hand. I don't believe in so much sympathy because that don't feed or clothe you. Why I say that, there is so many people [who] speak encouraging for you but never show they are willing to do anything. Like everything now all I can say stay as long as you can. When you can't stay any longer you are welcome back home. Listen Ralph when they require you to discontinue in School, the School is compelled to give you your fare back home aren't they? If not let me know so I can ask out for that. For I wouldn't want you to ride back like you went. I hope nothing like that won't occur. Everybody is feeling very well. Hope you are feeling fine and your Stomach don't give you any more trouble. The Douglas High School Boys went to Tulsa today to play football. Ralph, the Douglas School is some nice School as far as I've seen. I haven't been all through it. Cab Calloway and his Cotton Club show is here at the Warner Theatre. We have another Big Store here in town, the name of it is J.C. Penny. I'm sure you know they have a string of stores. Excuse me for changing ink. I started this letter before I set off from work. Oklahoma City hasn't changed. Only have the new Santa Fe Depot finished it. Very nice. I know by this time the old town would look good to you, after staying off so long. Your Mother sends Love and for you to write her. I see Tom Brown and his family every once in a while, they all are well. Herbert is helping around Jim Randolph, also he still have a little job at Glaubers cleaning up. We don't have more East Fourth Car line, they have taken it and Running Busses instead. I belong to the aging Choir at Avery Chapel, Dr. Haywood is still chorister and he still keeps time with the music with his whole body (smile). I guess I've said enough for this time. I remain as ever a friend and Stepfather,

John Bell
812 N Stonewall

Here is a little Souvenir $1.00 for you. I wish it was $100.00. I hope you will enjoy it.

To Ida Bell
TUSKEGEE INST
JAN 3, 1935

Happy New Year Mamma,

And I hope it brings you much joy and happiness. I received your letter and its much content. Thanks very much. Things were very dull here so I spent most of my time with my Music being very glad when school started. I received both of the nice cards, they cheered me up quite a bit. I don't get the paper anymore so you'll have to let me know what's going on there. I heard from Mr. Hebestreit, you know, the German music teacher. You didn't tell me anything of Malcolm. How did you all spend the holidays, Herbert, Mr. Bell? I hope he will find a job soon and that there was some way I might help but the Lord will make a way I'm sure. I'll write more next time. I don't feel so good tonight. Be good and give my love to the boys.

Love
Ralph

To Ida Bell
TUSKEGEE INST ALA.
JAN 13, 1935

Dear Mama

Was very glad to receive your last letter. I enjoyed it very much. I am glad that the Harrises are moving with you, I think this was a gift from God. I was worried about you and feel better now that I know you are able to get along. I received a card from Maxine and Malcolm, and Dyes, I was trying to tell you last time that I received a card from Mr. Hebestreit, the German Music teacher. You know I didn't remember your birthday but I would like to see your hair. What do you think has caused it to change? Can't you have Mr. Berman make a good picture for me. I would like to have a good large one of you. When you receive my grades, please send them to me. I want to save them. I stay busy now with my lessons, and spend all my time either in some class or practice room. I work at night and am studying French, in my spare time, with Mr. Williams. He is about the only person I spend any time with other than Hazel Harrison, the head of the piano dept. These are the two most interesting people down here and both mean a lot to my development. They both want to know you and I am sure both would be well liked by you.

I didn't get Herbert's letter until today but he writes that he is out of school. Why is he out and what is he doing now? I haven't heard from Miss Harris or Mrs. Cook yet but maybe I will later on. Did Mr. Bell get his job? It was too bad about Dorothy Cox. I thought she was all well and then came the news that she was dead. I am glad to hear that the Randolphs are well and I hope that will remain so. Tell the Harrises hello for me and I hope every thing will run smoothly and well.

Please try to send me a pair of gray checked or plaid pants—get the kind called "slacks" at May's if possible. Ask for Sol May and tell him you're my Mother and ask to see a good pair. You know they will have to last a long time (smile). Please send as soon as possible, the only ones I have left are growing thin and I can't wear my uniform trousers because they have stripes upon them.

I hope you won't work too hard and will keep well for me!

Love,
Ralph

To Ida Bell
TUSKEGEE INST ALA
FEB 1, 1935

Dear Mama,

I received your letter and my box the other day and I was very much pleased with it. Every thing was fine but the pants which are too tight in the legs and waist. The shoes, socks and sweater I am wearing every day but I am sending the pants to be changed. I'm sorry to cause you this extra trouble but I couldn't do anything with these because they can't be let out enough. I will send my measurements enclosed. I have been fairly well this week, but last week my stomach was out of order. There is nothing of interest here at this time but a few basketball games.

I am kept busy with my music and work from eight am to nine p.m. every day and of course the band work is included. Mr. Williams received your letter. How is Herbert? Tell Mr. Bell thanks for me and tell him I will write soon. Are you well? Please don't work too hard—it isn't worth it. Give my regards to the Harrises and my friends if I have any left, smile. Be good and pray!

Love,
Ralph

To Ida Bell
TUSKEGEE INST ALA.
APRIL 27, 1935

Dear Mama,

I must ask forgiveness for not writing sooner. The picture is the most appreciated thing you have sent since I've been here. I showed it to Walter and Hazel Harrison and they both think it, and you to be quite nice with the gray hair. It was a surprise because I couldn't imagine what it was, and when you looked up at me from the frame—well I felt very strange, it was the next best thing to seeing you. I am busy as usual. I am getting ready for the spring recital and that means hard work added to this I have already but just one more month of it and then it's all over. I wish you would tell Mary Lee that I had forgotten her, and hoped she had forgotten we had ever known each other. I have had no pictures made since coming here and have sent no one pictures of myself. My first year here, as I remember, Vivian sent me a picture of herself but I had forgotten since it stays always in my trunk.

When I do have pictures made, if ever I do, and I hope I shall, you shall be the one it's for, not Vivian.

The coat arrived, and need I say in time? It is a bit too large but I have found a student tailor who can cut it down to fit my five foot ten, and hundred sixty pounds. Give Wyatt my thanks and best wishes and Mrs. Slaughter and Sis likewise. The spring is beautiful here as always and the air is filled with the scent of honeysuckle while the nights are filled with singing voices of mocking birds Just why they wait till night to sing I cannot say but one waking in the early morning would think it long past noon day. I hope you are successful in getting Herbert in Hampton this year, however don't try to send him here because he would be unhappy here and the trades dept. is rotten! I am sending a program of last Sun. enclosed. Show it [to] Herbert and Mr. Bell. Please tell them hello for me. I must try to write them before school is out. I must close now and thanks again for the picture. I think it will help me to keep my balance. Be good.

Ralph W. Ellison

To Ida Bell
TUSKEGEE INST. ALA.
MAY 27, 1935

Dear Mama;

This is the first chance I've had to answer your letter. The closing days of school found me very busy trying to finish my examinations and fill all my engagements with the band and brass quartet. However I finished successfully and tonight I am at work at the library. I wanted to come home to see you this summer but it would not be the best thing just now because I could not make any money there and if I should leave here I would be unable to return. I don't know just what my plans for next term will be but I shall let you know in two months at the least. There are possibilities that I won't stay here next year at all but shall wait until I am better informed before I can tell you more. Although they made a mistake and mentioned me as a freshman in the new catalogue, I am a junior and have only two years before I receive my degree. I would like very much to see you and the others but I don't think I want to stay in Oklahoma City very long anymore. I don't think I would enjoy it very much. This is a lonesome place as there are fewer people here now than last year this time and they are still leaving. I haven't been down to Pensacola yet but I hope to make it later on. There is something about the place that has tied itself to me and I can't forget. Maybe it was because I was so tired of this place when I went down there and was so very glad to get away for a few days. Are you still having the terrible dust-outs there? Here it is acting very strangely; the days are very hot as is normal, but the nights are cold as those of Denver, and quite a number of us are suffering from colds and this one I have is extremely unpleasant. What's going on out there? You quit writing after you sent the picture, which was very nice but you know even your picture won't talk and it's lonesome down here! Has Herbert grown anymore? Does he have any kind of a job? How is Mr. Bell and the Harrises? Find out who sent me an invitation to the "prom." It was sent from 521 No Laird but I don't know anyone who would live there. Tell Saretta that I met a Hattie Diffay who knows her and that I think this Hattie is some girl (smile). Where is

Frank Mead and his mother? If you received my grades for last quarter will you send them by return mail and I don't have any underwear or pajamas. Thanks for the one spot in the last letter and please answer soon.

Ralph W. Ellison

To Vivian Steveson
P.S. You might surprise me and send a snapshot?
TUSKEGEE INST ALA.
JUNE 1, 1935

Dear Vivian;*

Had I more faith in certain phenomena I should not have been surprised to receive your letter, but as it were I was not faithful and so, was surprised. Some times it pays to give heed to little "feelings." Well, Miss, this is the month of brides and beautiful dreams of happy endings of a spiritual nature to pacts usually inspired by fleshy stimulation. But despite the endings, the brides, even the ugly ones, seem beautiful, glowing with the charm of them who heed Cupid's spell. Beware Vivian, June is a month to watch. Some one might lead you to the altar or whatever it is they lead one to. By the way, don't expect my spelling to improve, it won't; I'm too lazy. Right now this is the most boresome place you can imagine. Most of the students have gone and the same is true of the teachers. Living at such a high nervous tension during the term makes it very hard to adjust one's self when the sound and fury of school is over. Had I the courage, off I would go on one wild spree to quiet my nerves. Next week I hope to write you from that place, which, warmed by the sun and cooled by the Gulf's sweet breeze, to me is heaven. Really I think its quite unfair that all whom I know and like and all who think the same of me, and all the bored people in boresome towns, can't find their way with me to Pensacola town.

There is something healing about the sea I think, as others, something charming that makes one forget all he would forget and fills his mind with that which is the sea. There I hope to bathe in the lagoon at midnight with just enough of Italy's wine to keep me warm, and make more real the gleam of tiny phosphorescent lights which dot the water where it is disturbed. Forgive me if I have been guilty of boring, you must learn to love a place before you understand my crazy yearnings.

* Ralph's one surviving letter to Vivian Steveson, his old flame in Oklahoma City.

Tis very still as I sit here and write as though they who frequent here-abouts to seek the wisdom old and new had found them better ways to spend the sultry afternoon, but let them go, I'll sit and try to write you of this place we call the South's great pride. I finished up my work and was, I think, successful in my quest and now I'm tired. You write I am a stranger to you, and I must say that you are that to me. But I don't think we are the strangers we will be when once again we shall finally meet. I had tried to make some things easy for you when I did know things which knowing I wished I had never had the luck to know but since you choose, and influenced by me, to wake the dog who soon forgot his bone he lost, in sleep, tis well. Through you all I know of sleeping fitfully, then would you gladly let me lie asleep. I find myself often thinking of you and will I see you yet again, or will each new year find me still more distant than the last and the last more stranger than the first!

I wrote last time that would not find myself that way in spite of mama's strong desire that I should cloud her door again. Perhaps next year will find me there, but this has not revealed its will. I shall let you know in time should I not be here, my stomach is still bad and has me eating first one meal in just one day when [I'd] like so much to digest three (smile). I don't know what to write about just now. But please don't write of Fergeson to me. I have reason to find it's quite odious and think the sum of what I know to unfitting both to yourself and to me.

Write me wherein lies your main delights because only in such case [can] we keep friendship and I will learn enough to try to understand. My latest love is modeling at which I have been successful enough to have offers to sell pieces to the Motons and others. This piece is a woman's head done in plaster. I have tried to express myself in this art and people <u>here</u> think I have talent for it but in spite of all Music remains my love, Be good,

Ralph

To Ida Bell
[OCT. 1935]
TUSKEGEE INST. ALA.

Dear Mama,

I received [your] letter and was very pleased with it. I am glad that you and the rest are well and still able to look forward to tomorrow with confidence. I myself am fairly well but I suffer with those colds in the head again, and I think I will have to start using a spray if they don't stop soon.

I am glad to hear that Mr. Bell is working again. I hope he will find a better job soon because he does deserve one.

I received the pants and I like them very much. They fit and are just the kind I need. You know I'll have to wear them every day. I am sorry to hear Mrs. Slaughter is ill, if you see her tell her hello for me. I am sorry Mrs. Breaux got the grades because they will expect too much when I do come back there and I am still the lazy good-for-nothing I was when I left. You see I won't even take time to spell (smile). But if what she did will inspire some of the boys, well, I am glad to be of some use although it will be a long time before I even start to satisfying myself.

Is this Christeen, the same person who was given to the white lady? Write and tell me all about her and your uncle. You know I have the idea that he is a very light man. If I get a chance to go to Atlanta I will look her up. I stay busy but not so much that [you] have to fear for my health. I work from six thirty to nine at night and the rest of the time I go to school and practice. It keeps me busy and leads me to stay up late to read or to talk. You know they serve breakfast at 6:30 so I have eaten before 12:00 in a long time. Most of the time I only eat one meal a day, it's all I can do to digest it since the food is so coarse. Mr. Williams usually invites me up to drink milk or chocolate and to eat a snack after work. Friendships between members of the faculty and students are frowned upon here but we don't let that stop us, I was able to learn a lot from him that I won't get in the classroom, and besides we like the same things, books, music, poetry, pictures, etc.

Old Son doubtlessly feels someone will steal Bert (ha ha). Tell all the folks hello for me, and tell Herbert to write me why he wants to leave home and give up school. Be good and stay good and thanks for the stamps.

Love
Ralph

To Ida Bell
TUSKEGEE INSTITUTE
JAN. 2, 1936

Dear Mama;

I guess you think I forgotten your address, or that something just as bad has happened but I hasten to assure you that this isn't quite the case. I haven't written because I have not had anything to say that would make things seem brighter. I received the paper and mailed it back so I hope you have received it by now. One of the school officials is trying to see that I be allowed to stay here and enter my classes but I won't know how it will come out until after these holidays are over. I have been ill and spent most of the holiday in bed; even today finds me there, so you can guess what Christmas has meant to me. I asked you, Mama, to see Mrs. Breaux about the state aid, not Mrs. Haywood who doesn't know what she is talking about. You needn't say anything to Mrs. Breaux now or anyone else because I'm seeing to it myself. Next time please see the persons I ask you to if possible; if not don't see anyone as I have reasons when I do ask you to do something of the kind. I do hope you all are well and I wish you all the best things for this new year. Don't worry about me as I feel better and I think that as soon as I am able to study again I will feel fine

Yours as ever
Ralph

To Ida Bell
Tuskegee Institute
JAN 12 1936

Dear Mama;

At last time permits me to answer your letter. I am feeling better now than last time I wrote but of course the old stomach still lets me know its very tender; so much so that I don't eat meat anymore. And now a bit of good news: I have been allowed to enter the college again and I am attending classes. However there is a catch because I entered so late I won't be given credit for the work I do when I take examinations it next year. Dr. Patterson, the president here, is trying to secure a loan from the school to me, for money to finish without any interruption. If he is successful I will have to pay the school after graduation. He is working on my case now and in the meantime he gave orders for me to be allowed to attend school. I told you Mrs. Haywood didn't know what she was talking about. I wrote Mr. Dunjee about the matter and he attended to it. He had Mr. Duncan send me a new application that I am to send back as soon as possible. I hope this goes through because I need all the money I can get my hands on. My shoes are all wore out and there are other things I need. I appreciate all you are doing and trying to do but you mustn't worry about me. Thanks for the dollars, they always come in at the right time. I heard from Maybelle just about the time I received your last letter. She is well and wanted to know how I am getting along, and she also asked about you and the others. I will write you how everything turns out here so let's hope it will all be good, or at least, for the best.

How are you and Herbert and Mr. Bell? Well I hope. Here the weather, for the last ten days, has been like early spring, and the same might be said of the nights. I didn't have money to send cards this year but I did receive about five, one from Maxine. Will you do this, please ask Herbert to ask her for the books I loaned her. They are valuable and I wouldn't like to lose them. Thanks. I must close. I have lessons to get now, so answer soon.

Ralph

To Ida Bell
TUSKEGEE INSTITUTE
FEB. 26, 1936*

Dear Mama,

I was very glad to receive such a swell present. It was quite unexpected and I couldn't guess what on earth the box contained.

It is really too nice for the room in which I live. It came in handy this week because it turned cold after a heavy rain, and now it isn't necessary to use my overcoat on my feet.

How are things there, the people and all. The examinations have started and I feel funny since I don't have to take them, and I wish I had to.

Things are quite dry and I spend my spare time reading. I shall start collecting books for my personal library as soon as I finish school because books are far better friends than most people. I have one Mr. Williams gave me to start with and it will be worth some money some day as it is a first print.

You know we should be rich because it seems that everything I like to do demands (Money!) (smile).

Did you receive my last letter, the one in which I asked about the shoes?

How is Herbert and Mr. Bell? Did the Branams answer his letter? I wrote them myself but up to now they haven't answered.

Where did you get the picture? I wasn't sure whether you had it or Vivian. Now I am glad you do and thanks a lot for the print.

---

* This letter was dated "Feb. 26, 1933"—obviously the wrong date because Ellison was not at Tuskegee until June 1933. Because of his concern about shoes in his letter of January 12, 1936, we are dating this one 1936.

Tell Mr. John I hope he is well and lucky. Remember school starts on the fifth and I'll have to be registered by then. I hope you are keeping well strong. Be good.

Your Son
Ralph W Ellison

Tuskegee Institute Ala
APRIL 29, 1936

Dear Herbert,

I was very glad to hear from you in spite of owing you a letter for last time. However I think you understand how busy and lazy I am during this season. Are you sure you saw me in the picture? I wasn't playing cornet but was back in the drum section. I am the second fellow and only my head is shown. Is that where you saw me, if not look again for that is where I am. I wish you could have heard us that night. I'm sure you would have enjoyed it as the music was beautiful and the choir at its best.

You ask about those pictures, and I am sorry to say that I don't have them yet. However, once they are photographed I shall send them to you. Sculpture is very difficult to photograph and though one piece has been attempted it was unsuccessful. No I am not in the school of music this year. I missed out because of many matters, and have had to take the regular college course. It was a bitter pill to take at first, but as with everything else I became used to it and now the time I put on arts and other things. Too bad about Lloyd isn't it? Tell Whit I have a reason for not writing him but expect a letter soon. I noticed how much you had improved in your last letter; that's fine but watch your tenses and endings, don't write fool when you mean fooling or fooled. All it takes is time and good habits. Make good habit and it is as strong as a bad one. I was in Atlanta last month and I learned Walter Sneed was thrown out of school for not attending classes. He did not finish. Don't be so hard on the gals. Just remember they are silly at best. Yes I saw Dr. Haygood and Reggie while they were here. Have you decided about Cleveland? How will you work? I am glad that Mama is working and I hope you will find a job when school is out. I will write and let you know where I shall be this summer. I don't intend to come home however. Tell Frank hello if you see him, and for the last time what about my books?

So long till
next time
Ralph W. Ellison

To Ida Bell
TUSKEGEE INSTITUTE ALA
MAY 18, 1936

Dear Mama

I suppose you wonder what has happened to me for the last month. Much to tell the truth I have been busy preparing for and taking examinations. I am glad to say I was successful. Too I have been waiting to see if I would be able to give you some idea as to how I would spend the coming vacation. Today finds me just as much in the dark as did a month ago. I want to go to New York and work on the boats but I have been unable to see how I shall live until I am able to find a job. If I stay here I am sure I won't earn very much money as they are no longer paying as they did the last two years. I do know I don't wish to come there for the whole summer! It would kill me. I have been working on a survey with a friend who works in the Records and Reserve dept. (did) and it's been my duty to interview numbers of families that were hit very hard by the depression. If you feel you are having a hard time, just thank God that things aren't as bad as they might be. I know just how bad things can be! I made the dean's list for good grades last quarter and I have reason to believe I shall make it again this quarter as I made, out of the three exams I had to take, two A's and one B. I received the shoes and you don't know how useful they have been these last two weeks. Last Friday we had our Junior-Senior Prom, an affair at which I had a very good time. What plans have you for the summer? I intend writing several schools to see if I can get a scholarship for next year because I don't think Tuskegee's new program will suit people interested in things I am; however, I can't say definitely what I shall do or where I shall be at this time. I would like to go New York; it offers so much I need to help my education. I didn't hear from Dunjee, but the state sent a blank to be filled by the register, however I don't know what will come of it! To date I owe the school $60.00—how I shall pay it I don't know.

How are you and the others still working? I hope all is well. By the way I heard from Mrs. Lewis who sent me a $1.00 bill, she hasn't answered my letter; mention it to her when you write. Herbert also owes me a letter. Try to answer before school is out, and if anything develops I'll write to tell you of it. I hope you are well.

Love,
Ralph

To Ida Bell
JUNE 1, 1936

Dear Mama;

I am very sorry that you are still ill and that you are alarmed because of my little indisposition. It is uncalled for (the alarm, I mean). The tonsils had just gotten to the place where they could remain no longer so they had to come out. Friends arranged for a specialist to do it very cheaply, and this is the best time of year for it. Even though you don't feel that way about it. I'm also sorry that I couldn't come to Dayton,* but you see I'm not that sick and I have a job to hold here. You know I can't run home every time I feel bad. Gee but you got excited over nothing.

I think we had reached a final understanding about, Vivian. You seem to feel that I miss her. This is a nice romantic way to have things happen: but in this case it's hardly true to life. There are two or three others who have come my way since she did and I must confess that I miss either of them much more than I ever did miss Vivian, and I would much rather see anyone of them any day than that little lady. You must understand Mama that I don't feel just as you do about things. That which bound me to V is gone and I don't have time to be sentimental about it. Perhaps you'll be disappointed to hear this, but the truth is the truth. My bad feeling and drive to travel come from different sources and have nothing directly to do with anyone but myself, so please don't mention V feeling to me. If she misses me it's best that she forget; I hope she has. Otherwise I'm not interested. As you say I know more about people now. What's more I know more about myself and I must settle my own affairs and alone. Certain things have to happen at just the right time or else they last forever. I hope I've been clear about this. What I said about Ferguson was all in fun, not that I didn't believe what I said, but you see I had no feelings one way or the other about the matter.

I hope you're better by this time and you must take care of yourself. So with no hard feeling, I'll stop till next time.

Ralph

---

* This is the first mention of Ida's going to Dayton. She and Herbert had moved to Cleveland in early spring, and quickly moved on. Mr. Bell stayed in Oklahoma City for unspecified reasons.

To Langston Hughes

JULY 17, 1936

Dear Langston Hughes,[*]

This is just to follow up the little job I did for you. I delivered the M.S. and left your visa restrictions. I mailed the wrapped books, and later, the one I borrowed as well. I trust they arrived safely?

I met Barthé and he has taken me as his first pupil much to my surprise and joy. I had seen one of his pieces before but when I visited his studio I remembered your opinions. There is something there the others don't have.

I'm following your formula with success, you know, "be nice to people and let them pay for meals." It helps so very much. Thus far I've paid for just two dinners and the others check out so late I don't need breakfast leaving only my lunch to be paid for.

I've met a composer, white, whose done an African ballet that he intends doing into a play. He told me that his producer had spoken of having James Weldon Johnson do the book but so far he isn't sure that it will appeal to Johnson and is waiting to see him before going to work; besides he needs lyrics for inspiration and so is tied up until the book is started. Now suppose Johnson can't be had, would you be interested? The fellow's a good friend of Barthé. His name is David Guiney, the composer of Wagon Wheels, Chloe, etc. I'll let you know how the Johnson thing comes out and will have Barthé put him in touch with you if you're interested.

C. Day Lewis[†] has me interested in the left since I found his poetry and essays appealing. Don't be surprised if you see me on a soapbox next time you're here. Let me know if the last book didn't arrive as I had insurance on it.

Ralph Ellison

[*]   Ellison's first letter from New York, written to Langston Hughes, whom he encountered in the Harlem YMCA on July 5, 1936, the morning he arrived from Tuskegee.

[†]   C. Day Lewis (1904–72) was an Anglo-Irish poet whose poetry, especially in the thirties, fused a lyrical voice with a politics of radical reform.

To Ida Bell

SEPT. 3, 1936

Dear Mama;

IT is very pleasant hearing from you after such a long silence. Herbert told that you had been very busy so I understood why didn't write sooner. I am glad to know you both are working and that you like Dayton.

As I told Herbert, I am working and studying. When I arrived I had letters to one art teacher and many friends of a friend of mine at Tuskegee, and too, I had few dollars in my pockets. I registered at the YMCA and spent the first week looking for a job. In the meantime I got in touch with the artist, Augusta Savage is her name, who offered to let me work at her studio, but was too busy to give much instruction. I was very thankful for this and resumed looking for that much needed job. The second week found me working extra at the YMCA cafeteria at two dollars a day.

It was while working here that I met Langston Hughes the writer who was living at the Y, and he told me that he wished me to know Barthé, the sculptor. I then remembered that I knew Barthé through correspondence and that he had sent me pictures of his work etc. . . . I found his address and went down to see him. We talked all of eight hours the first evening and in no time we felt like old friends. He saw pictures of my things and because they have feeling in them, he offered to teach me. Since I admired his work more than I did Miss Savage's, and since he had more time to teach I took his offer. Later on the work at the Y became too nasty and took up too much time; so he started asking his friends about a job for me. As luck would have it he found one right off. I quit the Y and I now work for a well-known Dr.* I work from eight thirty until one o'clock, and use the rest of my day working at sculpture. I have only to keep people from disturbing DR. Sullivan, to answer all phone calls and keep his appointments straight. It is a very pleasant job, and my boss is very nice. He has helped many Negroes along, and upon learning of my interest in music he offered to help pay for my instruction as soon as he clears some of the debts he has incurred in buying and rebuilding this

---

* Dr. Harry Stack Sullivan, the renowned and well-respected New York psychiatrist to whom sculptor Richmond Barthé recommended Ralph. Hired as a receptionist, Ralph did more than just reception work, including making editorial suggestions on excerpts from the book Sullivan was writing. Sullivan was respected for his dedication and generosity to the people of Harlem, as well as for his reputation in the psychiatric community.

residence, which by the way is one of the finest I've ever been in. Just now I get $12.50 per every five days which isn't bad, recently I moved into the studio with Barthé, with whom I share expenses. Food here is very high but now I'm here, Barthé uses some of the knowledge learned while a butler in New Orleans and cooks for the two of us, and let me add that he does a good job of it. So you can see that things aren't as bad with me as they might be.

You asked if I had seen Walter yet. Yes I have. He was in Albany when I arrived, came down later. He refuses to return to school though they want him to, and this in face of the fact that he has no work. He would rather starve than return to live in that hell again, and though Walt is like a child I can understand how he feels about the place. He did some very fine work down there that wasn't at all appreciated. He is all down in the mouth because he is out of work and left here, where he was living with relatives, to return to Albany. In the mean time we are looking out for a job for him, and I think he will have something pretty soon. I hope so because I would like to return some of the many favors he did me in Ala.

I don't think it is likely that I return to Tuskegee this year as I don't have the money necessary and I am yet in their debt up to $60.00, and I feel a year away will do me good. I hate the people down there anyway.

I'm gaining weight, 170 lbs. now. How's that for one who came here to starve? I keep busy all day, but at night we attend plays or movies. Visiting some of Barthé's friends or reading takes up the rest of the time.

Jewel James is here studying the dance and her mother was here for a visit. Then there was Maxine, Tom, and Hetty who passed through on their way from Canada. They were very surprised to see me and still more so when they learned that I was studying Sculpture. They seemed well.

I must stop now, so write about these new found people of ours, I can't get anything out of Herbert other than that they are cousins, two of whom are in business.

Are you living at a different address from his? Tell me everything.

Love,
Ralph

P.S. I hope you can read this awful typing. I'll learn soon though!

To Hazel Harrison
236 W. 14TH ST.
NEW YORK CITY
OCT 23 1936

Dear Friend:[*]

I am very pleased that you liked the little head and that you noticed the improvement in my work. Dr. Locke was in for a moment last week and gave me your message. He also looked at the piece saying a few kind things about it. I have reasons to respect his judgment and I hope to have things to show him on future visits.

I followed your advice concerning Mrs. Patterson even to sending the snaps. Please inquire in your next letter if she received them as something seems to happen to most of the letters I mail down there I would appreciate any opportunity to have that hole investigated.

No I am not studying with Pious, but I do see him sometimes. I had planned to study with him but that was before I met Barthé[†] who is making me draw as well as sculpt. Frankly I have paid no attention to Dr. Curtis's letter. When I first arrived Pious was one of the few Negro artists whom I met. He gave me advice that helped me to avoid many insincere Harlemites, and had much to do with my casting my lot with Barthé. He himself is one of the most sincere people I've ever met and is sure, in time, to make a name for himself. Whenever two people fall out I think it a good idea to hear both sides before forming an opinion. I heard Pious' side and I feel that you won't think him such a blackguard once you are aware of the causes behind his actions. All I feel free to say here is that his being married caused a great deal of the trouble, in fact most of it, though it should not have, had certain people been wise enough to leave the man's private life alone. Gee it seems my morning to disagree with you. However I don't agree that character isn't reflected in drawing and modeling as in music. If you'll reflect, you will remember that some of the products of these two arts are cold while others are warm, some trite while others profound. Even when they are treated in a pictorial sense they reveal

---

[*] Hazel Harrison, the renowned classical pianist, was the head of the Music Department and a teacher of Ralph's at Tuskegee; she was also his mentor and friend.

[†] Richmond Barthé, the up-and-coming sculptor to whom Langston Hughes recommended Ralph as a student.

much of the artist, a painter does more than just draw lines and play with light and shadow, he reveals himself in the amount of meaning he reveals in his work. One painter might paint a landscape and produce a lifeless, meaningless scene, while another because he understands, and feels the greatness and enigmatical intelligence of the force which arranged the composition, will catch some of this in his lights and lines and transmit it to those who review his picture. An artist must with objective materials produce a correlative for the particular emotion that he wishes to arouse, and I don't feel that he can do this successfully unless his intelligence and instinct makes him aware of the meaning behind these emotions.* As I write I can't remember of having ever heard "stingy" or "mean" music although I have heard music that was poor and shallow, and empty and meaningless. This is true of some compositions as well as of some inter- pretations of compositions of which the above most certainly cannot be said. After saying all this I wonder if the artist isn't above this character thing? Character evaluation grows out of environment and environments are temporary and ever changing while it is the aim of the true artist to be infinite through the universality of his art. And too we must remem- ber that though the artist who goes in for Bohemianism is living up to a certain conventionality that governs his own small group even if he does detach himself from the conventions and moral standards of middle class and Puritan ideal groups.†

To Ida Bell

DEC. 1, 1936

Dear Mama;

I received your very interesting letter some time ago, but unexpected events arising have kept me too busy to get much writing done. I have been looking for a new place to live and have not had much luck. The stu- dio is becoming too crowded for Barthé and myself so it is necessary that I move, and the problem comes in that I am trying to find another place near this one so that I might be near my job and here where I study. It is

---

* Ellison's early concern with composition suggests James Joyce as a possible influence on his developing artistic sensibility, especially Stephen Dedalus's aesthetic speculations in the last chapter of *A Portrait of the Artist as a Young Man.*

† This letter was unsigned but likely sent.

in a white neighborhood and it is very difficult for a Negro to find a place. So far nothing has turned up, but some of my Jewish friends want me to go in with them and take a large apartment. I don't know whether we will do it or not, but at any rate I am going to move sometime this month and I will let you know the new address.

Herbert will get over his love affair most likely and I wouldn't worry about his not going to church if he is living a straight life. I guess he is pretty sick of his relatives, but he must learn to overlook their smallness and be larger than them. I guess he is like myself in that if I don't like you, your age don't count at all; it is really funny. Maybe the girl "done him wrong." So far I've had no time for love affairs, and most of the women whom I know are much older than myself and though I admire two of them a great deal, I wouldn't think of them otherwise. I might as well tell you that one of them, as are many of my friends here, is white. Both are very smart people and I'm sure you would like them . . . Speaking of marriage; I hope some day to marry but that day is, I hope, a long way off. I must learn to earn a living first and have finished my formal education. To get married without some income would mean to fail before I started out; besides I have yet to meet a person whom I could live with every day of my life.

I am very sorry about the picture and I will have another print made and send it to you. The postal department would do nothing about it here and it was not insured. Has Herbert received the one I sent him? Perhaps the hair is not so bad as I had thought, and brushing did have something to do with it.

I hope you do go to Cleveland in the spring it is a much more liberal place to live than Dayton . . . Did Mr. Bell arrive?

I was very sorry to hear of Mrs. Whitby's death. I don't hear from Okla any more and so had had no word of it. I have written Mrs. Breaux but as she didn't answer I did not waste more stamps. I find that most people are interested in you only when you are close by and able to help them in some manner. I might send them Xmas cards. At first I was able to save 2.00 a week, but now things are so high that it takes all I earn to live on. However I still have a few cents left in the bank.

Thanks very much for the information about Daddy and the plays. I found it all very interesting and can understand why I have a tendency to buy books I can't afford; only last week I had to do without food because I bought a book the day before pay day. A woman whom I know and who is interested in hands tells me that there has been a very famous surgeon in my family strain somewhere, and though I don't believe in that kind of thing I promised to ask if you knew anything of it. I told her if it were true it must have been some of the whites who are mixed in the family. How much of the Ellison gang were white, if any? I doubt if you two got your genius but every one thinks I'm a little odd and a bit gifted, and though I can't see it just now, they think I shall be successful. I have starting taking music lessons again, and I feel much better for having done so.

I have seen a few plays this season and a friend gives me free tickets to concerts so I manage to entertain myself. Money is the big problem here as everywhere and I don't see half the things I would like to.

Please let me hear from you soon. I must close for it is now time to leave here. Give my love to the others and tell Herbert to forget that shameless woman (ha, ha).

Love,
Ralph

To Ida Bell

APRIL 20, 1937

Dear Mama,

It seems the Spring has come to New York at last, and no one seems to object to its arrival, though for myself I feel it will be a very uncomfortable time. Closed up in [a] factory nine hours out of twenty-four is bad enough when there is the frost, the wind and rain outside, but to stand inside and look at the ships sailing up the East River as it sparkles in the sunlight, and all the birds flying and birds singing and with memories burning in my head like molten lead, it is apt to being the hellish season. Sometimes I wish I had the nerve to go on and take a boat and go until I grow tired. Daddy no doubt felt the same way when he ran off to the army, and so did Langston. I don't think it's lack of nerve that holds me back for I find myself fighting to stay put. Nor is it only in the Spring I feel these impulses, but in the dead of winter, at parties, when walking along the streets, early in the morning and in the dead of night. Especially in the night. Nights on which the skies remind me of southern moons which used to turn me soft inside. Sometimes I wonder if I shall ever grow out of this way of feeling about things. For so far there seems to be no hope. I had a long talk with Langston about it, in fact we had many talks and he tells me there is no use, and isn't even to be desired. He said he had the same trouble and was surprised to discover I was going through the same experience. I suppose this has made us friends, all for which I am very glad. You see in spite of my confidence in desiring to become a musician, so many things happened in school and here that I've become a little bewildered. And the urge I feel within seems not to fade away but become more insistent for expression, and I have yet to discover just what form it will take. Let us hope I shall soon find myself. This state of things leaves me very worried and unhappy.

Tell me how things are going out there and why Herbert is out of work. I received the Easter greeting with much pleasure. Too I heard from Maybelle last week. She asked me to come to Detroit and live with her but that is out of the question. I shall write her soon. She gave me the address of some of the Ellisons but I haven't had time to look them up.

I don't know what to think of Mr. John, perhaps he will show up soon. Nor do I remember the Koste you wrote about. Who was he?

Try and answer soon and forgive me if I don't write as often as before because this job takes quite a bit from me. Nights find me asleep as soon as I enter my room.

Goodbye and watch out for the spring fever.

Ralph

To Folks

Dear Folks.* I know I have waited a terribly long time to answer your letters. But right after I went back to work, the paint factory† went out on strike and it kept me busy. Now, however, we are back to work with a union and things are improved. The operation was successful and already I am reaping its benefits.‡ Langston just sailed and I am returning home from seeing him off. If my plans work out I shall be out there before I take a job on a boat, if I get it. I will write you about this later. It seems I just must do it. Be good and don't worry. Ralph§

---

* "Folks" refers to close family and friends in Oklahoma City. This letter is undated, but if the Hughes reference is accurate, it was probably written early in July 1937.

† When Ellison's job with Dr. Sullivan ended at the close of 1936, the father of one of Dr. Sullivan's patients got him hired as a laboratory assistant at the A. C. Horn Paint Company. The Long Island paint factory later provided a rich seedbed for Invisible Man's experiences in chapter 10 of *Invisible Man*.

‡ Perhaps Ralph refers to medical treatment for his acute attack of tonsillitis that spring.

§ See references to the job on the boat in the August 5, 1937, letter to his younger brother, Herbert.

To Herbert Ellison
AUGUST 5, 1937

Dear Herbert;

You confuse me with all these letters, one today and one last night. You ask me to come there and help you. That I would like very much to do, but don't you remember that I wrote you that I was out of work and now I've been thrown out of my room for non payment of rent. I haven't worked in almost a month, and the government won't give the papers to take the job on the boat. They are holding up all fellows my age because they think we are going to Spain.

Now you might as well understand this; I've told you the truth. I have no money and am dependent on Langston's aunt and uncle for the very food I eat; secondly, if I came to Dayton would things be any better? Do you have a job for me, could you feed me if I came there? How would I get there anyway?

You must understand this, Herbert. I know people here who are trying to get me a job and I am still trying to get a job on that boat, but I can't get the job without the proper papers. I can't take the papers if they won't give them to me. Please take time and tell me just what is wrong with mama.* You said she needs an operation, for what? What are the relatives there doing to help? You must remember that such things as these happen and we have to face them, you should have realized that when you undertook to leave Oklahoma City. Where is John Bell? Have you written him? Tell mama to write me herself and tell me what has happened. I feel bad as hell because there is nothing I can do to help just now but it's a fact. I spent what money I had in the bank to pay for my operation and my expenses doing the time I was not working. If coming down there would help things I would come by freight; but it won't and I have better chances here where people know me and are interested in me than there where I am unknown. I am trying to find work, and when I do I shall send

---

* Ida had taken a severe, painful fall shortly after Herbert wrote Ralph. Yet her letter of August 10 is very different from Herbert's: "I don't have to have an operation," she writes. "I didn't know what Herbert wrote you. I have a strained ligament and Rhm from bad teeth and last Sunday night I slipped on the steps and sat down on one hip and that is why I can't walk and this is why I am feeling so much better today and I think I will be up and round real soon now. . . . I do wish it was so you could visit with us. . . . I haven't had a letter from him (John) since May. . . . I don't want to see him again. . . . When you can, come see us. I am better. Lots of love."

you some money. However I can't send that which I don't have. This is just one of those things wherein everything goes bad at the same time and becoming excited wont help matters a bit. So take your time and write me just what is wrong and all the latest developments, and don't waste your paper telling me that I have to come down there; I'd like to but that takes money and as I've told you I'm broke!

Tell mama not to worry, it won't do any good, and to write me herself. I'm very sorry I have no money to send but until I find a job it will have to be so.

Your Brother
Ralph

To Ida Bell
MONDAY, AUGUST 30, 1937

Dear Mama,

I haven't written because there really hasn't been anything new to write about. I am still living with Lang's aunt, but since her fall season has started I fear I'll have to find another place to stay. She is a very busy dressmaker, and people come in at all hours making my presence some-what an inconvenience. They thought I would have had the job on the boat long before now, so I can't impose on them much longer. The job has failed to materialize due to the strike situation and I have no idea as to when it will. In the meantime I am trying to go on relief in order to get a job on the W.P.A. This has its own set of difficulties, the most important of which is to establish residence. I received your letter with the dollar which certainly was needed but you must not try to send me anything as long you yourself are unable to work . . .

I am very disgusted with things as they are and the whole system in which we live. This system which offers a poor person practically noth-ing but work for a low wage from birth to death; and thousands of us are hungry half of our lives. I find myself wishing that the whole thing would explode so the world could start again from scratch. Now one must have an education in order to get most any job, yet they don't give us opportu-nities to go to school. Look at your own life. You've lived these years since Dad died toiling from morning to night, toiling and praying from morn-ing to night. From Okla. City to Gary, to Okla, only there was no work in Gary, only prayer and those dimes with the holes which we filled with lead, then to McAlister where things were about as bad, and then back to

Okla. City, and now in Dayton. You've seen Herbert and myself grow up, and neither of us has a job. All those years and all that work, and not even a job to bring a dollar a week. The people in Spain are fighting right now because of just this kind of thing, the people of Russia got tired of seeing the rich have everything and the poor nothing and now they are building a new system. I wish we could live there. And these rich bastards here are trying to take the W.P.A. away from us. They would deny a poor man the right to live in this country for which we have fought and died. You should see New York with its million of unemployed, the people who sleep in the parks and in doorways. The rich old women strolling down Fifth Avenue carrying their dogs which are better cared for than most human beings. Big cars and money to burn and right now I couldn't buy a hot dog. I'm sick thinking of the whole mess and I hope something happens to change it all.

It is rainy weather here and for the last few days the skies have been gray with mist falling whenever it isn't raining. The water lies in puddles and you have to pick your way if the soles of your shoes are not the best. The fall is coming and the boys will soon be returning to school and I hope they leave a few jobs behind. I would like to be in a car riding up through Illo just now while the trees are beginning to turn deep red, and yellow, and purple and you can see the birds flying southward in the distance, soaring away, soaring away, and the apples on the trees, and the hay stacks in the fields. You can see the sun rise in the early morning blending the color of all this foliage into one sparkling mass of natural beauty with the dew upon it all. Sometimes you can see the harvesters already working in the fields and you think of the stories of the big meals they are supposed to serve and eat, and you visualize the big prize pies and home cooked breads, and sometimes you become hungry thinking about it all. Especially when you are hungry as I am now. I missed my lunch.

The city is so different in the fall. The only change here is in the skies which on some days are grey and misty and rainy; and you wonder where the people who sleep in the parks will spend the long night to come, the cold nights to come, and if you'll have to join them.

The kids are now flying kites but they haven't started playing marbles. Those who can afford them are still wearing summer clothing and there is some talk and much talk of hope of buying new overcoats. Over the tops of flats and buildings you can see the kites sailing, and dipping, and rising like gulls riding the wind over a blue gulf, and you can hear the cries of the boys floating down, floating down to the street, like when you were around Look Out Mountain and you heard people climbing above you. On the streets are picket lines of people fighting for higher wages and shorter hours, and when you walk down some of the streets you wonder how some of the people are able to eat. If you walk down Eighth Avenue you can see the curb markets and fruit stores and see food joints and if you come by around mealtime when the poor people are eating you can smell the fish frying and the hog maws and home fries. On the stands you see plenty of tropical fruit: mangoes, guavas and plantains, melons and yams. And on the corners you can buy bananas and fresh fish from vendors of pushcarts. All the fruit and fruit smells and fruit colors become all mixed with smells of washed and unwashed bodies and perfume and hair grease and liquor and the bright and drab colors of dresses and overalls, and that which the dogs leave on the sidewalk. I like to walk on such streets. Life on them is right out in the open and they make no pretense of being what they are not. The whore, the pimp, the ditch digger, the likker head, and the down-and-outer are all here trying to get along. It makes me very angry to think of the causes behind all the misery in the world, and the way it's all concentrated here in Harlem. I hope something happens to change it all.

Please let me hear from you soon, and you must remember not to worry about me. Tell me how your hip is doing and if you are able to walk.

Tonight's the night of the fight between Joe and Farr. Already you can see the excitement rising and the police gathering. Just now a regiment of patrol passed all in blue and yellow trimmed uniforms and you can hear the horses' feet going cloppity clop, cloppity clop on the asphalt sounding all out of place amid the smacking whirr, smack, smack whirr of the rubber tires. Tonight there will be hundreds of cops in Harlem and much shouting of excited Negroes and most of the whites will stay out if Joe loses and if he win, they'll come up to see the fun. I'll write later. So until next time—

Love,
Ralph

P.S,
I heard from Herbert this morning and he told me where you are, and about the policy. So to save it I have put my horn in pawn. I hope it reaches you in time.[*]

Ralph

---

[*] Ellison added this handwritten postscript to the typed version of his letter.

To Ida Bell

Dear Mama;

I haven't written lately because there has been nothing to say. I am still unemployed and walking the street looking for work. It is becoming cool here and the nights come very soon. I often wonder if the winter will catch me still looking for a job. If I had a room of my own, I might go on relief, but just now I am using the living room of some friends, and that is not just the arrangement the E.R.B. considers. Once I do receive relief I have a good chance to go to work on the W.P.A. However none of this will help until it happens.

I heard from Herbert Monday and he was planning to take a job out in the country, or to be exact, ten miles out of town. He did not say just what kind of job it was. I do hope he gets something worthwhile. He told me you were still having a lot of trouble with your hip. I hope it has stopped by now. He still talks about your relatives, whom he doesn't like. He thinks that relatives should be nice generous people. Too bad he had to find them different.

I really have no inspiration this morning so I wont bother you with any such long letter as my last. Herbert called it a <u>book</u> when he wrote me. I will let you know when something turns up, so in the meantime don't worry as I manage to eat and sleep, and even to keep clean. My laundry man stopped me yesterday and got after me for failing to bring in my stuff, each week, and made me promise that I would bring it in today.

Please let me know how you are feeling and write me of any new developments.

Love,

Ralph

To Folks
DAYTON, OHIO
OCT 17, 1937

Dear Folks;[*]

I arrived in Cinn. on Friday[†] at 5:45 p.m. to find my mother leaving and then in such a condition that she was unable to recognize me. At 11:00 o'clock next day she was gone. She was in such pain that she knew no one. It is the worse thing that has ever happened and I can't explain the emptiness. It is difficult to be grown up, and my brother and I are trying very hard to keep things under control. We walked to a movie today and ate candy and talked of old times on the way home. I was very glad the movie was dark.

I should have explained my presence in Dayton. I came up here Sat. night in order to transact the business necessary on such occasions. You must forgive me this disorganization. I shall write you later when all this is over. Then I shall tell you my plans; no doubt I'll return there. This morning we drove out into the country. The trees and hedges were nice in their fall colors. There were many people with baskets of red apples along the road. It was sunny and we passed a Scotty farm. (I almost write Kiltie Farm.) Tonight it is trying to rain; it is fitting.

Baldo Ravel.[‡]

To Richard Wright
OCTOBER 27TH, 1937

Dear Dick;[§]

I have intended to write you for some time but most intentions are neglected in face of death. Even good ones.

I lost my mother the day after I arrived in Cinn. The funeral was over

---

[*] Unidentified family and friends whom Ralph and his mother were close to back in Oklahoma City.

[†] October 15, 1937.

[‡] Perhaps a pun on the kidding Ralph got due to signs of premature baldness.

[§] Richard Wright was on the rise to literary prominence when he and Ellison met and became fast friends in July 1937. At the time Wright had published "Big Boy Leaves Home," which became the lead story in *Uncle Tom's Children* (1938), and was Harlem editor of the *Daily Worker*.

in a week's time and my brother and I are now here in Dayton transacting all final business. This is the end of childhood for both of us. I used to pretend this was so when I came to New York but now I know it was just pretense and nothing more. This is real, and the most final thing I've ever encountered. I feel very sorry for my brother as he has never been away from her before and though he tries to hide it, he is hurt very much. We spend a lot of time at the movie here eating candy like we did quite a while ago and then go along the streets that are very much like those of Oklahoma City, home. I say home because much from Okla is here. Sometimes we kid each other but we avoid talking of certain things and I see that he spends much time away from me so as not to mention these painful things. It is terrible. He needs her very much and I am able to help so little. Too I know that as the pain that holds us becomes a little blunted the antagonism between us will come alive and then things will be very difficult to manage. We are so utterly different.

You must write and tell me of the magazine* and if possible I should like for you to send me copies. It might be that I can secure a few subs. I go down to Cinn. where my aunt lives and I might try there. There is no *Daily* nor *Masses*† to be had here, and I've only today discovered this very old Typewriter. I spend most of my time in the woods that surround the town with a friend's young hound and a 22 rifle. Most of the time it is very cold in the woods and the rabbits stick very close to their beds making it very difficult to see them, so close do they merge into the fall scene. I walk along thinking, rifle ready, eyes supposedly looking for the cotton tailed gents but lost in the color of leaves the variations and designs from which I've been away a long time, then suddenly the sound of fast falling feet and mister rabbit is laying tracks up the hill to beat hell and the bullets which usually I'm unable to send into him. I lack the discipline which enables the eyes to pick the small live black eyes of mister rabbit out of the leaves and grass which are so much like his coat, but in a week or so he'd better beware. And anyway the season will be open then. And I will be able to use a shotgun. But who knows, perhaps I'll be back in New York by that time and someone else will bring these elusive dinners down to dust with metal sticks which roar and into flame do <u>bust</u>. (How's that? mo/Marvel, Eliot, Hemingway.)

---

* *New Challenge*, which had recently published Ellison's first review and to which, at Wright's urging, he submitted his first story, "Hymie's Bull."

† The leftist periodicals *Daily Worker* and *New Masses*.

Yesterday we picked a bushel of pears growing wild in the woods and Sunday we brought in two sacks, "gunny sacks" full of walnuts and fine full flavored butter nuts, which are new to me, and which I find very tasty. I don't hold Rousseau in very high regard but nature in fall dress is nice. You cannot say as in the Spring "Aint Nature grand," but a belly full of apples, pears, and nuts is very swell, and no pun is intended. What are you doing about the girl's girls? Had to give up the type. If the syntax is bad, blame it on my mother's great-aunt who is near a hundred years old and who is trying to tell me of her childhood as I write. She spends most of these days there back in Va. and Georgia. Seems that I come from a line of Niggers that liked to run off to the Yankees. I am unable to decide whether she approved or not. She's a fine old lady and quite spry despite the age. Just now she's telling me (for the fiftieth time) of my Grandma who "always spoke up to the white folks." Dick I feel this a large enough dose of this for you this time, so try to answer soon.

Ralph

To Richard Wright
NOVEMBER 8TH, 1937

Dear Dick;

It was very nice to receive your letter out here in my exile. Yes, in spite of its shortcomings I do miss the old town and the few choice people who go to make up its personality for me. Since I wrote you I have suffered from a severe cold and have found it necessary to give up the woods for a while. When I do go out it is to the village movie and afterwards to either of the two decent eating places of which the town boasts. Here I sit with my brother and a friend and comment upon the approximate pleasure the various maids could bring doing sexercise, and the other more abstract qualities of their beauty. They do have a few very neat looking little ladies hereabouts, and there is one in particular whom I might let run away with my imagination. But you know Dick we live life at its hardest, no illusions, or at least none of the old ones, and its hard to take advantage of naiveté. This little kid is so nice, so brown, so firm and so smilingly naive that I must avoid her or act disgusting to keep my values warm. Gee but its swell to be the man of the world in a small town, and quite, quite amusing.

Sunday I went over to Richmond, Indiana to inquire of the hunting, the season of which opens today, and while there I inquired of the CIO and was asked if that wasn't the railroad. Where in hell is the revolution?

What is going on, all I have here is the *New Republic* and the radio. The village rag carries all the tripe by Tin drawers Pegler, Boake Carter, and Dorothy Thompson, but very little international news. The *D.W.* and *N.M.** is unknown. Speaking of the *D.W.* won't you send me the review of the mag[†] that it carried? I am still waiting on my copy. I have Hem's new book[‡] that I read the first day and regretted it wasn't longer. If you wish to read it let me know.

I think its a goddam shame about your ms. It seems that some of those dam fools would realize that they had something good. Why not try Scribners? Try to stick it out a little longer and remember that though N.Y. is not proving very satisfactory just now it is the best we have and being there does save postage.

I can see you running out on Mr. John Davis's little party. What did happen there? I've scanned the Courier and the Defender but the information was nil. I would like very much to talk with you about the events come to past. What happened to Harry and his wife. The last and the second time she saw me she kissed me. I stopped by the drug store to insure myself in event I met her a third time. Mr. Wright would you rape easy? Would Mr. Ellison? Perhaps that is where she gets her knowledge of Negro culture. Would you be cultured, would you fathom the Nigger mind, would you know the language the tom tom speaks? If so write Miss M.S. If a Negro suffering from a loss of racial memory, see Miss M.S. by all means. All things are revealed in bed! Don't know when I shall return Dick, though I hope it won't be long. Flit is good for bugs and Sol. I would like very much to see the mag. I wish you would see if I turned in a subscription for Barnical (that isn't the way its spelled, but you know who I mean; Leadbelly's mama) and if I failed to do so please see to it that she gets a copy and I will send you the buck. I might have sent it in, but I can't be sure, so let me know if I didn't and I will send you the money. Writers of the World Must Write!!!!

Ralph

---

[*]   *Daily Worker* and *New Masses.*

[†]   *New Challenge,* the periodical whose first issue published Ellison's first book review, which was of *These Low Grounds,* the first novel by Waters Turpin.

[‡]   Ernest Hemingway's 1937 novel, *To Have and Have Not.*

To Marie Toynet Howard

DECEMBER 16TH, 1937

Dear Marie;*

I was very glad to receive the letter even if it did come long after I expected it. Anyway I thought you would drop me a Xmas card and was just waiting; we all learn to wait in time, if that we want is worth it.

Yes, I am in much better spirits than when I wrote, in fact I was so low at that time that it is impossible to remember just what it was I said to you. Perhaps there was much said that would not have been said had I had better control of my self. You ask what it was I addressed you as, and I must say that I have no control over what is inside me, except to keep it down, and to abort its more foolish expressions; and then not always successfully. I might have called you Marty, but that does not account for the "D". "M.D." could only have been MY DEAR? MY DARLING? No doubt it was MY DARLING, and if it was, consider that a glimpse inside me; besides, who can stop who from dreaming, even over the typewriter and under the disorganization and stress of other more somber emotions? I must explain the wavy effect of this machine. Here is the season of snow and temperatures of eight above and sometimes below, making it impossible to hunt, or anything else that requires venturing out into the open for any length of time. Hence I remain inside and try to write away the hours and my more morbid self. But one day even that would not suffice and the keys on the machine proceeded to stick and act nasty in a general way, so I takes me a screwdriver and a pair of pliers, and much steam for cussing, and a bottle of machine oil; and in twenty minutes I had taken apart that which in three days I have been unable to put together completely again. Except for the oceanic effect though, I think I did pretty well because as you can see it does work. Seasickness is apt to result if you read too fast, or on too full a stomach, so beware; though I suppose you think that if I were a considerate person I would have warned you at the start.

Marie, I'm very sorry that you didn't mail the letter anyway as I did need it bad as hell. There is little that I can answer to your LITTLE MAN WHAT NOW? I have been waiting here for the insurance co. to pay off the remaining claims on my mother's policies; this for a month's duration, because I should have been back in New York weeks ago. If and when the

* Marie Howard was a young woman Ralph had been close to at Tuskegee.

money comes I shall go back there and try to pick up where I left off. I made arrangements to be in Montgomery for Homecoming, but even then my funds were too low. Just now I am enjoying the hunting Dayton has to offer along with its snow with the bright red cardinals flashing across its whiteness, and its quietness except for the sound of the partly frozen streams tumbling over the stones and ice coated vegetation.

I speak now of a country, where I spend most of my time. I hate the little city. Here in town is where I spend my time writing, some of it in going to the movies, and a very small part of it drinking not wisely but quite well.

I read that you had a guest at your home for the game. It must have been very nice with the S'KeG victory and all. You won't appreciate the old place in its brighter aspects until you have been away and the brightness is freed in your mind from the all too plentiful ugliness. The pettiness, the ignorance, the provincialism et al. will fade into insignificance before the memory of honeysuckle, the low moon, the mocking birds, details of a few memorial dances and the richness of a few choice friendships. I know all this and I shall never forget it any the significance of you, you not always near, but always there. IT is the thing remembered that counts; always remember that.

Don't worry because you failed to write—Major Bowes' hour is on now and an Irish tenor is singing YOU DONT KNOW WHAT YOU'RE MISSING, that includes a line about kissing, There is much I'm missing. Anyway, one is apt to be at a loss of words when such things occur, and grief is such a formless thing, even that of friends.

But now my grief has been relegated to a more balanced position in the scheme of things and you must write of yourself in whom I am very interested, about the job, and the dozens of things you mention in your letter, and please, please make it soon.*

> *the folks who live on the hill on the top of the hill*
> *just a slight wavy effect hills wonder why people love*
> *the tops of hills*

---

* The original letter ends here without punctuation; the two quasi-poetic lines follow down the page without a sign-off.

To Langston Hughes

JANUARY 20, 1939

Dear Lang:

After all this time it takes some little optimism to any longer expect the mountain to come to Mohammad; so I, Mojammad Ras De Terror, come to the mountain. Louise tells me you expect to return by April so I thought it best to hurry into the mail before you start back. It might have been that yuh jus don fo'got ma adress agins the reason yuh ain wrote, or perhaps its the effect of June in January?

The *Afro-American** of this week carries a story on *St. Louis Woman* and its coming performance. Good luck! It is a dam shame that things here had to jam as soon as they lost the sustaining force of your presence. I hope they aren't completely shot before your return . . .

There is really little that I can tell you Lang. I spend all of my time trying to make a writer of myself and outside of a concert now and a play then I have no social life. I heard Marian Anderson and saw Odets' *Rocket to the Moon,* which I think a good play despite its conceptional faults. It had some of the most effective dialogue I've ever heard, and incidentally Luther Adler is worth seeing any day.

On the labor front the Tories are still after our jobs. However, we were able to keep dismissals among the Negroes down to the low number of four, while some forty remain. We do not yet know how things shall be now that Congress has passed the cut. Keep your fingers crossed . . . Wright is polishing up his novel,[†] trying to meet a March deadline. It's wonderful stuff . . . Gee I almost forgot: I have at last got my hands on a machine of my own, a Remington noiseless, and I would like to know what to do with your machine; shall I keep it till you return or shall I leave it with Kit? I've had it so long that it seems strange to be using any other machine. It seems likely that it could be used for twenty years to come with good results. I am highly grateful for the use of it.

Try and get back in time to see Ethel Waters in Mamba's Daughters, the

---

* The previous year, 1938, after quitting New York and his leadership of the popular Harlem Suitcase Theater in order to go to California, Hughes had signed a contract with the Federal Theatre Project to work on a musical version of the play *St. Louis Woman.* Although the Baltimore newspaper *The Afro-American* wrote optimistically about this plan, nothing came of it.

† *Native Son,* published to national acclaim in 1940.

critics have given reams of space to her performance. Maybe the Suitcase Theater could use the gal, huh?

Guess this is all. If you ever do those songs for TAC don't forget us. Rose says hello.

Sincerely,
[Ralph]

To Harry Brooks
FEBRUARY 5TH, 1939.

Dear Harry:[*]

Boy I was surprised to learn through Mike Rabb that you were still at Tuskegee. I wrote you twice last year but received no answer, and somewhat later some fellow from down there told me that you had gone home to Georgia. What I cannot understand is what happens to the letters I mail down there; no one seems to receive them. Perhaps this will fare differently. Mike tells me you are still in O.D. Hall. I thought of the old room many a time during the winter of 1937–38 during which I was stranded out in Dayton, Ohio. At a time when the temperature registered 8 above zero I was forced to sleep in the back of a car in a garage through which the wind swept with the force of a pile driver from the time I dropped off to sleep until it froze me into wakefulness some time around five o-clock in the mornings. But the thing that made it all so bad and that made me remember No. 4 O.D. was the fact that I barely had money to buy food and spent many of these nights on an empty stomach. On such nights I would lay in the back seat of the car, covered with my overcoat, and dream of a certain night on which I went to sleep hungry and you came in with millions of chicken salad sandwiches, chocolate cake, and even some wine. You had come in late from serving at a party out to the Government Hospital just in time to save my life. Brooks, I guess the memory of that night saved life many a night in Dayton, and though you didn't appear in the flesh, you are still due my sincerest thanks, so thanks for my life.

I came through the winter all right, came back to N.Y. in the spring and found a job. During last fall I married a woman[†] who, would you believe it, could not make piecrust! However, I must say that she does dam

---

[*]   Harry Brooks, Ralph's roommate and good friend at Tuskegee.

[†]   Rose Poindexter Ellison, whom Ralph married in September 1938, separated from in 1943, and divorced in April 1945.

well with most everything else. Well anyway, today a pie was baked in our apartment, and although it is said that too many cooks spoil the cooking, this pie is dam good. The good Lady Ellison made the filling and I remembered your instruction and made the crust. Hope that we live after it. Of course she wanted to know from whence came my knowledge and I had to tell her of you and Matt Hicks and all the boys. If you have time you could send along your recipes for sweet potato pie and anything else that might strike you as interesting. We have a pretty complete kitchen, and since my stomach has become so bad that its almost impossible to eat at restaurants, the wife experiments a lot at preparing foods.

What the hell are you doing now; have they made you an instructor? And how is the trumpet coming? I put mine aside sometimes early in 1937 and picked it up only once right after my return to the city in March, when I [played] the score for a modern dance ballet. The orchestra consisted of two trumpets, drums and percussion effects, piano and conductor. The dam things was composed by a friend of mine, Alex North, who is well known and considered quite a composer, but take it from me, there are few Dawsons; incidentally North is a Jew. For the trumpet I guess I left Tuskegee one year too late. If I had left in "35" before they refused to allow me to enter my class despite the guarantee of the State of Oklahoma that my bills would be paid, I might have gone on and graduated. Even after coming here I studied composition with Wallingford Reigger until forced to stop for an operation,[*] following which I lost my mother in Dayton where she had moved about the same time I left Alabama. Now writing takes so much of my time that I find little time to do more than keep my lips hard and my fingers loose. Though who knows; I might have to make my bread and meat with the old horn after all. How is Capt. Drye? I wrote him once or twice but no doubt he didn't like the tone of what I had to say, as he failed to answer. I meant no malice and it is quite possible that he just had too many things on his mind to get around to writing. Say hello for me, please.

Harry, it looks like I'm just rambling on and on, and I'm about to stop. Not, however, before bothering you about my trunk. Write about what it will cost to get it from the campus to the station plus the charges to express it to N.Y. In turn, I will send you a money order for the amount you name plus a few dollars for your troubles, or if you don't need the money I'll send whatever present you might suggest. You see, Brooks, there are

---

[*] Perhaps related to the tonsillitis attack in spring 1937.

pictures of my mother in the old trunk and a few other things, though worthless to anyone else, that are of importance and value to me. Please let me hear about this as soon as possible.

One more thing. In Dayton I met a fellow who knew you, one of the owners of a cafe. There was something familiar, I thought, about the fellow's face, and it finally occurred to me that I had seen him somewhere in New York. It was during the hunting season and my brother and a friend of ours, since there were no jobs to be had, were making our bread by supplying the cafes and groceries with rabbits, and the rich whites with quail, which we shot illegally at the risk of a twenty-five dollar fine for each bird shot— some days we took as many as a dozen and a half a piece. Well my curiosity concerning this fellow led me to take advantage of our contact as dealer and buyer of illegal goods to question him about himself. He was, as you say down there, a "regular nigguh" and it turned out that he was from Tuskegee as well as from N.Y. His name was "Smitty," who you'll remember as the basketball ace of a few years back. He left school and went to N.Y. where he was for a time the instructor at the Y.M.C.A. gym. I sold him many a rabbit before the season closed and had many talks about the school. There are many of the boys out there, not to mention Big Stuff, who is now a quietly married man. It's a dam small world I suppose, eh Money?

O.K. Harry, I'm signing off till I receive your answer, and news of yourself.

Very truly yours,
Ralph

Apt. 4-D
470 W. 150th St.
New York, N.Y.

To Herbert Ellison
MARCH 4, 1939

Dear Herbert:

Thanks for the birthday greeting, it came as a surprise. It made me feel very good to receive it. The clipping of John was interesting. Its too bad that he can't find a job off W.P.A. but there are millions here just as he is, wanting to do jobs that no one will give them. Many of us will lose our jobs around April, and then there will be many more. We are fighting for the sustenance of the W.P.A. through our union, but though we have won many battles up to now, it remains to be seen how we shall come out. We threw all our strength behind Roosevelt against Big business, but there are so many who should have likewise, who didn't, that it's is difficult to tell just how Congress will react. Something will have to happen. I hope you find the job you were speaking about. If not, hold on to what you have until it becomes warm.

I would appreciate it if you would let me know just how much the policies are behind, as I would like to pay them up. For while it is a nuisance to keep them paid, it's good to have them in case of death. You see it is the only policy that I have and if I die you and Rose would be in a hell of a spot. If you haven't time to take care of this, please get in touch with Dorfman and have him transfer them in his office or at least have it returned to me.

Have you moved yet? If not, try and be sure of whom you are moving in with. In one of the places I lived they stole and destroyed my papers and books.

I'm sorry, Herbert, that there are no pictures of Rose just now. She is supposed to have some more made, and when they are ready you will get one. Rose is well and says hello.

Well, Herbert, there really is no more news this time so this will be all until next time. Oh yes, what did you mean when you said you lost money the last time you went down to see Annie and Fred? Was it stolen or did you lose time from work? Try and let me know about the policies as soon as possible.

Sincerely your brother,
Ralph

To Joe Lazenberry
NEW YORK
APRIL 18, 1939

Dear Joe:*

You have no idea how glad I was to hear from you again. I mailed the card in spite of having been informed that you were deceased, like Mark Twain,

---

* This important letter is the fullest account Ralph wrote of his time spent in New York, Dayton, and again in New York after leaving Tuskegee at the beginning of 1936. It is both a factual and meditative version of his life and his mind's development during these self-fashioning years in his mid-twenties. Joe Lazenberry, whose letter Ralph answers, was a close friend at Tuskegee.

and I assure you that more than mentally my heart was in my mouth. It was like this: I happen to know a girl from St. Paul, Zelma Jackson, who gave me this information with a very positive assurance that it was true. I didn't know what to think; she was positive and I couldn't accept. I started to write your mother but decided that it would be too painful; after all the damn gal might have known what she was talking about. Well, I thought, that guy couldn't leave without giving me a chance to cuss him out for failing to answer my letters, he's bad, but not that bad. Then last month I wrote Rabb asking him about you and he answered that if you were dead it was only from the neck up. So with that hope I sent out the feeler. I am glad we are no longer out of contact. I suppose it takes some such incident as this to make one realize you don't miss your water till your well runs dry. I've known a slew of people since the Tuskegee days Joe but none I would rather have as a friend—and alive.

In broad outline it is surprising how similar the patterns of our lives have been. The following brief list of events will explain what I mean.

As you will remember, 1936 found me working for the psychoanalyst about whom I wrote you. Incidentally you might get an idea of the type of research they wished to have you do by reading *After Freedom*, the new book by Hortense Pondermaker who is an associate of Sullivan and much affected by his school of thought. Anyway, the job ended in Jan. '37 and I went to work in a paint laboratory, testing paint for the father of one of the patients whose friendship I had made while at Sullivan's. Only Negro in lab. incurring much wrath. Saved little money and stuck it out until July when bad tonsils and the desire to take part in the Spanish conflict made it necessary for me to leave. Bad tonsils out and by Aug had applied for passport. So many fellows going without much money that State Department had become suspicious. Department agents examined me, trying to crack my story, but lied out of it, making it necessary that they use technicality of my limited funds to keep me this side the Atlantic. Somewhat set back by this; the bastards waited until the morning I was to have sailed to investigate. Decided to try a tramp steamer to Mexico and thence to Spain. Took part in strike, picketing with union at a time when scabs had to be carried to and from the boats under the protection of a squad of New York's Finest, and there were goons.

I kept this up, my funds growing short and my pride long, sleeping in the Harlem office of the *Daily Worker*, eating at the home of friends who paid my transportation to meals and away, until October when I received word that my mother was very ill in Cinn. Went there. Lost her the day after I arrived. After funeral went to Dayton where she and my brother had made home about time I left South. Had to wait there for insurance to pay off. Funds faded, that General Motor's town without work, plants having closed down. Hunted with a friend all season shooting quail and rabbits, the quail illegally, which got old for food. This was all well and good as long as the season lasted. But then Dec. came and with it ice and hunger. Friend's wife, already the mother of three, became pregnant with child she could not bear lost her mental balance. Thought brothers were receiving charity from husband when it was really the other way around since we had given him our last funds to pay her physician. She insisted that we move—perhaps we were absorbing too much heat. We did. Snow on ground. Wind. Ice. Slept in his old Ford sedan in garage, slipping in after 12 in the darkness up to which time we loafed in pool halls, lobby of Y.M.C.A. Lived on doughnuts, milk which brother was able to charge at store where Mother had traded. Finally he got keys to tailor shop where he had once worked. Warm there, steam all night. Slept on coats piled on floor. About this time I helped fellow in cafe with his social security reports and on strength of this and the insurance money it seemed we would never receive, he allowed us to run up a bill. This lasted till latter part of Feb. when money did arrive. Left there, and my brother, who likes the dam place, on Mar 2 for NYC. Lived with white friends off Central Park, regaining faith in human nature. Looked for work. No work. Met wife at friend's house. Led with my chin. No jobs. Relief and W.P.A. Lived in sin for seven months, then civil ceremony. Still on W.P.A. and despite of what the bastards in Congress say, there are still no jobs. Not even at this horses ass of a Worlds Fair!

Hope you can find your way through all this Joe. It is important only because it is a sort of rough blueprint of my maturing. I had lost my friendship with W. B. W.[*] because of my political views—of all things—in the winter of '36 but the Dayton experience tested these views and made for strength to survive through it without bitterness. I came back to the city with a sort of strength, a feeling of lyrical self-confidence. Not a feeling that this was the best of all possible worlds, but I could survive no matter what the circumstances.

I suppose the very fact that I got married proves something unusual happened. It took nerve for a broke guy to go after my wife in the manner

---

[*] Walter B. Williams, a librarian at Tuskegee who befriended Ralph and is mentioned in Ralph's 1930s letters to his mother.

in which I did. She is a former member of Black Birds, the 1929 version, which she joined at fifteen and went to Europe. She left show in Berlin and toured the continent for six years, leading a band and singing, returning here in '35. Has broadcasted and worked nightclubs and Broadway shows, etc. Is not an intellectual, but possesses a sensitive intelligence, looks well, cooks well, and is skillful at all those things a man is interested in finding in the woman he marries—and this statement is no mere compensation. Most of all Joe, she's politically alive, thanks to having been present when Hitler entered Vienna; is no respecter of bourgeois conventions, being both politically alive and an actress, and possesses a good supply of what is called, "guts," a quality very necessary these days. Damn! It sounds like bragging to me; don't it? Forgive me the heat of my blood, the mist of mine eyes, the lyricism of my groom-hood.

But you Joe! How the hell did you bring yourself to marry after the disillusionment of Tuskegee? I respected your moods and opinions more mature than mine, and thus more preeminent than mine in those days, and as a result I believed you would never have the confidence to marry. I'm dam glad to know it wasn't true. I'm glad you weren't so certain of things, for now I've come to suspect people whose grasp of the world is such that they solve all contradictions, all problems so soon. I hope some day that we'll meet the girl. Was there anyone who saw things in their correct perspective in the twisted environment of Tuskegee—unless it was you Parker, and myself, who were aided and sustained by lemon juice and the liquor of the moment? I think not. Where is that guy? I'll never forget the time he purchased Ceeley Williams for me and my surprise that it could be so tight. Then there was the time we went to a gambling joint and he almost got in a fight—I won't forget that either.

TUESDAY, APRIL 25TH, 1939.

It seems, Joe, that I can never finish anything these days without interruptions; even when it is rushed as this is. After reading the first two pages I think you had better send me a list of questions so that I might clear up any confusions.

The idea of your trip sounds swell from certain angles of vision. After the romanticism of the attempted Russian venture, however, I wonder if the possibilities that occur to me are the same that makes it so attractive to you. Incidentally, I have been talking of a trip to Mexico for some time, but of course there is the money angle. Wright, too, who has just won a Guggenheim fellowship, is thinking in the same channels. Perhaps I should explain the statement concerning Russia. To have entered in such a manner would have resulted in almost certain imprisonment. You, my friend, would have been taken for a spy. Since the widespread sabotage and wrecking which resulted in the recent trials, it has been extremely difficult to enter the U.S.S.R. through the regular channels. The Russians would have thought that their enemies, knowing of their friendliness to American Negroes, had resorted to sending you as a capitalist wolf in naive sheep's clothing. Why don't you try through official channels? Go back to the trip. It seems to me that with your knowledge of sociology that it would provide excellent opportunities for research. Something more scientific and more penetrating than the things done by Margaret Bourke-White and Erskine Caldwell and others, who have offered indignation and pity rather than analysis—even though I think the camera and text have combined to give a picture lush with implications and of undoubted social and artistic value. No one has approached Negro life in this manner and it seems a fertile field. No doubt a publisher would jump at such a book. About Mexico I think that here too, you could do a valuable piece of work. When considered from the point of view that the cultural and economic condition of the two peoples are so very similar, it becomes astonishing that there is practically no contact between them; no one interested in interpreting each to the other. Langston Hughes knows the language but fails to see the important job he could perform, he has no vision in this direction. If we are ever to attain independence in the Black belt, or rather, if that independence comes to depend upon armed uprising, then these people will be our logical allies; their history is such that they could not help but be sympathetic, could not help but offering some help. They are fighting now for their independence from American capitalists and in time—if they keep their present political direction—they will be come an important factor for democracy in the Americas. You might perform an important job without becoming involved with anybody's politics; the facts and the nature of the material is such that it would not be necessary. Of course this takes money, but living is cheap in Mexico. There is also the possibility that you might obtain a job teaching there. I am told that sociologists etc. are needed. No doubt they would jump at the implications of having an American Negro working with them.

You say you plan to "enjoy to the hilt what this life has to offer to two individuals etc." Malraux in his *Man's Hope* has a character who has been put the question "how can one best make the best of one's life" answer:

"By converting as wide a range of experience as possible into conscious thought." Conscious thought has a way of leading to action. In fact the action is the consciousness—unless one is a fool or a knave, or both. Be that as it may, I believe in the answer and as I remember you I think you will agree.

One should live at the height of his time intellectually, one should be able to pick apart every experience, examine it and relate it to his whole world-view. In short a man should possess his experiences and not be possessed by them. Such thought becomes creative. And these times of social consciousness the resulting action is likely to become social action. This is rough as hell but likely as not you know what I'm trying to say even better than I do myself. Now: Today life in the U.S, seems to offer some pretty bitter experiences, so much so that, unless you're rich, for the believer in democracy it offers only disillusionment; so much so that through all strata of our population you find people forging weapons to protect themselves: labor unions, C.I.O. and the League of American Writers etc. The intellectual has fared no better than the worker. His world has become one of social action. To live life to the hilt as you put it has come to mean living with an alertness to the social forces operating in the world today; there is no escape, nor through art nor through literature— just finished Steinbeck's *Grapes of Wrath*—nor through music. What I'm trying to say, Joe, is that if you take the trip do by all means take it "to the hilt,' deep and wide but then convert it to conscious thought; make a book of it. A mocking bird sang each night on the post office building at Tuskegee, in the moonlight and shadows scented with honeysuckle. It made an impression on me. One summer I helped you make a survey of a cooperative farm a few blocks from America's largest Negro school, where people who could not read or write worked bare-foot in the Alabama sun. This too, made an impression, though a bewildering one. At that time I believe I put the more value upon the moonlight and mocking birds; now it is the other experience that has become the more meaningful. Conscious thought has converted it into an impulse to creation; in these times it is the positive reality. One sucks experience through the body into the mind and there makes something of it to change, improve the realities from which the experience came. You are certainly lucky to have a wife who will go along with you. Older Negro women had the pioneering spirit, even one of adventure, but the younger crop reach too readily for the shadow of *Security*, perhaps it should be SECURITY. The two of you should be able to influence the consciousness of the entire next generation of Negroes.

It is that that we here are attempting to do. At present it is still un-formed organizationally, but the consciousness is here. Wright already has one book and another to be published in the fall. Theodore Ward has *Big White Fog* that was produced in Chi., and is working on another. I am mapping a novel of the Negro college. I believe, Joe, that all Negro institutions should be examined and exposed for what they are in the light of world events. It will be muckraking of a sort, but we hope, constructive in its very power to disintegrate. Perhaps there won't be an organization but we will have a group in contact with one another who know what they are about, the direction in which they are traveling. Frankly, we are angry; but not so much so that we can't see. The standards are high—Wright is rated with Hemingway, is an important figure in the League of American Writers. We have overcome the cultural and intellectual isolation that has been characteristic of Negro writers. Let me know what you think of it and I'll go into it more fully next time. I guess I've written enough to start you to debating, then the both of us shall discover what the other has been thinking these last years. Perhaps you've done a book—how the hell would I know? My best wishes to Mrs. Leroy Francis Lazenberry and success to you both.

Ralph

Letters from the Forties

———

THROUGHOUT THE 1940S THE SPOKES OF RALPH
Ellison's letters radiate out from the hub of New York City.
At times, though, he continues to be a peripatetic correspondent. Several letters, written in March 1945 on a dangerous merchant marine voyage "somewhere at sea" in the
wild Atlantic, then anchored on the Seine in the French cathedral town of Rouen, place the sea's elemental, agnostic
reality against the uncivilized behavior of human beings.
During the summers of 1945 and 1947, Ellison's getaways
from Harlem's din into the peace and quiet of Vermont
motivate him to take a look at nature that is at once lyrical
and appreciative, cold-eyed and critical, from an incestu-
ous, sequestered, rural corner of an old America. There
are also penetrating, caustic riffs, written from Quogue, on
Long Island, in 1946 during a retreat to compose *Invisible
Man,* that expose the peculiar manners and preoccupations of a well-off class of post–World War II professional
Americans, a goodly number of whom are black.

Though memories of his beloved "dear folks" of
Oklahoma still stir his blood and bones, Ellison becomes
a New Yorker—and not just a New Yorker, but a citizen
of Harlem. All during his marriage to Rose Poindexter,
which effectively ends in 1943, throughout 1944, when
he and Fanny McConnell meet, fall in love, and commit

to each other, Harlem is home, and it remains home until the end of his life.

Together as well as one by one, the more than sixty letters surviving from the forties sweep over the hills and valleys of his consciousness, revealing a defiant intelligence and an unwavering commitment to individual personality. These letters are testing grounds for Ellison's self-shaping of mind and heart, while at the same time tracking the ups and downs in his life.

Familiar faces reappear from the thirties letters: his younger brother, Herbert; Richard Wright, to whom he writes the lion's share of the letters here; Langston Hughes; and others. New correspondents emerge as well: critics and writers Stanley Edgar Hyman and Kenneth Burke; friend and patron Ida Guggenheimer—to whom Ellison will later dedicate *Invisible Man.*

His first wife, Rose Poindexter, is here: "Dear Winchy, wenchy, wench," he begins his 1940 letter. Little is known of Rose, and what we do know fascinates. But in any case it seems impossible not to like a woman able to inspire a man such as Ralph Ellison to such moments of playfulness. There are three letters to Sanora Babb, fellow novelist, soul mate, and, briefly, lover—rich, fascinating letters that fill in what might otherwise seem an intimacy missing from Ellison's life at this time. Of their intense days together in November 1941, he writes to Babb several months later when she is back home in Los Angeles: "It was no 'rare holiday' but the start of a new phase of my life."

Most of all, there is Fanny McConnell, whom he meets in June 1944 and marries as soon as they are free. From the first she supports him in every way, and perhaps believes in him and his talent in a more unconditional way than he does; always she is present in ways that go deeper than it is possible to know.

ELLISON'S LETTERS TO HIS BROTHER, Herbert, and close friend Richard Wright illuminate the different passions, pitch, and depth found in these intense brotherly relationships. The kinship of Ellison and Wright grows up between two self-made men determined to explore and solve the labyrinths of the world and their own souls. Meanwhile, the fraught brotherhood of Ralph and Herbert flows in strong, sometimes sluggish currents of blood and years of close yet difficult family life.

Like earlier and later letters to Herbert, the two from the forties reveal a person prone to jams. Through Ralph's lens Herbert sometimes seems almost a cartoon of the proverbial younger brother: Herbert's fierce passivity pulls the strings of his older brother's sense of responsibility. He sometimes activates in Ralph an exaggerated man-of-the-world stance doubtless linked to an old desire to act like the long-dead father his younger brother never knew. Ellison is loyal to Herbert in a detached though unconditional way. It is an allegiance formed from ties of genetics and common upbringing rather than the spontaneous connection that flows from words and experience outside family affiliation, such as the allegiance Ellison developed with Richard Wright.

Certainly, some of the emotional boundaries Ralph marked off between himself and Herbert may have been compensation for the loss of personal privacy and independence that comes with sibling obligations. Yet Ellison's resistance to Herbert's requests for money he does not have only magnifies his generosity, as if acknowledging that a younger brother has a right to expect his older brother to protect him from some of the consequences exacted by immature and reckless acts. That said, the more Ralph offers to help, the less Herbert accepts help, as if refusal is the one stubborn act of independence a younger brother can muster against the older one. Still, Ellison's unconditional love comes through paradoxically in the modest conditions he attaches to the personal advice and financial help he extends to Herbert.

In stark contrast are Ellison's twenty or so letters to Dick Wright from 1940 to 1949. (Curiously, the two from 1949 are notes written to Wright in France, where he has been living permanently for almost three years. The first, brief and cryptic, is from Ralph; the second Fanny writes for Ralph, who is, she politely tells Wright, too swamped to attend further to a request of Wright's. These notes do not mark the end of the Ellison-Wright correspondence; there are letters back and forth in the early fifties about the publication of *Invisible Man* and Wright's *The Outsider*. Yet it is hard to imagine Ellison having anyone else—even someone as dear to him as Fanny—answer even the most prosaic query from Dick Wright in the earlier phases of their friendship.) In any case, the Dick Wright to whom Ellison writes long meditative letters throughout the forties was perhaps a stand-in for an imaginary older brother (Wright was six years Ellison's senior), someone Ellison wishes could provide for him the forceful presence he tries to be for his younger brother, Herbert.

Yet Ellison fledges more boldly than Wright intends or expects. For example, while Wright is away for considerable stretches in Mexico, Canada, or France, Ellison stands in for him as his friend, almost his man Friday, at various charged gatherings among the artistic and political movers and shakers on the left in Harlem, at which Wright's *Native Son* and *Black Boy* come under frequent, sometimes hostile examination.

In the early forties Ellison stakes out and clarifies to Wright more fully than he does to anyone else the approach he is moving toward in the related domains of art and politics. In an April 14, 1940, letter he writes this particularly salient passage:

> As I study Max's speech [at the end of *Native Son*], it seems to me that you were struggling to create a new terminology, i.e. you were trying to state in terms of human values certain ideas, concepts, implicit in Marxist philosophy but that, since Marx, and later Lenin, were so occupied with economics and politics, have not been stated in humanist terms of Marxist coloring. This lack I am trying to get at is indicated by the almost total failure on the part of Marxist-Leninist literature to treat human personality.

Less than a month after writing this, Ellison writes his friend that attending the National Negro Congress "was the most exciting thing to happen to me." The piece that follows, "A Congress Jim Crow Didn't Attend," is featured on the cover of the May 14, 1940, issue of the *New Masses*. In an important confession of faith, Ellison writes the essay in the first person and describes the thrilling epiphany he experiences when "I suddenly realized that the age of the Negro hero had returned to American life."

A year later, immediately after reading *12 Million Black Voices** for the first time in print along with photographs, Ellison writes an unusually powerful, confessional letter to Wright. "Writing is an act of salvation," he announces.

> I felt so intensely the fire of our common experience when reading *12 Million Black Voices* that I felt the solder of my discipline melt

---

* Richard Wright's *12 Million Black Voices: A Folk History of the Negro in the United States* was, in Arnold Rampersad's words, nothing less than "the autobiography of a race" that moved Ellison to deep contemplation of the complex contradictions of black lives in the United States.

and found myself opened up and crying over the painful pattern of remembered things. . . . I am sure now more than ever: that you and I are brothers. . . . We are the ones who had no comforting amnesia of childhood, and for whom the trauma of passing from the country to the city of destruction brought no anesthesia of unconsciousness, but left our nerves peeled and quivering. We are not the numbed, but the seething. God! It makes you want to write and write and write, or murder.

A few years later, in July 1945, just before the American atomic bomb dropped on Hiroshima rocked his mind and heart, Ellison writes the audacious words "We have become the fathers of our elders." In early August he recounts an encounter with mutual acquaintance Eugene Holmes on a Harlem street:

"So you and Wright are together?"

"No, Wright is by himself and I am by myself. We are individuals."

UNTIL WELL AFTER WRIGHT moves to Paris in 1946, Ellison's letters continue to be those of a brother whose feelings of fraternity and friendship go deeper than blood and bone. In his last actual letter in the decade, a long, full one from February 1, 1948, Ellison speaks of mutual acquaintance Roi Ottley "going around dismissing me as simply 'a disciple of Dick Wright's'—which doesn't bother me, feeling as I do about your work." He is glad Wright on his own has found, read, and liked the "Battle Royal" chapter of *Invisible Man* in *Horizon*. He also writes of wanting the inaugural issue of the new pan-African quarterly *Présence Africaine,* which includes Wright's "Claire Étoile du Matin," which Wright has sent or promised to send but has not arrived in New York. After passing on his and Fanny's best wishes to Wright's wife and daughter, Ellison returns to what he wants most from Wright: his latest writing. He closes with simple words having a hint of urgency from a close friend who, above all else, is a fellow writer: "Be sure that I get *Présence Africaine.*"

Whatever may follow, as the intensity of their friendship ebbs in the years before Wright's death in 1960, Ellison's many long, intense letters during the forties show him becoming and being a brother to Wright based on fidelity to what, adapting Ellison's own phrase, we might consider that "very stern discipline" born of friendship and art.

LESS INTENSE AND INTIMATE but equally as compelling intellectually are several letters to the literary critic and folklorist Stanley Edgar Hyman,* whom Ellison later calls his "old sparring partner." The accuracy of the phrase is embodied in critical comments Ellison makes about Hyman's vantage point on folklore's influence on literature, especially the novel—an influence Ellison finds too academic, too beholden to questionable tenets of current anthropology and sociology. As usual, Ellison's frankness is hidden in plain sight.

The same is true of a different frankness expressed in a long letter to Kenneth Burke in November 1945—a year, I should note, in which Ellison's letters comprise an especially rich, inspirational trove. He starts by thanking Burke for a recommendation, then calls his gesture "a little bit ridiculous" given that "my real debt to you lies in the many things I've learned (and continue to learn) from your work and that perhaps the greatest debt lies in your courage in taking a counter-position and making your 'counter-statement.'" Ellison then makes a counterstatement of his own against thanking "a thinker for having courage," and ventures into a territory of eloquence that is personal.

For when a man, in battling for his life, has given birth to works which enlighten and inspire, is it not a mistake to confuse the matter and attempt to thank him? It's like thanking him for being a human being. I suppose the only adequate expression of gratitude in such an instance lies in work, real hard work that comes of a similar struggle as that which has inspired or set off the chain reaction in one. So, if in the little things I write from time to time you observe anything of value, then to that extent am I able to express concretely my appreciation for what you have done. That is a debt I shall never stop paying and it begins back in the thirties, when you read "The Rhetoric of Hitler's Battle" before the League of American Writers, at the New School (I believe you were the only speaker out of the whole group

---

* Ellison's lifelong friendship with Hyman, which biographer Arnold Rampersad rightly called "one of the most significant relationships" of his life, began in December 1942. Hyman secured a lecture at Bennington College for the little-known Ellison and invited him to lead a discussion on Joyce and Wright in his class. He was a dedicated reader of Ellison's drafts of *Invisible Man*—it was a watershed moment when Ellison came across Hyman laughing out loud at a passage he'd given him to read.

who was concerned with writing <u>and politics</u>, rather than writing as an <u>excuse</u>—and that in a superficial manner.)

Abruptly, Ellison takes a risk, which, if it had failed, might have seemed arrogant enough to be worthy of attention from the goddess Nemesis. (Remember, he has been at *Invisible Man* for a mere three or four months, though its mighty theme and form have been gestating far longer.) "Anyway," he concludes, "I am writing a novel now and perhaps if it is worthwhile it will be my most effective means of saying thanks. Anything else seems to me inadequate and unimaginative."

Ellison's friendship with Burke follows from writing and reading each other's work. Until Burke's death, five months before Ellison's, their exchanges test and extend the meaning of that same democratic equality and fraternity that drew them together in the cauldron of the thirties.

IN THE VULNERABLE TERRITORY of love, Ellison's surprising frankness is both heart-stopping and heart-quickening, for in the end it arms as well as disarms him. Fanny moves in with him soon after they meet in late June 1944. Soon after, while she's in Chicago speeding up her divorce proceedings, Ralph writes her for the first time—a strange letter full of demonic self-doubt and anxiety as he teeters on the edge of love's precipice.

> You've been gone a week today and I've waited all day for a letter . . . Like a lovesick fool I've been unable to sleep since you've been gone, food is uninteresting to the point of nausea: and I've two deadlines staring me in my paralyzed face. . . . Darling, I <u>resent</u> the way I feel. I don't want to be this way. It is a dependence I've never known before. . . . Even my imagination, which has been my friend always when I've been unhappy, now has turned against me. Instead of consolation it gives me fears.

Slowly a touch of equilibrium returns. Gradually, beneath the floorboards of language, he realizes his demons are fears belonging only to him; although on the loose, they have nothing to do with the other human being, the person who is Fanny. So he writes that he is "stopping this right here"—falsely, because immediately his feelings overflow the dam of his will and become words that flow truly again: "Not," he writes, tasting his own wit uncertainly, "because I have no more to say, but because it's a hell of a first letter. Especially since I had such things, such heartfelt things, to tell you those first days of these years you've been away."

Immediately, he experiences a sea change. His demons fade into the shadows—at least for the time being. He breaks off the inadequate, dishonest close he's begun, and dives down to an extraordinary counter-statement of love that embraces the autonomy he and Fanny possess and bring to each other: "So goodnight—not 'my love' but you whom I love."

THE DEFIANT MIND AND PERSONALITY he brings to his fiction are poised on the cusp of life with Fanny. Other of his letters to her also forge the new meanings that can follow from breathing the heart's simplicity into old, tired words. In March 1945 he writes her at home in Harlem while "somewhere at sea" in a merchant marine ship in constant danger of deadly torpedo attacks from German U-boats. There he stows away his demons, and under the influence of his demon he imagines the ship as "the symbol and the fact of man's consciousness, intellect and courage." Watching the Allied convoy "curving across the ocean through storm and calm," he describes the ships' wakes as "paths of <u>humanized</u> nature." Always attuned to the vernacular, Ellison pairs the speech of a "West Indian Messman" with his own lyrical prose to evoke the "continuous present":

> "Well, O'll be damn Maan! We're right here in the same place we was yesterday." And so it seems. The same sun rising from the same green sea, the same sea birds flighting through the sun into and through a foamy wave tip, like a small white and silver butterfly.

Soon—after cold-eyed reference to petty politics and racial strife on board—he ends, but not before an even-keeled declaration to Fanny:

> Anyway, I love you enough to spend my life with you doing things both very foolish and even a few very wonderful too.
> Man's Fate is a strange thing, honey.

From Rouen, a cathedral town that wartime censorship prevents him from mentioning by name, he writes a charming description of the people, whom he likes, in particular the little ones: "You should see the fat babies! And the two or three year-olds, with their knee length socks, their berets and their short length coats which leave their fat little bottoms exposed.

They go along in their carriages pushed by their mamma and looking just as superior and supercilious as any Park Avenue baby."

In his last sentence and closing salutation Ellison cuts to the chase:

> And I want to see you Fanny-Mae, so badly I ache.
> I am very much in love with you,
> your
> Ralph

ELLISON WRITES EIGHT LETTERS from Winhall Station, Vermont, from mid-September to mid-October 1947. The whole purpose of his stay there is for him to take advantage of Ida Guggenheimer's gift of a rent-free cottage for a month to write like hell in solitude on his novel. Though older than Ida Bell Ellison would have been, in her maternal affection Ida Guggenheimer must have brought back memories of his mother. In his letters Ellison's respectful frankness is constant. He does not tiptoe around matters they disagree on—matters having to do with race and the doctrinaire party line promulgated by the Communist Party USA that it expected members and supporters alike to follow and that she followed the letter of more strictly than he did. Ellison's letters to Ida help the reader understand her ambivalence toward his dedication of *Invisible Man* to her, and also why her differences with the novel's satiric take on the Marxist left would fray but not break the bonds of their friendship.

In any case, the month in 1947 is not the first time he's had the run of the Guggenheimer cottage in Vermont. Yet, arriving alone, he finds the place "empty and full of the atmosphere of houses that are not regularly lived in, and you [Fanny] were not here with me so that we could bring it alive together." Briefly, he finds the little house's former "magic for writing was gone," but he chases that demon away and settles into a faithful routine of work.

The letters describe his daily habits. He cares for Fanny's rascally terriers, Red and Bobbins, especially Bobbins, who badly loses a fight with a porcupine. "I had to muzzle her and actually kneel upon her the pain was so great when we removed the barbs and there she lay looking so reproachfully out of her eyes."

Bobbins's mishap prompts him to write Fanny about the personality of her other dog. Not realizing Red is outside one evening, Ellison heard someone knocking on the kitchen door like a man and went with my flashlight to see who it was. But when I got there I had a strange feeling for the garage doors were still closed and the knocking definitely from the kitchen door. And it was then that Red began bawling me out for leaving him in the dark. He almost talked. Up here in the cold mornings I've seen that grin you spoke about, he seems filled with joy, and when I return after going into town in the later afternoon I swear that the little dog expresses pure love when he greets me.

As if explaining cryptically to himself as well as Fanny what the story of the little terrier has to do with the travails of the novelist of *Invisible Man,* he writes succinctly: "I go on and on, but this is the only way of being with you and it's the only thing I've written today." In these letters Ellison's antidote to his words and story going dry in the well is to write. And write he does: of life with Fanny's dogs; the changing weather; cloud patterns at dusk and early morning; the northern lights at night; changes in temperature; meals in the adjacent house with the Amsden family; his walks into town to the post office and the country store; Fanny's most recent letter; and a fine account of Faulkner's "Old Man," apropos of a short story she is writing: "Another thing to remember is that the flood, the river, the 'Old Man,' against whom the Convict fights is not so much a naturalistic river as a flood and river within his mind."

When he does write Fanny about *Invisible Man,* Ellison's touchstone is not his novel's journey from his mind to the page; it is the unfolding story of the novel beginning to be visible in the world. A week before returning to Fanny in New York, he writes her about good news from his agent: '*48: The Magazine of the Year* ('47 renamed) has made a fine offer to publish in its pages the "Battle Royal" chapter from *Invisible Man,* which has just come out over in London in Cyril Connolly's distinguished quarterly, *Horizon.* Best of all, word from the agency is that "several people said that mine was the most compelling piece in the American issue of *Horizon.*" In character as usual, Ellison dismisses such praise as "flattery," yet his pleasure and excitement are palpable. He cannot wait to settle in with Fanny and complete the long haul with her at his side in the midst of such encouraging auguries.

Perhaps it is fitting to end (or at least stop for a moment) where the decade and the letters of the 1940s end: on notes of expectation and uncertainty, and exhale in a "pause for contemplation." For once novelist

Ellison crosses the point of no return with *Invisible Man,* its outcome is up in the air, as it would remain until publication two years into the 1950s. Though Ralph Ellison had not yet come up with the question that would end his novel, the line belongs here—as an actual rather than a rhetorical question: "Who knows but that, on the lower frequencies, I speak for you?"

John F. Callahan

To Herbert Ellison
New York City
FEB. 6, 1940

Dear Herbert:

Believe it or not, this is my first letter of the New Year! As usual, I have had every intention of writing before now, especially with Rose giving me hell to write you, but other things have, until now, managed to get in the way. First it was being without a job, then trying to get back on the W.P.A., which by the way I finally managed to do. I went back to work in December and since then we have been scrambling around trying to get caught up with our bills. At the same time I have been trying to do some writing. Rose is about recovered, but has not found any work; though she did take part in a show last Sat. night in which they burlesqued "Gone With The Wind." She's out now at a meeting and will probably be surprised when I tell her that I've written you at last.

I hope that it is not as cold as it was out there. We have been having the coldest winter since I've been here; plenty of snow and cold winds. But here at least we have the tall buildings to knock off some of the wind and the subways, which are usually warm, to travel in. You say that it is 8° below now; remember that week we slept in John's car when it was 8 above? I'll never forget it! How is John? I received a letter from Jessie last week; she seems as sick of Dayton as you are. If you see her tell her that I am answering her letter soon. What happened to her musician? Is that why she wants to come back to New York? She'll probably be shocked when I tell her that I am married. I don't know if I told you last, but Alonzo Townsend is here in the city and drops in to see us sometimes. There is also the girl Etta, who used to live on Stonewall Street, Etta Lawrence it is. She's living here with Page, the musician and his family. Charlesetta Sandborn is here, married, but I've failed to bump into her, not that I wish to in

458 W. 140th St,
New York City,
Nov, 3rd, 1941.

Dear Dick:

Despite my having read 12 Million Black Voices in M.S., I have just found reading the published book a deeply emotional experience; I spent the afternoon living through it and brooding over the photographs. Now it is displayed on the mantel piece for all who come to see.

Reading it I was torn between anger, tears and laughter, pity indignation and joy. I found it impossible to read it critically. Anyway, but something else. Each little critical thing I try to say is really not criticism at all, but a stroke, no matter how feeble, in our battle. And Dick, when I see the whole thing summed up as you have done it, I am rendered incapable for the moment of that controlled kind of fighting we must carry on. For it calls for exaltation--and direct action. My emotional drives are intensified and reorganized in such a manner that the only relieving action would be one through which all our your shame and wrong would be wiped out in blood. But this is not all. After reading your history--I knew it all already, all in my blood, bones, flesh; deepest memories, and thoughts; those which are sacred and those which bring the bitterest agonies and most poignant rememberances and regrets. After reading it and experiencing the pictures, the concrete images, I was convinced that we people of emotion shall land the most telling strokes, the distructive- creative blows in the struggle. And we shall do it with books like this!

Part of my life, Dick, has been a lacerating experience and I have my share of bitterness. But I have learned to keep the bitter- ness submerged so that my vision might be kept clear; so that those passions which could so easily be criminal might be socially useful. I know those emotions which tear the insides to be free and memories which must be kept underground, caged by rigid dicipline least they des- troy, but which yet are precious to me because they are mine and I am proud of that which is myself. Usually we Negroes refuse to talk of these things; the fact that I mention them now is an indication of the effect which your book has had upon me. You write of the numbness which our experience has produced in most of us, and I must say that while I was never completely numbed myself, I have had to rigidly controll my thawing, allowing the liquid emotion to escape drop by drop through the trap doors of the things I write, least I loose controll; least I be rendered incapable of warming our frozen brothers-- which all good writing must do. Writing is an act of salvation..., I felt so intensely the fire of our common experience when reading 12 Million Black Voices that I felt the solder of my dicipline melt and found myself opened up and crying over the painful pattern of remembered things. Not tears of self-pity--although the bitter searching journeys of my mother and my own early childhood, jerking from Georgia to Oklahoma, to Indiana, back to Oklahoma and finally to Ohio, are all here to justify a few. No, they were tears of impatience and anger. When experience such as ours is organized as you have done it here, there is nothing left for a man to do but fight! Here is

matter how poignantly we might wish it were not so. We have for a
long time lost our sense of brotherhood. Sure, we fling the term
"brother" around but it is meanless, a carry-over from times when our
experience was common and the stoolpigeon was not one of our national
types. I believe we need to enter a period of public testimony in
which our essential oneness might be confessed and our brotherhood
acknowledged and accepted. I believe you book makes a good start. I
have know for a long time that you have suffered many things which I
know,and that the truths which you have learned are Negro truths.
(Thats one reason I have always been amazed by those who distrust you.)
I guess it is because we have shared this experience that we do not
often speak about it in personal terms. As between Sue and Johnny-boy,
as was between my mother and I, speech is not necessary. We are
immersed in the same flow of reality. Of this, however, I am sure
now more than ever: that you and I are brothers. Back when I first
knew you, remember, I often speculated as to what it was that made the
difference between us and the others who shot up from the same region.
Well, now,(and it is this which makes us brothers), I think it is
because this past which filters through your book has always been
tender and alive and aching within us. We are the ones who had no
comforting amnesia of childhood, and for whom the trauma of passing
from the country to the city of distruction brough no anesthesia of
unconsciousness, but left our nerves peeled and quivering. We are
not the numbed, but the seething. God! It makes you want to write and
write and write, or murder. Like most of us,I am shy of my naked personal
emotions, they are too deep. Yet one gets strength when he shared his
deepest thoughts and emotions with his brother. And certainly you could
have found no better way to share your experience with the rest of
us . Of course you will write auto-biographies some day, but when
you do the accent must of necessity be upon those factors which made
your life your individually own. Now however, I think it more important
to make Negroes aware of those things which make them brothers. It
would have been fitting to have dedicated the book to you little one.
Certainly it tell all he would have to know about his father.....Dick
you asked me what I thought and here I am telling you what I feel. But
you see, all the wandering, all the bitter hopes and terribly sad and
painfully direct and simple yet profound sense of life revealed here
is part of myself. My family, our friends, the fields of the South, the
streets and traps of the city, I've lived it , know it all. You've
caught it here. Be proud to place your book beside <u>Native Son</u>, For
while in the novel you sliced deep and twisted the knife to open up
the psychic wound, <u>12 Million Black Voices</u> seizes hold to epochs and a
continent and clears them of fog, and it squeezes out of us what
we leave unspoken. Some could deny N.S. but all but a few have come
along that pathset down here...Not strange to us who have a sense of
the tragic, the book makes me feel a bitter pride; a pride which
springs from the realization that after all the brutalization, starvation,
and suffering, we have begun to embrace the experience and master it.
And we shall make of it a weapon more subtle than a machinegun, more
effective than a fighter plane! Its like seeing Moe Louis knock their
best men silly in his precise, impassively-alert Negro way. I think it
signific nt that I can feel pride of this kind in a Negro <u>book</u>. For us
such pride has been confined so long to humble Things. Let the other
boys, the not-yet-quite-transformed boys, sift this gold for ideological grains of lead. Like the mystic whose ability it is to controll
his mystic states, I am overjoyed to now be able to hold my life
in my hands, turn 152 pages and see the course of it, my past and
the outlines of my future, flow past before me. To controll reality the
scientist must be able to manipulate it, to weigh and balance it, to
test it. This is also necessary for the writer when he approaches
experience--and for the scientific politician as well. I hope our

.8

political leaders will realize what is here made available for them. Here is their statistics given personality; here, I believe, is the essence of what they must work with; all Marx and Engles, Lenin and Stalin wont help them unless they understand this part of the theroitical word made flesh. That is what I think and I could be no prouder had I written the book myself. Which is not suprising, since it belongs truly to our 13 millions, and instead of simply fustrating the misplaced sense of rivalry of those of us who try to write, it should make us all better writers. It gives me something to build upon, my work is made easier, my audience brought a bit closer. I'm a better man for having read it. Yes, and a better Marxist. I've taken all this space to say "thank you", Dick, because deeply moved. Its barely grammatical and I hope the meaning comes through. Surely it had enough force behind it. As my mother used to say when life pressed her closely, I felt like yelling " Lord, I'm filled up! I'm full!"

Sincerely,

Dick, this will amuse you. I have held this up about a week awaiting the outcome of a report from Mrs. Wetham that you had been in the U.S. for two weeks. Seems some gal who had just come over called them and announced herself as the girlfriend of a French psychiatrist and announced that you were in town. Because Fanny had gotten the enclosed bloodbank material together, I checked with Reynold's office. Seems you don't have to make news, it's made for you.

the least. I saw Ed Weaver (from Langston) the other night and he tells me Virgil Chandler is working on one of the railroad lines and comes in town over the weekends. Ed said that he was looking for me, for what reason I don't know, remembering our dislike for one another.

How is the N.Y.A.?* You must be careful and keep your ears open for there is a group at Washington who would like to see the country enter the war, and if we did the N.Y.A. boys might be called to fight. I understand that some senator is asking that the N.Y.A. lists be given over to the War department. Let no one fool you into the army, or navy, even if they promised you an airplane or a battle ship. The chances of getting away from a dull town like Dayton are far greater than those of getting away from a war, once the bullets are falling around you, or the mines brushing the sides of your ship. Here there is much crying about aid to Finland. They're raising money and giving benefits. But none of the people who are so hot about Finland are saying a word about the 3,000,000 homeless, foodless sharecroppers we have in this country, let alone the millions of us who don't have decent jobs. Wonder why nothing is done about conditions here at home?

Let me know how things are going with you. I hope things will be so that you can leave Dayton next summer. If Rose is working by that time we might be able to give you a hand, at the least. Be good.

Your brother,
Ralph

To Mr. McGruder
NEW YORK CITY,
MARCH 26, 1940

Dear Mr. McGruder:

Your is a very difficult letter to answer, since it contains information and charges which, even if they came from a friend, would be hard to accept without further clarification. By this I do not mean to imply that I believe your statements to be untrue, but that simply out of fairness to Herbert, to you, and to myself, I must have more information about Herbert and the charges you have made against him.

---

* The National Youth Administration, part of the Works Progress Administration, was a New Deal agency focused on providing work and education for Americans between the ages of sixteen and twenty-five.

Frankly, your letter seems to have been written under an emotional strain, with the results that all you seem trying to say does not quite come through. For instance, on page one you state that Herbert has lived at your home for over a year and that he paid rent for only five months. You state further that he did not try to get work all last summer, but you do not say why you tolerated this. It raises the question for my mind: What is, or was, the relationship between Herbert and yourself? Were you friends before he began living in your residence, or did you befriend him after you found that he could no longer pay his rent and had no place to go? May I also ask if Herbert was a paying roomer in your home at the time you saw fit to send your nephew away, and if so, just why did you decide in favor of an outsider over one whom I assume is a blood relation? You say that Herbert "shares no interest in my house. He lets dirt collect in corners and makes no attempt to clean up only in the middle of the room." What, in this instance, is your main complaint: is it that you would have considered his keep earned if he had been fit to reciprocate by seeing to it that your household work was done with some measure of pains? I am asking these questions, Mr. McGruder, so that I might have some perspective as to the background of the trouble. As you seem aware, Herbert is legally of age and I cannot understand his being treated with such indulgence, nor can I understand his reacting to your kindness in the manner that you indicate. May I suggest here that since he is still under your roof and is not receiving aid from the N.Y.A. that you insist upon payment for his room; I see no reason why you should allow his debt to you to increase.

You say that Herbert steals your ties, has he stolen other things as well? What does he do with your ties, sell them? If he helps himself to your ties and wears them publicly, then perhaps he does not intend to steal, but is merely being too free with your possessions. No doubt he does not understand that the same indulgence that you extend him in matters of rent does not extend to your personal effects. The mail is more serious. Can you give me reasons as to why he would do such a thing, surely he knows it is against the law. Are you accustomed to receive money or other negotiable paper through the mail, and if so, has he taken any of these? And the people above you, have they any proof that he has stolen from them? Tell me please what is it he is supposed to have taken? You say "things"; how does he dispose of them; and have any of these people attempted to trace their belongings to the pawnshops?

Why on earth if you knew Herbert had $23.00 didn't you make him pay his bill? There must be laws to take care of such situations. It is not for you or I to say who he should go to bed with—we can only [hope] that he has sense enough to know that there are laws against such things—but you must hold yourself partly at fault that he threw away that sum and ignored his obligation to you. He must have been very ungrateful to have done such a thing.

You ask me what should you do. I in turn must ask, what do you expect of me? One thing is clear; you want $20.00 for a suit that he purchased on your account. I will be willing to help, once I know more about the facts: since we are perfect strangers I must have some confirmation for some of your statements, a thing I'm sure you will understand. This is purely a matter of business, since I appreciate your goodwill in writing.

You say that your sermons to Herbert are futile, but yet you have hope. Hope for what? That you can reform him? In your P.S. you say that you'll keep him there, but you hope for a solution. Do you mean a solution in the form of a settlement of his debts; that I take some steps to remove him from your home; or that I try to effect a change in his conduct? Please let me know specifically what it is that you wish, and I will let you know how much I shall be able to do toward bringing it about. However, I don't know just what impression Herbert has given you of me, and I must assure you that there isn't much that I can do just now. Briefly, I'm on W.P.A. and I have a wife. This is not, however, an attempt to evade any responsibility I might have as Herbert's brother. On the other hand, as I said before, he is a man—only a few years younger than myself in fact—and I do not consider his welfare my responsibility; there would be very little that I could do about it even if I did. This does not mean, of course, that I won't try to reach some understanding with you, or that I would allow you to take more interest in him than I do myself. Had I known of his indebtedness to you I would have written you out of my own gratitude even though I think from your letter that your kindness has [not] had the best effect upon him. That, of course is not your fault, but his.

In reply to your request that I keep your letter secret, you must realize now that with such serious charges being made against my brother that I cannot do just that. He will have to know that this information is in my possession if I am to do more than remain aloof. And even if I pay the balance on the suit, what about the more serious charges of theft and seduction? Further, if we reach an agreement concerning the matter of the suit, he will have to know for otherwise he will take it as just another instance of your indulgence and will take no moral responsibility in the matter whatever. What I can do so as not to embarrass you, is to withhold any attempt to question Herbert until after I've heard from you. I think you can appreciate the position in which I find myself; I have not seen Herbert for several years and have only a vague idea of his activities during that time. Now your information, your startling information pains, and though I do not dismiss it, it contains too many inclarities for me to take any immediate action. In order that we might arrive at a quick solution won't you please answer my questions point for point and as soon as possible.

Sincerely,

Ralph Ellison

To Richard Wright

25 HAMILTON TERRACE

NEW YORK, NEW YORK

APRIL 14, 1940

Dear Dick,

I have been trying to get this off to you for several days, almost two weeks in fact, but aside from encountering difficulty in locating your lawyer I was held up by the Daily for I wanted to send you its review of *Native Son*,* that I am enclosing.

I contacted, finally, Mr. Malcolm Martin of 284 Quincy, Brooklyn, who has promised to give you whatever information he might have; I have prepared him to expect a letter from you. I am enclosing an excerpt from the *Public Hearings on the Condition of the Urban Colored Population* of New York: this I copied rather hurriedly while doing my project work. There are nine volumes of their reports and I'm sure they will yield other material of this nature. If Martin is unable to give you what you want perhaps I can find time to go through the whole set of the reports. If you decide upon this, please give me a good idea of what you want, even to the manner in which you plan to use it so that I may exercise some sense of selection. I learned the other day that women who line the curbs of the Bronx Slave Market are often accosted as prostitutes by white men who drive there in their cars. Thus many women who go there for work fall into prostitution. There are of course women who go there for that

---

* Wright's thunderbolt of a novel quickly became a bestseller on publication in early 1940— a novel much revered and feared on the American literary scene. Ellison read some of its pages as it flowed from Wright's typewriter in the Harlem office of the *Daily Worker*, and became its champion in many late-night gatherings of Harlem artists and intellectuals.

purpose alone. These men hang in doorways and attract the attention of the women as they stand in line. Hope this is food for your imagination.

You were a wise guy, Dick, for getting the hell out of here when you did, for I'm sure you would have had to commit murder had you stayed. *Native Son* shook the Harlem section to its foundation and some of the rot it has brought up is painful to smell. I have talked about the book, trying to answer attacks against it until I am weary. I am enclosing a review from the *Afro-American;* practically a very garbled opinion expressed in the piece but been expressed by Berry or Basset,* both of whom should know better. Ted and I talked with these two from 9 one night till 3 the next morning, trying to explain what fiction is all about, but I doubt if we had much success. It is very amusing to hear them state that your "Blueprint for Negro Writing" is an excellent piece of work, very correct, but that you didn't follow its plan in NS. Seems to me that we had a discussion with them one night that at that time they disagreed with most of it.

As I write, opinion on the book seems sharply, violently divided. I have attended two discussions, one led by Berry and the other by Ernier Garlin, where it was violently denounced and violently defended. This, I think is good; the assumptions of many CP members have been challenged. It is interesting to note that many reject the humanist implications of your choice of a character like Bigger, which means that they reject—or do not understand—the humanist implications of Marxism. Reddick tells me Herndon was horrified by the murder of Mary! This and other reactions on part of CP leaders makes me question to what extent they are emancipated from bourgeois taboos . . . From a literary standpoint, however, the book has raised several interesting problems for me, though I haven't bothered to put them on paper, or even to think them out fully. One is: how far can the Marxist writer go in presenting a personalized, humanist version of his ideology? Both Gorky and Malraux attempted this and both ran into mysticism and criticism from the politicians and theoreticians. Then again, does the writer who accepts Marxism have the freedom to expound a personalized philosophy? As I study Max's speech, it seems to me that you were struggling to create a new terminology, i.e. you were trying to state in terms of human values certain ideas, concepts, implicit in Marxist philosophy but that, since Marx, and later Lenin, were so

---

* Theodore Bassett and Abner Berry were fierce antagonists of Wright who, according to Ellison's biographer Arnold Rampersad, "seemed obtusely unable to distinguish between propaganda and good fiction." Rampersad, *Ralph Ellison: A Biography* (New York: Knopf, 2005), 131.

occupied with economics and politics, have not been stated in humanist terms of Marxist coloring. This lack I am trying to get at is indicated by the almost total failure on the part of Marxist-Leninist literature to treat human personality. Am I shooting up a blind alley in this?

I have had several talks with Victor Zeller, he is a very interesting guy: thinks differently from anyone I know. Glad you introduced me to him. Rose sends regards to all. We envy you the Mexican sun after a night of rain, sleet, and snow three days back: the city was white. But now it promises to become warm and then we'll have the heat in common. If there is anything I can do just let me know.

Sincerely,
Ralph

To Richard Wright

APRIL 22, 1940

Dear Dick:

For once I'm glad I made a carbon copy of a letter. I wrote you on the 14th, sending a number of clippings and part of the information you wanted. Some of this is in the carbon, which I am enclosing. That it did not reach you is your own fault: you gave me as your address Madero 62 Colonia Naval, Cuernavaca, Mexico, leaving the Mor—what ever the hell that is—completely out. I went back through the reports I mention in the carbon and copied Martin's testimony verbatim and then mailed it to you a few days ago. Since I remember the facts here they are: Upon an investigation into the condition of domestic workers in Brooklyn it was discovered that a white garage owner, who operated a fleet of trucks between here and the South, had been taking advantage of his contacts with people who stored their machines in his garage to offer them cheap help willing to work long hours for little pay. This they could have for a small consideration to the garage owner. He received many orders. To supply them he sent his trucks into the Carolinas and Virginia, offering young girls 17, 18, and 19 years of age free transportation to New York and a job when they arrived. The girls of course got into the trucks and were brought here. The trips were always to reach the city around 2 A.M. to avoid publicity. Once here the girls were placed on a job and told they would have to stay until their transportation fees had been paid. They were closely guarded, never allowed to leave the house unless with some member of the family, and were allowed no contacts with city Negroes. Later the garage owner opened a "night club" to which the girls were allowed to come in cars supplied by himself. At the club they were allowed to run up bills which left them broke at the end of the week, and—as I read between the lines—were laid open to moral exploitation. In many instances after the girl had paid her transportation fees she had to leave her job penniless. Some were forced to get back to the South as best they could, while others hung on until they found some other slave-jobs. They could not get on relief because they could not establish residence. There are other details and I think I'd better copy the testimony and send it to you. In case you can't decipher the carbon, the guy's name is Malcolm Martin of 284 Quincy, Brooklyn.

Any country that can put out a postage stamp like the one on your letter must hold wonderful promise: it's a work of art after those of the U.S. Hurry up and learn the language. And say, them there bulls must have a rooting, tooting, farting, shitting, bloody hell of a time with those Mexicans. You got in something Hemingway missed, or is it that the bulls in Spain are better mannered? Rose read the letter and screamed when she got to your description.

I sent you Ben's[*] review in my second letter. The talk goes on. I review, or rather discussed the book with a group of female government employees last Friday. Spent the evening in a beautiful Village apartment patiently explaining to the nice, if insipid, bitches just why Bigger felt like laying Mary when he had a hand full of breast. They seemed fascinated by that part. I was the only man present and might have been afraid if there hadn't been so many of them. The book is like the Bible, it seems to hold some kind of satisfaction for all.

I was in to see Ben a few days before his review appeared. He asked me my opinion and I told him right off the bat I didn't agree with some of the criticism of the book. He sounded like a broad scholar of deep perception after Berry and Basset. But the main difference was that he sees the necessity of defending Negroes like Bigger while they didn't. They called Max's speech a plea for class collaboration, while he saw it as mysticism and NAACP in character. I agree with you, the level of awareness is low as hell! They call themselves Marxists and fail to see the dialectics of ethical judgments involved in *Native Son.* They refuse to see the revolutionary significance of Bigger and while professing to be revolutionaries they have yet to rid themselves of their worn out Christian ethics. They worry

[*]   Ben Davis, the Harvard-educated lawyer who headed the Harlem bureau of the *Daily Worker.*

about whether you justify Bigger; but as Clarence Wienstock pointed out in a letter from Texas, the book cuts through all that. They fail to see that what's bad in Bigger from the point of view of bourgeois society is good from our point of view. He, Bigger, has what Hegel called the "indignant consciousness" and because of this he is more human than those who sent him to his death; for it was they, not he who fostered the dehumanizing conditions which shaped his personality. When the "indignant consciousness" becomes the "theoretical consciousness," indignant man is aware of his historical destiny and fights to achieve it. Would that all Negroes were psychologically free as Bigger and as capable of positive action! As for Max's speech, I have little hope now that it will be understood for some time, these people don't think in such terms. They do not see that in the speech the whole ethic of moral justification is swept aside in the realm of ideas as Bigger has swept it away in the realm of action. It is not a matter of "justice" but of necessity. People like Ben are not free, nor in failing to see Bigger's necessity they do not see their own, and for the Marxist, freedom is the recognition of necessity. Hence a Hicks or a Bates jumps off the train when the USSR signs a pact with Germany. No doubt there will be similar sharp turns in the course of history relative to the Negro question, and these people will be caught short . . . Clarence had an interesting thing to say: "I think that Wright wanted us to understand Bigger's name as a pun upon itself. What he does is so much bigger than himself. And the bourgeois feel this inwardly. They hear the voice of doom: The revolution is the easiest you can pay for oppression! That is why their answer is not simple "justice" but revenge." . . . I have been doing a lot of reading since this book's been going around, boy! I have to keep up with the silly questions. I'm convinced that the only thing to do is to study until I can quote Marx till I'm blue in the face. In the "German Ideology and The Holy Family" he has treated problems similar to these you have raised when he criticizes Eugene Sue for making proletarian characters models of bourgeois morality. These bastards here are hollering their heads off because Bigger became a man rather than a political puppet! To hell with them. What I meant above was that the only way you can impress the politicians is to quote Marx until you're blue in the face.

No more news of the stage since an item in the gossip column of the Sunday Times which stated that Robeson, Eddie Dowling and Marc Connally were interested in it. Personally I've been optimistic about everything but I can't see it on the stage or screen unless distorted; I hope that never happens. Have been waiting to see what *Life* would have to offer; perhaps you're too anxious.

Too bad that Dhimah* had to get herself bitten and I hope she's recovered by now. Rose is well and as full of piss and vinegar as ever. As usual, I have been bothered with this goddamed stomach. I am still trying to write a novel. Read Sheldon over again, discovering, I think, some of the reasons why he was valuable to you. His working picture of the mind is useful, as well as some of the psychological insights. I plan to go back to it later. I have it from Keller. Interesting guy, Keller. I'm intrigued by attachment he has for his wife; she seems to fulfill a profound need in him. Perhaps it isn't fair to say this since I've seen them together only three times, but a writer keeps his eyes open; they're swell people. What do you know of Hegel's *Phenomenology of Mind?* I've been running across references to it recently and I'm trying to get my hands on a copy. Let me know if you're familiar with it.

Now about the clippings and reviews: If you'll furnish the change I'll be only to glad to oblige. Prices are so high here that I've had to give up my magazines. I suggest that you attempt to trace my two previous letters, since I gave my return address and so far have heard nothing of them. See if there is a Colonial Naval address. Yes, I can get that copy of the *Journal of Negro Education;* however, it'll require sending to Washington.

Speaking of your Jew, you should hear some of the chauvinism NS has uncovered. Basset brought a guy named Harold Bolton to a party discussion of the book and the dam fool embarrassed even Basset with his obvious bias. Then too, that same evening Audley Moore, she of the big ass, gargantuan breasts and bad breath—who had not read the book—seized upon the incident where Bigger observes a man and woman cohabiting before their kids and proceeded to deplore your vulgarity in presenting such an incident. Because Negro women did not do such things! She was a Negro woman and she knew. Rather than do a thing like that before their children, Negro women denied themselves the pleasures of the bed! Above all it was amusing, she is evidently an earnest soul. Fitzgerald said to have included such an incident meant to say that 12,000,000 Negroes observed papa and mama at bed and thus become psychologically flawed. Boy, how they resist admitting their psychological kinship with Bigger.

---

* Dhimah Rose Meadman, whom Rampersad describes as "a tall, commanding dancer of Russian Jewish ancestry," was Wright's first wife; they married in 1939 and divorced a year later.

Why the hell should I go on with this, these cockeyed reactions will continue until after the revolution, which gives us plenty of time to talk. My only fear is that timid writers who want favor and who believe it possible to write profoundly and "safely" at the same time will take these controversies on their face value. I understand that there is talk of requiring all writers to submit their ms. for inspection before publication, which I am not against—if the inspectors are people the writers can respect. However, I understand the suggestion originated in Harlem! . . . One more thing: No one here seems aware of how really nationalistic NS happens to be. It is NEGRO American lit, this aspect has been ignored.

Write soon,
Ralph.

P.S. Am going to Washington D.C. to cover Nat. Negro Congress for N.M., will send material when I return.

Notice stamps on envelope, that's supposed to make you feel hopeful and contented.

Ralph

To Richard Wright
New York City
5/11/40

Dear Dick:

Glad you received the letters, and you were right: it <u>was</u> Dhimah who gave the address. Incidentally, I'll be very interested to hear if you discover that image of woman's thought process. No doubt it will come from Biology: they seem never to stray afar from biological reality—even when they cloak themselves with intellectual sheep's clothing—and I think men make a mistake to expect them to do otherwise; since men are somewhat responsible for that condition. Anyway it's apt to prove disappointing. Sometimes they seem to represent the conservative, irrational potential in human life. And in the movement they waver between their biological craving for security, which manifests itself as fear and inaction, and the emancipation, both sexual and spiritual, that is there to be achieved. In many instances they don't give a dam about revolution at all; only to throw off their girdles and let their behinds expand. Dam man's inhumanity to man—and woman! Incidentally, I saw Ellen at the National Negro Congress. She asked me for your address, but I stalled in order to ask your opinion; should I give it to her? She seems to be living at a high pitch of tension, both nervous and emotional, made me wish there was something I could do to help her. Some one had told her that you were not happy— which made her the second person to ask me that question. As in the previous instance I replied that I had no reason to suppose that you were not happy. I intend to discover who it is that has raised the question, if you wish; I think it is Jane. Ted was the other to put the question. I told him that I had no interest in the matter and it was dropped. You can see why I suspect Jane, she being the person they both know in common. I hope I am not doing her an injustice. I hope you'll forgive me for mentioning this, for I have no personal interest in the matter.

I agree with you that there is little difference between Ben's and the *American Mercury*'s article. Ben is discussing the book at the bookshop tomorrow and I plan to be there to make him aware of that fact . . . The book seems to be holding its own. *Look* magazine this week is carrying photos of housing in Harlem along with a snapshot of you and references to NS. And Horace R. Cayton has a pamphlet on Negro Housing in Chicago that is highlighted with quotations from the book. I'll try to send you a clipping from the *Defender* that tells of a man named D. Ellison being saved from an eviction when the judge was reminded of NS.

Some of the boys seem over anxious to discredit the book. During a panel discussion on culture at the Congress, a young Negro girl got up and pointed out the necessity of explaining the book, and expressed some surprise that some people were against it, since it articulated her own experience as a Negro. Later I found her and she told me that doing a conversation with Berry, Carlton Moss and others, she had mentioned how dumb she thought the reviewer for the Afro must have been and was told by Berry that he agreed with the last statement in the review, i.e. we need writers like Wright but not books like NS. She said she had quite a row with them and concluded that Communists were kinda dumb. A little gal with her said, "See there, that proves that these ole white communists don't understand the Negro" and I had to explain that these were Blackreds who were making the fuss. You can rest assured that Negroes outside our circle of befogged Lennox Avenue understand the book, are accepting it and finding strength in it. Rosie's uncle, who had read no book of fiction since his childhood, read the book straight through. It's all he can talk about these days.

Well, the Congress was the most exciting thing to happen to me. I found in it the first real basis for <u>faith</u> in our revolutionary potentialities I have found. I know now that we don't have to worry overmuch about the stupidities of black CP leaders. Some morning they will be awakened from their "Marxist" fog by the people who think they are carrying out God's wishes when they fight for freedom telling them, "Comrades, us don't want to disturb youall, but us thought youall would like to know that us got the revolution going like youall been talking about." Once you wrote of Negroes celebrating a Joe Louis victory: "Say, Comrade, here's the wild river that got to be harnessed and directed. Here's that <u>something</u>, that pent-up folk consciousness. Here's a fleeting glimpse of the heart of the Negro, the heart that beats and suffers and hopes—for freedom. I guess what I am trying to say in the article I am enclosing, is that the "river" is harnessing <u>itself!</u>* For me, that is the soundest basis for emotional and intellectual optimism. You told me I would begin to write when I matured emotionally, when I began to <u>feel</u> what I understood. I am beginning to understand what you meant. I suppose that's why the experience of the Congress was almost mystical in its intensity. When will the Marxist psychologists explain the material-dialectical meaning of the mystical experience?

Now I want some advice. I am working with *New Masses* since I did the Congress piece and they want me to activate as many Negro writers as possible. I think there will be more coverage on Negro problems and that here is the chance to evaluate Negro life; of course as limited by magazine policy. Also, I think that here is an opportunity to bring the intensity of Negro experience to the problems of American life, and I plan to approach men like Franklin Frazier, Sterling Brown, Ralph Bunche, Gene Holmes and others for articles—under their own names or otherwise—which need not be limited specifically to Negro subjects. Or if they are too busy for this, I shall ask their opinions as to what particular angles of the Negro problem they think need be brought to light. I think you made them feel the need for a broader approach to Negroes, for recently the Communist has carried articles by Basset and Berry that make an attempt to get away from the old sectarian approach. Gingerly, they are touching some of the problems I raised in my article on the War. I wish you would

---

* See Ellison's "A Congress Jim Crow Did Not Attend," published in *New Masses,* May 14, 1940, and posthumously in *The Collected Essays of Ralph Ellison,* ed. John F. Callahan (New York: Modern Library, 1995). In "A Congress" Ellison tries to balance ideology and action, and is excited by blacks once more arising as heroic individuals in American society.

let me know what you think of the plan, and make any suggestions as to how it might be improved. I am planning articles on housing here in Harlem, in Washington, and Chicago—I might get a chance to go out there. Which reminds me: what about doing something on Mexico, something Hughes should have done but didn't? I know you're busy, but if it appeals to you why not knock something out? Now don't ignore this because it's all new ground for me and while I want to get something done I don't want to waste a lot of time. You doubtless will see possibilities which I have overlooked and there might be a possibility of raising the level of awareness revealed by *NS*, i.e., on the meaning of the Negro in American life . . .

Seeing quite a bit of Ted;* he has quite a bit more respect for your ideas these days and is fighting tooth and nail for the book. There's a hell of a lot of boiling and seething behind those small bright, quick eyes. He's worrying about "intellectual arrogance" but like myself, he's reading everything that will assist to a heightened consciousness . . .

I know this is as bad as M. Walker and I promise not to do it again. Give my regards to Dhimah and her mother and let us hear from you.

Ralph

P.S. I'm mailing *Look* to you.

To Richard Wright
NEW YORK CITY
5/15/40

Dear Dick:

I received your letter yesterday; the check from Reynolds came today. I shall start rounding up the stuff tomorrow.

This is to send you the address of Orson Welles and John Houseman, who are interested in dramatizing *NS*. It seems that they were in touch with Reynolds and were unsatisfied, so they got in touch with Carlton Moss in an effort to get in touch with you. Here is the story: they want you to write them if it is worth their while to fly over from California to discuss the dramatic rights with you. They seem to have been told of your wishes

---

* Ted Poston, a journalist and writer colleague of Ellison's at the Federal Writers' Project from 1938 to 1940.

that Ted* be in consultation with whoever does the job and this does not seem to be a hold back. I know that this doesn't give you much to go on, but for right now this is all I know. I shall question Moss in the morning, when he is to give me the address, and, if he knows more, I shall make a post-script.

Mike Gold is in Puerto Rico; it isn't likely that there will be any action on your article until he returns. Why the hell didn't you send it to *New Masses*? They have been going to town with the book. I wrote in my last letter that I was with them now and asked your opinion on several matters; have you received it? We are running three pages of Letters to the Editor on the book in this issue, I'll see that you get it. Why not send us the article anyway, or something similar? How about something on the highest plane?

What about Ellen?

There is really no news except the war. We are already in it; soon they'll hand us guns. I hope we know what to do with them. The fat Queen jumped on her bicycle and took a run-out powder, like the rulers of all the countries Hitler's pushed into. He's saving us a hell of a lot of trouble, only he doesn't know it.

Got to sign off now, bedtime. Sol asked me to include the note. Incidentally, I have also mailed you a letter that had hung around the Douglas Hotel for a couple of months. Ted picked it up. Postal service down there must be slow . . .

> Regards to all from
> Rosie and
> Ralph

P.S. Berry wanted your address and I told him I would have you drop it to him. I'm wondering if in some way he has got wind of your article to Mike Gold.[†]

P.S. Here is the address: John Houseman
> Sunset Bld.
> Los. Angeles.

---

* Ted Poston.

[†] Gold, whom Arnold Rampersad called "perhaps the most influential Communist writer in the United States," gave Wright and Ellison their due, Wright for *Native Son* and Ellison for his piece in the *New York Post* on the 1943 Harlem riots.

Dick, these guys did not tell Reynolds who they were so watch your step. Moss tells me that he has found Houseman to be a shrewd showman and he feels that he would be amenable to work with since they are liberal, more objective than are the usual showmen.

R.W.E.

To Richard Wright
NEW YORK
MAY 26, 1940

Dear Dick:

I've just finished your reply to Cohn in the *Atlantic*. It was a marvelous statement, one I believe important far beyond the immediate purpose. Cohn's hair must have stood up on his head when he read it; the paper fairly crackled, but aside from that, it was an important political statement. It was positive and optimistic, and in sharp contrast to recent statements by MacLeish, who has fallen back into the old muck of morality, phony spiritual values, and other such crap that he would not dared to have uttered a few years back. He accuses the writers of his generation of having disillusioned the younger generation of the glories of war, of having shown them the emptiness of carnage, and he complains that the writers gave nothing positive to take the place of these illusions. Which means, of course that this war is not the same kind of war as the last . . . but I'll just send along the clipping, or perhaps you've read this already?

Well, things are developing rapidly here. I've just heard F.D.R. in a Fireside chat giving the signal for a drive against anyone who opposes his war moves. There is also a bill just through the House preventing the hiring of Reds and Bundists on WPA. It's a black, nasty picture. Here is the same conjuring with religion, exploited by patriotism—Hitler. FDR is oh so religious these days. And that's no typographical error. Dies has become respectable in his sight and all our other fascists are held up as models of Americanism. The Negro press screams for the indiscriminate rights for Negroes to die in the Army . . . But the new men are rising, and this war will bring forward many more. Fellow up from the South tells me that their problem down there is to work rapidly enough to make the Negroes aware of the necessity of discriminating between white folks. He says it's dynamite. Consciousness of the necessity for revolution [is] growing rapidly. It would be interesting to see what'll happen when they are made soldiers and given guns. Well, one becomes so impatient in times like these that you could say a good word for anarchy!

As for Hitler, I'm hoping he'll be able to invade England and break the Empire. For in the same stroke he'll dig his own grave. I've never before realized how necessary it is that I write, and I assure you that I intend to <u>write</u> rather than fight. And from the appearance of things I'd better start doing something about it right away. This Trotsky business seems phony to me and I'm afraid all movement will be watched. But let me know what you can do. Meanwhile, I'm trying to get my affairs straight, such as they are. Incidentally, tell Dhimah that her brother has failed to pick up her valise. If he'll send his address I'll contact him here.

Haven't heard anything of Basset or Berry recently, except that my article was too "individualistic." I did not argue the point . . . I'll try to get out to see Martin myself. Saw a picture of him and know who he is. I'll also see Miller, this week. Victor lost your address, he'll write, Sillen's wife had a baby. He'll answer soon as he's used to the new arrival . . . I've been unable to get a line on Mike; I'll let you know when I do. You really should do something for the *Masses*. Do you receive it, and did you see the letter on *NS* that appeared recently? I'm sending clippings, but am having some difficulty in rounding up past issues of the Negro press. Mags are coming along also . . . I am also enclosing something from Sol* asking you for a piece of fiction. Well, let me know the lay of the land, the time to jump draws close.

Ralph

To Rose Poindexter
29 Hamilton Terrace
New York City, N.Y.
July 19, 1940

Dear Winchy, wenchy, wench:†

I notice that you left out of here without your tonic, what was the big idea? I'm sending it along with the make-up, as soon as I can get out of the house. And you had better take it!

---

* Perhaps Saul Bellow, later on a close friend of Ellison's, who at this time was involved with one or two journals in Chicago.

† Ralph's first wife, Rose Poindexter. This is one of his most playful letters and the only letter to Rose that survives.

I'm glad you're working hard and that you find the cast pleasant to work with, which should make things easier for you. It seems that things started happening here just as soon as you got out of town. It wasn't enough for me to be sick, now Dhimah is confined to bed with intestinal grippe and is under the doctor's care. Her mother is here cooking for us, and since she is about over her cramps things seem to be going smoothly enough. It seems that I don't have yellow jaundice, which I seemed to have had, and I have to go to the doctor at 4 o'clock for another examination. It will be my first time out since day before yesterday. We had to give up the two dinner dates planned for Wednesday and Thursday—which was just as well with me.

So the town is pretty and has good ice cream. Well, I wish I could have ice cream. All I can eat is cereal and starches and more starches. And, of course, fruit juices—sounds like your old diet doesn't it? Only I take mine without a lot of you-know-what! I'd like to see the town but I'm sure I cannot by Sunday, so you come down here for the day, can you? Could you sneak a little of that ice cream down?

I paid Dhimah the fifteen dollars, I plan to send Lee Bros. 2.50 when I go out, and I have to pay for the lights and gas. Dave, I'll leave to you and I'll send you $5.00. I hope its enough for I only have 27.00 left.

I won't see Carleton, Putney, or John, unless they come by. Maybe you'll see them Sunday if you come in. I'll try and write Herbert today. O.K. Keed, papa's behind is beginning to droop, so he's fixing to cut out. Take it easy and never mind that bed. I'll take care of the first time I hit that town. Don't spill out the kisses when you open the envelope.

Love,
Ralph

To Richard Wright
NEW YORK CITY
MOUNT SINAI HOSPITAL
JULY 29, 1940

Dear Dick:

This is just a note to let you know how to reach me if you should find it necessary.

It is my second week in the hospital with an attack of jaundice. It is quite likely that I shall be here a week longer.

I hope your work is going successfully.

Sincerely,
Ralph

To Richard Wright
29 HAMILTON TR.
NEW YORK CITY, N. Y.
SEPT. 23, 1940.

Dear Dick:

I am enclosing the lyrics for which you asked. Dorothy West's address is 131 West 110th Street. The apartment faces Central Park and the easiest way to get there is by taking a Fifth Avenue Bus. It is located, I think, between Lennox and 7th Ave.

I have inquired around for Mrs. Dean's address, but so far I've had no luck. However, I haven't been able to catch the boys over on Lennox, but I expect to in a day or two, and I will drop it along in the mail.

As for Ray Dee: I haven't been able to discover who he is. I did, however, learn the name of the guy who was making a dramatization at T.A.C. His name is Kine and he works at the Book Mart, a bookstore located on 7th Ave. near 53rd St. Carleton Moss tells me that some of the people around T.A.C. read his dramatization and found it competent. I'll look him up if you wish.

If Walter Anderson (the guy who wants the recommendation) sends you a drafted letter for your approval and signature, he does so at my suggestion as I thought it might save you time.

There's no news. Everyone here is fairly well, and I guess that's all. Hope your work is progressing. Perhaps I'll see you some night in a week or two. Greetings to Jane.

Ralph.

To Richard Wright
APRIL 12, 1941

Dear Dick:

Everything is moving smoothly here. The mail is piling up but most of it can wait until you return. Bigger is still dominating Broadway,* and I suppose he will for quite some time. I trust you have received the letter from

---

* Wright's novel *Native Son* was adapted for the stage by Paul Green and Richard Wright and produced by Orson Welles and John Houseman. It ran for 114 performances from March through June 1941.

Harpers quoting the number of sales on the published version of the play and the increased sale of the novel; I mailed this several days ago. Tell Ellen that there is a check waiting for her, twenty-six bucks is the amount. You must get up to Detroit, or have you been already? If it were warmer I think that I'd hop a freight and go up there.* I see by the papers that Walter White was there and had no more success in persuading the boys to come out than anyone else. There is the drama, the tragedy of this period: Negroes acting as the tools of fascism and the Negro middle class utterly helpless. I've been negotiating with the *Masses* to send me there to tell the story. They have made no decision as yet but I am afraid that they will be satisfied with what Joe North is able to give them . . . Rosie and the dog are o.k. but my eyes let me down in the streets the other day. The oculist tells me that I have an astigmatism of the right eye. I suppose by time you return I will have glasses. Hell of a thing, isn't it, to begin to pay the penalties of the writing craft before one begins to earn the advantages . . . There are clippings on *Native Son* here, along with a paper from Dr. Harris of New Jersey, in which there is published an interview. I liked the interview, especially what you said about the level of consciousness to be found in Harlem, the Negro middle class etc. So long. Hope you found your folks O.K. Nothing has turned up on the Brewer thing.

Ralph

To Richard Wright
453 W. 140TH ST.
NEW YORK CITY
NOV. 3RD, 1941.

Dear Dick:

Despite my having read *12 Million Black Voices*† in ms., I have just found reading the published book a deeply emotional experience; I spent the afternoon living through it and brooding over the photographs. Now it is displayed on the mantelpiece for all to see.

Reading it I was torn between anger, tears and laughter, pity, indigna-

---

* In the labor strife of the period the automobile companies successfully recruited unemployed blacks to work as strikebreakers.

† Wright's *12 Million Black Voices* and its stunning complementary photographs had an enormous impact on Ellison, moving him to a militant and compassionate reconsideration of his boyhood life in Oklahoma.

tion and joy. I found it impossible to read it critically. Anyway, I'm not really a critic, but something else. Each little critical thing I try to say is really not criticism at all, but a stroke, no matter how feeble, in our battle. And Dick, when I see the whole thing summed up as you have done it, I am rendered incapable for the moment of that controlled kind of fighting we must carry on. For *12 MBV* calls for exaltation—and direct action. My emotional drives are intensified and reorganized in such a manner that the only relieving action would be one through which all our shame and wrongs would be wiped out in blood. But this is not all. After reading your history—I knew it already, all in my blood, bones, flesh; deepest memories, and thoughts; those which are sacred and those which bring the bitterest agonies and most poignant remembrances and regrets—after reading it and experiencing the pictures, the concrete images, I was convinced that we people of emotion shall land the most telling strokes, the destructive-creative blows in the struggle. And we shall do it with books like this!

Part of my life, Dick, has been a lacerating experience and I have my share of bitterness. But I have learned to keep the bitterness submerged so that my vision might be kept clear; so that those passions that could so easily be criminal might be socially useful. I know those emotions which tear the insides to be free and memories which must be kept underground, caged by rigid discipline least they destroy, but which yet are precious to me because they are mine and I am proud of that which is myself. Usually we Negroes refuse to talk of these things; the fact that I mention them now is an indication of the effect which your book has had upon me. You write of the numbness which our experience has produced in most of us, and I must say that while I was never completely numbed myself, I have had to rigidly control my thawing, allowing the liquid emotion to escape drop by drop through the trap doors of the things I write, least I lose control; least I be rendered incapable of warming our frozen brothers—which all good writing must do. Writing is an act of salvation . . . I felt so intensely the fire of our common experience when reading *12 Million Black Voices* that I felt the solder of my discipline melt and found myself opened up and crying over the painful pattern of remembered things. Not tears of self-pity—although the bitter searching journeys of my mother and my own early childhood, jerking from Georgia, to Oklahoma, to Indiana, back to Oklahoma and finally to Ohio, are all here to justify a few. No, they were tears of impatience and anger. When experience such as ours is organized as you have done it here, there is nothing left for a man to do but fight! Here is something else: usually we Negroes are distrustful of each other, no matter how poignantly we might wish it were not so. We have for a long time lost our sense of brotherhood. Sure we fling the term "brother" around but it is meaningless, a carry over from times when our experience was common and the stoolpigeon was not one of our national types. I believe we need to enter a period of public testimony in which our essential oneness might be confessed and our brotherhood acknowledged and accepted. I believe your book makes a good start. I have known for a long time that you have suffered many things that I know, and that the truths which you have learned are Negro truths. (That's one reason I have always been amazed by those who distrust you.) I guess it is because we have shared this experience that we do not often speak about it in personal terms. As between Sue and Johnny-boy,* as was between my mother and I, speech is not necessary. We are immersed in the same flow of reality. Of this, however, I am sure now more than ever: that you and I are brothers. Back when I first knew you, remember, I often speculated as to what it was that made the difference between us and the others who shot up from the same region. Well, now (and it is this which makes us brothers), I think it is because this past which filters through your book has always been tender and alive and aching within us. We are the ones who had no comforting amnesia of childhood, and for whom the trauma of passing from the country to the city of destruction brought no anesthesia of unconsciousness, but left our nerves peeled and quivering. We are not the numbed, but the seething. God! It makes you want to write and write and write, or murder. Like most of us, I am shy of my naked personal emotions, they are too deep. Yet one gets strength when he shared his deepest thoughts and emotions with his brother. And certainly you could have found no better way to share your experience with the rest of us. Of course you will write autobiographies some day, but when you do the account must of necessity be upon those factors that made your life your own. Now however, I think it more important to make Negroes aware of those things that make them brothers. It would have been fitting to have dedicated the book to you[r] little one. Certainly it tell[s] all he would have to know about his father . . . Dick, you asked me what I thought and here I am telling you what I feel, but you see, all the wandering, all the bitter hopes and terribly sad and painfully direct and simple this profound sense of life revealed here is part

---

* Mother and son in "Bright Morning Star," the powerful, pitiful, pitiless last story in Wright's *Uncle Tom's Children*.

of myself. My family, our friends, the fields of the South, the streets and traps of the city, I've lived it, know it all. You've caught it here. Be proud to place your book beside *Native Son,* for while in the novel you sliced deep and twisted the knife to open up the psychic wound, *12 Million Black Voices* seizes hold to epochs and a continent and clears them of fog. And it squeezes out of us what we left unspoken. Some could deny NS but all but a few have come along that path set down here . . . Not strange to us who have a sense of the tragic, the book makes me feel a bitter pride, a pride which springs from the realization that after all the brutalization, starvation, and suffering, we have begun to embrace the experience and master it. And we shall make of it a weapon more subtle than a machine gun, more effective than a fighter plane! It's like seeing Joe Louis knock their best man silly in his precise, impassively alert Negro way. I think it significant that I can feel pride of this kind in a Negro <u>book</u>. For us such pride has been confined so long to humble things. Let the other boys, the not-yet-quite-transformed boys, sift this gold for ideological grains of lead. Like the mystic whose ability it is to control his mystic states, I am overjoyed to now be able to hold my life in my hands, turn 152 pages and see the course of it, my past and the outline of my future, flow past before me. To control reality the scientist must be able to manipulate it, to weight and balance it, to test it. This is also necessary for the writer when he approaches experience—and for the scientific politician as well. I hope our political leaders will realize what is allowed here made available for them. Here is their statistics given personality; here, I believe, is the outline of what they must work with: all Marx and Engle, Lenin and Stalin won't help them unless they understand this part of the political word made flesh. That is what I think and I could be no prouder had I written the book myself. Which is not surprising. When it belongs truly to our 12 millions, and instead of nicely frustrating the misplaced sense of rivalry of those of us who try to write, it should make us all better writers. It gives some something to build upon. My work is made easier, my audience brought a bit closer. I'm a better man for having read it. Yes, and a better Marxist. I've taken all this space to say "thank you," Dick, because deeply moved. It's rarely grammatical and I hope the meaning comes through. Surely it had enough force behind it. As my mother used to say when life pressed her closely, I felt like yelling "Lord, I'm filled up! I'm full!"

Sincerely,

Ralph

To Richard Wright
THE NEGRO QUARTERLY
One West 125th Street, New York, N. Y.
. . . . SAcramento 2-8650
MARCH 24, 1942

Mr. Richard Wright
Paul R. Reynolds & Son
599 Fifth Avenue
New York, New York

Dear Dick,

We wish to thank you for making it possible for *The Negro Quarterly** to reprint the "Men in the Making" section from *12 Million Black Voices*.

In order that we do not overstep the limitations of this privilege, we shall send Reynolds the proofs of the section we plan to use as soon as we go to the printers, sometime in May. I shall see that the same reaches you.

Sincerely yours,
Ralph
Ralph Ellison
Managing Editor
The Negro
Quarterly

RE: w

P.S. I've also sent our thanks to Reynolds and Best.

Ralph

---

* Ellison served as managing editor of *The Negro Quarterly* from March 1942 until the struggling journal's demise in 1943.

To Sanora Babb
THE NEGRO QUARTERLY
One West 125th Street, New York, NY
SAcramento 2-86500
APRIL 10, 1942.

Dear Sanora,*

My darling, even though I've taken some time to answer your letter I wish
I could tell you how relieved I was to receive it. A few days before it arrived
I had gotten to the fairly desperate point of calling Helen and asking her
if you were all right. She said that you were, and that she had received a
long letter from you only a few hours before. I don't have to tell you that I
felt better knowing that you were not ill or anything; yes, but a little hurt—
although I had no right to be—that you hadn't written. I suppose I've
been spoiled and had come to depend upon you more than I knew. I think
about you constantly. There is still much conflict in my emotions. Yet the
other day, riding along on a street car, slowly in the warm spring sun and
reading Karen Horney's soon to be published work on self-analysis,† I
came upon the words "a truly good, human, individual for whom every
individual seeks . . ." and found myself thinking of you. There it was in
a flash, a sensation of you as warm and as real as the spring sun and the
rocking motion of the car. Some day I'll get around to telling you just what
has been happening to me since I've known you. All that I can say now
with certainty is that it was no surface thing. It was no "rare holiday" but
the start of a new phase of my life. I am only just now getting back to the
point where I can write again, but rather than being discouraged by it I
believe that now my ideas are a bit more mature. Perhaps knowing you has
made me more human—but I've said all this before, it's only that it is not
a static fact, but a process, a process that makes itself felt in my reaction
to every subsequent experience. One doesn't say thank you for such . . .

---

*   Ellison most likely met Sanora Babb in November 1941 at a League of American Writers
meeting in Manhattan. At the time Babb, a fellow novelist, was editor of *The Clipper*, a radical
literary magazine on the West Coast. There was an immediate, strong magnetism between the
two. During Babb's time in New York they became lovers; after her return to California they
exchanged intense letters, and remained friends.

†   First published in 1942, Karen Horney's *Self-Analysis* remains a relevant book, exploring
the extent to which individuals can use psychological techniques to develop solutions to their
problems on their own.

and I don't thank you now, only don't cut yourself off from me. Should you do it will not be a matter [of] my disintegrating or anything romantic like that, but I find an important part of me unresolved. People like us don't go to pieces for long, nor do we crush easily; but we carry scars. My truly good human woman, blue eyed woman, my love, forgive me all the unhappy things I've written about malted milks, brief sweets; because you're really very basic to me. I've tried to be very honest about us, i.e. with myself. And though perhaps I'm a bit unwise to put it in writing—it's really a thing that should be said face to face (because faces are expressive and voices more direct than cold print)—I've been wondering if I was as brave about you as I might have been. And again, I wondered if this new sense of my own personality that you gave me might have aroused a subtle resentment within me. Resentment that by the very nature of American life only a white woman—I write with a deep anguish, Sanora, so please understand—could have appreciated those forces within me that I struggle so hard to develop. A truly human person, a woman who answers all my complex needs; a woman courageous enough and beautiful enough to become a human being is rare even for the most fortunate of the West, and for my own people, almost non-existent. That is a terrible thing and when discovered it makes for much chaotic emotion. Out of desperation man learns to cling to even his deformities because they are his own and he must have some stable ground on which to stand. I give up R. with reluctance because I understand the life out of which she was made and it's all we have. In some things we do not wish to hope. For some things we do not <u>dare</u> to hope; for, as with your entering my life, if realized it shakes up one's whole world. I once knew of a case where a Negro fell in love with an Irish girl and insisted that she wear a deep sunburn. He loved her as a human being, he tried to control the thing which made them different. What I'm trying to get at is not quite the same thing, yet the psychological pattern is similar. Sometimes we are oversensitive. We have a need for the best in human relationships and at the same time we often follow non-essentials to thwart the fulfillment of that need. This is morbid and I'm stopping right now. Action is much better in these matters than thought. All I know for certain just now is that were you here I'd remain with you night and day until you left. If you should perchance come and not wish it, then you must keep me unaware of your presence, lest I make a fool of myself and embarrass you.

It's strange that you ask me to be generous in recognizing that your novel is but a first draft. And stranger still that you should doubt that I might misunderstand true generosity to the extent that I might withhold whatever true criticisms I might have. I feel such a need for real criticism myself that I find it impossible to read your work and not hope in whatever way I can to help you make it better. I'll send you all my notes as soon as I am finished with it. Yes, you told me that Commins was out that way. I hope you have gotten back to the novel and that it is completed for fall publication. You <u>must</u>.

Thanks for the addresses. I've been terribly busy trying to get material and learning what has to be done. It's a strange world. I have to build an organization and learn it at the same time. But it's exciting and I see great possibilities in what we're doing. As you see, we're not confining ourselves to Negro writers. I think actually there is nothing to stop us from performing a real service both to American writing and social relations. So many writers have become aware of the Negro that I see possibilities of getting contributions from many to whom it has never occurred to publish in a Negro magazine. If Dick Wright, Doren Miller, and I can publish in *N.M.* then there's no reason why white writers can't publish in the *N.Q.* What do you think? Things are going very well, subscriptions are coming in and we've finally begun promotion.

I am enclosing a sub and a membership card to the Negro Publication Society. The sub will be much appreciated, but I suggest that you take out a regular membership in the society, which will bring you not only the magazine but a book as well. We are offering the *Negro Caravan,*[*] the book reviewed in the clipping I sent some time ago, which sells for 44.75. I think the book worth having at any rate. You might talk about what we're trying to do—and darling, if you should feel the urging of a Negro muse please give into it as I'd love to publish you.

Yes, I am feeling better, thanks to the removal of the tooth and your vitamins . . . Have you moved? Send me a picture, please. Did you receive *12 Million Black Voices?* I mailed it several days ago.

I've been saying some of the things we talked about recently. I've also been taking part in the League's readings from works in progress. Last time with Franz Weiscopf, Harry Slochwer and Klaus Mann, who is still pompous and aristocratic in his thinking. I don't know how much good I do but I keep on. I suppose I get more out of the experience than do those who listen

---

[*] *The Negro Caravan: Writings by American Negroes,* edited by Sterling Allen Brown, Arthur P. Davis, and Ulysses Lee (New York: Dryden Press, 1941), quickly became the most important, comprehensive, and influential collection of its kind.

to me . . . It's snowing, a rainy snow, and I'm a little tired. I would like to be in a warm big room before a fireplace with you. Green plates on the mantle, red pillows on the floor, books to read and smell of fruity apples and brandy. Music? Yes, but quietly. My darling. Write notes to me if nothing else.

I love you.

Ralph

To Sanora Babb

NOVEMBER 19, 1942

Dear Sanora:

I'm very sorry to think you haven't received my letters, but from your last I'm led to believe this is true. Only a week before you wrote I mailed you a note in reference to your ms. explaining that I had just moved and that it was on my desk to be re-read, since in moving I lost the notes summing up my opinion of it. I've just about finished the second reading and you'll have it definitely, direct from me—unless you still wish me to leave it at Random House.* Please, anyway look in the box—I did not know I was free to write your home—and see if my letters came through, as I'd still like you to know the things I had to say. No less than you, I want to feel free to write and to recapture our companionship. In my last letter I promised to mail you a carbon of a story I've been busy with; and, if you are interested, I shall mail it as soon as it's finished. I'd like to have your reaction. I wish I could talk to you for just one hour, Sanora. Because then I'd be able to clear up a lot of misunderstanding. Do you know that the merest note from you is far more emotionally disturbing to me than the novel I have occasion to read? That's rather poorly put, but the truth is that I find myself welling up to the point that I'm psychologically unable to answer. True, I'm very busy, but not <u>that</u> busy; it's just that I'm still in the middle of a conflict I cannot resolve. Perhaps I don't want it resolved; I don't know and don't suppose I shall, until I've seen you again—and perhaps not even then. So the confusion of feelings persist with the nostalgia (October's just past), the tenderness and, in some strange way, the hope.

---

* Ellison refers to Babb's first draft of *Whose Names Were Unknown,* her Dust Bowl novel, which Bennett Cerf of Random House planned to publish. However, when Steinbeck's *The Grapes of Wrath* came out in 1939, Random House reneged on its commitment. Although it is unclear which if any of Ellison's letters included this page of notes about the manuscript, the text in this letter of November 19, 1942, indicates that he had not yet sent Babb his thoughts. Therefore his comments follow as an appendix to this letter.

In re-reading your novel I had the same feeling of an emotional dense atmosphere I experienced during our first conversation, coming up Park Avenue in the dark that was more of Kansas and the plains than of a taxi and New York. Communication is ever a mysterious thing.

There is little to tell about myself. I've been busy trying to get out the magazine, which I find quite interesting, but not very satisfying to my own creative urge—a question that I believe was in back of something you said in a letter. We'll have another issue out in a couple of weeks and I'd like to know what you think of the last two. I had nothing to do with the first. If I stay out of the army long enough you'll see what a real publication it is possible to have with practically no money. To have shelved *The Clipper** was a great mistake. Incidentally, I'm still fighting that old battle with members of the board. Maltz should give you an idea of what's been going on.

I've moved my home, as I said above. It's a poor neighborhood now, with a folk church behind me and a bar in front of me, and excitement twenty-four hours a day. It's only a few blocks away from the old address but it's like living in another world. Here the people are alive. Boys stand beneath my window (I'm two flights up) at night and sing riffs from the latest hot recordings, the drunks roll past, fire trucks clang up the hill, and the building across has a copper roof designed with plumed gothic arches. I'll tell you more about it next time.

Dear Sanora, I hope you're finishing up your work in progress. And you're much too good a writer not to have your picture in all the papers— which would be a double treat. I've watched the trade journals with expectancy. Let me know how it is going . . . Was down to see H and T during the Summer and talked to her the other day. They're both well. You <u>might</u> write her. What else are you doing? And please don't worry about your book, you'll get it if it's the last thing I do.

Love,
Ralph

[ELLISON'S COMMENTS ON BABB'S DRAFT OF
WHOSE NAMES WERE UNKNOWN]

After reading your novel I found that my main criticisms of it were much the same as when I spoke to you: That it might have been made struc-

---

* In the early 1940s Babb served as secretary of the West Coast branch of the League of American Writers and edited the literary magazine *The Clipper* until its demise.

turally tighter had you dramatized your scenes more; that the whole would have had an even greater impact upon me had you organized it more closely around Julia's consciousness, since it is her "miscarriage" that foreshadows the 'stillborn strike' and the frustrations which lead up to the migration and accompany it; since her journey from bread (bakery) to breadlessness (pepper tea) furnished the pattern for the whole. This, I think, would have made unnecessary many of your own comments and would have intensified the splendid moods you've captured so well. I think after looking back through *Grapes of Wrath,* that you've captured the period and its meaning as well as he did, but that he organized his structurally and symbolically much tighter. Again, while he showed woman in the role of leadership of the family unit, you do a much more subtle thing because, consciously or no, your novel exploits, draws upon, the wide-spread fear of pregnancy, miscarriage, and the discovery of abortion, which weighs upon the consciousness of women during periods of drought and famine. Further, as a friend of mine has pointed out in an essay, Steinbeck was never for the workers in GOW, but was pleading subtly for the big shots to stop their wrongdoing. You, however, have been for the worker, showing his rebirth into a new consciousness. I'm glad you didn't overdo it, and it is ironical that one of the most mature novels of a strike was not published . . . I think Mrs. Starbuck one of your best characters, along with the old man, Julia, the kids Freida. Milt, for some reason is not as vivid . . . I keep coming back to dramatization: if at all crucial points, such as the beginning, and especially the end, you allowed the characters to take over, the effect would be terrific And allow the crucial scenes to develop at length. For instance, the incident of the snowbirds could have been keyed even higher. And the end should have been—listen to my 'should-have been,' well you asked for it—given in terms of <u>their</u> voices, <u>their</u> idioms, <u>their</u> emotions, not yours . . . There is a metaphor which intrigues me no end in this sentence, "The large owls scooped through the dark and settled on the tops of the frail country telephone poles like <u>blossoms</u>." Write and tell me why you chose blossoms, please . . . The discovery of the grocer's suicide is good enough to stand more dramatization and development, it's got plenty of visceral grip in it. And Mrs. S's trip to the bank is wonderful . . . Well, that is about all. I understand that this is a first draft that would be tightened in the next so I won't waste your time drawing your attention to things you would catch anyway. Oh, one other thing I like very much, the touch you've given the intimate scenes. They're nice and I envy them . . . Next time don't be afraid of the Negro, you know enough to give a deeper insight into Garrison even though he doesn't demand much attention. One final thing. Don't worry about not getting this book published. Reading it closely makes me feel sure that you will find an occasion to say your say about the same people and the same problems. The incidents might change, and the scenes, but your personal investment in their problems seems, to me, strong enough to produce not one, but several novels. If I ever see you again I'll tell you what the book tells me about you. I won't risk putting it down here because I might be wrong as hell. Anyway I had no idea of what a complicated, what a delicately complicated girl you were.

To Langston Hughes
NEW YORK CITY
DEC. 11, 1942

Dear Langston,

I delayed answering for a few days in hope that I could have something definite to say about the magazines, and something different to say about the proposed meeting. Unfortunately neither is possible. The magazine is at the bindery and Angelo* has decided now that it is not possible to go through with the affair at this time. Seems that we took a financial beating with the Golden Gate affair and can't afford the outlay necessary to arrange a large meeting. So I guess that's out.

   I'm glad to hear of the new draft ruling and I hope it applies to you; we need poets, us Negroes more than we need soldiers. You must tell me about the wreck, seems that you're missing all of the calamities these days. Keep it up and give my regards to Horace.

Sincerely,
Ralph

To Lloyd Mallan
TUES. FEB. 9, 1943

Dear Lloyd Mallan:

Due to illness I've been away from the office for over a week, hence the delay.

---

* One of the Scottsboro Boys of the early 1930s, Angelo Herndon was the founding editor of the newly launched *Negro Quarterly* in 1942.

In trying to set down my reactions to your poem, please forgive me if I say the obvious in several instances. And please understand that I do not feel that my ideas are dogmatic. I am quite humble and sincere in this and what I have to say is put in the spirit of one who stands with his feet in two cultural yards, that of my own people, on one hand, and that of the larger, American version of Western culture on the other. I am aware that the boundaries are vague in many places, but because your poem is offering in a sense to serve as a gateway between the two it would be well to see just how it would be used by the readers on the Negro side of the line. For unfortunately what might be intended as a gate for those on your side, might for those on my side appear like a barrier. Or worse still, a trap. This has nothing, necessarily, to do with intentions. It is only that the experience of Negroes has been so different from that of whites in this country that common Western concepts are clothed in drastically different forms. That is put rather clumsily. Here is what I mean: Amos and Andy are considered by many whites to be quite harmless humorists. But Negroes view them as vicious poisoners of the democratic mind. Their meat is our poison. So the point is raised as to just what might be considered the Negro concept of humor.

Now I believe irony, since you view the conditions which produce Mullato Mamma as 'hopeless' and draw certain contrasts, is the dominating mood of your poem. Thus you have raised the problem of just what is the Negro's concept of irony. What form of irony holds true for both white and black Americans? It is obvious that it must be broad enough to be meaningful to both groups if we here are to use it. But to leave this point a moment.

In quantitative terms, in terms of the unrelieved and detailed description of MM. she is a slut. You take more than two pages to tell us so. But the contrasting section (which is presented in abrupt transition and with such light strokes that the two there, mistress and lover, barely come through) is given only half a page. In fact, not half a page; for most of it is given over to recording naturalistic detail: smokestacks, cafe dancehalls, chairs, the city, etc. which in itself is no objection. But in the first section you present a portrait that is more or less well known to Americans; you are not presenting her in terms of your individual insight and vision. You're saying "See, this is the type I mean. You've seen her yourself." But if you are to give the reader new insight into this woman it seems to me that it would be necessary to be just as unmistakable as to what your insight is. I think your poem is unbalanced; and while the details of the last section are perfectly acceptable I feel that they are ineffective because they are not filtered through your own vision nor through the consciousness of any being within the poem—unless that of the dawn. And while dawn might terminate the nights of both, might turn off the screw, or screws, it can settle no issues nor make any strongly felt—except as you, M.M. or the other two figures are aware of it. This might be a hell of a way and a wordy way to criticize a poem, but it seems to me that one of the main things that such a poem, a poem of ironic contrast, must have is balance.

Briefly, I think that in order for our readers (Negro) to see the human core of the slut—and remember that they regard her so and shun her since they live on the white man's terms, for the most part—they must be made equally aware of the sluttish core of the mistress. Otherwise, while you might be aware that the two are sisters under the skin (or skirts), we will continue to be more aware of the horrible brutality of the one and oblivious to the brutal voluptuousness of the other. And worse, we might feel that your own attitude toward M.M. is sadistic rather than humanistic, or at least sympathetic, and you fail to emphasize her humanity through precise content.

Now for the problem of communication. In its use of American Negro folk music the poem is in the tradition of the Blues—But with an important difference: you write as an outsider who wishes to point out certain likenesses and contrasts between the Negro and white situations to readers identified with M.M. Like the blues, you present the brutalized and symbolically accept it. But because you stand on the outside and present the woman without any redeeming features, you make impossible that ambivalence of feeling which the blues arouse and which is the secret of their appeal. The blues are, in a sense, a technique of taking the spell off of the horrible in the Negro situation through the magic of laughter; a technique of transcending the situations named in the Blues lyric. But, and it is here I believe you go wrong, the blues come from the inside, from within the Negro group itself, and carry all those meanings, which, though critically unexplored, are felt or understood by Negroes . . . and by others who are able to identify themselves with the singer and the situations described in the lyric. In other terms, the Blues are a ritual through which Western values and social proprieties are rejected, or, at least, defied. This is true because the lives of those who create the blues are so different from the lives whose social, political, moral and esthetic values are protected by that complex of meanings, attitudes, manners, etc. which make up what the solid bourgeois considers the "respectable." As you know blues is a lyric; when sung, the I of the lyric becomes identified with the ego of the listener. Which again is an adjustment you do not allow the reader. Because your poem is not a lyric; it is descriptive; and though it too rejects the double standard of judgment usually brought to bear upon the two young women and attempts to affirm the humanity of M.M., it, by the intrusion of a sensibility (your own) which in the world of the poem does not take the oath of allegiance, does not take sides, bars the door to Negro entry. It sets up a Jim Crow sign, to put it drastically. It is the identification between the I of the blues lyric and the audience that makes for that kind of balance that your poem lacks. Perhaps, you'll say that the dawn in the poem offers this balance by bathing them both in the same grey light. But what Negro identifies himself with the dawn?*

The world of the blues, while brutal, even degraded, is a democratic world. It is like a lodge, a secret society whose privileges are available only to those who wear the official insignia. It is somewhat like the situation wherein Negroes refer to themselves as 'nigger' yet are outraged, even to the point of violence, when an outsider uses the term. Some Jews react this way to the term 'kike'; and yet when used within the group the terms sometimes convey emotional overtones of tenderness.

Yours is an objective point of view, Mallan; and I've said all this order to point out that the blues are never psychologically objective, even though they appear to be. You might probe your own wound and laugh at it and you might share that laughter with another who was also wounded, but for one uninitiated, to do so would be something quite different. Though you and I might start out from a common assumption concerning M.M., we wind up at quite different points because you do not allow me to enter the vehicle of your irony; it's too narrow to seat the broad bottom of my tender awareness that most white Americans believe M.M. is the product of absolute heredity, rather than a combination of heredity and environment.

Perhaps it is your overall method that makes for my difficulty. Eliot and Joyce used something similar, but they were writing at the end of a cultural phase, and of a world they felt to be breaking up. And they took the fragments of that world (especially Eliot) and exploited them for the emotional charge, the associational values, the affect, which they contained. But Mulatto Mamma, while moving through this world, and indeed cre-

---

* Ellison's paragraph on "the problem of communication" reads almost like an early version of his famous passage defining the blues in his 1945 essay "Richard Wright's Blues."

ated by it, was not _of_ it. Her world was never whole, say, in the sense of that of the lovely lady who stooped to folly and placed a record on the gramophone in Eliot's *Waste Land*. Because M.M. was never a participant in that Nineteenth Century world which produced the set of values which made folly for a lovely lady such an overwhelming tragedy—and which a hundred years later gave such poignancy to Eliot's fragment. Those values were never applied to her on a equal basis, because that would have meant that she should share in the economic and social rewards which those values protected. When applied to M.M. they were usually applied by those who stood above and pointed down, saying "look at you, bitch, Why aren't you as good as we?" Which of course is one of things you're writing about.

Anyway, I've used much too many words to say much too little and I'm going to stop. If you wish to continue the discussion I'll let you do the talking for a while. I won't, however, try to say how much of your poem is salvageable. That would be presumptuous. For the economies of the writer are unpredictable, as is the poetic vision when it gets into the groove and coordinates illusion and its reality. I do believe you're working fertile ground and I'd like to see what you bring forth. Frankly, from what I've seen of your translations (the Guilin piece and the new Latin-American anthology), I believe you capable of a much more empathy into Negro themes.

Which brings me to the final point of this letter. Thanks so much for sending the Guilin. I like it and would like to use it, but the others object to its length. Please let me know if you could bear to have us use only part of it—I hate to task you. And in the meantime I'll try to arrange to use it complete. Incidentally, the poem makes me feel like an ass for the crack I took concerning the work of the Committee—or at least your part of it. I'm sorry. If we use the poem it will be used in the next issue, which we hope to get to press this month. I'm pretty sure we'll use it, but give me your reaction to the extraction idea.

Please forgive me if my remarks seem to ramble, as I'm thinking on the typewriter in the midst of moving. I promise to make up for it in the rebuttal(!)

Sincerely,
Ralph Ellison

To Sanora Babb
306 W 141 St
New York City
july 4, 1943

Dear Sanora:

Although I thought I never would again, I was painfully glad to hear from you. It makes me glad that I failed to send the novel.* But let me hasten to say that I'm sending it this time, as soon as the post office opens after the holiday weekend. You've caught me at a moment when I'm giving up things, being so full of disgust, and sickness and despair that I'll part even with this thing which symbolizes so much that was meaningful and dear for so short a while. But really isn't as bad as all that. It is the fact that you've gotten another novel down that makes it possible for me to surrender this. You see, it's the only thing I had of you with emotion in it. Pictures? yes, but they are of other times and places and lyrical at that. Well, so I've given up a lot in the last six months and in time I'll give up even more. It's the giving-up without replacement that's bad; and that's why I'm glad you have the other book, which of course, you'll be too wise to allow me to see after all the struggle for this one; but it will be published and I will have it anyway. Sanora, if you felt adequate <u>without</u> writing books you'd have no necessity to write them. So don't worry about that anymore. Each book is a new encounter with experience; if you don't say it all at one time, then you're assured of something for the next—plus the experience of technique and emotion gained through the last attempt. Besides, you're more than a one-book author.

So I <u>will</u> take time to tell you what's been happening to me and what I'm doing. You know about the magazine. I went into it feeling that it was badly needed, since so little is understood about Negroes even by themselves or by those dedicated, supposedly, to leading us. I tried to translate Negro life in terms of Marxist terminology, hoping that by so doing to offer cues and insights to those whose field is that of action. (An unpublished editorial pointed to the significance of the zoot-suit before the

---

* Ellison refers to "Slick," his early unfinished novel of proletarian bent, begun in Dayton in early 1938 and worked on for some time in New York before he parted deliberately "with this thing . . . that was meaningful and clear for so short a while."

riots).* Well, I didn't get very far with those I thought I was working with. The usual distrust of a Negro who dares to think. I was accused of everything from going over to the "talented tenth" to being a Trotskyite! Simply because I was against the easy generalizations made concerning the Negroes' feelings about the war. Now that the riots are underway I wonder what those people who criticized me for not seeing the naive heroism of Joe Louis as pattern for my people think with Joe's hometown the scene of the worst riot in our history? It seems we can never support an issue without getting drunk and murdering off everything else we believed before. So now we're saying the Axis caused the riots—which is not even a half-truth.

Who believes this? Negroes don't, because we have been dedicated to riots and lynching as the bull of the Spanish bullfight is dedicated to the State. We can even <u>feel</u> these things approaching. It is the abyss, the volcano over which our homes are built. To tell us that agents had to come from abroad to start this national (not natural) phenomena is to insult us, Certainly it does not make for progress. It is easy to make nice neat explanations <u>after</u> the act, to explain it away in newsprint, or to make verbal noise to excuse Roosevelt of his responsibility. But who the hell believes it? What bothers me so is that these things could have been foreseen and were not. Today there is much noise made over a Madison Square Garden rally out of which nothing really concrete came; and what is worst is that my people want action desperately and attended the meeting not because so and so sponsored it, but came because some action would be forthcoming. Instead the riot came. And more will follow. You see, Sanora, it's the old issue of dissolving the League writ large. Always we throw away the medicine the moment the guarantee is relaxed . . .

Anyway, I'm not discouraged by the reception of the magazine—I came in with the second issue—for it was given quite a reception by those who grasped what I was trying to accomplish. I was willing to fight the detractors—who later would have accepted it opportunistically were it successful. Just now it is having a hard time. I had proofed the issue now long past due last month, after which I went to Vermont for my health. But when I returned it was still at the printer's. Herndon's job was to get the money—and perhaps you heard about Herndon. So that's a brief outline of the magazine. No great success, but it did convince me that I could get a publication of a fairly high quality—there was never anything

---

* Ellison will make important use of the early zoot suit passage years later in *Invisible Man*.

like it in Negro journalism—and that there was a need for the kind of material I chose to publish. It would never make Negroes run out into the streets shouting for a second front, but already a group of young writers were forming around it who listened to us where they had found others much too slick. It was meant as a long-term investment, but hell, R.W.'S aren't made in a day or by two line slogans . . . I'm saying all of this so that if you hear any of the funny little rumors that drift back and forth you'll know how I really feel. I can't write for NM nowadays because they say few things about my people that I can agree with—at least they never say enough. And would not allow me to. I hate to say it, but P.M. does a much more forthright job. Perhaps the day will come when I can function there again; I hope so. As mild as my last piece published there was, I hear some of the boys disliked it.

Wasn't it a sad little picture, and did you notice how my hair has gone? East and West of Loyang/Long has it been since we parted / Then there was snow like the flowers / Now come flowers like snow . . . but most of all I'm writing because you were always easy to talk with, even with all the distance in between. I started to write from Vermont to tell you how the country was.

When we went up the snow was still on the mountains and in the sunless gorges and the brooks swollen and the spring already green but late. We lived in a valley surrounded by mountains and the nights were cold and the days bright with fog in the morning that hid the tops of the mountain and hung clear over the top of the valley. Then after a week the apple blossoms and lilacs came and the bees; and in the mornings when you went out the rabbits left holes in the dew-wet grass and the squirrels made chattering targets on the wood pile. Then you walk up the hill to the old lumber camp, past the birches showing through the firs like girls in bright spring dresses, to the spring for water; and mark the flight of birds, the robins and swallows, imitate the chickadee's high, shrill call, frighten the snowshoe rabbit, gracefully clumsy, with feet made to flash across deep snow and not this spicy hill of trees; then, back to the old farmhouse and eat, and feed the baby, who is very silent upon first getting up and smiles only after her cereal is eaten. You would have liked her.

Most of the day I helped my friend repair the house, jacking it up in several places, knocking down the old plaster—150 years old—and replacing it with fiberboard and laying a floor. Then I fished for trout for the first time, alone with the noise of the stream and the flies and wrote much mentally of what I saw and heard and felt and altogether feeling sad that

I was alone and had no one to share it. My friends would have thought I was a fool—and no doubt I am. It was good for me though. I weighed 185 when I returned and had something of that complexion that girls used to admire when I lived in the sun and used my stomach for digestion rather than for keeping my emotions under control. I wish I had made pictures. I don't feel quite as good now. Then, I felt that confidence you feel when you find yourself adequate to conditions you had long since ceased to feel that you could control; the hard, clean life of the farm and the woods, of physical labor in the hot sun and the eating of rough plain food. Emotionally I must be a primitive, because that is the way I would have life; simple and direct even when brutal. Not that I would abolish the subtleties but prefer to feel their grain, without the timidity, or cynicism or callousness of some who call themselves politicians.

Well, now I'm back with the problems. If we get the dough the magazine will appear again. Just now we have brought out a series of pamphlets, some of which I edited, others that Herndon did himself while I was away. I'm writing again; now on my own. I'll never waste time with organizations again, but will write of the things I believe in and of what my people believe in, hope for and feel. If the organizations like it, wonderful; if not, I'll try to write with such honesty that, rejecting it, they will be forced to recognize the point of view. I don't want to do this, but I'm forced to do so. When a writer believes in an ideology to the point that he trains himself to articulate that ideology, adapting his ways of feeling and seeing and thinking and his ways or writing to that ideology and then finds it discarded by those for whom he wrote, then he must find more stable values upon which to build his work. For instance, as I've said before, my personality was organized and given direction when I first heard of the theory of a nation applied to Negro life. But today, when my people are prepared as never before, by India, Liberia, China, the USSR, to grasp that concept in living terms—nothing is said about it. It is like preparing a field for seed then throwing the seed in the brook. Emotionally I am prepared to write out of that concept, nationalism, as never before. But the right wouldn't want it and the left wouldn't either; War times are times of regression, and to abandon a concept just when it begins to bear fruit is <u>infantile</u> regression.

Negroes who once recognized some whites as friendly now arm themselves with knives when they go into white neighborhoods at night. They no longer trust white men; and all this over emphasis of Axis-inspired riots is meaningless. Don't be fooled if some Negro leaders voice it, they don't lead us anyway; they were abandoned by their masters and are more full of futility than you'd guess. I'm trying to map a new course for my writing, based upon those things that are abiding in Negro experience in the U.S. It will be much harder than before, there'll be no token fame to go with it nor pictures in *NM,* but I'll learn to write so that it will be read because it is true and perhaps now and then with a streak of beauty, but like some of the passages out of letters I wrote when homeless in Dayton it will have feeling of having been lived. Perhaps that is what you wish to see done. If so, you'll have at it . . . What else have you seen of mine since the NM? There is a short story* in *Common Ground,* Summer 1943. I'd send one, but as usual, I am broke. I am sending an unpublished manuscript though, which you can send back when through. It's just to prove that I'm doing something. Don't take it seriously as I'm very dissatisfied with it.

And write and tell me about your book and how you are. I enjoyed *Edge of Darkness*† very much. The war has helped Hollywood. Tell me all those things I'd like to know and even those I'm afraid to ask about. Got any snapshots? And thanks again for writing and for what you had to say about Detroit. As least you're standing firm and I'm glad I know you. (I had most forgotten: I watched out for your writer friend but he did not show up and our phone was cut off.) No, there will be no forgetting of friendship. Silence—and not too much of that—but no forgetting. There are too few folks to share one's feelings with for that, and whatever else happens there'll always be that big, warm wave of sympathetic emotion ever ready to do whatever it wills to do. Sounds irrational, doesn't it? But you know that it isn't. And even if you don't write again it'll still be true. I <u>know</u> it's true.

Love,
Ralph

---

* "That I Had the Wings," collected posthumously in Ralph Ellison, *Flying Home and Other Stories,* ed. John F. Callahan (New York: Random House, 1996).

† *Edge of Darkness* was a film adapted from the 1942 novel by William Woods. Set in Norway during the Nazi occupation, the Hollywood film is a gripping drama of collaboration and tragic resistance.

To Ida Guggenheimer
NEW YORK CITY, N.Y.
JUNE 26, 1944

Dear Ida,[*]

I did promise Bridie that I would come by and arrange the books, but when she called I was in the midst of a piece of work (the same upon which I was working when you left). And since then I have become ill—again! This time with an upset stomach and low blood pressure. Dr. placed me on a strict high vitamin diet, prescribed a lot of rest and sunlight, so I've taken the rest and the vitamins and the medicine and slowly I feel strength returning. In fact I feel well enough to sit at the typewriter, which I haven't done for a week. I finished the long Wright essay[†] only to discover that the magazine was already made up and had to cut it down from 5000 words to a thousand—which was very annoying, to say the least. They are publishing a little short story about the seaman in Wales in the July issue,[‡] and I am mailing you a copy along with this note. Hope you like it. Incidentally, my mail just arrived with a clipping from the Chicago *Tribune* in which Paul Engle goes way out on a limb by saying that "There is a remarkable story by Ralph Ellison about a Negro aviator in the United States army air forces. I think it's the finest thing in the book. The author, by the way, is a Negro now in the merchant marine. Which is very nice to me, but makes an awful fool of him. Before I became ill, I had lunch with a couple of *New Masses* people (perhaps that's why I became ill, it was very emotional although friendly). And one of them was simply furious, she said, upon first reading "Flying Home."[§] It seemed awfully defeatist to her, but with a further reading she saw something more. I was only amused . . . They, by the way, assured me that things were different and that they wanted me very much to enter a story in the Art Young Memorial Prize contest.

[*] Ida Guggenheimer was a wealthy widow who befriended Ralph because of their common love of literature, his talent as a writer, and their shared activism. When Ralph was strapped financially, she quietly helped him out. This is the first of his many letters to her in the 1940s. See Arnold Rampersad's excellent passages on her and their relationship in *Ralph Ellison,* esp. 172–231, 182–92.

[†] An early version of "Richard Wright Blues."

[‡] "In a Strange Country" was published in *Tomorrow* magazine in July 1944.

[§] "Flying Home" was published in *Cross Section* in 1944.

I told them that I might, but that it took a lot of deep feeling and think-ing for me to get as far away from them as I have, and it would not be an easy matter to come that close again. I talked as earnestly and sincerely with them as I've ever talked with anyone, trying to impress them with the human, moral, nature of any such movement as that of which they are a part. There was a time when I was willing to die in the interest of their ideas, my ideas, but now things are different. In the meantime there is work to do, the kind of work that I've been preparing myself to do. That will remain for a long time.

I haven't been able to see Buzzy, but have kept in touch with Clara, who says Buz is doing quite all right. I plan to pay her a visit as soon as possible . . . You must be having a time up there in the country. It is too bad that Sukey has to leave so soon. Is there no one to join you when she goes? Here the hot weather is beginning, so you stay there. However, had you been here last evening you would have gone to the Negro Freedom Rally . . . P.M. said that thousands were turned away. Certainly there is interest in such things . . . I have been reading a new book by Lewis Mum-ford, called *The Condition of Man.* It is a study of the development of Western personality from Greece to the present; and while I disagree with him frequently, I find it a very rewarding way to read history. As for *Cross Section,* I haven't read anymore of it. I shall have to look into Nat Turner. There is nothing recent been done on his life, I don't believe, and most of the old things are brief historical sketches. Thomas Wentworth Higgin-son did a good piece on Turner that appeared in the *Atlantic Monthly* dur-ing the Civil War period. I'll see what else there is when I get around to the library . . . I quite agree with you that the *Times* did Goshal* a mean trick; however, some reviewers were much friendlier. I'll have to read that also.

As for my teeth: no, I haven't finished that. I have one more to be filled—or is it two? Anyway, my stomach decided to go dead in the midst of all that and I haven't been back. I'm a little tired of the whole thing. The doc thought I had developed an ulcer, but it seems not. Blood pressure has fallen from its normal 130 down to 106, which takes the pep out of one to say the least. How I would like to join you there! But I'm afraid that the WSA† would not approve—as soon as I'm well enough to get down there I shall inquire. I talked with Clara today and she asked me to say hello

* Kumar Goshal, a native of India, was a prominent writer and lecturer in New York in the 1940s.

† War Shipping Administration.

as she would not be able to write just now. Perhaps she will have by time this reaches you. I hope that whether you sell the place or no, that you'll remain there for the summer. It's so very hot here. Please give Sukey my best and I'll write again in a few days.

Love,
Ralph.

To Ida Guggenheimer
New York City
JULY 13, 1944

Dear Ida:

I'll get to the urgent part of this note first: I'm flat broke and I need to borrow some money (1) for my rent—which can wait a while longer—(2) for my dental work—which has stopped altogether—(3) for my doctor to whom I went yesterday and discovered that instead of rising my blood-pressure had dropped four more points. I hated to admit to him that this was no doubt due to the fact that I hadn't been able to have one of the prescriptions he'd given me filled. My stomach has returned somewhat to normal, but it is hot here now and with the low blood pressure I find the afternoons extremely trying. Most of all, it stops me from working. It's a dreary tale, and if it were not so much the pattern of my life I'd find things extremely disgusting. I've tried to take care of these matters without bothering you, but with no success. Everyone seems out of the city.

The most irritating feature of being ill does not consist in the effect it has upon the above matters, but in the fact that it is stopping (or at least it slows me down) from getting down upon paper the most ambitious and conceptually mature fiction idea that I have ever attempted. I work on it during the morning, reading and making notes, feeding my imagination—but by afternoon and after I've eaten the heat knocks me out and I fell into a state of physical depression and troubled sleep. The main thing, I guess, is that I still feel like working. Incidentally, two more publishers are interested in my doing a novel, Little Brown & Co., and The Atlantic Monthly Press. There have also been two fan letters on the Wales tale—all of which is encouraging.

I'm sorry to learn that both Sukey and Bing are leaving so soon, it seems unfair both to you and to them. You should, however, remain there if you possibly can as the city is very unpleasant. By next Monday I shall know whether I may have permission to leave the city and I'll let you know. I've got to know definitely what my status is to be in relationship to the Merchant Marine, as I need very much to take advantage of the 1000 dollars that Reynal & Hitchcock are still impatiently offering me. A young Negro woman, a friend of mine, was by yesterday for a chat and was complaining that she didn't know where to spend her vacation. And while I didn't mention it to her I felt very sorry that I had not brought you two together. She is intelligent enough to be companionable, and handy enough to have been helpful. I guess I've never thought of introducing you because I seldom see her except when she hears that I'm sick. I'll see that you meet in the fall.

No, I've read neither Maugham nor Browder recently, but I shall get around to both as soon as possible. With this new project in mind I have been doing very specialized reading, however, and it will take quite some time. Granville Hicks reviewed Browder's book in the *New Republic* and of course did not like it. He says that Browder "tried to demonstrate that there is no opposition between his hopes and those of Eric Johnson, and I'm sure he is right. What I am looking for is an effective opposition to both of them. Until it appears, I agree with Arthur Koestler that "pessimism is obligatory." Which of course says more about Hicks than about Browder . . . Interesting to hear about George Murphy. I'm not surprised that he's doing that kind of work in the army. The army must have some pretty clever psychologists in charge of former radicals, their insight is sometimes singular. Put the pressure of a seemingly absolute force upon George and those like him, and they'll do most <u>anything</u> with enthusiasm. The great Negro Soldier, indeed! I am beginning to believe that nothing comes closer to justifying the fallacious theory of Negro inferiority than one Negro Communist. Which is a mean thing to say and I blame my saying so partly upon the heat . . . We've had our first near riot of the summer on Monday, when three gangs of young Negro boys shot it out among themselves and with the police. Several were critically wounded and one was killed—which almost precipitated riot action against the police force. It'll take more than a glib mouthing of words like Teheran to deal with these explosive and irrational elements. These boys are fighting among themselves just now, a little later with a little more desperate confidence and they'll strike out beyond the borders of the ghetto. I hope first, though, that they'll turn against some of our Negro politicians and hang them from the highest steeple in Harlem.

I'm surprised that you were annoyed with Bridie about the books. You know that I am glad to do whatever I can, and if you wish, as soon as I can I'll go down and arrange them. I would have gone long since, but Clara told me that Bridie had gotten married at last and had left the city for a while. By the way, I forgot to tell you that I went out to the Harbor*—Long Island—for the Fourth. And quite unexpectedly. Some friends picked me up. We stopped at the middle class Negro colony there, made up of New York and Brooklyn businessmen, social workers, professionals, and their wives and families. A typical Babbitt watering place, but for the day the people were quite pleasant and hospitable—and the seafood was good. I didn't get to the beach, but lay upon the grass in the sun and talked writing and politics with 'two fellow travelers.' The trip back was tiresome however and I returned a bit the worse for wear. Aside from attending two of the stadium concerts this is about all I've done. But with the European victories, and De Gaulle's visit, life is interesting to say the least.

This is all for now, Ida. Please give my best to the girls. Tell them there is a wonderful recording called 'G.I. Jive,' by Louis Jordan, which I hear sometimes about three o'clock in the morning when the traffic is gone and juke box in the bar on the corner is king of everything. It's such a good recording that I don't mind when it wakes me up, it's so much more interesting than most of my dreams.

And so, with love,
Ralph

P.S. Ida, just as I finished sealing your letter the phone rang. It was Richard Wright who informed me that he was trying to get in touch with a friend in Ottawa, to see if he and his wife could go there for their vacation. I, of course, told him of you and your problem. His reply was "Gee, if she just wants someone to keep her company, Ellen and I would be glad to keep her company and look after her too." I asked if he were serious and he said yes, that he was. So there you are, if you are interested let me know. His wife is Jewish, Marxist, and very nice. He has just finished a book and wants to go somewhere that he can do some physical work to harden his body up a bit and he doesn't want to be around many people. It's time you two met anyway.

R.

---

* Sag Harbor is a town on eastern Long Island across from Shelter Island on the way to East Hampton; according to Arnold Rampersad, "among black professionals in New York, Sag Harbor was the most prestigious vacationing spot within reasonable distance" of New York City (*Ralph Ellison*, 101).

To Richard Wright
306 WEST 141ST ST.
NEW YORK, 30, N.Y.
AUGUST 29, 1944.

Dear Dick,

I'll have to send the enclosed clippings for news, since for over a week now I've been flat on my back with a fever and cold. It's broken now, but left me so weak that I've been nowhere nor seen anyone. I even missed Horace. However, as soon as I can I'll get around to hearing what the latest stage of the controversy really is. I talked with Mrs. G. by telephone and found her all disturbed and quite exasperated with Minor and Sillen. I had told her what the possible reaction would be and she did not want to accept it. Now their smearing technique is so obvious that she <u>has</u> to accept it and she's quite sad. Said she was writing you. I hope if you do anything else along this line, that you'll make it analytical. Those guys are so bankrupt that they could answer nothing. They quote you against yourself, but so could you quote Browder against Browder, or in behalf of your own position. I thought Horace's article very well put—and of course Communist failures of the kind he mentions would fill a book . . . Let me know when you plan to return, and if it isn't too soon I'll keep you posted on what's being said. Give my best to Ellen.

Ralph.

To Richard Wright
306 W 141ST ST.
NEW YORK CITY N.Y.
SEPT. 5TH, 1944.

Dear Dick,

Thanks for reading over my contract* and returning it so promptly. I'm signing it this week and intend to get to work immediately.

I was finally able to get down to see Ida; she had asked me to read over a letter which she was writing you, but I was too weak to see it before she put it in the post. After reading it I was glad I hadn't. I would probably

---

* Reynal and Hitchcock had offered Ellison an advance of $1,500 spread over a year for a novel to be delivered by September 1, 1945.

have collapsed. She has encountered such a moral problem in this matter, torn as she is between her belief in the truth of your statements and her own need to believe unquestioningly in the boys, that talking with her about it reminds me of a psychiatrist in session with a difficult patient—which is complicated by the fact that I not only understand something of her need and the part which age plays in it, but also because I have a real respect for her aliveness and courage, and feel toward her a certain affection. Anyway, when I went down I read a copy of the letter, disagreed with her interpretation of your statements concerning the Trials, and spent the next four agitated hours reading the article to her, showing her (1) that your concern was not with a comparison between Ross's crimes and that of the wreckers, but with the motivating force behind the confessions; (2) that you upheld the Trials, rather than attacked them; (3) that explicitly you had not rejected Communism as a way of life, but had praised it in several places, and, (4) that you were concerned with, among other things, the morality of American Communism, and how it took its form from the nature of race relationships in our society etc. and her struggle to reconcile the faults which you write about with that which is vital about the philosophy and theory of action, was, in fact, an example of that morality in action.

Next day she phoned, very chastened, to agree with me. Dejected to the point of saying that if she made such a mistake she'd better stop trying to do something about the problem. She's very worried about what you'll think, and can't understand how she made the mistake. No doubt she'll write you again soon.

This thing seems popping all over. I ran into Scott, who tells me he heard Shirley Graham attacking you as a 'sadist,' 'politically confused' etc., in all of the boys' terminology. Is she a member? And I myself heard Attaway again (last night at William Steig's) making use of Ben and Sam's anti-Semitic argument. He accuses [me] in one breath of being much more of an intellectual than you, and in the next of making you my "only voice," whatever the hell that means. How righteous envious folks can sound! It was easy for me to explode his arguments, however. I did hear the rumor that you were neurotic again; first it was Bigger, and now you. "If you can't control a nigger, call him crazy," you know the technique. My reply was simply to ask if there were any sensitive individuals who in our time did not indicate some neurosis. Every one of us in the room did show some form of neurosis, so they shut up pretty quickly on that score. Let me hasten to say that I view the whole matter as a study in political psychology. I even wonder if you were not a little optimistic in hoping that any but a few would even understand what you were discussing. Americans are undoubtedly the most naive people alive . . . Incidentally, I've been reading a piece in *Direction* by Isadore Scheider, in which he admits that left-wing influence in literature is a weak thing, but he claims it was beaten down by the right, and by the so-called non-political critics who make political judgments in their criticism. He of course said nothing about the left's own bankruptcy in this development. He does admit that Cummings writes good poetry, but lays this to the poet's <u>bad</u> anti-left politics—which is the most honest statement by one of those guys I've seen in a long time.

I'm enclosing Ben's latest ravings, this time directed at Horace. This is what I would have received had I been fortunate enough to have published my article or review. I recalled our efforts to reach Yergan about the proposed meeting between Pearl Buck and a group of Negro writers the other day, when I learned that the Urban League is now sponsoring such a meeting—two, in fact—along with Harry A. Overstreet. He's a psychologist who has been running articles in the *Sat. Review of Lit.* on the Negro in American writing. So it goes.

I'll see you when you return.

> My best to Ellen &
> Julia,
> Ralph

To Richard Wright
SEPT. 30, 1944

Dear Dick,

Enclosed you'll find a copy of my contract with Reynal & Hitchcock. Please read it for jokers and let me know what you think of its terms.

One clause, that concerning the time of delivery, will be changed. I shall deliver the ms. within one year, rather than in the stated six months.

Especially would I like to hear what you think of the royalty percentage.

My agent feels that it is a generous contract, but I haven't discussed it with him to any length, and I won't until I hear from you.

Hope you and Ellen are enjoying your vacation. I've still no news on the controversy.

> All my best,
> Ralph.

To Fanny
301 W. 141 St.
New York City,
oct. 4, 1944

Dearest Fanny,*

You've been gone a week today and I've waited all day for a letter. Now night has come on and the only word I've had of you came when Winnie called to say that <u>she</u> had heard from you. It didn't make me feel any better—which is an understatement. Actually, I've begun wondering who the hell am I?

Like a lovesick fool I've been unable to sleep since you've been gone, food is uninteresting to the point of nausea: and I've two deadlines staring me in my paralyzed face. I've tried to retreat into sleep, but all through the night it's troubled dreams, or I lie on the razor's edge that is neither sleep nor waking. Darling, I <u>resent</u> the way I feel. I don't want to be this way. It is a dependence I've never known before, and it's not at all pleasant. Even my imagination, which has been my friend always when I've been unhappy, now has turned against me. Instead of consolation it gives me fears—and I don't have to tell you the shapes of these fears, we've discussed all that before. Your answer has always been, "But I'm with you," but now you're neither with me nor even willing to speak to me (I have a phone even though I discovered Mrs. Billie Warren† has not). I feel murderous and suicidal, the latter which I haven't known for years. I tell myself that you are very busy, but I can't help but feel that to endure your absence is not.

You're ill, or you have reconsidered our relationship, or, which is just as unfortunate, you're having a conflict over it. I started to try to fly out to Chicago this afternoon, but that would have been foolishly impulsive, and my health is not too good. But then, perhaps that would have been the last thing you'd desire. So here I am.

I know I shouldn't feel this way, but I do; and you're the only one who can do anything about it, one way or the other. Before you came I had a way of dealing with such things. Indeed they seldom happen when the armor of good sense and pride is buckled on. But with you I let it fall,

---

* Ralph's first letter to Fanny. They met for dinner at Frank's Restaurant in Harlem in June 1944 and fell in love that same night.

† Fanny's mother, whom she was seeing in Chicago.

gladly. Now the tender, uncertain flesh is getting burned—and I resent it. If, darling, you have doubts please write me and get it over with. When one has to die it's best to die quickly. There is enough suspense and tension in my life without your becoming the main center of it.

Fanny, I'm stopping this right here. Not because I have no more to say, but because it's a hell of a first letter. Especially since I had such things, such heartfelt things, to tell you those first days of these years you've been away. Perhaps it's good I told them only to your picture.

So goodnight—not "my love" but you whom I love. Wire me if you're all right and my fears only fears, and write me airmail if you've changed your mind. I would like to be far away when you return if you have.

Ralph

Add has returned.
Spinky's in town.
No mail of importance

To Ida G.
[MARCH 1945]
SOMEWHERE AT SEA*

Dear Ida;

This is just a note to let you know that I'm away again. Although I'm sure Fanny has phoned you by now. I tried to get you but had little time and failed. There is little to tell you now. I don't know where I am or where I'm going, I only know it's across the Atlantic. I'll have to wait and tell you all about it when I return. Meanwhile give my love to the family and my apologies—and you take it easy. There is such a lot of the world that needs changing that I'm afraid that you won't be able to do it all at once. But of course you'll try, and I, of course, underneath all my objections to how things are going, admire you for working in anyway you can for what you believe. I'll see you as soon as we return.

Love,
Ralph

---

* Written on the *Sea Nymph*, a merchant marine vessel bound for Rouen in France; its destination was top secret.

To Fanny
MARCH 1ST 1945,
SOMEWHERE AT SEA

Dear Fanny,

This is the first day out. The sea is calm and the ship alive and vibrating and slightly rolling. It is a broad, deep sea which might sound like a platitude. But it isn't. I have just been lying in my bunk thinking. The ship is all that lies between us and the terrific and uncontrollable and destructive nature of the sea. The ship is the symbol and the fact of man's consciousness, intellect and courage. It is, against the sea, the equivalent of man's sensibility against the madness of a world more irrational than humane. The amazing thing, however, is that anywhere that man's will and intelligence ventures, the irrational is organized and, to the extent that man is successful in discovering its inner laws of movement and organization, humanized! These convoy paths curving across the ocean through storm and calm, are paths of <u>humanized</u> nature.

Watching the convoy move is always fascinating. When the morning is bright and spring-like you come out on deck and watch the ordered lines of ships, each moving in its designated lane, the spray striking your face finely as you watch the bows slicing along, causing the blue-green water to foam fiercely white. Far away, many lanes of ships away, there is a haze and through the haze the ships, the farthest ships I mean, are transformed into distant industrial cities. Cities that like the eyes of certain portraits and billboard signs, seem to follow where ever you go. Actually, they are only the mast and smokestacks of the ships that, across the curved surface of the sea, rise high like distant buildings. You know they're not buildings, however, because they move along with you. And the ship moves, and yet at sea nothing seems to move until you're in sight of shore. (Perhaps there is no real sense of time without a sense of distance—or am I stumbling belatedly into a fact every high school student knows?) Anyway, here in the convoy time seems to have stopped; we are in the midst of a kind of continuous present. The West Indian Messman who works with me has a set joke for the moment when the pantry porthole is opened after the blackout is over each morning. "Well, O'll be damn Maan! We're right here in the same place we was yesterday." And so it seems. The same sun rising from the same green sea, the same sea birds flighting through the sun into and through a foamy wave tip, like a small white and silver butterfly. And out toward the far reaches of the convoy, the same destroyers, small dogs of war, armed to the teeth that appear like bell buoys gently rocking on the horizon. This morning I saw one that might have been a whale, a Moby-Dick, as it rolled in the swells, its white sides flashing in the sunlight.

Darling, that is much to say about the moods of the sea: how the formation of clouds affects the seascape, etc. But only men, ships and birds give it meaningful form. The sea is truly amorphous. And perhaps it is most intensely beautiful when it has almost swallowed up the sun, leaving only a few red rays to color the clouds and make weaving silhouettes of the convoyed ships. Because it is then that the subs come out to hunt us, picking off the boats as they stand out sharp against the horizon. But like God, the sea giveth as well as taketh: This morning I saw it give birth to the sun. There was no agony nor labor, only the slow flow of red light, light as beautiful as sunrise in the Rockies.

That's about all about the sea, I'd much rather recall it after I'm back with you. I was sick for the first two days, stomach. But now I'm O.K. The boat is like all boats, I suppose: Work and petty quarrels under the tension and of course petty politics and racial strife. We have one rather obscene Uncle Tom on board who presents himself as a militant union spokesmen, a very real bedbug of a clown.

I haven't been able to write thus far, perhaps I shall coming back. I hope things are straightened out over on Broadway, if not don't worry.

This isn't a letter in which I can tell you all the things I feel about not being with you (or even with Bobbins—has she learned to p.p. on the paper?) I dream about you doing the troubled nights and I reread your letter again and again. Once on that first night, hearing the engines pumping and the bells that mark the watch, moving and measuring us farther and farther apart, it was very painfully beautiful. Please keep your promise and remember that I look upon formalities, simply as formalities—dedication must come first, from the heart, as it has. The other, too, will come when I return, but you'll have no more than now—whatever that is. Perhaps at best it is no bargain—certainly it can't spell worth a damn—with or without the good housekeeping seal. Anyway, I love you enough to spend my life with you doing things both very foolish and even a few very wonderful too.

Man's Fate is a strange thing, honey.

See you later,

Love,
[Ralph]

To Fanny
MARCH 9TH, 1945.

Darling:

I've tried several times to get this letter off, but always something interrupts. Meantime I've heard from you—such a comforting letter—and from Ida. I certainly hope we'll be here no longer than you were given to suspect—though one never knows what actually happens. Nevertheless I hope I reach you even before this letter does.

I've often wondered what it was about this country* that stimulated such wonderful painters. Now I know, it is the country itself. Everywhere one turns is to be seen a natural picture setting. In the morning the air clears early and the distant hills, of which there are many, are a patch work of green of varied shades; the yellow, burnt orange, and variously weathered red of the roofs stand out against this, with their chimneys like well placed spots of color upon a canvas.†

To Fanny
MARCH 10, 1945

Dearest Fanny;

I received your letter several days ago at a moment when I felt rather low. It was like coming upon you on a cold night in the dark and feeling your polished little face pressing smoothly against my own. My spirits remained high for several days, but now I feel low again. We are in port now, but I've been having a spell of kidney trouble that keeps me from sleeping. This, incidentally, is the same trouble of which I have complained before but which none of the doctors take seriously. I went to the Army hospital here and was given a sulfa drug and a minor operation was suggested—don't get excited, it's really a minor operation though I must admit in a very major spot—when I return. I am bringing a statement from the hospital so the skeptics there won't think I'm faking. I return to the hospital tomorrow for another examination. Perhaps the drug will do the trick.

---

* Ellison's merchant marine ship had delivered its cargo of ammunition to Rouen, France, which Allied soldiers had liberated from the German army in late 1944.

† The letter is handwritten with no sign-off or signature.

I wish I could tell you something about the city* where we are docked, but I'm afraid I'll have to wait. It must suffice it to say that just now it is beautiful as so often described, and though the language is for the most part a barrier, I like the people. You should see the fat babies! And the two or three year-olds, with their knee length socks, their berets and their short length coats which leave their fat little bottoms exposed. They go along in their carriages pushed by their mamma and looking just as superior and supercilious as any Park Avenue baby.

This port was badly bombed and for a time was part of the front lines. Spires and masonry are all toppled down, and some of the buildings lean like the crooked house in the nursery rhyme. On the streets you see captured Supermen† already repairing damage they have made. And you see many of our Negro boys all over the place—but mostly doing the heavy, dirty, unrecognized work. Some mistake me for a foreigner on the streets, but usually I speak and they quickly smile in return. However, I don't feel the same enthusiasm in interviewing them as in England. The story is too dreary, and white troops are much better here—chiefly, it is believed, because the language makes it difficult for the whites to spread their anti-Negro propaganda. Then too from here the front lines are not so far away, and the near presence of death seems to clear up quite a bit of foolishness.

Nothing, though, seems to clear up the stupidity and chauvinism of white Americans. They are about just as contemptible toward these people as toward the English or Welsh. And the extent of their psychological disintegration as revealed in their sexual preoccupations is amazing. I don't mean the usual obsessions of men kept away from women for long periods of time, but of the specific forms of aggression as revealed in their sex attitudes. Look for very chronic post-war conditions at home when these return; political unrest, new forms of gangsterism, etc. It is exhausting to even think about it.

A letter from Ida came along with yours, it might be well that you go to see her. She sent clippings, and seemed to have the idea that I was having a wonderful time of it; "the Gulf Stream" etc. If only it were. I have been unable to do much writing, there being little privacy and quiet in a forecastle with three other men. They are quite a collection. One a consummate egoist a bit above the hep cat level of culture and intelligence; one a Puerto Rican who was discharged from the Army on a Section 8; and the

---

* Rouen, whose cathedral had been burned in the fighting.

† German prisoners of war.

other is the West Indian whom I described before. The last turns out to be very nervous, and between the three, things are exciting as hell, to say the least. Nevertheless, I haven't been entirely unproductive and I have read several of the Greek Tragedies, giving special consideration to their construction. I have also just about finished the 'Stephen Hero.' Perhaps I would write more, if as at this moment, I had a place to sit up and write, and a machine like this one of the Steward's, to write upon.

I am glad, dear, that you aren't worrying about the Board, things will turn out all right. It has caused me no end of concern though, that you had to go to L* about it. I hope he doesn't mind. What a horrible life, whenever one wished to make a step he must stick his head into another lion's mouth— and the undignified fact is that one has no other choice. I believe I would have more self-respect these days if I were in jail, but even that is a pitiful choice. I am more than ever convinced that as a people our horizon is narrow less because we are intellectually inferior, than because we need to protect ourselves from the chaos and indignities of our condition. And people like us are caught in the trap; somehow we opened our eyes for a second and the horror has kept them wide to ever more terrible and pitiful horrors.

But for me there is you dear, and that makes it worth while. Don't do too much in putting things to order, the spring is coming and we'll be on the move again—if there is any place to go. It is interesting that you ran into Rose[†] at Winnie's. Not so many nights before your letter came I dreamed of going in to Winnie's and she surprised me with you. You had just come from the Beauty Shop and your hair was done up crisp in a new style and I kissed you and your face was cool as it is at six pm when you come home in the wintertime. Give her, Winnie, my regards when you see her. And Dick and Stanley and Shirley and et. al. And most of all, tell Bobbins that man who used to be around all day will be returning soon so she shouldn't bite me. Tell her that I'm afraid she's right about Meatball—whose real name, incidentally, turns out to be 'Amos.' But she should remember that he is a Sea dog, doing his duty, whatever it is, to bring the war to a swift close. Certainly I'm for that. And I want to see you Fanny-Mae, so badly I ache.

I am very much in love with you,

> your
> Ralph,

---

* Logan Buford, Fanny's estranged husband.

† Ralph's first wife, Rose Poindexter.

To Stanley Hyman
JUNE 17, 1945.

Dear Stanley,*

I'm sure you understood at lunch yesterday that we had reasons for not listing our phone, since I was careful to make several of them clear. I'm sure also that you knew that I wasn't kidding. Therefore I was quite surprised and greatly irritated this morning to have Henrietta call and say that she'd gotten the number from you.

First, I couldn't understand why you'd give the number to <u>anyone</u> let alone Henrietta; for although she's a perfectly pleasant person she'll only interrupt my work as she did this morning. And you must have known also, that had I wished to see her I would have gone to pay her a visit.

To prevent this kind of thing it is now necessary to have the number changed—which is a needless lot of trouble. As soon as it comes I'll mail it to you, but please don't give it or the present one to <u>anyone</u> else.

Hope you get your books before you had to leave. I called Dick and Louise's this morning and since no one answered I presume that you had gone.

Give our best to Shirley, Laurence, Louis and Dick. I hope to see you soon.

Sincerely,
Ralph

To Richard Wright
306 W. 141 ST.
NEW YORK 30, N.Y.
JULY 22, 1945.

Dear Dick:

I read your letter to Ida last week but your card is the first direct mail I've received thus far. Perhaps the letter got lost, or misplaced in a carrier's pigeonhole. I hope it contained nothing urgent, if so please let me know. I

---

* Ellison's first letter to Stanley Edgar Hyman, an influential scholar who taught at Bennington College in Vermont. Hyman and his wife, the accomplished novelist Shirley Jackson, had become fast friends with Ellison and Fanny.

have been intending to mail the newspaper clippings, but the newspaper strike interrupted things and I have been trying to bring them up to date. I am afraid, however, that I'll have to send them as they are. Judging from the general quality of the discussion material you won't miss much.

Things here are all full of heat and the humidity brought by low clouds that had thundershowers. It has however been interrupted from time to time with spells of coolness. But all in all I've found it unfavorable for work. You're lucky to be away. We're looking forward rather uncertainly toward August, since we are uncertain as to where we'll spend it. I'll let you know wherever the hell it is. As it looks now, it will probably be back at Winding River, which, with Horace around, should be exciting enough, God knows.

Glad to hear that *B.B.** is still climbing, and I'll try here to give you the information I have on his course through the city. First: Dick Moore has the photos from *Life* on display on a bulletin board out in front of his store, along with a large autographed photo of you displayed in the window. They were attracting a lot of attention last week when I passed there. The book is still moving. Secondly: Old J.A. Rodgers had the book in his *Courier* column (I am sending this) and I met him on 42nd Street shortly after and engaged him in conversation about it. He said that he knew all the things you had written about and that he was implicitly attacking Du Bois, but had not read DuBois' review at the time so could not mention his name. I told him that DuBois had indeed said that the book was a lie, whereupon he said that he was going to do another piece in which he would mention the old boy by name. Rather amusing to see Edgar defending anything you write. Perhaps its because he's just Indian. There have been one or two letters-to-the-editor in the Negro press, pro and con, but of no real import.

Congrats on selling your book for publication in France. I heard indirectly about the *Mademoiselle* piece—or at least there was to be one—several days ago from Romare Bearden,† who has been asked to illustrate it (and herewith there is a confusion, because he was asked to do the illustrating for *Fortune*). Perhaps you know what it's all about. He says also that Willi Slamm (or Schlamm—I've met him) is doing a piece about you for *Fortune*. He's their political expert, I understand, and former member

---

*   Wright's important memoir-autobiography, *Black Boy*, published in spring 1945.

†   A prolific and more and more distinguished black artist who became a lifelong friend of Ellison's.

of one of the European left-wing parties. He writes a smart, anti-Soviet editorial for *Life*. I also hear from Bennington College that you were asked to deliver the Commencement Day address, but that you failed even to acknowledge the invitation so that they had to scramble around and supplement you with an obscure gent by the name of Mr. Justice Murphy, of the Supreme Court. That, I'm told, has been the campus joke this summer. I suppose it didn't occur to the boys up there that you might not be interested.

Saturday I received Bucklin Moon's Anthology *Primer for White Folks* containing your "Ethics of Living Jim Crow." I haven't had time to go through the book so I can't tell you anything of its quality.

Margaret Walker has popped up again—a couple of times. The first time when Tolson dropped in last week and told me that she had denounced you con brio until the wee hours of the morning when she lectured at Wiley during the Spring. Someone else—I don't remember whom—told me that Margaret had discussed *NS* very favorably during a lecture. Tolson, by the way, was funny. He said he had invited Margaret over for a talk after her lecture and after talking calmly for an hour, your name came up and M. jumped to her feet, her eyes flashing and began to walk the floor as she denounced you. She told him that she heard that you were writing an autobiography and that she was just waiting with a trunk full of your letters to strike back should you mention her. He, Tolson, said that she frightened him, she erupted so suddenly, going so far as to mimic what she termed your conceit, your regard for clothing, the manner in which she fingered the knot of your tie and your alleged mania for white women. Tolson was not taken in, but found it obscene . . . He is rapidly coming down out of his illusion. He had the notion that Harlem was a cultural center; now, after talking to the barren and lame-brained writers, and searching through the reviews of his book for someone who revealed that they understood what he was driving at, he's very appreciative of what we tried to tell him and a very, very chastened man. I felt both amusement and compassion. Despite his familiarity with Marxist concepts he had still to go through the process of deflation through which I passed years ago. You can't escape that process, I guess, which causes me to ache when I think of what this means for our people. These are strange times, Dick, really strange; and oh so full of irony. When Tolson came this time, his arrogance was left behind and he wanted to listen. He wanted to know this time what he could learn from Auden, instead of attacking Auden from a position a moon-distance away, and though he objected to some of my ideas he did listen. I couldn't help think of Ida coming to us for advice as I listened to him and I realized that we have become the fathers of our elders. The unquestionable authority of the left-wing politicians is tottering like a punch drunk prize fighter; now people are looking for someone who can answer questions and they are looking in our direction. Your prestige should rise by leaps and bounds now. And the wonderful thing is, I feel, that this will be because you dared to be simply what you are, an artist.

Others are anxious to talk nowadays, including politicians. Ida asked me if I would talk with Connolly of the ALP about conditions affecting the Negro. I did, finding him specifically interested in the failure of guys like Ben and ACP. As you know they refused to place Ben on the ballot and he indicated that the ALP was deeply dissatisfied with the boys and their failure to build a real organization in Harlem. He told me also that ACP had a very bad absentee record—one of the worst. Others tell me that it was because Hazel Scott was ill here in N.Y.C. indicated that Powell too was causing concern among the politicians (I don't mean only the Browder gang) and that they are faced with working out some disciplinary controls. All in all, it seems that the coalitions are breaking up and the white folks find themselves with a couple of black Frankensteins—or black elephants—on their hands. They aren't sure if they have leaders with followers behind them, or simply inflated symbols incapable of functioning in the real world. So now they come to folks like us asking if these obscene monsters they have created are real or imaginary. I'm having more talks with C. Incidentally DN is supposed to break with the Liberal Party; new groupings are fast forming. C. seems genuinely interested in building something real in Harlem. I'll believe it when I see it. Politics, politics! She was wasting my time by asking the same advice over and over again. She, like most Americans, seem to have no capacity for consciously accepting ambivalent situations; they don't believe in evil as far as it relates to their own inner being; nor can they accept the possibility that they are naive. Can it be our responsibility to remind them over and over again that to be naive is to be self-destructive? The more I think and try to understand, the more I tremble before the colossal responsibility we have as Negroes. Nevertheless, it won't be the first time in history that the slaves and sons of slaves have risen to positions of intellectual leadership. This hasn't happened yet, but certainly it is in the cards, the situation demands it. I'm beginning truly to understand the greatest joke, the most absurd paradox, in American history: that simply by striving consciously to become Negroes we are becoming and destined to become Americans, and the first truly mature Americans at that. Just as the biggest joke I know on you, is that after all the struggle to become a responsible Communist writer and spokesman, you became instead something much more important: an artist and articulator of the most vital possibilities of American life. For God sake don't show, or repeat this to an American Communist, he'll say I've become a mystic!

The latest here on the theater is that (a) Canada Lee has purchased the drama rights to B.B. and (b) some Broadway group is planning to produce Romeo and Juliet, with one of the conflicting families being played by Negroes! Doesn't that liquidate your bowels?

As for the theater (the serious theater, I mean) I've been reading some fascinating stuff out of France concerning plays written and produced there during the occupation. Kierkegaard has been utilized and given a social direction by a group there who have organized what is called the "Existential Theater," and from what I read their psychological probing has produced a powerful art. France is in ferment. Their discussion of the artist's responsibility surpasses anything I've ever seen, out of France, the Soviet Union or anywhere else. They view the role of the individual in relation to society so sharply that the leftwing boys, with the possible exception of Malraux, seemed to have looked at it through the reverse end of a telescope. I am sure that over there the war has made the writer more self-confident and aware of the dignity of his craft. Sartre, one of the younger writers, would have no difficulty in understanding your position in regards to the Left. He writes: "Every epoch discovered an aspect of the condition of humanity, in every epoch man chooses for himself with regards to others, to love, to death, to the world (Kierkegaarding categories, aren't they?); and when a controversy arises on the subject of the disarmament of the FFI, or of the aid to be given to the Spanish Republicans, it is that metaphysical choice, that personal and absolute decision which is in question. Thus, by becoming a part of the uniqueness of our time, we finally merge with the eternal, and it is our task as writers to cast light on the eternal values which are involved in these social and political disputes. Yet we are not concerned with seeking these values in an intelligible paradise: for they are only interesting in their immediate form. Far from being relativists, we assert emphatically that man is absolute. But he is absolute in his own time, in his own environment on his own earth. The absolute which a thousand years of history cannot destroy is this irreplaceable, incomparable decision, which he makes at this moment, in these circumstances; the absolute is Descartes, the man who escapes us because he is dead, who lived in his time, who thought in his time from day to day with limited data, who formed his doctrine in accordance with a certain stage reached in science, who knew Gassendi, Caterus and Mersenne, who in his childhood loved a shady young woman, who was a soldier and got a servant girl with child, who attacked not the principle of authority in general but the authority of Aristotle in particular, and who rises out of his time, disarmed but unconquered, like a landmark; and the relative is Cartesianism, that coster's barrow philosophy, which is trotted out century after century, in which everyone finds whatever he has put in it. It is not by chasing after immortality that we will make ourselves eternal: we will not make ourselves absolute by reflecting in our work desiccate principles which are sufficiently empty and negative to pass from one century to another, but by fighting passionately in our time, by loving passionately and by consenting to perish entirely with it."

The page has run out. Give our regards to Ellen and Julia. I'll send clippings separately. Fanny is fine.

Ralph

To Richard Wright
306 W. 141 Street
New York 30, N.Y.
Aug 5, 1945

Dear Dick:

This time I did receive your letter, although the others have yet to appear. Incidentally, I'd like very much to learn just in what way you associate me with the number 371. Such things are tricky and often revealing. It wasn't far off at that. However, even 306 will be incorrect after you receive this, for we are leaving Tuesday for Vermont. Write me in care of Mrs. Amelie Bates, Waitsfield, Vermont. We plan to stay there in the mountains until September. After that I don't know where the hell we'll live. The church is insisting that we move. I've learned that the pastor has asked the Edison people to remove my meters. He doesn't know what a fight he'll have on his hands if they do—though I don't believe they can, since I deal directly with them and have given them no cause to deprive us of service. Nevertheless you can see what we face on our return and there isn't a damned thing available.

There is little news. I mailed you the C.P. clippings by registered mail, so you are almost up on that. The latest development you can glean from the enclosed clipping. I have been telling people that the liquidation began in 1937* or before, but everyone except Wm. Blake disagreed. Now that Foster has stated that it developed over a period of ten years, they shake their heads and look blank. Ida is full of despair. This sickness, this inability to face reality, grows, widens, deepens with each new development; each new authoritative statement reveals new termite borings of easy, sheep-like belief, vacuity and lack of thought. And look at the authority they accept: only Browder, Minor and Ford have been shifted off the National Board, the rest of the gang with Foster are in the saddle. Browder ran the nag off a cliff, broke its legs, and left it moaning in the shallow water; Foster has told it the bones have mended, shot it full of dope and God knows what'll happen now. A broken, swag backed nag when the times call for tanks coordinated with jet planes full of high maneuverability and a speed faster than sound! Browder is as great an engineer as Hoover; Hoover only drained the country, Browder transformed a locomotive of history into a prairie schooner

Fanny and I attended the editorial session of the Newspapers Publishers convention to discover how they were thinking. It was pitiable. There is no level at all, nothing. Most of the time was consumed by a jerk from a government agency who showed a film concerned with clap and syf. The rest with crude jokes about it and a brief discussion of the tension in the South. Whites and Negroes in Birmingham are said to be arming themselves. I had hoped to take part, to learn, and to make a few suggestions; I kept my big mouth shut and got the hell out of there as quick as I could. Let Horace have them. The following day I attended the organization of a Negro magazine publishers assoc. Some ten or twelve magazines. They were more concerned with distribution than with rationale. Alice Browning was the driving force, and behind her stands Charles, her husband, who is strictly interested in the dollar. Two crackpots took up most of their editorial discussion period. I made a few comments with little effect, but spoke privately with a couple of reprint editors about the ethics of reprinting a writer's material. Both of these groups, for all of the potential power of the newspapers and their ability to make a noise, stand in the early dawn of publishing. They have only discovered the wheel, the laws of its functioning are yet to be discovered.

Partisan Review has a review of *Black Boy*. It is favorable and quite aware of the book's psychological organization. I'll send a copy along with

---

* Joseph Stalin's Great Purge, officially begun with the infamous "show trials" of 1937.

Horizon, which contains the material on France I wrote about last time. I am not surprised to see PR making a bid for you now; every time I think they've gotten over being a jerk outfit they break out with a rash.

And speaking of jerks, I talked with Blake recently who told me that Robeson now has a theory that Negroes and Africans (he makes little distinction between the two groups) have a special perception of reality which is closed to white men; a perception revealed in their sense of rhythm, their feeling for music and art. We had a long laugh over it. Here is your new Garveyism, this time wearing a Phi Beta Kappa key. Blake was concerned, puzzled over the liquidation of the party in the South (a thing by the way, which is causing Ben Davis a hell of a lot of trouble from his political opponents because he admitted that he knew about it but made no protest) I told him that I believed that it was to truncate any semblance of revolutionary consciousness in the new industrial frontier. I see it as part of the Myrdal study and the new rail rates given the South. Every thing you touch nowadays has been infected by the party's corruption. Blake expects only the blackest developments for the country.

Not only does Margaret have a screw loose, she also has a husband with a broken back. It happened in the Army, he is fully incapacitated, but instead of the Government giving his full compensation that is his due, they only wish to give him half. Too bad for M. Perhaps now she can get her mind off you. The following is crappy, but it's about you and you'd better know who's saying what about you. Last night we had some people in for a chat when Gene Holmes was mentioned. He had visited these friends the night before, and, while drinking, had given his opinion of *BB*. He disliked it—which is his right. But he had this to add: That a few nights before, you had called him to discuss some trouble you were having with your wife but that he had refused to see you. He did not want to see you because he would have to discuss *BB*: he could not understand why you wanted to see him, anyway; you really needed to see a psychiatrist. I was very glad to show them written proof that you were in Canada—which of course, is not important, because even if it were true, he should have told you those things, just as he cried over you shoulder when he got tripped up by Alberta Simms. There you have it.

I bumped into Gene myself the week before, in the crowded entrance of the Theresa. He asked what I was doing and let me know in the best Communist fashion that he had read the *Antioch* article. He planned, he said, to see how it compared with Burgum's discussion in *Science and Society.* Had I read it? "No. So you don't read *Science and Society* any more?"

"No." (Really I had) "No." Since the war those boys had nothing to say "Then what are you doing? Who are you with? Common Ground?" "No, I'm by myself." "So you and Wright are together?" "No, Wright is by himself and I am by myself. We are individuals."

He had no answer for that, not in the crowd; but was to get in touch with me. I hope he does. I'll hear what he has to say then give him a going over that he'll never forget. Not only are these things arrogant, they're full of spite and envy. As though I give a damn what Burgum thinks. I've never mentioned this because it sounds like trying to take credit I don't deserve: I was trying to deal with the tragic implications of Negro life back in 1940–41 when *Big White Fog* and Attaway's second novel were given to me to review. This was during the LAW and I discussed my ideas with Sillen and Burgum and partially because I was so damned inarticulate, and partially because they could not imagine Negro life offering themes for tragedy, they told me politely that I was nuts. I went into the problem of tragedy in a draft of my NM review and the *New Masses* asked me to cut it out. Several years later Burgum sees the implications when he writes of your short stories, and I'd talked with him before he finished one of those articles.

I'm glad you received the *Antioch,* and was pleased that you did not entirely disagree with the ideas.[*] I have to keep worrying the blues concept, though, until I can squeeze out all the meaning I feel waiting beyond its camouflaged walls—until I am as satisfied as you are that I have overrated it. There have been some slight reactions to the article already—mostly from those who thought to absorb it at one reading. Then too, the *New Republic* has asked me to do some reviews on the strength of it.

What you had to say about the contrast between my fictional and non-fictional prose is well taken; I have considered the possibility that I might not be a novelist myself. Nevertheless, I don't plan to stop for a while, even if the work in progress fails.[†] I want to give myself at least as much of a break as you gave yourself when you continued to wrestle with the form even after *Lawd Today* and *Tar Baby's Dawn.* I only hope my self-confidence is as justified as *Native Son* proved yours to have been.

Anyway, it isn't the prose, per se, that worries me; it's the form, the

---

[*]   Ellison refers to his essay "Richard Wright's Blues," which had just been published in the summer 1945 issue of *The Antioch Review.*

[†]   *Invisible Man,* begun July 1945 in Vermont. See Ellison's March 1981 introduction to the thirtieth edition of *Invisible Man.*

learning how to organize my material in order to take the maximum advantage of those psychological and emotional currents within myself and in the reader which endow prose with meaning; and which, in the writer, release that upsurge of emotion which jells with conceptions and makes prose magical. Its an uncertain battle on a dark terrain, but as you know, brother, the victory is the best, most satisfying thing a writer could achieve.

It is exciting even to hear you speak of getting to work on your long theme; it makes me both very dissatisfied with my own efforts and ambitious to work harder and learn to say the very best of which I am capable.

I suppose the explosion of the new atomic bomb has had repercussions in Canada. It has set my imagination awhirl. We've got to do something, to offset the C.P. sell-out of our people; and I mean by this, both Negroes and labor. With such power in the world there is no answer for Negroes certainly except some sort of classless society. Cheesecake optimism is all right to frighten non-men; give me the naked, cold realism of the blues, it's the basic bed-rock of any clearheaded approach to such events. The Loyalist soldiers could attack tanks with improvised bombs, but what could we do against such cosmic force, unless we concern ourselves with power? Here is the 'voice like thunder' of which you wrote; mankind must now move to intelligent, humane action, or be 'moved' clear off this god-forsaken planet. Men are coming into open conflict with the power of the universe again, and although the almost conquered force is in the 'control' of a few, it is so powerful that is an immediate threat even to them. Unity of peoples is more than a political necessity, it has become a matter of life itself—to hell with depending upon the 'intelligence' of the NAM. I'm going to smash me some atoms.

So long for now. We hope things are still pleasant there, and not as here, all rain. Give our best to Ellen and let us hear from you soon.

Ralph

To Ida G

Dear Ida:

This is the very first letter that I have had the energy to write.[*] The train ride here was long and crowded and when we arrived the woman whom I had engaged to meet us to drive us the remaining distance failed to show

---

[*] Though this letter is undated, the August 5 letter to Richard Wright outlining Ellison's plans to travel to Vermont suggests he would have written this one a few days later.

up. So there we were, Fanny, myself and the dog standing on this long empty platform with our luggage with no idea of how we were to get away. Fortunately an engine drew up to the siding causing the dog to bark back at the first locomotive she had ever seen. It was very amusing, and, with the news of atomic power whirling around in my head, somehow symbolic.

We didn't have to wait long though, until we engaged a taxi from Montpelier and finally were driven out to the farm.

The country is beautiful. Green things all around you and mountains surrounding you and the roar of swift mountain brooks whenever you go out of the house. It is such a change in tempo and atmosphere that we are thus far rather disorganized. We sleep far longer than we'd ever think of doing in the city: and our appetites have increased as though in place of normal human stomachs, we have suddenly unfurled cotton-sacks instead.

Food is a real problem here, far more of a problem than we expected. First, there is a shortage in the village, and secondly, we have no car to get in to shop. But most of all, or rather, worst of all, there is not a single drop of coffee to be had. Because it is such an essential item in my working day I wonder if you could have your grocer send up four pounds (Maxwell House preferred, but <u>any</u> brand is acceptable) and as much sharp American cheese as possible? Please understand that if you can't <u>have</u> this done, don't bother with it. If he will (your grocer) please have him send it parcel post to me, care of Mrs. Amelie Bates, Waitsfield, Vermont. I am enclosing stamps and a check.

There is little to tell you now. I had two cards from Richard just before I left; he seemed to have up plenty of steam after reading the discussion clippings. He feels that we should become the conscience of the Negro people, and of course I agree. In fact we've been that unconsciously all along.

The article* has begun to have a small effect: The *New Republic* has asked me to review a couple of books for them. Said several people had been recommending me to them. So it goes.

I must get this out to the mailman when he passes, so this will be all for now. I'll write you soon.

Ralph

---

* "Richard Wright's Blues."

To Ida G
WAITSFIELD, VT.
AUGUST 13, 1945.

Dear Ida:

I work now in the doorway of a barn that looks out across a field of uncut hay and goldenrod fringed by a grove of sugar trees to the mountains.

Beyond the mountains the clouds form ever-changing in huge, cottony amorphous masses, set in a pure blue sky; and when the clouds shift in the wind they make dark shadows against the mountain and shade the farms that rest serene against its rolling, day-dreaming slopes.

Only the typewriter chattering before me and an occasional plane sailing like a hard, white sliver of silver sun-flecked cloud recall the distant city.

In all directions the spaces are wide and the eyes become quickly adjusted to distance, resting here on a mountain, there on a cloud, yonder upon a clear, bright-green colored space surrounding a lonely farmhouse; and on—beyond and high above to rest upon a soothing swath of dark green timberland. It is truly no land for the near-sighted or the narrowly self-centered, and the rise of the mountains reminds of the depths to be inwardly plumbed in man to reach that inner balance from which springs the humanism so indispensable when man goes forth to wrestle Nature. This country was hewn out of the wilderness. The barns and houses are built of huge logs hewn from the virgin forest, squared into geometrical shapes by hand and built into dwellings intended to last forever. Then the men passed on, or moved to the westward, leaving the houses and barns to the birds and beasts and to be reclaimed by the mountain. We are not the same Americans now, and much that was won by those men must be re-won by us in our time; only now the battle is much more difficult. It's not so hard to win and become aware of one's dignity when one's strength is pitted against a mountain. In the city it is to be won against an opponent as elusive as charged electrons.

And here there is silence and silence and rustle of leaves to greet the ear in the break-of-silence, and in silence the drone of a bumblebee becomes the roar of a bomber. But when the breezes go the air becomes still as the noiseless flight of black butterflies above the sweep of meadow, then in the brooding hush that comes you hear the swift, bright rush of mountain brooks in the distance.

I'm told that there is quite a lot of incest in these mountains, the sign of a region gone to seed, a frontier exhausted and abandoned, but also influenced, perhaps, by the fact that everywhere one looks it is possible to imagine huge maternal women, such as Gulliver saw in his travels, reclining languidly, with their smooth mountainous breasts, nipples erect, to the hungry lips of the clouds.

Yesterday when we started down to the brook to wash in the icy water we saw two deer, standing alert and listening to our voices, then away they went, leaping in long, graceful dream-bounds over the meadow, to vanish swiftly into the woods, their white tails, lingering upon the iris of the eye, the only proof that they had really passed before us.

All for now. I guess you can see we like it here.

Love,
Ralph Fanny

To Ida G
AUGUST 14, 1945.

Dear Ida:

Would you please drop the enclosed letter in the mailbox? I have just received a request from my Draft Board for information concerning my employment status. I don't know why, for I am officially on shore leave; and all such information is usually gotten by writing the War Shipping Administration, the Government agency with which I am signed.

It seems this kind of stupidity will never end until after the war is over.

Incidentally, I have written you once since that first urgent letter, but did not explain that the first one was mailed after we arrived and discovered, contrary to what we had been told, that there was a food shortage. I think, really, that my friend felt a bit guilty for having his wife and children away in the country while he stayed in the city and sent us up to salve his conscience. This, of course, is quite all right for us—we object only because he did not give us a clear picture so that we might have come prepared. The prospect of being eighteen miles from the nearest store without adequate food cannot be sufficiently compensated for by the gorgeous scenery and climate.

You mustn't be concerned about any impression that you think I might have of your reaction to the article.* I thought yours was quite reasonable.

---

* "Richard Wright's Blues."

Because it is a difficult piece and would not have been worth the writing had it been crystal clear at one reading. And even with the most lucid exposition I believe that the concepts and the organization of the concepts are new and unfamiliar. I don't expect Dick himself to grasp it all without study—even when I consider that most of it might simply be tommyrot and speculation. Thanks for allowing Frazier to read it; I would like, when I see you, to hear his reactions more in detail. He is the authority on the Negro family, and I'm interested to learn his opinion of my statements concerning its psychological structure.

As for separate copies of the article, I believe that these might be obtained by writing Mr. Paul Bixler of the *Antioch Review,* Yellow Springs, Ohio; or if not through him, they might be reproduced by the off-set process (with his permission) at a reasonable cost. Try him first, though, if you're still interested, for they might still have the printer's plates intact and it could be gotten out with little trouble. What do you think could be done with it? I know that academic writers sometimes have such articles reprinted and bound in a simple paper folder for distribution among their colleagues. Certainly I would like to have a few for my own use, but beyond that it did not occur to me.

I'll think about the *Crisis* letter, though their circulation is very limited. If Wilkins wishes to reprint the piece as it stands he'd have to obtain permission from the Antioch people. I always run out about here. Keep well.

Love,
Ralph

To Richard Wright
WAITSFIELD, VT.
AUGUST 18, 1945

Dear Dick:

I work now in the door of a barn that—in the rhythm of the opening paragraph of *A Farewell to Arms*—looks out across a field past the trees to the mountains. In the field, the hay and goldenrod ripple in the wind beneath the flight of butterflies and flitting birds, and farther, beyond the trees begin a series of terraces which rise in ridges to steadily become a straight sparse fringe of balsam fringing the mountain ridge and stand like the teeth of a huge comb meant to clear the snarls from the fleecy clouds. Hemingway would gripe at most of that, but it's damn near true; anyway, when the poison of Harlem mixes with this pure mountain air anything's apt to come out of my typewriter.

We've been here since the 8th and I'm only just now becoming adjusted. I've worked a lot but have not answered any mail since I sent the letter in which I mentioned Gene Holmes. I hope it reached you. This, by the way is the same farm, belonging to John Bates' wife, that I visited year before last—only this time the only work I'm doing is on my typewriter. We plan to stay until the first, so write me here: c/o Mrs. Amelie Bates, Waitsfield, Vermont.

I'm glad to hear that the clipping came through all right. I also sent a copy of *Horizon* containing news of literary developments in France, and *Partisan Review* containing the review of BB. Better check if they haven't come through. About the discussion letters I certainly agree. They are one of the most brass confessions I've ever seen anywhere. Only men who are not only corrupt but whose corruption has frozen over and hardened can confess the things they do and still accept positions of leadership. They are dead men and unless they're controlled by public opinion and every other available force, they're as dangerous as Nazis. More so, because they still speak in the name of the only possible future.

I would like very much to talk with you concerning independence of thought. I believe we should serve notice on them that, goddammit, they are responsible to the Negro people at large even if they do spit in the faces of their members and that they must either live up to their words or face a relentless fire of mature, informed criticism which will use everything from the many forms of the written word to the platform and the radio. If they want to play ball with the bourgeoisie they needn't think can get away with it. If they want to be lice then by God let them be squashed like lice. Maybe we can't smash the atom, but we can with a few well-chosen, well written, words smash all that crummy filth to hell. You're right, they haven't changed, but they'll have to; and I hope you give them hell from one end of the country to the other. What the hell do you and I care about their hates, they hated us all the time. I'm prepared for their hate. The moment that I begin to peak and write like a man they'll use all their energy to jam me off the airways, because, like you, I'll be speaking on the wavelength of the human heart; on a station getting its power from the mature ideological dynamo of France and the continent. I thought those bastards were clever politicians; now I know they aren't even politicians. I could have formulated a more rational apology than all that crowd even though I have no interest in doing so and nothing at stake. Ida's right, a few good men <u>could</u> change that picture, but it would be folly to try to do it from the inside.

I see it this way: they have no conscience, being Americans, and the only force capable of awakening a conscience within them, and the only force politically capable of keeping them in line until that happens, are the Negroes. It is our job as Joyce put it, "to create the uncreated conscience" of the Negroes. And as for the Davises, Fords, Wilkersons, Yergans, yes, and Robesons, we can laugh those clowns to death. I've raved long enough, lets continue this when we return to the city.

You've mentioned several times that you're living in 17 cent. surroundings. That's how it was—to an extent—in Wales. The tempo of life was slower, the speech other worldly and charming and the coffee or rather the public house the main social center. But what you have to say about the architecture and cubism is very intriguing; especially from this part of New England. Here everything is severe straight lines, rectangles, cubes, squares and octagonal steeple—with square cupolas even on the magnificent barns. In the barn where I work you can see the skeletal structure of this architecture laid bare. They were rugged people who conceived it. This barn, like the house, is 150 years old and as far as the basic structure goes, strong as when it was first constructed. They tore the trees up from the soil, squared them by hand, put them together with pegs and erected them to stand forever. But something must have been dead inside those guys. Certainly it wasn't the mountains that caused all this straightness, for the mountains are all curves and sloping—unless it was because they had to battle the rocks so hard for an existence that they learned to hate even curved lines. Anyway they made these houses and barns to last, and they're outlasting them and outlasting the best things they had in their human culture. Last night Fanny and I went with a Farmer to a nearby town to see *Arsenic and Old Lace* performed by some kids from a summer camp, and to attend a dance. The kids did a good job, the play is the culture of Broadway, and they were New York kids. With all its facile glibness and gagging, there was a unity between performers and pattern performed.

But afterwards we went up stairs to the dance and it was depressing. The dances were principally square dances, the music by an orchestra consisting of a piano, saxophone and violin. This, by the way, was part of the several days' end of the war celebration, and for most of those present, a lighthearted, holiday occasion. There were cakes for sale in the hall, milk drinks and sandwiches, and a beautiful, handmade quilt was up for raffle. The music started, an anemic foxtrot that demanded a stethoscope to find its pulse. We said, This is not their medium, let's wait until they start the real dancing, the squares. We looked at the people, a seedy, washed out stock. These parts are sick from inbreeding and malnutrition. The stock is mainly English and sometimes during the evening I might have been in a Welsh village; except that in Wales the children are children who look their age, here they look like little adults. Their teeth are bad, and in a section where the broad spaces and clear atmosphere should make for sharp sure vision, their eyes are amazingly defective. They are a friendly people, despite their New England dourness; and in spite of their wrecked appearance, here and there in the bearing and expression of some farmer or his wife you can see peeping through signs of that gentility and sensitivity and inner balance which formed the understructure, the mass base of the Golden Day. The square dancing was dismal. Except for a few older people, and strangely enough these were mostly men—old farmers with a sense of rhythm and a grace that made you feel that they were dancing rather than simply hopping through half-forgotten patterns of hopscotch—except for these they had no sense of the symmetry demanded of such dances, the patterns were blurred until you couldn't see them, and for the most part they simply hopped about uncouthly.

I was so depressed. I've danced these dances myself when I was a kid, and later when I had grown ashamed of such things, I used to lie on Sat. nights in my room and look down into the lighted basement of the house next door where the country relatives collected and danced these dances with a joie de vie and a precision that made them truly a form of expression and revealed their foreshadowing of the mechanical dynamic of the Lindy hop very clearly, and what I missed was not simply the 'Negro 'rhythmical sense; I've seen whites in the West dance just as well. What I missed was a people's expression of its sense of life. It depressed me so that not even my winning of the quilt during the intermission could lift me up. I wonder how true this is of other sections? Thoreau rejected this pattern of life that now lies in ruin when it was still glowing with promise. His solution was inadequate, but his intuition was correct. The artist in America will always have a lot to learn from this: we must never be afraid to reject.

About the straight lines and the avoidance of the sphere, I believe that already when this country was first settled the tragic sense of life had been lost. Those Americans would not allow themselves to develop that ambivalence toward Nature that we find among other peoples. They fought with nature but instead of learning to love it as a benevolent antagonist, they learned simply to hate it. Hence the straight lines. They were trying to build a world of man by trying to exclude a most important part of man, Nature. The cubists, or at least the great cubists such as Picasso, worked through the phase of abstraction only to return to natural objects and events—although they learned through their explorations to present an essence of the real world, the plastic essences of people, of human figures. I think they forecast the development N. America must take; it points to a new humanism the need of which is stated most dramatically in the destructive-creative potential of atomic power. I think they're just a bit uneasy about using the bomb against Japan. Do you notice anything beside State Dept. bungling and reaction in the form of the surrender? Any sense of guilt? Air craft carriers against the spires and gleaming domes, what a picture! Its part of the larger picture I saw sailing down the placid Seine on top of a load of ammunition in a ship Armed to the teeth and saw the wrecks of German Tiger Tanks lying near the bomb shattered Walls of the Cathedral of Rouen and the topsy turvey streets near the square dedicated to Joan of Arc and bombers over the fields of Normandy such as Van Gogh painted and over the beautiful, well tilled hills where Flaubert saw the rains and mists come down when he wrote *Madame Bovary*. I saw the bombed buildings in London without a qualm—except, of course, for the human victims; what are the symbols and monuments of Britain to me, that I should feel a sense of loss? But in France it was different, even the negative symbols contain enough of their lost vitality to make one regret he failed to get there sooner. Certainly it provided me a new perspective through which to look upon the U.S. and, brother, the view is frightful. We are, we were born and became through our experience, the 'conscience of the Negro people' although they don't fully recognize it yet. But I think our destiny is something more than that; it is to become the conscience of the United States. I know that now, just as I 'knew' the other night and said so before the papers were drawn from the hat, that I would win the quilt. Out of the thirteen drawings, they called Fanny's name once and mine twice. It was a minor symbolic moment for me, aware as I was of the cultural decay of what had once been the most vital part of America. How fitting it was that some dame sent a man over to offer us six dollars for the prize! This is our country to an extent no one has yet set down. We might as well quit evading the issue and get busy to breathing the breath of real life into its half-alive form. A sense of responsibility based on a vision narrower than this is inadequate. There was a time when—and recently too—I hung back because of my poor education and clumsy writing, but no more. I'm stubborn enough to overcome some of this, and I find that when I have the broadest range for my passion it improves my writing although that is still sadly lacking. We almost always feel more than we are able to express; the break with the CP has allowed me to come alive to many things of which I was becoming aware during my bitterly isolated college experience. I'm reclaiming that now—with the stimulation of *B.B.** I might add—and forgotten passages of literature and repressed moods are becoming the wedges of insights. Some day I hope to do a surgical job on the repressive effect that CP sectarianism had upon my sensibilities along with the quickening effects of Marxism. I was never dead, but I was amorphous as hell, literally; and after my discovery of Marx too, too many questions, nebulous emotions and moods were left waiting breathlessly behind the doors of dogma. Was any of this true with you?

My novel is going well. I write much more freely here in the country. Harlem is killing me, I know that now. There my emotions are pulled in a thousand directions before I can have coffee in the morning. Here, even with four badly disciplined children hooting and yelling all day long I can work all day and feel that I've accomplished something. I don't know what it will be, but, boy, it won't be because I haven't worked. The only stable thing I have in all this sea of uncertainty is the raft of the concepts on which I lie as I paddle my way toward the shore. These, I think, are valid; and even though I fail they will be useful and will overlap with those being treated by anyone who truly writes in our time.

The theater sounds good—if it doesn't interfere with your long work. I don't dare look in that direction myself, I've too much to learn about the novel. And yet when you see the level of what is produced—

I haven't seen *Harper's* in several months, so I missed the reference to *N.S.* As for the *B.B.* article, Ida gave it to E.F. Frazier whom, she said, was impressed. I wish it had been written <u>after</u> that discussion slop, I would have kicked their so-called critics dead in the arse. I don't know if but that I'm ashamed for not having done so anyway. Isn't it odd that they always win allegiance of the <u>fear</u> in men, rather than their courage?

What you say about Ottley[†] is interesting. I read a letter he wrote Velasco in which he showed signs of an awakening awareness that there was a world beyond the bar, the bed and the table. Of course most of it

---

* Wright's *Black Boy.*

† Roi Ottley was an acquaintance of Wright's and Ellison's whose *New World A-Coming: Inside Black America* (1943) won the Life in America prize and was much discussed for its portrait of life in Harlem during the 1920s and 1930s.

was simply to empress Velasco, I believe—but when a guy like that gets to the point that he puts on paper that he has tried to find the meaning of life in sex and money, that's something. He also mentioned the new perspective he had won in relation to Powell and rejects him, verbally at least. He tried to give Velasco a picture of the developments in the European theater, and lo and behold, his idea of the theater was confined mostly to the movies! He did, however, describe a production of Julius Caesar in Greece, in which Brutus and not Caesar was the hero. He did not reveal despite this break in his brash shell anything like the alertness necessary to understand what he has seen. I do believe though that if the war has made fellows like him aware of their contrast with white Americans and conscious to the formulation of their own vague Negro personalities we have the first, almost invisible crystallization of something we can work upon. The education they have floats in their heads like pieces of driftwood but maybe now they will learn that they <u>are</u> only pieces of wood and not a ship. One thing is sure, many of them know now that the paddys, as they call the white boys, don't even have the pieces of wood. Maybe you should talk with Ottley—he'll probably betray you again, but what the hell—maybe you can suggest the meaning of much he has seen. He doesn't respect me enough for that.

God, you sound alive with all the things you want to do. And you will—if for no other reason than to keep from being bored to death. There truly isn't anything else to do. Nothing else is provided for us but to write and write. As for French, Fanny and I want to learn it too, it is a desperate need to keep from suffocating in the American desert.

As for non-fiction, I have in project a book of cultural studies of the Negro in American life; maybe in the form of a series of essays, or in the form of a criticism of Negro folklore and literature. Then too I have a notebook in fact, several notebooks, full of notes on psychology, in comparative literature and cultural anthropology which I plan to do something with, along with enough notes on the blues to make a book. My lecture this fall will be on Joyce and I plan to use *BB* to illuminate the *Portrait* and the *Portrait* to illuminate *BB*.* I think we should talk more about the kind of thing that's needed and compare notes. I have an unfinished essay on southern novels about the Negro that the Antioch people call brilliant that I'll send along when finished. I feel fine; I want to go out there on that

---

* Ellison lectured to Stanley Hyman's class at Bennington in November 1945 on the connections between Joyce and Wright.

mountain with the farm against its slope and scream like an eagle screams. Love to Ellen and Julia from me and Fanny.

Ralph

To Ida G
WAITSFIELD, VT.
AUG. 25, 1945.

Dear Ida:

At last the coffee and cheese arrived, yesterday, and this morning we had coffee for breakfast. It was a long time coming but we managed in the meantime; once by picking up stores in a neighboring town when we passed through on our way to visit a friend's farm. I thought I was going to help him hay for a day, but it turned out that he was mowing that day and only wanted us to see the place. It was very nice, situated upon a hill with wonderful views of the surrounding mountains and looking out across Waterbury Lake. Thanks lots for sending the stuff up. We were in a sort of panic when we discovered the food situation here.

The weather here has been rather gloomy the last three days, but even now, as I look out of the window, I see the sun coming through the clouds. This morning, when I went out to wash my face after making the fires, the clouds hung downhill behind the house to within about fifty yards from where I stood, hiding the tree tops and giving a new smooth curvature to the mountain. I couldn't even see the old logging road which cuts through the yard behind the house, nor the birches, higher up the hill, which show like girls in light summer dresses through the more somber dark green dresses of the spruce and pine, and nothing at all of the somber dark green dresses of the spruce and pine, and nothing at all of the old camp itself with its cabins, its garden with the huge squash plants that run down the hill from back of the horse barn and into the woods on the other side, nor the old cabin of logs, now fallen into decay, nor the smoke coming from the cook shack where Ida Tabor prepares the meals for the lumbermen and then goes to join them three miles up the mountain in loading the logs on the skids, rolling the logs into position, operating either the horse, Harry, or the tractor in snaking the piled logs over the narrow treacherous mountain road. It was all fog up there when I went out, but they were at work already. I could hear the angry puttering of the tractor behind the screen of fog. I'll tell you more of Ida Tabor later, she's close to your age, is one of the most skilled lumber woods <u>men</u> in the state and an authority on working horse flesh.

I'm very glad that you are getting to know Frazier so well. He is one of the few scholars of the Negro for whom one can have a deep respect. I shall be very glad to see him. Incidentally, Fanny knew him at Fisk and remembers him as one of the few teachers who inspired her to do any real thinking. You say he is detached; I'd say he is honest enough to develop a sense of irony and yet to escape the pit of cynicism, and irony is a mature attitude, allowing one to see, even though he remains aware of his own limitations in a situation.

The *Portrait of the Artist* is one of the books I shall discuss at Bennington College when I lecture there in the Fall. I'd like to talk to you about it. And I agree that no major novel can avoid the religious problem, on whatever form it presents itself; whether in the form of the orthodox church or the individual's struggle against other forms of the irrational that have not been institutionalized. This has been the failing of most left-wing novels, they looked upon the problem as solved. But it remains only its form is changed. Wherever there is human action that enlists the whole energies of the individual's complete personality, we move into those regions that for too long have been exploited by religion.

Join us by all means in being the conscience of the Negroes; I think that they (we) are the only hope of discovering the conscience of America.

Ralph Fanny

To Stanley Hyman
306 W. 141 STREET
NEW YORK 30, N.Y.
SEPTEMBER 18, 1945

Dear Stanley:

Sending you that check to cash was an act of desperation made necessary through the food situation on the farm where we spent our vacation. We had sent all our cash to New York and to Fanny's mother out in Chicago so that we could have food sent out to the farm, but the mails were so damned slow that we'd been here two weeks before the first package arrived and we were forced to use the remaining cash to buy food in Waterbury. It was a stupid situation. We then decided to return to the city early in order to avoid the holiday rush and left the day after the check arrived. This letter is over a half month late, but I was waiting to see if this apartment thing would allow me to get there on the first, and I wanted to send the mags at the same time. Thanks a hell of a lot for sending the money order—though I don't know why you (or was it Louis) failed to take out the postal fee, etc. I'll see that you get it when we come up.

I'm glad about the change in dates; it'll give me time to write a speech since I know only vaguely what the hell to say to a college crowd. But speak I shall and if you or Shirley have any ideas send them along. (Look, I was out drinking all night for the first time since you left N.Y. so if all this sounds confused it's because I am as woozy as a barrel of smoke.) As for the Joyce business I think I'd like to cross words with the little girls over *A Portrait of the Artist* and *Black Boy*. I made a lot of notes on the *Portrait* coming down on the train from which I should be able to say a few things—which you've probably told them already.

I am sorry as hell to hear about the criticism class. I had great hopes over what you could do with that. In our culture the good things cultural are always expendable.

I'm afraid I can't take credit for Moon's using Alphonse. I might have mentioned it to him, but then, he has a whole slew of publishing house friends who have at some time worked on the *New Yorker* and who follow both it and the "Negro question" very closely—any one of whom might have advised him, including Woodburn, Archer Winsten, Volkening. No one needed to urge him if he was looking, for unlike most *New Yorker* stories in which Negroes appear Alphonse succeeds in being 'about' the Negro child almost as much as it is about the cheap liberalism of the white kid's mother . . . Tell Shirley that I received a very nice letter from a man named Pascal Covici who wrote, by way of asking me if I had signed a contract with a publisher, that my essay on *Black Boy* was 'perceptive and revealing,' and, cynicism aside, I was pleased because he was Shirley's publisher and I told him so when I answered his letter. He <u>did</u> send along a book and God knows that's more than most publishers ever think to do when feeling out prospective writers. Tell Shirley she's lucky.

Yes, goddammit, my name is on that lousy little mag. In a burst of hope I gave the editor permission to use my name. But that isn't all of my shame, the little fool tells me that was I who inspired her to the venture! I'm glad you mentioned the rag; you've helped me in making up my mind to withdraw my name. I've tried several times to advise the woman as to editorial policy but she's a regular desert for ideas and will hear nothing I have to say. Another 'vanity' publishing venture, don't you know. I had hoped there were some new writers out in the west or born in the South who might send her some stories, but hell, she wouldn't recognize King Bear if it showed up in the mails signed by Joe Dokes without the a. Some fool did send her a well known short story in which he had clumsily made the character Negro and she published it. Only guys like Heider will benefit from the venture and I'm afraid that the mag is doing more harm than literature.

I've been looking for the Bentley job. What happened to him? I haven't read all of Blochower's book, but what I did read was solid stuff. I thought only the so-called left critics were making fools of themselves these days. Which reminds me incidentally, that Wright received a very glowing letter from Meltz, praising *Black Boy,* which, after Isadore and Dillen's obscenities, left Wright confounded for a whole day! I hope that this is unfair to write, but I wouldn't be surprised to hear that he had <u>dramatized</u> Wright's book and sent it along with a contract to be signed. Those guys, those guys! Some day I plan to look them up to see what they have to say for their literary opinions after all the confessing and breast-beating. No wonder Isadore felt W didn't want to see him at the Russian consulate. In case you haven't heard, they had liquidated the party in the South completely—only no one takes responsibility for that. Can you imagine, abolishing the 'vanguard of the working class' in the country's area now undergoing the most rapid industrialization? You say you <u>sold</u> in your friendship for Bentley, but look at me, I was eating and drinking and trying to achieve self-fulfillment with the lynchers of my people. They have done something far worse to the ideas of socialism than the Nazi did to the Jews—worse because so few understand just what has happened. A lot of good intentioned little people are now falling for Foster just as blindly as they fell from Browder, whose crimes they see abstractly as simple evil rather than a smooth job of political betrayal the repercussions of which shall be felt for the next twenty years or more.

Things are a-popping in a literary way in France, have you seen the last three issues of *Horizon?* If not look them up for some of the things they're doing over there sound exciting. Somewhere in the world men still believe in deep emotions, ideas and art. I was interested to see an interview of Malraux in *Twice a Year* in which he commented that American writing must need [to] undergo a process of intellectualization while at the same time holding on to its direct approach and its concern with the fundamental man. Do you remember my attempts to formulate the same ideas? Try to get the piece if you haven't already, it is very significant—despite Bunny Wilson's drool in the New Yorker. Wilson's getting to believe that all the leading writers of the world are concerned solely with proving <u>his</u> (Wilson's) psycho-political bias. Why the hell don't they place him in a microscope slide, stain him purple and dispense with him in one, short, neat paragraph in "The Talk of the Town."

"The man has made a complete spiral from artist, in which he externalized his fantasies, to critic (during which he explained with intelligence though with little depth, the work of superior men) and now he has come to 'convert' in the Freudian sense, all the world, all politics, all literature, into his own frightened little ego and became just the opposite of the artist, a lunatic. Why don't they turn the back of the mag over to you? Our love to Laurence, Shirley and Josephine.

Ralph and Fanny

To Kenneth Burke
306 W. 141ST S
NEW YORK 30, N.Y.
NOVEMBER 23, 1945

Dear Kenneth:[*]

At last after months and months of good intentions I am getting down to writing you. I started once before right after I received the Rosenwald Fellowship with the intention of thanking you for having recommended me. But when I had begun it occurred to me that the whole business was a little bit ridiculous; I was about to thank you for a minor favor while leaving the major debt unmentioned. For I realized then that my real debt to you lies in the many things I've learned (and continue to learn) from your work and that perhaps the greatest debt lies in your courage in taking a counter-position and making your 'counter-statement.' But then the problem arose of whether one really has the right to thank a thinker for having courage, and would not that be a misunderstanding and an embarrassment? For when a man, in battling for his life, has given birth to works which enlighten and inspire, is it not a mistake to confuse the matter and attempt to thank him? It's like thanking him for being a human being. I suppose the only adequate expression of gratitude in such an instance lies in work, real hard work that comes of a similar struggle as that which has inspired or set off the chain reaction in one. So, if in the little things I write

---

[*] Ellison's first letter to Kenneth Burke, whose work Ellison admired and learned from. According to Arnold Rampersad, Ralph "recalled a heated session downtown at the New School for Social Research" some time in the late thirties when Burke delivered an unusually controversial lecture, "The Rhetoric of Hitler's 'Battle.'" His "lucid fusion of Marxist and Freudian analysis . . . intrigued Ralph even as it infuriated many in the audience" (*Ralph Ellison,* 96–97).

from time to time you observe anything of value, then to that extent am I able to express concretely my appreciation for what you have done. That is a debt I shall never stop paying and it begins back in the thirties, when you read "The Rhetoric of Hitler's Battle" before the League of American Writers, at the New School (I believe you were the only speaker out of the whole group who was concerned with writing <u>and politics</u>, rather than writing as an <u>excuse</u>—and that in a superficial manner.) It took a war to reveal the illusion in which the boys were caught, but you must have known it all the time. I notice with more anger than irony that the NMU is recognizing the value of your work after the Science and Society farce. They might have learned from it effectively in those days but chose rather to murder it, as they did everything else that wasn't easily manipulated and cheaply exploited for their pathetically narrow interests.

Anyway, I am writing a novel now and perhaps if it is worthwhile it will be my most effective means of saying thanks. Anything else seems to me inadequate and unimaginative.

I am glad you found my article of interest.* I am, as you say, becoming quite at home in that amalgam of sociology, psychology, Marxism and literary criticism, and I'd go further and say that without it, coming from where I do in American society, I would not be at home in this rather cockeyed world. I suppose that is why I feel really indebted to you. Essentially the Negro situation is irrational to an extent which surpasses that of the rest of the world, though God knows that sounds impossible. Your method gave me the first instrument with which I could orientate myself—something which neither Marx alone nor Freud alone could do.

Which leads up to your preface for an ethic that is 'universal' rather than 'racial.' I certainly agree with you that universalism is desirable, but I find that I am forced to arrive at that universe through the racial grain of sand, even though the term 'race' is loaded with all the lies which men like Davidson warm their values by. Nationalism in the cultural sense seems a more accurate term, but the Fascists have rendered it confusing. I, for instance, would like to write simply as an American, or even better, a citizen of the world, but that is impossible just now because it is to dangle in the air of abstractions while the fire which alone illuminates those abstractions lies precisely in my being a Negro and in all the "felt experience" which being a Negro American entails. Of course this, when fully understood, reveals a task which seems overwhelming and a sense of responsibility that makes

---

* "Richard Wright's Blues."

Kierkegaard seem like a phlegmatic sleepwalker. It demands an ever alert consciousness and not because you are full of neurotic anxiety but simply because reality itself demands that you approach it from second to minute with your eyes wide open. Davidson's kind have been consciously concerned with blinding my kind for over 300 years and while he can smugly embody an unconscious culture, prejudice etc., I must, if I am to survive and struggle against them, be <u>conscious</u> of every idea, insight and concept that I am able to grasp, every second as though they were spread upon a parapet like so many rifles waiting to be fired. Being a Negro is (once one becomes self-conscious) very much like being a criminal. It "produces a kind of 'oneness with the universe' in leading to a sense of universal persecution whereby all that happens has direct reference to the criminal." I could continue quoting this passage of yours endlessly without violating the parallel. Hence, to throw away the concern with the racial (suppress national) emphasis would for me be like cutting away the stairs leading from my situation in the world to that universalism of which you speak.

For in the dialectical sense the two are one. And I would say that it is not a concern with race that has harmed American Negroes, but that they were not concerned with it enough.

How well I understand the possibility of civil war you mention! But don't you see the war exists already and its effects are in many ways more serious than any mere shedding of blood. It has warped our culture, truncated our ability to think deeply and broadly and schooled us to drop atom bombs on a defenseless city, and God knows what else is in store. And I sometimes wonder why Negroes haven't a larger responsibility in this matter than we suspect. Perhaps by not fighting, by not producing widespread civil conflict, we have done America and the world more harm than 'progress.' Perhaps what is missing from American tradition is a major internal conflict of such a nature as to make us aware of the dangers of arrogant power and an oversimplified and contemptuous approach to human life. I don't know, but I deeply suspect our responsibility as Negroes; for we call ourselves democrats as do white Americans and if we truly are, then we have the responsibility of fighting anything and anyone who threatens that democracy—and with the weapons at hand. Well, the Davidsons have lost the ability to face and grapple with reality, while we under the pressure of events are just now learning to do both. If this must come to civil war, let it. Violence is coming at any rate and perhaps if the conflict in our society is resolved we'll be so sobered that we'll think twice before starting another war. It might be too late. I fear what shall happen when the whites begin actually to feel the guilt and anxiety and 'color fear' which the use of the atom bomb has released within them. One thing is sure, Negroes now have a conscious sense of having been pushed into a corner and this time they'll fight, not with any hope of surviving but of 'carrying as many white folks with me as I can.' So you see this matter does not depend upon a rational equality of numbers, but the explosion of outraged humanity against an oppression that it can no longer confront with hope or optimism.

You are quite right about Carver: I deny that he ever existed! Carver, the myth, was a creation of Robert E. Park, the father of American sociology, who was adviser to Booker T. Washington and publicity director for that institutional creation of the compromise between northern capital and southern ruling class, Tuskegee Institute. Carver was inflated into the symbol of the achievement possible for Negroes who stayed in their place, bowed to the white folks, prayed to God and left politics alone. During my three years at Tuskegee I was unable to discover anything definite about the value of Carver's work and the younger men in science dismissed him as a glorified medicine man, more concerned with manner than with scientific investigation. But let us say that he was actually everything that he was supposed to be: of what value is that type of scientist to Negroes? So he smashed the peanut into a million products, has it kept a single sharecropper from living in fear and trembling? Has it put a single patch upon his exposed dignity? I don't think so. And the world is fast learning the results of a science that refuses to concern itself with values. When I see you I'd like to discuss this further. Carver was one of the most insidious hoaxes ever created by a ruling class to keep a people under control.

As for Wright's esthetic, I agree with you, and if I seem to back it unquestioningly, it is only because I feel the need to support the truth that it enables him to project. And while I do not believe it to be the only possible approach, I do think that it contains a fundamental approach based upon a self-acceptance that Negroes seriously need. In my own work, however, I am aiming at something I believe to be broader, more psychological, and employing, let us say, of twelve tones rather than one of five. Wright's work suffers from an esthetic over-simplification (his heritage from the hard-boiled culture he is fighting against). I should like an esthetic that restores to man his full complexity—that is why I wrote the *Antioch* piece. Much of what I put into Wright's mouth therein came out of my own brain; and as he recognized in conversation, it went beyond his book.

But now let me ask you a question: How will a Negro writer who writes out of his full awareness of the complexity of western personality, and who presents the violence of American culture in psychological terms rather than physical ones—how will such a writer be able to break through the stereotype-armored minds of white Americans so that they can receive his message? As I see it, the two racial groups in this country lack the accord of sensibilities of which Malraux writes and whites are unable to see Negroes as the reincarnation of any of the values by which they live. This is a crucial problem with me just now and I would like to have your opinion.

In my novel I've deliberately written in the first person, couched much of it in highly intellectual concepts, and proceeded across a tight rope stretched between the comic and the tragic; but withal I don't know where I'm going. For in our culture the blacks have learned to laugh at which brings tears to white eyes and vice versa, and that makes it hard as hell for a Negro writer to call his shots. Unless he takes Wright's method of transforming the liability into an asset.

But getting back to Wright and your note to Stanley, I think that what you have here is not just an arbitrary resistance to organization, but a problem in allegiance. Sketching it briefly, it goes something like this: First the Negro breaks blindly away from his pre-individual condition; next he discovers the organized discipline of communism, but naively believes that he has discovered a utopia in which blacks and whites are magically cleansed of their mutual antagonisms; the reality exerts itself and instead of revealing new forms of man he discovered the Negro communists wearing the psychological slave chains and the whites their psychological bull-whips, and a man like Wright begins slowly to discover that he has not escaped the nightmare which set him careening away from the pre-individual mass, but that he has found another of its many forms. At this point he must make a decision: Should he stay and accept the nightmare because it is more rational in this form than in the feudal shape it takes in the South—or should he denounce it. Should he remain loyal to a political party, accepting it for its stated aims, for its former rather than for its current action, or should he remain loyal to his people and to his own experience? I believe, for my part, that if one truly believes in communism one had the obligation to reject the course it has taken in this country since 1937 and that had more of those intellectuals who left it stated their reasons publicly, they might have saved the Left from becoming the farce it has now become. When it comes to breaking worn-out allegiances we Americans have a gangster psychology. For even when an organization goes bad, or when it persecutes us or maims us spiritually, we feel a strange need to keep silent about it. But that is an avoidance of responsibility and an indication of how far short we fall of true individuality. We are afraid to stand alone or to speak alone. And when we sneak away in hurt and outrage we hold our tongues and hope that things will get better with a 'change, in the political situation,' never facing the fact that we, each of us, is the political situation, or that the rejection of an organization is as much a function of belonging and belief as that of accepting its program.

Wright tried to speak out, but his *Atlantic Monthly* articles betrayed the fear and discomfort he felt in doing so. (See his Introduction to *Black Metropolis* for a mature statement of his position.) Nevertheless, he did the CP a service if he taught them that Negroes <u>will</u> reject their handshakes if real action is not forthcoming. And if they appeal to Negroes to join them on the basis of Negro suffering, then they must expect Negroes to reject them on the same basis. Meanwhile, I'd say that since all of us who pretend to think have now the obligation to resist and reject even while we participate in organization, it is an ambiguous solution, but hell, so is the situation.

My how I go on! But one final thing: thanks for the tip on the concordances of English poets; after the novel, if I have the nerve, I plan to try a book of cultural studies and that kind of charting will be useful. I find that more and more my black and white lore is becoming a study of white lore or a general examination of western culture. The most amusing development to date was my lecturing to Stanley's class on Joyce! But surprisingly even Leonard Brown (who completely charmed my wife and me) thought I had something to say. Maybe it is only through the attempt to understand the ghetto that one breaks free of it. Pardon me 'transcends it.' I went to Joyce for illumination of Negro life only to discover that it works both ways and that Negro life illuminates much of Joyce. From that single experience at Bennington I believe I have the key to a whole new system of Negro education. I know too much, however, about how this country is run to believe anyone would take an interest in doing anything about it.

By all means, let us get together before you are off to Florida. I will make it a point to be free every night except the 29th and any day you might suggest. My phone number is Edgecombe 4-6804.

I've been reading excerpts from your book. When does it appear? What I have seen is exciting and very suggestive and I can hardly wait to get it in my hands. Incidentally, if you find you can't get away I might come out to Andover, if it's convenient for you. Meanwhile, my best wishes and my sincere, though belated, thanks.

Ralph Ellison

To Stanley Hyman
306 W. 141 St.
New York 30, N.Y.
Dec. 12, 1945.

Dear Stanley:

As usual I'm late. Things here are still in an uproar, and I have been wait-ing to hear from Kenneth before I answered you. He hasn't, so I suppose that he has left for Florida. His book was announced for Monday, but so far no one seems to have it for sale.

I finally get in touch with Steig but was unable to persuade him to take the engagement. He's bashful as hell to begin with and has undergone some agony of an attempt to lecture and has sworn never again. He quite positively turned it down, but you might try. His address is No. 63 Cherise Street.

At the library the other day I happened to pick up your catalogue for 1944–45 and noticed that the Nazi film masterpiece *Triumph of the Will* was shown there. Having seen it recently at a private showing, I'd like very much to hear how the student body reacted to its imagery. I'd like to know also what Erich Fromm thought about it. Incidentally, if you get a chance you might send along that catalogue which we forgot to pick up when we left.

Tom Sancton read my NM piece and had a mild brainstorm in the winter book issue. He did, however, touch some of the things I intend to develop in my cultural book and I guess that's a warning for me to get it done—after the novel of course.

A little girl named anything seems to me a hell of a lot for your pains (I notice you ignore the initial pleasure). We'd like to hear more about her—and about your friend Laurence. Still talking to his Jess, I sup-pose?

No I haven't read the Heider piece, although I have it around. There's too dam much to read these days. Which reminds me of two things: Leonard Brown was kind enough to send me Clive Bell's *Civilization;* and that the name of the book I mentioned to Drucker is *Guines' Captive Mind,* British Anti-slavery Literature of the Eighteenth Century, by Eylie Wypher. It's published by Chapel Hill.

That's about all. Fanny is OK sends love. We're still in the old apartment, still fighting landlords. So when you come to town the old telephone number is still good.

Meanwhile let us know what's cooking.

Sincerely,

Ralph

To Herbert Ellison
749 St. Nicholas Ave.
New York 31, N.Y.
february 24, 1946

Dear Herbert:

I'm sorry that you feel you cannot talk with Loren Miller, and I'll try to explain my reasons for asking you to contact him:

Last month I received a letter from Langston telling me that he had met you, that you had been mugged and your eyes blackened. Otherwise, he said, you were all right (incidentally, he thinks you're a nice fellow, only like me a little "sad"). Now as it happens, I heard from you, after I received Langston's letter and you made no mention of having been mugged, nor of eye trouble. On the contrary you gave me the impression that you were working, and, except for your marriage, were doing not too badly.

Try then to put yourself in my place when your wire arrives: From here in New York it comes as a surprise; and for several reasons. In the first place, it is the first time I've ever received a request from you asking for money and the first time that anyone has requested such a sum. But more surprising, is the statement that you will go blind without glasses. Naturally, since you told me nothing about your eyes, I became suspicious. Eye glasses do not cost that amount, usually; and the demand for money today made me wonder whether the men who mugged you had not gotten hold of my name and address and sent the wire themselves. For if you remember, your wire gave a Ninth Street address which I understand is in not quite as nice a neighborhood as that of Paloma Street, which is the only address I have for you. So you can see why I was suspicious. Here I am thousands of miles away being asked to send money out there into God knows whose hands; perhaps yours, perhaps some thugs, so in order to learn details, to make sure where the money is going and to do so as quickly as possible, I phoned Miller, who is a lawyer and a friend and asked him to contact you. I then sent the wire to your own address, so that if someone was pulling a fast one, we could have them picked up.

In fact, I almost had the New York police get in touch with Los Angeles to investigate. Fortunately, I did not, for if you would not talk with Miller, certainly you would not want to talk to a policeman.

This morning when your answer came I was somewhat reassured, for at least you had received my wire. I am sorry that you feel you can't talk to the lawyer, however, because I must have more details and he not only could explain to me what your trouble is, but being there on the spot he can help you much better than I can. Strangely, I have just received a wire from him stating that he is unable to locate you at either of the addresses. What is going on? I want to send you the money, but I want to be sure that you get it. I should explain also that I am not able to sell much of my writing now; that I am working on a book, and we must live off of a fellowship, which gives me not much more than you make a month. So you can see that fifty dollars is not a sum that I have to toss around.

Please write me an AIR-MAIL-SPECIAL letter stating what is wrong with your eyes; whether the money is for treatment or for glasses or for both. Most of all, tell me whatever else is wrong, if anything. In fact, it would be more convenient for the way my cash is running if you would have your doctor contact me so that I could arrange payments rather than send the lump sum of fifty dollars. If you have difficulty in putting down these details, please see Miller, as I must pay him for his trouble now anyway.

I hope you understand why I am asking you to do all of this. Try to remember that although we are brothers, we haven't seen each other for eight years and as far as what has happened to us in the years between, we are almost strangers. Nor do I want to know any of your secrets for I consider you a man with your own life to live. If you are in trouble, however, I am ready to help to the extent that I am able. It is to protect both you and myself that I seek assurance that you and not someone else is to receive it.

Let me again suggest that if you can possibly change your mind, that you have to go to Loren Miller, and explain what has happened to your eyes. No more than that. He will write me and I'll send the money to you directly. If you do not plan to do that, then write me in your own hand and I will get the money to you.

Do not wire me; it is expensive and I do not keep much cash on hand and I cannot identify you through a wire. And if you must wire, don't waste money telling me to answer by Western Union, as I understand to do that anyway. And keep your messages as short as possible, as I would much rather give you the money than Western Union.

I am very sorry that this is taking so much time. That is why I asked you to see Miller. If you had, you would have had the money by now. Because I wanted to speed things up I called him long distance and since then have spent about $15 in wires and phone calls. So try to cooperate; by doing so you will save yourself further waiting and save us money that we need rather badly. As you know, I am married and recently we were forced, because of the housing shortage to take an apartment that costs us $25 more in monthly rent. This does not mean that we cannot send you the money; only that we must sacrifice in order to do so. I am only trying to explain why I must spend no money that is not strictly necessary. Miller, incidentally, is a nice guy. A few months ago he won the legal battle for the Negro movie stars when whites tried to put them out of the Blueberry Hill district.

Please cooperate with me, as I am very worried about you; in fact, since I received your first wire I have been unable to work. For us, this is very serious, as I am under contract to a publisher and I deliver my book on time. I hope your trouble is not as serious as it sounds and that everything can be done to correct it.

Please let me hear from you by return mail. Stamps are enclosed.

Sincerely,
Ralph

To Richard Wright
APRIL 4, 1946

Dear Dick,

Here it is. I hope it helps . . .

Ralph

The LaFargue Clinic was organized as the result of three men's aware-ness of the vast nervous and mental disorders found within the urban Negro community. The conditions which Frederick Wertham knew from his long experience as the psychiatric head of the mental hygiene clinics of two city hospitals and as a private psychiatrist, Richard Wright had ob-served both as a Harlem newspaperman and as a novelist who has given special attention to the affect of the urban environment upon the total Negro personality;* and what Wright and Wertham had seen through the techniques of their professions, Shelton Hale Bishop had learned as a pio-neer worker among the youth of Harlem, as the spiritual advisor to both youth and adults, and as the pastor of an institution outstanding for keep-

---

* Wright as an example of the fate and promise of juvenile delinquents, i.e., *Black Boy*.

ing alive the broad social tradition of the Negro church. Their coming together was most fortunate for Harlem.

For thus familiar with the ordinary routine of investigating, reporting and forgetting Harlem's crises, these three men knew that there is less need for investigations than for urgent action. Nor did they feel that the chronic condition could wait for the creation of an agency by the city or for a gift by private philanthropy. Instead, with two rooms in the parish house provided by Rev. Bishop and St. Philips Church, and with the professional skills of Dr. Wertham and a staff of psychiatrists and social workers who volunteered their services, they went into action. Out of their efforts has come the first institution of its kind, offering advanced psychiatric treatment to all who seek their aid for the small fee of twenty five cents."*

To William Haygood
749 ST. NICHOLAS AVE.
NEW YORK 31, N.Y.
APRIL 22, 1946

Mr. William C. Haygood
Director of Fellowships
Julius Rosenwald Fund
4901 Ellis Avenue
Chicago 15, Illinois

Dear Sir:

During her recent visit to New York I inquired of Mrs. Haygood as to the possibility of my obtaining an extension of my 1945 Fellowship, explaining to her that I found myself with far more work to be done on my project than I could hope to finish by the termination of my grant in June. It is thus at her suggestion that I am writing you.

The delay to my project arises in part to the following circumstances: During February 1945 while in the midst of my novel it became necessary for me to return to sea as a merchant seaman. While docked in Rouen, France I became ill and required treatment at the 167th U.S. General Hospital located there, and upon my return to New York, at the Queens General Hospital. As a result of this illness and the psychological wrenching

---

* These two paragraphs, including the words explaining his asterisk, are comments Ellison sent Wright on the LaFargue Clinic.

sustained from being torn from my work it was several months before I could concentrate upon my novel with any satisfactory results.

Thus I have only completed about two-thirds of my book, plus several scenes, sketches and developments belonging to later sections of the narrative. However, most of the continuous sections of my manuscript have been read by my publishers, Reynal and Hitchcock, and I am happy to report, accepted.

And now I come to the other cause of delay: After progressing this far I have discovered that the theme of my book requires a more extended treatment than I had anticipated. To the extent that it is possible to gauge such matters, I judge that I have about six more months of intensive work before the novel shall be completed.

Would it, in light of the above circumstances, be possible for me to receive an extension of my fellowship for this period?

I am enclosing copies of miscellaneous writings that I have published since receiving my Fellowship—some of which contain themes and notes to be treated at length in my next book, a critical study of the Negro in American culture. You will, also, find enclosed notices of lectures that I have delivered during the year before the faculty and student body of Bennington College and before one of its classes in literary criticism.

During the year I have, also, lectured on two occasions at New York University before a class studying Racial Contributions to American Culture; and before a group of psychologists, sociologists and writers called together by Miss Pearl Buck and Dr. Harry A. Overstreet at the East West Association, on the Negro in the aesthetic motivation of white Americans. Incidentally, this group, which was interested in combatting Negro stereotypes in writing, included Drs. Gene Welfish, Otto Klineberg, Gardner Murphy, G.W. Allport, Misses Pearl Buck, Rackham Holt and others. I realize that this might seem to be quite a bit of talking for one who is supposed to write; however, these lectures were based upon material which will form a part of my next book.

In closing, please allow me to express my appreciation to the Committee on Fellowships for making it possible for me to devote the major portion of my time to an intensive course of work and study which, despite all interruptions, has been most fruitful.

Yours very sincerely,
Ralph Ellison

Enclosures
P.S. Postage is enclosed for return of the attached material.

To Alex Morisey
749 St. Nicholas Ave.
New York 31, N.Y.
June 19, 1946

Dear Alex:*

It has been so long since I received your letter that I am ashamed to be answering now. I received your Xmas cards, and I had better stop right here to call your attention to my new address, so that we can look forward to another one next Xmas.

I have come across photography of yours in the Negro papers from time to time and I cut out one especially good reproduction of a group of girls on the Bennett campus to send you, but for the life of me I can't locate it. Our apartment is a maze of paper, mostly unfiled, and sometimes things get lost. Incidentally, I'm an old student of Orrin Suthern, of your music school. If you ever see him, give him my regards. The same is true of Eva Hamlin, whom I understand has gotten married. I'm still working on my novel and for the last two months have been living in a cabin out on Long Island. However, I shall return to the city during July and should you and Juanita happen into New York, please give me a ring. My number is Edcombe 4-6804.

Meanwhile, give our regards to Juanita and the children and good luck to you all.

As ever
Ralph Ellison

Mr. A.A. Morisey
Office of Public Relations
Bennett College
Greensboro, N. C.

---

* Alexander Morisey, the son of Alfred Ellison's daughter, Mamie, and therefore Ellison's first cousin.

To Stanley Hyman
P.O. Box 123
QUOGUE, LONG ISLAND
NEW YORK
JUNE 20, 1946

Dear Stanley:

Right after I read your Thoreau piece I went down to Long Island and found me a shack, not quite in the woods but close enough, and though near no pond, within earshot of the ocean. I have been there now close to two months at work on my book. I picked up your note when I came into the city for a weekend.

I didn't know what the hell you were talking about in reference to the Wertham circle until I saw Ralph Martin's piece of drool in the *N.R.* They turned down a very good piece on the clinic by Wright, then sent Martin out to do a story and what you read is the result. As far as the circle goes, Wertham is a friend of Wright's, etc.

I had intended to write you that I dropped into the American Academy ceremony and saw Kenneth stand to receive the applause of the audience, but I had to leave before it was over in order to leave town. Thus was unable to see him. As far our going down there as you suggest, I'm afraid that it is a little late now as we have taken care of the matter already. So let your mind be at ease. However, why don't all of us get together at Kenneth's anyway? If it is Okay with Shirley, why don't we arrange a date to meet there? I shall return to the city by July 1 and any weekend after that suits us.

I find the country very nice, though much too wet, and have been doing some fishing. Fanny and I were out in the ocean with some friends last weekend and caught some bass. I have observed the passion with which some fellows pursue fish and can see traces of those rituals that Jane Harrison explores in *From Ritual to Romance.** Speaking of folklore reminds me that I was told that during the folklore sessions that you attended here in the city something that I collected while on the project was read and was given credit by Botkin? Did you hear it?

Give our regards to Shirley and all we've got to say about those kids

---

* Ellison probably means Jesse Weston's *From Ritual to Romance.*

with their mouths full of teeth, is don't let them chew up the house before we get there.

Sincerely,
Ralph

To Richard Wright
Permanent address
Box 123
749 St. Nicholas Ave.—Apt. B Quogue, L.I. N.Y.
New York City
june 24, 1946

Dear Dick:

I suppose from the time it has taken me to answer your letters you feel that you might well have placed them in a bottle and dropped them overboard, leaving its delivery to chance and the currents of the sea. Nevertheless I received the first, which you mailed to my publisher, about three days later. It was then shipped to me out here on Long Island where I have been working on my book since the early part of May.

Which brings me to the matter of the pamphlet for Dorothy Norman: Since I couldn't get into town I had Fanny attempt to take care of it. She called Salzman, told him the problem and asked to be allowed to look for the pamphlet; but Salzman had not heard from you and he asked to see the letter. Now it so happens that you failed to sign your first letter. I told Fanny to drop it until later—after you had written Salzman. In the meantime she informed Dorothy that we were trying to get the material for her. During the weekend of June 14 I ran into the city and called Salzman, and read him your second letter. He said that your Washington Place apartment had been rented a few days after you sailed, that the cartons had been stored in a warehouse, and since there were several dozens of those it would take two or three days to go through them. He suggested that if Dorothy wished to get in touch with him, he would see if it were possible for her to go through the various cartons. I thanked him and told him that I would speak to D. as I was returning to the country at the beginning of the week.

The next day we were at the beautifully functional house of the Normans (where the lights don't click and the cans flush silently and your hands stay chilled from the cold drinks thrust into them by the hovering black and white uniformed maids) and I told D. what had happened. She was so disappointed that Fanny suggested that perhaps some of the cartons might have been taken to Charles Street and she would call Salzman at the beginning of the week to see if this were so. Of course it wasn't and she wrote to D. to that effect last weekend. I'll call her when I return to the city on the 29th.

Incidentally, the occasion for our visit to the Norman was a party given for the friends of the clinic. We thought it a rather nice party; Wertham seems to attract a decent group of people. Especially did it seem true meeting the group at the party only a few days after having been carried to visit Dr. Harold Ellis at his country place that is located a few miles from where I'm working. He has a small cottage set in acres of grass, seemingly well stocked with liquor, and close enough to an ocean inlet to see his boat anchored only a few minutes walk from his house. He has a new powerful outboard motor that must have cost him nearly the fee for one of his courses of electric shocks! We went there with our landlords, the Johnsons, and while we found his wife a friendly somewhat naive woman, he has all the cruder characteristics of his class. He made such infantile aggressive passes at Fanny that we were both embarrassed for him and the others present. I couldn't believe that the man was a psychiatrist. He acts more like a Washington civil service worker. This whole group is perfect example of the mechanized man. Life consists of money, the table, the stool, and for those still young enough, the bed. Being among them is like discovering oneself in the midst of an obscene nightmare. But, oh well, I see, I hear, I analyze and I record. And how they reveal themselves even in their play. I have discovered the pleasure (and some of the tragic emotions) of fishing since I've been down here, but I notice that they are interested only in catching fish, the more the better; they reveal no sporting sense, no desire to mingle, to take the fish with artificial lure, to pit skill and artifice against the instinct of the animal. In fact, they don't bother with fishing that requires skill, although they possess the tackle, the boats and the time to go where it is. Already Fanny and I have begun making excuses to get away so that we can fish by ourselves. They think it is only because we are young and desire to be alone.

I have given you my address above; as you will notice, it is two doors away from Earl Brown. Which reminds me that Brown is a brother-in-law to Dr. Cannon. I discovered this when a friend suggested that we mate our dog with the dog of a friend of theirs. The friend turned out to be Cannon, who came over to inspect our dog's pedigree. It didn't occur to me until later that this was the Cannon of the Quebec incident. I asked Johnson about him, and was told that Cannon is considered a very competent physician and a very courageous man whose actions are colored by his feeling that he is living on borrowed time. He was given up as a tuberculosis victim and is living with one lung collapsed.

Unfortunately, for your information and my amusement, I left town before your trip had hit the rumor waves, but on a trip in I talked with Velasco who told me that there was some such speculation concerning the political motives for your trip as you suggested. He said that there was some confusion over whether you had gone to Europe, to the Soviet Union, or Mexico. I talked with John Hammond, who asked about you and was interested in how long you would stay. I guess he had read the enclosed clipping from the *Pittsburgh Courier*. It seems that there is a bit of talk going around about my own work and he has been trying to get in touch with me for several months. Rumors have it that my book is finished (which it isn't) and our names continue to crop up in circles far outside the sway of the Left. My piece on *American Daughter* appeared in the *Saturday Review of Literature* this month under the title "Stepchild Fantasy." And I've been asked to do a piece for a special issue of *Survey Graphic* . . . I suppose Ida—who was much delighted over your letters—has written you that Ehrenburg answered some criticism of your political position with the remark that you were a great artist. It occurred while I was away so I can't give you the full story. There was also the piece by Norman in the *Post* that I'm sure she has sent you; if not, I'll send you my copy. As far as I know, the nature of your visit, nor the implications have yet to be reported by the Negro press. Perhaps Horace will have something to say.

A few days after you left I ran into Ted Ward and just for the devil of it I spoke to him. He lives in Brooklyn and is still wiggling on the hook of Communism, full of fear and trembling that he hides behind a mask of arrogant self-assertiveness and CP rhetoric. I broke through that as we stood at a bar while <u>he</u> downed whiskey after whiskey. He finally admitted that he too had been upset by the wartime policy; he had sold his business and refused to take part in any activity. Then he had decided that there was nothing else, who was he to question the party? He has aged visibly and the membrane of his lower lip is now a bright red; as I watched him, little old man that he is, I wondered if it came from too much whiskey or on the morbid side of mind if it was evidence of a suicide attempt. Hell, it's possible: He is not so sure of himself with me and shows a guarded respect for my ideas that he didn't have before. I could never understand the rituals of personal prestige that I see develop among people and I find it just as difficult to understand what you write about Aragon as I did back in the 30's when questions of prestige cropped up between you and Ted. As for Aragon, his message to you fits right in with his criticism of Gide. On that level, at least, there seems to be something in common between the psychology of American and French communists.

As interested as I am to hear you describe what you have found, I'm not at all surprised that you are discovering the naiveté of the French. From some of the things several of their really great writers have had to say about America (Gide in his *Imaginary Conversations,* for instance) I've had the feeling that they were speaking out of theories based upon personal experience which they applied to this country much in the way that one applies a metaphor to life. Because France has not become as highly industrialized as the U.S. but is of a much richer culture they manage to see the implications of our industrialism without experiencing it immediately. (It's like a man seeking in his male experience the equivalent of woman's childbirth pain and deciding that it is comparable to being kicked in the balls—which might or not might not be adequate; for while he makes the kick in his balls a ladder upon which he climbs to look over the fence of his male biology into the world of woman's pain, the woman is in pain; and while he might view the scene around her, he cannot grasp the ground upon which she lies as on a bed of fire, for it is beneath her and in her, and thus cut off from his vision. We live the horror that the French, even the most sensitive and cultured French, can grasp only through thought; and as the existentialists hold, how limited is thought!). To this extent I believe that we Negroes have an advantage over them, for all their admirable culture. For the world will not turn back from industrialism, but will go forward, and while the Frenchmen must plunge from the springboard of thought into reality that is hardly a problem of us who live too often beneath the surface and in the texture of that reality. One can master the meaning of his experience, but first or simultaneously one must act, must experience. There is also the fact that only a few men consciously grasp the intensities of experience; a Gide, a Valery, a Malraux no doubt experience the most intense tensions of their effort, while the average Frenchman moves along in the well-ordered patterns of their national rituals and traditions—until they found themselves occupied. The writers speak of lunging into reality, in truth, reality blitzed into them. It just happens that over here the average American is subjected to a more rigorous and intensive existence. But this could go on for hours. Remember how back in 1939 we listened to Benes and Thomas Mann during the League of American Writers Congress at Carnegie Hall and were almost afraid to believe that these leading Europeans could sound so naive about Hitler and the Nazis. There must be a psychological law that prevents men, once they invest in a particular way of life, from seeing the possibilities of other men rejecting their values and setting out to build a way of life based upon the antithesis of their most sacred ideals. Please write more about your observations and the ideas of those whom you meet. I'm very interested in Malraux and in any books of his and of others that you find interesting.

About the only thing I can say in closing is that I see no reason for you to hurry back here, it's still a madhouse and it gets crazier every minute. Give our love to Ellen and Julia and by next letter I'll try to have something to say about what's going on in the city.

As ever,
Ralph

To Richard Wright
NEW YORK 31, N.Y.
AUGUST 24, 1946

Dear Dick:

I've been putting down notes of things to write you about, but I've been so busy that I haven't found time to put them in a letter until now. Things here have gone to hell in a million directions. The lynchings that we were expecting have broken out all over the place; about eight in a month's time, with a lot of liberal & CP excitement being made over a vet whose eyes were gouged out by police nightsticks in North Carolina. Even the Village has its share of racism. It is now unsafe for a Negro to be found at least within a block of your Washington Pl. apartment unless he's armed to fight off a gang of Italian hoodlums. So many Negroes have been attacked that they are banding together for protection—mostly verbal, alas.

Which brings me to two closely connected items about you. Last month while visiting one of the Reynal Hitchcock boys we were asked if you and Ellen were together and informed that some Canadian writer had brought down the rumor that you were separated, you having left Ellen and gone to France. (Few people seem aware that you're a guest of the Govt.) Unfortunately, I don't remember the guy's name, but he was some one you had met in Quebec. I told my friends that I had seen you get on the boat together, and that as far as I knew this was a malicious lie. Later the *Daily Worker* carried a badly written article charging you with evicting an invalid artist from your Charles St. place, and of raising your rents to 150 bucks per month. The property was described as belonging to Ellen who was said now to be somewhere in Mexico. Of course you recognize the old smear, but the use of it in a newspaper article is particularly revolting. I even dislike passing it on to you. Thank God I am able to refute anyone who approaches me with such crap. Incidentally, several days after the smear I was approached again by the *NM* to return to their rag and boy did I rub their nose in it. These things put me farther apart from them than mere ideological or moral considerations.

I was interested in a piece on the French CP in *Colliers* that Duclos[*] was quoted as saying that "Russia is old-fashioned. It's a socialism. Our communist doctrine for France is a mixture of French materialism of the Eighteenth Century, of German Marxism and of the Modern British workers' movement. You can't imagine such a program turning France into a barracks. Frenchmen, the fathers of independence, can't be regimented." This seems like a fairly independent position to me and I wonder how it works out in action. Recently I went to visit a Jewish writer whom I knew before the war and met a French woman who knew Aragon and to whom I told of your experience with him. The Americans present refused to believe it was true, but this woman (whose former husband was a journalist who knew Aragon) said that he was a 'religious Communist, very strict' and this might have motivated his action. On the other hand, she said the French are sometimes very academic and that he might simply have been acting like an older man, with the privilege of having the younger man visit him. She said among other things that she was one of your many French fans and that it might be worth your while not to allow the incident to annoy you too much and see the guy anyway and ask him pointblank what the hell he means. She's a pretty interesting woman, almost incapable of understanding our obsession with race and feels that we should ignore it. If only we could! Since the CP went to hell the thing has pressed me wherever I've turned. We were out to Kenneth Burke's place in N.J. several weekends ago, where he gave me a letter he had written in answer to one of my own last year. He had tried to answer some of my opinions concerning the racial set-up and our culture, but was so dissatisfied with his answers that he could never mail the letter. In it he attempted to set down a formula for a Negro character who would incorporate all of the contradictions present in the Negro-white situation in this country and

[*] Leader of the French Communist Party.

yet be appealing to whites. He strived pretty much at a Dostoyevskian Idiot type, aware of contradictions, but clinging to the spiritual element of the Spirituals. Which certainly holds some possibilities (almost any broad play upon contradictions does) but I've always preferred another Dostoyevsky type, the Ivans, or Dmitris, rather than the Aloysas or Myshkins. All in all, it was a pleasant day. The Burkes make a fair attempt at sensible living. Well Ellen, Mary Chapin, the artist's wife sends regards.

Recently there has been a re-issue of Gorky's *Reminiscences of Tolstoi, Chekhov and Andreyev,* which I have found very good reading. Gorky had a tremendous tolerance for writers who were by temperament so different from himself, especially Tolstoi, and I'm struck by the warmth, almost tenderness, which existed among them. For all their disagreements they seemed aware of working for the same broad goals and thus had a regard for the precious abilities of the others. I was quite struck with this, since now with you gone I can't even talk about my problems with anyone who has the intelligence and the experience to understand. If you'd like the book, I'll send you one.

Which reminds me, I was in to Briggs' and he sends word that he has an unpurged first edition of Gertrude Stein's *Making of Americans,* if you're still interested. I suppose you've heard from Frank Taylor that they're interested in your doing a book on her. I talked with him about it and I think that not only would you do an important job, but that it would be a significant step toward teaching Americans to regard you as more than just a "Negro" writer. I hope that while you're away you will lose no opportunity to establish yourself as an international figure, as it will be important as hell when you return.

Interestingly enough, Fanny and I spent a weekend at Wading River where we sat around talking to Horace most of the time. He was supposed to break his analysis in July but it was extended six months and I think it has depressed him quite a bit. We've been told that he feels that people are laughing at him. He was quite concerned with what you could do next, in what direction you could develop, whether you'd return to the CP or go into the church. The old story of running up against the extremes of one's own sense of possibility and mistaking them for those of another. He says he's arranging a lecture trip to England for next year and I have no doubt that he won't. I left him feeling a bit sad. The guy needs justification. And while in my limited way I've always tried to justify that which I thought worthy in those I know—even while disagreeing with them on many levels— I find the most worthy thing about Horace (besides his charm) is his honesty. But with him honesty doesn't stop him from indulging himself or doing the things that he is honest about, so that in the end he is dishonest to himself. Just now he is at Yaddo, doing some writing.

This is all for now. I'm still writing my book. Father Divine married a young white Canadian, the country still stinks. Give our love to Ellen and Julia.

Sincerely,
Ralph

To Ellen Wright
749 ST. NICHOLAS AVE.
NEW YORK CITY
SEPTEMBER 23, 1946

Dear Ellen:*

We have just learned from Naomi that you have had an appendectomy. We hope that there were no complications and that you are now on the mend. We promised you that we would let you know when we legalized our name—so now you know. We finally got around to doing it. Can't say that it feels so differently but Bobbins says it is much nicer to be legal. I wrote Dick a month ago but with your illness I am sure he has been too busy to answer. Recently, Claude Roy, a young French writer, was in one evening and I took the privilege of giving him your address, since he seems so impressed with Dick's work. Tell Dick his old enemy, Harry Haygood, has been taken off the ash heap and is once more writing pamphlets on the Negro question. Ruth McKenney and Bruce Minton have been purged from the CP—the charge, "Infantile Leftism," which they repudiated in the press, stating that they are still loyal. The *New Masses* carries a self-righteous statement against them, charging that for a long time they have been critical of its editorial policy! What with Wallace thrown out of the Cabinet, things political have stepped up their pace. It all looks pretty dark.

Tell us about your French. Have you mastered it, so that you can keep up with Julia, who by now must surely have conquered it?

Tell Dick that Herndon ran in to see us recently (from Chicago). He looks well, is off of politics and has become a rather cynical businessman—

---

* This is a fascinating letter not only for its breezy feel of life on the left in New York, especially the doings of Angelo Herndon, a fire-breathing sometime Communist in the thirties and Ralph's predecessor as editor of the *Negro Quarterly,* but also because it seems a letter Fanny Ellison put her hand to as much as Ralph did.

insurance brokerage and women's clothing. Fanny was a little bit disgusted with his boasting about the extravagant profits he makes on fur coats which he sells on installment to poor women. Tell him also that the Schomburg Collection is asking for copies of his speeches and writings delivered in France. (We would like to have copies also.) But that I did not give them your address. We saw the piece on the clinic in *Free World*, part of which was quoted in the *Post*. It looked very good. There is an extra copy here should you want it.

Meanwhile, make the most of it and absorb enough of France for us.

Sincerely,

Ralph & Fanny

To Stanley Hyman
New York City 31
749 St. Nicholas Ave
JUNE 17, 1947

Dear Stanley,

I've been putting off writing until I had something definite to tell you. However, the only definite news I have is that my situation is still indefinite. I finally heard from Random House, in fact I met at Random House: Haas, Cerf, Linscott. They want my novel to the extent of buying up my old contract and offering me a $500 additional advance upon the receipt of three additional chapters. All of which is very nice—aside from the fact that I haven't pressed them to see how much more cash they're willing to put on the board. But here's the rub—I've discovered that there is quite a lot of bitterness between Reynal & Hitchcock and the Taylor-Erskine combine and that they might hold on to the book out of spite. The other possibility is that they might actually like it. I'm sending in part of the ms. today, so tell Shirley to hex 'em so they won't like it. Incidentally, just so you won't think I wasted my time up there, Random House thought the outline* was quite a piece of writing—which was an amusing surprise to me.

The other thing in the works is that Taylor is trying to get me into Yaddo for a while this summer, but what chances he has I don't know. Nevertheless I'd like to come back to Bennington for a weekend, at least, as soon as I hear from Reynal & Hitchcock. Indeed, if they take too long I'll have to come up [to] get away from the strain.

---

* See "Working Notes for *Invisible Man*," in *Collected Essays*, 343–49.

I've just about brought you up to date. Except that I'm finally over my cold; that Mary Hewitt and Atwood Woolf were up one morning; and that I'm glad you liked the snaps of Joanny. Those of you and Laurence were spoiled when a blast of cold air hit the wet negatives. Better luck next time—especially with you pushing a lawnmower.

Tell Shirley congrats on selling *Pillar of Salt,* and I'm very glad that some of my comments made sense to her conception of her novel. Oh, and you might tell Francis that I spoke to both Frank Taylor and Robert Haas of Random House about his work-in-progress and they are quite interested. I only hope I reported its contents correctly, having depended upon my memory of your description of it. I've got one thing right: pur-pose, passion, perception, the nature of rhythm—which God knows is a neat enough packaging for a profound commodity to make a publisher smack his lips. Francis should hear from them soon. If not, he should drop Frank a reminder—or he can write me and I'd be glad to remind him.

Finally, give my regards to Kenneth and tell him that the next time I'm up there, I hope I can stay long enough to have a chat with him.

Love to all,
Ralph

To Ida G
c/o STEIN
TWO RIVERS
SO. LONDONDERRY, VT.
AUGUST 16, 1947

Dear Ida:

We are finally getting around to writing on our 6th day here. It's almost unbelievable that we did finally arrive and the place is actually as lovely as we had been told.

Monday morning we set out bright and early to make the train but the baggage master at Grand Central Station insisted that before we could bring our dogs into Vermont we would have to have a letter from the Vermont Department of Agriculture stating that they could be admitted into the state. This, as we knew, was an unnecessary piece of red-taped maliciousness and in our anger and frustration we cancelled our tickets then and there and decided to forget about the trip. Then on the way up town it occurred to us that we might stop at the 125th Street station and try for a later train, which we did without any trouble whatever from the baggage master there. And we left, dogs and all, at 12:40 after calling Mrs. Stein to say that we were delayed. Knowing that we would miss the only bus in Londonderry, she drove the 35 miles to meet us in Brattleboro and from that moment on has been one of the kindest, most considerate people ever.

As you have probably heard, the cottage (which consists of two large rooms and bath and two verandas) rests upon a sloping hill overlooking the confluence of two rivers. We can look out across the rolling lawn past the noisy river to the big Stein house which gets its name, Twin Rivers, from the rushing waters.

We are absolutely isolated here, with plenty of quiet and no interruptions. I have managed to do some work and Fanny, when she is not cooking, is having something of a real vacation.

As for the Steins, they seem to be one of those rare rather large families in which all the members seem fond of one another. We have only this evening met Mr. Stein and the two boys, who just drove up. But the two girls seem quite alert and charming. Mrs. Gerda might well feel proud of them.

With all the running around and extra expense which the unexpected setback at Grand Central caused (taxicabs, extra tips, long distance phone calls, etc.), I find myself wishing that I had taken you up on meeting you at Clara's last Sunday. As it is, you will find enclosed my check for $42. Could you wire the forty-two dollars as soon as you've cleared the check; or before, if convenient.

If the days continue to fly swiftly, as they have thus far, we should see you very soon. The last few days have been terrifically hot and we hope that you spent them in air-cooled, perfectly magnificent movies.

Our regards to Clara and the girls.

Love,
Ralph and Fanny

To Bea and Francis Steegmuller
WINHALL STATION
SO. LONDONDERRY, VT.
SATURDAY, AUG. 23, '47

Dear Bea and Francis:*

We've waited until it's almost time to leave because we wanted to tell you everything about the wonderful vacation you've made so unexpectedly possible. In fact, my metabolism hasn't been the same since the arrival of Mrs. Gretchen Stein's first note. And let me tell you that anything that gives my old metab a filip is a momentous event. For one thing, it brought news which made it possible for me to avoid Yaddo to which I had reluctantly applied; for another it made it possible for the two of us to spend Fanny's vacation together.

I don't know why, I suppose because you are always so casual in referring to your 'little cottage,' but we were unprepared for its wonderfully functional spaciousness. We started catching our breath from the moment we glimpsed it as we rumbled across the bridge and by the time we had curved the drive and approached it full face we couldn't suppress our delight. Fanny's eyes haven't ceased to shine. Should you, by the way, miss your desk and milk jug, you'll probably find them at our apartment. They're quite nice.

Except for one or two rain-swept days the weather has been fine; and since one of those was spent at an auction we count it among the pleasant. We've read, we've eaten too much (cooking everything possible in this wonderful thick cream we get from the Amsdens), we've taken pictures, we've hiked and swam and seen much of the country from the Jeep Station Wagon.

But most of all—and certainly, Francis, you'll understand how much I appreciate this—I've been able to average five pages a day on my novel. It's as though a shackle had been removed from imagination. For now the stuff flows; I'm no longer elaborating a conceptual frame, but inventing. And I can leave the typewriter at the end of my working day without the fear that next morning I will have lost my inspiration. Indeed, I'm so

---

* Beatrice and Francis Steegmuller. Beatrice was a painter of some note, Francis a writer who gave Ellison the use of his Fifth Avenue office during some of the time he was writing *Invisible Man.*

delighted that I'm trying to arrange to remain somewhere in these mountains until the cold weather sets in. In musing over the difference between my ability to work here and my floundering at home, I've concluded that since I'm concerned a great deal with cloacal and subterranean imagery and symbolism, working in our little apartment (with its long, narrow entrance into a small, low-ceilinged room, dark and warm) is too close to what the imagination is struggling to transform. While here in a valley among mountains looking out upon a flowery hillside complete with spiders sinister, butterflies and humming birds, things don't seem nearly so desperate. Imagination is imagination again and I've regained some of the pleasure of writing.

Incidentally, I can now safely say that I've signed up with Random House. Right after you left I had a talk with Ted Ammonson, of Reynal & Hitchcock, and who though he seemed sincerely enthusiastic about my novel gave me the opportunity to buy up my contract without any of the nastiness that Frank and Albert had anticipated. In fact, he was so damned decent that I thought it over carefully for two weeks before I made the break. Random House came through with the new contract immediately, so it seems that once again we share a publisher in common. Maybe some day we'll make a good team to bash in his (incorporated) head. I hope, however, they've decided to take your novel as well.

By now we've met all the Edwin Stein family, had pleasant conversations with Barbara and Teddy, Paul and Mr. Stein, and been completely charmed, both of us, by Gerda. And last night, that silent little painter of monkeys and horses, Lucia, came up from Washington. But we shouldn't think of closing our letter without telling you how really very kind and considerate Mrs. Stein has been. Though very busy with her home and her canning, she has always found time to see that we haven't wanted for anything, whether it was to be found down at her place or in the surrounding villages; nor has her kindness seemed a mere matter of good form. And all of this without once violating the easy luxury of our isolation.

Don't stay in the southwestern sun too long Bea, and don't you, Francis get turned around what with Maupassant, Los Alamos and Corn Dances. It all sounds wonderful. We do hope Santa Fe proves to be as inspiring as Vermont's Winhall Station and we look forward to seeing you when you return.

Sincerely,
Ralph and Fanny

To Kenneth Burke
WINHALL STATION
So. LONDONDERRY, VERMONT
AUGUST 25, 1947

Dear Kenneth:

I was very disappointed to arrive at Bennington on your day of departure last June, for I had hoped to see you there. Especially, since until quite recently I've found it next to impossible to write letters that explains why you haven't heard from me. I did manage to use the telephone and was thus able to keep in touch with Stanley, but with you this wasn't possible; so I had to contend with my vain resolutions and bad conscience.

Since I've been here in the mountains I've written some seven letters in less than a week, so I suppose the psychological ice-jam has been broken. God knows it's been hot enough. But then, my novel has been going rather smoothly up here, and though the economic determinists would insist that it is because I've recently signed a new publisher's contract (having shifted from Reynal & Hitchcock to Random House) and am thus more serene in my gut life, I have a notion that the answer lies in the effect which the mountain has had upon my dream life. In Harlem I live out my horrors during the day: here I have my nightmares at night and by eight in the morning after watching the thick mist sweeping before the swift rising of the sun, I've achieved enough of a precarious tranquility to turn in a rather successful day of writing.

I suppose it's rather difficult when one lives in an apartment so high one must enter through a long, narrow (and oft times smelly) hallway, into a small and low-ceilinged warm little room, to deal facilely with the local and subterranean imagery with which I'm concerned in my book. For if art isn't life, neither is life art; and when your nose is bumped against your life too consistently and in too short an arch, there's no perspective in which the imagination can come to focus. I see no solution except to move. Or change my theme. Perhaps when upon mountains one should only write about holes; when in holes, only about mountain life. Think of what that might do for the imaginative quality of our literature.

What have you published recently? Just before leaving the city I hastily read your piece on Ideology and Myth and had it set off a few bells in my head. When I return I plan to give it a careful study, as it reawakens my interests in a piece I planned concerning the relations between our 'science' of sociology and racial ideology. Myrdal's *American Dilemma,* for instance, is full of rhetoric and ideological manipulations.

As for myself, I've just corrected the proofs on a section of my novel which is to appear in the American number of *Horizon* next October. It looks very strange in print, but it's too late to do anything about it. Connolly was enthusiastic enough in his letter however, saying that he threw out two pieces to make space for it, and asking to be my English publisher. I only wish the damn thing was completely finished, agonized over, learned from, and forgotten in the enthusiasm for my next.

Stanley tells me you are thinking of passing up Bennington next year, what are your plans?

Why can't you, the next time you're in the city, bring Libby and the boys up to dinner; we'd like to see you all very much.

As ever,

Ralph Ellison

To Langston Hughes
WINHALL STATION
SOUTH LONDONDERRY
VERMONT
AUGUST 25, 1947

Dear Langston:

We're here in Vermont living in the mountain summer place of some friends—all four of us. It's quite nice, much larger than our apartment and a million times quieter. I haven't heard the Lutcher woman yelling "The Lady's in Love with You" since over two weeks ago when she awoke me about two A.M.

There are no cats—either colored or feline to howl in the dubious ecstasies of fornication at midnight (is they ferking or is they fighting?); no sad voiced homeboys to stand outside the window at 4 A.M. and holler to someone above you: "Hey Joe! Hey Joe!" and then without pausing for breath to moo out, "Joe, getupandopenthedoorsoIcangetmykeyoutofyourwalletand gohomeandgetmesomesleep,please, Joe" as though rendering a recitative from a sad, sad opera; with Joe either gone away or dead, or sleeping like a rock,* or, like Richard, just too dam ornery to throw down the key so the sad-voiced son-of-a-bitch can leave and the evil, half-asleep neighbors can

---

* Perhaps a sly reference by Ellison to Hughes's well-known poem "The Weary Blues."

pull in their stocking-capped conks and stop their snide and loud-mouthed signifying. No, it's quiet here, and I've been getting more work done than in the city, and Fanny seems to enjoy every minute of the day

I was so busy for a month before we left that I forgot to get in touch with you. For one thing, Fanny's parents were visiting us from Chicago; for another, I was negotiating to go over to Random House (which I did with an additional advance) and trying to go to Yaddo, but which, fortunately, I was able to cancel when this opportunity came along.

Hope the summer is going well with you; give our regards to Aunt Toy, Emerson and Nat and we'll see you when we return.

Yours sincerely,
Ralph

To Fanny Ellison
WINHALL STATION, VERMONT
SEPTEMBER 17, 1947

Dearest Fanny:

Had I tried to write yesterday there would have been quite a few gloomy things to say, for my first day here, like yours there alone, was gloomy. Coming out of Brattleboro on the bus we encountered a terrific thunder-shower and drove through it all the way into Londonderry. Mr. Amsden was there to meet us, but when we arrived at the cottage it was empty and full of the atmosphere of houses that are not regularly lived in, and you were not here with me so that we could bring it alive together. Even after I'd built a fire and the dogs lay drowsing on the hearth it wasn't the same. And I found for a moment that its magic for writing was gone, but reminded myself quickly that I'd only just arrived and that the loneliness was to be expected. Anyway I was dog tired and you were far away.

Coming up was about as usual. The dogs were no problem after I'd checked them and a damned nuisance until I had. I found a seat in an air-cooled car that carried me straight through to Brattleboro. There was a mishap however: I had to leave the big bag in a small luggage room in the coach and when I prepared to leave I discovered that someone in moving it around had pulled out one of the handles. I discovered too that it was not leather, but a tough paper composition covered, if at all, with only a thin shell of leather. Being stored in that hot, dry closet wasn't good for it, nor was the over packing, slight though it might have been. I'm very sorry. To continue, trouble really started when we detrained at Brattleboro. The dogs just couldn't understand that a faulty handle demanded that they cooperate and not pull the hell out of the leash. I must have sweat a gallon in the first half hour while we waited for the bus. After that I tied them to one of its back seats and went outside to catch my breath. We left at three-thirty and all was well until the storm broke. People began piling into the old wreck and from occupying three seats we had to pile into two, and later when a crowd of wild high schoolers piled in, we were jammed into one and a half—the two dogs in my lap. I was very damn glad to see Amsden waiting at Cole's filling station.

Interestingly enough, your wire with the money arrived that morning—which is better service than that we get in the city. Thanks a lot. After the busman was paid I had about two-fifty, though I don't suppose there was any need of your being so prompt. Instead of going to the trouble of getting the lunch out of the bag I ate a ham sandwich on the train; thus for supper I had chicken and deviled eggs. Anyway, there was a chunk of baked ham in the icebox, along with eggs, butter, potatoes, and fresh tomatoes. I still have chicken and eggs, for last night after I had gone in with Mr. Amsden (at which time I got your letter—but neither of the boxes) I had dinner with them and two of their friends—a writer and her painter husband, he who painted the tray of which Mrs. A. is so proud. They brought along fresh corn from their garden and I was given some of that. I'm really quite well supplied. All I've had to buy has been milk, bread and crackers. However, if the box doesn't arrive this evening I'll have to get something for the dogs.

The mountains are for the most part still green, though up behind the Stein house there are patches of autumnal colors. Today the skies are deep blue with gorgeous clouds. Last night, when I had succeeded in getting away from the after-supper conversation (about eleven it had become very cold—forty by the thermometer—and when I went outside the sky was alive with Northern lights. This morning the horses, which are pastured where we took our evening walks, pounded by to awaken us about five and I looked out to see a heavy dew. When Mr. A. arrived with the milk he said it had reached thirty-six degrees. That isn't considered cold, however and frost doesn't form until it reaches thirty-two or below. Nevertheless I have a slight cold today and had to keep the fire going all morning. If only we had known that, you might have come up—if only for a day!

It is afternoon as I write this and I am out on the porch where I used to work. It is warm here, warm enough for me to sit with my skin bared to the sun. Let's hope it burns out the cold for I just couldn't get up enough energy to write earlier today—even though I set out first thing to write to you. I suppose that like last time it'll take me a few days to get adjusted and I don't have you here to help me. But adjust I must and get the writing done so we can be together everyday with no office to hold the day in suspense between nine and five-thirty. I think I'll like that. So don't you be too miserable because this time the separation is for us. I'm very excited about your story. By all means let me see it. You mustn't assume that aesthetic expression is the prime motive for writing; it is really only a means to the more profound end. So don't worry about it if you write out of sadness or hate or love—fear—or fascination, the important thing, if you wish to do it, is to write.

I mustn't go on with this darling, if you're to get it tomorrow, as it's about time for Amsden to go into Londonderry. I miss you enough to feel incomplete and being in bed is a bore—even in the deep night and bed the warmest place in the igloo. Come on down to my house baby, ain't nobody home but me—and the dogs. Right this minute to see you I'd be willing to allow you to bring Nellie Lutcher!

> Remember that
> I love you,
> Ralph

To Fanny Ellison
WINHALL STATION
SOUTH LONDONDERRY, VT.
SEPTEMBER 20, 1947.

Dearest Fanny:

Seems I am fated to receive your letters on gloomy days and to write you when the skies are clear. Don't get the idea, however, that the advantage of the weather is with me, for it is you who determines the climate of my emotions and I must say that neither of your letters goes well on a rainy day—nor, for that matter, with the bright days upon which I must answer. I hope by now you've received my first letter. I wrote you on the 17th, the same evening I heard from you. Unfortunately, it is impossible for me to mail my letters the same evening on which they are written, since they must be posted from the village and I am dependent for getting there upon the Amsdens who only go after 5 p.m.—much too late for you to receive the letter before you leave for work the following morning. I'm sorry, but it's the only way unless I walk up; and if I should, the day would be lost.

Incidentally, I received your letter of the 18th on the 19th. Thanks for the postal note. I didn't need it immediately, having most of the previous money. However, I ate the last of my butter and chicken last night and I'll need it soon. Thus I must ask you to wait a while for an estimate of my expenses. I think though that they will be much less than in the city, and I hope not amounting to much more than the pocket money I have there. There are still tomatoes, squash, string beans and some chard in the garden, making it unnecessary to buy vegetables for a while. Most of the money has gone instead to buy dog food as the package has yet to arrive. You might send me a carton of Pall Malls, I can't get them here and once on hand they should last a long while.

Ida sent up the roll of film I lost and enclosed two packs of Luckies that, since I'd just smoked my last, came in handy. And while on the subject of films—would you send up a bottle each of Super X33 and Replenisher? There was none in Brattleboro. I'll also need some 5x7 contact paper and M.Q. tubes to develop it in; but don't rush any of it as it's only to give me something to pass the long evenings. As for magazines, let me see if I can get them here. I have the *Look* with the Motley dramatization, so don't bother.

You ask about the cold. Yes, the nights are quite cold and the mornings require big fires until the sun breaks through the mist. Yesterday it rained after an uncomfortably humid night and this morning the mist clung to the rocks and grass in strands that shone reluctantly, backlighted by the sun, and there was an especially heavy dew. Already there is a marked falling of the leaves, and though there's been no frost, new splashes of color appear on the hills each morning. Today is bright and sunny, though cool. But yesterday went to hell with the rain. In all the cold I had trouble getting the fire to draw, and when it did and I had at last got to work—I missed the dogs. I called and called without even an answering bark. I went over to the Amsdens, but they hadn't seen them. I walked up toward Cole's filling station as far as the bridge, then back through the pasture where we watched the sunsets with the horses, now pastured there, following me. and begging for sugar apples. But still no dogs. Returning to the cottage I had lunch, then went along the old road that skirts the river where we swam and tried to track them. I saw small dog tracks mixed in with those of a large dog, but soon lost them among the tracks of the deer, squirrels, raccoon, and field mice that had gone along in the night—a regular nocturnal Noah's Ark procession. Finally except for the sharp pointed mark of the deer these faded out upon a harder stretch of the road and I gave it up and returned to the house with uneasy visions of babes in the woods befogged by my anger.

Two hours later they nonchalantly appeared covered with burrs and weed seed, but seemingly quite all right and even proud of something—what, I suppose I'll never know. I didn't beat them, as I was too relieved. I didn't reprimand them, because I was too amused at my own anxiety. Indeed, the son and bitch are gone right this minute, probably lunching off a deer they brought down yesterday. When they return I'll only greet them. I guess they can take care of themselves; certainly they know the way to come home.

So I suppose this prepares me psychologically not to allow their forays to interrupt my day, but the moods you express in your letters form a problem of another order. You must get over your gloom and anxiety, or at least wait until you see if there's a letter waiting you at home before you write. Once, a long time ago, I had the impression that when people were absent from you (and this includes me) they lost the major part of the reality, and that whatever the emotional ties that bound you to them were replaced by doubts and mistrust. It is unfair to say this now, but it is my response to your letter, and as unworthy as it may be I think you should know what it evokes. It's lonely here, and cold, and the beds are hard; but my reason for being here is neither warmth seeking nor comfort—except for my work—and since our mutual solitude is the sacrifice we make in the interest of a far more important thing, let's not either of us make a mockery of that sacrifice with our letters. Taking my own advice, I shall stop this business right here. Just remember that you're very important to me and that I wouldn't intentionally neglect you. If however, you don't for some reason hear from me as often as you think you should just—(since I see by the *Times* that a carrier was recently caught dumping mail down a sewer)—just call the Amsdens and have them call me over. Who knows, with the country going as it is, maybe the Whodunit boys are keeping an eye on everybody's mail.

Sorry that the boys chose to look me up just when I'm away. You might, I think, have been afraid of Alonzo rather than of Murray—though I guess both are harmless enough. Best keep everyone on the other side of the door, though, until you know for certain what they want. Tell Murray he can send his stuff up here should he wish me to see it.

Too bad about Dilly, give her my regards and hopes for her quick recovery. Anything from Frank or *Horizon*? Are you eating and getting rid of it regularly; from your letters I bet not. Me, I've still an annoying head condition, but am otherwise O.K. No sunbathing today though, too cool despite the clear sky . . . Red and Bobbins have come in now and insist that I tell you to check on their dog food as they're tired of *Pard*. I forgot to tell you that the big box came on the 18th, everything in it. What should I do about beds for these mutts, paper's no good and I'm getting tired of waking up in the middle of the night to get Red off the unoccupied bed. He's such a willful bastard; last night when I went to the post office he kept barking to go along which he couldn't in Amsden's car—and when I returned he had torn a hole through the screen door and was outside. Naturally, I beat his nose until his rear-end cried uncle.

Cheer up darling, I've written and written again, and I'll write because I love you. With that said, I'll now try to get back to work. How about some typewriter paper and envelopes?

As ever,
Ralph

To Fanny Ellison
WINHALL STATION
SOUTH LONDONDERRY
VERMONT
SEPTEMBER 21, 1947

Dear Fanny:

Just a note to tell you how pleasant it was to have you call today. I was taking medicine and had gone off to sleep over a magazine so that I failed to hear Mr. Amsden when he drove up. I was still a little dazed when I talked with you, waiting (as tense as any southern Negro who had just received a telegram) for you to tell me that some problem, some dam calamity had occurred. True, both of the Amsdens were seated right there and inhibited me somewhat, but I really thought something had happened.

Today I intended to devote to breaking this head cold, and I did take the medicine, but after I talked with you I didn't want to be here alone, so I went with him down near Brattleboro to pick up an engine he had bought at an auction. It was rather cool coming back and I was glad to accept their invitation to dinner. They had meat and all I have here are a few scraps of ham that I intended to make into an omelet. Well, tomorrow afternoon I'll go with them to a nearby town and there I'll pick up some kind of meat, maybe another chicken. Prices here are terrible as they are everywhere.

After we returned with the engine this afternoon, we picked up the oil stove and brought it over. It's quite handsome. I hope it's equally efficient, so that I can get started a bit earlier in the morning. I don't mind fussing with the fireplace, but on a cold morning it takes too much time. Anyway, I don't get going as quickly as when you were here to look after me—maybe because I still make four pieces of toast and eat them! The weather does require that one take extra nourishment, especially cold days like today, so I don't guess that I quite rate as a glutton.

But given a chance I could, right now, at this moment (and even with the cold) be a glutton about you, or for you, as it may be. But then, I hope you feel somewhat the same about me. It would be awful if you didn't. Maybe if I'm serene just before I drop off to sleep, I'll dream of you. "Dream of you"—that's a title of an old number by Jimmie Lunceford. So often up here I find my thoughts running to the melodies of old, sentimental songs. It isn't at all unpleasant, just means some more of my past has been bound up with you. Some of the songs are part of the loneliness and agony of adolescence which were all the more poignant because they had no definite object: now I have you, even though you're there and I'm here . . .

It's Monday morning now, and I went to sleep with the letter on the machine. During the night it was very warm and when I awakened it was raining. Looking out across the porch to the hill above the Stein house it is as though broad streams of orange and brown paint were running slowly down the hill. So far we've had one good day followed by one wet one, but now it seems we'll have two wet ones in succession. It doesn't really matter though, now that I'm sure that you're all right. So be sweet darling, I've got to get started to work.

> Love & xxxxxx
> Ralph

To Fanny Ellison
WINHALL STATION
SOUTH LONDONDERRY VT.
SEPTEMBER 24, 1947.

Dearest Fanny:

I received your most delightful letter on Monday afternoon and read it the first time while driving with the Amsdens to Springfield Vt. It made the whole day seem brighter and I read it the last thing before dropping off to sleep. I was sorry that I hadn't waited until I received it before writing the letter that you should have received by now—i.e. the first one . . . since the second was in response to your phone call. I needed that letter very much and now I suppose I need another just as revivifying.

For the cold here has become a problem in the mornings; I waste too much time getting the house warm and I discovered that the oil stove gives off fumes that make me ill so that I can't use it and must wait until the fireplace gets into action. None of which is any good for that morning mood out of which I was able to work so effectively in August. And thus, my work isn't going as well as I had hoped. Yesterday morning was particularly annoying, and then what should happen but I look up and here comes Bobbins limping to the house full of porcupine quills. Which might, on first thought, seem amusing, but far from it. As you'll note from the quills I've enclosed (don't stick yourself) one end has fine barbs, and these enter the flesh and the more the animal moves the deeper they are driven home. Thus when I rushed Bobbins over to Mr Amsden we were able to remove many of them with a pair of pliers, bringing spurts of blood from the barbs with each extraction and terrible pain, but we discovered that several quills had worked completely beneath the skin where we couldn't reach them. We then called a vet who told us that he could operate, but that it would mean cutting the dog's skin to shreds and that it was his practice to allow the quills to remain until they festered after which the body would push them out. Sometimes, he said, they work under one part of the skin and out through another. We took his advice, knowing nothing better to do; but poor Bobbins is in great pain this afternoon and cannot use the leg and shoulder where the quills are embedded.

I had to muzzle her and actually kneel upon her the pain was so great when we removed the barbs and there she lay looking so reproachfully out of her eyes. I felt like hell. I carried her home and placed her on the bed to sleep, but during the night she got down, which must have hurt something awful. If I had had a car here I would have packed and come home last night. I felt bad about Bobbins, then sorry for myself; and when I went down to the garden and found many of the string beans and tomatoes frostbitten and going to waste I actually felt like crying

Feel better this afternoon, though very tired. Mr. Amsden was so damned decent last night that when I heard them sawing wood with the engine this morning, I went over and gave them a hand. A nice experience, but it takes a lot from my softest muscles. Bobbins seems to be resting, though the pain is still very great.

How interesting that you should have a talk with Lipchitz; I had just that day been looking at a picture story on Washington Square that appears in the current *Harper's Bazaar,* and there among them was one of Lipchitz!

Your letter makes your visit very much alive. If only you could have gotten his picture.

Very good about your 35mm shots. I hope the girl is wrong about the enlargements, but had I placed them I would have requested a smaller size. Please don't bother to send the developers because I found some in Springfield. I haven't done any developing however, though I've taken a few pictures. Some were made in the little woodworking shop in the village, to which I plan to return and shoot in flash. I'm a bit tired of shooting the clouds and the morning mist—which isn't mist anymore, nor dew, for the frost is now quite heavy. You can send along some number two paper if you wish; there was only one pack in Springfield. I'd like some whiskey, darling, but you can't send it through the mail so forget about it. Maybe if you sent along some tomato recipes I would not get tired of them too soon. I've had stewed tomatoes almost every night; and since meat is so expensive I haven't bought any. This morning I had some of the little pork sausages and found them very good—with hotcakes. Tonight I'll try to get some macaroni, and you might suggest other meat substitutes. I've still a few string beans left and tonight I'll see what's at the grocery. If however, you care to can anything please do, since it won't go to waste. And send the cod liver oil for the dogs, I don't think they will mind it and it might make their coats look better.

Seems Ida has descended upon you, poor darling. I'll write her soon and maybe that'll take her off you. I don't see many advs. for Chester's book, how is it going? The one I did see had Dick and Horace plugging it, Horace declaring it to be a great work of art—as though he would recognize one if it blew up in his face! Voltaire and *Candide* indeed. Such romanticism at Ida's age. I hope she doesn't think I'm better than Voltaire also ... Your experimenting with Faulkner is apt to prove very rewarding if you don't give in to the emotion it evokes too soon. The thing to do is to reread it immediately after it takes hold of you. Remember that Faulkner had to absorb all of that emotion, had to dominate it, before he could control it in the story. Read it very slowly and remember that with Faulkner it is not mere repetition of words or phases that does the work, but incantatory sentence line. Notice too that he gets inside the character and sticks very closely to <u>his</u> impressions, to <u>his</u>, the character's, thoughts and emotions; and most of all notice the steady drone which is the rhythm of the story. I only wish I had it here so that I could be more specific. The repetitions are there, but not so much in terms of single words and in terms of ideas, and all enclosed in the long curving sentences. Another thing to remember is that the flood, the river, the "Old Man," against whom the Convict fights is not so much a naturalistic river as a flood and river within his mind. Everything, no matter how much in detail it is described, is inward. The flooding river becomes a metaphor for the whole of life and the world against which the convict struggles in order to return to the womb-like peace of the penitentiary. If you'll send up one of the books in which the story appears (I'd like the portable if you aren't using it), I'll try to analyze it on paper. And hurry up with your own story, I'm anxious to see it.

You ask about your dogs, and I've told you about only one of them. But Red is here too, sleeping before the fireplace. I haven't allowed him to get too far from the house today. He's a very ingratiating little son of a bitch and really almost talks sometimes. The other evening the winds were so strong that I went out and closed the garage doors then returned to my reading. I noticed Bobbins near the fire and 'felt' him in the room. Well in about thirty minutes I heard someone knocking on the kitchen door like a man and went with my flashlight to see who it was. But when I got there I had a strange feeling for the garage doors were still closed and the knocking definitely from the kitchen door. And it was then that Red began bawling me out for leaving him in the dark. He almost talked. Up here in the cold mornings I've seen that grin you spoke about, he seems filled with joy, and when I return after going into town in the later afternoon I swear that the little dog expresses pure love when he greets me. Somehow, he failed to get into the battle with the porcupine and I'm worried because he's still that lesson to learn. I only hope I get to him before the quills work beneath the skin.

I go on and on, but this is the only way of being with you and it's the only thing I've written today. I don't know, but with the cold and my missing you like I do, if things aren't going better by the end of next week, or at least by the first week in October, I'm coming home. I see no point in staying here if it doesn't increase my output. However, I've never been completely well since I've returned because this head cold is still active and it seems everywhere I sleep there's a draft on my head. I'm sure we couldn't and wouldn't want to spend the winter here; the heating problem is too great. Those artists who you ask about will pull out soon and return to their warm little apt in Brooklyn! (While I think of it, Paul's address is #68 Pemberton Square.)

Thanks for writing old Cipriano for me. I'll answer him from here; wouldn't think of taking his money though. And Fanny, if you intend sending the *Gide Journals,* don't. I'm not in a mood for Gide up here, but I would like to get into the Graphic Graflex Photography, and besides it is cheaper. But I warn you, should I come home next week it will <u>not</u> be because I'm interested in that book!

I must go now, Lady Good-Goodness. Write when you can, but please don't be too lonely, and please don't cry. Remember I'll be back in not too long a time and then we'll do for each other completely those things that dissolve all loneliness.

Ralph

To Fanny Ellison
WINHALL STATION
SOUTH LONDONDERRY, VT.
SEPTEMBER 29, 1947.

Dearest Fanny:

I'm writing this note just a little before time to go down to the village, so there isn't much time to say very much—though I don't suppose it matters too much, since I'll see you in a few days. It has been so cold here for the past three or four mornings that I'm quite sure now that remaining would be without meaning. For several nights the temperature has fallen to seventeen above, and though I haven't frozen it's still too cold for conditions here in the cottage. Yesterday the water was frozen and I had to wait a couple of hours after I'd had my breakfast before I could have my very much needed coffee; last night coming from dinner at the artist's house I damned near froze myself—even though yesterday and today were comparatively warm. I'm told that the cold has anticipated itself about a month and that this is November weather. November, Juvemver—I'm getting out when you come, so don't bother shipping anything else up.

And don't worry about Bobbins' shoulder, I take out a few quills every morning (thirteen or fourteen, thus far) and she's using her foot again, though somewhat gingerly. Red, is red, is Red; and what's more he's lifting his leg, but with gusto! Nothing is safe; I fear for my legs and when he's in that mood I keep moving so that he can't get himself set. Regardless of the trouble—and they are not the source of it, remember—they've been my companions and are, thus worth it.

I couldn't have that menu you suggested, there was no meat to be had, but I did have a good corned beef and potato dinner at the artist's. To-night I'm supposed to get a chicken from the Amsdens—if he remembered to kill it. The potatoes are all boiled for mashing, the string beans have been washed, and if I can get Bisquick I'll treat myself to biscuits. I hope the hen is ready, for I took a cold tablet last night and today I've felt a bit blah. If only the agony of the trip back was over and I was in your arms! I no longer have any wish to remain here and I can hardly believe it. Yet it has become a struggle, a drudgery to keep comfortable, and though it produces heat, it's words (and not simply curse words) that I'm interested in, returned here for. Don't, however, indicate any of this to Beatrice or Francis—or Ida. And don't tell her when I'm returning; I'll need rest once I'm home.

The cigarettes came and I told you that the recklessly sent seven came through, thanks again . . . Returning to Faulkner, look and see if the effect of flood and wetness aren't produced by describing the <u>results</u> of the flood; the raging river, the fleeing people, the debris sweeping and towering above the convict, the animals in panic and forgetting their instinctive feuds as they seek for safety from the river, the houses swept off their foundations, the boat moving over city streets, houses, past the tops of groves of trees; and within all this—and against its threatening destruction—the desperate strength of the convict? Against these disarrangements of nature and town, words like 'flood,' 'rain,' 'wet,' etc. are inadequate and academic. When a levee gives way and the Mississippi runs wild, who can be impressed by a few drops of rain?

Time to go, honey. I don't hear the engine sputtering and whining with the sawing of wood so I guess they're getting ready to leave . . . Cancel the dog food, please. They won't need it here. I can't wait for Friday to tell you of my love.

Ralph

To Fanny Ellison
WINHALL STATION
SOUTH LONDONDERRY VT.
OCTOBER 10, 1947

Dearest Fanny:

Your letter and the stationary arrived on the 9th, but either I misunderstood you to say that galleys would arrive from '47, or they are still in the mail. I spoke to the postmaster here about the missing package and she said you would have to trace it from that end. N.Y. mail has been very irregular, she says.

The news about '47* is very good; and if Henry is right about 10 cents per word, and if they use the same section appearing in Horizon, then the 5600 words should bring us close to $560.00. I hope he's right, and he should be, since that's his business. If their rate is ten cents, then I want the large sum and not the smaller one.

I talked with Frank's secretary before I called you and she tells me that several people said that mine was the most compelling piece in the American issue of *Horizon*. No doubt that's the kind of flattery they've cooked up in the office to encourage me to get the stuff out. Anyway it was kind for her to say so. Let me hear any comments, and you might look around in the papers to see if the press has had anything to say. I think they should, since implicitly, that issue constitutes an Englishman's criticism (or rather his evaluations) of our contemporary writing. I've loaned the issue to Mabel Amsden and am on pins to get her reaction. I'm 'fraid the stuff is pretty raw for her, but I couldn't very well have failed to let her see it. What do you think Bea really thought? I hope for God's sake that she doesn't think that I'm simply dishing up autobiography, or that she's reading mere realism!

Yesterday afternoon I took the dogs and camera and walked up to Susie Cole's and picked up some things, then back past the Vail's place and down the old road where Francis had trouble with the car. I flushed two grouse, and had only the shells I'd got at Coles but no gun. Next time I'll have a very alert cannon. On the way we ran into two dogs, and I must say that little Red is all dog; he kept advancing into them, and though he didn't fight he was quite ready for any attack. And coming back we met a great hound toward whom he ran barking only to make friends with the hound and for a few minutes, until I called him away, they had a fine time. I'm still pulling quills out of Bobbins. Otherwise she's fine.

Yes, I still have this damn cold. I've tried whiskey and cold tablets, but it simply hangs on. For one thing the frost has returned and it is quite cold in the night and early morning. If it gets worse I'll go over to the big house. That makes a problem, however, since there's no ice left over there. Though don't say anything to Bea about it, since she'll make it sound as

---

* In October 1947, '47: *The Magazine of the Year* reprinted the first chapter of *Invisible Man*, which had also recently been published in London in Cyril Connolly's *Horizon*.

though the house has become a desert. Nor must you mention it to Ida, who would put yeast into it for her own ambiguous motives.

I'm getting very tired of being away from you so don't expect me to remain here too much longer. I'll let you know before I start, but you mustn't be surprised if it's very sudden. There were too many people around when you were here, and with you here for such a short visit I was afraid to let myself go. Loneliness gets too much under the skin. Speaking of skin, I hope you're eating enough to keep yours filled out. You'd better. I want all of you that it is possible to have to love. Besides, I'll want to keep warm this winter. So eat up, you pretty lil thing, and write me,

> I love you furstest and
> mostest
> Ralph

To Fanny Ellison
<u>find check enclosed:</u>
Winhall Station
South Londonderry, Vt.
october 13, 1947

Dearest Fanny:

You certainly have fallen into the social life. I got your letter of the 10th; how did Ida's note get enclosed? Were you two on a drinking bout? Her note was keyed so high that at first reading I couldn't get what was going on; and yours had missing places. For whom are you to do letters? Bea or Mrs. <u>Gerda</u> (note the <u>d</u>)? Anyway, it sounds exciting.

Pass word on to Ed Stein that all I've gotten thus far is a squirrel and a porcupine (in revenge for Bobbins). However I'm taking his advice about the license—if you'll send along some money. I have only three bucks and I must clear up my milk and butter bill; it's been a month now. And, by the way, please look in my gabardine trousers for my ring, I can't locate it here. Hope you haven't sent them to the cleaners.

I've written Henry and '47, anything happening on them?

The weather's still fine, once the frost goes, and on Friday afternoon I walked up to the lake and took pictures. It was beautiful with wonderful color. Too bad traveling takes so long, it would have been wonderful to've had you here for the weekend.

The cold is not gone, but the long walks I've been taking with the gun have dissipated it somewhat. I still have bad dreams though, and it's a relief to get up in the morning—even to face the cold. By the way, I'm still living in the cottage; there is much less danger of the dogs doing damage up here. If the weather changes for the worse; then I'll have to sleep down at the big house and get my meals up here. I've damn near burned up all that wood we stacked in the garage. "I have known it, known it all, the mid-noon sunshine, the morning fogs, I've measured out my days in fireplace logs"—to paraphrase T.S. Eliot. To paraphrase myself, I love you, write me; I'm lonely; and envious of your old lovers, who for whatever pretext, have simply to walk up the street to see you.

Ralph

To Mrs. Stein
WINHALL STATION
SOUTH LONDONDERRY, VT.
OCTOBER 15, 1947

Dear Mrs. Stein:

Today I realized suddenly that I had been here a month and hadn't got around to writing you a letter. I'm quite ashamed, and I hope that your days in the hospital are flying by just as fast as are mine here at Two Rivers—and with none of the regret. Indeed they must be, for I hear that you're almost recovered.

The news that you were hospitalized came both as a shock and a disappointment: in the short time we've known you I had come to think of [you] exclusively in terms of health, boundless energy and well being; and we had looked forward to seeing the two of you and as many of the children as might have turned up. For as nice as the farm is, it is you, all of you, who give it its spirit of warmth and graciousness. Of that, being here alone has made me sharply aware.

Thanks very much for making your house available to me when the unseasonal cold descended; though, ironically enough, the weather has been so balmy since the very day that Bea and Francis and Fanny arrived that I haven't had to take advantage of it. It was as though they brought Indian Summer in their Lincoln luggage rack. However, the red room awaits me, and should the weather show the least tendency to return to seventeen above I shall hurry down to it.

I'm told that the terrific frost destroyed the really beautiful color to which you're accustomed here in the valley, yet I found it quite lovely even without the brilliant reds I noticed between Manchester and Bennington. Now the leaves are rapidly falling (the two Cottonwoods on your lawn are almost bare) and in the mornings after the frost has melted, the field outside the cottage is filled with the nervous running and penguin-posturing of Robins that thrust their red breasts forward and cock their heads at the least sound. There are also many songbirds I can't name, so I suppose this must be an important station on the route of their migratory flight.

And speaking of birds, tell Mr. Stein that the partridges hereabouts are, within the thick and ever present brush, the slickest things I've ever hunted—not excluding pheasants. Out of a dozen tries I bagged only one to show for my marksmanship. And while I can see that with a good dog they would make very exciting hunting indeed, for my self-esteem I think I prefer quail; there are more of them in a covey, and occasionally even the poorest shot wings his reward. When I pull the trigger they rocket into the bushes singing 'I'll Be Around,' and they mean it!

Evidently being here at your place is lucky for me. Since I've returned part of my novel (a rather raw and violent part) has been published in the *Art in America* issue of the English magazine *Horizon,* and has also been selected for publication in the January issue of '47. And as though this isn't enough of a good thing, word comes that it is being called the most interesting piece in the issue and has my publisher very pleased. I only hope that when the work is finished you won't regret having given it a push before the eyes of the astonished world.

My days here are slipping by as fast as the falling leaves and I shall have to return to the city very soon—perhaps this weekend, perhaps next week. So thanks again for a very splendid and profitable retreat, and my sincerest wishes for a speedy recovery.

Sincerely,
Ralph Ellison

To Richard Wright
749 St. Nicholas Ave.,
New York City 31, N.Y.
FEBRUARY 1, 1948

Dear Dick:

When your letter arrived I was in Vermont where I had retired to work on my interminable book. I remained in Vermont until the extreme dryness of the season brought threats of forest fires and sent me back to Harlem about the middle of November. I found your letter quite engrossing, but since you were on your way to the south of France and I was so busy, I thought I'd wait until you had time to return to Paris before I answered. Now that I've received your second letter I'm setting to. Actually I'm copying a letter which I had already begun, so I'll leave comment upon your second letter until the end.

For one living in these times I have very little news. It goes about like this: Fanny and I are still living in this tiny apartment, which in order to make a bit more livable we have painted ourselves. I see Wertham from time to time (who was very perturbed that he had not heard from you until he got your letter) and I am working on a piece describing the social conditions of Harlem that make the clinic a necessity. I've worked out a scheme to do it with photographs that should make for something new in photo-journalism—if Gordon Parks is able to capture those aspects of Harlem reality which are so clear to me. *'48* is publishing the piece and if successful we should get a few things said.* The clinic, incidentally, is expanding and beginning to have influence with the courts. In doing this piece I've been going through case histories, and though I've encountered nothing that I haven't conceived, just seeing the stuff in print is terrific.

Thanks for the encouraging words concerning the excerpt from my novel. I had hoped to send you a copy of *Horizon,* but you seem to have seen it before I did. Enclosed, however, you'll find the same piece as published by *'48;* it's somewhat censored, but essentially the same. They paid me ten cents a word, which ain't bad; indeed, it was the most I've ever received, and they're asking for more, and have informed me that it was their most successful piece. All in all, the reader reaction to both publications of the piece was pleasing and I would be extremely gratified if only the dam thing was finally out of my hands! It is a far more complicated work than the excerpt might lead one to expect, and I'm still going through the old agony of creation. Roi Ottley is going around dismissing me as simply "a disciple of Dick Wright's"—which doesn't bother me, feeling as I do about your work; it only reveals (as I pointed out to my informants) how insensitive Ottley happens to be. I'm getting some of the same reactions produced by *Native Son.* People look at me a bit differently now, and an

---

* Ellison refers to "Harlem Is Nowhere," an essay intended to be accompanied by photographs by Gordon Parks. In June, *'48: The Magazine of the Year* ceased publication, and the piece was not published until it appeared in Ellison's essay collection *Shadow and Act* (New York: Random House, 1964), without the Parks photographs. Parks's photographs and Ellison's drafts were exhibited together in a May 2016 show at the Art Institute of Chicago.

undertone of reservation comes into their voices. God, but how they fear one who can name a situation, who attempts to capture significance! Bill Attaway surprised me by his enthusiastic reaction, though he too, like so many laymen, assumes that I'm writing almost straight autobiography. And again I recalled Sterling Brown's[*] reaction to *N.S.* when Attaway said that if the rest of my book was anything like the excerpt, the rest of the Negro writers would have to go out and find jobs. You would think that by now they would have learned that no one but themselves can write their stories, and that writing is not a game of competition—unless with the great writers who came before us—and certainly I'm not interested in writing <u>better</u> than anyone, only in writing as well as I can with my own talent and my own intelligence. But how different was your reaction from Langston's. He read the piece, but has studiedly refused to discuss it with me—which would be O.K. with me, if he hadn't, while knowing how busy I am, called up to ask me to edit a pot-boiler he's getting together from his Chicago *Defender* columns(!) offering, of course, to pay me. What does one do with people like that? Well, that's enough of my egomania. It might interest you to hear that I've been coaching a Bennington girl who is doing her thesis on certain aspects of your work. I don't think she has anything very original to say at this point, but I'll swear that she's one young white gal who has made an effort to understand you. When she's done I'll try to get a copy to send to you.

I'm afraid my answer to your question concerning Chester's book[†] must be negative: a friend of ours who works at Knopf's tells us that although they early put money behind the book it laid an egg. As for reviews, I have only that from the NM which is enclosed. I understand the DW reviewed it much later and conceded that it was worthwhile knowing that some Negroes felt toward whites as did Chester's chief character. Unfortunately I missed the piece.

Personally I was disappointed with the book, having been led by the first[‡] to expect it to be quite good. Instead, I found it dishonest in its pseudo-intellectuality, and as false as Cayton's 'fear-hate-fear complex' in its psychology. Nor must you feel that I would have had him exclude any of his basic material, especially the political sections.

---

[*] Poet Sterling Brown, whose vernacular poetry is an inimitable part of the African American canon, was a longtime professor of American and African literature and folklore at Howard.

[†] Chester B. Himes, *The Lonely Crusade* (New York: Knopf, 1947).

[‡] Chester B. Himes, *If He Hollers Let Him Go* (Garden City, NY: Doubleday, 1945).

Rather, I should have liked to have had him write <u>more</u> politically, but with integrity. For I believe that when one writes of politics one is called upon to do more than cull a few terms from <u>materialism and empro-criticism</u> and scatter them dialogue-wise between episodes of a cops and robbers plot—no matter how gripping, or amusing, or hilarious some of those episodes might be. After all, if a writer is serious about his politics and its relationship to man, then he should at least attempt to master the ideas (artistic, technical, philosophical, metaphysical, etc.) which that political position embodies explicitly. And that is only the beginning, for the work of the novelist only begins here, his task is that of giving shape to the <u>implicit</u> which radiates about any philosophical position (and here I include political statements and tactics based upon that philosophy) like the invisible rays projected by a radioactive substance. Chester seems to have no conception of these, only a vague resentment against the Communists.

The other thing is that Chester jumped into a "genre" handled by such men as Malraux, Silone and Koestler—not to mention yourself, so very much closer to home—and thus he was called upon to write as comprehensively as they. If he were not such a mixed up guy he could have taken your *Atlantic* pieces along with *Black Boy* and learned enough to have written a compellingly serious political novel. And yet I believe he thought he was following your lead. For I believe that just as he has stated of Bigger that it was easy to prove Negro discrimination by reducing a Negro to less than human—a statement of rejection—just so did he analyze your recent work (though he <u>did not</u> state this to me)* as simple opportunism—missing completely the self-struggle with which you earned the right to publish those pieces. Well, if he wrote out of opportunism, he was disappointed. He told someone I know that he thought he had a best seller. I'm afraid that he misjudged the nature of the red scare and a lot of other related things. I shouldn't, out of fairness to Chester, allow this to end without saying that the character referred to as "Ellsworth" who argued with Lee concerning the maternal character of certain class divisions of the Negro family, actually refers to me and a conversation I had with Chester last year. It amused me to see him bring it into his book as he did, but, strangely enough, we haven't seen the Himes since. They called up about a party they were planning and then became silent, until they dropped us a Xmas card. They're still living in N.Y. but he hasn't even been by to pick up his rubbers in this worst of all winters since the 19th century. Could he

---

*   or to anyone else, that I know of. [*Ellison's own note. —Ed.*]

fear that I might put him in my book? If so, he should forget it; you put him in a book seven years ago.

Perhaps Chester accomplished the task of showing the communists what a Negro writer might do if he really started striking back at them; if so, more power to him. Recently they have been after me to reprint one of my old short stories in an anthology. I refused reminding them that in 1942 it was necessary, at the expense of much wrenching of emotions and intellectual convictions, to change the direction of my fictional efforts, and that I could see no reason to swing back over passed ground at this late date. Their answer was through a former friend, Charles Humboldt, who was 'surprised' at my 'hostility,' and who didn't think my story in *Horizon*, which he liked, showed such a change in direction; and why couldn't we get together. It's the same old pattern. To hell with associating closely with any kind of politicians. Recently *Partisan Review* has been after something from me (now that I have Connolly's good-house keeping Seal of Acceptability) and I've kept my distance. Yes, *N.M.* and *Mainstream* have folded, but they're starting something else I hear—with the same old art-hating goons in charge.

I suppose you've heard that Horace has married again. He is also reported to be suffering from diabetes. Drake is back, but intends to return to England. And Molly Moon has adopted an infant!

I have become so disgusted with politics that I hardly read the newspapers. Wallace and the third party movement hold the political spotlight, however. I don't know how Negroes regard him, although a few so-called leaders have endorsed him. Liberals like Max Lerner and the PM crowd are frightened pissless . . . The communists have either lost PV (which Yergan still controls) or their recent attack against it under Doxey Wilkerson's signature was a diversionary tactic. Nevertheless, the attack was bitter enough to have been sincere. And yet, they stand a good choice to survive and become a force again if the present trend of events continues long enough. Reality is becoming stern enough to make people reject anti-communist propaganda. We don't even have enough fuel oil to supply this country and prices are sky high.

Unfortunately *Présence Africaine* has not arrived. I'll give you my reactions when it does. As for the stuff for UNESCO, Fanny is collecting it, but it will take some time, since much of it must be culled from newspaper and magazine files. We'll send it along as soon as we have it . . . Look, why don't you stay the hell out of planes during bad weather? That was the god damnest trip I ever heard about—worse even than the time I was trying to get back to Rouen along the LeHavre road and the American soldiers kept trying to run me down in the dark. France certainly is exciting enough.

No, I've seen nothing of Peter Abraham's book.

I guess this is the end of this. I can't say "I wish you were here," since I know of nothing in particular that would make that worthwhile—except perhaps my own selfish interest in chewing the fat with you. Give our best to Ellen and Julia, and I'll try to find a decent picture of your sailing to send along next time. Be sure that I get *Présence Africaine.*

All the best,
Ralph

(over)*

To Frank Taylor
739 St. Nicholas Ave
New York City, 31. N.Y.
[july 1948]†

Dear Frank:

After reading and re-reading the script several times I can see your concern. Incidentally, in order to get this off I am doing the typing myself, so don't let my spelling get you down.

As for my general reaction, and before I make specific comment upon details, let me say that I feel the piece to be entirely too sentimental, and, as a drama of psychological race conflict, too much on the surface. The picture of the "white" milieu of the Carters (and I am aware that imagery and detail has been left for the shooting script, I refer to the writer's <u>conception</u>) are so shallow and puerile that it seems ironic that they endure such great psychological tensions for such feeble rewards. Being what I am however, I am naturally sensitive to such ironies. Nevertheless the adaptor seems oblivious to the great ironic possibility lying in the circum-

---

* This "over," apparently typed by Ralph in the original letter to Wright, suggests a postscript to follow, but if so, it has gone missing.

† The letter's probable date. Ellison's comments to Taylor at the end of this letter about *The Magazine of the Year*'s cessation of publication due to bankruptcy and his collaborating photographer being paid while he cannot even get the magazine's lawyer to return his article have the ring of a recent gripe. These proceedings were going on in May and June 1948; hence, the estimate of July 1948.

stance of Will and Melba's discovery of the essential oneness of values held by Negro and whites of this social grouping and level. This, I realize, is not his story, but whether he wishes to ignore it or not, it is part of his theme; and it is one which if developed even obliquely would make for a certain richness of conception.

The clue to what I feel is wrong with the piece lies in the drawing of Will Carter. The play takes a position against the narrowness of race seg-regation, making its point about the loss of human life stemming from the Navy's refusal to commission a man of Carter's skill; yet it fails to establish that Carter himself, as one who has lived on both sides of the color line and who is in a key position for seeing "people as people" has increased his humanity as a result. He has a Purpose (to gain the benefits of being 'white'), a Passion (to conceal his racial identity), which certainly are two important phases of tragic rhythm, or the 'rhythm of tragedy' if you will; but he lacks the third phase, Perception.* In its place we have a minister announcing a change in traditional Navy policy—a change which takes place in society, but not within his consciousness, and definitely not as a result of the dramatic conflict that has gone before.

I have no way of knowing whether the author is aware of his pun in naming Carter "Will," but <u>will</u> is exactly that ingredient of the heroic per-sonality that he <u>does not</u> possess. Here again is a Negro leading character who does not lead and who is not heroic because he is not capable of acting, but is always acted upon. (I am struck, Frank, by the consistency with which this turns up in the writings of whites about Negroes. It ap-pears that deep down, beneath the surface of liberalism, only whites are considered capable of true acts of will.) To demonstrate briefly: Carter doesn't decide to pass himself, his wife does it for him; he doesn't offer his services to the Navy, thereby risking his all for his love of country—he is asked; and when he is driven into the corner by the revelation of his true identity he does not "accept his fate" or fight back, or actively try to protect his children, but turns instead to drink. Take a look and you'll see what I mean. I suspect you have already.

This leads us directly into both the structure of the piece and to ques-tions as to its factual accuracy. I have not had time to read White's book, but I have read *Ebony*'s story of the Johnson family upon which the book is based, noting the following: Johnson (Will Carter) <u>did not</u> stumble into

---

* Ellison's letter to his agent, Frank Taylor, is notable for his use of Kenneth Burke's triad of "purpose, passion, and perception" in relation to the script he comments on.

passing, but according to *Ebony* his father before him "passed as white in Chicago to hold (a) job as real estate agent" (which means he was agent of restrictive covenants. You fill in the psychological implications of guilt, hate, etc. which would ultimately be involved). Johnson <u>did not</u> gain his practice in Gorman through the "Going-our-Way, Bing-Crosby, Barry-Fitzgerald" incident between Carter and Brackett, but "bought a going practice for $1,000" from a Gorham physician. I do not think, however, that the incident is invalid dramatically—providing the camera work is not as corny as the script.

These differences between the script and the facts are not in themselves important, but they do point up a major question of motivation <u>that is</u> important to the structure of the piece, to its psychological soundness, and to its documentary accuracy. I refer to the incident wherein Carter and Melba decide to pass.

I have no way of knowing whether White's book states that Johnson was turned down as an intern in a Negro hospital or not, nor whether Johnson gave White this information, nor whether Johnson was actually turned down; but I do know that the reason given is psychologically and historically false. For one reason it assumes that the mulatto is a <u>Northern</u> phenomena, rare to the South. Actually the mulatto is as Southern as the blue-black African type Negro. And not only are mulattoes plentiful, but during the Twenties and up to the Depression they were in a favored position—for many reasons unnecessary to consider here. But in direct relation to the play, because many Negroes tended to accept the magic properties which Southern whites believe to go with a white skin, the folk reveal this belief in such expressions as "white is right" in such verses as:

> *"If you white, you alright*
> *If you brown, you can hang around*
> *If you black, stand!"*

Both are statements of value and thus of acceptance though I am aware that they were sometimes to express irony and other attitudes. And not only were there, as now, mulattoes among Southern Negro professionals, they capitalized upon their whiteness, were proud of it. As for Atlanta, during the Twenties not only was it full of mulattoes, but John Hope, the president of Atlanta University [and] one of the most influential Negroes in the South, was definitely a man of white complexion. Johnson-Carter seem too innocent concerning the facts of race to have grown up in Chicago and, to quote *Ebony* again, to have worked as a "porter and dining car waiter to help pay his way through Rush Medical College."

This, I believe, is a crucial wrenching of facts. For in order to establish Carter's rejection by dark Negroes the author presents Carter and his wife's family as the only light skinned Negroes in their milieu, which is highly unlikely, and he ignores the fact that there are Negroes white enough to pass who do not elect to do so. The results of the failure to meet this artistic challenge is that Will Carter comes across not as a man who has a choice of action, but as a straw man blown along by the winds of his environment. Hell, the jerk didn't have to pass, he might have become— Walter White!

An attendant false assumption here is that mulattoes are rare in the profession of Negro medicine. Off hand I can name a half dozen among the physicians of my own hometown; and the most successful (a millionaire) is much lighter than the pictures of Johnson that appeared in *Ebony,* and he made his money within the Negro community and among Negroes. This is an important point, both as sociological accuracy and to dramatic structure. For, I believe, it indicates that Carter started on his career of passing not because he was rejected by darker Negroes, but because of an act of will. He <u>willed</u> (or at least Johnson willed) to attain the advantages lying on the other side of the color line. It seems to me therefore that it is in this act of will—however it is formulated and presented dramatically— that lies Carter's character which will win the audience to him and prepare it to accept him as he is at the height of his fortune, and as the malignant scapegoat of their sins when his fortunes unravel.

You see, rather than attempt to sell Carter as a man who suffers through no fault of his own, a man who is rejected by both Negroes and whites (Palmer makes dark Negroes the evil doers, because had they accepted Carter, he would have 'stayed in his place') I would appeal to the audience's American belief in the "go-getter," the man who "makes his own opportunities." I would manipulate its admiration for the skilled technician, the man with the "know-how" (hit 'em in their cliches, Frank, they love it); I would play upon the covert father-healer-wise consultant symbolism and magic with which we tend to endow our physicians. In other words I would present Carter in the role of the physician-as-hero, a sort of minor Macbeth whose flaw lies in his concealed racial identity. He is a man who has committed a crime but who sought to do good (actually a symbolic infanticide, since he kills the "white" identity of his children). And I say <u>crime</u> because I believe this is the name that an American audience will give Carter's act; for while it might be willing to see the justice of his going after better opportunities for himself and his family, its reaction will be ambivalent, because it also believes that a man should accept his own identity, and it tends to distrust anyone who does not. In any society the usurper, regardless of his justification is considered suspect, even malignant. And of course it will censor exposing his children to the awful fate of being a Negro (I can hear Negroes laughing like hell at this, but then everything can't be resolved in one picture).

Thus instead of attempting to draw the audience to Will and Melba on the assumption that "all the world loves a lover," especially good-looking, clean cut, young American lovers, I would take into consideration the socio-psychological fact that for large numbers of American whites this rhetorical appeal would be negated simply and exactly because these particular lovers are Negroes. Rather I would open with Will, Melba and their children living as whites completely unsuspected by their friends and neighbors in Gorham—and thus by the audience. I would paint them as loved by the town, as favored citizens, with Will wise and self-sacrificing, Melba gracious and full of "Civic virtues,"* and their brats (you should see pictures of the real Shelly and Howie!) slightly precocious, cocky and appealing. They would be the typical American family, but taking advantage of the concealed and often denied, American admiration for the aristocratic (as indicated in our love for the aristocratic, Roosevelt, and for England's assortment of dulled titles). I would make them slightly "better" than typical. In short, I would give them snob-appeal: in manner, speech, surroundings, "Family of Distinction" possessing the appeal of both the *Daily News* and the *N.Y. Times,* the *SEP* and *Town and Country.* I'd give them everything that would make possible the complete identification of the audience.

Only then, after this identification has been established—with of course, its undercurrent of impending doom—would I reveal the fatal secret: through flashbacks, hints, intonations, obsessions with and the avoidance of certain topics of conversation—and any other subtle devices of foreshadowing, especially the capacity of the camera to create mood and make shades of black and white meaningful—only then, as I say, would I lead to the dramatic scene of revelation. Not only do I believe that in this lies the true drama of the situation, but a further advantage of such a reorganization of the materials would be to allow a tighter unity of Howie's

---

* And by all means let her have big bosums, the bigger the better. [*Ellison's own note. —Ed.*]

story with that of his parents. Not only would he act as a surrogate of his father's good qualities and thus re-enforce Will's appeal as hero, he would also function as a sword of Damocles, bringing poignancy to Will's role by serving as the symbol of his fate, his justification and his tragedy.

With such a course I believe Carter would not only take on tragic stature, but would become believable and capable of playing the role of scapegoat that Palmer seems rather fumblingly to have allotted him. As now conceived, he falls outside Aristotle's category of a suitable hero. I would make him an admired and important man, the idealized image of the audience, who commits a fatal blunder—not the 'crime' of being a Negro, but that of denying his true identity—and who in falling takes some of the sins of the audience with him.

What is involved here is a conflict between racism and democracy; blood values versus human values. And just as Carter must represent, in his role of exemplary citizen and physician, democratic human values in which all Americans are supposed to believe, he must also represent in his role of usurper, of "nigger in the woodpile"—the terrible hypocrisy and pitiable waste and painful confusion that arises out of racial prejudice. It should not be missed (the audience certainly won't) that in passing, Carter gives implicit sanction to racial values; and indeed, by worrying that his child might be born black (what crap, what self-defeating crap on the author's part!) he gives <u>explicit</u> sanction to some shamefully reactionary nonsense. And, closely related to this, I wouldn't drag in poor Helen by her hair, simply in order that Joan and her parents won't have to face the problem of intermarriage. Better to let it hang, as Shelly (who to me is just as uninteresting and unappealing as Jane Withers, Gloria Jean, the later Shirley Temple, and all the dreary little snots they portrayed) is left hanging, a small question mark silhouetted far down the roving camera's depth of field.

Dear Frank, I hope this makes sense, because I'm stopping lest I find I've given away one of my best plots! Seriously, as now constructed, I don't care for the piece. Yet I believe it important and I would like to see it rewritten and produced with the seriousness it deserves. Right now I don't think it a fitting dramatization of a controversial theme. It calls for more than Palmer has seen in it.

I've told you Carter's troubles, now I'll tell you mine. After all the trouble I went to for '48, it has temporarily suspended. The amusing thing, is that while last time they delayed paying me for months, this time it seems I'll get nothing—not even my article back. Lauterbach tells me their lawyer refuses to release it. The other amusing thing is the photographer I brought in and whose work I directed, got paid because he worried the hell out of them for money from the very start. I'm afraid I'll end up with something like thirty cents on the dollar—if that much.

Meanwhile, Fanny is well. I'm still working and have a date with Albert[*] to discuss the material (not as much as I planned) that I turned in to him last Friday. My heart's in my mouth. At any rate, I hope to have more of the same for you when you return. We haven't heard from Nan concerning your friends, but I suppose we shall soon.

Good luck and the best from both of us.

Ralph Ellison

To Stanley Hyman

AUGUST 13, 1948

Dear Stanley:

I've been so busy with taking down the invisible man's discourse on what he calls 'the seven types of anti-invisibility' that I've had little time for anything else. It goes rather well, coming to over a hundred and fifty pages in seven weeks, and excluding those pages which I could not resist rewriting. Perhaps all that I need to become prolific is just such an elegant office as this;[†] where all the noises are impersonal, the telephone, for the most part, silent, juke boxes non-existent, and where to be reminded of the weird validity of my theme I have only to look up and see consternation and outrage on the faces of certain visitors to the roof of Radio City across the street when they discover me at the typewriter, which, to take advantage of the natural light, Steegmuller has placed near the window. With some it's as though they had looked across to see me doing number 2 out of the window—and I'll let you worry about the metaphor, chum.

Seriously, it has helped me a lot to be able to work away from home, though I don't know what I'll do when Steegmuller returns. There is, however, another reason why I haven't written: I wanted to say something

---

[*]   Albert Erskine was Ellison's editor at Random House. They worked closely together, especially during the stretch in the year and a half before *Invisible Man*'s publication in April 1952, the period when Ellison cut a quarter of the manuscript and followed through on his idea to create a separate prologue and epilogue to begin and end the novel.

[†]   Francis Steegmuller's Fifth Avenue office.

about your folklore piece.* I believe it to be as valuable an essay on the subject as I have seen in an American periodical and that it should do a lot to bring about a serious approach on to the subject. Certainly your <u>origin</u> <u>structure</u> and <u>function</u> triad gives the student something concrete to work with. I'm sorry that you had to give so much space to the junk you discuss in the first two sections.

Though I believe that you might have pointed out that guys like Lomax not only did not understand what they were working with, but that they were also under the spell of the racialistic conceptions of American folklore—which throws up the problem of <u>function</u> immediately, pointing in one direction to a partial explanation of the poverty of our folklore and in another to the pitiful condition of our scholarship in the field. It is my belief that it is not accidental that this field had been neglected, but in keeping with the character of our scholarship generally, for any delving into folklore brings the investigator into immediate contact with the painful and tragic elements which Americans have not been too anxious to touch. Pardon this lack of precision in my language, I planned to take more time with this but have decided to leave the sharpening until later. As for the triad itself, I'd say that for me personally I am more interested in <u>structure</u> and <u>function</u> than in <u>origin</u>—though, on second thought I guess I'm just as interested, only under the heading of <u>myth</u> and <u>ritual</u>, which do not require me to waste time pinning origin down to a specific culture in a specific country. For I believe that myth and ritual are always with us—if only we get the rational wool out of our eyes and see the pre-rational fleece (no plea for primitivism this, only that we recognize that very little of art, or anything else can be approached rationally as strictly rational). Besides, too great a concern with <u>origin</u> degenerates too easily into a concern with purity, and folklore is most impure. Which reminds me that I was amused by your concern lest an item in one of the books be "morally dubious" for children. Since I have not seen the item I raise no question concerning it specifically, but isn't one of the didactic functions of folklore that of dealing with the 'morally dubious' ambiguously? Isn't that one of the functions of its 'wit-work'? I can remember on the other hand that many of the double meanings in the folklore that I learned as a child were missed by me until much later, when my development brought into relief the lode of meaning embedded in the lore. Perhaps folklore presents an innocent face to all but the more knowing child.

---

* Ellison and Hyman often sparred in conversation and in print about the use of folklore in literature. See "Change the Joke and Slip the Yoke," in the *Collected Essays*, 100–112.

I know that it is fast becoming part of your task as critic to be annoyed as hell by ignorance and incompetence, but I don't think it necessary to take a swing at the Folklore section of the Writers Project simply because Botkin is a fool. Nor do I disagree with you that a hell of a lot of worthless stuff was collected; it was, and encouraged by Botkin. But there was also some quite valid material collected, which, as far as I know, has not seen the light. I do know that I myself ran into quite a bit of stuff, including the remnants of rituals focalized in children's games and still undergoing transformation and urbanization; animal fables, and a number of magic characters like "Sweet, the Monkey" a magic South Carolina Negro who could never be successfully imprisoned. There were other things, including sea chanteys and work songs, which might some day be of value to scholars, unless Botkin has thrown them out. I hope it doesn't come to that ever again, but who knows, perhaps it will be through the creation of another project that you'll get some of your most valuable work in Folklore. And, incidentally, what the hell have you against four flats . . . or the trey of hearts, for that matter? Seriously, didn't art song, symphony and opera all come about by trained musicians harmonizing the 'simple' melodies of folk-song in "four flats"? Perhaps I've misunderstood you, though I certainly agree that most of the attempts to adapt folksong are irritating to say the least. It is not, however the idea of adaption that is bad, but that individuals attempt it who have not the complexity of spirit or intellect necessary to do more than debase the original material.

The other thing I'd say about your comments on music is that, as you know, the sounds existed before the notation; thus it is sometimes for the transcriber to resort to complicated keys and modes in order to capture some of the harmonies with the greatest accuracy. You don't raise this question directly in your essay, but it is well to remember when considering singability as a test of an arranger's efforts. Perhaps some songs are singable only when the body dances out the rite?

I like also your comments on the "craze for anything 'folk 'or 'folksy'" with its implicit sanction of the negative conditions in which much of folklore was developed. I would not overlook, however, the yearning for a whole community which also marks this phenomena; not the desire for the primitive mistakenly understood as simple and uncomplex, but for the development of a broad, close community of human experience—otherwise, what lies behind your own interest in the material? . . . That's about all, and probably too much until I've read more in the field. Perhaps you'll think it arrogant for me to have said as much as I have. Well, you led with your chin for asking!

Incidentally (again) I read Shirley's *The Lottery* with a great deal of interest, though I did not think it as successful as most of her stories. I understand also that she upset the middlebrow readers who discovered there was something they knew little about. Good! Did you notice that their concern was with <u>origin</u> rather than with <u>function</u> or structure. My own objections, subject to revision when I've re-read the story, is that it has presented the rite in too specific a form for the contemporary reader, unfamiliar with such rites and the mystery they entail, [to] make the full identification between himself and the "dedicated and set aside" scapegoat. My other objection is over the understatement, for while I believe that the <u>ritual</u> may be understated (providing that the reader understands and makes the willing suspension of skepticism that marks belief) the <u>tragic action</u> can never be; as old man Aristotle points out in the *Poetics,* one requirement of tragic action is that it be of a certain proportion. Otherwise, while a situation of pity and terror may be reduced to a single sentence or phrase, its representation as action requires space in which the emotions may build to the required climax before it can rain down as catharsis. What do you think? It is a rich story, perhaps it is the placing of it in the form of a past situation rather than in terms of its contemporary equivalent that caused my trouble. If Shirley does anything else along this line let me know, we're beginning to work the same vein.

Yesterday I got a letter from Wm. Van O'Connor. Thanks for mentioning me, I'll try to come through with something a little later.

To tell you the truth, we had planned to forego a vacation until this tome of mine is finished. However I'd like to give you a definite answer next week when Fanny's vacation begins. I know she's interested in getting up there and I think I would too. I must warn you about the dogs, though, for while we care a lot for them, they can be annoying as hell. If we come, I'll do everything I can to find a place to leave them and will not bring them unless I find this impossible.

There's little news here; Frank Taylor is going to Hollywood, that's about all I know. Read Kenneth's piece in the *Hudson,* finding it OK, except that I expected something more exciting, being involved in my own imagery of killing, which I hope is the imagery that not only kills, but brings forth light and life. Having lots of fun reading anthropology these days, had some talks with *Life* concerning a photo-essay assignment with Gordon Parks in which I am not interested and against which Fanny is dead set, although, God knows, we do need the dough. Our best to Shirley and the kids. And I hope we can make it.

Ralph

P!S! I've just remembered your crack about my changing signature. Suffer me my phalanges, please; perhaps they're the only thing I have to hide behind or maybe they have to be conspicuous to take the place of my sloughed off <u>Waldo</u>. Ironic that I gave it up and grew the phalanges when I started trying to write. It's still there though, hiding in the loops, keeping the old type-tortures going.

To Richard Wright
NEW YORK 31, N.Y.
749 ST. NICHOLAS AVE.
OCT. 17TH, 1949.

Dear Dick:

I finally reached the other fellow whom I suggested and I found him interested. However I postponed going further until I could hear from you. Since he is to get in touch with me would you let me know your decision within the next few days—including, in case your answer is 'yes,' your wishes as to terms, credits, etc.

Regards,
Ralph

To Richard Wright
NOVEMBER 7, 1949

Dear Dick:*

This is a hasty note being dropped to you at Ralph's request. He himself is terribly swamped at the moment.

Your letter of acknowledgement came—but judging from its contents, we think that you must have misread Ralph's letter to you. The person

---

* We include this November 7, 1949, letter of Fanny Ellison's to Dick Wright because it explains Ralph's cryptic note of October 17, 1949, and because it illustrates how deeply involved Fanny was in the details of Ralph's life and work, personal and professional.

that Ralph saw for you and who could not set your poem to music was Teddy W. The person he saw who <u>could</u> do so was Josh White. He did not see Count Basie at all.

Hope this note is reaching you in time to prevent any mix-up.

The very best of luck on your film, and warm regards to you and your family.

Sincerely,
Fanny

Letters from
the Fifties

RALPH ELLISON'S LETTERS FROM THE 1950S ARE
commanding. For one thing, they challenge the stereotype
of that decade as a merely complacent, self-satisfied time
in American life. For another, he writes considerably more
letters in this decade than in any other. And he writes
from many places: New York City first and last, but in between from North Carolina, Alabama, Louisiana, Ohio on
the lecture circuit; from historically black colleges (Fisk,
Tuskegee, and Dillard) and historically white ones (Antioch, Princeton); then from Oklahoma on his conquering
hero's return home; from Rome while in residence at the
American Academy, and while there on stopovers to read
or lecture or participate in PEN International conferences
in London, Mexico City, Kyoto, and Karachi. But the most
distinctive thing is that more than a third of his fifties letters are written to his best friend: that vital, nonpareil literary bluesman born and bred in Magazine Point, Alabama,
another brother, Albert Murray.

Ellison crossed paths with Murray in 1935 at Tuskegee
when he was a junior and Murray a freshman. To call their
relationship in college more than a passing acquaintance
would be a stretch. Both men trace their intense friendship back to a chance meeting late in World War II "on
Seventh Avenue near 135th Street" when Ellison "was

making wartime Atlantic crossings in the Merchant Marine" and Murray was "a second lieutenant in what was then the U.S. Army Air Corps stationed at the Tuskegee Army Air Field where the 'Tuskegee Airmen' were being trained." As Murray would recall more than fifty years later: "It was that Seventh Avenue exchange that turned out to be the prologue to what became our lifelong dialogue about life, literary craft, and American identity."*

It should be remembered that as the 1950s begin, Ellison is a writer whose work is displayed in a few short stories and reviews of distinction, and a developing novel of great promise. From 1950 until *Invisible Man*'s publication in April 1952 his letters consist only of the seven he writes Murray. In them his voice belongs mostly to a wild man breaking through to revise *Invisible Man* from a novel-in-progress into a classic to be reckoned with—during the remainder of the twentieth century and, perhaps even more, in the twenty-first.

On January 24, 1950, Ellison writes his first letter to Murray, who is teaching literature at Tuskegee and writing a first novel of his own. Their exchange quickly becomes an intense, uninhibited, no-holds-barred ten-year correspondence. At the time Ellison is struggling with *Invisible Man,* a story whose telling acquaints him as well as his narrator with mercurial ambivalence. Ellison's name for his novel-in-progress in those days was "my you-know-what . . . a rock around my neck; a dream, a nasty compulsive dream."

Over the next year and a half, in one irreverent letter after another, he keeps Murray posted: "You are hereby warned that I have dropped the shuck" (May 14, 1951); "I cut out 200 pages myself and got it down to 606" (June 6, 1951). Finally, Ellison bursts out that his novel has become something of a picaresque, untamed Juneteenth ramble: "For me it's just a big fat ole Negro lie, meant to be told during cotton picking time over a water bucket full of corn, with a dipper passing back and forth at a good fast clip so that no one, not even the narrator himself, will realize how utterly preposterous the lie actually is. . . . As you see I'm more obsessed with this thing now than I was all those five years." Earlier in that June 6, 1951, letter responding to Murray's news that he's about to give the manuscript of his own first novel to the typist, Ellison repeats a generous hunch expressed

---

* Albert Murray, "Preface," in Ralph Ellison and Albert Murray, *Trading Twelves: The Selected Letters of Ralph Ellison and Albert Murray*, ed. Albert Murray and John F. Callahan (New York: Vintage, 2010), xxii, xxi–xxii, xxiii.

in several of these letters: "Who knows, perhaps we'll have books published in the same year."

Anticipating *Invisible Man*'s publication in another letter, he speaks about past labor, and perhaps a future creation: "I had chosen to recreate the world, but, like a self-doubting god, was uncertain that I could make the pieces fit smoothly together. Well it's done now and I want to get on to the next." Soon Ellison will embark on that journey of the next novel, haunted to an extent he likely did not anticipate when he came up with the conceit of the artist as a vexed, "self-doubting god." Like *Invisible Man* in the forties, his next novel will soon set the course of his life. Not surprisingly, a number of the 1950s letters to Murray and others illuminate the low visibility and erratic course of the novel-in-progress until an impressive fifty-page excerpt, "And Hickman Arrives," appears in the inaugural issue of Saul Bellow's *The Noble Savage* early in 1960.

In April 1952 *Invisible Man* enters the world to a reception so immediate, magnetic, and deep as to hint at the novel's longevity. Already Ellison feels stirrings of "the next." Even in the midst of "pre-publication jitters," he turns away from Ellen Wright's suggestion that he use Paris as a creative venue, writing that "my instincts tell me to go in the other direction: toward Oklahoma, where lies my destructive element, that substance I'm told the artist must dunk himself in."

In January 1953, informed he had won the National Book Award, he abstains from the usual boilerplate remarks in favor of an inspired address. Wittily naming his piece "Brave Words for a Startling Occasion," over five days and several drafts he hammers out a brilliant apologia for *Invisible Man* by way of the classic nineteenth-century American novel. In Ellison's mind, "its experimental attitude, and its attempt to return to the mood of personal moral responsibility for democracy" augurs a template for future novels he hoped would come from singular American novelists of all backgrounds.

"Brave words" and "startling occasion" soon take on other meanings as Ellison, beginning to mull his *next* novel, writes vivid letters about visits to North Carolina and Oklahoma. To Murray he expounds on giving the keynote that opens Bennett College's Homemaking Institute. In the vestry of the college's chapel he is flabbergasted when the president hands him a black robe along with a "printed card." Ellison looks at the card and on it sees "the order of the Methodist service and he was pointing to where it said SERMON."

Talk about conceits:

Someone had been so naive as to select "achieving peace through creative experiences" as the theme of the institute, and I knew I wasn't going to tell them that creative experience brought peace, but only a fighting chance with the chaos of living. I looked down there at those chicks, man and felt that I was a repentant Rinehart. I was full of love for them because they were young and black and hopeful and, like all the young, prepared to be swindled by another four flusher who had no idea of what it meant to be young, idealistic and willing to learn. I could hardly talk, but I tried to level with them; tried to direct them towards reality and away from illusion.

Turns out in "the days that followed the kids kept coming up to speak about it and to ask questions. And all I had done really, was to tell them to dig the world each for himself."

Ellison follows through on his plan to "scout the southwest" (meaning Oklahoma), where "I've got to get real mad again, and talk with the old folks a bit. I've got one Okla. book in me I do believe." In June he writes his brother, Herbert, that the trip "won't be for pleasure, however, but to refresh my memories and emotions, as I suspect that our lives there might have something to do with my next book. Anyway I want to return before all the old-timers are gone, or before I'm gone myself." He lets down his hair to Herbert more than usual, adding that it "would be wonderful if we could meet there, so if it's at all possible let me know and I'll do what I can to help you out. I thought I'd stick around for two weeks—if those Negroes don't make me angry all over again. Anyway, you write me airmail if you're interested and let me know the train fare from L.A.* and return."

No letter arrives. Ellison goes to Oklahoma City and stays three weeks, reconnecting with May Belle Johnston, his first cousin, the daughter of his aunt Lucretia Ellison Brown. As if to get his vivid memories down, the day after he returns to New York he writes at length to Murray of his impressions of Oklahoma, present and past:

But for the provincialism, I'd return there to live. I made it fine until evening, then I missed Fanny, the city, music, books or just conversation. Time would adjust that, I know, but then there's so little time . . . Boy, but the barbeque is still fine and the air is still clean and

---

* Herbert left Dayton for the army at the beginning of World War II and afterward moved to Los Angeles.

you can drive along in a car and tell what who is having for dinner; and it's still a dancing town, and a good jazz town, and a drinking town; and the dancing still has grace. And it's still a town where the eyes have space in which to travel, and those freights still making up in the yard sound as good to me as ever they did when I lay on a pallet in the moon-drenched kitchen door and listened and dreamed of the time when I would leave and see the world.

To keep the letter company he encloses "Deep Second," the gripping poem he wrote in Oklahoma while digging out how he felt then and feels now, returning.

IN THE MONTHS BEFORE *Brown v. Board of Education* in early 1954 Ellison puts together a speaking tour of historically black colleges and universities including Tuskegee, Dillard, Bethune, Howard, Coppin in Baltimore, and others. (In those days only a smattering of white schools such as Antioch and Princeton invited him to their campuses, though he'd been a participant the previous summer at Harvard's conference on the American novel.) Letters to Fanny and Murray offer rich helpings of observation about the differences and similarities between institutions, especially Tuskegee and Howard.

From the road that spring he describes in reassuring, vague terms initial attempts to get cracking on his second novel, remarks such as "I got some solid work done on my novel" to the upbeat, ever-encouraging Murray. By then he's begun to type out partial early drafts of scenes on thin yellow or blue paper, found after his death in the large metal cabinet next to the desk in his study at 730 Riverside Drive, across from the Hudson River and the blurry Palisades of New Jersey.

Ellison writes no more important letter than the one on May 19, 1954, to Morteza Sprague, his old teacher, librarian, and friend at Tuskegee, after he hears a radio bulletin announcing the Supreme Court's unanimous *Brown v. Board of Education* decision. For a while he rambles on, until—abruptly, no transition at all—words pour from his depths on the decision that declared segregation in public schools unconstitutional and affirmed integration as the law of the land:

> Well so now the Court has found in our favor and recognized our human psychological complexity and citizenship and another battle of the Civil War has been won. The rest is up to us and I'm

very glad. The decision came while I was reading *A Stillness at Appomattox*,* and a study of the Negro Freedman and it made a heightening of emotion and a telescoping of perspective, yes and a sense of the problems that lie ahead that left me wet-eyed. I could see the whole road stretched out and it got all mixed up with this book I'm trying to write and it left me twisted with joy and a sense of inadequacy. Why did I have to be a writer during a time when events sneer openly at your efforts defying consciousness and form? Well, so now the judges have found and Negroes must be individuals and that is hopeful and good. What a wonderful world of possibilities are unfolded for the children! For me there is still the problem of making meaning out of the past and I guess I'm lucky I described Bledsoe before he was checked out. Now I'm writing about the evasion of identity that is another characteristically American problem that must be about to change. I hope so—it's giving me enough trouble. Anyway, here's to integration, the only integration that counts: that of the personality.

Back in that Seventh Avenue conversation with Albert Murray, Ellison had uttered an idea vital to his literary sensibility: "Telling is not only a matter of retelling but also foretelling."[†] Not long afterward his first novel took off from the marshes of Jim Crow. From its epilogue through Ellison's address at the National Book Award ceremony to the molecules of his nascent novel-in-progress, his work lifted up readers' spirits over the cusp of integration. Brooding on the magnitude of *Brown v. Board of Education,* he imagines an American future "all mixed up with this book I am trying to write." He also admits ambivalence as he owns and welcomes being "twisted with joy and a sense of inadequacy," and meditates on the necessity of his fate "to be a writer during a time when events sneer openly at your efforts defying consciousness and form."

Then the light of the writer and citizen breaks the overcast. Once again he feels glad and finds "hopeful and good" the High Court's finding that "Negroes must be individuals," a responsibility across the color line that opens "a wonderful world of possibilities . . . for the children!"

---

* Bruce Catton's study of General Ulysses S. Grant's campaign in Virginia during the final year of the Civil War.

† Murray, "Preface," xxiii.

THIS AMERICAN LABYRINTH of circumstance makes his task—and problem—as a writer more urgent. He recognizes, more deeply than before, "the evasion of identity" as the fluid and true theme of the second novel, a condition that "must be about to change" in light of the integration decision.

IN THE MONTHS BEFORE Ellison goes to Rome in 1955, his letters have the improvising energy of those Sooners who jumped the gun on the official start of the land rush of 1889 and entered "unassigned [federal] lands" to claim their share of a territory that would soon become the state of Oklahoma. Like unsettled land to restless Americans, Ellison's theme is an abstract territory in his mind. Apropos of "the evasion of identity," he needs characters possessed of identity in the first place, however provisional. Accordingly, he writes in his September 1954 application for a Guggenheim Fellowship: "As for characters and levels of experience, it [the novel in his mind] is concerned with Indians, white folks and Negroes, with ideas and actions of the most articulate and of the barely conscious. It will contain adults and children; women, intellectuals and politicians; folk people and people of the elite."

He adds that this novel "is conceived not as a 'race' novel, but as a novel of ideas; which for me implies a novel of action, an exploration of the mysteries of existence, and the depiction of fabulous, unexpected turns of fortune which I see as typical of America at her best, and of the novel (as form) at its most interesting." Ellison's references to the novel-in-progress hover on the edge of territory he is just now entering, a world he is yet to create. In this vein it is not unsurprising that a number of letters during the time between *Invisible Man*'s publication and Ellison's two years in Rome seem gestures of reunion and reconnection, whether to boyhood pal Virgil Branam, his brother, Herbert, or Pat and Camille Rhone and the other kith and kin he addressed as "dear folks" in the heartbreaking note he wrote back to Oklahoma the day after his mother's lonely death in Ohio in October 1937. His conscientious outreach to the folks and places of boyhood in Oklahoma calls the past to the present and vice versa.

In a similar purposeful spirit he tells Fanny how it was speaking to contemporary students at Tuskegee: "I had Notes but ignored them and spoke from the hip or heart or wherever it is that sincerity and desperation are intertwined in one. The audience was so quiet that I became truly desperate and I found myself almost pleading with them to recognize that there was no longer any need to think of themselves as less than human. You know how I feel about these things."

The next day students surround him: "(I must have autographed 135 copies of the book [*Invisible Man*]) so that I know I had some effect." He leaves Tuskegee "with some reluctance, for despite the inroads into my writing time I received a great deal of satisfaction out of talking with students, and out of needling both students and teachers." Soon embers of his past begin to glow again at another historically black college, Dillard University in New Orleans: "Things have gone rather well as far as my contact with the kids is concerned. I'm told that they're stirred up, I hope so, they need a heapa stirring" (March 16, 1954, letter to Fanny Ellison).

ARRIVING IN ROME IN early October, Ralph and Fanny Ellison scarcely have time to unpack their bags or Ralph to finish "Living with Music" for *High Fidelity* before the director of the American Academy in Rome and his wife escort them and the other new fellows on a festive nine-day tour of towns and cities in Tuscany and Umbria. To his delight Ellison taps into a sensibility that originated in his boyhood and has smoldered ever since. "The Renaissance has sent my imagination on a jag ever since I was shooting snipes in Oklahoma," he writes Murray irreverently, with infectious excitement and enthusiasm, "but here it's around you everywhere you turn, the same sky, earth, water, roads, houses, art. And not only that, it's all mingled with the Romans, the Greeks, the Greco-Christians."

As soon as Ralph and Fanny return to their academy quarters in Rome, Fanny, though she speaks little Italian, lands a job with the Lampada della Fraternità, and Ralph considers the ruins visible outside the academy windows. Before long, the deprivations and poverty that are still so palpable in post–World War II Rome override the awe he feels at witnessing the magnificent, ambiguous remains of the old empire.

Architectural remnants and the timeless sense of ruin they embody both fascinate and depress Ellison. They intensify his consciousness of the social and cultural ruin everywhere in the present and increase the gravitational pull of hardship experienced daily in places in his own country he's left behind temporarily but not forgotten. "A man has, after all, to keep his feet on his home ground," he writes Murray in his first letter, clearly proud to "have the Academy ringing with Duke and Count and Jimmy Rushing."

Later that first year he writes Edna Slaughter a letter full of memories about his Oklahoma past mingled with keen impressions of the present he's living in Rome. When he thinks of Thomas Wolfe's famous epigram "You can't go home again," a counterstatement pops into his head: "One seldom ever leaves home for he carries home in the structure of his dreams wherever he goes."

Ellison's first letters from Rome are very much the letters of a man trying to find equilibrium between his work and a new, somewhat difficult, but alluring scene. For example, he writes his brother, Herbert, that Rome is "very very old and very, very beautiful," though he writes as the *responsible* older brother who is "much too busy trying to get my novel rolling to have spent much time sightseeing." To former patron Ida Guggenheimer, from whom he's been estranged since she took umbrage at the mordant satire on Marxist politics in *Invisible Man,* he sends an overdue letter assuring her that he feels "quite guilty over my neglect. Our differences have been political and only political and I have always felt that no political disagreement was worth the destruction of a friendship. . . . I just didn't know how to resolve the conflict so became silent."

Not until February 1956 does he bring up the second novel in a letter and then not to Al Murray but to Virgil Branam, an old Oklahoma sidekick to whom he sends "a snatch from my book to make you laugh—I hope." The "few riffs from old Cliofus"—a riotous character likely somewhat inspired by Branam—are similar to the excerpt he'd forwarded Murray the previous April. Each belongs to a wild tale from early Oklahoma-centered drafts of the novel-in-progress. Ellison composed these morsels back in America, and they are not really near the heart of the novel that now struggles for prominence in his imagination.

About the actual writing he has done or is doing on the second novel in what he calls "this infernaleternal city," Ellison mostly keeps his own counsel as he seeks the dramatic center of his novel-in-progress, and in so doing nudges its two principal characters out of hiding. In the meantime, his letters allow him to riff freely on impressions that fill his mind about the *scene* all around him. Long an admirer of Henry James's *The American Scene,* Ellison observes both Italy and America with such vividness, wit, and originality that from time to time his writing persona becomes Bre'r Ralph the Riffer.

March 16, 1956: "Spectacular scenery," he writes Murray about Ravello. Its elemental landscape mingles with the human in a place whose spirit suggests the paradoxes of history flowing into eternity:

Little towns clinging to the cliffs, lemon groves terraced upon narrow ledges in the almost perpendicular stone; old houses stacked literally one upon the other, foundation on roof; white walls, green shutters—all looking bravely and precariously out across the Bay of Salerno—from whence came the Moors who shaped the architecture, the boat loaded with loot from the New World, and most recently, the Americans.

In the same letter Ellison signifies about the black preachers who are leading the Montgomery Improvement Association's bus boycott and whose pictures he sees in the Italian and French newspapers:

But hell, they forgot to bribe the preachers! I saw some photos of those brothers and some of them look like the old, steady, mush-mouthed, chicken-hawk variety; real wrinkle-headed bible pounders; who in the pictures look like they've been to a convention where they'd caught some son of a bitch not only stealing the money, but sleeping with all their own private sisters! Yes, man! But they're talking sense and acting! I'm supposed to know Negroes, being one myself, but these Moses are revealing just a little bit more of their complexity. Leader is a young cat who's not only a preacher but a lawyer too, probably also an undertaker, a physician, and an atomic scientist. And they're standing their ground in spite [of] threats, assassinations, economic reprisal, & destruction of property. . . . Mose is fighting and he's still got his briar patch cunning; he's just a law, man, something solid under his feet; a little scent of possibility. In fact, he's turned the Supreme Court into the forum of liberty it was intended to be, and the Constitution of the United States into a briar patch in which the nimble people, the willing people, have a chance. And that's what it was intend[ed] to be.

April 1, 1956: A modest proposal to Albert Murray about the papacy:

I was down to St. Peter's this morning and heard the Pope and was in the crowd when he blessed everyone so maybe this will come through without delay. Anyway it was rather impressive, though I swear that if they'd just elevate them a Mose, preferably one converted from one of the storefront cults—which would take a miracle—

he would get in there and bring back some of the old vitality to the Church. He'd bring in some Negro Elks and Shriners with their drill teams and instead of having the platform at the top of the steps he'd elevate it up around the dome of St. Peter's. Most of all he'd have some real singing.

April 11, 1956: Ellison writes Edna Slaughter, in former days an inseparable childhood friend in Oklahoma City, of waking up in Ravello, after unseasonable spring "snow and snow and still more snow," to witness firsthand life sustained by a mix of contraries:

> I'll never forget how startled I was that morning I went to the window and found oranges and lemons showing through the snow. Maybe that was the most important morning of the whole trip: it was a demonstration that beauty and harshness could go together and that tropical fruits could grow despite snow storms.

April 12, 1956: Perhaps believing Fanny did not look hard enough in the Roman streets for the pickling spices he needs to cook a proper mess of pigs' feet, Ralph describes to Al Murray setting out on what he thinks will be an uneventful scavenger hunt:

> I must have covered every food store, market and drug store in Rome, trying to find the right jive. I went into stores and did everything from inventing new dances to standing on my head and pulling out my pecker trying to make them understand pickling spice and they dragged out everything from tomato paste to embalming fluid—everything and anything except <u>pickling spice</u>. Never in the history of the world did a mess of pigs' feet cause so much exasperation. I returned to the academy beat to my socks and prepared to assassinate the first person who spoke to me and fortunately no one did. Fanny just looked at me and went and got me a drink— which calm[ed] me enough to cook the trotters, but they weren't right, man. They were the saddest and I threw most of mine in the garbage.
>
> The next time somebody says something to me about Roman culture they're going to have to get a cop to stop me from talking, imagine a city without pickling spice!

May 4, 1956: In a letter to Saul Bellow,* Ellison imagines Hemingway and Faulkner reenacting the Civil War in Pamplona:

(Since Faulkner† seems bent upon organizing his poor Negroes to fight the North, do you think I could persuade old Ernest to organize a guerrilla squad to oppose them? I'd go along as impartial foreign correspondent to report the thing.)

Understand Faulkner has removed his granddaddy's Civil War uniform from the mothballs and is stocking up on mini balls. Seems he's been planning his strategy (ever the proper bourbon, of course) for a long time. Still, maybe this time we win—No?

September 15, 1956: As the Suez crisis heats up, Ellison writes to Al Murray, "You look in the Italian press and one day you see Egyptian belly dancers posing with rifles all set to blast at the French and British ... and the next day you see those crackers in Tennessee being stood off by the fixed bayonets of the all cracker National Guard." Murray is in Casablanca, in what is still the French colony of Morocco, and Ellison explores the global connections in a rhetoric of tragicomic absurdity:

What the hell do those crackers think they're doing? Mose is the only darker group who doesn't want to blast his kind from the face of the earth, who make any kind of allowance for their form of insanity. There was a time when the cracker's madness could be rationalized but now they're acting like a maniac chasing hell in an airplane loaded with the atomic bomb. Somebody, the Federal or State governments, I don't care which, had better straitjacket those fools before they wreck the plane.

THROUGHOUT HIS TIME IN ROME, Ellison's letters reveal an uneasy alliance, sometimes debilitating and sometimes synergistic, between the

---

* Bellow (1915–2005) is the only novelist to win the National Book Award three times. In 1976, he was awarded the Nobel Prize for literature. He and Ellison were pals at least from the early '50s (see Ellison's letter of January 8, 1952, to Albert Murray).

† In a March 4, 1956, article in *Life,* Faulkner had written "if it came to fighting, I'd fight for Mississippi against the United States, even if it meant going out into the street and shooting Negroes." In response, Ellison wrote Murray, "if the best can get so lost what the hell are the rest of us going to do?"

novelist and the man of letters. After a lapse in letters between him and Albert Murray—"one of our longest silences"—Ellison complains of having "been up to my ass in typescript and have only just climbed out of one level of the mess after another back to my novel."

It's April 1957, and the five months since his return from a professional trip to the PEN conference in Mexico City and a personal stopover of more than three weeks in New York have been fruitful ones for his novel-in-progress. In a letter at the end of January, Fanny proclaims happily to Saul Bellow that "Ralph has hit a high peak in his work, and the things coming out of it are brilliant and fine."[*] It appears that he has gotten well beyond the rough patch he described in a letter to Stanley Edgar Hyman before his and Fanny's trip to northern Italy, Switzerland, and France with the Murray family, and the ensuing months of almost continuous, often distracting travel.

Nonetheless, the 1957 letter to Murray delineates conflict between Ellison's sense of responsibility for *the* American novel and *his* own novel.

> Last year I made the mistake of agreeing to do an essay on the novel for an anthology edited by Granville Hicks and which will include people like Bellow, Wright, Morris & Herb. Gold. . . . But I got bogged down on the damn thing for two months, perhaps because I was resisting the necessity of leaving old Bliss and Cliofus and Severen and Love to deal with The Novel and those who say the form is dead.

Ellison is referring to Hicks's collection *The Living Novel* (1957) and his essay, "Society, Morality, and the Novel," one of the two major essays he signed on to write late in his first year of residency at the American Academy in Rome. "The other piece I probably mentioned is a piece on desegregation, which is still in the works. It deals quite a bit with literature and I'm hoping to make a short book of it at the suggestion of Robt. Penn Warren."[†] This essay Ellison began in response to his friend Virgil Branam's goading him in a letter, after the introduction in Congress of the Southern Manifesto of 1956, to "tell a man how it is." In its compositional history as well as its welter of form, "Tell It Like It Is, Baby" bears a resem-

---

[*]   Quoted in Rampersad, *Ralph Ellison,* 336.

[†]   Robert Penn Warren (1905–84) and Ellison became strong friends at the American Academy. Warren, best known for his 1946 novel, *All the King's Men,* and also "a poet of distinction," was named first poet laureate of Congress in 1986.

blance to the second novel; Ellison works hard at it in 1956 and drastically pares down and consolidates several drafts, but then he puts it aside and does not publish it until 1965.

Previously, Ellison wrote a revealing line to Saul Bellow about the challenge of his first year at the academy: "And underneath all this confusion like a sustained tone there was my novel and the need to discover where it was going." A rare elaboration comes seven weeks later in the letter he writes Hyman. "As for me, most of my writing is on the book, which is much more difficult than I had imagined," he admits before disclosing that at last he has gotten a hold on the novel's narrative and dramatic center.

> Still it's rolling along and I've become quite fond of the old preacher [Hickman] and his six-year-old revivalist [orphan Bliss] whose great act is an antiphonal rendering of the seven last words of Christ with the little boy sitting in a small coffin. Wild things arise from this, but I'm still having trouble in giving the book the dramatic drive I feel it needs. Will do, though; will do. Just learned that the kid preacher's name, Bliss, means rapture, a yielding to experience. Very American because of the overtones of progress and this guy really becomes Dick Lewis's* "mind in space." Having fun, as you can see. Today the old preacher is talking Aristotle (though unaware) as he tells kid just why coffin has to be of a certain size. So I guess if I don't succeed in making [the] book dramatic I can at least reveal the principles as they operate in life. Trick of course is to do both.

Perhaps Ellison looks to achieve the equilibrium between philosophical introspection and impassioned dramatic action his drastic revisions in the final year of composition brought to *Invisible Man*—an equilibrium, he might have said, between the shadow and the act.

Another crucial letter—Ellison's "first letter of the New Year" (1957), written to Harry Ford—identifies difficulties common to the essay "Tell It Like It Is, Baby" and the second novel. To Ford he readily admits to "sweating at this crazy book," meaning the novel. "It goes well at the moment but I can't count on it nor on anything else I turn my hands to.

---

* R.W.B. Lewis (1917–2002), author of *The American Adam* (1955) and distinguished biographer of *Edith Wharton* (1975) and *The James: A Family Narrative* (1991), was a close friend of Ellison's from Bennington days in the late '40s through his many years at Yale.

Everything goes to knots and tangles; like this essay I'm working on," he confesses before whirling into a wild riff about the out-of-control essay:

> I started out to do a simple piece on desegregation (for *Encounter*) but now it has become a monster of bastard form which sticks its demented head into matters of literature, politics, old Jamesian observations, myth, Gilbert Murray on Hamlet and Orestes, the *Ruggles of Redgap* of Charles Laughton, Malraux, Faulkner, the psychology of immigrants as regards the American Dream, the N.A.A.C.P., why Fiedler thinks Huck and Jim were practicing buggery on the raft (Huck sounds like that good old Elizabethan pleasure and hell, they were together in the dark, weren't they?), Jack Daniels Whiskey (how I wish I could lay this madness to drinking that!), cool jazz— ten penny nails and puppy dog tails. . . . About the novel I'll only say that some of the scenes are molto outrageous. If only I didn't require the gestation period of an elephant to bring forth my odd mice!

IT'S IMPORTANT TO NOTE that once *The Nation* prodded Ellison into submitting an essay of his choice for its centenary issue in September 1965, he got to work. He deleted, added, and shaped his drafts of the fifties into one of his most brilliant essays, in which the mixed rhetorical discourse brings a sense of completion to its disparate materials.

Ellison's riff on "knots and tangles" is keen commentary on what was happening with the mix of disparate rhetorical forms he was aiming to stitch together in "Tell It Like It Is, Baby," and perhaps a trenchant intimation of fears that he might not be able to fuse the stubborn shifting voices and narrative forms rearing their contentious heads in the novel-in-progress into a coherent rhetorical whole.

On a different level, that of the personal and intimate, "knots and tangles" seems an equally pertinent figure for the passionate, dangerous relationship he was about to enter in early 1957 with a woman other than Fanny. The most perceptive account of the shattering affair may be in comments made to Arnold Rampersad for his biography by a friend of Fanny's at the American Academy. Not identified by Rampersad, this person's "main worry was about Fanny, who was 'totally concerned with Ralph's welfare and success although she was also absolutely a fine person in her own right.'" As Rampersad notes, "The woman also admired Ralph's lover: 'She was stunning. She stood tall and had a wonderful, lustrous complexion. She was charming. It was difficult for her, too. She and Ralph had been struck by lightning. They really had no choice.'"*

In his 1957 letters Ralph keeps his counsel about the other woman, with two exceptions. On April 9 he writes to congratulate Saul and Sondra Bellow on the birth of their son, and Saul on his novel *Seize the Day*. After an intriguing aside on his own writing—"Things go slow with the novel for the moment. The Hicks thing came at the wrong time, it was like having to stop making a watch and go out to dig iron ore"—he shifts to an uncertain, intimate key.

> Now that we're conditioning ourselves to leave Rome has caught me up, off guard, out of position; poignancy and lost promises throb in the air. And, as you can guess, there's something eating my innards which I can't write about but if I don't crack by September I'll have to ask you for a friendly ear. I guess once in a while even old dogs like me discover suddenly that life has stirred up more anguish within them than they can keep down. Hope that I last until the fall.

Two months later he writes Murray a more unadorned, self-mocking version of what's going on: "Fanny and I are in a state of crisis at the moment and I might just be acting like a fool in his forties. That's as much as I can say now except that it's painful and confusing. . . . I don't know what our plans are at the moment."

Ellison's partial confidence to the Bellows shows vulnerability; it comes when his relationship with Fanny is brutally up in the air, an interval when he and his lover are seriously contemplating ending their respective marriages to begin a life together that would lead to children. His words to Murray are cagey; by the time he writes them things between him and Fanny are tilting toward a decisive break—she has just booked solo passage home to New York for late July.

Ellison writes two subsequent cryptic letters to Murray. On July 28 he notes tersely that "Fanny sailed on the 23rd." Three weeks later he adds the frail camouflage that she "left for home on the 23rd of [July] and must be up to her neck in getting adjusted because I haven't heard from her as yet."

During the rest of 1957, except for two notes about arrangements for his late August PEN International–sponsored trips to Japan and India and Pakistan, Ellison writes no more letters—except for six to Fanny.

---

* Rampersad, *Ralph Ellison*, 337.

From the first of these, written on August 12, until the last, October 23, ten days before he sails home from Naples on the *Giulio Cesare,* the letters are full of "knots and tangles." From one to the next, sometimes within the same letter, Ellison's feelings twist and turn—knots tie, then loosen and provide the string for further knots. Even without comparing Fanny's letters side by side with Ralph's, several things emerge vividly.

First, perhaps, is the complex pull of Ellison's passion, a force to which he has a certain defiant loyalty: "There was, I admit, some shabby aspects to what I did but then passion makes its own rules when it has to; the question is what is the hardest to forgive, the breaking of the rules or the existence of the passion itself," words followed immediately by "I can say that I miss you and that I do, and always have, realized how really good you've been to me." At times one has the eerie feeling that Fanny and Ralph, not to mention his absent lover, are mere bystanders, their particular persons figures destined to fade into the background of an impersonal, elemental dramatic frieze.

There is little question that when Ellison writes Fanny "that the old ties hold," he means it. Notably, in the letter of August 24, aware of the limits to words on a page, he cautions her (and himself) that "what needs to be said should be said face to face and with the possibility of our old, sweet resolution should words break down. If you hadn't been so insistent I could have told you that for me there is none better, nor do I expect there ever would be. There are other things to say but they must wait."

Finally, on October 9, he looks to the future with a mix of wariness, accountability, modesty, and respect for Fanny's personhood:

> Fanny, I got the impression that you feel that because of the way things went for me after you left that I have the notion that everything will go on with us as before. If so, then please understand that I know better and that I face the possibility that the basis of any lasting relationship might have been destroyed and that you might find it impossible to be near me for long; that all remains to be seen. Nor should you feel the need to be compassionate, since you have an honest right to rage, though I am grateful for it.

He ends on a downbeat note that is not a shrinking from what has happened or how deeply he has hurt Fanny so much as a long exhalation at the work that he, loving her, knows that he must do: "I'm discouraged, Fanny, and you're unhappy so let's hold off with this kind of thing until I get home. I want to say more but I just can't." He knows that words, even the most anguished ones, pale before deeds, as thought does before action.

There is a gap in the letters until the end of 1957. In February he writes his first letter of the new year to Albert Murray—who else?—about returning home "scrambled up inside" and since then "readjusting, not to my work, but to my place of work." He's vague about relations with Fanny except to say she's "well and sassy and keeping busy as hell." About his novel-in-progress he writes that he looks "to cut down some of the ambition of this job, but am in so damn deep that I've got to fight it through to the end. It might be an egg but it'll have to be the same egg I conceived two years ago." (Knowing what they know now, Ellison's readers might wish Murray had reminded his friend of the drastic pruning and revision he performed on the penultimate draft of *Invisible Man* the year before publication.)

Three weeks later Ellison kicks off a letter to Saul Bellow by growling, "Things ain't coming worth a damn." Presently he elaborates that he's "got a natural writer's block as big as the Ritz." On his lingering emotion over the affair in Rome, Ellison favors Bellow with the most telling and specific comments he gives anyone in writing: "Things Rome-wise are still snarled up for me and I guess there's nothing to change it. Time might dull the effect but I'll never forget and I know that your advice was good." Two weeks later, still in "the merry month of March . . . my birth month," Ellison writes plaintively that in "the ice and snow, and my stony work-in-progress, I have to be haunted by memories of last year's Roman spring. I'm old enough to know it'll never happen again, and I have no desire to go back at the moment but memories are hellishly clinging" (letter to Bellow, March 24, 1958).

For the rest of 1958 and 1959, Bellow and Murray remain Ellison's favorite correspondents. He accepts Bellow's invitation to live without paying rent or even utilities in what Bellow insists on calling his "wreck of a house" in Tivoli, not far from the Hudson River. Though sheepish about Bellow's insistence that the house is his to stay in, rent free, utilities included, Ellison accepts with pleasure and gratitude. In truth the place is a godsend—a stunning and authentic, if decrepit, seventeenth-century mansion—perfect to work in alone and hospitable to visits from Fanny on weekends. The place was a short drive from Bard College. There Bellow's intercession with friends in the English department paved the way to a job for Ralph with just enough teaching and salary to enable him to concentrate on his novel and the occasional essays on jazz he wrote during this time as a break from fiction. Ellison's letters show him taking a conscientious interest in the handyman work required to keep the house maintained in Bellow's absence (and somewhat in his presence). During his two years in Tivoli he enjoyed the solitude, hunting small game and walking the woods in the benevolent surrounding countryside.

While at Bard, Ellison's correspondence with Albert Murray touches on jazz, the civil rights movement, assorted literary gossip, and matters of craft as well as the many oddities of daily life that piqued Ellison's curiosity and led him to compose many humorous riffs. Appropriately, Bellow figures prominently in the last letter Ellison writes Murray in the fifties. It is a long letter that he begins in late June and returns to three weeks later; it's as intense and upbeat about the writing he's been doing as he was with *Invisible Man* early in the decade.

> I've been working frantically on the book, trying to complete a section while the emotion was still strong within me. I guess I must be nearing the completion, recently the typewriter has been drawing me like a magnet. Bellow has read book two and is to publish about fifty pages in a new mag that he is editing—*The Noble Savage*—of all things! I'm a contributing editor and it's paying 5 cents a word . . . I'll keep you posted on this as it develops.

The expansiveness and matter-of-fact intensity of the letter show Ellison to be as truly himself now as he was years earlier when he wrote letters about wrestling successfully with *Invisible Man*. Up to speed on his book, Ellison indulges his proud instinct to send proof to his friend that the novel so long in the works is tangibly progressing. As collateral he includes a mock-up of the logo and masthead of the soon-to-be-published first issue of *The Noble Savage*.

Characteristically, Ellison then playfully matches Murray's hilarious account of a military drill his friend has judged in California with uncensored, wild memories of his own, "marching in the moonlight" as a boy in Oklahoma to the commands of "that same type of mad drillmaster," suddenly alive and strutting again in his own imagination.

John F. Callahan

730 Riverside Drive
New York 31, N.Y.

May 19, 1954.

Mr. M.D. Sprague
Librarian
Hollis Burke Frissel Library
Tuskegee Institute,
Alabama.

Dear Mort:

 Congratulations on recieving such a wonderful batch
of prizes, they sound like the stuff librarians' dreams
are made of. I must admit that I was a bit confused by
the arrival of the unannounced,though familar,books but
was sure that an explaination was forthcoming--even if
I should find it necessary to remind you that she was
needed. I'm getting them off to the gentlemen immediately.

 I found the exchange most amusingly ironic and when
I mentioned it to Albert Erskine,my editor , we had quite
a laugh--all those wonderful items for ole Invisible!--
However when this was through he asked seriously if you'd
mind his quoting this information as publicity later on
when my work-in-progress goes into the works? Dont
rush to anticipate, I'm still a long way from having even
the first third of it done, and from the way I'm moving
I'm years away from the end. Anyway this reques' is not
important enough to cause you bother, so dont go to and
trouble if you think there might be objections. I wont
try to tell you how pleased I am that your donors asked
for IM.

 The reading list certainly would benefit by
addying the works by Howe and Baker and any others you
feel would help. Would you include James' The Bostonians
along with the others, please. As far Wilson's New
Yorkers piece of Nov.27, 1928, its his essay on Uncle
Tom's Cabin and I'll just bring it along and read from
it during my lecture.

 Now for Reid's question: Please tell him that
I feel that $ 500.00 plus expenses would be a bit more
reasonable. Otherwise I can see the five hundred bucks
vanishing in a lot of paper work which would not be to
my advantage. Certainly I would never eat fifty dollars
worth of food during any one week, not even at the Waldrof!
Thus I'd rather have the savings where they count--for me.

 Actually my lecture fee is(as it was in March)
$175.00 plus expenses; at which rate the lectures would
come to $875.00 for the five days --excluding expenses--
and I think the $500.00 figure plus roundtrip flight fare,
food, laundry, room board and minor incidentls (I itenize
because Flood left me holding the tabs for quite a number
of small matteNathithalpaEsyouppyteaclimakeeofay affairs
packageIdexpect to work like hell. Reid will find that

.2

total
this fee will to something around $635.00, but if he wants
a nice round figure to request,$600. is a good one. The
flight fare from here to Montgomery and back is 129.03, so
he can see where the bulk of the expenses lies.

Well so now the Court has found in our favor and
recognized our human psychological complexity and citizenship and another battle of the Civil war has been won.
The rest is up to us and I'm very glad. The decision came
while I was reading A Stillness At Appomatox, and a
study of the Negro Freedman and it made a heightening for su
of emotion and a telescoping of perspective , yes and a
sense of the problems that lie ahead that left me wet-eyed.
I could see the whole road stretched out and it got all
mixed up with this book I'm trying to write and it left me
twisted with joy and a sense of inadequacy. Why did I
have to be a writer during a time when events sneer
openly at your efforts and defying consciousness and form?
Well, so now the judges have found and Negroes must be
individuals and that is hopeful and good. What a wonderful
world of possibilities are unfolded for the children! For
me there is still the problem of making meaning out of the
past and I guess I'm lucky I described Bledsoe before he was
checked out . Now I'm writing about the evasion of identity
which is another characteristicly American problem which
must be about to change. I hope so, it's giving me enough
trouble. Anyway, here's to integration, the only integration
that counts: that of the personality. See you soon.

                              Ralph Ellison.

To Albert Murray
749 St Nicholas Ave.
New York 31, N. Y.
january 24, 1950

Dear Albert,*

I suppose by now you've received the information that Fanny had sent
you.† It was a rather impersonal way of going about it, yet it was one
way of insuring that you received the latest and most official directions.
Should you run into difficulties please let us know. The trip is much too
exciting to allow some fairly mechanical factor like a passport [to] cause
you delay.

As for passage, I've been away from close contact with the sea for so
long that I'm not up on such things; however I'm told that with the rush
for Europe come spring it's best to see about passage well in advance.
I would suggest that you try a cargo ship, since many carry passengers
and are apt to be cheaper and as fast. It's possible that once you decide, you might take a ship out of New Orleans and save yourself some
expenses. We're waiting expecting Virgil‡ to arrive from Japan any day
now and he'll have such things at his fingertips. You'll get it as soon as
he arrives.

Thanks very much for seeing to it that a few Negroes read my reviews;
I get the feeling that most times the stuff is seen only by whites and that,
I'm afraid, doesn't mean much in the long run. Although the reactions to
the piece by no means displeases me. Some day I'd like to have the time
and space to do a real job on the movies and not from any limited racial

---

* Murray had been a freshman during Ralph's third and last year at Tuskegee; they renewed
their acquaintance on a visit Murray made to New York in 1948 and soon became very close
friends. Throughout the 1950s the two men exchanged scores of letters, a correspondence that
Murray and John Callahan edited and published as *Trading Twelves*. The correspondence of
these two accomplished friends brings to bear on 1950s American culture what Callahan calls
"a vernacular intelligence, defiance, fervor, and, above all, style." The current volume includes
Ellison's letters to Murray from the 1950s, and all of Murray's end of their correspondence as
published in *Trading Twelves*.

† Fanny had sent the Murrays a letter full of information and suggestions about their coming
trip to Europe.

‡ Virgil Branam, a boyhood friend of Ellison's from Oklahoma City, now a ship's cook in the
merchant marine.

angle . . . The fellows on the *Reporter* are quite alert and on the lookout for competent stuff by Negroes, so you might send them something. They pay a little over ten cents a word and are yet in that formative stage where they are apt to print almost anything of interest. I have several things in mind for them but my you-know-what doesn't allow time for working them out, although two of the essays are in rough draft.

By the way, I took your tip and read Fiedler's piece on Montana and liked it. He's not bad, that Fiedler. And here's a tip for you: Get J. Saunders Redding's new novel *Stranger and Alone* which is to be published on Feb. 17th. I'm reviewing it for the *N.Y. Times*—a very short review unfortunately—but I think you'll find the book interesting. Not as a successful novel, but as a good and important job of sociological statement, and perhaps even more than that; for he has got ahold of some of the psychological motives operating in the Negro-hating mulatto types that collaborate with the white south in making such a travesty of Negro education . . . If I'm not careful I'll start my review right here! But see the book. I believe that at least we're going to have a group of writers who are aware that their task is not that of pleading Negro humanity, but of examining and depicting the forms and rituals of that humanity. But see the novel. And if I ever complete my endless you-know-what you'll get a chance to see what different things we make of a common reality. "You-know-what" indeed. It is a rock around my neck; a dream, a nasty compulsive dream which I no longer write but now am acting out (in an early section the guy is obsessed by gadgets and music; now I'm playing with cameras and have recently completed two high-fidelity amplifiers and installed a sound system for a friend); a ritual of regression which makes me dream of childhood every night (as a child I was a radio bug, you know, and take it from me after getting around with the camera bugs and the high-fi bugs and the model train bugs, you'll have no doubts as to the regressive nature of this gadget minded culture); or is it a kind of death, a dying? Certainly after it's all over and done up in binders I will have passed through the goddamnedest experience of my life and shall never be the same. Perhaps that is why it's so difficult to finish. Nevertheless I'm near the end and I'll be glad to get it over with. Perhaps as you say of my reviews there's a switchblade in it—if so, I'll be damned relieved to turn it against someone else for a while. Perhaps you've given me the subtitle: "The Invisible Man; a Switchbladed Confession."

Who knows, we might both have books during the 1950. Let us hope.

I've been asked to lecture on the sociological background of southwestern jazz at N.Y.U. in April. The director of course is a combination bopper and exponent of the Herskovits* myth-of-the-Negro-past-school of anthropology—<u>and</u> under contract to write a book on jazz . . . Well, I leave bop to Dawson† and Herskovits to who the hell wants him, and with my fear of having my poor little brain picked I probably won't say much of anything. So let that be a warning to you; if you have any ideas write them before you talk to these white boys, 'cause they're <u>all</u> eager beavers aspiring to win their spurs in *P.R.,*‡ *Accent* or anywhere else that will print a by-line. So write it before you talk it—if you plan to write it, and don't say too much even then.

That's about all, except to express my surprise that you got down to writing. Had you written before you came up last fall you might have had our apartment all to yourselves while we were having Parks's§ house all to ourselves just a few miles up the river at White Plains. Glad things are going good for you, Mozelle¶ and Mike,** give my regards to Bess and Mort and any old ones who would remember me; and we hope to see you in Feb. And you keep writing—all it takes is—shit, grit and mother wit—and a good strong tendency towards lying (in the Negro sense of the term).

Ralph

To Albert Murray

MARCH 22, 1950

608 FIFTH AVE.

Dear Murray:

What goes? Are you going abroad or not? I wrote you last month but received no answer. As you can see, I'm back in Steegmuller's office pounding away. Book almost finished—I hope. There'll be rewriting to do but

---

* Melville Herskovits, influential folklorist and anthropologist, author of *The Myth of the Negro Past.*

† William L. Dawson, conductor and composer under whom Ellison studied at Tuskegee.

‡ *Partisan Review.*

§ Photographer Gordon Parks was a friend and sometime collaborator of Ellison's.

¶ Albert Murray's wife.

** Murray's daughter, Michele, also known as Mique.

the main thing will be over. Right now it reads like a three-ring circus. All the anti-violence boys will blow their tops should it come their way. Regards to Mozelle from us two.

Sincerely,
Ralph

To Albert Murray
749 ST. NICHOLAS AVE
NEW YORK CITY 31
APRIL 16, 1950

Dear Albert,

We're sorry to hear of your difficulty and hope by now you've gotten passage. From our inquiries however, the problem seems to be general. A girl in Fanny's office was successful in getting early passage only after going through the complete list of merchant shipping offices freight shippers and then only because her husband, a former seaman, had connections. The only thing we found that is at all promising is a trip on the Arnold Berstein Line, but the sailing is not until July 5th. Let us know if you're interested. Meantime we're still looking, though it seems that the pilgrims have everything sewed up. Suggest you keep trying such ports as Baltimore, Mobile and New Orleans . . . Incidentally, you must be working a very smooth magic to get those boys to shell out that much dough (I mean 'squeeze,' such as dough) toward your expenses. I read the account of Founder's day; isn't it ironic that Drew* should lose his life on his way to take part; even so, if there are photographs or other materials around I'd like to see some of them just to revive my memory of the place . . . I see where Dawson's been waving his hands before some white folks. How did it go? The gal on the *Amsterdam News* writes a prose that is strictly from dietetic diarrhea, you can't tell whether she's trying to write criticism or simply suffering from verbal trots . . . Recently, at our first dance in years, we ran into a guy names Crouse or Krouse, who is married to a little yellow gal, a rather hard-bitten little thing, from Tuskegee or Greenwood, remember him, them? I think she is a relative of Peck Harper.†

---

* Dr. Charles Drew, pioneer in the preservation of blood plasma for transfusion, died in a car crash en route to a medical meeting at Tuskegee Institute, April 1, 1950.

† A student at Tuskegee.

No I haven't read *Beetle Creek*,* but I plan to. I have read *Idea of a Theater*,†
which I was unsuccessful in getting Random House to publish, and I think
as highly of it as you do. Yes, and the Hemingway; though I still don't know
what I think of the three installments I've read. In case you don't recognize
him, the writer he keeps needling is Sinclair Lewis, or seems to be. I knew
the lost young mistress referred to; she was very petite and smooth and attractive in mink coats and silly hats, and it was through her that we met and
had dinner with Lewis. So I guess that's my literary anecdote for today. I've
also read Auden's book on romanticism, but prefer something a little more
in my own frame of reference, or at least with more precision. Look at it
though, if you haven't. The piece on *Moby-Dick* is OK.

As for my review of Redding's novel—well. As far as novels go I found
it dead before it could get started, so I tried to place it as to archetypal
pattern and thus indicate how one might read it without being completely
bored. And to be frank, if my own nightmare of a book didn't touch some
of the same material, I might have handled him a bit roughly. But hell, it's
easy to knife a guy; the creative and difficult thing is to make him aware
of the implicit richness of the material as you see it. Then, if you're lucky,
you have shared your vision; if not, you still haven't wasted your time for
the Negro material will have been thrown into its wider frame of reference and the reader can pick it up and not only understand more of its
meaning but can, at the same time, judge it and demand that the Negro
writer quit fumbling around and get a good grip on his themes. Some
funny things go on in the symbolic level of *Stranger and Alone*. Redding
seems to be fighting a battle with color as he tries to designate a scapegoat;
and the black, razor-scarred boys were pretty charged up although it is
Howden who is the villain. Well, talking with an editor who'd seen an
earlier version I learned that Howden was originally a black boy. Black or
mulatto it seems that Redding was too much tied up to make him interesting, couldn't identify himself with the character to the extent of making
him come alive. Perhaps it is one of those books that are written simply as
research for some future writer.

As for Aleck Sander,‡ he is a bit of a bitch all right, and a eunuch, and a
denier-of-his-balls. But hell, what use has he of balls when he knows that

---

*   William Demby's 1950 novel *Beetlecreek*, about black life in rural Appalachia.

†   Francis Fergusson's 1949 study of ten plays and the art of the drama.

‡   A character in the movie version of William Faulkner's *Intruder in the Dust*.

his roly poly eyes are enough to get him in the movies? And what, by the way, do you think of Baldwin's piece on the protest novel* . . . Hell, I'm going to close this, it's Monday and after a week of rain and snow the sun is shining and I can use some sun. Only one final thing, I'm lecturing on western jazz at N.Y.U. next week and hope to get a publishable essay out of my notes. Marshall Stearns, who directs the course has received the first Guggenheim for a work on jazz. That's something to think about.

So . . . give my best to Mozelle and Mike and Mort and all.

Ralph

P.S. I've only one last big scene to go on the book.

To Albert Murray
749 St. Nicholas Ave.
New York 31, N. Y.
May 14, 1951

Dear Albert,

You are hereby warned that I have dropped the shuck.† About the middle of April, in fact; and strange to say I've been depressed ever since— starting with a high fever that developed during the evening we were clearing up the final typing. I suppose crazy things will continue to happen until that crowning craziness, publication. That hasn't been set and I'd like very much to see you in town so that you could read the ms. When are you coming up? With Duke's new band attracting attention and my recovery from my six hundred page obsession,‡ you certainly have excuse enough . . . Otherwise things are normal. Fanny is well and glad it's finished, I'm back at 608 Fifth trying to get started on my next novel (I probably have enough stuff left from the other if I can find the form.§

Our best
Ralph

---

* James Baldwin published his controversial essay "Everybody's Protest Novel" in 1949, arguing that Richard Wright's novel *Native Son* paralleled *Uncle Tom's Cabin.* Baldwin's essay seemed a repudiation of Wright, who had befriended and supported Baldwin.

† Ellison had finished *Invisible Man,* and he delivered the manuscript to Random House in the fall of 1951. It was published on April 14, 1952.

‡ In his revisions, Ellison cut the manuscript of *Invisible Man* from 810 pages down to 606.

§ This is Ellison's first reference to his second novel; his conditional "if I can find the form" seems an intimation of an ambition never realized.

To Albert Murray
NEW YORK
JUNE 6, 1951

Dear Murray,

I hope you get this before you start your hitch. Your news was a surprise, to say the least. I was expecting to look up and see the three of you any old day. It makes me kinda sorry that I didn't carry through during Nov. (?) when I called you and was all set to take a quick run down there. As luck would have it, it was during the big blizzard and you couldn't be reached—and I fell back into my old groove and decided that I'd better remain here and work. Besides, I would have had to borrow the dough. Come to think about it that was probably my last chance to see you in your natural habitat; after *Invisible* I'm just apt to be persona non grata—though I hope not. Anyway, I was having a little difficulty about that time and thought that such a trip might help, but I got over it and went on to turn in the book during April, having finished most of it at Hyman's[*] place at Westport. I went there just about the time Shirley[†] was doing page proofs of *Hangsaman*[‡] and it was just the spur I needed. I had been worrying my ass off over transitions; really giving them more importance than was necessary, working out complicated schemes for giving them extension and so on. Then I read her page proofs and saw how simply she was managing <u>her</u> transitions and how they really didn't bother me despite their "and-so-and-then-and-therefore"—and then, man, I was on. What I needed to realize was that my uncertainty came from trying to give pattern to a more or less raw experience through the manipulations of imagination, and that the same imagination which was giving the experience new form, was also (and in the same motion) throwing it into chaos within my own mind. I had chosen to recreate the world, but, like a self-doubting god, was uncertain that I could make the pieces fit smoothly together. Well, it's done now and I want to get on to the next.

Erskine and I are reading it aloud, not cutting (I cut out 200 pages

---

[*]   Stanley Edgar Hyman, folklorist and literary critic, whom Ellison called "an old friend and intellectual sparring partner."

[†]   Shirley Jackson, fiction writer and wife of Stanley Edgar Hyman.

[‡]   Jackson's 1951 novel about a young woman at a New England college.

myself and got it down to 606)* but editing, preparing it for the printer, who should have it in July or August. I'm afraid that there'll be no publication until spring. For while most of the reader reactions were enthusiastic, there were some stupid ones and Erskine wants plenty of time to get advance copies in the hands of intelligent reviewers—whatever that means. I guess it's necessary, since the rough stuff: the writing on the belly, Rinehart (Rine-the-runner, Rine-the rounder, Rine-the-gambler, Rine-the-lover, Rine-the-reverend, old rine and heart), yes, and Ras the exhorter who becomes Ras the <u>destroyer</u>, a West Indian stud who must have been created when I was drunk or slipped into the novel by someone else—it's all here. I've worked out a plan whereby I trade four-letter words for scenes. Hell, the reader can imagine the four-letter words but not the scenes. And as for MacArthur† and his corny—but effective—rhetoric, I'll put any three of my boys in the ring with him any time. Either Barbee, Ras, or Invisible could teach that bastard something about signifying. He'd fade like a snort in a windstorm.

Who knows, perhaps we'll have books published in the same year. I'm anxious to see what you've done and I've already told Erskine that you expect to have it typed by September. Come to think of it our writing novels must surely be an upset to somebody's calculations. Tuskegee certainly wasn't intended for <u>that</u>. But more important, I believe that we'll offer some demonstration of the rich and untouched possibilities offered by Negro life for imaginative treatment. I'm sick to my guts of reading stuff like the piece by Richard Gibson in *Kenyon Review*. He's complaining that Negro writers are expected to write like Wright, Himes, Hughes, which he thinks is unfair because, by God, <u>he's</u> read Gide! Yes, and Proust and a bunch of them advance guard European men of letters—so why can't these prejudiced white editors see it in his face when he goes in with empty hands and asks them for a big advance on a book he's thought not too clearly about? No, they start right out asking him about Wright-Himes-Hughes, with him sitting right there all cultured before them, fine sensibilities and all. The capon, the gutless wonder! If he thinks he's the black Gide why doesn't he write and prove it? Then the white folks would

---

* For a thoughtful and detailed account of Ellison's revision process, see Adam Bradley's *Ralph Ellison in Progress* (New Haven, CT: Yale University Press, 2010), 178–208.

† Ellison refers to General Douglas MacArthur, who, shortly after President Harry Truman fired him for insubordination in 1951, famously addressed a joint session of Congress with great fanfare and extravagant rhetorical flourish.

read it and shake their heads and say "Why, by God, this here is really the pure Andre Richard Gibson Gide! Yes, sir, here's a carbon copy!" Then all the rest of us would fade away before the triumph of pure, abstract homosexual art over life. Right now, poor boy, he demands too much; not only must the white folks accept him, recognize him, as a writer; they must recognize him as a particular type of writer—And that, I believe, is demanding too much of the imagination. Especially if it must be backed up with an advance . . . No, I think you're doing it the right way. You've written a book out of your own vision of life, and when it is read the reader will see <u>and feel</u> that you have indeed read Gide and Malraux, Mann and whoever the hell else had something to say to you—including a few old Mobile hustlers and whore ladies, no doubt. You've got to get it done by September—hell, I says this is only the point of departure, you can highball and ball the jack and apple jack in the next one, when you tell them about that philosophical, prizefighting, foot racing, chippy chasing, Air Force character you're going to meet up with in the next twenty-one months, name of Little Buddy.

Kidding aside I'm glad you've worked the hitch in with your larger plan in that you and Mozelle are getting that dream house. You've done so much since my days down there that I feel like a rounder. I never had much of a sense of competition (or at least I have a different kind) but with middle age staring me in the face I'm feeling the need to justify myself, or least Fanny's working and my thinning hair. So I'm trying to get going on my next book before this one is finished, then if it's a dud I'll be too busy to worry about it. I could use a little money, though, I really could. Anyway, just to put that many words down and then cut out two hundred pages must stand for <u>something</u>. I'll get you an advance copy if possible. Erskine's having a time deciding what kind of novel it is, and I can't help him. For me it's just a big fat ole Negro lie, meant to be told during cotton picking time over a water bucket full of corn, with a dipper passing back and forth at a good fast clip so that no one, not even the narrator himself, will realize how utterly preposterous the lie actually is. I just hope some-one points out that aspect of it. As you see I'm more obsessed with this thing now than I was all those five years.

Let us know where you're stationed should you transfer from Keesler and we'll be glad to see you, as always, the first time you can hitch a flight up here. We might go to Chicago during August but we're not certain. Meanwhile get the book finished. I want to learn more about Little Buddy and old Reynard, the more than life-size man-with-the-plan. Give our love to Mozelle and Mike.

Ralph

To Albert Murray
749 ST. NICHOLAS AVE.
NEW YORK 31, N. Y.
JAN. 8TH, 1952

Dear Murray,

Yours was really good news. I was beginning to think that you decided to sit on the egg six months or so longer, but now to learn that you've not only finished but are about to ship it up to us was just about the best Christmas greeting I've had in a long time. We were half way expecting you during the holidays—especially after old 'bass clef' Deren called to invite us to a party and suggested that we bring you along if you 'happened' to be in town. We went there looking for you in person but found you only in spirit. The chick was draped out in something like a sarong, her hair blazing, her feet bare with anklets of little bells that tinkled as she got into that Haitian groove. She really had the feeling for that stuff too, man—mostly in the shoulders though 'cause as she explained them Hateties don't fool around with bumps and grinds lessen its death dance.

But old Maya was shaking and tinkling with the feeling, and when we could capture her for moments in all that mob of people, talking with a great deal of insight. But it wasn't until around four a.m. when I happened to go back to the bedroom to get one for the road, that she broke down. She said, in the quietest, most confidential tone of the wild evening, "Ralph, what is a bass clef chick?" And I toppled, man, from the ankles, hit the flo' and rolled! He's here, I cried. He's arrived! Who, she said. What do you mean? Murrays, I said. And when I stopped laughing and looked up, man, there she stood without her anthropology on! Then I had to assure her that I was laughing at you not at her. Then as I grabbed for out coats I tried to explain what a bass clef chick meant to me—which took me into gut and bucket, blues and jive, meta and physic. So then she wanted to know what was meant by a chick calling somebody's name! And I said, He's here, he's truly been here! But what about calling his name, she said. And I said, Look, when the bass clef is grooving with overtones, earthing and skying, jooking and jiving, moaning and crying, doing-and-dying, penetrating and being penetrated and she hits him where he lives and he jumps bear or rabbit, bull or hound and begins to riff then, lady, his name has been called. She's still digging after it man. We left her digging, and I told Fanny who didn't hear most of it was damn shame what you had done to anthropology.

Seriously though, she's a nice person and I'm glad that we finally met. But you, man; I've been hearing about you from all over. You have taken that low-down southern cullud jive of yours and spread it all over western civilization. I was talking with Bellow* and he told me about you in Paris. He was both amazed and amused over your ease of operation. And I said, "Who, him? Hell, man, the world is his briar patch." If he didn't understand me he will when your book comes out. Hurry and get it up to us. I'll tell you whatever I can. And if Random is hesitant, I have a good friend at Knopf's who is anxious to see it.

Yes, maybe we'll have books published during the same year. I completed the page proofs in December and expect bound copies sometime in Feb. Publication date is set for the day after Easter. And the current issue of *Partisan Review* carries the prologue. Things are rolling, all right and I guess I'm not a slightly mammy-made novelist. There is quite a bit of excitement, with more calls for galleys than can be supplied, but who's puking and who's laughing I do not know. Keep your fingers crossed. I managed to keep in everything but that sour cream in the vagina that Ras the Exhorter talks about. It was too ripe for 'em, man. They called me and said, "Mr. E., that sour cream just naturally has to go." Maybe they know about "duck butter." So I guess I sold out. I compromised; all the stuff that really counts is still there, and I didn't dodge before they drew back to strike. In fact, I was so busy chunking myself I didn't have time. One thing both of us can be sure of is that whether our books are miscarriages or what not, this kind of labor of love is never lost, not completely lost, because just the effort to do what has never been done before, to define in terms of the novel that which has never been defined before is never completely lost. Hell, besides I'm trying to organize my next book. I've been a tired, exhausted son of a bitch since I've finished and I want to feel alive again. It's an awful life; for years now I felt guilty because I was working on a novel for so long a time, and now I feel guilty that I'm no longer doing so. Fanny's after me to do some stuff on Negro culture and perhaps I shall.

---

* This clearly indicates that Ellison and Bellow were acquaintances if not friends well before *Invisible Man*'s publication in April 1952.

We had a quiet Christmas, Erskine did not get to Europe but his wife did and they have been separated since her return. Steegmuller is back in his office I think to stay a while. I'm putting a hi-fi sound system in their apartment, for which a friend of mine has designed and is building a handsome room-divider bookcase. They're fine.

My copy of *Notes on a Horsethief* is no. 114. Your copy of *Invisible Man* will be numbered one of the first I can get my hands on. Give our love to Mozelle and Mique. And, MacNeil, be careful with the Mann's automobile!

Ralph

To Albert Murray

FEB. 4, 1952

Dear Albert:

It has taken me a hell of a lot more time to get down to writing you about the novel than it took me to read it four times. So without further delay let me say that we both think that you've written yourself a book.* I found it beautifully evocative and poetic (indeed, I'm not sure if it's a novel or narrative poem), especially those sections concerned with the past: Lil' Buddy, Luzeana, rabbithood, the womb, the nest—in the chinaberry tree. We found his discovery of his mistaken identity and encounter with L. Charley on the freight especially moving, poignant. For here I think your writing is saturated with the experiences, the rhythms, the texture, the 'signifying' in the broad colored sense of the term, the moods, the preoccupations (think you could get ole Deljean to sic my dog on her cat?) the search for manhood via adventure, and, of course, the search for the current self through the translation of the past into the meaningful focus of fiction.

All of this is rendered in terms of inwardness, yet because it is bathed in emotion and presented in terms of details: Dog fennel, water, smells, hollers (what the hell does 'tell the dya' mean?), speech rhythms, walking and dancing rhythms—all the complex interaction between sensibility and envi-

---

* Murray had sent Ellison the draft of a novel he was calling *Jack the Bear*. Ultimately elements of this novel grew into *Train Whistle Guitar* (Murray's first novel, published in 1974) and *The Spyglass Tree* (Murray's second novel, published in 1991). For a thorough explanation of how Murray came to divide this early draft novel into the later work, see Paul Devlin and Henry Louis Gates Jr., "Note on the Texts," in *Albert Murray: Complete Novels and Poems,* ed. Paul Devlin and Henry Louis Gates Jr. (New York: Library of America, 2018), 940–46.

ronment, it comes out whole. A balance is reached and dreamer and dream are made manifest, wheel within wheel to use an inadequate and mechanical metaphor. To put it in another way, while lying in bed he turns himself inside out—and we see the whirling world that made him, moving again in that wonderful process called boyhood. And of course there's that other dimension, the hero meditating on the hero theme at the same time as he seeks the hero's mission. And it is here that I ran into trouble.

For while I disagree with hardly any of his formulations of the nature of fiction nor with his theories of jazz, etc., I think the reader is deprived of his, the reader's, adventure because here you turn from presenting process to presenting statements. (Listen, I am probably too much involved in my own techniques of illusion to be a balanced critic, so take this with the knowledge that I have just emerged from a long period of madness.) Nevertheless I would like more Emdee, actually he's not as real as Lil' Buddy, though he's right there in the environment—or Jaygee, because with them Jack could arrive at his theories through conflict just as Stephen [Dedalus] arrived at his through talks, discussion, arguments with Cranly, Lynch, the dean, etc. His ideas are not the usual ones and I think much <u>unrevealed</u> revelation lies in the story of how he attained this kind of transcendence. Perhaps my desire to have what you choose not to present is proof of the success of what you've given us, still I feel the same about Eunice.

How 'bout that chick? Why does he go after Sugarbabe when she is his woman; what does Sugarbabe symbolize apart from bass clef, maturity, mama, or Daddy Bear's own darling that Eunice her dialectical opposite doesn't? And the reverse: For what value does Eunice stand?

Does she stand for unconscious fear of loss of manhood, Eunice= eunuch? If so, why? Man, you've got to watch that stuff! You're riffing over your own head. Certainly she is reality too. In short, I feel that Emdee, Eunice, Edison (look at how the E's fall in line, gate) and Jaygee form a sort of missing middle (you'll probably say a missing book which you had no intention of writing, so hush my big fat mouth) from the <u>process</u>, the unfoldingness of the novel. The hero is interesting and indeed is heroic (for he is a cultural hero in the milieu of the college just as L. Cholly is in the folk world of Gasoline Point), exactly because he mixes both of these sets of elements within his personality. Thus it seems to me that while he is saying yes, yes, yes to the complexity of the world, he is saying no, no to more than crackerdom and such asses as the doctor in the hospital. In order to think and feel as correctly as he does about so many things that mister has had to wade through a heapa hockey, illusion or whatever you want to call it. I know, 'cause I done a bit of wading myself. In fact, Jack speaks for me too and I'm dam glad you've taken on the difficult task of telling that part of the story.

Because, as you know, we've taken on in our first books a task of defining reality which none of the other boys had the equipment to handle—except Wright, and he could never bring himself to conceive a character as complicated as himself. I guess he was too profoundly dissatisfied with his life, his past life, to look too long in the mirror; and no doubt he longed for something, some way of life so drastically different that it would have few points of contact with what he knew or the people he knew it with. But you, hell, you'd eat chittlings at the Waldorf! Not because you wanted to brag or be different, because you know they're as good a food for the gut and poetry as any other, and I would too. More power to you. That's about all of this except for the following: If the publisher should want more wordage I suggest that you simply expand on what is already there. For instance, tell them how here as in the blues, sex means far more that poontang, but the good life, manhood, courage, cunning, the wholeness of being colored, the beauty of it (am I making suggestions or simply showing you that I see what is already there?) as well as anguish, and the deep capacity of Sugarbabe to stand for, to symbolize it all! The only other thing that I could watch and I had plenty to watch in this thing that I finished, are those rhythms from which you derived part of your style, I know how powerful they can be, indeed they can move a man to write, make him will to endure the agony of learning to think and see and feel under their spell—even before he learns what he must say if he is to achieve his own identity. Well, you have an identity and what you're saying no one but you can say. So watch the trailing umbilicus of rhythm. And I say this knowing full well that you might have consciously had Jack think in these terms by way of ironic comment on his literary approach to life. Intention does count, doesn't it?

Here finally is the only criticism that I make brazenly and without humility. (I) I don't think the stuff on page 92 <u>works</u> after you leave Pound. (II) I think it's a dam gone piece writing. Those Moses down there don't know what they're living with but you'll show it to them, articulate it for them.

I turned the ms. over to Erskine today (p. 31 was there all the time, but the pages slipped out of the binder and I was so damned irritated to have my reading interrupted that I wired you on impulse) and he said that he'd get to it as soon as he got a couple of other things out of the way. I'll keep you posted. Of course if they're interested he'll write; and if they're doubtful (though I can't see why they should be) I'll take it to Harry Ford over at Knopf; he's anxious to see it. You think that knuckleheaded Hamilton* is off somewhere writing a big book?

Man, you had me looking at photographs of that period in an effort to make Fanny see it as concretely as you made me see it, and there in the center of all the KIYI's† was old Gerald. I tried to find the portrait of Sprague, your son Mort, since you've writ him large, but I don't have one. Do you know by the way that I used to work back there in the stacks? High up? There's a sculpture of Booker‡ sitting on the floor, and other relics, and as the day turned to dusk in the late spring the outside light turned a deep indigo blue. The same old nest, the same old briarpatch. I only wish that I had known consciously that I was preparing myself to become something called a writer, rather than the aborted composer that I am. The bastards defeated me there, but I think they might have let well enough alone. Nimble is the word, they taught me to be many things in order to be myself. So I thank them although I don't forgive them and one of these days I intend to get hold of that kind of false artist, false teacher, for which Dawson stands.§ Just thinking about it makes me mad all over again.

I finally saw Ada Peters.¶ I spent an afternoon trying to give her something with which to make more than a provincial estimate of Wright. She was full of the old "he married a white woman" crap. I really don't see why she didn't talk to you and Sprague. At least she'd have a background with which to approach his work. Anyway I talked and I hope she does a good job.

Incidentally she mentioned *The Mark of Oppression,* let me know how the meeting comes out.

---

* Gerald Hamilton, a close friend of Murray's at Tuskegee whom Ellison considered a character.

† KIYI, a social club.

‡ A statue of Booker T. Washington, on which Ellison partly based the statue of the Founder in *Invisible Man.*

§ William Dawson, the famous composer and professor of music at Tuskegee whom Ellison revered and eagerly looked forward to studying with. While a student, Ellison could never win Dawson over, but after *Invisible Man* the two men more than reconciled. In the 1980s and 1990s, Ellison wrote several letters to Dawson that show a strong admiration for the composer and his achievements.

¶ Ada Peters, English instructor at Tuskegee.

As for the novel, I'm still sweating it out. Good things are being said and the publisher's hopes are high, but I'm playing it cool with my stomach pitching a bitch and my dream life most embarrassing. I keep dreaming about Tuskegee and high school, all the scenes of test and judgment. I'll be glad when it's over. The prologue has caused some comments, but I don't think Rahv[*] has decided what he thinks about the book as a whole. He does know that it isn't Kafka as others mistakenly believe. I tell them, I told Langston Hughes in fact, that it's the blues, but nobody seems to understand what I mean. But the thing is arousing interest. I've been asked to participate in a *P.R.* symposium on the artist and American culture, and *Commentary* has asked for some essays. You should submit something to them, they pay well and I think they feel that there's something not quite right about Baldwin and Broyard.[†] They're getting me a book on jazz to review, so maybe I'll have a chance to get some of this stuff from my N.Y.U. lectures down on paper.

Why don't you, by the way, do a short story about that bad cracker cop who got so puffed up with pride and recklessness that he kicked the keys off the piano? The son of a bitch, couldn't he see that was sacrilege? I'd have blown him down my damn self! Our love to Mozelle and Mique,

Ralph Tafe Edison
Ellison

To Ellen Wright
749 St. Nicholas
New York 31, N.Y.
MARCH 26, 1952.

Dear Ellen:

Forgive me for taking so long to answer but not only is life rather wild here at the moment, but after having put in such a long stretch at the typewriter I find it difficult to write anything—including letters. And what is worse, publication day is the 14th of April and my tension is building up at supersonic speed. Watch your mail, for in a few days you should receive *Invisible Man.* Tell Dick that I hope that I haven't let him down since it is the best I could do (aside for some cuts made necessary by publishing costs) up to now.

---

[*]   Philip Rahv, editor of *Partisan Review.*

[†]   Anatole Broyard, author, book reviewer, and friend of Ellison's. Broyard was of mixed racial descent and passed for white in the New York of the 1940s and 1950s.

I spoke to Random House about your agency and your interest in handling the book over there; however, they are now my agents as well as my publishers, and I'm told that they have some arrangement with Raymond Queneau and Gallimard. For you see after failing to hear from my former agent for about three years (doubtlessly he thought I'd never finish my book) I waited until I had turned in my m.s. and then proceeded to free myself of Reynal and Volkening.* It was done painlessly and we parted pleasantly. I then turned things over to Random House, quite willing to pay their slightly higher percentage of handling foreign rights.

This arrangement does not prevent me from having you handle short magazine stuff however, and I'd be only too glad to send you whatever I have. As soon as I calm down I'll send some things that I've been planning to finish. I hope this won't take long, I'd like to clear up such things before I get really working on the novel I'm trying to conceive.

Who knows, some day you <u>might</u> just look up and see us coming through the door. We wanted to come so very much a couple of years ago but were unable. Now my instincts tell me to go in the other direction: toward Oklahoma, where lies my destructive element, that substance I'm told the artist must dunk himself in; don't know, but I plan to give it a try. All this depends of course, upon whether we make enough money to stretch our legs.

Needless to say, we miss you and Dick very much, and like some others I know, wish very selfishly that you'd come home, if only for a little while. I shake my head when I think of little Rachel, what with a master of English for an old man and her knowing not a word of it! Send us photos if you can, we'd like to see how they've grown.

Meanwhile, as soon as I get over some of these pre-publication jitters I'll see what I can do about getting together some pieces for you to see.

All our best,
Ralph

---

* The publishing house Reynal and Hitchcock (through Ralph's first agent, Henry Volkening) originally bought the rights to Ellison's first novel, but Ellison was able to break with them in 1951 and transfer the rights to *Invisible Man* over to Random House and his editor Albert Erskine.

To Chester Aaron
749 ST. NICHOLAS AVE.
NEW YORK 31, N.Y.
APRIL 21, 1952

Dear Chester Aaron,[*]

Thanks very much for your refreshing reactions to *Invisible Man*. I must confess that your letter just about bowled me over, for I realized as I read that, although you might as you suggest change your ideas about the book the next day, I had at least made contact with you a reader who is capable of reacting profoundly.

I won't attempt here to go into most of the problems you raise but only to say that the book does not, believe me, arrive out of despair. I don't believe that I could have finished the book had this been true. Actually, it was something that had to be done in order to clear the way so that I could go on to other things. The great beauty of human life and its great tragic quality lies in the fact that, despite all, we are capable not only of enduring the most horrible conditions which we impose both upon ourselves and upon others but of transcending them. Art is that effective, I think, when it attempts to present both the fact and its transcendence.

This is beginning to sound very stuffy, so I am going to stop. I could not possibly say in so few words what I have not quite managed in so many. I shall look forward eagerly to see how you deal with these problems in your novel. Meantime, would you give our best wishes to Nan and the children.

Sincerely,
Ralph Ellison

---

[*] Author Chester Aaron had written Ellison regarding *Invisible Man* and to share his ideas about his own novel-in-progress.

To Hazel Harrison
749 ST. NICHOLAS AVE.
NEW YORK 31, NEW YORK
MAY 7, 1952

Dear Hazel Harrison,

I suppose by now you have received your copies of *Invisible Man* that I got off to you as quickly as I could. Unfortunately, I've been too caught up in the excitement of publication to answer your letter—which doesn't mean, of course, that it didn't give me the great pleasure that it did. It was one of the first to arrive and assured me, or at least gave me reassurance, that what I was doing had meaning. You have no idea of how pleased I am that you liked my book; for though I am aware that one can't really repay others for the hope and encouragement they give, it is nevertheless impossible not to wish that one could and to try at least to justify their faith. So you see, you shouldn't be surprised if you were one of the first to whom I sent the book. I don't have to tell you how miserable I was during so much of my stay at Tuskegee. (Much of it actually the result of my first real conflict with life.) So, naturally, when I was over my six years' ordeal of writing I wanted to be judged by those like yourself, Katherine—yes, and Walter Williams and Sprague—who were so generous and encouraging at a time when I could so easily have become cynical and been lost forever to any artistic pursuit.

How strange life is. All of you (who with a few others were the best of Tuskegee) just by being human and dedicated and kind taught me far more than I was able to learn in any classroom. Indeed, hardly without thought you (they) were preparing me for the faith in art and in people that has led me finally to writing. While Dawson, who had inspired me to come to Tuskegee, could see me only as some kind of irritation. When, ironically, had he been capable of approaching me with only one-tenth of the insight or disinterested humanity of you or Walter Williams, I would have turned out to be a musician today. But I suppose it is always the things that you do casually and which you don't regard seriously that are the most educational. But didn't I really start writing when Walter, Lazenberry and I began meeting once a week in his room where we read papers that we had written during the week as we drank coffee or wine? Well, so it was: the musician was stifled but a novelist was born. So I won't complain. Indeed, I am thankful that even one's negative experiences can not only be transcended, but if we keep trying, can be turned into an advantage—except, of course, I must confess, that I would have liked so much to have been a composer. So now I must make my music with words. But the important thing here is that you liked the book.

After some of the reviewers insisted on identifying me with the hero I was afraid that some of the college section would be misunderstood. Your reactions reassured me that those who knew me at Tuskegee and are familiar with the nature of my experiences as a student will understand that the college section, like the rest, is fiction and not fact. And what a different story it will be, or would have been, if it were the facts of my experiences that I was intending to present. There would have to be you and Walter and me and Portia and Dawson and Neely, and especially Neely, who was the real cause of my leaving when he refused to let me have a job during the summer of 1936, and the others Capt. Drye among them. Yes, and there would be our sessions in your studio, with all the talk and all the music, and Ella Haithe reading poetry, and Fanny Pittman playing. And that night when you and Allen Moton and I took the drive toward Montgomery with his talk of philosophy between drinks of whiskey and my looking down suddenly to see that we were travelling at 80 miles an hour on that busy road; and the concerts you gave down at Alabama State when you made the baby grand literally bounce across the platform as you played Brahms; yes, and there would have to be all of the candy you made which you used to give me; and Eva Sothern, and Hoskins; and the pianos pushed out into the narrow hallway and the thundering song of so many playing the Bach Inventions in unison on Saturday mornings. Yes, I guess there's a lot to remember and the amazing thing is that I've used so little of it in the book. All this must wait for an autobiography that will come much later.

Please give my regards to those who shared those days with me. Who knows but that before too long I shall visit Washington and we'll relive the rest of that time together. At any rate, I'll be able to autograph your book, which in my eagerness to get it off to you I failed to do. Explain this to Walter and Minnie Williams would you please, and give them my best.

Sincerely,
Ralph

Miss Hazel Harrison
654 Girard St. N.W., Apt. 414
Washington 1, D.C.

To Gerda Stein
749 St. Nicholas
New York 31, N.Y.
MAY 11, 1952

My dear Mrs. Stein,[*]

Since publication day events have swept me along at so swift a pace that here, days later, I find I've neglected to write you of the pleasure I received from your telegram. It was the first and arriving at the very beginning of what turned out to be the most delightfully exciting party I've ever had, or have attended—thus, especially meaningful. It was as though you had secured the success of the evening (we left sometimes after one A.M.) with your blessing. Thank you very much.

Since that wonderful beginning so many things have happened: There have been several parties given for us, I have been guest of honor at a *Time Magazine* editors' luncheon, have been interviewed by Harvey Breit, by *Park East Magazine* and the *Saturday Review of Literature,* and two radio programs, and have had the pardonable pleasure of seeing my book in many bookshop windows. Just recently I have been invited to take part in an American Library Association discussion on censorship (in June), and to address classes in fiction at Antioch College and at N.Y.U. All of which makes for quite a sudden and exciting break from obscurity, but nothing has been so important as that party which began the series. I suppose it is that, coming as it did before the book reviews, Fanny and I were made to feel that no matter what the outcome of publication, our friends were satisfied that I had persevered and completed the job. It was like receiving "A" for effort—and what an "A"!

Yes, and what a good omen! Much to our surprise the reviews have been far, far better than we'd dare dream. And only a few evenings ago the *New Yorker* editor told me that even their review would be a rave. It is somewhat bewildering as you can see—even though my pleasure in reading some of the flattering things said about the book does not extend to believing them. Indeed, I am now calming down into a feeling of

---

[*] Gerda Stein was a friend of Ellison's patron Ida Guggenheimer, and the mother of Beatrice Steegmuller, at whose Vermont cottage Ellison stayed and worked on *Invisible Man* in the 1940s.

thankfulness toward those like Bea and Francis and you and Ida* whose good wishes and aid we had over those seemingly endless years when I was fighting with my own uncertainty over my ability to communicate as much as with my inexperience. It would require a book fully as long as *Invisible Man* to begin to tell you how important this has been to both of us. Meanwhile I can only say thanks again for both of us as we wish you a speedy recovery.

Sincerely,
Ralph Ellison

Mrs. Gerda Stein
New York, N.Y.

To Alvin W. Gouldner
730 RIVERSIDE DRIVE
NEW YORK 31, NEW YORK
JANUARY 19, 1953

Mr. Alvin W. Gouldner
Department of Sociology
Antioch College
Yellow Springs, Ohio

Dear Mr. Gouldner,

If you judged from the long delay I have taken in answering your letter you would get no idea of how much I appreciated it. From Bear or Man, it was certainly a gratifying letter to receive. It gave me the feeling that I had reached someone who understood what I tried at such length to say.

You are quite right about my refusal to make the Brotherhood the CP. My idea was to attack the disease at large, not just one of the groups infected by it. Secondly, the attempt was to write a novel, not a polemic. The disease is widespread and I think that the action of the Republicans in killing off the filibuster rules change after their campaign promises carried out the same type of betrayal that I have depicted in the actions of the Brotherhood.

---

* In various ways Ida Guggenheimer and Francis and Beatrice Steegmuller were patrons of Ellison's in the years he wrote *Invisible Man*.

You are also quite right about the magic in the name, and I was very much amused to observe that even though I did not make this organization the CP, the Communists themselves assumed that I was writing about them and only them, and attacked me violently.

Actually, I do not believe that literature can come out of a simple class orientation; the "Proletarian Novel" is really a sad, mistaken dream, since literature evolves out of the abiding experience of a people. The proletarian concept depends upon a consciousness which is restricted almost entirely to a concept of class, an ambiguous thing of comparatively recent development, but the novel must come out of something far deeper, seizing upon those patterns of experience which are so abiding and so universal that they allow for a million variations and are recognized by people totally incapable of dealing with them on any profound level of consciousness. Thus, for example, by basing my book upon the historical pattern of Negro movement from South to North alone I was able to stir memories, certainly in Negro readers, which drew in their wake a great deal of the unformulated experience of the group, starting even before the Civil War. And the poetry itself is but an exploitation of speech rhythms and imagery which have been heard for years and years throughout the country wherever Negroes have been found—so that even when strained through my small vision, the average reader has a sense of being in contact with something much older and much bigger and deeper than my book. The mistake of the so-called proletarian writers was never to have learned that American writing is something that started hundreds of years ago. Thus, in order to be heard—whatever our political opinions—we must build upon that literature and speak with its deepest accents.

Yes, you are right about the period of which I was writing—between 1939 and 1943, but I doubt very much that those who preach the proletarian novel will ever accept me as one of their own.

Some day, in the spring perhaps, I shall come out to Antioch at the invitation of my friend Paul Bixler and we can go into these things at length.

Until then, my best good wishes,

Sincerely,
Ralph Ellison

To Richard Wright
730 RIVERSIDE DRIVE, APT. 7B
NEW YORK 31, NEW YORK
JANUARY 21, 1953

Dear Dick:

As you say, it has been a long time between letters. Somewhere along the way I have lost the delight of corresponding. Letters come with difficulty and I suppose it would take a psychiatrist to tell me why since there was a time when I was more myself when writing a letter than at any other time.

Thanks very much for the very nice things you had to say about my book. I am glad that you liked it.

As to your questions, I shall try to answer them in order:

1). The Party boys around Harlem have been afraid to say too much although Abner Berry* wrote an attack in *The Worker,* calling me all the standard names and saying that I had "sold out". Similar things appeared in other publications, always written by Negroes—but I am afraid that they only made members desire to read the book. There are a few Negroes of that group who still speak to me. I suppose that some of the stuff in the early section got under their skins so much that they could not completely deny the book.

2). Yes, there was a feature in *LIFE.* But, unfortunately, we ran into the presidential conventions and what was an eight-page essay was reduced to three pages which destroyed the effectiveness of what was, at best, a difficult job. Being a photographer and a writer, you will appreciate the tremendous difficulty of translating such intensified and heightened prose images into those of photography. At best, the essay turned out to be an excellent Ad.

3). I am told that for a first novel the book sold very well. It is now on its way to 15,000 and selling fairly well—180 copies the first two weeks of November. I think that the reception of the book caught my publishers a bit off guard. It was the most favorably reviewed book they have ever published, some of the reviews being extremely intelligent.

---

* Berry, a longtime leading figure among African American leftists in Harlem, had argued with Ellison years before about the politics of *Native Son.* In his review of *Invisible Man* in the *Daily Worker,* the newspaper of the American Communist Party USA, Berry harshly criticized the novel's failure to adequately critique the American capitalist system.

It has been very amusing to watch the reactions of some of the people who assumed that I was just kidding about writing. Some can't quite forgive me for having done a good book and others feel that I perpetrated a hoax. I ran into Reddick* at the Library Convention this summer and he insisted that this was not the book that I told him I was writing in tones which implied that I had somehow betrayed him.

4). I have been seeing notices of your publication date and I will be right at the bookstore on the 18th to get a look at the *Outsider*.[†] You say that you know Negroes will not like it, but without having seen it I would say not to be too sure. There were some who did not like mine—people like Ottley, and Ben Burns writing in *JET*. But despite them it has been widely read by Negroes and it is liked. Ironically, it got me placed on the *Defender*'s[‡] Honor Roll of 1952. I think that there is such a rapid change in our status, with money being more plentiful and racial restrictions giving slowly but steadily away, that more and more Negroes are coming to grips with their problems as members of Western Civilization and are seeing the broader problems behind their racial dilemma. Therefore they are looking for books, which relate them to this larger problem and though they might gag at the medicine they accept it in the end. Anyway, March looks like an exciting month.

I really have no idea when Fanny and I will visit France. I am working on a novel which demands that I go West, which will take about as much money as a trip to the continent. However, I am a little less enthusiastic about coming now than two years ago. For one thing, I am getting a little sick of American Negroes running over for a few weeks and coming back insisting that it's paradise. My answer to them is that my problems are not primarily racial problems, that they are the problems of a writer and that if a trip across to France would solve those, I would make it tomorrow, but after seeing them I am reluctant to believe that any such magic exists. So many of them talk and act like sulking children and all they can say about France with its great culture is that it's a place where they can walk in any restaurant and be served. It seems rather obscene to me to reduce life to such terms. But enough of that.

---

* L. D. Reddick, historian and curator at the Schomburg Center for Research in Black Culture.

† Wright's novel *The Outsider* was published in February 1953.

‡ *The Chicago Defender,* one of the important African American newspapers of the twentieth century.

What on earth has happened to Sartre? He's acting, from this point of perspective, as cockeyed as he looks. Is there any way that I can keep posted on the developments? Incidentally, we met your friend Dorina Silone and have seen her several times. This seems to be the year during which the widows and ex-wives of European writers have descended upon New York. Besides Silone, there is Mrs. Orwell, the ex–Mrs. Cyril Connolly, the ex–Mrs. Nabakov and the current Mrs. Chiarimonte.

We have heard that Julia has turned into quite a young lady and it is a little bit amazing to hear that she has now reached the age at which she studies Latin. Perhaps sometimes you will send us snapshots of both her and Rachel. It's good to know too that Ellen plans to come over this year and I hope you will change your mind and come along. After all, things move along here a bit from year to year and despite all, you are recognized as a leading American writer. I am very often asked about you by people who are interested in writing and, indeed, your name has come up on several occasions down at the Institute for Advanced Studies at Princeton where I go each week to take in Edmund Wilson's lectures on Civil War writing. (Incidentally, Negroes are now attending Princeton as a matter of course and as far as I know, no attempt has been made to capitalize upon the fact in the press.) The lectures, by the way, are very stimulating and I find it very significant that a man like Wilson has decided to re-examine that particular period. Its effect is certain to be good for the current state of American writing.

You asked about Langston. From the very beginning he publicized my novel—in his column and otherwise and has used every opportunity to advance it. After all his kidding me about never finishing it, he sent a wire saying in effect that the race goes not to the swift but to the one who continues writing until his book is finished. Only last month he recommended the book as a Xmas gift in his column. In short, he continues to like me and respect me, although few of his friends do. Toy* has been trying to get me down there so that she can fight with me about the book but I have so little patience with that type of foolishness that I dare not go. I would crush her.

I have run into Chester Himes after having lost track of him for several years since he published *Lonely Crusade*. I just finished reading his last novel *Cast the First Stone*. It is the prison novel that I think you saw and I am afraid it is not up to snuff. He writes mainly of homosexuality in prison but was unable to resolve it. He is now having a riotous affair with Vandy (he and

---

* Toy Harper—"adoptive" aunt of Langston Hughes—who "had fed and sheltered Ralph during his early years in New York" (Rampersad, *Ralph Ellison,* p. 262).

Jean no longer being together) and after a few drinks becomes insufferable. Recently with Horace Cayton* present he became so insulting that I had to threaten to take his head off, after which he calmed down, but I am afraid he will never forgive me. It gives me real agony to see a man so much in the clutches of the furies. Horace, by the way seems is much better shape and is leading a quiet life. At the moment he is very much interested in the problems of Africa. And while I am thinking of that group of people, did you see that John Woodburn died? And did you know that Sylvia (Wading River) too is gone? And that John Rothschild and Connie are no longer together?

By the way, James Baldwin was in to see me in September just before we moved (you will note that our address is 730 Riverside Drive—a nice apartment after almost eight years) and I had a long talk with him about writing and France, finding him very intelligent but very tied up. Recently, the publishers sent me bound galleys of his novel,† which is the best work on Negro religious conversion that I have seen thus far. I do think, however, that Baldwin could have gotten a bit closer to the material if he could have gotten rid of whatever it is that makes him feel the necessity of projecting such powerful material armored in Jamesian prose. I expect much better things of him in future books. Do you have other protégées floating around? One thing that I am a little sorry about is that right now I know of no young Negro writers here in the States with whom I can talk over the problems of craft and technique. On the other hand, I keep running into young white writers who are very eager. This is frustrating to me because I feel the responsibility of passing along some of the stuff which I learned from you and which I have to dig out for myself. The only young Negro writer I know of any promise is a fellow that I went to school with at Tuskegee. His name is Albert Murray and you might have met him in Paris last summer. He never ceases to amaze me because, while living at Tuskegee where he teaches, he remains alert to the latest literary and intellectual currents. Looks like a typical southern Joe College and yet is passionately involved with ideas.

I have a French publisher now—some subsidiary of Gallemard but I can't remember the name, nor do I know when they will publish it or who is to do the translating. Should you have heard who it is, please let me know. Gollantz brought the book out a few days ago in England.

---

* Cayton was a prominent sociologist who co-authored with St. Clair Drake the landmark study *Black Metropolis: A Study of Negro Life in a Northern City* (New York: Harcourt Brace, 1945).

† Baldwin's first novel, *Go Tell It on the Mountain,* was published in February 1953.

Meantime, good luck with *The Outsider* and our best to you and Ellen and the two girls.

Sincerely,

Ralph

To Albert Murray
WINSTON SALEM, NC
MARCH 18, 1953

Dear Al,

They've got the old rabbit back in the patch, wearing a black robe and trying to outdo ole Barbee!* All I needed was to have you in the audience to give me a few amens while I riffed. I'll write you from the Apple.

Rhine

To Stanley Edgar Hyman
730 RIVERSIDE DRIVE
NEW YORK 31, N.Y.
APRIL 1, 1953

Dear Stanley:

Hurray for the good news! I suppose by now you have received my card from North Carolina. I went to Bennett College at Greensboro to deliver the keynote speech for their Homemaking Institute—the theme of which was "Achieving Peace Through Creative Experiences." You would have had a big laugh to see me appear before the choir leaning against the pulpit and wearing a black robe. I wasn't able to tell so much about peace however, although I was quite pleased to find about as many bright girls as I used to find at Bennington. Bennet is also a girls' school and quite a nice one. Had a long talk with Robie MaCauley who teaches in the same city at Women's College.

Part of the time there was spent getting acquainted with cousins, many of whom I had no idea I possessed. I was pleased to see that they had done very well without me.

Yes, I would be quite glad to talk at Bennington in the fall. It would be

---

* Ellison (a.k.a. Rhine) refers to the Vespers keynote he gave at the opening of Bennett College Homemaking Institute in Greensboro on March 14 (see April 9, 1953, letter to Murray).

difficult before that time since the middle of this month will find me at Antioch College in Ohio and on to Fisk at Nashville and perhaps down to Tuskegee. There will also be a lecture at Princeton sometime during the spring and a trip to Oklahoma, all of which will make for a busy spring.

I don't feel so badly about the Hicks' review of Wright's book but what they did to him in *Time Magazine* was quite unfair, especially they're using me to beat him over his head for rejecting both Russia and America.* I suppose it was inevitable, since our positions on these matters are very much in opposition. Let me know what you think of the book, by the way, as I am writing a piece on "Negro Writing" for *Partisan Review* in which Wright's will be one of the books.†

Keep up the morale. Give Shirley and the children our love and if there is any possible break through which I or we can scoot to Bennington, I will be certain to take advantage of it.

> Sincerely,
> Ralph

To May Belle Johnston
730 RIVERSIDE DRIVE
NEW YORK 31, NEW YORK
APRIL 2, 1953

Dear May Belle:‡

Thanks very much for the birthday card and your letter. It is very good news to know that you and friends have helped the book. Until I received the clipping from the *Daily Oklahoman* I felt that no one in Oklahoma City except you and a few others knew about it, for I had received absolutely no mention of it in the *Black Dispatch*.

I remember very well reading the paper to you and being annoyed

---

* Granville Hicks's review of Wright's *The Outsider*, "Portrait of a Man Searching," had just appeared in *The New York Times Book Review* on March 22, 1953.

† *Time* magazine published a harshly critical review of *The Outsider* titled "*Native Son* Doesn't Live Here Anymore," claiming that Ralph Ellison had emerged as an "abler U.S. Negro novelist."

‡ The daughter of Lucretia Ellison Brown, sister of Ellison's father, Lewis Ellison, May Belle had accompanied Ralph when he was only three on a journey to the home of their grandfather Albert in Abbeville, South Carolina, shortly after the death of Lewis Ellison in July 1916. Here Ralph describes his recent visit to North Carolina, where he met with his cousin Alexander Morisey and Alexander's mother Mamie (Lewis's sister). This visit increased Ellison's desire to return to Oklahoma as he formulated early ideas for his second novel, some of which would emerge from his memories of his Oklahoma past.

by Bounce, just as I remember Dido and Sport and the bags of candy we used to consume together. There is so much about those days that I remember that I am sure you would be surprised. I remember not only the people who lived in the neighborhood but things which happened in the house, including the food which was eaten and the time we dug up the whiskey in the backyard and the bribe I was given so that I wouldn't tell Son.

I plan to come to Oklahoma City this spring or summer, so there will be ample time to reminisce. Please say nothing about my plan, however, as I would like to sneak in and look around for a few days as part of the book I am planning and I wouldn't want people putting on their Sunday manners before I look into a few things.

It was very nice of Grace to let you know that I was on the radio. Two weeks ago I was in Greensboro where I lectured at Bennet College and I was the guest at the home of Ethel and Ran Anderson, our cousins. I was also in Winston Salem where I stayed with Juanita and Alex and was at last able to meet Aunt Mamie. She was so much like your mother that I found myself carried back many years and was able to learn quite a bit about some of my own family traits. For instance, I recognized for the first time that some of Aunt Teat's humor and my own which I thought I had simply picked up from her is really part of the Ellisons' expression and was no doubt part of my father's. Certainly, you, Frances and Tom have it. I had planned to spend a day with her but was too busy with the college at Greensboro to get back in time. The first opportunity, however, I shall visit her again because I enjoyed talking with her very much.

It is good to know that Son and Frances are doing well. I look forward to seeing all of you quite soon. Herbert is in Los Angeles and as far as he will let me know, he seems to be all right. Unfortunately, Fanny and I have no pictures at the moment but I shall [have] one made very soon and will see that you get one.

Please give my regards to everyone who remembers me and I shall let you know when I plan to visit Oklahoma.

Fanny joins me in love and best wishes to you and yours.

Sincerely,
Ralph Ellison

Mrs. May Belle Johnston
1324 N.E. 10th St.
Oklahoma City, Okla.

To Alex and Juanita . . .
NEW YORK 31, N.Y.
730 RIVERSIDE DRIVE
APRIL 9, 1 9 5 3

Dear Alex and Juanita:*

Now that my visit with you has been long enough past for it to settle down
into the bright images of pleasure that it most certainly was I find myself
slowed down just enough to write you. Indeed, I was so caught up in
speechmaking and such that I finally got myself down with a bug and have
been forced to spend most of this week in bed. Perhaps it is just as well,
for I shall be at Fisk around the 22nd and for that stint I'll need the rest.
Certainly I'll need rest if I'm to be as stimulated by Fisk as much as I was
by Winston-Salem and Greensboro! I've had my friends laughing over my
experience with the black robe and the pulpit during vespers at Bennett,
not to mention my sitting up having tea with Jones and Bluford. They're
calling me Rinehart, but were seriously interested in my report on the
changes that I found in the South. Most were pleased, but there were
some, mostly Negroes, who prefer not to believe that there has been improvement. What an emotional stake some of them have in the old, harsh,
bitter, condition of Negroes. And when I tell them that there are perhaps
areas of Negro white relationships in which the whites are prepared to
move faster than we are pushing them, I am felt to be not only lying but
mad. I suppose the possibility of a real change in race relations frightens
them. So they will, I hope, be disappointed.

Alex, I read your material for the Nieman Fellowship and I see nothing
to add; however I plan to show them to Earl Brown as soon as I can find
him at home. He lives just two floors above me but is so busy that he's
rarely there except late at night. Perhaps he'll have some suggestions. It
occurs to me that you might talk with Allen Raymond about this project.
He just might have an idea or two.

I can't tell you how much I enjoyed being there; especially meeting
your mother, who along with Ethel opened up vistas of the past which I
thought forever closed. I thought, incidentally, that I had Ren and Ethel's

---

* Ralph's cousin Alex Morisey and his wife, Juanita, whom Ralph had just visited in North
Carolina.

address but can't for the life of me find it; please give them my regards and tell her not to forget to look us up when she visits her daughter. Fanny was very pleased to hear that her old friend Mrs. Malloy is a friend of yours as she is one of those at Fisk whom she remembers with highest pleasure. For myself I got a real kick out of old John Hauser, tell him that when he writes that novel I want to be one of the first to see it. I asked Teddy Wilson if he remembered John at Talladega and he said that he did. It was unfortunate that I had no chance to talk to Wilson before he came to Winston-Salem, as he might have looked you up. Tell T. Diggs that Spinky sends his regards, as of course do I.

Please give my regards to the rest of the family, especially the children. I'm sorry that I'm too dam beat to make this an interesting letter, the penicillin is getting in the way of my inspiration. However I'm enclosing my speech that might make up for it in part. Our plans for the summer extend no further than May 5th, when I shall, on my return from Antioch College in Ohio, lecture at Princeton. The general idea is that I, or we, shall get out to Oklahoma, but when, how, or by what route is still undecided. Perhaps I'll get back to pick up where I left off after all. I really hope so. At any rate it was wonderful being with you and thanks.

Sincerely,
Ralph

To Albert Murray
730 Riverside Dr.
New York 31, N. Y.
April 9 1953

Dear Murray:

Man, I hope you received my postal from Greensboro, as I was so close to the cotton patch as I have been in sixteen years, and I wanted you to know just in case those crackers jumped salty. As it was they treated me fine: plenty of newspaper space, photos, two interviews Winston-Salem and one in Greensboro; a TV show, during which I was interviewed by Robie McCauley (who incidentally, invited me to lecture to one of his classes at the Women's College—unfortunately I couldn't do)—in short, those people are acting civilized. Seriously, it was a most rewarding trip, especially meeting some of the very intelligent little girls at Bennett, where a young white instructor from Boston has done quite a job of introducing them to modern lit. There were also a few old heads who seemed to look ahead; indeed there were several who went through *Invisible* like trained critics. They reminded me of ole Eubanks, who discussed the book in terms of levels! Man, I'm not lying, I swear. Eubanks* says to me, "Ellison, you know you're a hell of a nigguh? This goddamn stuff is History, man. It's <u>history</u>! You read this shit one time and you get to thinking about it and you go back, and damn if you don't find something else. You got to dig that stuff man, 'cause it's loaded!" There was a little guy in Winston-Salem, a much more literate man, who kept me up all night talking about things which I aroused in him. He told me that I had completely bewildered Saunders Redding until he (John Hauser) and my cousin had straightened Redding out. He was so aroused that he swears that he (Hauser) is going to write a five foot bookshelf full of novels from things which I left for others to take off from. Man, that little Negro (he looks like a younger version of Brockway) is <u>extremely</u> gone! He's kind of a village atheist, only he's far more intelligent and forceful, who gets a bang out of shocking the <u>ignorant</u> educated Negros, with whom he refused to identify himself—although his job as manager of a housing project should make him a member of the club. It's always good to be the kindred soul.

In Greensboro I was twice a guest at the home of Eva Hamlin Miller. Little bouncy butt has two boys, is married to a successful dentist known as "Slick," and owns what is really the show place of the Negro side of town. On one visit I was guest of the Greensboro Men's Club, which is quite exclusive, I'm told. All I can say is that the Negroes were served some fine food that we gave no quarter, and good whiskey with which to wash it down. Beyond that we might have been an evening bullshitting with the boys on the block in front of Sage Hall. Up here, the big Negroes start out their affairs as pretentious as hell and have to knock out about a fifth of booze apiece before they settle down to enjoying themselves, but these Greensboro studs started preforming the moment they hit the door. I like that. Boy, but their local versions of some of the fancier men's fashions knocked me out; the cat who started that fancy vest business should be jailed, because there are one or two studs in Greensboro who have taken it and committed a crime against the western aesthetic!

But let me tell you what happened to me. On the 15th of March I made the keynote speech opening Bennett's Homemaking institute. Well, I had

---

* Tuskegee graduate, manager of food service at the Harlem YMCA, and friend of Ellison's and Murray's.

arrived at Winston-Salem on Saturday, where I spent the day and night with my cousin and his family, who drove over to Bennett about noon. First there was lunch with the student body and then Dr. Jones walked me over to his office, where a reporter and photographer from one of the local papers waited to interview and photograph me, after which I sat and talked with Jones a while. It was then that things started taking off. When it became time for vespers he hands me a black robe, which he tells me I am to wear. Man, I started to cut out right there, but as <u>he</u> was getting into his black robe I got into mine, then we went stroking out [along] the tree-lined walk [to] the chapel building, nodding to teachers and townspeople and young females all a-blooming and a-smiling in the spring sunlight. Well, in the vestry of the chapel Jones produces a printed card from his sleeve and say to me quite confidentially, "Don't let this bother you, but you speak right here." I looked. It was the order of the Methodist service and he was pointing to where it said SERMON.

Man, I really start to protest. But Doc looked at me as thought to say "come on, m.f., this ain't the time to start no shit." The next thing I know I'm walking with him, a preacher and a very young chick, back behind the choir stall where the machinery that drives the organ bellows was pounding away and snatching me back to years ago when I had played in such a passageway when I was a child. From then on it was a nightmare. We divided, the preacher and the chick going to one side, Jones and me to the other then to march ceremoniously upon the platform to come to rest, each group of us behind a pulpit! Behind me the organ, before the Gothic space and upturned faces. The organ is strictly brooding and upper register, and then in the distance, unseen and to the rear and above the congregation, sweet girlish voices began intoning the beginning of the Methodist ritual and the slow ho-ly, ho-ly, ho-ly ritual march beginning in the now opened doors on both sides of the chapel, sweet and ethereal down the length of the room and up to take their places behind us on the platform.

Well, gate, my past hit me like a ton of bricks. I know all the hymns, and the whole order of service and in spite of everything the emotions started striking past my defenses, not a religious emotion, but that of <u>remembering</u> religious feeling—that perhaps is little different. Anyway, there I was in a black robe, sharing a hymnal with the doctor (LL.D) with my throat throbbing and my speech notes rendered worthless because of the atmosphere. Someone had been so naive as to select "achieving peace through creative experiences" as the theme of the institute, and I knew that I wasn't going to tell them that creative experience brought peace, but only a fighting chance with the chaos of living. I looked down there at those chicks, man and felt that I was a repentant Rinehart. I was full of love for them because they were young and black and hopeful and, like all the young, prepared to be swindled by another four flusher who had no idea of what it meant to be young, idealistic and willing to learn. I could hardly talk, but I tried to level with them; tried to direct them towards reality and away from illusion. Once I heard my voice and, Jack, it was as sad and gloomy a voice as I've ever heard; and I knew then why even the most sincere preacher must depend upon rhetoric, raw communication between the shaman and the group to which he's spiritually committed is just too overpowering. Without the art the emotion would split him apart.

That's about it. Evidently I was effective. During the days that followed the kids kept coming up to speak about it and to ask questions. And all I had done really, was to tell them to dig the world each for himself. I took part in two of the workshops, one on creative writing and one on poetry. You should have heard me reading *The Wasteland* to those chicks! It's easy to make a fool of yourself around that many young gals.

Man, I must have a million cousins in N.C. I met one of my father's sisters and a cousin who knew my mother and father before they were married. What was more I got a chance to learn how many of what I thought were my own special characteristics are really family traits. My aunt, whom I've never seen before, started kidding me in my own dam idiom! Man, I come from a line of mad studs. I learned that my granddad stood up in the street in South Carolina and talked a mob of mad crackers out of lynching one of his friends. All I can say is that the old man must have talked the unknown tongue. Anyway, he got away with it because he lived to look at me when I visited him when I was four.

It's good news that you're winding up on old Lil' Buddy, let me see it as soon as you're done. As for no. 2 I've been busy laying the structural framework. Thus far it looks like a much more complex book than *IM* and there are several things to be gotten into focus. Incidentally, I'm doing a piece on the background of Negro writing for *P.R.,* in which I plan to touch on Wright and Baldwin, both [of] whom have novels. Take a look at their works, I don't think either is successful, but both are interesting examples of what happens when you go elsewhere looking for what you already had at home. Wright goes to France for existentialism when Mose, or any blues, could tell him things that would make that cock-eyed Sartre's head swim. As for Baldwin, he doesn't know the difference between getting religion and going homo. Here he is trying to write about store-front religion with a style that one good riff from a Negro preacher's sermon would smash like a bomb.

Boy, I heard about that Victoria. You be careful and don't confuse it with one of those sabre jets. Incidentally I talked with Dr. Pat on the first of March, he told me to let him know if I plan to be down that way this spring and I intended to; now, with the news of his resignation, I suppose that's out. Nevertheless I plan to drive out to Oklahoma this spring and I might take the southern route, in which case watch out. I shall be at Fisk from the 21st to the 25th, at Antioch on the 30th (of April) and at Princeton on the 5th of May; after that I plan to scout the southwest. I've got to get real mad again, <u>and</u> talk with the old folks a bit. I've got <u>one</u> Okla. book in me I do believe. (Hey, I said both of them, ghostwriter and ghost rider, both of them sanctified and gone!) Speaking of Tuskegee, Chauncey Eskridge was through here the other day and he's one cat who really knocked himself out over knowing a guy who's written a book. He tells me that the new chaplain at Tuskegee tells him that the people there are making a game of trying to guess who I was talking about. You should set up a class in adult education down there, man, because some of those cats sound too simple for pity. And please keep them out of the city.

How did the interview with Duke go? I was at his opening at the Band Box. We've become friends with his sister, Ruth, after I was on her radio program a couple of times and have seen Duke at parties. The first time he went for Fanny like a glad dog making for a meat wagon, so all I did was head for his old lady and he stopped that crap. He's damn nice guy nevertheless.

The Faulkner meeting was very brief. I had gone to Random House on the morning of the Book Award Ceremony to be photographed with De-Voto and MacLeish, when Saxe Cummins* told me to come place my coat in his office and meet Bill Faulkner. So I went in and there, amid several bags (suitcases, man suitcases!), was the great man. You've heard the crap about his beat up clothes? Well, don't believe it. He's as neat as a pin. A fine cashmere sports jacket, Tattersall vest, suede shoes and fine slacks, the correct tie and shirt collar rolling down! And I mean <u>down</u> down. Saxe says, "Bill, I want you to meet Ralph Ellison. He's one of our writers who's won the National Book Award."

"Glad to meet you, Mr. Ellison," Faulkner says.

---

* Faulkner's editor at Random House.

"Well, Mr. Faulkner, this really completes the day for me," I said.

"Yes," he said, "I guess this really is a day for you."

"Ralph's book is *Invisible Man*," Saxe said.

"Yes, I know," Faulkner said. "Albert sent me a copy almost a year ago."

"You know," I said, "you have children all around now. You won't be proud of all of them, just the same they're around."

"Yes," Faulkner said, "I was surprised to learn how many people like the stuff."

"You shouldn't be at all surprised," I said. But on this lame note I was snatched away by some publicity person to stand beneath the photogs' lights. Later I saw Faulkner at the party but then it was all small talk over bourbon. He was quite friendly and shy and his voice is soft, southern and courteous. Last week I saw him at the men's faculty club at Columbia at a reception for a visiting Japanese intellectual. He was even more uncomfortable than me as we stood around with cups of tea listening to the Japanese be polite through an interpreter. I think Faulkner, whose hands perspired all through the show, cut out even before me. It was raining like a bastard outside, but he was dressed down. You thinks he's been hanging around with Mose?

MacLeish and DeVoto are both easygoing and friendly men, nothing stuffed shirt about them. You haven't seen the photos. I've a bunch of them here when you come up. Mrs. DeVoto sent me a translation from a Yugoslavian paper in which it was stated that both MacLeish and DeVoto were Negroes. She said, "Move over"; I said, "There's room for many a thousand mo'." Life is strange, isn't it? I had no idea that when I bought DeVoto's book that I'd ever meet him. I met and was photographed with Justice Douglas, also, but *Ebony* killed the pictures. He's more like a rancher than a judge and I liked him. A spade photographer had us holding hands for about twenty minutes, it seemed, but he took it as a joke. I told him if I never received justice again this was one time I had held its hand. Then he startled me by asking me if I had graduated from the University of Oklahoma—me with my black head!* Man, I'm sounding off. I'll be writing you about that sound system next time. You take it slow and give our regards to Mozelle and Mique.

As ever,

Ralph

---

* When Ellison went to college in 1933, the University of Oklahoma was still segregated.

What's up with Mort? I was talking with Frank Taylor and Jim Agee about his attending Hamilton College and they, who both are graduates were surprised. Give him and Mike my best.

Speaking of M.D. reminds me that I used the Tuskegee library to point up to the kids at Bennett the kind of freedom that lies available in the south but which is too often ignored. I told them what a wonderful collection of books I found there through a few people's thinking and working not as Negroes but as librarians and scholars and who were building something of value to any human being with the intelligence and curiosity to use it. Naturally I was signifying, man; but I get a kick out of seeing Negroes from liberal arts schools puzzle over how a writer could come out of Tuskegee. I wish you could come up to Fisk, Bontemps hinted in the *SRL* that I had created another stereotype and I'm going to talk on minority provincialism as a problem for the creative writer. One thing I intend to do is point out where the so-called New Negro boys crapped up the picture. I don't know why those guys want to mess with a contentious Mose like me anyway; I done told them I ain't no gentleman, black or white, and I definitely ain't colored when it comes to writing.

> Tushhoggedly yourn,
> Elli

To Herbert Ellison

JUNE 5, 1953[*]

Dear Herbert:

I've been running around so much since January that I've found very little time to write anything, including letters. I suppose you know by now that my book won the National Book Award for Fiction, which carries no money but quite a lot of prestige <u>and</u> what is much better an increase in sales. As a result I've been to Greensboro, N.C., where, during March, I lectured at Bennet College for several days and had the pleasant experience of meeting our cousin Ethyl who lives there and who is old enough

[*] The 5 and 3 in the erroneous 1935 date on Ellison's carbon seem transposed, since all the details he briefs Herbert on took place in spring 1953. The brothers had not seen each other since 1938, when Ralph left Dayton to return to New York permanently. Herbert moved to Los Angeles after serving in the armed forces in World War II. In this letter Ralph catches Herbert up on relatives on their father's side, whom he's recently visited in North Carolina, and on their mother's side in Dayton. He also offers to pay Herbert's way to Oklahoma City in July.

to remember quite a lot about our father. She is the daughter of one of his older sisters, is married, and has herself three children. She is a very nice woman, very active in church work (she is an organist), and built like a small battle ship. But even more interesting, this trip allowed me to visit Winston-Salem where Alexander Morisey and his family and mother, who is our aunt Mamie, lives. She is an invalid now, having suffered a stroke last year and just recently an amputation of her left leg. She looks like a slimmer much better looking version of Aunt Teat, talks something like her, and despite her illness, laughed and joked with me and seemed very much like someone I'd known for years. She and all the others asked of you and I was embarrassed no end that I could tell them so little. Alexander is a reporter on one of the white newspapers and is a nice easy-going fellow whom I'm sure you'd like. He has three children, a fine young woman of twelve (she's quite large for her age) a boy of nine, and a little bitch whom I can't stand of five or six. I'm sure you'd find them interesting.

Well, that was one trip, later I went to Fisk, my wife going along this time, driving with me to her old school here where I had a seminar in creative writing. It was all very pleasant, but there were two surprises: just as I finished my lecture I looked into the face of someone whom I thought was John A. Townsend—it was his son! Later I had to go out to A&E, which is the state college for Negroes, and there I met Hilliard Bowed. Hilliard teaches there, is married and the father of a fine young daughter and is very much the guy I remember from Okla. You know, this must be my year to retrace my steps about the country, for not long after we returned from Fisk I was on my way to Antioch College, which is located at Yellow Springs, Ohio. The plane landed in Dayton and I went about trying to find our old friends, but in vain. Lawyer Stokes* is dead, Ferris Williams is dead and Leroy has sold out and moved away, the streets are the same but the people are very much changed. I couldn't even see old John Strange, although he is still there. I did see his wife, however, for when I went out to Gold street to take a look at the old place I couldn't find it, they had made a duplex out of it by moving in another house about the same size, so that in order to get my bearings I went on to the Johnigans—and that was the start of a real three ring circus.

When I walked up on the porch Ruby was talking on the telephone and upon seeing her gesture I opened the door and started in. Well, man, the

---

* W. O. Stokes, who generously allowed Ralph the use of his office to work and even to sleep in during the winter of 1937–38.

fool screamed, jumped up hysterically and told [me] to get out. I didn't know whether to slug her or to run, but instead of either I yelled "Hey, I'm Ralph Ellison!" Upon which she turned right around and ran up to me and kissed me, after which things quieted down—just for a minute. All the old folks are dead now and Ruby lives there alone, the other girls being married and having their own places. Even those two kids are away in college. They don't have the beauty school anymore, but that Bernice is married to a preacher and when she came over hell started popping. Ruby called everyone she could think of to come over to meet me. First came Mrs. Strange who now lives in the little house on the alley. She is very much the same, the same slow speech, the same disrupted house; although now the three children running around are those of Elizabeth, her oldest child. The other is about to be married and the little boy is now one big soldier boy over in Korea. She and John are divorced and he is married again. His foster parents have passed and I'm told that he inherited the property and is now in the contracting business. As I talked with her I recalled very vividly those cold nights we spent sleeping in that car because of her, though I don't hold it against her. She is a sad woman.

The others came together: Bernice, Mary Moon, and Betsy Camp. And if it hadn't been for that Bernice it would have been very pleasant. The two older ladies were simply interested in talking to one of Mama's boys, Bernice wanted to get her name in the newspapers. Before I knew anything that fool had gone upstairs and called the press. Suddenly a white girl and a photographer appeared to interview me and she insisted upon getting in the picture. It was very amusing because I really didn't care but I said nothing, just watched to see if she would come right out and say what she wanted—and she did. You would have laughed yourself sick to see that stupid woman go for that reporter. I think she embarrassed everyone but me. Unfortunately I had only a couple of hours in Dayton and there's little I can tell you. It is still more a place for my memories and I suppose it'll remain that way until such time as I can visit it for a long period, or until I write the memories out of my head. I learned that Aunt Annie had died some years ago, but could get no line on Frederick; if you have an address sent it to me as I'd like to look him up should I go through Cincinnati.

The next trip took me to Chicago, this time to receive a citation from the *Chicago Defender*. I wanted to look up Uncle Will and Aunt Minnie, but I didn't know where to start so from that point of view it was as bad a blank as the Walcott-Marciano fight. Though I think I must have caused that washout, for anytime someone gives me a fifty-dollar seat to a fight something is due to go wrong. Chicago is my wife's hometown and though she didn't go along everyone was nice to me because of her. The only Oklahoman I saw was Troy Jackson, whose son used to play football with me. They live in Oakland, I believe.

That is a pretty good idea of what I've been doing lately. I've made quick trips to Princeton University, where I [. . .] and another to Springfield, Mass. where I presented [. . .] an oil painting of what will be the jacket illustration of my book when it comes out in a paper backed edition (It'll be published by Signet, for fifty cents, so watch out for it.) to a leading wholesaler of books and magazines. That's it until the middle of the month, when I intend to visit Oklahoma City for the first time since 1935. It won't be for pleasure, however, but to refresh my memories and emotions, as I suspect that our lives there might have something to do with my next book. Anyway I want to return before all the old-timers are gone, or before I'm gone myself. It would be wonderful if we could meet there, so if it's at all possible let me know and I'll do what I can to help you out. I thought I'd stick around for two weeks—if those Negroes don't make me angry all over again. Anyway, you write me airmail if you're interested and let me know the train fare from L.A. and return. Incidentally, Langston Hughes is in L.A. now and has asked me for your address so don't be surprised if you see him.

Herbert, Aunt Mamie has asked to see a photo of you so if you find it possible—it need be nothing fancy, just one of those you make yourself in a machine for a quarter—I think you would give her a great deal of pleasure. She's paralyzed and unable to do more than read and think of the past and just a cheap photo means much to her. You might write her if you like, or send it along to me. Her address is 1823 East Third Street, Winston-Salem, N.C. c/o Mr. A.A. Morisey.

Well, that's about it; we are both fairly well and taking on weight. Mr. McGruder sent me that portrait of one made when I was about sixteen years old, and boy did I look different. Then I had too much hair, now most of it is gone from the top of my head. Well a man grows old and he loses the innocence from his eyes, fat clusters about his middle and gaps appear in his smile, he stays indoors too much and paleness takes the color from his skin and puts a wheeze in his breath when he tries to run— nevertheless there are worse things and I'm still trying to get a few things done. You take it easy and write soon.

Love,
Ralph

To Fanny Ellison
1224 N.E. TENTH ST.
OKLAHOMA CITY, OKLA.
JULY 2, 1953.

Dear Fanny:

I left Tuskegee on Monday, flying from Montgomery around four o'clock on a flight which carried me through Mississippi, La. and Texas; where at Dallas I changed airlines and proceeded, after a lay-over of about an hour, through the hot night sky, to Oklahoma City. We alighted about twelve o'clock and I took the limousine to the greatly expanded city, where I called my cousins. It was very amusing, for just as I stepped out of the car who should I see coming up the street smoking a cigar but Frank Mead, the boy who lived next door to the house where I spent some of the happiest days of my childhood. We must have talked an hour or longer before I realized that I was keeping my cousin waiting and grabbed a cab for her house. Since then I have been working during the hot mornings (not very successfully) and have gone around looking up old scenes and acquaintances during the afternoons and evening. I haven't seen too many thus far, but yesterday the Negro press learned that I was around and it won't be long before everyone will know it.

The city has changed, grown; but not so much that my dreams of it are invalid; for I can see the stages of metamorphosis undergone by many of the buildings, and sections, and even some of the people. I'll have to save most of this for later, especially the people, because I haven't seen many of the special ones. Of this I am certain however, one must return home after many years in order to learn some things about people, for it is only in one's home town, where we know the beginnings of personalities: childhood, adolescence, and now adulthood, that we can see them in any fullness of perspective. Already I can see the effects of sloth and ambition, indulgence and discipline, illusion and reality, and age and desire, sickness and health, defeat and triumph; the decline and fall of old stars, the rise and shine of new. For here, as in Tuskegee, I can see the harsh reversal in the lives of certain people who affected my own destiny in terms of such tragedy that I feel pity in my heart—even for Captain Neely,[*] a proud man

---

[*] Neely was dean of students at Tuskegee, known for, in Rampersad's words, "his weakness for young boys." Ralph harbored a deep resentment for many years over Neely's abusive treatment of him.

broken upon the wheel of his own arrogance, if ever there was one. But there are also those who have remained young and alive despite change of fortune and the ravages of time—and that too is part of the story. I'll tell you all about them when I return, for there are still so many of the important ones to be seen and talked with. I still don't know what will become of it but certainly there is enough working upon my memories (you'll really be surprised how good my memory is—along certain lines) and emotions . . . And I wish you were here and that you could see me now, for my skin has burned black again and you with your sweet madness would lie and say, "Darling, you're beautiful!" But nevertheless, I am brown and, I believe, much stouter than when I left home; though I'm not sure. For here there are so many people who haven't seen me in twenty years and who will re-mark upon my height and girth and width, until perhaps I'm beginning to see myself in their eyes. Speaking of time, I haven't reset my watch on this trip because it is a steady concrete, audible link-and-reminder that I am living twenty years in the past when I'm here. For only with you is that my reality: at six, you roll over, at seven arise, at nine, rush for the street and the subway stairs; at twelve grow hungry; at three pant in the heat of the afternoon; and at six roll home. Last night I grew lonely and thought of coming home, but that would turn the trip into an indulgence, since I've done so little of what I came here to do: still, the homing pigeon instinct is strong within me. What do you do, dear, in the dark of the night? In the quiet of the room? Last night I lay with moonlight falling across my bed and thought of you until I got up and lowered the blind upon the damned thing. No sense of the fitting, I'd say; and here it's so much larger, and so much lower than it's ever been over New York. Skyscrapers in the way, I suppose.

Fanny, you would have been amused to see me at Tuskegee, gently kid-ding those who predicted the chain gang for me, meeting the old tim-ers and/new-comers alike; and, most astounding of all, making the main speech during chapel services. Every one of my old friends on the faculty and administration were trying to get me to the new president, so that I ended up by seeing him at lunch and dinner on the same day. I'm to be asked formally to return there in the fall for lecture or a series of seminars, to be decided later, and there was some talk of a visiting professorship. I found the new man friendly and intelligent and not at all pompous. High hopes are held for him by Mort and Murray [and] some of the others.

Mozelle really took good care of me and I learned that you can't know her until you see her at home. I stayed with them, sleeping on Mique's bed while she slept in the living room. During the day I had the use of Albert's car while he was at work and was thus able to visit all my old haunts, and many of the new sections that have grown up since my days there. Chenault asked of you as did the Dawsons, who came out to Murray's as soon as they heard that I was in town and later I had dinner at their home; after which Dawson played tapes of music which he recorded when he was in Africa. You would have liked it, and as soon as it is possible we'll have to make the trip together.

I'm spending my nights and mornings now with Maybelle, whose husband (an older man) is a real Brockway, in the better sense of the term. We've been kidding one another since we were introduced and she says that he was predicting that I was coming a week before I arrived. Right now in the heat of the day he's outside without hat or shirt working in his garden and with his prize pigeons. He claims that I broke the drought that has lasted for some time, and which isn't really broken (although it did rain upon my arrival, as it did in Tuskegee) and he calls me Rainmaker. He's from Wichita and claims that he can make a tomato plant bear fruit in three days. I won't try to describe him, you'll just have to meet him— which I'm sure you'll do, since he says he intends to live one hundred and seventy-five years. I asked him why he kept moving around so much, and he said that if he sat down people would discover that he was dead. A real character, as you can see.

So much for that. The heat is getting me and I must go out and see some people. I don't know when to say I'll return; I've been so busy trying to finish the story that I haven't seen any of the older people and they're my main objective. However, hold out enough money from the check to pay for my flight fare plus eleven dollars overweight baggage (one stop flight, if possible), and don't worry about anything else; or of the money I started with I have about 302.00 left, which should be enough to keep me going. Should you find it necessary to call me, the number is Regent 6-7203, and there is usually someone here. The address is above. So take it easy, don't let the office get you down, and write me a note: especially if you run into trouble with the little man. I won't stay here longer than necessary, I'm trying to watch my diet (although I <u>did</u> eat some barbecue late the other night and paid for it (it was worth it, the sauce and flavor being just as I remember it, I'll try to bring you some of the sauce) and with the heat I'm getting a reasonable amount of sleep. If it's hot there, remember that the movies are cool. Take care of yourself, and remember that I love you.

Ralph

P.S. Please send me a picture of you, and Herbert's and Virgil's addresses. But especially the picture.

Random House's address
New American Library address

Oklahoma City, Okla
JULY 15, 1953

Dear Folks,

I've been here about three weeks and this being twenty years in the past is getting me down. Miss you all heap much. Write from heap big city where take big root with chief squaw. Night too lonely in homa Red Man, how!

Ellison

To Albert Murray
730 RIVERSIDE DRIVE
NEW YORK 31, N.Y.
JULY 24, 1953

Dear Albert:

I've finally returned from my jaunt into the past, somewhat tired but up to neck in experience. I don't know what the hell will come of it, but there's no denying that I've had it. I stayed in Oklahoma City a week and a day, and despite Phillips having contaminated the plane, the flight from Montgomery was without incident. I must have hung around the Dallas airport for over an hour before my plane came, then within another hour I was at home once more.

It's very amusing how things worked out, for once in the city proper I had no more than started removing my bags from the limousine than I looked up to see my boyhood buddy coming along smoking a cigar. It was as though he'd been sent as a welcoming committee, man. We must have talked for two hours before we realized that it was after two o'clock in the morning and that we'd both better be getting along, although at that hour the streets seemed remarkably full of Negro bellhops, taxi drivers and Indians. That's my hometown! My friend said he'd been talking about me constantly for over a week but that he had just returned from a trip, and thus didn't qualify as a welcoming committee, though he was damn glad to see me. Nevertheless, he was good medicine; it was as warm a return home as ever I've had (excepting, of course, my returns to Fanny, who this time greeted me with chilled champagne and glowing eyes).

Indeed, that's one town in which I just drip with <u>charisma</u>! Not only were most people glad to see me and buddies now from way back, having bitten the nipples on the same breast and bottles together, and shared the same adventures and loves and hates (though some such professors were at least as old as my dad) they all wanted to tell me what kind of guy I was and the good things they predicted for me. And there were newspaper stories and receptions given by the city libraries, with some of the Negro clubs (including the Tuskegee bunch) participating. And there were all the old teachers who many a rough day ago had wished me not only dead, but thronged with worms, now taking credit for having made me what I am today—whatever the hell that is! But that's life, I suppose, and that's the way it's supposed to be. So I forgive them their lies if they forgive me mine and say, "I'm your own dear baldheaded, tense-bellied, world-weary boy; thy very own!" Yes, and let them watch me like hawks and harpies, waiting to see if I'd grown a tail or spoke Shakespearean jive out of my anus, or walked on my elbows. Then, "Gee, you haven't changed at all. You still have your baby face!"

And bears! Man, that's the top town in the nation for the study of bearology. They've got all kinds, little, big, medium, monstrous and lil' biddy bears. And many of them my friends from way back, though others have become bears since I left home—which, God knows is long enough to do even Goldilocks in. But many are young bears with ideas and who have come up in the last few years. But boy, they're all authentic ... "Now don't tell me this is <u>Raf</u>... come on over here boy, and hug me (this from some fool I wouldn't have hugged even twenty years ago). You living in New York now I hear. They tell me you New York fellows is rough on women." Or "Boy, your wife sure don't know what she's doing, letting you come running down here by yourself. I'm liable to decide to keep you down here myself." (This from my lady King-Konga!) And from another while dancing, "Mr. Ellison, have your forgotten your western boy ways?" Or, "Raf, I bet you down here just giving these old nowhere-Okla City women a fit. I remember you, you that quiet, straight-faced kind. I got the dope on you. You better come and see me before I get in touch with the

Black Dispatch." And upon being introduced to another, who thinks I've forgotten her, "What's my name? I know you've forgotten me!" And then, when I've identified her, remembering what a bitch she used to be: "that's it, but don't say my name like that, honey, you make me nervous! Ha, ha, how'd you ever remember me? Done made a fine young man, too—How's that you said my name?" Bears will be bears.

And of course all the Negroes were busy waiting to see what would develop between me and my love of twenty-three years ago, wishing for some scandal, or perhaps hoping for some affirmation that true love never dies. Anyway, I met her husband at least a dozen [times] and he never once mentioned her name. Which of course was stupid, since she <u>did</u> come of her own regard for times past (she and my mother were good friends) to see me; just as I would have gone to see her had he been a bit less of a fool. Just the same, I'm not ashamed of my taste in women, even for those adolescent days—though how she let herself be sucked into marrying that joker is beyond me. No, don't tell the answer . . . let sleeping lovers lie, and lie, and lie.

I found that my memory of the city and the people extremely vivid, although both have changed. Some years ago a Mose who drove for the governor caused a lot of excitement by pitching him a ball in the blue room of the capital building, a formal boogie, man! Well, today Mose is living within spitting distance of the capital and the white folks are accepting our presence with a certain amount of grace. The city has expanded tremendously and there are several new additions financed by Negroes, and for the first time in the history of the city large number of Negroes are living in houses that were never the whites' to abandon. All in all, it's a prosperous town, too, and what with the continuous decentralization of our industry, should continue to grow. The people are still aggressive, though some of the old teachers are discovering that they really want segregation and are trying to discourage their students from attending the University of Oklahoma. They aren't getting anywhere, however, and I'm told that over three hundred Negroes are attending classes there. The old order changeth and a lot of asses are out in the cold wind of reality. But for the provincialism, I'd return there to live. I made it fine until evening, then I missed Fanny, the city, music, books or just conversation. Time would adjust that, I know, but then there's so little time . . . Boy, but the barbecue is still fine and the air is still clean and you can drive along in a car and tell what who is having for dinner; and it's still a dancing town, and a good jazz town, and a drinking town; and the dancing still has grace. And it's still a town where the eyes have space in which to travel, and those freights still making up in the yard sound as good to me as ever they did when I lay on a pallet in the moon-drenched kitchen door and listened and dreamed of the time when I would leave and see the world.

All in all, it was good to return, though so many, many of the old ones whom I'd hoped to see have died. And I couldn't see the old fellow who led the migration to what is the present Negro section because only a few days after I was there his wife (the mother of the jerk who married my old girl) was killed with his sister in a car accident. I've been asked to lecture at Langston* during the coming year so perhaps I'll see him then.

Perhaps one of the nicest things to happen to me came when the Randolph-Slaughter-Rhone clan (these are the "family" from which I was estranged when I learned that one of the wives has accused her husband of being my father, and to which up to that time I had felt as close, if not closer, as to my blood relatives) were called together for a Sunday morning breakfast. There were some twenty of us, including several lively children, and we ate tons of chicken and drank gallons of coffee and just played havoc with the hot biscuits and looked over old photographs (gad, but I was a big-headed brat!) and relived old times until well into the afternoon. The sad thing about it, of course, was that so many were missing: my mother and father (who I learned used to say that he was raising me for a poet? Poor man.) and their mother and father and grandfather and great grandmother, those to whom it would have meant more than it did to any of us, unless myself. So we broke bread together and there was forgiveness, even for her who caused me all that damn trouble. Which is what growing up is for and homecoming too. So, I came and there was much for me to be forgiven, though not so much from the clan and I received it. I suppose now that I'll spend the next twenty years trying to understand what happened and how, and what was real and what was imaginary. But that's my role and I accept it.

Just the same I didn't forget how wonderful you and Mokie and Miquie were to me and I never will. This time I look forward eagerly to return, so don't let Foster forget that he's committed. Tell him, by the way, that

---

* Langston University, the only historically black college in Oklahoma, founded in 1890 in what was then the Territory of Oklahoma.

Fanny does indeed remember his wife, and pleasantly. Fanny says that she's a fine gal. She also gave me the good news about your story, and Arabel* wants very much to see the novel version, which I hope you'll consent to, even though you might have reasons for not having it published. Certainly it can only help, for Arabel is quite taken with Luzana.† I better close this now because I'm working on a paper on the novel to be read at the Harvard conference on the contemporary novel on the fourth of August. There'll be Simenon, Frohock, Hyman, Katherine Anne Porter, Frank O'Connor, Pierre Emmanuel, William Sloane, and Carvel Collins participating. I'm to speak thirty minutes about the American novel that are apt to [be] thirty of the damnedest minutes I ever spent. This doggone integration thing maybe is going too fast. Anyway I'll write you how it goes, meanwhile take it easy and give my regards to Mike Rabb, Mort and Mann and the others, especially Mitch and Viv (that lovely woman) and tell Mort I'll write him soon and just to confound you I'm enclosing what came out of the typewriter when I sat down to test the keys upon my return. Guess the trip made me a little soft in the head. Just the same here it is.

Sincerely,

Ralph

P.S. I just talked to Laly and she says hi.

DEEP SECOND

> *Now when the plane-stirred winds drew down the enraptured*
> *   dawn*
> *I fell upon the slow-awakened past of joy*
> *Eagerly, eagerly, going forth to dawn-dance*
> *Diving blithely as a boy*
> *Plunging arrogantly twenty years through ordered space,*
> *And when to my older eyes the town appeared reduced and*
> *Dowdy as worn-out doll*

---

* Arabel Porter, editor of *New World Writing,* published by The New American Library of World Literature.

† Luzana, a guitar player in Murray's novel-in-progress, which, revised, would be published as *Train Whistle Guitar* in 1974.

Tossed into a corner of the newer city
There was only this to do; accept
Accept the smack, smack! of Time upon my flanks and
    plunge me boldly
Into that inner past to fit
The puzzle of now and then together
The girl and woman, man and boy;
Blue kites against the bluer sky and silver planes
Swimming beneath Arbuckle Mountain streams.
And learn that streets loom larger in the mind than ever
Upon the arches of the hills:
That kisses linger in the memory as indelibly as pain
Or harsh words thrown through the adolescent anger.
Fined too, the dream which went before the passion,
(That child father to the childish man) of him who
    dedicated me
That set me aside to puzzle always the past and wander blind
    within the present,
Groping where others glide, stumbling where other stroll in
    pleasure.
And now returning after all the years to crawl the paths
    most others
Had forgotten. My second coming into deep second, that
    frontier valley
Between two frontier hills, that world bounded by Walnut
    and Byers.
And then in the enraptured dawn at last possessing
That which all the others would now have lost;
The path still vivid, the old walks layered beneath present ways;
The inner houses behind the present walls revealed;
The earlier birdsong sound behind the now-dawn's awakening
    thrill.
And all the past was shaken up, and all the old speech singing
In the wind, and their once clear skins and once bright eyes
Looking through to see me in my passions venture.

Recaptured, held, their promise still promise and all their
    days dawn

In my awakened eyes. And me a red cock flaming on the hill,
Dying of the fire of past and present, and yet exalting
That in me and only me they live forever.
I who can give no life but of the word would give them all—
Their past unsullied and their present gleaming with
  child-smiles:
Their fathers rich with humanity and their mothers beautiful
And lovely: And their thoughts true and their actions wise;
And from that past we knew,
Would make for their children a dew-fresh world.
Oh, I would with them make of us all heroes and fliers,
Even now, though where once our blue kites dipped and sailed
I now plunge past in silvery planes—
Even in this Now, where derricks rise and engines throb upon
  our playing fields
And young girls laugh and glide within the room wherein my
  father died
And where my mother learned the grave transcendence of
  her pain—
Would make their heroes and world-makers and world-lovers,
And teach them the secret of that limping walk, that look of eye,
That tilt of chin, the world-passion behind that old
  back-alley song
Which sings through my speech more imperious than trumpets
or blue train sounds—
Yes, would heal the sick of heart and raise the dead of spirit
And tell them a story
Of their promise
And their glory.
Would sing them a song
All cluttered with my love and regret
And my forgiveness
And tell them how the flurrying of their living shaped
Time past and present into a dream
And how they live in me
And I in them

There it is, some of it sounds familiar, but for the life of me I can't be sure. Anyway, Deep Second is a block, or rather three blocks on East Second Street, wherein I spent much of my childhood and youth, and where I spent much of my time, talking and looking at the passersby upon my return. I was born not far from there, had my first job there, and my father died there in the old University of Okla. hospital building, which is now a Y.W.C.A. This ain't much but it's probably the first time anyone was mad enough to try to get Deep Two into a poem.

R.E.

To Albert Murray
FACULTY CLUB
HARVARD UNIVERSITY
CAMBRIDGE, MASSACHUSETTS
AUGUST 6, 1953

Dana-Palmer House

Dear Albert,

Up here you have to be pretty nimble, but there are a few fair squares, even here. We've had a fine, though rather hectic, time. Talk about the novel is running out of our ears.* Much of it too abstract and aloof. Which of course, left me a role to play.

To hear Anthony West, Frank O'Conner, Hyman, Simenon and all the rest boot the question of the "extended lie" around before about a grand of people is fun, if little else, yet I suspect that novel criticism will benefit. At least we all agreed that a more sensible terminology was necessary. This, by the way, might [be] an interesting place for you to teach. You'd be among peers, not dolts.

Incidentally, we're told that Henry James once lived in this house, which probably is true—I haven't been able to sleep in it.

Ralph.

---

* Ellison was invited to the conference on the American novel at the Harvard summer school. The event confirmed his confidence in his views on the American novel, and the experience was transformative for his sense of America and his relation to the country. See Rampersad, *Ralph Ellison,* 286–88.

To Jim and Madge Randolph
730 RIVERSIDE DRIVE
NEW YORK 31 NEW YORK
SEPTEMBER 18, 1 9 5 3.

Dear Jim and Madge:

Since leaving you I've been traveling so continuously that it looked as though I'd never get around to writing, or, for that matter, even to sending the copy of my speech that I now enclose. As planned we went to Harvard where we stayed for four days, taking part in the conference on the novel, the many parties, and spending our evenings in one of the faculty houses on the pleasant and tradition strewn campus. I was a bit awed over being asked to attend, but once we began the discussions I found myself on familiar, if not safe, ground and everything went well enough. Of one thing I'm certain: if we ever have a boy Harvard will be his college. The atmosphere there is so thick with learning, scholarship and freedom that most other schools I've seen are like imitations. As you can see I'm sold on the place.

That, however, was only the first of several trips. Later we visited friends in Williamston, Mass, and from there we went to Bennington VT, then up to Groton, Mass, and on up the state and eastwards to Cape Anne, spending most of a day at Gloucester before leaving to drive the coastline down to Cape Cod, where we spent our vacation fishing (quite unsuccessfully) for striped bass. The Cape is truly beautiful and even the Broadway-Coney Island aspect of its main street on Saturdays, when the boats run excursions from Boston, can't spoil Provincetown. Its quite old houses give you the feeling that the city didn't just grow, but was planned, carefully, from the very day the Pilgrims searched out the land and decided that Plymouth (or what they later named Plymouth) was a better land upon which to grow crops. As someone said, Provincetown is one town of which it can be truly said that there is nothing ugly about it. Even the lack of striped bass didn't spoil it and the only complaint I have is that we didn't stay long enough. For when we returned we ran smack into the hottest weather we've had here in years. We simply had to avoid the streets and all motion except the most necessary until the wave had passed. Now the weather is normal and I'm back at work, trying to clear up my correspondence, finish two essays, and work on my new novel.

There isn't time here to tell you how much being home again has meant to me, I can only say that you both had much to do with making it the deeply meaningful experience that it was. I only hope that Langston goes ahead and invites me to speak there this fall or winter, as they have threatened to do, so that I won't have to wait so long to see you again. If not, perhaps I'll have time from a planned trip to St. Louis to drop down. Meantime, until such time as I can bring me to Oklahoma, I'd like to bring some of Oklahoma to New York—I'd like to take you up on the offer to send me some chili. I'm enclosing a check for $10.00, if there's anything left just send me some Brown's Beauty Beans, which are not available up this way. Indeed, should you need more money to balance the chili with the beans and pay transportation costs, please wire me collect and I'll wire the money immediately. The more I think of chili the more homesick I become.

Please give my love to everyone and tell Sis that I tried to reach her from the airport the day I left, the last and most desperate of several efforts to remind her that she promised to have me a copy made of a certain photograph. Incidentally, I haven't yet stopped remembering things that wonderful breakfast in the country set off within me. Certainly nothing like it has ever happened to me before. I'm sure my friends are becoming a bit weary of hearing me talk about it; but then, when they ask me what happened on my trip I really try to tell them because I enjoyed myself. So now before I begin to bore you I shall call a halt and say goodbye with all my best wishes.

Sincerely,

Ralph Ellison

To Albert Murray
730 RIVERSIDE DRIVE
NEW YORK 31, N.Y.
SEPTEMBER 22, 1953

Dear Albert,

I had planned to wait until you returned from Cuba before answering your letter, but only today, while looking steadily and quite guiltily at the calendar, did I realize that you were not only back at Tuskegee but perhaps very much at work. We take it that you'll give us the high points of the trip when you get a chance.

As for us we've been very busy as usual. We spent part of Fanny's vacation up at Provincetown on Cape Cod, fishing unsuccessfully for striped bass; and besides trying to prepare a piece on the Negro and twentieth century fiction for *Confluence.** I've been converting my notes from the Harvard conference on the novel into an essay. (I see from your letter that I didn't go into details about that jaunt, thinking perhaps that the *Times* would carry a full report. Instead they gave the assignment to Frank O'Conner, with whom I clashed for hamming things up with his I-me-my Irish bullshit.) You'll notice that he doesn't mention me at all in his piece, but after I told him—over the air, though I didn't realize it at the time—that jokes were all very well, but that I hadn't realized that we'd been asked to Harvard as entertainers, otherwise I'd have prepared to tell a few jokes of my own, since I know a few good ones, he cut out some of the clowning and we were able to discuss a few ideas. Before that he was busy throwing his brogue and rep[utation] around, telling everyone how much better a writer than Joyce he was, sneering at every achievement of modern fiction, and when cornered, falling back upon theological arguments that were very much beside the point. Well, he does have an Abbey Theatre background and I guess that finding himself upon a stage before an audience of two thousand or more he couldn't resist going into his act. All he did for me was to get my Indian blood boiling and I went for him. I'm still hearing about how everyone was glad that I did. Besides if he is the champeen writer and intellectual of the century (incidentally I told him that a few of us knew who had done the real pioneer job of clearing the forest and sawing the wood from which his own work was able to take its meaning) then let the bastid act like one. Clowns? Hell, I've been teeing off on clowns all my life, and besides I don't think he's all that hell anyway. You should have been there, man, just to place a few good-sized hickeys on his ass. Anthony West revealed himself to be pretty much a creation of the library. When I spoke of the national framework of experience that affects the form of the novel, he confused it with nationalism as political philosophy; for a moment I thought I was arguing with Ralph Powe or Saunders Walker. Just the same it was a worthwhile experience and I did well enough to have them threaten to have me back next year.

---

* This became "Twentieth-Century Fiction and the Black Mask of Humanity." Ellison began this piece in 1946, then returned to it following his Harvard experience. There he made a strong positive impression on a young professor of government named Henry Kissinger, who edited *Confluence: An International Forum* and requested an essay from Ellison.

You asked if I finished the story for *New World Writing*.* I did to my satisfaction, but after sending me an enthusiastic letter and a contract, Arabel turned up with reservations at the last minute promising to let me know the cuts and additions they desired, but I succeeded in getting the ms. back only yesterday. Now they want the story for April but I don't know. I have the feeling that their desire for more exposition is motivated by their knowledge that the story was once part of the novel. At best the story is simply an amusement, but having taken so much of my trip to write it I don't feel like bothering further. I'm glad that they took your story and I'm glad to see you getting into print. This is a very necessary part of writing; until the work is printed it's still tied to your own subjectivity. Put it into print and the spell is broken and self-criticism is born. As for the problem of an agent I think that since you are so far from the city you might consider one. Don't, however, sign a contract with one; they work for themselves primarily and though they can place your work and perhaps get more money for it, they would hardly fall out with a publisher over one writer where they have other of his authors on their list.

Find who Arabel would suggest and let me check. Send her the old version of the novel, it won't hurt.

As for the hi-fi, three hundred is promising. There will be an audio fair next month and I'll look around to see the latest developments and send you a suggestive list. It's better to get the latest and I'll get you set up as cheaply as possible without sacrificing quality. Which reminds me that I promised Mokie a kitchen mixer. Tell her that I haven't forgotten and I'll get to her before long. That's it for now. I'm pooped and bound for bed. Give my best to all who deserve it and keep up the good work.

Ralph

To Albert Murray
Tulsa, Okla
oct. 16, 1953

Dear Murray,

I find myself back here in Okla. much sooner than i expected. I lost my cousin. Read ole Luz just before I left home and I found him fine in print.

---

* Ellison is referring to the piece "Did You Ever Dream Lucky?," an excerpt from the earlier versions of *Invisible Man*, which features the character of Mary Rambo. It appeared in *New World Writing* in 1954.

Wished section in which narrator discovers identity had been left in though. Regards to all.

R. E.

To Albert Murray
730 RIVERSIDE DRIVE
NEW YORK 31, N.Y.
OCT. 23, 1953

Dear Murray:

I've been back home a week today and I'm still a little tired. I dropped you a postal card from Okla. City, where I had gone to attend the funeral of that cousin who among my relatives was my best friend, and whom I visited this summer.* She'd had an operation, appeared for a week to be recovering, then she was no more. So I went back.

I went back a long way back, for she's buried not far from my father. I made my first trip to that burying ground when I was three, so I returned thirty-six years [later] to the place where much of my temperament was formed. Perhaps it is a low of civilization, of human life, that you must plant a man to make a man and the father's tomb become the second womb of the son. Anyway, that was thirty-six years ago. Then the place seemed far from town, now the city has grown up around it, has absorbed it as life always absorbs death, and as I have absorbed that planting of my father. Now it has taken on a gentle serenity of waving willows and bending sycamores that was not so years ago, when the sheer terror of death looked out of the raw red clay mounds, the crude granite stones, the wild countryside. Now there is grass and trees and flowers and the usual polished stones the familiar names—mostly of whites and Negro pioneer families, for now the Negroes have their own cemetery and only those who paid their first toll to death years ago still come here.

So we laid her down, this cousin of mine who was my father's favorite, and then went home. She was quite an interesting woman and I'll have to tell you about her some time.

I remained in Oklahoma from Monday to Friday, then flew out of there. I felt rootless and frustrated, I was living in that earlier time, living in that

* May Belle De Witt Johnston, with whom Ralph had recently rekindled his friendship (see letter of April 2, 1953).

old house where my cousin had lived when we were young, hearing the old rain in the night, the old thunder, the old lightning, and in the morning the hens sang soft beneath my window. The weather was warm, the Indian summer sad. And when I tried to live in the here and now there were the reminders of the joy of two months ago cut through with juke boxes yelling "She a Hand" and t.v. is the thing this year. Then everywhere I went I saw shotguns being oiled and guys preparing for the hunting season. Several whom I know took off for South Dakota for the pheasant season, and it was all I could do to remind myself that I couldn't go along. So I'm back at work, but somewhere out on the outer fringe of my consciousness I hear the bass music of shotguns singing. Look out pheasant, look out quail, here comes a bear in soldier's clothes, fire stick and all!

I'm lecturing at Antioch College the week of the thirtieth of November, so maybe I'll actually get another taste of hunting. At least I'll get down to Cincinnati to my mother's grave. Perhaps this has been my life's pattern: death, hunger, hunting and death. If so, then I'll be true to the pattern. Anyway, forgive me these thoughts. Enclosed you will find some memories of the summer. I'd have enlarged them but have no darkroom at the moment. Later, perhaps. I'm also sending shots I made of Sunny and his family whose names I can't remember—and they were so nice that Sunday morning. Please see that they get them with my regards. That's all for now, write when you can.

Sincerely,
Ralph

To Herbert Ellison
730 RIVERSIDE DRIVE
NEW YORK 31, NEW YORK
NOV. 14, 1953

Dear Herbert:

This is a letter that I should have written weeks ago but the sadness of its message has made me reluctant to write. Since I wrote you from Oklahoma City I have returned home and then returned to Oklahoma City once more. On Sunday, October 11, I received a call from a friend in Okla. City telling me of May Belle's death. I left here Monday at 5:30 and arrived there at 12 O'clock that night. She was buried on Tuesday, Oct. 13th, in the old Fairlawn Cemetery, where Aunt Teat and our father are buried. I remained in Okla. until the following Friday and returned home. May

Belle had many friends and her death, which came suddenly after what was thought to have been a successful operation, left everyone shocked. She, however, had told me one morning during July that this was perhaps the last time I'd see her alive, so I assume that she realized even then that her life was drawing to a close. At the time I left none of the family, Frances, Tom, Bert,[*] nor her husband, J.R. Johnston, knew what the operation was for, though I suspect cancer. Anyway, I was glad that I went home this summer and could spend some time with her. She, after all was my best friend among my relatives, our relatives, and it was like old times, when we lived out on Peach Street across from Orchard Park School. We had many a laugh about those times and she wished to see you very much. During my visit I often stayed out until after 12 or 1 o'clock and she'd stay half awake until I came in. She and her little dog, which was so old that he could hardly lift his leg when he went out to take a piss in the mornings. She cooked me a cake and some squabs, and warned me against the gossip of the town, treating me as though I were many years younger than I am or can ever be again. Yet I liked it and much of the great pleasure of being home came from staying out there with her and J.R., her husband.

I left Tom and Bert and the others, family and friends, O.K. I stayed at the old place with Tom and Bert this time. It's still very much the same out there, although they've changed the name of the street to Brauer and the school is now housed in a three-story brick building. Tom, who is now getting close to sixty, though you wouldn't know it to look at him, is very much the same and now that I've grown up a bit myself I can see that for all his bluster he is a very nice man. That is, he's generous, good-hearted and kind.

As for Frances I'm afraid that she'll always remain a stranger. She still lives at Claremore, where she and her husband, A.I. Davis, run a bathhouse. Certainly this was no time to get to know her. If you ever plan to go back for a visit, do it soon, we've reached the age when old friends die. Go too before the city changes too much, or before you lose interest—if you haven't already. There are still a number of your old friends around, who asked about you. And of course Frank and Mrs. Mead. Our little house on East 4th Street is still standing, but they've torn off the front porch and an oil well stands in what was the back yard and the houses where the Lawsons and the Rileys lived have been torn down and the land is

---

[*] Frances, Tom, and May Belle were siblings; Bert (Alberta Othello Brown) was Tom's wife.

taken up by an ice house. Most of the old teachers have been retired and replaced by younger if not better ones. And Mrs. Breaux, my old friend of years ago, was unable to remember me although she saw me for nearly an hour at her home and later came to the reception that the libraries gave for me. She was perfectly friendly but simply unable to remember. Actually she reminds me of her mother, Mrs. Paige at the time she was a Matron at old Douglass school. Incidentally the old school is now a warehouse for the board of education, the new one out on High St. has become too small, and they are now building a larger one out on the old State Fair Grounds, since the Negro population is spreading in that direction. The new fairground is to be out West, beyond the packing town. So the old town grows.

That's about all for now. I got caught in a blizzard last Friday evening as we were driving a hundred miles north of here to Barrytown, N.Y., where I was lecturing at Bard College, and though we made it in time for my talk I was so beat that I caught a doozy of a cold and have had to spend the last two days in the bed. You take it easy and don't forget that you owe me a picture.

> Love,
> Ralph

To Albert Murray
730 RIVERSIDE DRIVE
NEW YORK 31, N.Y.
NOV. 20, 1953

Dear Albert:

I finally heard from the school about coming down. These are the suggested dates: Jan. 17, 31; March 7, 14. Which of these seem the most interesting? (I've been asked to Bethune-Cookman for the nineteenth of March and I believe I could knock off Dillard around the same period. The important thing is to be at Tuskegee when things are most interesting. Incidentally, my note comes from Julius Flood.

Would you please find out if the entertainment committee understands that I do this kind of thing as a part of my living, especially since it takes time from my writing. Perhaps Flood understands this, but I'd like to make sure before I answer his letter.

There isn't much to report from here. I was part of a symposium on the art of narration at Bard College two weeks ago, along with John Berryman and Georges Simenon. Driving up Fanny and I were caught in a blizzard and I spent the following week in bed with the flu.

Still getting good reports on Luzana, and I had lunch with Arabel Porter the other day and her reports were likewise good. Just tell those dog-ass pseudo-critics that you are writing for Negroes with enough integrity to accept themselves and when you do that white folks are bound to like it just like they like jazz which originally was Mose signifying at other Moses. Naturally, like any real work of art jazz made a helluvalota white folks want to be Mose, simply because jazz is art and art is the essence of the human. Besides only dog-assed folks run away from that essence, so the hell with 'em. That's it for now. Try and let me have this information as soon as possible as I'd like to answer Flood.

Sincerely,
Ralph

To Albert Murray
730 RIVERSIDE DRIVE
NEW YORK 31, N.Y.
FEB. 1, 1954

Dear Murray,

Thanks for putting the needle to Flood. I suspect that he resented it but it produced action. I'm damned if I understand just what's going on down there, or why they want me. They sent me no idea of the format of their program, nor of theme; while I'm at no loss for things to talk about, it would be nice to try to integrate my remarks with whatever program they have.* Perhaps that's what they're leery of. Anyway, don't bother them with it. Mort was the guy who suggested that he would work something out, but as you say he tends to leave the field to shit artists like my boy Mike. He'd better make his weight felt or next trip he'll have Red Davis or Mike for president. And mind you, I'm fond of Mike and can't stand Davis, but what the hell has that to do with educating men and women? Mort's either going to have to make his values felt or quit. He was fine for us, but that was damn near twenty years ago and it's <u>now</u> that his quali-

---

* Ellison went to Tuskegee in February 1954 as the first stop on a series of lectures at histori-cally black colleges. He stayed with the Murrays and spent time with his old friend and teacher, librarian Morteza Sprague. Mike Rabb was the secretary of the Tuskegee Board of Trustees.

ties should be most effective. It's all right to hate ignorance in important places and brown-nosing and whatever that shit is that Walker and Davis put down, but hell, if his values aren't worth teaching to Foster—and even getting his head whipped a bit to get them across—then he's playing himself cheap. Not to mention those kids to whom he owes a responsibility by birth, by sensibility, by intelligence and by position. The whole thing depresses me. A man shouldn't let himself be boxed in and then pout about it. Well, more about this later.

Unfortunately Fanny, after quitting her job, took another recently and won't be able to come on the trip. She prefers to take the time off for the Salzburg trip. Thus I'll come down sometime around the eighteenth or nineteenth. Eubanks has been invited down for the following week. So I'm trying to get him to drive down when I go, but if he doesn't I'll be flying since my dates are too far apart to drive them in time without killing myself. I have a problem as it is, for after Tuskegee it looks as though I'll have an eighteen-day interval before I go to Dillard on the eleventh of March, to Southern on the fourteenth, to Bethune-Cookman on the nineteenth and to Howard on the twenty-second. I'd prefer to come home during the eighteen day period, but with the cost of flying what it is I plan to try to write somewhere between Tuskegee and New Orleans. Man, I'm getting out of this racket, the pay is bad, the colleges try to make it worse, and the result in terms of reaching the kids is dubious. I'm getting to look like a fat, baldheaded old fart fast enough; and little more of this and I'll start sounding like one.

I had the pleasure of seeing Bellow get the book award this year[*] that is encouraging for all of us. There ain't much originality, man, and they're waiting for you. Jack up old Jack, we need him. As for me, I'm in my old agony again trying to write a novel. I've got some ideas that excite me and a few scenes and characters, but the rest is coming like my first pair of long pants—slow as hell. Never mind, I'll get it out, it just takes time to do <u>anything</u> worthwhile. Incidentally, I just had a talk with Bellow and he's getting some of the same shit I received last year: the envy, the snobbery, the general display of lousiness, which some of the bright boys tried to pass on to me. He's shamed them both by winning something they want and by writing about them as they really are, without love, without generosity, sans talent, sans life. I thought they were simply reacting to my being a Mose, but hell, they can't stand for any-

[*] Saul Bellow won the 1954 National Book Award for fiction for *The Adventures of Augie March*.

one, not even one who's been around themselves (until he gets up and produces something that breaks their perception of style and form), to come along and try to leave his own agony on the heart of world. He tells me that years ago Greenberg* advised him that there was nothing more to be said in terms of fiction and that he, Bellow, should follow him and make a career out of criticism! Well, they ain't taking it gracefully. There is just as much sneering over Bellow's award as there was over mine, if not more. So I've learned a little more why Hemingway and everyone on back to Goethe, and probably back to Homer, have said to hell with critics. Today they see their world going to hell, all their standards fall flat and still they're afraid of anything that lets in the big wide contradictory sight see sound of the world. Stick to Mose. Man. He's got more life in his toenails than these zombies have in their whole bodies. As though you didn't know it.

Had quite a bit of fun hunting during the season and discovered that I could still hit them once in a while. I got ducks (none of which were good because they had eaten fish) quail, grouse, and squirrels. I hunted most of the time with Noble Simms' uncle and another old guy, who were fun enough in the beginning, but grew rather boring. They told no lies and had none of that old time humor, so next season I'm finding me some young studs and some kind of dogs. Those old cats had me walking my ass off, stirring up the birds—and then missing most of them. Indeed I've still to see one of them kill anything, and we hunted all season. He's the guy who took me out to have some fun at my expense only to have me imagine that I was back in Dayton in 1937 and started hitting every living ass. Poor man thought I'd tricked him although I never pretended that I was a stranger to a shotgun. Hunting is still a good way to live, man; and I'm glad that the instinct is still alive within me. It's much healthier than this backbiting and verbal murder, character assassination and bitchery that seems to be the current mode among the intellectuals. Tell Mokie that we're glad she found the machine useful—as I knew she would. One gadget you ought to avoid though, man, unless you want to work your balls off, and that's one of those floor polishers. I made that mistake and I'm about to end up with housemaid's knees from smearing on the goddamn wax! It's fun enough though, even if it does lead me to violate my taboo against work.

---

*   Clement Greenberg was a formidable art critic best known for his promotion of abstract expressionism and his championing of Jackson Pollock's work.

. . . I've run into some new bearisms which I'll report to you when I see you. Ran into a bear who was operating under F.D.R. with the stuff she had learned to work on Mose—and got away with it! Mau! Mau! Come up here if you can, if not I'll be down there in a couple of weeks and whatever happens don't go sour; you'll just have to do what the others aren't capable of doing, that's all. The world is changing so fast that most of these studs are going to crumble up before the very complexity of the freedom they thought they wanted and didn't, so forget them. It's the boys who'll call you papa, or at least will think of you as such even though they never give utterance to the thought, who'll inherit the earth. Be of good cheer.

Ralph

To Fanny Ellison

Tuskegee Institute, Ala

FEB 23, 1954

Dear Fanny:

I'm still here at Tuskegee, living at Dorothy Hall—as a guest of the school. Murray met me in Atlanta and as it would happen Dr. Foster had arrived just before me from Washington and shared the ride over here. It is a 135 mile trip, so we had an ample opportunity to talk and tell stories (though I'm afraid Murray and your old man took over that department). Anyway, he was amused and it was enjoyable rolling through the rolling Georgia farmland through the rain swept atmosphere. Certainly he is an intelligent man and if this school doesn't achieve something of reality under his administration it will be because of other reasons.

My luck held good for the talk on Sunday evening. I had Notes but ignored them and spoke from the hip or heart or wherever it is that sincerity and desperation are intertwined in one. The audience was so quiet that I became truly desperate and I found myself almost pleading with them to recognize that there was no longer any need to think of themselves as less than human. You know how I feel about these things. And when it was over there was much applause.

But more seriously, the students were after me the following day both on campus and during classes on literature and sociology (I must have autographed 135 copies of the book) so that I know I had some effect.

Monday morning at 8 am Mort, Murray and I had breakfast with the Fosters, where I met Vera, who seems a Vera fine person. She sends regards and said tell you that she's still working at social work. They're two fine kids.

I've agreed to return here in June for a seminar in American literature— which should help me to prepare my Salzburg material and they have agreed to pay me adequately—they'd better, because I'll be working with an unbelievable fool of a department head. Here during a time when integration is in the air, they have no courses in American lit.! I asked them how did they expect students to become integrated when they know nothing of the society into which they were to be integrated? It hadn't occurred to them that literature had anything to do with it. Anyway I've committed myself for June, five days, two hours a day.

Yesterday I had lunch with the Dawsons and a fine conversation about my speech and music, and Africa, naturally and the past, present and future of Tuskegee. He too is an admirer of Kathleen Ferrier and we talked of her art and then of music in general—really a very satisfying afternoon.

Naturally I've been seeing Morrell and Miguel and the Spragues, and Lily (she visited us last summer) who carried me through the Carver Research Center, explaining some of the research projects to me. Then the director, Russell Brown, took me through the polio lab, showing me the cancer cells in culture which they supply other labs for polio research. Once polio could be cultured in monkeys, but recently they discovered that the polio virus could be grown in human cancer cells The isolation of the cell was achieved at Minn. and the culture discovered at Johns Hopkins—but Tuskegee has become one of the leading centers for growing these cancer cells. Frightening, but they are getting things done. Carver was a lawyer now, but these guys and girls are scientists.

Last night I went with Albert to a dance for vets out at the Government Hospital where I played one number with the orchestra and danced with one of the nurses, and, ironically, had my photo made with some of the vets.

I plan to take advantage of their offer to stay here a while and try to rest and write, then continue to New Orleans for the Mardi Gras. So if you wish to write I'll be here. I'll have to wait to tell you about many things, conversations etc. Meanwhile I miss you very much. The spring is here is coming swiftly and even my blue ink has turned green. Monday morning early I was out walking over some of my old paths, listening to the birds and wished for you to help me deal with the deep mixed poignancy of it all. For a moment I felt what has been explained by all the endless old soldiers who return to pieces of their early battles since the legacy of time:

that the battles we lose remain more paramount than our brightest victories. I suppose it will always remain so, thus it is better to think always of the tasks at hand and of those which lie ahead. A little later, perhaps a couple of days after this deep rain, things will be glorious here. The moon will be low, the forsythia and violets will run riot and the birds will simply go wild with song—that's when I'll miss you and yearn to fly the spring home. Take care of yourself and remember that I love only you.

Ralph

To Fanny Ellison
DILLARD UNIVERSITY
MARCH 4, 1954.

Dear Fanny:

I started a letter in long hand while on the plane, but arrived so quickly that I had to put it aside. Later I'll try to finish it but until then it's better to tell you what happened the two days I've been here.

I arrived on the 2nd right in the turbulence of the Mardi Gras and have yet to get myself straightened out. First, this is a viciously Jim-Crowed city, and it took me two hours to get from the airport, simply because white taxis will not carry Negro passengers and the Negroes were slow in coming. Second, I could not find anyone at the college because it was closed for the carnival, thus making it necessary for me to depend upon the cabbie to select me a place to stay. Thus I spent the night in Shadowland, listening to the jukebox and the shouts of the dancers and the cries of the drunks. Next day I succeeded in reaching Gottlieb by phone only to learn that all the space at the school is taken up by visiting principals who are in conference. However, the woman on the switchboard here at Dillard happens to be the wife of Babel Pierro, who is a friend from Okla. City, and she had her husband come over to get me. He and Gottlieb arrived about the same time and he, after having me to dinner, took me to a nicer place to stay—it's niceness consisting of the fact that it is not adjoining a bar. A feature for which I pay $4.60 a day rather than the $4.00 that the other place cost me. Both have baths on the hall, so I'll do my bathing and crapping elsewhere. Perhaps after the 6th there will be room for me here in one of the dorms, until then they've promised to provide me with an office in which I may work undisturbed. I certainly hope so. I'm writing this at the Pierros, he having left to take his basketball team to Mississippi.

The address of the room is 2025 Iberville St.; the phone number Tulane 5609. This is for calls at night, otherwise send mail to Dillard, for I plan to spend most of my time here.

It's quite cold here, although it is quite green and spring-like. Many flowers are blooming and the campus with its white buildings and well-appointed grounds is quite handsome, and tropical. I've never been in a place like this city. Last evening Babe carried me down into the French quarter to buy fish and I was able to see quite a bit of it—though I must say that it has, for all its age and quaintness, a sucker-trap atmosphere like Broadway. Standard equipment for many of the joints is a dummy of a mammy with electric bulbs for eyes. Talking about weird! These things are worse than those little hitching post figures that, by the way, must have originated in this damned town.

The West Virginia thing seems impossible but I wired them that I was free from the 14th thru the 17th, on the 20th, and from the 26th thru the 30th. I just don't like the idea of dashing about more than I have to, even though we need the money. However if they offer me a free date I'll go. Did you send them the fee? I thought surely that would discourage them.

I left Tuskegee with some reluctance, for despite the inroads into my writing time I received a great deal of satisfaction out of talking with students, and out of needling both students and teachers. I like Vera Foster, who seems like a woman who can help Foster make a real college president of himself. There was a food show there last week, at which [I] sat at the speakers' table like a stuffed shirt, but afterwards the Fosters invited me to a gathering at a friend's place, where the husbands were to entertain themselves while the wives played canasta. Well, as it happened I was thrown—by design, I now suspect—with Foster for about an hour, during which we talked seriously about the school and its role in the period of integration and such related matters; and later I went home with him and Vera, where we talked and drank until 4 a.m. Mike Rabb was along and I'm afraid the two of us did most of the drinking. I was quite frank and ridiculed as many of those impossible features of the school and its attitudes as I could think of and praised those teachers and scientists and those features of its program that have already broken through the obscene provincialism which so cripples it. He took it well and gives the impression that he has many changes planned. I hope so. Nevertheless, I left because I wanted more time for myself. I was being entertained too much and didn't have enough character to refuse all the invitations, nor to stay in my room at night when there was a chance to ride out to watch the country Negroes dance in their roadside night clubs. Murray and Moselle were very nice and it is something to watch Mique's features changing mysteriously from those of Albert into those of Moselle. She's going to be a lovely girl one of these days.

Mickie cooked chitterlings for me and corn bread and waffles and it was all very good. She's teaching now, but still manages, like you, to turn out good meals. Incidentally, Foster's last words to me were an invitation for you to return with me in June. I hope you can, for you should see the place and the people should see you. Laly had me to dinner and she and Albert and I had an uproarious time laughing about old times. I'm still a bit upset (aren't I most of the time?) but I think a little quiet and a careful avoidance of onions will get me straight. It's only when I'm away from you that I truly realize how much your sacrifice of your onions and garlic help my well-being. I hope you're enjoying them in my absence. Yesterday just before the fellows came to pick me up I'd almost convinced myself that it would be quite the thing to come flying home until the 10th, I'm that lonely for you. In fact, I'm still tempted but resisting. These strange, empty beds are hard to take and I was not intended to live alone. You mustn't let yourself get out of order while I'm away, it'll only throw us that much behind when I return with my designs on you. So take it easy and remember how well it goes when we are in tune. That's what I remember at night in strange rooms in the dark, and if part of me seems dormant now that I'm away from you I know it'll awaken when we're together again and I'll know that's why I feel free to enter these exiles in the first place. We leave to return. I leave to return to you to be with you and beyond that all this wandering off is without meaning. Love me, darling and write,

Ralph

To Albert Murray
DILLARD UNIVERSITY
NEW ORLEANS, LOUISIANA
MARCH 6, 1954

Dear Albert:

This is a most difficult letter to write not only because of the news itself, but because it reveals the terrifying possibilities which often flow from what appear at the time of making them to be simple decisions. I tried to get Eubanks to come to Tuskegee with me over a period of months. He was committed to come and address the food show and to be honored, but some complex of motives caused him to decide not to and you know about his sending me the speech too late for me to deliver it and the jokes we made about it. Yesterday I received word that Eubanks was killed by a psychopathic dish washer over a wage dispute. He was both shot and knifed. Over and over my throat flexes with that old tragic cry "if only . . . if only . . ." and it's true, had he come to Tuskegee he'd still be there to relive the experiences of the visit.

I suppose the word has already reached Tuskegee. Martha Ann Sumpter phoned it to Fanny. If not, please pass it along. He was one of the good ones, and a rare one. I'll never have a friend with *his* combination of traits again, nor will you, nor will anyone who knew him. Should anyone wish to write his mother, her name is Mrs. Lillie Eubanks, Akin, S.C. Her phone number is Barnwell 3917.

I'll write you later about my trip here. Please give my regards to all.

Ralph

To Fanny Ellison
New Orleans, Louisiana
Dillard University
march 16, 1954

Dearest Fanny:

Just a note to get rid of the enclosed (there is more, but I forgot to take it with me and the Post Office is far) and to brief you on my movements. I leave for Southern tomorrow at 7:15 A.M. and shall lecture at 12 noon. Luckily for me the Pierros drove over on Sunday to see my friends from Oklahoma City who teach there because I shall have to return to New Orleans rather early on the 18th so as to make my plane to Jacksonville, from whence I go to Daytona Beach. I have reservations through to Washington, for there I shall head on the 20th or 21st—depending upon later confirmation. Anyway I'll contact you from Florida.

The weather has been very changeable and I'm sniffling. Hope it doesn't develop into anything. I've concluded that part of my trouble here comes from the water, which is unbelievably bad. Beyond these physical things, I'm simply tired of not seeing you and being there with you. I suppose I'll be popping my top by the time I see you—providing this thing doesn't become an energy sapping cold.

Things have gone rather well as far as my contact with the kids is concerned. I'm told that they're stirred up, I hope so, they need a heapa stirring. I am also enclosing a clipping from a local paper. And who do you think is working there? Tom Sucton, he was cordial, as was I, but another reporter did the interview. Small world.

Be sweet, lady, I look forward with eagerness to see you in Washington. Where you are is home. I love you.

Ralph

To William Dawson
730 RIVERSIDE DRIVE
New York 31, N.Y.
APRIL 12, 1954

Dear Mr. Dawson:

When I finally returned to New York and caught my breath I went searching for the recording by Inez Mathews as I promised you I'd do. There seems to be only one thus far, and I had it mailed to you, along with a recording of Carl Orff's *Carmina Burina* done by the Bavarian Radio Orchestra and chorus. I have the latter and thought you might find it of interest, if not musically, then as an example of the quality some of the engineers are getting into the recording of choirs. Please accept these as a gift from us to you and Cecile. I'm sorry that I waited so long to write because any recording purchased from Sam Goody may be returned for full credit if played no more than one time. Should you need other things please let me know as I rather enjoy scouting around the record shops.

Incidentally, I found the Mathews recording not only a good buy musically but also in terms of cash; I have no other record with so many numbers on it. I purchased three records for myself when I got yours, and between the twelve-inch by Inez Mathews and a ten-inch by Camilla Williams I had a house full of spirituals. Miss Williams, by the way, was appearing at Bethume-Cookman while I was there. I'll let you judge the voices, I'll say only that she's charming, very charming and not at all upstage. Hers was the only interesting voice I heard on my trip. I heard the choirs of Dillard and Southern but neither were impressive. They were not, however, in concert—which reminds me that while in Washington I had a chat with Hazel Harrison and Miss Pittman who asked of you.

That's it. I'm working on my novel, having gotten going very well in New Orleans; I should return to Tuskegee in June for a series of Lectures on American Literature if things go well. Meanwhile I shall try to find that series on the tape recording of choirs which I mentioned to you. They seem to have disappeared from around here but perhaps I can locate them at a bookdealer's. Certainly they should turn up by June. Until then our best to both of you.

> Sincerely,
> Ralph Ellison

To Albert Murray
730 RIVERSIDE DRIVE
NEW YORK 31, N.Y.
APRIL 12, 1954

Dear Albert:

After all the wandering I'm at home for a while. Last Thursday and Friday I was down in Baltimore, where I talked at Coppin State Teachers College and, the next morning, before a class in Negro Literature at Morgan. I suppose now I'll be free until June, when I'll return to Tuskegee if the boys haven't changed their minds. As much as I hate to leave I think I did the right thing in going to New Orleans, although I didn't see the parade because I couldn't ride in either the airport limousine or the white taxis and thus spent hours steaming. I called some white folks some unheard of mfers that day! Nevertheless, despite my anger over the JimCrow (they must have invented the hitching post nigger, for they have millions [of] life-sized figures of Negroes fishing), despite having to spend four nights in hotels that were hardly more than whorehouses, and despite the food, which put me in bed—I got some solid work done on my novel. They gave me an office to work in and I got down to business. They, meaning Dillard, which I found a most interesting school. They have the best lit. students and the most alert lit. faculty down that way, two white fellows and a Negro gal setting the pace. Southern is a bustling place, but I was there too briefly to get a real idea of what was going on. Except one night at a party at the dean's home the Negroes started needling me and I started asking questions and soon had everybody yelling at me, defending their right to be second rate! Naturally it was a Mose doctor and a Mose physicist who yelled the loudest. One Negro even drew his caddy on me! For a while there it was outrageous, then one of the women went upstairs and brought down her child and I turned to the father and asked if the child represented his attempt to produce a second class baby and he finally admitted that in some things at least Negroes had a responsibility to measure up to or to lead the field. It ended well enough, though, with one of the wives giving me a kiss as I, unrequested, left.

I keep running into people who were at Harvard last August. Three are teaching at Bethune-Cookman operating on a high level—although I believe this was the most uneven school of the tour. They do have the best college food I've eaten anywhere, the department being headed by a Tuskegee grad. But it was Howard that was the most disappointing. Those people ask the most provincial questions put to me anywhere. They spent most of the time trying to push me into an autobiographical corner and when I wouldn't budge things would get quiet and I'd have to give them another lecture. Brown, Frazier, Davis, Lovel and others were there but none of them would say a mumbling word—not even when I attacked some of their assumptions concerning Mose and America and culture.

Later at a party Sterling Brown was very friendly and came along to see what kind of strange creature I was, but it was sad. But it had to be an old friend who made me mad. After most of the guests had gone (fortunately) Walt Williams* started telling me that I was really developing, I mustn't pontificate too much (!) and that I should speak more like Matthew Arnold! I told him that it might be more entertaining to some audiences if I learned to sing, but that my interest lay in the quality and validity of my ideas. If he found them wanting I'd be glad to be corrected. No, I showed that I had thought a lot about these matters but I should remember that there are other ideas. What ideas and what were their value? I asked. You should speak more like Arnold, he said. That goddamn Howard is a graveyard, man. Holmes seems to do nothing but speculate on the sex lives of others, several of the bright boys are suffering from liquor impotence; we were told (Fanny met me there) that this was the first time that Sterling Brown had been seen in the home of one

---

* Ellison's friend and confidant from his Tuskegee days, who had once been the librarian at Tuskegee.

of his old friends in six years; another once-good-man who's taken the cure. Depressing. John Hope Franklin* seems to be the only real scholar and Margaret Butcher the most alert English teacher as well as the most socially conscious. The rest seem naked before the blast of reality. Can you imagine me standing up before a group of so-called leading Negro so-called scholars and saying that they had failed to define "Negro" except in blood terms, and not have one open his mouth? Maybe it's because they're afraid. The government has cut their funds again and there's talk of doing away with the school if integration comes and there they sit, the mask of illusion slipping down. And yet, when those boys see a guy like John Franklin functioning as an historian, writing papers, attending scholarly meetings, etc.—they think he crazy. Then one day he'll be appointed the head of the department in some big college and they'll think it's simply a fluke.

There were some funny things on the trip: the Globetrotters running out onto the Municipal Auditorium in New Orleans dressed in stars and stripes and the crackers applauding to raise hell. Goose Tatum ran out and tried to drag a white policeman in to arrest one of the opposing players and the cop must have brushed his coat sleeve compulsively for thirty minutes where Goose's big tar baby hand had gripped him. It was a minstrel show and magic, man, and the white folks were simply fascinated. I found also that the coach at Dillard was a Pierro, with whom I grew up. His wife also brought out the chittlings—though Mokie could teach her a few things. The amusing thing about Dillard lay in the fact that its chief backer is a Jew and he has put these Negroes in a stage set of a campus with white buildings of semi-plantation architecture! They left off the verandahs perhaps because they just couldn't stand to have these young Moses sitting around drinking mint juleps while the white folks rolled past and stared.

Before I forget it, will you please send me the name of the fellow who heads the English department? I have to write him about the lectures in June and I've misplaced my notes. I absolutely refuse to enter into correspondence with Sandy!

How are things going? Things here are well enough. The *New World Writing* advance copies are out and I had some sent to you to distribute

---

* Franklin was just emerging at this time as the most prominent and important historian of African American life in the nation.

to a few faculty members. I was allowed only a few. Incidentally, I tried to pay Sonny for driving me to the plane but he refused it. I didn't mean it as pay and would still like to do something for him. If you have any ideas let me know. Meanwhile, our love to Mique and Mokie and let us hear from you soon.

Ralph

To Morteza Sprague
730 RIVERSIDE DRIVE
NEW YORK 31, N.Y.
MAY 19, 1954.

Mr. M.D. Sprague
Librarian
Hollis Burke Frissel Library
Tuskegee Institute,
Alabama.

Dear Mort:

Congratulations on receiving such a wonderful batch of prizes, they sound like the stuff librarians' dreams are made of. I must admit that I was a bit confused by the arrival of the unannounced, though familiar, books but was sure that an explanation was forthcoming—even if I should find it necessary to remind you that one was needed. I'm getting off to the gentlemen immediately.

I found the exchange most amusingly ironic and when I mentioned it to Albert Erskine, my editor, we had quite a laugh—all those wonderful items for ole Invisible!. However when this was through he asked seriously if you'd mind his quoting this information as publicity later on when my work-in-progress goes into the works? Don't rush to anticipate, I'm still a long way from having even the first third of it done, and from the way I'm moving I'm years away from the end. Anyway this request is not important enough to cause you bother, so don't go to any trouble if you think there might be objections. I won't try to tell you how pleased I am that your donors asked for *IM*.

The reading list certainly would benefit by adding the works by Howe and Baker and any others you feel would help. Would you include James'

The Bostonians along with the others, please. As for Wilson's *New Yorker* piece of Nov. 27, 1928, it's his essay on *Uncle Tom's Cabin* and I'll just bring it along and read from it during my lecture.

Now for Reid's question: Please tell him that I feel that $500.00 <u>plus</u> expenses would be a bit more reasonable. Otherwise I can see the five hundred bucks vanishing in a lot of paper work that would not be to my advantage. Certainly I would never eat fifty dollars' worth of food during any one week, not even at the Waldorf! Thus I'd rather have the savings where they count—for me.

Actually my lecture fee is (as it was in March) $175.00 plus expenses; at which rate the lectures would come to $875.00 for the five days— <u>excluding</u> expenses—and I think the $500.00 figure plus round trip flight fare, food, laundry, room board and minor incidentals (I itemize because Flood left me holding the tabs for quite a number of small matters). I'd expect to work like hell. Reid will find that this total will [come] to something around $635.00, but if he wants a nice round figure to request, $600 is a good one. The flight fare from here to Montgomery and back is 129.03, so he can see where the bulk of the expenses lies.

Well so now the Court has found in our favor and recognized our human psychological complexity and citizenship and another battle of the Civil War has been won. The rest is up to us and I'm very glad. The decision came while I was reading *A Stillness at Appomattox,* and a study of the Negro Freedman and it made a heightening of emotion and a telescoping of perspective, yes and a sense of the problems that lie ahead that left me wet-eyed. I could see the whole road stretched out and it got all mixed up with this book I'm trying to write and it left me twisted with joy and a sense of inadequacy. Why did I have to be a writer during a time when events sneer openly at your efforts defying consciousness and form? Well, so now the judges have found and Negroes must be individuals and that is hopeful and good. What a wonderful world of possibilities are unfolded for the children! For me there is still the problem of making meaning out of the past and I guess I'm lucky I described Bledsoe before he was checked out. Now I'm writing about the evasion of identity that is another characteristically American problem that must be about to change. I hope so, it's giving me enough trouble. Anyway, here's to integration, the only integration that counts: that of the personality. See you soon.

Ralph Ellison.

To Alberta Othello "Bert" Brown
730 RIVERSIDE DRIVE
NEW YORK 31, NEW YORK
JUNE 8, 1954

Dear Bert:*

As usual I'm slow in answering, nevertheless I hope you don't feel that I wasn't pleased to hear from you. Indeed, I kept trying to write while I was down south, but it was one of the busiest months I've spent since finishing my book and I didn't get around to it. That trip took me to Tuskegee, Dillard (in New Orleans), Southern (in Baton Rouge), Bethune-Cookman (Daytona Beach) to Howard and to Coppin State Teachers College (Baltimore). Now I'm preparing to leave next week for Tuskegee again, where I'm conducting a seminar in American literature.† I'll be there only for a week, but I'm sure I'll be busy as the dickens, so I'm writing now. Tell Tom that I plan to drive and hope that I can run through Abbeville,‡ on my way down. I'm curious about the old home place.

I don't suppose I knew at the time I was there that we were going to Europe this summer but we are. I've been appointed to lecture at Salzburg, Austria for four weeks, after which we plan to spend a month visiting in Italy, Spain and France. I suppose we'll be away ten weeks altogether and utterly broke when we return but we plan to seize the opportunity of traveling while we can. I must say however that I'm going to regret missing some of the fine fishing that we've been doing the last few weekends. You know how interested I became in hunting when I was home, well, I returned here and brought me a shotgun and other necessary gear and made for the woods. Did very well too, quail, grouse, squirrels and ducks—quite a few ducks, but all had eaten fish and we had to throw them out. So now its fresh water fishing. We'd done salt water fishing for years, but I suppose seeing you and Tom with your poles gave me the idea of trying the lakes, so that now we both have spinning reels and are bringing in enough

---

* "Bert" was Alberta Othello Brown, the wife of Tom Brown, Ralph's cousin, with whom the Ellisons stayed in Tulsa occasionally on their travels.

† Tuskegee invited Ralph back for another visit in June 1954, to deliver the summer convocation address and lead a seminar in American literature for students who were English teachers.

‡ Abbeville, South Carolina, is the birthplace of Ellison's father, Lewis Ellison, and paternal grandfather, Alfred Lewis Ellison.

perch, crappies, etc. to supply not only ourselves but our neighbors. It's great fun, and we too use the *Fishing Encyclopedia*. We're glad you like it and were not at all bothered once we were notified that you had received it. It was my fault anyway, since I should have written that we were sending it. Incidentally, J.R.* asked me for a razor when May Belle was living and having promised him one I sent it. If you see him, please [ask] if he received it.

Yes, I did receive the picture you sent and thanks very much; it's the only portrait I have of Mom after the others were grown up, and the only one of Frances and John. As for J.R. and the home place, I think you'd both be less than fair to yourselves if you allowed him to get his hands upon it. I was very depressed by the bickering, to say the least. Certainly J.R. has nothing to do with that place and I hope you and Tom won't allow him to force you into selling. He's too old a man to spread the evil he seems bent upon and if the place is broken up through his efforts I shall start an investigation into whether he had anything to do with May Belle's death. I hope this isn't necessary; the place isn't in any way mine nor would I go through the muck such an investigation would entail, but I do know who worked, washed clothes and ran on the road to pay for that place and it certainly wasn't J.R. and it wasn't Frances and it wasn't May Belle. What's more the whole circumstances of May Belle's death, as described to me when I arrived, worries me. I hope you'll keep me posted on developments, for while I can't affect the outcome of the property quarrel I <u>can</u> as a relative, have the matter of May Belle s death looked into and I shall. Tell Tom that he can say this to Frances and to J.R. if he wishes. I realize that Frances was also grumbling about the place, but I know where she was when things were rugged on Peach Street. Someone should have J.R. committed; he's senile.

I've been getting the *Black Dispatch* and I read about Waller and recently about Lizzie Dyer. It's depressing, Waller was a good friend of mine from grade school days, when she watched my health and gave me good advice; and Mrs. Dyer was such a friend to May Belle and I'd known her since the days I lived out there and went to Orchard Park School. Should you run into Bunny Fant and Frank give them my sympathy. I suppose we've reached that time of life when friends die faster and faster. I lost a very good friend while on my trip. He was knifed to death, and the irony of it is that he was due at Tuskegee at the same time I was there but de-

---

* J. R. Johnston, husband of May Belle.

cided not to go. Of course it was the wrong decision for he was killed by a man he'd hired only two weeks before.

That's about all—Oh, yes, I had a call from Padie and promised to go to see her when I return from down south. She said she was well [and] asked of you and Tom.

I'll try not to wait so long before writing next time and I hope things go well for you. Lord knows when I'll get back to Oklahoma City, but one never knows. Certainly I'll make it as soon as possible. Meantime the both of you keep well and as happy as you can.

Love from us both,
Ralph

To Stanley Edgar Hyman
730 RIVERSIDE DRIVE
New York 31, New York
JULY 1, 1954

Dear Stanley:

Judging by the date we're getting old.

I was not in Austria when you put your letter on the way, but I was just returning from a ten-day trip to a red, hot Alabama (temp. 100.3 in the shade), where I conducted a seminar in American literature at Tuskegee. After lecturing two hours a night I must say that I'm a bit tired of the whole thing and have an increased respect for you guys who do it year and year out.

Nevertheless, I'm sorry that things didn't work out for Bennington but $25 just isn't right. I'd much rather meet some kids out at your place and just exchange ideas for drinks or kicks—I don't mean those frightful things taken with sugar and milk! Perhaps we can work something out for next year but to hell with Bennington's twenty-five bucks, I've learned too much during the last two years about college techniques of exploitation.

I'm very interested in the young lady's paper but I am scheduled to go up to Tamiment on July 20, for a lecture that I begged out of last summer and thus <u>must</u> fulfill. Why don't you mail me the piece, since I will probably be much more articulate about it on the typewriter than I would just shooting the breeze. I'll be responsible and take good care of it. The Tamiment people want me to spend some time up there (it's their summer camp located at a place called Bushkill, N.Y.) but I plan to come back as soon as possible, since we fly for Austria on the 19th of August and will have quite a lot to do. Perhaps I can return to the city before you have to leave for Bennington.

Thank Shirley for *The Bird's Nest* that arrived just as I was leaving for the South. I haven't had time to read it but will get to it soon, perhaps over the weekend. There's no news here of any consequences. My book was going well before the interruption and that's about all. Some odd stuff's beginning to turn up which should interest you once I have it shaped a little better. I'm certain that I embody a wild man.

Give my best to Kenneth and to all those Hymans; I hope we'll have a chance to get together before Europe. Fanny, who is in good shape, hopes so too and sends all her best to alla y'all.

Sincerely,
Ralph

To Albert Murray
730 RIVERSIDE DRIVE
NEW YORK 31, N.Y.
AUGUST 9, 1954

Dear Albert:

I was pretty annoyed with you and Mokie—but especially with you— because we had no word of how your trip went. Of course when *I'm* driving somewhere I'm the same way; I set out and arrive in good order and think nothing of it until the week or so it takes me to get my breath—then I write. I called Mokie, but she was busy and we were unable to reach her until Sunday, when she came up and spent the afternoon and part of the evening helping Fanny sew. It looked like a sweatshop when they got through, but Fanny's going to have some damn goodlooking clothes. Mokie, by the way, says that she has an idea who's being poppa and momma down there. Me too, and I suspect that Miss Mique has you well in hand. Give her our love. I'm disgusted with "This Lutherism"* you sent, it's the most inept piece of transparent crap I've seen yet. I had some hopes for the man but this, if it expresses his thinking, is as lame as the outpourings of any mush mouth who has convinced himself that his uncletomism is wisdom. All this and Walker too . . . I think Mort is doing the correct thing. I plan to write him. Meanwhile, I'm sure you'll give him the dope on our bull sessions. I've been working away at constructing

---

* A piece by Luther Foster, president of Tuskegee.

other organizing forms for this novel, which has led me to more reading in Faulkner criticism. I found the *English Institute Essays,* 1952, published by the Columbia University Press of interest. Most of the book is given over to Faulkner's *The Sound and the Fury,* but there are also three essays on rhetoric, one concerning Joyce, that are of interest . . . That Bear stuff in *The Confidence Man* is indeed gone. I guess I told you that the black image in *Invisible* was suggested by the figure of Black Guinea. That son of a bitch with his mouth full of pennies! I've also just read the galleys of Wright's book on the Gold Coast, *Black Power,* and though I'm somewhat annoyed with his self-importance, I think the book is important and I'm trying to work out a comment. Take a look at it; perhaps I could send you the galleys if I don't have to return them.

I'm glad the system worked out OK, and I think the kit idea the best solution. If I can be of help let me know, Sarser might well give you some kind of discount—only let me know before next week.

Things are getting frantic here over the trip. I've found a young writer who wants to stay here while we are away. His name is Alvin Copper and he has been working on a novel for several years. I don't know what it's like but it sounds sociological. Anyway, it looks as though he'll occupy the fort while we are away. As usual I've waited until the last minute before allowing the trip to become real for me, so that now I'm shopping and putting things in order and find myself short of dough even before I leave. If you still want to lend me something until I return, I can use any amount up to three hundred dollars, preferably the whole sum. This would be just the right amount of medicine to chase away that nagging anxiety of insecurity of getting busted in a foreign land. If you can send it and should you need it suddenly, don't worry, as I can always get an advance from my publishers—who would like to have me spending some of <u>their</u> money so as to be in a position to needle me about the work-in-progress.

I hope you'll get work done on your book and that you'll start turning out essays on jazz that can later be part of a book. You have the stuff and I think it'll do you good to have part of your identity anchored outside Tuskegee. Thus far you've stayed there and transcended its limitations. You've evolved the stuff, so now put it on the line. You're the only one I know who makes sense of all the ramifications and since it looks like no one is going to do anything with this material we might as well get started. I still think that that conversation we had with Maya one of the damnedest I've ever participated in! Tiger, rabbit, bear and priest (Campbell), strictly a jam session in metaphors and the jungle queen getting her butt kicked with each snap of her tail . . . Incidentally, I found that record, "Blue Monday," I asked you about. It's by Smiley Lewis and it's in the classic mold, a Mose singing triumphantly about hard work:

> *Blue Monday, oh how I hate blue Monday. Got to work*
> *   like a slave all day*
> *Then comes Tuesday, oh lawd Tuesday I'm so tired*
> *   I got no time to play*
> *Then comes Wednesday, I'm beat to my socks*
> *My gal calls and I have to tell her I'm out*
> *Cause Thursday is a hard working day*
> *And Friday I get my pay.*
> *Saturday morning, oh Saturday morning!*
> *All my tiredness has gone away*
> *Got my money, got my honey*
> *And I'm out on the stem to play*
> *Sunday morning my head is bad*
> *Boy it's worth it for the times I've had*
> *But I got to get my res'*
> *Cause Monday is a mess*

Boy, if I could sing that stuff the way Smiley Lewis does I'd run all these fancy singers out of the country. Call that primitivism if you want to. If you hear anything else by him let me know.

Back to jazz, I've heard enthusiastic reports on Basie from two other sources. I'm sorry we didn't get down to hear them together. I plan to make it before we leave. Take it easy, man. It's raining here and I've got to go out in it. Monday is, after all a mess.

Ralph

To Herbert Ellison
730 RIVERSIDE DRIVE
New York 31, New York
AUGUST 12, 1954

Dear Herbert:

I guess it's about time that I explained that bit of airline insurance which I mailed you in June: I had wanted to answer your letter before I flew down to Tuskegee, where I was teaching for about ten days, but just didn't have the time; thus when I took out the round-trip insurance for my wife I just took out a bit for you. Unfortunately, that kind of insurance is valid only for the extent of the trip so you can tear it up. However, we're flying to Salzburg, Austria, on the 19th (next Thursday) where I'm lecturing at the Salzburg Seminars in American Studies for a month, and I'll send you another policy. We will be in Europe for about two months as I have a few lectures in Germany after the seminar and then we go to Italy for a couple of weeks, then to Spain for a quick trip and then to France and home. We're already broke just from buying the tickets (I don't get paid for the Salzburg lectures, they just pay _my_ fare over and our expenses while we're in Austria—all I get is prestige and the opportunity of seeing Europe) but we decided that we'd better take advantage of the trip while we may. My wife is excited as all hell, but for the moment I can think only of having to run (except that story you saw) but I am at work on a long novel and that's taking up most of my time.

Doesn't time fly! And March 1st and June 14th continue to bring their yearly changes. I've started getting grey about the temples and very soon they'll start calling me "Baldy." Even my moustache has a few white hairs. I weighed the other day and I'm now 198 lbs., not a little of it around my middle. I would send you a photo but you've owed me one for years and done nothing about it so I'll just let you think about it. Don't you realize that I haven't seen you in sixteen years? John A. Townsend told me last summer in Okla. that you are larger than I am now, which doesn't surprise me, but I would like a picture of my closest relative. I'd pay for it if you'd have a photo made. Let me know.

Herbert, I hope you can get started on a home of your own but I know so little of your affairs, work, G.I. rights, etc., that I don't know how to advise you. Perhaps the winter will bring me some lectures out that way and I'll just come out there and have a talk with you. You know, we don't own anything ourselves, it took so damn long for me to finish my book that taxes knocked the hell out of my income, and there were loans to be repaid and furniture to be bought. Still, we want to have a place of our own and outside New York City and I guess that's our next project. When I was in Okla. City last summer I was amazed at the cheapness of the land out north east of the city. It's too bad neither of us wish to live there, though with the segregation thing changing so rapidly out there I might change my mind. However, my wife has never seen it and I doubt if she'd like it. Perhaps we'll try to drive out that way next summer. You'd be surprised at how some of the boys have turned out. Charlie Fields, for instance, owns three farms and raises hogs, and also owns a building on the east side. Several others have done just as well and just as unexpectedly. I'm enclosing a few snap-shots that I took. The guy under the flag with the straw hat in his hand is you. I didn't take it, Mrs. Slaughter did, the time when the Boy Scouts were encamped on their farm—which was a bit of a while ago. But now for those I made: moving alphabetically, the one with "A" on the back is the house in which you were born, on Byers street; "B" is a shot of how the school yard (Bryant) looks now with its oil wells and storage tanks; "C" is the new Tabernacle Church, which was erected on the same spot after the old one burned. It's quite handsome and was designed by a young Okla. Negro architect; "D" is the Y.M.C.A. located on Fourth Street about the spot where the Sheets lived, the small building this side of it is the office of Dr. Maurice Moore. The photo was shot looking West, toward Durland. You'll hardly recognize it with the porch gone but the little house in "F" is where we lived and had such wonderful times (I guess the best of <u>my</u> childhood) at 822 E. Fourth Street, and beside it is Frank's old home. They still own it but don't live there anymore, having another place on Sixth St. near Durland. On the corner to the left, where the Lawsons and the Rileys lived and the bootleggers who hid their whiskey in the alley—there is now an ugly icehouse of brick. All changes are not for the better. The tall tree under which we played and on whose apricots we stuffed our bellies has been cut down and replaced by that oil well you see above the Mead house. I didn't go down the alley, although I wanted to. Next door the Stewart house still stands but Mr. Stewart died last year, I believe. "H" is Deep Second looking downtown; "G" is 710 E. Second, where we were living when I hopped the freight for Tuskegee. That bit of fence you see on the left surrounds another oil well. "I" is the house on Stonewall, where you were living when I returned in 1935, and where you threw that cracker off the porch. Mama certainly had courage, moving in there and going to jail in defiance of that restrictive zoning ordinance. Do you remember the time she took us out to the zoo and took her time and showed us all of the animals before the cop came up to tell us we had to leave because we were Negroes? She knew that Negroes paid taxes to support the public parks and she meant for us to see the animals, law or no law. There was a time you were too young to remember, I think, when Negroes could attend plays and movies downtown and she always went. Well, I read in the *Black Dispatch* that this was once more possible and I thought how she would have enjoyed seeing that barrier fall. "J" is another shot of Deep 2, taken from beneath the awning of Jim's Drug Store. As you can see most of the wooden buildings are gone or now have brick facades. "K" is the Slaughter Building. I feel a little sad when I look at these scenes, they're all so familiar and memory filled and yet so small and distant. That's what happens when you grow up and go away, even the streets shrink and ghosts range in the mind. To look at these pictures you'd think that the City is a ghost town, but it's only that they were usually taken at midafternoon, when only a fool like me was walking around in the heat. And speaking of ghosts, do you remember the night we were afraid to go into the house because we saw something shining like eyes in the little house on Fourth Street? I do; Mr. Barbee who was a member of our church came by and took us in and showed us that the "eyes" were only the hinges on the icebox and told us never to be afraid of ghosts again. I always remember that when I'm afraid of unknown things . . . Did I tell you that Dr. Wiley was still alive, though an invalid shrunken to about a third of his original size? He is married to a nurse who takes care of him and they have a nice home . . .

Remember how when I called you Huck you resented it so? Well, I don't think you understood why I liked that name, but if you'll read Mark Twain's *The Adventures of Huckleberry Finn* (you can buy it for two bits in a paperback edition) you'll see why I always thought of him as a hero. I still do and it is a book I lecture about. So when we called you Huck it was for luck and adventure, a good spell. Like our belief, Frank and yours and mine, that if we called you "Rabbit Ears" the hucksters were sure to give you a watermelon, or peaches, or other fruit as they headed down Fourth Street on their way back to the country. For whatever reason it was, they certainly would pick you to give what they hadn't sold. I hope you're still as lucky and I hope also that you'll write more often. I don't care how well you put the words down, I'm interested in what you're doing and how you feel. I'll write you from Europe and let you know how things go. Meanwhile, take it easy and give regards to any Okies you happen to meet.

Love,

Ralph

To Albert Murray
AUGUST 19, 1954

Dear Albert:

Man, we're almost off, struggling with baggage and general anxiety. I forgot to tell you last night I was sending along the key to my new file (it's in the front closet) in which all of my papers are located. Should anything happen to us see what you can do with the junk. You and Stanley Hyman can play—or fight—at being literary executors. A hell of a thing to wish on anyone, but since we have about the same rifling that's what goes with it. Of course I'll try like hell to save you that problem. Take it easy, write your book, give my love to Mique and Mokie, and warm regards to the Mitch's and the Morts. This here is one monkey who's yelling at the buzzard to straighten up and fly right before he even hits the airport!

                                                              Ralph

R. Ellison
Salzburg Seminar in American Studies
Schloss Leopoldskron
Salzburg, Austria

To John Appleton
SEPTEMBER 4, 1954

Dear John Appleton:

Thanks for allowing me to see the galleys of Wright's *Black Power*. I found it of great interest, not only as a travel book, but as the attempt of a passionate intellectual to come to grips with the perplexing problem of Africa and modern power politics.

It seems to me that the value of the book lies precisely in Wright's ability to define the problem from the perspective afforded him by his dual identity as a black man and as an ex-Marxist intellectual. The first allows him to make a sympathetic but unsentimental identification with the aspirations of the Ashanti and to examine their lives free of the usual misconceptions often held by men of different colors and beliefs; the

second allows him to grasp the amalgam of Western political thinking and ancient ritual practices which has brought African nationalism
crashing into the once exclusively western councils where world power
spheres were decided. Africa, as the age-old saying of black men goes, is
at last stretching forth her wings. We are fortunate that Richard Wright
has traveled so far to report for us these her first, fumbling but porten-
tous efforts. Whether we like the developments reported in *Black Power*
or no, it is not a book that can be easily dismissed. Certainly it cannot
be safely ignored.*

Yours sincerely,
Ralph Ellison

Mr. John Appleton
Harper & Brothers
49 East 33rd Street
New York 16, New York

Ralph Ellison
730 Riverside Drive, 7B
New York 31, New York

STATEMENT OF PLAN

SOME PUBLICATIONS SINCE 1943†

My projected novel will be concerned with the problem of identity in
America, dramatized in terms of a young man's search for his father.

This search begins after a trip to Europe, where he has sought the relics of an intellectual hero of the thirties—when he realizes that he knows
very little of his own rather mysterious background.

Thus he returns to seek out his own identity as well as that of his father.
His quest takes him to Oklahoma, or one of the states last to represent the
American frontier; for it is here that he was born, and here he lives until

---

* This is one of Ellison's most pronounced commentaries on Africa, showing an interest in
that continent often overlooked by his biographers.

† Formatted like a letter, and part of his Guggenheim application, this is one of the most pro-
vocative early descriptions of Ellison's second novel, dated September 1954.

eight, when he is taken by a lawyer (who keeps his client's identity secret) and entered in an Eastern school for boys.

His break with his past is complete, for after living this far as a Negro he is told that he is white. His return is thus a plunge into the heart of his darkness, yet a fruitful one, for here he does discover traces of his father, a man as slippery as Proteus, and who manages to stay just one step ahead of him. Significantly, he discovers his father one day in Washington and confronts him with the question with which he (the young man) had as a child once moved folk-level Negro churches to poignant emotion, "Father, Father, why hast Thou forsaken me." To which the father replies, "Because you would have forsaken me."

This scope of this novel shall be broad, the level of consciousness and articulation high, and while the story of individuals and their most personal motives, it will also, I hope, throw some light on the nature of the American experience.

As for characters and levels of experience, it is concerned with Indians, white folks and Negroes, with ideas and actions of the most articulate and of the barely conscious. It will contain adults and children; women, intellectuals and politicians; folk people and people of the elite. In short, it shall attempt, in its symbolic way, to grasp the broad process of American life and explore it through the lives of individuals. Concerned with the broader meaning it will attempt to arrive at these through the specific personalities of individual characters. The main character shall, I hope, be of such diversity of experience and of such alertness of intellect, and so full of a passion to confront reality and understand it, that I should be able to define the nature of human experience in a manner as to create a novel of abiding interest to a variety of readers.

This is conceived not as a "race" novel, but as a novel of ideas; which for me implies a novel of action, an exploration of the mysteries of existence, and the depiction of fabulous, unexpected turns of fortune which I see as typical of America at her best, and of the novel (as form) at its most interesting.

To Pat and Camille Rhone
730 RIVERSIDE DRIVE
Apartment 7B
New York 31 New York
DEC. 7, 1954

Dear Pat and Camille:*

I've just had the sad experience of seeing last week's *Black Dispatch* with its tragic news. I've read it and I've been wrenched, and there's really very little that I can say about it. I learned from Jimmy that Little Pat† wasn't well but I'd hoped that somehow he'd survive his illness. Certainly when I saw him during October of 1953 I thought so, now I know that what I thought was a revival of his physical strength was in reality the strength of his spiritual courage.

It was in Jim's, and we had a quite pleasant talk about his grandfather, Jeff, and about those pleasant days over on Third Street, and we laughed a bit over his grandfather's stories. "What a fine young man," I thought. "And how much he has retained that poignant charm which he had when he and Jimmy used to go ambling up Stiles dressed in their blue overalls!"

For me one of the miraculous things about returning home was this maturing of your boy. It was certainly a shocking reminder of my own age, but somehow, seeing the fine quality of your young man allowed me to accept this not entirely happy awareness with a certain grace—as though through him some of the finer promises of my own life were redeemed. It was sobering even to think in this vein because it meant that I was surrendering certain youthful hopes, certain hoped for achievements of character, which I'd set for myself so long ago. Thus I suppose it was a recognition of failure.

We all experience these little crises, I suppose, and perhaps parents are fortunate in that they can more or less consciously pass along their ideals to their children and thus relive them and see their eventual achievement. Yet I suppose that it is through such young people as Pat that <u>all</u> of us, even those who, like myself, have no children, are a little better able to make these sad adjustments, and it is for this that we so deeply admire

---

* Pat and Camille Rhone, friends from Oklahoma City.

† Presumably the Rhones are "little Pat's" parents. See Ellison's letter to Virgil Branam of January 17, 1955, mentioning that "a little boy lived over on Third Street."

them. Unfortunately there are so few we <u>can</u> admire.—What I'm struggling to say is that Little Pat did something of this for me . . .

And while talking with him I was able to feel that in him that fine old couple who did so much to form my own sense of values had found a most worthy descendant. Thus here again I found in Pat an affirmation of some of the finest human qualities that it has been my good fortune to have known.

It has been quite a time since I've lived close enough to share your lives, my own having carried me to strange places to live among strange people, but the ties which were fashioned so long ago are still quite strong. Somewhere within us all there is that bright place (perhaps it's in the heart) where all of the best things—hopes, memories, a sense of nobility, honor, capacity for sacrifice and enduring friendship, and, still unspoiled despite my wanderings and all the scars of my growing up, that I tell you I share your sorrow and your loss.

I was too young when I left home to really know you and over the intervening years there was no opportunity, but when I saw your boys grown up I knew the kind of people you were and I was very proud to have known you. I've never tried to say such things before and if I do it too badly now, please forgive me. I could not have said anything like this to Little Pat, nor, perhaps to you, since we seldom give voice to what we truly feel. Perhaps it's just as well; nevertheless this is what I felt and I want you to know. Pat, and you, Camille, did your work well. Little Pat lived like a man and died with courage, and that is a great deal to say of any parents and of any child.

Please extend my sympathy to Pat's wife and to the rest of the family,

Sincerely,
Ralph

To Virgil Branam
730 RIVERSIDE DRIVE
New York 3 1, New York
JAN. 17, 1955.

Dear Virgil:*

We were damned glad to hear from you, though saddened by the news of your illness. The whole time we were in Madrid and Paris we kept

---

* Virgil Dodge Branam was one of Ellison's closest friends in high school in Oklahoma. They stayed in touch mainly through correspondence for decades until Branam's sudden death in March 1973.

an eye peeled for anyone of your general description, thinking sure that you'd turn up over there somewhere. I must say that in Paris I ran into several Colonials who were of your general darkness but as far as <u>bigness</u> goes, boy you are still the winner and still the champ! We could have had a hell of a time too; I walked poor Fanny bowlegged in both Madrid and Paris and if you'd been along the doctor would have had less work getting you reduced, your wife would have given a sigh of relief when she saw you and we would have enjoyed the whole trip much more for having had you along.

As you perhaps know we spent a month in Salzburg, where I was lecturing at the Institute in American Studies, after which we saw Frankfurt, Cologne, Ulm, Vienna, and traveled by car from Munich right up the Neckar valley, by car, to Frankfurt. After Germany we flew to Madrid, where I spent four days taking part in a conference with a few Americans and quite a few Spaniards during which we discussed North American culture. After that we remained in Madrid for fifteen days, then flew to Paris. I'll take the Spanish every time, though Paris is the more beautiful city. Since you've probably been both places many times I won't waste time telling you of things you've already seen, I'll only say that, generally, it knocked us out. eyes, pocketbook and all, including my right one.

Nevertheless, we were glad to get back home. Fanny is fine. I'm doing a little freelance journalism and working on another novel. Things are not too good just now, but neither are they bad enough to start complaining . . . I don't know when it was I saw you last, but I think it was after I had been home during the summer of 1953—well, I returned there the October of that year for my cousin Maybelle's funeral. Folks are dying away. Pat Rhone, who as a little boy lived over on Third Street across from the hospital, died recently and right afterwards Dr. T.J. Randolph* passed; Pat of a war injury, and T.J. from injuries received when he was gored by a cow some years ago. Hot Lips passed right after we returned from Europe and I saw quite a number of Okla. City and Kansas City people at the funeral, including Gladys' sister, who asked of you. I'll end this dark little passage by reminding you that Red has been dead some three years now, even though we sometimes speak of him as though he was very much alive. Bobbins is still O.K., living with friends in Long Island.

---

* Oklahoma City dentist, son of J. D. Randolph, one of the major father figures in Ellison's youth and a key citizen in black Oklahoma City during the time. Ralph worked for Dr. Randolph for a time, and also for his brother Jim.

Why don't you get the lead out and send me a photo of you and your family? We've been waiting at least to see that boy, who sounds as though he's living up to your great wrecking tradition. Boy, but I'd like to see him! Ol' John A. Townsend's boy is a senior at Fisk and Cabby's Boy is out at Langston. And man, you'd swallow your plate if you could see what a fine, good looking young woman that ugly little girl of Glad's turned into. She's married, teaches school, and has a great deal of poise. Glad and I had a real laugh over how she looked when we used to go there back in the old days. Her mother is in fine shape (Mrs. Spears) and so is Sing. I saw your boy Stephen Parker, who is about the only man in Okla City who is land poor. He has umteen run-down pieces of property and is bent upon getting more. Go back there when you get a chance, it'll do your heart good.

Take it easy Virgil, we're getting a little older—even I'm getting grey about the temples—so we'd better remember the advice of the old bull when he and the young bull were standing on top of the hill looking down at the herd of heifers.

"Come on," the young bull urged, kicking up his heels, "Let's run down the hill and mount us each a heifer."

"No, wait," the old bull said. "Let's walk down the hill and mount the whole herd."

Play it like the old bull, man. Anyway, the women like a man who takes his time!

Both Fanny and I send love and all the best to you and yours.

Ralph

To Paul Engle
730 RIVERSIDE DRIVE
APARTMENT 7B
NEW YORK 31, N.Y.
APRIL 10, 1955

Dear Paul Engle:*

Our mutual friend, Frank Taylor, suggests that I write you informally concerning a problem that has arisen out of my acceptance of the Prix de Rome Fellowship for next year in hope that you might find it possible to help ease the situation.

---

* Engle founded the University of Iowa Writers' Workshop program. In 1959, Engle would offer Ellison the position of writer-in-residence at Iowa, which he would decline.

Briefly—and ironically—I find myself in the ambiguous position of having accepted the Prix with its year in Rome at a time when we can least afford to deal with the financial obligations that accompany it. As you are probably aware, the Fellowship provides the following:

> Fellowship period—October, 1955—October, 1956.
> $600—travel expense, N.Y. to Rome and return.
> $300—European travel
> $100—each month from Oct. thru August; $150 in Sept.
> $150—for books and supplies.
> A bedroom and a study are provided free of charge.
> The candidate must pay for his own meals at the Academy at the
> rate of 200 lire per day or about $1.25; and must pay for his
> personal laundry.
> A candidate's wife may share his living accommodations free of
> charge, but meals, travel, etc. are not provided her.

These provisions seem quite wonderful to us, especially since wives are expected to come along with their husbands. But it is assumed, quite reasonably, that a candidate's affairs will be in such financial order that he can at least pay his wife's overseas passage and otherwise supplement the Fellowship where necessary. Unfortunately our affairs are not. Certainly if I were to go to Rome alone while my wife remained in the States at her job the Fellowship would be adequate, but a year is a long time to spend away from one's wife, especially so rare a year as one to be spent in Italy. And I believe that any experience upon which one is likely to feed for the rest of one's life should be shared with one's wife. Thus the prize that is meant as a balm has become a financial burden.

Ironically, our present financial situation came about through another honorary trip to Europe. Last summer I was invited to lecture at the Salzburg Seminar in American Studies, where my wife and I spent one of the most intense months of our lives, thoroughly enjoying ourselves though my work was hard—and went from Austria to Spain, where, at the invitation of the USIS, I participated in a conference of American and Spanish intellectuals.

As you know, such lectures bring nothing more than passage money and expenses, and the trip to Europe being itself worth the trouble. But while _my_ expenses to and from the USA and to and from Madrid were taken care of, my wife's expenses for all this travel had to come out of our savings plus borrowings of a few hundred dollars. All this was as recent as last October, and while we've managed to liquidate some of our debts, others are still holding on. Hence our total unpreparedness for this new trip.

Quite frankly, I have no savings to draw upon for my wife's fare, nor have we funds to sustain those inevitable expenses here at home—insurance, storage, etc. which must be taken care of in order to prepare for a year's absence. Nor will my wife be able to return and find her job (which has been our main support since our return from Europe) waiting as she did in October. To find it waiting after nine weeks was remarkable, but as valuable as she has been to her firm, a year is still a year and she expects to have to find something else.

On my side of this bread-winning team I am involved with a novel which I hope to finish by 1956 and we're hoping that it will provide an advance which will keep us floating until things are stabilized after our return—otherwise, we'll both be looking for jobs. For as you might guess, the royalty statements on *Invisible Man* have now become hardly more than a formality (a carrot placed before my nose twice yearly by my publisher to remind me of possibility); and my other writing income has slumped to a minimum due to the demands of the novel, which was interrupted for two months by the trip to Europe. The same is true of lecture income. I've had to refuse lecture dates, trying to get on with my real work. However, I've had no offers since the Rome thing exploded upon us. By now most college lecture schedules are fulfilled and I can't look forward to this as a source of income.

Fortunately, there is no real need for one writer to feel embarrassed by exposing the economic facts of his life to another writer, for I have followed Frank's advice to the letter: This is a frank and intimate baring of our situation. It is economic necessity at its most personal and fundamental level, and I know of no less embarrassing way of conveying it to you. Nor is there any way of hiding the fact that it is really rather absurd; for while most prizes are penalties, at least in part, usually we are saved this realization until somewhat later.

Indeed, I was aware that there are prizes which, like the ambassadorship to England, require financial independence on the part of the recipient, but in the excitement of being extended such a dazzling prize I allowed myself to lose sight of its less dazzling outlines. Otherwise, I would have soberly and regretfully refused it, making this really unfair request (unfair since the winner of such a fellowship shouldn't ever think of asking for more) unnecessary.

Nevertheless, my request is no less sincere nor our need less crucial, since we have the bear or prize by the tail, and anything you might do or suggest will be appreciated more than I could take of your time to tell you.

Sincerely,

Ralph Ellison

Mr. Paul Engle
State University of Iowa
Iowa City, Iowa
   cc: Frank Taylor

To Albert Murray
730 Riverside Drive
New York 31, N.Y.
April 12, 1955

Dear Murray:

Here are a few riffs from old Cliofus,* who seems on the way to out lie Sallywhite. This chok-drinking Charlie character appeared just as I was typing up this copy to send you, I don't know where the hell Cliofus got him but here he is anyway. As you see, the stuff is still crude—which means it's still building. Anyway, here it is.†

Things are all upset here, the damn prize‡ is something of a problem, for here we are still paying off our debts from the last trip and now we've got to prepare for another. The apartment has to be sublet (if the landlord approves). I have to do something about the car, and we've got to get money for Fanny's passage. Here we go again. I could take an advance, but this isn't good because we'll have to have something to live on when

---

* Important character in the "Hickman in Oklahoma" narrative of Ellison's unfinished second novel.

† Ellison's enclosure is what he called an eleven-page "Copy of [a] Working Draft" from his novel-in-progress. The excerpt is not included here but appears in *Three Days Before the Shooting . . .* , 865–92.

‡ Prix de Rome.

we return. I'm sure we'll work it out, but just the same it's a pain. I'd have had yours down to you but I discovered that $3000.00 of income which I thought I'd paid last year actually was received during this tax period—which literally knocked the crap out of our payment schedule. Nevertheless, I'll take care of you before Sept. 22—our sailing date.

What's happening with you Murrays? I've talked with Doris recently and she mentioned something about Europe but was very vague. Tell me something. How're Mique and Moque? Has spring shown? Man, I'd like to hit the road even though I'm sure I'd get disgusted with what they're not doing down there. But I always liked the place in the spring and I'm sure it would be as good for my soul as anything. Tell Nance incidentally, that I hope he got his fellowship even though I've neglected to write . . . I helped record the Ellington "Symphony of the Air" concert a few weeks ago and wished you were here to catch it. Don Gillis took up half the program but nothing happened until Duke started waving his shoulder, then the symphony started sounding like his band, strings and all. Even Don Shirley with his fabricated personality and cocktail lounge, white boy approach couldn't ruin it. We've caught a couple dances at the Savoy recently with Cootie Williams and Buddy Tate and I'm glad to report that the joint still jumps and the gutbucket is as full of rich life as ever. Let them look for white hopes of jazz as much as they will, the true stream still runs deep and blue. Tell Mitch* that when he comes to town, if ever, we'll have to go jumping. And tell him to hold down the Twenty-Nine† because I'll be back there the first chance I get. This is about it but before I drop it I should say that I hope you're not allowing those asses to turn you away from writing. The only mistake you ever made was, perhaps, to assume that they could ever really tolerate you among them. Man, you're a walking condemnation of everything they stand for; and though I'm sure you've done very important things for some of the students simply by being there, too much of your psychic and moral energy has to go into simply keeping the stink of some of the administration out of your nostrils. Now, with Mort away, it must be a real crapper. Well, the only way to stick them and stick them hard is by going ahead and publishing a book. A novel or a book of criticism, anything that expresses your sense of life—this is more important than

---

* Dr. Rudolph Mitchell, obstetrician and pediatrician, Murray's neighbor at Tuskegee.

† Roadhouse on Route 29, Macon County, Alabama.

the dough that you're going to have anyway, and you pointed out there's no contradiction between you having dough and writing. If you have something short, send it up to Arabel, she's dying for material and worrying the life out of me. But whatever and whenever—write and publish! End of sermon.

By the way, there's a Hemingway piece in the current *True,* which I haven't read. I'm catching up on the gal he recommended as worthy of the Nobel Prize, Isak Dinesen, whose *Seven Gothic Tales* I read down there during the thirties. I'm in the midst of *Out of Africa* and it's really very good. I understand that there are several others and I'm out to find them. I've also been having a once a week sessions with Bellow, listening to him read from his work-in-progress and reading to him from mine. For about thirty minutes we cuss out all the sons-abitches who say the novel's dead, then we read and discuss. Wish the hell you were taking part. If you fly up bring along some of the stuff and give it a try. It's the only genuine literary life I know these days; the rest is all cocktails and bullshit and the cocktails aren't always good. When I find myself at one nowadays I feel like asking with Choc-drinking Charlie,* "Where the hell's the <u>hat</u> that goes with these castrated pants?"

Take it easy, man. And write me. I'm in a violent agitated frame of mind and need a friendly voice. Give our love to Mokie and Mique.

Ralph

To Fred and Lucille Muhlhauser
730 Riverside Drive
New York 31, New York,
july 28, 1955

Dear Fred and Lucille:†

At last I've found the time and discipline to write. I've been intending to do so for weeks but yesterday after a long distance call from Tuskegee I knew I could wait no longer. For it turns out that you know Albert Murray, my best friend from college days. I learned that when I happened to mention that I had been visiting for a few days with friends in Cambridge

---

* A minor character in Ellison's novel-in-progress.

† Fred Muhlhauser directed the Salzburg Seminar that Ellison participated in back in 1954. In June 1955, Ralph visited Brandeis University and was reunited with the Muhlhausers.

whom we'd met at the Seminar, and he said "Not Fred and Lucille Muhl-hauser," and went on to tell me about your trip to Genoa. I'm sure you had a time with that adventurous character and it pleases me no end to learn that we have this further bond.

Murray is now a captain in the Air Force and will be in New York during the first week in August in order to sail with his family for an assignment at Casablanca. He told me to tell you that he intends to do Europe again as soon as he can. Who knows, perhaps we can all meet in some country in the fine spring weather. I hope so.

I had no trouble the morning I left you in the rain, although the streets dropping down to the river from the Square were flooded and there had been a bad automobile wreck in the night. I saw the cops sitting snug and dry in their car, writing down the necessary information as I went past. It was all very dream-like, with the rain drumming the top of my car and their faces remote behind the dripping glasses and windshields. All sound was muted. Down the road a couple of Harvard boys went zipping past in a hot-rod, going much too swiftly over the glistening asphalt as I rolled dripping toward Bennington.

I hadn't realized that I was running into the last two weeks of school, and found myself swung up into a round of my friend Stanley Hyman's classes (how frightfully brilliant some of those girls are!), faculty and student parties—a bastard whiskey sour was the popular drink this year, three drinks and you're ulcered out—Little League baseball games, concerts, art exhibits and plays. Finally there was the rather beautiful and simple graduation ceremony held under the morning sky. With sweet-voiced choir and concert of mellow hand-rung bells and the bright young faces beneath their mortarboards receiving their degrees on a lawn still perfumed by spring flowers.

I was taken in like the stranger at the wedding feast, and my old bones quickened to the challenge of so much youth and I kept going and enjoying myself to the end.

Just the same I managed to get some work done, to read some, and to engage in serious shoptalk with Stanley and Shirley. Naturally I played with my godson and with my older friends, his brother and sisters. I stayed on for two weeks, when business brought me home.

So now I'm back here working and being a bachelor. Fanny left last week for Chicago and I've been battling the heat alone and wishing I was back in Cambridge (when we return from Europe I intend to consider this seriously). I can't tell you just how much I enjoyed myself with you, only that it was one of the most refreshing visits in years. Thank you very much.

I told Fanny Linda's story about the uncles being chased by the bull and winning first prize in a foot race and she was greatly amused. Linda's quite a girl. We are sending separately some stamps for her, and you might tell her that if she ever wishes to send me a copy of one of her stories, I should be very pleased to receive it. You must say this very correctly for me, for I suspect that she's quite a lady; she'd [be] just about that age.

Fred, I read the essay by Miss Brumm, for whom I'm enclosing a note. She has a piece in *Partisan Review* that is just as good. Thanks for calling her to my attention.

Our time grows near and we'll soon be going so if we don't see you before we leave we'll write again, sending [our] address in Rome and any late news.

Thanks once again,
Ralph

To Dave Sarser
THE AMERICAN ACADEMY IN ROME
VIA ANGELO MASINA V, ROME 28,
ITALY.
OCTOBER 21, 1955

Dear Dave:*

I've been planning to write for quite some time now but things have gone so rapidly that I haven't had the time nor peace of mind. The trip took us eleven days for once we entered the Mediterranean the voyage became a cruise. We stopped at Algeciras, Spain for day, at Cannes, France for another and at Genoa for still another. Finally, and to our great relief, we docked at Naples. Here we were met by cars from the academy and driven to Rome.

But hardly had we been here a week and begun to adjust than we were taken on a guided trip through northern Italy. We were in Orvieto, Perugia, Urbino, Ravenna, Pisa, Florence, Siena, Assisi, Rimini, Todi, and several other towns where we visited the monuments, art galleries, churches and museums. We've been back here for three days now and I'm trying

* Dave Sarser, a friend of Ellison's since the 1940s and a fellow photography and camera expert, was also a violinist in the NBC Symphony Orchestra, led by Arturo Toscanini.

to get back in the groove. It isn't easy, after seeing so much great art one wonders what to do.

I've already changed over the machines to 50 cycles, bought a variable line transformer for myself and had one bought for the academy. The conversion seems to be successful except I get a small loop, about like this when I put the machine in the play mode but it's gentle and seems to cause no harm. I suspect there's a bit too much hold-back tension. On the other hand, the current here is very erratic so that I don't know what to expect when recording. Previous recordings were pretty punk but two of the composers, who know even less than I, make the tapes so I hope that I might improve things a bit. They had a 50-cycle kit when I arrived so I converted their machine when I did mine. No looping there. They're using a Phillips mike so I'm sure that my Altec will be an improvement. Incidentally, I made up a list of equipment that is needed here—headphones, splicing block, splicing tape, demagnetizer, etc., and suggested to the director that he have the New York office buy them from you, so when they do please include anything I forgot. They have absolutely nothing but a 600, 620, and a mike except the line transformer I had them buy. You'll probably be called by a Miss Williams and if so, include a kit of small parts for me; she'll take care of the shipping. I find that our standard of living is much smaller here than at home but if that stereophonic tape has come down within reason let me know; with all the composers and music lovers dropping in here Victor should put us on their reviewers list. We're badly in need of a sound system here and later I'll try to have them get a Musicians's, Audak, Components etc.

Dave, you'd simply go mad in this town, there are Lancias and Ferraris all over the place. Here at the academy there are three Volkswagens, one Singer, one Humber, two Hillman, and I don't know how many Fiats. One fellow has ordered an Austin Healy but it hasn't been delivered. I'm told that there is some way of having them delivered in France, driven 500 miles, at a price of 1500 dollars. It's a damn good thing that I'm broke, because you know what would happen.

That's the story for now. I can be reached at the above address within three days by airmail. In the meantime give my regards to your mother and tell Walter and the others up in Riverdale that I'm simply wordless before the magnificence of their country. Fruit, flowers, people, art all are wonderful. Take care of yourself and I'll write more next time.

Ralph

To Ida G.
AMERICAN ACADEMY IN ROME
VIA ANGELO MESINA 5
ROME 28 ITALY
OCTOBER 21, 1955

Dear Ida:

We have just returned from a trip to the hill country of north Italy—Oriveto, Perugia, Urbino, Assisi, Siena, Florence, Pisa, etc.—where we've been seeing as much of the great art as we could cram into nine days. Despite the damage of time and war it is still as awe-inspiring as you told me it was when you were last here. We went in a group guided by the director of the academy and his wife, eighteen excited people packed into three small European cars and an American station wagon, and carrying luggage and equipment for picnic lunches along the way. In the end we were quite worn out, but nevertheless, we managed to spend a day and a night in all of the important cities, and to stop briefly at many small spots in between. We by no means saw it all but our guides were wonderful and if and when we're able to return we have a good idea what we want to see. Since we're to be here a year I've a notion we'll be seeing some of these glorious cities again.

Ruins, architecture, art, palaces, churches and graveyards, my head is whirling with it all. I was somewhat reluctant to come here, but had I failed to do so I would have missed one of the major human experiences. Perhaps it is impossible to have a real idea of what human culture can be unless one visits Italy. Surely human aspiration found its most magnificent expression here, and certainly in terms of the individual. Here were so-called pagans who in their will to become godlike created cities worthy of gods. We saw magnificent art in the Prado during last year's trip to Madrid and in Vienna as well, but there is so much greatness here that the effect is simply stunning. Perhaps the secret of being truly human lies in aspiring to be <u>more</u> than human; certainly men concerned mainly with the stomach or self-glorification, or ideological correctness could not have created all this, and if in the end it was in vain (though I cannot believe it was) then one should have the courage to give one's energies to vain things. I only wish I could have seen this during the thirties, when I was searching so eagerly for patterns of self-transcendence. I'm sure its effect would have been even more liberating than it is now. When I was a boy I dreamt of Michael Angelo and now at last I've seen his magic hand.

Interesting enough, I had been thinking of you quite often on the trip; of the art to which you introduced me, and how really very generous you have been in sharing your experiences; the help you gave me. I thought of you especially in Florence in the Uffizi Gallery, and along the Ponte Vecchio where I came across little leather boxes like the one that used to sit on your cocktail table—which brought back memories of the pleasant times we used to have. Thus it wasn't too surprising to find a letter on our return that said that you had called.

Ida, I'm quite sorry to learn that you've been ill again and I hope that by now you've recovered. Miss Bond told me of your conversation concerning our relationship and I assure you that nothing has changed the deep feeling of friendship and indebtedness that I feel toward you, and, I feel quite guilty over my neglect. Our differences have been political and only political and I have always felt that no political disagreement was worth the destruction of a friendship. I certainly didn't wish to have all those wonderful years of warm human relationship poisoned; nor did I wish to upset you further with arguments and irritation. I just didn't know how to resolve the conflict so became silent.

The whole tempo of our life changed. First the trip to Salzburg of last year, then back for lectures and work on my book, then the sudden news that I had won the Prix de Rome and the extremely hectic preparations for the trip. Fanny told me that you called during the summer when I was away on a trip but I didn't reach you when I returned. Perhaps you were even then in the hospital.

Thus life goes on. First we were all good friends, you, Clara, and your grandchildren; then my politics made the children uncomfortable with me, then came my novel to increase that discomfort, then we lost Clara; if this is not too strong a word. But you were closest and I chose not to come around rather than lose completely what we had. I can't tell you how much it relieves me [to] write this letter, especially since I didn't wish my silence to be confused [with] Richard's. I think you'll understand without further explanation, so now I'll leave it.

As I mentioned above we'll be living here a year; in a huge villa which houses all the Fellows of the academy and their wives, and in which we eat and work and live. We have five rooms* that we are gradually making livable and I have a small one-room studio built against the old Aurelian wall that surrounds part of the estate. There are two large windows in it and

---

* More likely the "two" rooms he mentioned in his October letter to Harry Ford.

when not working I can look out on the beautiful garden where the Italian gardeners grow much of the fruit and vegetables which we eat, and all of the flowers for the large common room and for the tables. It is all quite Italian and quite beautiful, and being located out on the Janiculine Hill it is peaceful. Oddly enough, I've been so busy since coming here that I haven't started exploring Rome but soon shall; perhaps when I've learned a little of the language—which I'm studying at the moment. Fanny, by the way is doing quite well, though she <u>did</u> take lessons before we left home.

I shall close now and hope again that this finds you well. Don't use your strength in answering but simply call Miss Bond and give her any message you wish [me] to have and I'll write from time to time. She'll probably leave in January but another young woman, Miss Hicks, will have the place and she'll be glad to send along any word.

With love and warm
wishes from Fanny and
from
Ralph

To Albert Murray
AMERICAN ACADEMY IN ROME
VIA ANGELO MASINA V
ROME 28, ITALY
OCT. 22. 1955

Dear Albert:

I started this letter a few days before we left, but didn't have time to finish it so I'll pick up where I left off before going into the trip, etc. So as I was saying: I went into a store on Madison Avenue the other day and saw a slightly built, balding Mose in there stepping around like he had springs in his legs and a bunch of frantic jumping beans in his butt (pronounced ass), and who was using his voice in a precise, clipped way that sounded as though he had worked on its original down home sound with great attention for a long, long time—a true work of art. I dug this stud and was amazed. I was sitting across the store waiting to be served when he got up and came across to the desk to pay for his purchase and leave his address—when the salesman made the mistake of asking him if he wasn't <u>the</u> Joe (pardon me, Jo) Jones.

Well man, that definite article triggered him! His eyes flashed, his jaw unlimbered and in a second I though ole jo was going to break into a

dance. His voice opened up like a drill going through thin metal and before you could say Jackie Robinson he had recalled every time he had
been in this store, the style of shoes he bought and why he'd bought them
and was going into a tap dancing description of his drumming school,
politics, poon-tang in Pogo Pogo and atomic fission—when I remembered
what you had told me of his opinion of Alton Davenport and uttered the
name. Man, his voice skidded like a jet banking up there where the air
ain't air and he started stuttering. "Did you say Davenport?" he said "And
Birmingham, Tuskegee, and points south," I said. And he was off again.
In fact, he damn near exploded and the fallout must have swamped the
fat-ass Alton way the hell down Birmingham way. I thought I'd better get
him out of there to cool him off, so we moved out on the street with him
still blowing. I finally managed to tell him that I knew you and he calmed
down. He gave me his address to pass along to you so here it is: Jo Jones,
123 W. 44th Street, NYC Room 903. Judson 2-2300. What a character! I'm
afraid that he's not only a great drummer he is—in the colored sense—
also a fool. When we separated I followed him at a distance just to see
him bouncing and looking as he headed over to 5th Ave., and it was like
watching a couple of hopped-up Japanese playing ping pong on a hot
floor. Man, they tell a lot of wild stories about boppers but this stud is
truly apt to take off like a jet anytime he takes the notion. He probably
has to play his bass drum with a twenty-pound weight on his trap foot. In
fact as I moved behind him I expected any minute to see him re-react to
the outrage of Davenport's teaching music and run a hundred yard dash
straight up the façade of a building. Drop him a few calming words, man;
he needs them.

As you can see, we are here. It took us eleven days on the *Constitution*,
what with one-day stops in Algeciras (Spain), Cannes, and Genoa. The
food was lousy and the trip was a bore and [we] were damn glad to get off
at Naples, where we drove by car to Rome. We're about settled now, here
on the Janiculine Hill, in a huge villa where all the Rome Fellows and some
Fulbrighters live and work. We have a bedroom and a living room and I
have a study located in a one room cottage built against the old Aurelian
Wall, which surrounds part of the estate. My windows face the garden
that supplies our vegetables and flowers and I'm fairly remote from interruption and most workaday sounds. The only writing I've done however
has consisted of an article on music and some letters. For at the end of our
first week [we] were carried on a tour of northern Italy. We went by car

and saw the art of Orvieto, Perrugia, Urbino, Pisa, Assisi, Todi, Rimini, Ravenna, Florence, Sansepolcro, Sienna and many places in between. We were gone nine days and if we never see any more we've certainly seen some of the greatest. My eyes are still whirling and we simply must go back to some of the places to isolate and study those works which most moved us. If I had about one choice it would be Florence and the Uffizi Gallerie. I'm aching for a car now, just to get around at will. The Renaissance has sent my imagination on a jag ever since I was shooting snipes in Oklahoma, but here it's around you everywhere you turn, the same sky, earth, water, roads, houses, art. And not only that, it's all mingled with the Roman, the Greeks, the Greco-Christians. At a table I hear the Classicist talking the stuff, who did what, when and why and where, and I feel lost in a world that I've got to get with or die of frustration. We've got one of the keys, though, for here is where the myth and ritual business operates in a context not of primitive culture but beneath the foundations of the West. Some of the classical people here are snobbish about this mess but it belongs to anyone who can dig it—and I don't mean picking around in ruins, as important as this is. I've just read a novel titled *Hadrian's Memoirs** that is interesting in its reconstruction of the times, warfare, politics, philosophy, religion and the homosexual love life of the Emperor. It's really more of a scholarly synthesis than a novel but it's worth reading. As soon as I can discover who knows what around here I plan to get a reading list so that I can orient myself in relation to the classical background.

Man, I wish I could get over there with a tape recorder and copy some of your records. I bought that French set and it took up a good number of the reels I had so that I need a hell of a lot more jazz tapes to keep me on my proper ration. A man has, after all, to keep his feet on his home ground. As it is I have the Academy ringing with Duke and Count and Jimmy Rushing. I could just use a hell of a lot more. Books are a problem too; I'm only the fifth fellow in literature and they haven't built up much of a library. I guess I have to load up on my Penguins as soon as I can get down into the city. That Fanny is more like you, she's down there every day seeing all the sights. I've been only three times, and then on business. I'll catch up though. She's also speaking some Italian while I've only one lesson ...

No important news from home. We have friends living in the apart-

---

* *Memoirs of Hadrian* (1951), by Marguerite Yourcenar.

ment and since I couldn't sell the car I stored it. Which bothers me now; for I have been told that I could stay here two years if I wish, and perhaps three. Right now I'd trade it for a Volkswagen and a gallon of gas! Have a letter from Foster requesting ideas of what program of Tuskegee should be, I haven't yet written that self-liquidation is the trick.

How are things going with you, Moke and Mique? All three of you stay the hell out of the way of those bloody French. In fact, I suggest that you fly Old Glory everywhere you go. And by no means go around in anything white, because it's better to be shot for a Mose than an A-rab any damn day (as you can see I'm still learning how to operate this Italian typewriter). By the way, write me the price of those Moroccan scatter rugs; we have tile floors and we could use a couple in our living room. If they are cheap enough I'd be willing to pay the duty to have them here. Those I remember are white with brown, black, yellow etc. designs. Got to feather this nest, man. Now if I could just find me some chitterlings . . . Allen Tate's wife, Caroline Gordon, is here and as soon as I know her better I'm going to ask her. 'Cause sure as hell she's going to come up one day wishing for some turnip greens cooked with a ham bone and I have a notion that all the southerners in Rome have a joint which they keep secret. I met Snowden, the Negro cultural attaché at a party and he was operating semi-officially so I didn't bother him at the time. Incidentally, I'm still cutting my own hair; he has less than I have so I didn't ask him about an initiated barber. Nevertheless, I suspect old Snowden can speak the idiom and I'll bet my money that he's an operator. If not I'll find me somebody down around Bricktop's place. Some seamen from the *Constitution* promised to introduce us to that part of Rome when they came in next trip, so by the time you get over we'll have situation well in hand. Till then if there's anything I can do for you here or through friends in New York, just let me know. Kiss the girls for me and tell 'em us loves yall.

As ever,
Ralph

To Harry Ford:*
THE AMERICAN ACADEMY IN ROME
VIA ANGELO MASINA V, ROME 28,
Italy
OCT. 23, 1955

Dear Harry:*

I didn't see anyone who looked like you, donor or otherwise, but I saw myself some mighty fine Memlings last week in Florence. We were at the Uffizi Gallerie and there were just heaps of goodies which I wish you and Lebe had been along to enjoy. After an eleven day voyage which bored the balls off me and a week at the academy, where instead of really adjusting I worked like hell finishing up the piece for *High Fidelity,*† we were carried with sixteen other Fellows on a nine day trip through Northern art centers. We were in Orvieto, Perugio, Urbina, Rimini, Todi, Assisi, Ravenna, Pisa, Florence, Siena, and many small places in between. And the art books come alive: It was too much, of course and we'll have to go back to those places which really devastated us and spend as much time as possible. When the ship stopped for a day at Cannes we took a bus up to Antibes to see the Picasso museum there much to our disappointment. His best works are simply elsewhere. But any one stop on the trip more than made up for the wasted time. In Florence we had a room with a balcony overlooking the Arno and within a stone's throw of the old bridge; cheap too, and with good food. The director and his wife served as guides and managers of our four-car caravan and made the trip a sheer joy. The beauty of the scenery would have made the trip worth the bother.

So now we're back and boring in. Fanny went to be interviewed concerning her job today and we've both started taking Italian lessons. We have two rooms, one for sleeping and the other for entertaining, and I have a little study built against the old Aurelian wall that surrounds part of the Academy estate. Richard Wilbur had it before me and there are big sheets of paper pinned to the walls with words like NEB, RETICLE, CNTED, REPLEVIN, SHAMBLES, ELEMnOSYNARY, MANDIBLE, THAC-MATURGY, BRIT, and Dehiscent written on them. Imagine! I'm about

* Editor at Knopf.

† This was the essay "Living with Music," published in December 1955.

to put up a few of my own, like Rumpsprung, pisseyed, grannydodger and titfixed-moneygrabber. Dam if I intend to let a mere poet outdo me.

But there are more interesting traces of passed artists here. This morning Karl Milles' assistant took me through his studio and showed me the pieces he had just completed before he died, and it was quite impressive. There is a group for a fountain at the Met, consisting of the Muses riding on the backs of dolphins that I found quite dynamic and playful; and there was a monumental horse and rider that will grace a public building in Kansas City. This assistant, whose name is Tex, worked with the old man for thirteen years and now seems somewhat lost. Thank God I brought a few books. The place is lousy with artists, musicians and architects so that the library is full of art books, scores, classical studies and magazines on design etc., but dam little for a writing kinda fellow. I hear there's an English bookstore down in the city so I'll go down there soon and load up on Penguins. Nevertheless, I've been having fun with Graphis, Domus, Interiors and lord knows how many art journals. Fortunately I brought my own music because thus far the composers all seem on a 12tone kick and I got this nervous stomach. But I have hope.

There's little I can say about Rome this time, I've been down there only 3 times on business but next week I'm starting to explore. I'm already convinced that this is the navel of the world we know and I intend to absorb as much as I can. Tomorrow there's a group going down to Pompey and Naples but we'll pass it up so that I can get started writing . . . Drop me a word now and then and give our love to Elizabeth . . .

Ralph

To Herbert Ellison
THE AMERICAN ACADEMY IN ROME
Via Angelo Masina V, Rome 28,
Italy.
NOV. 12, 1955.

Dear Herbert:

Well, here we are in Rome. I had hoped to write before we left, but all the rush involved in sailing left me no time. Nevertheless, we left on the *Constitution* on September 22 and arrived in Naples on October 2, after stops in Algeciras, Spain, Cannes, France, and Genoa Italy. From Naples we went by the Academy station north to Rome, which is to be our home for the year. The Academy itself is a great Villa of more rooms than I now know, but enough to more than house, feed, and provide working space (the artist and sculptors' studios are as large as dance halls), a pool room, library, lecture rooms, etc. for over sixty people. And in addition there is a huge garden that provides our flowers and vegetables. My own working quarters consist of a small one room brick cottage (I've seen no wooden structures in this part of Italy, everything is stone or brick or tile) built against an old wall which was here in Biblical times. My windows look out across the garden and the sun comes in most of the day, making it a very pleasant place to work. I must admit, however, that I haven't yet gotten much done. The change in pattern is much too great in itself and we had hardly been here a week before all of the new Fellows were taken on a nine day guided tour to the North, where we visited the museums, ancient ruins and churches. We were in Urbino, Orvieto, Ravenna, Pisa (we were all around the Leaning Tower and it's still leaning), Sienna, Assisi, Perugia and Florence. It was all very wonderful and the trip through the beautiful country by car was in itself an experience I'll never forget. We've been back almost a month now and I'm still reacting to what we saw . . . As for Rome itself, I can only say that it is very very old and very, very beautiful, but I've been much too busy trying to get my novel rolling to have spent much time sightseeing. The academy is located on one of the seven hills that surround the main section of the city and I look down there from time to time but it is Fanny who has been exploring it. She has a part-time job, a rather difficult achievement for an American, and thus gets around quite a bit. I'm studying the language now and as soon as I'm able to speak a bit I'll venture out. Then I'll be able to write you about it. This place is full of painters, sculptors, musicians and people who write on ancient art, architecture and literature, and there is a poet, whom I knew back in New York and a journalist-playwright. I am the only novelist and, at present, the only Negroes are Fanny and I. Indeed, we've only met one other Negro couple since we've been here, and they were the cultural attaché of the U.S. Embassy and his wife. He formerly taught at Howard University but we saw them only briefly at a party so weren't able to learn much about them. Perhaps in time we shall. Anyway I suppose part of this experience will lie in living away from the Negro community for so long a time. I'm not one of those who want to be elsewhere but it will be interesting to see what the difference is going to be. If they only had some colored cooking once in a while!

I'm sorry that I don't have your letter at hand since I have an idea that you might have asked me some question. I'll try to find it and answer next time. I do remember that something was not quite right with your wife and I hope that by now it's straightened itself out. As for your wife's desire to give up working I sympathize with her and wish that mine could do the same, but if it isn't practical, it just isn't. You've never really told me of your physical condition, or whether you're working, or anything of that nature, but if you <u>can</u> take care of all expenses without her aid it might be a good idea to give her a vacation. If not, what can you do? And how about sending me a snapshot here? I know you won't, but take care of yourself and write whenever you can.

Ralph

To Albert Murray
AMERICAN ACADEMY IN ROME
VIA ANGELO MASINA V
ROME 28, ITALY
JAN. 30, 1956

Dear Albert:

I've been intending to write for quite some time now but first there was the holiday hurly burly then two weeks ago Fanny had an appendix attack, which though it did not require an operation, was very painful and has left her weak and has had us quite anxious. But the round of illnesses didn't stop there; I am just recovering from bronchial pneumonia after eight days in bed and a gallon of antibiotics. (Right now as far as I'm concerned they can give Rome back to the Etruscans. This whole joint is like a hospital most of the time. Americans don't seem to get the same energy from the food here and I'm told that it takes just about a year to adjust to the dampness of the climate and the germs that fill the air from the constant pissing on the street, monuments, churches, cars, and anything else these studs can lean on and direct a stream against. The dogs here run around in a perpetual state of confusion because their messages are always being scrambled by the human beings.) The best of Rome remains its past, I'm afraid, and I've given up any faint notions I might have had that the salvation of the world lay in Europe, just as I've learned that a lot of the crimes against taste which the Americans are charged with are just so much hokey. Hell yes, Hollywood is lousy but it just isn't powerful enough to be responsible for all the degeneration of Italian taste. Some of the stuff they show in the art galleries wouldn't be allowed to take up wall space in the states, and if you think television in the States is bad, man, you should see it here. Some outfit did a show called "American in Rome" in which I took part along with some of the others at the AAIR, and while at the station we had to observe an hour of their regular TV fare. Man, it was worse than a gang of fays trying to imitate a gang of Moses—like a vacuum full of crap! Well, the Italians are in spite of all this, a kind, warmhearted people and we like them and are making slow but definite progress with their language. I'm taking two lessons a week and getting down into Rome proper several times a week. Haven't been able to find any Negroes though, except the Snowdens, who are too much on the defensive. They're Boston and Washington, DC and you know what that means. The fays here resent him and insist that he <u>must</u> be a Tom, otherwise he wouldn't have been given the job. Actually he seems no more incompetent or competent than the US cultural attaches I've seen in other countries. Anyway, he seems under great strain and gives the impression of a man who wishes to hell that he had eyes growing in the back of his head. Madame Luce* is roundly disliked by some of the American colony, a great deal of which is pederast and ultra snobbish, not that one has to [be to] dislike La Luce. It makes for a very amusing though quite unsavory atmosphere because Americans away from home are the most insecure people in the world and become even more the victims of their status striving. So that here snobbism has become a prime value and they can't seem to see that the leaders in this farce are really the most ridiculous and insecure of the whole lot. When we see you I'll spell this out as it's truly instructive.

Thanks for the Faulkner, I'm sure I would have missed it otherwise. The library here is a farce except for classicists, architects, etc. No literature and magazines. That haul of books you've been buying makes me anxious. I've only picked up three beat old copies of Mencken's *Prejudices* and the biography of a civil war figure at the flea market. Ordered a study of the Ulysses Theme from England, which looks promising; have been reading Stendhal's journals and rereading the *Idiot* in a new translation and *The Sound and the Fury,* Sypher's book on Renaissance style, etc. This is the damnedest place, full of scholars but thus far no one knows much of literature or of the life out of which literature comes. I've also reread the *Royal Way* and now find it quite thin. It makes me sad but I'm sure that under other circumstances I'll feel differently about

---

* Ambassador Clare Boothe Luce, a former congresswoman from Connecticut, playwright, and wife of Henry Luce, publisher of *Time* and *Life* magazines.

it. Maybe I've reached the age when some of the things we loved grow wan. Of course right now I'm writing and searching for intensity and that makes me hard to please. That damn Russian though, he's got so much of it that he could reach you through the sound of a prizefight if you gave him half a chance. And speaking of prizefighting—Sugar Ray dug him up some religion and whupped hell outta Bobo.* His next role will probably be that of a preacher cause he is simply gotta have that limelight. I can see him whipping the hell out of the whole sinner's bench and thus making a short work of converting everybody. Billy Graham would be nowhere. Certainly it won't be the first time that such has happened and I'm sure ole Sugar would do it with great style.

What are we going to do about getting together? It would have to be this year, since I've now been told that my fellowship is only for one year (I suspect that writers are a bit too observant for the comfort of certain people here). So we'll have to see you during spring or summer. There is a possibility of my going to Madrid during March—which would put me closer. Spring isn't too far off and I'm told that it is a good time to visit Rome. Actually Fanny won't be able to travel until June, because her job will keep her tied up until that time. Let's make plans if we can . . . As for the rugs, hold off a while. If we get over there we could save you the bother and I'm sure that by that time you'll have all of the best getting places nailed down. A couple here know of a place in Tangiers, but we saw samples of the designs and were not taken with them. I could use some of those heavy leather shoes though, because all the floors here are tile and as cold as a well-digger's. No doubt the reason most of us are always full of cold. These I could use right now, having brought only a thin pair of traveling house shoes . . . Glad to hear that things have quieted down over there, the French have had illusions of grandeur for so long that they can't believe all that crap about their being citizens of France. And looks like a lot of that talk about absurdity was desperately serious; those boys and their system just ain't nimble no more. A case where good old, even brilliant ole wagon done broke down. Look up a book by Herbert Leuthy titled *France Against Herself.* He's a Swiss who has lived in France for a year and loves the country and from a piece published in *Encounter* knows it very well and spells out the nature of its crisis better than anyone I've read thus far.

Man, it goes on like this and spells out his disappointment at length and while you might reject his thesis he does make you think hard about the

---

* Carl "Bobo" Olson, middleweight boxer.

state of French culture and about that which is still valid in it. I guess the basic difference between French and American intellectuals is that Americans have always been aware of the flaws in our system and have never stopped raising hell about them while the French have been convinced that they were the leaders and that they always would be. One thing is certain and that's while you can argue about a machine civilization the only way you can beat it is to out produce it. What's more, the center of the world's cultural activities is no longer Paris but New York—art shows, music, opera, etc. and Louis Armstrong. That damn place generates creative tension and I never intended to be away too long—[and] see its kind of beauty before I leave. I owe a lot to France and despite my rejection of her intellectuals and their chauvinism, I'm not forgetting it.

If you have any word from Macon County, let me know . . . It's been raining here for two days and I made a big pot of chili for lunch and now my stomach is singing "the Wang Wang Blues." I've lost weight like a bastard, trying to eat this Italian grub. The French have them whipped hands down, both on food and wine. The Italians haven't recovered from rococo—although on New Year's we were introduced by [Alberto] Moravia and Paolo Milano to a traditional New Year dish which consisted of a stuffed pig's foot and peas and it was pretty straight, no fluff or cheese or wiggling . . . Tell Mokie and Mique we say hi and that we'd like to see them before long. Keep us informed of any changes and I look toward hearing from you.

As ever,
Ralph

To Stanley Israel
THE AMERICAN ACADEMY IN ROME
VIA ANGELO MASINA V,
ROME 28, ITALY.
JAN. 31, 1956.

Dear Mr. Israel:

Please forgive this tardiness, your letter had to find me here in Rome and quite some time later [than] would normally be the case, since my mail has to be sent over from my New York address which leads in some instances to quite lengthy delays.

It pleases me no end that you found *Invisible Man* of enough interest to subject yourself to it three times. Indeed, you make it almost impossible for me to disagree with you, for after all, you've read the complete book more than I have. Nevertheless, I'll try to answer your question—first, by pointing out that although my protagonist states that his invisibility lies in the refusal of people to see him out of a "peculiar disposition of the eyes," he is not being altogether honest. There is another dimension to the problem and a rather ironic one at that, because all through the book he constantly evades those acts that would have forced the unseeing ones to see him. To make himself visible involves an act of will entailing risks, humiliation, bruises to the ego; but these are inevitable if he is to create his own image in the eyes of the world. His whole life then, has been a refusal to run the risks of his own humanity and this continues up to the point where, in the coal cellar, he burns all the papers containing his old identities—those identities given him by others and passively accepted by him—no matter how painful they were. And it is only in this destruction of the old appointed roles in the interest of bringing light into his darkness, that he makes his first gesture toward defining his own experience and thus toward creating his own personality, his own identity. This he does by writing his memoir from underground, which I have titled *Invisible Man*.

As for my statement concerning one's "personal moral responsibility for democracy," that is my statement, not his. It is from a speech in which I attempted to state my testament of belief as an American novelist.* The novel is imaginary, a fiction, and perhaps an unsuccessful attempt to embody what I believe is my responsibility to the best traditions of American fiction and American democratic beliefs.

So I agree with you that my book is about a fairly universal American problem and was never intended to be any less than that, and I will say right here that I personally was never under the illusion that I was writing about the so-called Negro problem, though I must confess immediately that on the other hand I know of no universal human problem worthy of fiction which is not relevant to Negro American life on some level of meaning. One cannot, fortunately—or unfortunately if you will—have the universal in art without at the same time having to arrive at that universal through specifics. Thus for all its social, cultural and historical uniqueness, American Negro life is but yet another example of the diverse patterns of American life, and its predicament yet another example of the universal predicament of modern man. You see this and it's elementary

---

* "Brave Words for a Startling Occasion," Ellison's 1953 address upon receipt of the National Book Award.

but you'd be surprised at how many intelligent people do not. I think it is our heritage of racist thinking that made some book reviewers assume that I was writing about a race problem—a matter which I feel lies within the province of the sociologist rather than in that of the novelist. So let me put it this way: I was writing about what seems to me to be a common problem of modern man—his confusion as to his identity and as to his values. (Take a look at a novel titled *Cards of Identity,* by Neigle Dennis to see how an English writer depicts this same confusion, or Bellow's *Augie March*—which is another variant of the theme.) I feel that this one of the more crucial problems of the American, and that Negro Americans feel these matters with sufficient intensity to warrant my exploring it in terms of fiction. Unfortunately, perhaps, the novelist writes best of universal problems when he approaches them in terms of that segment of life that he knows most intimately. Thus I wrote of that which I knew best, but I tried not to cheapen it by treating it in terms that would rob it of its human immediacy. Personally I tend to dismiss the entire rhetoric of race as an explanation for human predicaments and though the reviewers can be confused by the true issues, I cannot, as a novelist, afford to be. And again, the muddy waters of race forced on me with all the viciousness of the old fashioned water cure, but I cannot, as a novelist, be forced to drink. Nor will I deny the universal humanity of Negro life simply because some would prefer to deal with it in the easy, futile terms of race.

Thank you for reading my book with such care, that you could do so is encouraging indeed. One of my great fears while writing the book lay in my awareness that much of what I was driving at would be lost, or at best, confused by the terms in which the story had to be told. You reassure me that here and there I was successful in pulling aside the veil of illusion and revealing some of the human reality that lay behind. I'm only sorry that my protagonist was not a bit more of an admirable man.

Sincerely,
Ralph Ellison

Mr. Stanley Israel,
1924 19 Lane
Brooklyn 14, N.Y.

To Virgil Branam
THE AMERICAN ACADEMY IN ROME
VIA ANGELO MASINA V,
ROME 28, ITALY
FEB 23, 1956.

Dear Virgil:

I knew you were bound to come over here, the question was <u>when</u>? And why the hell Nina didn't give you our address I'll never understand. Here we are way the hell over here suffering from over-integration (we're the only Mohawks in the wigwam) and you as close as Genoa! Hell, we might have come down there even if only for a few hours. In fact, the only thing colored around here other than us are photographs of Fanny's mother and one of you and your family. So that if we haven't been writing we have been looking at you and thinking about you. That boy of yours looks like he's in the old tradition and it was our intention to surprise all you homies by driving out there last summer, hitting Okla. City, then L.A., Oakland and San Francisco to see Herbert, you and especially that boy. Well, I was given the Prix de Rome fellowship for writing instead, and here we are. We've been here since Oct and, unless the fellowship is extended for another year, we'll be here until late Sept., when we'll return to the States. We'd like very much to see you, in fact to have you come up here so these fifty <u>fays</u> could see how we raise 'em back where we come from, so the next time you're in this part of the world give us advance notice. We'd hate like hell to be off somewhere on a sightseeing trip when you show up . . . We came over on the *Constitution* and tried to get word of you from some of the waiters but no luck. One was a character by name of Sugar Hips and another was a fellow from San Antonio, Texas named Paul Bourget. There is a couple here by the way who taught school in Frisco with the wife of a seaman known as Ghost Walker—who low mo sounds like one of your boys. If you know him tell him that the Goldins send regards.

As for news, you're probably more in the know than I am. I guess you know that Arvil has a little boy. I haven't seen him, but Arvil was over just before we left to pick up a camera I loaned him (boy, do I need it now! the one I have with me is busted and this fellowship money is so short that I can't stretch it far enough to get a new one, even with Germany just over the hill). Things go rapidly toward integration in Oklahoma City, according to the *Black Dispatch*—which is now partly owned by Saretta Slaughter's husband, a pleasant fellow named Finley. He's a doctor. Dunjee* had a heart condition last year and is now taking it easy. The folks gave him a big testimonial dinner around the first of the year and forked over enough dough to send him on a round-the-world voyage. It makes one feel pretty good to see that they appreciate him to that extent, because man and boy he's been one of the most authentic leaders I've ever encountered, a man with world vision who has done what he could in a d-a town. The Moses are building themselves a country club, integration or no; our good friend Dorothy's father, Dr. Cox went to join her in Jan. I saw him at a Shriners convention in Harlem a few years ago and again at home, when I was out there year before last. He and Frank Jr. had a clinic out on Sixth and Lottie and I stopped in to see Thelma who is still married to Ted and who at the time was working there. You know, I'm now in my forties and have gone far from Oklahoma City in my associations—and was never intimately involved with Dorothy, but I still find myself grieving over her death. I suppose in the broad sense that you hold friends dear and find them symbolizing your own youth and dreams and give a special tone to your shared experiences, I loved her. I loved her in that broad sense and I was enraged and am still enraged whenever I think of how unnecessary her death was; that tragedy of a fine human being lost in the crummy values of a small, provincial environment. She was a sacrifice to Negro education and everything bad in its social environment that the word implies. Well, her father and mother certainly made our lives pleasanter than they might have been had they never come to Okla. City. All in all I guess we had pretty good times in spite of being poor and all the rest. I tried to explain to one of my white friends just how things went, the parties down at your house, the dishpans full of chili and baked beans, the parties out at the Randolph's—he's dead, you know, and the house was sold to Victor Dunn, who opened a roadhouse in it and was closed up for operating without a license—Forest Park parties, etc. lets pretend. He found it rather strange and I think he was somewhat disappointed that there was another side to the picture, because if there were then he couldn't feel quite so much comfortable pity for Negroes. If you ever see the Ethel for whom we used to bottle that homebrew please give her my regards. I could use a few cases of that beer right now, because here whiskey is high as hell and I'm just too American and Colored to take a steady diet of wine. Speak-

---

* Roscoe Dunjee was the founder and editor of the Oklahoma City black newspaper, *The Black Dispatch.*

ing of eating reminds me. We live out here on the Gianiculum Hill, in a villa designed by Stanford White back in the late Nineties. The place is like a college dormitory, except many of the fellows are married. We eat together, however, and the food is a mixture of American and Italian— which is too much for me except for three evenings a week. The rest of the time I eat in our rooms, where Fanny is doing fancy cooking on an electric hotplate. Fifty people beating up their gums the first thing in the a.m. is just too much for me, because I might be evil and anyway I have to write my words, not waste them being pleasant to folks who're going to spend the rest of the day trying to figure out the measurements (original) of some old stones, or why Homer used one word instead of another . . . Fanny is working, we're both studying Italian and except for her having had appendicitis and my having just recovered from pneumonia, things are going well enough. I'm working on a novel and it's beating me to my d.b.a. but that's the usual way with me—a book's like a bad case of con- stipation, and I guess some would say that that's the way mine read . . . Well tell me something. I haven't forgot that Borsalina hat you promised me so now that I'm here where they come from I'm going to gift myself one in your honor. By the way, I went to Hot Lips'* funeral last year and ran into Gladys' sister and she asked about you. She's still living down at the Dewey Square and doesn't look much older. There were many people there from K.C. and Okla. City. It was quite sad. Anyway, here's a snatch from my book to make you laugh—I hope.[†] This is one of those old talking Moses who remembers everything and tells it in a hundred different ways, from perfect English to the most jived-up dialect, and he's filling in his boy on what's happened since he's been gone: "There was the big one in the union suit that Halloween," Cliofus said, "Who one time cried, 'Hey, Lawdy, Mama! In a crowd and caused a near panic. Just a little boy that time, but with a bull-frog voice, shouting" (with your permission, though I swear this isn't you or intended to be you. R.E.) "Here we is in the union station and all in our union suits! He's with his mama and his sisters and brothers and his mama damn near laid down and died. Then he went on reading off all the waiting room signs like a show-off foghorn. "Embar- rassed, see Harris, the Banker, Radiator leaky? See Puckett, the Tinker.

---

* Oran "Hot Lips" Page was a first-rate jazz trumpeter who played for the Oklahoma City Blue Devils in the late twenties, admired and listened to by Ellison and Branam.

† Part of the section of the novel-in-progress Ellison sent Albert Murray in 1955 (see letter of April 12, 1955).

Ladies, Do you have Bearing Down Pains? Loose the OLD BLOADED FEELING CHEW FEENE' MINT, TRY 666. TUBE ROSE. DRINK EVO. USE COCA . . . Look ayounder, Ma, Carters Little Liver Pills—My liver must be little, Ma. Kin I have some? And a lots of other stuff before his mama could clap her hand over his megaphone mouth. And she shook the fool so hard that his teeth threw sparks and it's like she'd busted a chockful bag, with old spinning tops, and cat eye marbles and rusty jacks and homebrew caps and a coupla railroad taps and a jackknife with a busted blade and a dried-out bird, a funky mouse, a ball of twine, a raw sweet potato with the teeth marks in it, one old boot jack, two black walnuts, a horned toad and a great big plug of Brown Mule—all of it spilling out on the waiting room floor. She was so upset, she hustled them out of there and took the Frisco . . . `'"

"Where and when was this, Cli?" Severen said.

"You remember, the Union Station. The Santa Fe Chief was rolling in, remember, and the chef cook hanging out the window with a big greasy bag in his ham sized hands (could've served either one with sliced pineapple, whole cloves and light brown sugar and you'd a had the real Smithfield—only spell it f-e-e-l, a waiter name of Shagwaugh said). Big Smith, the chef was lookin for his pretty little wife and his six little children to take home the bacon, and here they come busting through the door just as Jack and his mama and the rest were shooting out, and they're holding hands and looking for their railroading daddy who was looking into their pretty mama's big brown eyes and holding out the bag. Brought it from Chi, he said.

That's what makes the cheese more binding, she said.

I love you better that I do me, baby, he said.

You suppose to, cause aint these here your boys? she said

They she is, baby; that <u>why</u> I brings it all the way from Chi., he said.

And the six little children were licking their chops.

And that's when the steward stuck out his head.

There aint but one little thing I want to know, it's how could you bring it <u>from</u> Chi, when we took it <u>to</u> Chi? he said.

How could I <u>bring</u> it, Big Smith said. You talk like this is a one-way train. But just the same, I brought it from Chi, where they got more ham than this whole dam railroad. Cause it's the boar-hogs hangout and the she-pig's range. Besides, what you think I'm working for, with all these hongry mouths to feed?

And the six little children were licking their chops.

Just what the Santa Fe Railroad's got to do with how you spend your nights at home is entirely too dark for me to see, the steward said.

And ole Big Smith told him:

You said you wanted a wooking, well, that's me.

You said you wanted a study man—and that's me.

You said you wanted you a strong man who could bring it in the heat of summer and in the cold of winter, in the light of day and in the dark of night; in Oklahoma sleet, in Kansas snow and in Texas heat—and that's me too.

You said you wanted you a family man who had to stay on the job and on the ball and that's sho me. Just look at them boys, got appetites like six fullgrown tigers! So now if you know enough to want all that, it looks like me that you ought to know also that such a man's family just naturally got to eat!

Well, the steward who was a downhome paddy from Tennessee, stood there a while and shook his head with his face all red, and Big Smith looked back at him like an honest man, and they kept looking at one another till the steward started to grin, cause after all, they were both good Masons in the Thirty-second Degree. So he gave Big Smith the sign and locked up his store room and went on off. And the six little children were licking their chops.

Daddy, what you bring us home for supper, daddy, the six little children asked.

But Big Smith was holding their mama by her pretty little hands and looking in her eyes like a natural man. And their mama was smiling back. So they licked their chops some more and started making some wishes.:

I hope its roast beef, the first one said.

I hope its mutton, the second one said.

I hope its corned beef hash with giblet gravy, the third one said.

I could see me some sausage, the fourth one said—the Brookfield kind.

I hope it's round steak cooked tender as Jim Jefferies after Jack Johnson got through with him, and a great big bucketful of Bermuda onion gravy and a skillet of hot corn bread and some greasy mustard greens—just for me, the oldest one said. And he rubbed his little belly.

I don't care what it is, just long as it's some Virginia ham, the baby said, cause I got me a brand new tooth to try.

And that's when they got to yanking on their mama's pretty little arms, cause the engineer was starting to ring the bell.

Save it, I mean save it, pretty mama, Big Smith said.

I got to do it, she said. But you better give me your kind attention on your next trip through.

And if I don't I hope something big'll bite me, Big Smith said (I swear, man, these Branamisms just keep turning up!).

Ain't nothing that big around, she said. But you see me just the same and I don't mean maybe.

And he gave them the greasy bag and six jawbreakers and sent them hurrying on home while he rolled on down to Texas . . .''

Severen laughed, thinking, It's all true and it happened. Cliofus is telling it as just as he once told me stories when we were in the first or second grade. He's mixing it up but it's real. "Then what happened," he said.

"We watched them trains, remember, and when she hit a highball on that back of town grade, she came a huffing and a puffing and a ringing them bells and belching out pork chops, lamb chops, veal chops, beef steaks and crates of chittlings—which he <u>had</u> to get in Chi or else K.C., cause the Santa Fe Chief didn't serve no such special food as that. And those six little children would be hustling alongside those railroad tracks pulling their little red wagon and a-snatching and a-grabbing and a-gathering in the grub and singing in pure-dee barbershop style, "Our Daddy is a Railroad Man." And Big Smith would be waving out the dining car window with a tall white cap set on his head and a grin like new money on his shiny face—Hey! One of those boys is a doctor now and another one's a Government meat inspector, and the littlest one, he's a veterinarian. His ole daddy goes round telling everybody that he's a Ph.D. in Hogology. You remember them?"

Severen watched Cliofus staring into his face with demanding eyes as he wiggled a hair-tufted finger in one of his ears.

"Of course," he said. "Everybody liked those cute little kids."

Sure they did. And they had a bulldog named Mister Crump and a dominic rooster they called Big Boy, and a hen named Ginny, and a cat named Ribbons, and a garter snake called Tutti and another named Frutti, and a red-eyed horny toad named Booker T . . ."

There you are, if it were all in the vein I'd have no trouble, but it's only like this now and then and becomes quite complicated to write. I wish there was time and space to let you hear this Cliofus blow a while longer, because he really gets to riffing and lying but there isn't and if you're interested we can do it another time.

Meantime write me what's new, how Ethel is and how that boy is making it. He looks like he could whip you with one hand tied behind his back. I swear if he gives you a rough time it's just your sins coming home to rest. Too bad your mother—and mine too—couldn't have lived to see him. As for us, we're still trying and enjoying it and enjoying it even when we forget to try, but still no bambinos. If Herbert hasn't scored this clan is finished. He has children but I don't know whether they're his or his wife's. He writes now and then and is still living at 1917 Jefferson in L.A. If you get a chance take a peep and let me know what kind of man he grew up to be. I still haven't seen him since 1938 and he won't send a snapshot. What's with Calicutt? I saw Weber last year looking very thin. He'd been in Denver with his old man . . . There will be one of my short stories in *New World Writing* No 9,[*] which will be out this spring. Otherwise no news. If you ever get to Japan on any of your trips I'd like to send you the money to get us one of those little stove—hibachi—I think it's called. My workroom is in a little house set out in the garden and when it becomes warm we'd like to cook steaks out under the sky. Right now we've more snow in this country than in Alaska but I'm told that nothing lasts a̲lways. Fanny Mae said be careful and to write us a real letter next time. Meanwhile, give our best to Ethel and tell her that although we didn't send cards this Xmas we thought about you all and wished all the best for you. So take it slow, but take it.

> AND DON'T BE
> CALLING ME
> WALDO.
> Ralph

To Harry Ford
AMERICAN ACADEMY IN ROME
VIA ANGELO MASINA V,
ROME 28, ITALY
MARCH, 1956.

Dear Harry,

If haste in replying were any accurate indication of the pleasure we received in receiving your letter you might assume that the pleasure was very slight indeed. But of course you'd be wrong (which you know better than to be) because [as] we say in Harlem, you knocked us out. It's only that we've been busy and away on an eight-day trip to Ravello, where our

---

[*] "A Coupla Scalped Indians," published in 1956 in *New World Writing.*

host and hostess were so starved for talk that there was hardly time to do anything else. But more about that later. I'm glad you've been seeing Jean Douglas; I haven't written her a single line, though Fanny writes her quite often, and I'm quite guilty over having failed to have done so. She's one of my favorite people and I'm sure her scolding must have been rather like that of a rather perky little bird. (After the awful struggle against the snows we've been having here, the flowering trees in the garden are blooming and the songbirds are arriving in larger numbers each day, so that at the moment I'm quite bird-minded.)

As for Isaacson I've still no word, guess he crawled in and pulled the hole in after him. Anyway, the Martins went up to London or Oxford and bought themselves an instrument, so that problem is settled, and I've ordered my recorder directly from Dolmatch—which, in six months time, will settle that. Everybody else is turning up in Rome: Van Wyck Brooks is writer-in-residence for the moment; Calder has a show in a little gallery so small that the mobiles barely miss bumping as they move. If he ever comes in there tight and starts playing with them, as I saw him doing the other day (which is probably what they're meant for, being as meaningful as toys as objects d'art) these damn things are going to get mixed up and we're going to miss one of the greatest sequences from a Chaplin movie that Chaplin ever failed to produce. Bill Rogers of the A.P. was here for a hot minute along with his wife; Best of Viking is somewhere around; the Ben Shawns have been doing the city and various others are threatening. I had the pleasure of meeting Silone yesterday though my Italian is still too sparse to have made it really meaningful. It just occurs to me that either of his first two novels might be worth looking at again; might be even for Vintage.

And speaking of Books, I received *The Stranger, The Immoralist, The Armed Vision* and *The Hero,* from Pat—the last being especially appreciated because it led me back into what at one time proved to be especially stimulating patterns of speculation—but I haven't seen anything of your *American Democrat.* Books do get lost between here and the States—I've a suspicion that they frequently turn up at the Flea Market—but I'm hoping that it'll turn up soon. *I.M.,* by the way, has been given a very handsome publication, with a painting by Jacob Lawrence reproduced on the jacket and a retouched portrait which makes me look like a Fuzzy-Wuzzy on the back. Speaking of your wild publicity men, this Italian variety is absolutely without conscience. Not only did they try to make me look like Ethippia saluting the colors, they placed a band around the book stating that I had won the Pulitzer Prize as well as the Natl. Book Award! You know, that dam book is beginning to embarrass the hell out of me. Like these Photostats, which you were so nice as to send, and now these not-so-fine Italian publicity bands. What they need is for a few American sociologists and anthropologists to come over here and study these quite wonderful people, because they certainly are profoundly different from Americans. That poor Margaret Butcher just ain't no critic—as neither was Locke— and it's a pity that there was no one to give her a hand with that thing . . . I envy you all these operas, we've only heard the Vienna State Opera do the *Magic Flute,* which was our first time and, as far as I'm concerned, the last. I know the music and prefer it without the slack assed drama that the Vienna people served up with it. When those three lady wrestlers with knockers like basketballs descended on those goddamned golden swings I had to stuff a handkerchief in my mouth. There was good singing during the performance so I shouldn't burlesque it too much. We've been see- ing a sequence of old movies and that's been fun; and visiting old villas along with other academy people. A few weeks ago a group of us were shown through a villa that is now leased by the Belgian government—by the ambassador himself. A large kindly, and very witty man, he met us in the vestibule of the wonderful old house and shook us each by the hand; then as he showed us a most wonderful collection of Etruscan terra cot- tas and bronzes which were arranged in glass cases there in the vestibule, servants appeared with drinks and little sandwiches. He had made the collection himself, spending years to reassemble painting which had been separated and sold elsewhere; and there were three fine Memblings in a friendly room, and other rooms with Chinese art of the best periods and others given over to Greek classical sculptures. The man was so friendly and informed and wittily unpretentious that we all hated to leave and I'm sure you would have liked it. Friday we're going to Hadrian's Villa so <u>that</u> should be something.

Thanks for calling my attention to Mizener's piece; I got hold of it on the trip to Ravello and found it a real thought provoker. John Aldridge, who had been so persistent in his invitations that we went down to visit him and his wife, had read it and it served as the topic of conversation for several bull sessions. It seems that Styron had spent time at Ravello some years ago and convinced Aldridge and his wife that it was the next thing to heaven, so that they went down there to get away from it all and to write. Well, he's finished a book of essays and started a novel, but they're both going stir-crazy for want of people. I damn near had my behind talked off, even during the three days when it was truly beautiful (they're living in the house where part [of] *Beat the Devil* was shot, especially the part where Jennifer Jones walks down the stairs, though all I ever saw come down it was a lot of frozen <u>air</u>) but Ravello is up pretty high, in fact it clings to rocks and you can see the clouds keel off and touch the very blue Bay of Salerno below, and on the fourth day the sky threw snow at us with as little warning as that snow eagle in *Augie March* required to take a crap—and man, man! After that we just sat around the fireplace and drank (brandy, goddam it! no whiskey in the dam town) and talked and talked. Which was pleasant, but not always easy because I was determined not to fight with my host over some of his critical ideas. I was fairly successful, though I'm still amused that he wants to attack guys like Cowley, Tate, Ransom and Blackmur, and yet expects to have them pat him on the back and tell him that he's doing exactly what they did when <u>they</u> were young. But hell, how did he ever get <u>that</u> young? Anyway they were nice and we hope to see more of them. They took us over to meet Aubry Mennen, who lives in nearby Amalfi, where we had an haute cuisine luncheon and a very pleasant afternoon. Mennen lives with his male secretary in a new apartment that has been built in the sacristy of an old church (that's really seeking sanctuary!) and we were invited back for a discussion of American writing, but when the day arrived I was sick. It's just as well, because it seems that Mennen had really set the stage so that he could bait a couple of American writers and since I have no patience with that kind of thing, it might have been grim. He's never been to America, the profits from his American sales allow him to live like a king in a harsh, badly off part of Italy—and he hates the United States!

Your news of Stanley is very good indeed, he's just the man to do such an anthology and I wrote Pat that if Stanley had any suggestion of a project that I might do for Vintage I'd like to consider it. Unfortunately I have nothing in mind myself. Tell Stanley that I've been making notes for a letter to him that might well run to a small book. Problem is that they're in ink and nobody, not even I, can read them. I'll probably end up sending him a color transparency of his youngest . . . I'm certainly glad that John Hersey has gotten his talents in the right combination and I can't wait to read his new novel. The Jansons are rather strange. He's clever and perhaps the only real expert who has been at the academy since we've been here, but there is a blank spot somewhere. I like her but she will make bulldozing intellectual noises about literature and other matters which she just doesn't quite have authority for. One night she told me that I must be mistaken about people dancing to the blues, that she couldn't imagine anyone dancing to Jellyroll Morton's "Win'ing Boy Blues," and I had to tell her that it wasn't a wine-ing boy, but a winding and grinding boy that he was singing about and that it was possible to do some pretty effective winding and grinding while dancing—if one had the mind, the rhythm, and the backbone. Naturally that ended <u>that</u> conversation. She's still friendly though. I heard Peter give a very impressive lecture on Donatello recently and I understand that he is publishing a book on the subject very soon. He had a couple of the other classicists foaming at the mouth by pointing out some of the Freudian implications of the Neo-Platonist movement of Donatello's time. We pointed out also that several of the bronzes were originally intended as religious symbols and designated for churches, only to be taken over by the city-state as symbols of power. One of David was so used (a symbol of the state's determination to defend itself) and he demonstrated with photographs just how the sling was removed and, I'm sorry, just how the scroll was removed and the sling placed in its place. This involved quite a bit of scholarly detective work and along with several other matters made for an impressive lecture. At least it had some connection with life—which is far more than one can say for those people who count the number of times certain words turn up in Homer, or why more time is given to the description of one hero's arming for battle than to another—All very important I'm told. And you should see and hear them read from the original Greek. But of ritual, they know not; and of drama, they know not; and of the ways of oral folklore, folk literature they seem to know next to nothing, not even the very alive and creative scholarship in their own fields . . . I'm very glad you mentioned Murray's *The Classical Tradition in English Literature,** I've been looking for the Hamlet and Cambridge Ritualists thing but had forgotten where it appeared. Going right now to get it. I did too, though I needn't have rushed because the scholars here would never think to read it. The Hargaon is very good and I thought I had loaned it to you several years ago. The DeVoto on Twain† I read at Salzburg. Cantankerous as DeVoto

---

* Gilbert Murray's *The Classical Tradition in Poetry*, delivered as the Charles Eliot Norton lectures, was published in 1927, and uses Greek poetic concepts to analyze the English poetic tradition. Ellison had a strong interest in the writings of Murray and others of the Cambridge Ritualists.

† Bernard DeVoto was a scholar of American literature and an authority on Twain. His *Mark Twain's America* (1932) was in Ellison's library. When Ellison received the National Book Award for fiction, DeVoto was the winner for nonfiction for his major work *The Course of Empire* (1952). He died in November 1955.

was, he was a fine man and I think he'll be missed. For a popular study his book on fiction wasn't bad either. Last June when I was in Cambridge, Fred Muhlhauser asked me if there was anyone in Cambridge I'd like to see and I mentioned DeVoto; then that noontime I discovered that he had called DeVoto, whom he didn't know, and made a luncheon engagement at the Harvard Faculty Club. I was a little embarrassed that he'd done so and I think DeVoto was slightly irritated as well as puzzled, but he accepted and we had a fine lunch and good conversation. I'm glad now, since it was the last chance I was to have, ever.

Please keep me filled in on any interesting developments, because for all Rome's past greatness it's a rather provincial town; the present, with its irritating but creative tension is there; there, I believe, more than anywhere else in the world. There is the new in art, in music; and, God help us, in literature. There simply is more to do, to see, to hear, and to read in one day there than in a whole week or month in Rome. As you can see, I miss it; and although there is a possibility that the writing fellowship will be increased to two years like the others, I won't be at all sorry if we return in Oct. I'll know next month, when the decision will be made so I'll let you hear. Meanwhile give our love to Elizabeth and tell that Albert that he owes me a letter.

As ever,
Ralph

To Albert Erskine
American Academy
Via Angelo Masina 5
Rome 28
march 1, 1956*

Dear Albert:†

Thanks very much for letting me hear so promptly as we were both somewhat upset. Thanks even more for giving us the picture from that side, because there are so many rumors and so much free-floating hostility em-

---

* Misdated on letter; this has to be 1956, nearing the end of Ellison's first year in Rome, which began in September 1955.

† Erskine was Ralph's editor at Random House from *Invisible Man* through his 1987 retirement and up until his death in 1993.

anating from some of the elder Fellows and guests here that the Roberts as heads of the place take on the roles of very much abused scapegoats. So much so that it's difficult to always have an accurate idea of their real personalities. At any rate, he has returned and given me essentially the same information as yours and encouraging enough to say that we had a good chance and that he hoped we would remain. We're taking your advice and forgetting about it. Actually we don't and didn't expect the special ruling, we just wanted to make sure that if there was any possibility of remaining we wouldn't lose it through neglect. At any rate, since there are now to be two writing fellowships the various committees have a concrete instance to consider and I feel that beyond the needs of my own work a writer should be given the opportunity to stay two years since during the first year he's fighting the language, the problems of institution life and trying in general to get his bearings in relation to a completely different way of [living]. And if he's involved with a piece of work his chances of taking full advantage of his opportunities the first year are even less. I think also that the second year helps the financial side too, especially if there is a wife involved.*

As to the question about Lion Books, it grew out of an item I found on my Royalty statement: *Anthology* . . . Lions Books $25.00. What are they anthologizing and when? Speaking of Royalty statement, we were awfully sorry to see the general advance I received in September listed on my earning statement as royalties received. I'm afraid it's going to make a big difference in the tax we'll pay, for my actual earnings were only about $332; the $500 advance added also as earnings makes it tough for us since we file a joint return. I don't suppose it is listed erroneously?

I have a letter from Carlo Fruttero of Einaudi† who is the translator of the book, which he tells me is now being printed, though he gives no date of release. He wanted publicity material and photographs, etc. I'll let you know when the book appears—which will probably be <u>next</u> year.

Last night I received a copy of the new printing of I.M. and found it quite handsome. Will you have a dozen copies sent along and charged to me? I think that should be enough to fill any future requests for free copies, exchanges with visiting writers (Van Wyck Brooks who is currently writer-in-resident, has given me a copy of one of his many auto-bios etc.)

---

* Ralph pursued a second year of his Rome fellowship, and in April 1956 he was notified that he had been granted the extension.

† Italian translator of *Invisible Man*.

When you next talk to Red tell him how grateful we are. Even if the renewal does not come through, it has been gratifying to both Fanny and me to know that you two took our situation to heart and acted so effectively and speedily in our behalf.

Auguri,
Ralph

To Lou Bernstein
AMERICAN ACADEMY
VIA ANGELO MASINA 5
ROME 28, ITALY
MARCH 15, 1956
MR. LOU BERNSTEIN
415 LEXINGTON AVENUE
NEW YORK, NEW YORK

Dear Lou Bernstein:

I suppose that I'm the last person in the world whom you'd expect to hear from and especially from so distant a place as Rome. Still you'll probably recall my coming in to see you last summer and mentioning that I'd won the Prix de Rome in literature. That's the simple explanation; we're here living at the American Academy, where I'm spending this year more or less in finishing a novel. I say more or less, because with all the exciting sights this city has to offer I find it increasingly difficult to stay indoors. Everywhere one looks there is beauty and magnificence and thought-provoking reminders of the past. Statues, old palaces, slums, churches, monuments, and the ancient trees and fountains. The light, which is unlike any other light anywhere, falls down upon Rome's seven hills and throbs—literally screaming to the photographer, "Come out, come out, whoever you are and shoot!" And of course I'm a sucker for such a call; that is, until recently when my rather ancient Rollie, vintage 1937, began to have shutter trouble. So that now I'm immobilized, waiting to get up to Germany, if ever, to have the old box repaired.

In the meantime I've been looking at these people, so beautiful and challengingly human and thinking of a piece of advice you gave me some time ago: that I should learn to use the 35 mm camera. Certainly one needs its inconspicuousness to catch much of what demands to be recorded—if only not to insult them as so many tourists do. (Naturally, since I'm here for a year I'm above that class!) So here, some two years later, I've decided to do what you suggested. This is hardly the time to do so financially, since the money we receive on my fellowship is rather small, but I do have a small allowance for European travel and so I'd use part of it to document my visit. And it is here that I would appreciate your advice.

In looking over *Popular Photography* for March I see that Peerless is offering the Hexacon 35 with the Biotar f.2 for $119.95 along with a Zeiss telephoto 135mm for 39.95. The eye level reflex focusing appeals to me as does the all important price. The question is: Is this a first-rate camera? And would you recommend it? And is it available with automatic diaphragm?

My next choice would be a used or repossessed Nikon S2 if you have one in good condition, but it would have to be quite good, however, because Italian repairmen are not quite as reliable as one would wish. Nevertheless I'll leave this up to you. I've wanted one for a long time but the price always seemed out of my reach. Before I ask my final question let me hasten to apologize for taking up so much of your time. I am enclosing a page in the form of a questionnaire to make it as simple as possible for you. You can fill it out and return it to me. Final question: Would it be possible to place the order from here in Rome and save myself city sales tax and yet have you send the equipment over to the secretary of the Academy's New York office? She is coming over in May and I would be able to avoid the red tape and the tariff that goes with receiving equipment here in Italy. Incidentally, I will send you a check on my New York bank that can be negotiated before you turn over the equipment.

Lou, I'd like very much to see how your work is going as of now; by work I mean of course, your photography. Perhaps I'll be able to see some of it this fall, when it's possible that we shall return to New York. I'm not certain of this however, for there are chances that my fellowship may be extended for another year. In the meantime, I hope things go well with you and your family—your boy must be quite grownup by now—and I look forward to hearing from you as quickly as possible. Incidentally, I told Dimitri Hadzi, who is one of the up and coming sculptors who has just left the Academy for the States, to come in to see you. Do what you can for him, and if you're interested in seeing some of his work, he's being given a show by the Modern Museum very soon. You might even be interested in photographing some of it as it's quite interesting. Take care of yourself,

Ralph Ellison

To Albert Murray
AMERICAN ACADEMY IN ROME
VIA ANGELO MASINA V
ROME 28, ITALY
MARCH 16, 1956

Dear Albert,

Today I almost accepted a trip that, likely as not, would have brought me right down to Casablanca shortly after Easter, but I just couldn't make it. Anyway, it would have meant travelling without Fanny and using up the money that later on we may use together—perhaps when we link up with you and the Moque and the Mique. A painting fellow and his wife and baby are doing Spain and Tangiers and have been most persistent in urging me to come along: Easter week in the South of Spain, North Africa, the Prado again—everything I want to do. Perhaps if I'd been sure that you Murrays were going to be somewhere in the vicinity I would have taken them on—as Fanny urged me to. However a friend is driving down from Holland in May and I might get another crack at the trip. More on this later.

We've just returned from an interesting eight-day trip to Ravello, where we visited the critic John Aldridge and his wife. They were very pleasant, rather famished for conversation, book talk, etc., after having fallen for the old American escapist dream of romantic Italian isolation up on a hill, only to discover that they need people in the worst kind of way. So that we spent the time talking and talking. Fortunately we had something to talk about, because after a sun so warm that we were able to sunbathe on the beach of the nearby Boitano, that blue sky upped and threw snow and sleet at us with all the Satchel Paige virtuosity of that dam eagle in *Augie March* which didn't even have to tense its anus in order to blast the unsuspecting air.

The Aldridges are living in an apartment in an old palace and have only one fireplace, a bottle-gas heater, and two electric stoves—so that it was drink like hell and eat like Virgil Branam or freeze. He was rather amusing in that he's been calling the institutionalized critics like Cowley and Tate bad names critically and is surprised that they don't pat him on the back and approve his doing what he says <u>they</u> were doing when they were his age. (Aldridge hell of a sentence, but you'll get it.) Anyway, they're fighting back and he's indignant.

Spectacular scenery there, little towns clinging to the cliffs, lemon groves terraced upon narrow ledges in the almost perpendicular stone; old houses stacked literally one upon the other, foundation on roof; white walls, green shutters—all looking bravely and precariously out across the bay of Salerno—from whence came the Moors who shaped the architecture, the boat loaded with loot from the new New World, and most recently, the Americans. It's a rough land and until the tourists crowd in in the spring the natives live a hard, hard life.

Aubrey Mennen, the Indo-English writer who lives at nearby Amalfi had us up for a grand style luncheon, with young waiters in white jackets and gloves, at his place where he lives with his male secretary-housekeeper etc. Intelligent and thoroughly British as are so many westernized Oriental gentlemen, he made us warmly welcome and invited us back for a talk on the American novel. This for later in the week, when several painters and an American poet from Wyoming were to be present. Fortunately, I was ill on the appointed evening, because Mennen used the occasion to bait the Americans and I don't play that hockey—especially not with Europeans who've never visited the States. He comes to a harsh, suffering country, where on the profits of his American sales he can live like a king (and without the social disapproval of his home life which he'd get in London) and in easy access of little boys, and comes on with an attack against the only country that gives a damn about the condition of this country. As Fanny says to me, I will eat a man's food and then give him hell if he thinks that a meal entitles him to my agreement to some crappy ideas. He told Fanny that there was nothing new in America (our writing is simply an imitation of the British!) and that India was the new thing in the world. Fanny told him, "Yes, and a good American industrial assembly line would blast away some of those 'new' caste lines and oil up his mama."

Aldridge has just finished another book of critical essays. Tell you about him when I see you. Look up a book by R.W.B. Lewis, *American Adam;* I saw it down at Ravello and it looks interesting.

Van Wyck Brooks is here as writer-in-Residence and we've seen them several times. Naturally I took Hyman's book off the shelf lest Brooks see it and bust a gut.[*] He's very alert, despite his 70 years, and still writing away.

---

[*] Van Wyck Brooks was writer-in-residence at the American Academy in Rome in 1955–56. Stanley Edgar Hyman, in his 1948 study *The Armed Vision: A Study in the Methods of Modern Literary Criticism,* discussed Brooks's methods along with those of ten other modern critics. Ellison may also have been referring to Hyman's *The Critical Performance: An Anthology of American and British Literary Criticism in Our Century* (1956), which had just appeared.

That market place jive sounds fascinating, I'd like very much to hear one of those public liars riffing, you think they'd recognize my standing in that guild? Old Cliofus and Love and some of my other studs—including old Mary—would really like to pick up on some of their stuff. I've been playing around with the ideas for a story about a one-eyed cook who is always fighting and lying and traveling—maybe a cross between Falstaff, Coutee Brown (Q.T. Brown) and Branam, he would be just the guy to feed on that Marrakesh jive, that *King and the Corpse* brew. He's a real fool, fights with everything from a baby to a bear—she turns out to be mechanical just when he thinks he's taking her to bed and when they get through fighting just about half of her is in one corner and the other half in on the floor. This is slapstick but there's much more to him, mainly comic, and that's the way he'll stay. Maybe the white folks down in Alabama won't let him though, because I've been getting clippings and some of them make me see red. But maybe not.

I feel a lot better about our struggle though. Mose is still boycotting the hell out of Montgomery and still knocking on the door of Alabama U. So now the crackers want to withdraw their money from Tuskegee—which would be the best thing that ever happened—. Pat must feel like an ass because the crackers clearly reveal that their intention was to bribe the school into staying third-class. But hell, they forgot to bribe the preachers! I saw some photos of those brothers and some of them look like the old, steady, mush-mouthed, chicken-hawk variety; real wrinkle-headed bible pounders; who in the pictures look like they've been to a convention where they'd caught some son of a bitch not only stealing the money, but sleeping with all their own private sisters! Yes, man! But they're talking sense and acting! I'm supposed to know Negroes, being one myself, but these Moses are revealing just a little bit more of their complexity. Leader is a young cat who's not only a preacher but a lawyer too, probably also an undertaker, a physician, <u>and</u> an atomic scientist. And they're standing their ground in spite [of] threats, assassinations, economic reprisal, & destruction of property. Dr. Brewer of Columbus was shot and killed by a cracker recently over some issue of police brutality to another Negro. Something is happening and it's so very good to know that Mose's sense of life is too strong to be held in by the Pattersons or any of the other clowns at Tuskegee. Mose is fighting and he's still got his briar patch cunning; he's just a law, man, something solid under his feet; a little scent of possibility. In fact, he's turned the Supreme Court into the forum of liberty it was intended to be, and the <u>Constitution of the United States</u>

into a briar patch in which the nimble people, the willing people, have a chance. And that's what it was intend[ed] to be. Bill Faulkner can write a million Letters to the North as he did recently in *Life*,* but for one thing he forgets that the people that he's talking to are Negroes and they're everywhere in the states and without sectional allegiance when it comes to the problem. The next thing that he forgets is that Mose isn't in the market for his advice—for over three hundred years, only he's never been simply waiting, he's been probing for a soft spot, looking for a hole, and now he's got the hole. Faulkner has delusions of grandeur because he really believes that he invented these characteristics which he ascribes to Negroes in his fiction and now he thinks he can end this great historical action just as he ends a dramatic action in one of his novels with Joe Christmas dead and his balls cut off by a man not nearly as worthy as himself; Hightower musing, the Negroes scared, and everything, just as it was except for the brooding, slightly overblown rhetoric of Faulkner's irony. Nuts! He thinks that Negroes exist simply to give ironic overtone to the viciousness of white folks, when he should know very well that we're trying hard as hell to free ourselves, thoroughly and completely, so that when we get the crackers off our back we can discover what we (Moses) really are and what we really wish to preserve out of the experience that made us.

As for our travel plans, we'd like to make them fit with yours for the June period, because it seems certain that we'll miss the Easter in Spain. Fanny is working and I'm still tied up. If, however, I drive down in May, it might be possible to drop over to Casa even if I have to take a freighter back to Italy. As for June, we'd like nothing better than a trip with you [to] Spain, or to the north of here. Incidentally, I'll know in April whether we're to be here another year. It's being considered in New York and I'm told there is a possibility. After that I'll be able to make more definite plans.

I'm glad as hell to hear that you've taken up Photography; it's dam well time that those curious eyes of yours went on record. As for me I'm just like you, making notes on the U.S. and hitting and skipping here. But my camera went bad on me recently and I'm falling behind on my photo notes, I've just written the States to see what I can do about getting a 35 mm job, so if you're dissatisfied with the Leica why not give me a chance to buy it; or if any of your boys is selling, let me know. That 3M

---

* In the *Life* magazine article, Faulkner suggests that the civil rights movement may be moving toward desegregation and equality too rapidly, and advises the leaders to slow down and give white southerners time to think about it.

is a sweet camera. Anyway if you know of something for sale please write me immediately because I've got to do something soon. Like to be loaded when I got to Spain, if I go in May. I'd take some of my travel allowance so don't worry about the dough, because I'm spending so much time on this dam book that it'll take a pictorial record to help us make the most of my year here. You know me, I have to have something between me and reality when I'm dealing with it most intensely.

Damn, I've talked myself tired, so now I'd better hang up the phone. I'm homesick for some Moses for one thing, and I got no way to get any corn bread and these Romans think a chittling is something to stuff a sausage into. There is very little whiskey I can afford, <u>no</u> sweet potatoes or yellow yams, a biscuit is unheard of—they think it means cookie in this town—and their greens don't taste like greens. What's worse, ain't nobody around to speak the language. I'm up the creek. Fly up and see us. Tell Moque to drop off here and see us. Send Mique as a life-saving embassy. I know you won't, so give them our love and eat an extra helping of pie and real honest to goodness American ice cream for us.

Ralph

To Pat Knopf

American Academy

Via Angelo Masina 5

Rome 28, Italy

MARCH 19, 1956

Dear Pat,

Yours was one of the most pleasant and unexpected letters of the whole Roman visit—unless, of course, I include a most excellent letter from the quite unpredictable Harry Ford, who wrote shortly after you did. The two of you made me feel that I was still in touch with the better part of reality.

As for your list, there are indeed several books thereon which I think would be worthy additions to your Vintage series: The Unamuno, the Herzen, the Matthiessen, the Bodkin, the Gertrude Levy, the Ford Madox Ford, the Melville, the Lowes, the Dodds, and the Mirsky. These I have read, except the Herzen, which is referred to again and again as an important work.

To these I would add Unamuno's *Tragic Sense of Life; Themis* by Jane Harrison; *The Art of the Novel,* R. P. Blackmur's edition of James's *Prefaces to the New York Edition; Axel's Castle* by Edmund Wilson; and a work which so strongly influenced H. H. Tawney's *Religion and the Rise of Capitalism*—the title of which I can't remember, but which was written by Max Weber and is called something like *Capitalism and the Protestant Ethic*. I would also consider Gertrude Levy's *Sword from the Rock:* and a work on fiction which was very important to me when I started writing and which I still think serves as a needed antidote to so much abstract discussion of the novel as we've been getting: *Twentieth Century Fiction* by Joseph Warren Beach. You might also consider *Techniques and Civilization* and the *Culture of Cities* by Mumford. And what about Valery's *Variety* (s)? Back in the early forties when they were remaindered I couldn't find enough copies for my friends and several are still searching. I don't know John Aldridge's *After the Lost Generation* and it might be a real dog, but I happened to talk with him recently and learned that no one had reprinted it. As one of the few discussions of postwar fiction it might be worth considering. Finally, Fanny, my wife, suggests Malcolm Lowry's *Under the Volcano*. I remember it as a very fine novel. Certainly I would buy a few copies of that one.

As for a pet project of my own I simply haven't a thing in mind at this moment. But I'd like nothing better than to have a book in the Vintage series and if I have any bright ideas I'll hasten to acquaint you with them. On the other hand, if you have something in mind I'd like to hear about it; or if Stanley Hyman, who knows me and is very good at this kind of suggestion, has any idea I'd like to consider that too.

Thanks for the books, they're real lifesavers, for the Academy has very little of interest to a writer and thus they fill a real need. Could you, by the way, send me a list of the books that you had mailed? Sometimes books tend to disappear before they reach me and I'd like to check. I received the *Hero* by Lord Raglan (for which congratulations on broadening the influence of a first rate book), *The Immoralists. The Stranger* and *The Armed Vision*.

Things go fairly well hereabouts and after my bout with pneumonia, my work has begun to move again. I've also had the new experience of being present in a foreign country at the time a translation of *Invisible Man* was published. I must say that I have a sense of remoteness about it that is a relief after what I went through at home. Einaudi produced a very handsome book and now the reviewers are having their say.* This time,

---

*   The Italian translation of *Invisible Man, Uomo Invisible* by Carlo Fruttero, was published by Giulio Einaudi in 1956.

however, I'm not bothering to learn what their say is. Indeed, I almost left the other day for a month's trip to Spain, with some friends who were driving down. So you see, if I don't publish another book soon I'll lose all interest in anything I've written.

Thanks again for the letter and the books and please give my regards to all. If you come to Rome this spring or summer, please give us a ring. We'd like to show you this bit of transplanted America.

Sincerely,
Ralph Ellison

Mr. Alfred Knopf, Jr.
501 Madison Avenue
New York 22, N.Y.

To Albert Murray
[ROME]
APRIL 1, 56.

Dear Albert:

I've been waiting for several days to hear from New York about a camera I was interested in there. It is a single lens reflex called the Hexacon and I hoped to get it new with a f. 2 normal lenses and a 135 mm telephoto and case for $165.00, but for some reason the guy hasn't written and that dam M3 is working on me too hard to resist any longer. Get it, please, so I can have some peace! I need a telephoto and a wide-angle lens for inside work but they'll have to come later. I can't afford it but I can't afford to let this opportunity pass either. I'm enclosing a check on my New York bank to save you time and I hope it's no trouble. We don't have a bank here but I can send traveler's checks if you prefer. As for film I could use 35 mm Ektachrom and 120 color in any type you can get but how much depends upon the cost as now I'll really be cutting it thin. Here color's impossibly high and I just had to give it up. I'll also need a lens shade for the Sumicron, so send along the price for that too.

I notice that your letter was mailed the 23rd and arrived here on the 29th—which is longer than it takes to get to the states, I hope things move a little faster going over, though I swear you can never tell about Italy, these studs can be more casual than a Mose driving a white man's Caddy through a block where his boys are signifying at him from the sidewalk.

I airmailed some galleys back to the states and two weeks later the editor was raising hell because he hadn't received them. I was down to St. Peter's this morning and heard the Pope and was in the crowd when he blessed everyone so maybe this will come through without delay. Anyway it was rather impressive, though I swear that if they'd just elevate them a Mose, preferably one converted from one of the storefront cults—which would take a miracle—he would get in there and bring back some of the old vitality to the Church. He'd bring in some Negro Elks and Shriners with their drill teams and instead of having the platform at the top of the steps he'd elevate it up around the dome of St. Peter's. Most of all he'd have some real singing. Probably get old Bill Dawson out of retirement and that fool would have the whole city of Rome fighting to get up there to hear those righteous voices. Incidentally, I guess you know that Bill retired, I read it in the paper several months ago and forgot to ask you about it. Plan to write him soon, guess he saw himself getting nowhere fast with Foster.

That jazz lecture in French must have been something to hear, especially if you gave them "Dry Bones" in Parisian! Probably the first time many of those boys heard anything authentic about jazz. Keep it up because if we don't tell the story the fay boys will do to it what Stalin did to History. Better still is the news of the jazz novel. I've been seeing something of a fellow named Stanford Whitmore who has published a book titled SOLO that is about a jazz pianist. I don't know how it reads but if you see it around take a look as the British critics thought it had some importance as a study in individualism. Sounds bopish and Whitmore tells me that he derived something from me and I told him it's not what you derive from but what you make of it. Made me feel pretty good though to have him say that he was encouraged to finish his book and to believe in what he was doing after he'd read mine. He worked in the Laundromat for 23 bucks a week, then when the book was finished it was taken by a publisher and Hollywood—50,000—just like that, and he got married and cut out. Stopped long enough to buy him a Mercedes X.L. 190, which makes him enough like a Mose to warm my heart. Dig you later on the trip and other matters, this is really about the M3. If, by the way, you have any idea of how to get it to me before June, let me know. I'll try to learn what the customs are here in Italy, and think about it but I suspect that the duty would make it impractical. I suspect that you'll have better ideas on that end, perhaps someone reliable will be coming over. Anyway let me know.

The couple who tried to get me to go to Spain with them might come to Casa and if so I gave them your address and they'll probably look you up. He's a good artist (name's Walter Hahn) who has just discovered the *Golden Bough* and is flipping over it and trying to get it into his paintings, so blow him a few riffs. Take it easy.

Ralph

To Mrs. Edna Slaughter
American Academy
Via Angelo Masina 5
Rome 28, Italy
april 11, 1956

Dear Mrs. Slaughter,[*]

Here I am, late again with my answer. I work in a little brick studio that has been built into the old wall that was erected to protect Rome when Marcus Aurelius was emperor and which now surrounds part of the Academy grounds, and I sometimes misplace letters or even part of my manuscript between here and our rooms in the main building. Ofttimes things escape me thus for weeks and then, when the course of my work brings me back to that folder in which I've stuck them they reappear. Anyway, I'm glad that I found it before another month had passed. And even as I write I'm being distracted.

I am up fairly high above the garden here and just now a storm is ending. Twenty minutes ago the sky was overcast but whenever I looked out of my window I could see the two gardeners serenely making their beautiful geometrical patterns in the earth—setting out tomato slips, I believe, and pink and white blossoms showed bright on the fruit trees. Then with only a couple of dry rolls of thunder to give warning the sky broke and the men were dashing about like ants when a nest is disturbed. The Italians, who are expert gardeners, have an odd method of protecting young plants. A branch roughly a foot long and two inches thick is split down the center and filled with long lengths of straw until a kind of square fan, something like those which undertakers used to supply churches, is formed, and then the split branch is wired together. When young plants are set out they are planted in mounds about the size of those made by prairie dogs and these fans are

---

[*] Edna Randolph Slaughter was one of the Ellisons' closest friends during Ellison's boyhood years in Oklahoma City. Her husband was Dr. Wyatt Slaughter, who delivered Ralph. The Randolph and Slaughter families were prominent in black Oklahoma and figured significantly in Ellison's early years.

used to protect them. On a sunny day I can look out and see some hundred and fifty of them, each sticking in the earth near a plant mound. When the temperature falls the fans are placed down flat on top of the mound; when it rains, they are stood up and face forward in ranks like so many fuzzy head-stones; and when it is hot, they are stood at a slant to provide shade. Indeed, by looking at these one can judge what the state of the weather is. But not always. For this afternoon not only were the gardeners caught off guard by the rain, but as they rushed madly about the place the straw fans flat, they were suddenly bombarded by hail. It was as though the air was full of moth-balls. It hailed like it did in Oklahoma city in 1929 (how well I remember it, for that was the winter we found some old bakery tins and used them as sleds on the hard-packed snow that lay on the old Douglas School grounds. I think too that it was the first time I saw Sis wearing boots, which I thought quite elegant and romantic). The gardeners ran about with their coats over their heads and I could see the hail bouncing off them and filling the cinder paths and the turned earth with white pebbles. Then, just as suddenly as it came. the hail ceased, and then the rain.

But the garden plots are soaked, the tennis court has the appearance of a recently drained pool and many of the blossoms have been beaten from the trees. Just now I can see the boss gardener surveying the damage and trying with dramatically exasperated Italian gestures to make his work-men responsible for what, unless there is some truth to the talk that the atomic explosions are responsible for the unusual weather, is certainly an act of God. It is rather amusing to watch these violent gesticulations—their voices rise up to me as clear as bells through the rain-washed air—but it is also sad. Italy has had the worst winter of many many years. Spring is usually under way by February but this year the snows came in March and killed many of the crops. In such an exhausted country as this such can be a grave calamity foreshadowing a hard summer and fall. You have no idea how utterly harsh life can be for the poor of this country. And for all its age and beauty and the handsomeness and kindliness of the people them-selves, it is difficult not [to] feel a kind of despair for them. They certainly deserve to live better and I'm hoping that their growing industry will soon make it possible. Don't let me paint too somber a picture of the spring however, for it is a time of festivals, and optimism for the new year hangs high in the air. Last Sunday we joined the thousands in the square before St. Peter's Basilica to hear the Pope give his message to the world. It was quite impressive—I must send you a photograph of that majestic place. First there was music from choirs and bands broken by the speeches [of] high church dignitaries and then after a long wait the Pope himself* appeared in a high cardinal red draped window of the basilica. People were from all over the world and once his speech was finished the Pope greeted them in several languages and followed with his benediction, which the thousands of Catholics received kneeling on the ancient stones of the piazza and the rest of us standing with bowed heads. After that he left the balcony to the cheers and handkerchief waving of the faithful and the crowd broke up. We then made our way back to the Academy for a very special meal of lamb, which is the Easter dish here and quite delicious. Not only do the Italians believe in being washed in the blood of the Lamb they like to stuff themselves with it—and I hope that's not too poor a joke.

Things go well here for the moment, although our apartment in New York was recently burglarized, and my work is going fairly well. Last month we spent eight days at Ravello, which is some four hours to the south of Rome, where we visited a young American critic and his wife. They have been living there for nine months, having thought to leave the noise and tension of the States behind them for a while and enjoy the peace of a remote, thinly settled part of the world. Instead they discovered that they need people and the intensity of cities very much, so we went down to try to break their isolation. It was a pleasant visit although we spent our every waking hour talking and eating and drinking. The scenery there is spectacular, with the little towns—Ravello, Amalfi and Positano—clinging to the cliffs with their lemon and olive groves terraced upon narrow ledges in the almost perpendicular stone. The very old houses are stacked literally one on top of the other, like staggered blocks, with foundations of roofs rising ladder-like up the mountain with white walls, green shutters and low-domed roofs, and all looking bravely and precariously out across the Bay of Salerno. The architecture is strongly influenced by the Moors who were here during the Crusades, and when America was discovered these were all thriving towns with great castles, great families and beautiful churches. Traces of these glories linger since Stone dies slowly. But I'm afraid those great days are long past. Now it is a very harsh land of rock and wind and sun glare, and until the tourists appear in the spring the natives live a hard life indeed. Yet it is easy to see why tourists find it attractive. Three of the days we were there the sun gave us a taste of just how beautiful it can be. The sky was blue and the bay even bluer and the clouds like spun nylon. Our friends live in the old palace where

---

* Pope Pius XII, who served as pope from 1939 to 1958.

part of the film *Beat the Devil* was made, and we could take in the breath-taking view from their windows. When fishing is done at night there in the evenings the little fishing boats appeared on the water and their lights would shimmer like floating stars. We even spent one afternoon picnicking on the beach of a near-by Positano. Indeed, after the cold of Rome it was like travelling four hours into Spring. Ah, but then the weather turned its other cheek and we had snow and snow and still more snow. We spent the remaining days around the fireplace, yearning for the sun again but it never came so that we had to put that windswept eagle's nest behind us. Even so it was all very fine and I'll never forget how startled I was that morning I went to the window and found oranges and lemons showing through the snow. Maybe that was the most important morning of the whole trip: it was a demonstration that beauty and harshness could go together and that tropical fruits could grow despite snow storms.

You write that you wish some of the younger members of the family would do something outside the routine pattern and I know what you mean. But this seems to be the way it goes: the great grandparents take the desperate risks of pioneers and find and settle the new land; the grandparents establish a background and an economic base on which a fuller life is possible; their children then go on and learn to live with the freedom provided by a little security and to fulfill the social obligations inherited by the responsible leaders of a growing community; then <u>their</u> children grow up with their wings flexed for longer flights. If we're lucky, they have curiosity and ambitions that will carry them away from home, at least for a while, and they're apt to be less interested in possessing economic security than in using it to develop themselves and to make a lasting mark on the world. I have no doubt that Edasinna and Tuffy will travel in Europe and find their ways into many areas of American life that the rest of us came along too early or were too busy with other problems to explore. Each advantage carries its special disadvantage. Having grown up with no possibility of security during that period when I needed it most, I have been wandering into strange places myself and I have been lucky, but I do so at a price.

In contrast with many of those who stayed at home I have no children, I own no land, I am important to no community in any concrete way—although I do mean a little something in a literary way—and Wyatt or Finley or even Charlie Fields could lift my financial might with either of their little fingers. I'm not complaining either, for that money I've made thus far I've had to spend in order to buy experience, because for the writer experience is his capital and without it he is a dry well, a light without power. Well the group needs both kinds, the stay-at-homes who build solidly on their parents' accomplishments (perhaps my parents' only accomplishments were simply to take chances and to have faith in human possibility), and us adventurers, artistic or otherwise, who take the value of the community off to other parts and try to make something new of them there. At least I hope that this is true. I little knew that when Charlie Miller, who was about the last person I'd expected to be so important to my life, helped me on that freight train bound for Tuskegee he was also initiating me into a life of travel.* Nor did I realize that he was teaching me more in two weeks about the value of having confidence in one's own resources and faith in and respect for one's fellow man, no matter how unimportant he might be in the world's eye, than I was to learn in my whole three years of college. Certainly he helped to get me moving. I've lived in New York longer now than I've lived in Okla., and I've always moved where my fate seemed to direct me, and yet there is hardly a week that passes that I don't dream of home. Sometimes it's of one of your little houses in the 800 block on East Second (where we had one of Sheenie's puppies); sometimes it's 409 East Third and Grannie and Gran'ma Ret are quilting and Herbert and I are crawling under the frame, carrying them cotton or thread; or, most frequently, it is the little house at 722 East Fourth. Sometimes as I'm working for Jim again and having trouble growing up, and once in a rare while I'm working upstairs for Bud. (You know I can remember hearing T.S.E. Brown, flushed with pride of having a new baby boy, teasing Hettie and advising her to be generous to Doctor and bear <u>him</u> a son. It took me years to appreciate the irony of <u>that</u> incident or to achieve the pity for which it called. It must have been very painful for her.) Once not so long ago I was back there and you and my mother were taking Wyatt and Saretta† and Herbert and me on an evening window shopping trip downtown—just as you did years ago. Those were wonderful trips for me—far more than you can guess. Well, Thomas Wolfe titled one of his novels "You Can't Go Home Again," which is certainly true but I'd qualify this by saying that one seldom ever <u>leaves</u> home for he carries home in the structure of his

---

* Charlie Miller taught Ellison how to hitch rides on the freight trains, in order to make his way to Tuskegee to start his college career in 1933. Ellison described this journey in his unfinished memoir, *Leaving the Territory*. This experience, and the railroads in general, are the important setting and concern of his earliest short stories, "Boy on a Train," "Hymie's Bull," and "I Did Not Learn Their Names."

† Edna's two children, close to Ellison's own age.

dreams wherever he goes. I know this is true of me and I think it a good thing, although often painful.

When you mentioned Bud* in your letter I kept seeing two pictures, one of the gay, kindly man of sensibility and flair, who possessed the nice home in the country, with its lawns and flowers and fruit trees and chickens and cow; a man who laughed richly and who was kind to me and yet whom I knew even as a child to be a trapped man I don't have to say how or by whom, since you know this better than I ever could. But fortunately the perceptions of children are unsure and of the moment, for a child has no way of dealing with the harsher aspects of human relationships and must bury them in its unconscious. Otherwise the inevitable disillusionments of maturity would crush it, for it takes much living and learning before even an adult is able to put the tragic moments of experience in proper perspective. Thus I knew he was trapped and I <u>didn't</u> know, for I couldn't handle it. And for years it was the brighter picture of Bud that was dominant in my mind. Indeed, when I saw him last through the screen of my childhood it was in a sculptor's studio in N.Y. where I was studying. He, Hettie and Maxine were on a vacation trip and he seemed in good spirits and full of the old enthusiasm for life. I wasn't able to see him again until I returned home and that's when the second picture became dominant. My own cousin Tom took me for a drive to show me how the city had grown and, since we were in the neighborhood and I hadn't seen T. J., he drove on out to 23rd Street. As we drove along, Tom, whom I've discovered to be a very kind and well meaning man, told me of T.J.'s accident and said something about things not having gone so well for him, but I was unprepared for what I found. There was no one at home and I was glad, for when I looked at the place it told me what I'd see when I saw him. The trap had sprung and I knew it and I needed some time to contain the sudden coming together of that ghost perception of my childhood and the stark realization of the present. It was as though an unhappy prophecy had come true. I had loved that place and was always so proud that I knew someone who had the imagination and the taste and the income to have bought the ground and built upon it, cultivated it, and made it the promise of a home.

That it never really became a home was his tragedy. But it was a symbol to me of what was possible and I guess down deep inside I've always

---

* Edna's brother, Dr. Thomas Jefferson "Bud" Randolph. Ellison worked for Dr. Randolph in his dental office when he was a young teenager.

wanted such a place for my own. During my rather unhappy adolescence some of my best times were spent at parties there, and when I worked for Doctor I found it a special privilege to spend weekends there—although I always dismayed Hettie with the vast damage I could do to a pan of biscuits. What's more, I've decided that my profound recoil from Hettie's story that I was his son grew out of the guilty realization that I had wished, during those early days when I missed my own father terribly, that T.J. Randolph <u>had</u> been my father and that I could live in such a home. So when I tell you that as I saw that bright showplace in decay I felt something of my childhood shrink and die, you know that I'm not simply writing words. I was struck deep, down where my submerged emotions and dreams were buried. Then when I saw Tom and Hettie it was in his office and we sat talking superficialities, when I wanted to help, to do something. I didn't know how or what, but I couldn't even say anything comforting. There she was and there I was and the twenty years that lay between and the harsh reality were just too much. He wasn't a man you could pity and certainly she must have suffered too, so all we could do was sit there and look at eternity. I felt that I had failed him, for such a man should never be allowed to say, as he did, that he wished he could die. I had often thought of writing him when I was in college and later when I used to see his verses in the *Black Dispatch,* but because I didn't want to hurt her I never did. It was terrible. And even more terrible because even as he told the details of his goring by the cow and the awful time he spent impaled on its horn I knew that he had spent years, not hours, impaled on a far sharper and more destructive horn. Neither you nor I could have done anything about that, and I hope this gives you some comfort. Only he could free himself and he couldn't bring himself to do it and so he remained pinned there until it wore him out.

I'm thankful for the brighter picture I have of him, and I wish I could have done more in my relations with the two of them to have made it brighter. I suppose after one reaches a certain age, life becomes filled with those unfulfillable wishes.

Certainly I wish I could have done something besides play in the Tuskegee band before my mother died. She really made no demands of me, only that I do well at whatever I chose to do. Which was one of the greatest gifts she gave me, because in the light of the unhappy course of her own life she might have demanded security and safe harbors for me. It would have been most satisfying to have had her live to see that some of her faith was justified. Once in a joke she said that maybe she shouldn't let me work for "Bud Randolph anymore." and I asked her why and she said, "Because you're becoming as big a liar as he is." I'm sure now that she'd appreciate the joke of my having become a professional liar, since that, at rock bottom, is exactly what a fiction writer is. And T.J. could spin some yarns too, both to entertain and to get some of his patients out of his hair. But I'm sure that your father and Wade and Taylor and Jim and some few others, like Dr. Wiley, were quite an influence on my lie-telling. Especially old J.D. I can see him now, sitting with his legs crossed near the stove in the drug store and with a pipe full of Granger Rough Cut tobacco in his hand. Maybe it had rained or snowed and there were a few oldsters around—that's when the good talk flowed. Tall tales, jokes, state history, personal confessions, and more than a few outright lies. But they were lies told because it was realized that in the strange, contradictory nature of experience lies sometimes got us closer, not to the facts, but to the truth. Maybe right there, leaning with my elbows on a showcase, I was receiving my real education and it's a fact that I've done more with it than I've been able to do with all my years of music. So if you do get into that trunk please let me know what you find; I'd count it a great privilege to know. When I was home Ollie told me of the times at 407 E. First before I was born, when the women hid the guns on election day and the fight the men made for the right to vote. And the time your father gave Marmon Pruitt a beating on the Viaduct. I'm sure his notes will prove fascinating.

I should have told you in the first paragraph that I received your money order though we've done nothing about shopping as yet. Come June we plan to visit France, Switzerland and Spain, so if there's no rush we'll look around a bit before we send anything. For clocks, Switzerland is the country so we'll want to look there. On the other hand, if you have a particular type of picture in mind let me know because Rome has lots to offer. Thanks for bringing me up to date on the family and give them all our love. I know it'll be like pulling teeth for some (especially Jim—I don't know his son, 'Bi Jim') but I'd like very much to have snapshots of them and I'd trade them even. Meanwhile take care of yourself and I hope this doesn't tire you out for I find I'm long-winded today.

With love,
Ralph Ellison

To Albert Murray

ROME

APRIL 12, 1956

Dear Murray:

Just a quick one to learn whether you received my check for $212.00? I mailed it on the 2nd and sent it registered, but strange things happen to mail here and I'd like to be assured that you received it. I have failed to receive at least two packages of books sent to me from the States and thus far I can't even get an explanation, and before I wrote about my camera problems I had written a salesman friend of mine back in the states a letter in which I sent along a question & answer form so that he would lose no time in getting some information back to me. There was a good possibility that the guy would make a commission from the sale but I haven't heard the first word. It's very odd and I'm getting annoyed. There is a censorship here with the legal right to open mail but I don't think they have the right to hold my property without notifying me, nor to stop my mail and I'm getting in just the frame of mind to start writing about Italy in some of its less inviting aspects. I'd rather not however, as I'm too busy with my book to stop even for the money a series of articles would bring me. So let me hear as quickly as possible so that I can put a stop on the check.

Incidentally, I sent the letter to the address in the envelope, which was different from the first, being that of Melle Azoulay Reine/Rue de la Drome 22. I'm using the first address this time in case something was incorrect with the above.

It is still very confidential but I have just received the second year so it looks as though we'll spend at least part of next year in Europe. I'll let you know definitely later on, as I have also received a query from the President of Brandeis concerning my teaching there next year. They want a course in creative writing (fiction) and another in American Literature and have suggested that there would be no problem of Fanny's finding employment there, so you see I'll have to think about things. She doesn't want me to teach and I'd prefer to write books so most of the pressure is away from teaching job (I suppose) and the congenial atmosphere of the Waltham-Cambridge area. The only bad thing about this is that I've never been secure in an income kind of way and might not know how to live with it—especially in an environment in which there are no Moses. Maybe all

I really want is a little house within quick driving distance of New York, good bird hunting cover and a trout stream.

You would have laughed your ass off two weeks ago had you been here to see me trying to cook a mess of pigs feet here in Rome. Fanny found them easy enough but then she tried to find pickling spice—which just doesn't exist here. The poor girl walked her feet off trying to find them because she knew that I'd be an evil s.o.b. if I didn't have all the ingredients for this ceremonial dish, so that she came in late, with only some bay leaf and all-spice. And just as she expected I was fit to be tied. I wouldn't cook the trotters and spent the night cussing. Next day I set out myself. I must have covered every food store, market and drug store in Rome, trying to find the right jive. I went into stores and did everything from inventing new dances to standing on my head and pulling out my pecker trying to make them understand pickling spice and they dragged out everything from tomato paste to embalming fluid—everything and anything except pickling spice. Never in the history of the world did a mess of pigs' feet cause so much exasperation. I returned to the academy beat to my socks and prepared to assassinate the first person who spoke to me and fortunately no one did. Fanny just looked at me and went and got me a drink—which calm[ed] me enough to cook the trotters, but they weren't right, man. They were the saddest and I threw most of mine in the garbage.

The next time somebody says something to me about Roman culture they're going to have to get a cop to stop me from talking, imagine a city without pickling spice! I hope those Morocs have done better by you. We're thinking and planning about the trip with excitement now and will let you know how things are lining up. Meanwhile let me hear about that check; our apartment in N.Y. was burglarized 2 weeks ago and I'm rather jumpy.

Love to M&M,
Ralph

To Albert Murray
ROME, ITALY
APRIL 24, 1956

Dear Albert:

Man, did you take a load off my mind! Things go so balled up here postal wise that I thought maybe that check has gone AWOL. But now all the returns are coming in. I received six packages of books the other day, some of them a month overdue, so now with your news and that little registration tag I feel a hell of a lot better, I can hardly believe it. I've been bugging the boys in the camera stores here by going in and looking at that job, examining it, pressing buttons, sighting, exchanging lenses etc.—just so I'll have some familiarity with it. Prices here seem to take off from the listed price and zoom. One of these dealers will ask anything up to twice the value and you get the feeling that they think you think money is confetti. One character thinks that I'm finally going to buy and has come down 15% from his 50 % over price. Next time I'm downtown I'll go in and play with the machine just to see how much more he'll descend.

As for reaching me here at the academy, it will be easy enough by telephone, the number is 588653. If the call comes before noon I'll be out in my study, so should be given time to run to answer. All that is necessary is to tell the operator at the academy that the call is from you. As for the taxi fare from downtown, it's negligible, usually less than a thousand lire, and if I'm called I can be down in a hop, skip and a jump. Rome is fairly small. Unfortunately I know of no place to leave anything down there. I might, by the way, be able to have a friend bring me on a motorcycle. Whatever you pitch I'll be there like Mays . . . The Kodachrome price intimidates me, have they anything in bulk film? In the states costs are kept down by loading one's own cartridges. If anyone lands in Germany you could have them pick me up some cassettes for the camera and I'd be able to operate a little easier. The Plus X deal sounds fine. I'm certain that I can use a dozen of those boys . . . Don't worry about lens shade and filter, will manage that later. If they have a neck strap I could use. Plan later to get a 35 mm wide angle and a 90 mm long focus. Almost forgot the meter, get it; I'll send one check for the whole bunch of stuff, if it's all right with you. Anyway I hope you shoot up here yourself, if only for a hot minute. Plenty of fly boys shooting through this town. Spanish Steps look like Broadway and 42nd street most of the time. Not many in uniforms though, man, but you can pick em out.

Glad you got to Leuthy, I haven't located it myself though I've read the *Life* piece. Read a fairly engrossing novel about the Indochina situation called *A Forest of Tigers,** they speak of it in terms of *Man's Fate* and *For Whom the Bell Tolls,* but I'm afraid they're looking at it quantitatively, a little war a little novel and thus the three are war novels together . . . Faulkner wrote a letter to *Time* denying that Crap he dropped on the

* Robert Shaplen's 1956 novel. See letter to Harry Ford of May 15, 1956.

world, but the reporter stuck to his guns and insisted that he reported true. Which I believe he did. Incidentally, he's the same young Englishman who came up to talk with me last summer and brought along a novel that he had just published. I didn't get to read it though he told me some of the gossip of the royal family that was fairly amusing. Seems those two chicks were surrounded by capons all their lives as a matter of state policy. Shit, cried the King! . . . I've got to break this off because I want Fanny to put this in the mail today and she's giving me the rush. She sends the best, I send the best and my thanks . . . Roethke's here lecturing, I lecture on Thurs night, American novel, ethical core blah, blah, blah! There's a guy here from Mississippi on this series (Fulbrighter) who did a book on Faulkner, I hope he's in audience when I open up. Not that I plan to blast but I will call a turd a turd and our boy is pretty full these days.

Take it easy.
Ralph

To Saul Bellow
AMERICAN ACADEMY IN ROME
VIA ANGELO MASINA V
ROME 28, ITALY
MAY 4, 1956

Dear Sol:*

You were correct the first time, for in truth we're both in exile. And what's more, I think your exile is more attractive by far than mine. Rainbow trout and horses to ride—what more could a man want! Besides all this you've gotten over the hurdle of your divorce and that must give you quite a lift in itself, for I suspect that your emotions have taken quite a trouncing ever since you finished *Augie*. Of one thing I am sure and it's that you can't lose your interest in literature for long. You have too much invested in it and some of the rest of us have too much of a need for you to get your work done. Certainly I have a great deal to gain from just knowing that even way the hell out there in Nevada you're still pursuing the revivifying word. Go on back to those bootlegging twenties, what the hell, do you mean to keep

---

* One of Ellison's first letters to Bellow. They met no later than the early 1950s (see Ellison's January 8, 1952, letter), well before Bellow wrote one of the initial, glowing reviews of *Invisible Man* for *Commentary* in June 1952. Their friendship quickly grew, and they became increasingly close throughout the 1950s. For some reason Ellison's salutations to Bellow alternate between Sol and Saul, perhaps because Bellow was named Solomon at birth.

me in indefinite suspense? To hell with the bastards who think writing is done simply to keep the pockets of their Brooks Brothers Grey Flannel Suits stuffed with dollars, we know that it's the ride of the narrative and the all too infrequent rising flights into poetry that we live for. Hell, I'd rather be you than that prefabricated Fadiman any day, anytime and in anybody's history (if he goes down in history by the way it'll probably be for having corrupted more taste than Hollywood). You've got all the real stuff a writer needs, talent, technique, perspective, sensibility, a story to tell <u>and</u> the need to tell it. And while I might sound like Dr. Pep it's still true—So: let us sing like the birdies sing . . . You know, it was my plan to spend this year in Okla. and I still think it was a good plan, because while this place is interesting enough, so much of our stay here has been packed with trouble. First came the adjustment to the institutional way of life; learning to live with prying paranoids, to avoid the burbling old maids and the academic bitching at breakfast; developing the will to stumble to the john a mile down the hall at midnight; learning to sidestep the garlic, onions and other odd poisons in the food and to detour the carafes of sour wine and other dangers. Then the problem of language and learning one's way about the town—it took me months to learn that Rome is really a small city, the ruins, the age and the twisting streets had intimidated my sense of dimension. And underneath all this confusion like a sustained tone there was my novel and the need to discover where it was going. We solved the problem of the yakking at breakfast by eating in our room, then the work began to move—and then we both got sick. Fanny's appendix acted up and I had pneumonia, the two illnesses costing us over two months of precious time.

Now however, we're doing O.K. I've been making headway with the book although it's far from finished. But the point here is that even with Rome and the elections coming up and with Moscow only a hop-skip-and-a-jump away, this place has little of the creative tension so typical of New York. You can see more art hear more and better rendered music, and heaven help us, find more interesting writing, over there in a day than you can in months here. It's a very beautiful city and the people are handsome but I despair whenever I think of how they have to live and I'm forced to think about it every day. There is probably more hope for a Negro in Faulkner's Mississippi and all these ruins are but an ironic backdrop to the even greater ruin of the present. As you can probably overhear, I'm a bit homesick for the big city, subways and all. Primitive moment indeed, I suspect that right beneath our eyes Europe has become the most primitive spot on the face of the earth and I don't exclude Division St. Just the same, there is much to see here and to learn and we hoped that you and Sondra would come over and that we'd all go to Spain. I had to turn down a trip last month but Al Murray is bringing his car over from Casablanca next month and we're taking off for Switzerland and France and will try to get down to Pamplona in July for the running of the bulls. Which perhaps will be my sole Hemingway moment of this European year. (Since Faulkner seems bent upon organizing his poor Negroes to fight the North, do you think I could persuade old Ernest to organize a guerrilla squad to oppose them? I'd go along as impartial foreign correspondent to report the thing.)

Understand Faulkner has removed his granddaddy's Civil War uniform from the mothballs and is stocking up on mini balls. Seems he's been planning his strategy (ever the proper bourbon, of course) for a long time. Still, maybe this time we win—No? But back to reality, maybe you'll come over next year. If so we'll probably be here because after the sickness I got panicky and asked for a second year and I'm told that I'm very likely to get it. I just couldn't face the possibility of stopping my work and packing to come home. I hope we can stay, especially if the book isn't finished by Oct., because there is a lot of sightseeing and exploring which I've failed to do because of being so busy . . . I've seen Moravia—who has now gone to Moscow—several times, but find that I have less and less to say to him. Also met Silone. Paolo carried me to a press conference where Silone, Moravia and Carlo Levi were protesting the imprisonment of a very humanitarian priest in a manner that reminded me of the thirties. Only here it was a bit unreal, a bit tired—history as farce, as Marx put it in his book on the 18th Brumaire of Louis Napoleon. Silone's quite a word slinger and speaks such beautiful Italian that even I could follow him. Levi, on the other hand, is what you call a concrete milkshake. He works like hell at looking like an artist—purple shirts, a baggy head of hair, a smile that doesn't go with his calculating eyes. All three of those studs seemed to be looking over their shoulders to see whether History was approving their rhetoric. I left the conference amid the popping of flash bulbs feeling a bit sad. At least Phillips and Rahv knew that <u>they're</u> dead—as politicians, I mean—while two of these guys are good writers . . . Paole's been very nice to us here. He's introduced us about and has written a review of the Italian edition of *IM* . . . I must interrupt this to say that I have just received a cable from Fred Burkhart of Bennington College, offering me a job for a year during which one of the regulars will be away. I can't take it and I'm sending him your address. He offers $5500.00 and I think there is housing to go with it. I hope he contacts you because it's a good place and the kids are bright as hell ... I've also been contacted by the president of Brandeis about a job. They're expanding the Humanities dept. so if you want in there, now's the time to go about it ... The news about your new book is wonderful* and I don't think you should make a poor mouth about your stories at all, because while they don't give you the sense of accomplishment that comes from doing a big novel like *A. March,* they do amplify your general theme and readers like me like that. Let me know when it's ready ... Your boy Ted Roethke is here for a few weeks. He's been lecturing for the Fulbright people and while he's still a bad boy he's made some concessions to marriage. His wife is quite pleasant <u>and</u> good-looking. Gerald Sykes and Buffie Johnson were in town recently but have returned to Paris, where they're spending the year. Van Wyck Brooks has been here most of the winter and I've had some interesting talks with him. He's still writing and is still intellectually alive, which gives me some hope. You give me hope too, so keep writing. Yes, and kiss the bride for me and tell her we're very glad that things worked out so well so soon. When we <u>do</u> see you we'll celebrate with champagne, even if I have to rob a liquor store. Meantime fry a rainbow fish for me, the good life is where you find it.

Sincerely,
Ralph

To Herbert Weinstock
THE AMERICAN ACADEMY IN ROME
VIA ANGELO MASINA V,
ROME 28, ITALY
MAY 15, 1956

Dear Mr. Weinstock:[†]

Please by all means send me the page proofs for I'm sure that if both you and Harry Ford found *Le Partage des Eaux* a work of distinction I can't afford <u>not</u> to give it a looksee. Indeed, having just finished John Hersey's *A Single Pebble* and having been so impressed with its quiet blending of warm human insight and narrative art I can't help hoping that Knopf has hit a run of publisher's luck that will keep me delighted and moved and

---

* Bellow's *Seize the Day* appeared in 1956.

† A contributing editor at Knopf.

more creatively aware for at least the rest of the year. Certainly I'm glad to do whatever I can to help launch a good novel.

There is a minor problem however: we plan to take off around the first week in June for a short trip through Switzerland and then through the chateau country to Paris and I'd like to read the book before we leave. Could you get it to me by air mail? Books that come by boat sometimes take over a month. At any rate, if the proofs reach me in time I'll read them here, otherwise I'd like to have them along on the trip and I could send my comments from wherever we happen to be when I finish reading.

Rome is still as grand as ever and is now bursting at the seams with tourists, visiting American writers and fat cats beating the Income Tax. The season has opened at the Baths of Caracalla as yet but there is currently a group doing Brecht's *Three Penny Opera* down in the city that I'm told is quite exciting. We plan to see it ourselves next week. Tobaldi has been doing Tosca downtown with the usual license of interpretation demanded by Italian opera audiences. Everyone has a freewheeling good time!

Please give my regards to H. Ford & P. Knopf and my best to you.

Ralph Ellison

To Harry Ford
ROME
MAY 15, 1956

Dear Harry:

This is just a short note to thank you for the books. They arrived last week and I've read both the Shaplen and the Hersey with great interest. I liked the Shaplen* (he's here, by the way, and I'm seeing him on Sat.), although I don't think it gets into the *Whom the Bell Tolls, Man's Fate* class, but it is a damn good job that kept me interested straight through. I just wish he'd gotten the conflicting parties in contact before he did and with more amplification, because I feel that too often the suspense was allowed to piss itself away rather than build into explosions of insight. God, with that gal laying rich man poor man terrorist man and thief he could have had that action ringing like the anvil. And if she did a real professional job on one of those cats <u>he</u> would have made something give besides talk. Maybe it's

---

* Robert Shaplen, *New Yorker* columnist, journalist, and author of one novel, *A Forest of Tigers*, published in 1956.

the tyranny of Shaplen's reporter training which makes him wary of moving in close and thus instead of building tight forms he keeps too closely to things as they happen. But in this business a novelist's truth is a reporter's lie, while a reporter's truth for the novelist is simply unrefined ore.

Ah, but the Hersey!* I really surrendered to that one. I think it's his best book and without doubt it is one of the most important novels since the war—Civil War, that is. That old Master Joseph Conrad must be smiling in his grave over this one; for when you get on the boat with Hersey's young engineer you're moved wave, by wave, tug by tug, current by current not into the heart of darkness, but into the center of one of the most stony aspects of contemporary reality. And once you've negotiated the river the hard stone has turned into meaningful human experience. After reading the book I felt much better about myself, the value of what I'm trying to do and about the thinking of American writers. Frankly, Faulkner had depressed me, though I refuse to let his statement destroy the meaning that his works hold for me, but if the best could get so lost what the hell are the rest of us going to do?† Well, Hersey isn't a Faulkner but if he keeps this up we'll wake up one morning to discover that he's a very important writer <u>and</u> a deeply human individual as well. Certainly *A Single Pebble* should give back to readers that sense of wonder which is part of the old magic so often missing from fiction nowadays, and I think he helps us discover anew some of our own essential humanity.

O.K., so now I'll stop my little rhapsody with thanks, and if you find a line here that Bill Cole or some of the hucksters can use they're welcome to it. Though God knows Hersey don't need no boosts from R.E. . . . I've also read Caroline Gordon's new book‡ which is as full of pretentions as a Xmas goose. I'm afraid she's dug up Hart Crane so as to crucify him for his homosexuality and I don't know what else. He supposed to have been seeking God, and I suppose she is too, but I think here all she's done is to wade through crap up to her chin and He did not show himself. I guess the book is frightening though, because the main character has a writer's

---

* John Hersey, American journalist and novelist. His *A Single Pebble* was published in 1956. Hersey and Robert Penn Warren sponsored Ellison for the Prix de Rome fellowship.

† Ellison refers to Faulkner's infamous "Letter to the North" in *Life* magazine on March 5, 1956, in which Faulkner argued for a gradual resolution of the racial struggle in the South, one that could emerge only from the South and not be imposed by the North. He urged, "Go slow now. Stop now for a time, a moment."

‡ Gordon was a fiction writer and married to Allen Tate. Her novel *The Malefactors* appeared in 1956.

block that he goes into the Church to cure and ends up tending pigs—Chthonian symbols, you know. She can write too, but this one is rough, man, rough . . . I saw Peggy recently, looking quite matronly with her Irish poet of a husband. It was at a poetry reading so we didn't have a chance to talk much . . . No work of Isaacson, but that sure was good news about Fred and I'm dam glad they had someone like you and Lebo there to truly enjoy it . . . Looks like comes June we're going to drive with the Albert Murrays up through Switzerland and up through the chateau country to Paris and I'm looking forward to it with interest. I'll let you know before we take off. Things go well enough with Fanny and I'm still confusing myself with the way this book keeps taking off on its own. But the pile of paper is growing and <u>some</u> of it's bound to be publishable. Give our love to Elizabeth and scratch them cats for us and I'll write more next time. Right now I get to rush down to hear the spring concert of the academy composers; some of it promises to be ragged, but hell, we got to support our own—God dam em!

Ralph

To Albert Murray
AMERICAN ACADEMY IN ROME
MAY 18, 1956

Dear Albert:

With June leaping in on us it occurs that we'd better let you know our plan for the trip, which is truly simple because what it amounts to is that we're ready whenever you Murrays come up. The idea of going through Switzerland and then through the Chateau country sounds great to us and we've been putting some money aside in anticipation. If you've done your usual economic survey please let me know how much you think we'll need and by hook or crook we'll have it. As you see I didn't get back to Spain again and it's just as well, because if you drive down on your way back to Morocco it might just be possible to go along and take the boat back to Naples. Incidentally, Fanny is helping to organize an international conference that will take up the first week in June, so in case you get here during that period and want to keep rolling, I'll hop aboard and she'll catch us up the road a piece. What I'm trying to say is that we're ready and nimble, you just call the tune. We especially like the idea of doing Florence again, and Venice and Milan will be new worlds to discover.

The North of Italy is wonderful country and I'm sure you guys will like it, bring your picnic gear along because we'll probably want to eat lunch along the road and fill eyes and belly at the same time; that's what we did on the nine day trip we took with the new fellows last fall. Fresh bread, cheese, meat and wine <u>and</u> sweets can be had in most of the towns and the air and the sights transform it into something almost as good as fried chicken on the Juneteenth ramble in the woods. So whatever you care to do we're with it. We'll gather road information and choice-spot data from some of the old Europe hands here and we have some guidebooks and will get others—which, with your information ought to nail things down. So let's shake, rattle, and roll . . .

Ran into Artie Shaw yesterday and he told me that he's building a house at Bagur, Provinzia de Gerona, which is on the Costa Brava. Swears that it's to be his home from now on, so I guess he's here in Rome training to start through those Spanish chicks. Anyway, he invited us to drop in so it will be interesting to see him perform. Maybe we can dig him later because if I forgot to tell you, we're definitely going to be here next year. Got the official notice . . . Was also offered Brandeis job teaching creative writing and one course in American Lit, which I had to refuse; but the cat wrote back and said he'd cool it for me until Fall, '57. Looks like they're ganging up trying to make an honest man out of me, a lo mo, natural born hustler! Because just about the same time the man at Bennington wrote offering a job substituting for a cat next year at a take of $5500 plus housing. That one was right in my old briar patch, but looks like Brandeis will be the pitch because it's right in the Cambridge area and I'd like to operate among the Harvard brains a while so that I can see what they're really putting down. But, whatever I do, my main work will be writing novels and I'm making it plain to everyone. I'm thinking too that if I do go to Brandeis I'll get a critical book out of it, because I've watched you lit teachers long enough to know how to put students to work on the problems by way of learning what they find hard to understand. So just as with writing I learned from Joe and Sugar Ray (though that old dancing master, wit, and bull-balled stud, Jack Johnson is really <u>my</u> mentor, because he knew that if you operated with skill and style you could rise above all that-being-a-credit-to-your-race-crap because he was a credit to the human race and because if he could make that much body and bone move with such precision to his command all other men had a chance to beat the laws of probability and anything else that stuck up its head and if he liked a woman he took her and told those who didn't like it to lump it and that is the way true studs have always acted), here I'll also learn from your latest master strategist, the N.A.A.C.P. legal boys, because if those studs can dry-run the Supreme

Court of the U.S. and (leave it to some Moses to pull that on) I damn sure can run skull practice on the critics. Meanwhile I'm trying to get this dam book done so we can spend most of next spring traveling.

I've been looking out of the snap shooter since you wrote, but if it is troublesome to get up here I can jolly well wait until you come, I'm trying to get ready for it though and I've learned that the army was supposed to use an 85 mm fl.5 job called the Lithagon which is much cheaper than the Summerex and about as good. If you see one around let me know the price, I also know about the Nikon 105 mm f.2.5. That is very good, but it costs $152 stateside and that's a bit rough for the moment, though I need something for portraits and telephoto shots. As for film I can use a dozen rolls of that 135 Plus X 80 and six rolls of kodachrome type Aldridge, if possible because I understand you can use it in daylight with a conversion filter. I'm having a bulk of film loader sent over from home and plan to pick up some M3 cassettes so I can operate within my budget . . .

That's about it. "A Coupla Scalped Indians" is out in *New World Writing* No. 9 and I have a copy for you. Picked up abridged version of Kazin's *On Native Grounds*—which has a new postscript that mentions me. Also got Panofsky's *Meaning in the Visual Arts* (both Anchor books) that I understand is first class. Also reading Arnheim's *Art and Visual Perception* and a new Mentor titled *The Painter's Eye* by Maurice Grosser. As you can guess I'm now trying to dig where Malraux dug his digging and as one of the art historians here pointed out to me, a hell of a lot of his stuff ain't French but German—and not just Nietzsche either. I don't know where this will take me but it's damn interesting. Take it as you have to take it and as Louis said in his latest dispatch to the *Herald Tribune* from London, the Cats are still blowing and ain't shooting, and I hope that it'll stay that way—though I guess Louis hadn't heard about Cyprus. Tell them women folks hi! Fanny sends love.

Ralph

To Albert Murray
ROME, ITALY
MAY 22, 1956

Dear Albert,

Your letter arrived yesterday and I'm answering right back so as not to lose your mailing address. I wrote you on the 18th so you should have received that letter now . . . Thanks for getting the meter, etc., and don't worry about any other accessories because Germany is the place for them, and as I said in my last letter, I can wait until June for film—both black and white and color. So don't gamble on Athens.

As far as the trip goes we'll be looking out for you on the 24th and will have a pensione reserved for you up here near the academy if possible. You can then have your meals with us here when convenient because the food isn't bad—if you can digest onion and some garlic—and you'll find the place interesting and a good place to relax after the hurly-burly of mid-town, tourist-crawling Rome. We have a living room where you can stretch out and there is my studio for general all out bullshitting.

The schedule looks O.K. to us, though I suspect we'll find that we'll want to linger here or there a bit longer (Paris and Florence and no doubt the Loire region). Fanny says that she'll get to work on Italian hotels as soon as she gets rid of this conference she's running and meanwhile I'm checking with the people here. I've already arranged with a friend in Florence to use his influence to get us hotel rooms. We'll see who knows what about Venice—which we've been told is expensive as hell—and we'll write the hotel where we stayed in Paris to see what they have for those dates. So as for now we'll let the schedule stay as you have it.

Sorry to hear about Mique and I hope it's nothing too serious, especially not rheumatic fever. Friend's daughter here in Rome has had a similar fever but is recovering. I've got my fingers crossed too, so tell Mique that she'd better take it slow . . . When I first read your letter I read "Back" before "ankle" and said oh hell! But now I see that Mokie has had the easier part of the sprain business. Probably got it doing one of those down-home struts on those Casa streets. She'd better slow it too because the Ellisons have had enough trouble for <u>all</u> of us.

Yesterday just as your letter arrived I got a call from a friend who is going to introduce us to Isak Dinesen. She's the Baron[ess] Blixen so when I autograph a book for her I'd better use that name cause I sure as hell messed the pseudonym up above. I'll send you a report and I admit to be delighted.

Good to hear about your Mitchell, it's a damn good reel. I know you can get the rest of the gear in France and perhaps the Swiss will have something. I just bought a light rod here that was reasonable, though I haven't had a chance to use it. But those British Woolens intrigue both of us and we'll discuss them with you later. Would it be possible to bring a few items when you come? If so, we could use 2 jars of Pond's dry skin cream (large); 2 medium jars of 5-A-Day deodorant pads; 6 cans of silex ground American coffee; some bourbon whisky and some Kleenex. Could also use some kidney beans, but don't let any of this weigh you down. I'm enclosing a check for $25.00; if it isn't enough let me know; if more, just apply it to the film etc.

It just occurs to me that we might make Pamplona for the running of the bulls if we juggle a bit, think about it and we can decide later.

Over to you; I'm cutting it so as to get this to you before the address goes. Give our best to the gals.

Ralph

To Herbert Weinstock
THE AMERICAN ACADEMY
VIA ANGELO MASINA V
ROME 28, ITALY.
JUNE 21, 1956.

Dear Herbert Weinstock:

Thanks for allowing me the pleasure of reading Alejo Carpentier's *The Lost Steps*. Without, I hope, being too carried away by words in the rush to get under way for our trip, let me say that I found it most absorbing, both as a novel of ideas and as the unfolding of an engrossing narrative of adventure in which the ideas become at once image and action, character and scenery; yes, and in the end, dramatic perception.

I found it especially attractive that its hero is obsessed by those resonant questions that the Sphinx always puts to the Hare when old certainties are being shattered by change and the citadels of the mind have been shaken ajar to chaos. What is the meaning of human society? How must one live and act to achieve the creative life? What really, when he's stripped of the garments, the conceits and prejudices of his class and culture, is man? Not a little of my pleasure came, I think, because Carpentier's hero seeks his answers to these questions not only in the usual relationships, between man and woman, in the family, among friends, a work (each become another level of hell in its contradictions), but plunges back into those pre-literate cultures which are so often rejected because mistakenly regarded as primitive.

I liked it too that the hero, frustrated composer and anthropologist manqué that he is, sets out most significantly in search for a primitive funeral instrument—only to find himself swept along labyrinthine paths that lead him to a concern with those life-preserving motives with which men throughout the ages have asserted their humanity against the crush of destiny. In this lies not only the magic of the narrative's art (which has become much too rare) but at a time when the possibilities of rejuvenation which the art forms of so-called primitives have offered Western artists appear to have been exhausted, Carpentier suggests that a more <u>empathetic</u> examination of those sources which inspired Picasso and Stravinsky might reveal important secrets for our most needed resuscitation. Carpentier knows that here, as Stanley Edgar Hyman has suggested, the trick for the sophisticated artist is not the mere eclectic business of "looting" primitive art of its externalities, nor of attempting to become primitives ourselves (perhaps the only real "primitives" are found in great cities), but in learning once more to approach our own materials with that total inwardness of cultural vision which the pre-literate artist brings to the creation of his fetishes, his totems, his gods.

Besides, when we look at what has come to pass from all the looting and devastation of cultures, the least the artist can do—since he is a guardian of consciousness—to redeem those ways of life so thoughtlessly destroyed is to at least become consciously aware of what, in terms of universal culture, they meant. For here, perhaps, lies the secret of what <u>we</u> mean—or at least what, in the narrowed span of the world, we must come to mean if we are to survive.

These issues aside, I feel that if for no other reason than that it has brought the abstractions of anthropology under the significance-creating form of the novel and time lending them dramatic immediacy and creating a deeper perspective in which we may examine our problems, *The Lost Steps* deserves that high quality of attention which we have learned to bring to such works as Malraux's *The Walnut Trees of Altenberg* and *The Voices of Silence*. It is by no means lost upon me that the author of this "novel of cultures" is a French Cuban who writes in Spanish and I congratulate you for bringing such an important new talent before the North American reading public.

Please give my regards to Harry Ford and Pat Knopf and I hope there's a word in the above ramblings that you might find of use.

Sincerely yours,
Ralph Ellison

Mr. Herbert Weinstock
Executive Editor,
ALFRED A. KNOPF, INC.
Madison Ave.
New York 22, N.Y.
U.S.A.

To Stanley Hyman

ROME,

JUNE 22, 1956

Dear Stanley:

At first I didn't write because the letter I planned was long and I wanted to go into certain problems of my book with you, then there was sickness and I got too entangled with the writing to waste your time with my bird nest. But today I realize that I've been holding back because I didn't want to put a most painful question: WHAT'S HAPPENED TO THE BROOKLYNS? One advantage of being here I guess, is that I can't worry about them every day; the news is too slow and the radio here doesn't realize how important they are. So you give me the lowdown. I hated like the dickens to turn down Burkhart's offer for next year, but after our bouts of sickness I feared the further loss of time involved in moving before the book's done, so asked for and had already been notified that I would receive another year. I'm quite certain that you and Kenneth had something to do with his asking and I thank you very much.

As you can see, I haven't learned to use these damn envelopes yet— jobs have been coming my way just at the time I couldn't accept them. First there was an offer to give half of the fiction lectures at Bread Loaf, then Brandeis, then Bennington. Brandeis is holding the job for next year and I'll probably give it a try. God knows I wish I could have come to Bennington, with the novel out of the way I could have started working out the ideas for a book of criticism without a loss of stride. It seems unreal that it's been a year now since I've seen you Hymans and perhaps another whole year before I'll even be within telephoning distance. So tell Shirley and the kids that I miss you all and would even eat one of those phony peppermint cookies with you if I were granted my wish to see you. Rome is wonderful but I wear it badly because for all its beauty living here is like living right in the palm of the dead past and underneath every graceful curve there's a bone. Don't get me wrong, I'm no innocent American, it's just that the people here seem crushed by the weight of the past and terrible poverty of the present. As for the academy, it gives me a fine place to live and work, contact now and then with a first rate art historian or so and a lot of lil bitsy scholars who try to impress one another. The talk here ain't very good, until some character like Roethke, or R. Penn Warren (with whom I had a most interesting talk about KB, whom he admires) and I make up for the dead spots. There are many things to see and to do but I've really disciplined myself to keep up the day to day slugging at the book and so have missed most of the trips to nearby towns and even most of the tours to sites here in the city. I'm getting this to you now because next week we take off for a vacation, driving with friends to Florence, through Switzerland to Paris and on to London, where I'm to be a guest of the International PEN Club. We'll be in London the week of the 9th (July) so if there's any book scouting you want done drop me a card at Glebe House 62/63 Glebe Place, Chelsea, London S.W.3. Which reminds me, I'd like to send you some old coins but don't know what you'd like so let me know . . .

Ran into our old friend Elsie a couple of months ago. She seems a bit subdued now, with two children and separated from Ray. She must be back in the States by now while he has remained here. God, but she seems tiny! As though she has shrunk, physically with the long past but glorious days of the Woodside 'forties. . . . I'm waiting for your anthology, which Ford tells me is quite impressive and I've introduced Raglan to several of the classicists who are working on Homer and such but are totally unaware of the whole Cambridge school. Some of these cookies are from Amherst and Princeton too, so maybe you and Kenneth have given me a better education than I could even buy. It was, by the way, very pleasant to learn that Warren was as stimulated by *Counter-Statement* as I was. He Thinks K. is a great man, as do I. Eight months with dry as dust scholars foaming at the mouth whenever some amateur writes about Rome or makes a classical allusion, has given me an even deeper appreciation for that old rascal than ever before. I only wish now that I had his books here with me. Read your Freud piece in PR and found it so good that I'm amazed that they took it. Hope you're doing other things for them.

As for me, most of my writing is on the book, which is much more difficult than I had imagined. Still it's rolling along and I've become quite fond of the old preacher and his six-year-old revivalist whose great act is an antiphonal rendering of the seven last words of Christ with the little boy sitting in a small coffin. Wild things arise from this, but I'm still having trouble in giving the book the dramatic drive I feel it needs. Will do, though; will do. Just learned that the kid preacher's name, Bliss, means rapture, a yielding to experience. Very American because of the overtones of progress and this guy really becomes Dick Lewis's "mind in space." Having fun, as you can see. Today the old preacher is talking Aristotle (though unaware) as he tells kid just why coffin has to be of a certain size. So I guess if I don't succeed in making [the] book dramatic I can at least reveal the principles as they operate in life. Trick of course is to do both. Read Radin's *Trickster,* give it a look of you haven't. Tell Laurie that we're rooting for his side and a kiss for Joanne and hug for Sally, and an extra cone of cream for Barry the batboy. Tell Shirley [. . .]*

To Saul Bellow,
AMERICAN ACADEMY
VIA ANGELO MASINA 5
ROME 28
AUGUST 15, 1956

Dear Saul,

Just a note to say that we heard straight from the horse's mouth that no writer has applied for a Fulbright in Italy and that applications would be very welcomed. Deadline for applications in Washington is October 1. Pass the word along but by all means try yourself. It would certainly be fine to have you and Sondra here.

What the hell goes with you and why haven't you answered my letter? I haven't read your story in *Partisan Review* but I heard good things about it and plan to read it this weekend.

As for us, we've just returned from a trip to Paris, Munich, London where I attended the International PEN congress. Saw all the old farts and the younger English literary gangsters, fairies, floozies, and broken-down aristocrats slumming with the written word. It was fun and since I'll probably never get a chance again to freeload champagne cocktails at Clarence House with the Queen Mama and her little girl Margaret, I guess we can say that it was good for my writing. Seriously, they were both charming ladies. And that is saying a hellava lot for any two broads these days.

[Dear Saul, he seems to only have eyes for me. F.]

Saw the Kaplan family in Paris, ditto Jimmy Baldwin and Ann and Alfred whose little baby girl can stand on her tip toes and out-Kazin Kazin. She's a doll. We had driven to Paris with Albert Murray and his

---

* The last few words and salutation of this letter are missing.

family, so with such homefolks around we have to admit that we found Paris charming.

Let me know how things go, and if there are any new novels worth reading.

> Fanny sends love as do
> I to you and Sondra,
> Ralph

Dear, dear Sondra, It would truly be fine if you and Saul could come over. We are so lonely for the companionship of our "mature" friends and for their warmth. And besides there's Rome and the rest of Italy which I need not praise to you! Fulbrights are generous, it seems. Roethke was here on some sort of lecture arrangement and he and Bea seemed to have wonderful independence financially and Ted found time to write. Should you apply, tell us and we will report here that you have applied just in case it would help.

Tanti saluti ed auguri. Pensiamo a voi con viva simpatia,

> Fanny

To Richard Brown
AMERICAN ACADEMY
VIA ANGELO MASINA 5
ROME 28, ITALY
AUGUST 16, 1956

Mr. Richard K. Brown
Dept. of English, St. Peter's College
Hudson Blvd., Jersey City, N.J.

Dear Mr. Brown:

Your letter of April 12 was late in being forwarded to me at the American Academy in Rome where I shall be living until late '57. Moreover, I have been travelling and have only returned to my desk. I regret this long delay in answering your letter that outlines your interesting experimental course at Saint Peter's College.

As for my own attitude toward *Invisible Man,* I was more interested in the aesthetic problems involved in constructing the novel than in the socio-political nature of the material. Not that I underestimate the importance of what you call the "propagandistic" content. But I feel that all such materials are what the novelist starts with and that they are only a part of life. I believe that all major novels involve a great deal of conscious rhetorical manipulation, in that the writer is aware that his reader's vision of experience might not be his own and he cares since he knows that literature functions only when it is recreated by the reader on the basis of his, the reader's, own idea of reality. I work with the same reality, say, that Thurgood Marshall does, but the meaning which reality might have for him as a lawyer would not have the same meaning for me as a novelist. His approach is apt to be more analytical whereas mine insists that I not only analyze but that once the analysis is made I re-arrange it into a new synthesis so as to achieve form and significance.

You ask "was the symbolic value of the pushcart man . . . a deliberate intensification of the nightmare in which the hero moves or did it have some further point or was the whole concluding section on the Riot a conscious attempt to transcend the racial conflict . . . ?" I intended to have both. The discarded blueprints in the pushcart were a foreshadowing of a change in the direction of plot and of the hero's development. Among other things it symbolized the folk elements of the hero's past that were challenging him in the city. You will recall that in the Blues where the pushcart man sings is that of a chimera. As for the Riot section, if you go back to the beginning of the book you will notice, after the Prologue, that the action starts on a fairly naturalistic level. The hero accepts society and his predicament seems "right" but as he moves through his experiences they become progressively more, for the want of a better word, "surrealistic." Nothing is as it seems and in the fluidity of society strange juxtapositions lend a quality of nightmare.

Finally, let me say that at no point was I primarily interested in the racial connotations of this experience and was writing about a specific individual and his struggle through illusion to reality and it so happened that this individual was an American Negro. Thus much of the character of his world was affected by his racial identity. Nevertheless the perspective through which I had to approach the material was the perspective of Western culture. So I viewed the character and his life through the great form which we call the novel and which allows us to view our experience in a much more meaningful context than that of race, or even the struggle for Civil Rights.

If you can, try to secure a copy of *Paris Review,* No. 8, Spring 1955 in which there appears an interview mostly given over to *Invisible Man.* Write 2 Columbus Circle, New York or 3 rue Garanciere, Paris.

Thank you and best wishes,
Ralph Ellison

To Dave Sarser
THE AMERICAN ACADEMY
Via Angelo Masina V.
AUGUST 28, 1956

Dear Dave:

I've become as bad about not writing as you, hence this letter that should have been written two weeks ago. Perhaps by now Mr. Roberts, the director of the academy has contacted you about a sound system, if not, I gave him a list of what should be included and told him that you would see that he got the equipment available for his budget. (I didn't tell him that he might have to twist your arm to get it in time to bring it back with him.) Nevertheless, do what you can for him and I will see that it's set up on this side. If there are any special problems connected with the installation please send me the instructions and I'll do the rest. It occurs to me that I wrote you for some tape and spare parts for this bunch of machines you sold me—my speaker was bounced around by the servants and has a rattle—can you send me a replacement? If you can, do so and I'll send you a check by airmail. I also remember that you were to get me a few recording jobs, what happened to all that? Don't feel guilty as I've been busy as hell; however, I'm staying here another year so if there is any taping I can do please let me know . . . One further bit of business: I have a Leica M3 and I'd like to have a Nikon 105 m.m. lens for long focus work, have you one that you'd like to sell? Or an 85 m.m., or 135 m.m.? If so, quote me a price. Naturally it would have to be adaptable to the M.3., which I can handle on this side, since adapter rings are easy enough to get. If you don't have one for sale can you do anything about the price for a new f 2.5. 105 m.m.? Maybe we could do an article so that I can pay for it, ya got any ideas?

That said, what's happening with you? How is Mrs. Sarser, to whom, if you ever write her, my best regards. Did you get the 300AL? I was almost knocked down by one in London in July. That's a little job that I'd like to purchase for you and break it in before bringing it home. If you like, send check and I'll dash up to Germany and bring it back fully equipped with Telefunken mics and all. Seriously, I'll be glad to take care of anything that I can. Somebody is always coming and going to and from the States so it wouldn't be too difficult. We'll be home during the late summer or early fall of 1957.

By the way, I told one of last year's fellows here to look you [up] for some equipment. His name is William McDonald and he has just returned to teach at New Haven. He won't have the dough for the best but do what you can as he's a good guy. Things go well enough for us here. I'm working again after three weeks traveling in Germany, Switzerland, France and England. I went to London for the P,E,N, Club Congress, where I met the Queen Mother and Princess Margaret—along with fifty other people. Now <u>that's</u> a girl for you, really good-looking and quite lovely. Talked hi-fi with a lord something of the other and except for the Oxford English he sounded just like any other bug. <u>He</u> was in the process of building a corner cabinet. It made me homesick as we don't even have a crystal set and I've played my tapes until they bore me. <u>Can you send some of the latest pre-recordings and how much will they cost?</u> If you're too busy to write just send along something by leaving it at the Park Ave Office of the Academy and I'll send you the dough. I hope you'll send the lens information though, as it's very important. In the meantime take it easy, but take it.

Sincerely,
Ralph

American Academy in Rome
Via Angelo Masina V,
Rome 28, Italy

To Irving Kristol
AMERICAN ACADEMY
VIA ANGELO MASINA 5
ROME 28, ITALY
AUGUST 29, 1956

Dear Irving Kristol:*

The report <u>was</u> true. I had intended to attend the Paris Conference on the invitation of an American delegation, but since a new development in my novel might have made it necessary that I remain here until the last moment, I felt I could not fulfill my obligation to the delegation (which, by the way, was footing the bill). Since I would not only have had to arrive in Paris a few days before the conference but would have had to prepare a paper for discussion and later a report I regretfully withdrew.

Nevertheless, I am still interested in attending the conference and a report for *Encounter* sounds like a much more interesting reason for going; the problem now is getting to Paris. I've been enquiring for someone driving up about that time, but thus far no luck. Hence, all I can promise you at this time is that, if I am able to get there I'll do a report for you. Otherwise I suggest that you contact James Baldwin, who is now living in Paris and who might be attending. I don't have his address but H. J. Kaplan would know how to reach him.

Meantime I'm sorry that I can't be more definite about Paris but I can say that I have now a very rough draft of the desegregation piece which, as soon as I've gotten it organized a bit better, I'll submit to you.

Regards to Spender.

Sincerely
Ralph Ellison

Mr. Irving Kristol
ENCOUNTER
25 Haymarket
London, S.W. 1

---

* Kristol had requested an essay on desegregation in relation to the American civil rights struggle for *Encounter* magazine. Ellison worked on the piece for the next year, then largely set it aside until 1965, shortly before it was published as "Tell It Like It Is, Baby" in the centenary issue of *The Nation* in September 1965.

P.S. Thanks for the Alistair Cook's reports. I think he comes pretty close to making it seem as though it is the North that is responsible for what the South does to Negroes. Naturally that knocked me out. But not as much as his feeling that Martin Luther King (that slick villain who upset those simple-minded blacks, and a lawyer as well as a minister) invented the language of bureaucracy. Cook probably stopped off in South Carolina and had a few mint juleps with Jimmy Byrnes. Just enough, in fact, to make him imagine that he actually visited Storyville with its Blues singing whores hanging out of cribs during the 1930's—when, alas, Storyville was closed down during the <u>First</u> World War. It just goes to prove what I've always believed: what good journalism needs are a few heady hookers of imagination.

Don't get me wrong, because I think Cook means well; he just has a gift of being carried away by his own typewriter. As on the occasion when he introduced Sol Bellow as winner of the National Book Award, he became so carried away with his own voice that he came very close not only to insulting Bellow, to dismissing *Augie March* on religious-racial grounds as well. It was most embarrassing. The trouble with Cook's kind of glibness is that too often it twists him around his own corkscrew. Reminds me of a drunken conversation between a well-known white southern liberal editor and a Negro sociologist. The two had been out drinking all night, as old friends will do, and were watching the dawn come up over the Alabama hills. When suddenly the editor turned to his friend and said, "Hell, Joe, I know you think I'm a heel." "Who? What the hell you talking about, Roy," the sociologist said. "I'm talking about those editorials I write," the editor said, "that gradualism crap. I know you think I'm a heel because you know I don't believe it. But hell, Joe, <u>I have</u> to write that stuff. If I don't, the paper goes under. You understand me don't you Joe? You know I'm not really a heel, don't you? You understand my position, don't you?"

"Sure," Joe said, "Sure. Here, let's finish this bottle and knock off. It's almost daylight. Go on, man. Have another drink."

Hell, how do I know, perhaps Cook has a similar obligation.

R.E.

To Albert Murray
THE AMERICAN ACADEMY
ROME, ITALY
SEPT. 15, 1956

Dear Albert:

I'm getting this off at the last minute for I've been hung up with a piece of desegregation which I'm doing for *Encounter* and just haven't been able to write anything else. It seems that the trip up to London was just the beginning of a spell of dashing around, for after Wright's inviting me to come up to take part in the conference on African culture, I've been approached by two other groups to represent them there. One was the *Encounter* bunch, who wanted me to do a report and the other is an American group on Race and Caste, which offered to pay my fare there and back and to take care of expenses on a $35 per diem. At first I was willing to go for this group, only to learn that they wanted me to speak, to have a paper for publication, to write them a report and to be there a couple of days beforehand so as to hold conferences with the State department and others. Which was just too much for me, so I refused, withdrew; and the guy is still cabling me to change my mind. I guess the son of a bitch thinks I'm impressed by the little money he offered me. Certainly he can't understand that I'm simply not interested in racial approaches to Culture. Let him get hold of Dick Wright, he's on that kick, not me . . . Well, as if this wasn't enough, here comes a letter from the Congress pour la Liberté de la Culture asking if I'd be a member of the American delegation to Mexico City Conference on Cultural Freedom in the Western Hemisphere, with first-class air passage and expenses, and this time I've said "Yes." This is something I'm interested in, know something about, and which seems to hold some real promise. Besides I need to see my dentist and to take a look at the apartment in N.Y. so I'm off tomorrow and will be gone until the third week in October. I'll try to write from some point on the trip, which will give me some time in Paris on the way back, otherwise I'll write to you from Rome. I guess Fanny gave you the dope on the trip to London and I have little to add.[*] It was exhaustingly exciting and we were given special treatment; $21 per day rooms at the Ritz, platform seats on all social occasions, guided about by

---

[*]   Ralph and Fanny spent ten days in London in July 1956, with Ralph as special American delegate to the 28th PEN International Congress.

rump-sprung ladyships and slightly rummy ladyships; drinking the Lord Mayor's champagne, and her Majesty's liquor and God knows who-all's scotch and eating everybody's food. I was one of the lucky ones who were received by the Queen Mother and Princess Margaret, two very charming ladies indeed, the Queen Mother actually reads books and knows how to talk about them and Princess Margaret is the kind of little _hot_ looking pretty girl that our girl Laly* only _thought_ she was and who could upset most campuses, dances, club cars, bull fights, and three day picnics even if she had no title. No, I'm not about to do a Henry James but I was impressed by those two. I was also impressed by some of the writers I met, especially by Eliot, with whom we shared the guest of honor table the night of the closing banquet. I talked with him very briefly however because he was just recovering from a heart attack. All in all London was impressive and is, I think, the only city which in its massiveness and harsh sprawling conveys the idea of power. It is simply huge, a monument to empire which will remain long after the empire is gone. Full of art too, those damned Englishmen really have their share, with many private collections rivaling the Louvre in many types of art . . . I must say, however, that despite the language the only time I didn't feel exactly alien was one afternoon while we were having tea with the President of the House of Lords on the terrace of that House, and I looked across the Thames with its bridges and boats, to Westminister towering in the haze, and suddenly I was a child again and nursery rhymes were singing in my head. So London _is_ a sort of literary possession, but all the public ritual, the fading pomp and circumstance constitute a wall that's far thicker, because I understand the language, than anything I found in Italy or France. To be an American is to be many things but only the slightest bit English . . . We left there and went down to Munich to rest, to stuff ourselves with food (the British still ain't cooking) and beer. Stayed a week. I got the wide angle that I find very useful and I shot some of the Anscochrome, which pleased me very much, so I'm buying some in 35 m.m. bulk film so that I can load my own cartridges. $9.95 buys enough for eight rolls, which is much cheaper than Kodachrome. My Kodachrome came back fine, but I wonder how that roll came out that you started? The black and white was O.K. and I'm very impressed by your telephoto lens, which will be _my_ next buy. Indeed, I wish I had it for this Mexico City trip. Don't, by the way, forget that I'm interested in an Omnica bag for this stuff, as the one I have is simply too heavy and incapable

* Miss Tuskegee, 1935.

of being handily arranged. Right now I'm using a little plastic bag to hold a couple of rolls of film, my wide angle and some lens tissues. It's much easier to carry and it makes you less conspicuous. Some of the Venice stuff came out quite well, both in Kodachrome and Anscochrome . . . All in all the first part of the trip with you guys was the best and we're sorry that it couldn't have lasted longer. I still want to explore some of those towns we had to shoot though and to do the chateau country, so come on up next year. Picked up a Hemingway picture story in the barbershop the other day and was struggling to translate it, only to find it the next day in *Look*. He's still in there and I'd like to run into him now that he's doing Europe. I'm using that bit of dialogue from *The Sun Also Rises,* wherein Bill tells Jake that Lincoln was a faggot who was in love with General Grant and that he freed the slaves on a bet etc., in this essay I'm doing. The thing is beating the hell out of me because I have too much material, too many fleeting in-sights keep popping up which cannot be used in the short piece. I'll send along a carbon when I finish it as I'll probably extend it into a longer study of late 19th and early 20th century writing. I got to get the stuff out of me before I can have some peace. In the meantime I've written enough stuff for at least two further articles in the subject that I hope to sell. It is very odd how Mose seems to have thrown up his hands before this subject and here it is in the headlines. You look in the Italian press and one day you see Egyptian belly dancers posing with rifles all set to blast at the French and the British, in fact at all Christians, white folks and Jews, and the next day you see those crackers in Tennessee being stood off by the fixed bayonets of the all cracker National Guard. Thing about it is that the Egyptian belly dancer looked like Althea Gibson, the Harlem tennis champ, French ten-nis champ, and about sixteen other champs.

What the hell do those crackers think they're doing? Mose is the only darker group who doesn't want to blast his kind from the face of the earth, who make any kind of allowance for their form of insanity. There was a time when the cracker's madness could be rationalized but now they're acting like a maniac chasing hell in an airplane loaded with the atomic bomb. Somebody, the Federal or State governments, I don't care which, had better straitjacket those fools before they wreck the plane.

Life is running a series on desegregation but it hasn't appeared over here as yet . . . Man, that coffee which you brought us certainly improved our breakfast a hell of a lot. I don't know what the hell we'll do when it runs out because we're nearly been spoiled . . . There's no news in the States worth relating except book news. Vintage is bringing out two editions of James's essays, one on European and the other on American themes and Stravinsky's *Poetics of Music*. There will also be a two-volume edition of Gide's *Journals* and Hyman's anthology, *The Critical Performance*, Faulkner is working on a sequel to *The Hamlet*, one part to be called *The Village*, the other *The Mansion*. When we got to London we found a copy of Wright Morris's *The Field of Vision*, which is a quite good, quiet novel. That Morris is probably the most skilled of the younger novelists, he just won't open up with all he has . . . This is it, man. I'm getting packed to take off and by this time tomorrow plan to be heading to Paris. Tell Mike that I've learned to make more reasonable sounds on that recorder and that I promise to cook up some chitterlings just in case I find my way down there in the spring. Maybe with a belly full of that righteous cuisine— con cornbread, con buttermilk, con mustard greens. Speaking of which, reminds me that I've forgotten to tell you that old down home Mose and his wife have found Rome this summer and are walking over these ancient streets with the same deliberation with which they walk along an Alabama Road. Man, I liked to laugh out loud, I looked out of a shop on the Corso and there is old Mose wearing a billed cap, and his high-assed sport shoed buddy was wearing a cream colored silk shirt with a cravat that showed grimly beneath his round head. That mister was grim, taking no shit and seeing everything. In fact they were arguing with the women for getting tired just as we were arguing with Mokie and Fanny a few months ago.

You can't hold him man, he's on the move, all he wants is for the damn crackers to get the hell out of his way. I don't know where they got the money, but Brother, they are over here! See you. If you need anything from over yonder write me at 730 Riverside Drive or until the 26 of Sept. at the <u>Hotel Frimont, Calle Jesus Teran No. 35, Mexico City</u>.

Ralph Ellison

To Fanny Ellison
MEXICO CITY*
SEPT 19, 1956

Dear Fanny,

The trip was exhausting. Four hours after I left you I was in Paris, where I was picked up by Hunt and taken to have drinks with some of the Congress People, then at nine we took off for New York. It was the usual thing after that: Gander† at three A.M. then New York about nine. I had to hang around Idlewild Airport, so near and yet so far, until 12 noon then off we went, straight seven hours of flight for Mexico and the usual confusion of languages and custom inspection. Yesterday was the opening session with Norman Thomas speaking for the U.S. Farrell and Abe Harris didn't come down, so I'm here, I suppose to act as writer & Negro. Conference isn't well organized. I haven't received any money yet and am threatening to leave when I see the boys in a few minutes. So far only interesting thing here is Dan James who has been here all summer long so kind of reporting. We'll see more of him later . . . The speakers (except Thomas) all taking swings at the U.S. much to my boredom. I haven't heard a thing worth reporting but perhaps things will go better in the smaller sessions. The city is full of modern buildings and mean little old ones. It's taking me some time to get things in focus for my eyes are unadjusted to this American version of a European City. The contrasts are great with the Indian to be seen everywhere, and as with most Catholic countries, wealth contrasting with great poverty. Perhaps I'll like it later but as for now I'd just as soon hit it for New York. Yesterday I was so dam tired that I went to bed at 4 pm and slept till seven this A.M. Take care of yourself and don't worry as I'll see you as quickly as I can.

Love,
Ralph

---

* Ellison traveled to Mexico City for the Cultural Freedom in the Western Hemisphere conference in September 1956.

† Gander is the international airport in Newfoundland.

To Albert Murray
[POST CARD FROM MEXICO CITY]
SEPT. 24, 1956
CPT. A. L. MURRAY
CHEZ M. RAZZ
75 RUE DE REINS
CASABLANCA, MAROX

Dear Albert,

Been trying to see as much of this country as possible with all the yak yak coming from these Latin intellectuals. Mucho, modern, this city and as interesting as Italy. Rich past. Been going around with Dos Passos who knows the country from 30 yrs. ago. I'll write from New York. Love, to Mokie and Mique.

Ralph

To Fanny Ellison
730 RIVERSIDE DRIVE
NEW YORK 31, N.Y.
SEPT 28, 1956

Dear Fanny:

I received your letter in Mexico City day before yesterday and answered it, but was so tired and depressed that I couldn't send it after I had re-read it the next morning. The trip was long and tiring, the conference not well arranged, as I told you in my first letter (which I hope you've received by now) and the Mexicans are as fond of garlic as the Italians, so as you can see I've had it. I put in full time, attended all the sessions from first to last, almost drowned in the Latin rhetoric, restrained myself from firing back at the many unfair attacks at the U.S.A. and managed to say a few temperate words of my own. I learned that some of the Latin Americans expected me to join them in blaming every evil in their countries on this country but own some of them though I didn't. I'll have to tell you about the conference in person and will only say here that I saw a lot of Norman Thomas, Roger Baldwin and John Dos Passos, all of whom proved interesting enough to have made the trip worthwhile. I don't know how much real work was done there, or at least how much was accomplished through all the talking, but I hope a great deal. About all I know now is that there were motions for future meetings so there is hope.

The most disappointing thing was that I [was able] to see very little of that most interesting city. It is quite large—4 million, and full of modern architecture—and extreme contrasts between the rich and the poor. I did get to see little bits of it, some of which I photographed but there is so much to see that it'll take a special trip, which I hope will be possible someday. I lived in a small hotel, rather new and poorly constructed but the people were pleasant and there were many guests, native and foreign, coming and going giving the place a real international flavor. Unfortunately there was not much of a per diem—though I shouldn't complain considering what my fare cost the committee—so I couldn't take in much of the nightlife and I had to leave yesterday morning at 6 am following the end of the conference. Right now I'm staying at Sarser's. He's getting married soon and he and his girl are fixing the old place up so attractively that I hardly recognized it. I'll be there until Tues. when he has to take a trip to the coast. I'm writing from the apartment, and on the machine, which needs adjusting, since, as you can see, there are no periods functioning. (I'll take that back, the upper case period does work.) Charles has asked me to move in here and sleep on a bed that Liz left, so, as I have very little money and there is little in the bank I shall take him up when the time comes. I haven't been able to do very much here, only look over the apartment, which thus far, doesn't look too badly. Charles has shown me some nicks and scratches and I'll go over things carefully later on [in] the week but for the moment I have no real complaints—except that the place could stand a good dusting and airing. Evidently, Liz left plenty of old cigarette ashes, for the place reeks. I've talked with Harry, Albert, and Augusta and all are well. I'll see them when I get downtown. Jean's still here and Augusta said that Francis is in Rome and plans to return next week. Bea's here and I'll phone her before I go. Nina too is here, have talked with her and will see her in an evening or two. I'm writing before I've had a chance to get into the files, but the new one is very little damaged. I forgot the little one-drawer file near my desk and forget the key. Nor can I find the telephone number file, so can't call Langston or Parks. Did we leave the telephone pad here? It's rainy over here though not in Mexico—and I should have brought my heaviest clothing for this is fall, very much fall. Nevertheless I like being here . . . Incidentally, I was upset that you could not only forget that we saw *Johnny Chanen* together, during which you cried, but that you could see it again and go on to describe the plot to me. What gives? Having a boss named Miss Bevasqua, must, on the other hand, give you some comfort.

I wrote Al and Lottie a post card, thinking that you had heard from me—so go ahead and tell everyone that I was in Mexico having gone there from Paris—which is the truth. If there is anything I can do here for anyone, write me what it is and I'll do my best. I cannot bring anything home however. I brought Dan James' X-rays from Mexico. The poor guy has a rupture whereby his stomach has pushed up into his food canal and he wanted Arthur Logan to take a look at it before he allowed the Mexican physicians to operate. It's very tough luck because he can't do any work and must sleep sitting upright. Which means that his assignments there are not likely to be fulfilled.

There isn't much else to tell you at this writing. I plan to see Jones about my teeth and to take care of as much business as I can in the next few days and I'll let you know how things go. As for myself, I'm still tired and in need of sleep and somewhat depressed but expect this to pass with time. A letter is not the place to discuss such things so they must wait until I return to Rome. Let me know if there are other things you want done you can write here at 730 but don't wait too long as I can see that this is going to be another tense, swift visit.

Love,
Ralph

To Fanny Ellison
730 Riverside Drive
New York 31, N.Y.
October 6, 1956

Dear Fanny:

I've managed to let you get two letters up on me in spite of trying to keep you briefed on what's happening here. I've simply been going around on my ear, trying to get a few things done, checking the apartment, and having dinner with friends. I've had dinner with the Fords, the Dan James's, the K. Clarks, and night before last Jean had Harry and Lebo and Gavin to dinner with me and, after I had talked with him during the day, Sol dropped up after his class at the New School, bringing along Paolo Milano. Jean fed us all very well and, as you predicted, on roast beef. She's in good shape and plans to live in Rome in order to get away from Gavin and Mary's family. Gavin has not improved and she thinks he never will.

She was a bit miffed that we couldn't see Sholto when in London but I think she understands now. I also had lunch with Albert, who seems in good shape although he indicated that he still suffers from the Peggy episode. Nevertheless, he's still ahead on the stock market and looking quite healthy. There are still hundreds of people to see, including Arabel, who has been catching hell, with several operations and much pain, and Berny and Eleanor. I'm having drinks with Helen Frankenthaler this afternoon, will probably go out to Parks' tomorrow and plan to spend my last weekend here out at Kenneth's and Mamie's. All, naturally, send love. As far as my report on the apartment and Nina's I must say that after looking things over I must report that Nina was more accurate than I. The windows seem never to have been touched, the woodwork is filthy, the kitchen and bathroom full of roaches and grease over everything. The blind in the kitchen is unstrung and the blades bent out of shape; the arms and pillows of the upholstered chair are greasy and there are scars around the table that sits before the couch. As I knew when we discussed letting Liz have the place, she is as irresponsible as hell so now that the damage is done I feel that it is our own fault. Ramsey tells me that she had several people in here and that the night before the robbery there had been a party and argument between two people that became quite loud. Thus he thinks that the robbery was an inside job. I don't know but I plan to give Liz some very straight talk when I see her. I was in the office to say hello to everyone, including Harold, but it was the day before Mary Williams left for Rome so I had to make it a very short visit. Harold wants to have dinner with me so I'll try to arrange it for next week. Anna talked my ear off for the moment I was there very much concerned over the NAACP and the integration thing.

So things go. I bought a dacron and cotton suit for next summer but I certainly wish I had brought along an extra pair of slacks and that other sport coat. The weather is definitely fall, though lovely today—which is the third day of the World Series, with the Dodgers leading by two games. I dropped by the *Reporter* office to see Bingham, but he was at home tending Janet and their second child that appeared the night before. Kid was yelling like hell. Which reminds me that I had drinks and sandwiches with the Currys and heard all about Frances' sneak pregnancy and miscarriage. Jimmy was off to Maine the next morning, all loaded down with warm clothing and shotguns. He's been promoted on his job but our gal Frances doesn't carry her liquor any better . . .

Tell Al that I saw one of his cover paintings handsomely framed in the reception room of the *Reporter*. Also that he'd better hurry back if he wants to recognize any of that bum's paradise, Third Ave., because they're cleaning it up a mile a minute. Soon, with its fluorescent streetlights, it's going to be one of the best looking streets in the city. I haven't had my teeth done yet because I'm waiting for some money from the Academy that will be ready as soon as the two trustees sign the check. Lucky for me that I reserved a seat to return as late as the 27th, although I hope I don't have to remain here that long, for I too am in suspense, being in the apartment and yet not in it (Nina's little boy is nice but somehow strange, he sleeps entirely too much and seems a bit remote from things) and in New York and yet not here to stay, feeling the need to be working and being unable to do so. Then of course you're not here, which makes the idea of sleeping in this hard little folding bed all the more hard to take. When we do come back I think I'll throw out mattress and springs and start out new. I'm sure that Liz and Connie (who has some of my books, Liz says) have had too many creeps in this one for me ever to enjoy it again . . .

Sorry as hell I wasn't there to see the Murrays, I knew that they had a cruise in their plans but didn't realize that it would come so soon. Too bad that they brought the iron though, as I had planned to bring you that little G.E. steam iron. Let me know if you want to get rid of what you have, if so I'll bring the G.E. along. I won't be able to bring the overcoat though just my extra papers from Mexico City cost me five dollars. I'm leaving them here and pruning my luggage to the bone so as to bring those things we really need. My suit won't weigh much however; but there will be tapes and hand lotion and the heating pad etc. . . .

Glad things are going well at the Academy and that the new fellows are o.k. Give Sol's regards to the Arrowsmiths and write Chester that he can use my name as reference. Naturally I send regards of my own to all, including Mary Williams, whom I gave a big impulsive hug the last time I saw her. She _is_ a fine person and once in a while I too can be sentimental . . . Yes you did see Choncho with me, but I didn't mean to write that I thought Miss Drinkwater was your boss, but that it must be a comfort to have a boss with a cousin named Miss Bevaque . . . Anyway, I'll bring the letters back with me. You shouldn't worry yourself about forgetting that movie though, I find that I've forgotten the names of people I met only last year and that many incidents have become fused together. I suppose it's the pace we're living, the travel, and the inevitable aging. However if you'll think of what you were thinking when you wrote your first letter, the associated ideas, I mean, and those things you thought to tell me and those you thought might be annoying, then you'll probably have the answer. As for that wild sexual hunger just hold it down until I get back as I'll bring home quite an appetite of my own. I hope to rest up the last weekend just to have some physical reserve when I get there. Perhaps part of my tiredness comes from the added weight of the old hammer as much as from all the hectic running around; so save it, pretty mama, save it!

I weigh 189 with clothes on which means that I must be down to about 179 stripped. Plan to have a physical before I leave just to see how I'm doing. Eating O.K. and came in early last night and cooked pork chops, sweet potatoes, carrots, and string beans. Left half of it for Charles and went to a lousy movie in neighborhood, but he got up too late to cook the chops and ate the vegetables cold. He sleeps all day and has to rush off to work at Bickfords. I tried them for lunch one day and haven't had such poor food in years. I've also eaten some bad chili down without ill effect. Ruth and Dan have been very nice, telling me I can eat there whenever I want and I'm sure they mean it. She's very thin these days but they eat very well. What I'm trying to say is that I haven't been going hungry—at least not for food. Which reminds me that I've seen Velasco and told him about your black beans in Italy, which gave him a big laugh. He told me that Janice and Ted are divorced and called her to tell here that I was in town, so I went by to meet her husband to be. A very intellectual white boy, friend of Harold's, who is in for a rough time. Janice was wearing the same pajama top and step ins drinking hard and looking awful. I don't think she's in love with the guy but he's in business and she doesn't know how to take care of herself. Very weird. She has since moved but I don't know where. Ted is out of town on a playing date . . . I haven't called the Arters but will do; I want to be able to go by there for a while . . . Meanwhile, take care of yourself and keep me informed of what's going on around there and save it!

Love,
Ralph

PS. Where is your big camera?

To Fanny Ellison
730 Riverside Drive
OCT 26, 1956

Dear Fanny,

Just a quick note to say that I leave tomorrow at 7 P.M. for Paris. I don't know if they still want me to hang around there a couple of days, and if not I'll come straight to home. Needless to say, I'm tired and still somewhat depressed, but perhaps we can work this out between us. I hope so. Otherwise I've gotten one problem off my hand: I turned down Brandeis at $6500, which just covered enough for what I have to give them and the trouble I'd have to go through with the regular academic people. I hope you don't mind but I think Sacher thought he could get me for the same money that he'd pay some kid fresh out of school and still have the prestige which goes with my publicity value. They certainly wanted me but were simply too cheap. Edna and Max send love, as do Kenneth and Mamie and I'm seeing Ann & Callie sometime today. Everything is about the same at the apt; Charles will need supervision because he just ain't a cleaner. Says he's going to have a maid and I hope so because the place is a sight. I'm waiting for Dave to drive me down to the Academy office to leave my summer clothes and the hifi components. It's a cloudy day and like you a sty on my left eye. I'm sorry about my letters and I hope you'll help me out of my depression. Don't worry and look after yourself. Should you hear from Albert don't be surprised; he left for Rome yesterday.

                              Love,
                              Ralph

To Albert Murray
AMERICAN ACADEMY IN ROME
VIA ANGELO MASINA, 5
(PORTA S. PANCRAZIO)
ROME
NOV. 7, 1956

cable address
(am enclosing check for iron)
"Amacadmy"

Dear Albert,

I found your letter waiting for me when I returned on the 30th. I left N.Y. on the 27th and spent the 28 & 29th in Paris, where I gave my impression of the Mexico congress to the people who sent me over. Winter had come to Paris and I was tired so I described the ten days of Latin-American hot air, clichés, the strutting and posturing as great intellectuals that went on there, and came on down here to see Fanny and catch up on my home work. Those Latin Americans are wild and even the writers had nothing better to talk about than blame the U.S. for everything negative in the world and to mouth worn out Marxist slogans as the latest wisdom, there in one of the cities most given over to modern architecture and in a country in which there's an ocean's width between the rich and the poor, those bastards are fighting the machine! They, they say, are spiritual; concerned with personality, value, distinctions (subtle, of course) and hierarchy; while we North Americans are materialists and concerned only with building roads, bridges, machines, and in out-doing ourselves, so as you can see, I had it up to my ears. New York was such a relief that I was filled with a burst of energy. I felt like that middle-aged Mose you met in Paris: it's a damn good town. I stayed a month, having teeth repaired and cussing the bitch who made a pig sty out of my apartment. But what a bitch! Not only were things broken but she didn't replace a single light bulb, or, from what I could tell, dust a single piece of furniture. Blinds were busted and rusting, expensive plates, crystal cocktail pitcher and wooden salad bowl busted and cockroaches in everything. Even up front. So again I had it. But I did see a few movies, ate ice cream and was entertained by our friends until I was bowlegged. In Mexico I ate biscuits every morning until I saw the Mexican woman pouring hot cakes and brother—they are the largest and the lightest I've <u>ever</u> had. Those tortillas had prepared the Mexicans to really romp with Aunt Jemima! We'll have to jump down there with a car, man. That place is easily as interesting to me as Italy and in many ways with enough cultures rolling around under the surface and with a decided flair for things modern.

But back to New York. The changes in the city can be seen with some distinction after a year. More attention seems to be being given to neighborhood planning; 3rd Avenue sports the new fluorescent streets lights, is being paved and promises to become the most interesting street in the City. That El was messing up a hell of a lot of good space. The new Seagram's building on Park has been designed so that it offers a wonderful frame for the Lever building, which it faces at an angle. It's jumping and it's the liveliest city in the world—Well, that bastard Stevenson didn't even take the solid South. I hope that's the last of him—and I'm still a Democrat.* Maybe now we'll get rid of some of those crackers in Congress and the next time we'll get a statesman and not a jackass . . . Forgot to mention that I saw a lot of Norman Thomas, Roger Baldwin, & John Dos Passos in Mexico. Part of American delegation. Called me the 'Kid.' Boy, if we could only get in the position to use what we know and have learned by living in the groove of our circumstances! They're o.k. but they know the issues no better than we do and often not so well. I'll write more on this later . . . I was so busy down there that I didn't shoot up the place like I wanted to but did quite a bit. But brother, I picked up a Nikon 105 m.m. telephoto and have been reaching and gittin' it for a fare-thee-well around Rome. A beautiful optic that you'll have to try next trip up. I think I like the Rollie better for color although I brought back Anscochrome in bulk and am loading my own 35 m.m. at 8 20 exposures for less than $7. I find it better than EK and Gordon Parks uses nothing else. Sorry you didn't see the stuff from the summer, it was right there in the top drawer. I'll be sending you the money for the Omnic soon, because the bag I have to have is too heavy. Will the Leica bag hold a Rollie too, or will I have to have the larger size? Prefer the smaller one for its compactness. I don't expect to be buying any more lenses even though the new wide angle with the attachment looks very good. Just wish I'd waited to get the new meter, cause I'm traveling light as possible . . . Thanks for the tapes; they were equalized badly for my machine but by adding bass they sound good enough to hear until I can do better. Most of the stuff is good Duke

* Democratic presidential nominee Adlai Stevenson was soundly defeated by Republican Dwight D. Eisenhower in the 1956 presidential election.

and I'm starved for more of it. Missed him while in N.Y. but saw Ruth, who had a good down-home meal on the table—Yams, man! I told her I <u>knowed</u> <u>somebody</u> knew I was coming! Greens too, and all the fixings. That chick ain't Duke's sister for nothing. Anyway, if you can send more tapes, please do. My machine only plays 7½ inches per second and I suspect that the trouble with these is that the tape you used has different characteristics from the M.M.M. tape for which Ampex machines are equalized. *Scotch* is the brand name. I picked up the components for a sound system for the Academy while in N.Y. but they haven't come over yet; when they arrive and I've set it up I'll have the problem of classical music licked, but the jazz will still be missing. So send along anything that's good to you. Heard some Chico Hamilton out at Kenneth Clark's and liked it. They tell me he challenged Duke at a festival last summer and shook up those bored Ellington cats so much that they came storming back and outdid themselves. Which is pretty good for a five-piece group of so-called modernists. I only heard two discs, is he consistent? The Clarks send regards to you and Mokie. He's been advising Luther and still can't understand the place. He's also been asked to keep an eye on Derbigny's little blue-gummed gal* and is puzzled by her strange blend of naivete and sophistication (mainly verbal about sex and extra-marital affairs). Sounds like a campus-raised kid to me. What kind of person is she?

The Brandeis thing is all over; I turned it down after they only offered me $6500 and academic status. To hell with that; I could bring them that much in publicity—which they counted on—<u>and</u> I have a point of view which is fairly original. I certainly don't plan to go anywhere and start fighting with someone like Irving Howe at this late date. I'd rather go to a Mose school where I might keep some of the stuff in a briar patch. For $8000 I'd have taken it and would have worked like hell—which I've been avoiding all my life. I guess the man thought I would be taken in by the ofay set up, but hell, if I've got to have children I want them to look like me, they'd have some of the same things to write out of. The Man up there might not know it but there's a hell of a lot more knowledge and discipline in writing a novel than it takes to get a Ph.D. or at least <u>most</u> Ph.D.s and if he can't see <u>I</u> can. Anyway I've been living poor and avoiding the nets so that I could write and now [it] is too late to sell myself cheap; I'd rather write ads—which in its abuse of words is as low as whale shit . . . Writers around here at the moment: Warren and his wife, Eleanor Clark are

---

* Daughter of Tuskegee's administrative dean.

here; old Albert Erskine will be back from Madrid in a few days; William Arrowsmith of the *Hudson Review* is here on fellowship (he's a classicist who wants to write novels); Blackmur will be here to have drinks and dinner with us tonight; Allen Tate came in the other day; John Cheever is to be in Rome for a year, so it looks as though I'll have a few people to talk with during the winter. I didn't get to see Kaplan* in Paris, but heard his wife is seriously ill. Baldwin's down in Positano; Wright was still het up over the *Présence Africaine* conference, which he feels is of great future importance; says the American Negro is in the position to help them, which perhaps we are. But who the hell wants to live in Africa? Which reminds me, I hope no fool pulls the lid all the way off the mess we have in Egypt and Hungary, because I'm as sure as I'm setting here that the British will drop a bomb—if they have one. The Russians are threatening them and I think they've been pushed too far to give a damn, U.S. or no. Nasser is gambling too hard and too fast unless he intends to involve everybody. One thing is certain; he ain't the Jungle King. Poor Stevenson, he starts talking about the draft and bomb control just at the moment hell pops. We'd better prepare to jump and jump fast if that bear keeps farting because he'll head in our direction in spite of hell. If he does I hope we'll go for broke on his ass . . . Take it easy and give our regards to the girls.

Ralph

To Coran Palm
NOVEMBER 30, 1956

Dear Coran Palm,

If you were to judge by the time that it has taken me to answer your letter, you might suppose that it was dispatched to me in a bottle cast into the ocean rather than by plane. However in September 1955 I came to Rome as a winner of the Prix de Rome prize in literature and aside from re-arranging my life fairly completely, it also upset my correspondence and even the once rather direct route through which my mail always reached me. Well, better late than never, as the saying goes. Certainly this delay in no way indicates any lack of pleasure in hearing from you. In fact, my wife and I were both quite pleased.

---

* *Partisan Review*'s Paris correspondent H. J. Kaplan was a friend of Murray's.

We still look back upon that period in Salzburg* as one of the most stimulating and pleasant in our lives. I <u>have,</u> by no means forgotten our discussion of *Huckleberry Finn* that, by the way, I am re-reading at the moment, and I am quite pleased that you found some of the things I had to say useful. But even better is the news that you are now editing a magazine. I am myself quite busy writing another novel at the moment and trying to make about three deadlines on essays but I am very sorry that I did not receive your letter in time to try to do something about appearing in your publications.

I don't have any short pieces at the moment but there are two short stories that appeared during last year in *New World Writing* that you may find of interest.

Should you find either of these stories of use, I would be very glad to make it available.

Your news of Vilgot Sjoman was quite good to hear. Someone whom I met in Paris told me that he had become quite an important writer. Please give him our regards and we hope that before our second year in Europe ends next September we will find it possible to come up to Sweden, if only for a few days' visit.

Thank you very much for writing. Both my wife and I send you best regards.

Sincerely,
Ralph Ellison

Mr. Coran Palm
Uppsala, Sweden

To Harry Ford
JAN. 17, 1957

Dear Harry:

This is my first letter of the New Year. Since returning to Rome I've just been too busy fighting with the book and an essay that is insisting upon <u>becoming</u> a book that I've let my correspondence slide.† But not, thanks

---

* Coran Palm was one of Ellison's students at the 1954 Salzburg Seminar on American literature.

† The superb essay "Tell It Like It Is, Baby," which Ellison began in Rome but would not complete and publish until 1965.

to you, my reading. The books arrived right after Christmas at a time when I was reading Bruce Catton's latest book on the Civil War, so that I plunged into the *Peculiar Institution** without breaking stride. I found it most instructive and, I think, objective. Much of the material I was acquainted with, but had never seen it put in context. The whole package was first-rate, and though I missed the Hyman anthology the Jameses are keeping my appetite for criticism well under control.

Do not let me however, give the impression that all my time is being spent reading and writing, far from it. For it has been a writers' season. With R.P. Blackmur, Eleanor Clark and Robert Penn Warren, Dennis and Karen Devlin (he's the Irish Minister to Italy), Peter and Ebby Blume (he, alas, is the painter), John and Mary Cheever, Elizabeth Spenser (Mrs. Russian, husband's English), Bernie W. and, for a few weeks, Albert— with all these folks in Rome during the fall and winter we've quite a social life. Yes, and I almost forgot Eugene Berman and Alexis Heif; Heif is still around and Berman who has a studio in the city, will return later. Fanny took a color photo of Berman with the intention of sending it to you but it wasn't too good. Quite a nice man and all the others, good company. Indeed, I've been having the pleasant experience of talking with people who are not only intelligent but who don't give a damn about most of the petty matters that make living with academic people such a bore. We've seen the Warrens several times a week over the past few months and like them better every day . . .

That ghostly Robert drifted down from Florence with Jane and his mother during the holidays and we saw them at Bernie's apartment. God knows where <u>they</u> are now but I found his tough little mother rather charming. Methinks however that Robert wished her gone back to St. Louis. I got the impression that the little lady had given her laddie a hot foot of some kind—of some classical kind. Bernie said at the height of the party that all we needed were you Fords and all replied, Amen! . . Thus far it has been a good winter (only now turning cold) but soon the Warrens and Blackmur will leave and things will simmer down for us. Although Bernie and the Cheevers will be around to make us feel civilized. The rest of the time I'll be sweating at this crazy book. It goes well at the moment but I can't count on it nor on anything else I turn my hands to. Everything goes to knots and tangles; like this essay I'm working on. I started out to do a simple piece on desegregation (for *Encounter*) but now it has become

---

* Kenneth M. Stampp's 1956 book *The Peculiar Institution: Slavery in the Ante-Bellum South.*

a monster of bastard form which sticks its demented head into matters of literature, politics, old Jamesian observations, myth, Gilbert Murray on Hamlet and Orestes, the *Ruggles of Redgap* of Charles Laughton, Malraux, Faulkner, the psychology of immigrants as regards the American Dream, the N.A.A.C.P., why Fiedler thinks Huck and Jim were practicing buggery on the raft (Huck sounds like that good old Elizabethan pleasure and hell, they were together in the dark, weren't they?), Jack Daniels Whiskey (how I wish I could lay this madness to drinking that!), cool jazz—ten penny nails and puppy dog tails. Eugene Walter, who has to do with both the *Paris Review* and *Botteghe Obscure,** saw some of it and said that it sounds like a small book; I hope so, though God knows I wish the damn thing would quit running all over the landscape. Right now it has more leit-motives than a Wagnerian opera . . . About the novel I'll only say that some of the scenes are molto outrageous. If only I didn't require the gestation period of an elephant to bring forth my odd mice! Next time I'll play it *New Yorker* smart, I'll write the first and last scenes and let the reader guess the development. The novel will then have brevity spelled w i t, and mystery—gaining that when I won't know what the hell it's really about; understatement—to the tune of three or four hundred pages or 995%—and sophistication, spelled s h o r t n e s s. No more of this growing old and mellow with a theme for me. I'm going to assert my author i tee!

We had a nice card from the Daniels that we assumed you mailed us, for which thanks. Our regards to them when you write—and to Wright Morris, who has my permission to shoot Brendan Gill in his left nut—and to Gerry and Flora. We miss you and Lebo and I no less than Fanny for all my having seen you in October. Those were fine times and I hope when you come over we can get together, either here or in Paris. Meanwhile let us know how your new apartment turned out and give all those cats a scratch behind the ear, the livers of twelve fat pheasants and a deep drag of catnip each in honor of T. Stearns' new marriage.[†]

Ralph

---

[*] An Italian literary journal from 1948 to 1960.

[†] T. S. Eliot, whose famed poem *The Waste Land* was such a seminal influence on the young Ellison, married Esme Valerie Fletcher in January 1957.

To Jean Douglas

JAN 17, 1957

Dear Jean:

You must have concluded by now that I've fallen out of the world, lost my memory or encountered some other major disaster, while actually I've only been busy and, as always, negligent. I spent two days in Paris after leaving New York and returned to Rome exhausted; covering so much space and living at such a pitch of intensity simply took its toll of my energy and left me anxious that I might have lost control—such as I ever have—of my book. I hadn't but I required lots of rest and concentration to get things going again. Then, of course, Thanksgiving and the Christmas holidays tumbled down upon us—we're still digging our way from beneath all that—and we found ourselves caught up in even more social activities than we knew in New York. Rome is full of writers— R.P. Blackmur, Eleanor Clark and Robert Penn Warren, John and Mary Cheever, Elizabeth Spenser, John Ciardi, Bernie Weinbaum (a friend of the Fords) and countless others who drop in for a day or two. Then there have been the painters, Eugene Berman and Peter Blume and wife, and the composer, Alexie Hief—all the kind of people whom Bea would feel constrained to protect from her more plebian or underserving friends— especially naughty-naughties like me. With these bright stars mixed in with the poet and Irish Minister to Italy, Dennis Devlin along with his charming wife, Karen, and the regular Italian luminaries, Rome has been anything but the provincial city it seemed last year. Sadly but also fortunately, most of these will be gone by next month and we'll be back in our little academy groove . . . Which is just as well, since I have more deadlines than I can hope to meet. I guess being in New York gave me the illusion of having more energy than I possess. Perhaps you and your kindness when I was there had something to do with it, Jean, and I can never thank you enough. What will we do when you are here and we are there and with no prospect of your returning? I dread to think about it, and yet for all my silence I have inquired about a place for you here—though without too much success. I can tell you only that Perioli is a new section with modern buildings about which there are some of the same complaints that are charged against Manhattan House: thin walls, etc. and that many American Embassy people and middle-class Italians live there. But some of the buildings are heated with oil or coal and have wooden floors, quite an advantage during these bone-chilling winter days. Be that as it may, I'm told that apartments are not easy to come by for most are sold rather than rented, and that it is better to be on the scene than to try to negotiate at a distance. Laurence Roberts, the Director here, tells me that it would be far better for you to live in a pensione or a hotel while you took your time to look around; and that, in his opinion, some of the older places are much nicer than the modern buildings. There is no doubt that some of the places are most appealing. The Cheevers have an apartment in an old place on the Corso and it is magnificent—great rooms with high, painted ceilings, tile floors and walls so thick that with the blinds closed, the busy traffic just outside sounds miles away ... What are your plans? Are you still coming? And how is Gavin, and what of Ian? It's so frustrating not to be able to help, though I <u>can</u> listen if you care to write. As for us things go along well enough except for the fact that after all of Fanny's hard work in helping set us the organization she's been working for, they're forcing her out on the excuse that she doesn't speak German. The annoying thing is they gave her such short notice—not to mention the fact that little of the work is done in German. Thanks for your nice Christmas card and meanwhile I hope things are improved for you and that you're still the real, true, impish Scottish Jean. Both Fanny and I miss you and send you our love.

Ralph

P.S. Regards to Bea and Francis

To William Faulkner
AMERICAN ACADEMY
VIA ANGELO MASINA 5
ROME 28, ITALY
FEBRUARY 22, 1957

Dear Mr. Faulkner:[*]

I find myself very much in agreement with the first three of the committee's proposals and would be willing to do whatever I can to help make it effective.

---

[*] Ellison's only letter to Faulkner, who had written him about supporting a request to President Eisenhower to free the poet Ezra Pound. Pound had been in St. Elizabeth's, a mental hospital, since his conviction for treason because of Axis propaganda broadcasts he made during World War II.

I do not, however, agree to the freeing of Ezra Pound. Pound is, as you say, a great poet but I can't see this as a reason for freeing him any more than I could see the Rosenbergs freed because of their particular professions—whatsoever—even had they been the first in their fields. Pound committed treason and if what the Paris Edition of the *Herald Tribune* states is true, he continues from his rooms at St. Elizabeth's Hospital to encourage the treasonable activities of John Kasper. Thus, since his confinement does not interfere with this side of his activities, I cannot see why it should interfere with his creation of poetry.

It isn't easy for me to take this position because I myself have learned some little bit about literature from Ezra Pound; nevertheless, you know and I know that were I to wander into a situation where one of his more irrational disciples, such as Kasper, was beating the drums of hate, nothing (certainly no quotation of Pound's poetry, not even the most eloquent) could save me from a glimpse of death.

Isn't it a bit incongruous that the Pound question with its problems of hate and genocide should be connected with our efforts to help those who are trying to free themselves from that same type of evil, given the authority of the State, which Pound encourages?

Sincerely,
Ralph Ellison

Mr. William Faulkner
c/o Jean Ennis
Random House
New York, New York

To Albert Murray

CHECK ENCLOSED

AMERICAN ACADEMY IN ROME

via angelo masina, 5

(porta s. pancrazio)

rome

Cable address

"amacasmy"

APRIL 4, 1957

Dear Albert:

This has been one of our longest silences, which means that the world has really been too much with us. I've been up to my ass in typescript and have only just climbed out of one level of the mess after another back to my novel. Last year I made the mistake of agreeing to do an essay on the novel for an anthology edited by Granville Hicks and which will include people like Bellow, Wright Morris, and Herb Gold and which Macmillan will publish. But I got bogged down on the damn thing for two months, perhaps because I was resisting the necessity of leaving old Bliss and Clio-fus and Severen and Love to deal with The Novel and those who say the form is dead. Fuck Trilling and his gang, I know that a novel is simply hard to write, especially during this time when you can't take anything for granted anymore. Anyway I've finished that piece and I hope they use it. The other piece I probably mentioned is a piece on desegregation, which is still in the works. It deals quite a bit with literature and I'm hoping to make a short book of it at the suggestion of Robt. Penn Warren. I've begun to look closely at the novels of the twenties through the frame provided by today and the Civil War period and have dredged some interesting stuff out of Hemingway and Fitzgerald. The other writing news is that the Battle Royal scene has turned up in *A Southern Harvest* along with all those Southern big names, which amuses me to no end because it must mean that I've sold my soul to the crackers! "Flying Home," that long and not too smooth story is appearing in an anthology of writing edited by Charles Fenton of Yale, to be published by Viking (W.W.II, that is). I picked up a book on criticism published in England under the title,

Catastrophe & the Imagination,* which gives *Invisible* lots of space and picks it for a short list of novels which that wild stud thinks will be of interest a century from now. Surely the man must be on the weed. The other project is an interview of Warren for the *Paris Review*, which, if they don't cut it too much, should be one of their most interesting. Eugene Walter (Mobile white boy) an editor of the mag. helped me and we all got tight on some Pernod that Warren brought up to our place and we taped the whole thing. Sounded like a bunch of Moses drinking corn and I wished you could have taken part because for all the drinking we were axing straight through a lot of marbled-hard bullshit. I'm holding the tapes as long as I can so if you zoom up here you can hear them. Got to see Warren and Eleanor two, three times a week for two months and we became very fond of them and they of us. We knew them before but it took Rome to let us discover one another—which might be the most important thing to happen during these two years. I got to measure my mind against one of the best southerners and it's just like we've been saying, if Mose takes advantage of his own sense of reality he doesn't have to step back for anybody. Anyway, Warren is a man who's lived and thought his way free of a lot of irrational illusions and you'd like him. Maybe I told you that R. P. Blackmur was here most of the winter after being evacuated from Egypt. We saw a lot of him also and he has a capacity for night-owling and drinking that is appalling; and an elder statesman's tendency to dominate conversation even when he has nothing interesting to say that can sometimes be boring. Too much teaching and undergraduate worshipping, I guess. Nevertheless, when he's really riffing he reminds you of Buck Clayton, no straining and grunting just smooth, hot sound . . . MacLeish is here just now but I'll write about him later. Have talked to his wife about Hemingway during the twenties in Paris and it was dam interesting. So you see that writerwise this has been a year more interesting than the last.

That picture you give of Nixon and the old Mose knocked me out and I'm sorry I didn't get to see them when they <u>hit</u> here. Not only the air brass but plenty Moses back in the states must wonder what time of day it is. And the Democrat! If Ike wins the next election even Bilbo will rise up out of his grave and tell his boys to 'forget about white supremacy and git those damn nigras on our side' which reminds me that I've seen the Isaacsons twice since we visited them in Florence last July and each time he's

---

*   John McCormick's *Catastrophe and Imagination: An Interpretation of the Recent English and American Novel*, published in 1957.

given me a hurt puzzled look. I guess he's still puzzled by your little comments on Ike, politics, and the election. He still doesn't know whether you were just kidding or were damn serious and, I suppose, since I agreed that Stevenson couldn't win he doubts that I'm a Democrat, which I still am although I didn't vote for that weak sister.

As for travel we haven't been anywhere either and I don't see us going. We've just investigated getting down to Barcelona for Easter but found the fare too expensive. I did have the use of a car for a few weeks and we got to see a bit of the Roman countryside this lovely spring, but no Florence, no Siena, no where. We're waiting to hear from the freighter line about passage home. We want to leave here in Sept. and wander back with the tides, thus saving our dough and staying here to the very end. Thus far see no possibility of taking a summer trip. Incidentally, the gas situation here is O.K. Tourists get 300 liters a period, same as before. Don't worry about France, if you can bounce in here for a second before you start moving we'd like to see you. I haven't heard the idiom since Harlem in the fall.

Thanks for the bag for which I'm enclosing a check; it's the best ever and you may tell the young lady that I want to send her a book when we get back home, she was very nice and I'm sorry she hit here when I was a bit under the weather. But the bag has brought order into my equipment and beginning to get the hand of the Leica and the extra lenses. The 105 Nikon is a fine piece of glass and I've been using it to pick faces out of crowds as well as to do detail work on buildings etc. Fanny, by the way, is shooting some nice color with her old Rollei, in fact much better than most of my recent stuff. I've been giving my attention to black and white and having great fun ... Those tapes you sent are still sending the Academy. Sometimes I play them and open the door to find guys standing there bending an ear; so I say come on in, what this place needs is a little more Ellington. And man, we gave a party with another couple, got hold of some cheap but excellent French-style champagne to start them on before serving the martinis (we were celebrating the good fortune of those who were given a third year) then I put on Basie and Joe Williams and the whole building took off! People who had never danced before were trying to move and I was yelling never mind your feet, just bounce and let the rhythm tell you what to do! And some were doing it too. We went out to eat and they kept dancing in the restaurant to a guitar played by a Neapolitan character who must have gotten rich off of our party, then we came back and danced to Duke until everybody started falling down. As soon as the cartridge comes,

I plan to assemble it and then go find *A Drum Is a Woman** as I need something new to help me through the summer. If you have anything new you think I should have I would gladly pay for the tape and the cost of having it recorded. Let me know . . . I just received *The Town,* Faulkner's book on the Snopes, and Steegmuller's translation of *Madame Bovary.* Too busy to get to them at the moment but look out for them.

The news about the chapel was rather shocking; I guess I loved the old place; so much of what I hated about Tuskegee took place there as did so many of its lost possibilities come to focus there. Perhaps the burning is symbolic.[†] I had hoped to see it again, now it will become the occasion for some more stealing and more bad design and construction work and a hell of a lot of self-congratulation and pious bullshit when the new chapel is completed. One of these days I'm really going to put the bad-mouth on those scobes; here Africans and West Indians are taking over governments and Montgomery Negroes are showing their quality and <u>they</u> continue to act like this is 1915. Foster[‡] should be ashamed of himself. Well, man, world events are justifying our position and interests of the thirties, not those of the administration or the campus heroes and politicians; we are operating out of a different sense of time and on a different wavelength. Maybe Foster will see the light and be a man . . . Love to your girls from Fanny and me—Say, when do you go home?

Ralph

To Saul and Sondra Bellow

APRIL 9, 1957

Dear Sol and Sondra:

We couldn't be prouder if he were our very own.[§] We heard the good news through John Cheever just about the time <u>their</u> new son arrived and only my entanglement with the essay for Hicks kept me from writing for more details. Good things to the new Adam and tell him he's got a couple of new friends he's never seen. I should like to have been there just to have seen

---

[*]   Duke Ellington's ambitious musical allegory, recorded in 1956 and presented through television in 1957.

[†]   The historic Tuskegee University Chapel burned down on January 23, 1957.

[‡]   Dr. Luther H. Foster, president of Tuskegee from 1953 to 1980.

[§]   Sondra had given birth to their son, Adam, in January 1957.

your happiness, Sol. Cheever was like a child with a wonderful new toy and so delightfully proud of himself and of Mary. What a year for both of you, new books and new boys and all good. It's enough to make a duffer like me think of giving up both the pen and the bed . . . I hear from the Botteghe people that you have something wonderful going in the African adventure and I can hardly wait to see some of it, or all of it, since *Seize the Day* appeared in *PR* last year several people here have discussed it with me and have become interested in *Augie,* which seems to be unavailable in Rome. I'd like to give a copy to a couple of friends and thus would impose upon you for a signed copy. Their names are Meta and Leon Goldin and you can simply have the book sent to me here. I don't know the cost, so let me know and I'll send you the check as soon as I hear . . . Things have been fairly lively here this lovely spring. Writers all over the place: Blackmur, Eleanor Clark and Red Warren—with whom we had quite interesting times—Cheever, Arrowsmith, Elizabeth Spenser, and now MacLeish. I also spent a strange evening with the Malamuds but it didn't go so well after I declined to discuss my novel with him. I guess I get along better with the older guys, they know how to have a good time and it isn't strictly necessary to discuss literature with them, anyway not the first shot out of the box. Had plenty of literary talk with Warren though, when I helped Eugene Walter interview him for the *Paris Review.* There was talk here, by the way, that Elizabeth Spenser would probably get the NBA for *The Voice at the Back Door* but I was quite pleased that Wright got it <u>and</u> the thousand bucks.*
Looks like we got cheated! Incidentally, if you come across a book of criticism titled *Catastrophe and the Imagination* by a guy named McCormick, take a look see; he's a wild man but he thinks we're pretty good. Never heard of him myself. Things go slow with the novel for the moment. The Hicks thing came at the wrong time, it was like having to stop making a watch and go out to dig iron ore.† Nor has the spring helped, I simply want to goof about and dream. Now that we're conditioning ourselves to leave Rome has caught me up, off guard, out of position; poignancy and lost promises throb in the air. And, as you can guess, there's something eating my innards which I can't write about but if I don't crack by September I'll have to ask you for

---

* Wright Morris received the 1957 National Book Award for fiction for his novel *The Field of Vision.* Bellow's *Seize the Day* had also been a finalist.

† Ellison had agreed to write an essay for Granville Hicks, which would become "Society, Morality, and the Novel" and be published in *The Living Novel* in 1957, and included in Ellison's *Going to the Territory* in 1986.

a friendly ear. I guess once in a while even old dogs like me discover suddenly that life has stirred up more anguish within them than they can keep down. Hope that I last until the fall* . . . What's the good word? How does the novel grow? And is there a roof on the house, water in the well?[†] If you need hired man let me know, I'll probably have to take a job when we return. And what is this about your coming to Italy? I'm sure it'll be after we've left but if there's any information we can gather for you please let us know. That Senior Fulbright thing pays very well, by the way, and I'm pretty sure you could get it . . . If you happened to have reviewed Gill's novel tell me where as I'd like to see that faker keelhauled. One advantage of being here is that you don't have too much contact with that kind of character and you seldom get the opportunity to see their abuse of words . . . Regards to Herb and Helen and to Alfred and little Anna Kazin and don't forget to send the autographed copy of *Augie* as I forgot to say that one of my friends has read it and admires it very much. Sasha, you've made us very glad.

Ralph

Horace Cayton
AMERICAN ACADEMY
VIA ANGELO MASINA 5
ROME 28, ITALY
[SPRING 1957]

Dear Horace,[‡]

Please forgive my delay; your letter went to my New York address and then had to wait to be shipped over with other mail, only to arrive at a moment when I was under the most paralyzing deadline pressure. We were quite pleased to hear from you though surprised that you didn't realize that we have been living in Rome where I've been a fellow of the American Academy in Rome since October 1955. Well, time whirls so swiftly these days that by next September we will have returned and perhaps forgotten that we've ever been here. Though I hope not, for while I prefer New York, living here has been a most quickening experience. But about this when we see you.

---

* This seems to be an intimation of his "Rome affair" in its early stages.

† Bellow had received an $8,000 inheritance from his father and used the money to purchase the house at Tivoli, New York, where Ellison stayed the two years he taught at Bard (1958–59 and 1959–60).

‡ See footnote regarding Cayton in Ellison's January 21, 1953, letter to Richard Wright.

As for Chester I can only say that I saw him at Dick's in Paris last July and he seemed as tortured as ever, but I haven't seen or heard about his book. Let him have his aggressions because he has so little else. I am sorry to hear that he felt it necessary to do a job on Vandy though, but I suppose he'll go through the rest of his life pimping off white girls while hating them for being white then negating whatever justification (if there is any justification for it) he has in doin it by being such a cad toward them after he's exhausted the relationship. Anyway I hope he got in the fact that although he was threatening a woman with a butcher knife, he was too chicken to use it on a man. He's one writer who's too crossed up to give his talent a chance. In Paris I found that I could communicate only slightly with either Chester or Dick, although Dick is so much more intelligent, and Chester seems to hold me responsible because life in the U.S. has changed in relation to his conception of it.* The novelist is usually thought of as seeking reality out of chaos and illusion but Chester is so in love with a vision of absolute hell that he can't believe in change or in the fact that the world has changed in twenty years. He would impose further madness on the world instead of increasing our capacity for reality. We'll talk about this too when we return—And about Langston, who, I understand, got around to psychoanalyzing my personality in his autobiography—I am a hypochondriac, <u>he</u> says; which amuses me no end since Langston has as much talent for psychology as he has writing poetry of ideas; and I'm even more amused over the irony that for twenty years I've defended him against people who tried to analyze <u>his</u> personality, even though I didn't and don't care what his secrets are. Perhaps one day I'll write an autobiography and Langston will learn exactly why my regard for him has always been tempered by a great reservation—not based upon speculation or amateur psychologizing, but upon autobiographical fact, place, time and people. Nevertheless it probably doesn't occur to him that bad writing and phoniness and cheap sophistry and opportunism could possibly make one ill when one sees it in a former idol and an old friend. Well, I don't really have to write a public word about Langston, I'll leave it to the quality of my work to answer him.

Horace, we would be happy for you to have your painting back. Besides we aren't having the pleasure of seeing it just now. We'll be bringing several paintings back with us, so that the space won't go lacking. At the moment our apartment is in the hands of a friend but we'll send him a letter asking him to let you have it. You can send the money directly to

---

* Chester Himes and Richard Wright, African American novelists living in Paris in the 1950s.

us over here; we'll be glad to have it because we're slightly strapped. His name is Charles Justice (WA. 6-6804) and he works at night. Therefore the best time to call him is early evening, around 7:00.

Great things are, as you say, happening to old Mose, so much that at this distance we can't keep up with it; so if you have clippings of any of your columns which you think might help us, please send them along. In the meantime, Fanny and I look forward to seeing you in the fall.

Sincerely,
Ralph

To Bill Cole
AMERICAN ACADEMY
VIA ANGELO MASINA 5
ROME 28, ITALY
[SPRING 1957]

Dear Bill,*

Thanks very much for the reminders of my brief exciting moment with the great. I had never seen them and had forgotten that I had ever occupied the same compositional frame with either the great novelist or the admirable Justice. The photos remind me of a moment that I must either live up to or else I'll never live it down, at least not in terms of self-irony. Perhaps the unidentified woman is Fate, laughing at one of her little jokes.

Things go well enough in this infernaleternal city but we're gradually steeling ourselves to surrender it and its charms for those of New York, a thing which, during this lovely Roman spring isn't at all easy to do. But who knows, perhaps home is where life bangs loudest and grates the nerves most savagely; certainly part of Rome's charms lie in the fact that here one has few responsibilities, although the Vespa might be called a torture instrument on wheels. Anyway, we'll be seeing you in October at the latest.

Meanwhile thanks again and our best to Peggy and the little girls.

Sincerely,
Ralph

Mr. Bill Cole
Alfred Knopf, Inc.
New York, New York

---

* Bill Cole, editor and publicity director at Knopf.

To John Hunt
AMERICAN ACADEMY OF ROME
VIA ANGELO MASINA V
ROME 28, ITALY.
APRIL 23, 1957

Dear John:

Last evening I ran into Dennis Surat, the president of the International P.E.N. Congress and he mentioned the fact that the Congress would meet in Japan in June thus reminding me of our conversation last year. Surat told me that he hoped that I would be there, indeed, he said he thought it "important" that I be there and I, of course, told him that I'd like to go. Thus far I've heard nothing from Jim Putnam regarding this matter and Jim, I understand, was in England a few days ago. Have you any late word on this matter?*

I'm bothering you with it now because if I am to attend I will have to arrange my summer with this in mind, and there is also the matter of arranging passage for our return to the States, sometimes in or before September. Everything here is in a kind of suspense at the moment, for there is even a vague possibility of my remaining in Rome another year, though so vague a possibility that I'm forced to regard it out of the extreme corner of my eye, which I'm told, is the best way to see in the dark.

At the moment my work goes fairly well. I've heard nothing at all from the Pruves questionnaire, but I completed a long essay on the novel for a symposium which Ganville Hicks is editing for Macmillan, and for which people like Saul Bellow, Wright Morris and Herbert Gold have done pieces; though unfinished the essay on desegregation which I started for *Encounter* impressed Robert Penn Warren to the extent that he suggested that I make a short book of it, similar to his *Segregation;* I've joined Eugene Walter in interviewing Warren for the *Paris Review,* and despite the temptations of spring I'm still turning out my novel. I don't see myself finishing by September but all things considered I'm not complaining. *Botteghe Obscure* is interested in publishing a section of it in their next issue, so perhaps seeing it in print will speed up my creative metabolism. I do dread returning to the States with it unfinished because that will mean at least six months of lost time. Anyway, if *Botteghe* takes a section I'll send you a copy.

* Ellison would attend the PEN International Congress in Japan that year.

Thanks again for all the books, I hope your new novel goes well, and if we can attend to anything down here for the Hunts please don't fail to ask. Meanwhile any news one way or the other regarding Japan will be appreciated.

Sincerely,
Ralph Ellison

To Stanley Hyman
MAY 27, 1957

Dear Stanley:

I did indeed receive the carbon of your lecture* and while I didn't find in it the expected Hyman drive, I was by no means furious; it simply arrived at a moment when I was preparing for a lecture tour of my own, and I didn't have time to write. I returned recently and quite beat from fifteen days of one-night stands, strange beds and unpredictable food so I'm getting this off rather hurriedly and I hope <u>you</u> won't be furious at what will probably be too hasty judgments. Anyway, let me say here that I'm glad you've made this start and I hope you'll expand the piece into a longer essay. My questions center around the emphasis you give to what is really a dual tradition. As you probably anticipate, my feelings concerning Herskovits haven't changed too much, he takes you for an interesting safari and it is probably valuable; but when you take us on the same giro only to arrive at junction with Western myth, why go all the way to Africa? And when it comes to the question of the novelist can we discuss his relationship to tradition without considering the form itself—the form being itself a depository of absorbed tradition? Aren't novelists more likely to be influenced by other novels than either by life or a body of general folklore? Certainly this is true of me, for while I love the folklore and use it freely, my concern with the novel starts with other novels and my interest is the results of a literary culture, not an oral one. My sense of structure, form and character development came from books. True that I knew folk tales before I started writing but as a writer I came to them after discovering Eliot and I was aware of the trickster named Ulysses as early as I knew of the wily rabbit. After all I was named after Emerson and back in N.Y. there is my father's huge anthology of English poetry in which I made some of my first scrawls.

---

* See the last paragraph of Ellison's February 6, 1958, letter to Albert Murray.

I guess what I really want to see is more of an emphasis on the totality of human experiences as revealed in the joining of traditions. Thus I would have you point out the specifically American character of the figure or role that you identify as that of "darky entertainer." He is for all his Negroness closely related to Hemingway, that highly conscious artist who pretends to be a sportsman; or to Faulkner, who pretends to be a simple farmer; or even to Franklin, the skilled diplomat, scientist, lover, etc., who allowed the French to take him for a child of nature. Africa wasn't needed to supply this tradition, it was already here. Maybe that is how we started out in this country of American jokers. It's the first role that the Confidence man acted out, Black Guinea conning the passengers with his black makeup, his bent legs, and his mouth full of coins. As for my narrator, he comes out of Dostoyevsky's *Notes from Underground,* not Wright's *Man Who Lived Underground,* who is incapable of simple thought much less of philosophical articulation.

Incidentally, isn't the juxtaposition between intelligence and comic mask related to the incongruity between the violence of the battle royal and the desire of the protagonist to make a graduation speech? And isn't it related tradition-wise to the Hemingway hero, that sensitive man who refuses to think? American Jokery is the key, springing from that primitive country (in the beginning) with its government drawn up by politically and philosophically sophisticated minds. Yeats says somewhere that "active virtue, as distinct from the passive acceptance of a current code, is . . . theatrical, capaciously dramatic, the wearing of a mask. It is the condition of an arduous full life." The will puts a mask between this and the social circumstance in America and the mask is stamped "Made in America."

And in terms of the tradition of the novel the invisible man is another version of the young man from the provinces, like Pip, Mynkin, or the hero of *The Red and the Black.* Thus he is derived not from folklore immediately, but from the novel. And while you're correct concerning the role of the grandfather and Bledsoe, the hero is not simply playing dumb, he is in the grip of an illusion, not manipulating it to his own advantage. Clifton, on the other hand is selling the dolls out of his apartment over his discovery of the Brotherhood's duplicity. He does not, by the way, make the dolls sing (any more than Ras rides to his death) though I wish you had suggested this when you read the ms. for it would have been just the right symbolic touch to have him use a bit of ventriloquise.

Nor is the grandfather so much a smart-man-playing-dumb as a weak man who knows the nature of his oppressor's weakness. There is a good deal of spite in him (as there comes to be in his grandson) and the strategy he advises is a kind of jujitsu of the spirit, a denial and rejection through agreement. Samson, eyeless in Gaza, pulls down the house when his strength returns; physically weak, the grandfather sees conformism as leading to the same end and so advises his children; thus his mask of meekness concealed a denial become metaphysical, a profound rejection of a "current code."

And so with the Narrator; the final act of the book is not that of concealment in darkness but that of a voice issuing its little wisdom out of darkness as a result of a transformation through which the former rabble rouser becomes the author of a memoir. Confession, not concealment, is the mode. And his mobility is of two kinds, geographical as you point out and the psychological; so that all the while he is engaged in moving vertically downward (not into a sewer, by the way, but into a coal cellar, a source of heat, light, power and perception), he is in the process of rising vertically to a perception of his human condition. Besides, as regards the blues and restless mobility—it gets into them from the American conditions that gets it into Cooper, Melville, Hemingway, Wolfe, Steinbeck, as it got into those boys who moved westward to the Pacific. Restlessness of the spirit transcends geography and sociology.

I like your listing of blues themes but I hope you'll extend it, and get in all the irony of blues fantasy, all the laughing at the self, all the negative reassurance which, because it's sung, becomes positive, a transcendence. The most grandiose fantasy of the invisible man is his dream of being an educator, or a real leader of the Brotherhood. The fantasy in the cellar is ironic, the self-pity questionable because the motive behind the lightbulbs is spite and defiance; indeed, they don't exist, they are his metaphor to describe the extremity of his situation and thus rhetorical. That's it. I think you've been held back by the lousy material you had to work with and hope you'll forget us half-assed writers and really plunge into these blues. By the way, ain't us colored folks got no relationship to Jewish tradition? For Brandeis' sake you should have worked up a little of it, we do after all identify with the Hebrew children.

Things go rough here at the moment, too many spring parties, the tour, frustration over the work-in-progress, but trouble don't last all ways. Give our best to Shirley and all those other Hymans and thanks again for letting me see the piece.

As ever,
Ralph

To Albert Murray

Rome,

JUNE 2, 1957

Dear Albert,

Tapes received and everybody knocked out. With both Duke and Basie I couldn't hope for better word from home; and if they weren't enough, that character who calls himself King Pleasure is about to drive me crazy. The idea of him breaking off the story at that point. Did Moody blow everybody out of the place or did it go limp on him, or did everybody blast everybody else? Well, however it came out that King Pleasure sings more bop rhythm than anyone since Anna Randolph, who was singing and improvising her lyrics during the days when Dizzy and Monk were confined to Minton's Playhouse. Here's a fool who doesn't know you aren't supposed to sing prose, so he gets away with it . . . As for the bit from *Drum*, I like, but suspect that here again Duke fails to make the transition from the refinement of his music over to drama—or even over to words; so that what in music would be vital ideas comes over with a slickness and hipster elegance that makes you want to go and tell the man how really good he is and that he should do anything with that Broadway-hipster-Mose decadence but get it mixed up with his music. He should leave that element to Billy Strayhorn. Well, if we have to have that in order to get those diamonds, very well.

As for that Sugar Ray, I won on him against Bobo, would have lost on him when he lost to that meat-headed Fulmer, only the guy who bet me wouldn't bet, and I would have won on him this time if the guy hadn't gone back to the States. Somebody will have to whip Sugar Ray some day but I'll go along with him because he is an artist and I'll bet on grace and art when it's coupled with strength before I'd ever bet on simple youth sans these. And you never said a truer word about Jack, he is indeed both hare and bear, and he's bound to get you one way or the other.

Which reminds me that that heart thing worries me, I hope it's nothing serious. As for the weight, you can lick that by walking. I'm down to 181 with my clothes on, which means I'm lean and mean. I think I'll have a physical soon myself just to keep in touch with myself for this spring hasn't been too easy on me. I wish you were stopping here for a day so that I could talk about it. Fanny and I are in a state of crisis at the moment and I might just be acting like a fool in his forties. That's as much as I can say now except that it's painful and confusing . . . I don't know what our plans are at the moment. Fanny has to go home at the end of this month and I'm still waiting to hear if I'm staying here another year. A. MacLeish is doing something about it and I've been asked if I want to go to Tokyo & Kyoto in Sept. for P.E.N. I think I'll say yes but I don't know where I'll end up but it'll either be to Trieste, Milan, Turin Genoa, Florence, Naples, and Bari—which promises to be the extent of my travel this summer. I go through the ordeal of a lecture here in Rome on Friday and that'll be the end of that mess. It's worse than playing one-night stands and there is nothing amusing about it, because these people won't blow back at you.

I suppose you've gotten the check by now, Fanny had sent it along with a letter to Mokie which was returned but we used the last address you gave me, thanks for the bag, and as for the books, I have an extra copy of Faulkner's *The Town* and one of Steegmuller's translation of *Madame Bovary*. If you haven't picked them up yet, just let me know where to mail them. Faulkner has some amusing things, mostly reworked from some of the Snopes stories, but I haven't gotten around to the translation. I've really been too busy battling with myself and with this novel-of-mine-to-be to get much reading done. I'm going to whip the dam thing but it [is] giving me a tough fight; it just looks as though every possible emotional disturbance has to happen to me before I can finish a book . . . By the way, Hyman sent me a lecture he gave on Negro writing and the folk tradition, in which he writes about the blues, but it was a very disappointing piece. He's so busy looking for African myth in the U.S. that he can't see what's before his eyes, even when he points out that African and Greek myths finally merge in that similar figures appear in both. He sees what he terms the "darky entertainer" i.e. characters like Stepin Fetchit—intelligent men hiding behind the stereotype—as the archetypal figure to writing by Negroes—including mine. This figure, who he also terms a "smart-man-playing-dumb," he sees everywhere in Negro writing and I pointed out to him that wasn't African, but American. That's Hemingway when he pretends to be a sportsman, or only a sportsman; Faulkner when he pretends to be a farmer; Benjamin Franklin when he pretended to be a "child of nature," instead of the hipped operator that he was, even Lincoln when he pretended to be a simple country lawyer. But Stanley, being Jewish and brought up to wear his intellect like a crown of jewels can't see this at all; he thinks Mose had to get this mess from Africa when all he had to do was breathe the American air and he was ready to teach other

Americans how it was done. But even as sheer method Stanley's approach is weak because he tries to discuss the novelist and folk tradition without discussing the novel, the form which is itself a depository of folk and other traditions reduced to formal order. I knew Mose lore yes, but I didn't really know it until I knew something about Literature and specifically the novel, then I looked at Negro folklore with a shock of true recognition. I was trying to write novels in the great tradition of the novel, not folk stories. The trick is to get Mose lore into the novel so that it becomes a part of that tradition. Hell, Hyman don't know that Ulysses is both Jack the rabbit (when that cyclops gets after his ass) and Jack the Bear, Big Smith the Chef, John Henry and everybody else when he starts pumping arrows into those cats who've been after his old lady. Or if he does recognize this, it's only with his mind, not his heart. I was especially disappointed with his treatment of the blues, for while he lists a few themes he restricts their meaning to a few environmental circumstances: Mose can't rise vertically so he's restless; he can't get a good job here so he goes there—missing the fact that there is a metaphysical restless built into the American and Mose is just another form of it, expressed basically, with a near tragic debunking of the self which is our own particular American style. I really thought I'd raised that boy better than that. But hell, I keep telling you that you're the one who has to write about those blues. The world's getting bluesier all the time, as Joe Williams and Count well know, and even though those Africans have Ghana they still haven't developed to the point where the blues start. Well, what bothers me about Stanley's piece is that after all his work and insight it seems to reveal a basic failure to understand the nature of metaphor, thus he can't really see that Bessie Smith singing a good blues may deal with experience as profoundly as Eliot, with the eloquence of Eliotic poetry being expressed in her voice and phrasing. Human anguish is human anguish, love love; the difference between Shakespeare and lesser artists is eloquence but when Beethoven writes it it's still the anguish, only expressed in a different medium by an artist of comparable eloquence. Which reminds me that here, way late, I've discovered Louis singing Mack the Knife. Shakespeare invented Caliban, or changed himself into him—Who the hell dreamed up Louis? Some of the bop boys consider him Caliban but if he is he's a mask for a lyric poet who is much greater than most now writing. That's a mask for Hyman to study, me too; only I know enough not to miss my train by messing around over looking over in Africa or even down in the West Indies. Hare and bear [are] the ticket; man and mask, sophistication and taste hiding behind clowning and crude manners—the American joke, man. Europeans dream of purity—any American who's achieved his American consciousness knows that it's a dream so he ain't never been innocent, he's been too busy figuring out his next move. It's just that the only time he ever comes out from behind that mask is when he's cornered—that's when you have to watch him. Unless, of course, he's Mose, who has learned to deal with a hell of a lot more pressure. Write about those blues, and love to the girls from me and Fanny.

Ralph

Watch that heart!

To John Hunt
THE AMERICAN AVADEMY IN ROME
VIA ANGELO MASINA V
ROME 28, ITALY
JUNE 12, 1957

Dear John:

Thanks for your letter, I was just about to write you that I had heard from Jim Putnam and to correct a mistake I made in my letter: it was not Surat with whom I talked, but Andre C. the current president—through why or how I get the names confused I'll never know. Anyway, Putnam asked if we would like to go if they could raise the money, and I wrote him that we, one or both, would. The only problem is where he'd expect us to leave from, for I plan to remain here until Sept., even if I don't get a renewal for next year. I'm hoping for definite word any day now but am resigned to letting the fates work their way. If they raise the money in N.Y. I'll be ready. Perhaps I could find space on the plane that a group of Italian writers are supposed to take.

I envy you that trip to Provence and I'm sure I'll never get over the disappointment of failing to drive through France last summer. Perhaps I'll [get] another opportunity some day and I'll let nothing get in the way, certainly not a trip to London. After all these months of Italian food and wine I'd like to clear my palate and shake up my taste buds with a month or so of French cooking. Next time you're in the restaurant where you and your wife had me to dinner please have a portion of those wonderful little oysters for me, I'm simply starving for them and dream of them whenever a dish of pasta is set before me. Meanwhile, give my regards to all and I'll write you of any new developments.

Sincerely,
Ralph Ellison

Mr. John Hunt
Congres pour la Liberte de la Culture
Secretariat International
104 Boulevard Haussmann,
Paris-VIII.

To Albert Murray
ROME,
JULY 28, 1957

Dear Ole Albert,

Here I was thinking that you and the girls were sweeping over Europe and you've been grounded all the time. That business of a <u>mild</u> heart attack makes me feel like the time I got in the fight with that Ringer character down at Tuskegee, I was so busy hitting him and trying to knock him out that I didn't realize that what he was hitting me with wasn't his fist but a 12 lb. lead pig. What's more, I didn't realize that I was bleeding until my roommate came in and said, "Man, leave that sonofabitch alone, you're bleeding like a stuck pig." Well, I hit him again and left him alone and I'm lucky that I did because he just might have got my true range. Anyway, that sight of my own blood was a surprising sight indeed. Actually, it sounds very typical of you to be hit by a heart attack, confuse it with an upset stomach and keep on jumping. I'm glad they caught you in time because I couldn't see you keeping still otherwise unless of course they broke your leg.

Things here are slack for the moment. Fanny sailed on the 23rd and most of my crop of Fellows have taken off for the states. This morning I'm going to get visas for my trip to Japan and it looks as though I'll stop in India in my way back here to give a couple of lectures on American Lit. before some Congress for Cultural Freedom groups in Bombay and New Delhi. It makes me tired just to think about it but am fascinated as any Mose by the Japanese. I'll take off about the 28th and will be there for 10 days but don't know how long I'll spend in India. Incidentally, if there's any camera junk you're interested in in Japan let me know and I'll try to bring it for you . . . I'm still shooting but I've just about used up my supply of Plus X and I'm trying like hell to get a fresh supply before I leave here. Color wise I'm not doing so good; this Roman light is red as hell and I haven't been able to get the proper filters to cool it down. The other thing is that I want to control my color shot more than I'm able to do now and I have neither the time nor the money with which to experiment . . . I agree with you about Faulkner's *The Town,* the stuff was much better as separate stories. Here's ole Flem Snopes has become as respectable as Faulkner. I've been reading the papers of Dean Christian Gauss and have enjoyed his correspondence with Fitzgerald and Edmund Wilson. The correspondence with Wilson spans over thirty years and all of it interesting. We just didn't have teachers like that, man; and when I think of trying to write of some such relationship between a Tuskegee teacher and student, my mind, once M.D.* is excepted, flies swiftly to satire, to the Impossible Interview caricatures on the old *Vanity Fair,* to burlesque. Old Gauss must have been an unusually warm and intelligent human being. Been rereading *Moby-Dick* again and appreciating for the first time what a truly good time Melville was having when he wrote it. Some of it is quite funny and all of it is pervaded by the spirit of play, like real jazz sounds when a master is manipulating it. The thing's full of riffs, man; no wonder the book wasn't understood in its own time, not enough Moses were able to read it! . . . Speaking of jazz, I'm still knocking myself out with the tapes you sent. Indeed, more than ever, now that Fanny's gone; it's my only true atmosphere, yesterday the girl I grew up with from birth (she's the granddaughter of the old man in whose house I was born) showed up with her husband and thirteen year old son, and we spent the day talking about old times. Here some twenty-five years later she's trying to understand Charlie Christian and Lips Page and Pres,† who were all out there in the old days. She felt that their importance was an accident and thought that they didn't understand their influence, and I tried to explain how important they really were and how they were highly conscious artists. By birth and social status in the town she tends to look on jazz in terms of status, so I tried to get her to look at it as art and a universal language. Her husband, who is a physician and a good joe from Arkansas, can't understand

---

*   Morteza Drexel Sprague, the teacher of English literature at Tuskegee who was a signal influence on Ellison, and to whom he would dedicate *Shadow and Act* in 1964.

†   Lester Young, who became famous as a tenor saxophone player with Count Basie.

Louie's appeal, was nevertheless impressed by the fact that everywhere he's been in Europe he sees big photographs of Louis and hears Europeans trying to play like him. So I lectured him about the universality of the jazz language—really not trying to impress the father, but to get the thirteen-year-old son moving in the right direction. It was quite amusing and you would have appreciated the irony. We were having dinner under a trellis where there were several Italian families having a lomo down home go at the vino and the food. There was an accordion player and several cats who thought they could sing and sometimes the family joined in and sang folk songs, and once in a while one of the young fellows ripped up the summer quiet with an aria from Verdi. Posturing like a non-bullfighter before a paper bull—all very local color and, with the laughter and family togetherness, pleasant to observe. But there _we_ were talking about jazz and the world of music in which they'd lived but of which they'd been unaware. It's all the more ironic because she was a music major at Fisk and strove like a pilgrim striving for a piece of the true Cross to master that same music which the Italian family, including the little boys and girls, were throwing around with the same familiarity and impiety that you and I used to sing "Before I'd Be a Slave I'd Be Dead and In My Grave"—or "Funky Butt." Dignity lies at home, and that's a fact.

Well, they have loads of money—not n-rich, but <u>rich</u>, though you'd never know it by looking at them—and they're traveling and they have curiosity and are fast measuring their lives against what they see over here. That's all to the good for their lives will have become just a little more real. I spent the evening after they left playing Duke and went to bed feeling just a little less lonely. I'd heard the idiom and relived a bit of the past—which is really the same thing. One of the pleasant things I look forward to when I get home in late Sept. will be the chance to buy all those latest Dukes you've been writing about. The Shakespeare suite sounds intriguing. You know, one of these days I'm going to get ambitious and write an opera libretto and submit it to that guy. All the elements are floating around and I just might be able to write something wild enough and attractive enough to catch his attention. <u>Somebody</u> should do it because I'm sure that with a form to keep his imagination in bounds old Duke will surpass himself. <u>You</u> might think in those terms too. I'm going to give Weill a good hard look just to see what was really happening and I'm planning to get back to my old preoccupation with the ceremonial form of the Negro church to see if there's anything usable there. Recently I've been listening to a bit of Stravinsky every day and a bit of Webern and the younger boys who are on that kick. Listening to the latter it is easy to see why guys are trying to compose with tape recorders; much of what they do sounds like tape played backwards at a speed that is slower than that at which it was recorded. Well, outside my window there are a couple of birds making a sound like that of dice rattling away in a leather cup and I don't dig it; but maybe if I listen long enough I'll understand they're playing the dirty dozens or quoting the Empson of the birds—upon which feathers will sprout out from behind and I too will learn to fly; sans Pegasus, sans motor, sans rhythm, sans every dam thing . . . I've just learned about the fabulous father of a girl who graduated from high school in my class. When a young man he killed a man and escaped to sea, living on board ship for ten years without going ashore out of fear of capture. Later he came to Oklahoma (right after statehood), married and went to work at the packinghouse. Since then he's raised and educated two families and now, at ninety, he has a young wife and the first child of a third family. They tried to retire the old coot but he refused and works a full day and goes home at the end of the day and starts working on those baby boys he swears he going to have before he racks up his balls and stands his pool cue in the final rack! I thought I was simply lying when I started creating old Love, but here's a mister who is more fabulous than fiction!

If this goes on any longer it will become more seditious than a sedative, so now I'll stop it. Take care and rest, none of us can spare you for any serious bit of time and you're my most satisfactory correspondent. In fact I'm going through a phase quite like that I underwent at Tuskegee. I tend to push people away from me and I don't want to waste time with unessentials. You're the only one I really write to and, other than a wild, Russian chick of a girl who's now in the States and who wouldn't write home for eating change, my only friend. So rest, man and sketch out some more of those episodes. Love to lovable Mokable and Miqueable, from Ralphable.

As ever,
Ralph

To John Hunt
THE AMERICAN ACADEMY
via Angelo Masina V,
Rome 28, Italy.
JULY 31, 1957.

Dear John:

Your letter arrived at 5:30 o'clock and I'm answering immediately. I have indeed written Voyages Mercure, and I have also started the visa thing rolling. Interestingly enough, I had gone to the American Embassy for information and was told that I needed no visas for Japan and Thailand; nevertheless I shall apply for these visas as soon as possible—tomorrow.[*]

Which means that I buy your plan for the various stops. I should prefer, however, to talk about the place of the novel in the American experience rather that concentrate strictly upon contemporary fiction. In this way I can relate fiction to the larger complex of American culture and make for a less specialized discussion.

As for press conferences, I don't mind them either, but would prefer to stick fairly close to problems of literature rather than all do a lot of yakking about race relations in the U.S. I realize that some of this is inevitable but I'd like to avoid as much of it as possible. If this is agreeable to you please go ahead with your plans; I'll try to be in the physical condition which this little jaunt doubtlessly calls for. I like the part about your getting the expense money, 'cause, man, I am b-busted!

Best,
Ralph Ellison

Mr. John C. Hunt
Congress pour la Liberte
de la Culture,
Secretariat International: 1104 Boulevard Haussmann—Paris (8*)

---

[*]   Ellison attended the PEN International Congress in Japan and traveled to India in August and September 1957.

To Fanny Ellison
Rome,
AUGUST 12, 1957

Dear Fanny,

I'm writing in the hope that you've reached home at last and have been just too tired and or busy to let me hear from you.* I hope the voyage was restful and that you enjoyed the moods of the long sea voyage; certainly you have missed the brutal heat of Rome and, as I recall, little else of interest. The Finleys† were here for a few days and though I found them pleasant there was the remoteness of time and different values between us. They were disappointed in not seeing you—most people here seem to miss you—and it would have been interesting for me to hear the three of you recalling Fisk. Their thirteen year old is as tall as his mother, calls me "Uncle" and takes it for granted that I'm a Randolph. I wonder how far she would have allowed him to get with that uncle business had I remained a local boy? Still they were nice and unpompous and the recall of the past gave a bit of reality to the air of unreality which the academy has assumed since I've been alone. I felt unhappy about leaving you in Naples but couldn't see that remaining overnight would have helped improve the mood between us, so I went back to Rome hating myself. Since then I've felt physically lousy and now that I'm taking inoculations with the heat of August beating upon my head I feel even worse. Nothing is simple in this town and I realize, now that I am cooking and washing for myself, yes and shopping, how much you protected me from. I tried eating downstairs for three or four days but the garlic quickly undid me, so that now I man the skillet or I venture downtown. Nothing else happens. I've given up the parties and am trying to feel like a human being before the 28th, when I take off for Japan. I've been asked and have agreed to lecture or meet with writers in Beweint, Bombay, Calcutta and New Delhi, for the Congress of Cultural Freedom. Thus I shall have to return here before returning to the States. I have but the vaguest idea when I'll finish the tour, so I'll have to write you that information from the Far East (I sound like George and his "north woods"!). At any rate I won't be able to leave Italy before the end of

---

* Fanny returned to New York from Rome in late July 1957.

† Saretta Finley, née Slaughter, and her husband, Gravelly. She was the daughter of Dr. Slaughter from Oklahoma, a member of one of the most prestigious black families in Ellison's boyhood.

September. Continuing home from Japan would have been much simpler but since I'll be in that part of the world it seems a shame not to see some of it, the opportunity being mine for the asking. Too bad you couldn't have come along since you have far more interest in these places than I . . . There is little to tell you of the west coast; somebody's parent has cancer and there is much confusion and dashing around and much inner conflict of emotion. It would therefore be unwise for me to write you more than this because I simply don't know and I'd rather talk with you in our old setting; perhaps that alone would clarify what the situation between us actually is, or at least, what led to it. Perhaps you feel otherwise but I'd rather go over it with you just the same. There was, I admit, some shabby aspects to what I did but then passion makes its own rules when it has to; the question is what is the hardest to forgive, the breaking of the rules or the existence of the passion itself? I can say that I miss you and that I do, and always have, realized how really good you've been to me. More than that I'm concerned about you and I hope you'll take care of yourself and take things in easy stage, at least until I return.

As for news here, your friends, Eva and Erma, are both back from the hospital, one recovering from another operation and the other after having delivered herself of a baby girl. I haven't seen it and probably won't, for now there's no reason for my not telling the mother what a thorough bitch I think she is. The Laytons are in Boston, Saul must be in N.Y., the Stewarts are packing to leave sometime this month; Bill McDonald dropped in, looking very driven, indeed, like he's been hitting the bottle like a wine-o. He promises to give you a ring when he returns to the States. That's about all. Nina just sent regards from the Library; Jean has thankfully let me quite alone; and, other than the amusing fact that I went dancing at Bricktops with that amazing amazon, Edith Rickey (with George's consent, indeed, his urging—after a farewell party they gave) that is all the news. Tell me how you found things in the apartment, and if there is anything I can bring from Rome or the East, let me know.

Love,
Ralph

To Albert Murray
ROME,
AUGUST 17, 1957

Dear Albert,

Your last letter did a lot to cheer me up and then when Paul* blew in with the Plus X and reported that you were up and about I felt even better. I was on my way to get the second of my series of shots and thus had only a few minutes with him and his friend, both of whom wished to yak about Invisible. I was sorry that it had to be so brief but this trip is leaping forward now and any little simple thing becomes enormously complicated here in Rome. And it's all the more complicated now that Fanny is back in the States; I'm still getting my own meals and the shopping is the very dregs, you kill most of a morning just getting the stuff from the many small stores among which it's scattered. I'll be glad to get back to N.Y. and a little simple efficiency; yes, and a little honesty among merchants. Here you can spend loads of lire with a guy and he'll try to short-change you fifty lire. They don't seem to understand that Americans won't accept that crap. The amount of accepted corruption in this society is amazing. Well, it's their world and they deserve it, I'm getting further, I just want some dewy-eyed sonofabitch to tell <u>now</u> how superior Europe is . . . Anyway Fanny left for home on the 23rd of June† and must be up to her neck in getting adjusted because I haven't heard from her as yet.

Actually we didn't know where she would make port since she's on a freighter but I expect to hear as soon as the mail starts breaking the log-jam created by the long Italian August festa; as for me, I'm checking out of here on the 28th for Japan and I've already started packing to make for home, once I return here. Thanks for the film, I had just bought some medium speed Agfa that I haven't had a chance to try, however I understand it's pretty good and, in bulk it's not too expensive. I loaded my last Anscochrome and discovered that I only had three rolls, so I'm going to pick up some Kodachrome in Japan. This time I'm taking only the Leica and plan to do the best I can with it . . . I've been reading about the mess in Alabama and it appears that the crackers have gone a little more mad than

---

* Paul Brown, an old Tuskegee classmate of Murray's, was en route to Rome by way of Casablanca.

† In fact, it was the twenty-third of July.

usual. As for Ike and the Republicans, I'm afraid that they're playing some rather stupid half-assed politics. I'm getting quite sick of it and whenever I read about these southern senators being such noble characters, à la *Time,* I want to load up a sock with shit and go to work on the editors and publisher. There is something so immoral and rotten in those characters that any attempt to perfume them leads to the corruption of language; and if Russell of Georgia is the most skillful man in the Senate then it's because most of our political leaders don't have the guts to oppose him and are too busy fattening on the swill he's allowed to brew out of democracy. Now I read that Joe MC. is being praised in the Senate!

I've just finished a novel by James Gould Cozzens, *By Love Possessed,* which, except for a certain pompousness in the leading character, is well worth the reading. It hasn't been published yet but it probably will win the National Book Award. Cozzens is a pro and he's grabbed the forms of love and given them an examination that's right down the line, and he sees what I've had occasion to point out, that democracy is, or should be, the most disinterested form of love. I've also read Wright Morris' new short novel, *Love Among the Cannibals.* It's a satire and I think he's kidding the "novel-of-manners" boys, and the book isn't to be taken seriously . . . I've read several negative reviews of the Newport Jazz shakedown, it seems that they brought in that creep Eartha Kitt and some non-jazz dancers and Louis was wearing his ass instead of his genius. The whole circus sounds as though it was rather limp. I guess you can't throw too many musicians and hep cats manqué together too many times and have it come out listenable. Anyway, Duke wasn't there, I picked up a Columbia recording of his titled "Duke's Mixture," on which there is a version of "Do Nothing," "The Mooch," "How High the Moon," & "The Hawk Talks." Some are old, some new but all good Duke. Man, you just wait until I get my foot in Sam Goody's door again! Which reminds me, I'm writing for that belt for your turntable and I'll have them mail it directly to you. In the meantime, try washing the one you have; it's nylon. Actually, any piece of ribbon of that width should work until the real thing comes. If you're real desperate have Mokie sew together a piece of ribbon and simply turn the seam to the outside. They've only just gotten the cabinets completed for the set I'm putting together for the academy and I made the mistake of putting the business together temporarily last Sun. so that one of the composers could catch the broadcast of the Hindemith opera. I gave up my evening because I thought the sonofabitch was working and he comes late and with several friends. I was annoyed to say the least; but yesterday at lunch

I almost threw a plate of spaghetti in the fool's face when he insisted that I put the units together again just for him. I'm working on the thing so that it will be working and out of my hands before I leave for Japan but this punk thinks I'm going too slow—when I've been waiting to complete the thing since I selected the equipment in N.Y. last Oct. I was mad enough to walk the table. When done it will be a fine set but I've got to try to anticipate all the damn fool things such guys are apt to do to it because there are no dealers in Italy and I don't trust the technicians here. Their boys are going to wreck this system as quickly as they can but I won't be here to hear about it. My belly fills with acid when I just think about it . . . I'll try to write before I take off but if there's anything you want let me know before the 28th. As plans go now I will return here sometime about the middle of Sept. and get off for home as quickly as possible. I don't have the passage yet and I'm trying to save by going freighter, nevertheless I want to be back on the Drive by late Oct at the mostest.

Hi to Mokie and Mique

Best,
Ralph

To Fanny Ellison
ROMA,
AUGUST 24, 1957

Dear Fanny,

I suspected that you wouldn't answer my letter and now that I have only four more days, one of them Sunday before I take off I'm writing what might, given my favorite mode of travel, be my last letter. I received your wire and its abstract message and while glad to have its reassurance was nevertheless annoyed that it wasn't a letter. I still am. I was worried about you and the problems you might encounter and I'm still concerned about the apartment and all the other usual things. As for the other matter, I can tell you now that I was correct in telling you not to leap to conclusions concerning its immediate outcome. They are perhaps on their way back here now and the decision as far as decision is possible, was not to be cruel, not to cause the family pain and all the other traditional, respectable considerations were surrendered to. I, you see, suspected this; it is built into the other contradiction of the character. I don't know how I shall feel when I return here, but I tell you truly that I wish now that I hadn't accepted the lectures and had arranged to fly directly home from Japan.

I just have no desire to prolong what would be a sterile and painful situation. In these matters one must have faith and a certain amount of hope; mine are exhausted. I did not put the test to her, the circumstances did; that is why I would not insist upon a decision; I felt that if it was to be a life then the difficulties of making it a life would have to be faced, regardless of the cost and the costs were great. But for her the cost required that she move into strange regions of existence, that she violate one group of ties in order to embrace the unknown, give all for passion—or what not. It would have been a break with the ordinary if she'd been able but since she couldn't then I'm glad that there were no half measures taken; I need no added drag of indecision again. I don't know what I'll feel on my return here, but I do know that I don't want now what I wanted of her and anything else would be anti-climactic. A rather sad story; still, what I desired was good, and I wanted it badly enough to make the desperate attempt I made. That is <u>my</u> way of living and I'll always be sorry that you had to suffer in the apparent madness of my lunge toward which might actually be an abstract ideal. I don't know, it will take time to know this, whether it was abstract, I mean; though children, once they're yelling their little heads off are anything but abstract. Well, it takes only fertility to get them but it takes courage to have them and to bring them up and courage is achieved, not granted at birth and sustained by luck. <u>You</u> have courage along with so many other virtues and I hope you'll keep it and that you'll never panic ever again in this life, Fanny, you just have to let some things work their own way out. If you have done all you can do, then you must not push the other fellow or fight him into stances of decision he might otherwise reject. What you are, and what you can do, what you have learned, are important values and anyone concerned with values, and I am, will recognize what you are and act accordingly. I say this now without changing one bit of my belief that you were partially responsible for what happened here. You are a good woman who helped create that which caused you pain, when you might have held yourself in reserve and overcome the situation without stirring up all the limitations of our relationship. The point here is not who is responsible but that you are <u>you</u> and must have faith in you. Nor must you feel that I'm saying this after a defeat of my desires, it is not that simple for I haven't pressed nor persuaded or tried to give courage in a decision where I feel the other person must know her own mind; perhaps I could have helped, certainly I could have destroyed <u>his</u> happiness. No, I'm saying this after this brief separation, after missing you, and out of a desire that you do no further harm to your image of yourself. Right now I'm very tired and I don't like this indirection of statement, so I'll only repeat what I told you, that if I find that I'm wrong, I'll come and tell you. So now I'll tell you that the old ties still hold. Instinctively I find myself shopping for the apartment—or at least looking at things which would go well there—I've bought a chair and have had to restrain myself from picking up other things, and this even though I now question the value of such things. Maybe Joe Williams' The Comeback is for you after all. Who knows, perhaps it's up to you. I'm still leaving on the evening of the 28th (Wed.), flying a chartered plane out of Paris and arranged by Voyages Mercure. The plane itself is one of Air France. I'm worried about insurance that I haven't been able to get here but if I do I'll send it along. I should be in Tokyo on the 1st and remain there seven days, after which we'll visit Kyoto for three days. Leaving Japan I'll fly to Calcutta where I'll probably lecture, then to Karachi, Pakistan. I'll return here sometime after the 20th and I'll leave as quickly as I can for the States. I don't have passage as yet because of the uncertainties connected with the trip to the Orient, thus I would appreciate it if you would call Red and Eleanor's friend and see what you can set up by way of early passage. And I mean early because I don't want to be around the academy any longer than possible . . . I'm leaving my tape machine in charge of Anne Freeman should anything happen to me and I'll try to have as many things packed as possible, though clothing is a problem, since I don't know what the weather will be when I start back. Which reminds me that I haven't gotten travelers checks as yet, which I must do and I'll send you the numbers. There is also a check from "Flying Home" due here around the first* so I'll have Anne take care of all my mail and ship it to you if need be. I suppose that's all for business, if I think of anything else I'll send it along with the check numbers . . . Incidentally, won't you write MacLeish? I decided months ago that I didn't want to stay here another year and so didn't write him; besides, I was a bit annoyed over the unconscious condescension in his remarks about my intelligence. Why make a compliment out of the obvious, aren't most writers intelligent? Anyway, he's a good man and you tell him to use my essay in his classes but that he should avoid being squeezed by all the split infinitives. There has been no mail of interest. I did have lunch at the Villa yesterday, rather nice; the Louis Simpsons were there, and the Hebalds. Yes, and I ran into P. Milano one night at the Paris when I took Anne there for dinner, and

---

* Ellison's 1944 story had been reprinted in a Viking Press edition.

I looked up and saw Eugene at another table. He's away for the summer and I didn't learn just what Paolo is doing here; indeed, he stared at Anne so hard that at first I refused to introduce her; there's nothing like tossing something for the gossips to mangle. Otherwise, no news; I despise the same people, am indifferent to most and yearn for a change of scene. Take care of yourself, Fannymae; do what you have to do but don't do anything which will damage you needlessly later on. At least don't do anything rash in recoil from me, or at least not until you see me again. Still, if you need catharsis, you need it; just try to see that the good things, if there are any left, don't go down with the muck. You'll have to forgive the way this is written, what needs to be said should be said face to face and with the possibility of our old, sweet resolution should words break down. If you hadn't been so insistent I could have told you that for me there is none better, nor do I expect there ever would be. There are other things to say but they must wait. Don't worry about me if it crosses your mind to do so and be true to yourself. As for me, what was deepest and best between us still holds. [. . .]*

> Love,
> Ralph

To Fanny Ellison
AIR France En Plein Ciel LE
sept 20, 1957

Dear Fanny,

I'm on en plein ciel between Karachi and Tehran and should reach Rome by midnight. The India visa came so late that instead of spending 4 days in Calcutta, I went to Hong Kong for 3 days and lectured at Karachi University last night and set out again this morning.

The trip to Japan was wonderful and I found myself more at home than in Rome. The Congress itself was simply another convention, but the mixture of ancient and modern in Tokyo was quite exciting to me, especially as revealed in some of the smaller cities and in the private homes. I shipped some of the literature from Tokyo and it along with some of the photos that I'm going to have developed should give you some idea of the place. Hope things go well with you; I haven't seen my mail in weeks, so won't try to say anything important here. I do plan to leave Rome as

---

* The ellipsis indicates a short indecipherable passage before Ellison's legible salutation.

quickly as possible and will write you my plans as soon as I know them. That check of Hadzi by the way, was for deposit only as I had to [. . .]* in Japan. Take it easy and don't feel too harshly about us, if you possibly can.

Ralph

To John Hunt
THE AMERICAN ACADEMY
VIA ANGELO MASINA V,
ROME 28, ITALY,
SEPT. 27, 1957.

Dear John,

I hope that by now you're at home and done with lugging luggage and all the other irritations of travel. I haven't of course, since soon I'll take off for the States and am now involved in fitting too much into too few trunks. But at least the roar of the planes have at last died out of my ears.

Things went well enough at Karachi—or at least the first part of the lecture went fine, but then it came time for the Congress guy to lead off the question period and it became an irritating farce. I had talked about the relation between the American novel and the nature of the American experience: the problems posed by the conscious nature of the society, the problem of Europe, identity, etc.—all in relationship to the form of the American novel, nothing about the east or politics. But this character gets up and makes a speech almost as long as mine (which ran an hour) in which he attacked our skyscrapers, machines etc., and told the students how superior their spiritual atmosphere was to ours. I had to get up when he was through and point out that spirituality got into culture through the efforts of men and that there just might be as much spirituality in a skyscraper as in a sacred cow, but that at any rate I didn't care what the Pakistani did about their spiritual values, I only hoped that they would be better able to feed and clothe their people, and that certainly they should get them up off the sidewalks. We had been able to do a lot for our people because we did have a technology and while I hoped they didn't make the mistakes we have made and do make talks about abstract spirituality were certainly no corrective. Well he had the good sense not to answer me, and in the end the students let it be known that they didn't appreciate

---

* The four words written here in Ralph's hand are unreadable.

his performance (for performance it was, all full of ego and insincerity—S Broki was his name) for several were majors in American literature and one teacher had studied in the states. When the meeting broke up Syed Ali Ashraf invited us to continue talking in his office but Broki refused to go "back into your stinking little den," talked on for a few minutes longer (in his arrogant high British wog style (pleasant to me of course) and left.

I could have kicked his butt til his nose bled. Spender was here yesterday and I learned from him that this guy acts like that all the time. All I can say is that the Congress has to put up with some awful jerks. Nevertheless I think the talk did a little good, judging from the few questions that were put to me afterwards . . . Otherwise the trip was uneventful, although I discovered that Grindea had lectured in Karachi the evening before and I ran into him at the airport in Tehran. That guy gets around like a plane-hopping housefly.

I'm still impressed by Japan and Hong Kong and have been trying to imagine a way of getting back there. No luck so far.

Here is the ticket stub, I hope you can do something about it if we've been had. Since I haven't received word about my passage home you can reach me here for at least a couple of weeks, perhaps longer. Meantime take care of yourself and give my regards to all.

Best,
Ralph

To Fanny Ellison
ROME,
SEPT 29, 1957

Dear Fanny,

Your letter of the 25th arrived yesterday so here I am on Sunday morning once more on my perch in the garden trying to answer. Yes, and trying to get over my disappointment that Mayaloff could do nothing for me. As you may imagine my position here is painful and I would like to be off as soon as possible. Tomorrow I shall see what I can find and I'll let you hear at once. I received your first letter, by the way, and was waiting to hear about the ship. I had also sent other postcards and had a letter mailed from Iran when I stopped there on my way back. No, they didn't kidnap me in Hong Kong, but they did have two wonderful meals for the three of us who were traveling that far together, one being John Hunt of the Congress Secretariat and the other a Hungarian writer who had been imprisoned some six years prior to the revolution. The last meal was really a banquet with speeches. The only bad thing about that part of the trip was that I was on my own and had to pay my expenses there. Which reminds me that in my letter from Iran I wrote you that the Hadzi check was for deposit only, he gave it to me to bring him a lens. Any way I'm glad you used it and I'll have to give him his $80.00 change out of the $416.00 that I have here. I haven't paid my bills here and was quite surprised when the bank statement came showing only an 89.00 balance. I suspect also that all my last minute checks haven't cleared. If not, then I'll have to take care of them as well. The Mayaloff thing would have been a lifesaver, some kind of cheap passage is a necessity . . . So after Hong Kong I flew to Calcutta for an eight-hour stop, the Indians having refused me a visa until too late—thus Hong Kong—and it's just as well. For what with the summer's destruction, the news from Arkansas and all,* the sight of the terrible poverty, the thousands of people sleeping on the sidewalks, the filthy cows roaming the busiest streets of a city of eight million, the squalor, the crowds marching around behind the hammer and sickle, even the beautiful old things would not have sufficed to lift me out of my depression. Karachi was bad enough but being smaller did not present such a concentration of impact. Needless to say, I was glad to get out the following morning and head for Rome. Some of the misery in both countries is a result of the partition, the Hindu-Moslem conflict, which is probably more responsible for the condition of those peoples than all the years of colonialism. The British simply couldn't have created all of that . . . So I returned to Rome and its inefficiency after the modern world of Japan. The Academy is being painted and there is a great flurry of preparation for the new fellows, with new rules: no children under 18 are allowed except for the holidays; Thanksgiving and Xmas no furniture may be removed from a room, and fellows with children are advised that the academy can do nothing for them furniture-wise, and so on. There is much resentment over the harsh way in which the rules are phrased, and more over the report—for which I think him partially responsible—that Brickbauer instigated them. Nor is there good feeling over the report that Dave Jacobs has made it necessary to refuse furniture to fellows living outside because he had taken so much; when the fact is that the Jacobs children sleep on the floor and their apartment is as bare as any room I saw in Japan. My

---

* The "Little Rock Nine" struggle to desegregate Central High School in Little Rock, Arkansas, in September 1957.

cup runneth over with disgust. Nor did the word concerning Mary Williams cheer me up, though in my present circumstance it's merely a minor insect bite. I suppose of those of us whom I've damaged so deeply you show the lesser strain.

Perhaps I shall never look young again and she[*] is noticeably older, tense and sad, disillusioned with her mother's reaction, which evidently was without appreciation for the experience she is going through. She does so need to grow out into her own life but I fear she never shall. I didn't help things too by avoiding her and staying out of sight for two days, remaining in my room—only to bump into her at the top of the stairs—when she had had the strong feeling that I was somewhere in Rome. Someone had said that I wouldn't return until the 28th. Anyway, they left to pick up their new car and were gone a week, if only I had been able to leave. If-if-if, if I'd been a better man this mightn't have happened. If it weren't so painful I too would be amused and when I laugh now the laugh is bitter. So much for this just now, I hurt but the coming home. I beg your patience; I would have at least you happy . . . As for the job I'm glad that you took it and I no longer have the right to speak about your connection with the Lester crew. Anyway, you are working for Harold and if that is the job for the moment, thn that is the job. Too bad that your chance for an account came from a source you couldn't accept—especially since it had to do with my feelings about the past. I'm sorry . . . You poor girl, to have to go through the job of decorating after all of this. I hope Ramsay paid for it, he never has done a thing about that place and after his last letter I'm off him for good. I so wish you could have seen the Japanese houses, they're so striped and clean and neat. Everywhere you turn you see their sense of beauty, whether in the way a package is wrapped or in the manner they bind up the wounds of an injured tree. I find the country much more fascinating than Italy and would like to return. There is much to tell you and a few souvenirs, one a gift to you from a writer who admires my work. I sent tons of paper along by boat, some of it full of pictures of places I saw. I saw the Noh plays and the Kabuki players and visited temples and estates with marvelous gardens, and in Hong Kong we drove up to the peak and looked down upon the harbor full of ships and Chinese junks. The Chinese are quite a handsome people, more Western in their figures than the Japanese, and the women can be breathtakingly, head snappingly beautiful as they walk along the streets in sheathes cut to the upper thighs for comfort in the

---

[*] Ralph's lover, whom he saw once he was back at the American Academy in Rome.

hot climate. Graceful and unconscious, they make these Roman gals look artificial and their skins with little makeup are so smooth and clear, adding a feeling of tranquility that goes with their Buddhist faces. But back to reality, the Communists are heavily armed on the borders and I had the chance to go up to view them but declined. Also had the chance to visit Formosa, expenses paid but my lecture prevented this. And now back to Rome: I miss the little leather bound volumes that Laurence gave me—did you take them with you? And the brass and silver polishing cloths? (For some reason I'm reminded to tell you that I got a Burberry trench coat in Hong Kong, though now I know I should have saved the money and made the old one do. Nevertheless it was a good saving.) I've been struggling to pack for the last several days and it's been no fun. I still haven't done the books and I think I'll have to have a crate made for the large picture and for the frame of my chair. How did the cestino work out, for I think that I can have one made to order that would take care of the art and the books. Please let me know as soon as possible. I'm very sorry that you had to borrow from Al and Lottie because I would have sent you whatever was here, though it's good to know that they had it to spare.

Yes, I've been encountering the Arkansas mess on every hand. Italians in the neighborhood explode into rapid-fire descriptions of what has happened and the communists have used the photo of the girl being spat upon in posters throughout Rome. I've photographed them for you to see. Save all the stuff for me unless you have some good Lerners or Kemptons.[*] Time is my best news source, for the *Daily American* is quite its abbreviated same . . . Dilly seems to have no difficulty in finding someone to marry her, give her my regards . . . This must do for the time being. Tomorrow I'll take a look at the ship sailings and try to get out of here before I choke to death. Be kind to yourself and don't torture yourself about the new job. I'll come home as quickly as I can.

Love,
Ralph

---

[*]   Ellison refers to Max Lerner and Murray Kempton, columnists for the *New York Post*. They wrote perceptively and passionately about civil rights and desegregation issues for the *Post*.

To Albert Murray

OCT. 3, 1957

Dear Albert,

I've been back just over a week and have been so busy trying to ship out of here that I haven't had time to write. As it is it looks as though I'll have to stay here until the 3rd of Nov. when I'll ship for Naples. I had been counting on taking a freighter but it didn't pan, so here I am, on the pot but doing no business . . . Japan was so exciting that if I could go back tomorrow I'd leap. I spent 14 days there and took in as much of that modern-ancient civilization as I could cram. They're an efficient people—which is always a pleasure to encounter after these slackassed Romans—and damn near everything they touch takes on beautiful form. They've taken the Western way, especially the American, and done something of their own with it. When you visit one of their houses you realize what Mies van der Rohe and Philip Johnson are trying to get at with their frigid designs, but they miss it a mile. A Japanese house is austere but it's also warm; reduced to essentials not by hacking but by blending, brewing, testing until that which is left is not only the least that is necessary but also the most aesthetically satisfying. I'll have more to say about Japan later, right now it's enough to say that I knocked myself out (trading my Summaron wide-angle for a Nikon 35 mm fl. 8 plus $27.00) and that was the best part of the trip. And, because the smug Indians who make so many moral noises discriminate against writers, I had to skip my trip there except for an 8 hr. wait between planes in Calcutta; and went to Hong Kong. Spent three days there being entertained with two other Congress of Cultural Freedom writers and acting like a hungry dog on a meat wagon over all those beautiful women. I simply didn't know about the Chinese, man; those girls have figures that are the most beautiful I have ever seen, and complexions! Tell Mokie to keep you away from there, they'd drive you nuts. No kidding they <u>are</u> lovely and Hong Kong, is an exciting international city and I want to return. But as for Calcutta, no sir; too depressing with thousands sleeping on the sidewalks, cows wandering in the downtown sections of a city of 8 million, crowds parading behind the red flag. I was glad to get out of there, even though I was going to lecture in Karachi, which was only a little better, for it too has its refugees from the division between India and Pakistan. I lectured at the University in the late afternoon and returned to my hotel to be introduced to a bunch of white Fulbrighters from 'Bama and had a bitch from Montgomery try to tell me how wonderful things were there until the N.A.C.P. and the Supreme Court dropped the shuck. I then had to tell her that I was from down that way and how different the facts of life looked from our side of the line. She didn't like it but she started talking sense, or at least she tried. I won't say too much about Arkansas,* I've got a belly full of acid already and it isn't even nine a.m. I ran into it all the way back to Rome and I've been having guys stop me on the street to tell me how bad it is. The communists have used the shot of that girl being jeered and spat upon in a poster that they've plastered about the city. Well, it smoked Ike out and it showed that that Mose who put the question of the use of force to Stevenson out there in California was talking about a basic issue. Now I want to see someone charge Russell and those other wild talking motherfuckers with treason because it is exactly the name for what they're playing with. In the end tolerating those guys is as bad as tolerating communist subversion, for they are just as damaging. I flew with two fellows from Pakistan as far as Rome and they simply wouldn't have anything to do with whites—even though they were on their way to London for business. One told me that 'these whites don't like people of our color.' I didn't have the heart to argue with him, the news photos would have made me sound silly . . . So that's that. I shot some color in Japan and in Hong Kong that I'll show you when we get together again. Unfortunately it was raining most of the time we were in Kyoto, which is the old capital and most beautiful. Still I shot color there and in Bangkok, where I spent a day. You know, I've been seeing American tourists in Europe for several years now and I agree that some of us can be outrageous, but after traveling with a plane of Frenchmen the Americans rate as gentlemen. I've never been on a nastier flight, the plane disordered and filthy as a Macon County outhouse, pushing and shoving at points of boarding and landing; and general rudeness to their hosts. For a while I didn't even want to hear the language spoken again. Then I met Malraux's first wife and became friendly with her and had several conversations with her. She invited me to visit her and their daughter the next time I'm in Paris and introduced me to the Japanese writer at whose home she was staying, and he told me a drink-inspired confidence that he was the original of the character Kyo in *Man's Fate*. Later I was told that there was some truth in this and I wanted to talk to him further about those days but the next time he was sober and reluctant to talk. Clara Malraux is a pleasant woman and I shall look her up, as should you, when I'm in Paris again. She

---

* Governor Orville Faubus's resistance to the Supreme Court's desegregation order prompted President Eisenhower, finally, to send federal troops to Little Rock on September 4, 1957.

certainly served to remind me of the more pleasant side of France at a time when I was deciding upon which French jaw I would smash with my fist. Cotton field Negroes could teach that crew manners.

Hope things go well with you all. Fanny is fine and back at work with her old firm—and that's all there is to tell just now. Take care of yourself and give my love to the girls.

Ralph Ellison.

To Fanny Ellison
ROME,
OCT 9, 1957.

Dear Fanny,

I have been waiting an answer to my last letter but all that has come is a post card from Yonkers—which, nonetheless, was pleasant to have. In the meantime I've settled the sailing problem; I found that the freighter which you took would cost me $196.00 plus $6.00 tax, plus the cost of getting my things either to Leghorn or to Naples and that the sailing dates available were so close to the low season that it was foolish for me to consider spending almost as much money as tourist fare on a regular liner and having to put up with the uncertainty and the extended time on the water. I am therefore sailing from Naples on the 4th Nov., on the *Giulio Cesare* and should be in New York on the 14th. I'm still trying to pack and get all the things together for the Belle Arte, all of which is a great nuisance to me, especially since I must get some kind of crate so as to pack my chair and some of these books. Perhaps I'll get a smaller version of the trunk you took—how did it work out? . . . Things go their hellish little way for me here. Mary came over a couple of days after the new fellows and I told her at the big cocktail party that I'd heard that she'd been saying nasty things about me. She denied it, of course and I told her that I knew she wouldn't say anything nasty about me and so on—all in a kidding way. I like her and didn't want to make her uncomfortable. Anyway, I'm so guilty about what's happened and about being here so long that I just don't want to say anything lest I explode and set the whole place on fire. Besides, the seriousness of this thing is so much bigger than any gossip so we must ignore it and live life as it presents itself to us. I mustn't continue on this any longer for it's not yet nine in the morning and already I'm beginning to feel choked up. I met a *Newsweek* reporter named Ted Tompkins yesterday when I had lunch with the Hadzis (I'm suddenly liked by them, for some reason) and he promised to give you a telephone call when he made his return flight. He came over on the inaugural flight of T.W.A.'s new Jet-Stream so should be there by no . . . I also forgot to write from Japan that the secretary of their foreign minister might give you a ring when he was there with Mr. Fuijiyama. His name is Hayakawa, a very pleasant young man, who with his wife had me out to dinner. Kind of mixed up construction but you'll understand me. There is still so much to tell you about the trip and yesterday I received some of the color shots I took in Bangkok and Hong Kong, not the greatest photography but glimpses of those places nevertheless . . . Fanny, I've received your letter of the 4th and I'm quite disturbed that you haven't heard from me. I wrote about the 27th and mailed it myself from the big post office. I expected to hear from you yesterday so surely you will receive it before you do this one (I've just found the carbon of my last letter, it was mailed on the 30th so you should have it by now.) Yes, I received letters from you dated Sept 17th and 25th. I'm glad you received the mail from Teheran, I gave it to the Air France Stewardess and I was beginning to suspect that she forgot to mail it. Please try to be calm and avoid depression, I have enough of it here for both of us and it tears me even more to think of your continuing to suffer. You can be certain that you will decide what you want and we can at least try to help one another. So much will depend, it seems to me, upon our being once more face to face in familiar circumstances—at home. I'm afraid to go beyond that because so much has happened so fast that I can't keep it all separated. Things continue to happen as they must until there's resolution. So you cheer up, you're a wonderful woman and even this cruel thing mustn't flaw that. I'm glad that you're seeing some pleasant people; when I re-read your first letter in which I spoke of self-pity I realized that part of the unpleasantness it brought me came from your description of the creeps you had blundered into—Lurline, Dorothy, with her shitty reaction. Actually I found that as a piece of writing it was a good letter and part of my reaction to it came of your unhappiness and my guilt. The news about the possible new account is good indeed, I hope it comes through because you would have a reason to continue your Italian as well as testing yourself against all the new problems. Perhaps I should remind you that I do admire and am proud of your abilities. Please write.

Love,
Ralph

P.S. Your letter of the 5th arrived in the evening's mail so I'm adding this to this morning's letter, which I had intended mailing downtown in the morning. I was relieved to get this letter but also troubled by it. Fanny, I got the impression that you feel that because of the way things went for me after you left that I have the notion that everything will go on with us as before. If so, then please understand that I know better and that I face the possibility that the basis of any lasting relationship might have been destroyed and that you might find it impossible to be near me for long; that all remains to be seen. Nor should you feel the need to be compassionate, since you have an honest right to rage, though I am grateful for it. Still, if you think that this thing I'm going through and have put you through is simple sadism, then you have been observing quite another drama indeed. One thing is certain, I am not the same, you are not the same and M. is not the same, but neither are either of us absolutely changed and you should bear that in mind. I'm sure you still retain your spark and I can't imagine you without it though perhaps now it glows from the depths. I despair that we'll neither be able to forget what has happened, that's far more important than any harm to my career, but have no fear, I won't do anything to Mary . . . This is so hard to write, you've touched on so many things and your letter is full of just the kind of barbs that bring the acid to my tongue. You tell me things which you know I'll agree to: that I have no sense of money; very well, but you should also consider the possibility that if money had been more important to me I would not have wasted my time becoming a writer, I would have gone and made money and you would not have picked up your phone to call me. As for "hunting" you know that I wasn't hunting for anybody and I'm not the kind of man who would marry for money and you shouldn't imply that I am, even in a joke. Especially not in a letter in which you are asking how much money I need to get home. The money which I had here was here to pay my passage home, things went wrong with my lecture tour and I spent money for expenses in Hong Kong, the coat and a few gifts for you and people here. Besides I didn't think I'd be alive now and I spent more money to break the hell of the summer. Do what you can about money if you still wish to; another hundred plus that you intend to deposit on the 15th should get me through and if you can't do anything about it I'll find another way. And if you do I'll give it back to you in toto, even if I have to sell the car to do so. I'm discouraged, Fanny, and you're unhappy so let's hold off with this kind of thing until I get home. I want to say more but I just can't.

Ralph

To Fanny Ellison

Fanny: I'd like to bring you some gloves, what is your size?

Phones:

Cable address: 0040-0043

"Miyako Kyoto"   (7) 0036-0038

Founded in 1893

T h e M i y a k o H o t e l

K y o t o, J a p a n

ROMA,

oct. 23, 1957

Dear Fanny,

I've been expecting to hear from you for a week now, and since I haven't I suppose you're reacting negatively to my last letter. Well, I can only say that you gave me a most hopeless feeling and it hasn't left me. But our differences aside, don't you think you should let me know how you are? With this flu thing sweeping the world you just might be ill. If you are have someone send me a note. But perhaps you didn't get my letter, I mailed it to Oram's because I wanted you to get it as early as possible and marked it personal on the envelope. I do want you to be all right so don't refuse to write out of anger . . . There is little news here: the new fellows have just returned from the trip; Corda and Jack had a son, named Aaron and at two weeks Jack says he farts so loud that he thinks he has a dragon in his pants; the Rhodens are back, although I haven't seen them as yet. I'm having the rattan trunk made slightly longer than yours and, taking you at your word, I've written checks against the deposit you said you'd make on the 15th. If you were unable to do as you planned please let me know so that I can do something about it before I leave—Nov. 4, from Naples. Giulio Cesare. I forgot to tell you last time that as far as I know the Murrays are still in Morocco. I wrote Albert shortly after I returned from Japan but he hasn't answered. I'm sure I'll hear before long. Their plans for the summer were disrupted by his illness and at the time of his last letter he didn't know what they were going to do when his hitch came to an end. Japan seemed out of the question, since our forces are to be withdrawn. Incidentally, I ran into an Airman in Tokyo who knew him at Tuskegee, small world . . . I hope Miss Ann and Cally are O.K.—I dreamed recently that Cally wouldn't speak to me. And what about Billy and George? I shall cut this short-short and I suggest that we not lob letters containing warheads from here on in; after all, long distance fighting is too wild and I shall be back in N.Y. in a matter of weeks. I hope things go well with your job. Think well and look well, you're always at your best when you do.

Ralph

To Albert Murray
M/N *Giulio Cesare*
"ITALIA" 730 RIVERSIDE DRIVE
SOCIETA DI NAVIGAZIONE NEW YORK, NY
GENOVA
FEB. 6, 1958

Dear Albert,

Pardon this paper, I'm still trying to get my money's worth out of that lousy trip home on that lousy Italian Line—which I'll never do, because the only way to beat an Italian businessman is to kick his nasty ass. But don't let me get started on all that. I arrived on the 14th of Nov., dead tired, broke, and scrambled up inside. My personal life got fairly keyed up last year, which explains some of the scrambling but that must wait until you come here. The rest of it and most of it has had to do with readjusting, not to my work, but to my place of work; and to a certain modification of conception which returning home has forced upon me. As you can guess, I'm impatient to get through, would like to cut down some of the ambition of this job, but am in so damn deep that I've got to fight it through to the end. It might be an egg but it'll have to be the same egg I conceived two years ago. Otherwise, we're still here at the old stand, doing the best we can. Fanny's well and sassy and keeping busy as hell and I feel pretty good except for the fact that I'm losing that lean look I had when I returned— which isn't all to the good, because I felt much better. I've got to get some exercise . . . The news that you landed just where you wanted go pleases us no end, though I'd hoped that you'd land a little closer to New York. I'll watch out for your arrival and I'm damn sorry that I haven't been able to get the old New Yorker into operation so that I could pick you up, but insurance, battery and licenses are too big a load at the moment because they can't be spread out now that insurance is compulsory. I don't blame you for not investing in a new car, this whole business has gone mad. I've a perfectly good car but I doubt if I could get five hundred dollars for it on today's market; those fins have offended more than my aesthetic sense, they've clobbered my investment. In the meantime ship whatever you wish here and I'll be glad to take care of anything. Sorry I can't invest in any of those Gib clothes and it's dam lucky that I picked up a trench coat in Hong Kong because the wind around the building has no pity. Get the 2.8 Rollei over there, man, because even with all the competition here, they're much too high. I could have bought one with all the attachments from a friend for $200 two months ago but not only did I not have the dough, I'm concentrating on the 35 mm. Haven't been shooting too much here, though; too busy. We spent a weekend with Warren and Eleanor recently and I took a couple of rolls of the crowd of us playing with sleds but have still to have them developed. Actually, I'm waiting to set up a dark room so that I can save the costs. Perhaps I'll set it up at Sarser's, he's got a lot of free space . . . I know what you mean about the Cozzens,[*] I was enthusiastic to see a guy bearing down on that particular subject and though I had my reservations about his prissy hero and certain aspect of his style, it wasn't until I started to read the wild shouts of the reviewers that I got down off condescension and looked carefully at the book. He shot off his mouth about Faulkner and Hem, and that made me mad (I could forgive him his opinion of Negroes). He's not in their class and should know by now that anybody can shoot off his mouth but that you have to write a novel and after it's written people will know whether you can write or not and who your peers are. Certainly he's no moralist, and I suspect that he doesn't really realize what a shit his hero is even though he's professional enough to know that he had to let the guy undergo a reversal so that the plot could be completed. More about this when you get here. As for Warren I like him better the more I see of him. We spent a very pleasant time with them and I let Eleanor bluff me onto a pair of skis and found that I not only liked it but have a knack for it. I guess the sense of balance developed by hitching on to a car on roller skates, or standing atop moving boxcars remains with me. Anyway, I had enough of it to understand why people are attracted to it, it would be like me to get this old and start messing around with something I should have done ten years ago. Warren's fine and working on another novel. He'll probably win the National Book Award for his last poems.

You know, I'm sticking so close that there's little that I know about the ZI.[†] The crackers are still acting up and Ike and a lot of Republicans and

---

[*] James Gould Cozzens's novel *By Love Possessed* appeared in 1957 and was on the *New York Times* bestseller list for thirty-four weeks. See Ellison's August 17, 1957, letter to Murray.

[†] "Zone of the Interior," overseas military term for the United States.

Democrats would feel a lot better if they could just forget about Mose, but Mose is still pressing. I've heard that some of the leaders in the struggle are suffering from a lack of ideas of where to go after the legal struggle is won. There's been a letdown, and I suspect that they're really better at counter-punching than at working out broad strategies. But don't get me started in that, the sonsabitches are so provincial that they can't see that we have a hell of a lot of advantages beyond the mere legal. I received Foster's report from Tuskegee the other day, and they're talking of establishing a cultural center but from the sketch of the architecture they propose they haven't realized that they could really change the cultural life of Alabama if they'd forget the cracker bullshit and act like responsible, culturally advanced Americans—Not that many of them are, but they certainly could get people down there who are. Mann[*] just phoned from the Idle on his way to Africa. I suggested a few people whom he might see in Rome but I doubt that he'll have time . . . I was at a PR party recently and ran into Kappy,[†] who is now stationed in D. C., family and all. His son is permanently deaf from the fall he had. He sends regards. Bellow is on a ten weeks teaching stint out at Northwestern, and has been rolling smoothly toward the finish of another novel. He and Sondra have an old house up near Bard College and a handsome, intelligent 11 month old son, both of which I envy him a slight bit. We were there for a weekend and liked very much the manner in which they're working out their lives. They've been doing some of the work on the old house themselves (it dates from the 17th century) and are making it quite comfortable. Actually there's room for a least two families, and plenty of ground for the kids to play. There is quite a lot of game in that section and when we were there it was lousy for deer hunters . . . I think Lacy is someone I used to know but I'm not sure but will check . . .

As for me I'm working hard now both with the novel and on a piece which Hyman feinted me into doing.[‡] You'll recall my description on his piece of Negro literature and the folk tradition, well, he sent my letter to PR along with his article and I was placed in the position of writing a commentary or letting some of his glib confusion go unanswered. For some reason he thought I was furious about this goddam piece and it wasn't

---

[*] William Mann, an architect friend of Albert Murray's from Tuskegee.

[†] H. J. Kaplan, Paris correspondent for *Partisan Review*.

[‡] This essay, published in 1958 in *Partisan Review* as the last half of an exchange with Hyman, "The Negro Writer in America," became "Change the Joke and Slip the Yoke" in *Shadow and Act,* published in 1964. See Ellison's May 27, 1957, letter to Stanley Edgar Hyman.

until I saw it again after I returned to N.Y. that I understood why: If you label the archetypical role in Negro writing "Darky entertainer" you imply that this is also the symbolic role played by Negro writers. For to an extent a writer's characters are surrogates of his own personal preoccupations, symbols of his own psychological role. Stanley equates the 'darky entertainer' with a 'smart man playing dumb,' which is way the hell off too, and only reveals that he's so fascinated with the machinery of his method that he doesn't bother to see that in my own book at least, the narrator does any[thing] <u>but</u> play dumb, either vocally or intellectually. He writes a memoir, he orates, rants and sings for over five hundred pages. So now I am annoyed, not only because this is taking up valuable time, but because I thought this guy knew better. Actually he isn't at all interested in novels but in neat demonstrations that archetypical figures turn up in various places. I think that he's going to be hurt by my essay but I'm just dam tired of guys who are more interested in anthropology monkeying with the novel. These fucks are so impressed that Joyce used myth to organize *Ulysses,* and they miss completely the fact that for all a novelist's interest in folklore or myth, he uses it as a novelist, not as an anthropologist or a teller of folktales[*] . . . Hurry home, you all we miss you and it'll be pleasant if Mique, and Mokie can hit N.Y. with you. Give them our love.

Ralph

To Saul Bellow
FEBRUARY 26, 1958

Dear Saul,

Things ain't coming worth a damn, but it's good to have heard from you in spite of it. I had intended writing you my congratulations for having been appointed to the Academy or the Institute.[†] I've been so busy getting nowhere that I hardly remember my own name.

We had dinner with Charlie Marks and his wife shortly before he returned to France, and he told us that you and Sondra had been ill, but I had no idea it was so serious. I had pneumonia in Rome and I know how

---

[*]   Here and in other letters to Murray and Bellow (as well as to Hyman), Ellison is sharply skeptical of Hyman's tendency to impose assumptions from anthropology or sociology on the novel's very different perspectives on form. See the February 26, 1958, letter.

[†]   Bellow was elected to the National Institute for Arts and Letters in February 1958.

it can reduce one to a puffing bunch of bones. Thank-God you all came through it without serious loss.

I've been sitting here for a week trying to make a PR deadline on a piece commenting on an archetype-happy essay on Negro writing—folklore by Hyman. I didn't really want to stop to do it but someone has to bring some reality into the discussion. The guy has quoted from my book in several places but what he says the quotations mean is so fantastic that I had to go back and look at the text. I wish to hell the goddam anthropologists manqué would leave novels to hell alone. Hyman can't see that the novel devours archetypes as ruthlessly as Nature devours a vacuum. I've got a natural writer's block as big as the Ritz and as stubborn as a grease spot on a gabardine suit and when I have to write calmly in answer to this kind of foolishness I can do almost anything <u>but</u> write. I've had a hell of a day because on top of Hyman I made the mistake of looking at *Time* and there in the book section some schmuck of a reviewer had decided that in order to promote some white kid who's written a first novel about Negroes [he] has to tee off on me as a "jazzed-up, Joyced-up intellectual" who feels revulsion for Negroes. I could have kicked his nose til his ass bled. Why can't they have their white hopes with[out] dragging me into it? Come to think of it I really don't mind being smeared in a context of Joyce, jazz and intellect, though I plan to give Gissen hell when I see him next week.

Saul, you've missed a lot of lousy weather here but the last few days have been like spring and I can even believe that the time will come when I can help you put out the garden. I hope you and Sasha set out some tulips last Sept., I'm awfully soft for them . . . I still haven't made any dough so I don't have the car yet but I hope to be rolling by time you return. If not, I'll take the train. I've been playing recorder duets once a week with a *New Yorker* and have developed a little technique, perhaps by time you return I'll be worth listening to . . . Kappy was in town last month, we ran into him at Wm. Phillips. He's back for a stint in Washington. There's some kind of hassle going on between Hicks and the *Reporter* over Alfred's review of *The Living Novel,* which had the title "Ten Young Novelists in Search for Pity" (Feb 6). Alfred wrote that "The 'enemies' of the novel, though their pontifications may annoy and hurt, are utterly ineffective against the really powerful and original new novels that have come along in recent years—Saul Bellow's *The Adventures of Augie March* won several important literary prizes and awards, and sold a million and a half copies in the paperback edition. True, it did not win the Pulitzer Prize, but this failure used to be considered a distinction among American writers, at least two of whom turned down Pulitzer Prizes in the old days." Hick's comment was that he wanted it in the record that you made no such complaint. Kazin is still Kazin and a bit pompous but I suspect that Hicks is happy for the opportunity to drum up a bit of business* . . . Things Rome-wise are still snarled up for me and I guess there's nothing to change it. Time might dull the effect but I'll never forget and I know that your advice was good . . . †

To Stanley Hyman
730 RIVERSIDE DRIVE
MARCH 9, 1958.

Dear Stanley,

Here, more or less, is a copy of the piece.‡ As usual I was late getting it in and probably made changes here and there while on the subway taking it to Phillips. Certainly it is looser than I'd like it to be and there are a number of things missing from it which shouldn't be but this kind of thing requires all of one's time and I don't have it to give. I hope though that it starts some discussion. Later, when I'm not snarled up with other matters, I'd like to take another crack at this and see how much I can dredge up. It occurred to me yesterday that perhaps I've got enough scattered pieces to make the start of a small book, if so I'll have you to thank for getting this thing done.§

Things go so-so here, now that the weather seems to have let up with some of the snow. We went dancing with a bunch of writers last night, James Jones among them, and I must say that he picked a nice dancer. Both were pleasant. Everybody's pleasant these days but me. Fanny's well and sends regards and we both thank Shirley for the new novel that looks

---

* Granville Hicks's *The Living Novel,* which included Ellison's seminal essay "Society, Morality, and the Novel," appeared in November 1957. The literary critic Alfred Kazin wrote a negative review titled "Ten Young Novelists in Search of Pity."

† The letter stops here; because it is important we are including it.

‡ "Change the Joke and Slip the Yoke."

§ Ellison's first mention of the collection of essays, which would eventually emerge as *Shadow and Act* in 1964.

very good.* I plan to get into it after the coming week's Natl. Book Award madness is over. If you're in town give me a ring, I'm usually in the house except for the ten minutes it takes me to go down for the mail—around 10:30. Give our regards to all.

As ever,
Ralph

To Dimitri Hadzi
730 RIVERSIDE DRIVE
NEW YORK 31, NEW YORK
APRIL 14, 1958

Dear Dimitri,†

Greetings and my apologies for waiting so long to write. I've thought of you and Molly often and wondered at the progress of the baby but have been waiting until I could send you your money and the recording I promised you before I wrote. Now spring is here and though I haven't succeeded in making a satisfactory tape I <u>do</u> have your money and would like you to have it without further delay. I also promise to send the tape, perhaps a section of the new novel, as soon as I can. If, by the way, it is possible for me to deposit the money to your account on this side I'd like it handle it that way, for I'm a bit distrustful of what happens to money in the Italian mails. Nevertheless, I'll handle it as you wish.

There is very little news to tell you, I'm working on my book, which elates me and depresses me as the days come and go. I've been doing a few articles of dubious value, financially or otherwise, and I've been subjected to the usual hazards of seasonal colds and cocktail parties. I've seen few of the old academy crowd since Tex's rather successful show (except, of course, the Blaustines and the Hahns) but damn near everyone tried to be on hand for that one. Including Jim Hoffman from Washington, the Stewarts from Michigan and the Venturi, Marti etc. contingent from Philly. The gallery looked like an academy party of year before last—except that absence appeared to have made all our hearts grow fonder of one another. On the other hand I haven't run into the Laytons although I hear that Billy is winning awards and being [granted?] commissions. I thought of you a few weeks ago when we were visiting a friend and I looked up out

---

* Shirley Jackson, Hyman's wife, who published *The Sundial* in 1958.

† Dimitri Hadzi was an abstract sculptor of increasing note and a friend of Ellison's.

of the corner of my eye, and there on the mantle I recognized a Greco sculpture, a lovely nude of graceful, elongated and delightfully sensuous proportions. You had spoken to me of his work and I had seen photos of it which appeared last fall in *Domus,* but the last place I expected to see such a piece was in a friend's home—and despite the fact that this friend possesses quite a number of important modern pieces. He knows your work and no doubt I'll go there sometime and see a Hadzi. Speaking of art reminds me that I met Bertha Shaffer at a cocktail party recently and learned that she's to be in Rome in the coming weeks. She will be living in some hotel or pensione near the bottom of the Spanish steps, so tell all the guys to keep their ears open as she'll be there on business. I told her about the academy artists but she's just apt to go there without seeing anyone except some friend of the princepessa's, as in a recent instance.

How does the photography go? Which reminds me that I've failed to have the film I shot in your studio developed! I'll carry it downtown today, and if there is anything decent on it I'll send you copies. I'd totally forgotten it. Don't forget that if you wish me to handle anything along that line I'll be glad to do so—and I'll handle anything else within my powers, so don't hesitate to ask. Meantime, take care of yourself, good luck with the work, and our best to Molly.

Sincerely,
Ralph

To Saul Bellow
TIVOLI, NEW YORK*
SUNDAY, SEPT 21, 1958.

Dear Saul

I received your letter of the Fifth more than a week later, at a time when Jack Wheeler had the hallway all wet with varnish. This necessitated my waiting another week while it took its time to dry in this rather wet season, and it was only Friday that I could round up the box of clothing and ship it off to you. I hope I've sent the correct carton, this one was marked as you described, but while I was away in New York on business,

---

* Bellow purchased "a wreck of a house in Tivoli" in 1956. He invited Ellison to live and work in the house at his pleasure from 1958 to 1960. Fanny would often visit on the weekends, or Ralph would return to Manhattan. Many of the Ellison-Bellow letters of this period touch on the house they were sharing.

Hoffman was here to prepare his things for the moving men thus things were a bit moved around. I noticed another carton with what appears to be winter things in it, so if you need them just holler . . . And you might tell your little empress of a Sasha that she needn't be so damned respectful when asking me to look after anything here for I'll gladly do anything she asks, she should only remain lovable. Indeed, I'd just about ship the whole house—including Rufus and an odd dozen crickets—straight to Minn. if it would keep her there and you two in working(!) distance. I'm relieved and hopeful that she and Adam are still there for that is where they belong. At any rate, I've been telling the cautious meddlers that they were there anyway. Hivnor wanted to know as did the Dupees and I told them you were together long before I knew for sure. Bob called the other evening supposedly to ask me to dinner (it was the dinner hour ha-past) but really to get a line on the status of Leah and Jack. I told him I was not a good friend of the Ludwigs and let it go at that. I don't like it when these things are gossiped about, it only makes it more difficult to correct them. Let them find their drama in their own damn lives.

As for the house, there have been no major crises and, thus far no signs of a second floor leak. I did have a rather upsetting moment around the 1st, when I was still bouncing back and forth between here and New York like a ping pong ball's balls, which began with a call from Ted Hoffman to me in New York. He was here in the house through the intervention of Mrs. Dupee, who had gotten the key from Jack Wheeler. He wanted to round up his things, asked me to see that the truckmen left nothing behind, and wanted to know if I minded his taking his beds—which, of course, I didn't. He was somewhat agitated (his voice smiling) over the fact that Rufus was outside when they arrived and seemed frantic to get inside, and that there were several dishes of dried cat food and several chipmunk carcasses strewn about the terrace (actually the dishes were the remains of dog food left by Lizzie and no concern of Rufus at all) and he, Ted, felt the cat was being neglected. I refrained, although I can get awfully annoyed with people who jump breakneck to conclusions—and especially those who leap out of a misplaced sentimentality over animals, from telling him to mind his damn business. But what, after all can you say to a dramatist who doesn't use his eyes? Rufus, I suspect is far more self-reliant than Hoffman—as the animal carcasses should have informed Ted, so I simply explained that Adrienne was looking after Rufus and held my tongue. Anyone but Hoffman could see that Rufus is thriving, his coat is rich and thick, his pantaloons as full as a wealthy Turk's and his carriage quite arrogant. He probably tried to knock Ted off his feet out of sheer rudeness as an intruder who had no business in his house. Ted and Lynn are fine, as are their children, and he is enthusiastic over his new job. Unfortunately, he was to be here only for a day so would not be on hand when I arrived the following day.

Well, when I arrived my temperature began to rise. I discovered that someone had slept in the bed which Sasha had told me had been changed and readied for me—and (I still don't know whether it was to hex me or to encourage my writing through the displayed evidence of fertility) I found a barely wrapped and much used sanitary napkin (Kotex is a registered trademark!) smack in the middle of your desk!

That, as we used to say when bragging about some adolescent hot-rodding of a more than likely innocent girl, brought the rag; I almost flipped. Then I laughed at this display of one of the female mysteries and, with what I hope were the proper words, tossed it into the fire, washed my hands and began to unpack my manuscript. It might, after all, have been an emergency that brought it there. Certainly my subjective reaction was comical and I suppose it was really the shock of finding it on a desk, for I have seen countless of its sisters in my day. Kenneth Burke hints in an essay that poor Desdemona's handkerchief was blamed and she thus condemned, for its association with just such a feminine article. Napkin, it was called in the old days and "napkin" Othello called it when he accused her. It's a rich word, nap & kin kidnap and kinship and there is a little boat in it too—certainly it is a catchall for love's labors (sometimes) and for love's losses too. And love must nap after its labors, whether it produces kin or no. O.K, so I'll stop burking around. I only hope—even it was Lynn's, that it brings me luck.

But the surprises were to continue. That afternoon I stopped typing to hear a car coming up the drive and when I reached the living room I could see a young fellow get out of a car carrying a can and a can opener. When he saw me he became nervous and explained that he was a friend of Ted's and had come up to feed the cat (suddenly this reminds me of an old Minsky burlesque act "Who's gonna feed the Goddam Cat?"). I asked if he were a Bard student. No, he had come up from Poughkeepsie. But why? I asked him. Because no one was feeding him, he said. He had been up several times. Did I want the cat? Look, I said, this cat belongs here. This is his home. Hoffman hadn't been around so he can't know what's going on here. A woman down in Kidd Lane comes here and feeds the cat everyday I'm not around. And it isn't a question of my wanting him he goes with the house and he's <u>my</u> responsibility. How the hell does Hoffman know what's going on when he's supposed to have been only one day?

Well, the poor kid placed the can of cat food in my hand and cut out. I didn't know what to make of it and when I looked into the undergrowth beneath the chestnut tree I saw several empty cat food cans that had not been there before. I suppose old Rufus had been having a ball. Truly, it was an exasperating day. And that night I went to bed about 10 to be awakened by some dame who tried to give me the third degree over my identity. I was evil as hell and wouldn't tell her and even now my ears are just quivering to recognize that voice.

Next morning I was still agitated but working when I heard the thud of heavy objects on the porch and opened the door to find Wheeler, who was just then getting around to the hallways. I let him in to start his racket—which was all right, since the work had to be done when it could be done and the halls now look handsomely worth the trouble. But before I could settle down to adjust to the noise, I heard someone unlock the side door and a woman's voice rising up the stairs. This was Mrs. Dupee, who had had a key made from Wheeler's so as to let Hoffman's movers in. She apologized for entering the house without knocking but explained that she didn't know I was here. It was the first time, by the way, that I realized that for someone that fairly large Chrysler of mine could be invisible, which it must have been in this case, because Wheeler's station wagon has his name all the hell over it.

I was, to say the least, pissed off. I had forgotten that I had met her here and it was some time before I connected her face with her name and her name with her husband and I asked for her key, which she surrendered quite gracefully (she told me later that it was she who had the kid come over to feed the cat, and now that I think of it, he did <u>not</u> have an opener in his hand, perhaps he was carrying the key . . .). I thought that once the truck men were loaded and on their way I'd never see her again, but before leaving she invited me over to her house to work should Wheeler's noise become unbearable and since then I've been there for dinner. She's a good cook and except for the fact that I learned for the first time what an ass Dwight MacDonald can be in a discussion it was a pleasant evening. McDonald is *Lolita* happy.* He accepts it whole and thinks it great fiction, nothing like it in years, etc. He is teaching popular culture but had

---

* Vladimir Nabokov's novel *Lolita*, published in Paris in 1955, was published in the United States in August 1958.

little notion of the nature of the impact of *Esquire* magazine on kids in the provinces and tried to tell me that the important writers who appeared there were writing down. I mentioned some of Mann's essays, Hemingway's "The Snows of Kilimanjaro," Fitzgerald's *The Crackup* essays etc. and told him to consult the files, but he's so full of clichés that he thinks that he has only to believe a thing shoddy to make it so. Besides, even if Mann and Shaw and Hemingway and the others had written down for *Esquire* I still feel I was lucky to have my taste, such as it is, formed by second rate Mann-Shaw-Hem than by first rate McDonald—though fortunately Dwight had to leave to catch a train before I was irritated enough to bring myself to the point of telling him so. That's some place the Dupees have, or at least, some wonderful view.

Wheeler gave me his key when he finished buffing the floors and I hope no other keys are floating around. If there are, please let me know, because I'd hate to use the shotgun I brought up for the coming hunting season on some unsuspecting friend. I'm not so anti-social as this all might sound but I do have a thing about anyone coming into my lair, even when it's only a loaned lair.

Except for the note which I'm enclosing from your tree surgeon, describing the condition of the great tree out front—you could seal Phillips, Rahv, Fiedler and Delmore in the cavity along with a troupe of midgets and ivory-toting pigmies and only the annoyed ants and bees would suspect their presence—there is nothing more to report concerning the house. Tell Sondra that I've seen Adrienne only once, when she came last to return Adam's carriage and some laundry. She explained that her sister had been quite ill. She also said that she could only come here on Saturdays, which would be O.K. with me, but I haven't seen her since. She plans to do your silver soon, so I'll talk with her then. How much, by the way, should I pay her hourly? Don't worry about the condition of the house, for I'm used to cleaning the apartment in the city and have vacuumed and scrubbed and dusted and am quite concerned that the place be and remain shipshape. Hoffman just about denuded the guest room, so if you don't mind I'd like to fit it up with the bed from across the hall and get it set up for emergencies. I'm also finding a fire in the study fireplace not only practical these damp days, but a friendly prop for the music and my evening's bourbon. When I get into the city I shall shop for fireplace tools and I'm slowly getting some of the dust and crap that has settled onto your record player cleaned up. Soon that very wonderful collection of records will sound something like they were intended to. If, however, you get lonesome for the machine yell and I'll ship it up along with the records. I can throw something of my own together, or I can bring up my tape recorder. If there are drapes for the study let me know ... As soon as the rain ceases I'll give the lawn its final cutting and store the mower and the other tools in the basement. I shall also store the wood there, as much for the exercise as for the protection against the rain and the snow. Need tomatoes? The garden is running riot with them. However the dry spell ruined the corn and left the beets stunted and I simply won't discuss the jungle of squash.

So, as I say, things here are not bad at all—but why the hell didn't you tell me about Rufus? He is a pirate, a con-cat, and an arrogant bastard. He keeps trying to con me into feeding him three times a day, he races me for chairs and gets as indignant as hell when I win, he's destroyed two loaves of bread, boldly, in midmorning; and the other day, before I learned how to work a defective catch on one of the cabinets above the sink, he went in and dragged out a package of fig newtons and broke one of Sasha's large white cups and one of my own elegant Alpine ones which I had just brought up from the city. When I heard the noise I thought it was an electric glass kettle or a Chemex coffee pot, but was spared that. What about this character, and how does one keep him under control? I know about dogs; but how, pray, does one kick a cat's ass? Nevertheless, I find him a good companion and despite his insistence upon more I've been feeding him a bowl of milk for breakfast and a can of cat food for supper. Other than that we have a game we play: When I'm preparing my own meals, he stands up against the cabinet and tries to see what he can snatch off the counter with his great paw, while I in turn try to see if I can make him draw back a nub. Thus far, being fast as light for all his huge size, he has retained all of his members. Recently he's taken to calling me Henderson, what the hell does he mean?

Yesterday I went to the post office at Tivoli and inquired of mail as you suggested and was given a bunch of circulars and magazines. There are 3 issues each of the *New Yorker* and the *New Leader,* a copy of *Accent* which contains a study of your work and a copy of the *American Vegetable Grower* and, yes, a most interesting issue of *Scientific American* in which J. Brononwski has a piece on the Creative process, a piece very much like those he did for the *Nation* two years ago. Let me know what to send and she is done.

Things at the college are still strange to me but I'm learning. I finished my *Esquire* piece, which will be out in Jan., and the lead piece in the end of the month recording issue of the *SRL,* including the cover, will be mine.* I've moved my electric machine up here so if there's any fiction in me I'll soon be set here to get them out. From the way I'm running on in this letter the isolation is acting as a release—but hell, I can't talk with Rufus <u>all</u> the time, now play the recorder . . . I've found it necessary to make several calls to the city so you can send the bills to me, or I'll send you a check, as you please. Other than a cold and hay fever, I'm O.K. Fanny is O.K. and thriving, though I haven't seen her in about ten days. Take it slow and don't be afraid to hope, poison or no. Most of all don't try to answer all these words. Anyway I know by now that the only time you write and have little to say is when you're writing a letter. Most of the time I'm that way myself.

Best to all of you,
Ralph

To Albert Murray
Bard College
Annandale-on-Hudson, ny
sept. 28, 1958

Dear Albert,

The Ellisons are shook up like everyone else, I suppose, but otherwise we're about the same. I've been intending to write but ran into a busy summer of writing and fighting, of all things I don't need, the hay fever. I finished a long piece on Minton's Playhouse† for *Esquire*'s special Jazz issue, which is due in Jan. and that took quite a lot of time running around and trying to talk to those screwed up musicians, drinking beer so that I could listen to their miserable hard-bopping noise (defiance with both hands protecting their heads) and finally realizing that I could write the piece without their help; for after all most of them simply know that they're dissatisfied and that they want fame and glory and to be themselves (or Charlie Parker—which would be even better because most have only that which they've copied from him as miserable, beat and lost as <u>he</u> sounded most of the time—but hell, they believe in the witchdoctor's warning: If

---

* His lead piece, "As the Spirit Moves Mahalia," appeared in the September 27, 1958, issue of *The Saturday Review of Literature*.

† Minton's Playhouse was the Harlem jazz club that sponsored jam sessions, out of which emerged new dimensions of jazz known as bebop. Ellison's essay "The Golden Age, Time Past," on Minton's Playhouse in Harlem, was published in *Esquire* in January 1959.

Bird shits on you, wear it). And anyway they suspect, and rightly, that they ain't nobody. Man, I wished for you during the Newport festival. I was asked up to participate in the critics symposium and went up there and put the bad mouth on a lot of the characters. I wouldn't be a jazz critic for love or money, but I discovered that I have quite a number of fans who think that's what I've been doing for the *SRL*. So I had my say the first two days and spent the rest of the time looking and listening and a hell of a lot of it was simply pathetic. I finally saw that Chico Hamilton with his mannerisms and that poor, evil, lost little Miles Davis, who on this occasion sounded like he just couldn't get it together. Nor did Coltrane help with his badly executed velocity exercises. These cats have gotten lost, man. They're trying to get hold to something by fucking up the blues, but some of them don't even know the difference between a blues and a spiritual—as was the case of Horace Silver who went wanging away like a slightly drunken gospel group after announcing a blues. Monk, who is supposed to be nuts, got up on stage and outplayed most of the modern boys and was gracious and pleasant while doing so. But Bird had crapped on most of the saxophonists, who try to see how many notes they can play in a phrase and how many "changes," as they like to call their chord progressions, they cram into even the most banal melodic idea. There was even a cat there trying to play a Bird on a Tuba. He was spitting like a couple of tom cats fighting over a piece of tail and that poor ole tuba was wobbling like an elephant with a mouse doing a Lindy hop up and down inside his long nose hole. Taste was an item conspicuously missing from most of the performances, and once again I could see that there's simply nothing worse than a half-educated Mose unless it's a Mose jazz-modernist whose convinced himself that he's a genius, maybe the next Beethoven, or at least Bartok, and who's certain that he's the only Mose jazzman who has heard the classics or attended a conservatory. Duke didn't do much up there but it was easy to see why. These little fellows are scrambling around trying to get something new; Duke is the master of a bunch of masters and when the little boys hear him come on they know that they'll never be more than a bunch of little masturbators and they don't want to think about it. I was at a party given by Columbia Records at the Plaza recently, where they presented Duke, Miles Davis, Jimmy Rushing and Billie Holiday and it was murder. Duke signified on Davis all through his numbers and his trumpeters and saxophonists went after him like a bunch of hustlers in a Georgia skin game fighting with razors. Only Cannonball Adderley sounded as though he might have some of the human quality that sounds unmistakably in the Ellington band. And no question of numbers was involved. They simply had more to say and a hundred more ways in which to say it. I told Jimmy that I'd hoped to hear him sing with Duke but was afraid it would never happen. It was one of those occasions when the whole band was feeling like playing and they took off behind him and it was like the old Basie band playing the Juneteenth ramble at Forest Park in Okla. City. Duke left for Europe Mon. for the first time in about ten years and invited us to join the mob of fans, writers, and friends who were there to see them off. They served champagne, which helped offset the rainy morning but it didn't stop Duke from talking that gooie bullshit which he feels forced to spread. Great man until he opens his mouth. They did the number he wrote for the Great South Bay festival at the Plaza and it sounded well constructed and generally interesting. Watch out for it . . . This business of writing on jazz is quite interesting. Quite a lot of fan mail goes with it and while some of the younger "critics" are friendly, some of the others react as though I'm moving into their special preserve. Old John Wilson of the *Times* won't even acknowledge my presence at the various publicity gatherings—which amuses me to no end, since we aren't playing the same game anyway. At Newport, one of the critic-composers interrupted some remark I made concerning the relationship between Negro dance audiences and jazz bands, to say that he didn't believe that Jazz was connected with the life of any racial group in this country—but when one of his numbers was played by the International Youth band, a Swedish boy stood up and tried to play Bubber Miley on a trumpet and the voicing was something copied from Duke. I really don't have much patience anymore, Albert, and I didn't bite my tongue in telling this guy where he came from and who his daddy was—who his <u>black</u> daddy was. I don't fight the race problem in matters of culture but anyone should know the source of their tradition before they start shooting off their mouth about where jazz comes from.

It looks as though I'll have enough pieces before long to form part of a book and in the meantime it gives me a chance to earn a buck. *Esquire* is interested in anything I do, article or story. If you have anything you should send it to Harold Hayes and mention my name. There is a young crowd there these days who are trying to raise its standard and I think they should be encouraged—especially since they're paying damn well. On the ninth they're running a symposium on fiction along with Columbia University and I'm being paid fifty bucks just to be there just in case someone doesn't show—in which case I'll get five hundred and I'm not even bothering to prepare notes ... And what am I doing up here? I'm living in Bellow's house while they are away at Minn. and when I'm not struggling with my novel, I'm working on my notes for that single class in the American novel which I'm teaching at Bard College: I go to campus only once a week, and though it doesn't pay me much it does make it possible for me to stay up here most of the time. It's only two hours away from the city so that I can go down there or Fanny can come up here fairly easily. I'm a little desperate about the book so took this as a way to have the peace to get it over with ... Man, you'll soon have property all over the place, which seems like a good idea at that. Which reminds me that while I'm not yet in the position to send you all your dough outright, I <u>could</u> start paying you off at a hundred books a throw. In fact, I've been asked to let *Esquire* see some of the novel that I shall do as soon as I can solve a few problems connected with a certain section, and if they like it I should be able to send you the whole sum ... Had a call from Gwen Mitchell the other morning, she's up there at City College and Juilliard (this was down in New York) and tells me that Mitch is building at Tuskegee. I guess every fox has a hole but me ... What you tell me of L.A. is depressing but the next time you're there I'd appreciate it if you would drop over to 1917 Jefferson and see my brother Herbert and let me know your impressions. He works from 4:30 in the afternoon until late at night so you could reach him during the day. I'll tell him to watch out for you ... I know how depressing it is to see Negroes getting lost in the American junk pile and being satisfied with so little after all the effort to break out of the South. It makes you want to kick their behinds and then go after Roy Wilkins and that crowd who still don't see that Civil rights are only the beginning. Or maybe I should go after myself for not being more productive and for not having more influence upon how we think of ourselves and our relationship to what is truly valuable in the country. I'm trying in this damn book but even if I'm lucky one book can do very little. And wouldn't a damn nutty woman pick King to kill instead of some southern politician? I'm surprised that she wasn't torn to shreds right there on the spot.* The New York papers are reporting the gifts of money and letters of well wishers that the crackers are sending this bitch, a further indication of how depraved this southern thing can become. And they think we're fighting to

---

* On September 20, 1958, while in New York for a book signing, Dr. Martin Luther King Jr. was stabbed in the side by a mentally ill woman. The injury was nearly fatal, but King recovered in the hospital and at the Brooklyn home of a friend.

become integrated into that insanity! I almost cracked my sides when I heard that baleful voiced hypocrite [Arkansas senator] John McClellan lecturing Jimmy Hoffa with such high moral tone. Those sonsabitches don't even have a sense of humor. He doesn't see that with his attacks on the Supreme Court he's doing more to undermine the country than Hoffa is or could even if he was stealing a million a day and bribing every so-called respectable official with an itching palm—of which there must be thousands—that he could find in Washington. It would delight me no end if some reporter got to digging into McClellan's background and told the story of how he became such a moral leader, that would make interesting reading, because being a southern politician is by definition one of the most corrupt careers to be found anywhere. Everything about this mess breeds sickness, the bastard's lost his sons one right after the other and it's human to feel sorry for such misfortunes and indeed, it's the kind of thing which is apt to touch me most poignantly, since we have no children at all but hell, how can I sympathize with his loss when he's trying to deprive my kids of a chance to realize themselves? No, I hate him and his kind and I believe the world will be a better place when the last of them is put away forever. Certainly this country will have a bit more self-respect . . . I saw something of Norman Mailer during the summer and have been discussing Kerouac and that crowd with Bernie Wolfe* and I understand something of how far you got underneath that Greenwich Village poet's skin that summer in Paris. These characters are all trying to reduce the world to sex, man they have strange problems in bed; they keep score à la Reich on the orgasm and try to verbalize what has to be basically warmth, motion, rhythm, time, affection and technique. I've also talked to Bellow about this and it would seem that puritan restraints are more operative among the bohemians than elsewhere. That's what's behind Mailer's belief in the hipsters and the "white Negro" as the new culture hero—he thinks all hipsters are cocksmen possessed of great euphoric orgasms and are out to fuck the world into peace, prosperity and creativity. The same old primitivism crap in a new package. It makes you hesitant to say more than the slightest greetings to their wives lest they think you're out to give them a hot fat injection. What a bore.

Let me know what's happening with you. Are you still shooting? I've been too busy to do much but plan to carry a camera with me when I

---

* Bernard Wolfe, novelist and coauthor of *Really the Blues*, the autobiography of jazzman Mezz Mezzrow.

start hunting the countryside hereabouts. How's your health? Mine is weakened more than you'd expect by this damn hay fever but I look fairly well, am a bit more bald and taken to smoking a type of mild Conn. cigar which I discovered in New Milford this summer. Otherwise I haven't slowed much. Got drunk at a party recently and danced a young chick bowlegged, but hell, a rounder never changes. Love to them gals and let me hear what's cooking.

Ralph

To Herbert Ellison
730 RIVERSIDE DRIVE
NEW YORK 31, N.Y.
OCTOBER 1958

Dear Herbert:

It was a very pleasant surprise to hear from you. I had asked Virgil to go by to see you several times before but he had failed to catch you and I doubted that he would this time, thus my surprise and my pleasure. There was a disappointment in your letter, however, for when I read it I understood that you had enclosed a photograph—or at least had <u>intended</u> to enclose one—but search as I did I could not find it. Then, while I was down for one of my erratic trips to the city I received your photograph. I don't suppose you are aware of it but this is the first good look that I've had of you since 1938; and I must say that you've grown! Indeed, I'd even say that you've become a big, fairly rugged looking man. And more like our father than like mama—how tall are you? I'm five feet 10 ½ myself but am proportioned in such a way that I don't really look it. And you have all of your hair although, as you say, it is grey. I have very little of mine despite its blackness (I'm grey at the temples, actually) and Virgil meant that my hair is not only black but <u>back</u>—a way back from where it used to be. Indeed, should I live long enough I'll probably turn up with a head as bald and as shiny as our uncle Will's. Thanks very much for the photo, I shall send you one as soon as I have some printed.

I suppose you have received the magazines that Fanny mailed you by now. Mrs. Jacobson gave me the picture in which you appear when I was in Oklahoma City several years ago. It amuses me no end and I keep trying to remember the names of some of the kids but can't get very far. Wyatt Jackson, who appears in the middle of the second row, lives here in New York and the first time I catch him I'll ask him to identify them for me.

I recognize Calvin Caddell, Dutom, Otto, George Ragland, Kelly Smith and Gussie Lewis, Charlie, Christine Mitchell, Marcina Bunn—but the rest escape me. Perhaps you can do better but, man, that's been a long time ago. I plan to do a few more pieces on jazz and the musicians we knew back in Okla. and I'll send them along as they are published. In January there will be a piece in the special issue that *Esquire* magazine is devoting to jazz and I'll try to send you a copy. This, however, is not about Okla. but about Minton's Playhouse in Harlem, where Bebop was first publicized.*

I hadn't realized that you hadn't seen Virgil in such a long time. We've been seeing him almost every time he's in N.Y., except through this period when I spend so much time up at Tivoli, the little town about a hundred miles north of here where I spend part of my time writing a book and the rest at nearby Bard College, where I teach a class in the American novel. Virgil is seldom around for more than a few days and then he's chasing the girls but we hope to drive him up for a day or so in the woods. I have a friend's house up there, a fairly large house and it offers a pleasant change from life in the big city. As for Shep I don't recall <u>when</u> I've seen him, I suppose it's been about as long as it's been since I've seen you—in fact, longer. What's he up to these days? Virgil tells me that the town is full of Oklacitians but I can see that your routine doesn't leave much time to see them—and if I remember you correctly, you [don't] wish to be bothered with them anyway. Be on the lookout for friend of mine by the name of Albert Murray. He is a Captain in the Air Force who has been stationed recently at Long Beach. He is a very good friend of mine, and a very good guy, so when he drops by talk with him, for he can probably tell you more about what I'm up to and what I'm like than Virgil. I went to school with him at Tuskegee, saw him and his wife and daughter whenever they came to New York and as luck would have it, he was stationed in Casablanca during the same two years we were in Rome. Thus it was that in 1956 they drove up to see us and we drove from Rome to Paris where we visited together for a few days before we had to leave for London for a writers' convention and they had to head South for a few days in Spain before heading back to his duties in North Africa. He's very much down to earth with no crap about him so keep a look out.

You say in your letter that you'll send another photo made when you're not in your work outfit—from the looks of it you aren't working very

---

* "The Golden Age, Time Past."

hard—or at least your job is as clean as mine. What do you do? Langston Hughes told me that you worked for the County, but was as far as he could tell me. He said also that you were very nice to him and had driven him about in your car. I haven't seen him too much recently, in fact not since the Newport Jazz festival where I had gone to take part in a discussion; nevertheless he is O.K. and keeping busy.

I don't have much news of Okla. City these days, but I did see Saretta and her husband, Finley, and their son, the summer of 1957 in Rome. This year they visited Japan, I learn from the *Black Dispatch*. I also learned from Jimmy Stewart's column that Vivian,* who, as you know, is married to Virgil Chandler (that old pain in my ass) recently gave birth to a baby girl. It seems rather late to me but I'm glad for them because I'm sure she'll make a good mother. From the papers I see that the fight for integration continues to move quite successfully out there. Mamma should have lived to see so many of the things she stood for become an actual fact. Can you remember the time she took us to the zoo in defiance of the segregation law? I remember it vividly and the cracker guard telling her, "You'll have to leave, you and your chillun too," and her saying, "All right, I guess we've just about seen everything"; and our leaving the bench where we'd been sitting to go laughing to the street car line.† She certainly knew what was right and just along those lines and was willing to stand up for it—or go to jail for it if necessary, as she did out there on Stonewall St. I was in college then, but I remember the stories and your throwing the cracker off the front porch. He's probably foaming at the mouth over the changes which desegregation is bringing, but he should have known way back in the thirties that it was coming just as surely as Mamma resisted that crappy city ordinance. Come to think about it, neither of us should ever have any doubt as to what position to take in situations where doing the right thing requires suffering or inconvenience or the sacrifice of self-interest in the interest of the bigger issue of civil justice, Mamma was giving us lessons along that line almost from the time you could walk. Looking back at it now I guess Okla. City wasn't such a back place in which to be born; and although both of us have suffered from not having

---

* Vivian Steveson, Ralph's old flame from pre-Tuskegee years in Oklahoma City. See his letters from the thirties.

† Ellison recounted this experience years later in *The New York Times Magazine* of April 16, 1989, in a second-person narration titled "A World of Difference." The piece was published in *The Collected Essays of Ralph Ellison*, ed. John F. Callahan (New York: Modern Library, 1995), as "On Being the Target of Discrimination."

had our father when boys need a father most, the hard times we had were by no means the worst that could have befallen us. Actually we got much from the experience which we needed to face the life ahead and with what she had to work with I'd say she did very well—even though I know that I'm very seldom as good a man as she was a woman but I'll keep on trying and I'm sure you will too. I don't know Frederlake's address or anything but I'd like to do something about a headstone for her grave in Cincinnati. If you have this information please send it to me for I'd like to take care of a matter which should have been done six years ago, when I first made a little money. It won't be anything elaborate but it will at least be something for the obligation weighs on my mind.

My work goes on slowly. I'm trying to do a big and rather complicated novel and my teaching is really a way of keeping away from the city so that I can get it completed. I only teach one day a week and am paid very little. Previously I had turned down jobs at two more important colleges but it took a bit of desperation over the novel to push me into a classroom. Thus far I have no Negro kids in my class but most of my students are from New York and accept a Negro teacher as a matter of course. You'd die laughing to see me making like a teacher, puffing on a cigar, questioning them, trying to make them argue with me, kidding them in their own slang and giving them hell when they fail to dig into an assignment. Well, I couldn't teach a single one of them to spell or work problems in math, but I can teach them something of what American literature is all about and something of what the country is all about and I'm doing this as well as I can—not as well as I wish some of my teachers in Okla. and down at Tuskegee had taught me. Still, if I allowed myself to think about it I'd feel damn strange whenever I found myself standing before the class. I certainly didn't plan to be a teacher, college or otherwise, but here I am.

I forgot to tell you up above that I see Jimmy Rushing* from time to time and talk with him even more often. He's going great guns again and is currently in Europe. He has had a remarkable life and seems to remember everything that ever happened to him and wants me to do a book with him. I'm quite interested and if I can ever catch him still long enough I shall try to do so. I only wish that I'd been around Roscoe Dunjee, who is now retired and ill, for he has much important information about Okla-

---

* Rushing, the great blues singer (1901–72), was from Ralph's hometown, Oklahoma City. They knew each other growing up and kept up the friendship when each man moved to New York.

homa and its politics and such information shouldn't be allowed to go to waste. He, Dunjee, has written quite a lot of his autobiography in the form of editorials but little of it has been put together and I know of no one there who could give him a hand at organizing it. Life's a mess, if I had remained in Okla. I probably would never have learned to write and now that I have I could never live there long enough to put down some of the experience that has made the place what it is. Perhaps when I finish this novel I will go out there and see Tom Brown and the Randolphs and Slaughters, and write what I can before it is too late. I'd like also to drive out to L.A. to see you and your family, but that will take time and money. Last summer I was asked to come to San Francisco for a month with expenses paid, but couldn't break away, but from now on I'll be watching my chances. In the meantime take care of yourself and write when you can. Don't try to write such a long letter as this—unless you care to—but do let us hear from you. And give our best to your wife and children.

> Love,
> Ralph

To John Cheever
TIVOLI, NEW YORK,
NOVEMBER 12, 1958

Dear John,

I'm sorry that you and Mary won't be able to get up here to visit us, and even sorrier that you've sold the Fiat. There was such a fund of adventure tied up in its purchase, and I remember so vividly the agility with which you got it in and out of its parking place behind your Roman palace, along with the mysterious skill required to start it; and all the high, exciting parties it transported us to and from, and the frustration-killing jokes about the quality of Italian workmanship told at its expense; and it seemed such an integral part of the "American dream" aspect of knowing someone from home who could take a holiday in that grand apartment with its expansive living room with high humor and no stuffiness, that the news of the sale reminds me that another symbol of the gayer side of my Roman adventure has gone to join the truly dead past. Fanny told me last night, incidentally, that *Time* has once more referred to me as an expatriate living in Italy! Anyway, my feelings about Rome are, and were, terribly mixed, but many of the brighter memories have cars involved in them and I suppose I tend to think of such cars with something of the affection with which travelers of an earlier era thought of the horses which were so necessary to their journeys. Good old Fiat, I hope its new owners are kind.

I know what you mean about returning to Rome, for despite my mixed feelings about the place I find that during moments of distraction my thoughts go wandering there, and often in the middle of the night I hear the monotonous voice of one of the maids at the Academy calling, "Antimo, Antimo, Antimo," with all its sound of uninflected hopelessness. I suppose that I too shall find my way back there some day, compelled like a man to his mother or a dog to its vomit, by the sheer intensity and ambiguousness of the experience. Anyway, I only returned on the 14th of this month last year, which gives me at least another year in which to build up a good case of nostalgia. And let us confess it, spring there can be heartbreakingly lovely.

It's good to hear from a writer who finishes something, even though he thinks it's a dud; I seem to finish nothing these days—fiction-wise, at least—but continue to make more and more notes and more and more clutter for my desk, my pockets and my already untidy mind. If this continues much longer I'll either have [to] confess defeat or get the aid of a head stretcher—which, for me, would be much the same. Only the teaching goes satisfactorily, and that's no consolation at all.

Tell Ben that I've been hunting a bit and have taken two pheasants and enough squirrels for a stew, but that the ducks, rabbits and grouse have eluded me most skillfully. I had the pleasure of hunting with a man who has a fine Labrador pup but the birds were, unfortunately, elsewhere that day so that I missed seeing him go through his paces. Tell Ben also that I'm writing this in bed, the penalty of having eaten too many cookies on a drive back from Kingston—you may omit the fact that the complications started when I poured three old fashions on top of the damned things and when out with some of the teachers here and poured beer upon the top of these. Let us not slur the liquor, I say.

I am trying to stay put right here in Sol and Sondra's castle most of the time, with Fanny doing the traveling when she comes up on weekends. However I do have to go in once in a while and the next occasion I'll stop by to say hello. Meanwhile, give my best to Mary, Susie and Ben—and of course to Fred-luce-della-casa-Rico.

As ever,
Ralph

To Saul Bellow
November 27, 1958

Dear Sol.

I was finally able to get the tree people after waiting for them to appear for over a month. Two young fellows appeared early one morning and after a half day of scraping drilling and grunting they had the old tree laced into tight intersecting bolts like a fat lady in a corset. They painted the lips of its wound with pitch and its larger roots, located by probing the earth in a wide circumference with a crowbar, were fed with some high-powered plant food. The intention is to strengthen the walls of the wasted trunk until such time as it becomes practical to seal it with plaster, concrete or whatever it is they use. They left a small scoop that they used to mix their medicine, so I suppose we can expect them back before long.

As for leaks, I'm sorry to have to report that one has indeed appeared—or re-appeared, after about two weeks of continuous rain. It is an old one, located just before the window at the rear of the second story hall. I went above, into a graveyard of huge dead and dying flies, and tried to find the source, but it seems to enter from the outside, seeping through the outer wall and I was therefore helpless. However, the rain did produce Sarda—not to work, but out of conscience, or perhaps because I had told Andy Dupee that I doubted his existence. He turned on his bluff charm and explained that he had been very tied up with work and with the loss of his son to the army: and assured me that he would be over to work in three weeks time. This was well before election day but thus far, no Sarda. I am writing this in New York, of course, this being Thanksgiving, so he might appear while I'm down here. I do know that two weeks ago he was working at the Dupees' so perhaps in time he'll come over. High winds blew the other door from the garage and I managed to rehang them temporarily myself but they need more than this, and the rear windows need boarding since the windows have blown. I'll do as much as I can but if this bastard Sarda is to do the things he's supposed to do I wish he'd get started. The weather is freezing now and far too much heat is simply singing away though cracked windowpanes. Tell Sondra to give him the back of her hand.

To continue with household matters. I was confused over the fuel oil payments and sent them a check for the first delivery of oil at the time they sent over another, and they returned it with the explanation that <u>you</u> had taken care of it. Then came Sasha's letter with the electricity bill so I've simply rewritten the check that the oil people returned. I notice that it was overdue and it occurs to me that you might save us both trouble and delays by having the telephone bill turned over to me at the post office. You might do the same with that part of the utilities you wish me to be responsible for. At any rate now that the bills are coming in a bit of reality is making itself felt in my many-storied place of exile and it would be helpful if I had some idea of how much of my Bard money I should put aside each month. (While I remember it, your subscription to *Scientific American* is running out, and so is Sondra's *Gourmet*.)

For all its trails of rain, wind and cold, things go rather well with the house. One of the rubber shock mounts by which the back support of your typing chair is attached to the uprights came apart, but because they were badly designed and had led to many complaints, Fanny was able to get a set of new replacements without cost. I had them on within ten minutes and the chair is now a mite better than when new. Fanny also helped me improvise some drapes for the guest room, and since I spend most of my time there, I plan to get some heavy ones for the study. Sarda drooled at the idea of putting up storm windows all around, but the $600 he quoted is more than I'm likely to have and seems rather high. Anyway, the house is a nice house and for all its loneliness I find it a good place to be. Rufus, who insists that he is no more cat but a Fu-dog, thrives. I've been living to a large extent off my hunting and when he sees me preparing a piece of game he goes into a regular stomp down then tries to snatch it from me. I gave him a rabbit head the other day and the bastard went into a ritual dance, tossing it threatening it, accusing it, daring it to run. If you held your breath while watching him it became quite frightening. Yella Kid Wild, that's him.

The hunting has only been fair this year and poor Lensing's ass is dragging because he hasn't gotten a deer. I have no trouble seeing them, but that's because I don't hunt them. I am rather sad that I haven't seen any ducks within shooting range, but hunting has carried me over much of the land hereabouts and it is so beautiful that I feel fully compensated. Lensing and Dick Bard are sponsoring my application to the Rod and Gun Club and that elder Karamazov, Chandler Chapman has given me permission to hunt his land, so I suppose I'll get to know this country very well indeed.

I'm writing this on the electric portable I told you I planned to buy and I find it even faster than I'd dare hope. I hope Sondra was able to use the

Olivetti, but if not you might wish to trade it. If so, my dealer said that it was worth $55.00 here where they are in fairly good supply. Should this be impracticable don't worry about it, for I'm sure that I can trade it here in the city. Which reminds me that when it snowed the other day I really inspected your snow tires and found them definitely too small for my old bus. Which frustrates me no end since my $156 don't go very far. However Case called us in the other day to reveal that the college had been given $100,000, so it's possible that even so late a comer as I will get enough of an increase to pay for his snow tires. By the way, when I was looking over the tires I found a pair of charcoal slacks which, I'd judge from the waistband, are new. They seem more your size to me but could they be Greg's? . . . They are yours, I've just checked by telephone. Greg's O.K. One final item concerning clothing: How can Rene identify your shoes? She tried but the cobbler had forgotten.

Your report on the growth and variety of Adam's vocabulary amused me no end. And you're quite right about a little shit not hurting anyone, especially writers. But teach Adam the Smasher Ellison's law along with everything else, for not only is it simple and true and easy to remember, he is certain to find it useful along life's unfolding terrain: Shit flows up-hill.

Love to Sasha and tell her that I'm writing in the next day or so. What, by the way, did you two hot-blooded young things wear when you slept in that handsome icebox of a bedroom in winter, Eskimo parkas and baby bunting rabbit pants? The hounds of winter race through there now with no traces a-tall! No wonder Adam has all that energy; he had to have it to outrun those hounds. Regards to Jack and tell him they're still discussing his tenure at the college.

Love,
Ralph

To the Editor of *Time* Magazine
BARD COLLEGE,
ANNANDALE-ON-HUDSON,
NEW YORK
NOVEMBER 27, 1958

The Editor
Time.
Time & Life Building,
9 Rockefeller Plaza
New York 20, N.Y.

Dear Sir:

I was surprised to return from a hard afternoon of hunting the domestic cornfields around Tivoli, New York to learn from TIME'S Alien Corn piece that I am allegedly self-exiled in Rome.* May I inform you that your report is, to say the least, exaggerated? Actually, I returned to the U.S. a year and two months ago—not from voluntary exile, "for social and political causes," as Richard Gibson's rhetoric would have it, but from a stay at the American Academy in Rome; which was my privilege as winner of the 1955 Fellowship in Literature granted by the American Academy of Arts and Letters. Admittedly, two years may seem a long time to be away from this swiftly changing country even for purposes of broadening one's personal culture—which is the aim of the fellowship—but exile is, fortunately (and even for Negro Americans) largely a state of mind. As such I don't think it should be confused with the American's right to live wherever he wishes without having his feelings about this country put to question. Indeed, it is possible to live abroad for good reasons and to remain at home for bad ones.

My wife and I found living in Rome a wonderful experience and a welcome relief from the racial stresses of American life, but neither the artistic glories of its past nor the social felicities that were so generously extended us there got to us with quite the immediacy of the news that broke in Montgomery, Alabama. Yet during my time in Europe I had more than

* The November 17, 1958, issue of *Time* magazine contained a piece called "Amid the Alien Corn," in which Ellison and Richard Wright were each described as "Negro artists and writers" living in self-imposed exile. Ellison's letter was published by *Time* in the February 9, 1959, issue.

one white American tourist assume that he saw the stigmata of the exile on me and thus felt challenged to take a moral position toward my presence there. Some were apologetic, as though my presence in Europe was an accusation and a rejection of them personally. One or two reacted like a white Southerner trying to intimidate a Negro tenant who had packed up to try his luck in the North into remaining on the old plantation. And others felt compelled to give my assumed exile their rather hush-hush moral sanction. "If I were a Negro, I'd never go back to the States," they'd whisper. But in fact, my wife and I were so little concerned with thoughts of exile that we didn't even have our New York telephone disconnected.

On such matters as these, Gibson, whom I don't know, should speak for himself for the issues that claim one's heart and intellect are most personal. Thus while I sympathize with those Negro Americans whose disgust with the racial absurdities of American life leads them to live elsewhere, my own needs—both as citizen and as artist, make the gesture of exile seem mere petulance. Nor do I find Negro Americans who exploit the racial tragedy of our people for the entertainment of the French any less odious than those professional white southern literary men who go about Europe preaching the high value of that segregated and stultifying South in which they've avoided living since the early 1920s; both protest too strongly. As writers I should think the question of where one lives would be secondary to the question of where one is most creative. Faulkner writes with great creativity in Mississippi; Hemingway and Henry James wrote well in Europe; Richard Wright wrote better in Chicago and Brooklyn than he has in Paris. Let the writer go where he works well and if he goes stale in one place let him try another. Personally I am too vindictively American, too full of hate for the hateful aspects of this country, and too possessed by the things I love here to be too long away.

I am waiting for the publication of Gibson's novel with keen interest and I hope his life in Paris has allowed him to give full scope to his talents. Meanwhile I hope it will help his perspective to learn that even before I left Rome I was invited to join the faculties of Brandeis University and Bennington College; that on my return I was offered a position on the staff of a well-known national magazine; that I refused a position writing copy for a large electronics concern. I am at present a visiting lecturer in English at Bard College, a position that allows me maximum time for work on my novel-in-progress and for journalism, as well as affording me meaningful contact with a younger generation of Americans. This by no means solves the race question and its significance is for the most part personal. Yet the individual <u>does</u> count for something and these offers to one individual indicate that quite a number of institutions have made at least a token start toward eliminating those humiliations which revolt me, I assure him, no less than they do Gibson.

Sincerely
Ralph Ellison

Copy to Max Gissen.*

To Saul Bellow
MARCH 18, 1959

Dear Saul,

So much has happened since the arrival of your letter that I'm glad I didn't answer immediately. You shouldn't, however, believe for one moment that your *Times Book Review* piece had anything to do with my delay. Several of us who had read *Henderson*† had a big laugh at the Book Award ceremonies over your getting the jump on the critics with that that piece. And I must say that they fell straight into the trap. Anyway <u>I'm</u> primarily a writer of narrative, flimflam, and corn, and believe that if fiction possesses these symbols (or conscious symbolism) [they] are but a house without foundation; nevertheless, if we switch to music I find I like contrapuntal styles, where the chords (symbols) are accidental, emerging from the several voice lines sounding at once above the old narrative ground bass—no less than I like the hydrophonic forms, where the mingled melody determines the chordial structures which underlie it. I'd better stop right here before I think this through and tear it up. Anyway, as Albert Murray likes to say, argument is argument but a master is a fucking <u>master</u>; he mixes the modes and makes the materials bend to his masterly will. Beyond that a writer must, as you say, keep his shit about him. I had a great time with *Henderson,* thought it masterly performance and my only complaint is that I felt it came to its end too quickly. I wanted to continue reading, which, considering the fact that I had to read it while I was doing the last of the Book award pile, is quite a tribute; for I was damn near exhausted. I'm just back from the Middlebury lecture, where I took advantage of questions put me during the panel discussion to

---

* Gissen was the book editor at *Time.*

† Bellow's novel, *Henderson the Rain King* (1959).

give old *Henderson* a plug. Arthur Healy, who is an odd ball after my own heart, sends you his regards. It went very well up there, by the way, for which thanks as I was in great need of the dough. I've been asked to Bread Loaf come August, so it looks as though you've gotten me started on the circuit again. I won't go into the judging of the Book Awards here other than to say that most of the deliberations broke down to my arguing Alfred out of his desire to be fashionable. He sat there and turned on that great flow of words of his and was just about to convince himself that *Lolita* was just about the greatest novel and the most flawless novel he'd ever read.* Thank God <u>that's</u> over and I hope I'm hit with a typewriter if I get mixed up with that part of the award again . . . I was pleased no end that the biggest gravy train of them all had slowed down for you to hop on just at the time when you were about to take off on the yak-yak circuit for dough. I don't know to what extent this changes your plans, however I'm willing to stay with the house as long as you think it practical. Up until the trip in to New York for the book circus I was writing quite well, with new material flowing from the typewriter with that wild ease which makes me keep trying through the long periods of difficulty and uncertainty, so the place is definitely a good place for me to work. However, I now have some idea of what it costs to keep the place going during the winter and I feel guilty that you've paid for so much of my comfort here. Thank God I have the day at Bard to help things along. I've been more than earning my pay there, but I'm afraid that the place is so lax that little of it will mean anything. They allowed me to set up a two-semester course and then allowed students to drop out at the end of the first—which makes no sense to me, since the lectures are cumulative. Protect us from tired cynicism. Something has been said about my continuing next year but I've made no commitments. What I'd like to do is finish the first draft by August then see what kind of advance my publishers would be willing to lay out while I worked it into final shape. As far as the house itself things go well enough. Jack Wheeler is working on the stairs and the eighteen inches of snow which fell over the 12th and 13th seem to have done no damage other than that I would miss the Middlebury talkfest, but succeeded in getting a taxi at the last minute. I solved the problem of Rufus by feeding him heavily before I left and then placing dishes of food in various rooms with the doors closed just enough to require the added strength of hunger for him to open them—

---

* Alfred Kazin, the eminent American literature critic who served with Ellison on the judges' panel of the National Book Award in 1959. Although Kazin favored Nabokov's *Lolita,* Ellison argued strenuously and successfully for Bernard Malamud's *The Magic Barrel.*

which, being the gatto con il motto (Mange bene, caca forte, vida longo) he did and was in fine shape when I returned. If, by the way, the vet sent a bill to you it was a mistake and should have come to me. Rufus was coughing like a fat old man and I thought he might have worms so I left him to be wormed and boarded when I went into the city to help pick the award book; I've found it better to leave him there to be boarded than to depend upon the Staib kid or someone at the college. It costs me a buck a day and I don't have to worry about him being hit by a car. Anyway, I've only been into the city twice since you were there. So send me that bill and don't worry about Rufus, he had no worms and I suspect the coughing comes from the hair of small game or from the burrs which I've seen him pulling from his fur and eating. The news about Sasha was disturbing to both Fanny and I and terribly sobering. I'm glad nevertheless, that you know what it is and no longer have to clash in the dark. Just the same, I suspect that whatever its source you have need of Sondra's passion and intensity; the trick is to keep it in bounds. And surely we, you and I, must be as nutty as Cal Lowell or Berryman or Roethke, we just aren't the type to enjoy exploiting it. Mythomania compels me to seek extreme relationships as a means of affirming our reality. Thus we fight and argue and produce wild fictions inhabited by wild men. But perhaps we're really hopelessly sane, and our wives with or without lesions, can only take a bit of us without blowing their tops. But at least both you and Sasha have been productive during all your trouble and I think you should keep that in mind. By the way, I told Rufus that Adam was returning and he's been practicing climbing trees every morning. He got started when der Hagopian and her boy friend spent a weekend with us (it was his dad's caddy, and don't worry about it, they're rich as hell and the old man's a Federal judge) and brought their police dog along. Rufus chased him cringing up the stairs a couple of times, and once, under the dining table, he rose upon his hind legs and, using his paws like a boxer bent upon cutting an opponent to ribbons, slashed the great dog across his nose a couple of time. Outside it went the other way, with Rufus taking to the trees, finally to forget the dog and lie along a limb like a mountain lion in wait for an unwary deer. Sondra writes that you'll be here during late May and I can't wait to see Adam . . . You mentioned the typewriter but why make a settlement, why don't you take it in exchange for the ide box which you gave us? It's not quite fair to you but it would be less embarrassing to me. So if Sasha likes it, it's yours . . . Dammit, the cook isn't ready yet but I'll get him to you as soon as Fanny has time to type him. Remember, however, that he's quite rough and I'd like to work him over after you've read him—providing of course that you find him interesting. Thanks for the comments on the jazz piece, before long I'll have enough such pieces to make a small book and I'd like you to look at them critically when I start compiling. There is such a mixture of language in them that I'd like your opinion. Anyway, you can't really write about jazz without touching more important aspects of our cultural life—that's why Wm. Phillips and McDonald are so amusing when they write about popular culture. I've been outraging some members of my class by stressing that Mark Twain was a figure of popular culture and they're reacting as though I were trying to crap them. What a wonderful mixed-up bunch of self-deniers we are! By the way, after the semester at Bard the good manners of the kids at Middlebury—among themselves as well as with teachers—came as a shock. What's more, they seemed brighter than our poor schmucks hereabouts . . . I can't remember the title of the Tolstoi story you suggested that I read, what was it?

Now that I've time for my own reading I'd like to get to all those things you suggested, such as the Lawrence and the Walcott. I'm also thinking quite seriously of writing a short novel next time, something requiring no more than a year to finish. I was embarrassed as all hell when the M.C. at the book ceremony felt it necessary to credit me with a whole slew of books when she introduced me. Seriously though, I have several ideas that might best be handled in the shorter form without exhausting their possibility of being developed in later books. I'll talk with you about it later on. Meantime, let me say again that I'm happy for your grant and for the impact which *Henderson* is having. And most of all, let me say that reading it affirms for me some of things I'm trying to do and this is far more important to me than anything the critics might say, either pro or con. Doubtlessly, we're moving toward an emancipation of our fiction from the clichés of recent styles and limitations of conception. Just keep plunging ahead because there's no turning back and if only a few readers appreciate what you're doing it's only because they're trying to read the book they read ten years ago. You've done it neatly this time: you've written what you wanted to write in the way you've discovered to write it <u>and</u> you've moved on to tell them how to read what you've written. It's a shame that you have to spoon-feed literate readers, but they are, after all, literal-minded and we'd might as well accept this as a fact. For some the <u>critics</u> too, otherwise they'd all be heroes answering the riddle of the Sphinx. Love to Sasha and Adam.

Ralph

To Jack Ludwig
TIVOLI,
APRIL 23, 1959

Dear Jack,*

The news about the magazine, title and all, has me spinning. Keith was trying, for some reason, to get me in N.Y. so that when he called me here there was no time to tell me much—although in his best Madison Avenue style—and I've been waiting for Sol to show to learn the details. Surely there'll be something of mine in the first issue although the Sea Cook has begun to grow and is most unorganized. Saul's coming out here and we'll see at that time . . . As for developments concerning you here I'm very much in the dark. I have yet to attend a divisional meeting and although Fred Dupee says he hears you're out all I get from Artine are questions as to what you intended doing the coming year. Yesterday Ted W. asked if I would take on half time teaching the Russian Novel and four advisees. I'm still undecided. I did hear that Helen Chapman had tried to see you in Puerto Rico when she was there recently—whether for reasons of business or friendship I have no idea. As you may gather, I've tried to stay as far from the hot little underworld of the place as I possibly can. Man, but you've had a time of it these last months and I hope things have started flowing for the brighter shores. If there's anything I can do here please let me know. Once I had a fairly decent evil eye, though God knows things have been bad enough what with the loss of a co-ed in an auto accident and the loss of Orent in a fire. A firebug is suspected but developments are being kept quiet. Good luck with your work and regards to Les and Susie.

Best,
Ralph

---

* Jack Ludwig, a teacher at Bard, and others were starting a journal to be called *The Noble Savage*. Editor-in-chief Saul Bellow published the prologue and much of the Hickman and Bliss book of Ellison's novel-in-progress as the lead piece in the inaugural issue in 1960.

To Albert Murray
730 RIVERSIDE DRIVE,
NEW YORK 31, N. Y.
JUNE 27, 1959

Dear Albert,

I went through my commencement as 'teacher' on last Saturday afternoon and it's taken me this long to recover enough to get down to doing what I should have done months ago: write you a letter. It has been a most interesting year, full of irritations and discoveries; progress on the novel and a definite deep[en]ing of my perception of the themes which I so blindly latched on to. I guess old Hickman is trying to make a man out of me—at this late date. I've also been subjecting myself to the discipline of isolation, living alone most of the time doing my own house work and laundry; playing around with French cooking so as not to lapse into eating out of cans and, like a 19th century Englishman living in Africa, have been doing the thing completely, including wines with my meals and desserts which I made for myself. I was also splitting logs for the fireplace and hunting more or less successfully in the snow. Naturally Fanny came up for the weekends but I grew to dread the loss of time in the City and indeed, this is my first trip down in over three months. As soon as I can clean up some of the scenes a bit I'll send them along for your opinion.

For the better part of the year has been the way the novel has been going. I read publicly for the first time before students and teachers there, and at the end of two hours they were still in a trance. Old Hickman had them, man; the few Christians, the Jews and all. You would have laughed your ass off to see that old downhome Moses rhetoric work. It's not too difficult to observe when Mahalia cuts loose at such places as Newport, but most of the jazz fans don't possess the vocabulary to translate it into their own terms—since most have no religion, no sense of literature or art, no way of their own of focusing and coming to grips with profound feeling—but it's more difficult to reduce Hickman's sermons to mere entertainment; that old bastard knows how to get under even so initiated and tough skin as mine. He preaches gut, and that comes from depths and admits no absolute control. All I can do is ask him hard questions and write down his acts and his answers . . .

As for the teaching, I guess I'm beginning to learn some of the things you've known for a long time. It went rather well, but I was appalled with how ignorant some of these bright, progressive school products can actually be—not only in Literature, but of life. They wear beards and let their unwashed tits bounce around in their low-cut blouses and are still, literally, chewing bubble gum. I'm told that I'm a popular teacher, but if so I did it the hard way around. They all expect to be entertained but I played the dozens <u>at</u> them and signified about them in so many different ways that I don't think they found many places to hide from confronting the connection between their identities, social and personal, and the major concerns of the American novel. I wasn't nice at all. I hit them with their ignorance of the experience and their easy smugness towards the South, then tried to shake some of the shit out of their vague and inflated notions concerning the superiority of European fiction. I must say that they took it well enough—once they found that they couldn't out argue me, and following the last class they caucused at the rear of the room then called my attention to something they'd written on the blackboard "YOU WERE RIGHT ABOUT THAT DAMN CIVIL WAR!" I know Bard is something of a special case but the picture I get of what the American whites who matured during the thirties are doing to their children is frightening. We were, and are, penalized out of the irrationalities of race, but these poor kids are suffering from the excesses of their parents' sentimentality and utter lack of any grasp of the tragic sense. They have little discipline and they think that the world is simply waiting to pat them on the head. At least we got more than that out of Tuskegee, as bad as it was. When I see some of the Negro kids there—interestingly enough none signed for my class or stopped me for a conversation—imitating the whites I wonder where the country will be in thirty years. I signed to teach six hours next year, adding a course in the Russian Novel to the American—so maybe I'll make some contact with the Negroes and try to give them some sense of those things from their backgrounds which they must not lose.

Which reminds me of how right you are about Basie and the sound of his band, doubtlessly his arranger has been selected for him because he sure isn't any hell. I've been listening to jazz from two a.m. to 4, when I find it difficult to sleep and I must say that it's become hard listening. Somebody needs to come along and take the curse of Charlie Parker off the whole crowd because most of it is bird-shit. One of the kids at Bard who plays at being disc jockey came over one afternoon with a pile of records and I thought I'd die before he finished playing that pitiful blat of misplaced ambition and ego. I spent the rest of the evening play[ing] Duke to cleanse the atmosphere. I'm sorry that I don't have your letters here with me so that I could comment on the Jazz mags you referred to, I don't remember which they were, but I have been seeing the *Jazz Review,* in which I've found the interviews of older jazzmen valuable and most of the critical writing more useful for exposing the vapidity of the writers than for any insights it offers into the art. I'm still being asked to do jazz articles but at the moment I'm not at all displeased that I'm too busy to bother. Nevertheless I'm still planning to put together a book of essays. Right now I'm working up a piece on Negroes and Southern fiction, titled *The Seer and the Seen* for an anthology edited by some southern boys and scheduled by Anchor. If this goes well I'll use it along with the other stuff. I've been finding interesting things in Hemingway and Fitzgerald that might well work into a broader piece on the same subject. When you start lifting up that enormous stone, the Civil war, that's kept so much of the meaning of life in the north hidden, you begin to see that Mose is in the center of a junk pile as well as in the center of the cotton boll. All the boys who try to escape this are simply running from the problem of value—which is why those old Negroes whom I'm trying to make Hickman represent are so confounding, they never left the old original briar patch. You can't understand Lincoln or Jefferson without confronting them . . .

Mort mailed me some stories by one of the Tuskegee students, but they're mostly in longhand, which makes me more reluctant then usual to read them. I shall however, and I hope this kid is good enough to take such advantage. If he's not I intend to give him hell. And speaking of Mort reminds me that I have recently been to Hamilton College on two occasions, first to lecture at their art center a couple of months ago—which went so well that when we returned last week to attend the 79th birthday party of a most remarkable woman, the Dean greeted me with "Welcome home." No doubt part of my success there had to do with my speaking of my connection with Hamilton through Sprague and Frank Taylor, who is very active there now, and secondarily, through Pound and Woollcott (Alex). Taylor had been the favorite of Grace Root, whose husband's family has been so important in the history of the college (as well as in the government) and through him we've become warm friends. She's one of those alive, tough independent women who does what she wants to do, whether it's giving land, money, house and guidance for an art center, or going out of the way places in search for new species of primroses to hybridize, she's in her sixties now but last visit we put everyone else to bed while we sat knocking off bottles of red wine and discussing everything from Negro schools to religion. Her husband was Edward Root, the art collector who was so important to American painting, of which the house has excellent examples. We'll have to drive up there when you and Mokie come this way, it's most beautiful and Hamilton is a pocket of wonderful old American types who are amazingly alive as is the old lady I mentioned earlier. She is the first woman to attend Oxford, once taught at Hamilton herself and still uses a couple of the brightest students as readers—her eyes are about gone—who she proceeds to turn into first class scholars. I'm told she knows more about myth than Joe Campbell. Certainly she's one of the most alert and witty women I've ever met. I was placed at her left during the party—which was attended by people from all over the country—and I was never bored a second. Her husband taught chemistry and was the great hybridizer of peonies, a work and business that is still carried on by one of the daughters. It's amazing what you find when you break the confines of the New York literary world; up there some of the old Yankee strength is still expressing itself and thus far I've found none of that embarrassing phoniness which clings to the most authentic white Southern aristocrats. Memory is still alive, both personal and historical, and without the sickness which marks the south. I plan to explore such areas further. Now I know something of the Northern Jews and the Southern Jews of at least two generations, and something of all kinds of Moses so I guess it's time to get some idea of the various New England groups . . .

Which reminds me that you asked if I knew people on the West coast; unfortunately I don't, but Bellow said to introduce yourself to Gene Fowler* as his friend and that you would meet dam near every one worth knowing through him. The same goes for Henry Miller. I'm still working on this and will send you names as I come to them . . . What are you up to this summer? I hope you'll have time to get some writing done and it's good news that you've worked out certain problems. Why don't you get some of your jazz stuff down? *Esquire* pays dam well and they need such material. Incidentally, I've been asked to take part in a seminar on literature that they're running out at Iowa next fall; I'm part of the fiction faculty at Bread Loaf during August. Bellow has set up something for me at Chicago during the Winter—and I'm the chief American delegate to the P.E.N. congress at Frankfurt and Heidelberg next month. I'll stay no more than ten days and then right back and to work. I'm not sure but I think that being away from the interruptions of N.Y. and under the pressure of weekly lectures at the college I've gotten more writing done. I guess I'm

---

* West Coast journalist and novelist.

such a natural bum that if I took a job coal heaving I'd turn out a master-piece just so I could goof off. What we must do before too long is Spain; all of us with enough time to soak in some of it. I had my class roaring when by making some cultural point I told them about us and the luggage on the Lido: "Hell, man, we come from a long line of Red Caps!" which reminds me, if you ever think of teaching again this time it must be some-where where you can do some good and everywhere I go and they like <u>my</u> kind I bring you into it. You've got the degrees so it shouldn't be any trouble at all. I don't know how long I'll work at this game but I certainly don't wish to get in too far for all the good it's seemed to have done me. Bellow, who with his family is back in Tivoli, intends to continue teaching part time and writing the rest. He's very much sought after as a teacher and Min.* has made things very pleasant for him. Respectability is the very devil to escape these days but I go on outraging quite a number of people just by being me. One of the fellows in the English Dept. is married to an Arkansas gal who has been trying to make it as a jazz singer and who professes to love Negroes, etc. Well, last winter at a party he flipped when someone shook hands with him and left him holding an ice cube. Being a Mexican, he thought his manhood was being questioned and although a small man he wanted to break up the joint. So I sat on him and talked him almost sober—when his wife told me to sit down and, when I asked her what was wrong, she called me a nigger. No, I didn't kick her butt (he jumped sober as a judge, by the way), but I told her that I could quite calmly kick her all the way to Little Rock but instead I simply wanted her to kiss me. It was something and I'm sure she'd rather I had struck her or at least become angry, and realized later tha[t] I'd been pretty sadistic by remaining calm. It was all so unmotivated, seemingly, that the psycholo-gist at whose home the incident took place still hasn't figured it out. And oddly enough, I think he distrusts <u>me</u> because he doesn't know where I put that provocation. But hell, we grow up at some point and the poor woman wasn't striking primarily at me, she was trying to drag her hus-band. Poor woman, now every time she sees me she's in trouble.

Well, this shows you how my time has been going. I started this on the 27th and now here it is the 17th and I'm packing to unass the area this evening. In the interim I've been working frantically on the book, trying to complete a section while the emotion was still strong within me. I guess I must be nearing the completion, recently the typewriter has been drawing

* University of Minnesota.

me like a magnet. Bellow has read book two and is to publish about fifty pages in a new mag that he is editing—*The Noble Savage*—of all things! I'm a contributing editor and it's paying 5 cents a word . . . I'll keep you posted on this as it develops . . . Before breaking this off let me say that I went down to look at the delegates to the N.A.A.C.P. convention yesterday and I must say that the mixture is as before—only now the clothes are more expensive and there are more young people around. I don't know what I was doing exactly, but it was quite meaningful to simply stand there in the lobby and feel them moving and talking around me. Hell, I know what we want, I just like to hear the idiom. Fifteen minutes in a meeting with some of those studs and I'd want to start a fight, but just seeing them walk and pose and talk and flirt and woof—that's damn pleasant.

Take it easy, man; I'll write you when I return. Love to Mokie and Mique.

As ever,
Ralph

To Morteza Sprague
730 RIVERSIDE DRIVE
NEW YORK 31, N.Y.,
JULY 17, 1959.

Dear Mort,

I had quite a lot to say about you during a talk I gave at Hamilton College a few weeks ago. I had been invited there by Grace Root (who as you'll probably remember, is the widow of Edward), to lecture at the new arts center, and I was able to tie my career rather closely to that college. First there was you and our talks at Tuskegee, discussions of Pound and, I think, Alexander Walcott; then there was Frank Taylor, the publisher who gave me my first contract. Taylor, who is still our friend, introduced us to Mrs. Root and to many of the old timers whom you must have known during your time there. It went very well and we have since returned for the joint birthday party of the remarkable ninety-seven year old Mrs. Saunders— she whose husband was the authority of peony culture—and who at her late age is as alert and far more witty than most youngsters of twenty—and Mrs. Root. It is such a beautiful section of the state and the people are so refreshing that I feel sure that we'll return there as often as possible. I attended a class in the novel and I must say that the boys are quite bright, and much better read than some of my wild ones down at Bard College.

Thank God the whole country hasn't been blighted by the self-indulgent type of progressive education that is so common around New York City.

When Fanny told me over the telephone (I am spending most of my time writing up at Tivoli, N.Y.) that you had sent me some student's stories I was quite pleased and anticipated reading them when I returned to the city. Now, however, I am returning the stories unread—not because my interest in what a younger writer might be attempting is less intense, but only that I won't encourage a beginner to break one of the first rules governing the relations between writers and editorial readers: all mss. must be typed double-spaced. He might not realize it but even Faulkner observes this rule and I see no reason that he be excused. If he wishes to return his stories to me typed and enclosing a self-addressed and stamped envelope, I'll be happy to read his stories and give him my reactions. Indeed, I'll be as careful with his work as I shall have to be with my own students at Bread Loaf during August.

I hope things are well with you there and that I'll see you before long. As for me, I'm still fighting with my work-in-progress—which is well along now—and I'm leaving this evening for a couple of weeks in Germany,* after which I'll return, spend two weeks at the Breadloaf conference, and then prepare to return to my one day a week of visiting lecturing at Bard. I'm teaching a course in the American novel and another in the novels of Dostoevsky and Gogol. Some stuff this, and I suspect the intense reading which teaching requires is proving more rewarding to me than to the students.

I haven't heard from Albert in a few months, I've been too involved to answer his letter but I'm taking care of that this morning. I wish it were possible for the three of us to get together before long <u>somewhere</u> in this wide, wide country. Til then let me hear from you once in a while and please give my regards to the old timers.

As ever,
Ralph

To Albert Murray
[JULY 17, 1959]
This is just to show you that the mag is really in the works. I started this letter on the 17th, but had to stop in order to prepare 50 pages of my ms. for the first issue. I'll send you a copy when it's ready.

---

* From July 22 to 25, 1959, Ellison attended the PEN International Congress in Frankfurt, Germany.

AUGUST 1959

Dear Albert,

Your letter gave me much pleasure. It arrived while I was still up on Bread Loaf Mountain exhausting myself with two weeks of alleged teaching of alleged writers and an even larger gang who don't write but who hang around such conferences for the sake of entertainment. Of course they pay their dough and the staff is supposed to do everything to keep them happy. Nothing too demanding, understand. I worked my ass off for less money than I pull down, once in a while at least, for a single lecture; but even though Fanny's expenses were thrown in, the mountain was not bread, but a stone, I came down from there in a fairly sour mood, wondering how I had strayed so far on top of Robert Frost's Kilimanjaro; yes, and wondering why I ever had the idea that a porter's job was so undesirable. Then I found your letter with its fine description of your judging that drill competition. It snatched me back to Oklahoma to the time when that same type of mad drillmaster had the kids drilling on the school ground every late spring and summer evening when the weather was good. Sometimes we'd be there marching in the moonlight, and sometimes we'd be there to watch the men dressed in Knights of Pythan uniforms, going through their maneuvers on nights so dark that you saw hardly more than their plumed hats, their silverex belts, steel scabbards and the gleaming shapes of their swords, which they held blades forward against their shoulders as they moved. They were either members of the Odd fellows, the Shriners, the Uniformed Ranks (!) or the Elks—here I mean the drillmasters who grabbed us kids—it really didn't matter because most of those guys belonged to all the lodges anyway. And quite a number were vets of both the Spanish American and World Wars. As I write I realize why I lost my attraction for things military so early. Hell, by the time I was thirteen I'd had my legs drilled wrong side out and we knew so many fancy formations and had been threatened, cursed and cajoled so often that we might have slipped a West Point squadron on dress parade, and no one would have known the difference—except that we were doing all that swinging you described, even before we had any need to learn the Palmer house. Our ankles were still in good condition and only a few had corns (although most could have been called 'Stinky Dog' with justice and precision, since we lived in tennis shoes). Nevertheless, we had all the native movements, including the P.I. limp and the one-butt shuffle. We'd had it all drilled in, like Ivy League boys now have their white buck shoes with the <u>dirt</u> machined in. Those old guys were mad for drill, and no kid of a certain height was safe from their enthusiasm. I can see them now on some far distant dead occasion at Slaughter's Hall, dressed in white flannel, going through those pin wheeling formations over the polished dance floor; their canes (phallic rifles, magic wands) exploding against the floor like a fusillade of rifle fire whenever the drill-master turned, eyes closed like a magician disparaging the whole disgusting triumph over the low-down, ignorant, intractable material now transformed by the sheer Joycean mastery of a stud who in a world of justice would have been a five star general at the very least. Come to think of it, I probably embraced the difficult discipline of the trumpet just so that I could escape those cats. I didn't though, because after I joined the school band one or two would come over to the school ground to mess with us on late fall afternoons, teaching us formations we used between the halves of football games. Some of the granny-dodgers were as mad as Capt. Drye, only none had actually reached his rank in the armed forces. Our band used to accompany their drill teams to such battle-and-playing fields as Wichita and Topeka, and once as far as Denver. That time it was with the Elks, who held their Western Convention there and who featured two events, an oratorical contest—which was won by one of my classmates—and the drill contest. There was a woman's auxiliary too, man, and what with the drinking, the sweating and the signifying, it was truly a funky row. They shuffled and ruffled and danced and pranced; some were tight and others were clowning and kidding the whole idea of what they were doing to a military form, discipline, pose, you name it—so that the occasion had everything; comedy and satire well as the tension of tough competition. I can still see some of those tall, Watusi-looking Moses, wearing capes and fezzes and leaning on a pivot like a stagecoach taking a sharp curve, their shoulders touching, their faces skimming across a cymbal lightly. Yes, and the enormous hall now so quiet that even a deaf man could hear all that scuffing leather beneath the commands of the drillmaster. I suppose there was the usual Negro yearning for ceremony and identification in it, and a feeling of potentiality and a threat—along with the joy in formalized, swinging movement. Whatever, I'm glad I lived through that phase and you brought it all back again. The cream of it was, of course, you and the other judges knowing both idioms, the military and the Negro, and that made it an especially rich juxtaposition. Why don't we do something along this line for publication, perhaps as an exchange of letters? I'm sure it would be taken by someone, especially if we pointed out the relationship to jazz. Think about it anyway . . . I wondered where the hell you were, but I wouldn't have guessed the Panhandle in a million years. You want to keep loose, as old Satchel advises, or the AF will gain [on] you. Something always does; I went farting off to Germany for the P.E.N. and simply wasted my working energy; and teaching is a drag even though teaching the Russian novel along with a class in American lit. is rather stimulating. I've been terribly sick with the after effects of hay fever which has left me too tired to even enjoy the hunting season. I can see a flock of about fifty geese going over just now. We've had a very late summer here but with those boys going over in broad daylight, winter isn't far behind them. Anyway, don't let them tie you down too closely . . . I agree that Van Vechten is much more present in the fiction of the twenties than we stop to think nowadays and in fact Mailer would be quite surprised to see that the crap he's selling is actually V's leavings . . . I missed the *Anatomy of a Murder* records, but we've picked up the others and will soon get the newly announced *Back to Back* on which Duke and Rabbit* play the blues. He's still the best all right, while that poor Basie flounders around in that big tubby band like a fly tying to take off from a piece of flypaper. And most of the other stuff one hears is teen-age embarrassment and bird shit. When so many musicians can stand up in public and make their horns sound so miserable and self-pitying, castrated and flat, something awful must be happening in the country; something no one has named or even begun to grasp. The stuff sounds gutless and homo—like Lester† looked that morning I saw him switching down to 145th St., but not like he ever sounded. What's most distressing is that so many of these cats are Negroes who seem as much disorganized by a little acceptance as those L.A. Moses are by a little comfort. And just look at the color photos on the record sleeves. It's as though Van Vechten has moved out from his photo-castration of a few so-called poets and classical musicians and taken on the whole world of Negro jazz. It looks as though these guys are doing to themselves, out of self-hate and a child-like assertion, exactly what all the years of slavery and second-class citizenship couldn't do—they've killed their own rich Negro sense of life and become zombies. Thank God for Old Duke.

I've been thinking hard about getting out to see you and the girls, but thus far I don't see just how we'll do it. I've a lecture offered me at Chicago

---

*   Johnny Hodges, Duke Ellington's alto sax player.

†   Lester Young, saxophonist in Count Basie's orchestra and in combos of his own.

Uni in May and I might keep flying west at that time, and I've got to be at Iowa during the first week in Dec. for a gabfest by *Esquire*—but none of this would allow for Fanny to come along, nor, since I'll still be teaching, would there be sufficient time. I'll keep working on it because we'd really like to see you before too long and I'd also like to drop in on Herbert. Perhaps we could drive out during the summer, but my car is getting mighty old. We've been promised a larger apartment in our building and if it comes through we'll at least be able to put you up whenever you hit New York again. We've simply outgrown the present place and it has begun to drag me so much that I get depressed every time I go into the city. I try to have Fanny spend as many weekends up here as possible. Here I simply rattle around in all that space, smoke the endless cigars and talk to myself and the cat. He thinks I'm still crazy and by now he plays the dozens better than I do. Saul has offered to let me buy the house because his wife doesn't really like the country but not only do I not have the dough, I'm not so sure that Fanny would want to be this far from the city. So I'm enjoying it while I can. The air is winey now from the apple orchards, the herds of sheep drift into the meadow in front of the house as night falls and I've taken to puttering with the houseplants. The garden I planted in the spring turned out well under Saul's cultivation during the summer, and even this late I have more squash, eggplant, peppers and tomatoes than I know what to do with. But best of all, I'm able to get some work done. The only thing that's really wrong with it is that there are no Moses to keep me tuned in. Speaking of the West coast though, I'm afraid that I'd have the sense that I'd run out of space—unless I took some lessons in walking the water. Because just as a man has to have his own pony I have to have the feeling that I can still take off. Maybe that's what's bothering those L.A. Moses, they've run out of psychological running space. Tell Mokie and Mique to watch that stuff because one thing we can't stand is being crowded. By the way, I hear that Archie Moore is playing Nigger Jim, and I saw Althea Gibson playing a slave in the *Horse Soldiers,** so I guess pretty soon somebody will decide to do Faulkner's *The Unvanquished* and cast Wilt-the-Stilt Chamberlain as Ringo—and if that so-and-so, Sugar Ray wasn't so greedy he could have played Pip in the recent *Moby-Dick* . . .

Before I forget, we're asking for information concerning Mique's dance. I can't believe that she's in the 11th grade although the math thing sounds just like me. Next thing we know, she'll have grown beyond all recogni-

---

* A 1959 film directed by John Ford.

tion, certainly as far as the little kid we first saw goes. We'd better get out there fast. Take it easy and keep me posted on developments and I'll send you the news from here as it develops. Fanny sends love to you all, as do I.

Ralph

To Mr. Sydney Spiegel
730 RIVERSIDE DRIVE
NEW YORK 31, NEW YORK
DECEMBER 13, 1959

Dear Mr. Spiegel:

I hope you have endured your ordeal and I apologize for taking so long to write.

I must say that your letter is perhaps the most interesting that I have received concerning the effect of *Invisible Man* upon a reader. And not only interesting but, at this distance, hilarious. What a situation! Mrs. Ella Pride, who seems bent upon living up to her name but making a nuisance of herself, and a preacher who wishes to out-Bledsoe Dr. Bledsoe. The only suggestion I can make, since it is impossible for me to confront the lady on her own ground, is that you give careful consideration as to whether such people really should be introduced to education. I say this facetiously but the question is serious. I cannot ignore such people when I survey the world I know, but after I have written, I can only hope that they will understand and ignore them if they do not.

As for my racial identity, you may say to her that I am not only Negro but out of a Methodist home; that I did not intend to offend anyone, even her, but to present a picture of a certain phase of American life as I know it, with people speaking, thinking and acting in such manner as I know to be true. That if she believes that such people do not exist and that they do not exist even in Cheyenne, then her religion should take her out into the street and she should pray that her eyes be opened and that her ears be quickened and she have the courage to face the truth and the understanding which comes of charity.

As for Reverend Campbell, I know too much about the inner workings of an Afro-Methodist-Episcopal church to have even to be annoyed with him. It isn't pleasant to be called a traitor even by a man I've never met, but he should be very careful since it is just possible that he wouldn't stand up too well under scrutiny. Indeed, I'm made curious by his recklessness and his lack of grace.

At any rate, if the book is censored in Cheyenne, I shall turn the matter over to the American Book Publishers Association, who are well skilled in putting such petty censors in their places.

Naturally I did not write the book to degrade anyone and certainly not my own group, which would be to degrade myself. Nor did I write it to falsify reality or to present the kind of picture that might please Mrs. Pride or the Reverend Campbell. I wrote it in an attempt to give meaningful form to a body of experience which is much more chaotic and complex and tragically human and real than most of the solutions that are offered to deal with it— including that proffered by narrow, ignorant clergymen. I believe the picture presented in *Invisible Man* is a true one and that its statement about human life transcends (and was meant to transcend) mere racial experience. That on the broader level of its meaning it says something about the experience of being an American and that this includes all Americans, white or black.

Thanks very much for your letter and I hope you won't allow the Ella Prides and Reverend Campbells of this world to dampen your enthusiasm for teaching.

Sincerely,
Ralph Ellison

P.S. Should you care for me to comment on specific incidents in the novel I should be glad to do so.

Sydney Spiegel
1609 Converse Ave
Cheyenne, Wyo.

To William L. Dawson
730 RIVERSIDE DRIVE, 8D
NEW YORK 31, NEW YORK
DECEMBER 13, 1959

Dear Bill:

What a pleasant surprise to hear from you "cotton curtain" or no. Things go well for Fanny and me, both here and at Bard. At long last, we have a larger apartment in the same building and one that overlooks the Hudson. Next time you and Cecile are in the city, drop in for a view.

As for stereo, I have confined myself to a stereo tape machine that I have had for several years, but now that there is wall space I shall soon change over to stereo disks. I can't really advise you until I know the components that go to make up your present system. I will say, however, that the Fisher T-A 600 gives you an excellent stereo tuner and amplifier in one compact unit. There is also the Fisher 100T stereo FM-AM tuner with a master audio control 6 that is also excellent. As for a cartridge, the Shure is considered to be the best available at the moment. However, this is all rather abstract and if you will write me a description of your present components I would be very glad to suggest a way of converting them, if possible, to stereo.

I do go home for weekends and during the Christmas Holidays I shall be in the city. Here is our phone number in case you come up unexpectedly—WAdsworth 6-6804. You may also reach Fanny at LAckawanna 4-6700 during business hours. We will be very glad to see you.

Please give our regards to Mort Sprague and to Dr. Mitchell. It seems it is just about time for the whole bunch of us to get together again. We hear from the Murrays once in a while and things seem to go well with them. Our best to Cecile.

Sincerely,
Ralph Ellison

Mr. William L. Dawson
Tuskegee, Alabama

Letters from the Sixties

A S THE 1950S SLIDE INTO THE 1960S, ELLISON'S letters project a persistent ambivalence about his second novel. At first, the parallels with *Invisible Man* when its first excerpt appeared in print in the late 1940s were a promising harbinger. That novel—whose magical first sentence, "I am an invisible man," gives the whole work such artistic ballast—was yet to undergo Ellison's traumatic decision to cut more than two hundred pages. But *Invisible Man*'s true final course, though not precisely set, was somehow in the works; Ellison *knew* he could restructure and recast as well as rewrite on the way to the finish line. The auguries for the second novel were also auspicious, even more so perhaps when Ellison proudly wrote Al Murray in June 1959: "Bellow has read book two and is to publish about fifty pages in a new mag that he is editing—*The Noble Savage*—of all things!" That carefully selected and edited chunk of the novel, "And Hickman Arrives," came into the world on schedule early in 1960 to a strong buzz of praise.

Yet before and after publication of "And Hickman Arrives," Ellison's letters reflect a chronic indecision and uncertainty about his second novel. In his first letter of the decade he writes Saul Bellow, whose writerly mood swings he identifies with: "But as you say, almost anything is easier than the writing of novels. In fact I'm wondering right now as to how I ever sold myself the idea that it was the most interesting way to live. Let me write one good development tomorrow, however, and I'll give way to my old error."

Ellison writes this in January from Bard College, where he is teaching the Russian novel while awaiting the appearance in print of "And Hickman Arrives." Testifying to "that same pain, that same pleasure" of writing, he describes the unstable, sometimes turbulent relationship he's having with himself and the characters of his novel-in-progress: "I haven't been able to work for two weeks and I feel that I'm falling apart. I find myself in strange places in my dreams and during the days Hickman and Bliss and Severen seem like people out of some faded dream of nobility. They need desperately to be affirmed while I seem incapable of bringing them fully to life. I hope seeing some of the book in print will improve my morale and this shouldn't be long now."

Publication and the strongly positive critical response that followed do lift Ellison's morale, but the boost is temporary. A day after April Fool's Day he begins what turns out to be his last letter to Albert Murray by saying that he is "damned disgusted with myself because of my failure to finish" before assuring his friend that "I know nevertheless that it's better to publish one fairly decent book than five pieces of junk." Then he falls naturally into the grip of the stories within the story of his novel-in-progress:

> The work with old Hickman, Bliss and Severen goes on, with Hickman moving more and more into the role of hero and the old guy is so large that I've just about given in to him, some other crazy sonsofabitches have been boiling up out of the pot, one who sacrifices a fishtailed caddy on the Senator's lawn, and another who discovers that a coffin he'd been saving for 30 years or so had rotted away and decided then and there that the whole American government had fucked up and orders a case of Jack Daniels and a white cooch dancer to come to his house and flip her g-string. He loses his religion and his faith in banks—everything, but the old straight-laced granny dodger is so wild that I'm not sure that he won't blow the book to hell.

Ellison seems to end as he did to Murray ten years before about *Invisible Man*—or do his words reveal something alarming about his current proclivities of composition? "As you can see, deep down I'm mad as ever— insane, that is, but it seems to be my only way."

I should note that these letters to Bellow and Murray change key and continue without missing a beat on the tidbits of daily life. Ellison gives Bellow morsels from the recent symposium on contemporary writing at the University of Iowa, describing the antics of Norman Mailer,* who "avoided clashing with me on the White-Negro crap he's been selling— even though I gave him several opportunities." He also updates Bellow on continuing faculty votes of no confidence in Bard president James Case—"after three votes he threw in the towel." In the way one writes a friend who is away, Ellison moves easily from one thing to another: his ambiguous response to Bard's job offer for the next year, and a reminder of shoes Bellow left behind. Referring to "the nasty part of the business" of Bellow's estranged wife keeping Bellow from their son Adam, Ellison raises the flag of friendship to full staff and writes frank, felt, respectful words about Bellow's emotional hard times and the life that is in him: "Well, what is <u>is</u> and you're tough and flexible enough to put this unhappy thing in its proper place. Watch your health and seek life which always seeks those who would extend it. This you do and there's no question about it. For us life's a matter of pain and good cheer and there's no point in wishing it different."

To Murray, Ellison also moves quickly from brooding about lack of progress on the novel to things on his mind other than fiction—writes gladly, warmly, with robust affection. As if he hears Murray listening, Ellison declares he's "learning much more than the kids" in his "course in the Russian Novel"; and how "a lecture at Rutgers two weeks ago during a blizzard brought an offer of a job." He describes lecturing at colleges across the country: "The pay for these is quite good considering, but I'll earn it—what between functioning as a writer-teacher and having to talk about the problem. Which I can't very well refuse to do, now that young Mose is setting the pace for students all over the country."

As the sixties wear on, black students and some white students demand that Black Power and militant protest be addressed in lectures and talks in place of mere reflection on literature. Ellison's letters to Murray and others show an instinctive initial willingness to talk on campus and off about the brave acts of the black youths who integrated Central High School in Little Rock, Arkansas, in 1957 and the important and courageous lunch

---

* Norman Mailer (1923–2007), novelist (*The Naked and the Dead,* 1946) and innovative journalist (*The Armies of the Night,* 1968), whose "The White Negro" (1957) Ellison considered a facile discussion of race and sexuality.

counter sit-ins a few years later by black students (and a few whites), southern and northern. In that same extended April 2, 1960, letter Ellison explains his responsibility without fanfare: "I've been calling attention to the connection between social morality and literature so I can't do one without doing the other." Without transition he tells Murray he's doing the introduction to the Dell edition of *The Red Badge of Courage and Four Great Stories of Stephen Crane*. Rereading the "neglected stories," Ellison discovers Crane "often as indignant over the Negro thing as he was over the slums." Perhaps anticipating the raised eyebrows of Crane scholars, he ends by declaring what Murray already knows: "I won't ignore what I always preach—that the literary imagination of the Country (the first class imagination, that is) has to smuggle the black man into its machinery in some form, otherwise it can't function."

Satisfied, he shifts gears. "Beyond this the only news is that I've bought a Labrador pup that I've named Tuckatarby and hope to train for hunting." Riff after riff follows: "that Falcon" Murray's wife and daughter are seated in, "buzzing along all brown in that Hollywood whiteness"; "that fucking Rome, where I was anything but happy"; writers who rant over grants they didn't receive but remain silent about those they did; doing a piece on New York commissioned by *Esquire* "in which I used a switchblade on just about everything they hold sacred—especially white women—and they dropped it like it was cancer." He ends with a confession of faith that is also an expression of defiant pride: "I could have done the mood piece they wanted and made myself from eight to a thousand but I wanted them to look inside what makes a black Negro black." Then he goes off on jazz, praising Ray Charles for being "excellent proof of how vital the old voice remains." Having summoned Charles, Ellison brags a little about going to Adolph's, the local hangout at the edge of the Bard campus, "to eat and have a few drinks and there I dance from time to time with the students. Once in a while it works up to a mild swing—jukebox—but man, it's a sad substitute for the real thing and a real whiff of downhome funk would explode the joint. Write me."

This long last letter makes a reader sorry that long-distance telephone calls soon become inexpensive and easy enough to substitute for correspondence; it's a little like having margarine instead of butter. What Ellison observed and thought and *felt*, he was liable to share with Murray. In riff after riff this last letter, along with so many others to Murray, exemplifies and extends "what makes a black Negro black," and that "black Negro" is the very man who was writing: Ralph Ellison.

UNTIL DECEMBER 1967, there are few mentions of how the second novel is progressing, or not. In a letter to Stanley Edgar Hyman in March 1961, he writes, "I am still slugging and trying to make this mass of words mean something and am very weary." Ten days later to Bellow he notes wryly that he received a fan letter "that frightened me as much as it pleased me. Now I know how long it's been since I've published a book." The only other reference to the novel-in-progress until the Plainfield fire does its merciless work in November 1967 is a flat remark in passing to Nathan Scott[*] after publication of *Shadow and Act* three years earlier: "The book goes well, and the essays are receiving, for the most part, favorable reviews."

THROUGHOUT THE 1960S IN one paradoxical way after another *Invisible Man* is more explicitly present in Ellison's letters than the second novel. Nine of the thirty-five letters written during the sixties are about *Invisible Man*. In them Ellison answers queries, some from readers who know him, most from strangers. In reality none is truly a stranger, for *Invisible Man* has touched and changed every one of the readers who write Ellison. From the first year of the decade to the last, *Invisible Man* casts a lengthening shadow over Ellison; the book's presence calls him toward a former self—an implacable sun to the second novel's shape-shifting, changeable moon.

While Ellison parcels out pieces of his novel-in-progress to the quarterlies, *Invisible Man* emerges as a complex work of art in its fluid stability. Paradoxically, its experimental, picaresque quality of form and narrative provide Ellison and his readers a center; its chief actor and storyteller becomes a centripetal voice and force from which to take flight in centrifugal episodes and boomerang back to the stable ironic ground of invisibility. Both a finished novel and a National Book Award winner, *Invisible Man* is a daunting safe haven for a novelist now struggling to put several narratives into continuous relationship in a single novel. Part of the paradox was Ellison's aesthetic that once a novel enters the world, each reader recreates it according to the unique perspective, experience, and values he

---

[*] Ellison met Nathan A. Scott Jr., author of some two dozen volumes on modern literature and religious thought, during his 1961 stint at the University of Chicago. They remained friends until Ellison's death in 1994.

or she brings to it. Facing the labyrinth of his work-in-progress, perhaps Ellison took comfort in the fact that he had found his way out of the novelist's labyrinth in *Invisible Man*. Answering queries put to him by readers in these letters, Ellison writes in intense yet comfortable tones—the nonchalant frequency of a new relatonship, perhaps—as if he and his correspondent share ties to their mutual friend, Invisible Man.

For instance:

April 22, 1960: Ellison writes a young African American poet named Hayes that his letter "is undoubtedly the most interesting that I have ever received regarding the book from a fellow-Negro." His trenchant, incisive response to Hayes's "interpretation of Bledsoe and Lucius Brockway" calls for renewed attention and discussion in our time: "Each of them is my way of rejecting the notion that Negroes are mere victims of the racial situation; we are participants. In their respective ways, they are 'underground men' but neither has gone so far underground and emerged with as purified a vision as Trueblood. All three, however, were trying to tell the poor blundering hero something of the true nature of reality. Unfortunately, it took him much running before he began even to suspect that there was a message involved." Of Hayes's comments on Trueblood, Ellison writes: "It is not often that I think about Jim Trueblood these days and I must say that you are one of the few people who has seen beyond the incest to the human quality of the man. Thanks for reminding me of one of my more daring efforts."

April 25, 1963: To Florida State undergraduate Patsy Brill, Ellison confides "the necessity of discovering that my racial identity was not fundamental to my problems as an artist . . . Being a Negro has helped my work very much as the background and cultural identity of any literary artist is helpful. It gives some form, some specific shape to the chaos of life and it presents me with a specific set of circumstances, experiences, characters, dilemmas . . . that I must confront in order to discover who and what I am, what life is and what art is."

November 23, 1964: Neither is Ellison deaf to thoughtful criticism of certain choices he made in *Invisible Man*. In response to reservations expressed by Dostoevsky scholar and biographer Joseph Frank that a few passages in the "Golden Day" chapter are off-key and overstated, he muses: "Perhaps you are right, I tipped my hand too soon in the saloon scene. I had a problem of rhetoric and of some of the people. I was unsure of how the general reader would react to the intellectual level of the book, so I suppose I overdid it. I am pretty certain that if I were to do it now, that is to write that scene now, I would have held back more, would have been more implicit." Perhaps because Frank is also a friend, Ellison lets his hair down: "How good it is to hear that you like the scene between Ras and Clifton. It does indeed express quite a lot of what I feel about racism."

That same day he writes William Dolben, "The Founder is not a specific person, he is rather the personification of an archetype.... He is a founder, the dreamer who is also a man of action.... To some extent the pattern is heroic. Now, I am sure you can go on from there."

July 29, 1969: Ellison writes John Lucas, an admired friend (who is "doing something to raise the cultural level of some of our bankers"), a long and detailed letter answering questions about various cruxes Lucas intends to address in a lecture he is soon to give on *Invisible Man.* Ellison avers that the fact that *Invisible Man* "struck Ras in the jaws was a lucky accident and shouldn't be taken too symbolically"; perhaps half tongue-in-cheek, he confesses to "laying a false trail for my friend Stanley Edgar Hyman, who has great enthusiasm for Freudian speculation."

November 10, 1969: He answers Dolores Ruzicka's question about Dante's influence on *Invisible Man* with a denial that doubles as witty affirmation, and advice that is extreme understatement. "Unfortunately, however, beyond the Prologue I am afraid that any influence that I might have absorbed from Dante would have come through such writers as T. S. Eliot and Ezra Pound. Therefore, I believe that you are following a direction that would not be too fruitful."

Even apart from his illuminating specific comments on *Invisible Man,* Ellison stands on the high ground in a strategic position that requires little defense, unlike the uncertain, wary reinforcements he sometimes feels a need to deploy on the battlefield of his novel-in-progress.

OF RALPH'S FIVE LETTERS to Fanny during the 1960s, he writes four in a week from the Quadrangle Club at the University of Chicago in October 1961. Read one after another, these letters give the feeling they could have been written either at one sitting or as separate letters over a span of weeks, months, or even years, rather than in the single week that was the case. The letters have the feel, like so many others to Fanny, of a long relationship that has become a connection of blood and bone and nerves, one that is likely to continue indefinitely despite strains and fissures.

Ellison is at ease, his tone mostly comfortable and intimate. In the letters he finds a way to mention his stomach protesting the onions and garlic he's eaten unwittingly at restaurants or at the tables of friends. He also regularly fills in Fanny on his encounters with her mother and her ill step-father, George, for whom he does his best in Fanny's absence. He touches upon things you'd expect from a husband who misses his wife: when he gets a new room with a better bed, he writes, "Well, it's true and I rest better but I realize now that part of my trouble is the sleeping alone. You just hold on and we'll solve our problems together."

The "problems" he refers to center on her drinking. Here his nonchalance gives way to anxiety and alarm, palpably moderated because of what he knows is Fanny's lingering hurt, anger, and dejection over his affair during their time in Rome. For all that, he does not walk on eggshells: "I can't compete with the bottle." And he indicates his belief that in her case, abstaining from drinking is a matter of will and character, a problem that they can work out if both of them are committed to doing their part.

"Anyway, you should always remember that I'm not against your drinking, only against your getting drunk. It's the possible need to get lost, ossified, blotto—you name it—which upsets me. And it is real upset," he repeats, putting his vulnerability into the mix. "I've told you long ago of my anxiety of being unable to communicate with those I love." His concerns are in relation to both of them, rather than each of them in serial or isolated fashion: "Well, I have my fears and my ideals and that's one thing; but now that I'm here in Chicago and I see George and Billie I realize the tremendous job of self-creation you represent and I don't wish to see it flawed or undone by taking this easy way out of whatever it is that's causing your tensions." Perhaps more important than anything else is his assertion that "whether you believe it or not, I'm as proud of you as you are of me." Unwritten before, perhaps this unconditional declaration helped restore equilibrium to their marriage.

HIS MIND NEVER FAR from Oklahoma City in space and time, Ellison is "delighted" to hear from Hester Holloway, a treasured friend of his mother's back in Oklahoma City, and Edna Slaughter, daughter of J. D. "Grandpa" Randolph and Uretta Randolph. He has sent Slaughter *Shadow and Act,* and he is pleased she liked the book, especially the paragraph celebrating her father, the custodian of the law library of the Oklahoma State Capitol, to whom the white legislators turned for finer points of law not found in the books.

And he is mesmerized by memories of Oklahoma triggered by hearing from Miss Hester. They haven't been in touch since his mother's death in 1937, so he brings her up to date on his and his brother Herbert's lives since. Soon he stops short, realizing "that there's so much you could tell me of my mother and father and if there is the barest chance to come to Detroit I shall take it. I'd like very much to see you and bring the old times up out of the shadows." Most affecting is Ellison combining his boy's and man's perspectives into a single autobiographical story of the spring of 1921, when his mother was at her wits' end in Gary, Indiana, after a quick, ill-advised move from Oklahoma City: "Mama prayed and . . . you and Mr. Cook appeared the next day and took us back home." (In the unfinished manuscript "Leaving the Territory" Ellison describes the Cooks' "magnificent carriage with running boards and gleaming headlights, with spare tires on both sides and rear, a folding top and transparent side curtains against the rain.") The memory, perhaps partly a mirage perceived by the boy, intensifies the man's realization that the experience "was one of the most important trips in my life; because Lord knows what might have happened to us had we remained in Gary. Certainly I would not have grown up in quite the same way and so much of what I've become was formed in Okla."

Presently he remembers the Ferris wheel at a carnival in Oklahoma City "rising with its ropes of blue lights then moving so slowly in the early dusk as Mama walked me up Gary Street from the East Fourth Street car line." That Ferris wheel became an image of the wondrous light out in the world waiting for the adolescent narrator of Ellison's "A Coupla Scalped Indians" (1956). Now the grown man puts on paper a prayer of thanks to Miss Hester and by extension the "dear folks" he wrote to after his mother's passing. "Thanks to those like you," he continues in 1961, "I never had to apologize to myself, or make excuses to anyone, for being a Negro. That is much more than anything I got at Tuskegee or anywhere else. I couldn't have bought it <u>with gold</u>, and all that was necessary for me to get it was for you to be true to yourself. It's amazing, when you think about it."

FOR A WHILE HIS letters thin out. After *Shadow and Act* comes out, little dramatic happens until on November 29, 1967, a fire destroys the 250-year-old house Ralph and Fanny Ellison had purchased outside the tiny Berkshire town of Plainfield, Massachusetts. They had moved in that June and for a time Ellison found a rhythm as he worked to recast and revise Book II of his novel. Nine days after the conflagration, on December 8, he writes Charles Valentine of Washington University to tell him politely if firmly and definitely that because of the fire he will not be able to write the foreword to Valentine's forthcoming book, *Culture and Pov-*

erty. "The loss was particularly severe for me, as a section of my work-in-progress was destroyed with it." Remarkably, Ellison is composed and in full control as he spells out the task ahead: "Fortunately, much of my summer's work on the new novel is still in mind and if my imagination can feed it I'll be all right, but I must work quickly."

Again, paradox haunts his work on the second novel. He seems altogether more upbeat and confident writing on the "higher frequency" of what is to be done—of necessity, now, immediately—than on the "lower frequencies" in other letters that characterize what he actually has been doing or not doing on the second novel.

Complementary to Ellison's short letter to Charles Valentine is a long one written to his increasingly close friend Charlie Davidson. In the summer of 1968 he and Fanny stay at the Newport, Rhode Island, summer home of the Davidsons during and after the Jazz Festival. From there, the Ellisons make their way back to the Plainfield house for the first time since it was destroyed in the fire nine months before. Deep in Hawthorne country, he describes the landscape in Gothic terms: "The sheer devastation of what had been a quite lovely old house and grounds now reduced to a scene of desolation. A forlorn chimney standing stark and crumbling above a cellar-hole full of crushed and rusting appliance, broken crockery, ashes."

Neither Ellison fusses or dithers. "Fanny was able to contain the shock and sadness of it fairly well, and we set about trying to find a plumber and electrician to restore lights and water," as if the best way to mourn is to "try to make the cottage livable." Explaining from his desk back in New York why they did not return to see the Davidsons as they had intended, Ralph writes: "I've been working well however and I hate to think of breaking off." The letter continues in fullness, its riffs resembling in their energy those he formerly wrote Al Murray; only now a mute is attached to Ellison's trumpet.

The 1960s are almost over. In 1969 Ellison's letters answer queries about his reading, about his writing—that is, *Invisible Man*—and about young James McPherson's collection of stories, *Hue and Cry.* Don't worry, Ellison assures Edward Weeks, the editor of the Atlantic Monthly Press: "He is a writer of insight, sympathy and humor and one of the most gifted young Americans I've had the privilege to read."

By mid-1969, almost two years after the Plainfield fire, Ellison had rebounded enough to finish and publish "Night-Talk," an excerpt involving the novel's two principal characters, Reverend Hickman and Senator Sun-raider (formerly known as Bliss), that Ellison's prefatory note describes as "an anguished attempt to arrive at the true shape and substance of a sundered past and its meaning." Thirty-five years later, perhaps harking back to "And Hickman Arrives" (1960) and "Juneteenth" (1965), Arnold Rampersad will call "Night-Talk" "probably the strongest single section of his novel-in-progress to appear in his lifetime."

John F. Callahan

To Saul Bellow
TIVOLI,
JAN. 19, 1960.

Dear Sol,

I've been tied up down in the city for nearly two weeks, partially with work on the apartment and partially with lousy health. I'm back here now, where it snows and snows and snows. Things go well here, except that I've never been able to get a local man to deal with the roof. Right now this isn't crucial, because the roof has had snow and ice on it for damn near two months and no one can do anything about it until the thaw comes. I'm in touch with a guy so as soon as possible I'll have him up there. Since I've started out with this let me say that I'd be willing to take care of anything around here that I can; so if you want to send dough so that I can take care of bills here fire away. I'm sure that it'll improve your state of mind not to have so many bills coming to you from Minn.

 Your trip seems to have hit you as mine usually hit me, with a physical fading away and loss of tone. But this only lasts for a while and I'm sure you'll feel much better by time you're heading back. The planes sound exciting and a hell of a lot more interesting than most flights I've made since the days when barnstormers around Okla. City would circle you over the city for five bucks. You were furnished goggles and you sat there in the rush of air looking down and trying to pick up the old familiar land-marks and some envious friend at whom to wave. But as you say, almost anything is easier than the writing of novels. In fact I'm wondering right now as to how I ever sold myself the idea that it was the most interesting way to live. Let me write one good development tomorrow, however, and I'll give way to my old error. I haven't been able to work for two weeks and

August 10,1968

Dear Charlie:

]   I've been waiting until some of the slides which I
had duplicated were returned before answering your letter.
There was some kind of slip-up and they were finally returned last Sat. So now here they are. I must say that I
didn't come up with anything impressive, but after all,
one shouldn't try to shoot that type of event while sitting
on his ass--which leaves me the excuse that if I had been
running around I would have seen far less of you and
Terry. Besides that I <u>was</u> trying to see what I could do
with the telephotos.
    We too had a splendid time and there's no question but
that our time with you and Terry marks the high spot of
this summer. It is regretable that we didn't follow you on
to Boston because we stood in the ferry line until 7:45
and arrived in the Plainfield area well after 12 p.m.
where we spent thenight in an inn. Spending the time with
you was more important than you might guess, for when we
reached our place it was dreary as hell. Not the weatherm
but the sheer devastation of what had been a quite lovely
old house and grounds now reduced to a scene of desolation.
Aforlorn chimney standing stark and crumbling above a
cellar-hole full of crushed and rusting appliances, broken
crockery, ashes.
    Fanny was able to contain the shock and sadness of it
fairly well, and we set about trying to find a plumber and
electrician to restore lights and water. Our pump and storage
tank were ruined and since there's now no housing for
the pump I've had to replace both with a far more expensive emmersible type. It's a drag and Lord knows when
we'll be able to have the junk hauled away, the chimney
collasped and the hole filled in. But one thing is certain,
we wont try to rebuild right away. Rather,we'll simply
try to make the cottage livable and make do until we're
convinced that something has been done about fire protection in the area. Getting things statted was difficult
because everyone is so overloaded with summer business,
and it wasn't until a few days before we left that we
located people to do the job, thus making a drive to Boston
out of the question. They only finished the job last week
and we'll run up the first chance we get. I've been working
well however and I hate to think of breaking off.
    Otherwide things were pleasant there. We were guests
of theRichard Wilburs and that's usually a joy. You'll
have to meet them and if possible come down to Portland,
Conn, to one of their big parties. Usually it's black tie
with a live and not too square orchestra and a lot of
amusing academic and literary types--<u>and</u> dam good food.
They have a big rambling house, which <u>makes</u> it possible to have
sucn a variety of guests that you have to work pretty hard
at it to be bored; while they are themselves interesting

enough and humorous enough to make things swing. I'll work
on this and try to get him to come in when he's in Boston.

Charlie, that Sunday morning when I went to look for that
guy with the Thunderbird I knew the moment I saw him that he
was someone you had to keep an eye on. He just seemed to be
operating in anothier dimension of reality--and despite
the bright sunlight. In fact , he seemed to be wearing
some kind of invisible gas mask--which warned me that al-
thought I was only your messenger I had better watch myself.
But who the hell would have suspected that the bastard
had a goddamned race horse hadden in the trunk of the car?
And a horse named 'Porkchopper' at that!
It's wild! It's mad! It's crazy! It's exactly right!
I told Al about it and he flipped over the telephone. We'll
have to get up there as soon as possible to have a look at
that noble animal. Actually I envy you the freedom of
spirit which allowed you to grab him, because a couple of
years ago Vance and Tina Bourjayly--who own a whole heard
of horses out in Iowa--tried to give me a wonder little
prancing pony named Kerry, a little jet-black jewel who
pulled a cart with the stlye of a trotter. He had been
the pet of their daughter who was killed in a car accident
and thus very painful to have around, but although I
wanted him badly I floundered before all the problems of
bringing him east, finding him a stable, etc., so I
refused. Well, so now I have two goddam friends who own
race horses. One is Luna Diamond, one of Roger Steven's
secretaries down at the National Foundation on the Arts
(her husband was a law partner of Abe Fortas) and now
you. Next thing I know you'll be out doing roadwork by way
of getting in shape to ride, and I'll open the sports
page of the Times to redd "DAVIDSON TAKES THE BELMONT
STAKES ON THE PORK CHOP"
I'm reminded that I was born around horses and had become
quite familar with them by the time,three or four years
after my father's death, when my mother got rid of the last.
This was a mare with the then baffling name of 'Steve'
and the extremely willful ways of a rather spoiled pet.
She was as steady as an old rocking chair and delighted
in sticking her head through the kitchen window to beg for
snacks--sugar, apples, carrots; anything would do, and
she was without question my mother's delight. The other
horse, Fox, was a gelding which had to be destroyed during
my second Christmas when he slipped on the icy Okla.
City viaduct and broke a leg. Later I came to know other
horses and quite a few mules which were owned by friends,
employers and familar ice menx and hucksters. I learned
to ride them and drive them and the summer of my 16th
year I moved earth with them while working as a member of
a landscapegardening crew. And as a kid I used to spend
summer saturdays sitting on the wagon seat with old Uncle
Allen Watkins (a pioneer friend of my family who had
walked to Okla Territory from Tenn.) behind a team of
mules which he cursed roundly and with great style whenever
one of them made the mistake of letting a fart! Man, but
that was long ago! Take good care of Porkchopper and if
you have a photo please send it along.

3]

The news about the shoes is most welcome, so welcome in fact that my feet have begun to feelbetter. And as for the lense, I con't think that $95.00 is too bad a price. However, should you
However, should you find yourself in urgent need of a lense please let me know, because with the competition down here and the discount which I get from my dealer I'll probably be able to do almost as well as Charlier B. does in Japan. For instance, while the list price is certainly $175.00 the actual going price hereabouts is from $128 to $124.00-- which I was quoted on Sat, and this includes a gurantee. Used 105m.m. Nikkors go for about 114.00if you have the time and patience to look around. By the way, to whom should I make out the check? And before leaving this let me say that after having seen some of the shots made with the lense I'm quite pleased with its optical qualities and I'm nuts about the perspective it allows me. Now all I need to do is to learn how to make interesting pictures.I now have an 85--250mm zoom, an 50mm f.1.4, a 55mm micro Nikor, a 200mm tele and the 105. The next project is to acquire a 28 or 35mm wide-angle and I'll be throughx.
I'm sorry we didn't hear Clark Terry in Boston be- cause he wasn't up to par at the Festival. I suppose he was too busy trying to swing that load of lead. But if you have a casset tape player I'd like to send you a copy of a tape featuring Clark Terry and Shirley Scott. Titled Soul Duo, it's a gas. A recording engineer friend gave it to me a few weeks ago and there's hardly a day when I haven't played their version of This Little Light of Mine. By the way, do you remember Jackie and Roy's rendition of "Lazy Afternoon"/? I came across our recording of it the other day and found it still fresh and quite exciting.
Al's O.K. and is presently going through the excitement of owning a fine new stereo outfit. It's a Marantz tuner amplifier combination with Altec speakers and as excellent in visual design as it is in sound.He's as pleased as he can be. Yesterday a set of galleys arrived in which he has a short story and which I discovered that I had two short stories along with an essay. I gave up trying to write stories some time ago, but these two keep turning up; so perhaps I'll try my hand again and try to come up with a collection, since there are a few still floating around.
Charlie, since I don't know how to reach the Weins I've enclosed a set of duplicates of Joyce and Benny fpr you to pass along with my regards. Tell George and Charlie B. that I was too busy to do anything about the 'Dam News jerk and that I have a horror of writing letters to editors, but that I hope to write something about the festivals and theri import on my own--and this before too long. meanwhile, take care, give our love to Terry and I'll try to get up there as soon mas possible.

                                        Affectionately,

I feel that I'm falling apart. I find myself in strange places in my dreams and during the days Hickman and Bliss and Severen seem like people out of some faded dream of nobility. They need desperately to be affirmed while I seem incapable of bringing them fully to life. I hope seeing some of the book in print will improve my morale and this shouldn't be long now. We went to that handsome modern museum of Arthur and Elaine Cohn's for New Years and he's promised copies of the N.S. for next month. We're still getting publicity, by the way, and Esquire was nice enough to give us a mention in the brochure which they prepared for Iowa . . . You ask how it went out there and I'd say on the whole much better than at Columbia. Better questions, more participation—even though the positions of the speakers were more or less predictable. Dwight M. and Norman M. both tried to be as shocking as possible and M. Harris, who read a rather tame academic paper on the first day was brainwashed by Mailer at a party which followed and returned the next day to castigate himself for about a half hour and proclaim himself an "academic Beat." So you can imagine where this put me. Mailer chose to build his remarks around a point I made concerning the fact that writers had much to do with founding this country and he avoided clashing with me on the White-Negro crap he's been selling—even though I gave him several opportunities. I thought for a moment we would have a discussion of your work but it came late and Engle put a damper on it. Mailer is a nut of considerable charm, which he uses as he uses his adolescent shock techniques, to attract attention to himself. I doubt if he believes in anything seriously anymore except his ego. Although the kids were much taken with him I don't think they took his statements seriously but were rather glad for the excitement—much as they might have been upon hearing a judge, say, say shit at table. As entertainers he and Dwight make a good team <u>and</u> they're quite safe. One rails against what he calls mid-cult and popular culture and the other confesses his dissipations (mainly No Doz and benzedrine) and complains of the publishers, the foundation and the good old gravy train—but neither has much to say about the conditions which make true culture difficult to identify in this country or which make good writing difficult in any country. I found myself damned near disarmed by my sense of the seriousness of these matters. I guess the guy who wrote the piece for Newsweek expected me to go into some kind of racial war dance ala R. Wright, but hell, I have to save my own sense of life with all its complexity regardless what the other guys do. One of these days a bunch of us will get together and discuss these matters seriously and it's apt to prove quite shocking and deadly to the culturebullshitmasters. Maybe it'll be something for the *Savage** to work on.

Engle asked me to stay over and participate in the poetry and fiction workshops, for which I was paid, and some of the fellows saw to it that I got in some hunting. I suppose my new hat frightened away most of the pheasants (I had no hunting outfit along) but we knocked down some quail along a railroad cut. All together a fine trip. Harris, by the way, has sold the head of his department on hiring me, but I have no idea of getting that far away from New York until the book is done . . . Besides, I'm discovering how rugged the academic life can be. Case[†] finally backed himself into the position where almost all of his tenured people voted against him and after three votes he threw in the towel. Now we have a fundraiser as acting president, the board is mad at the faculty (our friend Sam has stayed out of it, damn him!) and the newspapers have painted us as a bunch of ingrates who did in a noble educator! The story is too long to tell here but I'm sure Jack would be pleased with the outcome.[‡] There is still a question of whether we'll continue next year, but then there was no certainty that Case and the trustees would have raised the necessary dough had he stayed. $4000 was the best the trustees could do last year. The division is putting pressure on me to stay next year and the needs of the department would make this logical, but right now I feel negative as hell. Only the house makes the region attractive . . . By the way, your shoes are here, and I've been keeping your books, some four, as they arrive. Let me know if you wish it this way. Up to now no books have come from Poland but I'll hang on when they do.

That's about it. I've no word from Minn. and if none comes soon I'll have Fanny call Esther. It's hard to be here and not think about Adam several times a day.[§] This is the nasty part of the business and I find it difficult not to resent the fact that this is one of the ways that women usually react. Well, what is is and you're tough and flexible enough to put this unhappy thing in its proper place. Watch your health and seek life which always seeks those who would extend it. This you do and there's no question

* Bellow's soon-to-be-launched renegade journal, *The Noble Savage*.

† James R. Case, the beleaguered president of Bard College, where Ellison was teaching in 1959 and 1960, resigned after the third vote of no confidence by the faculty.

‡ Jack Ludwig, friend of Bellow's and fellow editor of *The Noble Savage* journal.

§ Bellow's young son by his wife Sondra Bellow, from whom he was estranged at this time.

about it. For us life's a matter of pain and good cheer and there's no point in wishing it different. Fanny sends love and we await your return.

Ralph

P.S. If you get a chance please look into whether I have any royalties there. They published *Invisible Man* about 1954 and I haven't heard a thing from them—not even a request for permission. If I have it you should spend some of it.

To Albert Murray
TIVOLI, N.Y.
APRIL 2, 1960

Dear Albert,

I had Fanny get off a copy of the *Noble Savage* to you a couple of weeks ago, but have been so busy that only now am I getting around to the follow up letter. I hope it gives you some idea of what we're up to—although I'm not a very active editor at the moment—and I hope you'll let us see something of what you're writing. There is quite an interest in the mag and a few detractors have sounded off against the title even before the paper was available. At any rate, we're out to provide a magazine that will make it unnecessary for a good writer to even think about *P.R.* or *Hudson,* or any of the other academic house organs, and any criticism we publish will be by writers, not critics. Best of all, we have a top word rate of 5 cents per—which ain't bad at all.

I'm very glad to hear that you're underway with a book and very anxious to see anything you wish to send. But never mind about showing your face without ¾s of a book, most of what's being published shouldn't be, and although I'm damned disgusted with myself because of my failure to finish, I know nevertheless that it's better to publish one fairly decent book than five pieces of junk. The work with old Hickman, Bliss and Severen goes on, with Hickman moving more and more into the role of hero and the old guy is so large that I've just about given in to him, some other crazy sonsofabitches have been boiling up out of the pot, one who sacrifices a fishtailed caddy on the Senator's lawn, and another who discovers that a coffin he'd been saving for 30 years or so had rotted away and decided then and there that the whole American government had fucked up and orders a case of Jack Daniels and a white cooch dancer to come to his house and flip her g-string. He loses his religion and his faith in banks—everything, but the old straight-laced granny dodger is so wild that I'm not sure that he won't blow the book to hell. As you can see, deep down I'm mad as ever—insane, that is, but it seems to be my only way . . . I'm also lecturing away. My soph. course in American Lit is the most popular on the campus (!), some forty kids in a school where 14 is about tops; my course in Russian novel is intense and most useful to me, but I'm learning much more than the kids; a lecture at Rutgers two weeks ago during a blizzard brought an offer of a job—which I rejected—paying 9000—better than a full prof here about. I go to Washburn College in Indiana on the 14 &15—I tell you this so I won't miss you should you make it out this way—and in May I'll be at the University of Chicago for four days. The pay for these is quite good considering, but I'll earn it—what between functioning as a writer-teacher and having to talk about the problem. Which I can't very well refuse to do, now that young Mose is setting the pace for students all over the country. I've been calling attention to the connection between social morality and literature so I can't do one without doing the other.

I'm also doing an introduction to a paperback collection of Stephen Crane's work.* I hadn't paid much attention to him beyond following Hemingway's recommendation of the *Red Badge,* "The Blue Hotel" and "The Open Boat"—but I've been reading the neglected stories which haven't been anthologized so often and in which Crane is revealed as not merely the technical link between Twain and Hemingway, and thus the first of the 20th Century American writers, but in which he struggles with Mose just as hard as Mark Twain and which mark him as the last of the 19th century moralists. John Berryman gets some of this in his biography, but he was so busy psychologizing the work that he underplays the fact that Crane was often as indignant over the Negro thing as he was over the slums. More, the little bastard was from a long line of preachers and both sides and when we consider this some of the mystery of how he came to think and feel as he did is dispelled. That damned Methodist fire and brimstone along with all that hockey-assed hypocrisy had the boy running like a puppy with high-life on his balls from a very early age—very much as Henry James's old man's theological interests got to him, or Joyce's Catholicism got to him. The critics have praised Crane for the verbiage

---

* Ellison's introduction to the 1960 edition of *The Red Badge of Courage* became "Stephen Crane and the Mainstream of American Fiction" in *Shadow and Act.*

he left out, while refusing to see that he wasn't leaving out the religious background of his thought. The other thing that fascinates me [are] the parallels with his own life: not only the Methodism but the resentment of the church folks' shittiness at an early age, the early death of the father, and the strict mother. Read the *Monster* and you'll see where Faulkner got part of the idea for Benjy in *The Sound and the Fury*. Dilsey's line to Luster, "Quit projeking with his flower" appears here with Henry Johnson, the Negro hero, telling the little white boy, "I done tol yer many's th'time not to go a-follin' an' a-projeckin with them flowers." When Henry dashes into the burning house to save the boy, his face is destroyed by acid that looks like flowers in the flames. And as you know, Benjy's flower stands for Caddy's maidenhead . . . Anyway, I'm having some fun with the thing and at least I won't <u>ignore</u> what I always preach—that the literary imagination of the Country (the first class imagination, that is) has to smuggle the black man into its machinery in some form, otherwise it can't function. I wouldn't want to have to prove this in each instance, but for the 19th century boys it's just about true. Beyond this the only news is that I've bought a Labrador pup that I've named Tuckatarby and hope to train for hunting. I still have hopes but as of now it seems that I've got myself a shit machine, but if blood counts he should be a fairly decent dog . . . Fanny and I have been talking of coming west this summer, but we've decided nothing since we're still trying to get the apartment in order and there simply isn't money enough for a car.

How about that Falcon! I can just see Mique and Mokie buzzing along all brown in that Hollywood whiteness. My own old wagon is still batting along so I have to look at every new car that passes out of the corner of my eye. You'd better be careful, now that Mique's reaching college age, because the kids here use Falcons strictly as campus cars. Fanny and I frequently recall the 1956 trip and especially the excitement Mokie and Mique caused in Siena. That's where Mokie was breaking in those nasty-zippered harem pants and the Italians were bug eyeing all over the streets. I wish we could make another such trip, perhaps in Spain as we'd planned to do that summer. I'm teaching Hemingway and my nostalgia is compounded. Sometimes, in fact, I miss that fucking Rome, where I was anything but happy. I guess the trick in enjoying any part of Europe is to avoid large concentrations of Americans or at least stay cut away from them. I've been turning down trips on the cultural exchange, one that would have gotten me to Russia and the other to Berlin. I lose too much time and there is so much bullshit talked at these conferences that I simply can't bear it. Anyway, I work my ass off and all I get from it is the trip and I've made enough such trips . . . I'm pretty pissed off with *Esquire,* which in the publisher's column of the March issue, carried a report on the Iowa conference in which I was described as being 'complacent' concerning foundation grants to writers—this after Mailer launched an attack against them as buying the writers off. My point was that I was more interested in improving my writing than in the possible corruption a gift of a few thousand dollars could do me. I get sick of that childish crap since I see no point in complaining about money you accept on your own free will. *Esquire* missed the irony that with all the grants available I've had only the Rosenwald. I didn't ask to be appointed a Fellow to the American Academy in Rome, that was a prize and if I have any complaint to make, it's that I didn't have the strength to refuse it. The National Book Award was another prize, for which I received a gold plaque, not a thousand bucks given today. I've never had a Ford, Rockefeller, or Guggenheim, or any of the lesser gravy. No *Kenyon,* no *Sewanee,* nor *PR,* no *Hudson,* or any of the numerous grants which are doubtlessly designed to aid rather than hinder the writer and which a number of writers who are much less talented continue to receive. But what really angers me is the discovery that the little shit at *Esquire* assumed that because we were paid $500.00 for the time out there I was going to turn myself into a clown like Mailer. I talked seriously and I gave him the opportunity to meet me on my ground but he chose not to tangle. Yet the *Esquire* character is so awed by the phony Mailer image of the outlaw that he couldn't see what was happening. But there's more to it than that. I was asked to do a piece for an issue on New York which should hit the stands soon, and I did one (they guaranteed me two hundred whether they took it or not) in which I started back in Okla, went to Tuskegee and then described what New York meant to one of such a background, and in which I used a switchblade on just about everything they hold sacred—especially white women—and they dropped it like it was cancer. I could have done the mood piece they wanted and made myself from eight to a thousand but I wanted them to look inside what makes a black Negro black.

Those guys make a man almost sympathetic to a group of boots out in Chicago who presented a film titled *The Cry of Jazz* recently to a Cinema 16 audience and before which I appeared on a panel to discuss it after the showing (Marshall Stearns, Nat Hentoff and Mark Kennedy and Ed. Bland, the script writer and musicologist who made the film, were the other panelists). These guys made a pitifully bad film to advance the idea that whites had killed Jazz, that the American white had no humanity and that they must turn to the Negro to save themselves. The scene was that of an interracial jazz club—no Negro chicks, man, the studs all had white gals—during which one of the Negro intellectuals expounds on the relationship between the Negro environment and jazz and in which he argued that jazz was dead because the Negro community was limited by Jim Crow etc., a thesis which he tried to prove by some very questionable musicology. I pointed out that Jazz had the formal characteristics of most American art forms, but they were so busy trying to make a political point that they couldn't deal with it. Nor could they deal with the cinema. I told them that I was very glad to hear them give voice to their disgust and thought it good that the audience could hear what at least one group of Negroes felt, but wished they'd demonstrated their superiority by at least making a competent film. They are some arrogant and most half-educated studs—the same who've done their damnedest to kill off Louis and to make Jazz middle class. They showed scenes of shouting Negro congregations, with women crying and swooning and dancing, but they didn't put it on the sound track, they were too ashamed; they presented it to the sound of some most uninteresting bebop. And when I questioned them about this they answered that jazz and Negro church music was all the same. To which I said even if that were true what about the fact that a Negro church is not a nightclub or a dance hall? They wanted to cut my throat before it was over, but they were so wide open in their arguments that they were cut to pieces from the floor. The sad thing is that some of their ideas are worthwhile, but they really want jazz to be dead simply so they won't have to deal with it as Negroes while still having the pleasure of beating white folks over the head from having killed it. I wished I had your remarks concerning Ray Charles at hand at the time because he's excellent proof of how vital the old voice remains. He was well liked at Newport, but as much for his blindness as for his musicianship. You still have to be among such groups as you describe out there in order to have any full appreciation of an art that's moving in the deep complex stream of the old American chaos. Just reading your description makes me homesick. On Wednesday nights after I've taught all day, I sometimes go to a local bar to eat and have a few drinks and there I dance from time to time with the students. Once in a while it works up to a mild swing—jukebox—but man, it's a sad substitute for the real thing and a real whiff of downhome funk would explode the joint. Write me.

Ralph

To Paul Engle
TIVOLI, NEW YORK
APRIL 4, 1960.

Dear Paul:

What a relief to receive a pleasant reminder of the Iowa symposium! I had such an exciting and even inspiring time there that I retained the glow for weeks—until Rust Hills' report in the March issue of *Esquire* was called to my attention. Since then I've fumed and stewed in my disgust. For although I assumed that we'd been asked to go out to a center where writing and writers are taken seriously in order to discuss serious matters, *Esquire,* or at least Hills, really thought it was hiring a bunch of clowns and foils for Norman Mailer. He certainly has a greater belief in the power of money—if five hundred dollars can be called 'money' nowadays—than I, and I was most surprised to see part of my remarks concerning the foundations described as 'complacent,' when it simply seems bad form to ask for money, spend it and then complain about the donor. The irony of my statement was, of course, that I've received only one of the many foundation grants, the Rosenwald, back during the war and at a time I was still going to sea. I didn't ask for the Prix de Rome, I was selected; and the Nat. Book Award consisted, at the time I received it, of a gold plaque. I've received no Guggenheim, Ford, or Rockefeller grants, nor any of the lesser *Partisan Review, Hudson, Sewanee* or *Kenyon* awards which have been helping writers to get their work done. Nevertheless, I've no complaints and I still find it difficult to understand writers who're afraid of being corrupted by $3000. Forgive me shooting off this way, but I've just received a copy of Philip Roth's NBA acceptance speech and find him quoting (in disapproval) from Hills' report, and thus am in the midst of a very slow burn.

As to coming to Iowa next year, I've given it very serious consideration and concluded that prior commitments would make it impossible at this time. I'm still trying to reach the end of my novel and there are certain obligations owed to my colleagues here at this unhappy college. I'm sorry that this has to be my answer, not only because such opportunities are rare, but also because I liked Iowa, was impressed by the workshop, the students <u>and</u> the hunting. Indeed, I've just bought a Labrador pup and would like nothing better than to have him learn his trade out where the tall corn grows all those pheasants. I enjoyed the time I spent at your home and I hope it won't be too long before I see you and Mary again. My best to her and to you.

Sincerely,
Ralph Ellison

To Mr. Hayes
730 Riverside
New York 31, New York
April 22, 1960

Dear Mr. Hayes:

Thanks very much for your letter.* I hope you will understand me when I say that it is undoubtedly the most interesting that I have ever received regarding the book from a fellow-Negro.

You revealed such an alertness to the nuances of the plot, its imagery and its gestures that I could not help but be impressed and delighted. There is no doubt about it: one does enjoy being understood and sensitive readers are quite rare.

I was quite touched by your pilgrimage to 42nd Street. Although the spot where Clifton met his Tod is imagined, the newsstand was the one in the center of the block. But, as you know, the important thing was the action that I was imitating.

As for Norton's gift of $100 to Jim Trueblood, I am not quite so sure anymore as to just what was going on there. Certainly they are united by a common attraction [to] that chaos which threatens in the complex relationship among fathers and daughters. Trueblood has violated a powerful taboo but has faced up to his punishment manfully, thus becoming for the white community a sort of negative cultural hero. The irony of course is that Norton would simplify his relationship to Trueblood's and to the tragic impulses of his own nature (as revealed in his attraction to his daughter) through a gift of money. So it is not simply that men fear death but that men feel compelled to over-step the bounds of their social and human limitations to crash the frontiers of rationality and to confront the unknown. The irony here, it would seem, is that Trueblood has stepped off into the darkness, suffered and returned, and the whites have reduced

---

* Hayes had written Ellison in September 1959 to praise *Invisible Man*. In the letter he offers several interpretations of key characters from the novel including Trueblood, Clifton, Brockway, and Bledsoe.

his tragic agony to the level of entertainment; they would drain his life of its tragic meaning. For them there is nevertheless an aura of magic about him. He fascinates them, but because they fail to identify his humanity with theirs, his gift of sacrificial knowledge is wasted and the land remains in chaos. Thus although the southerners laugh at <u>him</u>, the Northerner is shaken. Trueblood becomes a sort of unrecognized bard narrating his tragedy freely through this for any who would hear. Norton does learn something of the true nature of his relationship to the college and to the Negro community—thus the pathetic nature of his gift to buy toys.

Your interpretation of Bledsoe and Lucius Brockway seems to me quite correct. They are indeed related in several ways, and each of them is <u>my</u> way of rejecting the notion that Negroes are mere <u>victims</u> of the racial situation; we are participants. In their respective ways, they are "underground men" but neither has gone so far underground and emerged with as purified a vision as Trueblood. All three, however, were trying to tell the poor blundering hero something of the true nature of reality. Unfortunately, it took him much running before he began even to suspect that there was a message involved.

It is not often that I think about Jim Trueblood these days and I must say that you are one of the few people who has seen beyond the incest to the human quality of the man. Thanks for reminding me of one of my more daring efforts.

I am sorry I have no lectures scheduled in the city within the near future and I am confined for the most part to my classes at Bard College. Nevertheless, I shall be in the city from time to time during the summer and if you find it convenient you might give me a ring.

Sincerely yours,
Ralph Ellison

To Richard Stern
Tivoli, New York
MAY 23, 1960

Dear Dick,

Life was finally getting back into its old groove after the Chicago trip when I realized that I had to go to Yale for a morning talk and a further day of visiting with friends. It went fairly well but was much less impressive after the pace you put me through out there and I was very glad to return here to work. Naturally, I still miss Chicago and regret I couldn't stick around to see more of it. Nevertheless I'm sure that my being there must have complicated your life a bit and I wish to thank you again for making everything move so smoothly. I hope next time there won't be all the pressure and we'll have time to see your Second City and to gab with Nathan Scott, whom I found intriguing, and to see some of the places Saul talks so much about. He, by the way, is in good shape and his play goes well, the weekends have begun to bring visitors and the season is on. Please let me know when you're due here as Fanny and I would like to be around. If not, give us a ring in New York.

This morning I had Fanny put a set of bound galleys of the Gaddis book* in the mail that you may keep or dispose of as you wish. I have another copy that I found in the Flea Market in Rome. Let me know what you think of the guy once you're through all that mass of words (look who's talking!) for while I found the first part amusing I soon lost my way. One day before too long I hope to have another look at it, so if you are interested enough to chart any path I should like very much to follow. Meantime I hope you've simmered down over the lousy review in the New Yorker and that all the rest have been favorable. I've ordered the book[†] and intend to put everything else aside when it arrives so I can see what you've got cooking. Saul says you've got stuff and that's good enough for me. Please give our regards to Gay and the children, who gave me as much pleasure as I found anywhere else in Chicago. I suppose it takes a childless man to really appreciate such nice kids as yours, card games, dancing classes, piano and all, and I'll remember them many a wistful day.

I don't know in what ways I might be able to return any of your favors at this distance, but if you have any idea just let me know.

Sincerely,
Ralph

P.S.: I'm enclosing my travel voucher and such receipts as I have. These things always bewilder me.

R.E.

---

*   William Gaddis, American novelist known chiefly for *The Recognitions* (1955).

†   The book is probably *Galk*, Stern's first novel, published in 1960.

To Robert Penn Warren
730 RIVERSIDE DRIVE, 8D
NEW YORK 31 NEW YORK
SEPTEMBER 7, 1960

Dear Red,

You seemed to have dropped out of sight but having received your book of poems* I can see why. Thanks for sending a little poetry our way.

Fanny has read them and likes them very much, and Saul tells me that the volume contains some of the very best you have written. I am looking forward to reading them.

I see by the postmark that you are in the beautiful wilds of Vermont. We were in Vermont ourselves when your book arrived in New York but I do hope that this late acknowledgement will reach you still.

Give our best to Eleanor and the children and Fanny and I hope that before another year goes by we will see you all.

With best wishes,
Ralph

Mr. Robert Penn Warren
West Wardsboro, Vt.

To Walter Goldfrank
730 RIVERSIDE DRIVE,
NEW YORK 31, N.Y.
[DECEMBER 1960?]†

Dear Mr. Goldfrank

I shall try to answer your questions in the order you listed them:

1) I have no idea of the number of copies of Invisible Man have been sold to date. Several years ago the hard cover sales were about 25,000, and it still sells an average of 200 copies per annum. The first paperback

---

* Most likely Warren's collection of poems from 1957 to 1960 titled *You Emperors, and Others,* published by Random House in 1960.

† Goldfrank had written Ellison with a series of questions about *Invisible Man* on December 26, 1960.

edition was some 350,000, not all of which were sold, since these tend to disintegrate in warehouses, to get lost in shipment and to disappear in other mysterious fashions. A new paperback printing was issued last spring and seems to be selling well. The book was also published in eight foreign countries.

2) Somewhat.* I refer you to the position taken by the president of Alabama State when his students became involved in the protest movement. The Bledsoe type president is perhaps a bit desperate these days, now that his existence is threatened. The new president of Langston University of Oklahoma insisted recently (although he offered no proof) that integration of colleges had led to a falling off of the number of Negro high school graduates and college applicants—a scare tactic through which he hopes to keep his own enrollment up.

3)† I think the general movement is away from such a regard for the individual—at least at those points where it becomes important. At the same time I believe this society provides more opportunity for the average citizen to achieve his individuality than any other, while pointing out that a society cannot disregard the uniqueness of so many individuals as comprise my own group without lowering the value of the individual generally. I would say in addition that a democracy is a collectivity of individuals, ideally at least, and that the individual is inevitably in conflict with the group, especially during times of national crises. Nevertheless I believe that one of the prime obligations of the American is that of insisting that his individuality be recognized. This isn't easy because we must achieve, define, our uniqueness, and far too often Americans turn from the loneliness and difficulty that this demands.

4) No,‡ I think we are simply becoming increasingly aware that the effects of 'peaceful' oppression are far more damaging than the direct physical assault dramatized in the ritual of lynching. I think we are less patient with inequalities today, even though we are better off economically and socially than ever before. We feel more intensely than ever precisely because we realize that improvement is more possible than ever before.

---

* Goldfrank's question: "Does the 'Dr. Bledsoe' approach to Negro higher education continue to impede progress today?"

† "Do you feel that American society has moved toward or away from the regard for the singularity and uniqueness of the individual that *Invisible Man* demanded?"

‡ "Would you agree that the idea that the Negro is exploited and oppressed is less intensely felt by Negroes today than in 1952?"

5)* I don't think that the Black Muslim movement has much of a future, since the main thrust of Negro American protest has never been racist as such, but constitutional; an insistence that we be allowed full participation in American life. Ras was the projection of a mood and attitude which I found in Harlem. Elijah Muhammad and his movement represent another form of that same mood and attitude and they express in an extreme form much of the rejection and disgust which many non-Muslim Negroes feel over the continued inequalities, the humiliation and the anti-Negro racism which mark their predicament.

6)† Since it is through the writing of fiction that I have my most meaningful relationship with life I can't take Mr. Ford's statement too seriously. Obviously, he is not interested in art but is more concerned with civil rights, personal gain and fame. He imagines the true novelist has far more freedom in choosing what he does than is actually true. As with all artists, there is a good deal of obsession and compulsion involved and as far as I myself am concerned, I must write novels whatever my experience as a Negro happens to be. My best way of expressing my Identity as a Negro is by being a good novelist. Personal [honor?] has little to do with it—except as I might deal with the question of honor as part of the complexity of life that makes for the texture of serious fiction. Not only is it possible that the best art makes the best propaganda, but Negroes suffer a serious lack which cannot be fulfilled by propAGANDA and I refer to that exploration and projection of the meaning of their experience which is the province of literature and through which alone we might come into conscious possession of those values which define us and as a unique people. Neither propaganda nor sociological studies prepared us for the children of Oklahoma City, Little Rock, for the Montgomery boycott or for the college sit-inners. For a foreshadowing of this you must turn to the sound of jazz, to the aggressive style and graceful style of Negro athletes and to a few poems and even fewer novels.

---

* "The similarity between Elijah Muhammad and Ras the Exhorter strikes me with great force. What are your feelings about the policies and activities of the Black Muslim movement? Do you think the movement has a future?"

† "In what I regard a pretty poor book, Nick Aaron Ford in 1936 wrote: 'since the Negro novelist has not produced even a first rate novel, is he not justified in laying aside the pretensions of pure artistry and boldly taking up the cudgel of propaganda? Could he not produce much greater results for the cause of his race and bring more honor to himself by open warfare of this nature than by secret subterfuge? I am inclined to think so.' Do you have any comments on that paragraph?"

One final word: I believe that writers must have a sense of realism not only about the life around them, but concerning their own capabilities. Negroes are not excepted and if they give themselves time to learn their craft and to discover their sense of life and their sense of life's values, then they should have realized that they belong to a minority which cuts across race and nationality. For these fame is <u>not</u> the spur, but the mastery of [a] bit of life through art form. The public might not be prepared to acclaim you when this is done, as they were unprepared to acclaim *Moby-Dick* back in 1851, so he'll have to turn to other members of this sub-minority for whatever praise they are willing to grant him. If this is too lonely a way for him, then let him become a civil rights lawyer, a specialist in race relations, or a sociologist. It is unlikely that he'll become rich but the Negro press will praise him, he will have the certainties offered by the statistical method—not to mention the encouragement to be had from the knowledge of the important role sociology played in the Supreme Court decision on Civil Rights.

That's it—all in a rush. I hope it helps and that your project turns out well.

Sincerely,
Ralph Ellison

Mr. Walter Goldfrank
Kirkland G-24
Harvard College,
Cambridge 38, Mass.

To Stanley Hyman
Tivoli,
MARCH 10, 1961

Dear Stanley,

I finally located the enclosed so now one big daddy may have the dope on the other . . . I was sent bound galleys of your book* which I read with an engrossment such as criticism has failed to arouse in me for quite some time. You're very good at clearing the perspective and I must tell you that if once in a while I've felt that you'd lost your interest in the work of the

---

* *Poetry and Criticism: Five Revolutions in Literary Taste* (1961).

poetic imagination as such, your book leaves no doubt that your criticism is rooted in a deep love of the poetic act and that your analytical system is basically a means of making that love manifest. I really felt that I was back twenty years [. . .] and just discovering poetry and criticism with all the excitement of that discovery. Any book that can do that for an old character like me is a very good book indeed. I wrote Mike a little note of comment and I've begun spreading the news to all my friends.

Things go about the same with me, I'm still slugging and trying to make this mass of words mean something and am very weary. I'm also thinking of giving up the country when Bellow returns in May, since now I get as much work done there as here. Fanny is fine and life proceeds without event. Tell Shirley that I hope she's back at her typewriter and although I've never said it, she should know that her productivity has been a source of strength to me as I creep along at my snail's pace. Tell her also to take a look at *The Gouffe* by Joachim Maass. I've read a third of it and believe she might find it intriguing.

Hope to see you soon although the weather has inhibited my readiness to travel.

Yours,
[Ralph]

P.S. Here's a dog song I heard my mutt singing:

> *Well, the cats are in the Catskills*
> *Sharpening up their peckers with their paws*
> *And when they get them sharpened,*
> *They'll try them on their maws . . .*

This was sung with a great deal of malice and dogged ambiguity but was too much for me. I'm not even sure that I've spelled paws or maws correctly and he refused to explain, saying only that it was a traditional song. Perhaps you can place the origin.

To Saul Bellow
Tivoli, N.Y.
MARCH 20, 1961

Dear Saul,

I hope by now you've adjusted to the heat and noise of Puerto Rico, if not perhaps there's a bit of consolation in the fact that had you been here you would have been subjected to the noise of the elements and to the other extreme of temperature. About the time your note arrived there had been a blizzard that dropped the thermometer to 28 below for several days and since then there have been several heavy snowfalls and indeed, the fields are still heavily white. During the freeze things became so bad for the wild animals that I saw a red fox hunting mice beneath the hard crust of white that covered the meadow out front, doing his little leaping death dance at high noon. Once I was snowed-in down in the city and the rest of the time I've had to depend upon Claude to plow out the drive and drag me out of the stuff. Of the three I've spent here, this is the worst winter of all. Right now I'm dam sick of it.

Aaron tells me that you're worrying about your house—which is unnecessary, since you must know by now that if anything goes seriously wrong I'd write you immediately. As for minor matters, I'm too busy with my own work to worry you with them; I'll simply take care of them and you can change them when you return. I still keep the house locked and try to keep the grounds free of the uninvited from Tivoli and Rhinebeck. On the other hand, if you feel that you can no longer trust me to look out for things please be practical about it and let me know and I'll turn it over to whomever you suggest and no hard feelings about it. Why should <u>both</u> of us worry? Or tremble? . . . Now to the house: Except for the roof, which is leaking a bit in your bedroom but not out above the second floor stairs (and which Holt had been notified about) the only damage has been the bursting of the copper pipes which rise to the bathroom within the wall to the right of the kitchen door. This occurred during the blizzard when the temperature in the house couldn't quite rise to fifty-eight degrees, but fortunately the only damage was to the pipes, not to the wall. I cut off the water and the pump and once the Holts were able to get to us, they cut out the burst sections and sweated in new lengths of pipe and that was that. I took the liberty of having a valve put in the hot water line and would have done so for the cold if the arrangement of the wall hadn't made it too difficult. Now when the weather is severe you'll have more control of the water to the second floor. Holt assured me that no damage was done to the inside of the wall because the water simply flowed down the pipe and was absorbed into the earth beneath the kitchen and dining room floors. Nor was it necessary to damage the wall-paper to get at the pipes, they simply removed the pine boards at the bottom, cut the pipe and lifted it out above in the little alcove off your study where, in the corner of the cabinets where your records stand, the pipes are exposed. Now the water works fine and the Holts have been paid.

As for the rest of the house, it's as you left it. After I caught Rufus on the bed, I closed your bedroom and hooked it; I work and sleep in the guestroom and this time you'll find only your own books and mail in your study. Shula called for the T.V. and I returned it to her last month. Outside, the last heavy snows snapped boughs from the pines in the back and to the roadside of the house, but thus far your big tree still cleaves the sky and confronts the lion of March with grace. Rufus is fine, the kitchen no longer smells of cat shit (maybe that's why it snowed so damned much). So that's the report on the house; there's been some lost gleam from the waxed floors, but I'll correct that when the thaw comes and the ground is dry. So enjoy yourself and save your worry for your soul and for your work. I'm gradually returning my effects to the city in anticipation of the time when I'll return to city living. Until then, however, and until you return, I'll be spending most of my time at Tivoli.

Things go O.K. with me, I'm working hard on the book, my classes are heavy and I've lectures which will carry me to Coe College, in Cedar Rapids and to Iowa City next month, along with close trips to Boston and Yale. Bard is coming apart in its English division and they're hoping I'll stay but I've had it. I'll be stopping off in Chicago to have a talk with Simpson and Stern when I'm on the Iowa trip and I recall that you once suggested that we might coordinate or at least work out some kind of continuity between our lectures. If you're still interested, I am and would be pleased to hear your ideas. I plan to give some attention to novel criticism and relate it to the Civil war background but will know a bit more about it when I consult Dick as to the most useful point of attack.

I received a nice little fan latter from George Rosenfeld the other day that frightened me as much as it pleased me. Now I know how long it's been since I've published a book.

Take it easy and regards to Susie.

As ever,
[Ralph]

To Saul Bellow
730 RIVERSIDE DRIVE
NEW YORK,
MAY 7, 1961

Dear Saul,

Sorry that the bills keep slipping through the hands of your Tivoli friends and landing with you. As for things at this end, I've finally got the Holts in to look at the roof and to clean the gutters. They send word that if you plan to paint the roof, now is the time to do it—which means, I suppose, that with the spring finally arriving they won't be so busy with frozen pipes and unsound heating systems.

I was indeed surprised to hear of Esther's death and yours was the first word I received. I suppose that Sondra has received the photos by now. I posted them before I went to Iowa and Chicago last month. I insured the stuff for a hundred bucks so I assume it got through.

I had already spoken to Claude about plowing and was told that with the weather so uncertain he preferred to do it around the middle of the month. We had freezing weather last week so he's in no rush. Nor is there enough grass in the back at the moment to do his kind of cutting, though by the time you arrive it'll probably be shooting up. Nevertheless, I'll pass the word along.

Iowa was frantic but pleasant. I met Phil Roth and got along with him well enough, Chicago was even swifter, or I at least was moving faster, so wasn't able to see Cogan but found the Sterns in fine shape. They're already getting the publicity together for your trip there in the winter and the dean is as enthusiastic as ever.

This continues to be my period for traveling and yakking. I go to Yale next Wed., was at Boston College last Sat. and will probably double back to Howe's hangout next week.

That's it. Things around the house are about as you left them and the fields are turning green. Fanny sends regards.

Best,
Ralph

To Horace Cayton
730 RIVERSIDE DRIVE
NEW YORK 31, N.Y.
JULY 15, 1961

Dear Horace:

After quite some time of wondering when you'd turn up again I was asked by way of fulfilling some of my contributing editor's obligation to the *Noble Savage,* to read your manuscript. I couldn't have been more surprised or pleased to learn at last where you are and that you're at work getting some of your autobiography down on paper. Indeed, I had recently been telling Saul Bellow something of the wide variety of your experience and what an important social document I felt an account of them would make; now, even though the editors were unable to accept your contribution in its present form, Saul agrees with me and it is at his suggestion that I write you my ideas for giving the piece the sharper focus which its contents demand.

First, let me say that while even the most casual can see that your story is most interesting, the reader aware of your background as scholar, sociologist, director of institutions and newspaperman, would realize immediately that the incidents which you report here are loaded with more meaning than they confess to any but the most fully informed. There's gold here but as the piece stands it requires more skill to claim it than most of our miners possess. Part of the trouble lies, it seems to me, in your use of understatement, which certainly has been an element in some of the most effective literary styles. But as you've used it here it makes for a loss of emotional force and intellectual significance. A number of important elements seem either to have been omitted or are so underplayed as to cause a lack of sharpness, a slackness of implicit tension and an erratic tempo. (Now don't stop reading at this point, I'm writing in this manner because I feel that what you have achieved is important and can withstand such scrutiny.) For instance, I don't get a sharp enough image of your family to place them vividly against the background provided by the fourteen year old state on the fading frontier, and though I know enough of the general Negro background to fill in much of what is missing, most of our readers could not. And don't forget the pleasure to be derived from learning how other people live, what they make of their environment. I'd like to see something of the family furniture, am curious about the size of your house, to hear what you thought of the horses, of your neighbors and Nish. You're writing at this point of family pride, so let's have it. What value did all of this represent to you who are, after all, the center of the piece. You had it good and you lost it and that's part of the story, so build us up for the fall.

Your last section is centered around your adolescence and I am forcefully reminded that while most of adolescent experience is hellish, Negro adolescence is hell <u>compounded</u> because of its inevitable entanglement with the confusions of race and color. Nevertheless, this shouldn't be allowed to blur the form through which it is presented; the confusion must be in the mind of the boy you were, not in your portrait of him. Which leads me to observe that while I can see adequate reasons for your feelings of rejection, they seem too much of a <u>social</u> matter with their main sources outside the family. Part of this is due to your understating the emotional tone of your family life (I don't mean your religious or cultural activities or the moment of racial fear, these are all very much here, but the quality of warmth, friction, love, conflict, harmony or dissonance etc.) which must have reinforced your feelings of rejection and/or acted as a buffer and source of comfort from outside pressures.

And what were your sisters like? And were there consequences flowing from your firing the big firecracker without the little brother who bore your distinguished grandfather's name? Let us have something of their personalities. You make the most complete presentation of your father, but I'm struck by the fact that you take so little advantage of the opportunity to make the reader <u>see</u> your mother. I have no idea of her height, her size, her voice, her idiom of speech or her color—only of her social activities and her fear. I would think that during that period the whole question of color as a specifically Negro value would have far more importance, both socially and aesthetically, than you indicate. And along with this I'd like to know more of your grandfather—of course I do, but from other sources—but here is a fine opportunity to fill in the reader's knowledge of a phase of American history which is only beginning to reveal its true importance. Technically, you can do this while documenting more fully the reasons for your family's feelings of distinction, of possessing a tradition. A reader would like to know if you ever saw your grandfather; were there photographs of him displayed in your home, etc. The bit about the Johnson letter is excellent and of historical importance. Why not heighten it with a fuller account of your grandfather's career? Were anecdotes about him told the children? And let's face it: wouldn't the social force of snobbery be operative in such a picture, just as it is in most family pictures where status is a concern? I sense it here and a frank discussion of it would do a great deal to point up the pity and terror of your parents' loss of social position, just as it would underscore your father's courage in accepting the role imposed upon him by the social changes in the town. For wasn't he, in a way of speaking, lynched socially and politically for reporting a lynching? The whole section describing his loss of his paper is damn good, and I believe that a fuller description of your parents' relationships within the family and the atmosphere in which you lived, would convey more of the meaning and emotion implicit within the incidents.

To switch our approach a bit, it occurs to me that your narrative falls into the pattern that someone had described as a "fall from high estate." This is a most meaningful socio-psychological experience—and far more so than such sociological descriptions as "a loss of class status," or "a loss of class identification" would suggest, and it links up with a mythic pattern which underlies much of literature. It also underlies the lives of many writers, especially novelists, among them Melville and Joyce. One thing is sure, you had no need to invent an African chief to give you a sense of prestige, you had the real thing and most rare, a U.S. senator for a grandfather. Tell us more of what it meant for a Negro child to have had one.

As to the form of your piece (which I hope is part of a longer work) I feel that it would help, for magazine publication, if you could give it more structural integrity. Since it ends with your taking off for Alaska—much as Huck Finn takes off for the Territory, or the hero of Joyce's Portrait for Paris—I'd build toward this development from the beginning; I'd get Alaska into the picture as quickly as possible. It was a period of northerly movement for Negroes. Your father went to Seattle seeking opportunity, responsibility, identity; others went to that farther frontier seeking the freedom that was gold. Thus you could use Mr. Walker to point the direction of your "plot" just as he actually pointed the direction of your Alaska adventures. Formally his possibilities are many; he stands for adventure, Negro daring, wealth achieved through adventure, for the possibility of escaping the limits of race. He is a man of integrity, intelligence and humor, etc. Why not allow him more freedom to function more fully in the role he seems to have played. Thus, while I don't insist that he functioned as a kind of father figure, I cannot ignore the fact that your decision to follow his path to Alaska was made after you received your father's ultimatum.

As you can see, I'm making a distinction between one's experience and the literary organization and techniques that we employ to endow the incidents of our lives with communicable significance. And I'd even extend this to the manipulation of chronology if necessary for formal effectiveness. Facts alone, strange and exciting events alone do not make good autobiography. Autobiography is a <u>literary</u> organization of facts and incidents. Form must be <u>imposed</u> upon life so that we may discover the true meaning of events and the connections between our own lives and the old, intricate, human story. The threads which hold the episodes of our experience together and which shape our emotions and our character provide, through their repetition and endless variety, the themes for literature. Our problem is to become aware of them, to observe how their specific quality lines up with the general human pattern, then shape them meaningfully and project them eloquently. You're very lucky, you were born with an interesting heritage, a hard head and an adventurous spirit which has kept you struggling with some of the most interesting themes of the human condition.

Take a look at the theme of women: There are your mother and sisters and your mother's mother—all too sketchily described; then there is the woman in the story of the ex-slave and his former owner and Mr. Walker's comment on the man's motives. Entwined with this theme is that of miscegenation, which raises its head in the incident of your little princess Nelly and the mother who didn't wish you to be making explosions of <u>any</u> nature with her little daughter. And again, there is the white girl with whom you were not allowed to dance and the Negro girl who designated as the limit of your choice of partners. Just as Dick Gregory is reported to have said, you apply for a job digging ditches and the white man asks you if you like white women and you know right away that he's got you stumped. If you say no, he rejects you as a damn liar and unreliable. If you answer yes, he rejects you as a potential rapist. Seriously, what fascinates here is that through this complex of frustration and desire, adolescence and race, there emerges not only the theme of social rejection but also a theme of filial guilt, the feeling that you had betrayed your brother. Man, this is powerful medicine, and I believe it needs only a few preparatory touches in the beginning—women, color, sibling rivalry, the question of racial and filial betrayal (described more than discussed) to shatter the reader with that power. Incidentally, the theme of betrayal and guilt is quite possibly operative on other levels of the experience: in your parents being more fortunate that the other Negroes, in your being better dressed, spoken, and indeed, being closer to the white norm both in the way you lived and the way you looked than most of the other Negroes. Perhaps it attaches itself to your grandfather's role as a leader. At any rate, I am not advising an explicit discussion of these psychological matters, only that you describe the situations in which they arise more vividly.

Now let's take a look at the general movement of your piece. On one level it moves from your birth into a distinguished family, through its fall from high estate, to its acceptance of a "Negro" identity as Seattle became more "Americanized" under the influx of southern Negroes and the acceleration of 20th Century social change. As personal history, it describes your movement from infancy, through puberty, to the discovery of the meaning of color during adolescence; from the passive, dream-state of the unawakened child protected by family and circumstances, to the trauma of racial rejection and thence to a phase of frustrated self-assertion and to final escape. I find it extremely interesting that you chose to negotiate the "murderous White Pass" lined with dead men, animals and discarded equipment (not to mention the dead hopes and dreams) as a means of escaping and asserting your manhood. How did you formulate your decision to yourself? Did you think to seek Mr. Walker's advice at that time? But to continue: As the history of a family's aspirations, the piece moves from the hope of participating fully and responsibly in the life of Seattle and thus in the life of the nation, and it reflects the Negro's post-emancipation hope of that manhood and citizenship symbolized by the figure of Senator Revels. It then takes us through the changing racial relationships within the city and the nation, and we see your father moving in this sea of change from an identity that placed him as a more or less integrated leader of the local G.D.P. to that of a Negro leader within a white dominated party.

Indeed, you have here one of the key moments of American Negro history: the hopes of Reconstruction with your grandfather symbolizing the possession of a spirit of freedom and responsibility which few Negroes since his time have dared even dream of possessing, and the suppression of those manly aspirations by the powers that be and the elevation of Booker T. and his policy of accommodation. And there you were in the center of it. This is what makes this phase of your life so interesting, so turbulent and so important to be repossessed in writing.

I've gone on far too long and I hope you'll forgive my presumption in writing as though you were unaware of what you were doing; I've gone on this way so that you will be assured that I understand what you're putting down and appreciate its value, and to give weight to my suggestions for making the piece useful for the *Noble Savage*. One further suggestion and

I'll close: Yours is a far more interesting experience of childhood than was Dick's and your account of it shouldn't be restricted by following too closely the powerful but quite limited image which he provides in *Black Boy*. You were born to a much wider horizon of possibility and you were, and are still, more exuberant in your approach to living. Dick play-acted at this but he was basically more often afraid and ill at ease than not. So let us have more of you, who were never a Bigger Thomas, whatever your frustration. So lay it on the line and on the level and let us look at your life as endowed with all you know and honestly feel. Then a reader who doesn't know the background will sense, nevertheless, the wonderful and intriguing humanity of your most American story. It is very important that it be published and I'd like to see it appear in the N.S.

Thinking of Dick reminds me that with you gone to the west coast and with Vandy and Dick gone to join Silvia Safford and with Chester in Paris and Jean gone God-knows-where—a period of my own life has come to a definite end. Isn't it a crime that so much of our experience—and the most interesting and complex of experience at that—never finds statement in literature? It is sadly true and that's one reason that I'm so happy that you're beginning to get some of yours down. Good luck and if I can be of any help let me do whatever I can. Fanny joins me in wishing you all the best.

Sincerely,
Ralph

730 Riverside Drive
New York 31, N.Y.

To Fanny Ellison
THE QUADRANGLE CLUB
OCTOBER 7, 1961

Dear Fanny:

It was damn good to get your note; your leaving has left an emptiness and I think I've had just about enough of Chicago for a while.[*] Indeed, I don't know what you find so interesting about the Quadrangle Club

[*]   Ellison had been named to the prestigious Alexander White visiting professorship at the University of Chicago, where he would also be the first participant in the Celebrities in Residence program. He resided for the quarter in the Quadrangle Club near the campus.

when you have so much in apt 8D. I miss it very much ... Sunday I went with Billie and Tobey to see George and we found him transferred to the Chest Building, where passes are required and where only two may visit at a time.* George was still very thin but he seemed stronger and enough himself to repeat every statement six or seven times. Now he's dramatizing his illness and speaks of himself as receiving "surgery without a knife," i.e. they're removing fluid from his lung with a rubber tube and injecting some sort of powder or dust (probably an antibiotic) beneath his skin. He's as intense as ever and says that the doctor told him that what he has is definitely curable. "Ralph," he told me in triplicate, "I'm recovering from a <u>severe</u> case of pneumonia; a <u>severe</u> case." I drove Billie home immediately afterwards because I had to attend the party at the Sterns which was given for one of J.F.K.'s assistants and your husband. It was O.K. but between us I'm getting bored with seeing some of the people so frequently. I went out afterwards and had some Chinese food and then to bed. I'm still running into onion and my temper's going quite bad ... It isn't made any better by the enclosed notice from the characters who are financing the car. Would you please take a look at the insurance and see if they aren't mistaken about the collision coverage. For years we've had $50 deductible when we didn't need it, considering that the car was worth so little. Now when we have a new car they seem to have removed it. I hope it's simply a mistake but if it isn't, ask them to correct it—No, you don't have to be bothered with it, I've called Allstate and have been told by a Mr. Giordano that he'd correct the mistake. Any little thing to drive you nuts! Thanks for doing the letters for me, I've yet to write DuCournet but I'll do that soon ... I've received my first check and as soon as possible I'll send you some money and will deposit some of it in Red Hook. I want to get that bank off my neck as soon as possible. By the way, I'd like to give Billie and George something, but you send it from there or give it to them when you return here and thus things may be kept in perspective. I'm having lunch downstairs with Zita and some friends of theirs today. They've invited me to the dunes but I fear there'll be no time for it. My first lecture is on the evening of the 20th and the damn Chancellor's wife wants to have cocktails and dinner—beforehand. I guess I'll have to go along. By the way Zita tried to have a conversation about Saul but I didn't encourage it. She says he's been having the same trouble since he was in high

---

* Fanny's mother, Willie Mae McConnell, and her stepfather, George, lived in Chicago and Ellison would visit them periodically. Tobey was a friend of George's.

school, which doesn't surprise me. I spent a couple of hours on Sat afternoon talking with Nathan Scott. They send regards and have invited me to Thanksgiving dinner. I don't know but I'd like to go to see Tucker . . . unless you're in town by then . . . How did it go with the Murrays? I've yet to write but tell Al that I'll do so as soon as I've had a chance to talk with Mort Sprague. That's about it since I've got to go out for a while. George liked the candy so much that he's demanding more of it and, naturally in this confused world, the store is out of it. Take care of yourself and see that doctor for a checkup. Many nice things are being said about you by those who met you here and not only do I agree with them, I know many more and I love you.

[Ralph]

P.S.
Careful on the office matter, let those who hold the responsibility do their own dirty work.

To Fanny Ellison
THE QUADRANGLE CLUB
OCT. 10, 1961

Dear Fanny,

I've been waiting for the letter that you mentioned over the telephone but now assume that it was lost. I hope it contained nothing important even though you said it was "incomplete." Nevertheless I've inquired here at the desk and at the Faculty Exchange, which distributes mail about the campus, in vain. Perhaps it's lying in some dark corner in a New York Post Office . . . There is little to tell you so far: I've met my class three times and managed to keep talking on each occasion; I have a decent enough room here at the club except for its noise; I eat lunch here, breakfast down the street on 57th, and dinner at a nearby restaurant, or with the Sterns.* Last night we had Chinese food over on 63rd. I've been having trouble with onions and garlic, and indeed, have been quite upset on two occasions yesterday morning being one of them. I had dinner with the Nathan Scotts on Sunday and I think I picked up garlic there. Monday I was

---

* Richard "Dick" Stern, professor of English at the University of Chicago, had arranged Ralph's professorship there.

kept close to the bathroom all morning and thought I'd miss my class I was so upset and so wet with perspiration but it cleared up in time and I learned that the weather had become suddenly quite hot . . . As you can see I'm just about the same. Sunday afternoon I spent a couple of hours with George and Billy, who seem in good shape. She's still trying to adjust to her store teeth and he's still repeating himself like Little Sir Echo but all in all they're OK . . . I'll see them whenever I can but I got the impression from George that they're cooling off on Mrs. Norton who, it seems, borrows too often to suit G. So I dare not telephone them ahead . . . Things are slow getting underway here. I was given an office yesterday but I've yet to get organized at the library and my identification hasn't come through. I understand that the college hasn't had to deal with visiting profs before so no routines have been worked out. I haven't been able to do much of my own work either but that should straighten itself out during the next few days. I feel the need to keep it moving toward completion and am trying to keep interruptions to a minimum. I fly to St. Louis for my lecture there on the 18th after which I shall return here immediately. I had planned to drive but was told that it's a six-hour trip each way and thus would be too tiring. The car, by the way, has worked beautifully and I've already put eighteen hundred miles on it . . . Bourjaily wrote the other day that Tucker is doing well so don't worry about him. I'll try to get up there to see him around the end of the month. They had him in the kennel with their little Beagle bitch so I guess by now he's humped some of that stuff he drips all over the place out of his system. He can get nowhere of course but at least he has the illusion of possibility . . . I had a late breakfast and a long talk with Ruth Waters, which was interesting and somewhat sad. She tells me that Finley is a miserly type and that Saretta's life has been one of frustration. Their son is an obvious homosexual type and an object of gossip who is doomed to suffer the longer he remains there, but that Finley is unable to see what is happening. Ruth herself has been married twice since I saw her and now has another child; this by her last and present husband, who she describes as a fine man, although I get the impression that she was in N.Y. on some restless little side adventure of her own. She has more intelligence and imagination than most people I knew in Okla. but you needn't send such visitors to get in touch with me here although my talk with her was interesting. Use your own judgment as to how important it is that I see them . . . I hope you'll write me what's happening there because not only is telephoning expensive but it has been my bad and depressing luck to catch you after your cocktail hour has begun on each occasion I've called you. Indeed, I'm still depressed over the last call and was quite saddened that you'd drunk so much with Mique in the house. Lord knows what she'll begin to think of us. I realize that you don't regard this as serious but for me it is, and becoming increasingly so. Fanny, I won't fight with you about it but I'm very serious when I tell you that you should think very seriously about the matter and realize that I consider it a problem that can completely destroy our relationship. I mean this and I'm sitting here at one in the afternoon feeling sick over it. Nevertheless, I can't compete with the bottle and if that's the way you want it, if it's really that important to you, then I think we should get it over with because I can't deal with it. Why don't you consult a physician? I have no doubt that there is something bothering you which you've never talked to me about and perhaps it's something which you haven't thought too much about. If I can help I think I should be given the opportunity, if not then at least you should go to someone who can. One thing seems certain, this thing is destroying our marriage and I think it a crime and an obscene waste. You'll forgive me for writing this way but I don't want this thing to break us up and I want you to know how I've come to feel about it . . .

Let me know if the rug came and if the painters have done their work. I'll send some money as soon as I'm paid for the St. Louis lecture. Meantime, I'd appreciate it if you'd send me the Murrays' address and if you'd forward any mail of interest.

The Sterns are in fine condition, the older children bright and intelligent and the three-month old baby boy is following in the same pattern. Indeed, Chicago appears to be a very good place for children. I've met three families, including the Scotts, and all have good-looking, intelligent kids. I took part in a touch-football game with a crew of them one afternoon and they ran me ragged. It was a beautiful day, as most of my days here have been, and I missed you very much. I needn't say that I miss you in the night and that here, unlike Tivoli, I find it terribly difficult to live and sleep alone . . . Don't forget to send me the cost of your flight fare because I wish to include it in my moving expenses allowance. I'd also like to know when you plan to arrive because there is a shortage of rooms here and I'd like to prepare in advance. Don't rush yourself but keep this in mind. One thing is certain, I don't want you at George and Billy's because he still hasn't an extra place to sleep. He embarrassed me explaining what they had done with the gift money, which they used, as they should have, for things that were more important to them. Still he'd have to give up his bed for you, I couldn't (and have no wish to) stay there and insist that you stay with me. So let me know in time. I've got to take off for the bookstore and the Dean's office now and thus must close this. Meantime think seriously about what I've said above and try to remember that I do love you.

[Ralph]

To Fanny Ellison
THE QUADRANGLE CLUB
OCT. 11, 1961

Dear Fanny,

This is just a note to get the enclosed cards to you. Please sign then and return as soon as possible. I took out the account so that I could handle expenses without the necessity of carrying around so much cash. After my bill here and my advance came out there isn't so much left, but there'll be more in December and I won't have to pay rent for the entire month.

The day is bright and sunny here and all it needs is you. I don't feel too peppy but I'm damn sorry that I didn't take off for Iowa on Thursday. This morning I was passing a military ceremony down on Drexel and 50th and stopped to watch, and there they were, the World War I vets, the ROTC boys, the Elks, the VFW's and drill teams of younger boys and Cub Scouts. There was also a band of seven pieces and the usual drum corps of youngsters, but only three girls; young ladies who marched with the ROTC and who wore a similar uniform. I missed the speeches but arrived just in time to see a short, heavily mustached young Negro of haughty but impressive military bearing, four youngsters decked out in Air Force blue, white spats and helmets, through a precision drill which had all the precise and contained and jazz-like rhythm you'd expect if the old Four Step Brothers had decided to do some of the favorite dance patterns of the Jose Greco dance troupe. The leader complained to me later that he didn't care for the grass (we were in a park) and I could understand him because much of the <u>stampada</u> of the Spanish dance would have been lost here and these kids were doing exactly that—even to clapping their white-gloved hands between steps. It started with the commander—dressed mysteriously in a fatigue uniform with a First Lieut's emblem on the front of the cap—shouted orders with far more style than the ROTC people, with the boys repeating while standing at attention, then he tossed them a salute in a hup-huping voice, spun on his heels and headed for the side-lines and they were off at high speed. They held this speed throughout their maneuvers and ended with a salute thrown as they fell to one knee. It was the best and most hopeful thing I've seen from Negroes during the whole trip. There was, of course, the old military yearning that was so much a part of my own boyhood, but now the elderly men in overseas caps are mainly from the AEF rather than the Spanish American War. There was a sadness about it too, but perhaps that's merely personal and because I'm tired.

Your letter about Connie's call was quite funny and there's no need denying it, despite the sadness of having Jimmy lose his mother. She was doing the <u>right thing</u> at the right time and feeling proud of it, but the right thing was not enough to kill the vulgarity or the comedy—or the drama.

I'm glad that you and Billie patched things up and you should know that she was quite neat last Sunday . . . That pompous ass Hill* called me to make a date to discuss the piece he wants to publish, but thus far he hasn't called. Which is just as well, since I haven't read the edited version. Would you call him and have the original returned? Ramsay is stalling and I'm getting tired. If you get no action let's take it to the rent control people. There are a hundred things that could be done to the apartment so keep adding to it each time you make a list. Should I write him?

I'm glad the Murrays were not too much trouble this time and I hope you can go there for Thanksgiving. Wish I could join you. Too bad Mique is too old to be adopted, you could have her about all the time!

I guess I told you that I have a new room and that it has bookshelves and a softer bed. Well, it's true and I rest better but I realize now that part of my trouble is the sleeping alone. You just hold on and we'll solve our problems together.

> I love you,
> [Ralph]

To Fanny Ellison
THE QUADRANGLE CLUB
OCT. 14, 1961

My darling Fanny,

Your letter arrived this morning (Sat.) and I am answering during the late afternoon of a day that began quite gloomily with a drop in temperature

---

* Herbert Hill, editor of the anthology of African American writing *Soon, One Morning,* published the Mary Rambo excerpt "Out of the Hospital and Under the Bar" from a draft of *Invisible Man* in 1963. This unpublished section from Ellison's draft gives a fascinating glimpse at Ellison's broader conceptions of the Mary Rambo character.

and what I'm sure was a swirl of snow. Now it's cool but bright and I'm sure that no one around has any doubts but that fall has begun. This afternoon I called the hospital to check on George and was told that he was not critical, although he does have pneumonia and has been complaining of a pain in his chest. This time I called for ward 45 directly rather than asking for him by name and thus was able to reach him. I'm sorry about the mix-up but it was the hospital's not mine. Be that as it may, I called Mrs. Norton and asked her to tell Billie that I would pick her up at one-thirty tomorrow afternoon so that we may be on hand at two p.m., when the visiting hour begins. I didn't talk with Billie but I have no doubt that Mrs. N. delivered the message. She's quite intelligent and aware of the worry that Billie is going through, and I quite agree with you that we should ignore George's bullshit. I'll give them some sort of present and be glad to do it. Billie didn't tell me what had happened in such detail as she did you, not even that she had been at the hospital when G. was given tests. Nevertheless, she knew that I had been misled by the information people (and the nurse and physician) out at the hospital and insisted that I call them again. Don't worry, I'll let you know in time if there's real necessity for you to come before you planned. By the way, you mentioned the last 4 or 5 days, do you wish to make this more definite? It will make it easier for me to take care of housing arrangements. Don't worry about it, because if nothing is available here there will be other hotels in the neighborhood. You might wish, under the circumstances, to stay with Billie, toward which, for all my designs upon you, I couldn't possibly object. And if you don't think I have designs, then you have no idea how out of place, lonely and restless this trip has made me. Perhaps there's something in the complaint I heard made by an older fellow years ago, when I shined shoes in the municipal building in Okla. City. "Damn," he complained, "that woman of mine must have measured me and is wearing it around her waist" (the bastard <u>had</u> to be bragging, now that I think of it, since as thin as he was his member couldn't have been long). "What you mean?" someone said, and he explained, "Hell man," he said, "She must've measured me because I ain't raised a hard in three days!" Make it two weeks and you've got me in a nutshell! . . . I'm sorry you didn't get to the Malamud party—even though the book is a dud, from all the reports from Saul, Dick Stern and others. Nevertheless, you should try to see the Blums even though I can't join you. They're a lot of fun and you'll see people whom we like there. Anyway, you should always remember that I'm not against your drinking, only against your getting drunk. It's the possible need to get lost, ossified, blotto—you name it—which upsets me. And it is real upset. I've told you long ago of my anxiety of being unable to communicate with those I love. Perhaps you should call me. I'm usually here at five-thirty, which is six-thirty N.Y. I want you articulate, or if inarticulate, then I want to be there to share the confusion directly. But don't miss the point, if you have problems that make liquor necessary, then I want to know them, or at least, I want you to go to someone who knows what to do to help. I might be the cause, after all . . . Your letter had the rhythmical swing (I'm referring to the long one) that I've been trying to suggest for your appeals. To hell with that Gil Harold will know that he didn't write what you've created. Anyway, true rhythms in a piece of writing is a result of a tension between one's desire, compulsion toward expression and one's emotional involvement with the ideas, the values, etc., which one would express. You are <u>really</u> involved with the old man* but Gil is probably simply involved with his career . . . I'm going in a few minutes to a party given by Arthur Heisserman and his wife—he's the man who drove us down to the section where Billie and George used to live—and I'm really not up to it. I'm still suffering from the onion and garlic, but they're nice people with three beautiful young daughters and a jumping jack of a young boy. The other evening I again had dinner with the Sterns, but this time Dick's agent, a young and for me impossible Italio-American woman who is now an associate of Russel and Volkening's was present, and at one point during the flow of food and liquor, I heard Dick say that he wished Saul would go for her instead of Susan. Well, I've long since ruled myself out of bounds in Saul's affairs of the bed—of the heart—but if I've any judgment, I'd say that he'd do better by sticking his balls where the monkey stuck his tail—in the rotary lawn mower! . . .

Your description of your adventures with Mique and her friends was first-rate. Let's face it, she's of another generation as are they. Nevertheless, there are certain human considerations that are important. You were right to be annoyed <u>and</u> correct in leaving the whole business to Mique. They're adolescents and they have still to learn to be human. As for your cigars—I, at least, didn't raise <u>that</u> problem. What I'm concerned about is the maintenance of an image of you that is very important to me and the

---

* Dr. Gordon Seagrave, the American doctor who was born in Burma and headed the American Medical Center for Burma, where Fanny was now working as executive director.

lack of control that the too frequent drinking brings about is destructive of it. You often forget what's happened during these moments and you don't really see the danger implicit in them. Well, I have my fears and my ideals and that's one thing; but now that I'm here in Chicago and I see George and Billie I realize the tremendous job of self-creation you represent and I don't wish to see it flawed or undone by taking this easy way out of whatever it is that's causing your tensions. And whether you believe it or not, I'm as proud of you as you are of me and I don't wish this recent development to spoil you . . . I broke this off on Sunday and intended finishing after I had seen George, but it didn't work out that way. I drove down to pick up Billie and Tobey was there to go along so the three of us found our way to the County Hospital. There was a mob going in when we arrived and the parking spaces all taken but thanks to Tobey, Billie was convinced that it was better for them to go in and take advantage of the visiting hour than for her to go with me to park the car. I was able to find a place four or five blocks away and by time I found the ward, they were already there and, I hope, recovered from the shock. He's in a men's ward full of very ill old fellows and a few youngsters, who when they were not being visited lay looking about them out of the remoteness of their sickness. Various religious groups were moving from bed to bed distributing tracts and little groups of Negro nurses moved from bed to bed, in consultation and then I spotted George, lying with his shrunken cheeks and several days of beard, talking with Tobey and Billie. He had lost weight and was obviously ill but said that he felt much better and that he had received excellent care. I had already learned that he was not on the critical list and, after Tobey had shaved him he did appear much better and something like himself. I've been kicking myself as being partially responsible for his illness: Sunday before last after we had been for a drive I treated them to cigarettes and a bottle of bourbon and I suspect that he might have gotten himself overheated after a bit of drinking. At any rate, he is recovering and I'm hoping he'll soon be able to leave that squalor, that gloom, that Civil War prison hospital atmosphere. I suspect that George was feeling the ultimate possibility of his predicament as he lay there. Tobey's presence reminded him of their boyhood and I noticed a tear when G. recalled some old friend who had died there, and there were several of his repeated references to Sam, who has lost his pension. I tried to give George and Billie as much privacy as was possible in that large ward of hollow eyes and then, when they were ready to leave, I left them and went for the car. On the way back,

I asked Billie if G. had been eating and she said that he hadn't been eating very much, so you were right. I'll do what I can to remedy this when he returns home. At least I'll see that they have plenty of food. Tobey is a nice man who has some understanding of G's character, his stubbornness, his power of will. I suppose he had to, otherwise their friendship would have ceased long ago. I left them at 36 Fl. and returned here, still upset in my emotions and uncomfortable from my stay in that overheated ward. I was too tired to write and yesterday I woke up with a cold, which I'm sure I picked up out there. I met my class however, and I've been taking it easy so that I'll be able to deliver my lecture tomorrow morning at 11 a.m., in St. Louis. I should be back here in the evening, or even sooner if plans to [do] a television interview fail to come off . . . So once more, don't worry about G. and I'll keep you posted . . . My classes are taking on momentum and I'm beginning to feel that I'm getting something done. Tucka is O.K. Vance said that he'd been on his first snipe hunt and had been very disappointed when both he and Tina had missed all their shots. I plan to get up there in November when the pheasant season arrives and then we'll see . . . From all I hear, the Malamud book is a dud, so don't feel that your judgment has to be wrong . . . Hurray for the Olmansons! Hurray for their dog! Come to think about it though, I've done without something very important for far more than 64 days but I won't go into that here . . . You will stay with me, here in my room, it's all arranged, but let me know a day ahead. We'll do something about your flight fare when you arrive, I don't want to get myself all irritated by trying to deal with the elderly secretary who should take it off my moving expense account. She's wrapped as tightly in red tape as the bowels of Washington D.C. I'll settle all this with Simpson when my time here is completed . . . I'm going to break this now. Give my regards to Virgil, tell Erskine I'll write him, say hello to Mique and send me their address. Meanwhile take it easy and don't forget to do something about that lock. I've been reading the reports in the N.Y. Times about the arrest of those black nuns for panhandling and am reminded that they're just like Willie, who is probably just as fraudulent. I wouldn't trust her as far as I could throw her . . . Give Ramsay my regards and tell him to get on the ball . . . Tell Macy's to take that rug and ram it and you be good, don't withdraw too much and remember that I love you.

[Ralph]

To Miss Hester Holloway
THE QUADRANGLE CLUB
NOV. 28, 1961

Dear Miss Hester,[*]

You have no idea how delighted I am to hear from you. I am indeed the oldest of Brownie's two boys and the same who drove with you from Gary to Oklahoma City during the Twenties. I had intended writing you summer before last after John Scruggs dropped in to visit us in New York and said that he knew you. But although he gave me your address I lost it before I could write. I then asked Jimmy Rushing to get it when he went to Detroit but I'm afraid that Jimmy forgot to do so. Well, I'm sure that if my appointment here has done nothing else worthwhile, it <u>has</u> brought us together again after all the long years and I am most thankful.

When Mama died I lost contact with most of her old friends and most of her relatives and I had often wondered where you were and how you were. Herbert knew very little more than I so he was of no help. I still keep in touch with Mrs. Slaughter and I visited Oklahoma City during 1954 so have some idea of what's happened to our friends there.

But let me tell you briefly what happened to us after Mama died. Because her death was accidental—she fell off the porch and fractured her hip (but was not x-rayed) with the results that her death from tuberculosis of the hip and blood poisoning was ruled accidental and thus a double-indemnity—we were forced to wait for seven months before the insurance claims were paid and thus I remained in Dayton until March, 1938. I then asked Herbert to come with me to New York, where I had lived for a year, but he preferred to remain in Dayton, where he had made friends and that is actually the last time we've seen one another. He was called to the Army at the time men were being taken for six months and was not released until after the war. He then settled in Los Angeles, where he married a girl with two children and now works for the County, owns his own home, car, etc., and from all the reports from friends who've seen him there, has turned out quite well. It makes me quite sad to think that Mama made all her sacrifices and didn't live to see that at least <u>some</u> of them were worthwhile. I correspond with Herbert and we talk over long distance telephone at least once a year.

---

[*]   A neighbor from Oklahoma City who was friends with Ellison's mother; only Ida's closest friends and family called her "Brownie."

As for me, I returned to New York in 1938, went to work on the W.P.A. Writers' Project, where I learned something of my craft and soon began to publish articles, book reviews and short stories. (I did not finish Tuskegee, but left in my junior year to seek work in New York and there decided I couldn't take any more of the south.) In 1939 I married a young entertainer but that went bust after three years. During the war I worked in the Merchant Marine as a Second Cook and Baker, and in 1944, back in New York between ships, I met my present wife and married her as soon as I was divorced from the first. In 1945 I started a novel which changed my life and which is indeed responsible for my presence here at the University. It was published in 1952, won the National Book Award in 1953 and is still being sold, read, talked about, taught in college English courses, and, I'm afraid, confused with the facts of my own life. In 1955 I won the Rome Prize, with the results that Fanny and I spent two years living at the American Academy in Rome. We returned in late 1957 and now live at 730 Riverside Drive, New York 31, N.Y. Since then I've taught literature at Bard College in Dutchess County N.Y. and have worked on a long novel that I hope to publish next year. My wife is quite good looking and extremely competent. In fact the little colored gal is the fundraiser for Doctor Gordon Seagrave, the Burma Surgeon and founder of the famous hospital in that country. Unfortunately, we have no children but our lives are full of activity and we try to make the most of things. That's about it. I'll send you some photographs when I return to N.Y. I think you'll recognize me because for all my baldness, my grey temples and moustache, I still have something of my mother's look.

You'd be surprised at how much I remember of the early years around Aunt Sue's restaurant—I was a bit afraid of her you know—and your place at First and Byers. I can even remember some of the moving pictures that Mr. Cook presented, and the sights and sounds of the carnivals that you used to bring to the East Side. It's quite a long time now and the world is much changed. Okla. City is much changed too, and yet so much of it is alive in my mind. I gave a talk before the Divinity School last week and I found myself telling the students about the hard time we were having in Gary and how Mama prayed and how you and Mr. Cook appeared the next day and took us back home. I remember so much of it; the car with Anderson driving, the spring floods along the way, the little suspension bridges, the snakes clustered on a dried tree trying to escape the rising waters; how Herbert and I were allowed to sleep under the car one night outside Jefferson City, Missouri. You were terribly nice to have helped us and I realize now that that was one of the most important trips in my life; because Lord knows what might have happened to us had we remained in Gary. Certainly I would not have grown up in quite the same way and so much of what I've become was formed in Okla. When I think of it I realize that there's so much you could tell me of my mother and father and if there is the barest chance to come to Detroit I shall take it. I'd like very much to see you and bring the old times up out of the shadows. Having reached this age I have become very curious about my parents; for I know that whatever I am, so much of it came from them and people like you who influenced me even before I was aware of what was going on. You were freer and more full of life than many people I grew up around, and now I realize that you and Mr. Cook, like Mama, must have been quite young. And I suppose the same is true of my father, who I remember as a child with a very long memory remembers. Still I'd like so much to hear what you recall of Mr. Bob and Brownie. I remember the day he tore the ulcers in his stomach because I was with him as he delivered ice to Mrs. Salters' grocery store. And I remember trips around the city with him and my dog; his giving me a bath and allowing me to play in the bath water while Mama and Adele Grant went to see a play. I remember much more too, but they are a child's memories and I'd like to get your picture of things. I don't have to tell you that I remember Charles and Sing and the McGrews and the Wallaces (he was a meat inspector and they left for Chicago where he was to study medicine while I was still quite young) and many others—so we'll have much to talk about.

Come to think of it, I learned where you were about 1952 from Mr. Love Townsend, who at that time was living with his son out in Brooklyn, but he was unable to give me your address. I also tried to get it from my cousin Maybelle when I went back home the following year. Perhaps you haven't heard but Maybelle passed not long after my visit. She was my favorite cousin and I returned for her funeral. As you know, she had lived for some time in Detroit and returned to Okla. only after her husband John had died. He was no longer John Carrol in Detroit but "Dr. DeWitt." I would have loved to have seen him in operation.

Recently I had a letter from Mrs. Slaughter, who was recovering from a bout of sickness and I shall tell her that I've found you at last—or rather that you found me. Many of the old timers are gone now, either to California or to their last resting place but a few hold on. I have come to appreciate them now, their good qualities and their bad and in some ways they are much better people, more daring and idealistic than their sons and daughters. I saw Saretta and her husband and child in Rome and, though I like her as one likes an old friend, she's made so very little of her opportunities. Indeed, Edna Slaughter is much more alive. Edna tries to push them to live a bit and to travel so that the child may get some fuller idea of what is possible for a human being in this world. So they are trying and they have the money to do it but I'm afraid their hearts are not in it. Finley, her husband, is a very successful doctor but I'm afraid that he's been bitten by the same money bug that bit Dr. Slaughter and helped make Edna's life miserable. In fact, I'm told that Finley is trying to prove that he can make even more money than Doc. Well, I've got nothing against money, but I do wish that they could see that the Negroes who went to Oklahoma were interested in doing much more and that those of us who were born there have some obligation to move a few steps farther along the path which you blazed. Mama always told Herbert and I that we were supposed to do something like that and, although I can't live in Okla. now, I do try to remember that I have the obligation to live up to the sacrifices she made for me. I also remember that there was more to it than that. That you were adventurous people and that you reached out for some of the joy of life. I've seen a lot of places, countries, and people from places in this society whom if someone had told me I would grow up to know and observe I would have thought they were trying to kid me; but for all of that, there are few of them who impress me as being more interesting or more human or imbued with a greater feeling for life than some of you. This has come to mean a great deal to me and I know that I've been extremely lucky to have grown up in that place and in that time and thus around you. Thanks to those like you I never had to apologize to myself, or make excuses to anyone, for being a Negro. That is much more than anything I got at Tuskegee or anywhere else. I couldn't have bought it <u>with gold</u>, and all that was necessary for me to get it was for you to be true to yourself. It's amazing, when you think about it. I remember the others too, the teachers who made you ashamed and the professionals who thought Herbert and I weren't good enough to play with their children, and the rather cruel women (there were two of them) who when their sons had died cried out in public that they couldn't understand why the Lord hadn't taken Ida Ellison's boys instead. I remember and understand and forgive but I can't forget the pain that some of this type of thing caused Brownie. Thank God she had you and Mr. Cook for friends for you made the foolishness utterly unimportant. What's more, that movie house back there on the alley, and the carnival when it appeared with its lights and acts and ferris wheel, spoke to me of another world and if it didn't get into my blood to the extent [to] charge me to run off to join a circus, it <u>did</u> get into my imagination and it gets into the things that I write. I can still see the ferris wheel rising with its ropes of blue lights then moving <u>so</u> slowly in the early dusk as Mama walked me up Gary Street from the East Fourth Street car line. We had been downtown and as we walked up the street in the light we saw it looming there like something magical and dreamlike. It has loomed and turned in my mind ever since and with it the sound of the acts and the generator supplying the electricity, the cables stretched across the street, and the white men running around, and the smell of kerosene and hamburgers and the cotton candy Yes and even the little alligators that were sold and a squid, or devil fish, which Charles or Sing—or <u>somebody</u> used to have in a tank on the back porch of your house. All this is precious stuff for a child to have contact with and I know now that had I been white or rich or whatever, I couldn't have had a richer time of it. Nor do I forget how impressed I was in my child's way, that you and Mr. Cook, my own people, were in charge; that it was on your property and that you brought all the wonder and excitement to the town. I'm sorry that you left before I was old enough to have drawn more strength from your presence but I'm thankful that I was alive and kicking while the city was still your home. And while I'm at it, let me tell you that your letter arrived at a moment when I was feeling depressed here and a bit worried over my first big public lecture. It was all I needed to lift my spirits and very much as though my mother was encouraging me through her best friend. My life has been influenced by you, my heart is still full of you and I thank you from its deepest depths.

I must stop here though there is much more I'd like to say. This is much too long a letter and I beg of you not to try to answer at such length. This is an outpouring of the heart and all it needs is some word of how you are and how things go for you. Meantime, although I don't intend to do much lecturing after I finish here on Dec. 16th, I shall try to get at least one talk near Detroit so that I might drop in to see you. I'd like that very very much. Who knows, it might just happen that way.

With fondest memories

[Ralph Ellison]

To Horace Cayton
730 Riverside Drive
New York 31, New York
November 2 1962

Dear Horace:

I'm glad to know you're still at it.

You of course may use my name as a reference for a Guggenheim to finish your autobiography and I wish you all good luck.

We half expected to see you in New York and were sorry you had to cancel your plans. I am assuming that you did cancel them for I hope you would not come to New York without getting in touch with us. Both Fanny and I had looked forward to that opportunity. She, I think, wanted to hand you your painting, rather than go to the trouble and expense of having it crated and shipped out to you, and I wanted to hand you your short story which required a great deal more comment than I had the time to put down on paper. Perhaps you will still come our way.

I am going to Chicago on Sunday for a four-day conference at the University. When I return I'll begin a teaching assignment at Rutgers. Between it and my book I expect to be a little busy this coming year.

Keep in touch with us. We are always glad to hear from you.

Sincerely,
Ralph

Mr. Horace R. Cayton
7387 Soqual Drove
Aptos, California

To Patsy Brill
730 RIVERSIDE DRIVE
NEW YORK 31, NEW YORK
APRIL 25, 1963

Miss Patsy M. Brill
Box U-1380
Florida State University
Tallahassee, Florida

Dear Miss Patsy Brill:

Your questions are far too complicated for the space of a letter, but let me attempt to answer them briefly.

1. As a member of a minority group my work has been affected in two ways; first, by the necessity of discovering that my racial identity was not fundamental to my problems as an artist; that even if the problems of my minority status were rectified, I still would have to wrestle with the problems of an artist.

2. I cannot give any specific instances where being a Negro has hampered or helped my popularity as a professor though I have no doubt that some people read my work simply because I am a Negro and others would never think of reading it because I am a Negro. Being a Negro has helped my work very much as the background and cultural identity of any literary artist is helpful. It gives some form, some specific shape to the chaos of life and it presents me with a specific set of circumstances, experiences, characters, dilemmas . . . that I must confront in order to discover who and what I am, what life is and what art is.

3. Racial prejudice has given me an ironic perspective on life.

4. The only obligations I feel toward my race is not to be ashamed of it and to be courageous and to affirm its humanity. I do not feel that this is an obligation that should take precedence over my obligation as a novelist. Nor do I feel that being a good novelist who depicts the truth as he sees it could possibly violate my racial loyalty.

Please feel free to quote any of the above comments.

With kind wishes,

Sincerely yours,
Ralph Ellison

To Robert Penn Warren
730 RIVERSIDE DRIVE, 8D
NEW YORK 31, NEW YORK
DICTATED JUNE 1, 1963

Dear Red:

I heard your speech at the Academy ceremonies last month and tried to catch you once the drinking started. But evidently you avoided the crush. I suppose we might have seen you at the Cheevers that evening had it been possible to get away but Fanny had just returned from Chicago where she had lost her mother and we were not quite up to the drive.

We would like to see you and Eleanor and the children—if not before you take off, if you are taking off for the summer—then as soon in the fall as time permits. With the rapid developments in the South I am sure there will be much to talk about.

Our best to all.

Sincerely,
Ralph

P.S. I still think that your letter to the Century Assn was one of the most generous that anyone has ever written about anyone and I am most grateful.[*]

To Horace Cayton
730 RIVERSIDE DRIVE, 8D
NEW YORK 31, N.Y.
JUNE 4, 1963

Dear Horace:

I am returning herewith the manuscript you sent me earlier this year. I am sorry for the delay on this and I am sorry again that it is not the type of episode that would fit in with the material we are slowly collecting for the anthology.

I asked for a piece in which you would write of your experiences with

---

[*]   Warren was one of those who nominated Ellison for membership in the Century Association. The nomination carried and Ellison was voted in at the general meeting in November 1964.

people like Embree because I think this would get you into an examination of the role of such figures as they function in the society and in the total context of the society. Our problem is to collect enough manuscripts by Negro writers that will provide a perspective that is not limited by the usual provincialism of Negro thinking. Our assumption is that Negro life provides perspective of American civilization that has not often been explored.

I am quite irritated with all the requests I receive from people who would have me stop what I am doing in order to write something which they consider important. Thus, I am quite apologetic in having to return your manuscript to you. The important thing, however, is that you have added this section to your autobiography and that I think is all to the good.

What has happened with the Guggenheim? Did you get it? If so, what are your plans and how does the book go?

Things have been hectic here what between trips to Rutgers* and the fulfillment of various lecture engagements around the East. We did have an amazing experience, which would have amused you no end, of going to Tuskegee for a week where on Founder's Day I received an Honorary Doctorate degree along with General B. O. Davis, Jr. Wish you could have been there. It was ironic and yet quite moving. And things are changing there. Since then we have suffered the loss of Fanny's mother in Chicago, and the rest has been mostly work.

Not too long ago C. L. R. James' ex-wife came up and spent quite a bit of time interviewing me about Dick and I have heard of other studies about him that are in the works. I hope that you will have something to say about him in your own work. If not in your autobiography, in terms of an essay. I have no doubt that you saw him under many revealing circumstances and regarded him without the sentimentality of which others seem to be the eternal victim.

We hope things are going well and disappointed that you did not show up during the spring as we understood you would.

Sincerely yours,
Ralph Ellison

---

* In the fall of 1962 Ralph became the first writer-in-residence at Rutgers University. He worked two days a week in a campus office on his novel-in-progress and gave several readings from the work. He remained in the position for two academic years.

Mr. Horace R. Cayton
814½ Laine
Monterey, California
 <u>We also returned Fiction n 85</u>

To Morteza Sprague
730 Riverside Drive
New York 31, New York
june 7, 1963

Dear Mort:

I received the notice that Sandy Walker[*] was to read from his novel at 10:30 at night. I trust you were there to undergo that marvelous experience. However, if you are still on speaking terms with Luther Foster you should suggest that having such announcements broadcast about the country as originating from Tuskegee is doing the place no worldly good. Indeed, friends of mine who were rather impressed with Dr. Foster when he spoke recently at Old Greenwich, Connecticut would be quite aghast if one of Sandy's announcements landed in their hands. There is no doubt about it, he must be one of the damnedest individuals to have come out of Birmingham. Thank God he doesn't get as much publicity as Bull Connor.

Fanny and I are still enjoying some of the glow of our visit and are only sorry that it had to be so short. We hope things are going well with you and Ellen, and if you get up this way you must come by to see us.

The Murrays are well and we are keeping busy.

Thanks very much for all your kindnesses. I don't know what Tuskegee will do if it ever loses you.

Sincerely,
Ralph

Mr. Mort Sprague
Tuskegee Institute, Ala.

---

[*]   Saunders "Sandy" Walker was a Tuskegee classmate of Ellison's to which he refers several times in the letters with wry amusement.

To Fanny Ellison
DEDHAM, MASS
SEPTEMBER 9, 1963

Dearest Fanny,

I received your fifth letter yesterday after somehow missing the 4th. I've written you at Namkham* and am sorry that you've failed to receive them. But please don't worry, I miss you very, very much and have worried that things might not be going too well for you. Now I won't worry anymore and I hope you won't worry about me. I was a day late in arriving here and have been talking and listening every [day] since. There have been bouts with the seasoning but for the most part I'm O.K.: learning something and am told that I've contributed something to the conference. This time my remarks were recorded and you may hear them when you return. I spent a day and night with Nancy and Dick during the Labor Day holiday, returned home and took off the next day for Dedham. Judy and Isham McConnel, with whom I had dinner the other evening, send their regards, and so does Tucker who is in a kennel in Lexington, and the bird, who is here with me. It seems that not only am I doomed to travel with a mass of gadgets but I must also take a zoo along. Noah, Noah, me! ... You are really seeing the fundamentals of life there and I envy you some of it. I've never seen a delivery but watch those village idiots, they're smarter than you think; I know, since I'm a village idiot.

There are about sixty of us here on this beautiful estate, talking and arguing and demonstrating apparatus, and although much of it is interesting I yearn for quiet. There's simply too much of it, but the food is decent—the breakfast is a delight—and there is endless liquor in the evening. But we are here for work and we are indeed working ... I called George as you requested and he tells me that you misunderstood him; his idea being that if you were coming through Chicago, he meant to come out to the airport to have a chat. He has written you at Hong Kong so you'll get the details from him. He sounded well and assured me that things were O.K. So don't worry about George and try to save your mind and emotions for the trip. I admire your line: "Everything beautiful deserves to be experienced in isolated places," but anxiety shouldn't be. Thus I guess this is the place

---

* A town in northern Burma. The American Medical Center for Burma, run by Dr. Seagrave, was located here, and Fanny traveled here in 1963 to inspect the center's hospital.

to say what you already know, that I didn't mean it when I wished that you'd go to Burma and stay or whatever the mean thing was. Forgive.

I wrote you that Sarser had found a 105 mm lens for the S.P. and that you were not to bring it but the 105 auto Nikon was still desired. I could use two 52 mm Nikon Skylight filters but don't allow any of this to become a nuisance. . . . Ligon and Winnie were in town over Labor Day and telephoned, sending you greetings. What a time I have explaining your being there, it's as though it were the most unexpected trip in the world—and perhaps it is. You don't have to question whether I think of you "occasionally," you're too much a part of my life to be so easily dismissed. But I did want you to have the experience of being on your own in a strange country so that you could learn a little more about yourself. I admit that I worry about you but only that you might become ill or encounter some unpleasantness as you go about learning what you have to know in order to do your work. As for me I find the house empty and I'm sure that if you were not a part of it I'd move and very quickly. I wrote you that I had refused to answer the phone for five days after you left and when I finally answered who do I get? Gwen Mitchell asking why I hadn't answered the query of a real estate dealer whom they'd given our names as reference! I must rush this downstairs so that it may be posted as soon as possible and I hope it reaches you in Hong Kong.

Love,
Ralph

To Theresa Ammirati
730 RIVERSIDE DRIVE
NEW YORK 31, NEW YORK
OCTOBER 23, 1963

Mrs. Theresa Ammirati
538 Seneca Street
Bethlehem, Penna.

Dear Mrs. Ammirati:

Thanks for your note; it is pleasing to learn that you found *Invisible Man* of personal meaning. And I assure you that when one writes as slowly as I, notes such as yours serve to remind me that communication is possible and worth all the slow effort and the doubt.

As for your question concerning the light bulbs, it has been so long ago that I can account for only a part of it: When I was a boy in Oklahoma, players of the illegal lottery known as POLICY always played the numbers 3-6-9 after dreaming of fecal matter. These figures were listed under this reference in the "dream books" designed for players of this game and money bet upon them was sure to bring a "hit" or win. I doubt very seriously that the publishers of such dream books knew much of Freud but they were aware of the symbolic relationship between the cloaca and money. For my part, I suppose that the underground in which my imagination was operating in that section of the novel dredged up that bit of the sewer quite naturally. Enough of Dr. F.

The conscious motive of the 1369 bulbs was to see if the concentrating of such a blaze of light upon the reader's eye could produce a kinetic effect from the page of a book. I felt that given such a concentration with a dark enclosure I should be able to reinforce the thematic content of the character's situation and make it resonate with overtones of withdrawal, alienation and that self-possession into which one comes when one has plunged into chaos and refused to be destroyed. The bulbs were a conceit as well as part of a scene. I have no delusion that I've explained the mystery of the lights but this is the best I can do beyond noting that by the time the scene in question developed in the course of the action, I had been building imagery of blackness and whiteness, see-non-seeing, and lightness-and-darkness, at such a pace that I'm sure that many other motives which are now obscure to me were present. Unfortunately, I don't have a book on hand and thus am unable to take a further look. I hope, however that this may be of some use to you.

With best wishes,

Sincerely yours,
Ralph Ellison

To Pierre Brodin
730 RIVERSIDE DRIVE
NEW YORK 31, NEW YORK
DECEMBER 23, 1963

Monsieur Pierre Brodin
Dean of Humanities
Ecole Libre des Hautes Etudes
52 East 78th Street
New York 21, New York

Dear Monsieur Brodin:

Please accept my deep apologies for my long delay in responding to your letter of September 18th. However, in brief reply, I have been influenced very much by the fiction and criticism of Andre Malraux, by Stendhal, by some of the writings of Andre Gide, and by two volumes of essays by Valery, the first and second series of *Variety*.

As a boy, I read many of the stories of Maupassant and, naturally, *Madame Bovary* was to prove important in forming my ideas of what a novel should be.

Following the Occupation, the works of Jean Paul Sartre, Albert Camus, along with the work of Simone de Beauvoir, claimed some of my attention. However, during the 40's before Existentialism became a vogue I had been introduced to such ideas through Malraux's *Man's Hope* and following the clue of his characterization of Unamuno, I was to read Unamuno's *Tragic Sense of Life*. I went on from there to the writings of Kierkegaard.

For me, beginning to write when I did, Malraux was and continues to be, a revelation.

This is by no means a complete list of the French writers whom I have read but these I have consciously read, and to great benefit.

Sincerely yours,
Ralph Ellison

To Edna Slaughter
NOVEMBER 23, 1964
MRS. EDNA R, SLAUGHTER
ROUTE 4, BOX 385
OKLAHOMA CITY, OKLAHOMA 73101

Dear Aunt Edna:

I am so pleased that the book arrived* and that you like it, and especially did I want you to see the short paragraph in the Library of Congress talk in which I mentioned your father. One of these days, if I shall ever justify it, I shall write an autobiography, and much of it will have to do with life at the Randolphs in town and country and in all the various houses around Oklahoma City in which they lived and where I played and learned.

I can't quite put it in perspective, but so much of my childhood was spent with your mother and father. And that brief period during my teens when I was with him at the Capitol, much happened which I want to get down. Somehow it's all mixed up in my memory with Uncle Allen and Aunt Ellen Watkins and their big house up on Styles Street with its old-fashioned back stairs. It's amazing how so many rooms and so many old houses cling to my mind. And while I am at it, what was the name of the horse which your father kept for so [long] at 409 East Third? I think of him as a very splendid animal, which he certainly was, but also symbolic of a period which was rapidly running out, even so early as the late 1920's. Then, too, I remember the once handsome rubber tire buggy which we used to own and which I watched decay as it stood in the alley near the parsonage of the old Avery Chapel Church.

It was much to my surprise to read in Jimmy Stewart's column that my father gave Jim his first job. I suppose I should get back there before too long and ask a lot of questions. Please give him my regards and, in fact, to all the family. And give my special regards to Wyatt's daughter and tell her it's time some other writers develop out of Oklahoma City.

I must say that the family has scattered. The last I heard of James Rhone I believe he was living and working in Denver. I doubt that I shall get to Oklahoma soon, but I sometimes get out to Yellow Springs where at one time, some years ago, I was briefly writing resident at Antioch College. Please

---

* *Shadow and Act,* Ellison's landmark collection of essays, was published in the autumn of 1964.

tell Camille and Pat to send the boys my regards, and give them our best. Would you please send me Ollie's address? I am able to fly to Washington in just about an hour and I would like very much to see her. Indeed I am in Washington quite frequently, but I've never known quite where to start in looking her up. It's sad to hear that she sold the place. There, again, I had good times, and in fact I remember visits to Chicasaw when they had the drugstore there so many years ago. I especially remember that they raised rabbits. When I was at home in '54 Ollie gave me some photographs of Wayne, herself and my mother that were made about 1919. They were quite gay those young people in those photographs, and I take them out every once in a while just to remind myself that mama's life was not all sadness— but you have known that all along. Speaking of Ollie, I saw the announcement of Heddie's death, and for all of the misery she caused me during my adolescence I found myself quite sad. She was a part of growing up, and in my life she was never simply alone; she was always counter-balanced by Tom, and he did have a certain largeness of gesture and openness of feeling for life. These are rare, and I feel lucky to have known him so well.

Please give our regards to the Finleys, and tell Zerretta that we are jealous that for all their trips to Europe they've failed to get in touch with us when they have reached New York. Nevertheless, here's Herbert's address: 5742 Mullen Avenue, Los Angeles 90403. I suppose I told you that we visited with Herbert and his family when I was in Los Angeles last April for a series of lectures.* I hope the Finleys will look them up just so they can report how things are going with him. He is a very interesting man. I find I must say, and more like me than I ever realized when we were growing up. We are going to try to have them visit us here during the Fair of next year and hope that can come off.

You are quite right about Fanny. She is quite wonderful, and not because of me by any means. As you know, she is connected with the American Medical Center for Burma and has, for about two years now, been its executive director. She is devoted to Dr. Seagrave and the work that he carries on in Burma. A great deal of her energy goes into raising money to supply his needs. I hope that some time during next year you will be able to re-establish the acquaintance you had so long ago at Fisk.

Finally, let me say that I was quite surprised to get your note about the

---

* Ralph traveled to Los Angeles to deliver the Ewing Lectures at UCLA in April 1964 and met with Herbert. It was the first meeting of the two brothers since Dayton in the winter of 1938–39, following the death of their mother.

"Today" show. I have been on television many times now through the years, but this is the first incident wherein the show reached other sections. Thus, I have been receiving notes from the Deep South, from the West Coast, Chicago, and from you. So I suppose now I can't be too irritated with what I sometimes see there, but it does serve a function of giving the viewing audience some idea of what the strayed sheep have come to look like.

I will be writing you again soon, and I will fill you in on some of the things that are happening as a result of this belated book. In the meantime, please give our regards to everyone, and I hope things go well for all.

Sincerely,

Ralph Ellison

To Jacob Cohen
NOVEMBER 23, 1964
MR. JACOB COHEN
275 SEVENTH AVENUE, 11TH FLOOR
NEW YORK, NEW YORK 10001

Dear Jerry:

Pardon the delay in answering your letter concerning Al.* Actually I find it very difficult to write about him. I suppose because I have known him since our days at Tuskegee and because our contacts since that time have been so constant and our assumptions about so many matters in such close agreement that I really don't have the proper sense of perspective. But I can say this that I feel that out of any given social, cultural and political circumstance, during any historical period, you get only a few people who respond with a certain adequacy to the influences that are dominant during that period. And in the United States there are so many influences and so many ways of avoiding them that few people are able to respond with anything like adequacy. The problem becomes even more difficult where Negroes are involved. So much of American experience is geared to deflect us away from that which is meaningful, and such overpowering efforts are made to encourage Negroes to think of themselves in the narrowest of terms and to dull their sense of possibility, whether socially or imaginatively, that very frequently we live in our times but are not of our times. And I say this because as I think of all the Negro intellectuals whom I have known, including some of our well-known leaders, few strike me as having the grasp of events and of the culture that Al

* A letter of recommendation for Albert Murray.

Murray has. Without doubt, he is the only Negro intellectual of my acquaintance who would not be out of depth if he were suddenly placed in a position of national leadership. He has the imagination which allows him to project himself into the centers of power, and he uses his imagination to deal with serious problems seriously and as though he were a responsible participant in the affairs of our nation and our time. This is not limited by his position within a social frame, which <u>would</u> limit him to things Negro. This is quite rare, and I suppose it is possible because Murray has always accepted himself and his background, and has found ways of using it as a source of insight and inspiration, as against the tendency, common to many Negro intellectuals, to regard their backgrounds as something to be rid of as they seek to move into the broader areas of American life. He uses his experience as a clue to the experience of others in other social areas. He has been able to possess such ideas of culture, politics, sociology, science, etc., as have claimed his mind, as a means of enriching his own humanity. And better still, he uses it not only to orient himself but as a basis of judgment and as a means of arriving at value. Thus, his judgment is to be trusted because it is based upon a firm sense of reality and because he has little patience with the false and pretentious.

As you must know, Al's education has been in literature. I am not certain of how many degrees he holds, but I do know that he has studied in many of the larger universities, both as an English major and as an officer in the Air Force. You know, too, perhaps that he has taught Geo-Politics in the Air Force ROTC and that he has served on an administrative level [in] instances where millions of dollars and highly technical operations have been involved both abroad and in this country. He could fill you in with the details of this. What I wish to say about it is that each of these assignments have not only been duties but they have been learning situations, situations wherein he was conscientiously concerned with enriching not only his own experience but that of his wife and daughter. He has never been the type of American airman who spends most of his time with Americans. His range of interests from jazz to art, to architecture to ideas, has always been a functioning part of his existence.

The other thing to be said, and of this I am sure you are quite aware, is that this man has a quality of exciting enthusiasm which is quite rare. When something claims his attention it must be shared with others. And he has an amazing ability to move people, who would be only mildly interested, to participate with passion in those things to which he has moved their attention. He is in the rarest sense of the term a <u>teacher</u>. He loves to explain, to explore and to guide. He is articulate and eloquent.

The final thing to say is that as we plunge deeper into the complexities of an America in process of integration there will be an increasing need for those Negroes who on their own, who through their interest in life and in the affairs of culture and politics have prepared themselves when it seemed even foolish to have been interested—Al Murray is such a person. If there is a wisdom that has grown from the long and complex experience of Negroes in the United States, then there surely must be those men of my own generation who have partaken of that wisdom, despite all tendencies to deny its existence—Murray is such a person. But better still, he possesses a complex sense of contemporary affairs, and he has the ability not only to bring that wisdom to focus and to fit it to the most fruitful ideas current during our times, but he has also the ability to make others understand the connections. He has the ability to tell hard truths humorously, and to give pleasant truths extensions that do not at first meet the eye. I can't see how you would go wrong by introducing him to anyone, and I am quite certain that he will have as much to offer developing your magazine as anyone you are likely to find.

That's about it. I'm not sure that this is what you want. If it isn't, please let me know and I will try to have my say. Most of all, be certain that I wish to do all I can to help both you, Al, and your project.

Sincerely,
Ralph Ellison

To Joseph Frank
NOVEMBER 23, 1964
MR. JOSEPH FRANK
57 RUE AUGUSTE LANCON
PARIS 13,
FRANCE

Dear Joe:*

Your review† did a great deal to dispel the suspicion that I was absolutely incapable of communication with the critics. There have been many reviews, most of them favorable (except a front-page *Herald-Tribune* review

---

* Joseph Frank, scholar of comparative literature and Dostoevsky's biographer, whom Ellison met during his two years at Rutgers.

† According to Frank, his review of *Shadow and Act,* commissioned and accepted by *Partisan Review,* for some reason was never published. However, he sent Ellison the unpublished manuscript.

of Podhoretz,* who decided that I knew nothing of the art of the essay, and who chose to defend Irving Howe somewhat belatedly), but far too often they seem to miss the point, or they pretend that whatever insights I might have they possessed all along. One man made a point of not understanding the title or the sectional divisions. I shall see to it that he sees what you have done with the structure of the book. Others have sought to treat the book as a work of art, which all but amazes me; and several assume that this is simply an extension of Invisible Man. You can understand then that I am a bit amazed.

I am so pleased that things are going well in Paris with you and the book, for as you know I am very, very eager to study Dostoevsky. Perhaps you have seen the announcement of Blackmur's book of eleven essays on the European novel, a part of [which] are studies in Dostoevsky. You might want to take a look. If so, they are published by Harcourt, Brace and World. If you are interested, let me know, and I will be pleased to see that you are sent a copy.

You asked about Langston Hughes. No, I don't think he is living in Paris but was probably there on his return from the Berlin Festival. I have no idea either how close he is to the Africain group, but I wouldn't be surprised if he is. I think his work is inseparable from the notion of negritude. I don't think you missed anything by not hearing that lecture. He probably had to tell the French, under the guise of discussing the problems of Negro writers, how difficult it is for Negro writers to be served hamburgers in Mississippi. Lord knows what he will be saying next year, because despite all of the violence, the bombings, and church burnings, the white citizens of McComb, Mississippi have decided to quietly desegregate. One hopes that the rest of Mississippi follows their lead, then maybe Negro writers can turn their attention to the problems of craft and of culture and get on with the work of contributing something of real literary value to American culture.

I couldn't tell you when we [were] having coffee down at Rockefeller Center what was actually happening to me. For a while, it was true that I spent a bit of my time with members of the New York Foundation, in recommending that they turn their attention to such people as yourself. I

* Norman Podhoretz, intellectual and editor of *Commentary*, had published one of Ellison's essays ("On Becoming a Writer") in 1964. He then wrote one of the few negative reviews of *Shadow and Act* the next year, the first of several critical writings about Ellison, culminating in Podhoretz's 1999 article "What Happened to Ralph Ellison," in which he dismisses Ellison's second novel as "archaic."

discovered at the end of the conference that they were interested not only in my advice but in offering me a grant. So, no, I am not at Stony Brook, rather I am this year a visiting fellow in American Studies at Yale,[*] and the best of it is I have to visit very seldom. The idea being that I produce some more fiction. I am very interested in what you have to say about *IM*, and I envy you being able to read it, because I am absolutely incapable.

Perhaps you are right, I tipped my hand too soon in the saloon scene. I had a problem of rhetoric and of some of the people. I was unsure of how the general reader would react to the intellectual level of the book, so I suppose I overdid it. I am pretty certain that if I were to do it now, that is to write that scene now, I would have held back more, would have been more implicit. As for the obscurity of the pink hospital scene, I understand very well how this happened. Originally, the hospital scene was a section that introduced the character of Mary who was working in the hospital and who aided the narrator in his escape, and upon his escape, put him up in her house in Harlem. Altogether I cut some 225 pages or more between the explosion in the factory and the hospital experiences, and it was in this long section that I developed the folk experience that sustains much of Negro life and sanity in the big city. So there is a complication of perspective at that particular point. One of these days, I shall find a way to publish that missing section because I think it might well stand on its own. How good it is to hear that you like the scene between Ras and Clifton. It does indeed express quite a lot of what I feel about racism. It will interest you also to hear of an incident which occurred here this fall wherein a retired white policeman shot down a Negro in the West 40's who was selling just such dolls as Clifton was killed for selling. I know that life frequently imitates art, but this is much too close for comfort. And quite a number of people associated the incident with that scene in *IM* and sent along clippings.

Yes, I have heard Leon Bib sing and I would say he is quite a good singer. I don't know him, however, but I am sure he must have been a lot of fun. Oddly enough, our singers and musicians—that is, classical musicians—but especially our singers, seem to cut through so much of the sociological fog in which Negroes are forced to operate and frequently find their way to real artistic insight. From what I've seen of Bib, he must

---

[*]   Following the end of his Rutgers visiting professorship, Ellison received a yearlong fellowship at Yale in 1964–65, funded by the Rockefeller Foundation, and arranged by his good friend Robert Penn Warren.

have had some training on a far more sophisticated level than that of folk music.

You asked about Saul's novel.* I have read it, but I must say in all honesty that I feel I am much too close to it to be objective. The most I can [say] is that he finished it and that it has been for several weeks now number one on the bestseller list. My difficulty comes from being so close to the characters and from my having absolutely no patience with anti-heroes. Still I shall re-read it once all of the noise quiets down in order to discover what I really do think about it. As of now, I can only say that it [is] by no means an act of the imagination such as he achieved in *Henderson* or *Augie*. I am enclosing Stanley Hyman's review from *The New Leader*.

I am surprised to hear that Charlie Marks is back in Paris. We tried to get together over the summer but it didn't work, and I just noticed that his friend Atlion has shown here in New York and had intended to call Charlie to talk with him about it. Please give him our regards.

As for our getting to Paris this year, it seems unlikely. If by some miracle I have this novel put away by the summer, don't be surprised if you see us coming.

I have no news about Rutgers, except that things seem to be going very well and that I have been replaced by La Sontag,† whose piece in the current *PR* on Campus [Camp] will have you rolling in the streets. I don't know what's happened to *PR*, maybe everyone is taking goof balls down there. You'd better hurry back, Joe. Whenever you get a chance, write us and please let me know about the Blackmur book.

Our love to you and Gigi.

Sincerely,
Ralph Ellison

---

* Bellow published *Herzog* in 1964.

† Presumably Susan Sontag, then a young fiction writer and essayist who held the one-year visiting writer fellowship at Rutgers after Ellison. She published an essay on contemporary drama and film titled "Going to Theater (And the Movies)" in the spring 1964 issue of *Partisan Review*. Her breakthrough essay "Notes on Camp" appeared in the winter 1964 issue and may be the piece to which Ellison refers here.

To Nathan Scott*
NOVEMBER 23, 1964

Dear Nathan:

This is to acknowledge *The Climate of Faith in Modern Literature*† and to say hello to you, and Charlotte and the kids.

I am getting into the book slowly, and I am finding it very useful for my own purposes. Sometime ago, I became concerned with the relationship of modern theology to literature but really had no way of approaching it systematically, and I find that your book is providing the necessary orientation, and between it and the *New Orpheus* I am getting quite an education, and indeed I don't know what's happening to me. I've gone back to reading Teilhard de Chardin after having given up his phenomenon of man while living up at Tivoli. Altogether, I am being forced to think in different channels and I find it to my advantage.

The book goes well,‡ and the essays§ are receiving, for the most part, favorable reviews. It makes one wish that he were a better writer and had been more careful. But then we have to do what we can in the time that we have and keep pushing the old stone up the hill.

I don't know whether Leslie remembered to tell you that I called on my way back from Wisconsin. I became upset physically and decided that it would be unwise to spend the couple of days in Chicago that I had intended. I hope to have better luck next time.

I hope things are going well with you, and we hope to see you soon.

Sincerely,
Ralph Ellison

* This seems to be Ellison's first letter to Scott, and one of very few he ever wrote him. Ellison met Scott in the winter of 1960 when Ellison visited the University of Chicago for four days of lectures and classes, and they deepened their relationship in the fall of 1961 during Ellison's period as visiting lecturer. Scott, a brilliant professor of literature and religion, and the author or editor of twenty-five books, would become an influence on Ellison's thought in the decades to come. Scott taught at Chicago from 1955 to 1977, and then assumed the William R. Kenan Professorship of Religious Studies and eventually the chair of the Religion Department at the University of Virginia.

† Scott's book of this title was published in 1964; his book *The New Orpheus: Essays Towards a Christian Poetic* was also published in 1964.

‡ Presumably Ellison's novel-in-progress.

§ *Shadow and Act.*

Mr. Nathan Scott, Jr.
5242 South Greenwood Avenue
Chicago 15, Illinois

To William Dolben
NOVEMBER 23, 1964

Dear Mr. Dolben:

The Founder is not a specific person, he is rather a personification of an archetype. He is one through whom the element of myth gets into the novel. He is a founder, the dreamer who is also a man of action, and I hoped he would give some validity to the Negro's great hope in education.

One way of understanding him, of course is to examine the pattern of his life as projected in Barbee's speech.* To some extent the pattern is heroic. Now, I am sure you can go on from there.

Sincerely,
Ralph Ellison

Mr. William W. Dolben
Lehigh University
Bethlehem, Pennsylvania

To Angus Collins
730 RIVERSIDE DRIVE
NEW YORK, NEW YORK 20031
MARCH 6, 1967

Mr. Angus R. Collins
12, Circular Road
Withington
Manchester, 20, England

Dear Mr. Collins:

I am sorry to have been so long in responding to your letter of January 31st but it was necessary that I consult some old files to complete the short

---

* Reverend Barbee's speech or sermon in *Invisible Man* mythologizes the Founder and his founding of the Negro college.

story bibliography listed in your letter and the files were not readily accessible.

Please add to your list of short stories the following:

"Afternoon," *Negro Story Magazine,* Vol. I, No. 5, March–April, 1945.

"Out of the Hospital and Under the Bar," *Black Voices,* ed. Herbert Hill, London, 1964. British reprint of *Soon One Morning,* New York, 1963.

Your list of published extracts from my work-in-progress is complete.

The short story mentioned in the *Paris Review* interview as having been 'bumped' from *New Challenge* was never published and I doubt that I would allow it to be published in the future.

In response to your two questions, I did not read Céline before the writing of *Invisible Man* but read him several years later. "The Death of Clifton," published in John A. Williams' *The Angry Black* is from *Invisible Man.* The story published in Dorothy Sterling's *I Have Seen War* is entitled "In a Strange Country" and was first published (as you yourself have noted) in *Tomorrow,* July 1944.

You might be interested to know that *Horizon,* edited by Cyril Connolly (London), published in October 1947, under the title "Invisible Man" is a section from that novel which I was to complete in 1952, and that it was the first published extract to appear anywhere. Later, in January, 1948, the same section was published under the title "Battle Royal" by *48, The Magazine of the Year,* New York.

The most extensive bibliography of my work—fiction and non-fiction—was recently sent to me by a graduate student working on his Master's thesis at the University of Tennessee. His bibliography not only lists the fiction which you have listed but many reprints of that list of fiction, and the non-fiction section lists every essay and review that I have published since 1937. I, of course, am not at liberty to forward you a copy of his work but should you wish to write him directly I will send you his name and address.

With kind best wishes, I am

Sincerely yours,
Ralph Ellison

cc: Maurice English

To Charles Valentine
730 RIVERSIDE DRIVE
NEW YORK, NEW YORK 10031
DECEMBER 8, 1967

Mr. Charles A. Valentine
Department of Sociology-Anthropology
Washington University
St. Louis, Missouri 63130

Dear Mr. Valtentine:*

Since receiving your letter of October 17th and the copy of your October 4th letter that you were so kind as to duplicate for me, bad luck has fallen upon us. On the late afternoon of November 29th our home in Plainfield, Massachusetts was destroyed by fire. The loss was particularly severe for me, as a section of my work-in-progress was destroyed with it.

I write this to say that as much as I had hoped to write the foreword to your forthcoming book *Culture and Poverty,* under the circumstances I don't believe I can take time out now. Fortunately, much of my summer's work on the new novel is still in mind and if my imagination can feed it I'll be all right, but I must work quickly.

Perhaps, if your publication deadline is not too close, I could write a comment for use by your publishers, if they so desired. I shall, therefore, send a copy of this letter to Maurice English, at the University of Chicago Press, so that he can inform me of the deadline and send me a copy of your book when it is put into galley form.

Believe me, I am indeed sorry to miss the opportunity of writing your foreword but I have no doubt but that you will understand my situation.

With every best wish, I am

Sincerely yours,
Ralph Ellison

cc: Maurice English

---

* This is an important letter. It is Ellison's first comment in writing about the November 29, 1967, fire that destroyed "a section of [his] work-in-progress." This sentence and the next paragraph indicate clearly the extent of the loss, and Ellison's clear and timely assessment of what would be required on his part to recover what was lost.

To Charlie Davidson

AUGUST 18, 1968

Dear Charlie:[*]

I've been [waiting] until some of the slides that I had duplicated were returned before answering your letter. There was some kind of slip-up and they were finally returned last Sat. So now here they are. I must say that I didn't come up with anything impressive, but after all, one shouldn't try to shoot that type of event while sitting on his ass—which leaves me the excuse that if I had been running around I would have seen far less of you and Terry. Besides that I <u>was</u> trying to see what I could do with the telephotos.

We too had a splendid time and there's no question but that our time with you and Terry marks the high spot of this summer. It is regrettable that we didn't follow you on to Boston because we stood in the ferry line until 7:45 and arrived in the Plainfield area well after 12 p.m. where we spent the night in an inn. Spending the time with you was more important than you might guess, for when we reached our place it was dreary as hell. Not the weather but the sheer devastation of what had been a quite lovely old house and grounds now reduced to a scene of desolation. A forlorn chimney standing stark and crumbling above a cellar-hole full of crushed and rusting appliance, broken crockery, ashes.[†]

Fanny was able to contain the shock and sadness of it fairly well, and we set about trying to find a plumber and electrician to restore lights and water. Our pump and storage tank were ruined and since there's now no housing for the pump I've had to replace both with a far more expensive immersion type. It's a drag and Lord knows when we'll be able to have the junk hauled away, the chimney collapsed and the hole filled in. But one thing is certain, we won't try to rebuild right away. Rather, we'll simply try to make the cottage livable and make do until we're convinced that something has been done about fire protection in the area. Getting things started was difficult because everyone is so overloaded with summer business, and it wasn't until a few days before we left that we located people to

[*]   Albert Murray introduced the Ellisons to Charlie Davidson (tailor and owner of the Andover Shop in Cambridge, Massachusetts) and his wife, Terry.

[†]   Ellison's first and fullest description of what he and Fanny found when they visited the site of their burned-out house in Plainfield some eight months after the fire.

do the job, thus making a drive to Boston out of the question. They only finished the job last week and we'll run up the first chance we get. I've been working well however and I hate to think of breaking off.

Otherwise things were pleasant there. We were guests of the Richard Wilburs and that's usually a joy. You'll have to meet them and if possible come down to Portland, Conn, to one of their big parties. Usually it's black tie with a live and not too square orchestra and a lot of amusing academic and literary types—<u>and</u> damned good food. They have a big rambling house, which makes it possible to have such a variety of guests that you have to work pretty hard at it to be bored; while they are themselves interesting enough and humorous enough to make things swing. I'll work on this and try to get him to come in when he's in Boston.

Charlie, that Sunday morning when I went to look for that guy with the Thunderbird I knew the moment I saw him that he was someone you had to keep an eye on. He just seemed to be operating in another dimension of reality—and despite the bright sunlight. In fact, he seemed to be wearing some kind of invisible gas mask—which warned me that although I was only your messenger I had better watch myself. But who the hell would have suspected that the bastard had a goddamned <u>racehorse</u> hidden in the trunk of the car? And a horse named "Porkchopper" at that!

It's wild! It's mad! It's crazy! It's exactly right! I told Al about it and he flipped over the telephone. We'll have to get up there as soon as possible to have a look at that noble animal. Actually I envy you the freedom of spirit which allowed you to grab him, because a couple of years ago Vance and Tina Bourjaily—who own a whole herd of horses out in Iowa—tried to give me a wonder little prancing pony named Kerry, a little jet-black jewel who pulled a cart with the style of a trotter. He had been the pet of their daughter who was killed in a car accident and thus very painful to have around, but although I wanted him badly I floundered before all the problems of bringing him east, finding him a stable, etc., so I refused. Well, so now I have <u>two</u> goddam friends who own racehorses. One is Luna Diamond, one of Roger Steven's secretaries down at the National Foundation on the Arts (her husband was a law partner of Abe Fortas) and now you. Next thing I know you'll be out doing roadwork by way of getting in shape to ride, and I'll open the sports page of the *Times* to read "DAVIDSON TAKES THE BELMONT STAKES ON THE PORK CHOP"

I'm reminded that I was born around horses and had become quite familiar with them by the time, three or four years after my father's death, when my mother got rid of the last. This was a mare with the then baffling name of "Steve" and the extremely willful ways of a rather spoiled pet. She was as steady as an old rocking chair and delighted in sticking her head through the kitchen window to beg for snacks—sugar, apples, carrots; anything would do, and she was without question my mother's delight. The other horse, Fox, was a gelding that had to be destroyed during my second Christmas when he slipped on the icy Okla. City viaduct and broke a leg. Later I came to know other horses and quite a few mules that were owned by friends, employers and familiar icemen and hucksters. I learned to ride them and drive them and the summer of my 16th year I moved earth with them while working as a member of a landscape gardening crew. And as a kid I used to spend summer Saturdays sitting on the wagon seat with old Uncle Allen Watkins (a pioneer friend of my family who had walked to Okla. Territory from Tenn.) behind a team of mules which he cursed roundly and with great style whenever one of them made the mistake of letting a fart! Man, but that was long ago! Take good care of Porkchopper and if you have a photo please send it along.

The news about the shoes is most welcome, so welcome in fact that my feet have begun to feel better. And as for the lens, I don't think that $95.00 is too bad a price. However, should you find yourself in urgent need of a lens please let me know, because with the competition down here and the discount which I get from my dealer I'll probably be able to do almost as well as Charlier B. does in Japan. For instance, while the list price is certainly $175.00 the actual going price hereabouts is from $128 to $124.00—which I was quoted on Sat, and this includes a guarantee. Used 105m.m. Nikon go for about 114.00 if you have the time and patience to look around. By the way, to whom should I make out the check? And before leaving this let me say that after having some of the shots made with the lens I'm quite pleased with its optical qualities and I'm nuts about the perspective it allows me. Now all I need to do is to learn how to make interesting pictures. I now have an 85–250mm zoom, an 50mm f.1.4, a 55mm micro Nikon, a 206mm tele and the 10 5. The next project is to acquire a 28 or 35mm wide-angle and I'll be through.

I'm sorry we didn't hear Clark Terry in Boston because he wasn't up to par at the Festival. I suppose he was too busy trying to swing that load of lead. But if you have a cassette tape player I'd like to send you a copy of a tape featuring Clark Terry and Shirley Scott. Titled "Soul Duo," it's a gas. A recording engineer friend gave it to me a few weeks ago and there's hardly a day when I haven't played their version of "This Little Light of Mine." By the way, do you remember Jackie and Roy's rendition of "Lazy

Afternoon"? I came across our recording of it the other day and found it still fresh and quite exciting.

Al's O.K. and is presently going through the excitement of owning a fine new stereo outfit. It's a Marantz tuner amplifier combination with Altec speakers and as excellent in visual design as it is in sound. He's as pleased as he can be. Yesterday a set of galleys arrived in which he has a short story and in which I discovered that I had two short stories along with an essay. I gave up trying to write stories sometime ago, but these two keep turning up, so perhaps I'll try my hand again and try to come up with a collection, since there are a few still floating around.

Charlie, since I don't know how to reach the Weins I've enclosed a set of duplicates of Joyce and Benny for you to pass along with my regards. Tell George and Charlie B. that I was too busy to do anything about the damn *News* jerk and that I have a horror of writing letters to editors, but that I hope to write something about the festivals and their import on my own—and this before too long. Meanwhile, take care, give our love to Terry and I'll try to get up there as soon as possible.

Affectionately,
Ralph

730 Riverside Drive

To Edward Weeks
New York, New York 10031
FEBRUARY 17, 1969

Mr. Edward Weeks
Consultant and Senior Editor
The Atlantic Monthly Press
8 Arlington Street
Boston, Massachusetts 02116

Dear Ted:

Thanks for allowing me to see the short stories of James Alan McPherson.* I not only enjoyed them but was left feeling more hopeful concern-

---

* McPherson's first book of stories, *Hue and Cry*, was published in 1968.

ing the possibility of American literature becoming enriched through the special contributions of young writers who combine the Ivy League experience with the rich and complex general experience of Negro America. Now, at last, we appear to have a writer who knows how to combine the two so as to make one illuminate the other.

Better still, with this collection of stories, McPherson promises to move right past those talented but misguided writers of Negro American cultural background who take being black as a privilege for being obscenely second-rate, and who regard their social predicament as Negroes as exempting them from the necessity of mastering the craft and forms of fiction. Indeed, as he makes his "hue and cry" over the dead-ends, the confusions of value and failures of sympathy and insight of those who inhabit his fictional world, McPherson's stories are in themselves a hue and cry against the dead, publicity-sustained writing which has come increasingly to stand for what is called "black writing."

Unlike those who debase their talent in this manner, McPherson will never, as writer, be an embarrassment to such people of excellence as Willie Mays, Duke Ellington, Leontyne Price—or for that matter, Stephen Crane or F. Scott Fitzgerald. He is a writer of insight, sympathy and humor and one of the most gifted young Americans I've had the privilege to read.

May his career be as long and as productive as your own.

> With warm
> regards,
> Ralph Ellison

To John Lucas
730 RIVERSIDE DRIVE
NEW YORK, N.Y. 10031
JULY 29, 1969

Dear John:

I've been so busy and disorganized, what with trips out of the city and going through the chaos of having the apartment painted—that I've had no time to answer my correspondence. So now let me apologize and say that I'm glad that you're back in the U.S. and that you're doing something to raise the cultural level of some of our bankers. They're quite fortunate because I know a hell of a lot of professors, poets and novelists who could benefit from the course you've described—not to mention a number of my friends among the "serious" musicians. I did a brief turn at Carleton a few summers ago, working with prospective vice-presidents of A.T.& T. and found it challenging and well worth the while.

It is quite gratifying to me to have you find *Invisible Man* still interesting and useful for your lectures, but I must admit that I haven't read the book through again since I corrected the page proofs, therefore I'll have to answer your questions without having had the time to check in detail. Nevertheless, I'll do the best I can.

Now to the smile. As I recall it Clifton's smile is a complex emblem signifying among other things his recognition that the Brotherhood had sold-out both Harlem and himself. And that he, in his naive idealism and eagerness to lead, had himself been an accomplice as well as a dupe in that sellout; and (2) that there was little possibility of his ever explaining his position to the protagonist, since he saw in the invisible man a reflection of his former (and now rejected) role of naive, figurehead leader, and one too full of illusions to face up to the Machiavellian nature of political reality.

Clifton's selling of the dolls was a consciously symbolic action through which he expressed his rejection of his former dedication to the Brotherhood. By selling them he acts out a decision to punish himself by embracing the negative stereotypes as a means of cleansing himself of any shreds of hope in the promises of Brotherhoodism. Clifton is, in effect, washing his hands; and is indicating that he knows that more was involved in his experience than the simple black & white matter of selling-out or being sold-out. He had, in other words, learned irony; a bitter, masochistic irony, and a cynicism that sent him into mid-town New York to manipulate the false, racist values that he once sought to destroy.

Perhaps there is also embodied here an acceptance of Ras' rhetoric of the night of the street fight—in the smile, that is. I'd better stop right here before I make the damned smile far more ambiguous than it could possibly have been—But have you noticed, by the way, the resemblance between Clifton's dolls and the gollywog appearance of our current crop of instant-Afro militants? I have and, man, it amuses the hell out of me!

My answer to your next question is affirmative. I do believe that the protagonist does indeed lock Ras' jaws with Ras' spear. Since the weapon was thrown in an attack it becomes a "free-floating" agency that the protagonist uses in turning violence against a violent opponent who, up to that moment in the action had confined his antagonism to angry rhetoric. Since the protagonist was yearning for reconciliation both with social reality and with Ras, it seemed right that he wouldn't wish to kill him but would try somehow to stop him from exhorting the group to hang him. That he struck Ras in the jaws was a lucky accident and shouldn't be taken too symbolically.

I suppose some few actions in the novel should be viewed simply as acts in themselves and without symbolic extension. However, I should confess that I was not above throwing in such a detail as the conjunction between the spear and the jaws as a means of laying a false trail for my friend Stanley Edgar Hyman, who has great enthusiasm for Freudian speculation. During the time the book was being composed ole Stanley regarded all fighting taking place in fiction as a form of covert fucking! Seriously though, there seems to've been a striving for symmetry involved. Both men are rabble-rousers, both have reached the end of a phase of their respective careers and the conflict between them has reached its most significant point of tension. Thus it would seem fitting that the protagonist should strike Ras in the area where he was most effective and most to be feared. For the protagonist sensed that in his capacity for transforming society through military action Ras was, potentially, far less effective than Dupre, the building burner.

As you probably know or suspect, the name "Dupre" was fairly common wherever there were many families from Louisiana and there were many in Okla. I used it not because of any desire to make a direct allusion to the Blues but because it sounded right for the character, his scene and his act.

The same goes for the name "Maceo," which, during my childhood, was also common. This doubtlessly because of the Southern Negroes' fascination with Spanish America, a fascination which goes back to slavery, became intensified with the Cuban revolution of 1895 and which reached a peak during 1898 with the Spanish-American War. I suppose that a number of the "maceos" whom I knew were named in honor of the Cuban general, Antonio Maceo, a revolutionary leader who, in 1896, was ambushed by Spanish government troops and killed. Perhaps all these Maceo Browns, Greens, Thompsons etc. in the Negro community had been dedicated to some kind of heroic action. I knew an A. Maceo Smith who is still a widely known civil rights and insurance figure out in Okla. and Texas, and Maceo Pinkard, the old-time theaterical agent (still operating in Harlem) was known to me long before I was conscious of the Blues-involved Maceos.

With *Buddy Bolden's Blues* you came close to the mark. I've owned Jellyroll's recording for many years, but I'm also aware that it is a cleaned up, jelly rolled version of an older, scatological jingle titled "Funky-Butt" which went "Oh, I thought I heard somebody say, Funky-butt, funky-butt, take him away." I've forgotten the rest, all of which was unprintable, except a verse that went,

> *Oh, I know something and I'm bound to tell*
> *Oh, I know something and I'm also bound to tell,*
> *His ass-hole's stinking, Lawd,*
> *And the flies are giving him hell . . .*

You asked for it, John Lucas! But here, as was often true, Morton was working on traditional material, and since Louis Armstrong was just as steeped in the tradition I chose to stick with him as being more to my fictional purposes. Which leads me to remind you that "Peter Wheatstraw" like "Cootie Brown," "Doby Hicks" and "Jack the Bear" are traditional trickster figures of Negro American folklore, whose names and legendary exploits have been appropriated by any number of blues singers, pimps, gamblers, hoboes and hustlers. Whenever these names occur in my fiction they are drawn from oral literary tradition and not directly from living individuals. I first heard the Peter Wheatstraw, the devil's son-in-law bit as a southwestern "brag," a challenge thrown out by card, pool, craps, dozens or piano players as they tried to get a contest going. Peetie Wheatstraw couldn't even sing the blues as well as some of the gamblers down on "Deep Second" St. in Oklahoma City—which is where Jimmy Rushing was born.

I'm appalled to learn that I've supplied words to the "Harvard Blues" that aren't there, but thank God for scholarship anyway! Either I must have telescoped information or I heard Rushing or Mildred Bailey sing the line in person, or I was attempting subconsciously to give the blues an explicit range it didn't have. I'll have to ask Frazier about it when I see him again. I do recall that I learned about the "Rinehart" call to riot from Walter Williams, who was librarian at Tuskegee when I was a student there. Try looking into the Mildred Bailey—or even Helen Humeslead since it sounds like something you'd get in a feminine version of a Blues. Can't imagine either gal singing that she was a "most indifferent kind of a guy," if that's the line. Anyway, for me what was important was the fact that the name seemed to fit the character who was to personify and manipulate chaos. That it brought an undergraduate rite of rioting at Harvard into meaningful juxtaposition with certain shifty goings-on that I was creating in Harlem I take as an added dividend.

John, you have me dead on target: I not only think of *King Joe* as a disaster, I found Robeson and Wright not simply "ill at ease" before the subtitles (and crudities) of the blues, but far beyond their depths, opportunistic, embarrassing and ridiculous.* And I'll agree that there was nothing wrong with Basie; in those days he could do no wrong and besides, he was sticking to what he knew, loved and respected. But who the hell who knew <u>anything</u> about the Blues would try to take lines from Southern Negro boys' lore—scatological at that—and try to convert them into the Blues? All that conversation which Wright has going on between buttermilk, cornbread and beans was what was apt to come up on the school grounds or in a vacation tent when some kid let a fart:

Poooot!

"Hey, man! Get the hell out of here until that goddam Irish potato quits choking that bean!"

It's farting lore, John, farting contest lines and maybe Jellyroll might have made a Blues out of such odorous material but Wright only managed to dunk Joe Louis into a crock of juvenile crap. I have the record too, but every time I look at it I think with Buddy Bolden, "Open up the window and let that bad air out!" Damn!

That's it and I hope I haven't gone on too long. One final matter: the fact that I haven't been publishing fiction doesn't mean that I haven't been writing. I'm still working on a novel that I began in Rome and a good part of which I lost when fire destroyed our summer home during Nov. 1967. I lost all of my notebooks for the book and everything else, but I've rewritten much of it (Book I runs to some 365 pages and Book II is almost as long) and the stream of composition is still running strong. It's aiming at other effects than those attempted in *Invisible Man* but I think you'll find it interesting. I hope so. In the meantime I am indeed interested in seeing what you're doing in the lectures so if there are any copyright problems connected with their publication please let me know. Good luck to you and keep the poetry coming!

Sincerely,

[Ralph Ellison]

---

* *King Joe,* a musical tribute to boxing champ Joe Louis, sung by Robeson with Count Basie and his orchestra.

To Frances Steloff
730 RIVERSIDE DRIVE
NEW YORK, N.Y. 10031
SEPTEMBER 19, 1969

Miss Frances Steloff
The Gotham Book Mart
41 W. 47th Street
New York, New York 10036

Dear Frances:

It is difficult for me to decide which particular books influenced me most as a teenager, for I read haphazardly and voraciously anything and everything in print, including pulp magazines, boys adventure books, the family doctor book and an odd Bible in which the scriptures were conveyed in pictorial symbols. There was also, of course, the King James Version, and the Bible—as sermon, as song, as equipment for living, as stylistic example—was primary.

But the Bible was more or less imposed upon one and when I try to recall the vast conglomeration of books which came after the *Brownie Books* and the fairy tales of pre-adolescence my favorites were *The Boy Scouts Handbook, Tom Sawyer* and *The Adventures of Huckleberry Finn*—and the hero of which I admired so much that I nicknamed my brother "Huck" in his honor. Along with these works of Mark Twain I admired a boy's edition of *Moby-Dick,* Cooper's *Leather Stocking Tales* (especially *The Last of the Mohicans*), Sinclair Lewis' *Arrowsmith,* Albion Tourgee's *Congaree Sketches* (which to the dismay of my eleventh grade American lit. teacher I tried to convert to verse!), Edgar Allan Poe's *Tales,* which linked up with certain Negro American ghost stories and stories of hidden treasure; a book about a Spanish picaro, *Juan Cigarella,* whose adventures closely paralleled those of John, the slave trickster of Negro American folk tales, Jack London's *The Call of the Wild,* and the short stories of Guy de Maupassant. I also read and reread Dickens' *A Tale of Two Cities,* the *Arabian Nights,* Stevenson's *Treasure Island,* Ruskin's story, *The King of the Golden River,* and the *Adventures of Sherlock Holmes.*

But one of the most influential series of books read during the period of early adolescence were the plays of Bernard Shaw, which I discovered in the library of a friend's parents. The prefaces to the plays were especially fascinating and did more than any teacher to make me aware of how exciting non-fictional prose could be. They were also my introduction to the relationship between ideas, art, and politics.

To these works I would add *The Souls of Black Folk* by W. E. B. DuBois, *The Weary Blues* and *Fine Clothes to the Jew* by Langston Hughes, and a work with a title so long that although I became aware of it almost as early as I became conscious of the Bible, I must leave to the last: *The Golden Treasure of Poetry and Song: A Compete Fireside Cyclopedia of the Best Verse in the English Language Over Thirteen Hundred Complete Poems by Nearly Two Hundred Authors Comprising the Best Poems of the Most Famous Writers for Four Centuries, English and American, Including Poems of Humor, Pathos, Patriotism, Nature, Religion and Sentiment, Arranged under Appropriate Division with Author and Subject Index, Compiled and Edited by Henry T. Coates.* As handy as its title, this book belonged to my father but scrawled on one of its end papers is to be found one of my earliest attempts (unsuccessful) at writing my name.

Sincerely,
Ralph Ellison

To Dolores A. Ruzicka
730 RIVERSIDE DRIVE
NEW YORK, NEW YORK 10031
NOVEMBER 10, 1969

Miss Dolores A. Ruzicka
847 Exposition Boulevard, Room 303
Los Angeles, Calif. 90007

Dear Miss Ruzicka:

Thanks for your interest in my novel. I was rather flattered that you found in it traces of influence from Dante. Unfortunately, however, beyond the Prologue I am afraid that any influence that I might have absorbed from Dante would have come through such writers as T. S. Eliot and Ezra Pound. Therefore, I believe that you are following a direction that would not be too fruitful.

On the other hand, the picaresque novel has been very much an influence. Although less through specific examples of the form than through the direction and freedom with which the form has endowed the Novel generally.

Sincerely yours,
Ralph Ellison

RE: fe

To Jennifer Johnson
730 RIVERSIDE DRIVE
NEW YORK, NEW YORK 10031
NOVEMBER 18, 1969

Miss Jennifer Johnson
Centre College
Danville, Kentucky

Dear Miss Johnson:

Thank you for your interest in *Invisible Man* and for your letter of October 28th with its questions, which I shall attempt herewith to answer:

I believe that the central theme of Negro American history before the end of Reconstruction was for full participation in the social, political and economic life of American society. I believe that only after the violence attending the destruction of the integrated Reconstruction governments of the South, and the establishment of harsh discriminatory laws, did the problem of justifying Negro manhood become one of the central themes of our historical quest. The imposition of such laws and customs, made manifest through legal and extra-legal action, caused some Negro Americans—not all—to question their identity both as human beings and as citizens. Thus a most perplexing split of mind was imposed, although in much of his daily activity—on his job, in his churches, in his arts and through forms of oral expression—the Negro American defined himself as Western, American, and representative symbol of the most complex dilemmas experienced by the individual in this most democratic and difficult of modern societies.

On the other hand, he has found it necessary to engage in a ceaseless questioning of himself, his values, and his goals in an attempt to answer the indictment of his humanity by a society which has persistently refused to treat him as equal and which in many ways treats him as somewhat less than human. Thus, I think that today one of the main themes of Negro

American life is an attempt to define the precise nature of our identity as creations and creators of American history, politics and culture.

In answer to your second question concerning the future of race relations, I would say that I am optimistic, because I think that the rise and spread of a counter-racism among black Americans is forcing thinking Americans—both black and white—to recognize the futility of using racial concepts as a means for ordering and identifying social realities.

The greatest cause for hope lies now, as in the beginning, in the expanded legal basis for freedom that has been made possible by the broadening of constitutional rights. The greatest cause for despair lies in the tendency of many Blacks to decry the injustices and brutalities of the past while failing to take advantage of the new opportunities for achieving themselves, and in the parallel tendency of many whites to encourage them in this.

Good luck with your work and thank you for writing.

Sincerely yours,
Ralph Ellison

RE

Letters from the Seventies

THE 1970S OPEN WITH ANOTHER TURN OF FATE THAT seems to compensate a little for the 1967 fire's hammer blow. In June 1970, out of the blue, Ralph Ellison receives an offer of an endowed professorship at New York University, and he accepts. From that year until his retirement in 1979 he keeps up a regular teaching routine.

In very few of his letters from the seventies does Ellison mention either the fire or the Albert Schweitzer Chair in the Humanities at NYU. Likewise, although he clearly senses that the second novel is on others' minds, he keeps his preoccupation with the unfinished book almost entirely out of his correspondence. Instead, he answers queries about *Invisible Man* ("At the time I wrote *Invisible Man* I knew nothing of the Ras Tafari sect. 'Ras,' however, was a term used by certain Black militants during the 30's and 40's as a title of leadership") and occasionally about his short stories ("In a Strange Country" "was not conceived as part of a longer work"). When friends such as Nathan Scott and Leon Forrest are candidates for academic positions or promotion, he writes letters in their support, and he also takes time out to compose commentaries endorsing forthcoming books he admires, such as Daniel Aaron's *The Unwritten War*. In an act of percussive syncopation he also writes a wrathful, Old Testament–like jeremiad, eleven pages long, to the editor of *Life* dismembering a 1970 review purportedly about Richard Wright but really a vilification of Ellison, especially his politics, which the review's author characterizes absurdly as the "obsequious bleatings of white appeasement."

At the same time more than a few of his letters from the seventies show strong interest and generosity toward individual aspiring African American writers. On the cusp of the decade, in 1969–70, he collaborates with James Alan McPherson, the brilliant young author of *Hue and Cry,* on "Indivisible Man" (*The Atlantic,* December 1970), a superb and comprehensive essay/interview that brings out the best in both writers. Two years later he writes McPherson a fulsome letter about "Subjective Account of Something Very Old," an autobiographical piece about McPherson and his father by which both Ellisons were "deeply moved. I mean to tears," he confesses. Also in 1973, responding to Toni Morrison, then a Random House editor, he writes a foreword to Leon Forrest's* novel *There Is a Tree More Ancient than Eden,* calling the book "a source of delight" and "profound instruction." In 1976 he sends Jervis Anderson a letter recanting former "doubts about your project" and praising Anderson's long, important profile in *The New Yorker,* which vividly and shrewdly tracks Ellison's return to Oklahoma City in relation to his boyhood there. At about the same time Ellison writes Horace Porter, whom he met at Amherst College during Porter's undergraduate years there, a letter of encouragement about a piece of autobiographical writing sent his way. Singly and together, these personal letters show Ellison open, receptive, and generous toward up-and-coming generations of African American writers.

ALSO REVEALING IN ANOTHER important way are letters in which Ellison takes tentative stabs at merging the particulars and the feel of autobiography. Early in the seventies he writes movingly to Betty Cameron, a stranger who teaches at Classen High School in Oklahoma City and assigns *Invisible Man* and several of Ellison's short stories to her students. After a grace note of thanks Ellison jumps back to once upon a time, "years ago," when he lived "less than a half block from Classen High School." The leap shows how quickly his attachment to Oklahoma comes into sunlight from the shadows of memory. "The experiences depicted in

---

* Leon Forrest (1937–97), author of *There Is a Tree More Ancient Than Eden* (1973) and *Divine Days* (1993), became a close friend of Ellison's.

Invisible Man . . . are imaginary and not autobiographical," he notes, adding crucially, "The sensibility out of which I write was formed in Oklahoma." Multiple examples prepare for a rousing finale: "You might say to your students that, although I'm no longer in Oklahoma City, Oklahoma City is still very much within me and turns up frequently in my dreams and in the fantasies and memories that inform my writing. I consider this a strength and a joy."

Writing to keep in touch with boyhood friends from Oklahoma City, he quickly modulates from life in the present back to his formative days and ahead to the present. "Harold," he writes to one close friend in early 1971, "I know how you must feel upon going back to Okla. City. . . . I have been returning on the average at least once over the last seven years. And when I get there I'm like a ghost—or a Rip Van Winkle who has slept for twenty years and awoke to discover that his world has changed—But how! Thanks to Urban Renewal, most of the city I knew and loved has disappeared." He calls the roll of friends they have in common, using vivid moments from the past to contrast some poignant falling-off or decline in the present against the wondrous vitality that continues to flow in the presence of the "Great Big Black One," Virgil Branam. Branam, the catalyst and inspiration behind Ellison's extraordinary essay "Tell It Like It Is, Baby," was and remains, however vicariously, a centripetal and centrifugal force of rejuvenation. A 1972 letter to him flows so easily one imagines the two sidekicks sitting down in the present to talk about any and every damn thing as they did long ago and will do as long as they live. More and more frequently Ellison casts his cherished "Cold Oklahoma Negro Eye"[*] on the past by telling stories that salute one or another of the elders whose exploits, escapades, and manly kindness filled some of the void left by his father's passing. These stories young Ralph heard in the past, and recounts in letters as a middle-aged man, show boy and man as one, someone proudly sensing that he's passed tests of initiation from men whose presence and accomplisments he feels in the very self-containment they were able to abandon as the ten-year-old Ralph listened to them talk.

One senses echoes of this qualified austerity and self-containment in Ralph's letter to Herbert Ellison in September 1979. He encloses a check to cover his younger brother's round-trip fare from Los Angeles to Oklahoma City, and accompanies it with detailed instructions "to learn what's

---

[*] Ralph Ellison and James Alan McPherson, "Indivisible Man," in *The Collected Essays of Ralph Ellison*, ed. John F. Callahan, 367.

going on with Bert [Alberta Othello Brown], her physical condition, and the state of her personal affairs." Ralph also directs Herbert to find out from Bert if her late husband, the Ellison boys' first cousin Tom, left a will—"and if so, where is it?" Make sure, he tells Herbert, to collect "the photographs which Bert promised me plus old letters that were exchanged between our father and Tom's mother and any old papers, letters, documents relating to the Ellison family." He concludes in a tone and style perhaps more bloodless than his generous intention: "Beyond such items, whatever else intended for me is yours." In any case, the letter's stiffness reveals Ralph's high expectations for Herbert as well as a fierce passion to secure and possess the history of his paternal ancestors.

Apropos of this passion, in a different key Ralph writes an enthusiastic letter to researcher Steward Lillard, who has disclosed his discoveries about the life and times of Ralph's grandfather Alfred Ellison in Abbeville, South Carolina. "Your information placed me in something of a dream-state," Ellison acknowledges. Lillard's revelations set the mature Ellison's imagination flowing with memories of his rail journey to Abbeville and the days he spent there with "Big Alfred" and his family a few months after his father's death in July 1916. The "dream-state" becomes a marker revealing rigorous standards of human conduct: "I'll make you walk the chalk-line," Ellison remembered his grandfather saying. Near the end of his own life he made his grandfather, who as a rare black sheriff in the post-Reconstruction South faced down white and black citizens alike unwilling to walk that line, the center of his memorable 1992 address to the Whiting Foundation.

TWO OTHER LETTERS DESERVE special mention. One is the last of many Ellison wrote over twenty-five years to the man he called in print and in person his "intellectual sparring partner," the critic Stanley Edgar Hyman. Written May 29, 1970, the letter is an unwitting valedictory essay in which Ellison takes issue frankly and passionately with many of the views expressed by his old friend in a recent *Atlantic* reconsideration of Richard Wright. "My objection," Ellison writes, "was to such generalizations as 'There can be no doubt that Negro hatred of whites is close to universal' . . . I believe that you make our Negro American attitudes and emotions toward whites far too simple. You allow us no contempt— a quite different emotion than hate—no irony, no forbearance, no indifference, no charity, no mockery, no compassion, no condescension—not to mention that ambivalence of emotion and attitude that you see so readily in the Blues."

Ellison rejects brilliantly Hyman's compulsion to insist that Wright was Ellison's necessarily primary influence: "Like yourself, I existed in a <u>field</u> of influences, both personal and environmental; but despite this obvious fact you go on reducing the complex field to a single writer and implicitly to the <u>race</u> of that writer."

Ellison discusses many things besides his and Wright's work—the blues, racial identity, Frank Yerby, Phillis Wheatley—before saying loud and clear, so Hyman will hear him: "Race and culture, culture and race!" A reader pricks up his ears for Hyman's imaginary rejoinder, knowing that the two friends have hashed out these and other things many times during many long liquid evenings and expected to do again many times in the future.

But they wouldn't. Two months later Hyman dies suddenly of a heart attack, and shock is Ellison's portion. Fortunately, his ironic, affectionate closing passage serves as a farewell, characteristic of the two men's angle of friendship: "Well, I guess this is enough abuse from one who seldom writes this type of letter anymore. I'll close by saying how pleased I am to see that our earlier hassle over these matters has just appeared in BLACK LITERATURE IN AMERICA, A CASEBOOK."

The other letter Ellison writes to the bespoke tailor and jazz aficionado Charles Davidson. As suggested in the letter, the Ellison-Davidson friendship exists on the field of the vernacular. "The store" is Ralph's name for Davidson's high-class Andover Shop, just off Harvard Square, where he is tailor of choice to presidential candidates, senators, a governor or two, and several sartorially fussy top jazz musicians (Miles Davis among them), not to mention Harvard students who to this day stand outside 22 Holyoke Street, sometimes venturing inside to buy a tie or a handkerchief as they wait for a look or a word from the legendary Charlie. In the letter Ellison plays on his and Davidson's chosen turf—American social hierarchy. His riff on jazz piano player Bobby Short glories in Short's talents and social and artistic standing as displayed in Short's superb autobiography, *Black and White Baby,* a signed copy of which Davidson sent to Ralph.

Like other of Davidson's close friends, Ellison roots for and places an occasional bet on Davidson's thoroughbred racehorse, Porkchopper. As always, there is payback: in this case a resemblance between Davidson and Ellison's character Choc (Chalk) Charlie, the beer-drinking Choctaw tailor who, when ten doctors fail, comes to the hilarious rescue, armed with needle and thread, to sew back on that "most important piece missing" from the hero of the Oklahoma movie-in-the-making in *Three Days Before the Shooting . . .*

LIKE THE LETTERS OF previous decades, much is spacious and centrifugal in the seventies letters, including the feel of Ellison letting go to plumb mysterious personal and intellectual depths. If there is something missing, it may be a sense of tension, a sense of something about to happen. In the forties it was *Invisible Man;* the reader has no question Ellison will finish the novel, and waits patiently in the betting line ready to wager on its success. In 1960 publication of the long section from the second novel in Saul Bellow's *The Noble Savage* and "Night-Talk" in 1969 creates an impression that Ellison, however quirkily he's dodging around corners, has the whip in hand and is likely somehow to drive his second novel past the finish line.

In contrast, the seventies end in hiatus. The last letter to his old friend Jimmy Stewart in Oklahoma speaks of what has happened: Ellison has retired from NYU, has received emeritus status, has just returned to Plainfield from participating in the Ralph Ellison Festival at Brown University, which Ellison says "turned out to have been quite a serious, dignified and, in a sense, an historical occasion." (This last refers to the fact that the festival also honored Dr. Inman Page, the first Negro graduate of Brown, who was Ellison's principal at Douglass High School in Oklahoma City.)

There is little forward motion, little strong sense of what is happening or will happen. If in previously published excerpts from the second novel—"And Hickman Arrives" (1960), "Juneteenth" (1965), "Night-Talk" (1969)—one senses narrative drive as well as a luminous, haunting, melancholy power, between the lines of the seventies letters there is an edgy fear that the second novel as a whole may be approaching the status of missing in action.

John F. Callahan

730 Riverside Drive
New York, New York 10031
March 5, 1973

Dear Jim:

Here the 5th of March has arrived and I find that I haven't
gotten around to thank you for sending the article and tape recording.
This hasn't been, I assure you, because we haven't been talking and
thinking about you, but is the result of the disarray in my affairs
that comes from trying to teach and write at the same time. Nevertheless, I want you to know that Fanny and I have read your Subjective
Account of Something Very Old and were both deeply moved. I mean to
tears. I mean to cartharsis and thus to a feeling of redemption through
being allowed to recognize the terribly complexity of unfolding life.
Indeed, we were so moved that I urge you to give us more, much more.
And I don't say this to flatter, I simply feel that you have such a
hold on your material that you could expand it into a significant book;
one which by its sensitive subjectivity would counteract much of the
empty sociological rhetoric which keeps getting in the way of any real
understanding of the impact of our social and cultural conditions upon
individual human beings. Yes, and because I suspect that such an approach
as yours is the only effective antidote to the dehumanizing abstractions
(well intended though they be) that so many black writers are projecting
as images of our situation. Your description of your father's difficulties
alone conveys more of reality than a whole book-shelf of sociological abstractions, because he comes across as a most complex human being. His pain
resonates and your regard for his predicament comes through with the mute
power of understatement. I should add that your description of working with
him at his electrician's trade and his difficulties over fulfilling contracts
not only told me much about you, but it caused me to re-live some of my own
job experiences and to recall relationships I had with older men whose low
social status was in contrast with their great value as mentors. In the
judgement of the community several of these were "failures" or worse, but
for me they were instructors to whom I owe far more than I do to some of
my official teachers.

I also liked your handling of the details of the cultural and historical background which operates in the relationships between blacks and whites
in Savannah. While others generalize about "The"Black man and "The" white
man, you've stuck to thorny human realities and individuals, some of whom
triumph and some of whom fail, but most of whom are caught with the abiding
confusion of good-and-bad. Thanks especially for giving us Mr. Simms, and
forgive me for envying you for having known him and his. Your little thumbnail sketches of your relatives and of the families in your neighborhood were
so effective that I was forced to make my own mental survey of families I
knew and the boys and girls I grew up with. Considering the circumstances,
a hell of a lot of them turned out so very well that any easy cynicism
concerning the prospects of their children and grandchildren is not only
uncalled for but obscene. And that includes a few who were assumed to be
heading either for early death, dismal failure, or the electric chair.

-2-

Isn't it ironic that white southern writers like Faulkner or Warren would understand your point about Flannery O'Connor and the Pullman porter and the California hustler and the cop while Ravh could not? He knows too little about American society, especially that of the South, and too damn much about books, while they, knowing both, would never allow the abstractions of literature to blind them to the snarl of human relationships out of which great literature emerges.

Back during the 1950's, when I interviewed Warren for the Paris Review, he related an anecdote in which an old Louisiana Negro man had killed a woman for badmouthing his grandaughter. When he decided to act, his victim was engaged in a crap game and the old man waited patiently until a friend could win back six dollars he'd lost to the offending woman, and this accomplished (I believe it took half an hour) he proceeded to blast the woman with both barrels of his shotgun. As Harry Morgan said of the black Cuban gunman in To Have And Have Not who had shot-and-machinegunned a bunch of men to death, that old man was "some nigger"! More confounding, he was a man of honor who felt that anyone, man or woman, who badmouthed his beloved grandaughter deserved to die. And although there were many witnesses, he refused to plead guilty, despite that fact that he could hara escape the death penalty by going for a charge of manslaughter. It took his friends three days to persuade the old bastard to plead Not Guilty and before they did he had shaken the town to its moral foundations. I guess he took the old code duello concern with honor far more seriously than anyone expected a Negro to do and so sent everybody out of their righteous minds. Now he didn't have to wait as long to act as your hustler's daddy did, but he was the same kind of deadly-patient old Southern Boot. That kind of black man will do what he feels he has to no matter how much he confuses socially accepted notions of justice. To my mind, you've got a hell of a fine story just in the old man's postponing his revenge until his last child had been educated. Tell us, Jim, what the hell went before!

I don't know what the hell is bothering Gaines, but his puzzlement over my Uncle Remus crack seems a waste of mental energy. I was simply trying to get those high-flying intellectuals to come down to earth and think a bit. So I mentioned calculus by way of emphasizing Uncle Remus' role as "teacher" as against his accepted role of "entertainer". There they were, accepting the notion that race blocked the writer from dealing with experience which takes place across racial lines and I was suggesting that their notion was false. Because human experience is human experience and it is the writer's role to use his craft to penetrate its mysteries wherever it seizes his imagination. Hell, everybody recognizes that under the surface of those animal tales Remus was teaching philosophy and guiding that white kid to identify with the human essence of social drama. So if that is true, it is possible that he was also teaching some math and we just weren't told about it because Joel Chandler Harris either didn't understand the abstractions or didn't find it significant enough to mention. But whose to say that those animals, abstractions for human qualities all, weren't also metaphors for mathematical relationships? Do we have to be limited by Harris' vision? Faulkner confesses that Mrs. Caroline Barr taught him all manner of things along with his social manners, and George Washington Carver taught all kinds of white folks botany and agricultural chemistry — even though he approached them socially with hat in hand. I'm riffing now, but a writer

-3-

as gifted as Gaines shouldn't have to be told any of this, all he has to
do is think!

    I must apologize for not having really studied the tape of your
mother but I have been waiting until spring vacation, which comes near the
end of the month. At that time I plan to isolate myself and play it until
I've absorbed what she has to say. I'll do the same with Ernie's reading, although that won't be as new to me since I heard, and enjoyed, his
reading down at the Library of Congress.

    In the meantime, please tell ole Mike Harper that I'm watching
him and give our regards to the Honigs.

    Thanks again, Jim, and keep up the good writing.

                       Sincerely,

                       Ralph Ellison

Mr. James A. McPherson
34 Fort Avenue
Cranston, Rhode Island 02905

To Revels Cayton Jr.
FEBRUARY 12, 1970

Dear Mr. Cayton:*

My wife and I are ever so grateful to you for your letter informing us of Horace's unexpected death in Paris.

We last heard from Horace a few days before he left California; he sent us an Xmas greeting that contained his photograph and a brief note saying he was leaving for Paris December 22nd. And then on January 22nd we received a letter from Michel Fabre,† one of Horace's friends in Paris, saying that Horace had taken ill at his home on January 18th, that he had called a doctor and the doctor had said it was no more than a cold aggravated by his diabetes and "usual heart disease." My wife wrote Horace immediately expressing our concerns and urging him to take special precautions against fatigue and the dampness of Paris, but he died before receiving the letter. Not that it would have helped but we would have liked him to know we were concerned about him.

Since then Michel Fabre and George Baguet have both been in touch with me. I gather they have extended themselves to the utmost in the situation—even locating Horace's address book, that the embassy had overlooked, and finding your father's address so that he could be notified. A friend of ours is going to Paris on Monday and we will send personal messages to M. Fabre and M. Baguet with our appreciation and to determine if there is anything that we can do.

We knew Horace for many years. My wife knew him in Chicago as early as 1937. I suppose we kept in touch about as much as people do these days who live in different parts of the States.

Now we would like to keep in touch with you and urge that you get in touch with us should you come this way, and we will do likewise when we come to Berkeley or vicinity.

Yes, I knew about Horace's planned biography of Richard Wright. We had talked about it last year. I would like to think that he had advanced enough with it for the possible publication of his notes but I suppose that

---

* Revels Cayton was the grandson of author Horace Cayton, a longtime friend of the Ellisons, with whom Ellison corresponded significantly in the 1960s.

† A French scholar who was friend and biographer of Richard Wright and who also wrote several essays on Ellison's work.

is too much to hope for, and a definitive biography of Wright is yet to be written.

I think it is admirable that Horace wanted his papers to go to the King Institute and I hope that the Institute will have the proper facilities to preserve them and to prevent exploitation by the dilettantes.

By all means, please keep us informed of any important developments and we'll be of help in any way that we can.

Yours sincerely,
Ralph Ellison

Revels Cayton, Jr.
1640 Milvia St. #4
Berkeley, California

To Thomas Griffith
730 RIVERSIDE DRIVE
NEW YORK, NEW YORK 10031
MAY 12, 1970

Mr. Thomas Griffith, Editor
LIFE Magazine
Time-Life Building
New York, New York

Dear Mr. Griffith:*

I would like to call your attention to an example of editorial shoddiness appearing in your issue of May 8, 1970 that does damage to *Life*'s reputation for accurate reporting and damage to my reputation both as a writer and as a man of integrity.

In a *Life* book review titled "Native Son Strikes Home," the assertion is made that Ralph Ellison and "James Baldwin after him both helped to create the image of [Richard] Wright as a novelist too much given to

---

* According to Rampersad, "Ralph threatened to sue *Life* and Clifford Mason. When advised that the First Amendment would prohibit his winning, he accepted an offer by *Life* to publish a rejoinder . . . he tried to boil down his response [and] gave up" (Rampersad, *Ralph Ellison,* 469). The letter seems to stand now as a rejoinder, and we include it as Ellison wrote it, sending it shortly after he read the flagrantly hostile review. Griffith and *Life* chose not to publish Ellison's letter in whole or in part.

social protest, too preoccupied with one level of black society and too constrained by the limitations of his brutish protagonist really to qualify as a master."

I am calling this matter to your attention not only because the assertion is untrue but, since it was preceded by a charge characterizing my politics as "obsequious bleatings of white appeasement," it was of libelous and defamatory intent. Since I am a black American it is obvious that such a characterization was meant to discredit me in the eyes of those who have no personal knowledge either of me, my politics, or my writings. And I find the charge of 'white appeasement' especially distressing, for in certain parts of the black community it is as damaging to the individual as the charge of 'nigger lover' would be in bigoted areas of the white population or as the charge of being pro-Hitler would be to a member of the Jewish community.

Considering the mounting turmoil of racial antagonism that is helping to tear our country apart, I simply cannot understand how such charges failed to arouse the attention of your editorial staff before they were published. That they did not leaves *Life* open to the speculation that either it does not regard such matters with seriousness or that some of its editorial staff is guilty of complicity in a conscious enterprise of character assassination and racial polarization.

I have no idea where you found your reviewer but I can assure you that he knows even less of my politics than he knows of my relationship with Richard Wright or of my writings. For not only have I kept my politics a matter of my own private concern, I have resisted being drawn into an area of activity in which, as a writer, I have no special competence. As for *Native Son*, I have never characterized its hero, Bigger Thomas, as "brutish" nor judged Richard Wright as "too preoccupied with one level of black society . . . to qualify as a master." What is more, it is a matter of record (see Constance Webb's recent biography) that I was a friend of Richard Wright, the best man at his first wedding—which occurred about the time *Native Son* was published; I had a minor role to play in the events leading to his final marriage, and during the 1950's I was a visitor to his home whenever I was in Paris. It is highly unlikely that our friendship could have sustained any such attack upon his skill as your reviewer attributes to me.

As your editorial staff could easily have discovered, I have at no time written a review of *Native Son,* and the two references that I made to it in print before James Baldwin wrote the first of several essays devoted to

Wright were anything but condemnatory. These references occurred in an essay-review of *Black Boy,* titled "Richard Wright's Blues," which appeared in 1945 in the *Antioch Review.* The first was a brief allusion to the dedication [of] *Native Son* to Wright's mother and the other was made during the course of discussing the "eroticism" frequently attributed to Negro American expression:

> "The 'eroticism' of Negro expression springs from much the same conflict as that displayed in the violent gesturing of a man who attempts to express a complicated concept with a limited vocabulary: Thwarted ideational energy is converted into unsatisfactory pantomime, and his words are burdened with meanings they cannot convey. Here lies the source of the basic ambiguity of *Native Son,* wherein in order to translate Bigger's complicated feelings into ideas, Wright had to force into Bigger's consciousness concepts and ideas which his intellect could not formulate. Between Wright's skill and knowledge and the potentials of Bigger's mute feelings lay a thousand years of conscious culture . . ."

Between the time the above was published and my next reference to *Native Son* there was an interval of sixteen years. In the meantime, James Baldwin was to publish, in 1949, his famous essay "Everybody's Protest Novel," an essay in which he took issue with Wright and about which I'll have only this to say: It would require an enormous strain upon one's imagination to see Baldwin's essay (really a credo <u>manifesto</u>) as having been inspired by my brief references to *Native Son.* That *Life* has published a reviewer who does so suggest that it has discovered an individual who possesses more competency for fantasy than for fact, more taste for malicious mischief than for critical evaluation.

Be that as it may, my next remarks on *Native Son* were published in 1961 when, during an interview with novelist Richard G. Stern I was asked if I had been "dissatisfied with the sort of work Wright was doing" at the time I was reading drafts of *Native Son*—which it was my good fortune to read as they came off the typewriter. My reply to Stern was:

> "Dissatisfied? I was amazed with watching the process of creation.
>
> I didn't understand quite what was going on, but by this time had talked with Wright a lot and he was very conscious of technique. He

talked about it not in terms of mystification but as writing know-how. 'You must read so-and-so,' he'd say. 'You have to go about learning to write <u>consciously</u>. People have talked about such and such a problem and have written about it. You must learn how Conrad, Joyce, Dostoievsky get their effects . . .' He guided me to Henry James and to Conrad's prefaces, that kind of thing. Of course, I knew that my own feelings were different, but that was not even a matter of question. Wright knew what he was all about, what he wanted to do, while I hadn't even discovered myself. I knew only that what I would want to express would not be an imitation of his kind of thing . . ."

To Stern's query as to "What sort of thing did you feel Wright was not doing that you wanted to do?" I replied:

"Well, I don't suppose I judged. I am certain that I did not judge in quite so conscious way, but I think I felt more complexity in life, and my background made me aware of a larger area of possibility. Knowing Wright himself and something of what he was doing increased that sense of the possible. Also, I think I was less interested in an ideological interpretation of Negro experience . . . When I came to discover a little more about what I wanted to express I felt that Wright was overcommitted to ideology—even though I, too, wanted many of the same things for our people. You may say that I was much less a social determinist. But I suppose that basically it comes down to a difference in our conception of the individual. I, for instance, found it disturbing that Bigger Thomas had none of the finer qualities of Richard Wright, none of the imagination, none of the sense of poetry, none of the gaiety. And I preferred Richard Wright to Bigger Thomas. Do you see? Which . . . directs you back to the difference between what Wright was himself and how he conceived of the individual; back to his conception of the quality of Negro humanity . . ."

Here, as you can see, my judgment had to do with a dimension that I found missing in the fictional character but which I found very much present in Wright himself; nevertheless, my judgment was neither reductive of Bigger Thomas nor made with malicious intent.

During December, 1963 and February, 1964 I published in the *New Leader* an exchange with Irving Howe in which I objected to what I considered Howe's over-emphasis of what he considered Wright's influence upon my own writing. To Howe's insistence that Wright was the spiritual father of Ellison and Baldwin I made the following denial:

"Wright was no spiritual father of mine, certainly in no sense that I recognize—nor did he pretend to be, since he felt I had started writing too late. It was Baldwin's career, not mine, that Wright proudly advanced by helping him attain the Eugene Saxton Fellowship, and it was Baldwin who found Wright a lion in his path. Being older and familiar with quite different lions in quite different paths, I simply stepped around him.

But Wright was a friend . . . and a personal hero in the same way Hot Lips Paige and Jimmy Rushing were friends and heroes. I felt no need to attack what I considered the limitations of his vision because I was quite impressed by what he had achieved . . . Still I would write my own books and they would be in themselves, implicit criticisms of Wright's; just as all novels of a given historical moment form an argument over the nature of reality and are, to an extent, criticisms each of the other . . . While I rejected Bigger Thomas as any <u>final</u> image of Negro personality, I recognized *Native Son* as an achievement; as one man's essay in defining the human condition as seen from a specific Negro perspective at a given time in a given place. And I was proud to have known Wright and happy for the impact he made upon our apathy."

One final quotation, this time from the March 1967 issue of *Harper's* Magazine. Please note, by the way, that here, as in most of the instances given, I am replying to questions put to me by interviewers at their own initiative. In this instance one of a group of young black writers said, "I notice that you mentioned, quite some time ago, that you learned a lot of skill under Richard Wright. Do you find that he gauged his craft to the great writers of the world?"
My answer:

"He certainly tried to do so. He was constantly reading the great masters, just as he read the philosophers, the political theorists, the social and literary critics. He did not limit himself in the manner that Negro writers currently limit themselves. And he encouraged other writers who usually rebuffed him—to become conscious craftsmen, to plunge into the world of conscious literature and take their chances unafraid. He felt this to be one of the few areas in which Negroes could be free and as equal as their minds and talents would allow. And like a good Negro athlete, he believed in his ability to compete. In 1940 he was well aware that *Native Son* was being published at a time when *The Grapes of Wrath* would be his main competition. Nevertheless, he looked toward publication day nervously but eagerly. He wished to be among the advanced artists and was willing to run the risks required."

None of the material quoted here is scattered in obscure journals. In fact, except for the *Harper's* interview they are to be found in *Shadow & Act,* a collection of essays that I published in 1964 and which are still available in hard cover as well as in paperback. With such easy availability I can see no excuse for their having gone unconsulted either by your reviewer, your book editor, or your research staff. And since they are required reading in many colleges and universities they should be familiar to any teacher posing as an expert on Negro American writers. Inasmuch as the reviewer must surely have seen them, I can only conclude that he has chosen to ignore evidence that contradicted his fantasy of allegations.

It is not that I should be attacked by a young man seeking public attention that surprises me, for such is the price one pays for a public reputation—indeed, such attacks are a form of negative compliment whereby one is elevated in order to be struck down. What does surprise me is the ironic display of editorial insensitivity that allowed such a piece to appear in an issue dominated by the portrait of Vice President Spiro Agnew! Perhaps it is just such editorial insensitivity (and irresponsibility) that has made the news media vulnerable to his attacks by providing him grounds for his rhetorical appeal. Thus, as I see it, there is far more here at stake than an ill-founded attack upon Ralph Ellison, and most surely it requires your attention and correction.

As indicated earlier, I am forced to wonder at the motives of those who would throw open the pages of a renowned magazine to the conveyance of misinformation no less than to the character assassination of those whose writings and politics its book reviewers might happen to dislike. The reviewer in question is listed in your pages as a teacher and critic—roles that apparently he regards with a criminal lack of seriousness. But as I see it, a book reviewer is also a reporter in that he tells us the who, why, what, when and where of the books and authors assigned to him. Thus, since the novel *Native Son* was published thirty years ago a reviewer reporting on its fate and welfare is expected to supply the reader with at least a minimum of background information—a point on which your reviewer not only fails quite miserably, but substitutes instead a pseudo-event fabricated for the most part from misreading and malicious fantasy.

Those readers of the *Life* review who are unfamiliar with the facts would have no idea that Wright's *Native Son* (like his *Black Boy*) was no less a financial than a critical success. Nor would they glean that it was a Book-of the-Month Club selection that was considered for the Pulitzer Prize. Nor could they suspect that it has been translated into many foreign languages, been issued in numerous editions, including the Modern Library, and in various paperback editions, and enjoyed as a play a successful run on Broadway. But instead of supplying such background information *Life*'s reviewer chose to use *Native Son* as an agency for attacking Ralph Ellison and as an excuse to impute a naked political and racist motive to those writers, editors and critics of the Herald Tribune Book Week Poll who found *Invisible Man* a novel of distinction. Not only were these well-known and even distinguished authors denied the possession of any serious concern with literary aesthetics but the reviewer also ignored the fact the critics who gave *Native Son* such world-wide acclaim were just as white as those who praised *Invisible Man*. Nor did *Life*'s reviewer bother to acknowledge that it was a white critic, Irving Howe, who began championing the virtues of Wright's fiction over that of Baldwin and Ellison long before he broke so wrathfully into print.

But black racism like white racism insists upon having it both ways: What contradicts its distorted view of reality it seeks to suppress, to deny and when possible, to destroy. Howe began asking for a re-evaluation of *Native Son* as early as 1963, but in his passion to present the *Book Week* authors as a gang of literary racists and Wright's novel as the victim of conspiratorial neglect, *Life*'s reviewer found it necessary to ignore not only Howe but a number of other critics, many of them white, who found Wright a writer of continuing interest. Evidently, in *Life*'s reviewer's eyes no white man can do anything positive as regards writers who are black. Therefore those white critics who praised *Native Son* so extensively and enthusiastically that its jacket design could consist of a collage of their accolades are treated as though they were guilty of an act of anti-Negro racism. Therefore, a black writer whose work receives high praise must, in this view, be guilty of sacrificing the honor and freedom of his people for personal gain. There, Ellison must be made a figure of such satanic power that two hundred white critics are converted to white racism in a conspiracy to destroy Richard Wright.

It doesn't worry me in the least that many readers might prefer Wright's novel to my own, nor do I care that *Life*'s reviewer believes that *Invisible Man* was honored by the *Book Week* Poll more for what he considers my politics than for its aesthetic qualities. It does upset me, however, that this "reviewer," the "teacher" and "critic" failed to note that in the *Book Week* Poll neither color nor racial background were criteria. If they had been, my novel would not have been considered. And if politics had been a factor in that poll, surely my book would not have been singled out, for not that many of the writers polled—if indeed any—are so anti black that they would push aside their devotion to literature to make a racial point, no matter how Machiavellian.

If you ask me, there is a rare and strange dialectic operative here and I pity the students who are being subjected to its spell. What does this "teacher" teach? And where? Is it for such as this that we clamor for courses in black studies, for more black teachers on college faculties? All living things are critics, it has been said, and *Life* has affirmed that it believes this critic alive by welcoming him to its pages. But that, I'm afraid, is about all it has affirmed. For there is a smell about this enterprise, an odor rank of enclosed rooms of the mind, a stench revealing a fear to face up intellectually to the complications of literature no less than to those of a multi-racial, pluralistic society. It is a fear that would reduce important conflicts of vision to petty motives and all complexities of culture and personality to the rank over-simplifications of racial hostility. Never in this view could a black American be judged worthy of recognition as a leading American writer, for to do so demands a mind open to the possibilities which exist within this racist society despite its racism and its perplexing contradictions of caste and class. Being an American, Henry James has written, is a complex fate; and being a black American is more complex than even that finely honed mind could ever have suspected. Because for blacks freedom is always hedged with traps and contradictions, and one of the saddest aspects of being a black American who strives for freedom of expression is that one's assertion of freedom often frightens one's fellow blacks far more than it frightens even the most bigoted whites. Unfortunately, this has rendered blacks easy victims of divide-and-rule techniques since slavery times and bigoted whites have made use of such techniques even unto this day. I must say that it is appalling to find evidence of this at work in the pages of *Life*.

To my mind, it takes an insular, unformed and worm-like sensibility, and one given to fantasies of boring from within, for a critic not to see that imputing a purely racial motive to those black critics and writers of the *Negro Digest* who selected Richard Wright as the most important black American writer of all time is to do them dishonor. For surely most of them must have picked Wright because they respected his qualities as an artist no less than his passionate advocacy of black freedom. And yet, your "critic" has managed to do exactly that. But there is nothing new in this, black racism usually ends up by being more detrimental to blacks than to whites just as the major victims of black violence are other blacks. *Life*'s reviewer has somewhere along the way become so segregated in his own mind that he doesn't dare embrace the freedom of discussion available to him in its pages by attacking the subject—if *Native Son* was indeed his true subject—of Wright's relationship to his times and to his peers. A serious critic would have examined *Native Son* in the context of *To Have and to Have Not, For Whom the Bell Tolls,* and *The Grapes of Wrath*—Wright in the context of Hemingway and Steinbeck. Nor would he have overlooked Faulkner of *The Hamlet* (1940) or *Go Down, Moses* (1942). Wright wished to be judged against the best of his times, for him this was one of the criteria of artistic freedom; but in your "critic's" hands he is subjected to a segregation more rigid than what he knew in Mississippi. And all because *Life* threw *Native Son* into the hands of a reviewer who hides incompetency behind a phony militancy. It makes one feel that what Wright won in his own time as been lost in *Life*.

Still, as a document of its times *Native Son* will stay alive as long as the human conditions to which it was addressed remain unresolved. Arguing about it will not improve it nor destroy it, but what can be destroyed is the quality of discussion that Wright sought to uphold when he attempted to elevate an abiding theme of American society and its politics to the level of serious literature. *Native Son* was not written as a lesson to black writers. Neither was it written to bootleg black nationalism before the public in the guise of Marxism, nor as an attack upon the Communist Party. It was written as a literary accusation of American values and the quality of American life. It is for this that it remains valuable. It is for this that it has remained alive.

In closing let me say that I expect *Life* to correct the damage that I have received at the hands of its reviewer and to be more circumspect about whom and what it publishes, especially in the torturous area of race relations.

Sincerely,
Ralph Ellison

RE:fe

To Stanley Hyman
730 RIVERSIDE DRIVE
NEW YORK, NEW YORK 10031
MAY 29, 1970

Dear Stanley:

Thanks for the encouraging words concerning the Bearden[*] piece; as you probably realize it is my first attempt at art criticism and I undertook it with fear and trembling. I hope you'll still find some of it valid once you've seen Bearden's work. There are several here in the apartment at which you and Phoebe are welcome to have a look-see whenever you're in New York. But now to remove a few of the needles you inserted with your kind words.

When we discussed your essay on Wright at the Mitchells either I was drinking faster than you, or you were three sheets in the wind: therefore since both are possible let me hasten to say that if you thought that I was objecting to your using such terms as "Negro artists," "Negro American experience," etc., you were mistaken. My objection was to such generalizations as "There can be no doubt that Negro hatred of whites is close to universal." For if Negro hatred of whites were so universal such black militant writers as Jones wouldn't have to go to such frenzied lengths in their efforts to arouse that hatred. I also objected because I believe that you make our Negro American attitudes and emotions toward whites far too simple. You allow us no contempt—a quite different emotion than hate—no irony, no forbearance, no indifference, no charity, no mockery, no compassion, no condescension—not to mention that ambivalence of emotion and attitude that you so readily see in the Blues.

---

[*] Ellison's introduction in the catalogue *Romare Bearden: Paintings and Projections* done for an exhibit at the Art Gallery of the State University of New York at Albany, November 25–December 22, 1968 (reprinted in *The Collected Essays of Ralph Ellison*, ed. John F. Callahan, 688–97).

As I see it, Negro American art style, from that of the folk to the most sophisticated individual expression, embodies a transcendence of raw hatred or any other "raw" emotion. Indeed, as with any cultural expression worthy of the name, it is transcendence and sublimation that define it as art. And despite the prevalence of stereotyped notions of Negro spontaneity and instinctually, our life-style—at least as it has evolved in the South—has been shaped by a determined will to control violent emotion (we seldom run amuck) as a life-preserving measure against being provoked into retaliatory actions by those who desire only to destroy us.

One of the functions of such emotional control has been the preservation for ourselves of a maximum freedom of decision in selecting the moment and circumstance under which retaliatory action would be taken and aggressive emotion released. Such control has been often interpreted as apathy and fear by sociologists both black and white, and by those who view us from a distance or who tend to congratulate themselves as being of a superior and nobler race because we avoid easy provocation, but we know better because we cling to our own sense of values and have never been sold on Sir Walter Scottish notions of bravery, cowardice, honor, etc. Such values have a class and race aspect and woe to a minority that forgets it. For here questions of life and death are always just beneath the surface of the simplest confrontations between the races. But another function of such emotional control springs from our will to humanize a hostile society in our own terms and to convert that control into a source of pleasure and affirmation by transforming the threat of social existence into forms of self-definition and triumph.

Thus our resistance to provocation has acted as a life-preserving discipline—which in turn has reinforced our tendency toward stylization, not only in art but in the processes of everyday life, from work to worship. What is so ironic about our efforts at literary (as against musical and choreographic) projections of our life-style and experience is the fact that we've seldom achieved a formal control—or control of literary forms—commensurate with the control cum flexibility that is so characteristic of Negro American expression at its best. I refer to Negro American idiom as it finds expression in oral tradition, and in physical movement, whether in work or play, sports or ceremonial activity, in dress and cosmetic culture; and to the essence of which we hear in Jazz.

But how could I have objected to your use of the terms "Negro artist" or "Negro American experience"? I use them not only in the Bearden piece but in almost everything else I've written about American culture.

I have, however, tried to see that the meaning that is conveyed is not primarily racial, but <u>cultural</u>. I try to make the terms convey something of the complexity of Negro American life and expression along with their intricate connections with the broader culture of the United States. Because far too often they are used in a manner reductive of that complexity and slighting of those interconnections. When I refer to the plastic possibilities of Negro American experience I am giving recognition to such features of physical identification as hair and skin texture, facial structure, skeletal structure and variation of skin color, etc. Over the centuries, so-called 'primitive' African sculptors have made much of these possibilities in terms of their tribal and religious values from the most subtly observed naturalism to the abstract manipulation of forms that in the West we recognize as cubism.

In a predominantly white society where so much vicious nonsense has been imposed upon blacks in the name of European (I almost said "Aryan") standards of physical beauty, the problem of what to do with the given physical features of people who are culturally and visually Negro American became a special problem for the plastic artists of that background. All too many attempted to find a solution through the language of naturalism, when the answer lay, as it lay for most western artists, in the direction of abstraction—very much as it did in the choreographic and literary arts. But since in the fields of painting and sculpture the greatest activity of black Americans came during the Depression and under the auspices of the W.P.A. at a time when agit-prop theories of art were the rage many black artists got hung up on the notion of "content" at the expense of mastering form and technique. But you know all of this.

My reference to Negro Americans depending upon narrative was not meant to imply that other Americans had not so depended; it was to point out that for a people lacking a class with broad formal education as it fought for a positive definition of itself in a society in which an inferior status was imposed upon it by force, violence and anti-Negro stereotypes (the time I referred to, or meant to refer to, was the period of slavery and the early period of emancipation) narrative played a special role. (Yes, I know the narrative function of stained glass windows, items presenting national iconographics, and such, in developing religious and national identities for those without literal skills.) The Negro American's conception of himself was seldom supported by an articulate philosophy, or by conscious theology, or by any of the specifically analytic forms of the mind. Note, too, that I referred to narrative forms that were simple and graphic, and this because the majority of my people were at the time unlettered and, for a great part of that time, enslaved. This was not true of most whites, and at the time that our great American folk archetypes were being created white American intellectuals, with very few blacks participating on a conscious intellectual level, were extending and testing the ideas and ideals of the Enlightenment. The spirit of those ideas and ideals was indeed present among the slaves and free blacks but for the majority of slaves, as for many uneducationed whites, they required simplification and indeed sloganization. As you damn well know, I view my people as American and not African, and while our experience differs in unique ways from that of white Americans, it is never absolutely at variance with the dominant American mode. Diversity within unity is the confounding reality ... Nevertheless, no Negro has ever headed the Stock Exchange, been President of the U.S., Chief of the Combined Armed Forces, or even president of Harvard, Yale, or General Motors. Second, plots and pastoral motives are indeed present in the American drama of blackness and whiteness but here it is prudent not to let one's self be carried away by abstractions.

And now, since you've managed to needle me into type (!) concerning your Wright essay, let me say that I found it a useful piece <u>despite</u> my objections. What's more, it gives me special satisfaction because it gives the lie to the character in *Life* who would make all literary judgment a matter of racial prejudice. You were taking Wright seriously long ago and as far as I know only Irving Howe beat you to the popular press with a re-evaluation of *Native Son*. I am enclosing a more recent piece on yours truly and Wright* in case you missed it. Modern Fiction Studies Vol. XV No. 4 <u>Winter</u> 1969–1970.

And now back to my carping. I do by no means agree with your statement that "The Man Who Lived Underground" "is the perfect metaphor for Negro identity in life under the streets in a sewer that is the formulation of <u>ecclesia supra clocam</u>." Cloacal, yes; Ecclesia, no; metaphor, yes, but perfect not at all. Here I feel like the soldier who was questioned by his captain after being observed shaking his head throughout a lecture on sex devices, in which the captain stated that an orgasm was no more than a form of relief from muscular tension and very much like taking a crap.

---

* See William Goede's "On Lower Frequencies: The Buried Men in Wright and Ellison," *Modern Fiction Studies* 15, no. 4 (Winter 1969–70): 483–501.

"Captain," the soldier said, "I wasn't shaking my head out of disrespect, I just meant that either <u>you</u> don't know nothing about fucking or <u>I</u> don't know a damn thing about shitting!"

Seriously though, my objection is to what Wright did with his metaphor. I find it too mechanical and his character too limited in mind and sensibility to make it come alive. That is why I continue to reject the notion that *Invisible Man* was inspired by Wright and insist that my character was inspired by the narrator of *Notes from Underground*. My narrator, like Dostoevsky's, is a thinker, and this is true despite the fact that my character doesn't think too clearly or too well. Nevertheless, my protagonist does possess a conscious philosophical dimension and is, since he lives by ideas, an intellectual.

In reading your piece I was amazed to discover you involved with the notion of a "racial" line of continuity in fiction by Negro Americans, a notion for which I raised hell with Irving Howe. Why is this notion so compelling, is it that you overlook the fact that such fiction is written by <u>Americans</u> and that black American writers are no less the heirs of all the world's fiction than any others? I get the feeling that if ninety-nine Jewish and Irish American writers had used the metaphor of the underground at the same time as Wright and I had read them all you'd still trace my use of it back to Wright. What about the multiplicity of influence available to those who seek for a way of doing things in this country? And what about the fact that books are so ever-present for those who've learned to use them? And magazines? I was reading Babel in issues of *International Literature* before I ever met Wright and I still have the copy of Kafka's *The Trial* that I read in 1937. Nor is this simply a matter of reading European fiction, there were metaphors of the underground right in my own cultural backyard. I had heard the Blues sung and played all my life and an inescapable line was to be heard any day as I made my visits to back alley joints and houses as a delivery boy:

> *If you don't believe I'm sinking*
> *Look what a hole I'm in . . .*

I was also familiar with stories of being buried alive, and I saw my father put into the ground when I was three years old and remember it vividly. Considering your psycho-analytic bent, surely this would be a more crucial source for my attraction to the metaphor. There was also the story of Lazarus, and Dante's "notes from underground" as well as the various connotations that the term "glory-hole" evoked when used in my community. The point is that, like yourself, I existed in a <u>field</u> of influences, both personal and environmental; but despite this obvious fact you go on reducing the complex field to a single writer and implicitly to the <u>race</u> of that writer. Well, to convince me that you're correct you must come up with proof that Wright possessed more imagination, or a <u>richer</u> imagination than my own.

Anyway, "The Man Who Lived Underground" and *Invisible Man* no more made "a later serious imaginative literature possible" for Negroes than the Biblical story of Jonah made possible *Moby-Dick*. Nor do I believe that Hawthorne alone made Melville possible. It is not that writers don't influence other writers but that talent and imagination and instinctive knowledge of how to use <u>all</u> that is available to the writer makes the difference. And I don't care what James Baldwin says about the influence of *Black Boy* on his own writing. I don't know when Baldwin conceived *Go Tell It on the Mountain* but I do know that he was working on a novel before Wright went to live in Paris and it was for the completion of that novel that Wright got Baldwin the Saxton Award. Nor did Baldwin meet Wright in Paris, he came to Wright's attention in Harlem, or at least in New York. I recall Wright showing me a picture story in *P.M.* for which Baldwin had done the captions and Baldwin was working on a novel at that time.

You say of the black militants that they "have taken at least one life-giving position, the 'Black is beautiful' emphasis on pride in Negro identity" and that "in Wright's time this was not possible, and all he could do, in such later work as *The Outsider* was to affirm a self which transcended Negro identity."

Perhaps you're right, but only perhaps. Such slogans as 'Black is Beautiful' were in the air during Garvey's day and before; during the thirties pictures of Christ and the Holy Family as Negroes were common in Negro homes, business places and Sunday Schools and songs like "Underneath the Harlem Moon" that praised the beauty of Negro women were common on juke box and radio. Going farther back, the first popular song among Negroes that I can remember being taught (circa 1915–1917) carried the boastful line, "I'm dark brown and chocolate to the bone."

Evidently you see the possibility of one writer influencing another as a one-way street, because if Wright had wanted to avail himself of one literary character's "life-giving emphasis on pride in Negro identity" he could have found it in Chapter 17 of *Invisible Man* where you'll find Ras exhorting Tod Clifton with the words, "You're six feet tall, mahn. You're young and intelligent. You black and beautiful—don't let 'em tell you different!" These lines were published, as you well know, sometime before *The Outsider* and I can assure you that Wright had read them. So evidently what was "not possible" for Wright was indeed possible for a sensibility that was attuned novelistically to what was present in the emotional atmosphere in black America.

You wrote that "for this brief period of four or five years, Wright had an aesthetic mastery over his passions. Earlier, he had not yet attained that control, and later he lost it. If a Negro writer never strives for this sort of control, or rejects it as not worth having, he may end as an artless racist demagogue on the order of LeRoi Jones; if he over contains his emotions, he becomes a white Negro writer, in the long gray line from Phillis Wheatley to Frank Yerby."

How would you translate this if the writer in question were a Jew? The equation bothers me because as I see it, even when granted your assumption that the Negro writer's main problem is the successful transformation of racial hatred into art (an assumption that I reject) it would appear that the writer who fails or over-contains his emotion does not become as you say a "white" Negro writer—unless in this instance you mean "white" to be inferior—he just becomes a poor or inadequate writer—or a first-rate writer of fiction who is empty of that vibrancy which stirs the reader to new perceptions of reality and a quickened perception of the possibilities of art.

In Yerby's* case, isn't it the form in which he chose to work that determines what his work has become? Isn't it quality, rather than what he has done, or not done, with racially inspired emotion? Yerby is a practitioner of a form of fiction characterized by its thinness of emotion and by the slight demands that it makes upon the writer's personal passions, obsessions, or what not. Nor is there any literary law which holds that Negroes are not free to work in this field of fiction. Nor is any moral law violated when he chooses to do so, unless it is the morality of choosing an inferior aesthetic form for the expression of one's talents. And anyway, how do we know that Yerby has any passion to express?

What I'm trying to say is that racial identity does not dominate individual culture so absolutely as you would seem to believe. Nor does it over-

---

* Frank Yerby (1916–91) wrote *The Foxes of Harrow* (1946), the first novel by an African American to become a bestseller. Yerby wrote romance novels of the antebellum South, and later historical novels set in Europe from the time of Pericles to the Dark Ages.

ride the individual will in the aesthetic realm as certain sociology-minded critics and black militant theorists would have us believe. Accidents of birth, geography, personal contacts, the availability of models, cultural examples, individual psychic dimensions and the cultural climate in which the individual comes to consciousness can, and often do, play a more important role than racial identity—when that individual begins to function as an artist. However, as citizen, as member of a minority group living within a racist society, the role of the individual writer's racial identity is inescapable in most situations where he is anonymous, or his role of artist unknown, or regarded as of no importance. Said a young white professor of English lit. to me after a lecture out in northern Illinois, "Mr. E., how does it feel to be able to go places where most black men can't go?"

Said I to him, "What you mean is, how does it feel to be able to go places where most white men can't go."

My point was that I was no abstraction in the black and white division of American society, but an individual with countless connections that over-rode my status as a "Negro." For while my status and statistical identity is that of a black, I am also an individual with an individual destiny, and an individual past. Besides, why should I let a teacher assume that simply because he was white all doors were open to him? There are plenty of black doors that are closed to me, no less than they'd be to him; he simply couldn't imagine that such existed.

Race and culture, culture and race! Why demand (if that's what you're doing) that Phillis Wheatley's racial identity produce a type of poetry that was alien to her personal culture? Why demand that she feel emotions that nothing in her life or the codes of the society in which she grew up prepared her to feel? After all, she was no more 'southern' than George Washington or Ben Franklin; therefore it seems to me unreasonable to treat her as though she were denying her heritage when, in effect, she was giving expression to the only heritage of which she was aware. She couldn't write out of the Negro American folk culture that was thriving in the South because she had no contact with it. And like most of our early New England poets she was probably more British in her personal culture than "American." After all, the poor woman was born in Africa in 1753 and died in 1784. She was brought to New England at the age of seven and grew up and was educated in a white household at a time when the Wesley-Whitfield revival was sweeping the region. Her problem, or the problem of her poetry, was that she took Pope as a model, and it was this that made her work so arid. Phillis Wheatley's failure was a failure shared by most early New England poets; she came on the scene before Americans had learned how to express the Americanness of the budding culture. I don't believe it valid to criticize her for having failed in her sheltered Boston slavery, with her smattering of classical education, to embody a Negro American tradition to which she was alien. For her it was not a question of being a "white Negro" writer or expressing controlled anger, it was a question of being the kind of writer she was (which was not a very competent one) or of being no kind of writer at all. You might well have criticized her for not having written in the language of Senegal, French or Arabic, from which she was separated at the age of seven.

Well, I guess this is enough abuse from one who seldom writes this type of letter anymore. I'll close by saying how pleased I am to see that our earlier hassle over these matters has just appeared in BLACK LITERA-TURE IN AMERICA, A CASEBOOK, published by Crowell. I hope you've been paid and that things go well for you and Phoebe. Fanny sends love,

Yours sincerely,
Ralph

To Michel Fabre
730 RIVERSIDE DRIVE
NEW YORK, NEW YORK 10031
JULY 15, 1970

Dear Mr. Fabre:

Shortly after our return from a brief vacation in New England the postman brought us your gift. Puzzled and enchanted by the beautifully stamped envelope, we were more than delighted when we found the Nadar* inside and the small family picture that had been taken by your wife's grandfather. It must have taken many weeks of walking and searching to find the Nadar and we want you to know that it will always give us pleasure as will the small photograph which your wife was so generous as to part with. We thank you both so very much.

Meanwhile, I have talked with both my agent and publisher concerning your request to reprint my short stories. Their advice is that a French collection should not precede the publication of the English collection

---

* Nadar is the pseudonym for Gaspard-Félix Tournachon (1820–1910), a French artist best known for his photographc portraits and much admired by the Ellisons.

which has been in the planning for some time but not been done because they are waiting for me to write two or three new stories to be included.*

Nor can I decide concerning the Wright letters. Although I don't have a complete file of this correspondence, I still don't know what I want to do with such letters that I do have. I hope that Ellen will understand when you explain my indecision. However, I appreciate your interest.

I hope that you will keep in touch with me and we shall always be pleased to see you and your wife whenever you are in this country. With every best wish, I am

Sincerely,
Ralph Ellison

To Harold Calicutt
730 RIVERSIDE DRIVE
NEW YORK, 10031
FEB 3, 1971

Dear Harold:†

What a pleasant surprise to hear from you! I had just begun to cuss the mailman for delivering a load of boredom and there <u>you</u> were after all these many years. The only thing to flaw the pleasure was the realization that you had been right here in the Apple and only the lack of our telephone number kept us apart. So it goes; and no matter what you do, circumstances conspire to defeat you. By which I mean: that we left our number in the directory precisely for such old friends as you, hoping that should you venture here you'd have the time and interest to look us up. Had you called it would have made up for the endless interruptions we get from total strangers, cranks and crackpots—not to mention the telephone-hustlers trying to sell magazine subscriptions and a variety of other junk.

Since the *Atlantic*‡ piece—which, thank God, you saw—all kinds of people from all kinds of places have called us, but none of the distant

---

* Apart from several episodes from his novel-in-progress Ellison did not finish or publish any new short fiction after the date of this letter. His *Flying Home and Other Stories,* edited by John F. Callahan, was published posthumously in 1996; a second international edition appeared in 2012.

† Harold Calicutt was a close friend and classmate of Ellison's at Douglass High School in Oklahoma City.

‡ "Indivisible Man," an essay/interview by James Alan McPherson and Ralph Ellison, came out in the December 1970 *Atlantic.*

friends whom we'd like to hear from again. No, there's one exception: Reginald Thomasson saw it and called from the Kennedy Field where he was waiting between planes (he's still at South Carolina State), but no one else. Late one night a woman called from Denver and when my wife asked if she could be of help, the chick said no, that she was checking to see if the magazine had been telling the truth! The only thing I can say is that she was curious enough to pay for the call. Which reminds me that the article has also led to a lot of bad manuscripts being sent to me by people wanting to get into the writing game. I don't know what they think I'm doing with my time—what with struggling with my own writing, with teaching and with involving myself with various civic responsibilities which, considering how naturally dogasted I used to be about such matters, takes quite a bit of effort on my part. Still, I shouldn't complain, really, because out of all the undesirable responses I did at least hear from you.

Harold, I know how you must feel upon going back to Okla. City. I was back there twice last year, having lectures at Stillwater and at Norman, and I have been returning on the average at least once over the last seven years. And when I get there I'm like a ghost—or a Rip Van Winkle who has slept for twenty years and awoke to discover that his world has changed—But how! Thanks to Urban Renewal, most of the city I knew and loved has disappeared. That includes schools, places of work and the various houses I lived in when my father was alive and soon, I suspect, the house at 407 East First where I was born will disappear. Now even the old Aldridge Theater is gone, Deep Second is no longer a center of community affairs and Slaughter's Hall hasn't heard the sound of happy feet for over a decade. When I'm there an obsessive refrain sounds in my mind: "Where have they all gone? Where, oh where" . . . Everyone's now off to the northeast and all the old grooves have been erased—not worn out like the grooves of a fine old recording that has been played until the tune is more in the memory than in the phonograph, but simply erased, torn down, uprooted and junked because some strangers who never knew the magic, the wonder and inspiration of living in those old dear grooves decided that they were no longer to exist. So what do we have now? An East Side without a center, a hometown that exists more in the memory than in the landscape. It makes me sad as hell. Not that I would deprive our old friends and acquaintances of their fine brick ranch houses. I just wish that a few of those shotgun cottages had been left as witnesses to the hard good life we knew as kids. I wish too that someone had had the insight to see that Durland Court was a gracious spot, what with its giant trees and lack of automobile traffic, for anyone to live in. But evidently they didn't recognize what they had—or no one had the courage to make a fight to preserve some of the scenes that make for a continuity of experience, tradition and memory.

Well, let's face it, we were told that you can't go home again and its true—Except in dreams, memory, and through the recollections one shares with friends, old friends. So when I go back I hang around Randolph's Drug Store just as I did years ago, whether working or idling away the time. I talk with Gladys Spears and with Jim Randolph and I latch onto any other familiar face who happens to come through the door. Sometimes I see Dillon Bunn or Floyd Alexander, Henry Butler, or Jimmy Stewart (he comes here often) and reminiscing with them over drinks helps kill some of the pain of times lost and scenes vanished and even restores some of the ghosts from the past. Everyone remembers vividly something that has grown dim for the rest and the talking brings the old days alive again.

And of course everyone remembers something connected with the Great Big Black One, and as the talk builds you and I and Cabbie Mitchell, Red Atkins and company are sure to come into the recalling of some incident that took place at school, work or play, most of them really funny or outrageous and having to do with Virgil.

He drove through there summer before last, I think it was, and kidded himself into believing that no one would recognize him. And as a matter of fact one of his best friends did not. Gladys told me that he came into the drug store looking like a Baptist bishop and started asking her intimate questions and acting such an imposing ass that she had cussed him out before she recognized that the fool was pulling her leg. Lord knows how many sedate, middle aged ladies he outraged as he swung through the town by going up to them displaying the same blank expression and insinuating voices that he'd used when they were hot young girls and saying, whispering, out of the side of his mouth, "Hey, baby, step over here and let me see if your pussy's wet."

Now don't get me wrong, no one told me that he actually pulled that old jive again, but I wouldn't put it past him; and if he did, I bet he got away with it just as he did years ago, with those beat-up broads flattered as all hell! While if you or I should try something like that they'd have had their husbands, little children, dogs, pastors and the police on our butts. Virgil always received the special privileges granted to those who have the nerve to play the fool (true fools being ignored as having no sense of right and wrong), and because he did, I lived during a most painful part of my adolescent confusion in the reflected light of his outrageous glory. Even today I'm in his debt for teaching me so much about the difference between the public decorum of females and their private possibilities. And that's to say nothing about the fun we had dancing to the phonograph down at their place on First Street.

You ask if I've seen Raymond Leek, Webber or Harold Brown. Raymond I haven't seen for over fifteen years. The last time was on the subway and I quickly discovered that despite my pleasure in seeing him something had gone dead between us. I don't know what, whether the times, changes in our circumstances or the desire on his part to cut certain ties to the past. I do know that there was no quarrel. Since then in all my wanderings about the city I've never lain eyes upon him, and when Herbert and his family were here for the World's Fair I would have given a lot to have brought those two together again, but I had no lead.

Two years ago I had drinks with McGowan at a bar and restaurant he was managing on 125th St. near Seventh Avenue, and about the same time I caught up with Tackhead (Edgar Giddings, in case you've forgotten his name). Tack, who is an official in one of the waiter's unions, owns a cleaning and pressing shop and some other business up about 139th St and Seventh Ave, but his hours are such that he's difficult to contact. He wanted a copy of a photograph I have of the old football team on which we played and after having it reproduced I made several trips to his shop hoping to give it to him in person, but I was never able to catch the bastard. Finally I mailed it but I have yet to hear from him. I can tell you this about him though: Tack is no longer the hard, lean, little flint-headed fellow we once knew, but has become a hefty _fat_ fellow. Very much as has Tom Waddkins, our old quarterback boy-friend of Charlesetta Sandborn, who is now back in Okla City. He couldn't get into his old clothes with a greasy shoehorn and a ramjet engine! Time, man; time; it does the damnedest things to men, women and cityscapes and very little of what one might have expected.

Of Brown, I have no news except—according to McGowan and folks back home—that he had gone a bit to pieces on the sauce. I hope this is exaggerated because I admired him and had some fine times with him.

But I do talk with Arvil Lovette from time to time, and a couple of years ago he had me over to talk with a class of students at the Brooklyn school where he teaches. The last time we talked he, his wife and two children were doing fine. I also had a pleasant surprise three years ago when I went to Baltimore to talk to a group of musicians whose formerly segregated unions had been merged and there saw Tracy McCleary. He has been leading an orchestra there for over twenty years. His business card bears the legend: *Tracy McCleary and His Royal Men of Rhythm, Sensational Swing Band/Red Hot Music Makers for All Occasions.* His address is 2656 Lauretta Ave. and his telephone number is WI 7-5611. He looked fine, a little heavier, and his brother Willard is teaching at some Texas college but I've forgotten just where. Following this line, you might run into Mac Henry Norman somewhere in L.A.; as is Bernard Sheppard, the Sanborn gals—Zelma is the principal of a school there, though I don't know her marital name. Find one and you'll get a line on the rest.

Last night Herbert called and said that he'd like to see you, so the next time you're free in L.A. give him a ring. His address is 5742 Mullen Ave, L.A. 90043, and his phone number is Axminister 5-5674. He's doing O.K., has a wife and two kids and is still a loner and as skeptical as ever.

I saw him last during December of 1969, when we met in Okla. City to attend Mrs. Slaughter's funeral. She died, by the way, at age 86, and was alert right up to the moment she keeled over while playing bridge. Not only that, she was still going on hunting trips to Colorado and South Dakota with Wyatt, Jim and her nephews and <u>she</u> doing the cooking. She was one of our mother's closest friends and had had the kind of helpful involvement in our lives that one hopes for from blood relatives but which, alas, isn't always forthcoming. I should add however that our own blood relatives, Tom Brown (the old 'Frisco brakeman) and his mother, who was my father's sister, did indeed help us over a number of rough spots—and he still would if it proved necessary.

But looking back over all these years I can now see that Mrs. Slaughter and her family played a very important role in my own family's morale, and that our regard for her was based upon more than yearning for more affluent relatives. Nor was it for vanity or social climbing that we called her mother and father (the older Randolphs) "grandpa" and "grandma" or her maternal grandmother, Mrs. Foster, "granny." I was born in her parents' house and after my father's death they served in the place of the grandparents who were never to know that such offspring's as Herbert and I existed. She was a fine, tough-minded lady and now with her gone one of the last close links to my mother is forever broken.

Slowly, slowly—and too often not so slowly—we all go into the dark. Mrs. McFarland is still with us but only partially so. A few years ago her daughter gave a dinner for my wife and me, and the old lady was quite alert. But when I saw her at Mrs. Slaughter's funeral she barely knew me. The same thing occurred during the 1950's when Mrs. Breaux came to a lecture I was giving there at the old Dunbar Branch Library. This lady to whom I'd been so close, had to ask John A. Townsend whether I had been one of her "little men"! How sad that was for me. She had been so kind and inspiring, and just at the moment that I had hoped she could see some of the results of all her time and patience, I learned that I had slipped completely out of her memory.

Well, I suppose that people who dedicate their lives to inspiring the young receive their greatest and only sure satisfaction in the process of helping them, not in waiting around for the little bastards to grow up and return home all eager to show themselves off for their admiration. Besides, for her there were so many! So I guess that the only way one can repay such debt is to pass along some of the inspiration they gave us to some other young jerks. I try to do some of that, but today with all the edgy generation gap and black rhetoric it isn't always easy. Imagine, some of the young black radicals who know nothing about me treat me as though I was brought up rich and safe and know nothing of the harsh aspects of Negro life. But then I forget that they are a new people, the Blacks, born only a few years ago out of the mouth of a Malcolm X! And, I'm sad to discover, they treat people like us, who had to scramble around to read and see whatever novels, magazine and plays were available, with contempt. We, they say, were trying to be white. I always thought we were simply trying to become the best selves possible for us to be, so to hell with such attitudes.

As for me, I guess for all the hard times we had during the Depression some of our luck was good. At least we weren't confused about who and what we were, and we had a few good teachers and a social life that often offered a great deal of satisfaction. Certainly we didn't spend much time, if any, wondering what white people thought about what we were doing. So that now, whenever I want to measure the success of some fancy dance or dinner or bull session, I always fall back on our old vanished good times back home. And I ask myself, "Is this party really as productive of good feeling as some of the times we had back home?" And surprisingly, only a few measure up. So, Harold, I'm glad you were there to share and give your special dimension to some of the good-bad times I shared, I'm glad you took the time to write to me, and before I bore the hell out of you with my long-winded typewriter I shall stop with this final word on the Great Big Black One: We heard from him around Christmas, from all places, South Africa—where one of his many ships had taken him. Here is his message from the back of a postcard that displays the Cape Town War Memorial Gardens with Table Mountain showing in the background:

"So busy with these dam cards can't visit the city, but I want to let every-one know I got here—V.B." I guess we'll hear from him bye and bye and when we do I'll pass along the word . . . By the way, James Alan McPher-son, who wrote the article in the *Atlantic* has a fine book of short stories, among them two about the experiences of dining car waiters. Take a look. I think they'll amuse you.

Finally, I'm enclosing a copy of a photo that appeared in the *Black Dis-patch* of Jan. 21. Maybe you'll recognize some of the cats from long ago. They're raising money to equip the Douglass High School band with new uniforms and you might wish to mail them a buck. So, until the next time, keep well and let us hear from you. And please, <u>please</u> don't try to answer these long ramblings of mine, just let me know about you. All the best . . .

Sincerely,
Ralph

To Hank Wilson
730 RIVERSIDE DRIVE
NEW YORK, NEW YORK 10031
MAY 18, 1971

Mr. Hank Wilson
Coordinator of Community Relations
Office of Student Relations
Southern Illinois University
Carbondale, Illinois 62901

Dear Mr. Wilson:

Thank you for writing me concerning your projected thesis study, "Toward a Model with Rationale for Black Studies Curriculums."

I don't believe that I can be of any assistance to you, however, since I have never taught Black Studies as such. It is my opinion that disciplines such as history and literature when taught must include Negro American reality but that it cannot be taught separately since it did not evolve separately.

Thus, when I teach American literature I include Negro American folklore and the writings of black authors—but always with the context of American literature. This has been my approach since 1945 when I first began lecturing before student and faculty groups.

Sincerely yours,
Ralph Ellison

To Charlie Davidson
730 RIVERSIDE DRIVE
NEW YORK, N.Y. 10031
JULY 10, 1971

Dear Charlie:

Last Friday evening after spending a pleasant hour listening to Bobby Short performing and being interviewed over the radio, it occurred to me that despite my best intentions I hadn't thanked you for sending me his autobiography. Last month I had tried to reach you by telephone but you and Terry were away and I had simply left my name with one of the girls. It made the fourth time I've missed you although the other calls were to the store and though disappointed I figured that you were probably looking after Porkchopper.* Despite my tardiness in thanking you for the book I found it thoroughly enjoyable. Indeed, I was disappointed that it hadn't continued for another hundred pages or so. For not only does it offer insights into what makes Bobby Short tick, it is highly entertaining and an important contribution to American cultural history. With popular entertainment being a mixture of high culture, low culture, family and neighborhood culture and personal talent, how nice it is to learn something of how a highly successful product of that mixture came to be!

Listening to Short on the radio caused me to think, What a gifted, charming and insufferable little rascal of a man and what a gifted artist! He's good, he knows he's good and he means to see to it that neither the interviewer nor anyone else misses the fact that <u>he knows his own high value</u> . . . Which is as it should be. He could probably charm a steak out of the jaws of a hungry dog and then have the poor animal dancing to his piano. In short Short is long on class, the kind of class that causes George Frazier to flip his typewriting lid. And as for those sociologists and half-assed politicos who've been filling the air and bookstores with vapid, dehumanized nonsense about what they term "The black experience," Short's account of the background of an individual Negro American of mid-western origins, gives a richer sense of the general Negro experience

---

* The name of Davidson's legendary competitive racehorse. For a fuller account of Ellison's important friendship with Charlie Davidson, see his August 18, 1968, letter, in which Ellison writes vulnerably and painfully about his and Fanny's first return to the Plainfield house months after it was ravaged by fire.

than all their pronouncements. It restores some of the sense of complexity, wonder and diversity that I recognize as part of my own life. Against the dreary, reductive, paper-thin images of Negro American life-style and personality that are now so fashionable it was a pleasure to recall many of the details of my own life in Oklahoma. The aspirations, folkways, manners, hard-and-good times of his mother and her friends were a duplication with variations of those of the people I grew up among. It makes for a strange and volatile mixture and if you try to class angle it, you're dead. Short is younger than I am and I grew up in a completely segregated state while his was deceptively unsegregated, but the sense of promise that his people shared despite the racism and other disadvantages (and others that were merely apparent) kept them fighting and trying to move ahead. So it's good to read a man who appreciates the human and cultural richness of what was more often than not an economically under-privileged background. And I'm sure that had Short failed to respond to and against that human and cultural richness (including the goddam phonograph and radio!), he wouldn't have been prepared for the economic good-times that lay ahead. In this country one thing leads to another—no matter what the other turns out to be. And if we stop living to give ourselves over to complaint the best we can expect is more frustration. His sister's "Social Aristocrats" club might strike some readers as quaint, but those chicks were teaching themselves the felicities of social conduct, and I'll bet you that the food they served was as good as their dancing. One such girl I knew back in Oklahoma has been operating on high levels in Washington for years and her style comes from just such clubs.

So I consider the photographs of his family and friends precious documents. They capture the pathos, the aspiration, sense of style, age and youth of a given moment of our under-evaluated history. I've seen photographs of my father's sister dressed very much as his mother did when young—hat, suit and mutton sleeves. Yes, but all I can say about his father is that the cat was damn elegant in the hat! Should Bobby Short publish another volume of his autobiography (and I hope he does) I hope his publisher will send it to me early for possible comment. In the meantime, you can believe that I am recommending *Black and White Baby* to all my reading friends. Especially to those literary intellectuals who take their ideas of black Americans from such as Pat-of-the-monkey-hand and Jimmy Baldwin. I want the bastards to contemplate, if they can, the wonderful mystery of American experience made manifest in the phenomena of such an elegant and sophisticated artist as Short emerging from Black Danville.

Recently, in the June issue of *Vogue,* I saw Short was photographed with a group that frequents Elaine's restaurant. It was a good photo by Irving Penn, a photographer whom I admire a great deal, and at least three of the fellows are friends of mine. Nevertheless I couldn't help but feel that the magazine might have served its readers to a more instructive effect had it given the space over to an excerpt of Short's book. The magazine operates on the mystification of social hierarchy—Jet Set, Beautiful People and all that—as well as of fashion, but for its readers there's a far more intriguing mystery in the little brown skinned man with moustache standing near the center of the photograph.

Things go on here as usual, I'm still writing and trying to make life meaningful. I miss seeing you but can't seem to get up to Boston anymore. Plan to do something about that this fall. Meantime give our warmest regards to Terry and if you get down to this nasty fun city please give us a ring.

> Sincerely,
> Ralph

P.S. If you don't have a tape of Flip Wilson telling the story about the preacher and the Go-Rilla let me know as I'd like you to hear it.

To Stuart Omans
730 RIVERSIDE DRIVE
NEW YORK, NEW YORK 10031
SEPTEMBER 14, 1971

Professor Stuart E. Omans
Department of English
Florida Technologial University
P.O. Box 25000
Orlando, Florida 32816

Dear Professor Omans:

Thank you for your kind and generous letter of August 6th. I am happy to know that you are getting along with *Invisible Man.*

As to your question, no, I do not have a published collection of short stories. I have written only eleven or twelve short stories, all of which were published in the '40s and '50s—with the exception of one published in the late '30s and one published in 1963. "Flying Home" and "King of the Bingo Game," both written in 1944, were published in five, or more different anthologies during 1970.

It has been my plan to publish a collection but not until I write more stories. I'm hoping that will be soon.

Sincerely yours,

Ralph Ellison

To Betty Cameron

730 RIVERSIDE DRIVE

NEW YORK, NEW YORK 10031

FEBRUARY 2, 1972

Mrs. Betty Cameron

American Literature Class

Classen High School

1901 N. Ellison

Oklahoma City, Oklahoma 73106

Dear Mrs. Cameron:

Thanks for your interest in my writing. I can't tell you how pleasant it is to learn that your class has not only read my novel but is familiar with some of my short stories. Since I've published so few stories such familiarity is, I suspect, quite rare. Writers remain alive as writers through the interest of their readers; therefore it gives me much satisfaction to learn that my work is taught to a younger generation of readers. This in itself would be quite enough to earn my gratitude, but the fact that it is occurring at Classen High brings me an added pleasure.

Years ago, when there was a streetcar station at Classen Boulevard and 16th Street, my mother took care of a series of apartments which were located above the shops on the west side of Classen between 16th and 17th Streets. Behind the shops, going westward on 17th Street, there was a wide lot with empty frontage, at the rear of which was located a series of garages where the tenants of the apartments stored their cars, and above the garages there was a small apartment. This apartment, or "servants' quarters," was provided for the caretaker of the apartments, and thus it came about that I lived with my mother and brother less than a half block from Classen High School. The time was the middle Nineteen Twenties and in keeping with the social arrangement of the day the schools were segregated. I could not, therefore, have attended Classen even had I been of proper age (I believe I was about eight). Nevertheless, I was quite familiar with your school. Sometime later, it was my special privilege to attend concerts there as the personal guest of Dr. Ludwig Hebestreit, the director of the Little Symphony Orchestra. Dr. Hebestreit, who was the supervisor of public school music, also taught at Classen High and he gave me lessons on the trumpet in exchange for cutting his lawn. So it is that I owe a part of my training in music to your school.

If your students will take a look at my book of essays, *Shadow and Act,* they'll find many references to my life in Oklahoma City. In an interview titled "That Same Pain, That Same Pleasure" they'll discover a reference to my friendship with Henry Bowman Davis who lived on 18th Street in the vicinity of their school. Henry and I were drawn together by our interest in radio, and since I knew no Negro boys in the immediate vicinity, [he] also made up for many of the friendships I had left on the East Side upon coming to live on 17th Street. It was an interesting neighborhood for a young boy, and even though living there required walking a long distance to reach my own school, I recall those walks as both pleasant—especially in the springtime when the lawns were green and the birds and flowers arriving—and instructive. For along the way I learned something of the processes of business and manufacture (I was sometimes late for school) and was afforded a close-up view of how a more affluent section of the city went about its living. Even the shortcuts through various alleys provided some measure of education, what with views of backyards, gardens, and the interesting objects which wealthy whites could afford to throw out in the trash.

So yes, I am indeed a product of the Oklahoma City school system. And except for the third grade, when I studied at the old Orchard Park School on Peach Street (now Brauer) and the seventh which found us living in McAlester, Oklahoma, I was a pupil at the old Douglass High School, located then at Walnut and California. The last time I was at home the building was being used as a warehouse by the Board of Education, but I began there in the first grade; played in, and was student director, of the band, and a member of the varsity football team, then known as the "Red Machine"; and it was from there, in 1931, that I graduated.

As for the relationship between the experiences depicted in *Invisible Man* and my own life, I must say that they are imaginary and not autobiographical; just as the section in which the fictional action is set is not

Oklahoma, but an imaginary deep south. I should add, however, that the sensibility out of which I write was formed in Oklahoma. My interest in books and music began there, and it was there that I sold newspapers, shined shoes (often in the downtown section). waited on table (at the Skirvin, the Huckins, the Oklahoma and University clubs) and ran the elevator at the old Lewinsohn Clothing Store on Main Street near Broadway.

I was born at 407 East First Street and lived any number of places on the East Side. My father was a construction foreman for the company which erected many of the city's early steel and concrete structures, including the Colcord Building—which, by the way, I hope has escaped the fury of urban renewal! As you might suspect, I loved the city in which I grew up. My parents came to the city shortly before statehood. Many of my old friends, schoolmates, employers and teachers are still residents there, as are the relatives of whom I'm fondest, Mr. and Mrs. L.T. Brown.

You might say to your students that, although I'm no longer in Oklahoma City, Oklahoma City is still very much within me and turns up frequently in my dreams and in the fantasies and memories that inform my writing. I consider this a strength and a joy. Good luck to you and your class and good reading.

Sincerely yours,
Ralph Ellison

RE:fe

To Dr. William Halloran

FEBRUARY 17, 1972

Dr. William F. Halloran
Associate Dean
Humanities and Communication
College of Letters and Science
The University of Wisconsin
Milwaukee, Wisconsin 53201

Dear Dr. Halloran:

I have known Nathan Scott for well over a decade, during which time we have shared a friendship marked by numerous visits, a stream of correspondence and many lengthy conversations via long distance telephone.

During the late 1950's, which marked the beginning of my several lectures at the University of Chicago, and during the fall of 1961 when I occupied an academic chair there, I came to know Scott and his family on their own home ground and thus it is out of this background that it is my pleasure to offer you my opinion.

Nathan Scott is a prolific writer and critic who has been in the forefront of those thinkers who would reveal to artists and laymen alike the unique ways in which the concerns of contemporary art and literature coincide with those of the more creative of present-day philosophers and theologians. His has been an effort to make us aware of the many ways in which current literature is locked in an agonizing struggle to give new formal structuring to insights and intuitions which have long been regarded as the sole province of religious thinkers. In this it is my interpretation that he views the artist as moving toward reassuming under a new guise a role long ago rejected; that of sacrificial priest; a role in which worldly secular manipulators of artistic forms struggle painfully toward creating a new vision of the sacramental dimension of human existence.

Scott's love of the arts and literature is profound. He brings to them a mind steeped in history, philosophy and theology which enables him to bring into focus the continuity of idea and form linking earliest art to that which in these chaotic times is undergoing a process of creative metamorphosis. Here I am reminded that Scott was one of Reinhold Niebuhr's favorite students and that recently Mrs. Niebuhr had occasion to describe him as "one of the family." She was referring of course to the close friendship which Scott has shared with her family since his student days, but she might well have been implying something more: that Scott, like her late distinguished husband, is also a dedicated and learned man. Certainly he is one of the very few of my fairly wide circle of friends who could be so described without a certain embarrassment. However, lest this sound too solemn, let me add that he is also a sophisticated and convivial man whose high good humor and warm sympathy is a delight to his friends. He is also a gracious host and his wife, who is accomplished in her own right, is charming.

But let me return to Scott's humor. He is so lacking in the pompous self-regard so often associated with one of his role and attainments and so aware of the endless ways in which the comic and tragic modes are intertwined in the human condition that had he been of an earlier generation of Negro American ministers I am certain that he would have been among those in whom religious exaltation took the form which the Negro folk designated as "holy laughter." This is by no means to make light of his priestly role but to point to its warmly human emphasis.

Scott spins a good yarn. His conversation is engaging, wide-ranging and informed by an intellect that, without advertising itself unduly, endows even his simple observations with the nuances and resonance of a well-informed subtle mind. I must, however, add this warning: Nathan Scott can hardly be said to suffer fools gladly. For nonsense of any kind, issuing from any level whatsoever, simply brings out the <u>scorn</u> in him— and along with it an expertise for invective and a high eloquence for denunciation.

He is, as I've indicated, no less a man of ideas than a man of God. He takes his dedication to the forms and processes of the intellect and his role as teacher as seriously as he does his role of priest. There is no question of his qualification either as writer or teacher. Nor should the quality of his attainments be confused by questions of his racial identity. His professorship at Chicago came long before the current rush to extend at any cost the color spectrum of university faculties. Nevertheless, because your consideration of him comes during the present state of affairs I feel it proper to offer you my views as they touch upon this situation.

Nathan Scott is a prime example of the high quality of intellectual achievement of which American society is capable of producing when one of Negro-American heritage seeks actively to transform his individual and group experience into conscious thought and technical mastery. Far from seeing his identity as a member of a racial minority as a hopeless hindrance or as an excuse for rejecting his obligation to explore the widest possibilities of his individual mind and talents, he has sought to test himself against the very best intellects and achievements within the fields to which he has dedicated his life. As I see it, he regards his background as the endless source of intellectual and spiritual insights with which, as a form of modern, democratic American experience, one would expect it to provide all those who have the willingness to probe its mystery.

Thus in this day of noisy and often empty assertions of Blackness Scott seems never to have experienced the need to question either his identity or his manhood. Rather, he has gone about doing his work, and it is by the quality of that growing body of accomplishment that he insists upon being judged and it is this he offers up as self-definition. He has refused to be put on the defensive by present-day racists, whether white or black; perhaps because he learned long ago to see through and around the dilemma of identity on which today so many young blacks are wasting their energies. He knows that what counts in the sphere of individual self-awareness is not so much the irremediable fact of one's racial heritage as what one makes of it; of the insights into the human condition it provides or the maturity and amplification it offers one's talent. He has accepted the challenge of his pluralistic cultural heritage with grace, and as an American intellectual he asserts his humanity by striving to come into conscious possession of as much of the world's culture as he has the intellect, energy, and talent to command.

Scott's range of experience is so broad, spanning that of parents brought up in Alabama, a Detroit childhood, education and training in some of the best colleges and universities and twenty-six years of teaching assignments both here and in England, he has much to bring to any faculty. But there is also the further value of his example. He is a "role model" whom students, both black and white, might observe as they go about the business of achieving themselves in a society of conflicting and rapidly shifting values; a suggestive example of how to go about achieving the promise of being an American. Having had extended conversations with various of his graduate students, it is my impression that he has had a high measure of success in affecting their sense of direction and value. Not that they had shaped themselves into images of Scott (he is too uniquely himself for that) but that they were alert, informed and thinking individuals. This, I take it, is no small achievement.

In closing, let me congratulate you in even considering the possibility of bringing Scott to Wisconsin. It is testimony to your concern for the quality of your faculty. I wish you all success and I am sure that Chicago's loss will be Wisconsin's gain.

Sincerely,
Ralph Ellison
Schweitzer
Professor of the
Humanities

RE:fe

To Clarence Major
730 RIVERSIDE DRIVE
NEW YORK, NEW YORK 10031
APRIL 10, 1972

Mr. Clarence Major
11 Waverly Place 3 J
New York, New York 10003

Dear Mr. Major:

Thanks for your letter but I regret that I can't be of help.

In recent years I have recommended a number of people for Guggenheim fellowships, and on several occasions with success. This year—sad to say—neither of my two recommendations were so fortunate, leaving me to suspect that the tide, for the moment at least, is running against me.

There is also the reason that I feel myself incompetent as a critic of poetry and in keeping with this I have been careful to recommend only writers of fiction and criticism, with the exception of one painter whose work I have known for many years and about whom I wrote an essay.

This is by no means a negative judgment of your suitability, as I am sure you will understand, but to suggest that another reference might be to your advantage.

Good luck to you and I sincerely hope that you will receive a Guggenheim.

Yours truly,
Ralph Ellison

To Passport Office
MAY 31, 1972

Passport Office
Los Angeles, California

Dear Sir:

I herewith submit to you this sworn statement that Herbert Maurice Ellison is my brother.

My brother was born June 14, 1917 and I, March 1, 1914[*] in Oklahoma City, Oklahoma. Neither his birth nor mine were registered however.

Our father, Lewis A. Ellison, was born March 4, 1877 in Abbeville, South Carolina, and died in Oklahoma City July 19, 1916. Our mother, Ida Milsap Ellison, was born in White Oak, Georgia in 1884, and died in Dayton, Ohio in 1937.

As supporting documents I am enclosing a copy of our father's Death Certificate, and a passport issued to me in 1959. Although the passport has expired, I assume that it is adequate for identification in this instance since it will be accepted as proof when I apply for a new passport.

I am also enclosing as proof of my identity a proof sheet from Who's Who, a curriculum vitae, and copy of a news release from the New York University News Bureau announcing my appointment as Schweitzer Professor in the Humanities at New York University.

Very truly yours,
Ralph Ellison

---

[*] These dates are each wrong by a year. Herbert Ellison was born June 14, 1916, and Ralph Ellison on March 1, 1913. The source of confusion has to do with the fact that Negro births were not registered or recorded in Oklahoma City at this time in history. By all accounts, Herbert Ellison was five or six weeks old at the time of his father's death, the date of which was recorded as July 19, 1916. Likewise, Ralph Ellison's references to his age at this time put him at just over three years old, raising the question of where the 1914 date comes from.

Fortunately, Arnold Rampersad's biography provides the clue. In 1943, to get into the U.S. Merchant Marines, Ralph needed proof of his birth. According to Rampersad (*Ralph Ellison*, 167–68), James Randolph, Ellison's old employer in Oklahoma City, "organized six persons to provide affidavits that they had known Ralph Waldo Ellison since he was a child. Only Randolph swore that Ralph 'was born in Oklahoma City, Okla., on March 1, 1914.' (The others cited no year.)" Time was of the essence to Ellison in New York City. If he had changed the date on Randolph's affidavit, the affidavit would have been denied, and perhaps worse. Thus it is easy to see why Ellison let the matter go. In any case, from then on he allowed the 1914 date to stand. It is fortunate that Rampersad—and before him Lawrence Jackson—corrected the date of birth and helped get to the bottom of why the error occurred.

To Virgil Branam
[SUMMER 1972]*

Dear Virgil:†

Since I keep thinking about you I guess I'd better drop you a note just to let you know that we're still here. It has been a summer of work for us with no vacation. I've been trying to finish my novel and thus we've stuck to the city.

Your last letter with the news that you've retired to the railroad crossing left me with mixed feelings. I was glad that you could retire, but somehow I've thought of you as my adventuring buddy, one ever on the move to strange, foreign places; one who could report authoritatively on the wine, the women, the food, dances and songs of other lands. I came to think of your capacity for the new and the strange as inexhaustible beginning from those days back in the thirties when you left Oklahoma City, went west and continued many times around the world. There wasn't to be too much of that for me, but as long as you were experiencing the wide world I shared in it. It was a matter of knowing someone who had managed to stay untangled, who had escaped the snares and set out see the variety of life with his own fresh, curious vision. You'll never know how important this was to my own vicarious sense of life, but I assure you that it was very important. Your reports, your tales (and reports on pieces of tails) added to my sense of the possible and afforded me some idea of how someone of my own background might react to the great variety of life. So that now you've come to rest I feel even more deprived than I came to realize I had been after you no longer made port in New York. Now I'll have to fall back on the store of your stories which are stored in my memory—some of them going back to those days in Kansas when you worked on the harvest, knew George and Julia Lee, roamed in the joints around Eighteenth and Vine. Whenever I hear certain old songs or see the Mills Brothers on T.V. I recall the days down on First Street and how much your mother and Adah provided for the pleasure of your friends. Recently I read the galleys of a

---

* Branam dies in March 1973 and Ralph mentions his June 1972 commencement address at William and Mary in the letter and puts the summer of 1972 in the present, hence the editors' date of summer 1972.

† Virgil Branam, Ellison's boyhood friend in Oklahoma. A letter written in 1972 probably in September refers to Branam as "the Great Big Black One."

book about the experiences of old Professor Whittaker who was the principle of Douglass school when he was a cadet at West Point and it brought back so many of the things that occurred when we were students. I didn't realize how long ago it had been until I saw a picture of Albert Alexander this summer and that bastard is now sporting a snow-white beard! I have no idea why Lola puts up with it but neither do I know the color of the hair hidden beneath her wig. But one thing is certain, we've all grown older and some, like Leslie Filson & Lattrell Robeson who recently died, have left the scene . . . Whittaker's story, by the way, is quite interesting. He was appointed to West Point from South Carolina during the Reconstruction, spent six years there and was attacked by his class mates who tied him to a cot and cut a piece out of his ear. The case became a cause celebre throughout the country, led to the dismissal of the superintendent of the Point, and involved two Presidents of the U.S. It was a matter of racism and in the end Whittaker was forced to leave without graduating. Later he returned to South Carolina, studied and practiced law and engaged in the real estate business, all before going to Oklahoma as a teacher. My mother told me a part of the story when I was a boy but the book, which I learned about a couple of years ago when I was giving a [lecture] at West Point, is so interesting that I'll send you a copy when it is published.

Herbert and his wife spent a bit of time with us this summer on their way to and from Europe. They're in good shape and enjoyed their first trip so much that I suspect that they'll try it again next summer. They're still living in L.A. Herbert and Bad Boy visited Oklahoma City last winter and he tells me that Bad Boy wants to move back there. Herbert's been trying to get in touch with Shep for about two years but with no luck. If you run into him please give him my regards. He's about the only Okie that Herbert is interested in seeing and he's the only one who seems to have dropped out of sight.

As for me, I'm keeping busy writing and holding down the Schweitzer professorship at New York University. I'm unable to take many outside lectures these days and thus have cut down on the traveling. However I did give the commencement address at William & Mary last June and received an honorary degree. I felt pretty shaky about it but the reports were favorable . . . We haven't yet rebuilt the house in Mass., which we lost a few years ago to fire, but a contractor is supposed to be adding a couple of rooms to my studio this fall and we hope to have the use of it next year. Our place is in beautiful mountain country with broad vistas and quiet, clean air and I hope you'll be able to spend some time with us there. It is located in a village of fewer than three hundred people but we have enough friends in neighboring villages to make life interesting.

Ralph

The Foreword to Leon Forrest's Book[*]
As I began to get my bearings in the reeling world of THERE IS A TREE MORE ANCIENT THAN EDEN, I thought, What a tortured, history-wracked, anguished, Hound-of-Heaven pursued, Ham-and Oedipus-cursed, Blake-visioned, apocalypse-prone projection of the human predicament! Yet, simultaneously, I was thinking, Yes, but how furiously eloquent is this man Forrest's prose, how zestful his jazz-like invention, his parody, his reference to the classics and commonplaces of litera-ture, folklore, tall-tale and alum-street jive! How admirable the manner in which the great themes of life and literature are revealed in the black-white, white-black American-ness of his characters as dramatized in the cathedral-high and cloaca-low limits of his imaginative ranging.

So I read on, bouncing between moods of tragic contemplation and bursts of hilarious laughter, between speculations upon the shifting re-lationships between the American myth of democracy and everyday re-ality, brooding over his evocations of those dilemmas bred of Christian faith and racial conflict, of social violence, family friction and dramas of a peaceful kingdom. And when, all too soon, I put the book aside, I thought, <u>Well now, here is the beginning of a novelist in the grand man-ner; one who is unashamed to be serious, philosophical—even religious. Here is a black American writer who, having rejected the stance of cul-tural self-segregation, reveals himself as eager to pit his talents against the achievements of the great masters of the form. A word-possessed (and word-possessing) imaginative man from the Negro American briar patch, whose way with words is as outrageously and inventively stunning as this outrageous America which gave him birth!</u> In other words, it was impos-sible not to be amazed.

But now in calmer mood, it is my opinion that Leon Forrest demon-strates in his first published work a knowledge that has been resisted by some of the most talented of American novelists: That it is a cowardly waste of time for the writer to rail against the chaotic and surreal nature

---

[*] In January 1973, Toni Morrison, then an editor at Random House, inquired whether Ellison would be willing to make a comment on the galleys of Forrest's manuscript. His full and gener-ous response prompted Random House and Forrest to use the piece as the novel's foreword.

of American society as outrivaling the form-creating powers of fiction. For rather than confining his efforts to projecting a neat, minor slice of life, he seems to assume that, whether we like it or not, the day to day, here and now life of American society is the only life we have to live, and that as such, it is the writer's challenge and his task. Therefore, Forrest has given his considerable energies and talents to the discovery of the literary means and angles of vision necessary to reduce this confounding, pluralistic society of ours to eloquent form. That he has done so with such a large measure of success in his first novel provides us not only with a source of delight but with one of profound instruction.

Ralph Ellison
February 8, 1973

To Jim McPherson
730 RIVERSIDE lDRIVE
NEW YORK, NEW YORK 10031
MARCH 5, 1973

Dear Jim:

Here the 5th of March has arrived and I find that I haven't gotten around to thank you for sending the article and tape recording. This hasn't been, I assure you, because we haven't been talking and thinking about you, but is the result of the disarray in my affairs that comes from trying to teach and write at the same time. Nevertheless, I want you to know that Fanny and I have read your "Subjective Account of Something Very Old" and were both deeply moved. I mean to tears. I mean to catharsis and thus to a feeling of redemption through being allowed to recognize the terrible complexity of unfolding life. Indeed, we were so moved that I urge you to give us more, much more. And I don't say this to flatter, I simply feel that you have such a hold on your material that you could expand it into a significant book; one which by its sensitive subjectivity would counteract much of the empty sociological rhetoric which keeps getting in the way of any real understanding of the impact of our social and cultural conditions upon individual human beings. Yes, and because I suspect that such an approach as yours is the only effective antidote to the dehumanizing abstractions (well intended though they may be) that so many black writers are projecting as images of our situation. Your description of your father's difficulties alone conveys more of reality than a whole book-shelf of sociological abstractions, because he comes across as a most complex human being. His pain resonates and your regard for his predicament comes through with the mute power of understatement. I should add that your description of working with him at his electrician's trade and his difficulties over fulfilling contracts not only told me much about you, but it caused me to re-live some of my own job experiences and to recall relationships I had with older men whose low social status was in contrast with their great value as mentors. In the judgment of the community several of these were "failures" or worse, but for me they were instructors to whom I owe far more than I do to some of my official teachers.

I also liked your handling of the details of the cultural and historical background that operates in the relationships between blacks and whites in Savannah. While others generalize about "The" Black man and "The" white man, you've stuck to thorny human realities and individuals, some of whom triumph and some of whom fail, but most of whom are caught with the abiding confusion good-and-bad. Thanks especially for giving us Mr. Simms, and forgive me for envying you for having known him and his. Your little thumbnail sketches of your relatives and of the families in your neighborhood were so effective that I was forced to make my own mental survey of families I knew and the boys and girls I grew up with. Considering the circumstances, a hell of a lot of them turned out so very well that any easy cynicism concerning the prospects of their children and grandchildren is not only uncalled for but obscene. And that includes a few who were assumed to be heading either for early death, dismal failure, or the electric chair.

Isn't it ironic that white southern writers like Faulkner or Warren would understand your point about Flannery O'Connor and the Pullman porter and the California hustler and the cop while Rahv could not? He knows too little about American society, especially that of the South, and too damn much about books, while they, knowing both, would never allow the abstractions of literature to blind them to the snarl of human relationships out of which great literature emerges.

Back during the 1950's, when I interviewed Warren for the *Paris Review,* he related an anecdote in which an old Louisiana Negro man had killed a woman for badmouthing his granddaughter. When he decided to act, his victim was engaged in a crap game and the old man waited patiently until a friend could win back six dollars he'd lost to the offending woman, and this accomplished (I believe it took half an hour) he proceeded to blast the woman with both barrels of his shotgun. As Harry Morgan said of the black Cuban gunman in *To Have and Have Not* who had shot-and-machine-gunned a bunch of men to death, that old man was "some nigger"! More confounding, he was a man of honor who felt that anyone, man or woman, who badmouthed his beloved granddaughter deserved to die. And although there were many witnesses, he refused to plead guilty, despite that fact that he could escape the death penalty by going for a charge of manslaughter. It took his friends three days to persuade the old bastard to plead Not Guilty and before they did he had shaken the town to its moral foundations. I guess he took the old code du-ello concern with honor far more seriously than anyone expected a Negro to do and so sent everybody out of their righteous minds. Now he didn't have to wait as long to act as your hustler's daddy did, but he was the same kind of deadly patient old Southern Boot. That kind of black man will do what he feels he has to no matter how much he confuses socially accepted notions of justice. To my mind, you've got a hell of a fine story just in the old man's postponing his revenge until his last child had been educated. Tell us, Jim, what the hell went before!

I don't know what the hell is bothering Gaines, but his puzzlement over my Uncle Remus crack seems a waste of mental energy. I was simply trying to get those high-flying intellectuals to come down to earth and think a bit. So I mentioned calculus by way of emphasizing Uncle Remus' role as "teacher" as against his accepted role of "entertainer." There they were, accepting the notion that race blocked the writer from dealing with experience which takes place across racial lines and I was suggesting that their notion was false. Because human experience is human experience and it is the writer's role to use his craft to penetrate its mysteries wherever it seizes his imagination. Hell, everybody recognizes that under the surface of those animal tales Remus was teaching philosophy and guiding that white kid to identify with the human essence of social drama. So if that is true, it is possible that he was also teaching some math and we just weren't told about it because Joel Chandler Harris either didn't understand the abstractions or didn't find it significant enough to mention. But who's to say that those animals, abstractions for human qualities all, weren't also metaphors for mathematical relationships? Do we have to be limited by Harris' vision? Faulkner confesses that Mrs. Caroline Barr taught him all manner of things along with his social manners, and George Washington Carver taught all kinds of white folks botany and agricultural chemistry—even though he approached them socially with hat in hand. I'm riffing now, but a writer as gifted as Gaines shouldn't have to be told any of this, all he has to do is think!

I must apologize for not having really studied the tape of your mother but I have been waiting until spring vacation, which comes near the end of the month. At that time I plan to isolate myself and play it until I've absorbed what she has to say. I'll do the same with Ernie's reading, although that won't be as new to me since I heard, and enjoyed, his reading down at the Library of Congress.

In the meantime, please tell ole Mike Harper that I'm watching him and give our regards to the Monigs.

Thanks again, Jim, and keep up the good writing.

Sincerely,
Ralph Ellison

Mr. James A. McPherson
34 Fort Avenue
Cranston, Rhode Island 02905

To Stewart Lillard
LINCOLN HILL ROAD,
PLAINFIELD, MASS
01070
AUGUST 28, 1973

Mr. Stewart Lillard
864 Delverton Road Ext.

Dear Mr. Lillard:

If I delay acknowledging your letter much longer you'd be quite justified in considering me (if you haven't already) rude! I apologize with the explanation that your startling research arrived at a very hectic time—near the end of school year at NYU, following which my wife and I had to come up here to Mass., where we've been struggling with a contractor, plumber and electrician since the middle of June. After having lost our summer house some six years ago to fire we began last October to adapt a small cabin which I had used as a studio to the broader needs of living. We've added two rooms, cooking facilities, and a bathroom; very minor improvements indeed, but given the scarcity of workmen in this area and allowing for the independence displayed by workmen when they're in a monopolistic position, we might well have been building a mansion! Fortunately, now that the Labor

Day weekend approaches they've taken their tools and gone, leaving me the quiet in which to catch up with what for me are more important matters—like working on my book and answering your questions.

I must say that your information placed me in something of a dream-state. (Yes, Alfred Ellison was my grandfather and Lewis Alfred my father.) Some of it I had encountered as a child through listening to my father's sister, Lucretia, who was as proud of her family background as any member of a FFV. From her I heard that my grandfather had been some kind of town official, and that although unlettered he knew more about local and state politics than most people who could read. Often she stressed his ability to interpret the private motives at work behind the public contentions of politics, the relationships between kinship and private interests and public issues. From her I also learned that my grandmother Harriet looked like a white woman and that when she lost her life in a fire she had the distinction of having her death reported in the white newspaper. When I began paying attention to such stories I was too young to grasp the fact that my aunt was speaking of a time frame that included the Reconstruction, and later when I learned something of that period I did not connect my grandfather with the stereotypes of black legislators then current. From all I had heard about him he was simply not that type of clown—as you'll see from what follows.

Upon coming to New York in 1936 I learned from my father's cousin, the Reverend William Ellison, who pastors a church in the Bronx, that a relative, Henry Ellison served in the South Carolina legislature but took it with a grain of salt. I had, after all, been warned by my mother that the Ellisons took their background much too seriously. Now that I've read your findings, however, I shall ask William Ellison whether or not the young William Ellison whom you mention as my grandfather's ward and brother was not in fact his (the Reverend Ellison's) own father. I suspect this is true, because his father and my grandfather were brothers.

At any rate I heard or overheard other hints about the South Carolina past of the family, but as was frequently the case with black Southerners who had left the South, there was a conscious effort made to focus the minds of the young toward the future. Nevertheless I was impressed that my grandfather was a man of stern principles and of considerable courage—as was illustrated by the account of his refusing to leave Abbeville after one of his friends was lynched. It was said that he walked the streets of the town with his hands folded behind his back in defiance of the order to leave. "If you're going to kill me, you'll have to kill me right here," I was told he said, "because I'm not leaving. This is where I have my family, my farm, and my friends and I don't plan to leave . . ." This was strong stuff, admirable stuff—which I could understand because racial violence was no stranger to Oklahoma. Needless to say, I hoped that I had inherited such courage.

My aunt also liked to recall her father's strong part patriarchal control of her brothers. When they were rebellious she said that her father's favorite phrase to them was, "I'll make you walk the chalk-line, sir!" On two occasions following my father's death, Herbert, my younger brother, and I lived with her and her three children, and there were frequent occasions for her to warn us of punishment with the same phrase. Incidentally, this allows me to correct a bit of your data: only one of the Ellison daughters preceded my father and mother to Oklahoma. This was Janie, who went to Fort Sill in the employment of an army officer. Later, as the wife of a career army man, she made her home in the Philippines. Lucretia and her children were in fact brought to Oklahoma by my parents and lived with them until my aunt, an excellent laundress—really an artist—was able to set up house for her family. I'm told that her husband, from whom she was by then divorced, was a surveyor.

Now back to South Carolina: The deed through which my grandfather transferred ownership of the family property to my father listed the names of my brother and myself, thus upon the deaths of my father and grandfather we became the titular owners although our uncle Jim was in actual possession. Since, however, my mother had no idea of returning to the South to live, there was never a question of Uncle Jim's right to do with the property as he saw fit. As for me, the property was something that would be mine when I came of age.

But for years I puzzled over the relationship between General Sam McGowan and my grandfather. What lay behind the juxtaposition of the names of a Confederate general and a former slave? Years later I came across a brief account of General McGowan's career while reading Freeman's *Lee's Lieutenants,* and thus learned of his career as Chief Justice of South Carolina—but this only deepened the mystery. Perhaps, I thought, it had something to do with my mysterious grandmother Harriet; a matter of yard chillun, perhaps. Now I'm amused that your research indicates that instead of being a matter of blood the connection was political! What is more, I learn that the man whom family legend projected as intensely interested in politics had in fact <u>been</u> a politician. Nevertheless I'd suggest, if I may, that there is still an interesting mystery behind the figure of my grandmother because she was never talked too much about, and when she was it was always with a guarded air. Perhaps it centers in her maiden name of <u>Walker</u>, which is that of a family once important in South Carolina. I have no doubt but that the light skin, blue eyes and reddish hair which have turned up in the family spring from her, but that is more common than not; as a novelist who has learned much from Faulkner I am interested in the linkages, in the hidden sources of the confluent blood.

Another point of correction: I have indeed been to Abbeville, where I spent a short time on the old home place and met my grandfather, Aunt Belle and Uncle Jim. (Robert and Eddie were long since dead.) This was not long after my father's death, and either just before my cousin Tom Brown (Lucretia's son) had gone into the Army or just after his return from France. Because it was Tom and his sister, Maybelle, who took me there so that my grandfather could have a look at his son, Bub's boy. Considering my age at the time I remember some of the details quite vividly: the approach which the train made over a bridge or trestle which spanned the river of red, clay colored water; Uncle Jim waiting for us in his horse-drawn carriage; the large quantities of vegetables that were being harvested, the great fireplaces of the old house, into which I could walk and see the light filtering down the chimneys; a grove of pecan trees which Uncle Jim told me had been planted by my father when he was a boy, and from which for years each Christmas a bag of nuts was sent to us in Oklahoma; a ruined church that had been converted into a chicken house. Quite impiously, the stained glass windows had been left in one of the walls, thus creating a disturbing effect in me as I watched the chickens roosting beneath in the filtering of the colored light ... I'm not certain that this was in Abbeville itself, but if not it was somewhere close by. From your photographs (for which many thanks) I'd suspect that the house I visited was on my grandfather's farm, but I don't forget that I was only three or four years old and that was long, long ago.

The Reverend William Ellison tells me that at one time my grandfather and his brothers contracted for building railroad trestles for the Southern Railroad and that later several of the younger Ellison clan had worked as porters or, like my cousin Tom Brown (who retired only a few years ago as a brakeman for the Frisco Railroad) performed the chores of brakemen but were paid the wages of porters. Others, I'm told, were hostlers, i.e. men who serviced and repaired engines in the roundhouse.

Which leads to the connection between my mother's first husband—whose name, by the way, was not Mass Watkins, but Maston. I was told that railroading Negro families often visited one another up and down the line thanks to the railroad passes available to them. The Watkins owned a home in Atlanta which my mother kept until the early 1930's, and it was on one such visit that my mother and father first met. Maston was a fireman on the Southern and was killed along with his engineer when a group of white youngsters placed a skiff across the tracks. And so, also, it was out of such pathetic circumstances that I came to be born!

As for my father's service during the Spanish American War: He did indeed serve out of the country. He was a member of Company F of the 24th Infantry and was among those black troops who got Teddy Roosevelt off of San Juan Hill. When I was a youngster in Oklahoma several veterans of that engagement told me that my father had actually gotten into the blockhouse. Later my father served in the Philippines and was sent to China during the Boxer Rebellion.

By the way, my father did not join the construction firm in Oklahoma. This occurred in Chattanooga, after he had failed in operating a restaurant. According to family friends, who continued to talk about his cooking well into my high school days, he was an excellent cook. Be that as it may, he worked as a construction foreman with this firm—whose name escapes me—and had a part in building the first steel and concrete buildings in Oklahoma, Arkansas, and Texas. Despite the ravages of Urban Renewal some of the buildings are still standing in Oklahoma City, notably the Colcord Building, of which I possess a photograph of the topping-off ceremony. It was all of twelve stories, but in those days a miracle on that flat land . . . As a foreman he was to hire a number of boys who've now become prominent businessmen as water boys. On a recent trip to Oklahoma one of them, a man who gave me one of my jobs, drove me around to the sites of several of the buildings. Only after my birth did my father give in to my mother's objections to his being away from home and abandon construction work. From that time until his death he operated an ice and coal business, supplying both White and Negro homes and grocery stores. All of three years old, I was with him when he collapsed while mounting a ladder to place a block of ice in a grocery refrigerator.

As to the passing of the family property into other hands I can add the following: Sometime during 1937 I received in New York, a letter from Uncle Jim that had been forwarded from Oklahoma by my cousin Maybelle. In it he informed me that the old homestead was in danger of being lost for non-payment of taxes. The sum was minor, but at the time I was unemployed and possessed no friends capable of making me a loan. Thus it was through such miserable circumstances that the property passed into the ownership of the Reverend J. S. Belcher. It was the only real estate that I thought of as my own and there was a time when I dreamed of trying to buy it back but had neither the money nor the hope that I could ever, given my outlook and temperament, live in South Carolina in peace. I do recall however, and with amusement now, that I aroused the hostility of a group of black expatriates in Paris in 1954, when upon being asked how things were going in a racial way back home I answered that they were improving and that I imagined that during my life time it might be possible for me to live in my father's old home in South Carolina without too much difficulty. For that rash prophecy I was denounced as an uncle tom agent of the State Department!

I can't tell you how much I appreciate what you've turned up, but it's like having vague family legends turn out at long last to be a bit more fact than fantasy. I didn't consciously associate the grandfather in *Invisible Man* with Alfred Ellison but perhaps they shared a similar sense of the complexity of the human condition. I do know that pride and stubbornness were two of the Ellison characteristics of which my mother warned my brother and me—and yet I must confess that whenever I regard the faded photographs of my grandfather, father and uncles I am proud of being a part of those proud and rather handsome rascals. And should you find your way to New York I'll show the image of the Robert Ellison who lies beneath the grave marker—along with those of old Alfred, Lewis Alfred, Eddie and Jim.

When I told my friend and editor, Albert Erskine (a white Tennessean) that you'd dug up the record of a black Ellison dating back to 1790 his laconic reply was, "Well, you're lucky that General Sherman didn't get up that far!" Which is of course quite true; but I'm personally lucky that you, Mr. Lillard, have an interest in rooting down into that soil below the social pyramid and if there's anything I can do to help please ask. In the meantime I'll have a talk with William Ellison and with another cousin, Mrs. Ethel Anderson of Greensboro, N.C., who spends part of her time living with her children in Harlem. Which reminds me that when Mrs. William Ellison died last May a number of people from Abbeville attended her funeral and told me that they knew my folks. Perhaps William Ellison will put me in touch with them and I'll try to record whatever they have to offer. Good luck to you in your effort to put this minor part of Southern history together again.

Sincerely,
Ralph Ellison

To Ashbel Green
LINCOLN HILL ROAD
PLANFIELD, MASS. 0107
AUGUST 31, 1973

Mr. Ashbel Green
Managing Editor
Alfred A. Knopf, Inc.
201 East 50th Street
New York, N.Y. 10022

Dear Mr. Green:

Thanks for allowing me to read Daniel Aaron's *The Unwritten War*. I found it (for whatever my opinion is worth) one of the most impressive and disturbing works of literary history that I've ever encountered. Certainly I know of no more thorough account of the manner in which 19th century American writers, both major and minor, responded to the events and issues culminating in the Civil War. Nor am I aware of any work that spells out more ruthlessly the instances of equivocation, bad faith, failure of nerve and betrayal of the responsibilities of art and citizenship with which those writers, with few exceptions, sought to escape the artistic and philosophical challenges poised by that war.

In light of the obiter dicta which would see in poets—novelists, critics, historians—the "antennae of the race" or "unacknowledged legislators" of a nation's morality, Daniel Aaron offers crushing evidence that most writers of the period fell dismally short of such exalted roles. Some of the most gifted were not only malingerers who, dodging the war both as citizens and as artists, allowed men of lesser gifts to meet the challenges of art and governance which it was their own responsibility to confront; worse, no one succeeded in converting the war and its aftermath into artistic forms commensurate with its tragic dimensions. There is no wonder then, that the splintered nation which was forced to seek a new basis for unity in the confusion and destruction left by the war, the betrayal of the Reconstruction and the murder of its President, found little literary guidance as it began to flounder along with those problems of national identity, equal distribution of wealth, authority and justice that have harassed American society since the moment the guns fell silent at Appomattox.

Given this failure of poetic vision, perhaps only the nation's great natural wealth, the flexibility of its structure, the vitality of its original promise—and sheer good <u>luck</u>—have saved it from total self-destruction. At any rate, Aaron makes it clear that not until the advent of William Faulkner was the Nation to be blessed with a writer possessed of the breadth of talent and capacity for tragic statement necessary to even begin to give structure and detail to a predicament which General Sherman in a resonant word termed "hell"!

For me *The Unwritten War* stands as a corrective to the excesses of Edmund Wilson's *Patriot Gore*—a work with which it is destined to be compared, but one which, thanks to Aaron's objectivity and steadfastness of moral vision, it far surpasses. I feel certain that this work will take a place of first importance in those courses in American history and literature which by coming forthrightly to grips with the past serve to refine our vision of the present.

Sincerely,
Ralph Ellison

(Copy to Daniel Aaron)

To Lee Brawner
730 RIVERSIDE DRIVE
NEW YORK, NEW YORK 10031
FEBRUARY 24, 1974

Mr. Lee B. Brawner
Executive Director
Oklahoma County Libraries
131 Northwest Third Street
Oklahoma City, Oklahoma 73102

Dear Mr. Brawner:

Your letter of January 4th found me most grateful and, I must confess it, reassured. For until I had read its contents and received the architectural drawings (which soon followed), I had cautioned myself that the library project might well be more dream than reality. I knew of course that out there in my distant birthplace something marvelous had been set in motion, and that I, of all people, had been chosen for a prominent role in its symbolism. Of this there was no question. You yourself, Mr. Walter Gray (to whom my regards) and Mayor Latting had written me, Jimmy Stewart and my cousin Tom Brown had told me orally, and my reading of the *Oklahoma City Times* and the *Black Dispatch* had confirmed it in black and white. And yet this news had struck me as so unreal as to be even more startling than winning the National Book Award.

Without too much exaggeration I could say that so exhilarating was its effect that I dared not dwell upon it lest I awaken to find that I had either misread, misheard, or been beguiled by a mischievous dream. But I hasten to add that I viewed neither possibility with chagrin: quite the contrary. Since the earlier letters from home belied my having been guilty of so narcissistic a dream, perhaps I had simply misinterpreted their contents. But if this proved true my excitement had by no means been totally misplaced, because I consider having my name associated with such a remarkable flight of the civic imagination an honor beyond my wildest imaginings. As such, I had allowed the rare pleasure, the positive thrill, of knowing that Oklahoma Cityians who prize the world of books most highly had deemed my work worthy of a role in their drama of city planning. "And if it comes to nothing more than this," I told my doubting self, "if no bulldozer rolls nor rite of ground-breaking comes to pass, you can't take that away from me!"

Now for me this was no mere matter of consoling a tender ego. Given my memory of the early history of our city library system's relationship with the citizens of the Eastside, I had to consider the sheer announcement of such a project a most significant gesture, and this would be true whether that gesture remained immanent in the realm of the symbolic or soared in time to become an architectural reality dedicated to the preservation and distribution of books. There was no need to confuse the relative values of symbolic gestures and steel and stone when I recalled that during my growing-up even a <u>symbolic</u> gesture of such magnitude would have been inconceivable. Therefore I could not help but view the project as a positive manifestation of change, an earnest of goodwill, a justification of the faith in the possibility of advancement demonstrated and taught by such citizens as Roscoe Dunjee and Mrs. L. S. McFarland—Yes, and as a matter for profound gratitude.

Nevertheless, I was also aware that although there are those like yourself whose high regard for the role of books in society leads them to conceive marvelous projects for the public good, they must of necessity depend upon the commitment and support of those who legislate, allot budgets and assign contracts. A circumstance making for those possibilities that I dared not think about. I could not easily ignore that such supporters are by the nature of their roles all too capable of defaulting on their commitments. Whether this be due to changes in the political climate or to shifts in the tides of economics doesn't matter. The unhappy fact is that when they change their priorities (and they are supersensitive to all manner of pressures), our brightest civic visions, especially in the area of culture, all too frequently go by the board. Besides, how could I ignore the fact that here in New York the valuable Schomburg Collection had suffered from decades of neglect, or that the great New York Public Library—one of the city's glories—has itself been enduring years of financial difficulty? From such a perspective your plans for the expansion appeared so remarkable as to render the possibility of their being aborted lamentable but by no means a cause for disillusionment. Rather, it was a cause for hope; at least for me—even though I can imagine that the abortion of the project would have aroused a good deal of cynicism among those who still make their homes on the East Side of the city.

I hope all this doesn't contradict my saying that I dared not think too concretely about these matters, for although suppressed as I waited the word which you've so generously given me they did, nevertheless, play about the edges of my mind like so many distorting ghosts bedeviling a television screen. And while by no means lacking faith I am, after all, a novelist and haunted as such by what Henry James termed the "imagination of disaster." Thus, unhappily, I am conditioned to anticipate the stale disappointment of the expected more often than the heartwarming delight of the unexpected. By outlining difficulties overcome and positive progress made you've reassured me that in Oklahoma City at least, the unexpected continues to win out. I am delighted.

I am little skilled in interpreting architectural drawings, but I like both the design and scale of the library and, in light of your forecast for its completion, I join you in hoping that all goes well and according to schedule. Nor was your word concerning the old Dunbar Branch without its rewards, for it saddened me to think that the familiar little building might fall to the bulldozer of urban renewal. As you might be aware, my first library books were borrowed from the improvised branch that was thrown together in the Slaughter Building in rooms once occupied by a pool hall, my last (at least in Oklahoma) from the Dunbar Branch; a place I remember fondly for having been the source of so much pleasure and instruction, and a primary influence upon what was to become my life's work. Thus it comes as a relief that the old building is not to disappear as have so many of the buildings and houses that occupied the scenes that I hold dear and to which, again and again, I return in dreams of home, but will find continuing life in the new structure. For in the realm of libraries (as in the realm of culture generally), continuity is all and the essence of a library lies not in buildings but in the books they make available.

I, too, have news of Mr. Wilson: A few weeks ago he dropped by to discuss his part in the project, and sometime in March, after his return from Oklahoma, he plans to begin his work. Much to my surprise it turned out that I had met him a few years ago while lecturing at his university in Binghamton. I had wondered what the sculptor would think when he laid eyes on his subject but he had the advantage of already knowing. I only hope that I prove worthy of his skill. Your long-distance judgment was correct, I found him a quite pleasant individual.

Again I thank you for your informative letter and my wife and I are looking forward to the dedication. In the meantime if I can be of service, I am at your call.

Sincerely yours,
Ralph Ellison

To Dr. James Randolph
730 RIVERSIDE DRIVE
NEW YORK, NEW YORK 10031
MARCH 1, 1974

Dr. J. L. Randolph
331 N.E. Second Street
Oklahoma City, Oklahoma 73102

Dear Jim,

I've delayed so long in acknowledging your gift that you probably consider me most ungrateful. If so, please forgive me because I so much enjoyed receiving your gift (and in so unexpected fashion) that it would pain me to feel that my delayed response had soured your pleasure in the giving. My excuse for delaying is the pressure of work and certain complications of an economic nature that have made it necessary for the contents of the large suite of offices that were occupied by the professorship which I hold at New York University to be relocated in two tiny rooms on another part of Washington Square. If you can imagine having to cram your drugstore into Tom's old dental office and reception room you'll have the picture. I guess I should have had the foresight to have followed T.J.'s urging and become a dentist, or taken your example and become a pharmacist. And yet, I suspect that dentistry and pharmacy have their own problems—or would have if I started messing with them. Anyway, Jimmy Stewart carried out his mission immediately he arrived in New York, and despite my delaying until last week I finally purchased the cigars. They're quite fine: Maria Mancini Clemencaaus, with seven-inch pre-Castro fillers and Honduras wrappers, hand-made in Tampa, Florida. With these in the humidor I'm reminded of an expression I heard originally when I worked for you at the drugstore: "Man, I don't want to be a rich man, I just want to live like a rich man . . ." So thanks to you, I've been doing just that.

Even so, my temporary wealth hasn't spoiled my continuing pleasure in seeing the snapshots of you and Madge in the *Black Dispatch*. They snatched me so far back in time that I recalled people and incidents that had almost faded from memory. One was an occasion when our beloved Cute and Camille had taken Herbert and me out to your parents' farm for a weekend and Easter morning egg hunt. Wyatt and Sis had driven out in the buggy behind Bluebell and you arrived later in what was perhaps one of the cars in the *Black Dispatch* center spread. Then as you rolled into the driveway, I upped and jumped onto the running-board, so delighted for the opportunity to steal even so short a ride as to be that reckless.

Well, when you came to a stop, my delight came to an explosive end! As I recall it, everybody except Herbert (who was capable of doing much talking at the time), your Mother, Granny, Cute—my beloved Cute—and Camille and especially you, gave me so much hell that it's a miracle that I ever again found the nerve to hop on a moving vehicle. And that goes for the many freight trains I had to grab years later when that old master, Charlie Miller, was instructing me in how to hobo my way to college. Perhaps that verbal blistering led to my inability to eat hard-boiled eggs without suffering blinding headaches. On the other hand, it might have been due to an allergy. If so, I outgrew it.

Still, I've never outgrown my love for cars and seeing pictures of those early East Side wonders reminds me of such matters as the Franklin owned by Mr. Taylor, the Englishman who owned the Blue Front Grocery Store, and my learning to drive the drugstore's Model T Ford when I was twelve, and your hair-raising account of a trip a group of you made to Chicago taking turns driving John Cooperwood's machine. As I recall it, it was while returning late at night, worn-out from the trip and all asleep but the driver, that upon approaching the city limits somebody opened his eyes to find the car bowling along at fifty miles per hour with ole John negotiating that series of curves around the State Capitol with all the confident skill of a Barney Oldfield. You were making good time and soon you'd be home and relaxing in bed—or so at first it appeared.

Because then you took another look and discovered for all his dancehall swinging of those curves, Ole John was dead asleep at the steering wheel.

Talk about being in a tight place: You were moving too fast to jump, you couldn't slow the car down, and if you laid a hand on John you were afraid that a drizzling fit would hit the man (and everybody else) and in the excitement he'd wreck the car. They say that everybody gets religion on the battlefield and I'd guess that the same was true of everybody who was forced to sit there and watch ole John zip around those narrow curves. And doubtlessly it paid off. Because not only did ole John manage to get you safely home, he had parked the car, turned off the engine and settled down to catch up on his sleep before the rest of you came out of your state of shock and realized that you'd lived unharmed through a driving miracle. There was no question about that, because all of you lived to tell the tale. I must confess, however, that while I believed your account, I always wondered if that in the telling you weren't giving away your true blood relationship with ole Taylor by stretching the details—if only a wee bit. But hell, it really didn't matter, because even if you had it was such a fine story that I still recall it with delight.

In fact, it suggests to me that the *Black Dispatch* might well have included photographs of John Cooperwood, Al Kerr, Buddey Bunn, and Oscar and Reggie Pittman, because they were all legendary drivers—whether cadillacing slowly down Deep Second during a Sunday afternoon promenade or burning up the highways on long distance trips. And come to think of it, I'd like to see a photo of Sticks Walker, the mechanic who died of blood-poisoning after trying to doctor his burned hand with a pocket knife. Back there we certainly had our share of fine drivers and mechanics. And among the drivers I'd list at least one woman: Mrs. Zelia N. Breaux. And what about Professor Bruner and Rich Walker, who shared a love for fine cars as well as a glamorous wife? Still it was good to see that picture of Halley Foster and his horse again. I remember him vaguely, if at all, but a copy of the photo hung in your father's house. If I'm correct, he owned the first motorcycle on the East Side and my mother told me that she had created a mild sensation by accepting his invitation to take a ride on its rear seat . . . And then there was that fleet of cars owned by S. D. Lyons, but I won't go into that. If the *Dispatch* had printed photographs of all the automobiles I remember there'd have been no space for anything else.

Yes, but how delightful to see a photo of such men as Tilton Willis,

Sol Dunn and, especially, Mr. Bob Williams, whom I liked very much. When you were living on the corner of Third and Phillips, the Williams lived up the street near the Bill Prices, and I seem to recall that he rode a bicycle with his trousers carefully clipped to his legs as he pedaled back and forth from his job at Jenkins Music Store. Oddly enough, I remember his daughter Helen quite vividly but her sister has become vague; was her name Rachel—or am I thinking of Rachel Moore? How memory fades! There was a time when I could remember every family on that block but now the best I can come up with are Randolphs, Bowens, Baileys, Haywoods, Bethels, Hyatts, Youngs (I.W.), Sanders (Lizzie) Williams, Crawfords, Price and McCleary (they later took over Dr. Young's house. I do however remember your mother's story about Hilliard Bowen:

Once when she and Granny were cooling pies on the windowsill young Hilliard saw them and got so excited that he went yelling to his sister, "Hey, Zenobia! Hey Zenobia: Run around the house and smell!"

It took me years to realize that there was an unintended pun hidden in someone's asking a young girl to run around and smell—although there were quite a few older ones running around doing exactly that! At the time my innocence focused my attention on the pies, for I knew their quality from having eaten them and I sympathized with Hilliard's having to content himself with the mere aroma.

But wait! While my memory is still in that block, did I ever tell you what happened in 1966 when Tom Brown dropped me by the Prices' home for a quick visit? If not, here it is: When we arrived Bill Price and a friend were relaxing in the shade of the front porch, and after Tom had introduced me as someone Bill used to know, Bill looked me up and down with the grimace of an outraged judge and then allowed, gruffly, that yes, he remembered me as Ellison-the-ice-man's boy. Whereupon he lumbered into the house and returned with an old photograph in which a group of early settlers posed impressively in their lodge uniforms, asking if I could identify any of them. I suppose he thought my father was among them. Unfortunately he wasn't, but I did manage to recognize several of the men; having no difficulty at all with Dr. Bethel because a very young Allen stood by his side. After that we talked awhile of the good old days and ole Bill expressed satisfaction that I remembered so much and had managed to reach manhood without getting my brains knocked out. To which I replied, with respectful modesty that I had just been lucky. Then, as Tom and I prepared to leave, I said with a surge of sincere emotion, "Mr. Price,

I'm delighted to have seen you again and to have found you in such vigorous health." To which sentiments he cleared his throat and said,

"Why, yes, boy, I'm doing pretty good." And then with rising voice he added, "All I really <u>need</u> is another three inches on my dick!" Now I needn't tell you <u>how</u> he said it—which was <u>molto basso profundo</u>; from the very soles of his big feet and from the porch beneath his feet—and LOUD: In fact his voice was so thunderous in the quiet of that Third Street afternoon that everybody on the block <u>had</u> to have heard it. And not only did they have to have heard it, they had to know who had said it and could not possibly have misconstrued what precisely the hell he was bellowing about. In fact, he might as well have stood up and stretched his apparently inadequate member to the north, the east, the south, the west, or to wherever it was he'd been trying to score and have done with it.

He didn't but I can tell you this: Before the echoes died away you could hear the block exploding with the sounds of windows coming down, doors slamming shut and all kinds and ages of jellyroll being placed under lock and key. And if ole Bill meant to shock a naive youngster he surely succeeded—although not by what he said. For from the street-knowledge I'd picked up working for you and in being Tom's cousin, I had learned too much about human character not to know that some very old hound-dogs can still go on the hunt and tree. And old tomcats too. What shocked me was the contrast between the enormity of his ambition and the lateness of his age, because he must have been all of eighty at the time. Every time I think about him I crack up, but I still can't help but hope that whatever it was that Mr. Price had absorbed from Oklahoma's climate, good food or bad whiskey to give him such vitality had been absorbed to some extent by me. But, man! <u>Three</u> more inches? Well, now after long and careful consideration I'll leave such ambition to Wyatt and Taylor, the rascals.

Here in the East I've told this story many times and always to gales of my listener's laughter. But it was sometime long after 1966 that in thinking about the situation in which Bill Price had made his unexpected statement that I came to a conscious awareness of his motive in making it—and thus to a conscious appreciation of the adult's privilege of laughing with and/or at his elders as well as his peers. Such a privilege can't be granted, it must be earned; and in time I came to see that Mr. Price was not merely trying to shock me. He was also giving recognition to my having attained manhood. I recalled that while making his statement he studied my face to see how I was taking it, and since instead of panicking or blushing with

embarrassment I had roared with laughter I passed his test. He had initiated me and in his sight I became right there and then a man among men.
Other things being equal, he would probably have offered me a drink of
whiskey—straight. Never before during my residence in Oklahoma City
had the privilege of such laughter been mine. And certainly not when I
was a kid tagging along after Uncle Allan Watkins; if it had, there was a
memorable occasion when it would have saved me a great deal of physical
discomfort and ethical disorientation.

I refer to an incident that occurred long before I had reached adolescence (I was seven or eight) when I was riding with Uncle Allan behind
his team of mules. It was a hot, airless summer afternoon and the wagon
was weighted down with a load that we had hauled all the way from the
fair grounds. A streetcar had passed us moments before and now rumbled
far in the distance, leaving us in a silence broken by the sound of harness,
wagon wheels and hoof beats thudding dully on the asphalt. All of us—
man, boy and mules—were wet with sweat, and I was eager to get on to
Uncle Allan's place and to some of Aunt Ellen's lemonade. I dreamed of
peace and shade, but then, just as we were creeping our way westward
on East Fourth Street between Gary and Stiles—one of the mules was so
indelicate as to let go a great, resounding fart.

It was quite a blast, and for an instant I just sat there, feeling Uncle
Allan swaying on the seat beside me and unable to believe my own ears.
Even given the anatomy of the mule this was a blast to suspend the sun
in its westward journey and my instinctive reaction was to fill the interval
with laughter. But it was here, precisely, that my youth and inexperience
presented a problem. Because that mule had done far more than broken
wind: she had blasted hell out of one of the most rigidly enforced taboos
associated with toilet-training, and one that by symbolic extension was
tied up with such matters as good manners and the difference in social
initiative which separate men from boys. Being no less in secret rebellion
against such generation-based distinctions than any other average boy, I
wanted simply to laugh my ass off. But there in the presence of Uncle
Allan Watkins, a friend of my late father and an associate and friend of
Grandpa Randolph, I was frozen with inhibition. I associated Uncle Allan
with an unassailable adult dignity and with an authority that rested no
less upon his age and the high respect and homage paid him as a pioneer
citizen, than his honored place among the dignitaries of Tabernacle Baptist Church. He symbolized all those virtues that I was being exhorted
by my mother, teachers, pastor, and family friends to make my own. And

among them being that control over one's primitive instincts which alone made for public order, provided a clear distinction between good and evil, and marked the contrast between the attitudes and manners displayed by gentlemen of high moral purpose and those flaunted by low-lifers, hustlers and out-and-out rounders. Therefore, I wasn't <u>about</u> to earn Uncle Allan's displeasure by honoring his mule's violation of proper decorum with one of my own. Which was exactly what I feared Uncle Allan would judge my laughing to be.

Actually, things were going too fast for me to have thought this out in such detail, but in my confusion I became more and more certain that my laughing at a mule-fart in Uncle Allan's presence would have been, in effect, an even more repulsive sort of farting than the mule's. A sort that, while doing no violence to his sense of smell (the mule's was already raising hell with mine) might well scandalize his finer sensibilities. You can see how things stood. One of the effects of my father's early death was an inclination to endow the male adults whom I loved and respected with all kinds of finer sensibilities. And this, whether they be farmers, train porters, packinghouse workers, ministers, teachers, or men of medicine. Unfortunately, this contributed to the hard time I was having in measuring up to what were considered civilized standards, which, considering the times, the frontier character of Oklahoma and the irreverent attitudes of the wild Negroes, both juvenile and adult, whom I moved among, was already difficult enough. But at the moment my pressing problem was what to do about the conflict between the mule's blast (still echoing in my head), Uncle Allan's inscrutable presence, and the pressure of suppressed laughter now becoming physically painful. I was aching for him to signal me, provide me with a a form of acceptable reaction, but as we rocked along through waves of asphalt heat it was as though Uncle Allan had gone stone deaf. So to contain myself I concentrated desperately upon the lazy action of the mules' great toiling rumps and watched the offender's tail swishing flies. And as I held my breath against the billowing product of the mule's magnificent effort I could feel the laughter sizzling inside me like high-pressured air rushing into an inflating inner tube. But still no sign from Uncle Allan.

Reaching Stiles now, we turned the corner into the welcome shade cast by that hospital which loomed on the west side of the street, and there, unable to stand the suspense any longer, I stole a quick glimpse at Uncle Allan's face—Just in time to see him let fly a stream of tobacco juice. And as he lashed out, giving the mule a slash across the butt with the ends of the reins, Uncle Allan broke his silence:

"Now you cut that out, you filthy whore," Uncle Allan said.

You could have knocked me off the wagon-seat with a jaybird's feather. For in bland contradiction of the fact that kids my age were forced to pass through the Grand Avenue red light district every time we went to school, I wasn't supposed to have even heard of a whore, but I did; and hearing a man of Uncle Allan's decorum curse his mule for a <u>filthy</u> whore struck me as even funnier than the mule's impropriety. Things were <u>really</u> getting out of control. With the pressure of repressed laughter about to burst my britches, I was now further inhibited by the necessity of pretending that I was ignorant of the term <u>to</u> which Uncle Allan had given such forceful expression.

Nor did he provide me any relief. As the mules clopped along I stared vainly at the flashing of his profile as it knifed through shadow and shade, but still he signaled me neither aye nor nay. In fact, his face couldn't have been more composed, decorous, or remote had he been sitting in his pew in Tabernacle Baptist Church listening to Reverend E. W. Perry castigate his congregation with St. Paul's strictures against the evil, hound-dog ways of the Corinthians.

I was damn nigh hysterical. My gut was about to bust, the tears had begun streaming down my face, and in trying to hide them, all I could do was stare at from whence had come all that great volume of sound and wonder at the circumstance which had turned what had first appeared an occasion for laughter into an ordeal. And how I envied the mule her freedom of expression! Uncle Allan could call her any kind of whore he could think of, but she knew it for a physical fact that there was simply more room out than in, and now she was acting on said knowledge with the regularity of a ticking clock and the imperturbability of a duchess—and how.

By the time we'd traveled another half-block I saw Uncle Allan reach up suddenly, snatch off his hat and begin fanning the air, trying to get rid of the effect of the mule's latest venting of her windy prerogative. And this time Uncle Allan wasted no time in expressing his opinion.

"Doggone that whore," Uncle Allan said, "she's gone and done it <u>again</u>!"

And now, watching him lash the mules into a chain-jangling trot, I threw caution to the wind and laughed. I was still afraid that I'd get thrown off the wagon seat, but I laughed. I laughed all the way around Stiles Park and was still laughing when we reached the lot behind his house and began unhitching the team. And Uncle Allan? He went about removing the mules' harness in silence. I could see him looking at me from time to time but if he cracked a smile I failed to see it. Not that he acted offended, he didn't. I suppose he just wasn't going to waste his good breath on a fool boy's cracking up over a mule-fart.

God bless Uncle Allan's soul. I realize now that he probably knew exactly what was going on inside of me and was having as difficult a time keeping a straight face. That he did so successfully was simply the result of his having had far more practice in the art. If he hadn't been a religious man he'd have made one hell of a poker player. And who knows, who's left to recall, perhaps at one time of his life he had been. But although I shall never know for certain what was going on behind that bland, patient, tobacco-chewing face, I suspect that it was right there that, following his example, I began learning to control my own.

I guess that after all this spate of words you wish that I'd learn to control my typewriter if not my memory of days long past. If so, it's what happens when I smoke good cigars and you have only yourself to blame. Besides I don't intend to answer even though I'm always happy to hear from you. So there.

I talked to Tom recently and he told me that except for the harassment of thieves things are O.K. with you and that Madeline is doing fine. May the good things continue and I hope the time for dedicating the new library—the one which should more fittingly bear your father's name than mine—will come soon, for my wife and I plan to be there and look forward to the opportunity of seeing you all again.

Take care of yourself and my love to all the family and to Tom and Bert.

Sincerely,
Ralph Ellison

To Edward Stanley
730 Riverside Drive
New York, New York 10031
September 27, 1974

Mr. Edward Stanley, President
Laboratory for Research in Relevant Education
145 East 69th Street
New York, New York 10021

Dear Ed Stanley:

I am quite impressed by the high quality of the proposed series. It strikes me as no less entertaining than educational, and it should make a major contribution to our American awareness of who and how we became whatever it is we are, by its dramatic presentations of the options taken, or rejected by representative Americans and the choices left to those who would build upon their efforts. The quotations from Dr. Morris and Dr. Peterson are very much to the point. This said, I offer the following suggestions:

Perhaps the conception of "leaders" should be broadened by way of recognizing the fact that not all of those who have shaped the nation were politicians nor were they all involved directly with government. A number were writers and even publishers. I think immediately of Emerson, Mark Twain, Thoreau, Melville, Henry Adams, Stephen Crane, writers who created aspects of American character and explored various dimensions of American identity, moral and cultural, in works which developed American vernacular language, style and wisdom in works of literature. Nor would I overlook those who influenced the values of the Nation through works of popular culture—not excluding the minstrel show, the writers of Tin Pan Alley dittys, radio drama, motion pictures and popular musicals. Recall that President Lincoln was killed while watching *Our American Cousin*. I stress these possibilities because these "unimportant" arts have a profound influence upon our values, and as projectors of myth they have done much to cloud our perception of our history and our moral predicament.

Beyond this, I'd suggest that some outline of a program concerning the life of a woman, a member of an ethnic minority, or of the Negro group. Of the latter, Frederick Douglass and Booker T. Washington come most readily to mind. Finally, why not a program on the work of that important popularizer of ideas, the published Haldeman-Julius whose Little Blue Books and *Appeal to Reason* contributed so much to the literacy of the provinces? And what about Harriet Beecher Stowe, Paul Cuffee—the wealthy black New England shipper and colonizer of Liberia—Richard Allen, who founded the Afro-American Episcopal Church? Jane Addams?

In closing, let me slip a pin into Mars Jefferson: He did indeed have a lot to say about slavery in his first draft of the "Declaration of Independence" but by way of making a scapegoat out of ole George Third, whom he accused of being responsible for the peculiar institution—when, in fact, the colonials, both north and south were exploiting it as hard as they knew how. See Catherine Drinker Bowen for more on that soft-shoe shuffle.

Good luck,
Ralph Ellison

RE:fe

To Mr. Lee Brawner

JANUARY 7, 1975

Mr. Lee Brawner, Executive Director
Oklahoma County Libraries
131 Northwest Third Street
Oklahoma City, Oklahoma 73102

Dear Mr. Brawner:

Would you be interested in acquiring for the Ellison Library a copy of the various translations of *Invisible Man*? They number about twenty, although a few are second and third printings of a particular language. I would be glad to make such a gift to the library if you wish to have them and if there is space to accommodate. Let me know, at your convenience, and we will ship them out at our expense.

I might also provide single copies of some of the journals and literary magazines that contain essays, short stories and chapters from my work-in-progress. However, I would be anxious to avoid duplication of any items you might already have since I have only two or three copies and other libraries want them. My wife will provide you with a list, if you are interested, and she will no doubt suggest other items that may be of use, depending on the objectives and range of your projected needs. We do not wish to encroach in any way so please feel free to be perfectly frank.

We are faithfully kept in touch with library's progress through news clippings from the Oklahoma press and conversations with Jimmy Stewart. All seems to be progressing and I hope the problems are at least foreseeable.

My wife joins me in best wishes for the New Year to you, your family and your colleagues.

Sincerely
Ralph Ellison

To Jervis Anderson
730 RIVERSIDE DRIVE
NEW YORK, NEW YORK 10031
DECEMBER 12, 1976

Dear Jervis Anderson:

I've received so many favorable comments regarding your profile of me that I can only conclude that you've been highly successful. They have come from friends and from strangers and from several people whom I haven't seen for years. There have been a number of letters and several local and long distance telephone calls. Jimmy Stewart phoned from Tuskegee, where he'd gone in an effort to recruit engineers, to say that friends in Mexico had seen your piece and liked it, and the very first letter to reach us here came from a white Virginia banker who found in the view which you provided an affirmation of his own American faith. He saw in the contents of the profile a lesson for his own son, a young lawyer with ambitions to become a writer, and he gave me the impression of having discovered certain unities of American experience that exist beyond the obvious divisions of race, class and geographical region. If true, and I believe that it is, you've achieved that feat of communication that is a constant challenge to the American writer.

So now, after my doubts about your project, I am glad that I trusted your opinion rather than my own. I suppose that I'm simply too close to me to even glimpse what you've trained yourself to see. From my point of view, my only interesting aspect lies in my two published books and the imagination which they embody. You saw something more, and for that I thank you. And not only for your seeing, your perception, but for the writing. A number of people came up with such enthusiastic comments that I was forced to remind them that, since I was merely your subject and the art yours, their comments should, more properly, be conveyed to you, and I hope that they, and other readers, have written you their reactions.

As for myself, I can only say congratulations and, again, my thanks for a job well done.

Sincerely yours,
Ralph Ellison

Mr. Jervis Anderson
The New Yorker
25 W. 43rd Street
New York, New York 10036

To Horace Porter
730 RIVERSIDE DRIVE
NEW YORK, NEW YORK 10031
DECEMBER 22, 1976

Dear Mr. Porter:

Thank you for your letter and for allowing me the privilege of reading your moving essay. Thanks also for making me aware that, despite the temper of those times, my small effort at Amherst was not a total bust.

Yes, I remember very well my friend Cal Plimpton's jokes about our relative drinking capacities. Indeed, every few months or so we meet at a club of which we're both members and engage, mano a mano, in that talk-lubricating pastime. And on more than one occasion I've reminded him that shortly after offering me a teaching job at your old college he upped and took off! Considering the tensions of that period, I really don't blame him, but the idea of him throwing me to the tigers of wrath in the guise of a dark horse of instruction and then resigning still gives me a laugh or two.

Looking back I'm glad that I had that opportunity to talk with Amherst students and I'm pleased that, despite your unhappiness, you stuck out your time there. I suspected that much of the discomfort which Afro-American students were going through at that time was simply the anguish of the initial college experience (any college) and was not essentially different than that I experienced many years before at Tuskegee. Perhaps the difference was that during the '60's students had been given a facile name for their unhappiness, and one which provided many of them an excuse for rejecting academic discipline. Those who worked on their studies while they protested I could respect, but what on earth could I do about the many who appeared to be throwing away a much better opportunity for an education than that which my mother and I had had to make such great sacrifice. No ideological catch words could blind me to the fact that they were wasting a valuable opportunity for learning how to convert their anger into forms of conscious thought and creative action. The need to control and transcend mere anger has been our lot throughout our history, and for many years failing to do so, as the saying goes, got you dead. Nor are things essentially different today, for no matter the headiness of our slogans, an unthinking indulgence in anger can lead to a socially meaningless self-immolation and to intellectual suicide. From your essay it strikes me that you were most fortunate in your background because it kept you from wandering too far from your chosen goal. Even your religion appears to have served you well by providing channels for your emotions and giving support to your hopes and aspirations. I'm reminded that during my own college days my mother's religious faith was a firm support, even when I was so entranced by the ideas of Bernard Shaw that I went two weeks without food while working in the school kitchen. I was getting drunk on ideas but her faith helped to keep my feet down there on that red Alabama clay. But then, even for a doubter, faith is a gamble on the future and a compass against chaos and, as you discovered, bending the knees isn't the only way to pray.

I smiled when you referred to the experience of being in an environment where for the first time you could use a vocabulary previously confined to your reading and thinking. In my case I knew many words that I couldn't even pronounce, words I hadn't bothered to sound simply because there were no occasions for using them without appearing pretentious. Once I shocked a white man whose shoes I was shining by revealing that I was familiar with Freud's theory of dreams, but neither of us were prepared to communicate on that level, for it would have placed too great a strain on the arrangements of social hierarchy—and on the two of us! But the freeing possibilities of books is so obvious that I continue to be amazed that so many of our young people avoid them. And yet, wherever books find attentive readers and no matter how unlikely the place, marvelous transformations of possibility occur; for you in Georgia, for me in Oklahoma.

Speaking of Georgia, I once played dances at a hall located on the top floor of the building which housed Lunceford's Drug Store, drank beer at a beer garden operated by a Miss Outlaw, and visited the home of Dr. Brewer who, you might recall, lost his life during a civil rights incident in Columbus. It might interest you to know that I, too, am familiar with kerosene lamps, horse and mule teams and the rest—even though I never lived in the country. In fact, when I left home for Tuskegee we had a corral in the back yard which my mother rented to a landscape gardener who kept his livestock there. During the summer of my sixteenth year I had so much trouble working with his team of mean little Spanish mules that I came to understand why it is said that many of our preachers were called to the ministry after a hard day of looking a mule in the behind. Speaking of making up our faces and our minds, perhaps the mule connection is precisely what's missing in the experience of many who see protest as the only means of doing something about racial injustice. It's considered bad form to mention such matters (i.e., the first Negro to do this or that), but when the returns are all in it might well be observed that while I was being criticized for being inactive I was actually exploring in places where no blacks had been before but where today, thanks to such venturing, it is fairly common to find us. I've always felt that Americans by definition are frontiersmen. Whether we see the frontier as geographical, as intellectual, as hierarchal, or as a combination of all three—which they most often are—we are obligated to explore and master new areas of living. Yes, and thinking. And this is even more true of Afro-Americans who have been prevented from knowing many of the most important processes of this society. Thus, if we would change society it is imperative that we possess some concrete idea of its complexity. I wouldn't have believed that I'd ever see the day when that old line about "Free schools, white schools and dumb boots," would apply to the Ivy League, but dam' if it didn't! Anyway, for us to remain in one narrow groove while ranting about "freedom" strikes me as an affront to those who endured and sacrificed to enable us to become better prepared for our continuing role in the struggle for freedom. There are many ways of participating in that struggle and I'm consoled that Dostoyevsky found his most meaningful outlet for gambling not in the streets or at the roulette wheel but in putting pressure on the form of the novel.

I'm delighted to hear that old Lee Willie Minifees'* act of arson was instrumental in your friend's discovering the pleasure of bird-watching. Last week I saw a mocker doing damn well along cold, wind-swept Riverside Drive—which suggests that a southern trickster can make it up here as successfully as the Yankee trader did down south. Some years ago when R. W. B. Lewis and family were spending the summer on Cape Cod a mocking bird that had drifted up that way caused all kinds of confusion by riffing from the perch he'd made of their T.V. antenna. Passersby thought that they were hearing an electro-mechanical gadget. The rascal was imitating everything from a whole song to snakes in the grass. I think I actually heard him taking off on James Brown.

It is good to learn that you are working in the American Studies department at Yale and I hope you're in touch with Michael Harper and Robert Stepto. Recently they interviewed me for an issue of the *Mass. Review* and I have the impression from them that much lost time is being made up at Yale. Good luck with your writing and teaching—in that order—and

---

* The jazzman in "Cadillac Flambé" who burns his prized white Cadillac convertible on Senator Sunraider's lawn to protest the senator's references to the Cadillac as a "Coon Cage" in a senate speech (see *Three Days Before the Shooting*, 1085–97).

rather than try to make a date during this rather hectic period, why don't you give me a call the next time you're in New York? I'll be glad to see you and so will my wife, who found your essay most moving.

Sincerely yours,

Ralph Ellison

RE:fe

To G. A. Smith

MARCH 20, 1977

Mr. G. A. Smith, Head
Department of General Studies
Wulfrun College of Further Education
Paget Road
Wolverhampton, WVS ODU
England

Dear Mr. Smith:

"In a Strange Country" was written as a short story during World War II, and published in the now defunct American magazine, *Democracy* in July 1944. Although imaginary, it was an attempt to give fictional form to some of the American racial conflict that was to be observed in the European Theater of Operations at that time, and to suggest the perspective of irony afforded a young Afro-American by a voyage to Wales.* As a merchant seaman I became slightly familiar with war time Swansea, Cardiff and Barry and used Swansea as a setting for my fiction. The fact in the fiction, however, does not lie in any personal experience of racial difficulties encountered there, but in my having shared the warm hospitality of a few private homes—one of them the quite Victorian residence of a collier owner—and a memorable evening of drinking in a men's club where the communal singing was excellent. I was also familiar with a club operated by the American Red Cross in a village a few miles north of Swansea. I recall that it was frequented mostly by Afro-American GI's, and that the Welsh ladies who prepared the food not only did amazing things with

---

*   For a second Ellison story set in Wales, see "A Storm of Blizzard Proportions," unpublished in his lifetime and included in the second Vintage International edition of *Flying Home and Other Stories*, 2012.

powdered eggs but prepared a delicious salad from the flesh of hares. My seaman's rating was that of Second Cook and Baker and I assure you that I found much to envy in the culinary resourcefulness of those ladies.

It has been years since I've looked at the story, but it was not conceived as part of a longer work and the form in which it was reprinted is as complete as I was able to fashion it under the wartime conditions which inspired it.

You might consult Afro-American newspapers for accounts of Black American G.I.'s in Britain. At the time our armed forces were segregated the black newspapers were duly attentive.

Sincerely yours,
Ralph Ellison

To Robert Alexander

MARCH 21, 1977

Professor Robert J. Alexander
Department of English
Point Park College
Pittsburgh, Pa. 15222

Dear Professor Alexander:

At the time I wrote *Invisible Man* I knew nothing of the Ras Tafari sect. "Ras," however, was a term used by certain Black militants during the 30's and 40's as a title of leadership. It was adapted from an Abyssinian title meaning 'Prince,' and the militants who used it identified quite strongly with the Ethiopians.

You will note that when my Ras is in his 'destroyer' phase he wears a lion skin and carries (and uses) a spear. These are details he picked up from watching newsreel filming of Haile Selassie's fight against the Italians. That war aroused great interest in Harlem, and in projecting his ambitions for leadership Ras seized upon this means of 'naming' his role.

It was as simple as that. I suspect, however, that Ras wouldn't have known what to do with the Ras Tafarians. He was a proper West Indian gentleman at heart!

Sincerely,
Ralph Ellison

To Cyrus Colter
730 RIVERSIDE DRIVE
NEW YORK, N.Y. 10031
NOVEMBER 23, 1977

Professor Cyrus Colter
Chester D. Tripp Professor of Humanities
Northwestern University
Evanston, Illinois

Dear Professor Colter:

When I was asked to read the galleys of Leon Forrest's first novel, *There Is a Tree More Ancient than Eden,* his publishers asked my permission to use my wildly enthusiastic comments as a foreword. Having met Forrest but once I wondered how he would react to what might well have been taken as an imposition, but on the assumption that if <u>he</u> did not object <u>I</u> would be honored to be even so tenuously identified with his impressive talent I consented. Since that time I have come to know Forrest personally, have read other of his writings, both critical and fictional, and after engaging in numerous exchanges of ideas with him I am even more impressed. Briefly, I think of him as one of the most talented and morally engaged American writers.

Forrest is an experimental writer, both as to material and as to form. Much of the life he recreates has gone untouched by novelists, and I consider the fact that he has attempted to bring it to formal order an act of artistic courage and responsibility. One might say that both his material and his methods are unconventional, and yet his experiments are anchored securely in a firm grasp of the culture of the form in which he expresses himself— A fact that can confound the inbred conservatism of critics, testing both their perceptiveness and their reliance upon received conventions.

Nevertheless, Forrest sees with his own eyes and speaks with his own voice. His imagination and talent are fed by precisely that vernacular mixture of traditional native folk elements (street argot and Shakespeare, the dirty dozens and Elizabethan epithet, Afro-American cultural lore and pragmatic narrative techniques, etc.), that American writers have played upon experimentally since Mark Twain's direction-pointing feat of capturing the wry "Americanness" of American experience.

Also impressive is the fact that Forrest has embraced the duality of his identity as Afro-American–American forthrightly, and used it to brilliant creative effect. He knows that the secret of projecting the essence of the Afro-American background's potential for literature lies not in merely imitating, say, a blues, a slave narrative, or a spiritual in what too often amounts to but an empty assertion of racial pride, but in appropriating and combining whatever elements of that vast array of intellectual concepts, oral and literary stylistic devices that comprise his heritage as a modern American writer. Indeed, he uses all that is available to him with a gusty humor as he strives to render eloquently his complex vision of human experience. Abstractions, compression, and wildly incongruous juxtapositions mark his method. His style is highly personal, combining the comic and tragic modes to covey the turbulent eclecticism that marks the drama of American social hierarchy. Thus he draws upon his own group's ancestral styles while using Melville, Mark Twain, Conrad, Dostoyevsky, Saul Bellow—or anyone else whose contributions he finds of aid in projecting his own unique vision.

As a fellow writer I am delighted that Forrest's novels reveal the play of a mind that enjoys the challenging confounding and revelatory process of fictional creation. In other words, Forrest is a <u>happy</u> liar in the interest of truth. For him telling an engaging tale is no mere matter of entertaining the reader, nor is it one of demonstrating to his peers that he has mastered the latest fashions in novelistic communication. Rather, it is a matter of achieving clarification, or sharpening the reader's perceptions through the vivid projection of a complex moral vision arrived at through a careful attention to the way things happen. Thus at his most comic he is a perceptive teacher, and at his most tragic he exhorts us to embrace the fullness of the human condition with courage. In my opinion Northwestern is most fortunate in having him as a member of its community of scholars.

Sincerely yours,
Ralph Ellison

To John Callahan
730 Riverside Drive
New York, New York 10031
January 17, 1978

Dear Mr. Callahan:

The "historical frequencies" phrase of your essay's title so intimidated me that I began reading it in fear and trembling. This, perhaps because

I've deliberately kept myself only vaguely aware of my preoccupation with history—or at least with the intricacies of its American uses and misuses. Nevertheless, remembering your book on Fitzgerald, I plunged in, became intrigued, and must now confess that you caught me fair and square. Indeed I'm amazed by much of what you've discerned in my writing, and especially by the manner in which you make clear its thematic continuity. And while I can't say that I've grasped all of what you've written, I <u>can</u> say that I shall re-read it many, many times.

Which is only as it should be, for not only is the writing first-rate in itself, it is also one of the most perceptive and appreciative criticisms to come my way. And while this has done wonders for my morale—not to mention my ego—there have been more practical benefits. Thus I am in your debt for your comments on "Society, Morality and the Novel" for a quite practical reason. For some time now Mike Harper, James Alan McPherson and Al Murray—among others—have referred to the piece, but it was your citation that finally persuaded me to see just what their comments were all about. Having put it aside after it was rejected for inclusion in *Shadow and Act* (1964), I was in for something of a surprise. And not only by what you made of what I had struggled to say, but also by its brashness and ineptness; what with its mixed metaphor whereby I have touchstones inflating (Perhaps I was thinking of expanded micas) and becoming wandering rocks! But now, despite its howling defects (which can, I hope, be corrected), I'm thinking, thanks to you, of including it in the collection of essays I'm toying with putting together.

And again, thanks to you, I was able to locate the transcription of the Southern Historical Association's exchange on the novel and history. That was a most pleasant interval in New Orleans, and upon reading the exchange I found myself roaring with laughter over the vividly recovered memory of Bill Styron's slapping away at the persistent attacks of his impassioned "<u>bete noir.</u>" Given the position I took in that exchange, it was as though Bill's gadfly had been set up just to give substance to my arguments. Of course he hadn't been; besides, such passion is evoked only in those who are inspired by a "sacred" cause. Our common racial identity notwithstanding, I'd be afraid to mention Nat Turner in the presence of such a man.

Returning to your essay, I was reminded dramatically of the fact that a writer can never anticipate or be fully conscious of where his imagination will carry him. Nor can he anticipate into what thematic territory that has been earlier and more artfully explored he might, all unknowingly wander. Therefore I was just about knocked out of my chair by the connection which you draw between the dream sequence in "Tell It Like It Is, Baby" and "My Kinsman, Major Molineux." Suspecting that you were perhaps being more creative than critical (if that is possible), I grabbed up Hawthorne's stories—and I'll be damned if you weren't right on target. I only wish that I'd had your insight when writing the essay because I'm sure that I would have made it more of a piece. Since I had forgotten the essay your examination was meaningful both for what you say and for having restored it to a place in my working memory. What's more, I now realize just why I forgot it: After I had given it to a usually insightful friend to read his exasperated response had been, "Well, I read it, but what the hell is it?" So rather than try to spell it out for him—and myself—I simply banished it from memory. And this, perhaps, because I was aware that when one attempts to mix literary modes in the interest of making disparate materials into rhetorical wholes one runs the risk of leaving structural holes—YET! I knew also that most of my essays tend to be somewhat "mammy-made" or eclectic, so my friend's annoyed reaction led me to conclude that the piece was a total failure. Now, its holes and tatters aside, I'm pleased to have raised it back to consciousness. And so, all things considered, you've made this a most redemptive holiday season and I am most grateful.

Incidentally, I am delighted that you approved of the Harper-Stepto interview's reference to Fitzgerald. I've touched on him again in an essay published in the current issue of *The American Scholar*, and if you haven't seen it I'd be pleased to mail it to you.

In closing, let me say that I remain disappointed that I missed the opportunity of having a real talk with you and your wife when I was out your way, so should you come to New York and have the time I hope you'll give us a ring. Our number is WA. 6-6804.

Sincerely yours,
Ralph Ellison

Mr. John Callahan
Department of English
Lewis and Clark College
Portland, Oregon 97219

To John Taggart
FEBRUARY 27, 1979

Dear John Taggart:

Now that our apartment is more or less back to normal, with heat, hot and cold water and the absence of distressing midnight calls warning of more burst pipes—I'm at last getting around to thanking you and Mrs. Taggart for your kindness during my trip to Shippensburg. Despite my tiredness and my dissatisfaction with my performance, I did, thanks to you, enjoy myself.

Usually such jaunts leave me exhausted, but this time I <u>arrived</u> exhausted and it was your talk of your days at the University of Chicago, of mutual friends and of jazz that served to revive me. I only wish that there had been time to really listen to your stereo system while exploring your record collection. In fact, I would have enjoyed even hearing your comments on that mass of Coltrane!

Which is to say that I'm always interested in the play of a poet's mind, and especially when it recognizes the richness of jazz. Unfortunately, the majority of poets I know are most uneducated—and uninterested—in this area of our culture: Thus the fact that you were able to collect so many poems inspired by a single jazzman was for me a most pleasant and instructive experience. Writers of my generation seem to make little or nothing of the fact that both Louie and Eliot were washed by ole man Mississippi, while you appear to have been born knowing that, despite its many divisions, American culture is of a whole. Anyway, perhaps it's no accident that both Eliot and Armstrong were great quoters and masters of the art of juxtaposition: men who knew how to use whatever there was to use, and in original ways. I guess I could go on and riff awhile on that notion, but this is not the time, so I won't. But I'm sure you understand.

Please give my regards to Miss Bontempo and her friend for getting me to the airport under such difficult conditions. Tell her that I apologize for not having thanked them in person. Unfortunately, upon our arrival we were a bit too pushed for time to observe the amenities, I had intended to check my ticket and return to the car, but I was told to go immediately to the loading area, and then when I started through the security checking apparatus my coins, watch, metal pens, pencils and keys started that electronic device beeping so insistently that soon, in the process of divesting myself of offending metal, I had resurrected the old Cha-cha-cha much to the guards' amusement and my annoyance. And once I was through the mercifully silent gate and had collected my belongings it was too late to return to the gracious young ladies. Come to think of it, I encountered not a single snotty student, a fact that I consider quite remarkable.

Thanks again for your kindness and should you find yourselves in New York my wife and I would be pleased to see you.

Sincerely yours,
Ralph Ellison

Mr. John Taggart
Lyceum Committee
Shippenburg State College
Shippensburg, Pa. 17257

To Herbert
LINCOLN HILL ROAD
PLAINFIELD, MASS, 01070
SEPTEMBER 18, 1979

Dear Herbert:

Here enclosed is the check for your round-trip fare to Oklahoma City and back. I hope that you'll be able to learn what's going on with Bert,[*] her physical condition, and the state of her personal affairs. I feel there's a certain urgency about this, considering her recent operation and weakened condition. Therefore I suggest that you ask her directly for answers to the following questions:

> Did Tom leave a Will, and if so, where is it?
> Did he have a lawyer, and if so what is his name?
> Who precisely is Carmen, and what is her legal status in relationship to Tom's estate?
> If there is a Will ask her if it has been probated.
> And ask her about property, taxes, debts and mortgages, whether she has a Will and who her heirs are.

---

[*] "Bert" refers to Alberta Othello Brown, the wife of Tom Brown, Ralph and Herbert's first cousin. Ralph hopes she will be able to supply important information about the condition in which the recently deceased Tom left his personal affairs. For this information we are indebted to Ralph's cousin Muriel Morisey's excellent but thus far unpublished recent memoir, "Ellison's Kin."

As I understand it, Carmen's mother was Tom's father's daughter, making the mother Tom's half-sister. Thus, there is a question as to Carmen's legal designation as a niece. Tom told me that he had fallen in love with Carmen's mother and when he informed his own mother that he wished to marry her she revealed their blood relationship, which made marriage impossible. It would seem, therefore, that there is a question as to Carmen's legal status as a niece. Should any contention arise over Tom's estate, these facts should have a bearing.

I'm sure that you've thought of these and other questions on your own and I offer them so that you'll know my thinking on this matter. Most of all, you might keep in mind that Bert has been of strong spirit and has undoubtedly lived with the reality of death for years. Therefore I think that you can talk quite frankly about these matters, while stressing that you've returned home to help in any way that you can. If Bert does not have a Will, ask if she wishes you to get a lawyer to draw up a Will. A Will will prevent confusions after she's gone.

I'm sure that you'll get Jim's advice on how to proceed if there is anything about which to proceed. I think it very important that you learn if there is a Will and Carmen's position.

That's about it. As I told you in the spring, I have no desire for anything out there except the photographs which Bert promised me plus old letters that were exchanged between our father and Tom's mother and any old papers, letters, documents relating to the Ellison family. Beyond such items, whatever else intended for me is yours.

Please give our love to Madeleine and Jim, and take care of yourself and let us hear from you.

Yours sincerely,
Ralph

Mr. Herbert Ellison
5742 Mullen Ave.
Los Angeles, Calif. 90043

To Robert O'Meally
LINCOLN HILL ROAD
PLAINFIELD, MASS. 01070
SEPTEMBER 28, 1979

Dear Mr. O'Meally:

Please forgive the delay.

I have crossed out two of the quotes from the unpublished sections of my interview with Hollie West. The first because it might give the reader the impression that I solicited an introductory letter to Miss Savage.* I did not, therefore I object to the way you've put it because it slights the role played here by Miss Hamlin. She wrote the letter out of her own enthusiasm for my prospects as a sculptor and by way of encouraging a student who was far less interested in that art than in music. Thus while the fact that she did so is of minor significance in a "book of literary criticism," in the briar patch of my autobiography her generosity was most meaningful.

The second quote contains a distortion that is much more serious. When I presented Miss Savage with Miss Hamlin's letter she explained that her duties as a supervisor on a W.P.A. arts project made it impossible for her to instruct me, and that was that. I was never her student. Thus my study with Mr. Barthé had nothing to do with the quality of Miss Savage's work, with my opinion of it, or any dissatisfaction that I could have had with her as a teacher. Actually, I had learned of Mr. Barthé from Mr. Hughes and Dr. Alain Locke, both of whom were enthusiastic, before I presented Miss Hamlin's letter to Miss Savage, and it was after learning that she was unable to instruct me that I asked Mr. Hughes to put me in touch with Mr. Barthé.

These are the facts and I hope you will make the necessary corrections.

Sincerely,

Ralph Ellison

---

* Augusta Savage, a prominent sculptor in Harlem when Ellison went to New York in 1936.

To Jimmy Stewart
LINCOLN HILL ROAD
PLAINFIELD, MASS. 01070
OCTOBER 8, 1979

Dear Jimmy:

From the nineteenth to the twenty-first of September Brown University held a most unlikely event which they labeled 'The Ralph Ellison Festival." When I was approached with the idea both Fanny and I were struck with horror, and all the more so because of our awareness that only last year Brown had so honored the memory of Dr. Inman Page. But what could I do? It was a great if intimidating honor and besides, Dr. Page had never allowed me to get away with anything when we were students; therefore, suspecting that he was giving me an order from beyond the grave, I agreed.

Well, for all our fears, it turned out to have been quite a serious, dignified and, in a sense, an historical occasion. Dr. Page, as you know, was the first Negro graduate of Brown where he was the orator of his graduating class. This accounts for his having been honored last year, and since I was one of his students there was thus an historical link between last year's and this year's festival. Therefore as a bridge between the two occasions, things began with my being presented with Richard Yarde's study in watercolor of the oil portrait of Dr. Page for which he was commissioned last year by the university.

The presentation took place in the Rockefeller Library with both the study and the finished oil exhibited on easels surrounded by flowers. It was a most moving occasion, during which I shared some of my memories of Dr. Page with an enthusiastic audience. The oil now hangs in the library and the enclosed is a Polaroid of the study that hangs temporarily on the wall of our summer place here in Plainfield, Massachusetts. I felt most inadequate to be placed in the august company of Dr. Page, but since there is no question but that he was a root influence and father figure for us all I steeled myself and tried to make the most of the opportunity by describing something of his and Mrs. Breaux's creative roles in the educational and cultural affairs of Oklahoma and, ultimately, of the U.S.A.

Judging from all reports, things appeared to have gone very well, and if true there are now quite a few students, both black and white, who are a little more aware of how, starting with Dr. Page in 1877, ideals, ideas, and educational techniques which he discovered at Brown continued to influence receptive minds in Oklahoma. If you ask me, they were two teachers who triumphed over both racism and the backwardness of some of our people simply by doing that which they elected to do even under the most difficult of conditions. Certainly I know of no one other than Mr. Dunjee who did more to make American ideals and a sense of American possibility manifest in the lives of young Oklahoma Negroes.

One is seldom afforded the opportunity to pay homage to those who touched his life so profoundly as Dr. Page and Mrs. Breaux, so while the critics and scholars devoted their time to analyzing and discussing my writings, I concerned myself with that famous son and daughter. Incidentally, the theme of Oklahoma and 'going to the territory' (both Indian and Oklahoma) was sounded throughout the three days discussion, so you might say that it was as much a celebration of Oklahoma as it was of one of its sons. Thanks to the good doctor we all inherited some of the spirit and the ideals which he picked up at Brown, and that in itself was enough to justify my being there.

Incidentally, the entire program was organized by Michael Harper, a young Negro poet who is a professor at Brown and not in Black Studies but in the Department of English.

Strange things continue to happen. I retired in September from New York University, having become sixty-five last March, and after those amazing days in Providence, I returned to find a letter informing me that I had been granted the title of Professor Emeritus! Mr. Page must have chuckled over that one and recalled how he once chased me off the campus of old Douglass.

We shall return to Riverside Drive at the end of October, so the next time you're in New York come by and see the portrait. In the meantime, let me thank you again for locating Bert for us. We had spent a great deal of time trying to reach her with no success, and although there's little that we can do for her at this distance, now thanks to you she is at least aware that we're anxious to do whatever we can.

Take care of yourself, give our regards to May Lois and we hope to see you soon.

Sincerely,
Ralph

P.S. I would appreciate your informing Lee Brawner about the Brown occasion; it might be useful to the Ellison Branch library.

To John Callahan
730 RIVERSIDE DRIVE
NEW YORK, N.Y. 10031
NOVEMBER 19, 1979

Dear John.

This brief note is to assure you that I'll be more than happy to recommend you for a Guggenheim. Their material arrived in this week's mail and I'll get to it promptly. Meanwhile, I asked Harper, who called earlier, to convey this message to you, as I expected that he would be in touch with you sooner than this note could reach you.

I must say, I had no idea of your full academic background and I'm most impressed by what I learned. You are one smart cookie. Power to you! In all the colors of the rainbow!

Thank you for your print-off of ". . . Images of Kin" and for your letter. We'll talk it all out when next we dine, and we're going to miss seeing you this holiday and perhaps next summer too since we take off for Plainfield as soon as the ground is dry enough to plant. However, we hope some business will bring you this way sooner.

Fanny says, yes, we will welcome the pears. Pears are one of the few fruits that I can eat with comfort and with appetite. We hope the chore of packing and shipping will not be too burdensome. Do what you can conveniently.

Although Michael sent you a Xerox of my "Perspective of Literature," I am enclosing a printed copy for more convenient reading.

Until next time, all the best

Sincerely,
Ralph

Mr. John Callahan
Lewis and Clark College
Portland, Oregon 97219

Letters from the
Eighties
and Nineties

FOR SIXTY YEARS, FROM 1933 TO 1993, RALPH ELLISON'S letters echo the seasons. In the thirties and forties an uncertain, restless, ambitious young man casts the intense light of springtime. During the fifties and sixties the brightness deepens and expands through a long high summer. Gradually, Indian summer arrives with its palette of warm, hazy colors. All the while the earth continues its revolving journey as the last slanting light of autumn brings tinges of wintry blue.

In the last decade and a half of his life, until pancreatic cancer brought on a swift death in April 1994, Ellison worked to restructure, fill in gaps, and write transitions that he hoped might bring together the parts of his ambitious, tragicomic second novel. Unfortunately, he did not succeed. He does not directly address why, yet between the lines of these wonderful letters he tells the story of his work and life with an intensity that extends and enhances the reach of the Ellison canon.

IN JUNE 1979 ELLISON retires from the Albert Schweitzer Chair at NYU and enters the homestretch of his life. Some of the letters he writes in the eighties and early nineties have the autumnal, even wintry quality he increasingly associates with his novel-in-progress, particularly its hero, the Reverend Alonzo Hickman, who in fiction, like Ellison in life, grows older as he tells his story.

In the "Completion of Personality" interviews conducted by John Hersey in 1974, again in 1982, and published with final revisions in 1987, Ellison invokes "that aura of summing up, that pause for contemplation of the moral significance of the history we've been through, that I have been reaching for in my work on this new book." * Reading through Ellison's often contemplative, scrutinizing letters in the order he wrote them in the eighties and nineties, one senses a man heeding time's passing—and sometimes alarmed, as if he himself is now haunted by the riff Invisible Man's grandfather invented for those endless envelopes peopling his grandson's disturbing dream: "Them's years," the old man warned.

Them's years, and the letters written in the eighties are more numerous than those of any other decade save the fifties, as if the autumn of Ellison's life answers summer breath for breath. In many of the later letters Ellison seems to answer an inner call that urges him to take stock of what Yeats called "heart mysteries": his ever swelling novel-in-progress; the people and places left behind in Oklahoma; the vernacular challenge posed by his fiction and his experience of American culture; the vulnerability involved in negotiating the disappointments and pleasures of friendship; and Ellison's strong compulsion to set the record straight on matters of the heart and mind, ranging from the particulars of his relationship with Richard Wright to distressing mistakes made in print about his life and words by those who ought to have known better.

UNTIL THE EARLY 1990S the novel-in-progress hovers over the letters—sometimes a swollen moon struggling to enter its last phase, other times a barometer able to register literary morale and moods from gladness to dejection. Sometimes the work-in-progress seems a task Ellison's assigned himself, as when he responds to Jacques Barzun's congratulations on the thirtieth edition of *Invisible Man* by noting his "dismally low rate of publication . . . at a time when I'd hoped to have at least two more novels in print" before he adds with a touch of wistfulness and melancholy hope, "I still have a chance." A year later, in 1983, he tells Kenneth Burke he would "have no desire to undertake" a sequel to *Invisible Man,* since he's "hav-

* " 'A Completion of Personality': A Talk with Ralph Ellison," in *The Collected Essays of Ralph Ellison,* ed. John F. Callahan, 821.

ing enough trouble just making a meaningful form out of my yarn concerning a little boy preacher who rises to high estate and comes asunder."

A meaningful form: those words lead him to characterize the steep climb
facing him in the second novel. "There are all kinds of interesting incidents
in it, but if they don't add up it'll fall as rain into the ocean of meaningless
words." Perhaps Ellison has in mind Burke's narrative schema, "Purpose
to Passion to Perception"—the rhetorical trajectory that helped him shape
Invisible Man—when he muses: "I guess what's bothering me . . . is working out a form for the NEXT PHASE of which you write." Then he ends
in a simple, charged assertion: "Anyway, I'm still writing."

Them's years . . .

With their passing, a reader hears notes of futility. In February 1986,
after a long and generous letter devoted to a detailed criticism of Horace Porter's draft of a first novel that included marvelous commentary on
Fitzgerald's *Gatsby*, Ellison refers in passing to "my notorious novel-in-
progress." Two months later he declines Bill Ferris's invitation to speak
on Faulkner at the Center for Southern Culture with a resigned confession that "work on my long overdue novel seems to progress as slowly as
ever." One imagines the author of *Invisible Man* shaking his head as he acknowledges his "own unruly demon." In early 1987, after the exhilaration
of publishing his well-received collection of essays, *Going to the Territory*,
he writes *New York Review of Books* editor Bob Silver that he's "unable to
work on my novel," and shortly thereafter he tells Gilbert Jones that he's
"taking a beating from my writing."

Yet!

Let that one word Ellison was fond of be a counterstatement against
exaggerating his melancholy. For the old, strong, satisfying writer's confidence returns in a late October 1987 letter to John Kouwenhoven. We
"hoped that we'd make it north to see you," he closes. "But as things
turned out my writing reached a point that I dared not interrupt, no matter the sweltering weather." Ellison's tongue-in-cheek allusion to fate and
necessity in relation to the unfinished second novel recalls the fire in his
belly when some thirty-five years earlier, during 1950 and 1951, he moved
heaven and earth, inside and outside himself, to finish *Invisible Man*.

Even more upbeat is his answer to a letter his longtime friend Jim
McPherson wrote in May 1989 and sent along with a story by a student at
the Iowa Writers' Workshop. Ellison reads the young writer's description
of "teenagers bopping downtown D.C. with boom-boxes" and laughs out
loud. Not, he makes clear, because it brings back the past in the form of

the memorable zoot suiters he put into *Invisible Man* but rather because in the present moment he feels himself the young woman's contemporary *as a writer*. "For it so happened that when the clipping of her story arrived I'd just been editing a scene in my work-in-progress wherein an old white-haired Negro trickster (like me, he's too old and full of Afro-American folklore and guile to've become a born-again African on such short notice!) . . . goes slow-dragging along a downtown D.C. street toting a radio from which the <u>Jelly-roll Blues</u> is blaring. I don't know whether the coincidence was a matter of life imitating art or of art imitating life, but whatever the case may be I took it as hilariously affirmative."

Vividly hailing his novelist's living vocation, Ellison holds his ground and invokes the stance he takes throughout the novel-in-progress that tragicomedy is a bold guide to the black (and white) American scene: "Our sense of comedy is one of our hard-earned weapons of survival, the American blackness of our laughter our saving grace."

FROM THEN ON THE LETTERS in the last years of his life, from June 1989 through June 1993, are silent about the novel-in-progress; this despite the computer discs, printouts, and typed and handwritten partial manuscripts mounting up in his study, and despite the interview he gives to David Remnick, two months before his death, that testifies to substantial composition and revision of scenes and passages indisputably part of the second novel.

Yet Ellison's letters before and after 1989 show plenty of other unfinished business preoccupying him. Some of the things he continues to brood over and determines to put right are matters having to do with friendship and the literary record, especially "the controversy over my relationship with Dick Wright," a recurring fishbone in his throat "so annoying that I'd just about decided that those involved in promoting it are either incapable of understanding the complexity of friendship or have deliberately distorted matters in the interest of their notion of an artist-intellectual father-son relationship between Wright and myself."

In 1982 Ellison uses French scholar (and Wright biographer) Michel Fabre's request for comments on a manuscript Fabre has written as an occasion to offer his own perspective. "Things were bad enough when my warm memories of the relationship were chilled when I learned of entries in Wright's journal in which he wrote of my father as having committed suicide and of myself as having been under psychoanalysis. . . . But having been long familiar with Dick's exaggerations and his tendency to project his own feelings of inadequacy upon others, and having no way of reaching him beyond the grave, I could only hope that in time some of the truth would come to light." Rehearsing several professional and personal actions of Wright's, which surprised him at the time and which remained vivid and apparently painful, Ellison tells Fabre that long ago "I concluded that whatever they were, the contradictions went with our friendship."

Ellison has grown to accept Wright's "contradictions" and lapses of loyalty as the baggage of friendship. Yet distortions by others of the "quite complex" friendship he enjoyed with Wright continue to disturb his peace and quiet. A 1988 letter in which he chastises scholar Robert O'Meally for using sources carelessly and mistakenly is a case in point:

> Therefore be warned that your information leaves me damn near as annoyed with Garson and Pierson as I was with you when I reached page 48 of your *Craft of Ralph Ellison* and found my phrase regarding Richard Wright, "too driven or deprived or inexperienced" distorted into "too driven or deprived or depraved." For I consider this distortion of my meaning (how the hell does one equate, misread, or debase a lack of experience into depravity?) as being so blatantly insidious—especially when attributed to me as a friend of Wright—that it couldn't possibly have escaped either your eye or that of your editor. Therefore the fact that it got past both of you left me baffled, and I still wonder if I wasn't used to voice an opinion regarding Wright that was not my own. I needn't remind you that it has been picked up and used against me as proof of my alleged anxiety over Wright's influence.

Ellison then proceeds to offer meticulous clarification on important matters of biography and folklore. Along the way he offers his view that "when it comes to scholarly accounts of my life and work the details of my own lived experience are to be preferred to another's uninformed speculations. In fact that is why I'm taking time to respond to your letter. Besides that, I consider your explorations of the blues more important than my annoyance. May they be successful—and scholarly!"

In effect, without yielding his point or flinching from conflict, Ellison forgives past lapses in favor of betting on future possibility. What matters is *the work, the work*—the writing to come, not past errors or "annoyance." (A year later Ellison's austere generosity becomes unstinting praise for O'Meally's *New Essays on Invisible Man:* "I'm also grateful for your giving some of the novel's history, much of which I'd either ignored or forgotten." Clearly O'Meally's collection, in particular his fine introduction, puts him in Ellison's pantheon of "home-boys" who *have* learned to do their "home-work.")

Perhaps Ellison lays the ghost of Richard Wright to final rest in a letter to Michel Fabre early in 1989 occasioned by Margaret Walker's tendentious biography of Wright. Explaining his own childhood fascination with France and his debt to the fiction of André Malraux, he writes simply, scrupulously, of the reciprocity governing his and Wright's friendship: "Which is not to say that I learned <u>nothing</u> from Richard, because I did, and for that I am most grateful. Nevertheless, and as is usually true of such relationships, ours was a free-wheeling exchange of ideas and experience in the process of which he learned a few things from me as I learned quite a number from him."

For Ellison, mutual learning is an important tender of friendship. And in this more and more autumnal decade friendship is on his mind. A 1987 letter to his old friend Richard Wilbur testifies to the strong pull the ethics of friendship exerts on him, and calls to mind Cicero's famous treatise "De Amicitia." For Ellison the apparent issue at stake, a mutual acquaintance's homosexuality, is a smokescreen, a convenient distraction from facing and keeping faith with deeper, timeless matters of duty required by friendship—duties he views as close to those of citizenship. On point here is Ellison's response to being called a patriot in print by another scholar, also a close friend. Agreeing, Ellison makes sure to take the trouble to refine the matter properly. "My problem," he replies, is "to affirm while resisting," and perhaps there is no better example of the complexity that he insists is the marrow of human relationship.

Ellison continues to take pains to keep in touch with old friends from Oklahoma City and from other points east, west, north, and south with whom he struck up friendships over the decades. His letters to old friends in Oklahoma City about the past might have made notes for an autobiography.* They also exhibit a healthy interest in and tangible grasp of the present lives led by those he writes to and their families—the kind of conscientiousness that keeps friendship alive as time slides inexorably by.

Hearing from Odette Harper Hines, an old friend from the Federal Writers' Project during the late 1930s and early 1940s, Ellison confesses to concluding that "I had failed you by not taking part in the marches etc." The pleasure he takes at her awareness of *Invisible Man* and the news

---

* The closest Ellison got was an unfinished second-person draft manuscript called *Leaving the Territory.*

that she herself is a published writer cause him to "realize that you hadn't given up on me entirely, but that indeed you were aiding in my part of the struggle. It will amuse you to learn that certain younger friends now tease me by recalling that they first came across such slogans as 'Black is Beautiful' and Jesse Jackson's 'rainbow' notion—which they find on page 291—in *I.M.* As Fats Waller said, 'One never knows, do one?'"

Trenchantly signified by Waller's virtuoso "incongruous juxtaposition of elevated and vulgar styles," Ellison's allegiance to the vernacular is another abiding, animating presence in his correspondence. In a fine 1984 letter to the young Henry Louis Gates Jr., Ellison recommends that "you try not to load too much of your erudition upon the backs of us slender reeds. Rather, reveal to us dummy's the extent, if any, that ole Mose is hiding in Henry James's word-pile."

Certainly Henry James having a wordpile is an idea to conjure with, and a year or so later Ellison does just that. Writing Hugh Kenner to thank him for sending *Jamesian Travesty,* a witty computer simulation of Henry James's style, Ellison excavates James's wordpile, only to find a vernacular stash of his own. "Some of its phrases remind me of Afro-American folk idiom and suggest the possibility that that form of American speech was always sounding beneath the sonorities of old Henry's prose; and this much in the manner that the issues of the Post-Reconstruction might possibly have found their way into works less concerned with public matters than *The Bostonians.*" Surely no one doubts the elevated style of James, but where, oh where is the vernacular? After the pause of a paragraph break Ellison comes to the rescue: "That's wishful thinking, I know, but the phrase, 'She rare woman' suggests the Harlem street kids' 'She be <u>fine,</u> man!'" And Ralph Ellison is just warming up:

> I hear overtones of bawdiness that I'm sure—but not <u>too</u> sure—that Henry James, who disdained the "unutterable depths of the bastard vernacular," would have found outrageous:
>
> "She rare women, he had something so tremendous after ashes of light . . ."
>
> Could the computer mean that Chad (or was it dear Strether—I daren't look at *The Ambassadors*) had "hauled" the good lady's "ashes"? I ask because here sex is as understated as the theme of abortion in Hemingway's famous story.
>
> ". . . But it's very right to go on with a cynicism of courage—from something to thing."

Finally, Ellison booms out: "Amen! And with a courage born of cynicism—if need be!"

From his renewed, computer-inspired joy at James's vernacular, Ellison flips to James Joyce, that Black Irish master of vernacular, and a passage from his precious signed copy of *Anna Livia Plurabelle,* which he bought in a bookshop on Harlem's 125th Street in the late thirties for a buck twenty-five.

Whom but Ralph Ellison can one imagine riffing this way and that on behalf of the American vernacular, all the while in cahoots with a computer?

THESE LAST LETTERS—THESE LETTERS from the eighties and nineties—will not unravel the mysteries or solve the Sphinx's riddle of why Ralph Ellison did not finish his second novel. However, they do show him regaining the "delight of corresponding," something he told Richard Wright he had lost after *Invisible Man*'s publication. Although vibrant, this delight is no longer a young man's delight, but the subtle, rich satisfaction of a man savoring the smoldering, melancholy fire of age.

Intriguingly, soon after his last words to Jim McPherson in June 1989 about the novel-in-progress, he writes Claire Thiebault, a perfect stranger, thanking her for "reassuring [him] that *Invisible Man* still casts a spell," but not before assuring *her* that "a novel is like a rocket which the novelist shapes to the best of his ability" until "each reader recreates a different book by playing his or her own variations on the writer's all too limited picture of reality."

In the dozen letters of his last four years, though he is hard at work on the second novel, Ellison does not mention his writing. His letters are to Bill Dawson about Tuskegee days; to Lowry Ware about that man's exemplary work on (and Ellison's own boyhood memories of) his grandfather Big Alfred Ellison, a former slave; to Dick Lewis, praising his original storytelling biography of the James family and the mysterious territory it has opened to Ellison; and, last but not least, to Willie Morris, swapping tales about memories revived by the contradictions of reality, past and present.

Day to day it seems likely that Ralph Ellison knows he is giving himself to a novel he would not live to complete. Yet he does not break. Instead, the last letters feed a silent spring of creativity that spurs him to carry on as far as he can with his life and his novel-in-progress of more than forty years.

John F. Callahan

Ralph Ellison
Star Route 91-A
Plainflied, MA 01070

Mr. Romare Bearden
357 Canal Street,
New York, NY 10013

Sept. 8, 1986

Dear Romie:

Your letter was forwarded to me here in the Berkshires and I was both pleased and surprised. Pleased, because you liked the essays, saw how they link up, and recieved a laugh or two (thank God you busted no stiches!), and surprised because while you're the Bear-den who told me about Brer Rabbit's adventure in a bear's den ("Don't a mother move, Brer Rabbit cried"), I can't recall recieving a letter from you before. Greeting cards with your own art, yes--and some still grace our walls--but over all the years I can't remember a single letter. I'm also glad that you required no surgery and assume that by now you're back at your painting.

It might interest you to know that the essays are being reviewed all over the country, and for the most part quite favorably. True, a few reviewers complained that the book wasn't a novel,but then they reviewed the collection for whatever they perceived it to be. One thing is certain, it was assigned to quite a number of Negroes, all good writers, so if it comes to nothing else it gave them something write and think about. It even made the bulletin board of the local post office,which reminded me of the many time I was warned that if I didn't stop lying and messing around I would end up in the boy's reformatory, and probably graduate from there to McAlester, which meant that I'd land in the Oklahoma State Penitentiary. So you

1

can be sure that when I saw my photograph on that post office wall I was relieved that it hadn't been placed among the Ten Most Wanted! The essays, incidently, are already schedueled for paperback next year and I hope that they will indeed be counted among the most wanted.

Thanks for the clipping from the TLS,which I found quite interesting. Mellers is an insightful critic and after reading him I'd like to see Porgy_and_Bess again. Its text renders it cold for Fanny, but every now and then I find myself humming its Lullaby and whistling Bess' love aria to Porgy. Thar's good black artistic gold in them stereotypes, so instead of being thrown off by the crap it's best to seek it out, learn from it,and transcend it.

Because,like it or not, it is the vitality of Afro-American artistic and cultural style which lends such work its interest and endurance. After all these years some of us are still beefing over Huckleberry_Finn—which raise questions as to what makes it an enduring work of literature, and surely it's not because of its epithets. I'd like to give such people the advice given a mouthy,knuckle-headed character in an early musical (probably by Bert Williams):

"Brother,go 'way back and sit down!" To which I'd add, "And while you're at it, do yourself some reading!"

We hope things go well with you and yours, and again my thanks.

                                             Sincerely

2

To Herbert Ellison
LINCOLN HILL
PLAINFIELD, MA. 01070
AUGUST 28, 1981

Dear Herbert:

I am sure that by now Michael has told you that we have been trying to reach you. In fact since last winter we've tried many times to phone you, and the same is true of Jim and Saretta, who tried to reach you a couple of weeks ago when she was in L.A. Could it be that you've put all of us down?

If so, you might have at least done us the courtesy of dropping us a postcard to let us know it. And if not, you might have notified us that you were giving up your telephone, thus saving everybody a lot of worry and wasted time. When the operator told us that your phone had been disconnected we were alarmed; which, given the fact that our last exchange had to do with your having been robbed, is fairly understandable. And all the more so since our only indication that you had received the money for which you asked was our cancelled check, and that not until the following month when our bank statement arrived. We thought this most unlike you and when you failed to respond in any way regarding the three sweaters that we sent you shortly after our last talk, we were indeed most upset.

Nor were we the only ones upset by your sudden silence. I know that Jim tried unsuccessfully to phone you many times before learning your phone was disconnected, and that he tried to make contact with you through Badboy. This went on for months during which we wondered if you were ill or in some other kind of trouble. Finally, two weeks ago, Jim called us here to say that Badboy had at last made contact and that you were all right. And since Jim had told Badboy of our concern, Fanny and I assumed that you would give us a call but that was the extent of our news until Fanny discovered that the number through which we had tried to reach Michael was not the same as that recorded in our 1980 Calendar. Thus we were able to reach Michael, who assured us that he had seen you recently and that you were okay. We were pleased and most relieved but I'd be less than candid if I didn't add that I am also annoyed.

Obviously you have your own reasons for suddenly going silent, but while I respect your privacy I still think that you're showing less consideration for those who care for you than any of us would have suspected, especially since none of us has knowingly offended you. That is at least my opinion. It isn't like you, or hasn't been, to return a favor with silence and I'm not referring to money but to the sheer matter of politeness and of your failing to communicate.

But be that as it may, what I'm really writing you about is to tell you that during our talk of two weeks ago Jim informed us that Madeline had undergone an operation for a brain tumor, which was evidently the source of her long illness. As would be expected he was terribly upset but still took time out to tell us that he was still trying to reach you. I haven't heard from him since and when I tried to reach him last Sunday to learn how she was progressing he was at the hospital. Thus failing to reach him, I called Saretta and Finley, who told me that Madeline's possibilities of recovery were most pessimistic (Jim told me that she was partially paralyzed and failed to recognize him). I myself feel terribly concerned at this development but it is possible that you've turned your back on all of us to such an extent that you're not interested, but if not I suggest it might help Jim if you gave him a call and if need be you can send me the bill. Incidentally, he has finally given up the drugstore and is carrying on with a reduced schedule in Finley's building, with no change in either his business or residential phone numbers. You might also phone Sis, who had also undergone a recent spell of sickness. In the meantime we hope you're well and coping.

Sincerely,
Ralph

To Michael Harper

SEPT 3, 1981

Dear Michael:

Thanks for all the goodies, and especially the copy of R.W's letter.* She is indeed a fine reader and I appreciate the opportunity for seeing how fluent she has become . . . Since Monday morning when I drove Fanny to Northampton for her monthly bus ride to NYC I've had one hell of a time. My typewriter had gone out on me so after dropping her at the bus station I hauled it down to Springfield to I.B.M. for repairs, I then drove to Westborough, a suburb of Boston to an electronic lab where a friend had been holding a rack for my audio equipment. A professional item,

---

*   Perhaps Rosanna Warren, daughter of Red Warren and Eleanor Clark.

it is very heavy and unconsciously hi-tech, but once the stuff is installed in it a thief would have one hell of a time getting it out. Well, three of us managed to get it <u>into</u> the back seat of the car, but when I returned here I discovered that there was no way of my undoing that which had required three of us to do; therefore I left it in the car for the night and decided that I'd be much better at solving mechanical puzzles after a drink, a meal and a good night's sleep. I was wrong. After two hours of sweating and cussing I concluded that there was no way that one man was going to get the dam thing out so I took drastic measures. No, I didn't use TNT but I did the next best thing: I removed the door. It worked but it remains to be seen whether I succeeded in replacing the door correctly, nevertheless, I matched cake of oil and grease with cake of dust and grease, torqued the bolts and slammed it shut. My next trip will test it . . . I've reread C. Davis's piece and wonder how he concluded that Baldwin and I were ever friends. We were cordial but never close—and I mean in <u>any</u> sense of the term. But while he and W. were friends, and W. and I were friends we were never a trio. In fact I can't recall ever being in the same company with the two of them until 1954, and that was in Paris. The first ever heard of Baldwin was back in the 40's—when Wright told me that he was trying to get a Saxon (?) award for a very talented young writer. Which makes Davis wrong again; Baldwin and Wright were friends <u>before</u> 1946 . . . C.D. writes that *The Outsider* was a new departure for Wright, but if so it didn't arrive at the philosophical high point where Davis places it. Can you imagine a D.A. playing psychological cat-and-mouse games with a boot* killer? I can't—or at least Wright failed to convince me that one could. Perhaps there's something wrong with my imagination, but if I know anything about the NYC cops of that period they would have kicked Cross Damon's butt so hard and fast that he would have confessed to killing Abe Lincoln—and been damn glad to do it. Then he would have come up with something more resonant than, "A man alone is nothing." Maybe something like, "How did I ever think I could get away with this bullshit?" W. aimed at a moment of tragic perception but his plot was too absurd to create pity and terror and thus too trivial to give resonance to his hero's statement. If you ask me, Davis read a much better novel than W. wrote.

As for the Flip Wilson tape, don't worry about it. I tried to make you a copy but failed because of a mismatch between my mono and stereo ma-

---

* African American slang for "black."

chines, so it will have to wait until I'm back in N.Y. where I can dub from one stereo machine to the other.

I liked both the Callahan and the Stepto* and shall reread when less harassed . . . Please thank Rachel for the poems. I wish someone had introduced me to Frost when I was her age. Tell her also that there was a Black billed Cuckoo hanging around the garden for over a week but now seems to have left the area, perhaps heading south. He was a handsome fellow and unusual for these parts . . . We had dinner with the Wilburs and O'Malleys last Sat. eve. Much drinking and dancing, good food, conversations. O'Malley played tapes of some of his own compositions, reminding me that he is something other than a lawyer . . . Your news of Roland's cussing reminds me of the summer of my sixteenth year when I worked for a landscape gardener. He was also a Baptist deacon who became so upset one day over the misbehavior of his team of little Spanish mules that he forgot God for a moment and gave them hell in a display of Elizabethan cum down home colored cussing style. He was a past master of the art and after that I kept hoping that one of the crew would annoy him enough to make him show what he could do by way of the dozens. I mark my own cussing from that summer . . . Had a postcard from John† but must wait till he returns to learn what the hell he said.

Love to all from Fanny
and R E.

To Michel Fabre

MARCH 3, 1982

Dear Michel Fabre:

Here are some of my thoughts upon reading your essay,‡ along with a few suggestions and corrections.

---

* Ellison most likely refers to essays by John F. Callahan and Robert B. Stepto published in the winter 1980 *Carleton Miscellany.* This issue was mostly devoted to papers and poems presented at the Ralph Ellison Festival held at Brown University in September 1979. Callahan's essay "Democracy and the Pursuit of Narrative" (in *Moby-Dick, Huck Finn,* and *Invisible Man*) and Stepto's "Literacy and Hibernation: Ralph Ellison's *Invisible Man*" were adaptations of papers delivered at the Brown festival.

† Probably Callahan; almost legendary for his indecipherable, left-handed handwriting.

‡ Most likely Fabre's "From *Native Son* to *Invisible Man:* Some Notes on Ralph Ellison's Evolution in the 1950's," in *Speaking for You: The Vision of Ralph Ellison,* ed. Kimberly W. Benston (Washington, DC: Howard University Press, 1987), 199–216.

Let me begin by saying in all frankness that the controversy over my relationship with Dick Wright has been so annoying that I'd just about decided that those involved in promoting it are either incapable of understanding the complexity of friendship or have deliberately distorted matters in the interest of their notion of an artist-intellectual father-son relationship between Wright and myself. Things were bad enough when my warm memories of the relationship were chilled when I learned of entries in Wright's journal in which he wrote of my father as having committed suicide and of myself as having been under psychoanalysis. For the truth is that my father died of ulcers and I have never been psychoanalyzed. Thus I realized that I had been cast into that fantasy world which led Dick to describe Horace Cayton as fearful of white women (including Dorothy Norman)—Cayton! Who had been the lover of Chicago heiresses long before those areas of society were available to Dick and who was a worldly, sophisticated man by any standards. But having been long familiar with Dick's exaggerations and his tendency to project his own feelings of inadequacy upon others, and having no way of reaching him beyond the grave, I could only hope that in time some of the truth would come to light. Until then I could only wonder as to why it was that none of those involved in the controversy bothered to notice the extent to which my writings and thought were different than Wright's. Perhaps your essay will prod them in such a direction.

As you are aware, my relationship with Dick was fairly complex even when our friendship was most intense. From 1940 on, for instance, I did not show him any of my attempts at fiction because he had become upset by a short story of mine, the style or content of which he saw as an invasion of his territorial claim. After a long interval of silence I had found it necessary to press him for an opinion and his reluctant reply was, "This is my stuff," I was startled by his reaction but I respected his sincerity, and since I was trying like hell to develop my own "stuff," I decided not to bother him with what I regarded as mere five finger exercises in my effort to learn the art of fiction. After that I showed him only my attempts at essays; which, more often than not, he found cluttered with too many ideas for his taste. However, I don't remember him as ever indicating that these were a threat to his territory. I do recall, by the way, that when he read my published review of *Black Boy* he remarked that I had gone . . . "Way beyond the book . . . way beyond the book" . . . I didn't press him as to exactly what he meant because I realized that I had skirted, though ever so tentatively, the area of personal psychology and had tried, as a critic, to suggest what I considered a more fruitful approach to his autobiography than that provided by a stress upon the mere sociology of racial relationships. So in a sense I <u>had</u> gone beyond the book.

As I say, our friendship was quite complex and I was sometimes surprised by Dick's contradictory actions. I had accompanied him when he went to inform his fiancée that he could not marry her, had been his best man when he married Dhima, and had been instrumental in reuniting him with Ellen after his first marriage failed. But when he and Ellen were married I was neither notified nor invited to the wedding. Since I considered him my best friend I was quite surprised—and all the more so when I learned that Ben Davis, whom Dick viewed as an enemy, had taken part. It made me realize that Wright's personal and political lives were mixed in stranger and more surprising ways than I had realized, and that even for a man who took a small boy's delight in surprising his friends. It raised the question of what was conscious, what compulsive, and I concluded that whatever they were, the contradictions went with our friendship.

That said, here now are a few notes that I jotted down while reading your essay.

Page 11: If I was an ideological writer at the time, that ideology was a product of my own intellectual grappling. Nevertheless you're correct in stating that my perspective emphasized the Negroes' rather than the workers' point of view. How could it have been otherwise given the fact that most unions discriminated against us? Over the years things have changed but relatively few Negroes are to be found within the top leadership of the unions. In those days a cousin of mine had been performing the task of a railroad brakeman for many years but his classification (and salary) was that of a porter. In the New York building trades one seldom saw a skilled Negro workman even though there were scores to be seen once you crossed the Mason-Dixon line. So there was no way for me to accept the Communist notion that workers and Negroes were united without a large dose of salt(s).

Page 10: The farm was the property of John and Amelie Bates.

Page 12: I believe that it was a convention of war that the prisoner of highest rank in prison camps became the spokesman and leader of his fellow prisoners.

Page 21: I was not pretending. I respected Wright's freedom to see things as he saw them, but this did not mean that I saw life exactly as he did. After all, we were of different regions, different backgrounds, and different familial circumstances. And don't overlook the fact that I admired what Wright had made of himself. That he could make himself a powerful writer did indeed increase my sense of the possible. But remember also that I had studied with William L. Dawson, the composer and conductor, and with Hazel Harrison, a pupil of Busoni, and that I knew George Washington Carver—all of whom were examples of high possibility. Wright, being close to my own age and having less formal education, simply reaffirmed a sense of possibility that I already possessed. So if I admired him and took his side in controversy it didn't mean that I agreed with him absolutely. I also admired Dr. Carver but I certainly had my criticisms of his personality and of many of his social attitudes.

Page 22: The correct quote is "Between Wright's skill (not Bigger's) and knowledge of the potentials of Bigger's mute feelings, etc. . . ." I'm sure that you will have caught this error, but after having O'Meally misquote me as having written that Wright was too "depraved" when I wrote "deprived" I am a bit sensitive.

Page 23: I probably wrote "least" but I meant "lest" and I'd appreciate it if you would make the correction.

Page 24: You write that "this can be understood to mean that the act of writing equals the actualization of murderous impulses"—and it can, but I meant that writing was a way of <u>transcending</u> such impulses.

Page 25–26: I think there is a difference between the Communist notion of books as weapons and what I meant in this particular instance. I certainly didn't mean a weapon used by someone acting under orders from the Central Committee.

Page 27: I think it would be more to your point if you indicated that Wright granted me permission to reprint "Men in the Making"—which I did.

Page 29: Although Reynal & Hitchcock gave me my first book contract they did not publish *Invisible Man*. For after the death of Mr. Hitchcock a dispute developed between Eugene Reynal and my editors, Frank Taylor and Albert Erskine. When Taylor and Erskine joined Random House my contract was purchased, and thus it was that Random House published the book.

That's it and Good Luck to you.

Sincerely,
Ralph Ellison

Mr. Michel Fabre
c/o Edward Margolies
141 East 3rd Street
New York, N.Y. 10009

To Jacques Barzun
MARCH 23, 1982

Dear Jacques:

For some thirty years now I've been haunted by a a growing sense of the absurdity of being a fairly well-known writer despite my dismally low rate of publication and now, at a time when I'd hoped to have at least two more novels in print, this thirtieth edition business* has fallen upon me and I have neither the will nor a way to escape it. It's as though during some unguarded moment in the past I made a brash wish to become famous and was heard by the gods who soundlessly laughed and said, "Okay, but you won't like it," then proceeded to educate me in the tricky ways of absurdity and wishing.

Actually I am aware that I alone am responsible for this state of affairs for I brought to writing a fledgling musician's sense of form and perfection, I was also badly educated, as stubborn as hell, and in awe of the sheer power of the great novelists. Yes, and perhaps a bit chicken before the possibilities of failure. Thus hearing from you is not only a pleasure but a source of reassurance. For if your way of writing is anything like mine— and I am familiar with some of your many books and had studied Berlioz on instrumentation on my own when still in high school—I still have a chance. At any rate, I'll keep on cooking.

It so happens that we, too, shall be denied the pleasure and/or pain of the Fool's Day meeting, for in order to escape the hubbub of the publication 'event' we're down here in Key West where we own a spot of earth; therefore we won't make it back in time. Speaking of absurdity, being here is like leaping from the frying pan into the fire, but although the weather is in the upper eighties it is quite bearable, the foliage is lush, and there are plenty of writer friends on the scene. We look forward to seeing you in May and in the meantime Fanny and I send you our best regards and thanks.

Sincerely,
Ralph Ellison

---

* Ellison refers to Random House's decision to publish a thirtieth-anniversary edition of *Invisible Man* in March 1982. Though a chore at the time, Ellison's long introduction to the edition is his fullest retrospective statement on his novel's composition, context, and theme. It precedes the text in all editions today.

Mr. Jacques Barzun
Charles Scribner's Sons
597 Fifth Avenue
New York, N.Y. 10017

To Silvia Saunders
MARCH 28, 1982

Dear Silvia Saunders:

There have been many, many responses to Mitgang's piece in the *N.Y. Times*[*] but yours has been all the more delightful for being the most un-expected.

And this is <u>not</u> because we never think of you and your mother; we do indeed think and speak of you both every summer when we're gardening in the Berkshires. Thanks to seeing your peonies years ago we've managed to grow a few ourselves and in reading the literature we frequently come across the name of your father, whom we regard in a legendary light for having brought so much beauty in our lives. Two years ago while still under the spell cast by your garden we planted the peonies, but as of now not a single blossom has appeared. So last fall when we prepared them for the winter I told them that if they didn't do something soon I'd report them to you and they'd be sorry. I hope you'll forgive me for taking your name in vain but if it works—and I'm certain that it will—I'll let you know.

We came down to Key West to escape all the to-do that seems to come even with a special edition of a book that has been in print for thirty years. Fortunately though, we have a small condominium here and enjoy the lush foliage of this tropical isle. The place is full of writers and artists so it isn't at all surprising that we should run into that old Hamiltonite, Frank Taylor, at a recent party. Should we run into him again I'll give him the good news of our hearing from you.

---

[*] "*Invisible Man*—As Vivid Today as in 1952"; Mitgang's article was published in *The New York Times* on Ellison's birthday, March 1, 1982.

Thanks so much for remembering me, and my wife joins me in sending you our best, and, indeed, our appreciation for the Mitgang clipping.

Sincerely,
Ralph Ellison

Miss Silvia Saunders
Griffin Road
Clinton, New York 13323

To Steven Kellman
MARCH 28, 1982

Dear Mr. Kellman:

Thanks for letting me know that I have readers in Soviet Georgia, and for your role in increasing their number. It gives me some of that delayed pleasure which I imagine one receives upon learning that a message launched years before in a sea-borne bottle was actually fished up along a faraway shore and enjoyed by a sympathetic reader. Till now whenever I thought of the possibility of any of my writings finding readers in Russia it was in terms of hunting with a shotgun in thick cover. You fire the gun's broad pattern of pellets in the direction of what is at best a vaguely seen target, and if you are told of the results in the form of royalty payments—well, that's history. But if you missed, or were unable to hear a thud or count a kopek—that, without question, is mystery. And a mystery of international publishing wrapped up in a political enigma at that! Thanks to you, at least some of that mystery has been dispelled.

It might amuse you to learn that back in 1958 when teaching at Bard College I had the gall to offer a course on [the] Russian novel. It turned out to be a fairly popular course, and this despite the fact that I knew nothing of the original language and had to teach from translations. However, I had read, enjoyed and learned a great deal from the Russian novelists and was thus able to translate many of their characters' customs, motives and dilemmas into what were more or less satisfactory American equivalents—even when the closest examples I could arrive at were from Afro-American experience; slave for serf, plantation owner for Russian aristocrat. Things were very lively in that incongruous classroom, and I learned a lot from our little forays into the realm of comparative humanity and culture. Therefore it pleases me immensely to learn that the Georgians find my own writing of interest.

Several writer friends have informed me of their having met Soviet writers who were familiar with my novel, but none were able to tell me how this had come about or if there was an edition of *Invisible Man* available in Russian. I was intrigued because I had known since 1954 that the novel had penetrated another sector of the so-called Iron Curtain. This came at the conclusion of a series of lectures at the Salzburg Seminar when a student who had been silent throughout my several weeks of effort approached my wife and me and proceeded (with tears in her Slavic eyes!) to present me with a copy of the Slovak edition. After weeks of misinterpreting her silence as a sign of ideological disapproval you can image my surprise.

And not only because my novel had been translated into her language as early as the French and German editions, but that its ideological implications were apparently of less importance to those who governed her country than whatever literary merits it was deemed to possess. Thank God for the unexpected. I'm reminded that Malraux held that art, in its broader connotations, is an assault upon logic. Perhaps it is also an assault upon ideology and thus able, once in a great while, to communicate a vision of human experience across the division of politics. I assume that some such thing occurred with the Yugoslavs and if true your letter confirms that the process continues—if only among the Georgians.

At any rate I am most grateful for your thoughtfulness.

Sincerely,
Ralph Ellison

Professor Steven G. Kellman
College of Humanities and Social Sciences
The University of Texas
San Antonio, Texas 78285

To Committee on Admissions, NYU
APRIL 2, 1982

Committee on Admissions
Undergraduate Division
Department of Romance Languages
New York University
19 University Place
New York, N.Y. 10012

I am writing in the interest of a young friend, Sophia Baldwin Lewis, who has expressed a desire to become a member of your student body. Sophie, as she is familiarly known, is the daughter of my old friends Nancy and R.W.B. Lewis. During Sophie's lifetime her father (who is the official biographer of Edith Wharton and an outstanding critic) has been a professor of American Studies at Yale University, and I have known her mother since her undergraduate days at Bennington College. By way of indicating the intricate nature of my relationship with Sophie's family I should add that I am the godfather of her older brother.

Sophia Lewis is a graduate of Connecticut's very fine and demanding Hopkins School that she attended for five years, and while she was by no means one of its leading scholars her work was competent and she was without question one of its most popular students. Perhaps it is the sheer intellectual quality of her background that has been responsible for Sophie's casual attitude toward many of her studies; thus as is often true even of students possessed of the most exceptional abilities her grades are a less than reliable index of either her intellectual abilities or her capacity for hard work. However, I am moved to write on her behalf because I believe that her grades in languages offer a truer indication of her ability to pursue a successful career at New York University.

I am especially impressed by her work in Italian. She has spent many summers in Italy and over the years has acquired more than a classroom familiarity with the Italian language. This became quite clear during the fall of 1981 when she, a sixteen-year old high school senior, more than held her own against junior and senior college students studying Intermediate Italian at Yale. Inspired by this achievement she now wishes to continue her studies in the Department of Romance Languages at New York University. It is my hope that she will be able to do so, for given her intensified interest in her studies and her desire to test herself in a region beyond the immediate beck and call of her family, I don't believe that she could have made a better choice.

Sophie is a fine and rather attractive young woman and I'm sure that you'll find her worthy of your most serious consideration.

Sincerely yours,
Ralph Ellison
Albert Schweitzer
Professor Emeritus in
The Humanities

To Michael Harper
RALPH ELLISON
730 RIVERSIDE DRIVE
NEW YORK, N.Y. 10031
APRIL 30, 1982

Dear Michael,

Thanks for the material on your great-grandfather.* I am delighted to have it and I'm sure that it will resonate in my unconscious whenever I'm trying to conjure up the complexity of his times—and ours. But I'd like to know a little more about <u>his</u> daddy and those Chippewas. It looks as though you're rooted more deeply hereabouts than in the Africa wherein he devoted so much of his energies. Considering all of his traveling it's no wonder that you keep bouncing around; it's in the genes! He was a remarkable human being and I think all of us could profit from knowing more about him.

Williamsburg† was beautiful and we were glad that the meeting came in April rather than in May because it gave us a few weeks head start on spring. But as usual the social activities that accompany our work there were a bit overpowering. I ate too much, drank too much, and didn't sleep enough. And all of this was intensified on our last night there because of the reception for Joseph Cullman's retirement from the board. He's a

---

* Michael Harper's maternal grandfather, John Albert Johnson, an African Methodist Episcopal Church bishop and missionary in South Africa from 1908 to 1916.

† Ellison was the first African American elected a trustee of the Colonial Williamsburg Foundation; he served with dedication and distinction until his mandatory retirement at age seventy in 1984.

resourceful man, well liked, and we'll miss him. However, he was replaced by Edgar Topping, the historian—which makes our board one of the few that has willingly allowed itself to be spooked by the presence of <u>two</u>.

I had hoped that our two trips would get us out of some of the 30th anniversary hoopla—and it did—but we returned to find letters, phone calls and other interruptions. Still there were articles in the papers from coast to coast so I guess a little something will come of it. Incidentally we can't tell from your letters whether you received your copy or not. Thus Fanny wants you to know that she had the publisher mail it to the English office at Brown. So if you didn't get it let us know. Naturally I expect to inscribe it when I see you.

And don't forget to let us see your shots of the library out west. I tried to photograph it myself but the light was bad and the streets too full of traffic to allow for a decent perspective . . . Talked with Leon, who called on my birthday, and advised him to get himself an agent. After all, it's a bit much to expect another writer to look out for his interest, no matter how interested she might be, when the fact of it is that they're working the same side of the street. I don't know what happened with his new ms. but after the egg laid by Angela Davis the publisher might have been reluctant to take another chance with a writer who's as experimental as Leon surely is . . . Thanks for John Wright's review of O'M,* it's hardly what I would have said, but John has no reason for being as subjective as this ole ass-kicker me. Give him my regards . . . If you get down for the doings at the Academy-Institute on May 19th we expect to see you here along with the rest of the liquored-up poets, etc. After that we hope to head for the hills and the woodchucks. Incidentally, if you're wondering what the hell happened to my typewriter, the answer is nothing. I'm doing this on a word-processor—which, to tell the truth, is word-processing me!† I'm trying to master the damn thing as a means of speeding up my rate of production. It appears that it'll take a bit of time to do so, but I'm getting there. I've just finished editing an interview that I did with John Hersey down in Key West but, alas, poor Fanny still has to do the final copy on her typewriter as per usual.

---

* Robert O'Meally's *The Craft of Ralph Ellison* (Cambridge, MA: Harvard University Press, 1980).

† The first letter Ellison wrote on a word processor. From here on almost all were done on his computer.

Our love to you and Shirley and all those chillun, and we look forward to seeing you.

Ralph

To James Randolph
RALPH ELLISON
730 RIVERSIDE DRIVE
NEW YORK, N.Y. 10031
MAY 2, 1982

Dear Jim,

I've called you over the past few months but have been unable to reach you. So knowing something of what you must be going through, I decided to bide my time. Because I also realized that Herbert had also tried to contact you with no more success, even though we'd both called on occasions when the line was busy. But finally, a few days ago, I received a call from Herbert and he gave me the good news that he has spoken not only with you but with Madeline as well. Fanny and I were much relieved and we hope that Madeline's recovery continues.

Fanny and I have been going through a bit of hurly-burly here, thanks to the publication of the thirtieth anniversary edition of my novel, a most unexpected event despite the fact that there have been many editions since it first appeared in 1952. Yet there have been far more interviews than I can recall from the days it was issued, and I'd be a liar if I said that all the new publicity didn't please me.

There have been reporters and photographers, an appearance on the *Today Show*—all apparently set off by an interview in the *New York Times* which appeared, all unknowing to me, on my birthday. All of the new attention is somewhat bewildering but nevertheless satisfying when I consider all of the crap I had to take from some of the so-called Black Radicals during the late '60s and most of the '30s.[*] Still, we tried to escape at least some of the to-do by spending a couple of weeks down in Key West, where we own a small house. The weather was quite a contrast with that of New York, being in the upper eighties, but we enjoyed the tropical lushness. But then we returned here in time for the blizzard and it was as though we hadn't been away. Fortunately, we were able to go south again shortly

[*] Probably Ellison means the '70s here.

afterwards, this time to Colonial Williamsburg, on whose board of directors I've served for a number of years. So there we found spring again, with the foliage in blossom and the birds singing their heads off. It is a lovely part of the country and by now we've become accustomed to working out problems with the likes of old Virginians and the heads of major corporations with whom I'd never dreamed I'd even come within speaking distance. Well, we have and the one thing I've learned is that people are only people and once we are able to come into neutral contact there is much to be learned and much to share, and that included pleasures as well as problems. You should see Fanny by candlelight during a formal dinner in what was once a great plantation mansion! She looks like she was to the manor born—only it took a hell of a time to get her there.

Seriously though, I've learned something of how things really go in this crazy country and I've come to believe that the real root of many of our problems is not race so much as the contention over power. Of course this is but to say the obvious, since the mystique of race is used to confuse the issue, and none are more confused than some of those who would elect to lead us, many of whom know less about how the country operates than a skilled bell-hop or a quietly observant waiter. Americans are contenders for power and in the contending we often become confused as to how our interests coincide, and thus the common human aspects of issues become clouded in terms of who's black and who's white. It's really a miserable bore, but that's what history stuck us, and we'll remain stuck until we realize that there's a hell of a lot more to our predicament than race . . .

Anyway, we're back in our crowded apartment again, living our same old life, and looking forward to the end of the month when we'll take off for the Berkshires and start digging in the earth to get a garden started. Last year our harvest was a bit meager, thanks to two winters of light snowfalls that reduced the level of the water table so drastically that our neighbors had to haul water from other sources. We once had trout in our spring-fed pond, but last summer the water fell so low that one morning when I went out to get the mail I saw foot prints in what had been the bottom of the pond and all that was left of the trout were a few scales and bones. Last winter there were several feet of snow up there, so we're looking forward to a steady flow from the spring and, if we're lucky, we'll restock it with trout.

What has happened to the *Black Dispatch*? They have sent me a complementary copy for years and I miss it. And that's true despite the fact that the guys who're trying to edit don't seem to know their business. I hope it hasn't gone under and would be more than willing to subscribe if they're still active. Poor Dunjee, he must be whirling in his grave! Things certainly change. I saved the photo of the Slaughter Building that was published when you closed the store and I was amazed that they couldn't even get the ownership straight. I really felt sad because, as you know, so much of my life and education took place in that unspectacular building. I can't tell you how much I appreciate what you contributed to whatever I've now become, but I do want you to know that I am aware that you did more than you probably realize. One doesn't often get the opportunity to say thanks, so I'm saying it now. Meanwhile, our love to you and Madeline, and God bless you both.

Ralph

To Charles Etta Tucker
RALPH ELLISON
730 RIVERSIDE DRIVE
NEW YORK, N.Y. 10031
MAY 9, 1982

Dear Charles Etta:

Hearing from you was indeed a surprise, but I am most pleased that you wrote. Not long ago I was thinking of the coincident of your sharing a family name with the president of Wake Forest College, Dr. James Ralph Scales. He too is an Oklahoman, a historian, and an ex-president of Oklahoma A&M. A tall, handsome man, he admits to being 1/16th Indian (I forget the tribe) but he looks like a full-blooded chieftain. When I questioned him about his name he told me that people with that name were to be found all over the state. So, recalling your summer trips to Anadarko led me to wonder if but that somewhere in the dim past there might have been a connection. I find it an intriguing idea, there being so many hidden connections, thanks to racial mysticism, but he, like the rest of us, probably got his name from some Anglo Saxon. What's important is the fact that he's made it what he wants it to mean.

Still, at this stage of my life I find myself confronting things as mysteries that I'd never really stopped to think of before. For instance, whenever I bought penny candy from your grandmother's store I always connected her with the scales above the counter, thus making a child's unconscious connection between her person, the weighing device, and my hope of receiving full value for my coins. Oddly enough I think that I remember your grandfather, but for the life of me I can't bring him into as clear a focus as I do your grandmother. Nevertheless, I remember the rest of the family in detail. Including your mother and father, your aunt and uncle who owned the restaurant, Benny and his parents and Teddy, whom I secretly regarded as one of the best looking older girls in the entire city. Yes but here I falter, for while I remember her jolly sister I can't remember her name.

But why shouldn't I recall them? I was born just up the street at 407 East 1st, went to church and attended kindergarten up at the other end of the block, and played, fought (with Toy Henderson and others), delivered ice cream, medicine and Lord knows what else, all over the area. If prodded I'm sure that I could recall most of the kids who lived in your block, including the Buns, Wilson "Duke" Douglas, Princess and her sister, the Burnetts, and the Youngs—Joe, Amanda and Ran—who lived on the south side of the street. Doubtlessly most of us share the burdens and/or delights of such memories, but for me the scenes and the smells and the sounds, wry incidents, volatile moods, strong emotions and painful defeats have become an inseparable part of me, thanks to Time's having blended them, as only Time can, into something precious. As a writer I don't know what I'd do without them, for they constitute, in their garbled way, my first contacts with the mystery of being alive. Never again will I find people so open in their reactions, and never again will human situations be so fresh in their impact.

That is why I share some of your distress upon returning home. I resent what has happened to that section of town in which we grew up, and I have difficulty relating to the sections to which our population has shifted. I hunted my first rabbits and quail in the vicinity of 23rd and Eastern and felt especially blessed whenever I came upon a tree loaded with ripe wild persimmons. So that now not even the honor of having a library named for me in the old area can quite compensate for the loss of the old wild country that clings to my mind.

And yet I'd rather have kids devouring books than hunting rabbits. Besides, there are more of us now, many more, and they have to have places to live. I only wish that something had been done to preserve those sections in which we once lived. Because all things considered, and my personal poverty notwithstanding, most of us had an interesting childhood and were in daily contact with adults who gave us the courage to dream. The scene that I recall so vividly, even the shacky houses, the squalor of the tenement where Charlie Christian lived, and the railroad tracks were all part of that which makes me me. So it pains me to return to find so much of it fallen into decay. Who would believe that the Deep Second of today, neglected and inhabited by so many who appear hopeless, was once a place of excitement, hope and aspiration? Looking back I realize that it even had more style and order than anything I saw on my visits to newer areas. I'm referring here to the business sections not the residential areas, some of which I found quite handsome. But so were some that are now destroyed. Durland Court was a gracious example of residential planning, I don't care who happened to live there. And so were the houses in which the Whitbys, the Youngbloods and the Filsons lived. And as for excitement, I've danced in a number of cities, both here and abroad but never have I found anything to match Slaughter's Hall on a good night with a good band playing. And the proof that it was extraordinary lies in the fact that by the '40s the music and dance that were partially created there had found fans throughout the world. Even the Africans were stomping and calling it "Swing"!

Well, change is ever with us and will continue after we're gone. Which is one of the irrevocable aspects of the so-called "human condition." Still, regret is also an inescapable part of that condition, and when I read of Lola's death I was saddened. During the winter I had seen photographs taken at the time of her retirement and was alarmed because she appeared unwell. But then I forgot about it until I happened upon a clipping that I'd taken from an old issue of the *Dispatch*. It was a memorial to Mrs. Tillry and I came upon it shortly before I read of Lola's passing. I clipped it because as a youngster I had visited their home and later, as an adult, I realized what a marvelous job she'd done in raising all those girls; an achievement that was most meaningful to me since she, like my mother, was a widow. At the time I came across the clipping I amused myself by imaging how shocked Jack (excuse me, LOWELL) would have been to learn that I had a photo of her mother on my disorderly desk. This because while Lola and I got along very well, Lowell and I were most often at odds. Nevertheless their mother was a part of my childhood too, so why shouldn't I honor her memory?

Since Lola's passing I've kept an eye peeled for news of Albert, but thus far I've seen nothing. I'm hoping that he's bearing up for I know at close hand how painful such a loss can be. Herbert's wife died several years ago, and hardly had he begun to adjust to it than he lost his son. This was just a few months ago in Los Angeles, where he continues to live.

I know that it's depressing, but while I'm on the subject I should mention that Mrs. Mary Fields passed in December. You'll recall that she was the mother of James and Charlie and a sister of Mrs. Canty and Mrs. Sheets. Another sister, Adel Grant, has lived in L.A. since we were children, as does her younger sister, Georgia. My parents were friends of the Cantys and Adel and my mother were quite close. I remember being left with my father on a snowy evening while the two ladies went down town to see a play. I was between two and three years old at the time, which makes it long, long ago. I'll always remember Georgia with warmth because my first encounter with the "belly-rub" came when I saw her dancing with Theodore Wells in the family parlor down in the 700 block on East 1st. They were dancing to the phonograph and what a laughing, shaking, good-smelling, good time they were having. I couldn't have been more than three or four at the time, but I knew right then and there that such dancing was for me!

You ask if I remembered Lorraine Sanders and William Hoskins and the answer is yes. Virgil Branam loved to tease Lorraine so I remember her vividly—even the color of her hair. And as for Hoskins, I not only played on the football team with him, but once I went with him on a trip to his father's farm where we ate the hearts out of about a half dozen vine-sweet watermelons. Those were the days! Please give them both my regards.

I wish that I had such news to pass on to you, but I haven't been an Okie in quite some time. Tack Giddings operates a business in Harlem but although we talk once in a while by telephone it's been years since we've met face to face. And the same is true of Arvill and Garnetta Lovett. Last year we missed an opportunity for seeing them by not being able to attend their daughter's wedding. So it would seem that the pattern of our life does as much to keep old friends apart as does mere distance. For although Brooklyn is much closer than Okla. City I have little more contact with friends living there than with others who live in Europe. I tried to reach Elvira and Charles Townsend for years, but even Arvil couldn't manage to do so and they both lived in Brooklyn. Some years ago I made an extended effort to reach Elvira, not only because I wished to talk with her about my mother, who drove to Ohio with them back in '36, but because I had need for photographs from our days on old Douglass. As I recall, most of you girls kept albums, while few, if any of the boys had the sense to do so. I regret that I didn't because so much is preserved in those snap shots which is only vague in my memory. But so it goes. Not only is it impossible to really go home again, change being change, but too often it is impossible to resume friendships that were begun at home. And that's all the more reason for my finding your letter so welcome . . .

Yes, I have been back home twice since the library opened. The first time was after I'd been lecturing in St. Louis and decided to make an unscheduled visit to surprise my cousin, Tom Brown and his wife. Which was fortunate, because within a few months I had to return for his funeral. However, it was a brief visit because I was still teaching and thus failed to see many of those whom I would have liked to see. Since then I've retired—although not from writing—and the next time I get out there, if ever, I'll make every effort to look up our dwindling survivors. Please give our regards to any of those who remember us (we keep up with Badboy through Herbert), and especially Zelma and Booker, my old Tuskegee homie. Incidentally, his idea of your renting a car when you return home is excellent, for by doing so you'll be some insulated from the shock of change. And besides, it'll save your feet!

Fanny joins me in warm regards.

Ralph

P.S:
I almost forgot my one piece of news: the other day I received a phone call from Sherman Sneed, whom I haven't seen since I left home during the '30s. He is now Lena Horne's manager and is involved in her highly successful show. I haven't seen him yet but plan to do so before spring becomes summer. Let an Okie leave home for a while and there no telling what he'll turn up doing. Look at you and Booker! Hell, look at me!!

Mr. and Mrs. Booker Tucker
517 Caldwell Street,
Compton, California 90220

To Kenneth Burke
RALPH ELLISON
730 Riverside Drive
New York, N.Y. 10031
NOVEMBER 7, 1982

Dear K.B.:

I'm delighted that you are taking time out from your important work in order to give a wider dimension to the Yale boys' project.* I'm not in very close touch with them but they seem quite enthusiastic.

The point that I was trying to make in all of the din around the bar the other day had to do with the narrator's encounter in the factory basement. You write that he gets into a "furious fight with his white boss," but in fact he gets into a fight with his <u>Negro</u> boss, Lucius Brockway. You'll note that Brockway's idiom is Afro-American and that on page 158 his face is likened to a withered black walnut with shrewd, reddish eyes. The narrator reacts as he does because Brockway symbolizes that type of old southern Negro who would enforce a pattern of conduct upon the youth that white southerners imposed upon the group as a means of maintaining their form of social order. Such elders drew upon a form of filial authority that grew out of the family and the church and used it to protect the group's members and to control their conduct. However their authority rested ultimately upon the white's willingness to use physical force. Thus once a young Negro rejected the filial piety upon which the oldster's authority rested they realized that such authority had little bite. Indeed, it had no more bite than Brockway's false teeth. And in the industrial North, where the religious ties that were a source of in-group order were weakened, it had little bite whatsoever . . . Coming upon the old guy in the basement after his encounter with Kimbro and the union members, the narrator is confused and angered by Brockway's suspicion and his insistence that he [had] an important role in the plant's social hierarchy. This reminded the narrator of Bledsoe's assertion of <u>his</u> dominant role in that power structure which linked his college to southern order and northern philanthropy and the narrator had been treated badly by both. Talk about

---

* Ellison may be thinking of Kimberly Benston's solo project, *Speaking for You: The Vision of Ralph Ellison* (Howard University Press, 1987), to which Benston and Ellison each strongly encouraged Burke to contribute.

the black dimensions of white power! This probably has little to do with the point toward which you're working, but I thought I'd call it to your attention . . . Incidentally, both Bledsoe and Brockway have achieved a limited <u>individual</u> transcendence within the limitations of their areas of assertion—or at least <u>they</u> thought so.

As always, it was a pleasure seeing you at the Academy. In fact you're the main reason we try not to miss the meetings, and when you don't show both Fanny and I are disappointed.

Love,
Ralph

P.S.
While looking up your quote of my reference to B. T. Washington's crab metaphor I kept reading and came upon your remark concerning the possibility of 'rejoycing' hidden meanings out of a text. This led to my recalling how I had transformed a bawdy verse that I'd learned in my teens from a respected pharmacist.

His version went:

> *Did you ever see Miss Margaret make water?*
> *She pisses a wonderful stream,*
> *Seventeen miles and a quarter,*
> *And you can't see her twat for the steam.*

You can see what I did to those noble lines on p. 179 of *IM;* it's far inferior to the original, but what can one expect when the context of situation—rhetorical, psychological and physical—forces his narrator to transform a pee-party into a tea-party?

R.
P.P.S.
I've always tried to turn your insights back to the necessities of fiction.

To James Roark
730 RIVERSIDE DRIVE
NEW YORK, NEW YORK 10031
NOVEMBER 23, 1982

Mr. James L. Roark, Associate Professor
Department of History
University of Missouri
8001 Natural Bridge Road
St. Louis, Missouri 63121

Dear Professor Roark:

I have read yours and Professor Johnson's manuscript with engrossed attention and find it most fascinating. Never before have I found the experience of the free slaveholding caste of antebellum Negroes brought to life
in such vibrant detail. To be able to detect what Henry James called the
"density of felt experience" behind the enigmatic details of the letters is
indeed a scholarly achievement of a high order and, I think a contribution
to all who would grasp the complexity of our American past.

Thanks to your imaginative research and reconstruction, the William
Ellisons, their families and friends can no longer be regarded abstractly
as traitors to a racial identity which they shared with many slaves, but
must now be viewed as ingenuous human beings who possessed a unique
cultural identity and who lived and grappled with the complex problems
posed by a specific period of our turbulent history. The very fact that
they were able to travel, the law notwithstanding, back and forth between
South Carolina, New York and Canada comes as an intriguing surprise,
and I can imagine Henry James passing them on his strolls up Broadway—
with the great master of the novels of manners being totally unaware of the
mocking "American joke" being acted out before his unseeing eyes. Their
color was their fate—yes, but their culture—most southern and yet most
American—was an assault upon the logical illogic of racism. Truly there
was much more to their kind than met the color-blinded eye.

Bearing such a surname, it has long been my fate to have individuals
who become belatedly aware of my South Carolina lineage to attempt
to thrust kinship with that ambiguous caste upon me; specifically, a presumed kinship with William Ellison. Thus there was a time when my notions of racial loyalty led me to deny it outright. Later I confessed that I

truly didn't know of such a kinship but that I was more than willing to let the past retain its mystery. In fact I was quite amused whenever I found my white Southern friends electing themselves aristocratic backgrounds that were pieced together out of little more than the moonlight and magnolias of movie and historical romance. For I suspected that history operates in the present in far more interesting, and subtle, ways than they could ever devise and that at best they were but exercising their American freedom to make art of a past that was oft times squalid.

Still, as a novelist concerned with the morality of our American experience I was forced to conclude that whatever the facts turned out to be, there was no more disgrace in one's being related by blood to a <u>black</u> slaveholder than to those who happened to have been designated "white," (designation by others having so much to do with which side of the color line one landed on in the first place)—which, like so many Afro-Americans, I most certainly am; and this on both sides of my family tree. Nevertheless, the possibility that I <u>might</u> in fact be related to William Ellison left me uneasy, for as the saying goes, I had enough troubles of my own and no need whatsoever to give myself aristocratic airs. Besides, I had come to accept the fact that most attempts at moralizing history in retrospect are a risky business, and to do so is to find oneself up to one's neck in myth and in questions of morality that are most difficult to answer. The closest I have been able to come in any basic way is to say that slavery was a crass violation of the ideal democratic compact upon which this republic was erected, and that all else flows from that initial fall from a transcendent ideal.

So, as I say, if the question of my possible kinship with William Ellison still leaves me somewhat uneasy your revelations have given him a richly human dimension. And if it should turn out that my grandfather happened to have been both William's blood relative and his chattel, nothing will have changed. The murky mystery of blood and race, color and property will remain and I'll still have the task of giving my own individual content to the Ellison name. Here, what is important comes to me through my knowledge of, and contact with my immediate family, and I being in Oklahoma with Ida and Lewis Alfred . . . But enough of such speculation and on to your question:

Unfortunately, C. Vann Woodward was mistaken in assuming that when I spoke of my South Carolina background I was referring to the William Ellison family. Actually, I was referring to that of my paternal grandfather, Alfred Ellison of Abbeville Court House District, who was neither wealthy nor a holder of slaves. Nevertheless, it might interest you to know that he did play a small role in the drama of South Carolina Reconstruction politics, during which he served as a constable, as a marshal, and as village magistrate. He was also a friend and political ally of Henry H. Ellison, the Radical Republican State Representative and ran unsuccessfully for such a seat. Family legend has it that Alfred and Henry were brothers, but here again this might well be the result of their common surname. However, during the 1970's my father's cousin, the late Reverend William Ellison of the Bronx, N.Y., told me that as far as he knew Alfred and Henry H. Ellison were kin. All I know is that Henry and my grandfather were associated with General Sam McGowan, who had been one of General Lee's officers and who was later to serve as the Chief Justice of South Carolina. Both of the political Ellisons of Abbeville had business dealings with the General and my grandfather purchased property from him. This was located at the foot of Recession Hill and I find it ironic but somehow symbolically right that I should have inherited it from my father and then lost it to taxes.

Following the decline of Radical Republicanism, my grandfather was instrumental in gaining Negro support for the General, and thus helped return the Democrats to power. No doubt he had learned something firsthand about the limitations of the art of the possible, not to mention the baffling incongruities imposed by his times and the necessities of politics. Nevertheless, he ended his days as a farmer and drayman, well known but no longer a political force. Should you come across any information concerning him, I'd be most pleased to have it.

I doubt that any of the above will be of use to you, but perhaps the following might: During the 1970's Mr. Stewart Lillard became curious about my South Carolina connection and looked into some of the old records of Abbeville and was thus able to substantiate much of the family talk that I'd heard from my father's older sister when I was a child in Oklahoma City. It was from her that I learned that my grandfather had been a political figure, and I possess a deed to the old family property, but such verified details as I possess I owe to Mr. Lillard. You may get in touch with him at the Everett Library, Queens College, 1900 Selwyn Avenue, Charlotte, North Carolina 29275. I don't know whether he has published his findings but I'm sure that he will find your project of interest and might well be of assistance in tracing the Ellisons across county and racial lines—from low country to high.

I allow myself to be hopeful at this point because in looking over materials sent me by Mr. Lillard I noted one possible link between the Ellisons of Fairfield District and Abbeville Court House. He wrote that "by 1860, Mrs. Mary Ann Ellison, then a seventy-seven year old grandmother from Fairfield District, lodged with her granddaughter in Abbeville. She subsequently died leaving an estate of twenty thousand dollars that included thirteen slaves. And a young farmer with the same family name, his wife, and infant son resided in Donaldsville Township. Following the War Between the States, the *Abbeville Press* newspaper announced the marriage of G. W. Ellison to Mary A. Millford on October 11, 1865. William Ellison, farmer, was listed on the militia enrollment of 1868."

These would appear to have been white Ellisons, but perhaps Mary Ann Ellison's background in Fairfield District offers a clue to the connections you're seeking.

Mr. Lillard also found the will of Mrs. Louisa Ellison (1836–1916), who was known in my father's family as "Aunt Lou," along with records that listed a Lucy Ellison (Negro) who was born about 1790 and who was living during 1870 in Long Cane Township of Abbeville County. Incidentally, I had difficulty in finding either Fairfield or Stateburg on the several maps I possess and was able to locate them only after consulting Volume XXV of the Eleventh Edition of the Encyclopaedia Britannica. Perhaps you might wish to do something about this in your final draft.

Meanwhile, if you have questions I would be most willing to try to answer them. I am most thankful to you for the privilege of reading your manuscript and shall rush to acquire the finished work the moment it appears.

I wish you every success with your project.

Sincerely,
Ralph Ellison

cc:
Stewart Lillard
Queens College
Charlotte, N.C.

C. Vann Woodward
Yale University
New Haven, Conn.

To Ron Burke
RALPH ELLISON
730 RIVERSIDE DRIVE
NEW YORK, N.Y. 1031
DEC. 10, 1982

Mr. Ron Burke
American Business Products, Inc.
155 North Dean Street
Englewood, New Jersey 07631

Dear Mr. Burke:

Please find enclosed my check for $265.00 in payment for one (1), Comm-Pac modem, as offered by the Osborne Computer Corporation through ABP, Inc.

Thanks for sending me the information on the modem, it was most appreciated, for despite the fact that we own two Osborne computers the company has been remiss in keeping us in touch with its new products and developments. Therefore we have no idea of what would be involved in the updating of our machines to double-density etc. and would appreciate such information as you are able to supply us.

I realize that our lack of information is not the fault of your organization for we purchased our first machine from a Computerland outlet located in Huntington, Long Island. This was done on the advice of a friend who lives in that area, but after we obtained our machine our relations with Computerland proved less than satisfactory. Not only is it difficult to get there for consultation, but when the original keyboard was updated they managed to leave the "?" and "/" characters off of the updated keyboard. This was by no means fatal, for both my wife and I type by touch. But then, as I mentioned to you via telephone, for no apparent reason the updated keyboard went haywire.

I was working one Oct. afternoon in Plainfield, Mass. when suddenly the machine began talking gibberish. This occurred shortly before we returned to New York; where, hoping that the trip back might have restored the keyboard's sanity, I tried the machine again. But alas, after performing normally for a paragraph or two it lapsed again into idiocy. However, before giving up I <u>did</u> try the computer section with the keyboard that I purchased from you and it worked successfully. I am assuming, therefore, that the trouble lies with the keyboard and not the electronics, and as soon as time permits I shall bring the ailing computer across the George Washington Bridge for your attention.

In the meantime I look forward to receiving the modem and I wish you a fruitful holiday season.

Sincerely yours,
Ralph Ellison

To Mr. Burgess
RALPH ELLISON
730 RIVERSIDE DRIVE
NEW YORK, NEW YORK
FEBRUARY 28, 1983

Dear Mr. Burgess:

It has been so long ago and my motives were so mixed at that time that I am unable to give you an exact answer to your question concerning the 1369 light bulbs. Which is to say that I was trying to orchestrate my themes in such a manner that symbolism that might well be missed by readers of one background would be easily grasped by those from other backgrounds. I was trying to cover my bets, so to speak. Thus since my own background spans both the Afro-American folk and the fairly sophisticated area of the literate American I found myself alluding, sometimes consciously, sometimes only half-consciously, to symbolism from my childhood background in Oklahoma.

During the 1920's and 1930's the illegal gambling game of Policy—which is similar to today's lottery known as The Numbers Game, wherein bets are placed on a series of three digits taken from the daily stock market reports—was so popular that there were quite a few dream books available to those seeking advice on how best to transform their dreams into cash. It so happened that in such guide books the numbers 3-6-9 were assigned as the numerological symbols for dreams of feces, and the reader was assured that when he had had such a dream a bet placed upon that occult numerical sequence was a sure formula for transforming simple merde into a more negotiable coinage.

As you can see, the idea was quite childish, but the built-in ambiguity of such numbers-magic was so inescapably amusing that "3-6-9" became a most convenient part of our vernacular speech. We could use it in caution, in intimidation, in anger or in fun, and indeed it could be used in certain areas of polite society without censor. As in "Hey, watch it, man! You're about to step in that 3-6-9!" Or, "Listen here, buddy, don't be trying to snow me with any of your old, cold 3-6-9!" Or, "How'd you like to get the living 3-6-9 kicked out of you?"

I suppose that it was the sheer logic—or illogic—of symbolic thinking that led me to the strategy of having a narrator who was trying desperately to transform his nightmares into prose try to illuminate his efforts with 1369 light bulbs. And it is possible that I enlarged the original numbers as a teasing clue for those who might have been amused upon discovering the old dream book symbolism lurking in such an unexpected—and ambiguously well-lighted—place. There was, however, a more organic motive, for since the narrator was writing from underground I also hoped to add further overtones to the fertility-decay symbolism which was at play through [out] his narrative.

But as I say, in attempting such writing one's motives are so ambiguous that one trope spills over without warning into another. And this is such an instance, for on a quite different, and serious, level I was simply experimenting to see what kind of kinetic effect might be achieved by my concentrating in such a secluded and narrow space such an intensity of light upon the reader's eyeballs. And I was hoping, more or less consciously, that should his nose miss the joke hidden in the cloacal reference his eyes would suggest nevertheless that something less obvious was at work in the background. It was as simple and as complex as that, and if you find my answer offensive I apologize—And may James Joyce forgive me!

Sincerely,
Ralph Ellison

Mr. F. Burgess
123 West 92nd Street
New York, N.Y. 2313.

To Miss Messenger
RALPH ELLISON
730 Riverside Drive
New York, N.Y. 10031
MARCH 7, 1983

Dear Miss Messenger:

I haven't read *Nausea* in many years and have no time to do so at the moment, but since questions of artistic influence can be quite tricky the best I can do by way of answering your query is to offer you the following dates:

Nausea was first published in this country in 1949, four years after I began writing my own novel (1945), and two years (1947) after the "Battle Royal" section was published in the English magazine, *Horizon,* and a year after the same excerpt received its first American publication in the now-defunct New York-based *Magazine of the Year.* This by no means disproves the possibility of the influence which you perceive but it does take on significance in light of the fact that my command of the French language was (and still is, unfortunately), too inadequate for me to have read Sartre's novel before it was made available in an English translation. True, *Nausea* was first published in 1938—in France, that is—but Sartre did not become famous until the winter of 1944–45 when his drama *No Exit* was staged. It took some time for his fame to flare in the U.S. and therefore it was hardly likely that I would have known much about him. The main point here is that I was well under way with my novel before Sartre made his American debut.

Perhaps the question of influence arises because the Occupation forced the French to a sense of estrangement such as was the lot of American frontiersmen, seamen, and slaves, which is to say that the experience of Nazi occupation compelled French intellectuals to name and explore in their own terms an aspect of the human condition that is at least as old as the *Book of Job.* Melville was concerned with it in his own time, as were the creators of the Blues in theirs and Hemingway in his. But since the human condition is abiding it must be constantly rediscovered and made a conscious possession of those who think and act. I became consciously aware of existentialism (lower case) during the summer of 1936 when I read Malraux's *Man's Fate* and *The Days of Wrath* for the first time. From them I became aware of the existential elements in American and Afro-American cultural expression. Then, during 1938 I discovered Miguel Unamuno portrayed as a character in *Man's Hope* (*L'Espoir*) and was led to read *The Tragic Sense of Life*. This put me on the trail of Kierkegaard, and thus it was that that by the time Sartre made his appearance I was familiar with quite a number of works on existentialism. Indeed, when Sartre became such a rage among American intellectuals I was quite surprised. After all Malraux was far better known and to my mind a superior novelist. This is not to say that I didn't read anything of Sartre that I could get my hands on because I did; as did Richard Wright, who was to become a friend of Sartre in Paris. I even met Sartre when he visited New York sometimes during the mid-1940s, but as far as I am aware his influence upon my writing was limited to the general intellectual excitement which marked the post-war years and to which he was without doubt a most important contributor.

Cordially yours,
Ralph Ellison

To Michel Fabre
730 RIVERSIDE DRIVE
NEW YORK, N.Y. 10031
JUNE 7, 1983

Dear Michel:

I appreciate very much your sending me the transcription of my 1971 University of Iowa talk on Richard Wright. It would have been disastrous to have published the transcribed version for it hardly represents the lecture I gave. Either the microphone placement was faulty and made it impossible to record much of what was being said, or my diction was such that the transcriber ended up with innumerable errors and misinterpretations. And added to this is the fact that I spoke extemporaneously from notes rather than from a prepared paper.

As you know, there is quite a difference between a public talk, during which one's presence, one's gestures, intonations and diction give extension to one's words, and a lecture written primarily for the eye. Thus I have never agreed to have a talk published unless I had the opportunity to "translate" it into a readable form. Something is lost in the process but, let's face it, we're dealing with two distinct forms of communication. Fortunately, however, I was able to find my original notes, and although it has taken up time that I really couldn't spare, I've worked them into a paper that I think you might be able to use.

Needless to say, if it should turn out to be too lengthy I will understand your not using it. And if not, it won't be the first time. For I had given editors of *New Letters* permission to publish the talk back in 1971, but Charlie Davis refused to release it to them. But knowing how I feel about unedited talks I suspect that I must have worked on the piece before I gave them permission. If so, I don't know what has happened to it, and I hope that the version I'm sending you will have a better fate. You should know, incidentally, that I have a new collection of essays in the works and I shall send a copy of "Remembering Richard Wright" to my editor for possible inclusion. God knows that after all the work that has gone into it (we should have gone to our summer place two weeks ago!) it should receive some kind of public exposure—which, without your efforts, it probably wouldn't have.

You set June 18th as your deadline and I am rushing this to you well before your deadline. In any case, please be so kind as to write me, by return mail if possible, of your decision.

> With every best wish,
> Ralph Ellison

Michel Fabre
Universite de Paris
Paris (V) France

To Kenneth Burke
730 Riverside Drive
New York, N.Y. 10031
June 20, 1983

Dear Kenneth,

I don't know what the hell happened. Some say that it was the sound system, some say that it was me, and someone suggested that some of my remarks might have been perceived as being anti-Jewish. But whatever it was I wish I had stuck to my original rejection of the honor-bestowing role. Frankly, I'm tired of those who wish to turn the ceremony into money-and-medal-throwing riot in which all seriousness is forgotten. As it is I take part mainly to see old friends, old friend and mentor, and as far as eating and drinking goes I'd just as soon do it at home with serious thinkers who know the proper relationship between food and drink and the world of ideas.

I'm enclosing an edited version of my remarks—the editing consisting of extensions which I hope will make up for some of the meaning lost in translating to print—and a deletion of a bit of dialogue which I conceived as comic. You can judge for yourself for I am including it. The best I can say for the damned thing is that I was trying to get at some of the underlying drama of social hierarchy which was taking place, if only in <u>my</u> amused eyes.

I hope by now that you've heard from Benston, the Yale prof who's editing the collection.* I called him right after I heard from you and he said that he'd get in touch. Since then I've been so busy editing a bungled transcript of a speech on Richard Wright that I gave back in 1971 that I've had no further contact with the guy. I prefer to give a talk from notes or a loosely structured draft because it sounds more like conversation, but after the Academy fiasco and the Wright business—which is to be published in France—I think I'll write and read the writing and save myself a lot of trouble.

As for my old novel and its <u>summing up</u>, I have no opinion. But I do know that while it dealt with a period when black mayors of cities like Detroit, Chicago and Philadelphia were impossible, the <u>idea</u> of their being such was not. Indeed, we'd already had a Negro communist on the New York City Council, and Adam Powell Jr. was already becoming a powerful congressman. Poor guy, his slogan was, "Keep the faith, baby," but he forgot the old warning against pride and got his arrogant butt humbled. A hell of a thing to happen to a Baptist minister who probably knew as much as anyone about American rhetoric . . . You're probably right about a sequel of I.M. being impossible, but even if it were I'd have no desire to undertake it. I'm having enough trouble just making a meaningful form out of my yarn concerning a little boy preacher who rises to <u>high estate</u> and comes asunder. There are all kinds of interesting incidents in it, but if they don't add up it'll fall as rain into the ocean of meaningless words. I

---

* Previously cited as a note to Ellison's letter of March 3, 1982, to Michel Fabre, Benston's *Speaking for You* remains an essential collection of work on and about the life and times and writings of Ralph Ellison.

guess what's bothering me right now is working out a form for the NEXT PHASE of which you write.

Anyway, I'm still writing—or will be at it again as soon as we can get out of the city and up in the Berkshire hills . . . Hope things are going well with you and I'll get in touch with you from up there.

Our best to youse 'n
yourn,
Ralph

Enclosed: Gold Medal for Malamud Presentation talk.

Kenneth Burke
154 Amity Road
Andover, N.J. 07821

To John Hersey
730 Riverside Drive
New York, N.Y. 10031
June 20, 1983

Dear John:

Thanks so very much for your note and for your student's comments on my Library of Congress reading. I was quite unprepared for the size of the crowd, and especially for the many young people. Many of them were "Blacks" whom I would have expected to have been turned off by the pounding I took during the Sixties and Seventies. But no, there they were along with the whites and they seemed no less enthusiastic. I guess that's one of the benefits of being a survivor. Nevertheless, it <u>does</u> make for a dilemma, because I don't really know whether they were applauding a "performance"—a reporter was kind or reckless enough to mention Mark Twain—or responding to my cockeyed prose. So I guess I'll have to accept it as a gift and reserve my worrying until such time as the book is published.

We too were sorry that you and Barbara couldn't join our little get-together, but we understood. I needn't tell you that you're welcome whenever you have the time.

You'll note from the above address that Fanny and I are still here in the humid city, thanks to my having to edit a talk I gave back in 1971 in time to make a pressing deadline. I was also under pressure from Maggie to get my remarks to her in a printable form. Incidentally, by way of saving paper I wrote my loose "speaking draft" on the back of what I thought was disposable information sent me by one of the boards on which I serve. And it <u>was</u> from such a board, but when I reached the Academy-Institute I discovered that the sheets contained confidential information that would have been disastrous had it fallen into the hands of outsiders. Thus instead of turning in my remarks immediately after they were delivered I had to transfer them to more innocent paper.

Which didn't really matter because my speaking-writing ain't my reading writing, and Lord knows that my speaking-writing didn't go over any too well during the ceremony. So you win some and you lose some. Which is to say that your note helped to put things in a more realistic perspective. At any rate I'm enclosing a copy of my remarks so that you'll know that despite the outcome I was trying to say something meaningful.

We hope you and Barbara are enjoying the summer and look forward to seeing you whenever we can.

Sincerely,
Ralph

P.S. The computer on which this is being composed is an Osborne 1, and the printer is a far from letter quality Epson. It has by no means improved my spelling, but it has certain advantages over my typewriter. I can't wait until Fanny has mastered hers!

John Hersey
R.F.D. Box 144
Vineyard Haven, MA 02568

Enclosure: Presentation of Gold Medal (talk)
to Bernard Malamud.

To John Callahan
AUGUST 12, 1983

Dear John:

When the Coolidge sign imposed itself upon my bewildered eyes it was leaning against a house located in a no-parking zone on Route 9 that leads into Northampton. It is a 45 mph zone and at the time I thought that either I was seeing things or some old timer had blown his top from nostalgia. The other day when I returned to photograph it for you it had been moved to the edge of the lawn where no passerby could possibly miss it, but in the heavy traffic it was impossible to get a shot. Now it doesn't really matter because the incongruity of its presence has been dispelled, and you can see it in the current issue of *Time*. I had forgotten—if I ever knew—that ole Cal was once mayor of Northampton, then a state senator, and later Governor of the state. He hardly missed a step on his rise to the presidency, and after choosing <u>not</u> to try for a second term in the White House, he returned to live in Northampton and died there in 1933.

Now, fifty years later he's undergoing something of an apotheosis. Down in "Hamp" they're knocking themselves out with memorial ceremonies and crying jags, and I'm sure that there are those who'd like to dig him up, brush him off, and fly him back to Washington. Perhaps, with Reagan stealing ole Cal's long-muted thunder (or his "cool") it's a feasible idea. But then, heaven help us, the Hooverites, Wilsonites—even the Nixonites—would get into the act and we'd have a reversal of that process of rehabilitation and elevation by which movie actors can start their careers playing thugs, outlaws, or bums, and end up years later playing J. Edgar H., Abe Lincoln, G. Patton, or maybe even God. Then all an ex-prexy would have to do is resurface and then—buoyed up by gains ill gotten from hawking patent medicine on TV—begin frowning the right frowns and smiling the right smiles while taking care not to smell either too rank or too deodorized while honing his skills in intoning bullshit in sonorous timbres of different voices before different audiences—and he'd have it made.

'Cause aint this the land of the second chance? It can happen, John, because too many Americans simply can't distinguish between snake shit and snake oil. So given a chance almost <u>any</u> old moldered ex-president could end up stinking up the White House again and hardly anybody would know where the stench was coming from.

You think I'm kidding? Just take a look at that masterpiece of the taxi-dermist's art who's got this memory-less nation by its absentminded balls today. So let the Hamptonians put some TV makeup on ole Cal-the-cool—hell, even on ole Warren Gam-G., Herbert Hoo., or Dick Outhouse Nick—and any one of them could have another shot at messing up the high seat, Tea Pot Dome, Jazz Age booze, Great Depression or Watergate notwithstanding.

Maybe the so-called "primitives" who shun the camera out of fear that their souls will be seized are not too far off target—only it aint their souls that they have to worry about but their bison-biting minds. Magic lives, man! And it's by no means all black; it's technicolored and so effective that it appears that if given enough exposure to optics, chemicals and electronic disseminated double-talk (What did the Indian chief say in de-scribing the Oklahoma Negro who conned him out of his liquor money? "Him tall like pine, black like crow, talk more shit than the radio") that the average American is apt to be so befuddled that the most transparent fraud can take his land, his gold, and even his good wife's jelly-roll and be praised in the name of progress, the Golden Rule, and supply-side economics.

But enough of this ranting or I'll start sounding like Jason Compson . . . Thanks for the copy of your essay; reading it makes me wish that I'd got-ten the proper grounding in math and physics that would have allowed me to continue my early enthusiasm for science.* Spurred during my teen days by an enthusiasm for building radios and my playing around with chemistry sets I read so many articles on popular science that, much to the annoyance of my teacher, Mrs. Berry, I'd take over the class. But as time went by an ineptitude for math, a lack of up to date lab equipment, and a bumbling physics teacher—I remember the guy best for his pride in his Brooks Brothers suits and his habit of squelching our whispering by striding back and forth in front of the blackboard while intoning, "Those whom the gods would destroy they first make mad!" No wonder I cooled off and became absorbed by my first passion for music. Later my interest in Marxism brought me back to science but in a way that was too abstract and focused on sociology to be really useful. I've subscribed to *Scientific*

---

* Ellison refers to an earlier version of Callahan's essay, "Tradition and Innovation: Evolving Paradigms in *The Structure of Scientific Revolutions* and *Invisible Man*," in *Beyond the Two Cultures: Essays on Science, Technology and Literature*, ed. Joseph W. Slade and Judith Yaross Lee (Ames: Iowa State University Press, 1990).

American for years but much of it is over my bald old head. Now, thanks to you, I'll have a go at Kuhn.

At any rate I understand something of what you're saying about the manner in which the processes of science and fiction writing are related. Indeed, I recall my puzzlement during my music days over the ease I had in solving harmonic equations—a kind of mathematical skill, I'm told— and the fact that I had to rely on my fingers and toes in dealing with math. Talk about anomaly! I don't remember how conscious I was in playing with the anomalies of science and technology, but you've made me aware of the extent I was doing so. I guess I was playing beyond my game and having fun. But perhaps, to paraphrase Faulkner, when a tinker goes to work knowing knows before theory formulates. For if the beginning is in words, or terms, it is also the violation of the word. And when terms produce technologies, a questioning of the authority of scientific theory often leads to the discovery of new techniques, and thus to the modification and metamorphosis of theory. I guess tinkers make their scores by monkeying around with theory as it finds concrete existence in machines. I'm reminded of the cotton-picker's reply when the boss man told him, "Sam, you can lead a hoss to water, but you can't make him drink." "Yes, suh," Sam said, "I been hearing that every since I can remember. But somehow they got that wrong..." "What do you mean? Everybody knows that's true." "I know," Sam said, "but if you lead him to that water and put enough <u>suction</u> on his ass, he'll drink!"

Your point about patriotism is well taken, I've never been able to dismiss democratic ideals so easily as have some of my colleagues whose racial background make the rewards of democracy more easily available. Therefore I would affirm the principles while insisting that they be extended to all and on the basis of equality. It ain't the theory which bothers me, its the practice. My problem is to affirm while resisting. That is why I joined the <u>Merchant Marine</u>—not the Coast Guard, as you have it on page 15. During the war I wanted to do my bit, but not in an army in which I would have been considered less than equal. In the merchant marine I was a civilian, and even when our ship entered the war zones there was a certain protection from the union, of which I was a member. Incidentally, there's nothing like being shipbound on an ocean with German submarines aiming at its butt to make white Americans forget some of their racial prejudice. For who knows, when a torpedo strikes, the guy in the position to give you a helping hand might well be a Negro. Of course the reverse is also true: some rabid racist might well forget his hate and save a black man's life. Melville knew what he was doing when he isolated American democracy on a whaling ship . . .

***

IT WOULD HAPPEN THIS WAY, I was working on this a little while ago when your letter containing the Coolidge clipping arrived and I learned that I was telling you something that you already knew. So what the hell, I'll leave it anyway—if only because I've got it on the computer. You asked about the cost of this contraption but since I don't have the figures at hand I can only say that at the time it was about $1800.00, plus $700 for the printer and $125 for the monitor. It is an **Osborne 1,** which has since been upgraded so that it has twice as much memory and certain other improvements. The company has also released two more professional models, the **Executive 1 & Executive 2,** either of which should you decide, is probably the way to go. Since I acquired mine the competition in the computer market has brought prices down, making it possible to buy a superior machine for just about the price I paid for mine. Look round, see what the damn things can do, and wait for the Xmas come-ons before you buy.

Things are still bumpy here. I had to shoot a couple of raccoons and a woodchuck, mail delivery has been restored, but the roof still leaks in the bedroom. Otherwise we're fine and rolling with the alternate periods of 90-degree heat and driving rain. Not much of a garden this year, but your strawberries are still coming in. Heard from Harper who's writing and trying to keep out of Shirley's family hassles. I'm working away on the endless novel and that's about it. A fellow who teaches at the University of Texas at El Paso sent me a copy of his recent work of Faulkner criticism, titled *Faulkner's Search for a South.* In it gives me a certain amount of credit but I found it of interest for other reasons. For one thing he's a white Mississippian and has a fairly cold eye. Take a look when you have the time. Meanwhile our love to you and yours. I'm enclosing snapshots for the girls* of a couple of young bandits who were inspecting our garden site a few mornings ago.

Sincerely,
Ralph

---

* Callahan's daughters, Eve and Sasha, who enjoyed several family visits to the Ellisons in Plainfield.

P.S. Of course we want to see you for lunch, but let's leave the logistics for later.

RE

P.P.S. Thanks for the Fitzgerald quote, it's most revealing and I'm sure that you'll make insightful use of it.

R.E.

To Allen Ballard
RALPH ELLISON
STAR ROUTE 91-A
PLAINFIELD, MA 01070
AUG. 24, 1983

Dear Mr. Ballard:

Your letter finally reached me here in the Berkshires after being forwarded to my New York address and then undergoing further delays due to the Postal Department's computerized forwarding system. I am sorry for the delay and I hope my reply reaches you in time to be of use. However, before attempting to answer your questions I must warn you that my Ellison files are in New York and I am forced to rely upon a very sketchy memory.

Yours is the first reference to the Phoenix riot to come my way, therefore I have no idea of its impact upon my father's life. I do know that my father left Abbeville at the age of twenty-one to serve in the Spanish-American war. He was a member of the Twenty-fourth Infantry, Company F., served in Cuba, the Philippines and, according to my mother, was in China during the Boxer Rebellion. I don't know exactly when he returned to Abbeville but I am informed that at some point before or after the war he and a friend operated an ice cream and candy store near the big church (that of the Calhouns) located in the center of town. I know also that my mother and father moved from Abbeville to Chattanooga, Tenn., where after failing in a restaurant venture he joined a white construction firm as a foreman. During the early 1900's this firm erected the first steel and concrete buildings in Oklahoma, Arkansas and Texas, and it was only after my birth that he left the firm to remain in Oklahoma City where, during the early days of Statehood, he had established residence.

I would have to check my files to give you the name of my grandfather's friend who was the lynch mob's victim. Nevertheless I have the impression that it occurred earlier than that which took the life of Mr. Crawford, and I seem to recall that my grandfather's friend was a Mr. Anderson. I'll add, for what it's worth, that I was taken to visit my grandfather shortly after my father's death in 1916 and that to a small child's eye the village was quiet and peaceful.

According to a newspaper clipping which came to my attention a few years ago, my grandfather died in his bed at the age of seventy-six, sometime in 1918. I wish I could be of more help, but as you know the Post Reconstruction did far more than destroy lives, property and hope; it imposed a terrible disruption of memory. I can't tell you how gratifying it is to learn that someone who springs from the same soil as myself is doing something to heal the gap in our historical memory. During the fall, when we return to New York I'll provide you with the few further details I possess concerning my family background.

I am most grateful for the copy of the Union League petition. It is the second official document having to do with my grandfather's civic activities to come to my attention. And it is of particular interest to me because, as you'll note, its right hand column lists the name of Henry Ellison. Henry was my grandfather's brother and served in the State Legislature. As a child I overheard such guarded talk about my grandfather's political activities, but only recently has it begun to be substantiated by documentation. My aunt, who also lived in Oklahoma City, was quite proud of her family background but seldom spoke of it directly to me. And by the time I reached my teens I dismissed what little I had overheard as sheer mythology. Now I know that much of her talk was true. My grandfather had served as a local magistrate, and like his brother had run for the legislature—although unsuccessfully. In your future research you might look into his relationship with General Sam McGowan, a man with whom he had business and political dealings during the period when political power shifted from the Republicans to the Democrats. McGowan was to become Chief Justice of South Carolina and appears to have been a friend of the two political Ellisons. Perhaps that friendship had something to do with the, for me, surprising fact that court house records list my grandfather as still voting at a time—the 1880's—when I had assumed that Negroes could no longer exercise that right.

As I say, your copy of the Union League petition came as a startling and appreciated surprise. But no less surprising was the information concerning your Aunt Lula. I do indeed remember her from Tuskegee and I regret that during that time I failed to learn that she came from the Abbeville-Greenwood section. At the time I shared the Tuskegee experience with your Aunt I began to correspond with my cousin Alex Morisey, a son of my father's younger sister, and had I known your Aunt Lula well enough I might have brought the two together and thus learned things about my "roots" that would have been most supportive in my attempts to orient myself in the social hierarchical chaos which seems to be typical of college life. On Tuskegee's campus she was a lady of high status and I'm sorry to learn of her death.

Good luck with your book, the publication of which I look forward with high expectations.

Sincerely,
Ralph Ellison.

Professor Allen B. Ballard
Dept. of Political Science
City College of New York
137th St. and Convent Ave.
New York, N.Y. 10031

To Mark States
RALPH ELLISON
730 Riverside Drive
New York, N.Y. 10031
AUG. 24, 1983

Dear Mr. States:

I'm afraid that I can be of little help regarding the political affiliations of Langston Hughes. When I came to know him, Hughes was internationally famous, some twelve years my senior, and had far more friends and acquaintances, both white and black, among writers, entertainers and political activists than I could possibly have come to know. He introduced me to quite a number of people, including Carl Van Vechten and Mr. and Mrs. Arthur Spingarn, but in the shifting alliances between fellow travelers and communists of various stripes it was often difficult to decide who were friends or who were foes. Being a poet who had made his name during the Harlem Renaissance Hughes knew many whites from a more romantic and less sectarian period of the Left, and no doubt continued his friendship with many of them long after more rigid lines were drawn by the Stalinists and Trotskyites. I'd remind you that the old *MASSES* was a far more romantic expression of rebellion than the *NEW MASSES,* and that the revelations issuing from the Moscow Trials separated most of the romantics from the hard-liners. But the trials notwithstanding, not all friendships were shattered by differences of political opinion.

Nor was there such a definite division between what you term the "White" Left and the "Black" Left, if indeed such a division existed. As an expression of a generalized attitude the Left was a form of integration, an attempt to resolve certain divisions of class and race as they related to what were considered basic social and political issues. A. Philip Randolph, for instance, was a socialist, as were a number of other Afro-Americans who were left of the N.A.A.C.P., but as socialists they were allied with whites of the same political views. Richard Wright was something of a Negro nationalist, but his world-view was Communist-Marxist, and thus most of his friends were white. And although I was closer to Wright than to Hughes I had no idea of what persuasion many of his white friends happened to be.

Hughes was by no means an intellectual (a group toward whom he shared a Moscow-inspired bias. See his correspondence with Arna Bontemps.) He had little interest in political theory—or in literary theory, for that matter—and often he teased me for my passion for such. Which is to say that his approach to political issues appeared to be emotional rather than philosophical, and was determined by what he viewed as being in the best interest of Negroes. About this I could well be mistaken, but I do know that during the time when I was publishing in the *New Masses* I was considered a young outsider—which I was—and thus not privy to the nature of Hughes' relationships with the magazine's editors, nor to the degree to which he embraced their ideas and programs. I admired him as an older, more worldly friend, and as a literary [man] from my grade school days, but being unaware to the exact nature of his political alliances, I have no idea of when, if ever, he changed them.

Why don't you examine the content of his writings that were published after the period with which you're concerned, including the *New Masses* files, his *Simple* columns, his poetry and journalism? He was a poet so most likely the clues you're seeking are in his poetry. At any rate, his papers are at Yale and available to scholars.

In closing, it comes to mind that I saw two prominent Negro Communists, William and Louise Patterson, at Hughes' private funeral, and since they were both Party officials it would appear that his relationship with two old friends extended beyond the limitations of death and dying. I would suspect that the same was true of at least <u>some</u> of his white friends who also remained true to Moscow.

Sincerely yours,
Ralph Ellison.

Mr. Mark States
1929 Delaware St. #-C
Berkeley, CA 94709

To Erskine Caldwell
R A L P H   E L L I S O N
STAR RTE. 91-A
PLAINFIELD, MASS. 01070
SEPTEMBER 20, 1983

Dear Erskine Caldwell:

In 1936, a few weeks after my arrival, I saw my first New York stage play, a version of your *Tobacco Road*. I was fresh out of Alabama where I'd just completed my junior year at Tuskegee Institute, and had by no means adjusted to the wider, but unchartered, freedom of the Big Apple. Which is to say that I was excited by its possibilities but quite aware that although I was out of Alabama, Alabama was by no means out of me. Thus while I was engaged in exploring the city I was going about it gingerly, as with a recently mended arm that still felt insecure without the restraining protection of its plaster cast.

Beyond the borders of Harlem I tended to view New Yorkers through the overlay of my Alabama experience, contrasting the whites I encountered with those I'd observed down South; weighing class against class and southern regional styles against their opposites. Then suddenly, there in a darkened theatre, I was snatched back to rural Alabama, and when Jeeter Lester and the horsing couple went into their act I was reduced to such helpless laughter that I distracted the entire balcony and embarrassed both my host (Langston Hughes) and myself. It was a terrible moment, for before I could get myself under control more attention was being directed at me than at the Lester family. I apologize but there was nothing I could do about it.

I laughed and laughed, and although aware of what was happening there was no way of explaining even to Hughes that you were to blame. For by giving artistic sanction to a source of comedy which in the interest of self-protection I had been forced to deny myself you had released me from three turbulent years of self-restraint. I had seen Jeeter's type in Macon County but there their capacity for racial violence would have been far more overwhelming than their comical wrong-headedness. Indeed, they kept crowding me and I had been tempted to armor myself against their threat by denying them their humanity as they sought to deny me mine.

Which was one of the southern Negro's strategies for dealing with poor whites. The child's jingle, <u>My</u> <u>name</u> <u>is</u> <u>Ran</u> / <u>I</u> <u>work</u> <u>in</u> <u>the</u> <u>sand</u> / <u>I'd</u> <u>rather</u> <u>be</u> <u>a</u> <u>nigger</u> <u>than</u> <u>a</u> <u>poor</u> <u>White</u> <u>man</u>, sums up the attitude. But while such defiant boasting allowed for a release of steam it was frustrating because it was dangerous to convey it to its proper targets. Keeping such sentiments to oneself became a life-preserving discipline that was observed by countering provocation with "cool." Thus I became hysterical in the theater because by catching me off guard and compelling me to laugh at Jeeter you also forced me to recognize and accept our common humanity. For weren't there aspects of Negro character that were just as outrageous? And wasn't the "horsing" scene symbolic of my own frustrating situation as a healthy young man whose sexual outlet was limited to "belly-running" with girls met casually at public dances? So you had me both coming and going, and under such pressure that laughter was my only relief. But more important, by making me see the comedy and allowing me to express it openly you told me something important about who I was, and thus helped initiate me into becoming, if not a "New Yorker," a more tolerant American. And thus you eased some of the conflict I was having in dealing with my southern experience.

For that unexpected liberation I am no less grateful than for the laughter and it's damn well time that I told you so. During the Forties I met you at what was my first Park Avenue party and wanted to do so then but was much too uneasy. Therefore I'll do it now as I wish you Happy Birthday. May there be many more during which you'll go on teaching us how to laugh at, and think through, the absurdity of our outrageous human condition.

Sincerely
[Ralph Ellison]

Mr. Erskine Caldwell
P.O. Box 4550 Hopi Station
Scottsdale, Arizona 85258

RE:fe

To Linda Morris
RALPH ELLISON
STAR ROUTE 91-A
PLAINFIELD, MA 01070
SEPT 22, 1983

Miss Linda G. Morris
4230 Flowerton Road
Baltimore, Maryland 21229

Dear Miss Morris:

Your letter was forwarded and reached me on the 22nd: I hope my reply reaches you in time.

1. You are correct when you state that I graduated from high school with Tracy McCleary in 1931 but mistaken as to my having received a music scholarship to Orangeburg State College. Perhaps that was true of Reginal Thomasson, who later became bandmaster there. My scholarship was to Tuskegee Institute.

2. No, I was not a saxophonist but a trumpeter. However, I did have the privilege of borrowing Mrs. Breaux's soprano sax but used it only for self-instruction. Yes, I played in the Douglass High School Band and was for a time its student band-master. We did indeed perform at the Aldridge Theater.

3. Yes, I remember the Belvedere occasion quite well. I had flown to Baltimore V.I.P. style along with J. Caesar Petrillo, an official emeritus of the national union. Even for a member of the National Council on the Arts this was somewhat incongruous, thus my perspective was somewhat restored when I discovered Tracy taking a leading role in the merging of formerly segregated musical organizations.

4. If you'll take a look at the introduction to my *Shadow and Act,* you'll see that I make much of a group of boys whom I refer to as "Renaissance Men." Tracy was one of those boys and when a segregated library branch was set up in our community Tracy, his brother Willard and I ran through the so-called boys' books, westerns and detective stories in a rapid sweep and were soon devouring such adult books as we could get down. I read my first Freud, A.A. Brill's translation of *The Psychology of Dreams* that I by no means understood—during that exciting period. Tracy, Willard Bowen (another member of the group) and I studied Latin together, and

although we were all fairly good students, Tracy and I were frequently thrown out of class for deliberately triggering Bowen's easily provoked but uncontrollable laughter. We were also conspirators in a hilarious noon-hour put-on during which we'd exchange sonorous Latin phrases learned from our music instruction textbooks as though we were carrying on erudite conversations. He, as I recall, was Signore Allegro; I was his colleague, Signore Andante. The game was no big deal but far more mystifying to our listeners than mere Dog Latin.

I recall also that our gang not only read books from the Public Library branch (now desegregated and named for me, by the way), we bought such books and magazines as we could afford and used the garage attached to the house in which the McCleary family lived on East Third Street as a collective library from which any of us were free to borrow anything that caught our attention. And yes, I'd almost forgotten: I had heard of Tracy and Willard sometime before I came to know them, thanks to a friend of my mother's who owned the house in which the McCleary family was living at that time. My mother's friend, Mrs. Hester Cook, was amazed, if not outraged, by the extensive cussing vocabulary of such young and innocent-looking boys. Fortunately, they had other virtues and thus my mother saw no reason for forbidding our association. I must admit nevertheless that I do owe something of my fondness for wordplay, both sacred and profane, to our shared experiences. Yes, and one of the tragedies of my growing up was our losing touch.

In closing I'll say that Tracy struck me as having the finest mind of all our group and I am pleased to know that you are bringing him to the attention of a wider public. I'll be delighted to learn what happened to him during those long years since our rather interesting boyhood.

Sincerely yours,
Ralph Ellison

To John Callahan
RALPH ELLISON
730 RIVERSIDE DRIVE
NEW YORK, NEW YORK 10031
NOVEMBER 5, 1983

Dear John:

I've been trying to write you for weeks but things continued to go foul even after we left last Sunday morning. First we had the roof to the bedroom repaired and then discovered that with three people stomping around up there we had lost electricity in the bedroom, in the bathroom and in Fanny's study. I was unable to discover exactly where the disconnection lay, but when the handyman roofer returned the next day to repair a burst pipe in the shower his banging around restored the current to all of the disrupted outlets. Then we took the circuit box apart to inspect the wiring, the outlets in all of the affected rooms, and every damn thing else we would think of but with no success. So there was nothing else to do but to disconnect the circuits and appeal to an electrician.

Well, if you've seen the bastard I've seen him. In fact he didn't even return my call. Thus we were without service until we left and spent the rest of our time there worrying about fire. Then, in storing my tiller I strained my back and by the time we made it back to the city I was so exhausted that I haven't been out of the house since I got the car into the garage and made it back to the apartment. Things are better now, thank God, and I can bend without pain. Better still, we've gotten most of our junk out of the middle of the floors and are able to make our way about the apartment without breaking our necks. So now I've storing up energy for next week's board meeting down in Colonial Williamsburg—a chore I would forego but for the fact that one of its favorite members is retiring. After that I hope to return and get back to working with my editor on the essays and then back to my novel. Yes, and preparing myself for whatever the hell it is I'm expected to do at the MLA. I can't say that I look forward to it but seeing you and the big H[*] will make it worthwhile. In the meantime don't worry about your essay for I'm sure that it will give that mob something to think about. In fact, I'm sure that it will give me something to think about and I'm eager to hear you.

Fanny is well, as always, and we send our love to you and yours.

Sincerely,

Ralph

---

[*] Originally coined by Fanny Ellison in response to Michael Harper's poem calling Ralph the "big E," Ralph affectionately turns the moniker back on Harper.

To Allen Ballard
RALPH ELLISON
730 RIVERSIDE DRIVE
NEW YORK, N.Y. 10031
NOV. 21, 1983

Dear Professor Ballard:

We returned to the city at the end of October but I've been so harassed that it is only now that I am able to thank you for your letter. The country is fine until you have to pack up and leave it, and then once again you learn how formidable the city can be when confronted after several months of peace and quiet. Perhaps my parents should have remained in South Carolina—where I'd have other matters to complain about. Geography is fate—or is it the other way around? After all it was in a Northampton bookstore that I stumbled into your *Education of Black Folk,* a discovery I made only a moment ago in the course of typing this letter! So now I'll learn more about you.

The church you visited is most likely the one attended by my relatives, for they were in fact Afro-American-Episcopalians—which is quite a mouthful, but so I was baptized. And yes again, the gravestone you mention is probably that of my father's brother, R.H. Ellison. Robert died in March, 1912, and If I'm not mistaken I have a photograph of the plot. I also have photos of my grandfather and of three of his other sons, including my father, but none of his daughters except for the second oldest, my aunt who lived in Oklahoma City. I met another daughter when I visited Abbeville after my father's death and came to know the youngest in Winston-Salem during the 1950s ... But what intrigues me in the graveyard connection is your mention of there having been a Wideman family. For while I had heard of the Lomaxes and the Smalls, I don't recall that name. Is it possible that the novelist, John Edgar Wideman is a member of that clan? I understand that he was born in Washington, D.C., but it's possible that his folks got out while the going was good as did mine. It would be most interesting if it should turn out that both Wideman and I have our roots in the South Carolina hills. Which reminds me to thank you for the transcript of the Lomax affair. Most likely my grandfather was indeed among the group who guarded him. The two families were friends and I understand that Henry Ellison was elected to Lomax's seat in the legislature following his unexpected death. Lomax was a farmer and successful merchant and I think that it was from him that my grandfather acquired his property. It would appear that Lomax, who was born in 1832, was to die shortly after the events recorded in the transcript.

It was also interesting to see the name of Robert Smalls for not only have I heard and read much about his activities, I also attended school with members of his family who settled in Oklahoma City. The girls were quite good looking. Here I'm reminded that when Mark Twain completed *Huckleberry Finn* in 1883 he left Huck thinking of lighting out for the Territory. Well, it would appear that quite a number of South Carolina families had the same idea, among them Johnson C. Whittaker. Whittaker had been a slave and was a blood relative of the family celebrated in *A Diary from Dixie,* recently re-edited by C. Vann Woodward. During the 1870's he was appointed to West Point where his experiences led to the dismissal of the Point's superintendent. Later he practiced law in South Carolina, served as president of South Carolina State, turned up as the principle of my grade school, and after returning to S.C. served once again as president of S.C. State. My mother knew him in S.C. and told me, when I was a child, of his difficulties at West Point: He looked white—as he damn well should have—and when his classmates discovered that he was Afro-American in culture and status several of them tied him to a cot and slashed a notch in his ear. This sadistic bit of magic sprang from the Point's tradition that only the physically perfect were eligible for graduation. Well, eventually they got rid of Whittaker but in the process they stirred up a national cause celebre and made possible for a bit of West Point to enter the segregated school system. Some time ago I lectured at the Point and learned that one of its officers was writing a book about the incident, thus making available a bit of American history that professional historians chose to ignore. You're quite correct about the power of historians to distort our views of our own history. Last year during a symposium at the New York Public Library I had occasion to remind a New York intellectual who contended that history should be left to the historians that the W.P.A. folklore projects had turned up far more of our group's history than several generations of historians. But given the American insistence that we have no history historians have acted more as mythmakers than recorders of complex socio-political events. Thank God for the camera and the tape recorder! And I hope that the madness of the '60s and '70s which led our young folk to put down their elders has faded, thus making it possible for them to discover the past for themselves . . . Incidentally I think the name of my grandfather's church was St. James A.M.E., and the Calhoun's church was Trinity Episcopal . . .

That's all for now. If you wish to reach me you can do so at the above address. In the meantime I hope things go well with your book. Come December and I'll begin working with my editor with a second book of essays.

Sincerely,
Ralph Ellison

To Ron Polito
RALPH ELLISON
730 RIVERSIDE DRIVE
NEW YORK, N.Y. 10031
NOVEMBER 22, 1983

Professor Ron Polito
Chairman
The Art Department
University of Massachusetts
Harbor Campus
Boston, MA 02125

Dear Professor Polito:

In attempting to answer your query of Richard Yarde I find myself in the embarrassing position of admiring such examples of his work as I have seen while knowing very little of his skills as a teacher. Personally, however, he strikes me as being gifted, sincere and dedicated to his chosen art. And I am told that along with fulfilling his duties as a teacher he is highly productive. This suggests an intensity of motivation that is revealed in his fascination with Afro-American history, which appears to be a major source of his inspiration. In some artists such a preoccupation might well result in mere illustration, but Yarde appears to have transcended that possibility by allowing his fascination with history to guide his explorations of color and three-dimensional form. Thus in his examples of as-semblage he uses the details and legends of his ancestral past as "found objects" that inform his manipulation of form and design.

In this regard Yarde reminds me of Romare Bearden, who is also fascinated by, and gifted at, narration. Both are concerned with the details of contemporary experience no less than with the myths, legends and plastic details of times long past, and both seem bent upon using the discoveries of such modern masters as Picasso, Brague, Duchamp and Dubuffet to make concrete details of experience that have been ignored or willfully repressed in official versions of American history. In this both appear bent upon forcing the viewer to a more informed vision of American experience through the resources of experimental art. In this enterprise Yarde, like Bearden, makes use of his knowledge of art history, of water color and painting, of silk-screen techniques and collage, of photographic values and the expressive possibilities of mixed-media—an example of which is his recent "set piece" reconstruction of the Savoy Ballroom and its atmosphere; a lively artistic evocation of a cultural institution which had a seminal influence upon the arts of music and dance, both popular and classical, in this country and abroad.

Thus while basically concerned with painting Yarde seeks not only to make us see in fresh ways, but to make us grasp the complex connections between aspects of reality and the historical forces which shaped that reality. Surely this preoccupation must be of great value when conveyed to students. But as I say, I have no idea of Yarde's skills as a teacher, and therefore I can but suggest that if he has pleased you and your colleagues thus far it seems to me that he is well worthy of advancement.

Sincerely yours,
Ralph Ellison

To Michael Harper
RALPH ELLISON
730 RIVERSIDE DRIVE
NEW YORK, N.Y. 10031
NOVEMBER 24 & 25, 1983

Dear Michael:

It's Thanksgiving eve and I aint even smelt a chittlin'! True, I'm full of ox-tails, sweet peas, carrots and potatoes and other goodies, but somehow a man needs to be reminded by what's at hand of what was at hand. Fanny's been shopping and I've spied what looks like an off-spring of Purdue's eloquent nose and reminded myself that after all a turkey aint nothing but a burd. Nevertheless, I look forward to whatever she's going to conjure up in the kitchen and plan to attack it with gusto. I'm sure that you have similar plans. You'd better have, considering the formidable competition that you've arranged for yourself.

Things go on here as they did during the summer: the intercom is still driving us nuts, some of the tenants who've always been reluctant to pay their rent (they consider landlords as natural enemies, trouble-makers, and fair game) and so they're yelling louder than anyone else for a rent strike. The telephone rings too often with the voice on the other end speaking in Spanglish, and this late at night, when even Fanny has hit the sack. I spent too much money for a dozen cassettes—only to discover that midway through a recording the sound drops out and although the tape keeps turning it aint saying a damn thing that I've been able to hear. So it goes—Snafu!

You've asked me a couple of (times) if I had seen a book having to do with the Black Heritage of Oklahoma. Well, in retrieving a pencil I came upon such on the bottom shelf of a bookcase. Much to my surprise it has a portrait of me on the cover and inside I discovered to my great pleasure that Willie Stargell is an Oklahoman. It's not much of a history, if you ask me, but it has its uses—if you can get through the misinformation. I did not grow up on the West side, as it states, but on the East side, and the only time the North Canadian River ever threatened me was when I went swimming in it. In fact, the only time I was really frightened by it was shortly before my second birthday, when my father drove our wagon onto it so that he could fill the wagon bed with clean sand to use in the sand pile he was making as one of my birthday presents. I told Richard Wright of this incident and later it turned up in *Black Boy* as an illustration of his uncle's sadistic treatment of a child. Evidently Wright forgot that I had also told him that my father reassured me that there was no danger in what he was doing and that I should never be panicked by water. I didn't mind Wright's appropriating the incident, but I did resent his associating my father with his uncle.

Which reminds me that, thanks to a lady upstairs, I have begun reading the biography of Langston Hughes in which I've already discovered some unnecessary confusion: in a footnote Faith Berry questions the date of my first meeting with Hughes, apparently because she relied on Fabre. If she'd asked me I could have told her that the date was July 5, 1936, for I had spent the 4th in Washington with Mort Sprague's parents. Y'all just can't seem to get even the simplest things right! Perhaps I'm over-reacting, but I find the book depressing both in its conception and because of the sadness that underlays Hughes' charm.

I heard from Callahan who sounds in good shape and I look forward to seeing the two of you at the MLA. Meanwhile I'm keeping my fingers crossed to insure that you'll make it. If you don't I aint showing up! Spent part of Thanksgiving reading a copy of his essay and was quite pleased with the sharpness of his reading. At last someone has pointed out that one of the things *Invisible Man* is about is the nature of rhetoric, eloquence, and leadership! Better still, he sees that it is also about the nature of Afro-American leadership and I'm tempted to search for a rejected scene in which the narrator dreams that he and several leaders are taking turns in attempting to break the maidenhead of a tough-hymened young Negro woman. None are about to make a penetration, and when it came his turn he bounces around on her quite willing belly with no success until it occurs to him that the solution was to use his fountain pen. It's an outrageous scene and I'm sure that it would have provided the Freudians with a field day and gotten me lynched by the feminists! No wonder J. Edgar Hoover tried to scandalize Martin Luther King for being a cocksman. Fool didn't realize the stud-hoss role of black Baptist preachers. True, I don't know whether King resorted to a fountain pen but he dam sho did something that White, Wilkins and Grainger didn't! Seriously though, Callahan is a perceptive critic and I'm most thankful for his interest in my writing.

Hope you and yours are having a pleasant holiday and that the boys allowed you to watch the Lions and the Cowboys do their thing. I watched both games even though a malfunction of our TV set made it somewhat surreal. D'you ever see Too-Tall Jones squash a quarterback while standing on his head? Well, that's how it appeared on our tube, and Dorset was skittering through the line with his feet pounding the air. But I enjoyed every minute of it. In fact, I'm thinking of getting a patent on the process, organizing a company, and having a corp of technicians running around the country adjusting sets to make television programs more interesting.

Take it easy,
but take it!
Ralph

To John Callahan
RALPH ELLISON
730 RIVERSIDE DRIVE
NEW YORK, N.Y. 10031
NOVEMBER 29, 1983

Dear John:

I'm too busy for a letter but thought you might be amused by what I wrote Harper concerning your essay. So here it is:

I heard from Callahan who sounds in good shape and I look forward to seeing the two of you at the MLA. Meanwhile I'm keeping my fingers crossed to insure that you'll make it. If you don't I aint showing up! Spent part of Thanksgiving reading a copy of his essay and was quite pleased with the sharpness of his reading. At last someone has pointed out that one of the things *Invisible Man* is about is the nature of rhetoric, eloquence, and leadership!

Better still, he sees that it is also about the nature of Afro-American leadership and I'm tempted to search for a rejected scene in which the narrator dreams that he and several leaders are taking turns in attempting to break the maidenhead of a tough-hymened young Negro woman. None are about to make a penetration, and when it came his turn he bounces around on her quite willing belly with no success until it occurs to him that the solution was to use his fountain pen. It's an outrageous scene and I'm sure that it would have provided the Freudians with a field day and gotten me lynched by the feminists! No wonder J. Edgar Hoover tried to scandalize Martin Luther King for being a cocksman. Fool didn't realize the stud-hoss role of black Baptist preachers. True, I don't know whether King resorted to a fountain pen but he damn sho did something that White, Wilkins and Grainger didn't! Seriously though, Callahan is a perceptive critic and I'm most thankful for his interest in my writing.

That's it. I'll have more to say when I've read it again but as of now I'm bearing down on those essays which I spent the weekend at my editor's place discussing. Looking at the stuff left me uncertain that they're worth the trouble and I dread having to read them in order to come up with a plan of organization. I should never have listened to you and Michael!

Hope things go well with you and family, to whom our love.

Sincerely,
Ralph

To Linda Morris
RALPH ELLISON
730 RIVERSIDE DRIVE
NEW YORK, N.Y. 10031
DEC. 12, 1983

Miss Linda Morris
4230 Flowerton Road
Baltimore, Maryland 21229

Dear Miss Morris:

I was most pleased to receive your article on my old friend Tracy McCleary. I found it both enjoyable and informative. Informative because you brought back those exciting times when jazz fostered a now missing excitement and enthusiasm, and enjoyable because you allowed me an insight into what happened to Tracy during those years when our paths had parted. How ironic to learn that when he was blowing away at 'Bama State I was blowing away at Tuskegee. We were hardly forty miles away, but while I knew a number of 'Bama State students and saw the wife of its president almost weekly when she came to Tuskegee for piano lessons I missed Tracy completely. We were probably blasting back at one another from opposing bandstands during football games!

Still, that's life, and thus I'm pleased to have some of the blank spaces filled in. Indeed, I'm sure that there are a number of Tracy's old friends in Oklahoma City who would feel the same. Therefore I suggest that you submit your piece to Mr. Russell M. Perry, the editor and publisher of *The Black Chronicle.* The address is P.O. Box 17498, Oklahoma City, Okla. 73136. Telephone number: (405 424-4695).

Good luck to you, and I assure you that I shall get in touch with Tracy.

Sincerely,
Ralph Ellison

To Alan Nadel
RALPH ELLISON
730 RIVERSIDE DRIVE
NEW YORK, N.Y. 10031
JANUARY 27, 1984

Mr. Alan Nadel
17 Walter Avenue
Highland Park, N.J. 08904

Dear Alan Nadel,

Each time I've tried to respond to your manuscript* I've ended up writing little scatter-brained essays on matters that you understand all too well. So now I've decided that the only solution is to tell you that I am most impressed by your book, that I hope it will be published soon so that I can study it at leisure, and assure you that your thoughts on allusion are so intriguing that I shall read the (to me) unfamiliar works to which you refer as soon as possible.

For as you might have anticipated, by identifying certain of my strategies and giving a fresh theoretical rationale for ideas and allusions that I arrived at through sheer tinkering you have not only given me numerous shocks-of-recognition but provided me with a good measure of that rare pleasure which comes to a writer upon discovering that he is in communication with that most desirable of unseen collaborators: a sensitive, well-informed reader. I am especially pleased that you've pointed to the several ways in which I've attempted to "integrate" (and consciously "Afro-Americanize") our literature, whether by initiating dialogues with certain master-works of its pluralistic tradition or by using them as models.

Come to think of it, however, I might have had a different reaction. For you, in a sense, have blown my cover—think of the mixed emotions that Henry James might have felt if someone had solved upon first reading the still elusive mystery of *A Turn of the Screw*! But instead of being displeased with your exposure of my corny pranks and cony tricks I find myself delighted. You point to aspects of my work about which I had to remain silent lest I appear to claim for it subtleties that might exist less in the text than in my mind—Oh, Hermes! Where were you when I needed you?

---

* *Invisible Criticism* would be published by the University of Iowa Press in 1986.

"Ellison," the critics would have said, "you <u>talk</u> a good game, but you sure haven't written one!" And I would have had no answer. Henry James, fine critic and theorist that he was, knew when to talk and when to play it mum, when to wear the critic's top hat, and when to don the turban which marked him as a thirty-second degree magician. His trick (and challenge) was to keep his dual roles dissociated; thus where his own work was concerned he spoke to enhance the technical magic of his craft while being careful not to invade his fellow critics' territory. And a good thing too, considering what he did to Hawthorne!

But for hundreds of years writers and critics have been engaged in a game of hare and hounds, and until recently both have observed certain unwritten rules of the game. Hence with no Bloom-Hartman & Company waiting to defenestrate me I felt fairly secure in my amusement over critics who had no nose for the sources and objects of my manipulations. Sometimes it was as though I'd written an invisible text. Or as though they assumed that my work couldn't possibly have any connection whatsoever with what others had written. And it wasn't that I hadn't cued them with Captain Delano and Eliot's Harry and laid down a trail of other signs and clues:

> *THROW ME INTO THE BRIAR PATCH!*
> *THIS HEAHS A BLACK GUINEA BANK!*
> *HEY! TOD CLIF IS ON A CLIFF*
> *HE'S FATED TO FALL!*

But I refer mainly to my many debts to Joyce and Melville, Mark Twain and Eliot, not to mention the violence I've done them. But also ignored was my preoccupation with what I consider the distortions and omissions that characterize much of what passes for American history, literary criticism, and sociology. Talk about voodoo economics! Hell, the present gurus of the GNP learned it from historians!

Seriously though, I am especially grateful for your analysis of the "Golden Day" section of my novel. For some thirty years I'd waited for <u>somebody</u> to remark the extent to which Mumford's work was being attacked and argued with. For as you point out in fine detail *The Golden Day* is indeed the counter-text (a term that had little meaning for me at the time I was writing) to all that wildness that erupts in mine, and I feared that I was being so embarrassingly obvious that Mumford's supporters would be after me cheek and thigh. But much to my chagrin I was wrong.

Thus as far as I am aware you're the first critic to point out the outrageous extent that I was out to dynamite the illustrious gent's conception of American history and culture.

What an architect! What an untragic would-be tragedian! Why the way he stacked the deck reminded me of those log-rafts described by Huck Finn as being thrown together so larcenously that a hound dog could be sailed straight through their yawning cracks. In fact I was so incensed that years later I was still burning; and when I began writing the embers flared up again. Therefore I set out to give myself so much swinging room that I could not only send Mumford on a boomeranging course through his own gaping holes, but send him in and out and back again until he landed on his head.

But not really. I merely wanted to land the equivalent of a sharp, backhanded slap, the kind that's so quick and well-aimed as to do the maximum damage while escaping the attention of any but the most attentive eye. One of the beauties of literary allusion (and the same is true of melodic insinuation in jazz) is that it allows one to kick an annoying behind without breaking the basic rhythm of one's forward motion.

And yet it wasn't that I didn't admire Mumford. I have owned a copy of the sixth Liveright printing of *The Golden Day* since 1937 and own, and have learned from, most of his books. I was simply upset by his implying that the war that freed my grandparents from slavery was of no real consequence to the broader issues of American society and its culture. What else, other than sheer demonic, masochistic hell raising, was that bloody war all about if not slavery and the contentions which flowed there-from?

As a self-instructed student I was quite willing for Mumford to play Aeschylus, Jeremiah, or even God, but not at the price of his converting the most tragic incident in American history into bombastic farce. For in doing so he denied my people the sacrificial role that they had played in the drama. I can't thank you enough for pointing to my little attempt at undermining such "accepted" ways of "deconstructing" our common historical experience.

I must confess, however, that at the time of writing I was by no means prepared to go after Ralph Waldo Emerson in the manner that [I] went after Mumford. After all, I do have my pieties, and sharing his first names was inhibiting in more ways than one. Ralph-the-Exhorter was my father's favorite author—perhaps because being from post-Reconstruction South Carolina my dad found solace in Emerson's encouragement of self-reliance. So rather than going after Emerson's oracular stance, I went after some of the bombast that had been made of his pronouncements. This you make quite clear but I'd suggest, if I may, that it might help if you pointed up the distinction you make between my trustee "Emerson" and ole Waldo who strikes me, incidentally, as being as difficult to pin down as the narrator's grandfather.

At any rate it might amuse you to hear that on one of my book shelves there are two small bronze medallions and a small wooden plaque. The medallions are inscribed with images of Emerson and Lincoln respectively, and the plaque with an image of Janus. Janus sits between Emerson and Lincoln so that he can give them his divided yet unified attention. They appear to be communing, but although I've tried for years to grasp the drift of their deliberations thus far I've been unsuccessful. So for consolation I have a small photograph of Mark Twain, who hangs above my typewriter smoking a cigar and dressed in the academic regalia that he donned to accept his degree from Oxford. Being a word-man of Southern background, he encourages me sometimes by singing a spiritual, or by recounting a Negro folk tale. And once when interrupted by a yell of "Make it new!" from Ezra Pound across the room, Mark yelled back, "Hell, if you get some of <u>this</u> stuff in it can't help but be new! Didn't you hear Tom Eliot say that he speaks with a <u>nigger</u> accent? Well, dammit, to anyone who knows how to listen, he does!"

Which brings me to your insightful comments on the importance of *Huckleberry Finn* to my fiction. I read it so early and at so many points in my life that there's no way in the world for me to know when it is or isn't making itself felt in my work. Thus I wish that I could say that my allusions to fog, bridge, and river in the paint factory section were intentionally as extensive as you find them to be. I only know for certain that as a novelist I work not only from literary texts but from the sights and scenes around me. Of course these filter-and-feed back to books that have made a strong impression upon my imagination. And it is to these that I find myself turning, whether consciously or unconsciously, for clues as to how to give form to my observations. Fortunately, one can draw upon both sources at one and the same time. So Huck Finn, London Bridge, Ishmael et al. aside, one source of the scenic imagery came from observations made back during the Thirties when I crossed the Fifty-ninth Street Bridge twice daily on the way to my job in Long Island City and back. Whatever facts really are their symbolicity constitutes the stuff of fiction— But don't hold me to it . . .

And now on to the ten drops of black dope used in whitening the paint.

Here the initial allusion seems to have been to the Negro percentage of the total population; which in symbolic and political effect rendered the white population even "whiter." No blacks, no need for the pervasive stress on color. There was also the ironic implication that although the narrator failed to see that he was apparently only an insignificant black "drop" he was, nevertheless, as important to the general scheme of things to the illusion of a total whiteness of power as the white paint to the rank and aura of national myth and monument. Being <u>sticky</u> symbolic, paint is a most ambiguous agency of illusion; it reveals as it conceals, and if it streaks it doesn't "hide." Beside, there's always something behind it or beneath it. There's always something in the background, so that it signals the presence of that which it's used to deny. Thus the Negroes' invisible condition defines certain elements of illusion involved in America's flawed enactment of its democratic promises. Hence my riff on paint and perception focuses upon those personal and hierarchical motives that combine with historical complexities to whitewash our perception of reality . . . But I mustn't be taken in by my own playing with allusions and illusions. As a "word" paint is but a sign and symbol to conjure with. In the manufacture of <u>real</u> paint such drops of dope would probably serve as a drying agent, or as an aid to its viscosity and covering properties. But since I gave myself the options of surrealism I was free to transform the black dope into something more useful. I could make it "bleed" (a paint manufacturer's term) through its toughness and reveal that which it was meant to conceal. To the writer's good fortune—and especially to that of an Afro-American writer—symbols are as much a means of destabilizing reality as they are a means of making reality cohere to human designs. And when symbolism is really working poetically nothing—not paint, not machinery, not electronics, nor flesh and blood, or bone structure—can withstand its magic. For example, for all the stress placed upon Negro blackness as a sign of the negative it has served for hundreds of years to advertise excellence. There is more to it than that, however, since the black image also warns the buyer to beware—if not the product, at least the ambiguity of appearances. More confounding, it challenges us to contemplate the mystery of American identity as it taunts us, say, in the style and visage of Vanessa Williams. What the hell kind of make-up was used on her?

I don't know if the muses are still with us or not, but sometimes writing appears to me to be a process of releasing a genie from a symbolic lamp or bottle and then forcing it into an all too physical typewriter; or, as in this instance, a word-processor. But once the genie is uncorked all kinds of unexpected things begin to happen. Strange transformations occur—As when the foamy whiteness created by the confluence of two rivers leaps from one text to another to become transformed simultaneously into a symbol of freedom, a reversal of human fortune, and the contents of a paint can—While the turbulence set up within the can spills over to evoke the old forgotten song, Mose Kicked the Bucket, and to which the rampaging machinery in the basement roars out the refrain, "Old man Mose is dead!"

Isn't it amazing how little details can determine the direction in which our interpretations of an allusion will take us? On page 186 (by the way, your pagination is somewhat out of order) you refer to the "important victory" which the narrator speaks of having lost. Well, part of the intended meaning rests in Brockway's term, "young nineteen hundred Negroes." That epithet was once applied by Negroes born during the 19th century to those born during the 20th. Used negatively it implied a loss of both spiritual and physical stamina and good common sense as well. Used positively it suggested that younger Negroes were smarter than their elders and were more likely to be more impatient and militant in the face of racial discrimination. Brockway's usage was malicious, and thanks to the old guy's trickery the narrator lost far more than his job. He lost a generational struggle which he'd assumed to've been already decided: With his grandfather's riddle, with Brockway's slavery-inspired ignorance and suspicion, and with Bledsoe's guile. Bledsoe—whose name is not "Herbert," as certain critics would have it, but "Hebert" and pronounced "A-bear"—had loaded him down with Bellerophonic letters directing the trustees to keep him hoping, wandering and wondering. But, thanks to young Emerson, the narrator lands in Brockway's basement where that tar baby of an unlikely Iobates "kills" him. Thus he is sent on to the next stage of his agon. Thus by blasting the hopes of our little young 20th century mantheMose Brockway also insured his resurrection as one who was a bit more aware of his folk heritage. And so he emerges from the hospital still struggling with the presentness of his past, but rid of certain illusions as he goes searching for the Pegasus that will help him confront his Chimera. Little did he suspect, poor fellow, that he would have to teach himself to fly—and in a hole in the ground at that!

But enough is enough. For as you can see you've got me playing with my own concoction again. Therefore I'll close with my heartfelt thanks for having paid my work the compliment of such careful, creative and insightful reading. And I say this while remaining fully aware that you might have used any number of novels to illustrate your theory of allusion. May you find early publication and the widest of readership.

Sincerely,

Ralph Ellison

To Henry Louis Gates

RALPH ELLISON

730 RIVERSIDE DRIVE

NEW YORK, N.Y. 10031

FEB. 2, 1984

Professor Henry Louis Gates

P.O. Box 3388 Yale Station

Yale University

New Haven, Connecticut

06520

Dear Professor Gates:

I am behind in our correspondence by a margin of four to one at the very least. Thus let me hasten to thank you for the Anthony Davis recording, for your essay and—although I'm somewhat dismayed to see it again—for the stuff that I published all those years ago in the *New Masses*. Somewhere in my files copies of the originals are falling steadily into decay, but it would appear that the sins and failures of one's youth have such tenacity as to be indestructible even though they were committed on the poorest of print-stock. If they fall to dust and silverfish in one's files they simply resurrect themselves elsewhere with the blessings of Xerox. Scanning through the stuff gave me a feeling similar to that which I have whenever I come across photographs made when I was an adolescent: a mixture of disbelief that I could ever have been so callow—what with my pimples and teen-age grin—and relief that I survived and will never have to go through all of that again!

As for the unsigned editorial from the *Negro Quarterly* that you sent along I'll have to confess that I wrote it. I hadn't read it for years and was surprised to discover that I had tried to probe the mystery of the zoot suit even earlier than I thought. Unfortunately, however, my file of the *Quarterly* has disappeared and thus I am unable to tell you if I am responsible for any of the others. If so, you've probably identified them by the style, such as it is, but if you wish further verification send them along and I'll take a look.

With the Bland piece there's no problem. Ed Bland was a young Chicagoan, and (I think) a self-trained intellectual. An acquaintance of Richard Wright, he appeared at the *Quarterly* office during my short stay there— 1942–44—with an interesting but rather unformed essay. I accepted it and what was published was the result of my fairly heavy-handed attempt at re-writing. In other words, the prose is mine but the ideas are Bland's. Shortly afterwards he went overseas to a soldier's death. This is most regretful because he night well have gone on to make a name for himself as a writer; in which case I would've denied my role in reshaping his essay. As to Arden Bland, I seem to recall that Ed did have a son, but whether he and Arden are the same I am unable to say.

It is good to know that the *Quarterly* has been reprinted. It owed its brief existence to Angelo Herndon's attempt to become something more than a Communist figurehead. By way of lending him a hand I left my job on the Writers Project, but there were endless money problems plus Herndon's conflicts with his comrades, so I left and joined the Merchant Marine. Sometime later Herndon took the magazine to California and I lost touch. It might be worthwhile if you could get hold of the files. I myself would be interested to see what the hell I had to work with but I have no idea of how to go about it. The last I heard of Herndon was that he became disenchanted with politics and was living in Chicago, where he was dealing in real estate. But for the cynicism spawned by his disillusionment with the Party, Herndon might have turned into an effective leader. Neither of us was much of an editor, but under the circumstances—the war atmosphere, the lack of a group of supporting writers, etc.—we did the best we could.

Thus even though my experience at editing was brief I sympathize with your ambivalent position regarding your two audiences. Perhaps you'll just have to keep writing as searchingly and as eloquently as you can and let your readers, whomever they might be, come up to your standards. Those who are serious will try to measure up and to hell with the others because they'll only bitch and hedge to protect their own sloth, no matter what you do. I've read the extract from your book with interest and shall read the entire manuscript as soon as I'm free to do so. Meantime I hope you'll find works to challenge your powers of analysis. And if none happen to be written by Afro-Americans—So what? You don't have to worry about that damn monkey because he has a thousand identities—probably the least interesting of which is "Shine," and that thanks to so many inept attempts at making his more significant than he could possibly be. Tackle Hermes, tackle Janus, tackle Yellow-Kid Wiell, even Jessie Jackson— they're all the same but for the scenes in which they operate. Or why not

Mark Twain, who spanned both major streams of American culture and offers the added advantage of having been a <u>literary</u> trickster. Or what about Reveren' Leroy? Of course all this is off the top of my head because I've met you only briefly and have yet to read your book. Nevertheless, I'd suggest that you try not to load too much of your erudition upon the backs of us slender reeds. Rather, reveal to us dummy's the extent, if any, that ole Mose is hiding in Henry James' word-pile. I'm very intrigued by this as a possibility, because unlike the black tricksters one hears so much about in pool halls, barbershops and bars, Mose is more subtle. He is most wary of calling attention to himself, and when he's working his tricks in language he's apt to turn up in the most unexpected of places.

Be that as it may, I've listened to the Anthony Davis recording, and I have to confess that I found your liner notes of far more interest than his music. Like most of the post-modern music I hear it struck my ear as unformed. It might be that I'm too old to get his message, or that I've had enough of unstable tonalities and rhythms. Or that I've been ruined by all those musical effects that nowadays composers feel that they can dispense with. But I happen to feel that good things should only be displaced for something better, and having an ear for melody and a foot for rhythm I have need for reassurance. Perhaps the early 20th century Russians could provide Davis with hints as to how to use all that old-time jazz that's still hanging around. But who am I, a dropout musician, to have such criticism of those who're struggling against such a powerful body of vernacular art? Still, very often a step backwards makes for a forward leaping. And if there's one thing certain about today's surrealist and electronic composers, it is that they've deliberately ignored a body of art that might well supply them with substance. Madame Boulanger is dead and gone, but she's still screwing a whole generation of American composers. Thank God that Duke didn't fall into her sterile trap! Otherwise his music might have turned out like the chatter of the chips inside this computer, interesting to other chips but not worth a dam to a jazz fan. Still, where art is concerned one must live in hope. Therefore with your encouragement I'll keep an eye out for more Anthony Davis.

Thanks again for your thoughtfulness in sending me the material from the *New Masses* and my regards to Mr. Benston.

Sincerely,
Ralph

P.S. Don't misunderstand me on Jackson, having him in the race is like having a trout in a pool of sunfish; he keeps them lively.

To Odette Hines
RALPH ELLISON
730 RIVERSIDE DRIVE
NEW YORK, NEW YORK 1031
MARCH 29, 1984

Mrs. Odette Harper Hines*
4415 Lee Street Ext.
Alexandria, Louisiana
71301

Dear Odette:

I can't tell you how wonderful it was to hear from you, but either your e.s.p. is working with precision or coincidence is outdoing itself by proving that it has its reality even through one is advised to shun it when writing fiction.

I say this because only a few days before your letter arrived Fanny and I were talking of you and our old days on the Writers Project, and this led to my describing your family place here in New York with its unique arrangement between the two branches of your family. Then came recollections of Lester Granger, Carlton Moss, Ottley and a number of others whose names we hadn't mentioned for years. I have often wondered how things had gone with you in the Deep South after the turbulent sixties, and have recalled my pleasant surprise at not only finding you there but happily married.

Of course I realized from your last letter that you had become an activist, and had concluded that I had failed you by not taking part in the marches etc. I regretted it but felt that there was more than one way to fight and that there was more than one front to the war. Now I realize that you hadn't given up on me entirely, but that indeed you were aiding in my part of the struggle. It will amuse you to learn that certain younger friends now tease me by recalling that they first came across such slogans as "Black is Beautiful" and Jesse Jackson's "rainbow" notion—which they find on page 291—in *I.M.* As Fats Waller said, "One never knows, do one?"

Nevertheless, your experiences with young people are similar to mine. I receive a new crop of fan letters with each new generation of students, and often from Europeans. Better still, some of those who attacked me most bitterly during the sixties and seventies have changed their minds about me.

---

* An old friend from Ellison's years with the Federal Writers' Project. See the introduction to "Letters from the Eighties and Nineties" in this volume.

Well, it's a big country and given its racial structure it is difficult for our young people to grasp how institutions and action relate. While I was . . . catching hell for not joining the rides and marches I was participating, and quite vocally, in the Carnegie Commission which produced the basic ideas for Public Television, serving on the National Council on the Arts, the Boards of the Kennedy Center and The National Portrait Gallery, Bennington College, and the New School, etc. There was little, if any, danger in these activities, but they did serve to bring something of our experience into areas where our interests are important. During the same period Fanny was working with the International Rescue Center, and later became the director of the American Medical Center for Burma, a group that supported Doctor Gordon Seagrave, the famous Burma Surgeon. So all in all neither of us were completely out of the struggle. I even held the Albert Schweitzer Professorship at N.Y. U., and am now a professor emeritus. Looking back it seems a bit nutty that my life should have gone in such a direction, but it seemed unfair to protest our lack of opportunities to play a part in the broader affairs of the country and then refuse invitations to participate. In these matters it is difficult to know how effective one has been, but if nothing else I've accustomed quite a number of white folks to exchanging ideas with a Negro. Perhaps those who come after me shall benefit from my little effort at pioneering.

But how wonderful to learn that even while you were engaged in the movement you were also having children! We are delighted, and perhaps just a bit envious since we missed that blessing. But learning that you are also a grandmother makes me feel like a Rip Van Winkle who took a nap and woke up two generations later to discover that time had leaped far ahead. Or perhaps we've simply been living on different time-tracks, and with you having found the Fountain of Youth. For except for your daughter, who bears your likeness, you appear in the photograph much as you did when I last saw you. Which is something of a miracle, for whenever I happen upon newspaper photos of old friends in Oklahoma most of them reveal ravages of time much as I do myself. I'm as lively as ever, but my moustache has turned salt-and-pepper (and more salt than pepper) while the thinnest of hair screens the baldness of my head. So that now whenever I find myself tagging some stranger as an "old fellow" I quickly remind myself that I am perhaps older than he. Some of us look old but don't feel it, while others feel it but don't show it. I guess I belong with the first group, but whatever the case there is no question but that time imposes its own perspective, as does race and geography. Thus I should say here that I was quite pleased that you had gone south to live. For I had the feeling that Harlem had little to offer you in terms of a suitable mate. I knew that this was but a reflection of my own opinion of the fellows I knew in Harlem and so I kept it to myself. Incidentally, I looked in Anderson's book to see if I could identify you and your brother but without success. Thank God that you grew up when things were jumping and then got out, because today it's a sad, sad place. Indeed it's worse than the neighborhood in which I grew up and these are now urban-renewed into super highways and the like. My old school is now a warehouse, the house in which I was born is gone, and the streets where I played and worked and grew up are now abandoned. American change can be both relentless and callous.

Even this neighborhood has changed over the more than thirty years we've lived here, much of it taken over by Hispanics. But there's still the river so we cling to the Drive and no longer go wandering about late at night. Nevertheless, Fanny and I still find much to enjoy in our lives. We have a shack in the Berkshires where, gardening and writing, we spend at least five months of the year, and some years ago we joined a number of writer friends in reclaiming a run-down compound in Key West, had it landscaped and rebuilt or renovated its houses, and so are able to spend part of the winter season in the sun . . .

Thanks for allowing us to see the photograph of you and your daughter, and we'd be delighted to see the rest of your family along with a photo of your portraiture. The news that you have become a painter was another surprise, and yessin' or no yessin' aside you've found a way to improve the southern scenery even as you added to its population and improved its civility. No wonder you're a happy lady!

Thanks for remembering my birthday, and our best wishes to you and yours,

Sincerely,
Ralph

P.S.
We were disheartened when we read of Lester's death and it is a relief to learn that he spent his last years with you.

P.P.S.
I am enclosing the photograph, not simply because you sent along a stamped, self-addressed envelope, but in hope that you'll [send] us others.

To Odette Hines
RALPH ELLISON
730 RIVERSIDE DRIVE
NEW YORK, NEW YORK 1031
APRIL 23, 1984

Dear Odette:

After seeing your snapshots of pony, swimming pool and happy children I know that you are the best of grandmothers. For although there was no private swimming pool in my childhood, I <u>did</u> have a friend who had both a pony and a billy goat. The goat had its cart and the pony its rubber tired buggy and saddle, and my brother and I shared rides with my friend and his sister in both buggy and cart. Your photos brought it all back for the first time in many years. Therefore, I have an idea of your children's good fortune and can appreciate some of the valuable lessons that they might have learned in their play.

The pony's name was Blue Belle, the goat's Billy. Blue Belle was a rather short-tempered Shetland mare who kicked and pitched when irritated by whip or rash tugs on her bit, and she taught me quite early a respect for animals that I'd missed when dealing with my father's horses. But so did Billy, who went into a rage of butting whenever an unwary posterior appeared within his range of vision. Both were touchy, but Blue Belle gave me the greater pleasure, including rides about the neighborhood and fairly long trips into the country on visits with my friend's grandparents. My friend's father was a physician and when wintry roads became unsafe for his car Blue Belle was harnessed and hitched to her buggy. Then with the good doctor dressed in great-coat and hard black physician's hat dwarfing the seat—much to the delight of neighborhood children and adults alike—she'd take him on his rounds. It took some time for me to accept the fact that strong little Blue Belle was not a <u>pony</u> but an adult horse, thus knowing her proved educational in a number of ways. Thanks for reminding me of such pleasant times.

And how nice to learn that Carlton is doing so well. He was among those who used the project to advance his skills and he rated far higher on my scale of values than, say, Ottley or Poston. Indeed, I considered him more of a friend than I did John Velasco, whom I saw mainly because he was Rosie's cousin. I enjoyed Carlton's jokes and stories (sometime I find myself quoting one of his jibes: "His head was knotty/And his nose was snotty") and had hopes that when the Depression was over he'd be able to continue his interrupted career in radio. I can't recall quarreling with him ever, but even if I had I'd no more ignore him on the street than I'd ignore my brother. If I passed him by it must have been because my mind was elsewhere and not because I wished to avoid contact. Besides, I found no difficulty in being civil to those with whom I held strong political differ-ences. And here I think of Ben Davis who was never a friend of mine, but I talked with him in public at least a couple of times after he was released from prison. And this quite some time after his group had attacked me for *Invisible Man.* He was living in this neighborhood at the time and when he saw me enter the drug store where he was having breakfast I had the impression that he thought I'd be embarrassed when he roared out, "Why there's Ralph Ellison!" I was surprised, but nevertheless, I went over and spoke with him and tried to get a line on Angelo Herndon, with whom I had lost contact during the war. As far as I was concerned Davis was an idealist who entered politics and got caught in an international bind when his comrades betrayed those in whose interest he had sought to act. He knew where I stood, so if he wanted to talk, why not?

War and politics do indeed make strange bedfellows, but it would seem that the communists were compelled to designate all those who disagreed with their politics as enemies. Worst, even those who weren't members of the group were infected with the virus. Then came the war, people who had come together on the projects were scattered, and when the war ended they went their separate ways, became involved in their various careers and seldom saw one another again.

This was true of a number of people whom I regarded quite highly. Bill Attaway, for instance. I haven't seen Attaway for years but even though I've tried to make contact it's as though he faded from the earth. For a long time I had no contact with Add Bates, who persuaded me to enter the merchant marine during the war. After the war our lives entered dif-ferent grooves and although I visited his cabinet-maker's shop several times our old friendship wasn't resumed. Then a few years ago Fanny and I decided to install a new kitchen counter and new cabinets so we called upon Add. He accepted the job and was a friendly as ever, but during the installation we noticed that he was having difficulty in remembering his measurements. He'd use his ruler, make careful notations but then in a few minutes he'd be repeating himself. Finally I decided that my presence was a distraction and made myself scarce. In the end he did a satisfactory job, was paid and left in a pleasant mood. We saw him sometime later at a party given by one of his friends, an occasion during which we noticed that instead of displaying his usual conviviality he sat quietly alone, observing the activities with the attitude of a dignified but mildly bemused stranger. That was the last time that I can recall seeing him, but then, last year, while attending a brunch given by a group of young business people from Oklahoma I learned from one of his old buddies that Add was suffering from Alzheimer's disease.

I won't go further in this vein, but should you write Carlton tell him that if he happened to've had an experience with Add similar to that which he ascribed to me it was due to a tragic illness, not some petty attempt at a put-down. Tell him also that I would like to hear from him.

But now to happier news. On April eleventh I received the first medallion presented by the City College of the City University of New York (what a mouthful!) in honor of Langston Hughes. The occasion marked the ninth Langston Hughes Festival, and was quite moving—at least for me. As you might remember, I met Hughes on my first morning in New York and at a time when I still considered myself a musician. Later he encouraged my writing while finding my intellectuality most amusing. Then in 1979 when correspondence between Hughes and Arna Bontemps was published there was revealed an exchange between them wherein they were amused by the slowness with which I wrote and a bit of annoyance with my concern with literary theory. Thus I can't help but wonder how they would have reacted to my receiving the Hughes medallion, but since both had a sense of irony I'm sure that they would have responded with good grace. At any rate, Langston had been a hero of mine since about the sixth grade and was responsible for my meeting many of those who would influence my career; perhaps the most important was Richard Wright. During the later years of his life we weren't as close as before but I respected him and am most proud to have been honored in his memory. It reminds me that there is continuity in Negro life, and that we when stick to our own ideals and do the best we can chances are that we'll encourage others to hope and take risks that might well prove to be creative.

I'll close by asking that you forgive the length of all this and by no means should you feel obligated to respond in kind. Any lil' ole word from you will be appreciated, and when there's time I'll send you a photograph or two. Keep well and don't spoil them youn'uns! Meanwhile our best to you and yours.

Sincerely
Ralph

P.S. This strange type results from my using a computer, which suggests that I'm as gadget-happy as ever!

To Bill Dawson
JULY 25, 1984

Wm L. Dawson
Tuskegee, Ala. 36088

Dear Bill:

We are most delighted to have the biography of Hazel Harrison, and I am especially thankful for the photograph of our old faculty. I recognize everyone except the lady who stands to Hazel's left, and it brought back many, many memories of those confused but hopeful olden days. As was usual when he was on his best behavior Captain Drye looks like little Jack Horner, but only the Lord knows who he was cussing behind his moustache! Probably Mr. Polk, if he happened to have been the photographer. My memory of friend Suthern is quite vivid, but I'd forgotten that he was almost as tall as Cap. Nevertheless, the photo is so evocative that I can even recall the perfume of some of the ladies.

After Nineteen-thirty-seven you, Hazel, and Mrs. Pittman were the only ones of the group whom I was to see again, and I saw Mrs. Pittman only at Hazel's funeral. I did run into Dr. Patterson several times some years ago when he was attending board meetings on Park Avenue, but I haven't laid eyes on his wife since Tuskegee. So life goes. We came together, things happened, and except for memories and whatever I managed to learn, it was all over. Thus since I retain so little from all that was offered, I thank God for my still serviceable memory.

Incidentally, the publishers sent me the galleys for the book some time ago, but I withheld comment not only because it struck me as a bit thin, but because they had published a number of my short stories without permission. I am sure that you will understand my reaction. Nevertheless I appreciated the authors' effort, and had they gotten in touch with me I would have been only too willing to make suggestions that might have given the book a wider range.

But why complain? We have it now, and when and if some future scholar becomes interested it will be there to build upon.

Seeing Hazel standing beside you I recalled having accompanied her and Allen Moton as their somewhat incongruous chaperone on a trip to Montgomery and back, during which Allen drove the Motons' sixteen cylinder Cadillac at unbelievable speeds while trying to impress her with his knowledge of philosophy. Naturally, he had been drinking and handled that big truck of a car as though he was trying to thread some kind of a crooked needle. Only my youth prevented my hair from turning white, and I swore right then and there that if I made it back to the campus alive I'd let that May and September affair take whatever turn it was fated to take without my assistance. So now, years later, I learn that it took the turn of marriage and a quickie Mexican divorce! The last time I saw Moton was on 125th Street and he looked like a wino. How terrible that with all his opportunities and (I've been told) talent he chose the role of imposter, "Doctor Ravel" was the title he used to impress Harlem's filles de joie who, being realists, were far more impressed by his easy-come-easy-go flow of money.

In closing I must tell you that your gift came as a good omen, for in the same batch of mail I also received an autographed copy of Handy's *Beale Street Blues*. A white friend college professor who served on President Johnson's staff found it while going through his deceased father's papers and decided that I would appreciate it. Which I most certainly do, and all the more because arriving with Hazel's biography it reminded me once again that the currents of art like the extremes of life often come together in moments of illumination.

We're still caught here in the heat and noise of the city but hope to make it to the country by August. In the meantime our love to you and Cecile.

Sincerely,
Ralph

To John Roche

[John Roche
15 Bay State Road
Weston, Mass 02193]
NOV. 6, 1984

Dear John:

Your gift and note made for one of the few bright spots of our late and now departed summer; therefore I feel terrible for having failed to tell you so much earlier. But despite our resolutions we were held here in New York by changes in our building's management, by breakdowns in service, and by a rent strike. Thus after planning to be off to the hills by the first week in June we remained to be assaulted—for the first time in years by Manhattan's heat, hounded by Latino-beaten bongo drums, and left sleepless by the dreadful noise broadcast so relentlessly by the new-style portable juke-boxes (Japan's latest revenge upon this volatile and gadget-happy nation) which every little bastard in Washington Heights appears to own, and which they insist upon sharing with us poor deprived ones even at four o'clock in the morning! Fortunately, I was able to preserve my sanity during the day by working on a new book of essays, and after nightfall by relying on double bourbons for nightcaps. Fanny, being the more civilized, managed simply by being beautiful, cheerful and patient.

Finally, we made it to the hills in October, but only for one hectic week during which we were able to correct only a few of the damages done by last winter's rigors and were able to survive by hauling water from our fairly distant neighbors. But then, why waste time and money repairing pipes that will probably burst by the time we arrive again? Obviously, we'd lost a round in our struggle against nature; with winter, weeds and woodchucks having done their thing; and so, come spring, we'll make a new beginning. It's all a part of the game—or am I simply being bemused by a lyric set to a melody composed by Vice-President Dawes?

Anyway, after this unforgivable delay let me hasten to thank you for the *Beale Street Blues.* I am absolutely delighted to have it in my collection of precious things, and shall treasure it along with my signed copy of Joyce's *Anna Livia Plurabelle,* and parts of manuscripts by Malraux and Silone which Fanny gave me years ago. I took it as a good omen that the score arrived in the same batch of mail that brought a biography of the late Hazel Harrison, who was a teacher friend from my days in the Tuskegee music school. For Hazel, a fine classical pianist who arrived on the scene too early to be granted nationwide recognition which now comes relatively easy for Negro artists, was a prize pupil of Busoni and herself a powerful example, both as a performer and teacher. Sad to say, it is not much of a biography but by arriving along with the Handy it served nevertheless to remind me of how constantly the two streams of culture out of which I come have merged, been transformed, and merged again to bring me influences from distant places. Hazel was a friend of Prokofiev and Percy Grainger, neither of whom I was ever to see in person, but through her stories and demonstrations on the piano I was able to widen my range and relate more closely with their music.

With Handy, however, it was different; for I had grown up with his music and legend, and during the late nineteen-forties our apartment was but a block away from his. He was blind by that time, but I often saw him walking through the block where he lived on Convent Avenue and thus was able to greet him and wish him well. I really wanted to talk with him about music but wasn't enough of a reporter to ask for an interview. Besides, he knew me only as one of the many admiring voices heard in the street and therefore I satisfied myself with the knowledge that I lived near a great composer.

Years earlier, when I was down-and-out in Dayton, Ohio, I attended a football game between two Negro schools which began with the home team's band playing "America." But then, after paying it their solemn respects, they bridged smoothly into "The Saint Louis Blues" as though it were an even more exalted "national" anthem. At first I was startled but then quickly realized that, in a sense, it was indeed a national anthem and quite fitting for inspiring emotions needed for a football game—or any damn thing else of national significance.

Those were the days when the only way I could read a copy of the New York *Times* was by walking a mile or so from the Negro section into downtown Dayton—which I did daily so that I could read Hemingway's dispatches from the Spanish Civil War, which I studied for style as well as for information. For me it was a period of disorientation in more ways than one. For at a time when I was making my uncertain transition from music to literature I had rushed to Ohio because of my mother's death. Then, being broke and unable to find work, I was forced to remain in an area that seemed to have little connection with the world I'd left behind in New York. There I had been involved in the agitation over the war in Spain, but the Ohio papers gave it as little coverage as they gave racial relations. In brief, I was at loose ends in a world that had fallen apart. But as Malraux has written, art is an assault upon logic. Thus hearing the "Saint Louis Blues" juxtaposed with our national anthem not only worked wonders for my morale, but told me something of where I was politically while suggesting that even for a writer the example of a folk-based art such as Handy's could not only transcend the divisions of race, politics and geography, but could speak—at least to my own sense of the national experience—with far more force and resonance than Samuel Francis Smith's "America." Perhaps I exaggerate a bit, but whatever the truth may be there's no question but that Handy lifted me out of a deep depression and I'm most grateful to have a score inscribed by his hand.

That's all for now because I want to get this into the mail, but after election day perhaps you'll tell me what the hell is happening to this country. Meanwhile our love to you and your lady from me and mine, and once again my thanks.

Sincerely,
Ralph

P.S.:
Since I'm tied up with my essays and my too-long-in-progress novel, both of which are under contract to my publishers, I'm doing no lecturing for the time being. However, once they're out of the way I'll come a-calling.

To Herbert Ellison
DEC. 3RD, 1984

Dear Herbert:

I thought that you might find looking at the enclosed amusing. Fanny made copies of the various papers that rounded out my service on the Williamsburg board. The sheet with the map gives the order of events that took place during the meeting, the names of the board members and spouses who attended, and the places in which we were housed.

The other material is the best we could do in making a copy of the menu, which was excellent, and I'm sorry that there is no way to convey to you the atmosphere in which Dan* and I were "roasted." The best I can do is to say that it was emotional, amusing and when the trumpeter took off with his <u>wha-wha</u> mute in that old plantation mansion, it was historical. I only wish that a tape had been made of the entire proceedings because I was too moved to keep it straight in my mind. For to tell the truth, I don't know what the hell I said in my little farewell remarks. One thing is certain, and it's that Fanny and I will miss those twice-yearly junkets to Virginia and the friends we made there. Besides, where else in the world could we not only have the illusion of living like millionaires for a couple of week-ends a year, but <u>actually</u> living and working with some

---

* Daniel Boorstin, historian and Librarian of Congress, with whom Ellison served on the Colonial Williamsburg board.

of the most dedicated, generous, and socially responsible people in the country? Nevertheless, for all the dreamlike aspects of our involvement they are all of that and more; so that after all my doubts as to the wisdom of becoming involved with powerful white folks—and especially in a setting where it was once of no more consequence to lynch a Negro than to kick a hound—I'm glad that we took our chances and became pioneers. But after all the complaining we do over our not being able to participate in the nation's affairs it would have been hypocritical <u>not</u> to have risked discomfort, uncertainty, or downright insult. But as it turned out we integrated the board and its social life so successfully that there are now two Negroes to take up where we left off. So once again Mama was right: we have to take chances and have faith in all our dealings!

That's all for now. We're both O.K. and hope things go well with you.

Love,
Ralph

To John R. Brown
RALPH ELLISON
730 Riverside Drive
New York, N.Y. 10031

Professor John Russell Brown
Department of Theater Arts
State University of New York
At Stony Book
Stony Brook New York 11794-5450
DECEMBER 26, 1984

Dear Professor Brown:

When your original letter regarding Mr. Amiri Baraka was forwarded to me I tossed it aside as a joke. Now that I have your second query in hand I must apologize for having done so.

For since it is fairly widely known that over the years Mr. Baraka had made me a target of his displeasure, I assumed that rather than seeking information you were making available to me the news that Mr. Baraka had achieved considerable success at boring from within the groves of academe, and that I (who was under the false impression that he had become a born-again Christian—or was it a Titoist?) would be made uncomfortable. Clearly, I was far off the mark but, nevertheless, I acted accordingly—which was presumptive of me but, I hope, understandable.

For after all, this is a nation of practical jokers, and one in which the most hilarious of booby-traps are launched from behind the soberest of facades. Thus it was that I responded to your original request as I had to Mr. Baraka's unprovoked attacks—with silence.

Now, however, the unquestionable sincerity of your second request places me in a position which is, to say the least, ironic. For as a retired teacher who regards the instruction of the young as a serious moral responsibility I find myself challenged to rise above any personal resentments that I might have entertained in the past by offering you a serious evaluation of your candidate, and that I honor that responsibility as being of far more importance than Mr. Baraka's opinion of me or mine of him, and thus overrides the honorable possibility that he might well consider even a favorable evaluation from me distasteful. Such possibility notwithstanding, I was challenged to convince myself that my concern with the education of the young rendered me capable of the necessary objectivity, and thus I proceeded to give serious thought to your request.

As I proceeded, however, it was here precisely, that I became aware of a problem that, unfortunately, I find insurmountable. For it is a problem (or joke of circumstance), which arises not from my possible opinions, either negative or positive but from my general ignorance of your candidate; a state of affairs that denies me any firm grounds on which to respond in any way that is honest and constructive.

Which is to say that I have been in the presence of Mr. Baraka (even when he was still Mr. Jones) fewer than a dozen times, that I have read none of his recent books or plays, and that I know nothing whatsoever of his abilities in the classroom. Thus I must leave to speculation as to how I would have responded had I possessed the knowledge necessary to be of your assistance and close with the hope that your decision will be of the best interests of Stony Brook and its students.

Sincerely,
Ralph Ellison

To Hugh Kenner
RALPH ELLISON
730 RIVERSIDE DRIVE
NEW YORK, N.Y. 10031
FEB. 20, 1985

Mr. Hugh Kenner
103 Edgevale Road
Baltimore, Maryland 21210

Dear Mr. Kenner:

You are indeed most tactful and by no means mistaken. For I am probably the same R.E. whom you assumed that I would be. At least I <u>think</u> I am, if only because I'm guilty of having published a couple of books.

Thanks very much for the *Jamesian Travesty* and for the Beckett, both of which are giving me much pleasure. I must confess, however that true to its author's way with words the Beckett has been playing hide-and-seek somewhere in the piles of papers on my desk, while the James has been teasing me into trying to make sense of its "nonsense." Some of its phrases remind me of Afro-American folk idiom and suggest the possibility that that form of American speech was always sounding beneath the sonorities of old Henry's prose; and this much in the manner that the issues of the Post-Reconstruction might possibly have found their way into works less concerned with public matters than *The Bostonians*.

That's wishful thinking, I know, but the phrase, "She rare woman" suggests the Harlem street kids' "She be <u>fine</u>, man!" And *Travesty*'s way with the Master's diction also reminds me of Fats Waller's incongruous juxtaposition of elevated and vulgar styles in his phrase, "One never knows—do one?"

Indeed, one never do; so having a dirty mind and gutbucket ear I swear that I hear overtones of bawdiness that I'm sure—but not <u>too</u> sure—that Henry James, who disdained the "unutterable depths of the bastard vernacular," would have found outrageous:

"She rare women, he had something so tremendous after ashes of light . . ."

Could the computer mean that Chad (or was it dear Strether—I daren't look at *The Ambassadors*) had "hauled" the good lady's "ashes"? I ask because here sex is as understated as the theme of abortion in Hemingway's famous story.

". . . But it's very right to go on with a cynicism of courage—from something to thing."

Amen! And with a courage born of cynicism—if need be!

It is most intriguing, and with all the "plashing" and "stream(ing)" around I'm reminded of lil ole Anna, down whose soft cheek a pearly tear did flow—Anna Livia, the plurabella:

> "But she were stream . . ."
> "She <u>stream</u> (?)"
> "She certainly."
> Then what happen, man?
> "She certainly and then stood up and lost her lap!"

Joyce would have loved that!

It was marvelous to find those "Stiff cabinets" turning up in *Travesty*'s Daliesque time-warping of prose: stiff cabinets with gaping drawers, and, I suppose ("by the bush"). It reminded me of a lady with prominent dentures who was called "Miz Acid Bath," and faintly of Joyce's epithet for Rebecca West; which was, if I'm not mistaken, "Chilly Bum-bum." Incidentally, that "slim ass rain" in the Joyce segment sounds as Afro-American as the epithet which Isham, the Negro character in Faulkner's "Delta Autumn" applied to Boon Hogganbeck—which was "narrow-assted." No wonder Boon tried to kill him!

Travesty's "She charmed with him so." is lovely, and I hope, truly, that "he caught."

If words and letters vibrate their messages, so too does the ear as it responds to linguistic styles other than those to which it's been tuned. I suppose that's why one must read James with such close attention. Perhaps not, but years ago when I first began trying to read him I floundered so often in his tidal waves of qualifications that I had to repunctuate his prose by way of speeding him up and slowing him down—A contradiction, I know, but by "Hemingwaying" him a bit I was able to get a little "jazz" into his music. After that I was prepared to learn a bit from his prefaces, a process still in progress . . .

But this has gone on far too long, so I'll close by pointing to something serious that I've gained through the play you've provided: The computer's circling back and forth over James' prose affirms the extent to which his acts, scenes, agents, and agencies blended one into another to create both his subjective and objective effects. Congratulations, and thanks for teaching even while you play. I'd love to have more of *Travesty*.

Sincerely,
Ralph Ellison

To Jimmy Stewart
RALPH ELLISON
730 RIVERSIDE DRIVE
NEW YORK, N.Y. 10031
MARCH 3, 1985

Dear Jimmy:

Thanks for allowing me to read your segment about Dr. Slaughter.[*] It brought back the days when I held the good doctor in awe and viewed him as a rather distant example of what was possible if I worked hard and saved my money.

I say "distant" because while his wife and my mother were close friends and her parents (in whose rooming house I was born) treated me like a grandson, my relations with him were fairly formal. He was my physician, from time to time our landlord, and one of the most energetic and imposing of community leaders. He was also the father of my two oldest friends, kids with whom, as a child, I had often shared holiday dinners and trips to their grand-parent's home in the country. But since he was a busy man I seldom saw him in his home. Later, at the age of thirteen, when I went to work for Dr. T. J. Randolph, whose office was in the Slaughter Building, I saw him daily, and continued to do so during the period when I worked in the drug store—including the three years I spent accumulating money for college. But although he played an important role in my life I never felt that I really knew him. And unlike yourself, who grew up to join him in community leadership, I left home too early to even <u>begin</u> to reach that state of maturity that might have allowed me to approach him as, shall we say, man to man. As a result our relationship remained that of a youngster to an important adult, and while I frequently exchanged ideas with Mr.

---

[*]   Ralph's old Oklahoma City friend Jimmy Stewart had sent him part of his manuscript about some of the significant black men they had known as boys in Oklahoma City.

Dunjee and had the benefit of his advice, I was never on such terms with the doctor. Thus it is that your anecdotes have provided me insights into his character which were denied me by time and circumstance.

And yet, through family ties and friendship—yes, and through the need of a fatherless boy to find examples upon which to pattern his manhood—he continued to puzzle me. But by the time I returned home as an adult he had died, and thus I missed the experience of seeing him as the master of the great house he built while I was away. This I regretted much in the way that one regrets missing the last episode of an interesting movie. For during my childhood he appeared to have been so busy accumulating property that there was little time left for the enjoyment of the fruits of his labor. The same seemed true of his wife, whose life seemed to me far more restricted from the felicities of living than was warranted by their wealth. And so I had hoped that once he had reached his goal, whatever <u>that</u> was, I would have the pleasure of seeing him enjoy life in terms that I perceived as being in keeping with his financial status. In other words, I thought that he should at least get as much fun out of life as my cousin Tom Brown, Fulton North, or some of the fast-living hotel men and waiters.

That was most naive of me, for obviously working and accumulating wealth <u>was</u> his pleasure. It was an end in itself, and thus it was left to you and others of our generation to combine the styles of living, responsible yet gracious, which I perceived as proper for Oklahoma Negroes. But each generation has its pattern, and while older might lead the younger to the mountaintop not all of its members are inclined to venture into the newfound land. S.D. Lyons, for example, built his now historical mansion long before Dr. Slaughter got around to building his, but it was so alien to his style of living that he and his first wife lived in the basement. And until she died and he remarried, the well decorated and expensively furnished floors were left unused except for company. This I know because I often made deliveries there, and later gave his grandson music lessons up in the unused rooms above. No wonder guys loafing in the barber shops spent so much time discussing in great detail the ways in which <u>they</u> would have spent Lyon's and Slaughter's money!

In closing I'd suggest that you might include in your account such characters as A. B. McDonald, Fred Witlow (co-owner of the Aldridge), Tom McNeely, Mr. Burnett, the grocer, Dot Flynn and Mr. Jacobson, the haberdashers, and Heywood James, who owned the Climax news stand. Perhaps Bill Fant and Dewitt Miles or other taxi-men would be of interest. There is also Deck Fuller, who was a police department detective long before Al Kerr joined the force. (Incidentally, Virgil's last name is spelled "Brannam.")*

As I think back the Eastside appears to have been packed with characters, and the same must have been true, if to a lesser extent, of the Westside. At any rate, there was such a variety that you should have an endless source of material. My only other suggestion is that you consider presenting them as much as is possible in a serious as well as a comic light, for what you perceive of your subjects will reveal much of your own values and attitudes. Thus ultimately your memoir will constitute a portrait of you. In other words, give us as much of the complex Jimmy as the private "Jimmy" can stand!†

Thanks again, and regards to May Lois from the Ellisons.

Sincerely,
Ralph

To H.B.O. Davis
RALPH ELLISON
730 Riverside Drive
New York, N.Y. 10031
MARCH 7, 1985

Dear H.B.O. Davis‡

Hearing from you was a highlight of my holiday season and for that many thanks. And as for our addressing me as "Ralph"—forget it! For not only do my friends (and many total strangers address me so, you had no other with which to label me. On the other hand, your old nickname has been the key term for one of the most interesting of my boyhood experiences, and if you had addressed me otherwise I would have been rebuked and embarrassed.

For although ours was all too brief a relationship there was nevertheless a bit of Tom Sawyer and Huck Finn about it that I've treasured. So the

---

* Ralph seems to be in error here. In his letters Virgil spells his name "Branam."

† Ralph's shrewd advice to Stewart applies to his own letters to Oklahomans in the 1980s.

‡ Henry Bowman Otto "Hoolie" Davis was a pal of Ralph's in Oklahoma City. The lasting importance of the friendship is clear from the rush of memories that comes to Ralph as he is writing the letter and the trouble he goes to in order to track down someone he hasn't seen or been in touch with for some thirty-five years.

fact that I remembered you only as "Hoolie" helped to preserve an aura of that time, place and circumstance. Perhaps in our country that is one of the functions of boyhood nicknames; they preserve the precious democracy of boyhood and undercut the formalities that society imposes later to divide us as adults. Thus I remember the good things and have quite forgotten the fire that marked our last meeting. Anyway, without "Hoolie" in the old memory bank I would have lacked an identifier for one of the kindest ladies of that entire period, for she lives in my memory not as Mrs. Franklin Davis but as "Hoolie's mother."

Indeed, if I hadn't had your nickname to mention to the Yale chaplain who presided at the christening of my godson I probably would have never been able to get in touch with you again. Fortunately, the champagne served during the post-christening party loosened my tongue enough for me to tell him of my surprise in discovering that as an Afro-American Episcopalian I was familiar with much of his ritual, and then went on to tell him of our old friendship. This led him to get in touch with the historiographer of the Oklahoma Diocese, and he in turn sent me your family name. (Incidentally, I mentioned the incident in a book of essays, and if you haven't seen it I'd be pleased to send you a copy.)

All in all, that christening that launched a new life on its course seems to have been a fateful moment in which several strands of my own were drawn together. The baby's father's father was, like yours an Episcopalian minister, and his mother, a half-Jewish-half-Christian Southerner, was a student at Bennington College at the time I gave my first lecture before a college audience. And suddenly I was talking nostalgically of Oklahoma. But when I realize that the babe who made our getting in touch a possibility is now a junior at Yale I am appalled that the process was interrupted and hung fire for so long. Yes, and I am amazed that it was your son who turned in on what had been set in motion and managed to keep it going through my literary agent. How odd that it all began so long ago when we exchanged used ice cream cartons on which we were simply concerned with winding radio coils.

But what a coincidence it is that while you continued our boyhood interest in electronics to become a professional, we should both end up as writers! I had thought about you often and wondered what would have happened to me had I continued living in your old neighborhood. Perhaps I, too, would have tried to make it in electronics, but probably not, because not even World War II could revive my old interest. (How could it, with me serving as a second-cook and baker on merchant ships?) But as things worked out, my mother quit her job out there and we moved back to the Eastside, where I put most of my energies into music. And, after finishing high school and working a couple of years to earn money for college, I hoboed to Tuskegee (1933) and did no further tinkering with radio until 1949.

By that time, however, I had switched from music to writing, and had been publishing enough fiction and criticism in various magazines to keep me hopeful. I had also gone through a marriage, been divorced, and married again (this time it has lasted forty-one years) and then, quite unexpectedly, our old interest loomed in my life again.

Always a music lover, I had become interested in high fidelity, and upon coming across an article on the Williamson amplifier in *Audio* magazine, I studied the circuit and decided that I remembered enough from the old days to build it—which I did. And then, having done so, I was bold enough to get in touch with one of the fellows who had adapted the English circuit to American components and asked him to check it out for me. This he was kind enough to do and in the process we became and continue to be good friends.

What is interesting about all this is that my friend, David Sarser, was born in Kansas City and his relatives who still live in Perry Oklahoma. At the time I made the contact he was a violinist in the N.B.C. Symphony, the famous orchestra which he joined after studying at Julliard, and it was through him that I soon found myself not only wiring room amplifiers and assisting in the installation of hi-fi sound systems, but having the delightful experience of accompanying him to the home of Arturo Toscanini to assist (in a very <u>minor</u> role I assure you) in the transference of many of the Maestro's early recordings to tape.

Let me hasten to say that I write this not by way of name-dropping, but to illustrate the extent to which Dave has served me as a sort of reincarnation of Hoolie. I associate the two of you not only because he was later to turn from music to electronic engineering, but because in each instance my knowing you began with casual contacts that turned out to make y life more interesting. Radio formed the linkage and was to prove more important in your lives than in mine. In Dave's case, however, it is as interesting for what it <u>didn't</u> do as for what it <u>might</u> have done had he been more interested in business than in experimentation.

For as it turned out his *Musician's Amplifier* played such an important role in what became the high-fidelity industry that had he been concerned with its financial possibilities he might have become a very rich man. As his associate the same might have happened to me, but I doubt it. Still, such possibilities notwithstanding I believe both Dave and I have been otherwise compensated, each in our separate ways. For me as a writer it proved important to have even a slight acquaintance with a science. And while Dave is no Avery Fischer, he has done important work, owns a few patents, and has inherited oil land in Oklahoma. Fortunately, the armatures who did ground work for the personal computer such as he performed for hi-fi-reaped both the pleasure <u>and</u> profits from their hobbying—Or at least <u>some</u> of them certainly have. But then, life is a matter of chance—that puts you scientists in the business of keeping it under control. And I'm sure that there is great satisfaction for Dave in knowing that his play has long since become not only the livelihood for thousands but a source of pleasure for millions.

But how ironic that technological advances have curtailed your own knowledgeable tinkering even as it has brought an end to mine. Never long on theory, I was simply too busy writing and teaching to make the abrupt transition from vacuum tube to transistor. As a result I no longer enjoy the pleasure of hanging around surplus electronics stores, checking out new circuits, or stinking up the house with soldering flux. Indeed I have yet to look inside the computer that I use for word-processing, I no longer build Heath kits, and my roof antenna has been missing two elements since autumn. Years ago I did collaborate with Dave on an article describing multiplexing, and on another in which we advised hi-fi bugs to save their new discs by transferring them to tape.[*] Those were the days of reels, with the cassette revolution still waiting in the wings. But since that time I've left such subjects to you who are experts. Nevertheless, I am still a reader of *Scientific American* and would be delighted to have some of your own writing.

With that I'll close, hoping that all my stirring up of the past won't discourage you from replying. And in the meantime my regards and heartiest thanks to your son.

Sincerely,

Ralph

---

[*] The article in question, "Tape, Disco, and Coexistence," was published in the March 1955 issue of *High Fidelity* magazine. In the months after Ralph's death in 1994, David Sarser was enormously generous and skillful in carefully working to put Ellison's many computer discs in good order.

To Camille Rhone
730 RIVERSIDE DR.
NEW YORK, NEW YORK
10031

Until 3/29/85:
727 Windsor Lane
Key West, Fl. 33040
MARCH 18, 1985

Dear Camille:*

Well over a year ago Jim gave me your address over the telephone, where-upon I jotted it down and then managed to misplace it. And since I was certain that it was somewhere close at hand I was reluctant to ask Jim for it again. But it was only last week as I prepared for this trip to Florida that I came upon it. Quite logically, it was attached to one of Madge and Jim's Christmas cards.

And so it is that I am able at long last to write to you, way up there in Ohio, from way down here in Key West. Years ago I spent a brief period in Yellow Springs while serving as Writer-in-Residence at Antioch College, and thus I have vague memories of the town. But for the life of me I can't imagine you in any other setting than Oklahoma City. As you might recall, Mamma and Herbert were living in Dayton when she passed on during the fall of 1937, and it was while waiting for the accident clause of her insurance policy to be settled that I came to know Dayton. That was during the economic crisis of the so-called Recession, and with little money and no jobs available Herbert and I were finally forced to give up her house, sleep in a neighbor's garage, and hunt rabbits and game birds for a living.

Fortunately, I had been hunting since I was eleven and so by joining up with a local friend who was also unemployed, we were able to manage. Naturally, we used shotguns, but I assure you that I was never so thankful to your mother for having loaned me the .22 rifle with which I had my first lessons in marksmanship than during that dismal Dayton period. Once during another hard winter (both our families were living on Stiles)

---

* Camille Randolph Rhone, the daughter of J. D. and Uretta Randolph, and her sister Iphigenia ("Cute") were "like older sisters to the Ellison boys." For an excellent account of the Randolph and Slaughter families' impact on young Ralph, see Rampersad, *Ralph Ellison*, 13–17.

when Mamma was working and I was unable to keep a fire going in our little monkey stove, your Mother and Grannie saved Herbert and me from freezing. So years later in Dayton it was as though she had come to our rescue again. For it was she who helped get me started toward the skills through which we survived.

That sad Dayton fall and winter we hunted all over what have long since become thickly settled residential areas and were guilty, sad to say, of breaking the law to stay alive. For while we ate the rabbits we bagged and sold the rest to neighbors (one of whose remarks—"I'm a dear lover of rabbit," I'll never forget), there was still a dire need for money. Therefore we shot numerous quail that we sold to General Motors executives who had homes near the city. And with them abetting us in crime to a cost of six bits a bird this "dear lover of quail" was unable to taste even a single wing.

We hunted all that season from dawn to dusk, and when the season ended and the temperature dropped to eight below zero we had to resort to sleeping on piles of soiled clothing left in a cleaning and pressing shop owned by a man for whom Herbert had once worked. Still we kept our troubles to ourselves, and then Mr. Stokes, a lawyer whose son Rembert was later to become the president of one of the colleges in Xenia, befriended me and allowed me to use his typewriter for my writing. He was a kindly man, and upon learning accidentally that Herbert and I had no place to stay (we were too proud to tell him) he insisted that we sleep in his office and make use of its bathroom facilities. It was a cruel time of testing, what with Mama gone, but once we had weathered it and kept our self-respect we were both convinced that we had earned the right to be considered grown men. And with Mama's affairs finally settled I returned to New York to begin my career as a writer, while Herbert remained in Dayton and was inducted into the Army.

Herbert and I talk between Los Angeles and New York about once a month, and frequently you, Cute, and your parents are recalled as indispensable parts of the old good times that are now long gone. These include the holiday dinners, the various houses in which you lived, and being picked up by you and Cute to be taken for weekends on the 23rd Street farm. The last time I was there Jim was kind enough to drive me out to see the old homestead, and did that bring back memories! We also talk about the task we had of crawling beneath the quilting frame to retrieve needles and thread that were dropped when your mother and Grannie were quilting, of the fun we had licking the dasher after the delicious ice cream was frozen, of our helping with the canning, and our assisting in the beating of cake batter and kneading the dough for home-made bread and rolls.

Herbert was saying the other evening that your parents were the only grandparents that he'd ever known, and I agreed. For although I had met our father's father on a trip to South Carolina shortly after our father died, it was your parents and grandmother who filled that important gap in our lives. In brief, we loved them and count ourselves lucky that they were so generous with their time and affection. Incidentally, it turns out that during the Reconstruction period our grandfather, Lewis Ellison,* was something of a political figure, a fact that has come to light recently in at least three historical studies. Nevertheless, I saw him only once and for but a brief visit; thus, it was Jeff Randolph who took his place and played an important role in shaping my life. That has been most important to me, and I want you to know how much I appreciate it. Indeed, I've often regretted that neither he, your mother, Grannie, nor Mamma lived along enough to see that I didn't go <u>completely</u> to the dogs—but that's life. One does what one can, and the rest is left to the young whose lives are touched.

And speaking of going to the dogs, I'm reminded of the time during the sixties when my wife and I went to visit Ollie in Washington, D.C. It was Sunday morning and thus we had to track her to church; where, completely unaware that I was sitting beside her. she graciously shared her hymn book with a young stranger. Then, during a lull in the service, I whispered to her, "Do you mean to tell me that you don't recognize who's been sitting beside you?"

And it was then that she gave me a long hard look, almost cracked up, and said, "Why you dirty <u>dog</u>!"

That Ollie! Yes, and that Wade! Both were important to the picture. And come to think of it, you, too, had an important role in getting me started. For after all it was you and Cute, if I remember correctly, who taught me to stand up and walk like a man. Which must have been quite a job, considering the fat little blob of blubber who was photographed sitting in a washbasin outside 407 East First St.! I treasure that photo along with another in which your parents are sitting on the front porch and you, a tiny girl, can be seen staring out bashfully from behind the screen door.

Every time I look at such pictures, or recall the old days on Third St. with you and Pat and your baby boys, I become so enraged with what

---

* Alfred Lewis Ellison, otherwise referred to as "Big Alfred."

Urban Renewal has done to the area in which I grew up that I curse them roundly for having been so callous and stupid. Because no matter how poor we were, or how humble our dwellings, those were the scenes in which I was formed and therefore I love and value every stick, stone and weed of them. Still, in this country it is in the nature of things to change and rapidly. Therefore it is the task of memory to preserve the lovable parts of the past with all its complex workings. Having reached my seventies, I now appreciate the uses of memory and the part you've played in mine. I only wish that I could see you so that we could bring the past alive again in person. But since that isn't possible, at least not for the present, this rambling letter is the best I can do.

My wife and I are down here for the annual meeting of the owners of a compound of condominiums we share. Ours is but a tiny house but quite pleasant and we'll enjoy it for a couple of weeks before returning to New York. Later, should the winters become too much of a problem, we'll probably spend at least three months of the year here in the sun. For as you might have guessed, I've retired from New York University and am now a "Professor Emeritus" a nice title, but I'd rather have the salary which went with my chair. However, when I say that I've <u>retired</u>, I only mean from teaching. I continue to write, have contracts for a couple of books, and am still being read—at least in universities all over the world— And with that I'll close. Drop me a line if this doesn't exhaust you—or simply send me your telephone number on a post card and I'll give you a ring at any time you suggest. In the meantime our regards and best wishes to you and yours.

Sincerely
Ralph Ellison

Mrs. Patrick Rhone
1314 Carry Street,
Yellow Springs, Ohio 45387

To Charles L. Brown
RALPH ELLISON
730 Riverside Drive
New York, NY 10031

Mr. Charles L. Brown
Chairman of the Board
AT&T
550 Madison Avenue
New York, NY 10022
APRIL 10 1985

Dear Charlie:

Over the years I've received many letters from readers of *Invisible Man,* but I assure you that none has been more unexpected nor more welcome than yours. For in my business, as in yours, the name of the game is "communication," and the realization that you've reached out and touched someone is its highest compensation.

But not only am I grateful that you would take time out from your busy schedule to give me your reactions, it so happened that your letter arrived at a time when Fanny and I were just beginning to feel a post-retirement depression induced by the spring-brought realization that our bi-annual visits to Williamsburg have come to an end.

Thus hearing from you evoked some of the pleasurable memories of what began as a reluctant acceptance of a pioneering-type challenge, but which turned out to be a most self-fulfilling education in democratic possibility. I suppose one of the unstated—and perhaps unrecognized—functions of C.W. is precisely that of providing men and women of good will (but disparate backgrounds) an unhampered opportunity for working together in the interest of a transcendent cause. At any rate, I've never felt so "American" as when doing whatever I could to further that effort. Nor have I come to the end of an assignment with such feelings of regret, or been more relieved to discover, thanks to you, that all such cherished lines of communication between ourselves and the group are not completely severed.

But then it seems that you have a way of allaying such pain. As on the rainy morning when I drove with you and your wife to the airport. I was feeling pretty low at the time, and the pleasant talk we had enroute did much to lift my sagging spirits. My thanks to you both for that—Yes, and for taking time out to encourage a rather nostalgic ex-trustee and author.

Our best to you and your wife from Fanny and yours truly, who bears the hilarious "historical" distinction of being the first of our kind to be "roasted" at Colonial Williamsburg!

Sincerely,
Ralph

To Miss Muldrow
RALPH ELLISON
730 Riverside Drive
New York, NY 10031
APRIL 10, 1985

Dear Miss Muldrow:

At the time your letter arrived in New York I was on a trip to Florida, thus by the time I returned your deadline had passed even before I realized that you had written. For this my regrets.

Had there been time for an answer I would have written that the time frame of *Invisible Man* is, roughly, the 1930s and 1940s. There are, of course, references to earlier periods, including slavery and Reconstruction.

Yes, there are many everyday happenings in the story, but all are transformed according to the needs of the plot and to the tenor of my imagination. Novels are a fictional way of telling certain truths, and a mode of make-believe.

And yes, you failed to encounter a name for the narrator because it is his intent to keep his identity secret; perhaps in hope that the reader will use his or her own experience in bringing the action alive. But I refused to give him a name out of respect for <u>his</u> desire for privacy, and out of my writer's need to project his story as an account of "Everyman." Thus the title of the novel is *Invisible Man* rather than "The" Invisible Man.

Thanks for your letter and again I am sorry that my answer is too late for your project. Incidentally, it might interest you to know that my paternal family originated in Abbeville, South Carolina. If you are ever up that way and are given to inspecting headstones, you'll find their graves in the old burial ground. Yes, and if you're interested in recent studies of South

Carolina history you might well come across the names of some of them in recently published accounts of our struggles.

Sincerely yours,
Ralph Ellison

Miss Cheryl Muldrow
Route #7, Box 55
Florence, SC 29501

To Todd Jones
RALPH ELLISON
730 Riverside Drive
New York, N.Y. 10031
APRIL 10, 1985

Mr. Todd Jones
Butler University
629 West Hampton Drive
Indianapolis, Indiana
46208

Dear Mr. Jones:

Before I attempt to answer your questions, allow me to point out that the title of my novel is *"Invisible" Man* rather than "The Invisible Man"; nor is it a collection of "stories," but an attempt at that larger fictional form called the "novel." Nor is *Shadow and Act* a collection of "stories"; it is, rather, a collection of essays. And if you'll approach it as such you'll probably learn far more about me and my background than is possible to convey in a short letter. In calling this to your attention I don't mean to offend, but to suggest that forms of writing reveal their meaning at best when read according to the conventions in which they are written. Otherwise it is as unproductive as applying the rules of football to a game of tennis. And now, with that out of the way, I'll try to answer your questions:

I wrote *Invisible Man* out of a desire to tell an interesting story that would make some artistic sense of the motives and attitudes that were current during the times in which the action unfolds. In other words, I wished to create a fictional context in which the narrator's hopes, moods and experiences would come vividly, and meaningfully, alive. And I hoped to do this in a manner that would hold my readers' attention and encourage them to identify with my hero's (the narrator's) situation by undergoing an imaginary excursion into such aspects of Afro-American experience as I sought to depict.

But most of all, I hoped to encourage my readers to <u>think</u>; and to compare their own situations as human beings and as Americans with that of my leading character. For I believe that a serious novel should not only provide the reader with entertainment, but that it should also offer him instruction in comparative humanity.

My answer to your second question is that I described the environments presented in I.M. (you'll recall that there are several that are determined by geography and racial attitudes) because they were the only scenes in which I could imagine the course of the action as <u>believably</u> unfolding, and because I believe that in fiction the scenes in which one's leading character acts become aspects of his actions. They are not all-powerful, but they do determine, more or less, that which he does and does <u>not</u> do. Thus along with the institutions, opposing characters and conflicts of interest found within it a fictional scene constitutes the social framework in which the hero makes his assertions toward those goals which he identifies as desirable forms of freedom. If you are seriously interested in such matters, take a look at Henry James's *The Art of the Novel*.

The answer to your final question is that I am currently working on other essays and other novels.

Good luck to you, and success with your paper.

Sincerely yours,
Ralph Ellison

To Charles Etta
RALPH ELLISON
730 Riverside Drive
New York, NY 10031
APRIL 22, 1985

Dear Charles Etta:

Thanks for your letter and the surprising clipping—which is the first indication that my birth date is of newsworthy interest. But then, as Fats Waller quipped. "One never knows, <u>do</u> one?"

Anyway, your letter arrived with other interesting items; among them a note from a young Dartmouth professor who has paid me the honor of overloading his poor little new-born son with "Ellison" for a middle name, and the other was from the daughter-in-law of Camille Rhone, who is one of my earliest and oldest friends. Camille now resides in Yellow Springs, Ohio, where following the death of her husband Pat some years ago she moved to join her son Mitchell and his family. You'll probably remember Camille as the youngest daughter of the J.D. Randolph family, and Pat was for years the linotypist for the *Black Dispatch*. I hadn't really been in contact with her since attending the State's 1966 celebration of its 60th Anniversary—at which, incidentally, the Governor presented medals to Maria Tallchief, Roy Harris and me as representative Oklahoma artists. Then, last year, I heard that she had been ill, and so after years of silence I decided to write. I waited far too long, for now I've learned that the after-effects of a stroke have left her unable to reply in person. However, her son's wife informs me that Camille is otherwise healthy, mentally alert, and was pleased that I had broken my silence. I learned also that she reached the age of eighty last August, which pleases me all the more to have word of her.

She is, after all, one of the surviving members of what I grew up regarding as my extended family, which relationship grew out of the circumstance that I was born in her parent's rooming house which was just to the east of your old home. And it was there that she and her sister "Cute" (Iphigenia) taught or tricked me into learning to walk. That was at the rather shaky age of six months, and came about, I assure you, <u>not</u> because I was intellectually precocious, but because I was born with log-like legs and a vicious appetite for candy and cookies. I'm told that the two young girls simply sat me down in a little chair, stood across the room with a goodie, and said, "Come and get it," and I took off!

Later, when they were in high school, the two young women took Herbert and me on our regular weekend visits to their parents' farm out on what was then a rather distant West 23rd Street. And with all the exciting things to do there we came to associate the two with pleasure. Years later, when she and Pat were married and began raising a family (three boys) they lived next door to her father, mother, and grandmother, and since Herbert and I were close to them she continued to provide an important link between their generations and ours. Sad to say, she and Jim are the last of the immediate family, and when they're gone an important part of my own life will have ended. As of now, however, both are well and at least once a month one of the Ellisons is in touch with Jim by telephone.

As you can see, your letter did indeed arrive in a most welcome delivery of mail. You helped rekindle memories of our school days in Oklahoma, and that from Camille's daughter-in-law stirred even earlier memories. It also reminded me of the fateful role which the state of Ohio has played in my life. For it was there that my mother and Herbert were residing when she died in 1937, and it was there in Dayton while waiting some seven months to settle her affairs that I wrote some of my first published writing. It was also in Dayton that Herbert and I last lived under the same roof, for while I returned to N.Y. and joined the W.P.A. Writers Project he remained. But then, during the Fifties, Ohio asserted its influence again and I found myself returning to serve the first of my stints as a Writer-in-residence in various colleges. And where else but at Antioch—which is in the town of Yellow Springs where Camille now lives. So in a sense Ohio marked the end of one phase of my life and the beginning of another. And considering the circumstance that my mother is buried in Cincinnati and the fact that Camille once played at being my mother-surrogate, Ohio would seem to be a part of some mysterious pattern. Even so, I wouldn't take that too far because it's possible that states with names that begin with the letter "O" are simply out to bug me . . .

But how amusing it is to learn that you and Booker share with Fanny and me a common interest in gardening. Last month we spent a good part of two weeks in Key West trying to do something about an "orchid" tree (so called for its lovely cattleya-like blossoms.) The problem is that it casts so much shade and shed so many leaves, petals, and bean-pods that explode button-shaped seeds with the velocity of shotgun pellets that it's damn near ruining the wooden deck on the front of our little house. Worst, its roots are damaging the stone wall which gives us privacy from the street, and it deprives our hibiscus and passiflora from needed sunlight.

However, our major problem in Key West springs from the fact that we have little space for personal cultivation. This is because our property is part of a condominium that a group of us formed out of what had been a dilapidated compound in the Old Town section of the island. Nevertheless, the grounds that we share with our friends and neighbors are landscaped with lovely tropical plants, trees and flowers. Though I must add that the thump of oranges and avocados on one's roof can be quite shocking.

I should also explain that my amusement over our mutual gardening hobby arises because I felt that Booker, like myself, had escaped the pressure exerted by Tuskegee's old regime to convert each and every student, and no matter his or her interest, into some kind of farmer. But now, years after Booker had made his way into the mysterious world of medicine, and I had blundered into the mad-man's world of writing, <u>both</u> of us find solace and pleasure (I hope) in working the soil. To my surprise I am even thankful that during the year I attended school in McAlister I took a then required course in agriculture!

So now, after rushing south to meet the spring, Fanny and I are back here in New York's fickle weather, and with each day's mail bringing seed catalogs which carry exhortations urging us to SPEND! PREPARE! DREAM! GET SET TO BRING FORTH FINER FRUIT AND VEGETABLES COME SUMMER AND FALL! Well, my mother was a former Georgia farm girl who kept a kitchen garden back when we lived next door to Frank Mead on East Fourth Street. She also raised chickens, sweet peas and guinea fowl. So with all that in my background I guess it was inevitable that gardening was sure to surface somewhere along the meandering path of my life.

But who'd ever have believed that I'd own a tractor, a tiller, and a plow? A lawnmower, maybe. But a shredder-chipper and pruning saws? Hell, the man must be out of his shook-up mind! So tell Booker that while I've never lived on a farm, somehow a long dormant farming gene seems to have taken over. Not that I'm complaining, because there's nothing like eating the fresh green products of one's own and one's wife's labor. Maybe it's also a form of revenge against the supermarkets and a retort to those who refused to give our freedmen grandparents their promised forty acres and a mule!

You asked if I am still teaching and writing: Writing, yes, teaching, no. I retired from NYU in '79 and the only thing I miss is the income. But my writing continues with a couple of works-in-progress giving me holy hell.

And yes, I knew of Albert's marriage through reading the *Black Chronicle*. It is interesting that he should visit Lola's sisters, but not surprising. For after all, he was part of that family for many years, and such being the case I don't find it at all unusual that he'd want his new wife to meet— and perhaps win the respect—of those with whom he'd been so closely aligned. Maybe it was his way of saying, "Although Lola's gone and I've remarried I still value your esteem" . . . Come to think of it, <u>my</u> ex-wife's family liked me much better <u>after</u> I had remarried, but that's quite a different story.

I think of Babe from time to time, especially the poignant image of times past which he and Lowell made as they danced during our class reunion, and I'm glad to know that he's still afloat, booze or no booze. If I'm ever in Atlanta again I'll try to look him up . . . Thanks again for writing, and Fanny and I hope that things go well with you and Booker.

Sincerely,
Ralph

Mrs. Charles Etta Tucker
517 W. Caldwell St.
Compton, CA 90220

To Herbert Ellison
RALPH ELLISON
730 Riverside Drive
New York, N.Y. 1031
APRIL 25, 1985

Dear Herbert:

I don't know whether the news has reached California, but on Tuesday, the 23rd, I was one of twelve artists to receive the first National Medals of Arts. It is quite an honor, but since there were many far better known writers to choose from I was both surprised and a bit dubious. Especially after I saw that the letter which notified us was dated for April Fool's Day. Nevertheless, after a formal notice arrived from the White House I accepted and Fanny and I flew down to Washington to take part in the ceremonies—which proved to be quite exhausting.

First came a Pre-Awards party during which we stood in a receiving line for over an hour pumping the hands of guests and mumbling replies to their words of congratulations; a tiring routine in itself, but one which resulted in our missing the food and drink we damn well deserved. Still it was pleasant to find ourselves being feted along with the likes of Leontyne Price and Jose Ferrer, between whom we stood while the guests filed past. And at noon the next day, during the presentation of the medals at the White House, I sat at the President's table next to Martha Graham, who was on his right, and across from Miss Price, who was on his left. He talked with all of us, told anecdotes, and was the man of personal charm that he is said to be. Best of all, he hosted a fine meal. Not that it was better than those we had during Lyndon Johnson's presidency, but one that proved that in that area at least the quality remains first rate. The same was true of the service; which, as during the days of Kennedy and Johnson, was in the hands of what appeared to be a whole regiment of dignified Negro waiters. Finally, when the medals were presented, the President gave a short speech, and as he called our names each approached the podium in turn. Mrs. Reagan read the citations, and we were presented with the beautiful wooden cases that contained the silver medals. Fortunately, the President had to rush off to a discussion of his budget so there were no speeches demanded of us—and a good thing too, because each medal and its case is so heavy that some of the older awardees were unable to lift much less than stand holding them while thinking of something fitting to say. Nevertheless, they're handsome and an honor to receive—as can be seen even from the rather poor photographs which I am enclosing.

So much for the main ceremony, but that evening there was more. This time from the Congress, which passed the bill that made the awards a possibility. This time our host was Senator Kennedy, and the site was the Botanic Garden. There we were able to eat and drink and view more orchids than we've ever seen before, and talk with friends with whom I served on the original Council on the Arts and the Board of the Kennedy Center. We had thought to remain in Washington the next day taking it easy and visiting some of the new museums, but were both too exhausted and so returned to NY. So we're here trying to get back to normal while attempting to put things in perspective. And as usual when something like this happens to me I regret that Mama was unable to share what she made possible . . . That's all for now, and I hope you'll find the enclosed of interest.

We both send our love.

Ralph and Fanny

To Mamie Rhone
RALPH ELLISON
730 Riverside Drive
New York, NY 10031
APRIL 30, 1985

Dear Mamie Rhone:

Thanks so very much for your letter. It was informative and the best reply I could have hoped for in view of Camille's condition. I am happy that she is there with you and Mitchell, and absolutely delighted to learn that you named your son after Taylor, that dear old rascal whom Wyatt called "my lying uncle." As you know, novelists are liars who take tricky trips around Robin Hood's barn in an effort to tell whatever it is they perceive <u>truth</u> to be, and I loved Taylor for his ability to remember incidents concerning his family that occurred before I was born or when I was away, and to elaborate them in ways that imparted a touch of magic and glamour. Whenever I return home his absence makes for a sense of incompleteness, perhaps because in certain ways, and especially in his gift for talk, he was more like his father than any of the others.

Am I correct in assuming that Jimmy and his family are also living in Yellow Springs? I ask because somehow I associate him with the Sloan-Kettering Institute (or some such Kettering organization), and recall attending the opening there of one of its labs during which Mr. Kettering danced every dance and seemed quite unbothered by the cement dust which whirled with each step of our dancing feet. I also remember Aunt Edna's dinner and my meeting with you of the younger generation. I had been away from home so long that it was quite shocking to realize that Jimmy and Mitchell, whom I'd last seen as little boys, had become young adults. Once while on a trip with the Douglass marching band to Topeka or Wichita I saw Cute and Jimmy (or was it Mitch?) and recall that in referring to Maxine he pronounced her name as "Max-a-mean," a delightful play on words by a very cute little boy!

Since receiving your letter exciting things have happened to us here, and by way of sharing it with Camille and your family I am enclosing photocopies of some of the newspaper accounts. Tell Camille that strange things continue to happen to one whom she and Cute taught to walk. Thanks again for writing, and our best to all.

Sincerely,
Ralph

1314 Corry St.
Yellow Springs, Ohio 45387

Enclosure: set of materials for National Medal
of the Arts publicity & luncheon & reception.

To John Callahan
RALPH ELLISON
730 Riverside Drive
New York, NY 10031
MAY 12, 1985

Dear John:

I found your chapter 6* so interesting that I can hardly wait to see the completed manuscript, footnotes and all. It goes without saying that I was fascinated by your analysis of the role played by eloquence in the structuring of IM, for you focus upon one of the major shaping forms which is at once a means of keeping the plot moving and the main agency through which the narrator carried on his struggle toward perception. I know of no critic who has explored this area with so much insight and am delighted.

But as you suspected I do have problems with the Wright section— not because of what you make of "The Man Who Lived Underground" per se, but because of the manner in which you relate it to *IM* and me to Wright. Here I realize that I risk being overly subjective, but I'm confident that you'll accept or reject my comments as you see fit. And since there's no honest way of avoiding a certain amount of subjectivity I'll begin with a bit of autobiography that you might well have read elsewhere but overlooked when you set about structuring your chapter.

Sometime during 1940 I presented Wright with a story for criticism, and after much delay he finally told me that he didn't like it because it showed too much of his influence. "This is my stuff," he said. And his response was so emotional that I was taken aback, for up until that moment I had regarded him as my mentor and had taken it for granted that my fiction would reveal his influence. Indeed, I would have been surprised if it hadn't; and that would have been true even though I thought that I had formed my story out of my own observations and personal experiences and had attempted to use Hemingway's techniques to shape them. Still Wright made it clear that he felt that I was invading his turf, so after his outburst I decided quite consciously that from that moment on I would prune my stuff of any suggestion of his influence. I was hurt by the encounter but realized later on that it had freed me to go on my own way,

---

* An early draft of "Frequencies of Eloquence: The Composition and Performance of *Invisible Man*," revised and published in Callahan's 1988 book, *In the African American Grain*.

exploit my ear for speech, my eye for significant detail, and my bent for tragic comedy. We remained friends and continued to discuss ideas and technique, but I no longer showed him my efforts—Not only because I didn't wish to offend him, but because I couldn't conceive of myself as his rival. Moreover, I was attracted to a broader range of techniques than he found necessary. (Technique is both vision, and a way of achieving vision—at least in fiction—and I saw differently because I had lived my own life, not his.) There were also our differences of temperament and my own strong sense of what I wished to achieve in fiction. For although I was young as a <u>writer</u>, in terms of experience I was twenty-six years of age, married, and had studied the musical arts since childhood.

Which is to say that as a musician with ambitions to become a composer I had already reached quite high for my artistic standards and I continued to do so after switching to fiction. Thus long before I met Hughes and Wright I had found my artist heroes in the likes of Bernard Shaw, Richard Wagner, Beethoven, "Hot Lips" Paige and Louis Armstrong; in Melville and Twain, the Dumas' and Dickens—not to mention my later discoveries such as Eliot, Pound, Hemingway and Malraux. I had been a bookish kid, and despite the realities of racial segregation I saw nothing incongruous in identifying with artists whom I considered to be the best, no matter their color, nationality, or where they operated beyond the color line.

For instance, I stumbled upon Shaw's plays in the library of a friend's parents, and through reading his essays I found Wagner and Nietzsche, and although I was too innocent and ignorant to grasp the broader implications of their work I identified with their literary and musical eloquence. (Incidentally, a German conductor whose lawn I mowed taught me orchestration by analyzing Wagner's scores.) My point is that I was young enough to use my freedom to make simplistic identifications with those whom I saw as heroes, so that by the time I met Wright I had my own high, if uncritical, standards. (As I write this I recall that about the time I discovered Eliot at Tuskegee I was still numb from the emotion generated by my reading of *Wuthering Heights,* that cast an even more powerful spell than I experienced two years later when reading *Native Son* in ms. Different scenes, different characters, techniques and points of view, but even as a musician I responded to literary power and artistic skill rather than to the writer's color, nationality, or philosophy.) Nor was the fact that most of those who seized my imagination happened to've been white due to any rejection of my own group. Instead, it was out of my search for that art which most moved me. The same standard applied when it came to sports, jazz musicians, and classical musicians. If my taste was to develop, the necessity for some form of hierarchical rating was inescapable. Some athletes and jazz musicians were obviously overshadowed by others and there was no escaping that fact. How else could I establish standards for my own ambitions? And since there were few, if any, major Negro poets or novelists (I knew quite early that the Dumas' were not "Negroes" but French, and that Pushkin was a Russian, no matter how often they were claimed by Black race men), where else could I turn but to the power of the works I read?

Thus the obstacles to my integration as an American citizen notwithstanding, my aspirations as a reader and aspiring composer goaded me, willy-nilly, to integrate myself symbolically with the best that came to hand, eye, and ear. One could say that segregation <u>forced</u> me to live in the sphere of imagination, both as compensation for what society denied me and as an assertion of my will toward personal freedom.

Nor could I reverse that process of imaginative integration after Wright inspired me to try my hand at writing. I am most grateful for what he did, but my standards were already formed, and there was nothing that I could do, or wished to do, about it. For our bonds of friendship notwithstanding, his fiction would have to undergo comparison with all I'd read; and that, to be fair to Wright, was how he wished it to be. His standards, like mine, were universal, and he was determined to be compared with the best. Thus in getting his act together he drew upon the likes of Dreiser, Mencken, Dostoyevsky, Sartre, Camus, Malraux, and Gorky, etc. Which brings me to the connection which Wright's MWLU and my IM have with that great seminal treatment of the underground as a metaphor for the psychological condition of a fictional character: Dostoyevsky's *Notes from Underground*.

I like your phrase, "cryptic cagey," by the way, but in truth I was by no means suggesting that *IM* derived from Wright's story. If anything, I was correcting Howe and suggesting that my story, "Flying Home," which appeared in the same *Cross Section* also contained protest, and this despite the fact that it differed in style and approach from that of Wright. Although I had been searching for my own voice since 1940, Howe insisted upon seeing me and my fiction through Wright's, but I was damned if I was going to allow him to impose his narrowness of view upon whatever the hell I wrote. Nor would I allow him to restrict my artistic freedom to choose models or limit my freewheeling mixture of literary styles. But lest this become too boringly defensive, I'd better return to the text at hand.

You write that my Iowa statement led you to examine *TMWLU* "both as an ancestor and a relative of *IM* (because) although their fates diverge . . . Fred Daniels and . . . *IM* share a common passion to speak to people about the kinship between the official world and the unacknowledged underground reality of both self and society." And you go on to speculate that "Surely, Ellison acknowledged and built upon Wright's parable of the unshrewd, oblivious, fatally undouble conscious voice of Fred Daniels . . ." And it is here that I must disagree, not only because this is all too deterministic, but because by focusing on my relationship with Wright you overlook the debt which both Wright and I owe to other novelists and forms of fiction. What's more, it's like assuming that because a goose and a swan happen to occupy the same barnyard, swim in the same pond, and are friends it <u>guarantees</u> that the goose will follow the swan's example and instead of laying eggs that produce goslings it will bring forth cygnets. But while there's no question that both goose and swan will lay eggs(!) their respective offspring will be determined not by their proximity but by their genetics. A bee pollinates great varieties of plants (here let Dostoyevsky be the bee) but each will produce its own flowers and fruit in kind. True, a critic might decide to slip a swan's egg under the goose's butt, but while this might stir up arguments as to whether the hatchling which comes forth is a goose, a swan, Daffy Duck in drag, or some kind of Frank Perdue fuckup that has too little black meat or too much white to be a proper "oven-stuffer" the egg will produce a cygnet that was signed and sealed—if not incubated—by swans. But all joking aside, I know, John, that you're not that kind of critic, therefore I suggest in all seriousness that you take a fresh look at *Notes*.

If you do and then look at the prologue to *IM* you'll see that the opening rhythm (or riff) alludes to *Notes*:

"I am a sick man . . . I am a spiteful man. No, I am not a pleasant man at all. I believe there is something wrong with my liver . . ."

—Notes from Underground

"I am an invisible man. No, I am not a spook like those who haunted Edgar Allen Poe; nor am I one of your Hollywood-movie ectoplasms . . ."

—Invisible Man

And what the hell is <u>Poe</u> doing here? Forget it! But if you'll test the characteristics shared by my narrator and the "author" of *Notes* you'll see that both are talkers who employ irony and that both address the reader as <u>writers</u>. You'll also note that just as Fred Daniels is far from effective as a speaker, he has absolutely <u>no</u> identity as a writer. It wasn't at all necessary that he be so lacking in eloquence—the vernacular is rich with such possibilities—but instead of allowing him an eloquence fitting of his background Wright looped a rope around his neck and tried to animate him in the manner that Tod Clifton animated his dancing dolls. Had Daniels been a swan or a goose the poor guy would have been incapable either of dive or flight, no matter the ability and passion of his creator. Thus he'd have done no better against predators of sky and water than he does against the cops.

I suspect that here, as in *The Outsider* Wright was so fascinated by Raskolnikov's verbal dueling with a law official that he tried to use the same device but failed to endow Daniels with the proper equipment. In *The Outsider* he took a pattern from *Crime and Punishment* but ignored the difference between 19th century Russia and 20th century America with results that were quite unreal. For in his chosen setting white cops wouldn't have wasted the energy of a district attorney by allowing a Negro criminal to get to him, much less wasted his time playing psycho-philosophical games. Instead, they would have gone up side his damn fool head with pistol barrels. In Dostoyevsky Wright chose a hell of a pollinator, but not even ole Fyodor could prevent an earwig or doodle-bug from screwing up the pollination. Fiction is composed out of other fiction, but the writer has to be careful as to what he takes and what he leaves alone.

The "author" of *Notes* and the narrator of *IM* are characterized, each in their respective ways, by styles of ironic self-consciousness; but to my mind Daniels is near lacking in a true sense of self—Not because he couldn't have been depicted realistically as possessing such, but because Wright didn't allow him to express himself in terms of his own background and culture. In other words, there is too little of Wright—the conscious, thinking eloquent individual—in Daniels; while there is too <u>much</u> of society's racially biased wrongs. This springs, I think, from Wright's Marxist philosophy and from his insistence on depicting the Negro as victim. At any rate Daniels is overwhelmed by circumstance because he isn't given enough aggressive humanity to make the convincing case that Wright intended. To me this was like cutting off a corpse's head by way of fitting him into his coffin—Or of making him so mentally defective that he was ripe for victimage even <u>before</u> the cops erased him.

Here, it seems to me, you've strayed from the goal toward which you are headed (which is a discussion of eloquence as a dramatic agency) and become involved with a discussion of environment or scene. And not only with the scenes in which Daniels and my narrator act—or fail to act—but the scene in which their <u>authors</u> acted. Thus the fact that both Daniels and my narrator spend time underground (note here that most of IM deals with events taking place <u>above</u> ground) leads you to lose sight of the agency through which they would assert themselves or with which they <u>fail</u> to assert themselves—which is the spoken and written word. In other words, by overlooking the difference between the two characters and becoming snarled up in the relationship between Wright and Ellison you become deterministic: Wright and Ellison are Negro writers who occupied the same social scene, Wright was an established novelist before Ellison, ergo Ellison built his *IM* upon Wright's *TMWLU.*

But for me this raises the question as to why the narrator of IM isn't a descendant of Bigger Thomas, a much more assertive character? Or why isn't the invisible man a descendant of "The King of the Bingo Game"'s central character? They did spring, after all, from the same imagination. For even if Wright had intended for Daniels to come across as deranged, the narrator of IM would still be closer to the king of bingo if only because their respective situations are somewhat surreal, and because they are assertive in ways that Daniels isn't . . .

John, I'm going on at such length because I think that you leave me fewer choices in telling my "lie" than I actually had. Which is to say that I feel that in restricting me to the single influence of Wright you bar me from drawing upon the far more accomplished fiction of Dostoyevsky. But if that is true, doesn't it reflect upon my literary taste and resourcefulness? And isn't it contradictory to credit me with being "cryptic cagey" and, by implication, full of "shit, grit, and mother wit," and then overlook the possibility that I might have drawn <u>not</u> upon Wright's fiction, but upon Wright himself? Why take from the artifact when the genuine article was at hand? Wright did, after all, write of his troubles with the communists in *The God That Failed,* was an eloquent speaker, <u>and</u> a writer who went to fairly extreme lengths to communicate his vision. I'm not saying that my narrator was by any means intended as a portrait of Richard, for as a model his example would have been too limiting of my imagination. Nevertheless, I <u>will</u> suggest that Wright was far more suggestive than Fred Daniels, and the same is true of Ben Davis, Angelo Herndon, and quite a number of other ambitious communists. For as you well know novelists are also half-assed sociologists who abstract and make use of any and everything they observe in the process of constructing fiction. So I ask again, why take from the flawed artifact when the man himself is right at hand? And especially when you're concerned with an assertion of eloquence that leads through passionate struggle to ironic perception?

In closing I leave you with the suggestion that you follow through with your insightful observation that eloquence in *IM* is a major agency with which the narrator keeps his plot unfolding—Much as Daniels' lack of verbal skill keeps *TMWLU* spinning in an environmental rut. Wright believed sincerely that "freedom is the recognition of necessity"; thus it is ironic that he failed to allow his character even a glimmer of that recognition. I realize that this is to be hard on Wright, but it seems to me that this particular fiction failed because he refused to endow Daniels with even that smidgen of his own consciousness that might have allowed him to express a redemptive perception of his fate.

Please forgive the length and repetitions and feel free to continue our discussion. In the meantime Fanny and I send our love to you and your three lovely girls.

Sincerely,
Ralph

P.S.

This damn thing is already so long that you might as well have the following from an earlier draft:

When I read your interpretation of *The Man Who Lived Underground* I asked myself if it were actually true that Wright intended it as a contribution to the "literature of necessity." I did so because it would seem to me that if such was his intention Wright would have endowed his character with the basic agencies for dealing with his opponents; a brain and a certain amount of eloquence. Because no matter how extreme his condition he needed something more than a desire to express himself in order to communicate his vision. He needed more than a purpose and a passion to fire that purpose; he also needed an agency with which to achieve his will. And he needed these even though he's doomed to fail. Thus it seems to me that Wright focused his argument more on Fred Daniels's environment than upon his character, and upon the forces that crushed him than upon his possibilities of communicating his view of social reality. Freedom, in Wright's ideology, was the consciousness of necessity, and that necessity involved a revolutionary change in the order of society; but

Daniels arrives at no such consciousness—or Wright doesn't allow him to—and thus becomes a victim of that failure of perception which you describe.

In light of your concern with eloquence, I find this most interesting. For while you're concerned with eloquence and the perception of reality obtainable through rhetorical communication, you seek to argue your case through a character who is, for the most part, inarticulate. And then you contrast him with the narrator of *IM*, who despite his flaws is nevertheless able to express himself.

RE

John Callahan
Box 8
Bard College
Annandale-on-Hudson, NY 12504

To Ben Rosenbaum
RALPH ELLISON
730 Riverside Drive
New York, NY 10031
MAY 20, 1985

Dear Mr. Rosenbaum:

Unfortunately, my reply to your question must be a bit more extended than the space you assign for an answer, and this because the choices you present are more limiting than my view of the relationship between a writer and his possible readers allows. My answer, in brief, is that for me both skilled and unskilled readers are important, and for the following reasons:

As one who depends upon his writings for a livelihood I find anyone with a mind open enough to read—and, even better, to buy—my work important. They needn't agree or disagree with what I have to say, but it is most important to me that they lend me an eye and an ear. To me this is important because I write by way of attempting to communicate my view of the human condition. Indeed, my need for communication is such that I would continue to write even if few readers were interested in that which I seek to communicate. I know this sounds as though I have been asked whether I eat to live or <u>live</u> to eat—which, since I do both, would leave me no room for a clear cut answer!

But it is precisely because of my need to achieve maximum communication that I am eager to reach, in your words, "the reader who is very familiar with literature and literary criticism." Writing, and especially poetry and fiction, is a form of art and thus <u>artificial</u>. As such it depends for its effects upon a body of conventions that have evolved as means of informing the reader (or listener) that a "made-up" story is about to be related, and informs him that he is not to take it as literal truth but as an exercise of the fictional imagination; or, if you will, a "lie" through which an attempt will be made to arrive (in a lively and entertaining way) at some recognizable aspect of truth as we know it.

A writer's art consists of his ability to manipulate the conventions of his craft and he does so on various levels of meaning; which he seeks to hold in synthesis much as a juggler keeps his Indian clubs or apples rhythmically flying to-and-fro from hand to air and back to hand again, according to a predetermined pattern of action which arouses his viewers' fear of failure even as he fulfills their need to be ever reassured that human skill and intelligence can conquer the law of gravity. Of course writing is far more complex because the writer seeks to convey ideas as well as images and actions. Moreover, he tries to make his ideas emerge <u>through</u> his arrangement of images and actions as they come to focus in details that describe the scenes, physical struggle and psychological processes that continue to bring his characters and their emotions alive in the minds of his readers.

It is here, therefore, that he values the informed reader—or the reader who is skilled in reading—because he is limited to communicating with nothing more than mere words on a page. He has no scenery, spotlights, nor sound system as with stage drama, the movies or television, and thus he achieves communication by encouraging the reader to cooperate in his effort by using his, the reader's, own imagination and knowledge of other fiction and forms of story-telling to help bring the unfolding story alive on that mental screen, sensitized by literature as by living, which we call the "mind." When he is successful in persuading the reader to feel that he is "experiencing" the story, the writer feels in turn that he has been successful in communicating his artistically formed vision of experience. Therefore it is for this reason that I value the reader "who is very familiar with literature and literary criticism" . . . Because in most instances it is he or she who is best able to understand what I am about. What's more, such readers make my task a bit easier because, by approaching my work in an informed way, they grasp that which is implied (or left understated) as well as that which is vividly presented and given emphasis through stresses upon such devices as rhythm, repetition, and such universal emotions as exaltation and sadness, pity and terror that shape my story.

In other words, the act of reading brings writer and reader together in an act of creative collaboration, and thus it is the trained reader who challenges the writer to make the most of his talent. In trying to meet that challenge writers maintain both the standards of literature and their craft and discover unrealized possibilities of both their talents and the form through which they would communicate. But as I say, both the trained and untrained reader are necessary to the writer, and if he is serious and thinks that human life is of a whole despite its variety—yes, and writes to eat—he values all who'll lend him (if only for a few pages) an eye and an ear.

Sincerely
Ralph Ellison

Mr. Ben Rosenbaum
4620 Dittmar Road
Arlington, VA 22207

To John Callahan
PLAINFIELD, MA
JULY 15, 1985

Dear John:

Your chapter and letters arrived at a time when we were still struggling to repair the damage of two severe winters, hence my delay in replying. For awhile we had neither electricity, water, nor telephone—so you'll get the idea. I've mowed around the house but most of the ground is still claimed by grass that looms ass-high to a tall elk; and while I've tilled enough of the old garden site to allow Fanny to do some planting, we have doubts as to its outcome because the weather has been cool and lacking of rain. But no matter, we'll still have the peace, the quiet, and the exercise.

Thanks for allowing me to see the chapter; which, beyond all questions of personal interest, I found engrossing. And so much so that there's no way for me to give you an orderly reaction. Therefore I'll have to content myself with a few rambling notes which I made after my second reading. [Come to think of it, trying to deal with the narrator, the "Ellison" I was when I wrote the novel, the "Ellison" I'm identified with today, and with what you've made of all three is as confusing as trying to interpret the logo on your letterhead. Who the hell is the <u>brown-skinned</u> guy—Lewis or Clark? If it's a Meriwether it would seem that someone other than ole T.J. had been playing around in the slave quarters. Maybe Meriwether went west to integrate this mess—Or to escape it! A plausible theory, perhaps, but on re-examination I see that the name "Lewis" is closer to the white profile while the Clark is closer to the brown—Which knocks my "theory" back to a brown square intersected by twin profiles of shadowy identity.] Anyway, here are my notes and speculations:

The word "fabulous" in the second paragraph of your tenth page seems ambiguous; thus it might annoy a reader who finds my introduction fabulous in the sense of being "made up" or invented, but not at all in the sense of being "marvelous." You can, though, keep your readers alert by having it both ways. Incidentally, sometime when you're in NY I'll show you the notebook in which I wrote the opening lines of the prologue. And if you were ever around when I'm making the morning's coffee you'd find that I'm thronged with a whole insane system of disembodied voices, any one of whom would make ole Invisible sound taciturn.

The point about my patriotism is well put. I am indeed, but on my <u>own</u> terms; a most uncomfortable condition which leads me to participate in such of the nation's affairs as I am able, even when I have grave doubts as to the wisdom of so doing.

When the narrator goes downtown to lecture on the "Woman Question" is he "hustling" or simply carrying out orders in his usual naive way? To hustle the situation he'd have to be more cynical than I recall him to have been at that point in the action. I'd say that he was still reacting rather than taking initiative. And that goes for his getting involved in the "ass struggle."

In the funeral section you rely on O'Meally—whose book I don't have here to consult—but I'd say beware of anyone writing of music who doesn't know the difference between an euphonium and a saxophone!

And while I'm on the subject of music it occurs to me that although Murray and Neal are quite close when they refer to the influence of music on the form of *IM* they might well have stopped a bit short of the mark. For it is quite possible that the over-all form is less blues than symphonic.

Or at least that was my intention; because as I see it blues forms are fairly limited for the expression of complex ranges of experience and emotion. Perhaps that is why Ellington went in pursuit of larger forms. Which was not, I assume, out of any disloyalty to folk or vernacular forms, but out of his need to be more broadly expressive. But perhaps Murray was not thinking of a "big band" but of a symphony orchestra. Whatever, it's amazing to me how certain critics (Black) embrace the folk forms but are reluctant to venture further. And yet artistic forms proliferate and shack up with those of other arts. The novel took off from tragic drama, as did symphonic form, and the Italians, Germans, Czechs (I think of Dvořák's use of folk themes), the English and Russians have all built upon, and transformed, folk forms with a vengeance!

Of course a novel can no more be a symphony (or a blues, for that matter) than a lyric can be a tragedy. Nevertheless, it can be as inclusive as a symphony, and its potential is wasted when it isn't. For it has the capacity to include a variety of "smaller" forms by way of articulating its characters and themes as it strives to achieve formal completeness. The "novelty" of the novel lies in its play upon its own formal possibilities as it goes about revealing patterns, ever old yet ever new, of human experience. The American novel is experimental not because American novelists are hung up on art-for-art's or technique-for-technique's sake, but because given the social and historical circumstance out of which it arose it was forced (and still is) to revolutionize its base, methods and modes; and this out of the sheer necessity of recording and keeping pace with American change. Here it became a paradigm-smashing affair, and Melville and Twain <u>had</u> to improve by way of adapting the form to America's social conditions. (As you can see, you and Kuhn are forcing me to rethink this mess!) But I'll keep going:

On the page containing footnote #14 you say that "Ellison suggests that [*IM*] was generated by an attraction between persons of rather opposite values—his and Invisible Man's . . ." But here <u>I</u> would make the following distinctions: the narrator is Ellison's projection of a <u>character</u> who was attracted to other <u>characters</u> who possessed opposing value. If not, then where the hell was I—off somewhere paring my nasty nails? And on your fifteenth page you write; "Becoming a writer . . . he released the power of the spoken word and the energy of action in the ironic self-conscious, symbolic and potential action of his literary, vernacular narrative—his and Ellison's (and our) novel." This is well said so I hope I'm not quibbling when I suggest that while it is indeed "Ellison's (and our) <u>novel</u>, it is, nevertheless, the narrator's <u>memoir</u> or autobiography. In this sense *IM* is a novel in the form of a memoir. And thank god, because otherwise the narrator would be in complete control and there'd be no need for my getting into the narrative act. As it is the narrator blew <u>his</u> riffs and I blew—and orchestrated—both mine and his. And by the way, it isn't Invisible Man who discovers the ambiguity that you quote from *Shadow and Act,* that was Ellison, who, was, and remains, a writer: but who despite all his lecturing was <u>never</u> a rabble-rouser.

I like your plotting of the narrator's struggle with eloquence and the way his words kept having the opposite effect from that intended. It reminded me that Anthony used reverse Latin to telling effect against the conspirators. What Burke terms "the power of the negative" is implicit in language, but unfortunately I couldn't allow the narrator Anthony's command of words. Instead, he was commanded <u>by</u> words. And as you make clear, he is too vague as to the nature of his audiences to sway them to his will.

He should have paid more attention to Shakespeare—or at least to what ole Booker was doing behind what he appeared to be doing.

Bravo! for your pointing to "mythic past, magic and miracle" in Barbee's sermon. Imagine the bastard suggesting that a god-like figure descended to earth to save the Founder!

Surprised to find the quote from Holmes, with whom I was acquainted back during the forties. The narrator is indeed undergoing a rite of passage, and in it even such minor characters as Brockway, Mary, the doctors and the Blueprint man serve as celebrants. Damn near <u>everybody</u> does something to keep the bastard running. I'm afraid that there was a heap of Candide in that fellow! Yes, and as there was trickster in Anthony and Booker T. As for Invisible Man, don't forget Ford Maddox Ford's warning against first-person narrators; who, dumb or smart, tell the truth as they see—or want the <u>reader</u> to see it.

In your discussion of the Sambo dolls you might make clear in what way they are "look-alikes of Invisible Man." True, they're stereotypes and he enacts certain stereotypical roles, my question is does he <u>look</u> like them?

That's it, John, and I close with the suggestion that you make no major changes because of anything I've had to say. It is an insightful and well-argued chapter and I'm most pleased to have had you as a reader and critic. In the meantime August isn't too far away so if there's anything in these notes that you consider worth discussing, we'll do so when you come this way.

Our love to you and yours,

Sincerely,

Ralph

To Carl and Mary Humelsine
RALPH ELLISON
730 Riverside Drive
New York, NY 10031
SEPTEMBER 6, 1985

Dear Carl and Mary:

We were thrown together by historical fate when, as you will recall, President Johnson appointed me to the original Bi-centennial Commission of which you, Carl, were an important member. Then by way of carrying out your commitment and providing a group of the new commissioners with a concrete idea of the Nation's past whose celebratory year we were to structure, you were so kind as to invite a group of the commissioners to Colonial Williamsburg. There I met the two of you for the first time and was introduced to CW/s visionary setting, its educational activities, and gracious hospitality.

I was most impressed, and although concerned as to what my contribution to the commission might be, my Williamsburg visit left no doubts that being a member of the committee offered an excellent opportunity for an American novelist to discover important details of the nation's past of which he was ignorant. And this enlightenment could be achieved while participating in the conscious process through which the nation's history is brought to bear on the present as it is shaped by the ongoing collaboration and conflict between the Government, the private sector, and business. More important, it was also a rare, integrative opportunity for a Negro citizen to bring the details of his group experience into that process of "consciousness raising," and thus it was even more of a challenge. Meeting you strengthened my determination to do my best, but then, perhaps to instruct me in the complex relationship between History and politics—at least as perceived by two chiefs of state—Fate struck again.

This time it was in the shape of President Nixon, who came into office and immediately threw me off the commission—which was not surprising. But that the president could be so unperceptive as to get rid of you

Carl, a man who was dedicated to preserving and teaching the nation an appreciation for its historical past, and thus lose in that nationwide effort to resuscitate America's historical memory, <u>Mary's</u> infectious charm and social skills all in one fell swoop—<u>that</u> I found most surprising indeed.

Fanny and I took my own dismissal as a joke, but Carl's struck us as a bad omen. For if so experienced an actor in the drama of quickening the country's historical memory could be so summarily dismissed—and even before the props were arranged and the cast selected—surely a farce was in the offering. Therefore we decided that it was just as well that my own small walk-on role had been cancelled. For after all, in performing their roles in the epic of the nation's history Presidents are like playwrights who are charged with structuring and directing a given set of scenes and actions which are drawn from that master-script we call the Constitution. So they do their best and then depart while under a new director the epic goes on unfolding. Thus when presidents change the script is modified and mistakes like that in which you, Carl, were given the bum's rush, are made. Having had but the briefest exposure to your low-keyed style, I felt disappointed that this could happen. Yes, but little did I suspect that you had your <u>own</u> compact with American history, or that in fulfilling your mission you were beyond being limited by presidential decision. Thus when historical fate struck at me a third time—and with <u>you</u> as its agent— I was damned certain that I had been elected the butt of an historical joke, and a subtle, Southern Carl Humelsine version at that.

Thus when you suggested that I join you on the Colonial Williamsburg board I suspected that you were challenging my courage before the class and racial mysteries of the Tidewater Republic. And as it turned out you had me at least three ways: As a citizen I believed that I was obligated to serve this country to the extent of my ability, and as a writer I believed that I should know as much about its affairs as was possible for me to experience; and as an individual who had grown up complaining about the lack of opportunity for Negroes I was obligated, now that you had opened the way, to undergo whatever risks that were involved with what I suspected would be a formidable and hostile bunch of Virginians. I was reluctant, but since neither Fanny nor I are given to backing away from <u>real</u> challenges I accepted, and you know the rest.

What you might <u>not</u> know is how much Fanny and I appreciate the uncondescending manner in which you and Mary handled our initiation into what was then a strange, if not alien, world. You quickly made us feel at home, and that feeling was solidified by our reception by the members of the board, their wives, and the entire CW staff. At first, Carl, I thought that after having conned me so successfully it might be a matter of your having conned your associates to put up with me, but then I came to realize that they, like you, were concerned with curing the nation of its historical amnesia and that all they expected of me was to contribute whatever I could. With you as their leader they were bent upon resuscitating the past by way of enriching the present so that the nation could move a bit closer to those ideals that were first given voice in Williamsburg. I soon discovered that in that enterprise, you were the goading voice of old American promises; practical, daring, given to endless improvisations, capable of creative con, and a hard-headed idealist who, abetted by Mary's aplomb, had been performing in the private sector to make our democratic ideals manifest with a success that would cause any senior American diplomat or president and their ladies to turn green with envy. During the years that followed we came first to admire and then to love you. Indeed, it has been but months since I retired from the board but already Fanny and I feel as though we have been cast out of Eden. That's how much we miss the work and play to which you introduced us.

We're delighted that although you've come to the end of your official involvement with Colonial Williamsburg you will still be present at the grand place where you've done so much to bring America's historical past into vibrant and creative alignment with the present. May you long enjoy your new home and the fellowship of those who love you.

Sincerely yours,
Ralph Ellison

To Carl Carlisle
RALPH ELLISON
Star Route 91A
Plainfield, MA 01070
SEPTEMBER 9, 1985

Dear Carl:

This is terribly late for me to be responding to your letter of May 1st, and I apologize. Since July we've been here in the hills; where, having missed the summer of '84, we've had to contend with a collection of burst pipes and cold solder joints from the past two winters. There were also electrical problems, a last minute request for an introduction to a literary collection that is to be published by the National Endowment for the Arts, and a long essay for a collection of my own which is scheduled for release in the spring. But as you might suspect, our disruption really began with the Washington affair that was so exhausting that it wrecked our schedule for the entire spring and summer—

Beginning with the evening before the awards ceremony, which found us standing in a receiving line for over an hour and a half shaking hands and mumbling appreciative mumbles to the congratulatory mumbles of miles of guests. Which, for the first half hour, was interesting but soon palled as guests kept arriving and disappearing into another room where food and drinks were being served and the decibels kept rising while we, poor honorees, had to keep pumping hands and smiling. This went on for so long that I soon found myself hoping that you and Mary would appear to bring a bit of humane consideration into the affair.

If this sounds ungrateful it's not that it was unpleasant to have the well-wishes of so many strangers, or uninteresting to chat with La Price and Jose Ferrer, between whom Fanny and I were stationed, it's just that at CW you accustomed us to seeing such affairs handled with so much more panache.

But despite the evening's having evoked visions of bursitis and dying of starvation and thirst midst plenty, the next day's luncheon not only went off without a hitch but provided me, along with the handsome medal, with at least one other surprise. For although I had been to the White House a number of times, had swapped hoboing experiences with L.B.J. in the Oval Office, and had once been seated at dinner with Mrs. Johnson, the Shah of Iran, and [the] Duke [of] Ellington, this was my first time to be seated at a <u>President's</u> table. Thus when directed there by a secretary I recalled that the notice of my appointment had arrived on April Fool's Day and steeled myself for the unexpected.

"Stop, Look, and Listen, and then count ten before you pull <u>any</u> verbal string," I told myself; "and remember L.B.J.'s advice to the group of civil rights leaders who were complaining about President Nixon's policies: '<u>You</u> might think he's a so-and-so, but <u>he</u> doesn't think he's a so-and-so—So go <u>talk</u> with the so-and-so!'" I knew also that I am enough of my mother's son not to be impolite to my host in his own house, but the problem was that I didn't know if the <u>President</u> would know what to make of the first gent of color to be roasted—at least in recent times—at Colonial Williamsburg. How, I asked myself, will he react when confronted by Banquo's ghost at his table? But as it turned out there was no need for such concern.

Presiding at a table for eight, the President sat with Leontyne Price on his left and Martha Graham on his right, while I was seated next to Miss Graham and just opposite La Price, who engaged the President in such a lively flow of conversation that there was no <u>way</u> for me to make him uneasy. Indeed, both gave excellent performances of the respective roles of "President" and "Diva," and he lived up to his reputation as a man of a certain charm by telling anecdotes and including us all in his conversation. Best of all, he hosted a fine meal of which the service was expert, and asked for no speeches from the awardees when he and Mrs. Reagan presented the medals.

All in all, it was a memorable occasion and indeed an honor to have been selected as a member of such a distinguished group of artists and patrons of the arts. <u>And</u>, like you, I was glad that there were no Whittaker Chambers-types included. I was also pleased that the Congress asserted its own role in creating the awards with a party hosted by Senators Kennedy and Pell, that most influential friend of the arts. This came during the evening and with the Botanic Garden as its setting. There with the main ceremony behind us it was quite pleasant to eat and drink and talk surrounded by more orchids than we'd ever seen. Nevertheless I'm afraid that despite this testimony to the bipartisan nature of the awards they are still misunderstood (and willfully) by people who should know better.

As with a writer friend of ours who is herself the wife of a very distinguished author (and himself the recipient of honors sponsored by the White House) who allowed herself to tell me that I should have <u>rejected</u> the medal! Presumably because she disagrees with the President's policies. I told her that I accepted the medal not as a vote for the President, but because it was endowed by the American Government, and because I hoped that the Government would continue its bipartisan involvement in the arts. She has known me for a long time but evidently forgot that I received my opportunity for becoming a writer by working on the Federal Writers' Project, and that I was charter member of the old Arts Council and had sat on the board of the Kennedy Center and would, therefore, have far more than a personal interest in the success of the National Medal. For as I see it Presidents will come, do their thing, and depart; but if those who select the honorees do their work objectively and well the medal program will go on as long as there's a nation. I had nothing to do with establishing the award, but I do have an obligation to make other Afro-American writers aware that the Government will reward their talent. And that, it seems to me, is far more important than making a far too facile (and questionable) political gesture.

Which brings to mind a comment made years ago by the late critic, Stanley Edgar Hyman when I wondered out loud if I hadn't been given an award simply because I happened to be a Negro.

"Ralph," he said, "I've never heard you grumble when things were going against you, so why the hell are you complaining now that something good has come your way?"

Well, this time I didn't and am quite satisfied to let the future decide whether or not I deserved the award. In the meantime I value your opinion and can't tell you how much I appreciate your congratulations.

Carl, I realize that this is far too long a letter to impose upon a busy executive, but we miss the hell out of you and Mary and it is one way of compensating for the vacuum that retiring from CW has made in our lives. Call us whenever you're in New York and we'll rush to see you. We hope that your new home is going well, are quite certain that its design and craftsmanship will be excellent, and look forward toward that visit.

Thanks again for your letter and our love to you and Mary.

Sincerely,
Ralph Ellison

To Neil Ortenberg
RALPH ELLISON
730 Riverside Drive
New York, N.Y. 10031
OCTOBER 19, 1985

Mr. Neil Ortenberg
Thunder's Mouth Press
P.O. Box 780
New York, N.Y. 10025

Dear Mr. Ortenberg,

Congratulations on your decision to make Langston Hughes' *The Big Sea* available again. It is a valuable segment in the history of Afro-American literature and I am surprised that it was allowed to lapse from print. Fortunately, the short sightedness of its original publisher is your opportunity and I feel sure that it will be a successful project.

This said, however, I must decline your offer to write an introduction for the following reasons: I am in the process of completing a book of essays (scheduled for publication in June) while trying at the same time to complete my long delayed second novel. Thus I am under too much pressure to sustain the interruption necessary for writing a proper introduction. And then, to be more precise, there is a more personal reason:

When *The Big Sea* was first published I reviewed it for the *New Masses,* and in the course of my review I offered certain criticisms regarding what I considered its lack of intellectual range. Hughes, who was a friend and hero of mine, was hurt by my remarks because he felt that I made demands of his autobiography that went beyond his intentions. I, in turn, was distressed by his reaction, and so, out of respect for his feelings I declined to review *I Wonder as I Wander*—as now, out of respect for Hughes' memory, I must forego what would be a second encounter with *The Big Sea.*

In closing I would suggest that you consider Mr. Arnold Rampersad,[*] who teaches in the English Department of Rutgers University. He is a serious critic who has published a number of papers on Langston Hughes, and is at work on a critical biography. I suggest him because of the several critics of Hughes who have come to my attention he is the most sensitive and knowledgeable.

Sincerely,
Ralph Ellison

To Michele Higgs
RALPH ELLISON
730 Riverside Drive
New York, N. Y 10031
OCTOBER 19, 1985

Miss Michele A. Higgs
Howard University Press
2900 Van Ness Street, N.W.
Washington, D.C. 20008

Dear Miss Higgs,

Thanks very much for the complimentary copy of *A Case of Rape.* It is, I think, the only work of Himes with which I was unfamiliar. I began reading Himes when he was published in *Esquire,* and continued to find his work of interest during his period in Europe. Come to think of it, there was a time when we hunted squirrels on Long Island, and during the '40s

---

[*]   Rampersad would later write the first complete biography of Ellison (2007).

and 50's my wife and I exchanged many a pleasant visit with Chester and his first wife, Jean.

Which is to say that I knew both the man and his writing and find it regrettable that he was unable to give his theme—which is, as you suggest, abiding and therefore most important—the extended treatment it demands. As it stands, however, it strikes me as a sketch rather than a fulfillment of his intentions, and one that suffers from the psychological sketchiness of his characters, men and women, white and black. For me their motivations lack convincing orchestration; and thus, being all flaws and no heroism, they provide me with no point for sympathy or identification. This is especially true of the men, who have little to redeem them. And while Himes makes the case that the woman's ravagement by social attitudes was more deplorable than her physical assault by drugs and sexual savagery, the recording sensibility through which the plot is presented (presumably that of a newspaper man or writer) he remains outside the action, and thus fails, at least for me, to establish his moral authority. Instead, Himes has an established novelist investigate the pathetic incident and then has the narrator dismiss him as being too blind and prejudiced to see the true complexity of what has happened. The heroes of Hammett and Simenon, who accept the physical and psychological risks of their moral postures, would call this cheating At the least it is a mistake of fictional strategy.

Nor are these fictional shortcomings remedied by allusions to Richard Wright on the dust jacket and in Mr. Herndon's comments. Not that his analysis is without merit, but that as used here it serves to impose a question of promotional morality upon the morality of a fictional situation. Rape is a universal phenomena, but in literature the universal must be achieved through the eloquent articulation of specific characters, psychologies and incidents. Here excesses of pride and failures of judgment lead to disaster, and this at those points where human arms become too short to overcome the universe as it finds expression in social custom, prejudice and injustice. But while flawed characters, whether black or white, heroes or fools, are indispensable to literature (Oedipus did, after all, kill his father and marry his mother, and John Henry died of excessive pride in his physical strength), when it is implied that such flawed fictional characters are drawn from those of real people not only does it suggest that the author has failed artistically to give his characters the attributes necessary to motivate, sustain and give authenticity to their action, it raises an ethical problem—at least for me—which has to do with the relationship between fact and fiction And I say this while recognizing the gossipy appeal of romans a clef.

Who, for instance, is the "Himes" character in the fiction, and upon what other men of flesh and blood are the characters directly involved in the rape based? And if such exist why drag Wright into the fictional squalor while allowing them their privacy? Many black men have died, and innocently, when accused of rape, but here by way of compensating for one author's failure to raise his fictional rapists above the threshold of banality we have something that comes close to the rape of a deceased and respected author's reputation—Which strikes me as the most unkindest rape of all.

Having said all this, I should add that Wright was for many years a friend, and thus it is possible that I am over-reacting. If so, I hope you'll understand my frankness. I am grateful to you for the book, wish Howard University Press success with its publications, and hope that it will discover and publish many talented writers.

Sincerely,
Ralph Ellison

cc: Mr. Charles Harris

To Camille Rhone
RALPH ELLISON
STAR ROUTE 91-A
PLAINFIELD, MA 01071
OCT. 22, 1985

Dear Camille:

Yesterday a neighbor brought an Episcopalian minister who lives in this area to meet us and I was reminded of you and the church on Third and Lindsey. I can still see Pat marching down the aisle as he took part in the ritual, and even see him kneeling as he faced the altar. But although I can recall the time when Father Kilpatrick was the minister who sponsored an official Boy Scout troop I no longer remember the name of the church. And yet I can visualize the house where you lived on the corner of Third and Phillips and can see quite clearly where the homes of the

Haywoods, the Bowens, the Williams, Bill Price, Dr. Young, the Bethels, and my mother's friend, Lizzie Sanders, were located. So it would seem that time and distance are taking their toll. On the other hand, a church is more than a name, it's really its minister and congregation; thus since, you, Pat, and my cousin Maybelle were part of the congregation I still retain something of what is important. And that's enough of that!

I hope all has gone well with you and the family since the last time I wrote and will so continue. Fanny and I have had a busy summer, with my making progress on my novel and completing a book of essays that will be published next June. Indeed, we were so busy that our only garden crop was string beans! We find this amusing, but they are a delicious purple variety that grew in such abundance that we'll be eating them for weeks to come. There were also a few lilies, impatiens, peonies, and delphiniums to delight the eye and attract the butterflies, bees, and humming birds, but little else except wild flowers, some of which were plentiful. So we've promised ourselves that next year we'll arrive here sooner, have things under more control—especially the weeds—and do better with our gardening, both vegetable and floral. In the mean time we console ourselves with the fact that the weather here was so irregular that even the professional farmers had less than a successful season.

It is a sunny day, here in the mountains, with the light made golden as it falls through the leaves of the trees outside my study windows. These towering, ancient sugar maples line an old stone wall which curves away from the house into the woods, forming an avenue of sweeping branches above a sloping lane, and now in the bright afternoon sunlight the air glows with color as far as the eye can see. I try to force myself to ignore it, but with little success. For our house stands on a plateau which drops abruptly into a steep ravine, making for an intriguing view, and when I look below to where the trees have lost most of their leaves, the tall trunks and branches give the light a silvery cast. A few years ago we sold off some of the timber by way of improving the grove and now the clearing has a deceptive way of promising views of wild life that are seldom forthcoming. Yes, but I keep looking!

Until the recent frost it was barely possible to see the sky there because of the thickness of the leaves, which provide a favorite nesting spot for such shy birds as Scarlet Tanagers and Hermit Thrushes. They've migrated now and we miss the music, but when I look up in the other direction to the park-like area where apple, pine, wild cherry, aspen, and maples are slowly encroaching upon the meadow, the seasonal display which draws thousands from other sections to view the glory of New England's fall is still with us, showing orange and red, gold and brown through and against the green of pine and white of beech and aspen.

There are, incidentally, many, many sugar maples here, some so old that they must have been planted during Revolutionary times, and in early spring many are tapped for making maple syrup. We once had a deal with a local farmer who tapped some of ours in exchange for the several gallons which we used ourselves and gave to friends; an arrangement which came to an end when failures on his farm forced him to take a job in a factory. So now surrounded by these magnificent trees we buy our syrup from others.

But whether tapped or not, the maple woods make a fine sight, even as now when the scarcity of birds is a sure sign of approaching winter. Until a couple of weeks ago we could see several broods of wild turkeys and their chicks working the meadow which faces the house, but no longer. And the deer and fawns which we've watched with pleasure seem to have known instinctively that the hunting season is approaching so they're no longer to be seen browsing and flashing their nervous white tails. One might say that the deer have gone like the spots from the coats of their now maturing fawns.

And so it will soon be with the Ellisons. We're packing to return to the excitement of New York and the readjustment that the noise and density of people requires after four months of country quiet. We like it here and are reluctant to leave, but once we're back and settled we realize once again why we chose to live in all the clamor. Besides, it's the "getting place" of my profession, and with so <u>much</u> to see and do we learned long ago to be selective. However, it does have its disadvantages. We have many friends there but none whom I've known so long and well as those at home. Nor are its streets and buildings so full of personal associations and memories. Therefore the memories and knowledge of people that support my writer's imagination are for the most part back in Oklahoma. I often wonder what life would have been had I been able to return to Oklahoma after college, but then I have to face the possibility that if I had I wouldn't be the "me" I am today. So as it is I thank the stars that I had what I now realize was a rich and varied experience, and to that experience and to those who shared it I try to be true.

I talked with Herbert last week and found him well. He said that he had called Jim but after three poor connections they were unable to talk. I suppose that earthquakes and stormy "Gloria" interrupted communication all over the country. We were spared most of it except several hours without electricity. Herbert sends his regards, and my wife and I send our best regards to you and yours.

Sincerely,
Ralph Ellison

To John Callahan
RALPH ELLISON
Star Route 91-A
Plainfield, MA 01070
OCTOBER 25, 1985

Dear John:

We're packing and preparing to leave no later than Monday and while Fanny has kept on top of things and managed to keep clutter to a minimum, I'm somewhat up in the air. I finished the Caldwell essay (now titled "An Extravagance of Laughter"), but in our rush to Conn. for a weekend editorial session there was no time to correct misspellings, etc. Erskine and I made corrections on the spot so that the ms. could be sent to the copy editor; thus I don't have a decent copy to send you. However my agent called yesterday with word that he had received a corrected copy— now being read by the editor of the Sunday NY *Times* Magazine—so in time you'll be able to see it.

Unfortunately, "Tell It Like It Is, Baby" got lost in the editorial shuffle, and since you present such an eloquent argument for its inclusion I regret that I didn't have it to show Erskine; who, by the way, had problems with the dream section. That wasn't the only problem of selection, however, because there are so many interviews with relevant materials, and with the sixty page Caldwell being the only unpublished piece included it will take up the major space of what will be a *Shadow and Act* sized collection. The title, as of now, will be *Going to the Territory;* the contents: "Little Man At Chehaw Station"; "On Initiation Rites and Power"; "What These Children are Like"; "The Myth of the Flawed White Southerner"; "If the Twain Shall Meet"; "What America Would Be Like Without Blacks"; "Going to the Territory"; "A Portrait of Inman Page"; "An Extravagance of Laughter"; "Remembering Richard Wright"; "Homage to Duke Ellington on His Birthday"; "Romare Bearden"; "Society, Morality and the Novel"; "A Very Stern Discipline"; "The Novel as a Function of American Democracy"; and "Perspective of Literature."

I had thought to include the introduction to the 30th Edition to *IM*, but was persuaded that it is to our economic interest to let those who are interested buy that edition.

Which brings me to your problem with the dolls;* here I think you were tricked by a bit of understatement and indirection. The fat man explodes with laughter and the crowd is repelled <u>not</u> because the narrator looks like the dolls, but because in his sudden sense of betrayal he feels his "throat constrict [and] the rage welled up behind the phlegm as I rocked back on my heels and crouched forward." It is at this point that you were thrown off by a telescoping of the action which presents its results: "There was a flash of whiteness and a splatter like heavy rain striking a newspaper and I saw the doll go over backwards, wilting into a dripping rag of frilled tissue, the hateful head upturned on its out-stretched neck still grinning toward the sky." Psychologically, the narrator's consciousness lags behind his reaction, he records his having spat on the doll after the fact, and it is the vehemence and unexpectedness of I.M's reaction that leads the pot-bellied man to laugh and point out to the crowd that it is I.M. who had flattened the entertaining stereotype with spittle. You'll note that it is after this that the crowd backs away and laughs hysterically as the irrepressible dolls resume their dancing. I.M. tries unsuccessfully to destroy the damn (and damning) doll twice: once with spittle and again by crushing it with his foot. His first attempt produced a multiplication of dolls, and his second is frustrated by an old lady in a blue polka-dot dress who cries out and leads him to pocket the doll instead of crushing it. So he tries <u>three</u> times, once by water, once by crushing, next time by fire in his underground darkness—and you take it from there!

Your plan for your next book looks intriguing and I'll do my best when contacted by the G. people. But whether they are forthcoming with cash or not I think you should write it. Why the hell should a foundation keep you from writing something that <u>I</u> am anxious to read? You've already made a start with the autobiographical material in your Hurston section, so keep going!

Harper was here for an overnight visit, during which we had much lively talk and brought to an end our summer's entertaining which began with you and the three girls. The sun is bright today but it's raining leaves with all the commotion of a 19th century lady getting out of her slips and

---

* Ellison refers to a passage in Callahan's revision of his book chapter on eloquence in *Invisible Man*.

corsets. It's a flashy display but now that it's time to make tracks I'm glad we won't be around to see the trees all bare. Tell the girls that Fanny will bring them up to date on Porcupine Jones,* who was last seen disappearing between the barn and the garage, when we're settled in New York. Meantime our love to you all.

Sincerely,
Ralph

To Camille Rhone
RALPH ELLISON
730 RIVERSIDE DRIVE
NEW YORK, N.Y. 10031
DEC. 2, 1985

Dear Camille:

Thanks for the (belly) laugh. Those elusive crappies remind me of the time Fanny and I spent our vacation surf-fishing off Cape Cod. I had good equipment and was fair at surf-casting, but while fishermen on both sides of me were bringing in 30 and 40 pound Striped bass all I could reel in were Sea Robbins—and it didn't matter that I was using the same bait or selection of lures. I threw them an assortment of lead-weighted goodies but they kept shaking their shaking heads.

I'm returning the clipping along with one from the *Washington Post* which I came across last month when visiting Williamsburg, Virginia. The heavenly fellow who does the talking is probably right—having been given hands, the monkeys are indeed messing up the earth, and those monkeys are <u>us</u>!

Even so, and for all his wisdom, the heavenly personage appears to have forgotten that dolphins were once <u>land</u> animals that became so disgusted with earth's state of affairs that they said to hell with it and went to live in the oceans. Heap much intelligence floating down there.

I'm also enclosing a clipping announcing my Nov., 1984 retirement as a member of Colonial Williamsburg's board of trustees. It's not much of a photograph but you can see how bald I've become, and you might find it interesting that two Okies sat on the board; the other being Daniel Boorstin, the Librarian of Congress, who grew up in Tulsa. I served there

---

* Porcupine Jones narrated several charming children's stories in letters Fanny Ellison wrote the Callahan girls, Eve and Sasha.

for fourteen years and now that it's over Fanny and I shall miss our twice-yearly junkets into the nation's past. Should your grandchildren be taken on trips to the South, Williamsburg would be a most interesting (and educational) experience.

As you can see, all kinds of strange things have happened to your old friend. A little over a decade ago I became the first Negro to be appointed to the Williamsburg board, and now there are two.

Twenty years ago the State of Virginia was putting up "massive resistance" to the new civil rights legislation; today an Afro-American has been elected Lieutenant Governor. I don't know how it all fits together, but the climate of racial relations is quite different than it was when we became affiliated with Colonial Williamsburg, and I suspect that Fanny and I have played a minor role in that change. That's what you get for tying me in that baby chair!

After a morning of high winds and rain the afternoon here is bright and sunny, but when I look out I can see white caps on the Hudson River and the gulls flying low over the roiling water. The weather reports forecast snow, so I guess winter is finally heading this way. Take care, keep working on your printing and before you know it you'll be writing <u>writing</u>.

Love,
Ralph

To Mamie Rhone
RALPH ELLISON
730 RIVERSIDE DRIVE
NEW YORK, N.Y. 10031
DEC. 3, 1985

Dear Mamie Rhone:

Thanks for your letter and the *Dayton News Magazine* article, which I found most informative. I was aware of the Dunbar Dayton connection, but knew nothing of the link between Yellow Springs and Virginia Hamilton. I've also received a word from Camille in the form of a comic verse about fishing for crappies. As a former fisherman I appreciated the poet's exasperation with the finicky taste of non-biting fish, but my real pleasure came from the message that Camille printed on the clipping. It was short and a bit unsteady in execution but I had no difficulty whatsoever in grasping her message. This I take as a good omen, for just as the verse makes evident that she's lost none of her sense of humor, the message indicates that she's making progress in regaining her writing skills. To paraphrase the old joke having to do with the difference between reading print and reading scrip—(or reading <u>reading</u>, as against reading <u>writing</u>), she might be unable to write <u>writing</u>, but she's well on her way to writing <u>printing</u>!

Oddly enough I had just been thinking of Saretta when your letter arrived, although in a far different mood than that sparked by your news of her accident. For two weeks now my wife and I have been living with two huge five-drawer files that take up most of the space in our vestibule. Brought up from the basement after the Fire Department insisted that it be cleared of all property belonging to the building's tenants, these two monsters dominate our living space like as couple of moving vans crammed into the rear seat of a small Japanese car. It's hard to get around them, impractical to climb over them, and impossible to crawl under them. And while it is bad enough that Fanny and I are forced to question ourselves a dozen times a day as to how we came to such an impasse, the meter reader, porter, and various delivery men react by giving us looks as if to say, "What kind of odd-balls would live like <u>this</u>?" and then get the hell out of here as quickly as possible.

The looks on their faces remind me of Saretta's when, years ago, she and Tuffy dropped in to see us unexpectedly. We had just moved from a smaller apartment on the floor below, and while waiting for new shelves to be installed were forced to contend with hundreds of books piled all over the study and living room floors. Sis gave me a look which seemed to say, "Well, well—I always thought you were some kind of nut, but now I'm sure of it!" Lord knows what she'd think (she's too much of a lady to <u>say</u> it) if she saw these files! Having once suffered a broken arm, I know how painful such breaks can be; therefore I'm glad that the pleasant memory came before I knew of her present accident. And yet, when I consider the rigors undergone by two friends who've had hip replacement surgery, Sis is lucky that it was only her wrist.

Which leads me to say how much I appreciate your taking the time to write. At last there's <u>someone</u> in the far-flung clan of Randolphs, Rhones, and Slaughters who writes (and answers) letters! Neither Jim, Taylor, nor Wyatt would bother, and dear Sis limits herself (at least as far as I'm concerned) to Christmas cards. Such, I suppose, is the difference between generations. For whenever my mother and Aunt Edna were in different cities they kept in touch—And thank God, because during times of trouble they could at least advise and console one another. But somehow that civilized custom waned with the younger generation; thus for all the many things that have happened to Fanny and me which I'd like to share, I don't—And only because writing letters that go unanswered is like shouting into a deep dark well—You're bored by hearing the echo of what you already know. Being fascinated by the mystery of my background, and eager to keep up with what's happening to those whom I've known all my life I find such silence regrettable. For while I realize that they're all busy people with their own concerns, I still feel that an exchange of news fires memory, keeps important details of the past alive, and helps us gauge the meaning of experience as viewed by those who "knew us when." On the other hand, it might just be that my letters are just too damned long!

In a previous letter you mentioned that a colony of writers lived around Yellow Springs; and now, thanks to the *Magazine* article I shall look out for their work. (I'm enclosing a *New York Times Book Review* ad for a Virginia Hamilton collection.) In fact, I recognize two names mentioned in the article with pleasure: Paul and Norma Bixler. When editor of the *Antioch Review* Paul accepted my essay-review of Richard Wright's *Black Boy,* and I take it as a tribute to his editorial taste that it keeps turning up in anthologies forty years later. I ran into Paul a few times here in New York and once had a pleasant visit with the Bixlers and their big "naughty boy" of an English bulldog in Ohio. Should you run into them please give them my regards. Judson Jerome is another name I recall, perhaps from my stint at Antioch and, of course, from his poetry.

It turns out that the Yellow Springs writers group formed the year before I arrived in Dayton, and when I read of its help to younger writers I realize how ironic it was that I, who was so much in need of someone with whom to discuss the craft of fiction, knew nothing of its existence. Nevertheless, I <u>did</u> receive what was perhaps a more vital form of aid and encouragement right there on Dayton's East side, and from a most unexpected source.

My benefactor was Lawyer Stokes, one of whose sons was to become the president either of Wilberforce or Central State. We were brought together through the kindness of an old friend of his daughter. This was Marian Minus (a Dayton native whom I met through Richard Wright), who upon learning that I was going to her old home town wrote a letter of introduction to her old friend, Marie Stokes. I made myself known to Marie and she in turn introduced me to her father. As a result, some of my earliest attempts at writing fiction were done in his office and on his typewriter and stationery.

Nor was that all, for later when my brother Herbert and I had lost our living quarters Lawyer Stokes allowed us to sleep in his office and make use of its toilet and bathing facilities. He was a man of great curiosity who put much effort into learning just what made me tick, enjoyed arguing with me, and appeared not to mind when someone the age of his youngest son scored telling points; which, considering that I was a young radical and himself a Republican County committeeman, made for a most incongruous and instructive friendship. I shall never forget his kindness during what seemed a period of hopelessness, and when I weigh what I received from him with what I <u>might</u> have gotten had I known members of the writers group I'm sure that knowing him was more desirable. Not that knowing those who were concerned with the same problems of craft with which I was struggling wouldn't have been to my advantage, but while I would come to know many writers in New York, Dayton was the only place where I could have known someone with Mr. Stokes' experience. During my hour of despair he was, in a sense, a figure of hope who appeared out of nothing more substantial than a letter. Here too, as with so many things, in the beginning was the word . . .

You are most kind to write me, and I hope you'll continue whenever there's news that you consider of interest. But <u>please</u> consider me enough of a friend of Elmore Mitchell's family to address me simply as "Ralph." Meanwhile, all the best from me and mine to you and yours.

Sincerely,

Ralph

To Muriel Spence
RALPH ELLISON
730 Riverside Drive
New York, N.Y. 10031
FEB. 2, 1986

Mrs. Muriel Spence*
171 Burlington Street
Lexington, MA 02173

Dear Muriel:

It was pleasant to finally bridge the time, distance, and generational gaps between us, even though only by telephone, and I hope we'll keep in touch.

The titles of the books I mentioned are: *No Chariot Let Down, Charleston's Free People of Color on the Eve of the Civil War,* edited by Michael P. Johnson and James L. Roark. The University of North Carolina Press, 1984, and *Black Masters, A Free Family of Color in the Old South,* by Michael P. Johnson & James L. Roark.

The first volume consists of an exchange of letters between members of the William Ellison family and their friends that were found during the 1930's by a group of little white girls while playing under the porch of what had been the Ellison mansion. With the passing of time this collection came to the attention of Johnson and Roark, who grasped the letters' historical value, edited them, and then set out to reconstruct the social, political, and cultural background out of which they were written. They performed an admirable job of scholarly detective work, and I'm sure that you'll find the results fascinating. Your great grandfather, Alfred Ellison is mentioned in many notes.

As you might well be aware, many of the southern Negroes who settled in Philadelphia after the Reconstruction came to its violent end were from Abbeville, S.C. Allen B. Ballard, a professor of political science at CUNY has written of this phase of our history in *One More Day's Journey,* which was published in 1984 by McGraw-Hill. I thought enough of Ballard's ef-

---

* Muriel Morisey Spence was the daughter of Ellison's first cousin Alexander Morisey; by 1986 she was a lawyer in the Civil Rights Division of the Department of Justice. See note to Ellison's September 18, 1979, letter to his brother, Herbert.

fort to say in a blurb that "(it) is important to all who would possess fresh insights into the roles played by southern freedmen and their descendants as they [went] about shaping northern no less than southern history. I recommend it highly to all who would add to their knowledge of American history. It is dramatic and revealing of much that has been omitted from so-called official versions of our nation's history."

That's it for now. I'm enclosing the clipping that made me aware of what you've been up to. Our best regards to you and your husband.

Sincerely,

Ralph

To Horace Porter

RALPH ELLISON

730 Riverside Drive

New York, N.Y. 10031

FEB. 29, 1986

Dear Horace:

I hope your trip to the west coast went well for you and Carla, while taking it for granted that his grandparents were delighted with Zack. Breaking with our custom of spending the final weekend of the year with my editor and his family in Conn., we spent our holiday season at home alone, greeted the New Year with the old ancestral ritual fare of pigs feet, ears, tails and black-eyed peas, cornbread and dry champagne, and found it a relief not to be involved in the usual series of parties. Other than that we kept to our regular pattern of work and struggle with disorder.

For months we've been intimidated by a couple of five drawer legal files that were removed by order of the First Department from their decade of storage in the basement, and the effect upon this already crowded apartment is unbelievable. We've made space for one of the monsters, but its mate remains in the vestibule where it forces anyone who would enter to squeeze past, startled cheek by dusty jowl, while it assails the nose with emanations from the long-buried but ever-stirring past. And once the victim survives that encounter with encapsulated time he must then run the risk of stumbling over piles of books, magazines, scholarly journals, and stacked transfer files that groan with their loads of events that go back to the 1940's and beyond.

We're doing our best to impose some kind of order on the chaos but the very mass and variety of the stuff, and the temptation to check out old happenings and make reevaluations that it invites, makes for slow going. And of course there is the continuing pressure of my notorious novel-in-progress, on which work was interrupted by our return to N.Y., plus such extra obligations as required by writing a grant-seeking statement for a friend, and commenting on a work of criticism that touches on some of my own writing. But despite such interruptions I managed to complete a long essay for my collection that is scheduled for June, and with the galleys now on hand I've been working with the copy editor over all kinds of petty (to me) details that are a necessary part of being published.

As you can see, I've been busy as hell, and that explains my slowness in responding to your ms. Nevertheless, I've read it not once but twice; the first time by way of giving myself over to the narrative, and the second in hope that I'd have something to say that you might find useful. I'm afraid, however, that what I have to say is rather disorganized; therefore I'm sending along what started out to be an orderly statement along with the jottings made in response to the unfolding narrative. You'll find many repetitions, but that ideas that were blurred in one attempt will be stated a bit more clearly in the other.

As you know, reading a novel is always a subjective process, but reading an <u>unpublished</u> novel while working on one of one's own is not only subjective but confusing. Thus I found it necessary to remind myself that the techniques and assumptions that guide my own efforts aren't necessarily yours, and that your way of feeling and presenting your material is a product of your own experience, vision and artistic goals. Therefore with this in mind I must remind you that the best I can do is to give you my reactions with the understanding that you will take anything that you might find valid and ignore the rest. Most of all, you should consider the possibility that the story that I read is not the book you wrote; that is a possibility arising out of the circumstance, or convention, that places the reader's imagination and the writer's text in a collaborative relationship. For while he is guided by the writer's narrative directions and evocative skills, the reader must bring the fiction to life in his own individual imagination, and this on the basis of his own experience and vision of social and psychological reality. The degree to which he reads "creatively" and perceptively depends upon the strength of the writer's poetic, rhetorical, and analytical skills. For while certain novelists may disavow the use of rhetoric, rhetoric is inherent in linguistic communication and plays an important role in inducing, building, and sustaining the fictional spell. Thus no matter how powerful and vivid the story might be in the writer's mind, his reader must still be <u>persuaded</u> to willingly suspend his inclination toward <u>disbelief</u>. For while he wishes to be transported and entertained, shocked, horrored, even chilled, he is so conditioned by experience and by his life-preserving need to distinguish between illusion and reality, between shit and shinola, that he clings to his own vision of reality. Thus even then he surrenders to a work of the imagination most willingly when the author bases his illusion, his "lie," upon the highest degree of that which Henry James termed "felt life." And that "felt life" must encompass such matters as terrain and weather, social customs and manners, and the realities of race, class, and religion, etc. He wants social reality to be dealt with in an imaginative way, but while he will accept and enjoy fantasy, he will <u>not</u> accept it when presented in the guise of fictional realism—Unless, of course, the writer exercises the skills of a supreme trickster and overpowers his resistance. He is willing to place himself in the hands of the writer, but in doing so he wants to feel that those hands are reliable. And when the writer's strategy is that of providing him with a narrator who tells the tale, he wants that narrator to at least <u>appear</u> reliable; even when, as in the work of Ford Maddox Ford, said narrator is <u>intended</u> to be unreliable by way of testing the reader's powers of attention and perception. (Forgive me for going on about matters with which you're familiar, for I do so as a means of getting my <u>own</u> rusty ideas in some kind of order.)

I say all this by way of making the following suggestions: I think that you have a worthy tale to tell, and I read it with interest, but that you've given it over to a narrator, Oscar Montgomery, who is incapable of structuring your narrative to its potential advantage. Oscar tells me that he is a prize-winning journalist, and I say "O.K." but I take his statement as a promise to be fulfilled. He has aroused my expectations, and while I've read enough fiction to know that by way of keeping my attention as he advances his plot he must also frustrate some of my expectations, I am by no means prepared to be frustrated <u>before</u> he establishes his credibility.

Therefore I expect a journalist to exhibit the skills of a journalist, to have an eye for significant detail, a knowledge of political structures and relationships. And since Oscar has been given the role of central intelligence in what is his "memoir" and your novel, I expect him to fulfill the obligations of a novelist. I expect him to structure your plot in a manner that will grip my attention from its beginning, through its middle, to its climax and end. I expect him to make me see, feel hear, and small the atmosphere and action. In other words, I expect him to possess, and exercise those dramatic skills that are an important part of the novelist's bag of tricks. Most of all, I expect him to have a compelling curiosity about his fellow characters, their motives and acts, and the agencies through which they act, and the scenes in which they assert themselves. And I expect him to demonstrate that he knows that his characters are consubstantial with their antagonists as with their allies, and that the scenes in which his protagonist acts are as much a property of this (the protagonist's) character as his most private hopes and passionate desires, or the air he breathes.

Because from its exposition through its agon, to its unraveling a plot should be a living organism, and its central intelligence, the voice which manipulates and dialectically arouses, fulfills and frustrates my expectations, and which ultimately rewards me with a perception into the meaning of all the sound and fury that makes up a story, is one into whose hands I have surrendered my own intelligence, imagination, and sense of life. And when that central intelligence assumes such responsibility and authority but fails to deliver, he violates my trust and embarrasses the author for whom he acts as surrogate.

(All this is off the top of my head but I would guess that I'm trying to get at the morality involved in choosing one's central intelligence.)

At any rate, I expect Montgomery to get Diamond into action gradually but with a strong impression—Much as does Nick Carraway, his fellow Yalie, in presenting and projecting Gatsby—So now the cat is out of the bag! But it seems impossible for a reader familiar with *The Great Gatsby* to read a narrative written by another Yale man and not compare Montgomery with Carraway. Famous texts have a way of imposing themselves on those that come later. Thus such a reader would expect a Yalie narrator, whether white or black, to provide the main character with enough mystery and attraction that he is eager to spend the time necessary to learn exactly why the narrator finds him of interest. My problem with Montgomery is that he himself isn't interesting enough to make Diamond interesting. He doesn't convey enough of an emotional involvement with Diamond's fare to induce me to become concerned. And this, I think, is because he provides me with a flat character who is presented, for the most part, in flat, unfocused scenes. Only now and then do we hear him speak, and too often we hear Diamond through Montgomery rather than through his own dialogue spoken in scenes wherein the dramatic issues are given emotional urgency. I would expect also that he would give me a more definite idea of his own background and values during the early part of his exposition; that, in a word, he would lay enough of his cards on the table to allow me a better idea of where he's coming from, and a clearer grasp of the forces that are in opposition, both within himself and in the experience he narrates. If he says that he is an old childhood friend of the protagonist, I want to know the level of that friendship. If he says that Diamond is witty, I don't want to take his word for it, I want to experience the scene and feel Diamond's mind at work as it gives utterance—And this through dialogue which I can hear as if listening to an exchange between actors on a well-lit stage.

When I am told that the hero is a politician in pursuit of the gover-norship of a southern State, I want to know more of his motives, of his knowledge of party alliances and of his connections with those who wield political power as it interlocks locally and nationally. I want to know some-thing of his because Montgomery mentions historical dates and events that provide a timeframe for his plot's development. And since that timeframe includes Jimmy Carter and the racial turbulence of a historical period it is important that I know something of the moves and tradeoffs and possibili-ties that would motivate a Black politician to enter the contest. Otherwise Diamond strikes me as involved in a free-floating fantasy. And all the more so, because Montgomery fails of concreteness in aligning his forces. Here you might think of the reverses suffered by the Democrats thanks to the Kennedy machine's antagonism toward Johnson and Carter ...

In Montgomery's presentation Diamond comes across as being as much of a buffoon as his hero, Julian. Indeed, I wonder why Montgomery, Diamond's non-speech-writing speechwriter, doesn't advise him to get rid of such baggage. For while introducing the career of Col. J. is amusing as provocation, in the real world of southern politics it would be coun-terproductive—at least to my mind. I hope I'm not haggling, but while I'm willing to involve my mind in an imaginary political contest, reality presses in upon me with questions as to why a Georgia-born Negro would limit his white aides to two northern Catholics. By the widest stretch of the imagination he might have managed to win a primary election, but in the Bible Belt it is unlikely; even today which finds an Afro-American successful in the race for the Lieutenant-governorship of Virginia. I know some of the whites who were involved in that historical feat and it was a reversal of expectations that far outdid most of what fiction has offered. But, then, politics constitutes, for better or worse, our national form of drama; therefore if Montgomery would convince me of Diamond's vic-tory in a Georgian primary he'll have to provide me with a more rationally imagined explanation as to how it came about.

(Incidentally, Montgomery muddles his plot and wastes an opportunity for arousing interest and tension by waiting so long to introduce Midnight's role in Diamond's decision to abandon the contest—itself a disillusioning letdown. Midnight and the crucial shooting of Dr. Brown should have been introduced earlier as a foreshadowing of things to come. And, since money is the grease of political machines much as rhetoric is their gasoline, so should Rev. Sales as the source of Diamond's finances and his instructor in the art of persuasion. Plots are like bombs, their ingredients have to be assembled and carefully weighed lest at the decisive moment they produce a sputter instead of the expected explosion. Big bombs require long fuses, little bombs may do with shorter ones; but whether large or small, for them to be effective the narrator must be careful in his timing.) Returning to *Gatsby,* Carraway gives us scene after scene, and is careful in making his transitions from scene to scene. And in the process he prepares us for the entrance of Gatsby. But in the process he reveals significant details of his own background through the manner in which he interprets and comments on the scenes. He reveals his own values, his prejudices, his ignorance and his wonder. He stresses his emotional and intellectual involvement and the effect wrought upon his intelligence as he learns more about Gatsby. Far from dumping his passages of exposition upon us, he modulates them by filtering them through his own reactions. He presents what he learns of his hero in scenes, being careful to use their lights and shadows for maximum effect. He describes his conception of Gatsby's motives, his purposes, and the shadowy agency through which he seeks to achieve his goals step by step, as Gatsby moves toward and away from his goal. And, most important, he does not allow his hero to abandon his goal before the promised clash of forces and fate have reached a climax.

Gatsby wants Daisy beyond all bounds of reason, and he goes after her until he is killed for being a wrong-headed man in the wrong place at the wrong time. Gatsby strikes me as being just as illogical in his goals as Diamond is in his, but he pursues his goal with a logic which instead of defeating the plot makes it succeed., He gets his money illegally and his misperceives the milieu from which he would snatch "the golden girl," but as with the heroes of classical tragedy his criminality and blindness are in the interest of an ideal. In presenting his account of Gatsby's quest for Daisy, Carraway provides us with an extended comedy of manners. We are allowed to enter the atmosphere of Gatsby's parties, Tom and Daisy's home, the Wilson parlor. We hear the various dialogues as well as the lyrics to then popular songs. He appeals to our sense of smell, as to our sense of hearing, and allows us to feel the scenes and emotions he ascribes to his characters. Most of all, he allows us to see and experience the significant details of the scenes in which he projects his characters, and in doing so he keeps off camera as much as possible—quite unlike Montgomery who impedes the eye and blurs the forward pace of the action. Most significant for the artistic shapeliness of his narrative, Carraway does not waste time on unnecessary details. He moves with scenic economy from significant scene to significant scene, and doesn't frustrate the reader by saying again and again, "I bit my tongue."

Because he knows that the last thing the reader wants is for him to stop the flow of information that keeps him afloat in the stream of action. The reader wants him to increase the emotional tension and make his scenes as vivid and life-like as possible so that he, the reader, may participate more fully in the action. And when Carraway doesn't know enough of, say, Tom and Daisy's motives, he describes enough of their gestures, facial expressions, conversation to allow us to fill in something of that which he finds puzzling.

The same is true of his treatment of Gatsby. Initially he knows far less about Gatsby than Montgomery knows about Diamond—but that precisely is the source of his narrative's engrossment. He is in search of Gatsby, and the reader becomes involved because of the quality and intelligence of Carraway's curiosity. In pursuing his interest Carraway, the mid-western bonds salesman, becomes the surrogate for Fitzgerald, and thus a "novelist." I return to this idea because I think that Montgomery is in the same ambiguous position. It isn't enough that he tells us that he is a journalist (Gatsby tells us little about selling bonds), he must present his narrative like a journalist who is exercising the skills of a novelist. And while he might wish to keep his own emotions out of the picture, he should not make the mistake of depriving his readers of every possible opportunity for experiencing the emotion generated by the plot.

Carraway cares about what happens to Gatsby. He makes him interesting, he makes him daring as well as wrong-headed and romantic. He is a romantic fool who dies of love, but we care about his fate because Carraway makes him an ingratiating figure. Diamond, I'm sorry to say, is something else. Not because the idea of such a character doesn't seize my imagination, but because Montgomery refuses to develop his potential. I read of his life with a certain interest, but I don't really care about his political adventuring, his marriage, his romantic affairs, his fate. And the responsibility for my frustration (and I assure you that I want to be moved by Diamond) rests with Oscar, who gets in the way of the compelling story you have to tell. Perhaps things would go better if you used a different central intelligence

and presented your narrative in the third person. It would require an exploration of other techniques, and a refinement of your hero's motivation; but
since "motivation (as we are reminded by Kenneth Burke) is identical with
structure," it might result in a tighter, more effective plotting.

Horace, this is the best I can do at the moment so I'll stop. Take what
you find usable and junk the rest, but before making changes in your manuscript try it out on other readers. For as I said earlier; the book I read
might be quite different than the one you've written.

[Ralph]

To Bill Ferris
RALPH ELLISON
730 Riverside Drive
New York, N.Y. 10031
APRIL 16, 1986

Mr. William Ferris
The university of Mississippi
Center for the Study of Southern Culture
University, MS 38677

Dear Bill Ferris:

My wife has just informed me that in the more than usual disorder attending getting a book of essays to my publisher and fulfilling long-standing
commitments for readings and lectures I had failed to respond to your and
Mr. Harrington's invitation to participate in next July's Faulkner Conference. For this I apologize even as I express my regrets for being unable to
participate in so important a conference.

As things stand, however, the conference takes place at the time of year
during which I am able to write with the least interruption. Thus it is that
June finds my wife and I taking off for the Berkshires; where, if lucky, we
remain until November. Our place is fairly isolated, the air and water clear
and clean, and the telephone mostly silent. In brief I find it a pleasant
place in which to write fiction. Not that it speeds up my rate of production. Indeed, work on my long overdue novel seems to progress as slowly
as ever, and this despite the fact that the quiet of the hills makes the tolling
of bells even louder.

I am most grateful for the honor which is implicit in your invitation, but
as one who has long tried to follow the example of that great writer whose

accomplishments will be the focus of attention I must continue to do so by struggling while I can, and as I can, with my own unruly demon.

Good luck with the conference and with the transformations of American culture in which you're engaged. I assure you that even in so short a time it has far surpassed Richard Wright's wildest dreams.

Sincerely yours,
Ralph Ellison

To Mamie and Mitch Rhone
RALPH ELLISON
730 Riverside Drive
New York, N.Y. 10031
JUNE 22, 1986

Dear Mamie and Mitch:

Thanks for sending me the memorabilia of Jim's funeral. The sad news had already reached me by a telephone call from Mrs. Harry Youngblood, leaving me so upset by its possible effects on Camille that until now I've been unable to respond. Jim was one of the most important figures in my adolescence and I owe more to him than I can ever say, other than that having him gone leaves me greatly diminished.

During the Fifties, when I returned home after a long absence, Jim told me that before I was born my father (who had been a foreman for a Tennessee firm which erected many of the early steel and concrete buildings in Oklahoma, Arkansas and Texas), had given him his first job. Then he drove me around the city and pointed out the many downtown buildings (the few that remain are now historical landmarks) on which he'd worked with my dad's crew as a water boy. Years later it turned out that Jim was to give me one of _my_ first and most meaningful jobs; therefore I much appreciated his making me aware of the linkage, both economic and symbolic, between himself, my father and me.

Jim was a kind and tolerant boss who allowed his young employees to stuff themselves on free ice cream and candy, taught us to deal patiently and politely with a sometimes ornery public, and served me personally as an example of tolerant, responsible manhood. Thanks to his efficiency as a businessman I can't stand the tacky, slip-shod efforts presented by most so-called Negro businessmen here in New York.

Come to think of it, by sending me on deliveries all over Oklahoma City and into contact with dealers who supplied his drugstore with everything from tobacco, to fountain supplies to cosmetics and pharmaceuticals, Jim did much to continue the extra-curricular education which my father initiated as soon as I was able to sit erect on a wagon seat. Thus on trips around town with my dad I was introduced to the mysteries of blacksmith shops, breweries, bakeries, ice and ice cream plants, and to many areas of the city's life that most Negro kids would never know. During my employment with Jim I thought I was merely working, but later I realized that I was being further educated in the processes of industry and business—not to mention the ways of white folks!

Please tell Camille that thanks to matters having to do with my newly released book of essays Fanny and I are still stuck in New York, but that once we've attended my editor's daughter's wedding—which takes place next week—we'll head for the Berkshires. I'm enclosing a Polaroid shot for Camille's amusement. The "Territory" in the title refers to the old Oklahoma Territory into which the Randolphs put down stakes so long ago, but the "Red men" posing with the book are Hopi Kachina dolls, members of our collection, who were kind enough to stand in for the Oklahoma brothers. Few, if any, Indians turn up in the essays, but Mitch's grandfather is mentioned in the last. Perhaps that's having it both ways, but ole J.D. was heap much Indian, and even I, on my mother's side, am a wee bit Creek!

We hope that things go well and send our warmest regards to all.

Sincerely,
Ralph

Mr. & Mrs. Elmore M. Rhone
1314 Corry Street
Yellow Springs, OH 45378

To Richard Dixon
RALPH ELLISON
730 Riverside Drive
New York, N.Y. 10031

Mr. Richard C. Dixon
Box 87146
Chicago, IL. 60680
SEPTEMBER 6, 1986

Dear Mr. Dixon:

I am most grateful to you for sending me the review (which I hadn't seen) of my book of essays, but even more for your own writings. They were a pleasure to read—especially *Sage-Advice, Softening-up-Chinatown,* and the *Laughton.* Actually, I like the entire lot and it gives me great satisfaction to learn that I had even a small role in your decision to return to writing.

And not only because we need as many good writers as we can get, but because I, too, have had to reject the thoughtless discouragement of those who would impose their own narrow sense of possibility upon my desire to gamble for a broader area in which to define myself.

"Boy," I was told by a Tuskegee dean, "you walk around this campus with that horn and all those books when you'd do better if you took some agriculture and made something useful out of yourself."

And later, in New York, a writer friend reported that a good part of a social evening was marked by laughter over my to them hilarious belief that I could become a writer. Having worked with several of the participants on the Writers Project, I had thought that they, like myself, were using it not merely as a means of earning a living, but as an opportunity for developing more writing skills. Now it was plain that they regarded my ambition as so unrealistic as to be threatening to their own complacency and unearned cynicism. So I reasoned that they were reassuring themselves with laughter at my expense. Well, I was chagrined to hear it, even at second hand, but it didn't deter me. For a few years earlier something of the same had happened when the news got around my hometown that I planned to hop freight trains to get to college: The wise guys cloaked their fear of the unknown with laughter, but in a year I had become the student leader of the Tuskegee Band.

This comes to mind because of your word about the rejected copies of *Shadow and Act* that is, I'm pleased to say, still in print. So in this regard my advice—which you obviously don't need—is to keep reading and writing, because in our situation the prizes go to him who dares the possibility of snagging his ass, which is a constant of the human condition. Incidentally, your reference to Dostoevsky's *Gambler* reminds me that my wife and I once visited Wiesbaden where the great man himself experienced a frenzy of gambling. Oh, but what literary capital he made of the experience! Several of my quick-witted, clever-handed Oklahoma schoolmates took up gambling as a profession, but while I had neither their skill, nerve, nor inclination I did share enough of their spirit to stake my life on becoming a writer. And I would do it in my own mammy-made fashion. Which brings me to Dr. Colter's review.

He seems to have forgotten that just as every good-bye don't mean gone, and that every shut eye don't mean sleep, a writer's failure to publish doesn't mean that he isn't writing. There is such a thing as self-criticism and a regard for the standards set by the best that's been written . . . But enough of that, I appreciated his review and consider it one of the best of a surprisingly favorable lot. Besides, it's clear that he had a fine time writing it, particularly when analyzing "An Extravagance of Laughter," and rapping with me through my persona. He's also the only one, thus far, to reveal a familiarity with the old laughing barrel joke. But you were correct when you underlined your "not so" of disagreement. I didn't expect the reader to take me literally, not after making it clear that as a boy I had worked in Negro barbershops and was therefore a literary descendent of a slew of yarn-spinners. As such I felt free to take my incident of embarrassment and exploit it <u>hyperbolically</u> as I dramatized the action.

But hyperbole ain't necessarily hype, certainly not when it's obvious; and on the serious level of the essay I thought to demonstrate the dynamic of that type of Afro-American humor in the process of using myself as scapegoat. In other words, I tried to fashion a form to fit the content and make the form identical with its function. And like a jazzman caught up in a flight of improvisation and trying to stay a step ahead of his riff, I was snatching and grabbing at any and everything that would help me get my message across.

Dr. Colter might know the absolute boundary between truth and falsehood, fiction and non-fiction, but as a writer I'm not so fortunate. Nevertheless, I <u>am</u> concerned with truth, both in my everyday life and in my writing, but here's the rub: Novelists are natural-born liars who regard "truth" (here I'd prefer "reality") more highly than those who would reduce the chaos of human experience to the neat formulae of religion, sociology, psychoanalysis—or proper expository form. There's a contradiction here but it springs of ole Adam's inadequacy before the protean task of applying language to the things of this world. Like his descendants, Adam was unable to reduce life to a word-pile but at least he got some of it right; so whatever "truth" happens to be it surely must encompass both his success and his failure. Moreover, he had no manual of style to guide him and therefore was forced to break rules—and suffer—in order to find them. We're more fortunate in realizing that while literary forms vary in felicity (with some being more desirable than others) life itself is in constant motion and thus ever evasive of the literary forms which we would impose upon it. Isn't that a reason for *Huckleberry Finn*'s identity as an American novel?

As for me, writing is as burdensome as when I first began but most of what I've presented to my publishers has been published. So let's say that I insist on doing things my way, and if you're so inclined—or not so inclined—I hope you'll do your writing and publishing your way. In either case I wish you the best of luck, and thanks again for your thoughtfulness.

Sincerely,

Ralph Ellison

To Charles Etta Tucker
RALPH ELLISON
Star Route 91-A
Plainfield, MA 01070

Mrs. Charles Etta Tucker
517 W. Caldwell St.
Compton, CA 90220
SEPTEMBER 7, 1986

Dear Charles Etta:

We had anything but a "nice and relaxing" summer, what with having remained in New York until the third of August when, finally, we made it here in the hills. So we steamed and cussed in one breath and reminded ourselves in the next that we were fortunate that there was enough interest being stirred by the new book to keep us in the city. And there were other compensations.

Among these was the pleasure of seeing the fairly attractive but somewhat neglected section of Riverside Park which faces our building land-scaped anew and planted with hundreds of flowering plants; a joint project of the Park Department and neighborhood groups who decided to reclaim it from the dogs and litterers. And then, much to our surprise, it was suggested that it be named for me. I say "surprised" because for years most of the tenants of the building where we've lived since the Fifties had no idea that I was a writer, and since the anonymity made for privacy we preferred it that way. So while pleased with my new status I declined the honor and suggested that the space be named for Eugene Ramsey, our former landlord who integrated the neighborhood and sought to maintain its quality.

My rejection was accepted with grace, but thus far I've no idea as to whether they'll name it for the pioneer realtor or not. I hope they do because his taking over a building occupied by whites and making it accessible to Negroes shouldn't be dismissed as a mere business venture. Ramsey, who is now deceased, was a West Indian immigrant who began as a day laborer and learned the real estate business while working as a chauffeur. Thus during a summer when attention was being focused on the contributions of immigrants it would have been most fitting had his been remembered.

Our other compensation for being stranded in the city came with the Tall Ships, which converged on its waterways in celebration of the Statue of Liberty. We have, thanks to Mr. Ramsey, a view of the Hudson River from every window of our eighth floor apartment and thus were able to spend a glorious day watching the tall masted vessels course up the George Washington Bridge and down again with sails, emblems, and bright banners proudly astream in the wind. We watched and took photographs for hours and ended the day with a feeling of having relived a graceful moment of a not always graceful past. Hope you saw them on television, which provided an even broader view.

I am most grateful to you for sending the review of my book of essays (which I hadn't seen) and, though it saddened me, for Henry Bridges' obituary. As coincidence would have it, some time during July when going through my books on jazz I had come upon Henry's photographs as a sideman in jazz orchestras and received a pleasant shock of recognition. I knew him from having lived in the seven hundred block on East Second, but at the time I left home he had yet to undergo his transformation into a musician and thus remained in my mind as J.D.'s younger brother. Seeing his photographs and reading the tributes to his skills as a soloist

I marveled once again at the influence which Mrs. Breaux, our school music program, and the presence of so many excellent jazz musicians had upon our lives. It appears that Henry was not only an excellent musician but a responsible and highly respected citizen, and so handed on some of the lessons and examples to which we were exposed as kids to a younger generation. If you are in touch with J.D. please give him my regards—and that goes for Zelma, Shep, Gladys and other Okies who might remember (or <u>wish</u> to remember) a schoolmate who strayed to the east.

I'm sorry to learn you had trouble on your trip to China, but during these days <u>any</u> trip can be trying—what with plane crashes and terrorists. At our age moderation is the best policy, so I hope that you and Booker will continue as you've described. In the meantime, ask Booker to please give my regards to Frank G. and other Tuskegeites, and let me know if you hear anything of Tackhead Giddings. And yes, we plan to be in Oklahoma City during the middle of November for an event which I am not at liberty to reveal but of which I hope you are aware. You probably are, given the way secrets tend to get out, and it will be a pleasure if you are there to take part.

Sincerely,
Ralph

To Romare Bearden
RALPH ELLISON
Star Route 91-A
Plainfield, MA 01070

Mr. Romare Bearden
357 Canal Street
New York, NY 10013
SEPT. 8, 1986

Dear Romie:

Your letter was forwarded to me here in the Berkshires and I was both pleased and surprised. Pleased, because you liked the essays, saw how they link up, and received a laugh or two (thank God you busted no stiches!), and surprised because while you're the Bear-den who told me about Brer Rabbit's adventure in a bear's den ("Don't a mother move, Brer Rabbit cried"), I can't recall receiving a letter from you before. Greeting cards with your own art, yes—and some still grace our walls—but over all the years I can't remember a single letter. I'm also glad that you required no surgery and assume that by now you're back at your painting.

It might interest you to know that the essays are being reviewed all over the country, and for the most part quite favorably. True, a few reviewers complained that the book wasn't a novel, but then they reviewed the collection for whatever they perceived it to be. One thing is certain, it was assigned to quite a number of Negroes, all good writers, so if it comes to nothing else it gave them something to write and think about. It even made the bulletin board of the local post office, which reminded me of the many times I was warned that if I didn't stop lying and messing around I would end up in the boys' reformatory, and probably graduate from there to McAlester, which meant that I'd land in the Oklahoma State Penitentiary. So you can be sure that when I saw my photograph on that post office wall I was relieved that it hadn't been placed on the Ten Most Wanted! The essays, incidentally, are already scheduled for paperback next year and I hope that they will indeed be counted among the most wanted.

Thanks for the clipping from the TLS, which I found quite interesting. Mellers is an insightful critic and after reading him I'd like to see *Porgy and Bess* again. Its text renders it cold for Fanny, but every now and then I find myself humming its Lullaby and whistling Bess' love aria to Porgy. Thar's good black artistic gold in them stereotypes, so instead of being thrown off by the crap it's best to seek it out, learn from it, and transcend it.

Because, like it or not, it is the vitality of Afro-American artistic and cultural style which lends such work its interest and endurance. After all these years some of us are still beefing over *Huckleberry Finn*—which raises questions as to what makes it an enduring work of literature, and surely it's not because of its epithets. I'd like to give such people the advice given a mouthy, knuckle-headed character in an early musical (probably by Bert Williams):

"Brother, go 'way back and sit down!" To which I'd add, "And while you're at it, do yourself some reading!"

We hope things go well with you and yours, and again my thanks.

Sincerely,
Ralph

To Eve Schaenen
RALPH ELLISON
Star Route 91-A
Plainfield, MA 01070
OCT. 8, 1986

Miss Eve Schaenen
Associate Publicist
Oxford University Press
New York, NY 10016

Dear Miss Schaenen:

Since reading excerpts that were published back during the forties I have yearned for *The Complete Notebooks of Henry James*—and now, mirabile dictu, not only are they at last available, but you and Leon Edel have entertained the possibility that I might have something helpful to say on their behalf! For this I am most grateful and hope that some bit of the following might prove useful:

To read *The Complete Notebooks of Henry James* is to enjoy a startling look behind the scenes and over the shoulder of that great master of dramatic, exquisitely crafted novels. For here, far more than in any of his nonfictional writings, access is provided into the creative interplay between James' artistic consciousness, his concern with the moral implications of fictional techniques, and his struggles with the nature and responsibilities of an essentially American form of sensibility and conscience. Even better, the reader is guided and cued through the intricacies of James' world, actual and imaginary, European and American, by the expert commentary of Leon Edel and Lyall H. Powers.

For through their enlightening but unobtrusive editing James' world comes alive and the reader is enabled to explore at leisure one of modernism's great creative workshops. Functionally the hitherto private "book-of-books-behind-the-books" out of which the many short stories and novels of this most prolific artist emerged, the *Notebooks* reveal something of the agony and the ecstasy, the surprising uncertainties and enviable joys, that went into James' life-work and informed his search for the meaning and possibilities of being a conscious American.

The *Prefaces* to the New York Edition of James' works constitute one of the great seminal essays in the craft of modern fiction, and are indispensable to all writers and lovers of literature. Now it is our good fortune that they have been joined by *The Complete Notebooks.* Which, in their fascinating revelation of the subtle ways in which a great writer struggled with his conscious experience and endowed it with eloquent form, are of the same supreme order. To my writer's bias they are even more fascinating than the recently published sketchbooks of Pablo Picasso, an artist with whom James ranks as master architect and champion of transcendent artistic form. (Yet!)

Yours sincerely,
Ralph Ellison

To Walter Grey
RALPH ELLISON
730 Riverside Drive
New York, NY 10031
NOV. 28, 1986

Mr. Walter Grey
The Grapevine Gallery
Box 132, Oklahoma City,
Oklahoma, 73101

Dear Walter and Dan:

We are enjoying the Kachina, your gift prints, and the rug—which arrived much faster than it takes to get a letter from one part of New York to another, and thus in plenty of time for Fanny's Thanksgiving Day of a birthday. We also received your data on the prints, and once the holidays are over we'll follow your instructions as to their framing.

Although it's been over a week we're still reliving our exciting experiences in Oklahoma, and I regret that thanks to my confusion over the day of my departure my last visit with you was limited to drinks. For after you drove me back to the Stewarts I learned that while I was enjoying your conversation (and wishing that I could come away with certain kachinas in your personal collection!) Fanny had called to remind me that my plane would not leave on Wednesday, but on Thursday. I was surprised, but not totally; for some years ago Fanny and I got our wires crossed over the date of my departure for an extended lecture tour and I found myself in Chicago a day earlier than expected. Talk about confusion!

But though exhausted, both physically and emotionally, by the excitement of my homecoming I regret that my mistake led to a shorter visit at the Grapevine than was necessary. I had thought to get in touch the following day, but spent it relaxing with the Stewarts and going over old times with my brother. This was all to the good, for while I talk with Herbert once a month I hadn't seen him for seven years.

Thus the extra day was indeed a blessing, for it eased the disquieting fact that for the first time in all my returns home I failed to see a single member of our extended family, the Randolphs and Slaughters, and blunted some of my dismay over finding so much of the city in which I grew up destroyed. As you, say tempus fugits; and in its process so many people whom we hold dear turn up missing. For instance, I've just learned that three days after I left, Camille Randolph Rhone, who taught me, oh so many years ago, to walk was returned home from Ohio for burial and had I known of her passing I would have remained even longer.

Thus the delay provided time in which to evoke much of what is now forever lost in reminiscing. So we talked and lazed about and talked some more, and there was time the morning of my flight to present that huge blowup of our baby picture to the Ellison Branch Library.* Which was fortunate in that it has far more space in which to display it (or store it) than either of the now long-vanished little kids it captured.

All in all it was a wonderful visit that still echoes so vividly that each night since our return I've dreamed that we were still there. Miss that quiet! Miss being with so many of those who knew us "when"! But dreams, alas, are dreams and reality consists of such things as the traffic noise of the Westside Highway, beat boxes, and the familiar clutter of our apartment. Therefore I'll end this—and Fanny joins me—in thanking you and Dan for having done so much in making our brief mixture of dream and reality so memorable. I won't even mention the role played by the only decent martinis I had during the entire trip!

Sincerely,
Ralph

---

* One of the honors of which Ellison was most proud was the Ralph Ellison Library, named for him and opened in an official ceremony on June 25, 1975, in Oklahoma City that was attended by Ralph and Fanny.

P.S.:

I finally remembered the name of an acquaintance of mine who had advised retaining the Cowboy institution in its present location: Dillon Ripley, the former head of the Smithsonian, and a man for whom I hold the highest regard.

To Bettye Thomas
RALPH ELLISON
730 Riverside Drive
New York, NY 10031

Miss Bettye J. Thomas
3104 N.E. 15th Street
Oklahoma City, Okla. 73117
DEC. 4, 1986

Dear Miss Thomas:

Although I've long followed a self-protective policy of not reading unpublished manuscripts—and especially those of strangers—I've read yours and found it interesting if somewhat puzzling.

I say "puzzling," while you label it a non-fiction novel it made more sense to me as an essay in criticism, or as an imaginative interpretative reading of *Invisible Man*. Interesting, because within it I caught glimpses of a fictional narrative that was striving to assert itself in its own terms. This I found frustrating, for while Bercha Rhodes was going on about *Invisible Man* (about whom I know far more than I would ever write) I wanted to know more about her. Who was she? What was her conflict with Wanda? And why, since she writes with a certain eloquence, does she arouse my interest but then fail to fulfill my expectations?

And why do you, who can form meaningful sentences and paragraphs, fail to let yourself go and give full structural form to a narrator who, if given a chance, would probably say, "To hell with those broken rungs," and simply fly out of her hole? The dominant characters in successful fictional actions move (and move the reader) from a situation in which they elect and act in the assertion of purpose, and in their passionate attempts to achieve their stated purpose they arrive at (and allow the reader to achieve) a perception of what all the sound and fury of action is all about.

(From purpose, through passion, to perception, is the formula. Or, in other words—and you'll forgive me for restating that which you obviously know—basic narrative consists of a beginning, a middle, and an end.) But as I read *The Rung That Broke* Bercha has sidestepped the obligation of providing the reader with a clear sense of the scene in which she finds herself, and has left him unclear as to her purpose. And I see this as the result of her relying upon the reader's familiarity with *Invisible Man*. Yes, I realize that novels are made out of other novels, much as successful surgical operations rely upon operations that have gone before. But a surgeon cannot cure the patient at hand simply by recalling other patients who were restored to a certain wholeness through the skill of another surgeon. No, the operating surgeon must deal with the individual patient who lies as it were, "etherized upon the table," and in terms of that particular patient's physical and psychological structure, and in terms of his own intuitions and mastery of his craft. Otherwise he's like a lawyer who is fluent in quoting precedents but fails to sway the jury to react in the interest of his client.

Touching briefly on narrative structure: You write that I presented Invisible from an "omniscient point of view," but if you take another look you'll see that I actually wrote from the narrator's point of view while the narrator wrote from his own, first-person, point of view. Thus there is a covert form operating within an overt form, and while I wrote a novel, the narrator wrote a memoir. A minor point, perhaps, but it is through such manipulating of viewpoint that certain effects are possible.

You draw a parallel between the darkness in which Bercha finds herself and that of my narrator, and she writes of the difference between her handling of the situation and his. Perhaps it might help if you stepped back a bit and looked at my narrator's predicament in the light cast by an old parable: that of the frog in the churn of cream.

Leaping after a fly which ranged beyond his tongue, the frog lands in a thick white substance and thinks he's about to drown. He scrambles in a circle seeking a way out, he croaks for help which is not forthcoming, he looks desperately for the equivalent of a ladder—runged or rungless— with which to free himself, and is on the point of giving up—When, lo and behold—he realizes that his random kicking is keeping him afloat. And now as he kicks with conscious purpose he feels the cream turning into weight-sustaining butter that allows him to hop from the churn.

And so with my narrator. He kept kicking and churning the events of his experience around in the form of words and images until they became a pattern of symbolic action; which, despite the fact that he remains noncommittal as to how it was accomplished, he managed to have published.

True, there is a mystery here but one that would require another novel to dispel. The significant point however, is that both Brer Frog and my narrator found themselves imprisoned in a dangerous substance, cream for one and a symbolic blue-blackness for the other, and that each hit upon a common strategy for freeing himself. For both kept on kicking until the butter came.

Which is to say that each in his own way achieved an act of transformation. One by kicking his destructive element into good frog-flavored butter, and the other by reducing his darkness to a patterned structure of words and actions that provided the reader with a certain amount of illumination. Thus if he failed as a political leader (his broken rung) he wound up having some success by switching from rabble-rousing to furtive writing.

Along this line of thought perhaps it would help to consider the possibility that symbolic falls make for symbolic ascensions; no plunge to or beneath the earth, no rise into the heavens. No fiery flesh, no spiritual smoke. No symbolic darkness, no symbolic light. So no matter what made my narrator so black and blue (and he was author of much of his unhappiness) its symbolic purpose was narrational. It prodded him to make a story of his experiences. Yes, and to transcend his emotional condition with wry humor—much as Ishmael went a-whaling and transformed <u>his</u> travail into a great novel. My narrator's fall was by no means so fortunate, but at least he tried. Incidentally, you write of the angel rolling the stone away from the tomb of Christ—Well, there I can only suggest that in our turbulent times angels take many forms, and therefore I'm not about to mess with them. On the other hand I believe that the Spirit continues to help those who help themselves, and that it makes itself felt in writing which is sincere and risk-taking. Thus, since I am only a writer I am willing to keep writing and let spiritual matters take care of themselves—which is a form of faith. One thing seems clear: if I don't write—and publish—neither the Spirit nor that mysterious force known as the muse will have a chance to speak through me. Therefore I would be in a far more hellish hole than the character you refer to as "Invisible."

Perhaps the same holds for you; and if so, I would suggest that you continue doing that which you do very well—which is writing. And that you do so <u>without</u> that elusive good-housekeeping seal of academic approval. Mark Twain, Hemingway, and Faulkner, to name only a few, did very well without a Ph.D., and so can you . . .

As for Miss Rhodes, I would suggest that the one thing she shouldn't do is to get her mind so fixed on Invisible or any other fictional or real-life character that she allows herself to become mesmerized into inaction. Instead, let her write her own story and remember that Old Bad Air is part of a total experience. Life is of a whole, therefore we can't achieve the good without coming to grips with the bad. Nor should she allow the kidding around of Buddy Bolden in the old blues fool her; because he knew very well that in order to have a good transcendent dance there has to be the stressful odor of excited bodies as well as exciting music. Here there is no difference between the dancers, the dance, or the outpouring of musicians. No funk, no fun; no decay, no rebirth . . .

Good luck to you and
to Bercha Rhodes,
Ralph Ellison

P.S.
My line of Ellisons originated in Abbeville, S.C.

To Robert Silvers
RALPH ELLISON
730 Riverside Drive
New York, NY 10031
JANUARY 28, 1987

Mr. Robert Silvers
The New York Review of Books
250 West Fifty-Seventh St.
New York, NY 10107

Dear Bob:

When you spoke to me about the Du Bois I realized that it would be difficult to fit it into my busy schedule. But you were persuasive and I was intrigued by the challenge of rereading Du Bois after all the years and so thought to give it a try. But then details from my personal past reached out and grabbed me.

Hardly had I begun reading and making notes [when] it was necessary to fly out to Oklahoma City (my home town) to introduce an old classmate upon his induction into the Oklahoma Hall of Fame. Thinking to work on the review during my six days there, I took the book along. But then to my surprise it turned out that I, too, was to be honored by the Governor with a State reception, by the Library System with a book autographing party, and by old friends with a rash of reunions; all of which left me with little time to sleep, much less than read with the critical attention which I'd hoped to give the Du Bois.

However, on my flight back to New York I did return to the task and kept at it while trying to recover from the physical and emotional stress of the trip and recapture the interrupted mood of my novel-in-progress. But then came another interruption, this time in the form of an earlier commitment to read during a two-day tribute staged by Seton Hall University in honor of Kenneth Burke. And though far less tiring than the Oklahoma jaunt this too proved to be an emotional occasion because Burke is an old friend who has been an influence on my thinking since 1937; and indeed, a far more important influence than Du Bois has ever been.

Fortunately, the Seton Hall commitment was but a one-night stand, and I was able to get back to my work—if only long enough to be again interrupted. This time by the appearance of a crew of workmen who came to install new windows in all the rooms of our apartment. And although they worked efficiently in well coordinated shifts I'm sure you get the picture: The shifting of furniture, books, files, heating devices; the noise, the gusts of ancient wood dust and blasts of cold air from the Hudson River. And naturally there were delays due to mismeasurements and the recent storms. So now we are still living in what looks like the aftermath of a cyclone, I am still unable to work on my novel, and have quite lost the concentration required of the Du Bois. I am, therefore, returning the book with my sincere apologies and regrets to you and to its publishers for having made such a botch of an opportunity for discovering what I might make of an important scholar whose unexplored "Americanness" I find as intriguing as that of Audubon or George "Krazy Kat" Herriman's. Thanks for the opportunity; and, again, my regrets.

Sincerely,
Ralph Ellison

P.S.: A friend sent me a copy of Alfred Kazin's recent piece, which I found amusing—if somewhat puzzling—in its reference to me. Alfred seems surprised that I am a member of the American Academy and Institute into which I was inducted a mere short year before himself. Thus he has seen me there, and since I haven't had a new suit since 1974 he must have seen the one I was wearing many times before. I thank God that he wasn't criticizing a book, because what he interpreted as a snobbish reaction to his suit was actually my relief at seeing him looking so fit after I'd heard that he'd undergone a dangerous heart by-pass operation!

Nevertheless, I shall pass the piece along to my long-retired tailor, Pat Silvestri, in the hope that he'll appreciate the fact that an old piece of his handiwork withstood the evaluation of such an esteemed critic. I guess that my old and respected friend Alfred remembered that I once assisted a men's clothing store's window display man in dressing show window dummies and decided to hit me with a bit of <u>teufelsdrockh</u>. Devilishly clever, but was it shit or shinola?

R.E.

P.P.S. I am returning the Du Bois under separate, First Class cover.

To Harold Bloom
RALPH ELLISON
730 Riverside Drive
New York, NY 10031
JANUARY 29, 1987

Dear Harold Bloom:

If my response is somewhat delayed it's because I'm still a-reel from triple shock. First, from arriving in all innocence to participate in Seton Hall's homage to Kenneth Burke to find myself being given a book with my own dour image on the cover. Surely, I think, there's been a mistake . . . But then came the second and most pleasurable shock of learning that the book had been edited and introduced by Harold Bloom! I couldn't have anticipated such a development during even the wildest whirls of my imagination; but there it was, in my hands . . .

So I thought, Burke and Bloom? Bloom and Burke? Who's joyce-ing me around in Jersey? And then the shocking sense of affirmation which came of my realizing that the alphabetical critical linkage had been there all the time. That the same dear old Kenneth (whose work had provided me with a basic orientation when I was trying to place such elusive matters as the relationship of Marx to Freud, literature to politics, and rhetoric to dramatic form in a workable perspective) was your Rabbi as well as mine!

(So you thought I was <u>only</u> a goy?)

Truly, Harold, with a single stroke you made whole <u>years</u> my day, and although I'm still spinning like a top, I am most grateful.

It might interest you to know that I first became aware of Kenneth at the New School, during a 1937 League of American Writers Congress meeting to which I was invited by Richard Wright. It was an event that I'll never forget, for while Kenneth's reading of "The Rhetoric of Hitler's Battle" brought sneers of protest from many of the Leftists in the audience, it cast a brilliant light upon what for me had seemed to be a world of utter intellectual and political confusion. So while they yelled and sneered as though K.B. was a mad man (several *New Masses* editors and writers among them), I sat stunned as by a lightning stroke of revelation.

And indeed it was a stroke that led me to read all the Burke that I could get my hands on, and one that became even more illuminating with the terrible revelations of 1945. Needless to say, his analysis of Hitler's rhetoric told me much about that insidious linkage between word-magic and political power that made my own life so vulnerable. More, he pointed directions that made it possible for me to understand and exploit the rich rhetorical resources of my cultural background. He also encouraged me to think for myself; therefore when certain critics complained that Burke's method could be applied to anything and every kind and quality of literary and artistic expression, I responded with a loud "Amen" and laughed my twice-emancipated head off! Later (in 1942, I think) Stanley Edgar Hyman introduced us, and since then I've considered Kenneth one of the most precious of my friends. As I say, it is good to know that I share some of his insights and inspiration with you, and I am most grateful for the surprising "bloom" that you've given my work.

Sincerely,
Ralph Ellison

Professor Harold Bloom
Yale University
New Haven, CT 06520

To Leon Edel
RALPH ELLISON
730 Riverside Drive
New York, NY 10031
FEB. 9, 1987

Mr. Leon Edel
3817 Lurline Drive
Honolulu, Hawaii 969816

Dear Leon:

Hearing from you was such a pleasure that I wish that you were here so that we could have drinks and a chat. Yes, but when I look out upon all the snow on the palisades and ice on the Hudson I'm glad for your sake that you're there where it's bright and sunny.

"Here," fortunately, is Manhattan; because our Plainfield place is habitable only in the summer and fall, after which we hurry back to this crowded old nest where we've lived for over thirty years, and to the bitter-sweet attractions of the city.

I can't tell you how pleased I was for the opportunity of having even a small bit to say about James' *Complete Notebooks.* How fortunate we all are that for you—who appear to've been fated to find that long-lost chest of magic in the bullrushes—there'll be no retiring! And all the more since every time I look around I'm stumbling into something new, instructive, and entertaining from Edel.

As when browsing through Edmund Wilson's *The Fifties,* I came across your background notes to his Gauss Seminars. It made me recall that, thanks to Saul Bellow, I too had attended several of the series. Indeed, and despite Wilson's delivery, I found them so interesting that I broke the law speeding down the icy Jersey Turnpike getting to Princeton. And afterwards, during the parties that followed, there'd be the good talk with the likes of Bellow, the Dick Lewises, the Berrymans, and Mel Tumin; and, on one occasion, with the Roethkes. So, thanks to you, all kinds of forgotten scenes returned to mind.

Like the sight of the ex-Mrs. Blackmur performing a modern-dance version of an odalisque shimmy in Bellow's bedroom while a couple of graduate students literally drooled at the sight of her rather mechanical pelvic gyrations. Then came the scene in Dick and Nancy's apartment, during which Ted Roethke was giving me a hard time for not knowing Sugar Ray Robinson, Joe Louis, or a single member of Detroit's then notorious Purple Gang. It was as though he assumed that all birds of a certain color flocked automatically together. I was told later that prior to my arrival Roethke, drunk and in one of his manic states, had been gobbling grapes faun-like by the bunch, had attacked a large soft cheese with his naked paw of a hand; and that then, by way of badgering the distinguished critic, had pinched one of Wilson's generous cheeks and asked where he'd gotten all that "blubber."

"And what," Wilson was said to've replied as he stared up into that petulant, babyish face of Ted's, "do you think you are, some kind of half-baked Bacchus?"

Then there was the epic, no-holds-barred domestic version of civil war during which I saw Delmore Schwartz attack his wife as though bent upon giving dramatic substance to Wilson's lectures. Starting at the rear of the first floor hallway of Bellow's apartment, they exchanged punches through the bedroom and into the parlor; then out of the parlor back into the hall; then out onto the porch and across the icy lawn, throwing furious punches all the way. And I must say that blonde Betty was giving as much as she took, and grimly holding her own even as they drove away, still fighting, in their battered car.

Such post-seminar high jinks aside, I got a lot from hearing Wilson lecture and was grateful to have him examine the conflict through which my ancestors had been liberated. Later, however, when given an opportunity to review *Patriotic Gore* I found his conclusion so far at odds with the impression I'd gotten from his oral exposition that my background as the grandson of a South Carolina freedman and Reconstruction politician asserted itself and made it impossible to carry out my task with objectivity. If the contenders whom Wilson seemed to admire had won the war I wouldn't have been able to attend his lectures. So while agreeing that Lincoln was far from a saint, I could never lose sight of the fact that he signed the Emancipation Proclamation. Nevertheless, I had long admired Wilson and still have most of his books on hand to consult whenever there's a need to evoke his period.

I managed to publish something in the *New Republic* while he was still there, but never in the world would I have expected to find myself mentioned in a book by Edmund Wilson. Therefore coming across his reference to the Kazins' party gave me quite a laugh; both because my exchange with Alfred had completely slipped my mind, and because Wilson, whom I'd thought engaged in another conversation, had been so ironically observant.

Fanny and I saw the Kazins fairly frequently during that period, with Alfred ever striving to impose his knowledge of literary masterpieces upon my gropings. Still, our talks were always lively and I learned from them; but by contrast with the exchanges I had with Bellow they were usually a bit one-sided. Perhaps because Alfred seemed to see all people and experience as shaped by the books he'd read, while Saul saw experience as a thing for wonder, and as material to be explored and shaped by fictional technique. Thus ours were exchanges of personal experiences cum speculations about literary form and technique. And this from the perspectives provided by our experimental concern with fiction. Accepting (and respecting) our diversity of backgrounds as a given, neither attempted to impose his views upon the other. Instead, we shared a mutual concern in seeking fresh ways for transforming experience into imaginative art. I should add, however, that Alfred has had good things to say about my novel, and on a number of occasions.

Thanks for including photographs in *The Fifties,* especially that of a grown-up Reuel;* whom I myself had been forced to photograph while on assignment to do his mother's portrait for a book jacket. It was the only way I could get the chubby, freckle-faced little rascal (whom I suspected of playing hookey by faking illness) out of the room. Dressed in the white, footed pajamas worn by youngsters, he looked indeed like Bunny Wilson's lagomorphous offspring. But at the end of the session, when B.B. arrived, he damn near gave me a stroke by demonstrating a certain Hamlet-like aggressiveness as he challenged his languid stepfather to a sparring match. And this with a prize-fighter's stance, foot-work and feints. And there sat poor, exasperated B.B. trying to shoo that bobbing blob of freckled motion with washerwoman swings of his arm . . .

But lest I bore you by way of expressing my appreciation for your post-retirement doings, I'll stop right here! In the meantime keep well, keep writing, and I hope to see you come May.

Sincerely,
Ralph

---

* Reuel Wilson, son of novelist Mary McCarthy and Edmund Wilson, whom Ellison photographed while on assignment to do his mother's portrait for a book jacket.

To Paul Martiani
RALPH ELLISON
730 Riverside Drive
New York, NY 10031
FEB. 11, 1987

Mr. Paul Martiani
24 Main Street
Montague, Mass., 01351

Dear Mr. Martiani:

I too am somewhat vague as to when I first met John Berryman. It might well have been through Saul Bellow, because until he moved back to Chicago Saul and I were fairly close, and I visited him several times at Princeton. In fact, it was through Saul that I attended some of Edmund Wilson's Gauss lectures, and there is no question but that Berryman was at Princeton at that time. The gap in my memory lies in my being unable to pinpoint the beginning of Saul's stint there. It may have been during the fall of 1951, and if true I could have seen John during the Christmas season. Here a check of Blackmur's sabbatical might be of help.

However, I am certain that I saw Berryman during Wilson's seminars, and that I had known him prior to the 1952 publication of *Invisible Man.* On this my memory is firm because shortly afterwards, when about to enter the northern entrance of the New York Public Library, I ran into Berryman and Alfred Kazin and was amused when John implored me rather emotionally to reassure him that the incidents in my novel hadn't happened to me!

Your information concerning Bard College is, in part, correct; I saw Berryman there and noted that he and Pearl Kazin were making numerous telephone calls during which they dramatized, but didn't explain, what appeared to be a deep anxiety. Finally, during a gathering at Jack Ludwig's, they revealed that Dylan Thomas was dying—or had died—in New York's St. Vincent Hospital. It was then that John relieved himself of a rather drunken recital of "Do Not Go Gentle into That Good Night" that left me feeling almost as mournful for Berryman as for Thomas.

But although my wife and I drove Pearl and John back to New York, I did not enter the hospital; perhaps because their grief was so intensely private that it would have been intrusive of one who did not share their friendship with the marvelous Welsh poet. Later I read that the intensity of John's friendship with Thomas was more poetic than actual, and possibly an imaginative thrust toward an ideal relationship. Evidently he had a whole circle of such "friends," most of them poets.

Thus it is good to learn that in his letters Berryman referred to me as a friend, but while we're both Oklahomans, were born the same year, and I had lived in McAlester during the year Berryman's father killed himself (1926), it would be decades before we'd meet; and even then, given our differences of background and temperament, there was little opportunity for a close relationship. There are, of course, various levels of friendship, and beyond our common geographical origins and mutual concern with literature there was the fact that my own father had died (of natural causes) when I was three. But although my father's death left a terrible void in my life, I was far from being as tormented by my loss as John by his. This did make for a certain sympathy, and as a young writer it was a comfort to know that Berryman, who was already famous, had first seen the light in a city where I had once roamed and sold newspapers—Even though by the time I arrived he had long departed the scene. Call it hope by association based on a primitive magic of place, but it is often by seizing upon such slim co-incidents and identifications that we seek to deal with our uncertainties. Thus the best way I can put it is that Berryman and I were friends-through-friends, geographical origin, and literature. Beyond that I admired both his poetry and his criticism and found him always interesting, if often explosive, to be with. John's was a charismatic, death-haunted personality but he made life exciting.

I can't tell you how frequently I saw Berryman, but given our mutual friends, our membership in the American Academy Institute, and the many parties given by writers and their friends it was inevitable that we'd run into one another. I also knew two of his wives, the first from his Princeton days, and the last during the end of his life.

And during the period he was writing *Dream Songs* I grew to expect his drunken (sometimes) telephone calls. in the course of which he'd read from work in progress. The copy of *77 Dream Songs* which he gave us is inscribed "To Ralph & Fanny/Affectionately & with thanks for help on 68" (line, I suppose, 17). I can't recall how many such calls there were, but usually he wanted my reaction to his uses of dialect. My preference is for idiomatic rendering, but I wasn't about to let the poetry of what he was saying be interrupted by the dictates of my ear for Afro-American speech. Besides, watching him transform elements of the minstrel show into poetry was too fascinating. Fascinating too, and amusing was my suspicion that Berryman was casting me as a long-distance Mister Interlocutor—or was it Mister Tambo—whose temporary role was that of responding critically to his Mister Bones and Huffy Henry. Whatever, I would have advised a lesser poet to abandon the dialect business, but never one so gifted as Berryman. In the course of writing this I've just discovered that he referred to me in Professor Berryman's *Crack on Race* as his "colleague."

Unfortunately, I can't recall ever having received any letters from John; but my wife, who keeps our files, promises to take a look, and if anything is forthcoming I'll let you know.

Thanks for the good word about *Territory* and *Invisible,* and good luck with your project.

Sincerely,
Ralph Ellison

To Richard Wilbur
RALPH ELLISON
730 RIVERSIDE DRIVE
NEW YORK, NY 10031
FEB 24, 1987

Mr. Richard Wilbur
715 ® Windsor Lane
Key West, Florida 33040

Dear Dick:

The main focus of your letter reminds me of an incident that occurred when I was about five years old. About block and a half from where we had recently become next-door neighbors, I ran into a friend of my own age who sat on his tricycle in the middle of the sidewalk bawling as though his heart were breaking. When I asked what had happened he said, "My mamma is dead."

Not having met his mother but assuming her alive, his answer produced a shock of sympathy. And since I had lost my father two years earlier, I shared his parental loss by pushing him up the hill to his home. Then came another shock; when, within a matter of hours, I learned that his mother had been dead for at least two years, and that the actual cause of his tears had been a spanking administered by his father after finding him so far from home base. I was, to say the least, amazed. Not by his fib, but by his eerie resurrection of his mother to account for his tears. Was it because he'd been shamed by my seeing him cry, or did he believe that all of his unhappiness was due to his mother's death, and that every time he disobeyed he was punished again by the loss of his mother? And if so, did this mean that he felt responsible for her death? What had he done to have set such a terrible cycle in motion? Was this what the preacher meant by "eternal punishment"? And was it possible that I had done something similar that caused my own parent's death?

As you can imagine, I was quite upset by the sheer metaphysics of his crying, and only my short, child's attention-span saved me from prolonged suffering. Nevertheless, as we grew up I continued to regard my friend with a sense (sometimes amused) of wonder. In time, however, I came to recognize that there was a certain logic in my friend's explanation: If his mother had been alive she would perhaps have seen to it that he remained near the house; but since she was not there to restrain him, he had wandered away and gotten his little butt blistered. Looking back and remembering that it took me over ten years to accept the reality of my own parent's death it seems possible that my little friend had come to associate all of his unhappiness with his primal loss, and that the loud dissonance of his crying arose from its painful ground bass of upward and/ or downward spiraling overtones. Nevertheless the fact remains that such reverberations of mother-loss were set off by a spanking, and the immediate cause of his unhappiness was a smarting bottom brought on by his adventuring too far beyond the reservation defined by his father.

I mention this because your letter poses a similar question of cause and effect as regards the Ellisons and Frank Taylor: The Ellisons had been friends with the (heterosexual) Taylors since the '40s; in 1983, Frank, who had earlier accepted and revealed his homosexuality, lived in the Ellison's Key West house, during which time they came to a parting of the ways with dear, sexually courageous Frank—Ergo, the cruel Ellisons broke with Frank because they were prejudiced against homosexuals.

Well, Frank <u>might</u> have chosen to occupy our house because he is homosexual, but I find that explanation far too simplistic and reductive of the circumstances, Frank's personality, and our motivation, to ascribe the break in friendship to an assumed objection on our part to his choice in lovers. To do so is like assuming that I abhor all physicians because I lost my mother to the incompetence of a single practitioner who failed to order an X-ray after she broke her hip in a fall. But I've been a member of a scapegoated group too long to be guilty of such foolishness; and, having grown up around dentists, physicians (and various quacks), I am too well aware of their variations in skill and dedication to make such a mistake. So while it is true that we broke with Frank, it had nothing to do, at least not directly, with sex. Incidentally, I've never said or written a word to Frank about what happened in Key West and I write this only because of your concern.

So while I won't bother to deny it, I doubt that I accused you of saying that I was anti-homosexual. Nor am I about to get into a who-shot-John exchange about the matter. However, I do know that neither Fanny nor I are prejudiced against homosexuals, whether in the open or in the closet. And as far as Frank is concerned, you should note that in 1981 I mentioned him in my introduction to the 30th anniversary edition of *Invisible Man.* I did so because Frank gave me my first book contract and it was a convenient way of recognizing his role in the publication of my novel. Since this was long after his so-called emergence my doing so was hardly an indication of prejudice on my part. Had I been prejudiced I would have revealed it as early as 1958 after being told by a reliable friend that Frank had approached him homosexually. At the time Fanny and I assumed Frank to be a happily married heterosexual, but I assure you that the news did nothing to lower our regard for him. Instead, I resented my friend's having passed along information which I had no desire to know.

You should also know that although I was hounded out of college by a homosexual dean of men (yet!) the experience did nothing to prevent my associating with or being a friend of homosexuals who did not, as you say, force one to be aware of their sexuality. Therefore I am surprised that you are so certain that Langston Hughes was homosexual. For during the long extent of our friendship he never once revealed it to me. Indeed, he always struck me as asexual. It's true that I heard speculations back in the '30's, and that last year the question was raised in a woman's rather inept biography of Hughes, but as far as our friendship was concerned it wouldn't have mattered. For, just as my relationship with Frank centered on his role as a promoter and publisher, my friendship with Langston was based upon his identity as a poet and writer. Langston might have reduced too much of life's complexity to racism but hardly to any anguish he might have felt regarding his sexual identity. Thank God that even friendship has its boundaries and level of mystery!

But as far [as] our break with Frank is concerned there is no mystery. It began all unforeseen when on the recommendation of mutual friends we rented our house to a couple of elderly writers whom we'd never met. We did so, and although neither Fanny nor I was ever to lay eyes upon them, we found them good tenants. The following season, after his wife had died, the husband asked again to rent the house; and, being sympathetic and pleased with the care they'd given it we agreed with an arrangement that was to continue through the following season of 1984. It was when we heard from Mr. Roos, in August, 1983, saying that Frank and Steve wanted us to replace the bed in my study with one that was more comfortable that things began coming apart.

For although we had become aware that Frank and young Roos were companions, we were not told that they, too, would be occupying our house. In retrospect and given the father's age and loss of hearing, I am aware that there are those who would have found it logical that Frank and Steve would join him. But then nurses do exist, and being absent from the scene and having had no personal contact with Mr. Roos (nor knowledge of his financial situation) Fanny and I were far from being that insightful. Instead, being square, and holding on to certain old fashioned notions of friendship, we would have expected our old friend Taylor to've been frank about his intentions and told us in advance. Much as I, as a Negro, would have done had I intended to bring a white girl companion into a friend's house in a community wherein our interracial presence might have raised questions. And not because I give a damn about those who entertain racial prejudice, but because I would have felt that it was my friend's right (and my obligation) that he be told. The last thing I would have thought to do was present him with a <u>fait accompli</u>. Nor would I have felt that prejudice against racial identity or sexual preference could justify such an act.

But whatever his reasons, Frank failed to tell us that he was to be one of three tenants occupying our house (and at the rate we gave the widowed Mr. Roos). This we took as a form of distrust if not a callous violation of friendship. And all the more since we were under the impression that Frank and his friend were part owners of Key West property that, presumably, they could have occupied. That they chose instead to take advantage of our house, we took as exploitive. Nevertheless, we absorbed the shock and kept quiet. But in August 1983, Mr. Roos wrote of Steve and Frank as though our silence meant an agreement to their presence. Then Frank complained that the mattress of the studio bed in my study was uncomfortable (I suppose that he meant that it was too short), and mailed us a Sears catalog illustration of the type of bed he (they) had selected, and offered to bear half the expense. It was only then that we investigated and learned that Frank had lived in our house the year before and expected to live there in 1984. Thus after occupying the house without informing us, he proceeded to act as though he had no sensitivity to the fact that it was <u>our</u> house and that its furniture and decorations, such as they are, were an expression of our taste as limited by what was available and by our economy.

But be it ever so humble (and as Frank, given his past connection with associates of Harry Stack Sullivan, should know) a house, like a home, has its charge of affect. And this is especially true of the house in question. Because for the first time in her life Fanny was able (and without interference from me) to restructure a house and play with it, discover its possibilities, and shape it to her own taste. While I, in appreciation of her rare opportunity, made myself absent by way of sharing her experiment. So you'll understand that she didn't want me, or anyone else, telling her what she should do by way of making her house livable or aesthetically pleasing. Least of all did she want Frank suggesting that she throw out a piece of furniture that she'd found satisfactory. She did, nevertheless, inform Frank that he could solve his problem as he saw fit, but without our participation, and as long as <u>our</u> bed was back in place, and his removed, once he'd vacated our premises.

But then, after the Key West season was over, we began receiving telephone calls that were transferred to our New York number by Southern Bell from people who assumed that they were phoning Frank's residence. This I took as an invasion of privacy that he could easily have prevented had he been willing to inform us that he'd taken over our Key West number. That he did not enforced a growing feeling that we were not simply at odds with an unthinking erstwhile friend, but with a half-assed trickster who seemed to assume that his emergence from the closet endowed him with special privileges.

I could go further with this but I won't, except to say—and this is far more important—that since we thought that you and Charlee had come to understand something of the complexity of our break with Frank we were confounded when we learned he was occupying <u>your</u> place. This we took as a negative judgment of us on your part, for if our circumstances had been reversed our conception of friendship would never have allowed us to have even contemplated such a move. Therefore, when you spent a year abroad and didn't write, neither of you, I assumed that we'd reached the end of our friendship. Charlee said that she'd written, but as with the telephone lines between Cummington and Plainfield, over which we were receiving calls from all over the U.S. and parts of Europe at a time when she could seldom reach us, the mail avenues between us must have been haunted. And the fact that other friends <u>did</u> hear from you seemed to affirm a break. We regretted this and resented the idea that it could have come about because of someone like Frank, with whom we'd never been so close as with you.

As for your suggestion that we might have felt socially neglected by you in Plainfield, forget it. Being rather solitary, both Fanny and I are quite used to being by ourselves. Nor have we ever felt that we were being ignored by you. For we were quite aware that your web of friendships is as intricate as our own, and that not all of your friends would find the others (including us) acceptable. Therefore we never expected, nor would we have desired, to be invited every time you entertained. And especially to family gatherings, which we regard as intimate. So here you can forget my brush with Chris. He, thank God, has his own personality, which is quite different than yours or mine, and any encounter between us was a matter of the moment. Given our differences of age and interests I would no more expect to be a friend of Chris than I'd expect you to be a friend of my brother. The problem, if such it was, had to do with what we perceived as Charlee's feeling that she was in some way responsible for keeping us entertained. Not that we didn't appreciate her concern, but that between old friends it wasn't necessary. It was enough to know that you were nearby if needed, and we hoped that you felt the same.

I'll close by returning to my opening anecdote. My friend who confused a spanking with the loss of his mother was a child, but Fanny and I are far from childhood. Nor do we feel that we reacted childishly to our unpleasant encounter with Frank's manipulations. What some of our Key West friends and acquaintances seem bent upon making a matter of prejudice we see as a justifiable reaction to a violation of friendship and our rights as property owners. Perhaps we should have been more tolerant (or condescending), but how much painful confusion would be prevented if people didn't insist upon reducing complexities of scene and conflicts of motives to a matter of prejudice! And yet even those who suffer most from doing so are at some times guilty. Whites do it, Negroes do it, even sophisticated homos do it—All do it by reducing the reactions and motives of others to prejudices targeted at what they, themselves, seem to regard as their tenderest vulnerabilities. Thus in this instance that which began with the unauthorized occupancy of our house and a disagreement over a studio bed has been transformed into a nut bag masquerading as Pandora's ambiguous box. Therein lies our answer to the mystery of our break with Frank, and if further explanation is required, you'll have to find it elsewhere. And please don't misunderstand my mention of landlords' rights. We have, at least on two occasions, given the house rent-free to other friends, and had Frank asked our permission he could have lived there without arousing our resentment.

I hope this gives you a clearer idea of our view of the matter, and that reading it will provide a measure of the catharsis and sense of reconciliation that I've achieved in the writing. At any rate you may take the length of it as an indication of my concern that an ultimately trivial incident could do so much damage to our friendship. I hope also that you've fully recovered from your illness, and that all goes well with your family. Our thanks for the *Phaedra,* which in your translation brings much needed comfort as we try to deal with our own "frail estate."

Sincerely,
Ralph

To David Diamond
RALPH ELLISON
730 Riverside Drive
New York, NY, 10031
MARCH 3, 1987

Mr. David Diamond
249 Edgerton Street
Rochester, New York 14607

Dear David:

I've heard certain composers complain that writers' ears are numb to music: and writers say of composers, "Lyrics they'll read, and perhaps stage directions, but <u>never</u> an essay nor piece of prose fiction. And if by chance they're forced to read a dissertation, it must play second fiddle in musical notation."

I overstate a bit but since such erroneous but strongly held opinions do exist I'm all the more grateful to you for giving them the lie in the form of such a delightful gift! It has been years since I've received such a musical surprise, and since the tapes arrived our apartment has resounded with their sonorities.

And especially the clarinet quintet, that evokes my days as an aspiring musician, and a time when one of my best friends was an excellent classical clarinetist. His was a remarkable family in which his father (a dentist) and mother (a teacher and Christian Science reader!) and three brothers were all musicians with whom I spent many a Sunday afternoon listening as they played on their strings, piano, and reeds. So as I listen to Sobol and company I imagine my old friends arrayed in that spacious living room of an Oklahoma City house that no longer exists, swaying and blending as they give voice to your resonant sounds. But then comes the abrupt suspension of your quintet's conclusion—for which I'm never quite prepared—and I'm reminded to stop dreaming and give the music my fullest attention— Whereupon I reverse the tape and begin again. And then, when it comes to the end, I play the Harris tape and go on to the 2nd more challenging (for me) Violin Sonata. I hope you'll forgive me for the little dance step of recognition I do when the First reaches its percussive finale. Finally, I end up saying a prayer of thanks that after your studies with La Boulanger you retained your own unique lyricism. That, perhaps, is a measure of my own limitations as a listener, but I still believe that even the most abstract of music has need of the lyricism you manage to blend from dissonance.

But you should know that even the descriptive matter that came with the tapes is evocative. For it reminded me that during the celebration of its 60th birthday the State of Oklahoma saw fit to honor Maria Tallchief, Roy Harris, and me as Oklahomans who had done something in the arts; and that during the late 30's I took a few lessons in composition from Wallingford Reiger. Best of all, I recalled that during 1936–37 I attended a number of the Town Hall recitals given by the likes of Joseph Szigeti, Albert Spalding, Roland Hayes, and that marvelous singer with red hair Parvio Frisch (?), whose sheer artistry made one forget that her voice was fading. She, Hayes, and Escudero (who was still dancing in Paris during the 50's) confirmed for me the invulnerability of artistic mastery over physical aging. It delights me to think that I might have been in the audience at the time you were introduced to Szigeti . . .

I've missed you at the Academy and hope that work on your cantata goes so well that you'll be able to attend the May meeting. And not only because it would be a pleasure to see you, but because Time is cutting such a swath that the place is beginning to show signs of a discontinuity that it can ill afford. Malcolm grows increasingly feeble, Peter is not as feisty as he used to be, Glenway died a few days ago, and so many who gave tone to [the] organization are being replaced by those who have little respect for its traditions. You are needed, but as I see it the cantata is far more important—and you may take that as the considered opinion of one writer who reads and listens to music in respect for a composer who reads writing! I'm still toiling away on a rather wild novel, and when it's done I'll see that you receive a copy.

Sincerely,
Ralph

To Stewart Lillard
RALPH ELLISON
730 Riverside Drive
New York, N.Y. 10031
JUNE 7, 1987

Mr. Stewart Lillard
730 Heather Lane
Charlotte, N.C. 28209

Dear Stewart Lillard:

Here is the Hyman essay with the reference to the "Territory" (initially designated, at least officially, the "Indian Territory," and later "Oklahoma Territory"). Had I been more alert I could have pulled the record from the cabinet near where you were sitting and given you the source immediately. Nevertheless, Hyman's essay is of interest in itself, and since you are familiar with Columbia's rather extensive collection of Bessie's recordings you can take a look at the set titled *Bessie Smith's Empty Bed Blues* and on Side Two of G 30450 you'll find Ted Wallace's "Work House Blues"; which, given a few turns, will come forth with the lyric in question.

Incidentally, in re-reading Hyman's essay I was amused to find him making an error similar to those he points out in Paul Oliver's study. It was a slip, of course, since Stanley was quite familiar with Huck Finn's decision to light out for the Territory—that might have resulted from Twain's exercise of his heritage of Negro folk tradition. But given the fact that he set the scene of his novel "forty or fifty years" before its 1885 publication and thus some eighty years after Emancipation[*] and <u>during</u> the collapse of Reconstruction, there were ample contemporary reasons for Negroes to head west.

---

[*] Ellison's "eighty years after Emancipation" is misleading. In historical time that would have been 1945 or so, a hundred years more after its fictional time of 1835 to 1845, and long after the collapse of Reconstruction. He must have meant some twenty or thirty years *before* Emancipation and some forty or fifty years *before* the collapse of Reconstruction.

Hyman forgot that the Oklahoma Territory was also a part of the western <u>frontier</u>, but it remained so even after 1907, at which time it became the State of Oklahoma. Which is to say that the unstructured nature of the area made it attractive to many of the discontented, black and white alike, who were seeking a new beginning. So by 1887 there were ten thousand people (Sooners) in Oklahoma City, members of the Randolph clan— who formed my extended family—among them, and the economic and governmental structure for statehood was already in place. That's why Carrie Nation soon swept down from Kansas to attack the saloons of Guthrie, the Territorial Capitol, with her famous hatchet. And perhaps that is why, as a child, I associated her six feet, one hundred-and-seventy pounds of angry Temperance passion with the tiny, wash stick wielding old gal on the Old Dutch Cleanser label! I wonder how Huck Finn would have reacted to the likes of either.

It was wonderful to see you and to meet Raymond Frankle, and I am most grateful for the Oklahoma City *Bulletin*. Once again, as with your research into the Ellison family background, you've presented me with precious details of my beginnings.

Fanny joins me in sending my best regards to you, yours, and to Ray Frankle, and we hope that you'll give us a call whenever you're in these parts.

Sincerely,
Ralph Ellison

To Martin Williams
RALPH ELLISON
730 Riverside Drive
New York, N.Y. 10031
JULY 4, 1987

Mr. Martin Williams
The Smithsonian Associates
900 Jefferson Drive
Washington D.C. 20560

Dear Martin Williams:

Thanks for your most gracious letter, your book, and its dedication. It is encouraging to know that one so knowledgeable as yourself still finds my jazz pieces of interest. And all the more when I read the passages that you underlined in *Jazz Heritage*. Naturally I read them immediately, and I am now in the process of going through the entire collection and already I am being brought up to date on musicians and stylistic mutations that had escaped my attention.

Since you mention *Going to the Territory* you should know also that I possess a number of the Smithsonian recordings and others which I'm sure they inspired, and that recently I was able to direct both John Lucas and a couple of University of South Carolina librarians to Columbia's Bessie Smith series for verification of my statement that she refers to the Territory (first "Indian" and later "Oklahoma") in an old recording. Of course that old sanctuary for escaped slaves, post-Reconstruction freedmen, and freedom-seeking citizens like my parents turns up in Negro folklore, but since both Lucas and the librarians are blues buffs who questioned the Smith connection I was able to refer them to Bessie's rendition of "The Work House Blues." I learned of that number from Stanley Edgar Hyman years ago, but you should have seen my smirk!

I also own a copy of yours and Bill Blackbeard's edition of the *Smithsonian Collection of Newspaper Comics,* which these days I find myself consulting almost as often as I turn to the Britannica. Even more rewarding, I go through it for the art and its critical and cultural information no less than for its humor and power to sweep me back to my childhood.

Which is to say that it reminds me a bit of how I came to be whatever I've come to be, so if you ever wonder who your work is affecting you can be certain that I am among them and that it has been all to the good. Keep helping Americans to discover who they are and, once again, my thanks.

Sincerely,
Ralph Ellison

To Gilbert Jones
RALPH ELLISON
730 Riverside Drive,
New York NY, 10031
JULY 30, 1987

Mr. Gilbert Jones,
150 East 58 Street
New York, NY. 10155

Dear Gil:

I've been so busy fighting the heat and taking a beating from my writing that I've failed to thank you for sending along the review of my book of essays. I do so now, both for your thoughtfulness, and for making me aware of a publication that had escaped my attention. As you say, they're still trying to tell me who and what I am, and once in a while they say that I am a "conservative." Fortunately, they are careful not to add "neo," but they continue to overlook the fact that I'm simply an American! But what the hell, critics will be critics so I remind myself that I'm lucky that my books are still being read—and taught if not read!

In the meantime I'm still working on a novel and Fanny is bearing the confusion with her usual graciousness. Most of the time we're here, laying low in New York. However, we do spend a few weeks of winter in Key West and, usually, most of the summer and fall in the Berkshires. This summer, thanks to the pressure of my work, has been an exception but eventually we plan to escape to the hills.

Thanks again for your thoughtfulness, and we hope that all goes well with you.

Best regards from us
Ellisons,
Ralph

To John Kouwenhoven
RALPH ELLISON
730 Riverside Drive
New York, N.Y. 10031
OCT. 30, 1987

Dear John:*

Now that I've knocked myself out trying to cram your erudite dissertation on American culture into a Shasta can of a foreword I'm rather shaken in self-confidence but relieved that at last I can now acknowledge your letters. And all the more because if I hadn't taken courage from knowing that you were aware of my effort I would have written Johns Hopkins that I had done my best but failed. Perhaps after reading my attempt they'll agree. But however it turns out the effort has been all to my benefit, for in the course of writing I re-read both *Made in America* and *The Arts in Modern American Civilization* and checked them against the current scene. As a result I couldn't help thinking of the fun I might've had in the classroom by using your insights in discussing such recent phenomena as "funk," kinky-headed blondes, corn-rowed, cowrie shell-bedecked Negro girls, the chemical-curled hair of young black men, the worn, frayed look of blue jeans that was once the badge of work, sweat, thrift and age but now obtained with acid baths and machinery; so that a once humble but honorable item of vernacular dress can meet the demands of funky fashion and high price tag. (I'm reminded of those white buckskin shoes that were sold with dirt and scuff built in.) And there is of course the computer-abetted debacle of Wall Street. Such matters considered, Harvard can push *The Machine in the Garden* into whatever mystical past it likes but *The Beer Can* is where the action is. All one has to do is keep it in mind when walking the streets, watching TV, or reading the news.

Wouldn't it be wonderful if by way of confounding the author of *Civilizing the Machine* some researcher turned up with an Edison recording of Black Patti singing *Aida,* or of Stepin Fetchit reciting *Hamlet* in a clipped J.F.K. or Maurice Evans accent? Or if someone discovered a recording by the slave pianist, blind Tom, doing a rendition of Chopin in meticulous

---

* A cherished friend of Ellison's, John Kouwenhoven was for many years a professor at Barnard College. Like Ellison, Kouwenhoven was a champion of the vernacular. See Ellison's foreword to Kouwenhoven's *The Beer Can by the Highway* in the *Collected Essays*, 850–52.

19th century style? As far as I know only the Fetchit would violate the facts of our ambiguous history, but even with all the Afro-American opera singers around I doubt if Mister John Kanon (how dare he share your initials!) would know what to make of such foreshadowings from the past.

Hell, it wasn't a snake but the Adamic American who screwed up the garden, and he did it with saws and screwdrivers, hammers and nails, and with what were once called "donkey" and "nigger" engines! And speaking of engines, it was Northern engineers as much as anybody, soldier or politician, who freed the slaves. And the guy who writes about "civilizing" the machine can take that from this descendant of slaves who built railroad trestles, worked as round-house hostlers, and left one descendant (my father) who worked as a construction foreman on the first steel and concrete buildings erected in Arkansas, Oklahoma and Texas! Yes, and another (my cousin Tom) who died in 1979 at the age of 84 after serving for over fifty years as a Frisco Railroad brakeman. Instead of bemoaning the machine the slave craftsmen and mechanics probed their mystery by eye and by hand, while others made up songs that stressed the effect of machinery on human hopes and relationships. They were also aware that when it came to acquiring many of the techniques developed by American culture "slavery" was a relative condition. Just as the freedmen quickly discovered that "freedom" was the most relative of terms. Thus they recognized the connections between the spread of cotton-picking technology and the movement to the steel mills and assembly lines of Northern cities. And during the time when the boll-weevil was being blamed for messing up the realm of King Cotton, it was W. C. Handy (I think) who gave us the lines "From milkless milk to silk-less silk/And now you give me loveless love." Handy didn't mention it, but he knew damn well that rayon comes out of labs and factories, and that oleo isn't squirted from an udder—

As you can see, I'm still revved up from reading you! And from reading those Virginians who're going at one another over what to do about James Bland's "Carry Me Back to Old Virginny." But, unlike you, Leo Marx doesn't give me a hint that such a development was possible, still we now have a fight over how to "emancipate" those dear nostalgic darkies from Bland's lyrics so that the State can keep its favorite song. Next thing we know some iconoclastic black scholar is going to turn up insisting that Thomas Jefferson had a slave architectural engineer who actually directed the building of Monticello. Here the joke turns on the fact that Bland was no slave but an educated Northern songwriter—entertainer who played a "darkey" in his role as an American (mistakenly dubbed "Negro") minstrel. So no matter what solution today's Virginians arrive at Bland will still be there, laughing in his Golden Slippers over the censored words no less than at the mocking confusion caused by his pseudo nostalgic tune.

As you point out, American culture is most "American" in what lies hidden in its mixture of modes, thus it's hard to tell who the hell had his hand in the mixing. Come to think about it, it's getting harder and harder to figure out just who _is_ most truly American, because it seems to boil down to who was most modified by the democratic process, be they black or white, than a matter of allegiance to flag, region, social class or racial identity. Perhaps that's why many white Americans are so haunted by the possibility of a Negro turning up in the woodpile. And one of the worst things that could have happened to increase the panic on Wall Street was naming the day of its onset "Black Monday." Why not "Reagan Monday"? Or democratize it and call it "S.H.F. Day"? Or they could substitute "computer" for "F," as in fan.

Your words about ole Henry James are well taken, but I was reminded that for all his snobbery James is still important in teaching young writers something of the novel's aesthetics. And while he left folks like me out of his portrayal of American life he _did_ provide clues that help me tell my stories. Sure, Twain is my "ancestor," but for a novelist to be unaware of James' _Prefaces_ is like a medical man trying to become a surgeon without a knowledge of Gray's _Anatomy._ Anyway, if I'm not mistaken Richard Bridgman has some interesting things to say about James in _The Colloquial Style in America,_ so perhaps there was a bit of the vernacular hidden beneath his cultivation. In the beginning, even for James, there was our tricky American mixed-diction; which has its say no matter how much we would deny it. And it's apt to jump up at anytime simply because we are never quite sure who's giving us the ear—especially when we're writing. And I'm afraid that that's true, dear John, even of you, where you comment on the vernacular origins of cantilevered seats on agricultural machines during which I found your own prose teasing your argument. For suddenly you switched modes and abandoned the colloquial relationship between form and function—thing and thing names—sponsored by vernacular speech for the cultivated evasion of referring to the buttocks euphemistically as a "pear-shaped fundament!" That's when the following bit of doggerel (which comes from an example of vernacular advertising distributed during my boyhood) rang in my head. It was printed beneath a cartoon sketch of a man who sat meditating on the extreme south end of a lop-eared donkey who looked back, Balaam's beast-wise, at his burden

(who was bestride him fundament to fundament) and appeared a bit irritated by his rider's philosophical musings—which were:

> *As I sit on my ass on the ass of my ass*
> *A curious paradox comes to my mind:*
> *While three-fourths of my ass is in front*
> *Of my ass, the whole of my ass is behind!*

And as I sat on my fundament all overwhelmed by visualizing seats,
pears and fundaments, I was knocked plumb out of my chair.

So as Fats Waller warned, "One never knows, <u>do</u> one?" The best one
can do is watch out for such linguistic nodes, because as you are well
aware it is in such fleeting conjunctions of vernacular and cultivated style
that the comic, cathartic action occurs—at least to the earing eye and eyeing ear of a vulgar, vernacular-bred Oklahoman.

Getting back to your comments about the nonfunctional aspect of the
cantilever principle when used in the design of modern furniture I'll confess my liking for certain of the products that issue from what you describe
as the "pure playfulness of Mies van de Rohe's . . . cultivated aesthetic
playing solemnly with forms developed in the vernacular." For isn't that
what Henry James was doing when he smuggled vernacular understatement, pauses and rhythms into the dialogue of his cultivated characters?
And isn't that what you've been doing, in a scholarly way, as you've gone
about teaching us to recognize the interaction of cultivated and vernacular
styles? Having no emotional investment in the trappings of aristocracy
(and my connections with Colonial Williamsburg notwithstanding), I'll
admit to our having four Mies chairs, two Brno and two Barcelona. And
sometimes when at table I give my Brno a bounce and imagine that I'm
sitting on the cantilevered seat of my old tractor and working the earth like
my granddad instead of enjoying its bounty sans jeans, sans calluses, sans
salty sweat on my lazy brow. And it works both ways, this quirky mixture
of styles. For when I grow tired while mowing a meadow I caress my tractor seat with my "pear-shaped fundament" and imagine that I'm sitting in
my Brno having a beer.

O.K., John, I know that this has gone on far too long, but blame John
Hopkins for saddling me with such an unfamiliar task, and yourself for
stirring up my imagination. Fanny and I thought of you and Joan and the
Lynes quite often this summer and hoped that we'd make it north to see
you. But as things turned out my writing reached a point that I dared not

interrupt, no matter the sweltering weather. Our best to you both, and please don't let the length of this note discourage you from writing.

Sincerely,

Ralph

To Robert O'Meally
RALPH ELLSION
730 Riverside Drive
New York, N.Y. 10031
MARCH 11, 1988

Mr. Robert O'Meally
816 Elm Street
New Haven, CT 06511

Dear Mr. O'Meally:

Thanks for taking the time to check Paul Garson's quotations with me. For while I haven't read his book I can say flatly that the information given him by Leroy Pierson is false. I don't know Pierson, have never met him, and as far as I can recall I've never conversed with him nor conveyed information to him through third parties. Therefore any information that he might have received from my editor or agent was not checked with me, and, since both are responsible individuals and aware of my intense distaste for sloppy scholarship, false reporting, and irresponsible editing I doubt that Pierson had contact with either. Therefore be warned that your information leaves me damn near as annoyed with Garson and Pierson as I was with you when I reached page 48 of your *Craft of Ralph Ellison* and found my phrase regarding Richard Wright, "too driven or deprived or inexperienced" distorted into "too driven or deprived or depraved." For I consider this distortion of my meaning (how the hell does one equate, misread, or debase a lack of experience into <u>depravity</u>?) as being so blatantly insidious—especially when attributed to me as a friend of Wright—that it couldn't possibly have escaped either your eye or that of your editor. Therefore the fact that it got past both of you left me baffled, and I still wonder if I wasn't used to voice an opinion regarding Wright that was not my own. I needn't remind you that it has been picked up and used against me as proof of my alleged anxiety over Wright's influence.

Returning to your query, Pierson sounds to me like another of those free-wheeling yarn-spinners who so delight in having a role in the unfolding of a story that they'll do so even at the expense of telling outright lies. If asked what happened, say, between Ma Rainey and Georgia Tom Dorsey during the ides of March, 1922 they'll confess to having been present even if it were in a midnight blackened bedroom and proceed to come up with any details, no matter how absurd, that they hope will make their contentions convincing.

As when Pierson says that I played trumpet with Peetie Wheatstraw's band. Hell, I <u>never</u> played trumpet with any band in St. Louis, and that includes Barrelhouse Buck MacFarland's, with whose name and music I am unfamiliar. Nor have I ever participated in a recorded jazz session, whether in Oklahoma City or in those towns and cities of Alabama and Georgia where I did, in fact, play gigs with Tuskegee jazz units. And beyond passing through St. Louis and East St. Louis while enroute elsewhere by railroad I recall being in that area briefly when I was between six and seven years old, and again during the summer of 1933 when I was on a hobo trip, and many years later when I lectured at Washington University. But on no occasion did I hear about, or come in contact with, anyone who called himself "Peter Wheatstraw." And even if I had, the idea that I based the junkman in *Invisible Man* on the guitarist/singer who used that name is ridiculous.

There, my reply to your question, "is Pierson's data dependable," is No! And I'll add that Pierson strikes me as being of the type of individual whom you took much too seriously when researching your earlier book: Talkative types who when asked about matters of which they lack knowledge will proceed to supply the inquirer with irresponsible products of their own freewheeling fantasies. So it would seem that this time around you've run into two of the type, one who has supplied you with false details of my biography, and another who has abetted him by placing his lies between the covers of a book. Thus as the victim of such mythmaking I hope you can understand my annoyance. Yes, but as a writer of fiction and an amateur student of folklore I'm intrigued that trickster types who gave you false leads when you were a graduate student are still testing your gullibility as a professor. Nevertheless, the motives of those who manipulate the process of folk myth are worth more conscious attention. For while trivial in themselves they illustrate some of the confusion that can be wrought by the power of the verbal negative.

Sometimes such distortions of biographical fact originate with those who might possess a general knowledge of their victims' lives and characters, and are fabricated by way of suggesting more intimacy with the subject than the mythmaker actually possesses. I suspect that sometimes, as with those black tricksters who'll tell white folks—or Negroes of a different region or social class—anything that comes to mind, it is done out of the sheer joy of spreading confusion. And as an American phenomenon it issues from a national need to prepare the uninitiated for the ongoing uncertainty of our national existence. It can also issue from a desire to make the subject of the inquiry more admirable, while rendering the misinformer himself more interesting for having played—and this by mere word of mouth or line of type—the shaper and enhancer of his victim's image, and thus the bearer of hitherto unknown details of knowledge. Such catch-as-catch-can essays into the province of biography are not necessarily malicious, but they <u>can</u> be annoying, and especially when one happens to be a writer who reserves the right to tell his own story.

And here I must remind you that after I was willing to do whatever I could to help with what I understood to be a work of literary criticism, you included (and contrary to my request) details of my background, some true, some false, which you obtained from people who knew me during various periods of my life and on different levels of intimacy, but none of whom knew me, or <u>could</u> have known me during the entire curve of what has been, both geographically and intellectually, a widely varied experience. Thus it was with the aid of such unreliable informants that you launched into what borders on unauthorized biography.

An example of the misinformation that can result can be seen in your reliance upon the unchecked statements of Taylor Randolph. True, Taylor knew me from my birth and I was fond of him, both for himself and as the son of the man I considered my foster grandfather. Taylor knew me as a baby, as teenager, and intermittently as a young man, but he was always my senior. And having his own life to lead, there was no way for him to have known many of the significant details of my developing life; anymore than he could have known as much about my father as he might have assumed. For here the generational roles were reversed, with my father the adult and Taylor a junior whose oldest brother was my father's close friend. Thus while Taylor assumed that he was being helpful when he told you that my father's nickname was "Bubber," I could have told you that he had turned "Bub," a nickname acquired as the elder son of a large family, into one that would have been applied to a younger sibling. But such was my father's stature in our community that long after his death his friends referred to him as "<u>Mister</u> Bub," and the same was true of my mother. For in that time and place to address a friend by his or her nickname bespoke intimacy, the addition of a title to one's greeting bespoke respect. Such details are perhaps of no importance to your concerns, but they are nevertheless biographical <u>facts</u> and they echo with nuances of character, manners and social status. Incidentally, a friend of mine who was Taylor's favorite nephew often referred to him fondly as "My lying uncle," an epithet which I heard many, many times to the accompaniment of my friend's delighted laughter.

But to be serious again, biographical facts, no matter how trivial, can be thronged with effect, they ring bells that chime in one's ears with an intimate sense of self. They throb with nuances that tell us who we are, what we are, and what we've been. To outsiders they aren't important, nor, objectively, should they be. But to us they are subjective and, in our general scheme of being, definitive. Thus if we haven't committed such details to paper or tape any outsider who would know us must take the pains to ask what they mean to us subjectively. Hence my annoyance that you used supposedly biographical detail in your book against my wishes. Frankly, I think that even if I had given you my permission you still would have been far too unskeptical as to the reliability of your informants, whether it be of their knowledge, intentions, or memories.

As when you were told by Al Murray (who, despite the general impression, did <u>not</u> know me personally when we were students at Tuskegee but began our relationship later in New York City), that I was taught to cook by a boyhood friend. Which was, I assure you, a creation of Murray's myth-making imagination. The objective/subjective fact is quite different. For despite our boyish resistance to such 'girls' work my brother and I were taught not only to cook, but to wash and iron clothes and to sew, both by hand and by sewing machine, and to perform house work and other such tasks, by our widowed <u>mother</u>. She did this as a matter of imposing discipline on two rambunctious boys, and out of her insistence that we play a responsible role in sustaining our family's home life. Seeing that we did so required her constant attention, but she stuck to her program and we learned. Indeed, by the time when I was four or five I was changing and diapering my baby brother. And by the time I met the old friend whom Al Murray mentions as my mentor in the culinary art, I had been cooking for years. I had also spent much time in the kitchen of father's older sister, a great cook, and had helped my foster grandmother and her mother in the baking of breads, cakes, and cookies, and in the preparation of custards for ice cream. Murray knew none of these homey details, and for all his imagining of how things were during that phase of my life the friend he mentioned (who was lucky to have a mother who worked only at home), wasn't drawn to cooking until his late teens, and this after we'd both worked as waiters. Admittedly, none of this is of great importance, but I feel nevertheless that when it comes to scholarly accounts of my life and work the details of my own lived experience are to be preferred to another's uninformed speculations. In fact that is why I'm taking time to respond to your letter. Besides that, I consider your explorations of the blues more important than my annoyance. May they be successful—and scholarly!

So in closing let me add that as far as I know "Peter Wheatstraw" was not, and is not, a living individual, but a character born of Afro-American mythology. Unfortunately, I know nothing of his legend, nor of how it originated, but as a boy who had friends who were aspiring pool & billiards sharks I was familiar with "Peter Wheatstraw" as one half of a dual persona that was evoked in the form of a frontier brag (or boast) when players wished to challenge prospective opponents to combat upon the green cloth of pool tables. The name of "Wheatstraw"'s other half (by the way, he was never 'Peetie' but always 'Peter') was "Lord God Stingerroy." Thus when a challenger banged through the swinging doors of the pool parlor he'd stamp his boot and let out a belligerent roar that went:

> *My name is Peter Wheatstraw,*
> *I'm the Devil's only son-in-law—*
> *So who wants to play [or shoot]*
> *the Devil's Son—Lord God Stinsgerroy!*

That is the extent of my Wheatstraw knowledge, and the circumstance out of which I appropriated the name when I used it in my novel. In other words, I 'novelized" it, and you'll note that it appears at a point when the narrator is being challenged to draw upon his folk-based background for orientation and survival. The pavement pounding, piano playing, and whiskey drinking were added to urbanize and fill out the vernacular frame, and were invented (if not appropriate from a forgotten source) to fill out my "Wheatstraw's" identity. For me the likes of "Wheatstraw" are in the public domain, therefore I was free to use him for literary purposes. Just as I used that kindred creation of the folk imagination, "Jack the Bear." Here no violation of privacy or copyrights are involved, because for a novelist and descendant of storytellers such items of folk tradition are part of his inheritance and are to be used—much as the composers of music used the folk music of their individual backgrounds—in the expression of his own unique vision. They are part of the mother lode that supports his storytelling and are as free to be used by the conscious writer as they are by the oral tellers of tales.

Which leads me to suspect that whatever the true name of the individual who chose to call himself "Peter Wheatstraw" happened to be he was involved in a similar act of appropriation. In other words, he was a living individual who sought to tie himself to traditional legend. Given such tendencies of our Afro-American folk and their descendants I wouldn't be surprised if some guitar player, pool shark or expert at the games of Tonk or Georgia skin turned up calling himself "Sweet the Monkey," "Fuckum-up Jones," or "Ras The Scholar"—hoping thereby to give his performance an element of mystery, danger, and/or erudition. I'll end with a question: Why would a writer who could invent Proteus Rinehart and Trueblood have need to pattern a character upon a living individual, no matter how interesting that individual might happen to be? Good luck, and my thanks for *Tales of the Congaree*.*

Sincerely,
Ralph Ellison

To Alan Nadel
RALPH ELLISON
730 Riverside Drive
New York, N.Y. 10031
APRIL 19, 1988

Dear Alan:

After being intimidated by your juxtaposition of R.E. and the American Canon (which evoked an image of myself attacking a battleship with a pea-shooter!) I have been reading and re-reading *Invisible Criticism*. It is a most instructive experience, and while far too involved to serve as an unbiased critic I am, nevertheless, much impressed by your analysis and insight. And this even to the point of admitting—at least to my inner self— that from time to time I <u>have</u>, indeed, been so irreverent as to have played a sly game of the dirty dozens with the work of my literary betters. What's more, you've made it clear that I've Twained a few and Bakhtined a few even before I'd read Bakhtin! I'm reminded that during my last telephone

---

* O'Meally edited a new edition of Edward C. Adam's *Tales of the Congaree* in 1987.

conversation with the painter Romare Bearden he invited me to have a look at what turned out to be his last work so that I could tell him what he was up to. It was his joke on me in my self-assumed role of critic of painting, and I think of it now because you have indeed revealed quite a bit of what I've been up to in my jazz-like habit of allusion.

I think that you've produced an excellent, thought-provoking work of criticism, and I'm proud that you picked my small body of writing as your subject. What's more, I shall draw it to the attention of all my friends who teach with the utmost confidence that they'll find it both challenging and instructive. While I, myself, shall return to it from time to time for the pleasure of its argument, and when seeking clues to whatever might be working beneath the surface of my on-going attempts at creating meaningful fiction. Fortunately, a novelist doesn't have to be aware of <u>everything</u> he's doing or trying to do, and I've discovered that critics can be blind to matters that are obvious to those who're not encumbered by preconceptions imposed by their, the critic's methodologies. So I suppose that the best approach for the critic of American fiction, as for its writers, is to hang loose and expect the unexpected, no matter from what area of this irreverent society it turns up. You have done exactly that, and I thank you for paying my writing the respect of such serious attention.

Sincerely,
Ralph Ellison

Alan Nadel
17 Walter Avenue
Highland Park, N.J. 08914

To Benjamin Payton
RALPH ELLISON
730 Riverside Drive
New York, NY 10031
MAY 9, 1988

Mr. Benjamin F. Payton
President
Tuskegee University
Tuskegee, Alabama 36088

Dear Dr. Payton:

I share your regrets over my having been unable to attend Tuskegee's 71st Founder's day Convocation of last March, and you are most gracious in understanding the stress of work that made my attendance impossible. Nevertheless, I am pleased that the occasion turned out to be the glorious academic and historical event that I fully expected.

I say "expected" because one of my prized pieces of Tuskegee memorabilia is a battered copy of the May 1931 *Tuskegee Messenger*. This issue was devoted to the Fiftieth Anniversary of the Institute and one which with its many photographs, speeches and letters of congratulation from distinguished leaders of the nation, was to provide a young student (who enrolled barely two years later) with a vivid sense of Tuskegee's past and a vastly more hopeful vision of his future than the socio-economic conditions of the Great Depression seemed to justify. Now the honor that you've bestowed upon me seems to suggest that through the mysterious processes of time that hopeful vision has been confirmed. For although I did not achieve the goal of becoming a composer of music—the basic reason for my presence on campus—Tuskegee's library and the personal examples set by a few of its teachers who encouraged my creative bent did indeed have a great deal to do with my becoming a writer.

In retrospect there was a fateful irony at work in my imperceptible, and unintended, changing of goals. For while I was simply giving my attention to anything and everything challenging to my intellect there were those who were annoyed by my somewhat unorthodox attitude. I can now recall with amusement—though at the time I was far from amused—one member of the administration advising me to give up "that horn and all those books" for courses on the "Ag side"; from which, he suggested, I could "learn something useful and make something" of myself. An old Tuskegian who had served under Booker T. Washington, this man was devoted to the institution, but unfortunately his devotion was focused upon a frozen moment of its past. Thus he failed to realize that it was not simply in the trades divisions and academic classrooms of Tuskegee or through its cultural entertainment that its students were educated. It was in the totality of its atmosphere, academic, social and historical. For me at least some of its more important lessons were taught in the living rooms of Greenwood, along the surrounding roads, and in the public square of the town. And while I could not have articulated such a perception during my turbulent days on campus, I sensed that Tuskegee was a most important example of America's many testing-training grounds, and thus a place wherein its students were exposed to the influence of a transcendent vision. He might have doubts, but that vision was inescapable, what with the Washington legend, the buildings, the statuary, the photographs and historical papers—if one bothered to read them! And it was that vision which, ultimately, one was obliged to interpret in terms of one's individual background, personality and dreams.

For if Tuskegee shaped its students, each individual student shaped the Tuskegee of his time by reaffirming in his or her own terms its broader, historical mission. And in the process (it didn't matter if this were more by intuition than by conscious insight) they moved both themselves and the institute toward the fulfillment of that far-sighted vision of possibility out of which Tuskegee was founded. The challenge was of grasping that which was left unstated in the public projection of that vision along with that which those goals were stressed at a given historical moment; therefore, like countless others I did my best to grasp its broader implications and took my chances.

For one holding such ideas of his experience it would have been marvelous to have shared, some fifty years later, the occasion which marked the further realization of that vision, and even better to have received from your hands the medal which gives concrete recognition to my identity as a Tuskegee alumnus. The medal is both handsome and eloquent with echoes of difficult feats achieved and of promises, educational and socio-political, yet to be fulfilled. It is a high honor to have been presented such an award and I shall display it with pride.

Sincerely yours,
Ralph Ellison

To Charles Etta Tucker
RALPH ELLISON
730 Riverside Drive
New York, NY 10031
MAY 21, 1988

Mrs. Charles Etta Tucker
517 W. Caldwell St.
Compton, CA 90220

Dear Charles Etta:

Yours was the first news that I had of the *JET* item, for which my thanks. I seldom see *JET* these days so Fanny and I searched a number of stores before realizing that that particular issue was outdated. Fortunately our postman was able to supply a copy—Yes, and there I was, looking like old Uncle Jack caught unexpectedly in a cathedral pulpit. I would send you a transcription of my remarks, but since they were spoken out of the emotion of the moment I have but the vaguest idea of what I said. And the fact that I've been complimented by Bearden's wife and others leaves me all the more curious. Later we were told that the memorial service was recorded, so and if I can get my hands on a tape I'll type you a copy of my remarks. Bearden, whom I had known since the 30s, was a very fine artist and a most interesting human being whose talent we were privileged to observe as he worked toward the achievement of his highly individual style. But while we are proud to possess a few of his paintings they are far from compensating for our loss of a generous, insightful friend.

You ask if it's customary to receive copies of the material when one's picture appears in a magazine, and the answer—as far as I know—is not necessarily. However, when I give an interview I expect to check what I've said from the printer's proof sheet, and after the interview is printed I'm given several copies of the publication in which it appears. Incidentally, the *Guide* sketch* of me was drawn from a photograph that was taken a few years ago when I was far less bald than I am today.

I'm glad to hear that Shep and John Scruggs could combine their tal-

---

* "Television . . . Makes Us See One Another," *TV Guide,* April 23, 1988, is a perceptive sketch by the poet Roderick Townley that highlights Ellison's views of television and American culture in distinctive ways not found elsewhere.

ents, even for so short a time. And for anyone who remembers it proves that for them at least those manual training classes at Old Douglass were not in vain. I did know, however, that Shep, like Lloyd Lambkin and the Lounds boys, was clever with tools, and Herbert informed me some years ago that he was operating a commercial cabinet business in L.A. Nevertheless, the bit about Shep and John constructing props for Mrs. Breaux's operettas is news to me, even though I appeared in at least three of her productions. The first being *The Gypsy Rover,* in which Otis Talley took the leading male role, another was *The Bells of Cornville,* with Lonzetta Townsend the leading lady and Jerome Dowd the leading tenor. I can't recall the title of the last production in which I took part, but it was during my teens and in it (may heaven forgive us!) Dorothy Cox and I performed a tap dance that was taught us by Shag Jones!

I haven't seen John Scruggs since the fifties when he was visiting N.Y.C and stopped by to bring me a message from a friend of my mother's, Mrs. Hester Cook who lived, as did John at that time, in Detroit. Since my mother died in 1937 having a word from one of her closest friends was like receiving a message from beyond the grave. Naturally I was most thankful for John's kindness and wrote Mrs. Cook immediately—only to have my letter returned with the dreadful Post Office notice: "Addressee deceased" stamped on the envelope.

You might recall the Cooks as having operated a movie house that was located on Byers between 1st and 2nd Streets. And for a number of those segregated years they brought professional carnivals to the 600 block on 1st Street. These usually included a Ferris wheel, the lights of which could be seen for miles in the dark, the usual rides, sideshow acts, animals, freaks and cotton candy. Mr. Cook was also one of the first Afro-American electricians in Oklahoma, and the owner of a number of rental houses, one of which was occupied by Tracy McCleary's family.

And here I'm reminded that in 1921 after our mother took us to live in Gary Indiana (where one of her brothers worked in the steel mills) only to find that city in an economic depression, it was the Cooks who came to our rescue. Driving over from Chicago where they were visiting Mr. Cook's mother, they persuaded Mama to return to Oklahoma City, and the very next day we were off on one of the most exciting automobile trips back to our native briar-patch that any young boys could have imagined. So now you can blame the Cooks for your having had to grow up with such a pain-in-the-neck as myself!

And since I'm still wandering back in those early days I also recall that Shep and his cousin, Melvin Todd, were so amused by our attempt to imitate the feats of the movie stunt man, Richard Talmadge, that they nick-named me "Ralphie-Tal" and Herbert "Huckie-Tal." Remind Shep of this and give him my best wishes the next time you make contact.

Herbert had told me that Gladys' daughter was ill, but the news of her death is nonetheless saddening. I remember her as something of an ugly duckling of a little girl who grew up into a good-looking swan of a young woman. I can still see her playing on their Second Street porch with her grandmother, and can remember her musician father as well. And of course Gladys was one of my favorites among the older girls. Please tell her of my sympathy.

Charles Etta, the most pleasant surprise in your news filled letter is the word about your daughter! Since you'd never mentioned her before I had no idea that you and Booker were parents. Next time you write tell me more about her and any other little Tuckers whom you might have kept hidden.

And how wonderful that your daughter took you to visit Tuskegee! Yes, and that you found it still a handsome campus. I haven't been there in quite a number of years now, and last March when an opportunity arrived in the form of my being chosen to receive one of the medals issued in celebrating the 71st Founder's Day Convocation I was unable to be there in person. Still, after having seen what has happened to our old section of Oklahoma City I've dreaded the idea of returning to the old campus— now a university—lest there be nothing left that I could recognize. Thus your report on its appearance is reassuring.

However, you can tell Booker that I do keep in close touch with Mr. Dawson and that sometimes we've talked by telephone for over an hour. He is in his eighties but his mind and memory as sharp as ever. What's more, he's still bouncing about the country conducting choirs in colleges and churches. Last time we talked he was thinking of selling his Hudson sedan that is now so ancient and well kept that it has become a much sought collector's item. I'm delighted to have him for a friend and often find myself laughing at how a relationship that started so badly could turn out so well. I say this because during one of my first harmony classes with Dawson he asked me, who was not a pianist, to play a certain progression of chords on the piano. I made an attempt and as luck would have it I struck a wrong note. But then, failing to understand that I was supposed to return to my seat, and having studied harmony with Mrs. Breaux for four years and therefore quite familiar with the progression, I realized, and immediately corrected, my mistake. Whereupon Dawson, who wanted the next student to supply the correction, threw a piece of chalk at my head.

Well, I didn't like that worth a damn, and after class I went to his office and informed him, man to man, that anyone who threw at me should be thrown at in turn. Which was an unusually rash act for a Tuskegee student, and one that might well have gotten me expelled. But luck was with me, for although a man of quite volatile temper he apologized for his action and physical combat was averted. Nevertheless, until he finally accepted the fact this crazy little Oklahoma Negro was not only one of his greatest admirers but also a hard-working student I remained fairly high on his do-do list. Incidentally, his contacts with the likes of Malcolm Whitby and Gilbert Baxter, among other of her ex-students, led to his having great respect for Mrs. Breaux.

I can hardly believe that Zelma is a great grandmother, and much less that her son, who was only a small lad when I last saw him, is now a grandfather! As they say, tempus fugits fast as all hell, so I suppose there's a certain relief in living far way from the scenes of one's childhood. Otherwise we'd all grow old long before our time from the stress of so much change occurring in so short an interval. I have a fairly good memory of my childhood, but quite often I have to remind myself that the people I retain in memory have long since been modified—as have I myself by time and circumstance. You mention Garvis and Gladys Sparks, and I remember them vividly, perhaps because their father and mother were friends of my own. They were also members of our church, of which Mrs. Susie was one of its most active members. How sad to hear that Gladys and Garvis are no longer with us.

If you and Booker have been married for fifty years you must have grabbed him hot out of Tuskegee, and in doing so you demonstrated that you knew precisely what you wanted in a mate. I, on the other hand, made a mistake on my first attempt—as did my ex-wife—and was married for barely three years. But then I met Fanny, and we've been together for forty-two years, lived in the same apartment building for thirty-five, and are still finding each other worth the experience. So hurrah for you and Booker, and may you have many more years together. In the meantime, don't believe everything you read in *T.V. Guide,* because with all the junk we've accumulated over the years this apartment of ours looks like a storage warehouse, interesting to browse in but difficult to negotiate without a map!

Regards to Zelma and to all those other Okies.

Sincerely,
Ralph Ellison

To Roger Lathbury
RALPH ELLISON
730 Riverside Drive
New York, N.Y. 10031
AUGUST 18, 1988

Mr. Roger Lathbury
100 Cameron Mews
Alexandria, Virginia
22314

Dear Mr. Lathbury:

So seldom am I asked to sign a first edition of *Invisible Man* that when yours arrived I felt a sense of wonder. And all the more that you were able to find a copy and were willing to pay a price in the range of that which I hear book dealers are demanding.

But perhaps you had something of the good luck that was mine back in the Thirties when a friendly book dealer allowed me to buy the 347th signed copy of *Anna Livia Plurabelle* for the even then unbelievable sum of $1.25! This transaction took place on Harlem's 125th Street, and since the dealer was well aware of its market value I suspect that he allowed me to have a signed copy of Joyce at such a ridiculous price for the sheer pleasure of watching the expression on my face.

You ask whether I signed Paul Cubeta's copy at Bread Loaf, and the answer is that I'm not sure. I do remember Cubeta and it is quite possible that I signed his copy during the summer of 1959 when, thanks to my late friend, John Ciardi, I lectured and read manuscripts there in the Vermont hills. At any rate you should know that I began the novel in Waitsfield, Vermont, a village not too far from Middlebury and that it pleases me no end to learn the background of your interest.

Sincerely yours,
Ralph Ellison

To Arnold Rampersad
RALPH ELLISON
730 Riverside Drive, Apt. 8-D
New York, N.Y. 1031
october 23, 1988

Dear Arnold:

Volume II of your Hughes Biography arrived earlier this month and we are pleased to have it join its mate.

Learning the details of Langston's life of which I was unaware is both illuminating and saddening, for no matter to what extent Langston was the author of his fate, such a generous man deserved much better.

Clearly through your scholarship and grace you have given his life a perspective which can only enlighten the serious reader. We are pleased that you undertook this work that can hardly be surpassed.

Fanny joins me in best wishes in times to come and in appreciation for your inscription.

Sincerely,
Ralph Ellison

Mr. Arnold Rampersad
34 Riverside Drive, Apt. 4D
New York, New York 10024

To Michel Fabre
RALPH ELLISON
730 Riverside Drive
New York, NY 10031
JANUARY 12, 1989

Professor Michel Fabre
12 Square Montsouris
75014 Paris France,

Dear Michel Fabre:

I accept your apology and it is good to know at long last what happened to the DELTA issue. I am also sorry to hear of your illness and sincerely hope that it remains a minor matter.

I too have read Margaret Walker's book and was disgusted that such shabby writing could have found a publisher. Yes, and even more disgusted that they were so insensitive as to send me the galleys for comment! Therefore I have no objections to your quoting from my letters to Wright—providing that you send me copies of same. I ask this because the file in which the carbons of my correspondence with Wright are stored is not easily available, thus making it difficult for me to check the quotes to which you refer. I anticipate no problem here, but given the zaniness of some of Margaret's writer friends I'd like to forestall any that might arise once your comments are published.

Since I've known Miss Walker since 1937, when Wright introduced us, I've thought of her as the prime example of a woman scorned, but even after all these fifty years of her persistent bad-mouthing of Wright I was totally unprepared when she went so far as to charge him with bisexuality! Now I wouldn't be surprised to hear that she's telling Julia and Rachael that their father was an eunuch! I have no idea of what the hell Wright did or didn't do to that poor woman, but whatever it was it continues to bring out the worst in her. (Where, by the way, is Ellen? Last summer we heard that she was living in the U.S., but if so we've nothing more of her.)

As for using my letters to Richard regarding France, you have my permission, but here again I'd like to have copies so as to see the full context from which you quote.

It is ironic, but I find that scholars who have access to Wright's papers are bringing to light details of our relationship that I had long since forgotten. Which is, one hopes, all to the good. Because, unfortunately, there are naive critics who assume—and this despite their lack of any first-hand knowledge of our friendship—that by virtue of Wright's having been both older <u>and</u> a published writer he was automatically my mentor in all things intellectual. When the truth of it was, and as you correctly suggest, my interest in a number of areas of literature and experience preceded and extended beyond his own. My fascination with France, which began with my favorite cousin's return after serving there during the first World War, is an easy example.

Dressed in his soldier's uniform, he arrived home with his duffle bag filled with photographs and trophies and proceeded to regale everyone with vivid accounts of the broad social freedom he'd known in Paris. At the time I was only four years old, but I was to listen to his and to other veteran's stories for years. Later, as a bookish teenager with a head full of expatriate's adventures by cattle boat, I aspired to tour the continent and end up among those who found the Left Bank so glamorous. Then after becoming a young writer I was to read a number of French poets and novelists. I read *Jean Christophe* on my own at Tuskegee, and came upon Saint-Exupery's writings a little later. And although I was in Malraux's presence but once (he was in New York raising money for the Spanish Loyalists), I admired him and learned far more from his fiction and writings on art than was possible—at least for me—to learn from Wright.

Which is not to say that I learned <u>nothing</u> from Richard, because I did, and for that I am most grateful. Nevertheless, and as is usually true of such relationships, ours was a free-wheeling exchange of ideas and experience in the process of which he learned a few things from me as I learned quite a number from him.

Good luck with your books, both of which I look forward to, with interest, and Fanny joins me in wishing all the best for you and Gene Genevieve.

Sincerely yours,
Ralph Ellison

To Robert O'Meally
RALPH ELLISON
730 Riverside Drive
New York, NY 10031
APRIL 17, 1989

Mr. Robert O'Meally
816 Elm Street
New Haven, CT 06511

Dear Robert O'Meally:*

The other day while glancing through a copy of an MLA publication, *Approaches to Teaching Invisible Man,* I was reminded that I'd failed to thank you for your gift of the *New Essays.* I thank you now, and for your selections and introduction. For while I'm much too subjective to offer an unbiased criticism I'd venture that they're some of the best I've read, and I'm pleased that your readers will now be aware of my debts to the likes of Burke, Bergson and Yeats. I'm also grateful for your giving some of the novel's history, much of which I'd either ignored or forgotten. Perhaps after reading your introduction some of our lazy would-be critics will realize that we don't inherit an insightful knowledge of our ancestral lore through skin and genes but must pay it the respect of research and study.

Which is to say that even home-boys must do their "home-work," and that on both sides of the color line. And especially on the "white" side from which they've traditionally been excluded, and from which they segregate themselves through intellectual cowardice, laziness, and a tendency to leave the corporate responsibility for making sense of this American mess to whites. Nor are they much better when it comes to analyzing the American-ness of their own people—Whom they presume to know simply because of speech idioms, physical features, and skin tones shared in common. But isn't that how Brer Rabbit got done in by Tar Baby? How seriously can one take, as critics, young city types who were born generations after the slave experience and so far from the Negro south, church, cotton-patch, pool hall, and barbershop that they think that Peter Wheat-

---

* Robert O'Meally is Zora Neale Hurston Professor of English and Comparative Literature at Columbia University. He edited *New Essays on Invisible Man,* published by Cambridge University Press in 1988.

straw, Dobie Hicks, Uncle Bud, and Sweet the Monkey were single individuals instead of mythic figures who spring out of the mist of interracial, intercultural mythology? And how can they achieve molasses if they aint got no lasses, specific insight without general knowledge? And vice versa.

I wonder how many of those to whom I refer know how to belly-rub, stand the emotional strain of playing the dozens, have a taste for chitt'lings, or possess enough consciousness of their complex American background to appreciate the atmosphere of a 1930's Lenox-Avenue restaurant, where when a well-dressed customer ordered barbecued ribs the waiters and countermen would shout to the chef-capped cook, "Gimme a breast of Guinea hen!"

Being students of American culture out of sheer necessity those fellows made comedy of the contrast between their own vernacular bill of fare and the elite menus of posh downtown restaurants, and having worked in such they knew precisely wherein the comedy lay. This suggests that they realized that grasping the essence of their own group style required a familiarity with that of their "others"—Which is quite a different approach than that of critics who would reduce art to a matter of color.

And what would most of our black esthetic critics make of Negro headwaiters who could endow rich, upwardly mobile whites with status among their peers simply by treating them with deference? Or who could deny rich aspirants status by treating them with a polite but observable coolness? Yet this often happened, with the headwaiter taking over the role of arbiter of status and the whites acknowledging his authority by accepting his judgment—And this in the old South where manners served as an emblem of achievement and agency of power! Who says that the last can never be first?

Which suggests that while Jimmy Baldwin learned a lot from Henry James he failed to grasp as much as he might have from the old master's concern with the comic aspect of manners. Nevertheless, James, that aristocrat born into a democratic society, was preoccupied with manners for some of the same reasons that black headwaiters found them a rich field for subversive exploitation. For although they themselves were designated inside outsiders (as was James in his beloved England) they could, nevertheless, manipulate the social aspirations of their employers in ways that could have consequences even in the strictly segregated area of politics. For while a knowledge of the symbolic action of manners could help the white individual orientate himself and reach his desired place in the fluid and rapid shifting of American social hierarchy, the very openness of that hierarchy left him vulnerable to doubts that were implicit in the dubious color symbolism which provided order and helped maintain a certain stability in a democracy marked by glaring violations of its most sacred principles. (*PUDD'NHEAD WILSON*)

But as the old British saying goes, no man is an idol to his valet—Nor, I would add, to his black headwaiter. Thus the Civil War continued by means other than arms, and with former slaves playing a punishing—if shadowy—role in the arena of social manners. In the post–Civil War South cotton was the economic king, but he had an ally in King Color, and one whose realm extended through Washington into the post-Abolitionist North where he carried on a chaotic guerrilla action against the North's vulnerable sense of democratic morality. It was otherwise in the stable mono-racial societies of Europe, and thus James was led to set some of his richest studies of manners abroad. For it was there new world whites could confront the mysteries of blood and power which supported the old world's social hierarchies free of the questions poised by slavery and segregation. James expatriated himself from an important part of his subject, and thus from the darker side of some of his characters.

That French family into which Newman hoped to enter gave him a hard time in deed and gesture, but it was nothing to what he might have experienced had he stepped across the Mason-Dixon line and undergone an initiation at the hands of some Negro headwaiter who was expert at the role of teaching white folks to be "White" but whose real motive was to teach them to be American. So I'm afraid Baldwin echoed the style and rhythms with a certain grace but failed to recognize how pertinent James's vision was to the racial situation. Perhaps Baldwin might have benefited from a bit of on-scene southern exposure and a more functional knowledge of American experience as it finds expression in Afro-American folklore, humor, and social pranking . . . By the way, the difference between "woofing" or "barking at the big gate" and true Afro American "signifying" lies in the crudeness of the former and the latter's conscious subtlety. The same holds true, I think, between what is called Black criticism and that flexible, informed probing of literature which is true criticism . . .

Forgive me if these rambling digressions (which your book inspired) sound too Southwestern chauvinistic! At any rate I hope that the *New Essays* will find many readers, and that all goes well with you and yours.

Sincerely,
Ralph Ellison

To John Hersey

APRIL 24, 1989

Dear John:

Thanks for the *Horns of Plenty,* a publication of which I was unaware but to which I shall now subscribe. As you might be aware, I've been a fan of Burke's and student of his writings since 1937 when, thanks to Richard Wright, I attended a League of American Writers conference and heard K.B. read from "The Rhetoric of Hitler's Battle." I was dismayed when a number of those present hooted his analysis, among them Communists and fellow travelers, but I decided then and there that his was an eclectic approach that made sense of politics as well as literature. And then of course Hitler went into action and K.B.'s insights were verified—at least for me, because there were those who didn't change their minds until Hitler attacked the Soviet Union.

Later I came to know him personally and when I visited his New Jersey home and discovered—in his waterless outhouse (Yet!)—a Calder sculpture in the form of a wire hand holding the roll of toilet paper on the upraised finger of its second finger I was certain that I'd found my guide through the mazy mixture of vernacular and classical motives that made up my life and background. Give that old rascal a bale of hay and he'll spin you an atomic reactor, a S.S.T., and a Park Avenue condo, but never would he allow such truck [to] distract the irreverent working of his sharp Thoreauvian mind.

I'm sorry, though not surprised, that we've lost Malcolm* for although I was not drawn to him as to K.B. I published some of my first pieces in the *NR* and was made confident in my study of Faulkner (which began before Malcolm's resuscitation) through his efforts on Faulkner's behalf. How fortunate that he and KB were friends and remained so for such a long, productive time.

Thanks again, love to Barbara, and we hope to see you soon.

Sincerely,

Ralph

---

* Malcolm Cowley, an influential writer and critic who was also a longtime editor of *The New Republic,* died in March 1989.

To James McPherson
RALPH ELLISON
730 Riverside Drive
New York, NY 10031
MAY 4, 1989

Mr. James McPherson
711 Rundell Street
Iowa City, Iowa 52240

Dear Jim:

Thanks for the clipping from the *Washington Post*—which, but for the thoughtfulness of you and your friends, I wouldn't have seen. It would seem that in D.C., as in N.Y.C., the more things change the more they remain the same, <u>or</u> the worse they become. Nevertheless, it's good to have such a vivid example of the feedback which continues to flow between current racial relationships and my old novel.

Please tell your friend that when I read her reference to teenagers bopping downtown D.C. with boom-boxes I laughed out loud. For it so happened that when the clipping of her story arrived I'd just been editing a scene in my work-in-progress wherein an old white-haired Negro trickster (like me, he's too old and full of Afro-American folklore and guile to've become a born-again African on such short notice!) who goes slow-dragging along a downtown D.C. street toting a radio from which the Jelly-roll Blues is blaring. I don't know whether the coincidence was a matter of life imitating art or of art imitating life, but whatever the case may be I took it as hilariously affirmative.

Anyway, please remind your friend that in this democracy each individual is challenged to be <u>self</u>-defining, and this holds true even for whites who seek to make matters easier for themselves by treating us as though we were invisible. And all the more for us whom some whites would designate scapegoats in their drama of self-definition. So why debase one's own humanity as a means of striking back? Why not project oneself as one aspires to be while using our traditional comedy as a means for maintaining our complex sense of reality? Why not practice that old ancestral maxim on coping: Change the joke and slip the yoke? Our sense of comedy is one of our hard-earned weapons of survival, the American blackness of our laughter our saving grace. Therefore even if we chose to "wield the power of (our) image" guided by the worst that has been done to us rather than by our own conception of humanity we would still be slaves to the misconceptions of others. Of course there are times when force is called for, and when such times arise I am far from nonviolent. But even so, I prefer to pick the time and place in which I strike back. One of the hidden jokes in the Tar Baby fable is the fact that he looks black but is really white. So it's a waste of time—and dangerous—to be tricked into falling for his interpretation of reality. Step around the bastard and proceed to get your cornmeal made!

Hope things go well with you and your writing, and again my thanks.

Sincerely,

Ralph

To Claire Thiebault

RALPH ELLISON

730 Riverside Drive

New York, NY 10031

JUNE 7, 1989

Miss Claire J. Thiebault

1918 Palou Ave.

San Francisco, CA 94124

Dear Miss Thiebault:

It has taken me far too long to acknowledge your note of February 4th but I am no less grateful for your having written. And all the more for reassuring me that my novel is still tuned to the frequencies of readers like yourself.

For as I see it, a novel is like a rocket which the novelist shapes to the best of his ability then shoots into a dark sky and waits to see whether it produces a hoped-for pattern of meaningful pleasure or a barely discernible sputter of sparks. For once a novel is published it is out there on its own, and even though it might attract a bit of attention before fading from sight it is still important—at least to the launcher—that he have some idea of its effect on its observers.

And all the more when the novel in question has been circling for some thirty years. Because the novelist can never forget that his work can come alive only through the willing collaboration of his individual readers; each of whom helps bring it to life by bringing to it emotions and insights gained from their own unique experiences. Thus, in a sense, each reader recreates a different book by playing his or her own variations on the writer's all too limited picture of reality. And if a novel is to remain alive it must do so through time-wrought changes in attitudes and perception. It is here that he faces his real test, because even if he has dealt with believable characters, scenes and conflicts his only excuse for invading his readers' privacy is the evocative quality of his art. Thanks for reassuring me that *Invisible Man* still casts a spell.

Sincerely,
Ralph Ellison

To Nathan Scott
RALPH ELLISON
730 Riverside Drive
Apartment 8-D
New York, New York 10031
JULY 17, 1989

Mr. Nathan A. Scott, Jr.
1419 Hilltop Road
Charlottesville, Va. 22903

Dear Nathan:

I was delighted by your essay on Red Warren, both for its insights and for its sending me back to volumes of his poetry which I hadn't read for some time. It says much about Red's personal values and our old historical problem which much needed to be said, and is, I think, a valuable contribution to literary criticism. I wish that I were capable of saying even a tenth of what you've said with such clarity. The essay really belongs between hard covers so as to be available to scholars who are unfamiliar with the *Centennial Review,* and especially those readers who would reduce a gifted poet and rigorous thinker to the more negative aspects of his native region and its history.

In a more personal way, however, I value your essay for the memories it evoked of our days at the American Academy in Rome (1955–57). And especially '56, when the Warrens and their small children were Academy guests whom Fanny and I saw daily. Thanks to Albert Erskine, Red's old friend and our mutual editor, I had known Warren before he and Eleanor were married (he was the most distinguished writer to attend the book party given for the publishing of *I.M.*), but it was in Rome that we really became friends. For it was there that he became the companion with whom I enjoyed an extended period of discussing literature, writing, history, politics—you name it—exploring the city, exchanging folk tales, joking, lying, eating and drinking.

A vigorous man, he damn near walked my legs off as we covered miles of what for him were familiar historical sites, restaurants, and bars. And it was through such pleasurable roaming that any bars to our friendship that might have been imposed by Southern manners and history went down the drain and left the well-known Fugitive poet and the fledgling writer and grandson of Freedmen marvelously free to enjoy themselves as human beings.

That summer Fanny and I were the Warrens' guests at the old Spanish fort at Porto Ercole (Obertello), and I was pleased to learn from your essay that we were there during a period when some of the *Promises* poems were being written. Which is to say that for all our wide-ranging talk Red and I did <u>not</u> discuss our work-in-progress. It was, all in all, a magical summer and I thank you for giving us some idea of what Red was about in the seclusion of his study. (By the way, that was the year when I saw quite a bit of Allen Tate, Archie MacLeish, and that wonderful critic and talker, R. F. Blackmur. And while I'm name-dropping it might interest you to know that it was Warren and MacLeish who sponsored me for the Century, and thus set a precedent for <u>your</u> membership. Yes, it was two poets who integrated the Century!)

During the years when the Warrens hosted their famous black-tie parties Fanny and I were often among their weekend guests. Marked by good food, good talk, fine drinks, and live music for dancing, these were pleasurable occasions of a truly rare order. We were introduced to an array of people-writers, artists, curators, publishers, academics—whom otherwise we might not have encountered, and as a writer I found the gathering instructive in the irony with which American social change finds expression in modes and manners. Yes, and in unexpected places. For while the setting was a converted Connecticut farmhouse with native woods, aflame in the grates, thanks to Red and a few of his old buddies and their wives the atmosphere was comfortably Southern and yet cosmopolitan, intellectually sophisticated, but downhome friendly. I suspect that a few who took part were bewildered by the easy Americanness of the mixture, their talk of equality notwithstanding. For as far as we were aware no other writers gave parties that encompassed such a diversity of backgrounds and talent.

There were always surprises when we visited the Warrens. As when they enticed me to put on skis and have a go down the snowy slope behind their house (I discovered that the sensation of skiing was surprisingly similar to that which I'd experienced while standing atop a swiftly moving freight train.) Or as when we attended Rosanna's wedding and were delighted—though not surprised—to learn that the ritual would be performed by a Negro minister. The Warrens made no special to-do of this but saw it as fitting since the wife of the minister was a friend of the family who had known Rosanna from infancy.

Today, alas, the time of such parties has come to an end because of Red's failing health. Thus an important source of pleasure has gone from the lives of all who were so fortunate as to have been invited. But I'm sure the spirit that made them possible will continue through the Warrens' children's respect for tradition. Rosanna, as you might know, is a university teacher with two children of her own, and Gabriel is now married and working at sculpture. Knowing their love for their father and mother I have no fear that Red's personal values will fade with his passing. For, as you wrote, Red is indeed a man of "grateful reverence," both in his person and in his poetry. He celebrates the complexity of humanity in word and in deed, and for that I am most thankful. Just as I am thankful to you for your eloquent essay.

Our love to you and Charlotte and we hope you're having an enjoyable summer.

Sincerely,
Ralph

To Mrs. Robert Penn Warren
RALPH ELLISON
730 Riverside Drive
Apartment 8-D
New York, New York
10031
AUGUST 5, 1989

Mrs. Robert Penn Warren
West Wardsboro, VT 05360

Dear Eleanor:

When Fanny suggested that we send you a copy of my letter to Nathan Scott I was a bit hesitant because I realized that when a natural-born liar like myself starts recalling the past he's sure to stray into myth-making. And all the more when he's recalling fond memories.

Which is to say that I'm pleased that you like the letter (my first to Scott despite a friendship of over thirty years), and apologize for my mistake concerning the dance music. Maybe it was due to the lingering spell of bourbon because I was pretty sure that I'd seen Fats Waller holding forth on your piano. But since so many aspects of your parties remain so vivid in my mind my mistake was probably due to their own Warren magic.

So please feel free to send a copy to Blotner,[*] with or without your corrections. I'm only sorry that I failed to write Scott of the wonderful time that we had dancing in the Irish Embassy with the poet-ambassador and his wife (It's shameful that I can remember his nose but not his name!) However I do remember that old Albert[†] was in Rome at the time and that even he enjoyed it.

We still haven't managed to get to the country, thanks to the muddle of our affairs here and the fact that I haven't driven our garaged car for over two years. But if I can get it started we'll head for the Berkshires, and once settled we'll try to get up to see you. Our love to you, Red, and Rosanna— Yes, and to Gabriel and his expectant wife.

Sincerely,
Ralph

To William Dawson
RALPH ELLISON
730 Riverside Drive
Apartment 8-D
New York, New York
10031
SEPTEMBER 20, 1989

Dear Bill:

Let me begin with a bit of personal history: I first heard of you during the late twenties (1927, I believe), from a newfound friend who had arrived in our community from Kansas City. With great enthusiasm he was describing the wonderful band of his school there, and when I asked him the name of its director he said, "He's a wild son-of-a gun named Dawson."

---

[*] Joseph Blotner, biographer of William Faulkner and Robert Penn Warren.

[†] Albert Erskine, longtime editor and friend of Warren's and Ellison's at Random House.

And when I asked him why he called you wild he said, "Because if those guys make a mistake he'll pick up the first thing handy and go up side their heads!"

Well, I was far more impressed by his description of the excellent performers that you'd made of your young musicians than by his comments on your temper. After all, we had a few hair-trigger teachers of our own, I had dreams of becoming a composer and I was searching for a role model. Then in 1931 an older friend who had become a member of the Tuskegee band returned home and gave me a description of your musicianship, your organizational genius, and your personal style. He described your dress, your manner, your magic on the podium, and the exacting discipline which you demanded (and received) from your musicians. And then as though fate had taken a hand I was soon to hear the Tuskegee Choir during a broadcast from Rockefeller Center. All of which left me convinced that if I intended to continue my studies of music it should be under your guidance.

Two years later, being short of the money needed to journey by passenger train, I hopped a freight and arrived at Tuskegee where I became a member of the band and one of your students in the school of music. It was the beginning of our relationship and nothing that I had heard about you proved to be untrue. You were a strict disciplinarian, an inspiring teacher, a stylish dresser, and a magical conductor who transformed choirs of untrained voices into ensembles that phrased and soared like angels. And then to my awe and delight I heard the initial performance of your *Negro Folk Symphony* and knew that "Dawson, William L." would be magical words in my life—Yes, and my Kansas City friend was accurate concerning your temper, which proved true when I made a mistake in a harmony class and you threw a piece of chalk at my head!

But most important to me was the fact that you took my artistic ambitions seriously and had assembled a music faculty which did the same. And although it turned out that I would end as a writer rather than a composer, the discipline and encouragement that you provided was far more important in my development than I am able to tell you. For this I thank you, Bill, and my congratulations on this, your 90th birthday!

Sincerely,

Ralph

To Lowry Ware
RALPH ELLISON
730 RIVERSIDE DRIVE
APARTMENT 8-D
NEW YORK, NEW YORK
10031
SEPTEMBER 7, 1990

Mr. Lowry Ware
HC60, Box 115
Due West, South Carolina 29639

Dear Mr. Lowry:

I am most grateful for your gift from my grandfather's past.* For not only is it one of the most unexpected communications I've ever received, but it does much to fill some of the gaps in my vague knowledge of an ancestor whose story has intrigued me since my childhood.

I say "vague" because for years my mental image of my grandfather was overcast by a veil of myth-like incongruities through which I was barely able to imagine the man of flesh and blood. Much of this had to do with age, geography, and patriarchal authority. I heard of him first when I was a young child, and the idea of his being the <u>father</u> of my own father and aunt, both tall and vigorous people, caused me to view the abstract image which I held in my mind with an element of awe. He was the respected patriarch of a family whose oldest members had migrated to my birthplace in Oklahoma but lived worlds away in South Carolina. Therefore I knew of his existence only through older relatives who endowed his image with an aura of authority that I had no way of grasping. So while he was the head of my clan, the only way I had of imagining his role as my grandfather was by observing the styles and manners of elderly men who were close at hand. These were the grandsires of my young friends, but my attempt to give detail to the abstract image of my own grandfather proved ineffectual. While I could observe the grandfathers of my friends in the processes of daily action, mine remained a structure of mere words, and thus difficult to relate to the times and the life around me.

---

* See the reference to Ware's *Old Abbeville* in the note to Ellison's letter to Ware of June 17, 1992.

The difficulty arose in part because through having lived in Abbeville my older cousins knew our grandfather in person and informed me that he had been a former slave, which I could understand, because there were a number of former slaves living in our community. Still when my cousins went on to marvel over his knowledge of South Carolina politics and politicians I was totally confused. But they insisted that when the newspapers were read to him aloud he would order his readers to repeat passages that he found questionable. And despite the fact that the politicians involved were usually white he would then interpret the underlying clashes of interests, discuss the probable motives, and then explain his disagreement with the paper's account.

Here I must add that the newspaper items that you were so kind to send me are accounts of incidents that occurred long before my Oklahoma cousins were born. But since my grandfather had children and grandchildren close at hand I would assume that their mother was among those who did. Years later a cousin who lived in North Carolina told me that she had indeed read aloud for my grandfather's information, so I assume that he continued this custom until his death.

As for me, the very idea of my grandfather's political knowledge was baffling. For not only was I born far from the land where old time things are not forgotten, I was also too young to grasp the idea of his being what I would now describe as an "inside-outsider." By which I mean an individual who is aware of the values and functioning of a society in which he is denied most of its freedoms and guarantees. Such individuals still exist, and although illiterate they are often possessors of a sharp native intelligence and are capable of a certain wisdom born of experience, a retentive memory, and a sharp attention to the ways of society. I can't say that my grandfather possessed any of this, but his fragmentary "myth" suggests that he did. I also know that there is no necessary correlation between literacy and wisdom, for even today some wise men are illiterate.

Be that as it may, I do have proof that my grandfather had personal knowledge of some of those whose activities received newspaper coverage. For when I reached my teens I came to know that he had business dealings with a former lieutenant of General Robert E. Lee. This was Sam McGowan, who rose to the rank of General and served later as the Chief Justice of South Carolina. I learned of the personal relationship between the General and my grandfather around 1938, when I found among my mother's papers the deed through which property owned by General Sam McGowan was transferred to Alfred Ellison. Then only a few years ago I was amused to learn through the kindness of a white southern researcher that my grandfather had once arrested the future General and Chief-Justice of South Carolina for committing some boyish prank.

I wish I had more to tell you, but my closest link to the subject of your research was my Aunt Lucretia, who had migrated to Oklahoma shortly after my father and mother settled there. But even here I had problems.

For although my aunt possessed fierce family pride she was most guarded in what she said to my younger brother and me about our grandparents and the family's life in South Carolina. Perhaps because after having lived during the Reconstruction and the aftermath of the Hayes-Tilden Compromise she felt that the family had fallen from a higher estate and feared burdening us with the disappointed dreams and hopes of the family's past. (Incidentally, our mother, who adored our father and saw to it that his memory remained vividly alive, often warned us against giving in to what she considered the Ellison's sin of inordinate pride.)

Over the years, however, our aunt did drop bits of information through which I learned that our grandfather had once had a role in local politics, and that one of his brothers had served in the South Carolina legislature. But being ignorant of Reconstruction history I took this with a grain of salt. For since there were no Negro officials, either city or state, in the Oklahoma of my childhood, how could such a thing happen in South Carolina?

My aunt also hinted that my grandfather was of such unusual status, at least for a Negro of his times and place, that accounts of his activities had often appeared in the local newspaper. For this she offered no proof, but now at long last you, yourself, have provided printed evidence of the truth of her assertions. What's more, your evidence confirms that which I received from the researcher mentioned above. But as far as I can remember the only newspaper item that she described in any detail was an account of the death of her mother and baby brother whose lives were lost in a fire. Should you come across an account of that incident I would be gratified to have a copy.

To be brief, it wasn't until I reached my teens that my fragments of information concerning Alfred Ellison began to take on any semblance of reality, and this through reading historical accounts of the Reconstruction. But even then I was frustrated in my attempts to give order to my grandfather's ambiguity as former slave, law man ("magistrate" was the old English term of his time), farmer-politician, and insightful but unlettered citizen. The man of flesh and blood remained remote within his crossword puzzle of a legend, but I finally began making a bit of sense re-

garding my aunt's (aristocratic?) disdain for most of the Negro professionals who dominated the social life of our Oklahoma community. For me the
fact that she was a mere laundress made her disdain most puzzling, and
this despite the fact that her expert services were eagerly sought by upper
class whites. And while I respected her opinions and great skills as a cook
it was inescapable that she had none of the social status of our ministers,
physicians, real estate men, or teachers. Nevertheless, she maintained her
lofty attitude, kept to herself, and frequently reminded my brother and me
that we came from an important family and should, therefore, bear our
inherited name with honor and pride. For me this was like being told that
we had inherited a great fortune that we would enjoy once we found its
hiding place. Of course the next step in that perilous quest would be to
vanquish the guardian spirit of the faithful slave who had been slain and
buried after promising to give the fortune eternal protection. This pattern
I knew from hearing ghost stories of the Civil War, but who had been
the sacrificial slave, where was he buried, and how would I confront his
spirit? As I say, for me my grandfather was shrouded in myth, and only the
fact that my own father's memory remained highly respected long after his
death gave my aunt's assertions the least bit of reality.

In the meantime my brother and I identified with the friends of our
parents, most of whom had migrated to Oklahoma from the South, and
this whether they were working folk or professionals. Indeed it was among
these and the jazz musicians who soon followed that I found heroes and
role models as interesting as those I encountered in books. And while I
took an abstract pride in being the grandson of the mysterious Alfred Ellison he remained almost as abstract as the photographic image which I
found among my father's possessions: A brown-skinned patriarch with
veiled eyes and head of thick dark hair who faced the camera sporting a
white goatee that was carefully trimmed in the then current style.

I hasten to add, however, that my abstract sense of my grandfather's
personality is by no means due to my having failed to meet him in person.
Rather it was because of the gap between our ages, my ignorance of my family's backgrounds, and the rapidity of change that marks American history.
For shortly after my father's death I did indeed meet my grandfather.

This was through an incident that came about (or so I was told years
later), because Alfred Ellison had become curious about his recently deceased son's three-year old brat of a boy. And so it was that I came to be
taken to Abbeville by my older cousins, Tom and Maybelle, who were the
children of my grandfather's oldest daughter, my Aunt Lucretia Ellison

Brown. I have no idea of the length of our visit but it couldn't have been more than a month: because the adult in charge, my cousin Tom, was a Frisco Railroad brakeman. And since the Frisco made free passes available to its employee's relatives he probably arranged for the trip to take place during his summer vacation.

Be that as it may, it was through Tom that I spent a few days with Alfred Ellison and my Aunt Bell and Uncle Jim, the two adult children who lived with him on the old home place. And it is thanks to that visit that I retain a child's vivid but spotty memories of the family's old home and its owner. These include its fireplaces that were so tall that a three year old could step beneath the mantles and peer up the chimneys, my Aunt Bell's cooking, and the huge feather bed in which I slept. I also remember the fresh fruit, melons, and vegetables that were gathered each day and heaped on the back porch to be carefully sorted and arranged for the market—which suggest that my grandfather was still active as a farmer.

I also remember Abbeville's huge moths, its butterflies, and the swarms of fireflies that an older neighborhood boy taught me to catch and store in a bottle, and the fun of watching them twinkle and glow through the glass at nightfall. But best of all there were the tall pecan trees, which were said to have been planted by my father, and with the fruit of which I was distantly familiar thanks to Christmas holidays when my Aunt Lucretia was sure to receive a gunny sack filled with that delicious share of her old home's bounty.

Since I remember my grandfather as being as taciturn as he appears in the photograph mentioned above I have no idea as to what he thought of his grandson. He was said to have been quite proud of my father so I think he found me acceptable. At any rate we got along fairly well, perhaps because we were united in our mutual grief. And my only unfavorable memory of the trip has to do with a violent nighttime storm. The next morning the air was quite clear and as I accompanied my Uncle Jim on a walk to assess the storm's damage we came upon a nest of fledging birds that had been blown from their home in a tree.

> So around and about I had come
> Upon that which I had started from.

In closing I would suggest that you get in touch with Mr. Stewart Lillard whose address is 5122 Chadwick Place, Charlotte, NC 28226. Mr. Lillard, whose research I refer to above, is a librarian who became interested in my grandfather some years ago and has published certain details of my grandfather's life that you might find of interest.

Thanks again for your thoughtfulness, and I wish you all the best as you continue your research into Abbeville's historical past.

Sincerely yours,

Ralph Ellison

To Williard Espy

RALPH ELLISON

730 Riverside Drive

Apartment 8-D

New York, New York 10031

JUNE 5, 1991

Dear Williard Espy:*

The titles of the books by Constance Rourke to which I referred the other day are *The Roots of American Culture* and *American Humor*. To my mind they contain her best insights regarding the role of the vernacular in structuring American culture, but should you find the above titles of interest take a look at her *Trumpets of Jubilee* (a study of Henry Ward Beecher, Harriet Beecher Stowe, Lyman Beecher, Horace Greeley and P.T. Barnum), her *Audubon,* and her *Troupers of the Gold Coast* or *The Rise of Lotta Crabtree.*

Other insightful works that focus on the conflict between our "cultivated" and "vernacular" styles are *The Arts in Modern American Civilization, The Beer Can by the Highway,* and *Half a Truth Is Better than None* by Russell Lynes' good friend, the late (alas) John A. Kouwenhoven.

And, finally, I recommend the writings of Hugh Dalziel Duncan, who is perhaps the best on the subject. Take a look at *Communication and Social Order, Language and Literature in Society, Symbols in Society,* and especially his *Culture & Democracy.* Duncan's works should be required reading for anyone interested in grasping the tragic-comic mixture of American society!

I much enjoyed sitting in on the round-table exchange, and especially the remarks from you that prompted this note. My best wishes to you and good luck with your writing.

Sincerely,

Ralph Ellison

---

* Author of *An Almanac of Words at Play,* among other works.

To Dick Lewis
Delivered by Hand August 7, 1991 at the Player's Club
RALPH ELLISON
730 Riverside Drive
Apartment 8-D
New York, New York 10031
JULY, 1991

Dear Dick:

I received *The Jameses* on Saturday and since their arrival I have spent every available moment devouring their remarkable story. And this steadily and slow, as with a fine wine of excellent vintage. And in the course of being swept along by your narrative I'm learning new facts about the family and the chaotic freedom with which they struggled. As he noted, being American was indeed an arduous task, even for Henry James and his family. And for those of his background it was both an embarrassment of good fortune and a challenge to their subtlety of mind. So much to test and evaluate! Such a mixture of comedy and tragedy! Such a riot of diversity demanding reduction to meaning through eloquence of style and perception!

I'm reminded of my first encounter with James's fictional prose, which I found so measured and slow and yet so artful and intriguing that I, who was under the influence of Hemingway's bland understatement and jazz-like rhythms, became so frustrated that I resorted to the desperate act of typing passages from the master's fiction and re-punctuating them as a means of gleaning the subtleties of their meanings! Which is to say that I had to speed them up to slow them down, accelerate their rhythms to get at the range of their meaning—A contradiction, but one that worked—at least for me. What's more, it made my study of the *Prefaces* more rewarding and the subtlety of the fiction more available. And now, thanks to you, I'll even be able to deal with Henry Senior, who heretofore has devastated me with his quirky complexity.

Better still, you've woven the complex background of the family into a narrative that throbs and flows with the energy of insightful fiction; and although I've only read a few chapters, after each interruption I return as quickly as possible in my eagerness to learn what happens next. Yes, and always to the things unexpected!

For years I've argued that Henry James Jr. knew far more about everyday American life than he's been given credit for, and have often cited his eyeful wandering about the streets of New York and his knowledge of the Bowery. Now you've made its importance so clear that even Edel will be forced to do some rereading.

But who would has suspected that his finicky father had allowed himself the perplexing freedom of close contact with a Negro American? And especially one like Billy Taylor! Apparently Taylor served briefly as a sophisticated Jim to Henry Senior's freedom-enslaved Huck, which was exactly the mentor and anchor Henry Senior needed in coping with American reality. Too bad the relationship was so brief, for Lord knows what would have happened had it extended a few years longer. Perhaps our Henry might have come to know Taylor and gone on to rival Faulkner in analyzing the complexity of our racial relationships. Certainly he would have saved us decades of shameful evasion and hypocrisy. *The Bostonians* has implications that are still coming to light, but think what it would have been had James known the likes of old Billy!

Which brings me to the quote to which you called my attention. Dick, you are as reckless as generous! What will the Jamesians think when they see my poor words in what is sure to be rated as an outstanding study of Henry James and his family? Nevertheless it is an honor for which I'm most grateful. For as little as his influence shows on the surface of my writing I have considered James one of my most esteemed masters. And this since my first reading of his *Prefaces* to the New York Edition. You might say that he's hidden in the stuff of my writing much as the figures from Saint-Gaudens' sculpture were hidden in the lowly vat of plasticine.

Thanks for the book, thanks for the inscription and quote, and our love to you, Nancy, and the entire family.

Sincerely,
Ralph Ellison

To Lowry P. Ware
730 RIVERSIDE DRIVE
Apartment 8-D
New York, New York
10031
JUNE 17, 1992

Professor Lowry P. Ware
Department of History and Government
Erskine College
Due West, South Carolina 29639

Dear Professor Ware:

In apologizing for my delay in responding to the wonderful gifts of your letter, documents, and *Old Abbeville*,* I shall start with a trip to Chicago.

On the eighteenth of April my wife and I departed for the Windy City in a state of confusion that welled into what I can only describe as a time warp of dreamlike dimensions. For while my wife grew up in that city (which I first visited at the age of six, later as a member of the Tuskegee Band, and still later when teaching at the University of Chicago) neither of us was prepared for the changes, social, architectural, and political, that we'd soon encounter.

The occasion for our visit was dual. I was to receive the Chicago Public Library's Harold Washington Literary Award that is presented annually in conjunction with the city's Printers Row Book Fair. Washington, you'll recall, was the first Afro-American Mayor of Chicago, and the handsome library named in his honor is now the largest in the country. So in doing my homework I was delighted to learn that despite Washington's ward heeler's past he had been fascinated by the power of language and possessed a love for books that, for a politician, was highly unusual. What's more, in public address he delighted his audiences with a Twain-like mixture of modes in which proper English was mocked by phrases from Afro-American vernacular. In other words, he consciously Americanized

---

* Ware's *Old Abbeville: Scenes of the Past of a Town Where "Old Time Things Are Not Forgotten"* (1992) has a chapter called "Big Alfred Ellison and His Grandson, the Novelist," much admired and cited by Ellison in the last two years of his life.

his language in a manner that appears to have been both amusing and politically effective.

The morning following the Award ceremony it was my role to open the Printers Row Book Fair with a speech of welcome. But while prepared for both events and the social activity involved, it was during the Award dinner that past and present leaped out of phase and stunned me.

For before the presentation I was welcomed by Chicago library commissioner John Duff on behalf of Mayor Daly, that most unlikely son of his father, and was astonished when Mr. Duff announced that the Mayor had proclaimed that day, the Nineteenth of June, Ralph Ellison Day.[*]

Well, my wife and I made it through that surprising turn of events, I gave my speech of acceptance, and though left fairly exhausted was delighted by the task of autographing so many books. Then came dancing and drinking and much talk with friends and with strangers.

Next day as scheduled I gave the talk that opened the book fair and received a standing ovation, after which my wife and I sought to return to reality by taking a tour through the Southside neighborhoods where she had lived as a child. But again we found that time and change had made for startling surprises.

For as we wandered and searched for sites once familiar—apartment houses, dance halls, restaurants, and churches we were reminded that try as one will the possibility of returning to the past was as vain as attempting to retrace one's footsteps in fast flowing water. Which ancient wisdom I should have learned from trips to Oklahoma City, where most of the sites I knew as a child have long been abandoned. Nevertheless I had hoped for my wife's sake that such drastic change would be untrue of Chicago. But as it turned out most places where she had lived were gone, centers once famous for exciting entertainment had now disappeared, and the few that remained had been stripped of their glamour.

So for the rest of the trip we dreamed of the past and made the most of the present, dined and danced in the once racially restricted downtown area, and enjoyed the jostling and bustling. Yes, and the freewheeling style of windy Chicago. And in the process we told ourselves that once back in New York we'd try to return to our everyday reality. But don't you believe it.

Hardly had we unpacked and inspected our mail than, thanks to you, I found myself caught up again in the confusion of the past with the pres-

---

[*] June 19 is also Juneteenth.

ent. This time by wandering in my imagination through the streets and town square of Old Abbeville. But most of all I was quite overwhelmed by your book's portrait of my grandfather, Big Alfred—a moniker new to me and thus all the more startling and amusing. Big Alfred indeed!

And what an illuminating gift to receive after all my years of wondering about my grandfather's background and character. For except for my memory of visiting him shortly after the death of my father he had remained, at best, a photographic image surrounded by mystery; a man whom my Aunt Lucretia had often hinted, proudly but vaguely, as having been a figure of importance in Old Abbeville.

Which, all things considered, appears to have been true. But, given the distance in time, the distortions and mystery with which most historians of the Reconstruction have cloaked the lives of ex-slaves like my grandfather, this was far too complex for my grasp. Besides, during my childhood I had known quite a few Freedmen, most of whom were intelligent, hardworking citizens. Still there was a mystery about them that I viewed as a matter of manner and style. They seemed to expect far more from society than their freeborn descendants, and this gave them an aura of unreality. Thus as I read your account of Alfred Ellison's encounter with County Commissioner Jefferson, the past and the present flew together in a way most enlightening. And in recognizing traces of my Aunt Lucretia's style in my grandfather's way with opponents he sprang alive and I roared with laughter. And even more over the implications of class conflict cum sibling rivalry which underlay Big Alfred's business dealings with William, his educated brother.

Which is to say that as an historian you brought my grandfather alive with the skill of a novelist who grasps the importance of supplying significant details in aiding his readers to pierce the mysteries of history. Would that other historians possessed such illuminating skill! For then the past becomes a conscious part of the present, and the mystery made of history is no longer ungraspable.

During the days that followed I telephoned my brother in California and read him the section on our grandfather, and he too was delighted. Then on the Fourth of July I was again made aware of the presence of the past in the present, that volatile mixture of the positive and negative. This time by the Tall Ships a-sail on the Hudson; which, thanks to the fine view provided by our eighth floor apartment, we thoroughly enjoyed.

Yes, but then came the car-burning and looting that occurred a block east from our building, which is located not far from that in which David Dinkins lived before becoming our Mayor. Now the occupant of Gracie Mansion, he's busy making history by overseeing affairs involved with a Democratic convention in which two young Southerners are running for the top jobs of the nation. Can it be that now at long last this nation is finally accepting its regional and racial diversity?

Which reminds me: In case you missed it, you might take a look at a book titled *Black Masters, A Free Family of Color in the Old South,* for in it you'll find information on Alfred Ellison which your research has clarified and extended. The authors are Michael P. Johnson and James L. Roark, its main subject a free black named Ellison who was a prosperous manufacturer of cotton gins, and himself an owner of slaves.

When the book was first published, a white southern friend teased me about the irony of a black Ellison owning slaves, and I agreed. Then, after thinking it over, I pointed out that the irony might have been even subtler, in that Ellison's slaves might well have considered their being the property of a black man no worse than being owned by a white man. And that it was possible that what bothered them far more than Ellison's racial identity was his class status, which was as unusual as their being items of his property.

Thanks again for your gift of *Old Abbeville,* copies of which I shall purchase as gifts for my relatives and friends. Meanwhile, please forgive the length of this letter, again my thanks, and all good luck to you and your writing.

Sincerely yours,
Ralph Ellison.

To Willie Morris
RALPH ELLISON
730 Riverside Drive
Apartment 8-D
New York, New York 10031
APRIL 12, 1993

Willie Morris
408 East Northside Drive,
Jackson, Mississippi 39206

Dear Willie:

Yours is indeed a voice from the past, but one most welcome.* And especially when it comes at a time made sorrowful by our loss of Albert Erskine and John Hersey. Before his retirement Albert was my editor and our link to Robert Penn Warren, while in Key West Hersey and his wife were our next-door neighbors. Both Fanny and I miss Albert and John, and our knowing that we've reached that time of life when such losses are common does nothing whatsoever to relieve our distress. Thank God for memory!

Speaking of which, thanks for stirring my memories of times we spent together when you lived in New York. Those were great days, and while I understood your need to return to home base Mississippi's gain was the Big Apple's loss. At least for me, because your accent and background served to relieve some of the intellectual provincialism which made my share of literary life in the Apple so annoying. In other words, you made living among many of the northern-born writers I knew more American.

I look forward to reading your memoir of Manhattan and am pleased to have our friendship recorded. At this distance in time our adventures at Grinnell strike me as hilarious, but although I've racked my memory I've come up with nothing worth calling to your attention. Nevertheless, I'm haunted by the possibility that it was during the same trip that I crossed paths for my first and only time with Martin Luther King.† I've tried to

---

* Ellison's friendship with Morris was a wonderful reconnection at the end of his life. Ellison had admired Morris, a white Mississippian, and his books, starting with *North from Home,* published in 1967 while Morris was editor of *Harper's Magazine,* and up through his memoir, *New York Days* (1993).

† Ellison was on a panel discussion with Dr. King and half a dozen others, including Morris, at Grinnell College in Iowa in October 1967.

check with my files, but they're in such disorder that I decided to forget it and get on with this much delayed answer.

Anyway, I enjoyed your portrait of Hayakawa, Murrow, and Friendly. And I, too, was impressed by the contrast between McLuhan's writings and his presence. But believe it or not, I had completely forgotten my encounter with the cat in the black beret and black leather jacket!* And when I read your description I recalled that I was deciding the best position I could get him so that I could kick his arrogant ass until, as we used to say in Oklahoma, it was roping like overcooked okra. Fortunately, I grew up with fellows who delighted in playing the dozens. And while I refused to take part in their game of disparagement I was thus disciplined in controlling my temper. But like you I wondered how the kids and McLuhan were taking the message embodied in you, "a white Delta boy," and myself being so friendly.

Good luck with the book, give our warm regards to David, and should you get up this way please give us a ring.

Sincerely,
Ralph Ellison.

To Willie Morris
RALPH ELLISON
730 Riverside Drive
Apartment 8-D
New York, New York 10031
JUNE 16, 1993

Willie Morris
408 East Northside Drive
Jackson, Mississippi 19206

Dear Willie:

Yesterday after weeks of searching for your letter on desk tops, in folders, and under piles of computer printouts from my work-in-progress, it finally turned up in a place I least expected: After reading it and sharing with me her amusement over your question regarding the origin of Tucka's name,

---

* Morris's *New York Days* triggers Ellison's memory of a confrontation with a young African American militant who called him a "sell-out" and an "Uncle Tom" at a party after the Grinnell event. For more detail on the incident, see Rampersad, *Ralph Ellison,* 439–40.

Fanny tucked it away in her own pile of papers. Which explains my tardiness in answering.

We were delighted that both you and David—to whom our warmest regards—remember old Tucka after all these years, and were amused by your disagreement over the correct spelling of his name. Indeed, it's as though a play on words contrived years ago had suddenly borne fruit. But you are the winner, because Tucka was our diminutive for Tuckatarby, a name we conceived because it blended Tucka's Labrador blackness with echoes of Brer Rabbit's encounter with Uncle Remus's Tar Baby's stickiness. He was, by the way, an excellent retriever, whether of quail, ducks, rabbits, or pheasants. We miss him and are pleased to have him remembered.

In rereading your letter I'm reminded that my anxiety over its being misplaced was spurred by your dateline and your question regarding Martin Luther King Junior. But as it turns out I recall little of that encounter, perhaps because it was brief and I was a bit weary of traveling. Therefore I am relieved that my delay in answering was not as negative as it might have been had my memory been better.

How wonderful that you should have a black U.S. district judge remind you that he was the young man[*] whom you advised to study law and return home to the State of Magnolias! Let's hope that the Clintons remember him and find ways to make use of his knowledge and experience. One thing is sure, with your advice having such an effect in attaining the fulfillment of our democratic ideals you can say to hell with your detractors! And better than coming full circle your advice has spiraled upward and will continue to effect others through the example and counseling of District Judge Wingate.

Having experienced the failure of my first marriage it's good to know that you're happily remarried. Perhaps failed first marriages are actually rites of passage through which young males and females prepare and become inured for the stresses and the pleasures and pains of matrimony. But of one thing I'm sure: After living with Fanny for some forty-seven years I've never regretted that my first marriage went sour.

You asked if I were still doing lecture gigs and the answer is seldom.

---

[*] According to Rampersad (*Ralph Ellison*, 440), "A black student leader . . . broke up the confrontation" between Ellison and, in Morris's later description, "a big rousing figure, a young black man in his mid-twenties in a black leather jacket and a black beret" at that long-ago party at Grinnell.

The rigors of traveling and socializing after running my mouth for an hour or so has become too discouraging even though the fees I'm offered are often quite tempting. Nevertheless the main thing now is writing more books.* I remember the gig at Milsaps College with pleasure, and all the more because I associate it with Eudora Welty and the coincidence that my mother was a Milsap from a rural area near Savannah, Georgia.

Good luck with your book, and if it brings you this way—which I hope—let's get together, have some drinks, and exchange long thoughts about the old days.

In the meantime our best to you and your wife from Fanny and me.

Sincerely,
Ralph

---

* Intriguingly, Ellison does not mention the second novel that he was working hard on during this time. His last reference to his writing comes at the end of a fascinating note, written on June 7, 1989, in which he thanks a young woman for "reassuring me that *Invisible Man* still casts a spell."

Acknowledgments

We are grateful to the Library of Congress, in particular Alice Birney, Specialist for the Manuscript Division, for tendering informed and courteous help before her retirement; Barbara Bair, who has recently stepped capably into Dr. Birney's shoes; Donna Ellis, also retired, the archivist who supervised processing the Ellison Collection and writing its indispensable finding aid; and Jeffrey Flannery, Head of the Manuscript Division's Reference and Reader Services, and his staff for extending us courtesy and helping us find our way out of seeming blind alleys regarding the letters.

We also thank Ellison scholars, particularly those whose original papers at the two-day 2016 seminar in the elegant Ralph Ellison Room at the Library of Congress provided evidence of the importance of the letters to Ellison scholarship, and the need for a volume such as the present one. Other colleagues, from four different continents, made a similar case at the International Ellison conference at Oxford University in the fall of 2017.

Finally, we acknowledge the following individuals for specific contributions vital to *The Selected Letters of Ralph Ellison:* Jacqueline Ko of the Wylie Agency, and also Emma Herman; Zach Selling, Associate Head of Special Collections and College Archivist at Lewis and Clark College; Joanne Dearcoop, Literary Executor for the Estate of Sanora Babb; and Tracy Floriani, Professor of English, Oklahoma City University, who is writing a biography of Fanny Ellison, for the invaluable service of turning up Ellison's three letters to Sanora Babb at the Ransom Center at the University of Texas.

Arnold Rampersad, Professor Emeritus in the Humanities at Stanford University, deserves gratitude for his biography *Ralph Ellison*, whose rich nooks and crannies inform the footnotes to the Ellison letters many times in many ways. Personally, Arnold was always gracious, prompt, patient, and perceptive, answering many querying emails and phone calls. His frankness and more than collegial support have substantially improved this volume.

It is a special pleasure to thank Adam Bradley, Professor of English at the University of Colorado, Boulder, and author of *Ralph Ellison in Progress*, for his close reading and inspiring suggestions to drafts of the introductory essays to this volume; and to recognize Angie McGinnis's careful reading, typing, proofing, formatting, word-processing, editing—what didn't Angie do?—and everything else required to shepherd each section of the manuscript into readiness. And in loving memory of Rhoda Cummings, John Callahan's devoted partner, who gave John precious support and wise counsel throughout the book's editing but sadly did not live to see it published.

It is easy to be oblivious to the "very stern discipline" and talent required to turn the ambitious glint in a writer or editor's eye into a comprehensive, complex thousand-page volume. But the women and men at Random House have made that happen with *The Selected Letters of Ralph Ellison*. For example: in early days Nicole Counts saw ways to integrate images with language, art with text, and did valuable editing as well; later, Nancy Delia and her team of copy editors brought a generous, compassionate rigor to the manuscript; Rachel Ake and Barbara M. Bachman designed the stunning jacket and book's interior, respectively, so that design and language would speak to each other; and crucially, Chris Jackson, an editor's editor if ever there was one, approached the seven introductory essays eager to discern what their author wanted to say then urged, cajoled, and nudged him until he got that on the page.

In the end we have a book that belongs truly to Ralph Ellison and his readers.

John F. Callahan
Marc C. Conner

Chronology

1910   Lewis and Ida Milsap Ellison, newly married natives of South Carolina and Georgia, respectively, forsake the South for the new state of Oklahoma, formerly called the Territory of Oklahoma.

1913   Ralph Waldo Ellison is born on March 1 in the Randolph family's boardinghouse in Oklahoma City, brought into the world by Dr. Wyatt Slaughter and matriarch Uretta Randolph.

1916   In June another son, Herbert, is born to the Ellisons.

    A few weeks later three-year-old Ralph suffers a life-

changing trauma. Sitting on top of his father's ice wagon waiting for him to make a delivery, he hears a rumbling on the stairs
leading down to a dirt cellar. As Lewis Ellison topples over, a
huge block of ice hits his abdomen, aggravating damage already
caused by a stomach ulcer. Serious infection sets in, and on
July 19 a desperate operation to save his life fails.

Late that summer at the request of Ellison's grandfather,
Ralph's adult first cousin Tom Brown takes him by train to
meet "Big Alfred" Ellison in Abbeville, South Carolina.

In the last years of Ellison's life his grandfather figures
prominently in his letters and also in his last public address, a
talk to the Whiting Foundation in 1992.

After her husband's death Ida Ellison immediately becomes
sole support for her two young boys and herself. Her long
hours as a domestic require Ralph to step up and care for his
younger brother.

1919 Ralph enters first grade at Frederick Douglass, the K–12 segregated public school for black students in an Oklahoma City
fast becoming a Jim Crow town. He graduates from Douglass
in 1932, a year after his class.

1921 In search of a better racial and economic climate for her boys,
Ida tries her luck in Gary, Indiana, moving in with her brother,
who works for U.S. Steel's large manufacturing plant. Within
a few weeks luck turns against her: her brother loses his job
and she must pawn the little jewelry she has. In a merciful surprise old friends look in on their way back to Oklahoma City,
sense her desperation, and take the family home. The drive
goes through Tulsa, where Ida and the boys had stopped on
their way north to Indiana to see a cousin, Tom Brown. On the
return trip evidence is everywhere of the recent terrible Tulsa
riot of 1921, in which gangs of violent whites bomb, burn, and
all but obliterate the formerly prosperous black neighborhood
and businesses of Greenwood. Much later, haunting images
of the devastation eight-year-old Ellison witnessed, including
the Browns' elegant baby grand piano resting blackened in the
street, appear in a surreal passage of *Juneteenth*.

1924 Back in Oklahoma City, the family remains "poor as hell," in
Ellison's words. After the promise of a better job "in service" in
McAlester, a small town southeast of Oklahoma City, Ida takes

her boys there—very briefly, because the job falls through. Ellison puts this ambivalent family journey into "Boy on a Train," an early story he writes in Dayton after his mother's death.

In July Ida Ellison marries James Ammons, twelve years her junior. Before his untimely death a year and a half later, Ammons teaches his stepson how to track and hunt small game, skills Ellison puts to use in various venues in the decades to come.

1925-31 In his teen years jobs and music dominate Ellison's life. He delivers the influential newspaper *Black Dispatch*. Remembering vividly his many talks with crusading editor Roscoe Dunjee, in 1972 he writes and delivers an address posthumously published as "Roscoe Dunjee and the American Language."

During these years young Ellison works regularly for both Randolph brothers, dentist Dr. T. J. (Bud) and pharmacist Dr. James (Jim) Randolph. He becomes something of a lab assistant to Bud, learning "to cast inlays, pour plaster-of-Paris models, and make crowns and some of the simpler bridges." In addition to whipping up ice cream sodas and sundaes in Jim's drugstore, "his main task was to deliver medicine and other purchases to customers, and also to pick up supplies." Ralph "learned to drive when he was about twelve," and Jim Randolph soon trusted him "to use both the store's motorcycle and its Model T Ford."[*]

Barred by Oklahoma City's increasingly stringent Jim Crow laws from attending performances of German-born Ludwig Hebestreit conducting the all-white, award-winning Oklahoma Junior Symphony, Ellison redoubled his efforts to meet the maestro. Ellison's biographer writes that Hebestreit was taken with "this black youth's spunk and skill."[†] Ellison himself recalls Hebestreit offering him lessons "if I would cut his grass"; in fact, Ralph paid Hebestreit $2 a week for trumpet lessons, "but the contact is worth ten times as much to me."[‡] The lessons were in composing and orchestration. The classical emphasis existed sometimes complementarily, sometimes

---

[*] Rampersad, *Ralph Ellison*, 24.

[†] Rampersad, *Ralph Ellison*, 42.

[‡] Rampersad, *Ralph Ellison*, 42.

antagonistically to Ellison's intense, developing love for the blues and jazz, as he heard Jimmy Rushing at Slaughter's Hall and jazz artists "Hot Lips" Page, Count Basie, and Coleman Hawkins there and elsewhere in Deep Deuce. He never forgets listening, rapt, to Louis Armstrong in person, once in 1929 and again in 1931, at the Aldridge Theater.

Zelia Breaux, daughter of Inman Page, the first black graduate of Brown University and the principal of Douglass, gave Ellison harmony classes. "For more than ten years, Mrs. Breaux was a sort of second mother."* Under her watchful tutelage he became lead trumpeter in the Douglass High School band.

In December 1929 Ida Ellison marries again, to thirty-year-old John Bell. Although biographies speak of fractious times and Bell remains "Mr. Bell" to his stepson, letters exchanged while Ralph was at Tuskegee suggest a humorous fondness and respect between the two.

1931-33 Ellison does not graduate with his 1931 Douglass High School class. Dejected in Oklahoma City while waiting for his destiny to unfold, he is offered a job by Milt Lewisohn, owner of the fashionable Lewisohn's clothing store. At first he is janitor and elevator operator. Soon noticing Ralph reading George Bernard Shaw in slack moments, Lewisohn defies racial protocol and upgrades his employee's job description to include helping design the store window's displays of classy suits.

Misled by the band director of black Langston University, who Ellison was sure had promised him a place in the college band, Ellison considers his future. Urged on by his friend and former classmate Malcolm Whitby, he begins to dream of Tuskegee. In January, in a Pathé film, he sees and hears the Tuskegee Choir in performance at Radio City. When he learns that the choir's conductor, William L. Dawson, is about to have his Symphony No. 1, the Negro Folk Symphony, performed by the Philadelphia Orchestra, his focus becomes fixation. "Dawson spent years in school," he writes in his notebook. "Beethoven was somewhat a dumbbell until forty so there's hope for me."

His inquiring letters to Tuskegee go unanswered until May

---

* Rampersad, *Ralph Ellison*, 26.

1933, when word comes from Alabama that the orchestra is in urgent need of a first trumpeter. Alvin Neely, the school's dean of men and a future nemesis, tells Ellison to come in June. As soon as Neely drops the other shoe about the amount of cash needed to enroll and what employment would be available, Ellison scrapes together just enough—not including train fare. Somehow he cajoles Charlie Miller, a black sheep in the Randolph family, who could pass for white, to show him the ropes of hoboing and guide him part of the way over dangerous freight tracks to Tuskegee. Summoning all his moxie, twenty-year-old Ellison arrives on campus around midnight on June 24, a large bandage over his left eye covering the gash he received fleeing railroad bulls in Decatur, Alabama.

1933-35 After a fitful night's sleep Ellison writes his mother from his new room. This letter and the many that follow in a rush from Tuskegee are a far cry from the nonchalant, humorous letter he wrote on March 23 from the State Training School for Negro Boys, a reform school in Boley, Oklahoma, where he was investigating a job teaching music: "I'm <u>Mr.</u> Ellison out here and I forget to answer sometimes." Rare are the Tuskegee letters without intense requests for the money, clothes, or musical supplies he needs to stay afloat.

Poverty was a given for Ellison his three years at Tuskegee. While he works in the bakery, the library, and the dining room, he improves as a musician; in his second year he is asked to play several cornet solos and given a lead spot in the brass quartet.

Unlike his idol Dawson, who throws a piece of chalk at him when he blunders in a class recitation and routinely withholds the respect and affection Ralph craves, the famed pianist Hazel Harrison becomes both friend and mentor. She also gives him criticism that stays with the artist in Ellison: "I had outraged the faculty members . . . by substituting a certain skill of lips and fingers for the intelligent and artistic structuring of emotion that was demanded in performing the music assigned to me." Ellison will put Harrison's stern advice to use more than forty years later in one of his finest essays, "The Little Man at Chehaw Station": "'You must *always* play your best . . . even if it's only in the waiting room at Chehaw Station, because in this country there'll always be a little man hidden behind the stove . . . whom you don't expect, and he'll know the *music,* and the *tradition,* and the standards of *musicianship* required for whatever you set out to perform!'"*

Tuskegee was a place of friendships—with Hazel Harrison of the music faculty, Morteza Sprague in English, and for a time librarian Walter Williams as well as fellow students such as Joe Lazenberry, Mike Rabb, Harry Brooks, and Marie Toynet Howard, who all favored irreverent, strong doses of the vernacular. His only clash seems to have been with Dean Alvin Neely, who abuses his administrative power to exact degrading sexual favors in exchange for routine permission to leave campus for places other than home.

Good standing in the college band carried with it yearly travel possibilities, which Ellison took advantage of, especially Chicago. And there was travel in Keats's imaginary "realms of gold," especially with Professor Sprague, whom Ellison would call "a dedicated dreamer in a land most strange" in his moving dedication to *Shadow and Act* thirty years after he left Tuskegee for New York City in 1936. In Sprague's classes Ellison read *Wuthering Heights* and *The Portrait of a Lady;* students gave reports from extra reading such as *Crime and Punishment* and *Jude the Obscure.* Outside class Sprague urged T. S. Eliot's *The Waste Land* on an eager Ellison, who marveled at the echoes of Louis Armstrong's "two hundred choruses on the theme of 'Chinatown'" in Eliot's montages.†

Returning to Tuskegee for his junior year in 1935, Ellison feels he's left his Oklahoma City home for good, and begins to dream of New York as he dreamed of Tuskegee three and a half years before. Soon two palpable changes propel him toward New York. First, Tuskegee's curriculum shrinks music offerings in a way harmful to Ellison's ambitions; second, his mother abruptly pulls up stakes in Oklahoma to be near her many relatives in Dayton. She is sure her son will follow her, but he does no such thing. Instead at the beginning of June he buys a train ticket to New York to work in that city during

---

* *Collected Essays,* 72.

† The quote is from an undated meditation in Ellison's papers at the Library of Congress.

the summer and save enough money to see him comfortably through his senior year at Tuskegee.

JULY 1936–
OCTOBER
1937   Ellison begins the summer of 1936 in New York with the best of both worlds: a windfall in his pocket in the form of a belated scholarship check from the state of Oklahoma, and the knowledge that should he decide against returning to Tuskegee, his mother's move to Dayton (his brother, Herbert, went with her) removes any obligation to return to provincial Oklahoma.

After a stopover in Washington, D.C., Ellison arrives in New York on July 5. The next morning outside the Harlem YMCA he runs into Langston Hughes, whom he had met briefly at Tuskegee, and Hughes soon extends his legendary kindness: loans him Malraux's *Man's Fate,* recommends him to his friend Richmond Barthé for sculpture lessons (recently Ellison had taken up sculpture), and gives priceless advice: "Be nice to people and let them pay for meals."

Barthé accepts Ellison as a student and allows him to stay in a room in his Greenwich Village studio for several months until well-known psychiatrist Harry Stack Sullivan hires Ellison as his receptionist and he becomes informal editor of Sullivan's book manuscript.

In September Ellison decides not to return to Tuskegee. He moves uptown to Harlem in December when his job ends and goes to work in the A. C. Horn Paint factory across the East River on Long Island. A strike ends his employment in the spring. He dips his toe into radical Marxist politics in Harlem, and tries hard to ship out for Europe to fight in the Abraham Lincoln Brigade in Spain, but the effort is foiled by clamps imposed by the State Department.

He meets Richard Wright, whom the Communist Party USA has sent from Chicago to New York to take charge of the Harlem office of the *Daily Worker.* They become fast friends, and Wright takes Ellison under his wing. He urges Ellison to write a book review for his leftist journal *New Challenge,* founded with Dorothy West. Pleased with the piece, he publishes it and then presses Ellison to try his hand at fiction. He does so, and Wright accepts "Hymie's Bull."

Amid these positive developments, Ellison receives from a relative the shattering news that his mother is seriously ill in a Cincinnati hospital. He pawns his trumpet for expenses and takes the first train to Ohio.

OCTOBER

15–17,

1937   Arriving in Dayton Friday night, he finds his mother so delirious she does not recognize him. At the hospital early the next morning, she is unconscious; she soon dies, not seeming to know that he is there next to her.

OCTOBER

1937–MARCH

1938   Ellison and his brother, Herbert, devastated by their mother's sudden death, instinctively try to go back to boyhood, going to the movies, eating candy, and talking family matters, as they did long ago in Oklahoma.

Needing solitude and breaks from Herbert, Ralph often walks the woods outside Dayton; he writes Richard Wright about being comforted by the leaves and wild pears of autumn, and the stray bunnies in his path.

Fiercely he turns back to writing short stories, and by December, a novella called "Slick" becomes his first unfinished novel. Herbert, Ralph senses, is adrift somewhere beyond him, hurt that his older brother survives by going inside to places he cannot go.

The brothers leave the unwelcoming rooms of their relatives' home. A friend of Herbert's squeezes them into a corner of his house, but soon his pregnant wife insists they move out. During the freezing winter they wander the streets from one coffee joint to another, then sneak back and sleep in the friend's car in his open garage; later they seek shelter in a tailor shop where Herbert had worked briefly, sleeping in piles of clothes.

Soon things take a turn for the better. Lawyer W. O. Stokes, who made Ralph's writing possible by allowing him use of a corner in his office along with a typewriter and letterhead belonging to the county Republican Party, allows the two Ellisons to sleep and wash up in his legal quarters.

All through the frozen months Ralph's life is the half dozen stories he writes and keeps in a brown imitation leather folder,

"Ralph W. Ellison" blazoned on it in gold-colored letters. He bides his time until March, when he learns that with Richard Wright's timely help, he has been accepted as an employee in the Federal Writers' Project of the WPA.

MARCH 1938–
DECEMBER

1939   In New York Ellison reconnects with Wright, Langston Hughes, and others. He meets and soon moves in with vivacious Rose Poindexter, a singer, dancer, and actress, whom he marries in September. His day job flows into his writing; he collects folk songs and stories using the folks of Harlem as his primary sources. His reviews begin to appear regularly in the *New Masses* from 1938 on, and in 1939 he publishes his first fiction, "Slick Gonna Learn," an excerpt from the work-in-progress, in *Direction*.

1940   In late April the *New Masses* sends Ellison to report on the National Negro Congress in Washington, D.C. His piece, "A Congress Jim Crow Did Not Attend," marks a turn in his work. Though reportage, it has a narrative quality that brings elements of his character, personality, and experience to bear on the environment and events of the congress. In a preliminary way it anticipates some of the qualities, though by no means the most remarkable ones, of the protagonist of *Invisible Man*. The *New Masses* touts it on the cover of its May 14, 1940, issue.

1941   In the aftermath of *Native Son*'s publication Ellison becomes Wright's chief comrade in arms in disputations about the book among Harlem's literary and political radicals. Ellison's friendship with Wright deepens significantly after *12 Million Black Voices* puts him achingly in touch with his own experience of race in America.

Another soul mate—and more—at this time is radical writer Sanora Babb, whom Ellison meets at a November meeting of the League of American Writers. Their affair is as brief as it is intense, and their literary friendship will endure after his marriage to Fanny.

1942–43   Impressed by the first issue of Angelo Herndon's *Negro Quarterly*, Ellison severs ties with the Federal Writers' Project to become managing editor. Complementing Herndon's public presence, he does "the actual writing of most, though not all, of the editorials."*

The finances of the *Quarterly* are inadequate, and its winter-spring number of 1943 is its last. Late in May, Ellison leaves Harlem and goes alone to the Vermont farm of John and Amelie Bates. There he finishes "That I Had the Wings" in time for the summer issue of *Common Ground,* and writes several reviews for *Tomorrow.*

Late on August 1, 1943, after a stimulating evening at the Queens home of his new friends Stanley Edgar Hyman, *New Yorker* staff writer and critic, and his novelist wife, Shirley Jackson, Ellison walks from his subway stop at 137th Street into a riot fast becoming an insurrection. The rest of the night and the next morning he roams the streets. Asked by the *New York Post* to report what he saw, Ellison writes a powerful column prophetic of black rioters and police in decades to come: "It was as though they spoke different languages." If real changes did not come, he asserts, "new riots can soon be expected."

During the summer his important personal, literary, and political friendship with Ida Guggenheimer begins.

In September, as Ellison has been expecting, Rose leaves him for good. He joins the merchant marine later that month; in late December, certified as a second cook and baker, he steams out of New York Harbor as part of the crew of the Liberty ship SS *Sun-Yat-Sen* toward the Welsh port of Swansea.

1944 At sea and while the *Sun-Yat-Sen* was docked in Wales and, briefly, in bombed-out London, Ellison works on three stories he will finish back home and publish in 1944: "In a Strange Country," "Flying Home," and "King of the Bingo Game." A fourth, "A Storm of Blizzard Proportions," also set in Wales like "In a Strange Country," is published posthumously.

In June, Ralph and Fanny McConnell meet at Frank's Restaurant in Harlem. They fall in love over dinner and hours of intimate conversation about everything in their lives. Soon they move in together. In the meantime he accepts an advance from Reynal and Hitchcock for a novel he has in mind about a black

---

* Ellison to Mrs. Robert Polsgrove, January 9, 1969, quoted in Rampersad, *Ralph Ellison,* 153.

airman who is the highest-ranking American officer in a Nazi prison camp.

1945   In February he is assigned to the *Sea Nymph* on his second merchant marine voyage, one notable for a half dozen letters he writes at sea and while docked in Rouen.

Back in the States his divorce from Rose becomes final. He finishes "Richard Wright's Blues" in May and it is soon published in *Antioch Review*. The Rosenwald Fund awards him an $1,800 fellowship for the prisoner-of-war novel he has accomplished little on so far.

In June, Vermont beckons. His Wright essay comes out to critical appreciation that reverberates well beyond Wright and *Black Boy*. Even so, the piece is eclipsed by the first sentence of *Invisible Man,* typed out in the open doorway of a barn.

1946–49   Ellison's preoccupation is always *Invisible Man*. Indispensable is the love and multifaceted support of Fanny—she and Ralph marry in August 1946. That same year the estimable Albert Erskine becomes his editor at Random House.

He writes "Harlem Is Nowhere" in 1948 and "The Shadow and the Act," a review of the Hollywood movie adapted from Faulkner's *Intruder in the Dust,* in 1949. The latter appears in *The Reporter*, "Harlem Is Nowhere" sixteen years later in *Shadow and Act*.

Invisible Man, however, begins to fulfill its promise after publication of the first chapter in London late in 1947 and New York in January 1948, each time to a chorus of praise.

1950–52   In the homestretch, Ellison cuts *Invisible Man* by more than two hundred pages, including the word *The* from its title.

Partisan Review publishes "Invisible Man: Prologue to a Novel" in the January–February 1952 issue; Random House brings out the novel on April 14 to mostly admiring reviews and a few bitter denunciations, largely by Marxist or black nationalist reviewers. The Republic of Ireland bans the book for indecency.

The Ellisons are the first African Americans to lease an apartment in the Beaumont at 730 Riverside Drive.

1953–55   In January 1953 Ellison receives the National Book Award for *Invisible Man* and delivers a powerful address called "Brave Words for a Startling Occasion." In the spring of 1953 he lectures and reads at historically black colleges, notably

Tuskegee—his first time back since leaving in 1936—and Fanny Ellison's alma mater, Fisk University; he's also invited to Antioch and Princeton.

In July he spends a week in Oklahoma City making time to "talk with the old folks a bit" and test his conviction that "I've got <u>one</u> Okla. Book in me I do believe." Then he speaks at a summer conference at Harvard where young Henry Kissinger asks for an essay and Ellison dusts off "Twentieth-Century Fiction and the Black Mask of Humanity" for the journal *Confluence*. In October 1953 word comes that May Belle De Witt Johnston, Ellison's first cousin with whom he had joyfully reconnected in July, has passed away; he goes to her funeral and in November writes Herbert about his rush of feeling for May Belle and his lost boyhood in Oklahoma City.

In 1954 he receives an invitation to the Salzburg Seminar to teach classes on the American novel, folklore, and Negro expression. On the way home the Ellisons stop in Spain at the invitation of the American ambassador, then visit Richard and Ellen Wright in Paris. While there Ralph has his fortune read by a Gypsy woman who insists he must see a performance by the legendary flamenco artist Vicente Escudero. The upshot is "Flamenco," an evocative short essay *Saturday Review* publishes in December, followed in its February 1, 1955, issue by "February," a haunting piece Ellison wrote earlier about his coming of age in Dayton after the death of his mother.

The next year he applies for but does not receive a Guggenheim Fellowship. However, the statement of plans he prepares for the fellowship application becomes something of a lodestar guiding the novel that stirs in his mind and, increasingly, on paper. In January 1955 the American Academy of Arts and Letters awards him the Prix de Rome. He is uncertain about the structure of his new novel, and before he and Fanny sail for Rome they visit the home of the Hymans, where five years before Ralph seized on Shirley Jackson's effective, matter-of-fact transitions to escape the narrative jams he had gotten himself into with successive drafts of *Invisible Man*.

1955-57 After stops on the French Riviera and in Naples, the Ellisons arrive in Rome in early October. The American Academy's director and his wife take the new fellows and their spouses on a nine-day trip through Tuscany, a trip that for many years served as a movable feast for the two Ellisons. Back in Rome, Ralph settles into a secluded writing studio; Fanny works at a coveted but tedious daily job with Lampada della Fraternità (Lamp of Brotherhood).

Before turning to his novel, Ellison finishes "Living with Music," published in December by the *Saturday Review*. Still warming up, he resumes his correspondence, giving his impressions of the simultaneous ruin and grandeur of Rome to friends and his brother back home.

Not until 1956 does Ellison break new ground on the second novel and come up with Hickman and Bliss—the father-and-son characters and theme for his novel that also drive "Tell It Like It Is, Baby," an essay his boyhood friend Virgil Branam needles him into writing. Like the second novel, he takes the hybrid essay back to America unfinished in October 1957.

He never settles down for long in Rome, taking short trips to northern Italy, to Switzerland and France with the Murrays, to a PEN conference in London, to another conference in Mexico City, to New York for three weeks, and then to Paris on the way back to Rome. Curbing his restlessness, he buckles down to work on the novel: "a high peak . . . the things coming out of it are brilliant and fine," writes Fanny in early 1957.[*]

Then comes the affair whose passion has Ellison (and soon Fanny) in knots and tangles until their separate leave-takings, Fanny's in July and Ralph's in October.

During his two years in Rome his writing triangulates among fiction, essays, and letters. There he writes more letters than in any other comparable period; there he and Fanny also develop several lasting friendships, the closest of these perhaps with Robert Penn "Red" Warren and Eleanor Clark.

After a taxing trip to PEN International events in Japan and Pakistan, Ellison heads home to Fanny in New York and an uncertainty that soon becomes a mutual resolve to restore trust and friendship to their marriage.

1958–59 Ellison finds "readjusting" hard, "not [to] my work, but to my place of work." Soon he publishes "Change the Joke and Slip

---

[*] Quoted in Rampersad, *Ralph Ellison*, 336.

the Yoke," an exchange with Hyman on folklore and the American novel, in *Partisan Review*. Saul Bellow comes forward to offer his house in Tivoli in Dutchess County, New York. Ellison accepts, and for two years he teaches classes at Bard College while Fanny comes up on weekends from the city.

During these years Ralph publishes essays on musicians Charlie Christian and Jimmy Rushing, whom he has known since boyhood, and "As the Spirit Moves Mahalia," on Mahalia Jackson's profound vernacular spiritual voice.

In 1959 Bellow reads Book II of Ellison's second novel, pronounces it "every bit as good as *Invisible Man,*" and selects a long excerpt to lead off the debut issue of *The Noble Savage.* That summer Ralph and Fanny move into a larger apartment at 730 Riverside Drive with a fine view of the Hudson; in late July he goes to Frankfurt, Germany, to speak at the PEN International Congress.

In September 1959 Ellison enters his last year of teaching at Bard, while Fanny becomes executive director of the American Medical Center for Burma.

1960 He publishes "And Hickman Arrives," the first excerpt from the second novel to see print, and his introduction to Dell's edition of *The Red Badge of Courage,* "Stephen Crane and the Mainstream of American Fiction." That summer ends his time at Bard and his sojourn at Bellow's house.

1961–64 In 1961 he becomes a visiting professor at the University of Chicago, where his hopes for a permanent position are dashed but the friendships he strikes up with Richard Stern and Nathan Scott endure. Later he accepts appointment as a visiting professor of writing and comparative literature at Rutgers for 1962–63, an appointment extended for a second year.

"It Always Breaks Out," from the second novel, is published in 1963; his defiant half of an essay/exchange, "The World and the Jug," in response to Irving Howe's "Black Boys and Native Sons," is published in two parts in 1963 and as a whole in *Shadow and Act* (1964).

He and Fanny attend President Kennedy's 1963 White House dinner honoring the centennial of Lincoln's Emancipation Proclamation. Kennedy's assassination in November affects Ralph as "a horrific intervention by real life in his novel-in-progress, which itself turned on an attempted political assassination by gunfire."*

While putting together *Shadow and Act,* the collection of essays published in 1964, he delivers "Hidden Name and Complex Fate" at the Library of Congress, and also publishes "Blues People," a skeptical review of LeRoi Jones's book of that title.

In 1964 he is elected vice president of American PEN and to membership in the Century Association; that same year he becomes a member of the American Academy and the National Institute of the Arts, and receives a yearlong fellowship at Yale University for 1964–65.

While delivering the Ewing Lectures at UCLA in 1964 he sees his brother, Herbert, in person for the first time since 1938.

1965–67 "Juneteenth" is published in 1965; he also writes and revises "Bliss's Birth," one of the most accomplished and central chapters of the second novel, unpublished in his lifetime. Nine years after Ellison began his autobiographical/historical meditation, "Tell It Like It Is, Baby," in Rome, *The Nation* publishes the essay in its centennial issue in September 1965. In that same year *Book Week*'s poll of critics, writers, and reviewers names *Invisible Man* the most enduring work of fiction published in the last twenty-five years, and President Johnson names Ellison a founding member of the National Council of the Arts.

In 1966 Ellison is named honorary consultant to the Library of Congress; he is also appointed to the Carnegie Commission on Educational Television, a catalyst for the establishment of American public television. He receives an honorary doctorate from Rutgers University. In 1966 Fanny retires from her position at Harold Oram, and she and Ralph make two trips to Oklahoma City.

In 1967 *Harper's Magazine* publishes "A Very Stern Discipline: An Interview with Ralph Ellison" by an impressive trio of young African American writers: James Thompson, Lenox Raphael, and Steve Cannon. Ellison is also named to the board of directors of Colonial Williamsburg and receives an honorary doctorate from the University of Michigan.

In June 1967 the Ellisons purchase and move into a

---

* Rampersad, *Ralph Ellison,* 400.

250-year-old country home in Plainfield, Massachusetts. Ralph settles into his work of revision, most likely on what he imagined to be the last section of Book II. In October he interrupts his work to speak to a symposium at Grinnell College; while there he is on a panel with Dr. Martin Luther King Jr. Later at a party a militant young black man charges in and loudly accuses Ellison of being an "Uncle Tom."

Back in Plainfield, on November 29 the Ellisons return from errands to see their house in flames—the dwelling and their belongings mostly destroyed, including Ralph's precious notebooks and pages of significant revisions on his novel.

1968–69 During these years of recovery from the trauma of the fire, Ellison struggles to recapture the driving force of his fiction. A welcome distraction, deeply bound up with the novel's themes of home and fathers and sons, is the commission he is offered to write an introductory essay for the catalogue of the SUNY Art Gallery's exhibition of Romare Bearden's *Odysseus Collages,* later published as "The Art of Romare Bearden."

In 1969 President Johnson awards him the Presidential Medal of Freedom, and French minister of culture André Malraux honors him with the Chevalier de l'Ordre des Arts et des Lettres. More important and meaningful is his finishing and publishing "Night-Talk," a moving central episode in Book II of the second novel. Almost equally meaningful is the collaboration, begun in July 1969, with James McPherson on an essay/interview called "Indivisible Man."

1970 He publishes "A Song of Innocence" from the novel-in-progress. *Time* publishes his passionate essay "What America Would Be Like Without Blacks." Stanley Edgar Hyman, his friend and sparring partner, dies suddenly at the end of July. Ellison is appointed Albert Schweitzer Professor of the Humanities at New York University, effective September 1. McPherson and Ellison's "Indivisible Man" is given the cover in the December *Atlantic.*

1972 Ellison is named a trustee of the Colonial Williamsburg Foundation.

1972–74 Random House gives Ellison a second advance on the second novel, this time $125,000. Fanny Ellison types a complete version of Book I and as much as he has gotten done on Book II.

Awarded an honorary degree from William and Mary, he gives a brilliant, witty address in his tradition-breaking role as commencement speaker.

He is named to the advisory board of the National Portrait Gallery in 1972; publishes "Cadillac Flambé," another excerpt from the novel-in-progress; declines a tenured professorship at Harvard University in 1973; and is awarded an honorary doctorate at Harvard the next year, in 1974.

In 1974 Random House extends the deadline for the second novel from 1965 to 1975.

1975-79 In June 1975 Oklahoma City dedicates the Ralph Ellison Library, a branch of the Metropolitan Library System. Jervis Anderson of *The New Yorker* uses the occasion to write a skillful profile of Ellison's life to that point. The Ellisons also purchase a conch house in Key West, Florida, in the compound where friends and writers John Hersey and his wife and Richard Wilbur and his wife are neighbors.

Ellison publishes "Backwacking," a short offshoot from the second novel, written more than a few years before, in the autumn 1977 issue of *The Massachusetts Review;* more impressive is his powerful essay on the mysterious presence of American vernacular, "The Little Man at Chehaw Station," in the winter 1977–78 issue of *The American Scholar*.

The September after Ellison's retirement from New York University in 1979, his good friend Michael Harper, the poet, organizes a three-day Ralph Ellison Festival at Brown University; the major addresses and papers from this event would be published in the final issue of *The Carleton Miscellany* in 1980.

1980 Ellison receives honorary doctorates from Brown and Wesleyan universities.

1982 He buys his first home computer, an Osborne I, in January. (Introduced in April 1981, the Osborne was the first portable personal computer available in the United States.) From then on, he writes his letters, essays, and episodes of the second novel on the computer.

1983 Random House gives Ellison a $25,000 advance on an anticipated second collection of essays. He reads from the second novel as part of the Gertrude Clarke Whittall lecture series at the Library of Congress to a mostly black, standing-room-only audience. Of his performance *The Washington Post* enthused, "You would have thought it was Mark Twain." He also buys his second computer, an Osborne Executive model.

1985   On April 1 Ellison is the only writer among the twelve artists awarded the newly created National Medal of Arts by President Reagan in a White House ceremony.

1986   He publishes *Going to the Territory,* his second collection of essays, notable for the long autobiographical meditation "An Extravagance of Laughter."

1988   After he buys an IBM computer, his friend David Sarser transfers all files of the second novel to the IBM, in the process erasing all dates prior to 1988. Tuskegee honors Ellison as its most distinguished alumnus; on April 6 he gives the eulogy at Romare Bearden's funeral at the Cathedral of St. John the Divine in New York City.

1989   Ellison publishes "On Being the Target of Discrimination" in *The New York Times Magazine,* the last piece of his writing to see publication in his lifetime.

1990   At the National Book Award ceremony Ellison is moved when that year's winner, Charles Johnson, author of *Middle Passage,* unexpectedly uses his acceptance address to pay tribute to Ellison and his work, especially "the intellectual expansiveness and artistic generosity" of *Invisible Man.*

1992   He revises the "Hickman in Oklahoma" sequence of the second novel on his computer; he gives his last public address, at the Whiting Foundation in October.

1993   He revises the "Hickman in Washington, D.C." sequence of the novel on his computer; on December 30 he revises and saves the "Rockmore" segment of the second novel.

1994   On his birthday, March 1, Ellison responds to toasts at an intimate dinner in New York held to mark his eightieth (really eighty-first) birthday.

At the end of March he becomes gravely ill; admitted to New York Hospital–Cornell Medical Center, he is diagnosed with inoperable pancreatic cancer. He returns home and three days later passes away with Fanny at his side.

John F. Callahan
Marc C. Conner

Photograph Credits

Index

Aaron, Chester, Ellison's April 21, 1952,
    letter to, 303
Aaron, Daniel, *The Unwritten War*, 657,
    715–16
Abbeville, S.C., 799–800, 808–10,
    851–52, 891
    Ellison's father's life in, 799
    Ellison's grandfather in political life of,
        711–12, 783–84, 800, 848, 968, 969
    Ellison's visits to, 12, 361, 660, 712,
        800, 970–71, 977, 986
    Lillard's research on Ellison's ancestors
        in, 660, 709–14, 784–85, 971–72
    lynching witnessed by Ellison's
        grandfather in, 710–11, 800
    Ware's research and book about, 11–12,
        967–72, 977–78
Abraham, Peter, 252
Abraham Lincoln Brigade, 991
abstractions, 678, 679, 706, 708
Accent, 288
Adams, Henry, 728
Addams, Jane, 728
Adderley, Cannonball, 531–32
Adler, Luther, 98
Adolph's (near Bard campus), 570
Adventures of Augie March, The (Bellow),
    399, 409, 415, 434, 437, 454, 481,
    482, 521–22, 637
    National Book Award won by, 347–48

Adventures of Huckleberry Finn, The
    (Twain), 32n, 369, 471, 473, 479,
    651, 809, 819–20, 904, 907, 931, 932
Adventures of Sherlock Holmes, The
    (Doyle), 651
Africa, 312, 370–71, 491
African American folk tradition, 6, 44,
    931, 956–58
    Hyman's lecture on Negro writing and,
        486–88, 490–92, 519–20, 521
    idiom of, in prose of James and other
        white authors, 755, 838–40
    trickster figures in, 649, 651, 943–44,
        956–57
    white Americans' lack of familiarity
        with, 956–57
African Americans:
    "acting as tools of fascism" (1941), 143
    antebellum, free slaveholding caste of,
        782–83, 978
    "black experience" and, 692–93
    black studies curriculums and, 691
    college experience sometimes
        anguishing for, 731–32
    colleges and other institutions for, 108
    comic sensibility of, 960
    cultural and economic conditions of
        Mexicans compared to, 24, 106
    "darky entertainer" figure or role and,
        487

African Americans (*cont'd*):
depending upon narrative, 678–79
destined to become conscience of United States, 196
duality of identity of, 736–37
as easy victims of divide-and-rule techniques, 674–75
Ellison's only obligations toward, 622
emotional control of, 677
emotions of, toward whites, 660–61, 676
eroticism frequently attributed to expression of, 669
expatriation of, 544–45
"felt experience" of, in relation to universalism, 204–5
found to be individuals by U.S. Supreme Court, 270
Freedmen, 270, 360, 977
housing for, investigated in aftermath of Wright's *Native Son*, 135, 137
humor and irony as conceived by, 155
Hyman's generalizations about, 660–61, 676
identity questioned by, 653–54, 699–700
intellectuals, alleged to think of themselves in narrow terms, 632–34
Invisible Man and predicament of, 398–99, 593–94
journalism by and about, 136–37, 150
see also *Negro Quarterly*
leadership potential of, in radical Marxist politics, 182–83, 194
as mere victims of racial situation, 572
militants, 569, 647, 657, 735
next generation of writers, 312, 646, 658
novels vs. propaganda for cause of, 594–95
Poe's *Tales* and stories of, 651
popular songs among, 681
protesting racial injustice, 731–33
protest movements of, 594
"racial" line of continuity in fiction by, 680–81
special perception of reality ascribed to, 186
stylization as tendency of, 677
tragicomedy and, 752
transcendence of "raw" emotion by, 677
unemployed, recruited as strikebreakers in Detroit (1941), 143
unions' discrimination against, 764
and use of term "Negro artists" or "Negro American experience," 676–79
white southerners' imposition of social order on, 780–81
writers, dehumanizing abstractions and, 706
writings of whites about, 253
see also race; race relations
African culture, Paris conference on (1956), 453, 455
Afro-American, 98, 129, 135
Afro-American Episcopal Church, 728
After Freedom (Pondermaker), 103
"Afternoon" (Ellison), 640
After the Lost Generation (Aldridge), 420
Agee, James, 323
agents, Ellison's caveats on working with, 341
Agnew, Spiro, 672
Alabama State, 305, 593, 815
Aldridge, John, 408–9, 415, 416, 425–26
After the Lost Generation, 420
Alexander, Albert, 704, 777, 856
Alexander, Floyd, 687
Alexander, Lola, 704, 777, 856
Alexander, Robert, Ellison's March 21, 1977, letter to, 735
Allen, Richard, 728
Ambassadors, The (James), 838–39
"America" (Smith), 834
American Academy and Institute of Arts and Letters, 216, 772, 782, 791–92, 915–16, 922, 930, 999
Prix de Rome fellowship awarded to Ellison by, 400, 439n, 544, 586, 588, 996

American Academy in Rome, Ellison's
  Prix de Rome fellowship at
  (1955–57), 272–82, 383–517,
  544–45, 962–63, 996–97
  accommodations in, 386–87, 388,
    391–93
  art and culture experienced during,
    272, 383–84, 385–86, 389, 391, 393,
    394–95, 408, 410, 411, 416, 425
  books shipped to Ellison during, 407,
    420, 431, 432–33, 438–39, 480, 490
  essays written during, 277–78
    see also "Society, Morality, and the
    Novel"; "Tell It Like It Is, Baby"
  extramarital affair during, 8, 279–80,
    281–82, 481–82, 489–90, 499,
    502–4, 509, 515, 574, 997
  Fanny and Ralph's illnesses during,
    394, 402, 420, 435, 436, 520–21
  Fanny's job with Lampada della
    Fraternità (Lamp of Brotherhood)
    and, 272, 997
  Fanny's solo departure from, 280, 490,
    493, 498, 500
  fellowship extended for second year,
    411–12, 418, 431, 436, 441
  financial concerns and, 376–79
  guided tour through Tuscan and
    Umbrian hill country soon after
    arrival, 272, 383, 385–86, 388, 391,
    393, 996–97
  landscape at, 423–24
  length of fellowship and, 390, 396
  letters written during, 8, 272–82,
    383–515
    see also specific recipients
  living away from Negro community
    and, 393, 395, 400
  Murrays' visit during, 443–44
  paucity of literary offerings in library
    and, 389, 392, 395, 420
  photography during, 413–14, 418–19,
    421, 422, 431, 432–33, 442–43, 451,
    479, 494, 500
  possibility of fellowship being extended
    to third year, 485, 490, 492, 504
  return home after, 281–82, 481, 484,
    485, 498–99, 504, 505–6, 507, 508,
    513, 516, 517
  sound system installed at, 272, 384,
    389, 392, 451, 469, 501–2
  jazz tapes sent by Murray and,
    479–80, 489, 494
  voyage and travels en route to, 383,
    388, 391, 392, 400, 996
  work on his second novel during, 8,
    273, 277–79, 413, 435, 447–48, 453,
    472, 477, 485, 490, 997
American Adam (Lewis), 416
American Book Publishers Association,
  563
American Daughter, 219
American Dream, 3, 279, 473
American identity, writers who created
  and explored, 728
American Labor Party (ALP), 182
American Library Association, 306
American Medical Center for Burma,
  613, 626–27, 631, 826, 998
American Mercury, 135
American PEN, 999
American Scene, The (James), 273
American Scholar, 739, 1001
Amherst College (Mass.), 447, 658, 731
"Amid the Alien Corn" (Gibson), 544–45
Ammirati, Theresa, Ellison's October 23,
  1963, letter to, 627–28
Ammons, James (Ralph's stepfather),
  987
Ammonson, Ted, 229
Amos and Andy, 155
Amsden family (Vermont), 120, 228, 232,
  233, 234, 235–36, 237, 238, 239,
  243, 244
Amsterdam News, 289
Anatomy of a Murder records, 560
Anderson, Ethel (Ralph's cousin), 315,
  316–17, 323–24, 714
Anderson, Jervis, 11, 1001
  Ellison's December 12, 1976, letter to,
  658, 729–30
Anderson, Marian, 98

Anderson, Ran (Ralph's cousin), 315, 316–17

Anderson, Walter, 142

"And Hickman Arrives" (Ellison), 9, 267, 283, 567, 568, 577, 662, 998

Angry Black, The (Williams), 640

Anna Livia Plurabelle (Joyce), 756, 833, 839, 952

antebellum period, free slaveholding caste of Negroes in, 782–83

anthropology, 262, 445, 520, 521

antiheroes, 637

Antioch College (Yellow Springs, Ohio):
Ellison as writing resident at, 630, 846, 855
Ellison's lecture at (1953), 265, 269, 306, 308, 314, 317, 321, 324–25, 343, 996

Antioch Review, 198
Ellison's "Richard Wright's Blues" in, 157n, 164, 186, 187, 189, 191–92, 201, 204, 206, 669, 889, 995

Appeal to Reason, 728

Appleton, John, Ellison's September 4, 1954, letter to, 370–72

Arabian Nights, 651

Aragon, Louis, 220, 222

Aristotle, 257, 261, 278, 448

Armed Vision, The (Hyman), 407, 416n, 420

Armstrong, Louis, 397, 491, 495, 501, 587, 649, 740, 861, 988, 990

Arnheim, Rudolf, *Art and Visual Perception*, 442

Arnold, Matthew, 357

Arrowsmith (Lewis), 651

Arrowsmith, William, 470, 481

Arsenic and Old Lace (Kesselring), 194

Art and Visual Perception (Arnheim), 442

Art Institute of Chicago, 248n

"Art of Romare Bearden, The" (Ellison), 676, 677–78, 1000

Art of the Novel, The (James), 419, 853

Arts in Modern American Civilization, The (Kouwenhoven), 935, 972

Ashanti, 370

Ashraf, Syed Ali, 507

"As the Spirit Moves Mahalia" (Ellison), 529–30, 998

Atkins, Red, 687

Atlantic (formerly known as *Atlantic Monthly*), 165, 208, 250, 1000
Ellison and McPherson's "Indivisible Man" in, 10–11, 658, 659n, 685–86, 1000
Hyman's reconsideration of Wright in, 660–61, 676, 679–82
Wright's reply to Cohn in, 139

Atlantic Monthly Press, 166, 576, 645–46

atom bomb, 470
"cracker's madness" and, 276, 457
dropped on Japan, 115, 188, 189, 196, 205, 424
possibility of civil conflict in America and, 205, 206

Attaway, Bill, 170, 187, 249, 829

Auden, W. H., 181, 290

automobile companies, unemployed blacks recruited as strikebreakers by (1941), 143

Axel's Castle (Wilson), 419

Babb, Sanora, 148n, 993
Ellison's letters to, 13, 112
April 10, 1942, 148–51
November 19, 1942, 151–54
July 4, 1943, 159–63
Whose Names Were Unknown, 149–50, 151, 152–54

Babel, Isaac, 680

Back to Back (Ellington and Hodges), 560

"Backwacking" (Ellison), 1001

Badboy, or Bad Boy (Herbert Ellison's friend), 704, 759, 779

Baguet, George, 666

Bailey, Mildred, 649

Baldwin, James, 301, 312, 320–21, 448, 453, 470, 681, 693, 761, 957, 958
"Everybody's Protest Novel," 291, 669
Go Tell It on the Mountain, 312, 681
Wright's image and, 667–69

Baldwin, Roger, 460, 468

Ballard, Allen B.:

  Education of Black Folk, 808

  Ellison's letters to

    August 24, 1983, 799–801

    November 21, 1983, 808–10

  One More Day's Journey, 891–92

Bangkok, Ellison's trip to (1957), 497,
  512, 514

Baraka, Amiri (LeRoi Jones), 676, 682,
  836–37, 999

Bard College (Annandale-on-Hudson,
  N.Y.), 542, 569, 570, 582, 921

  Ellison appalled at ignorance of
    students at, 551–52, 556–57

  Ellison's lecture at (1953), 345, 346

  Ellison's teaching position at
    (1958–60), 282–83, 519, 529,
    551–52, 554–55, 556, 557, 563, 582,
    590, 617, 998

    course on American novel, 533, 536,
     538, 540, 543, 545, 547, 549, 584

    course on Russian novel, 550, 552,
     560, 568, 569, 584, 768–69

    departure at end of second year, 582,
     598, 998

    proximity of Bellow's Tivoli house to,
     282–83, 482n, 519, 582

Barr, Caroline, 708

Barthé, Richmond, 6, 21, 79, 80, 81, 82,
  83, 743, 991

Barzun, Jacques, Ellison's March 23,
  1982, letter to, 750, 766–67

Basie, Count, 263, 272, 389, 479, 489,
  491, 552, 560, 650, 988

"bass clef chick," meaning of, 295–96

Basset, Theodore, 129, 131, 133, 136, 140

Bates, Add, 829–30

Bates, John and Amelie, Ellison's stays at
  Vermont farm of (Waitsfield, Vt.;
  1943 and 1945), 7, 111, 160, 161–62,
  184, 188–200, 764, 952, 994, 995

Baxter, Gilbert, 951

Beach, Joseph Warren, *Twentieth
  Century Fiction*, 420

Beale Street Blues (Handy), 832, 833

Bearden, Romare, 3, 180, 810–11, 884,
  945, 948

  Ellison's introductory essay for
    exhibition catalogue ("The Art of
    Romare Bearden"), 676, 677, 1000

  Ellison's September 8, 1986, letter to,
    757–58, 906–7

  funeral of, 1002

"bearisms," 349

Beat the Devil, 409, 426

beauty, standards of, 678, 681

Beauvoir, Simone de, 629

bebop, 530n, 536

Beckett, Samuel, 838

Beer Can by the Highway, The
  (Kouwenhoven), 935, 972

Beethoven, Ludwig van, 491, 861

Beetlecreek (Demby), 290

Belcher, Rev. J. S., 714

Bell, Clive, *Civilization*, 209

Bell, Ida (Ralph's mother, formerly Ida
  Milsap Ellison), 3, 4, 5–6, 18–20,
  64n, 145, 146, 332, 333, 362, 368,
  427, 429–30, 574, 575, 619, 620,
  695, 702, 711, 714, 731, 778, 783,
  799, 809, 844, 846–47, 856, 858,
  888, 942, 949, 969, 985–87

  "Brownie" as nickname of, 20, 616n

  family's horses and, 643–44

  first husband of (Maston Watkins),
    712–13

  grave of (Cincinnati), 343

  Guggenheimer compared to, 119

  illness and death of, 6, 17, 22–24,
    87–88, 90, 92–93, 100, 103–4, 271,
    616, 834, 846, 855, 923–24, 992,
    996

  Lewis Ellison's first meeting with, 713

  as original keeper of Ralph's flame,
    12–13

  photographs of, 20, 47, 68, 69, 101

  Ralph's letters to, 12–13

    March 23, 1933, 29

    June 26, 1933, 18, *26–28*, 30–31

    July 16, 1933, *32–33*

    July 23, 1933, 33

Bell, Ida (Ralph's mother, formerly Ida
   Milsap Ellison) (*cont'd*):
 Ralph's letters to
   August 4, 1933, 34
   August 20, 1933, 35–36
   August 25, 1933, 36–37
   September 4, 1933, 38
   September 22, 1933, 38–39
   October 1, 1933, 40–41
   November 5, 1933, 42
   November 11, 1933, 43
   November 26, 1933, 44–45
   December 4, 1933, 45
   December 14, 1933, 46
   January 10, 1934, 46–47
   February 1, 1934, 47–48
   February 14, 1934, 48–49
   March 21, 1934, 50
   April 17, 1934, 50–51
   May 2, 1934, 51–52
   May 27, 1934, 52–53
   June 15, 1934, 53–54
   July 1, 1934, 54–55
   July 2, 1934, 55
   July 18, 1934, 56–57
   August 13, 1934, 57–58
   August 21, 1934, 58–59
   August 28, 1934, 59–60
   October 2, 1934, 60–61
   October 24, 1934, 61–62
   November 16, 1934, 62–63
   December 9, 1934, 63
   December 23, 1934, 63–65
   January 3, 1935, 67
   January 13, 1935, 67–68
   February 1, 1935, 68–69
   April 27, 1935, 69–70
   May 27, 1935, 70–71
   October 1935, 72–73
   January 12, 1936, 74–75
   February 26, 1936, 75–76
   May 18, 1936, 77
   June 1, 1936, 20, 78
   September 3, 1936, 21, 80–81
   December 1, 1936, 83–85
   April 20, 1937, 21–22, 85–86

   August 30, 1937, 22–23, 88–90
   September 30, 1937, 23, 91
 Ralph's relationship with, 18, 20,
   537–38
 religious faith of, 732
 remarriage of, to Ammons, 987
 remarriage of, to Bell, 988
 return to Dayton, Ohio (1936), 20, 78,
   80, 84, 990, 991
 salutations and sign-offs in Ralph's
   letters to, 18
 segregation laws disobeyed by, 537
Bell, John (stepfather), 5, 18, 22, 34, 38,
   73, 78n, 84, 87, 362, 988
 letters written to Ralph by (1934), 65n,
   66–67
 Ralph's letters to
   July 4, 1933, 31–32
   March 2, 1934, 49
   undated letter [perhaps written in
     response to Bell's February 5, 1934,
     letter], 65
 Ralph's warm relationship with, 65n,
   66–67, 988
Bellow, Adam, 480–81, 519, 525, 528, 543,
   548, 569, 582
Bellow, Saul (sometimes addressed as
   "Sol"), 3, 7, 140n, 296, 381, 454,
   477, 485, 519, 534, 554, 555, 591,
   596, 600, 606–7, 612, 737, 918, 920,
   921
 The Adventures of Augie March,
   347–48, 399, 409, 415, 434, 437,
   454, 481, 482, 521–22, 637
 "And Hickman Arrives" excerpt
   published in *Noble Savage* by, 9,
   283, 556, 567, 662, 998
 Ellison's letters to, 13, 282–83, 567–68,
   569
   May 4, 1956, 276, 278, 434–37
   August 15, 1956, 448–49
   April 9, 1957 (addressed to Saul and
     Sondra), 280, 480–82
   February 26, 1958, 282, 520–22
   September 21, 1958, 524–30
   November 27, 1958, 541–43

March 18, 1959, 546–49

January 19, 1960, 567–68, 569, 577–83

March 20, 1961, 571, 597–98

May 7, 1961, 599

Ellison's relationship with, 434n

Ellison's teaching job at Bard arranged by, 282–83

estranged from wife and kept from son, 569, 582

Henderson the Rain King, 546–47, 549, 637

Herzog, 637

National Book Award won by, 276n, 347–48

Seize the Day, 280, 437, 481

Tivoli, N.Y., home of, *see* Tivoli, N.Y., Bellow's house at

Bellow, Sondra ("Sasha"), 436, 437, 448, 519, 520–21, 525, 526, 528, 542–43, 548, 561, 599

Ellison's April 9, 1957, letter to Saul and, 280, 480–82

estranged from husband, 569, 582

PS to, on Ellison's August 15, 1956, letter to Saul, 449

Bellow, Susan, 613

Beneš, Edvard, 220–21

Bennett College (Greensboro, N.C.), 215, 316–20

Ellison's visit and keynote speech for opening of Homemaking Institute at (1953), 267–68, 313, 315, 316, 317–20, 323

Bennington College (Vt.), 179n, 181, 225, 230, 231, 249, 278n, 363, 364, 382, 770, 825

Ellison offered substitute teaching position at (1956), 436–37, 441, 446, 538, 545–46

Ellison's lecture at (1945), 116n, 198, 200, 201, 208, 214

Ellison's lecture at (1953), 313–14, 338

Benston, Kimberly, 824

Speaking for You, 780n, 792

Berman, Eugene, 472, 474

Bernice (friend in Dayton, Ohio), 325

Bernstein, Lou, Ellison's March 15, 1956, letter to, 413–14

Berry, Abner, 129, 131, 135, 136, 138, 140, 309

Berry, Faith, 812

Berryman, John, 346, 548, 584, 918, 921–23

The Dream Songs, 922

Bethel, Allen, 44, 722

Bethel, Rev. Dr., 34, 722

Bethune-Cookman University (Daytona Beach, Fla.), Ellison's visit and lecture at (1954), 269, 345, 347, 354, 355, 357, 361

Bib, Leon, 636–37

Bible, 651, 652

Bi-centennial Commission, 873–74

Big Sea, The (Hughes), 878–79

Big White Fog (Ward), 108, 187

Bird's Nest, The (Jackson), 364

Birney, Alice, 13

Bishop, Shelton Hale, 212–13

Bixler, Norma, 889

Bixler, Paul, 192, 308, 889

Black and White Baby (Short), 661, 692–94

Blackbeard, Bill, 933

Black Boy (Wright), 114, 180, 183, 197, 198, 202, 212, 250, 605, 669, 673, 681, 763–64, 812, 995

Ellison's essay-review on ("Richard Wright's Blues"), 157n, 164, 186, 187, 189, 191–92, 201, 204, 206, 669, 889, 995

reviewed in *Partisan Review*, 185–86, 193

"Black Boys and Native Sons" (Howe), 998

Black Chronicle, 856

Black Dispatch, 48, 314, 362, 368, 373, 400–401, 429, 537, 691, 717, 720, 721, 774–75, 854, 987

"black experience," Ellison's critique of notion, 692–93

Black Guinea, 487

"Black Is Beautiful" slogan, 681, 755, 825

Black Masters (eds. Johnson and Roark), 891, 978
Black Metropolis (Drake and Cayton), 208, 312n
Blackmur, R. P., 409, 419, 470, 472, 474, 478, 481, 635, 637, 921
Black Muslim movement, 594
black nationalism, 675, 995
Black Power (Wright), 365, 370–71
Black Power movement, 10, 569
blacks, *see* African Americans
black separatism, 10
black studies curriculums, 691
Black Voices (ed. Hill), 640
Blake, William, 185, 186
Bland, Arden, 823
Bland, Ed, 586, 822–23
Bland, James, "Carry Me Back to Old Virginny," 936–37
Bloom, Harold, 4
    Ellison's January 29, 1987, letter to, 916–17
"Blue Monday" (song), 366
"Blueprint for Negro Writing" (Wright), 129
blues, 301, 560, 649, 650, 661, 676, 789, 870–71
    concept of, in Ellison's essay "Richard Wright's Blues," 187
    Ellison's analysis of tradition, 156–57
    Hyman's take on, disappointing to Ellison, 488, 490, 491
    themes in *Invisible Man* related to, 488
"Blues People" (Ellison), 999
Blume, Peter and Ebby, 472, 474
Bohemianism, 83
Boland, Mr. (Oklahoma City), 65n
Bolton, Harold, 133
Bond, Miss, 386, 387
Bontemps, Arna, 323, 802, 830
Book Week, 999
boom-boxes, 751, 960
Boorstin, Daniel, 835n, 886
Bostonians, The (James), 359–60, 755, 838, 974
Botkin, Benjamin A., 260

Botteghe Obscure, 473, 481, 485
Boulanger, Nadia, 824, 930
Bourget, Paul, 400
Bourjaily, Tina, 643
Bourjaily, Vance, 608, 643
Bourke-White, Margaret, 106
Bowed, Hilliard, 324
Bowen, Catherine Drinker, 728
Bowen, Willard, 805–6
Boxer Rebellion, 713, 799
"Boy on a Train" (Ellison), 987
Branam, Virgil, 4, 7, 52, 271, 273, 277, 286, 374n, 417, 535, 536, 659, 687–88, 778, 842, 997
    Ellison's letters to
        January 17, 1955, 374–76
        February 23, 1956, 273, 400–406
        [Summer 1972], 659, 703–6
Brandeis University, 381n, 469, 488, 545
    Ellison offered teaching position at (1956), 431–32, 437, 441, 446, 466, 469, 538, 545–46
"Brave Words for a Startling Occasion" (Ellison), 267, 270, 995
Brawner, Lee, 745
    Ellison's letters to
        February 24, 1974, 716–19
        January 7, 1975, 729
Bread Loaf Writer's Conference (1959), 547, 554, 557, 558
Breaux, Zelia N., 40, 41, 58, 61, 73, 74, 84, 345, 689–90, 721, 744–45, 805, 901, 906, 949, 951
Breit, Harvey, 306
Brer Rabbit (trickster figure), 906, 956, 981
Brewer, Dr. (Columbus, Ohio), 417
Bridges, Henry, 905–6
Bridgman, Richard, *The Colloquial Style in America*, 937
Bridie (Guggenheim assistant), 164, 167–68
"Bright Morning Star" (Wright), 145n
Brill, Patsy, Ellison's April 25, 1963, letter to, 572, 622

Brodin, Pierre, Ellison's December 23, 1963, letter to, 629

Broki, S., 507

Brontë, Emily, *Wuthering Heights*, 861, 990

Bronx Slave Market, 128–29

Brooks, Harry, 990
Ellison's February 5, 1939, letter to, 99–101

Brooks, Van Wyck, 407, 412, 416, 437

Browder, Earl, 167, 169, 182, 185, 202

Brown, Alberta Othello "Bert" (Ralph's cousin), 344, 660, 741–42, 745, 779
Ellison's June 8, 1954, letter to, 361–63

Brown, Charles L., Ellison's April 10, 1985, letter to, 850–51

Brown, Earl, 218, 316

Brown, Harold, 688

Brown, John R., Ellison's December 26, 1984, letter to, 836–37

Brown, Leonard, 209

Brown, Lucretia Ellison (Ralph's aunt), 12, 64n, 268, 314n, 315, 689, 710, 711, 784, 969, 970–71, 977

Brown, Paul, 500

Brown, Richard K., Ellison's August 16, 1956, letter to, 449–51

Brown, Russell, 350

Brown, Sterling Allen, 136, 150n, 249, 357–58

Brown, Tom (Ralph's cousin), 64n, 65, 314n, 315, 344, 361, 362, 428, 539, 660, 689, 712, 717, 722, 727, 779, 841, 936, 970–71, 986
personal affairs of, at time of his death, 741–42

Brown & Co., 166

Browning, Alice and Charles, 185

Brown University, 744–45, 988, 1001
Ralph Ellison Festival at (1979), 662, 744, 745, 762n, 1001

Brown v. Board of Education, 4, 269–70, 360

Broyard, Anatole, 301

Brumm, Ursula, 383

Buck, Pearl, 171, 214

Buddy Bolden's Blues (Morton), 648–49

Buford, Logan (Fanny's estranged husband), 178

bullfighting, in Mexico, 131

Bunche, Ralph, 136

Bunn, Dillon, 35, 687

Burgess, Mr., Ellison's February 28, 1983, letter to, 787–88

Burgum, Edwin Berry, 186–87

Burke, Kenneth, 3, 7, 112, 203n, 209, 216, 222–23, 253n, 261–62, 446, 447, 526, 872, 899, 916, 917, 956, 959
Counter-Statement, 447
Ellison's letters to
November 23, 1945, 203–8
August 25, 1947, 230–31
November 7, 1982, 780–81
June 20, 1983, 750–51, 791–93
narrative schema of, 751
"The Rhetoric of Hitler's Battle," 116–17, 203n, 204, 917, 959

Burke, Ron, Ellison's December 10, 1982, letter to, 786–87

Burkhart, Fred, 436–37, 446

Busoni, Ferruccio, 833

Butcher, Margaret, 358, 408

Butler, Henry, 687

By Love Possessed (Cozzens), 501, 518

Byrnes, Jimmy, 454

"Cadillac Flambé" (Ellison), 733, 1001

Calder, Alexander, 407

Caldwell, Erskine, 106, 884
Ellison's September 20, 1983, letter to, 803–4

Calicutt, Harold, 406, 685n
Ellison's February 3, 1971, letter to, 685–91

Callahan, John F., 286n, 762, 812, 813
"Chaos, Complexity, and Possibility: The Historical Frequencies of Ralph Waldo Ellison," 737–39
Ellison's letters to
January 17, 1978, 737–39
November 19, 1979, 746
August 12, 1983, 5, 795–99

Callahan, John F. (*cont'd*):
  Ellison's letters to
    November 5, 1983, 806–7
    November 29, 1983, 814
    May 12, 1985, 860–67
    July 15, 1985, 869–73
    October 25, 1985, 884–86
  "Frequencies of Eloquence," 860–67
  Guggenheim applicaton of, 746, 885
  "Tradition and Innovation," 796–98
Call of the Wild, The (London), 651
Cambridge Ritualists, 410, 447
Cameron, Betty, Ellison's February 2,
  1972, letter to, 658–59, 695–97
Camp, Betsy, 325
Campbell, Joseph, 365
Campbell, Reverend, 562–63
Camus, Albert, 629, 862
  The Stranger, 407, 420
Cannon, Dr., 218–19
Cannon, Steve, 101
Cape Cod, Ellison's trip to (1953), 338,
  340
Cards of Identity (Dennis), 399
Carleton Miscellany, 762n, 1001
Carlisle, Carl, Ellison's September 9,
  1985, letter to, 875–78
Carmen (relation of Tom Brown), 741, 742
Carnegie Commission, 826
Carnegie Commission on Educational
  Television, 999
Carpentier, Alejo, *Le Partage des Eaux*
  (aka *The Last Steps*), 437–38,
  444–45
"Carry Me Back to Old Virginny"
  (Bland), 936–37
Carter, Jimmy, 896
Carver, George Washington, 206, 350,
  708
Case, James R., 569, 582
Case of Rape, A (Himes), 879–81
Cast the First Stone (Himes), 311
Catastrophe and Imagination
  (McCormick), 478
Catton, Bruce, *A Stillness at Appomattox*,
  270, 360, 472

Cayton, Horace, 7, 135, 154, 169, 171, 180,
  185, 219, 223–24, 240, 249, 251, 312,
  666n, 763
  autobiographical writings by, 600–605,
    621, 623–24
  biography of Wright planned by,
    666–67
  death of, 666–67
  Ellison's letters to
    [Spring 1957], 482–84
    July 15, 1961, 600–605
    November 2, 1962, 621
    June 4, 1963, 623–25
Cayton, Revels, Jr., Ellison's February 12,
  1970, letter to, 666–67
Céline, Louis-Ferdinand, 640
censorship, 306, 563
Centennial Review, 962
Center for Southern Culture, 751
Central High School, Little Rock, Ark.,
  integration of, 508, 510, 512, 569,
  594
Century Association, 623, 963, 999
Cerf, Bennett, 151n
Chamberlain, Wilt, 561
Chandler, Virgil, 125, 537
"Change the Joke and Slip the Yoke"
  (Ellison), 519–20, 521, 522, 997–98
"Chaos, Complexity and Possibility"
  (Callahan), 737–39
Chapin, Mary, 223
Chapman, Helen, 550
Charles, Ray, 570, 587
Cheever, John, 7, 470, 472, 474, 475, 480,
  481, 623
  Ellison's November 12, 1958, letter to,
    539–40
Cheever, Mary, 472, 474, 475, 481, 539, 623
Chevalier de l'Ordre des Arts et des
  Lettres, 1000
Cheyenne, Wyo., effect of *Invisible Man*
  on readers in, 562–63
Chicago:
  Ellison's trips with Tuskegee band to,
    35, 39, 40, 42, 62
  Ellison's trip to (1953), 325–26

Ellison's trip to (1960), 590–91

Ellisons' trip to (1992), 975–76

panel to discuss film *The Cry of Jazz* in, 586–87

see also University of Chicago

Chicago Defender, 135, 249, 310, 325

Chicago Public Library's Harold Washington Literary Award, 975–76

Chicago Tribune, 164

China, 162

Christian, Charlie, 494, 998

Ciardi, John, 474, 952

Cicero, "De Amicitia," 10, 754

City College of the City University of New York, 533, 830

civil conflict:

  race relations and potential for, 205–6

  see also riots

Civilization (Bell), 209

Civilizing the Machine (Kasson), 935–36

civil rights movement, 8, 283, 417–18, 480, 500–501, 518–19, 533–34, 544, 569–70, 826

  Cook's reports and, 454

  Faulkner's "Letter to the North" in *Life* and, 418, 433–34, 436, 439

  Montgomery, Ala., bus boycott and (1956), 274, 417, 594

  see also desegregation; integration

Civil War, 3, 276, 311, 360, 395, 436, 472, 477, 552, 553, 598, 818, 919, 958

  Aaron's *The Unwritten War* and, 715–16

"Claire Étoile du Matin" (Wright), 115

Clara (Guggenheim associate), 165–66, 167–68, 227

Clark, Eleanor, 469, 472, 474, 478, 481, 518, 997

Classen High School (Oklahoma City), 658–59, 695–97

Classical Tradition in Poetry, The (Murray), 410

Clinton, Bill and Hillary, 981

Clinton, Tenn., mob violence following school integration in (1956), 276, 457

Clipper, The, 148n, 152

Coates, Henry T., 652

Cohen, Jacob "Jerry," Ellison's November 23, 1964, letter to, 632–34

Cohn, Arthur and Elaine, 581

Cohn, David L., 139

Cole, Bill, 439

  Ellison's [Spring 1957] letter to, 484

college sit-ins (1950s), 594

Colliers, 222

Collins, Angus, Ellison's March 6, 1967, letter to, 639–40

Collins, Carvel, 334

Colloquial Style in America, The (Bridgman), 937

Colonial Williamsburg Foundation, 11, 771–72, 774, 807, 835–36, 850–51, 876, 878, 886–87, 1000

  America's historical memory and, 873

  Ellison invited to join, 874–75, 999

Colter, Cyrus, 903–4

  Ellison's November 23, 1977, letter to, 736–37

Coltrane, John, 531, 740

Columbia Records, 531–32, 931, 933

Columbia University, 322, 532–33, 581

comedy, African Americans' sense of, 960

Commentary, 301, 434n, 635n

Common Ground, 163, 994

communism, mutual antagonisms of blacks and whites and, 207–8

Communist Party of France, 222

Communist Party USA (CP), 119, 182, 221, 224, 675, 764, 765, 823, 959, 991

  Brotherhood in comparison to, 307–8

  conflicts in, described by Ellison in his letters to Wright, 169–71, 181–83, 184–85, 186–87, 188, 193–94

  Ellison's critiques of, 136, 197

  Hughes's political affiliations and, 801–3

  Invisible Man and, 307–8, 309

  leadership potential of Negroes in, 182–83, 194

Communist Party USA (CP) (*cont'd*):
liquidated in South, 202
Moscow show trials and purges of
1936–38 and, 106, 170, 185, 802
responses to Wright's *Native Son* in,
129–30, 135
Wright's troubles with, 169–71, 207–8,
219, 865–66
Complete Notebooks of Henry James, The
(eds. Edel and Powers), 908–9,
918
"Completion of Personality" interviews
(Ellison and Hersey), 750, 772
computers:
Ellison's purchases and use of, 14, 772,
786–87, 794, 798, 1001, 1002
James's style simulated by (*Jamesian
Travesty*), 755–56, 838–40
Condition of Man, The (Mumford), 165
Confidence man, first role of, 487
Confluence, 340, 996
Congaree Sketches (Tourgee), 651
Congress, U.S., 98, 102, 104, 468, 858,
877
Southern Manifesto of 1956 and, 7,
277
"Congress Jim Crow Did Not Attend, A"
(Ellison), 114, 135–36, 993
Congress pour la Liberté de la Culture
(Congress of Cultural Freedom),
455, 497, 498, 506–7, 511
Connally, Marc, 132
Connolly, Cyril, 7, 120, 230, 244n, 251,
640
Connolly, Eugene, 182
Connolly, ex-Mrs. Cyril, 311
Connolly, Marc, *Green Pastures*, 44, 47
Conrad, Joseph, 439, 670, 737
consciousness:
indignant and theoretical, 132
of necessity, 866–67
"consciousness raising," 873
conscious thought:
anger and, 731
converting wide range of experience
into, 107–8, 701

"felt experience" of being Negro
American in relation to, 204–5
Constitution (ship), 388, 390, 392, 400
Constitution, U.S., 274, 417–18, 874
Negroes' full participation in American
life and, 594
Cook, Alistair, 454
Cook, Hester, 68, 575, 806, 949
Coolidge, Calvin, 795, 798
Cooper, James Fenimore, 488
Leather Stocking Tales, 651
Copper, Alvin, 365
Coppin State Teachers College
(Baltimore), Ellison's 1954 lecture
at, 269, 356, 361
Counter-Statement (Burke), 447
"Coupla Scalped Indians, A" (Ellison),
406, 442, 575
Courier, 180
Covici, Pascal, 201
Cowley, Malcolm, 409, 415, 416, 930,
959
Cox, Dorothy, 68, 401, 851, 949
Cozzens, James Gould, *By Love
Possessed*, 501, 518
Craft of Ralph Ellison, The (O'Meally),
753, 772, 939
Crane, Hart, 439
Crane, Stephen, 584–85, 646, 728
Ellison's introduction to paperback
collection of works by, 584, 998
The Monster, 585
*The Red Badge of Courage and Four
Great Stories of Stephen Crane*
(Dell edition), 570, 998
Crime and Punishment (Dostoevsky),
990
Crisis, 192
Critical Performance, The (Hyman),
416n, 458
Cross Section, 164n, 165, 862
Cry of Jazz, The (film), 586–87
Cuban revolution of 1895, 648
Cubeta, Paul, 952
cubism, 194, 196, 678
Cuffee, Paul, 728

Cullman, Joseph, 771–72

Cultural Freedom in the Western Hemisphere conference (Mexico City; 1956), 455, 456, 459, 460–61, 462, 467, 468, 997

culture, racial approaches to, 455, 661, 683–84

Culture and Poverty (Valentine), 575–76, 641

Culture of Cities, The (Mumford), 420

Cummings, E. E., 171

Cummins, Saxe, 321–22

Daily American, 510

Daily Oklahoman, 314

Daily Worker, 6, 92n, 93, 95, 103, 128, 131, 221–22, 309, 991

Daley, Richard M., 976

Dante Alighieri, 573, 652, 680

"darky entertainer" figure or role, 487, 520

Davenport, Alton, 388

Davidson, Basil, 204, 205

Davidson, Charlie, 576

    Ellison's August 18, 1968, letter to, 576, 577–79, 642–45

    Ellison's July 10, 1971, letter to, 661–62, 692–94

Davidson, Terry, 576, 642, 692

Davis, A. I., 344

Davis, Angela, 772

Davis, Anthony, 822, 824

Davis, Arthur P., 150n, 357

Davis, B. O., Jr., 624

Davis, Ben, 131, 135, 182, 186, 194, 764, 829, 865

Davis, C., 761

Davis, Charlie, 791

Davis, Frances Brown (Ralph's cousin), 315, 344, 362

Davis, H.B.O. "Hoolie," 4

    Ellison's March 7, 1985, letter to, 842–45

Davis, Henry Bowman, 696

Davis, John, 95

Davis, Miles, 531, 661

Davis, Red, 346

Dawson, William L., 8, 35, 45, 47, 64n, 100, 288, 289, 300, 304, 305, 329, 350, 422, 756, 765, 950–51, 988, 989

    Ellison's letters to

        April 12, 1954, 355–56

        December 13, 1959, 563–64

        July 25, 1984, 831–32

        September 20, 1989, 965–66

    Negro Folk Symphony, 43, 966, 988

Days of Wrath, The (Malraux), 789

Dayton, Ohio:

    letters written by Ellison from, 6, 17, 23–24, 92–97, 163

    Ralph and his brother living in, after their mother's death (1937–38), 23–24, 93–94, 99, 101, 104, 616, 834, 846–47, 855, 889–90, 992–93

    Ralph's mother's illness and death in (1937), 6, 17, 22–24, 87–88, 90, 92–93, 100, 103–4, 616, 834, 846, 855, 923–24, 992, 996

    Ralph's mother's return to (1936), 20, 78, 80, 84, 990, 991

    Ralph's visit to (1953), 324–25

"De Amicitia" (Cicero), 10, 754

"dear folks" letters, *see* Oklahoma City

"Death of Clifton, The" (Ellison), 640

Declaration of Independence, 728

Dee, Ray, 142

"Deep Second" (Ellison), 269, 334–37

Delaney, Miss, 34

Dell editions, 570, 998

"Delta Autumn" (Faulkner), 839

Demby, William, *Beetlecreek*, 290

democracy, 797, 798

    as collectivity of individuals, 593

    Ellison's disillusionment with, 107

    "personal moral responsibility" for, 267, 398

Democracy, 734

Dennis, Neigle, *Cards of Identity*, 399

Depression, Great, 22, 77, 88–89, 125, 678, 690

Descartes, René, 183–84

desegregation:
  Ellison's essay "Tell It Like It Is, Baby" and, 7, 10, 277–79, 453n, 455, 457, 471, 472–73, 477, 485, 659, 739, 884, 997, 999
  Life series on, 457
  see also integration
Detroit, unemployed blacks recruited as strikebreakers in (1941), 143
Devlin, Dennis and Karen, 472, 474
DeVoto, Bernard, 321, 322, 410–11
Diamond, David, Ellison's March 3, 1987, letter to, 929–31
Diamond, Luna, 643
Diary from Dixie, A (ed. Woodward), 809
Dickens, Charles, 861
  A Tale of Two Cities, 651
"Did You Ever Dream Lucky?" (Ellison), 341
Diffay, Hattie, 70
Diggs, T., 317
Dillard University (New Orleans), Ellison's visit and lecture at (1954), 265, 269, 272, 345, 347, 350, 351–56, 358, 361
Dinesen, Isak, 381, 443
Dinkins, David, 978
Direction, 171, 993
Divine, Father, 224
Dixon, Richard, Ellison's September 6, 1986, letter to, 902–4
Dolben, William, Ellison's November 23, 1964, letter to, 573, 639
Donatello, 410
Dos Passos, John, 460, 468
Dostoevsky, Fyodor, 396, 557, 635, 670, 733, 737, 862, 865
  Crime and Punishment, 990
  The Gambler, 903
  The Idiot, 223, 395
  Notes from Underground, 487, 680, 862, 863–64
Douglas, Jean, 407
  Ellison's January 17, 1957, letter to, 474–75
Douglas, William O., 322

Douglass, Frederick, 728
Frederick Douglass High School (Oklahoma City), 40n, 66, 662, 685n, 691, 696, 704, 744–45, 805, 859, 986, 988
  drill team practice on grounds of, 558–59
Dowling, Eddie, 132
Doyle, Arthur Conan, *The Adventures of Sherlock Holmes*, 651
Draft Board, 154, 191
Drake, St. Clair, 251, 312n
Dream Songs, The (Berryman), 922
Dreiser, Theodore, 862
Drew, Charles, 289
drill teams:
  in Chicago parade, 610–11
  in Oklahoma City, 558–59
Drum Is a Woman, A (Ellington), 480, 489
Drye, Captain, 30, 34, 36, 61, 100, 305, 559, 831
Du Bois, W.E.B., 180, 914–15, 916
  The Souls of Black Folk, 652
Duclos, Jacques, 222
Duff, John, 976
Dumas, Alexandre, père and fils, 861, 862
Duncan, Hugh Dalziel, 972
Dunjee, Roscoe, 48n, 74, 77, 401, 538–39, 717, 745, 775, 841, 987
Dunn, Victor, 401
Dupee family (Tivoli, N.Y.), 525, 527, 528, 541, 550
Dvořák, Antonín, 871
Dyer, Lizzie, 362

East West Association, 214
Ebony, 253–55, 322
Edel, Leon, 908, 974
  Ellison's February 9, 1987, letter to, 918–20
Edge of Darkness (film), 163
Education of Black Folk (Ballard), 808
Egypt, Suez crisis and (1956), 276, 457, 470, 478
Ehrenburg, Ilya, 219

Einaudi, Giulio, 412, 420
Eisenhower, Dwight D., 468n, 475n, 478,
    479, 501, 512, 518–19
Eliot, T. S., 157, 246, 456, 473, 486, 491,
    573, 652, 740, 817, 861
    The Waste Land, 158, 320, 990
Elizabeth, Queen Mother, 448, 452, 456
Ellington, Duke, 272, 380, 389, 468–69,
    479–80, 489, 495, 501, 531–32,
    552–53, 646, 824, 871, 884
    A Drum Is a Woman, 480, 489
Ellington, Ruth, 469
Ellis, Donna, 13
Ellis, Harold, 218
Ellison, Alfred ("Big Alfred," Ralph's
    grandfather), 12, 314n, 361n, 660,
    756, 783–84, 808–10, 818, 891, 919,
    967–72, 971, 977, 986
    chapter in Ware's *Old Abbeville* about,
        12, 975, 977
    death of, 800
    Lillard's research on, 660, 709–14,
        784–85, 971–72
    lynching in Abbeville, S.C., witnessed
        by, 710–11, 800
    ownership of family property and, 711,
        784, 809, 968
    photograph of, 970, 971
    Ralph's visit with, 12, 712, 800, 970–71,
        977, 986
    in South Carolina politics, 711–12,
        783–84, 800, 848, 968, 969
    strong patriarchal control exerted by,
        711
Ellison, Belle (Ralph's aunt), 712, 971
Ellison, Eddie (Ralph's uncle), 712, 714
Ellison, Fanny McConnell (Ralph's
    second wife), 7, 185, 198, 216, 217,
    218, 223, 251, 261, 262, 268, 291,
    296, 300, 306, 315, 317, 321, 326,
    331, 332, 334, 346, 347, 354, 367,
    382, 407, 420, 431, 535, 539, 557,
    561, 563, 564, 583, 585, 591, 592,
    596, 617, 621, 623, 666, 706, 709,
    729, 744, 759, 760, 772, 794, 807n,
    827, 829, 833, 835, 850, 857, 869,
    884, 887, 907, 909, 920, 923, 934,
    951, 979, 981, 999, 1002
    Berkshires home and, 571, 574, 576,
        642–43, 882, 1000
    breakup in Taylor's relationship with
        Ralph and, 924–29
    Chicago trip of (1992), 975–76
    cigar smoking of, 613
    Colonial Williamsburg and, 874–75
    courtship and wedding of, 994, 995
    drinking of, 574, 608–9, 612–14
    Europe trip of 1954 and, 367, 374–75,
        377–78
    as Fisk graduate, 200, 317, 324, 498,
        631, 996
    gardening as interest of, 855, 856
    letters written to Wright by, on Ralph's
        behalf, 113, 224n, 262–63, 455
    at National Medal of Arts ceremony
        (1985), 857, 858, 876
    as original keeper of Ralph's flame,
        12, 13
    as photographer, 472, 479
    in preparation of manuscript for
        Ralph's second novel, 11, 548,
        1000
    Ralph's extramarital affair in Rome
        and, 8, 279–80, 281–82, 489–90,
        499, 502–4, 509, 515, 574, 997
    Ralph's letters to, 117–20, 269, 280–82,
        573–74
        October 4, 1944, 117–18, 172–73
        March 1, 1945, 118, 174–75
        March 9, 1945, 176
        March 10, 1945, 176–78
        September 17, 1947, 232–34
        September 20, 1947, 234–37
        September 21, 1947, 237–38
        September 24, 1947, 238–42
        September 29, 1947, 242–43
        October 10, 1947, 243–45
        October 13, 1947, 245–46
        July 2, 1953, 327–30
        February 23, 1954, 271–72, 349–51
        March 4, 1954, 351–53
        March 16, 1954, 272, 354–55

Ellison, Fanny McConnell (Ralph's
  second wife) (*cont'd*):
 Ralph's letters to
  September 19, 1956, 459
  September 28, 1956, 460–62
  October 6, 1956, 462–65
  October 26, 1956, 466
  August 12, 1957, 281, 498–99
  August 24, 1957, 281, 502–5
  September 20, 1957, 505–6
  September 29, 1957, 507–10
  October 9, 1957, 281–82, 513–15
  October 23, 1957, 516–17
  October 7, 1961, 605–7
  October 10, 1961, 607–10
  October 11, 1961, 610–11
  October 14, 1961, 611–15
  September 9, 1963, 626–27
 Ralph's relationship with, 111–12,
  117–18, 172–73, 224, 236, 238, 245,
  279–80, 281–82, 353, 464–65, 499,
  502–4, 505, 514–15, 516–17, 573–74,
  608–9, 997
 Roman sojourn and (1955–57), 272, 275,
  377–79, 387, 389, 393, 394, 396,
  402, 412, 415, 416, 418, 432, 434,
  440, 443, 472, 479, 489–90, 493,
  498, 500, 544, 962, 963, 996–97
 in Tivoli, N.Y., 282, 524n, 533, 540,
  542, 551, 561
 in Vermont, 189, 194, 226–27, 228, 232
 working for American Medical Center
  for Burma, 613, 626–27, 631, 826,
  998
 working with International Rescue
  Center, 826
Ellison, G. W., 785
Ellison, Harriet (Ralph's grandmother),
  710, 711–12, 818
Ellison, Henry (Ralph's distant relative),
  710
Ellison, Henry H. (brother of Ralph's
  grandfather), 784, 800
Ellison, Herbert (Ralph's brother,
  sometimes addressed as "Huck"),
  5, 6, 18, 31, 32, 42, 47, 54, 81, 86,
  89, 91, 268n, 271, 315, 400, 427,
  574, 616, 620, 631, 688, 689, 697,
  711, 714, 846–48, 884, 910, 969, 977
 birth and childhood of, 20, 64n, 695,
  720, 846–47, 854–55, 890, 942,
  985, 986
 Branam's visit to, 535
 deaths of his wife and son, 778
 "Huck" as Ralph's nickname for, 18,
  32n, 369, 651
 McGruder's charges against, 125–28
 money requested by, 210–12
 mother's illness and death and, 22,
  87–88, 93, 616, 992
 move to Dayton, Ohio (1936), 80, 991
 Murray asked to check on, 533, 536
 as person prone to jams, 113, 125–28,
  210–12
 photograph sent by, 535, 536
 Ralph and Fanny visited by (1972), 704
 Ralph's first meeting since 1938 with,
  561, 631, 999
 Ralph's letters to, 112–13
  September 4, 1933, 37
  October 11, 1933, 41
  April 29, 1936, 76
  August 5, 1937, 87–88
  March 4, 1939, 101–2
  February 6, 1940, 121–25
  February 24, 1946, 210–12
  June 5, 1953, 268, 323–26
  November 14, 1953, 343–45, 996
  August 12, 1954, 366–69
  November 12, 1955, 273, 392–94
  October 1958, 535–39
  September 18, 1979, 659–60, 741–42
  August 28, 1981, 759–60
  December 3, 1984, 835–36
  April 25, 1985, 857–58
 Ralph's May 31, 1972, letter to Passport
  Office on behalf of, 701–2
 Ralph's relationship with, 112–13, 211,
  406
 schooling of, 56, 62, 68, 69
Ellison, Ida (Ralph's mother), *see* Bell,
  Ida

Ellison, Janie (Ralph's aunt), 711

Ellison, Jim (Ralph's uncle), 12, 711, 712, 713–14, 971

Ellison, Lewis Alfred (Ralph's father), 3, 12, 84, 85, 113, 314n, 315, 324, 337, 342, 343, 361n, 429, 486, 575, 618, 630, 660, 702, 710, 711, 712, 714, 783, 784, 808, 812, 818, 970, 985–86

  in Abbeville, S.C., 799

  as construction foreman, 713, 799, 900, 936

  death of, 64n, 680, 702, 713, 752, 763, 922, 986

  Ida's first meeting with, 713

  military service of, 713, 799

  restaurant venture of, 713, 799

  supposed nickname of, 941–42

Ellison, Louisa (1836–1916, "Aunt Lou"), 785

Ellison, Lucy, 785

Ellison, Mary Ann, 785

Ellison, Mrs. Herbert (Ralph's sister-in-law), 394

Ellison, Ralph:

  addresses given by

    "Brave Words for a Startling Occasion," 267, 270, 995

    "Hidden Name and Complex Fate," 999

    for opening of Homemaking Institute at Bennett College (1953), 267–68, 313, 315, 316, 317–20, 323

  alleged to have expatriated to Rome, 539, 544–45

  annoyed by biographical inaccuracies and distortions, 743, 753, 765, 939–44, 952

  artist heroes of, 861–62

  artistic sensibility of, 21, 82–83, 676, 810–11

  as aspiring musician, 5, 86, 304–5

    see also Tuskegee Institute—Ellison's music studies at

  autobiographical concerns and, 305, 539, 602–3, 658–59

  awards and fellowships received by

    Chevalier de l'Ordre des Arts et des Lettres, 1000

    Chicago Public Library's Harold Washington Literary Award, 975–76

    National Book Award, 267, 270, 321, 323, 347–48, 407, 571, 586, 588, 995

    National Medal of Arts, 857–58, 876–78, 1002

    Presidential Medal of Freedom, 1000

    Prix de Rome, 400, 439n, 544, 586, 588, 996; see also American Academy in Rome, Ellison's Prix de Rome fellowship at

    Rockefeller Foundation fellowship, 636n

    Julius Rosenwald Fund fellowship, 203, 213–14, 586, 588, 995

  Berkshires home of, *see* Plainfield, Mass., Ellisons' summer home in

  bibliographies of works, 639–40

  birth of, 3, 12, 423n, 702, 985

  book of criticism considered by, 446

  as book reviewer, 93n, 95n, 187, 189, 266, 286–87, 301, 879, 991, 993, 994, 999

  both skilled and unskilled readers important to, 867–69

  boyhood in Oklahoma City, 3, 4, 12, 17, 143–46, 344–45, 695–97, 702, 805–6, 854–55, 942, 985–88, 996

  carbon copies of letters made by, 13, 130

  on college lecture circuit, 265, 269, 271–72, 378, 546–47, 569, 995–96; *see also specific colleges*

  college teaching positions, 657

    offered and declined in 1956 (Bennington and Brandeis), 431–32, 436–37, 441, 446, 466, 469, 538, 545–46

    see also Bard College; New York University; Rutgers University; University of Chicago

  computers purchased and used by, 14, 772, 786–87, 794, 798, 1001, 1002

Ellison, Ralph (*cont'd*):
on conscious thought, 107, 699
contrast between fictional and
    nonfictional prose of, 187–88
cooking and other household tasks
    performed by, 942–43
death of, 749, 1002
dogs of
    Red and Bobbins, 119–20, 226–27,
        232, 233, 235, 237, 239, 240, 241,
        242, 243, 244, 246
    Tuckatarby (Labrador pup), 570,
        585, 588, 608, 615, 980–81
essays written by, 10–11, 266, 729, 763,
    835, 876, 878, 893, 1001
    "The Art of Romare Bearden," 676,
        677–78, 1000
    "As the Spirit Moves Mahalia,"
        529–30, 998
    "Change the Joke and Slip the
        Yoke," 519–20, 521, 522, 997–98
    collections, *see Going to the
        Territory*; *Shadow and Act*
    "An Extravagance of Laughter," 10,
        11, 884, 903, 1002
    "February," 996
    "Flamenco," 996
    foreword to Forrest's *There Is a
        Tree More Ancient than Eden*, 658,
        705–6, 736–37
    "Going to the Territory," 10, 745, 884
    "The Golden Age, Time Past," 529,
        530–31, 536
    "Harlem Is Nowhere," 248, 995
    "Homage to Duke Ellington on His
        Birthday," 884
    "If the Twain Shall Meet," 884
    "Indivisible Man" (in collaboration
        with McPherson), 10–11, 658,
        659n, 685–86, 1000
    introduction for *Romare Bearden:
        Paintings and Projections*
        catalogue, 676, 677–78, 1000
    "The Little Man at Chehaw Station,"
        10, 884, 989–90, 1001
    "Living with Music," 272, 391, 997

    "The Myth of the Flawed White
        Southerner," 884
    notebooks with ideas for, 198
    "The Novel as a Function of
        American Democracy," 884
    "On Becoming a Writer," 635
    "On Being the Target of
        Discrimination," 19, 1002
    "On Initiation Rites and Power," 884
    "Perspective of Literature," 746, 884
    "A Portrait of Inman Page," 884
    "Remembering Richard Wright,"
        791, 884
    "Richard Wright's Blues," 157n, 164,
        186, 187, 189, 191–92, 201, 204, 206,
        669, 886, 995
    "Society, Morality and the Novel,"
        10, 277, 280, 477, 480, 481, 485,
        522n, 584, 738, 884
    "Stepchild Fantasy," 219
    "Stephen Crane and the Mainstream
        of American Fiction," 584, 998
    "Tell It Like It Is, Baby," 7, 10,
        277–79, 453n, 455, 457, 471,
        472–73, 477, 485, 659, 739, 884,
        997, 999
    "That Same Pain, That Same
        Pleasure," 696
    "Twentieth-Century Fiction and
        the Black Mask of Humanity"
        (Ellison), 340, 996
    "What America Would Be Like
        Without Blacks," 10, 884, 1000
    "What These Children Are Like,"
        884
    "The World and the Jug," 10, 998
    "A World of Difference," 537n
ethics of friendships of, 754
European travels (1954), 365, 367,
    374–75, 385, 714
European travels with Murrays (1956),
    418, 419, 436, 440–41, 443–44, 447,
    448–49, 457, 997
extramarital affair of, 8, 279–80,
    281–82, 481–82, 489–90, 499,
    502–4, 509, 515, 574, 997

first marriage of, *see* Poindexter, Rose

fishing enjoyed by, 216, 218, 361–62

French influences on writing of, 629, 789–90

gardening as interest of, 855–56

geography's impact on, 17

high school girlfriend of, *see* Steveson, Vivian

horses, pony, and goat in life of, 643–44, 661, 828

hunting enjoyed by, 93, 97, 101, 104, 244, 245, 247, 283, 343, 348, 361, 535, 540, 542, 582, 846–47, 987

illness and death of, 749, 1002

jaundice attack and (1940), 141

jobs held by, 988, 991

Key West home of, *see* Key West, Fla., Ellisons' conch house in

lecture fee of, 360

letters of reference or recommendation written by, 657, 697–700, 736–37, 770–71, 810–11, 836–37

literary influences on, 629, 651–53, 680–81, 789–90, 861–62

   question of Wright's influence, 248–49, 661, 671, 680–82, 860–67

as merchant marine, 7, 111, 118–19, 165, 167, 173–78, 191, 213, 252, 266, 702n, 734–35, 797–98, 823, 829, 994, 995

musical interests of, 355–56, 365–66, 380, 389, 468–69, 479–80, 489, 494–96, 552–53, 560, 586–87, 644–45, 649–50, 696, 796, 797, 824, 833–34, 861, 862, 870–71, 929–31, 932–33, 946, 965–66, 987–90; *see also* sound systems

Negro writers and subjects promoted by, 136–37, 150

   see also Negro Quarterly

on pain and pleasure of writing novels, 567–68

patriotism of, 5, 797–98, 870

philosophical thinking and, 183–84

as photographer, 8, 235, 240, 242, 287, 413–14, 418–19, 421, 422, 431,

432–33, 451, 456–57, 468, 479, 494, 500, 511, 512, 514, 518, 534–35, 627, 644, 920

political thinking of, 5, 22, 24, 88–89, 104, 105–8, 114, 129–30, 136–37, 139–40, 146, 162, 188, 249–51

preoccupation with history, 737–39

problem of identity explored by, 371–72

publishers interested in doing novel with (1944), 166, 167, 169, 171

radical Marxist politics and, 169–71, 181–83, 184–85, 186–87, 197, 202, 207–8, 222, 224, 251, 273, 307–8, 309, 991–92

reflecting on accomplishments in life, 426–27

religious matters and, 59, 200, 319, 584–85, 698, 732

remarriage of, 7, 224, 994, 995

   see also Ellison, Fanny McConnell

science and technology as interests of, 8, 796–97

as sculpture student, 6, 21, 72, 76, 79–83, 428, 743, 991

second novel by, 8–11, 267, 269, 270, 282, 283, 314, 315, 320, 326, 338, 356, 360, 361, 364, 367, 375, 378, 381, 386, 446, 523, 545, 571, 583–84, 635n, 637, 638, 650, 657, 729, 749, 750–52, 756, 792–93, 798, 835, 879, 893, 934, 982n

   "And Hickman Arrives" excerpt from, published in *Noble Savage*, 9, 267, 283, 556, 557, 567, 568, 577, 581, 583, 662, 998

   auspicious auguries for, 567

   "Backwacking" offshoot from, 1001

   "Bliss's Birth" chapter of, 999

   "Cadillac Flambée" excerpt from, 733, 1001

   Cliofus character in, 273, 379

   conflict between Ellison's sense of responsibility for *the* American novel and, 277

   early drafts found after Ellison's death, 269

Ellison, Ralph (*cont'd*):
  second novel by
    Ellison's ambivalence and, 567–68, 569, 577–81
    Ellison's association with Hickman character in, 750
    Ellison's outreach to folks and places of Oklahoma and, 267, 268–69, 271, 273, 302, 314, 315, 317, 321, 330–37, 339, 371–72, 996
    Ellison's reading from, at Library of Congress (1983), 1001–2
    Ellison's work in Rome on, 8, 273, 277–79, 413, 435, 447–48, 453, 472, 477, 485, 490, 997
    Ellison's work in Tivoli on, 526, 533, 536, 538, 547, 548–49, 551, 554–56
    evasion of identity as theme of, 270, 271, 360
    files transferred to IBM computer, 1002
    first public reading from, 551
    first references to, 291, 292, 294, 302
    Guggenheim application and, 271, 371–72, 996
    "Hickman in Oklahoma" sequence of, 1002
    "Hickman in Washington, D.C." sequence of, 1002
    "It Always Breaks Out" excerpt from, 998
    Juneteenth and, 9, 986
    "Juneteenth" excerpt from, 577, 662, 999
    Kennedy assassination and, 998–99
    "Night-Talk" excerpt from, 576–77, 662, 1000
    as novel of ideas, 271
    portion of, destroyed by fire at Ellisons' Berkshires home (1967), 9–10, 571, 575–76, 641, 642–43, 650, 657, 704, 709, 1000
    Random House and, 1000, 1001
    "Rockmore" segment of, 1002
    sections of, sent in letter to Branam (February 23, 1956), 402–5
    "A Song of Innocence" excerpt from, 1000
    Statement of Plan for, 371–72, 996
    Three Days Before the Shooting . . . and, 9, 379n, 662
  serving on boards and commissions, 826, 873–75
    Bi-centennial Commission, 873–74
    Kennedy Center, 826, 858, 877
    National Council on the Arts, 805, 826, 858, 877
    see also Colonial Williamsburg Foundation
  short stories written by, 639–40, 645, 658, 694–95, 695, 729, 831, 992–93
    "Afternoon," 640
    "Boy on a Train," 987
    collected in *Flying Home and Other Stories*, 163n, 685n, 734n
    "A Coupla Scalped Indians," 406, 442, 575
    "The Death of Clifton," 640
    "Flying Home," 164, 477, 504, 695, 862, 994
    French publication of collection, 684–85
    "Hymie's Bull," 6, 93n, 991
    "In a Strange Country," 164, 166, 640, 657, 734–35, 994
    "King of the Bingo Game," 695, 865, 994
    "Out of the Hospital and Under the Bar," 611n, 640
    "Slick Gonna Learn," 993
    "A Storm of Blizzard Proportions," 994
    "That I Had the Wings," 163, 994
  South Carolina ancestry of, *see* Abbeville, S.C.; South Carolina
  story about Randolph's paternity of, 429
  on symbolic action of manners, 957–58
  tonsillitis attack and (1937), 78, 86n, 87, 100n, 103

trumpet (or cornet) played by, 6, 23, 30, 31, 34, 36, 38, 39, 52, 53, 90, 100, 559, 696, 805
"Uncle Tom" allegations and, 1000
unfinished novella by ("Slick"), 159n, 992, 993
unpublished manuscripts read and critiqued by, 658, 893–99, 911–14
  Babb's *Whose Names Were Unknown*, 149–50, 151, 152–54
  Callahan's writings on *Invisible Man*, 860–67, 869–73
  Cayton's autobiography, 600–605
  Mallan's poem, 155–58
  Taylor's script, 252–57
unpublished memoir by (*Leaving the Territory*), 427, 575, 754n
Vermont sojourns of, *see* Vermont
"white appeasement" allegation and, 658, 668
in WPA Federal Writers' Project, 24, 98, 101–2, 104, 137n, 754, 823, 825, 855, 877, 902, 993
on writer's art, 868
writing as act of salvation for, 114, 144–46
writing career launched by, 5, 6, 24, 25, 98
Ellison, Rev. William (Lewis's cousin), 710, 712, 714
Ellison, Robert H. (Ralph's uncle), 712, 714, 808
Ellison, William (Alfred's brother), 977
Ellison, William, family of South Carolina (presumed antebellum kin of Ralph), 782–83, 785, 891
Ellison family:
  Christmas traditions of, 712
  Lillard's research on history of, 660, 709–14, 784–85, 971–72
  pride and stubbornness ascribed to, 714
  South Carolina past of, 710, 711–12, 713–14, 782–84, 808–9, 851–52, 919, 967–72, 977
  transfers of property ownership in, 711, 713–14, 784, 968

Ralph Ellison Festival, Brown University (1979), 662, 762n, 775, 776, 1001
Ralph Ellison Library (Oklahoma City), 11, 716–19, 729, 745, 806, 910, 1001
Ellison Papers (Library of Congress), 13
Emancipation Proclamation, 919, 931
Embree, Edwin, 624
Emerson, Ralph Waldo, 486, 728, 818–19, 821
Emmanuel, Pierre, 334
emotional control, Negro cultural expression and, 677
Encounter, 279, 396, 453, 455, 472, 485
Engle, Paul, 7, 164, 581, 582
  Ellison's letters to
    April 10, 1955, 376–79
    April 4, 1960, 588–89
English, Maurice, 641
Enlightenment, 679
"eroticism" of Negro expression, 669
Erskine, Albert, 225, 229, 258, 292–93, 294, 297, 302, 359, 411n, 470, 714, 765, 962, 965, 979, 995
  Ellison's March 1, 1956, letter to, 411–13
  final work on *Invisible Man* and, 292–93
  Murray's "Jack the Bear" given to, 299–300
Escudero, Vicente, 930, 996
Eskridge, Chauncey, 321
Espy, Williard, Ellison's June 5, 1991, letter to, 972
Esquire, 528, 532, 533, 554, 879
  Ellison's piece on Minton's Playhouse for, 529, 530–31, 536
  Ellison's piece on New York City for, 570, 586
  Iowa conference and (1960), 561, 569, 581, 586, 588
"Ethics of Living Jim Crow" (Wright), 181
Eubanks (good friend at Tuskegee and later in New York), 318, 347, 354, 362–63
"Everybody's Protest Novel" (Baldwin), 291, 669
existentialism, 183–84, 320, 789–90

Existential Theater, 183
expatriation:
  Ellison's assumed exile in Rome and,
    539, 544–45
  of Negro Americans, reasons for, 545
"extended lie," question of, 337
"Extravagance of Laughter, An"
    (Ellison), 10, 11, 884, 903, 1002

Fabre, Michel, 11, 666, 812
  Ellison's letters to
    July 15, 1970, 684–85
    March 3, 1982, 752–53, 762–65
    June 7, 1983, 790–91
    January 12, 1989, 754, 954–55
    "From *Native Son* to *Invisible Man*,"
      762n
  as Wright's biographer, 685, 752–53
Farewell to Arms, A (Hemingway), 192–93
Farr, Tommy, 23, 90
fascism, 139, 143, 204
Faubus, Orville, 512n
Faulkner, William, 279, 365, 395, 435,
    473, 487, 490, 545, 557, 675, 707,
    708, 712, 716, 751, 797, 798, 913,
    959, 974
  civil rights movement and ("Letter to
    the North" in *Life*), 418, 433–34,
    436, 439
  "Delta Autumn," 839
  Ellison's analysis of writing style of,
    240–41, 243
  Ellison's February 22, 1957, letter to,
    475–76
  Ellison's first meeting with, 321–22
  Ellison's imagined reenactment of Civil
    War by Hemingway and, 276, 436
  Go Down, Moses, 675
  The Hamlet, 458, 675
  Intruder in the Dust, 290–91, 995
  Notes on a Horsethief, 297
  "Old Man," 120
  The Sound and the Fury, 365, 395, 585
  The Town, 480, 490, 494
  The Unvanquished, 561
Faulkner Conference (1987), 899–900

"February" (Ellison), 996
Federal Writers' Project, *see* Works
    Progress Administration
Fenton, Charles, 477
Fergusson, Francis, *Idea of a Theater*,
    290
Ferrer, Jose, 857, 876
Ferrier, Kathleen, 350
Ferris, Bill, 751
  Ellison's April 16, 1986, letter to,
    899–900
Fiedler, Leslie, 279, 473
Field of Vision, The (Morris), 458, 481
Fields, Charlie, 368, 426
Fifties, The (Wilson), 918, 920
filibuster rules, 307–8
Filson, Leslie, 704
Fine Clothes to the Jew (Hughes), 652
Finley, Gravelly, 401, 426, 537, 608, 619,
    760
  Ellison visited in Rome by, 494–95,
    498
Finley, Saretta Slaughter, 64n, 400–401,
    427, 537, 608, 619, 759, 760, 888
  Ellison visited in Rome by, 494–95,
    498
First Amendment, 667n
Fisk University (Nashville), 44, 53–54,
    323, 376, 495, 631
  Ellison's lecture at (1953), 265, 314, 316,
    321, 323, 324, 996
  as Fanny's alma mater, 200, 317, 324,
    498, 631, 996
Fitzgerald, F. Scott, 477, 494, 528, 553,
    646, 738, 739, 799
  The Great Gatsby, 751, 895, 897–98
"Flamenco" (Ellison), 996
Flaubert, Gustave, *Madame Bovary*, 196,
    480, 490, 629
flawed fictional characters, Ellison on,
    880–81
Flood, Julius, 345, 346
"Flying Home" (Ellison), 164, 477, 504,
    695, 862, 994
Flying Home and Other Stories (Ellison),
    163n, 685n, 734n

folk forms and folklore, 679, 871
  Hyman's essay on, 259–61
  Hyman's lecture on Negro writing and,
    486–88, 490–92, 519–20, 521
  influence of, on literature, 116, 259n,
    486
  songs and, 261
  see also African American folk tradition
Ford, Ford Maddox, 419, 894
Ford, Harry, 7, 300, 419, 437, 447
  Ellison's letters to
    October 23, 1955, 386n, 391–92
    March 1956, 406–11
    May 15, 1956, 438–40
    January 17, 1957, 278–79, 471–73
Ford, James W., 185, 194
Ford, Nick Aaron, 594
Ford Foundation, 588
Forest of Tigers, A (Shaplen), 433, 438–39
Forrest, Leon, 657
  There Is a Tree More Ancient than
    Eden, 658, 705–6, 736–37
Fortune, 180–81
'48, The Magazine of the Year, 120,
    243–44, 247, 248, 252n, 257–58,
    640, 789, 995
For Whom the Bell Tolls (Hemingway),
    433, 438, 675
Foster, Luther H., Jr., 333–34, 347, 349,
    352, 353, 364, 390, 422, 480, 519,
    625
Foster, Vera, 334, 349–50, 352
Foster, William Z., 185, 202
foundation grants, remarks about,
    attributed to Ellison, 586, 588
Fowler, Gene, 554
Foxes of Harrow, The (Yerby), 682n
France:
  Communist Party of, 222
  Ellison aboard merchant marine ship
    docked in Rouen, 111, 118–19,
    176–78, 196, 213, 252, 995
  Ellison's description of landscapes in,
    176
  Ellison's rejection of culture of, 396–97
  existentialism in, 183–84

  literary developments in, 202, 220, 221
  rich culture of, 220
  source of Ellison's fascination with, 955
  theater during occupaton of, 183
  Wright expatriated to, 113, 217, 219,
    221–22, 225, 310–11
France Against Herself (Leuthy), 396–97,
    433
Frank, Joseph, Ellison's November 23,
    1964, letter to, 572–73, 634–37
Frankenthaler, Helen, 463
Frankfurt, PEN International Congress
    in (1959), 554, 557, 560, 998
Frankle, Raymond, 932
Franklin, Benjamin, 487, 490
Franklin, John Hope, 358
Frank's Restaurant (Harlem), 994
Frazier, E. Franklin, 136, 192, 197, 200,
    357, 649
Frazier, George, 692
Freedmen, 270, 360, 977
Freeman, Anne, 504
Free World, 225
"Frequencies of Eloquence" (Callahan),
    860–67
Freud, Sigmund, 204, 447, 573, 732, 805,
    916
Fromm, Erich, 209
"From Native Son to Invisible Man"
    (Fabre), 762n
From Ritual to Romance (Weston), 216
frontiersmen, Americans as, 733
Frost, Robert, 558, 762
Fruttero, Carlo, 412, 420n
Fulbright Program, 448, 482
"Funky-Butt" (song), 649

"G. I. Jive" (song), 168
Gaddis, William, 591
Gaines, Ernest J., 708
Galk (Stern), 591
Gallimard, 302, 312
Gambler, The (Dostoevsky), 903
Garlin, Ernier, 129
Garson, Paul, 753, 939
Garvey, Marcus, 186, 681

Gary, Ind., Ellisons' brief stay in (1921), 575, 616, 617–18, 949, 986

Gates, Henry Louis, Jr., 11
  Ellison's February 2, 1984, letter to, 755, 822–24

Gauss, Dean Christian, 494

George III, King, 728

"German Ideology and The Holy Family" (Marx), 132

Germany, PEN International Congress in (1959), 554, 557, 560, 998

Gibson, Althea, 457, 561

Gibson, Richard, 293–94
  "Amid the Alien Corn," 544–45

Giddings, Edgar ("Tackhead"), 688, 778

Gide, André, 220, 242, 293–94, 629
  The Immoralist, 407, 420
  Journals, 458

Gill, Brendan, 473, 482

Gillis, Don, 380

Gissen, Max, 521, 546

Go Down, Moses (Faulkner), 675

God That Failed, The (Wright), 865–66

Gogol, Nikolai, 557

Going to the Territory (Ellison), 11, 481, 751, 884, 933, 1002
  publication and reviews of, 902–4, 906, 907
  Random House's advance for, 1001
  selection of essays for, 884–85

"Going to the Territory" (Ellison), 10, 745, 884

Gold, Herbert, 477, 485

Gold, Mike, 138, 140

"Golden Age, Time Past, The" (Ellison), 529, 530–31, 536

Golden Day, The (Mumford), 817–18

Golden Treasure of Poetry and Song, The (ed. Coates), 652

Goldfrank, Walter, Ellison's [December 1960?] letter to, 592–95

Goldin, Meta and Leon, 481

Gollantz, 312

Gordon, Caroline, 390
  The Malefactors, 439–40

Gorky, Maxim, 129, 862
  Reminiscences of Tolstoi, Chekhov and Andreyev, 223

Goshal, Kumar, 165

Go Tell It on the Mountain (Baldwin), 312, 681

Gouffe, The (Maass), 596

Gouldner, Alvin W., Ellison's January 19, 1953, letter to, 307–8

Graham, Billy, 396

Graham, Martha, 857, 877

Graham, Shirley, 170

Grainger, Percy, 833

Granger, Lester, 825, 827

Grapes of Wrath, The (Steinbeck), 107, 151n, 153, 672, 675

Gray, Walter, 716–17

Great Depression, 22, 77, 88–89, 125, 678

Great Gatsby, The (Fitzgerald), 751, 895, 897–98

Great Migration, 308, 891–92

Green, Ashbel, Ellison's August 31, 1973, letter to, 715–16

Green, Paul, 142n

Greenberg, Clement, 348

Green Pastures (Connolly), 44, 47

Greensboro, N.C.:
  Ellison's visit to (1953), 316–20, 323–24
  see also Bennett College

Greenwich Village, New York, attacks on Negroes in (1940s), 221

Gregory, Dick, 603

Grey, Walter, Ellison's November 28, 1986, letter to, 909–11

Griffith, Thomas, Ellison's May 12, 1970, letter to, 667–76

Grinnell College (Iowa), Ellison and King in panel discussion at (1967), 979–80, 981, 1000

Grossner, Maurice, *The Painter's Eye*, 442

Guggenheimer, Ida, 7, 112, 164n, 169–70, 177, 179, 182, 197, 219, 235, 240, 243, 245, 306n, 307, 994
  Ellison's letters to, 119
  June 26, 1944, 164–66
  July 13, 1944, 166–68

[March 1945], 173
[August 1945], 188–89
August 13, 1945, 190–91
August 14, 1945, 191–92
August 25, 1945, 199–200
August 16, 1947, 226–27
October 21, 1955, 273, 385–87
Ellison's relationship with, 119, 164, 273, 386
Invisible Man dedicated to, 112, 119
show trials and purges of 1936–38 and, 170, 185
Vermont cottage made available to Ellison by (1947), 119, 226–27
Guggenheim Fellowship, 105, 291, 588, 621, 624, 701, 746, 885, 996
Ellison's Statement of Plan in his application for, 271, 371–72, 996
Guines' Captive Mind (Wypher), 209
Guiney, David, 79

Haas, Robert, 226
Hadzi, Dimitri, 414, 506, 508, 513–14
Ellison's April 14, 1958, letter to, 523–24
Hahn, Walter, 423
Haile Selassie, Emperor of Ethiopia, 735
Haithe, Ella, 305
Haldeman-Julius Publications, 728
Halloran, William F., Ellison's February 17, 1972, letter to, 697–700
Hamilton, Chico, 469, 531
Hamilton, Gerald, 300
Hamilton College (Clinton, N.Y.), 323, 553–54, 556–57
Ellison's talk at (1959), 553, 556
Hamlet, The (Faulkner), 458, 675
Hamlin, Eva, 215, 743
Hammett, Dashiell, 880
Hammond, John, 219
Handy, W. C., 834
Beale Street Blues, 832, 833
Hangsaman (Jackson), 292
Hardy, Thomas, *Jude the Obscure*, 990
Harlem, 17, 197, 230, 827
Ellison's first days in, 6, 991
as Ellison's home, 111–12

Ellison's observations on details of life in (1937), 22, 23, 89–90
folks of, as source for Ellison's folk songs and stories, 993
housing for Negroes in, 135, 137
LaFargue Clinic in, 212–13, 218, 248
responses to Wright's *Native Son* in, 114, 129
riots in (1943), 138n, 994
street violence in summer of 1944 in, 167
see also New York
"Harlem Is Nowhere" (Ellison), 248, 995
Harlem Renaissance, 801
Harlem YMCA, Ellison's encounter with Hughes at (1936), 6, 21, 79n, 80, 812, 830, 991
Harper, Michael, 11, 733, 738, 739, 745, 746, 798, 807, 885, 1001
Ellison's letters to
September 3, 1981, 760–62
April 30, 1982, 771–73
November 24 & 25, 1983, 811–13, 814
Harper, Peck, 289
Harper, Toy, 311
Harper's, 197, 671–72
Harpers (publishing house), 143
Harper's Bazaar, 240
Harris, Joel Chandler, 708
Harris, Miss (Oklahoma City friend), 62, 64, 68
Harris, Roy, 854, 930
Harrison, Hazel, 20, 21, 68, 69, 82, 356, 765, 831, 832, 833, 989–90
Ellison's letters to
October 23, 1936, 21, 82–83
May 7, 1952, 304–5
Harrison, Jane, 216
Themis, 419
Harvard University, 1001
conference on the American novel at (1953), 269, 334, 337, 338, 340, 357, 996
"Rinehart" call to riot at, 649
Harvey, Bill, 44
Hauser, John, 317, 318

Hawkins, Coleman, 988
Hawthorne, Nathaniel, 681, 817
  "My Kinsman, Major Molineux," 739
Hayes, Harold, 532
Hayes, Roland, 930
Hayes (African American poet), Ellison's
    April 22, 1960, letter to, 572,
    589–90
Hayes-Tilden Compromise, 969
Haygood, Harry, 224
Haygood, William C., Ellison's April 22,
    1946, letter to, 213–14
Healy, Arthur, 547
Hebestreit, Ludwig, 67, 696, 987–88
Hegel, George Wilhelm Friedrich, 132,
    133
Heider, 202, 209
Heif, Alexis, 472
Heisserman, Arthur, 613
Hemingway, Ernest, 108, 131, 290, 348,
    381, 457, 477, 478, 481, 487, 488,
    490, 528, 545, 553, 584, 585, 675,
    755, 789, 834, 839, 860, 861, 913,
    973
  Ellison's imagined reenactment of Civil
    War by Faulkner and, 276, 436
  A Farewell to Arms, 192–93
  For Whom the Bell Tolls, 433, 438, 675
  To Have and Have Not, 95, 675, 707–8
Henderson the Rain King (Bellow),
    546–47, 549, 637
Hentoff, Nat, 586
Herald-Tribune, 476, 634–35
Herald Tribune Book Week Poll, 673, 674
Herndon, Angelo, 129, 154, 160, 162,
    224–25, 823, 829, 865, 880, 993–94
Hero, The (Raglan), 407, 420
Hersey, John, 409, 439, 979, 1001
  "Completion of Personality"
    interviews with Ellison, 750, 772
  Ellison's letters to
    June 20, 1983, 793–94
    April 24, 1989, 959
  A Single Pebble, 437, 438, 439
Herskovits, Melville, 288, 486
Herzog (Bellow), 637

Hettie (Oklahoma City friend), 37, 428,
    429
Hewitt, Mary, 226
Hicks, Granville, 167, 314, 522
  The Living Novel, 277, 280, 477, 480,
    481, 485, 521–22
Hicks, Matt, 100
"Hidden Name and Complex Fate"
    (Ellison), 999
Hief, Alexie, 474
Higginson, Thomas Wentworth, 165
Higgs, Michele, Ellison's October 19,
    1985, letter to, 879–81
High Fidelity, 272, 391
Hill, Herbert, 611, 640
Hills, Rust, 588
Himes, Chester B., 249–51, 293, 311–12,
    464, 483, 879–81
  A Case of Rape, 879–81
  Cast the First Stone, 311
  If He Hollers Let Him Go, 249
  The Lonely Crusade, 249–51, 311
Hines, Odette Harper, Ellison's letters to:
    March 29, 1984, 754–55, 825–27
    April 23, 1984, 828–31
history and historians:
  Bi-centennial Commission and, 873–74
  Callahan's essay on Ellison's
    preoccupation with, 737–39
  Colonial Williamsburg's mission and,
    873
  Ellison on, 809
Hitler, Adolf, 105, 138, 139, 140, 221
  Burke "The Rhetoric of Hitler's Battle"
    and, 116–17, 203n, 204, 917, 959
Hodges, Johnny, 560
Hoffa, Jimmy, 534
Hoffman, Ted, 525–27, 528
Holiday, Billie, 531
Holloway, Hester, 4
  Ellison's November 28, 1961, letter to,
    574–75, 616–20
Hollywood, 394–95
Holmes, Eugene, 115, 136, 186–87, 193, 872
"Homage to Duke Ellington on His
    Birthday" (Ellison), 884

homosexuality, 754
  and break in Ellisons' friendship with
    Taylor, 924–25, 926, 928
Hong Kong:
  Ellison's impressions of, 509–10
  Ellison's trip to (1957), 505, 507–8, 510,
    511, 512, 514, 515, 518
Hoover, Herbert, 185
Hoover, J. Edgar, 813, 814
Hope, John, 254
Horizon, 186, 193, 202, 251
  excerpt from *Invisible Man* published
    in, 7, 115, 120, 231, 236, 244, 247,
    248, 640, 789, 995
Horne, Lena, 779
Horney, Karen, *Self-Analysis*, 148
A. C. Horn Paint Company, 21, 86, 103,
  991
Horns of Plenty, 959
Horse Soldiers (film), 561
Hoskins, William, 305, 778
Housman, John, 137–38, 139, 142n
Howard, Marie Toynet, 24, 96n, 990
  Ellison's December 16, 1937, letter to,
    96–97
Howard University (Washington, D.C.),
  393
  Ellison's visit and lecture at (1954),
    269, 347, 357–58, 361
Howard University Press, Himes's *A
  Case of Rape* and, 879–81
Howe, Irving, 359, 469, 635, 670–71, 673,
  679, 680, 862
Hudson, 261–62, 583, 588
Hue and Cry (McPherson), 574, 645–46
Hughes, Langston, 85–86, 88, 106, 112,
  137, 293, 301, 311, 326, 339, 461, 537,
  635, 743, 803, 830, 861, 953, 991, 993
  The Big Sea, 878–79
  Ellison's brief encounter at Tuskegee
    with, 21
  Ellison's first encounter in New York
    with (1936), 6, 21, 79n, 80, 812,
    830, 991
  Ellison's letters to
    July 17, 1936, 21, 79

January 20, 1939, 24, 98–99
December 11, 1942, 154
August 25, 1947, 231–32
Fine Clothes to the Jew, 652
Herbert Ellison's eye injury and, 210
I Wonder as I Wander, 879
political affiliations of, 801–3
psychoanalysis of Ellison in
  autobiography of, 483
St. Louis Woman, 98
sexuality of, 925
"The Weary Blues," 231n, 652
Langston Hughes Festival (1984), 830
Humboldt, Charles, 251
Humelsine, Carl and Mary, Ellison's
  September 6, 1985, letter to, 873–75
Humeslead, Helen, 649
Hunt, John, 459
  Ellison's letters to
    April 23, 1957, 485–86
    June 12, 1957, 492–93
    July 31, 1957, 497
    September 27, 1957, 506–7
Hyman, Stanley Edgar, 3, 7, 112, 179n,
  207, 230, 231, 277, 292, 334, 337,
  370, 382, 409, 420, 445, 472, 573,
  637, 648, 917, 933, 994, 996, 998
  The Armed Vision, 407, 416n, 420
  The Critical Performance, 416n, 458
  death of, 661, 1000
  Ellison's lectures at Bennington and,
    116n, 198, 200, 201, 208, 214, 313–14
  Ellison's letters to, 116
    June 17, 1945, 179
    September 18, 1945, 200–203
    December 12, 1945, 209–10
    June 20, 1946, 216–17
    June 17, 1947, 225–26
    August 13, 1948, 7, 258–62
    April 1, 1953, 313–14
    July 1, 1954, 363–64
    June 22, 1956, 278, 446–48
    May 27, 1957, 486–88
    March 9, 1958, 522–23
    March 10, 1961, 571, 595–96
    May 29, 1970, 660–61, 676–84

Hyman, Stanley Edgar (*cont'd*):
  Ellison's relationship with, 116
  essay on Oklahoma Territory, 931–32
  essay on use of folklore in literature,
    259–61
  lecture on Negro writing and folk
    tradition, 486–88, 490–92, 519–20,
    521
  "The Negro Writer in America" (with
    Ellison), 519–20, 521, 522
  Poetry and Criticism, 595–96
  reconsideration of Wright for *Atlantic*,
    660–61, 676, 679–82
"Hymie's Bull" (Ellison), 6, 93n, 991

Idea of a Theater (Fergusson), 290
identity:
  of Afro-American–Americans, duality
    of, 736–37
  evasion of, as theme of Ellison's
    second novel, 270, 271, 360
  Negro Americans' questioning of,
    653–54, 699–700
  problem of, explored in *Invisible Man*,
    398–99
  racial, inescapability of, 683–84
  racial, not fundamental to problems as
    artist, 622
Idiot, The (Dostoevsky), 223, 395
If He Hollers Let Him Go (Himes), 249
"If the Twain Shall Meet" (Ellison), 884
I Have Seen War (Sterling), 640
Imaginary Conversations (Gide), 220
immigrants, 473
Immoralist, The (Gide), 407, 420
"In a Strange Country" (Ellison), 164,
  166, 640, 657, 734–35, 994
India, 162, 416
  Ellison's trip to (1957), 280, 493, 497n,
    498, 504, 505, 508, 511
  partition of Pakistan and, 508, 511
individual:
  regard for singularity and uniqueness
    of, 593
  Wright's vs. Ellison's conceptions of,
    670

"Indivisible Man" (Ellison and
  McPherson), 10–11, 658, 659n,
  685–86, 1000
industrialism, 220
integration, 334, 463, 634
  imaginative, of Ellison, 862
  in Oklahoma City, 400, 537
  of personality, 4, 5, 11, 269–70, 360
  of schools, 8, 593
    Brown v. Board of Education and, 4,
     269–70, 360
    at college level, 593
    in Little Rock, Ark. (1957), 508, 510,
     512, 569, 594
    and mob violence in Clinton, Tenn.
     (1956), 276, 457
  study of American literature and, 350
  supported by both white and black
    Left, 802
  see also desegregation
International Literature, 680
International PEN, *see* PEN International
International Rescue Center, 826
Intruder in the Dust (Faulkner), 290–91,
  995
Invisible Criticism (Nadel), 816–22,
  944–45
Invisible Man (Ellison), 9, 25, 113, 116n,
  270, 283, 290, 300n, 359, 576, 601,
  617, 635, 673, 674, 681–82, 750,
  754, 755, 829, 911, 993, 999, 1002
  Afro-American vernacular in, 308,
    780
  "as big fat ole Negro lie," 266, 294
  Bledsoe's approach to Negro higher
    education in, 593
  blues themes in, 488
  Brockway character in, 572, 780–81
  Brotherhood in, 307–8, 487, 488, 647
  Burke's narrative schema and, 751
  Callahan's writings on, critiqued by
    Ellison, 860–67, 869–73, 885
  Clifton's selling of the dolls in, 487,
    636, 647
  Clifton's smile in, 647
  Communist Party and, 307–8, 309

contract for
  with Reynal and Hitchcock, 167, 169,
    171, 214, 225, 229, 230, 302, 765,
    994–95
  transferred to Random House, 225,
    229, 230, 232, 302, 765, 925
cutting and revising of manuscript,
    7, 258n, 266, 278, 282, 288, 291,
    292–93, 294, 567, 995, 996
"The Death of Clifton" story from, 640
dedicated to Guggenheimer, 112, 119
descriptions of environments
    presented in, 853
"Did You Ever Dream Lucky?" excerpt
    from earlier versions of, 341
earnings from, 378, 412
Ellison's answers to queries about,
    449–51, 562–63, 571, 572, 589–90,
    592–95, 636, 646–50, 652–54, 657,
    735, 787–88, 851–53
Ellison's experiences in Oklahoma
    City in relation to, 658–59, 696–97
Ellison's interpretations of key
    characters and scenes in, 450,
    487–88, 572, 589–90, 780–81,
    870–72, 885
Ellison's lack of desire to undertake
    sequel to, 750–51, 792–93
Ellison's motives for writing, 852–53
Ellison's name for his novel-in-
    progress, 266
eloquence and rhetoric explored in,
    813, 814, 860, 863–67, 872, 885
first excerpt published from (chapter
    one), 567
  in 1947 *Horizon* (London) under title
    "Invisible Man," 7, 115, 120, 231,
    236, 244, 247, 248, 640, 789, 995
  in *'48, The Magazine of the Year*
    (New York) under title "Battle
    Royal," 120, 243–44, 247, 248,
    252n, 257–58, 640, 789, 995
  reactions to, 244, 248–49
  in *A Southern Harvest*, 477
foreign editions of, 302, 312, 412,
    420–21, 436, 593, 729, 769

The Founder character in, 573, 639
"Golden Day" chapter of, 572–73, 636,
    817–18
grandfather character in, 487–88, 714
Hyman's essay on folklore and,
    487–88
identification of Ellison with hero of,
    249, 305, 871–72
interest in, at Classen High School in
    Oklahoma City, 658–59, 695–97
Italian publicity men and, 407–8
Italian translation of (*Uomo Invisible*),
    412, 420–21, 436
jacket art for, 326, 407
Jackson's transitions as model for, 292
junkman in, 940
literary allusions in, 817–21
literary influences and, 487, 573,
    789–90, 860–67
Mary Rambo character in, 341n, 611n
Mary Rambo excerpt from draft of
    ("Out of the Hospital and Under
    the Bar"), 611n, 640
Mitgang's 1982 article on, 767, 768
motive of 1369 light bulbs in, 627–28,
    787–88
names "Dupre" and "Maceo" in, 648
narrative structure of, 292, 571–72,
    912–13
Narrator in final act of, 488
Narrator without name in, 851
National Book Award won by, 267,
    270, 321, 323, 347–48, 407, 571, 586,
    588, 995
Negro speech rhythms and imagery
    in, 308
New Essays on Invisible Man (ed.
    O'Meally), 753–54, 956, 958
paperback editions of, 326, 592–93
parallels between Ellison's second
    novel and, 567
perspective transcending racial
    experience in, 398–99, 450, 563
prologue of, published in *Partisan
    Review*, 296, 301, 995
protagonist's invisibility in, 398

Invisible Man (Ellison) (*cont'd*):
   publication of, 121, 291, 293, 296, 301,
      306, 407, 412–13, 963, 995
   pushcart man in, 450
   question at end of, 121
   Ras character in, 24, 735
   Ras struck by protagonist in, 647–48
   reactions and responses to, 267, 272,
      293, 301, 303–10, 311, 314, 315,
      318, 322, 397–99, 434n, 436, 478,
      562–63, 571–73, 627–28, 634–37,
      636, 756, 813, 814, 816–22, 850,
      961–62, 995
   request to sign first edition of, 952
   Russian readers of, 768, 769
   sales of, 309, 323, 592–93
   satire of Marxist politics in, 273
   socio-political or "propagandistic"
      materials and, 450
   as statement about human life, rather
      than mere racial experience, 563
   "Them's years" riff from, 750
   thirtieth-anniversary edition of, 750,
      766, 767, 772, 773, 885, 925
   Thomas's manuscript and, 911, 912
   time frame of, 851
   title of, 851, 852
   Wright's writings as supposed
      inspiration for, 680–82, 860–67
   writing of, 7, 111, 117, 119–21, 187–88,
      190, 192–93, 197, 204, 213–14, 215,
      228–29, 230, 232, 234, 239, 241,
      247, 258, 266–67, 287, 288–89, 291,
      306–7, 751, 952, 994–95
   written in first person, 207
   zoot suit passage in, 159–60, 751
"Invisible Man: Prologue to a Novel"
   (Ellison), 296, 301, 995
Iowa, *see* University of Iowa
Ireland, Republic of, 995
Isaacson, 407, 440, 478–79
Israel, Stanley, Ellison's January 31, 1956,
   letter to, 397–99
"It Always Breaks Out" (Ellison), 998
Ivy League experience, 646
I Wonder as I Wander (Hughes), 879

Jaboro, Caterina, 63
Jackson, Jesse, 755, 823, 824, 825
Jackson, Lawrence, 702n
Jackson, Mahalia, 551
   Ellison's "As the Spirit Moves
      Mahalia," 529–30, 998
Jackson, Shirley, 179n, 201, 216, 225, 382,
      446, 596, 994, 996
   The Bird's Nest, 364
   Hangsaman, 292
   The Lottery, 261
   Pillar of Salt, 226
   The Sundial, 522–23
Jackson, Troy, 326
Jackson, Wyatt, 535
Jackson, Zelma, 103
"Jack the Bear" (trickster figure), 491,
   943–44
Jacobs, Dave, 508
James, C.L.R., 624
James, Dan, 459, 462
James, Gilbert, Ellison's July 30, 1987,
   letter to, 934
James, Henry, 279, 337, 456, 458, 472,
   545, 584, 670, 674, 718, 759, 782,
   817, 824, 937, 938, 973–74
   The Ambassadors, 838–39
   The American Scene, 273
   The Art of the Novel, 419, 853
   The Bostonians, 359–60, 755, 838, 974
   *The Complete Notebooks of Henry
      James* (eds. Edel and Powers),
      908–9, 918
   "felt life" notion of, 894
   manners and social hierarchies
      explored by, 957, 958
   Portrait of a Lady, 990
   Prefaces, 419, 908–9, 937, 973, 974
   A Turn of the Screw, 816
   vernacular stash in wordpile of, 755–56
James, Henry, Sr., 973, 974
James, Jewel, 81
Jameses, The (Lewis), 973–74
Jamesian Travesty (Kenner), 755,
   838–40
Jamie (Oklahoma City friend), 34, 48

Janson, H. W. and Mrs., 409–10
Japan, 507
  Ellison's impressions of, 509, 511
  Ellison's trip to, for 1957 PEN
    International Congress, 280, 485,
    490, 493–94, 497, 499, 500, 504,
    505, 506, 512, 514, 997
jazz, 8, 346, 365, 366, 380, 469, 494–95,
    530–32, 552–53, 560, 644–45, 661,
    677, 815, 818, 824, 862, 905–6,
    932–33, 940
  Ellison's essays on, 283, 549
    "The Golden Age, Time Past" (for
      Esquire), 529, 530–31, 536
    Ellison's lecture at NYU on (1950),
      288, 291, 301
    majority of poets uninterested in, 740
    Murray's lecture in French on, 422
    Newport Jazz Festival and, 501, 531,
      532, 537, 551, 576, 587
    panel to discuss film *The Cry of Jazz*,
      586–87
    tapes sent to Rome by Murray, 479–80,
      489, 494
    Whitmore's *Solo* and, 422
jazz critics, 531, 532, 553
Jazz Review, 553
Jean-Christophe (Rolland), 955
Jefferson, Thomas, 553, 728, 936
Jerome, Judson, 889
JET, 310, 948
Jewish tradition, African Americans'
    relationship to, 488
Jim Crow, 3, 19, 270, 587, 653, 986, 987
  in New Orleans, 351, 356
Johnny Chanen, 461–62, 464
Johnson, Buffie, 437
Johnson, Charles, *Middle Passage*, 1002
Johnson, Eric, 167
Johnson, James Weldon, 79
Johnson, Jennifer, Ellison's November 18,
    1969, letter to, 653–54
Johnson, John Albert, 771
Johnson, John H., 253–55
Johnson, Lyndon B., 10, 857–58, 873,
    876, 896, 999, 1000

Johnson, Michael P., 782, 891, 978
Johnson, Philip, 511
Johnsons (Ellison's landlords in
    Quogue, N.Y.), 218–19
Johnston, J. R., 344, 362
Johnston, May Belle De Witt (cousin),
    40n, 74–75, 86, 268, 314n, 329,
    344n, 362, 712, 713, 882, 970–71
  death and funeral of, 40n, 341, 342–44,
    362, 375, 618, 996
  Ellison's April 2, 1953, letter to, 314–15
Jones, Dr., 316, 319
Jones, Ed ("Too-Tall"), 813
Jones, Gilbert, 751
  Ellison's July 30, 1987, letter to, 934
Jones, James, 522
Jones, Jennifer, 409
Jones, Jo, 387–88
Jones, LeRoi (Amiri Baraka), 676, 682,
    837, 999
Jones, Shag, 949
Jones, Todd, Ellison's April 10, 1985,
    letter to, 852–53
Jordan, Louis, 168
Journal of Negro Education, 133
Joyce, James, 83n, 116n, 157, 194, 198, 201,
    208, 340, 365, 521, 584, 602, 645,
    670, 788, 817, 839
  Anna Livia Plurabelle, 756, 833, 839,
    952
  as Black Irish master of vernacular, 756
  Portrait of the Artist as a Young Man,
    83, 198, 200, 201, 602
  Ulysses, 520
Juan Cigarella, 651
Jude the Obscure (Hardy), 990
Juilliard School of Music (New York),
    56, 58, 533
Julius Caesar (Shakespeare), 198
Juneteenth (Ellison), 9, 986
"Juneteenth" (Ellison), 577, 662, 999
Justice, Charles, 465, 466, 484

Kafka, Franz, 301
  The Trial, 680
Kaplan, H. J., 453, 470, 519, 521

Kar, Vady Shaw, 47

Karachi University, PEN International event at (1957), 265, 280, 504, 505, 506–7, 508, 511–12, 997

Kasper, John, 476

Kasson, John F., *Civilizing the Machine*, 935–36

Kazin, Alfred, 448, 547, 915–16, 919–20, 921

  On Native Grounds, 442

  "Ten Young Novelists in Search of Pity," 521–22

Kazin, Pearl, 919, 920, 921–22

Keats, John, 990

Keller, 133

Kellman, Steven, Ellison's March 28, 1982, letter to, 768–69

Kempton, Murray, 510

Kennedy, John F., 858, 896, 998–99

Kennedy, Mark, 586

Kennedy, Ted, 858, 877

Kennedy Center (Washington, D.C.), 826, 858, 877

Kenner, Hugh, 4

  Ellison's February 20, 1985, letter to, 755, 838–40

Kenyon Review, 293–94, 588

Kerouac, Jack, 534

Kerr, Al, 721, 842

Key West, Fla., Ellisons' conch house in, 766, 767, 772, 773, 827, 849, 855, 934, 979, 1001

  Taylor's stays at, 924–27, 928–29

Kierkegaard, Søren, 183, 205, 629, 790

King, Dr. Martin Luther, Jr., 417, 454, 533, 813, 814, 979–80, 981, 1000

King Joe (musical tribute), 650

"King of the Bingo Game, The" (Ellison), 695, 865, 994

King of the Golden River, The (Ruskin), 651

King Pleasure (vocalist), 489

Kissinger, Henry, 996

Kitt, Eartha, 501

Alfred A. Knopf (publishing house), 249, 296, 300, 437–38

Knopf, Pat, 407, 409

  March 19, 1956, 419–21

Kodachrome, 456, 457

Koestler, Arthur, 167, 250

Kouwenhoven, John:

  The Arts in Modern American Civilization, 935, 972

  The Beer Can by the Highway, 935, 972

  Ellison's October 30, 1987, letter to, 751, 935–39

  Made in America, 935

Kristol, Irving, Ellison's August 29, 1956, letter to, 453–54

Kuhn, Thomas, 797, 871

LaFargue Clinic (Harlem), 212–13, 218, 248

Laly (Miss Tuskegee, 1935), 334, 353, 456

Lampada della Fraternità (Lamp of Brotherhood), 272, 997

Langston University (Oklahoma City), 333, 593, 988

Last of the Mohicans, The (Cooper), 651

Last Steps, The, aka *Le Partage des Eaux* (Carpentier), 444–45

Lathbury, Robert, Ellison's August 18, 1988, letter to, 952

Latting, Mayor, 717

Laughton, Charles, 279, 473

Lauterbach, Richard E., 257–58

Lawd Today! (Wright), 187

Lawrence, Etta, 121

Lawrence, Jacob, 407

Lazenberry, Joe, 102n, 304, 990

  Ellison's April 18, 1939, letter to, 24–25, 102–8

"leaders," conception of, 728

League of American Writers (LAW), 107, 108, 116–17, 148n, 150–51, 152n, 160, 187, 204, 221, 917, 959, 993

Leather Stocking Tales (Cooper), 651

Leaving the Territory (Ellison), 427, 575, 754n

Lee, Canada, 183

Lee, Ulysses, 150n

Leek, Raymond, 688

Lenin, V. I., 114, 129–30

Lerner, Max, 251, 510

Leuthy, Herbert, *France Against Herself*, 396–97, 433

Levi, Carlo, 436

Levy, Gertrude, 419
  The Sword from the Rock, 420

Lewis, C. Day, 79

Lewis, Nancy, 770, 918–19

Lewis, R.W.B. ("Dick"), 278, 733, 756, 770, 918–19
  American Adam, 416
  Ellison's July 1991 letter to, 973–74
  The Jameses, 973–74

Lewis, Sinclair, 290
  Arrowsmith, 651

Lewis, Smiley, 366

Lewis, Sophia Baldwin, 770–71

Lewisohn, Milt, 988

Liberia, 162, 728

Library of Congress, 999
  Ellison's papers at, 9, 13
  Ellison's reading at (1983), 793, 1001–2

Life, 133, 180, 181, 262, 276n, 418, 679
  desegregation series in, 457
  Ellison illustrated essay in (1952), 309
  Ellison's May 12, 1970, letter to editor of, 658, 667–76
  Faulkner's "Letter to the North" in, 418, 433–34, 436, 439
  review of Wright's *Native Son* in ("Native Son Strikes Home"), 658, 667–76

Lillard, Steward, 784–85, 971–72
  Ellison's letters to
    August 28, 1973, 660, 709–14
    June 7, 1987, 931–32

Lilley, J. H., 29

Lincoln, Abraham, 553, 715, 728, 819, 919

Lion Books, 412

Lipchitz, Jacques, 239–40

"liquor impotence," 357–58

Little Blue Books, 728

"Little Man at Chehaw Station, The" (Ellison), 10, 884, 989–90, 1001

Little Rock, Ark., school integration in (1957), 508, 510, 512, 569, 594

Living Novel, The (ed. Hicks), 277, 280, 477, 480, 481, 485, 521, 522
  Kazin's review of, 521–22

"Living with Music" (Ellison), 272, 391, 997

Locke, Alain, 82, 408, 743

Lolita (Nabokov), 527, 547

Lomax, Alan, 259

Lomax, Hutson J., 808–9

London:
  Ellison's impressions of, 456
  PEN International Congress in (1956), 447, 448, 452, 455–56, 997
  wartime devastation in, 196

London, Jack, *The Call of the Wild*, 651

Lonely Crusade, The (Himes), 249–51, 311

Look, 135, 235, 457

Lottery, The (Jackson), 261

Louis, Joe, 23, 90, 146, 160, 650, 919

Love Among the Cannibals (Morris), 501

Lovette, Arvil, 400, 688, 778

Lovette, Garnetta, 778

Lowry, Malcolm, *Under the Volcano*, 420

Lucas, John, 933
  Ellison's July 29, 1969, letter to, 573, 646–50

Luce, Clare Boothe, 395

Ludwig, Jack, 525, 550, 582, 921
  Ellison's April 23, 1959, letter to, 550

lunch counter sit-ins, 569–70

Lutcher, Nellie, 231, 234

lynchings, 221, 320, 593, 710–11, 800, 836

Maass, Joachim, *The Gouffe*, 596

MacArthur, Douglas, 293

MacDonald, Dwight, 527–28, 581

MacFarland, Barrelhouse Buck, 940

machine civilization, 397

Machine in the Garden, The (L. Marx), 935

MacLeish, Archibald, 139, 321, 322, 478, 481, 490, 504, 963

Macmillan Publishers, 477, 485

Madame Bovary (Flaubert), 480, 490, 629

Made in America (Kouwenhoven), 935

Mademoiselle, 180

Magazine of the Year, The, see '48, The Magazine of the Year

Magic Barrel, The (Malamud), 547n

Magic Flute, The (Mozart), 408

Mailer, Norman, 534, 560, 569, 581, 586, 588

  "white Negro" notion of, 534, 569, 684

Mainstream, 251

Major, Clarence, Ellison's April 10, 1972, letter to, 701

Making of Americans, The (Stein), 223

Malamud, Bernard, 481, 612, 615

  The Magic Barrel, 547n

Malcolm X, 690

Malefactors, The (Gordon), 439–40

Mallan, Lloyd, Ellison's February 9, 1943, letter to, 154–58

Malloy, Mrs., 317

Malraux, André, 129, 183, 202, 207, 220, 221, 250, 279, 294, 442, 445, 473, 629, 754, 769, 833, 861, 862, 955, 1000

  The Days of Wrath, 789

  Man's Fate, 433, 438, 512, 789, 991

  Man's Hope (*L'Espoir*), 106–7, 629, 790

  The Royal Way, 395–96

Malraux, Clara, 512–13

Mann, Klaus, 150

Mann, Thomas, 220–21, 294, 528

Mann, William, 334, 519

manners, symbolic action of, 957–58

Man's Fate (Malraux), 433, 438, 512, 789, 991

Man's Hope, or *L'Espoir* (Malraux), 106–7, 629, 790

"Man Who Lived Underground, The" (Wright), 487, 679–80, 681, 860, 862–67

Margaret, Princess, 448, 452, 456

Mark of Oppression, The (Kardiner and Ovesey), 300

Marks, Charlie, 520, 637

Marshall, Thurgood, 450

Martiani, Paul, Ellison's February 11, 1987, letter to, 921–23

Martin, Malcolm, 128, 130–31, 140

Martin, Ralph, 216

Marx, Karl, 114, 129–30, 197, 204, 436, 916

  "German Ideology and The Holy Family," 132

Marx, Leo, 936

  The Machine in the Garden, 935

Marxism, 119, 136, 159, 197, 222, 273, 675, 796

  humanist implications of, 114, 129–30

Mason, Clifford, 667

Massachusetts Review, 733, 1001

Masses, 802

Mathews, Inez, 355

Maugham, Somerset, 167

Maupassant, Guy de, 64n, 229, 629, 651

Maxine (Oklahoma City friend), 34, 41, 61, 67, 75, 81, 428, 859

Maya, 295–96, 365

Mays, Willie, 646

McCarthy, Joseph, 501

McCarthy, Mary, 920n

McCauley, Robie, 313, 317

McCleary, Tracy, 688–89, 722, 805–6, 815, 949

McCleary, Willard, 805

McClellan, John, 534

McConnel, Judy and Isham, 626

McConnell, Fanny (Ralph's second wife), *see* Ellison, Fanny McConnell

McConnell, Willie Mae (later Billie Warren; Fanny's mother), 172, 200, 232, 400, 574, 606, 608, 609, 611, 612, 614–15, 623, 624

McCormick, John, *Catastrophe and Imagination*, 478

McFarland, Mrs. L. S., 717

McGowan, Sam, 688, 711, 784, 800, 968–69

McGruder, Mr., 326

  Ellison's March 26, 1940, letter to, 125–28

McKenney, Ruth, 224

McLuhan, Marshall, 980

McPherson, James Alan, 691, 738
  Ellison's letters to
    March 5, 1973, *663–65*, 706–9
    May 4, 1989, 751–52, 756, 960–61
  Hue and Cry, 576, 645–46, 658
  "Indivisible Man" (in collaboration
    with Ellison), 10–11, 658, 659n,
    685–86, 1000
  "Subjective Account of Something
    Very Old," 658, 706–7
Mead, Frank, 327, 344, 856
Meadman, Dhimah Rose, 133, 134, 140, 141
Meaning in the Visual Arts (Panofsky),
    442
Melville, Herman, 419, 488, 602, 728,
    737, 789, 817, 861, 871
  Moby-Dick, 290, 494, 561, 595, 651,
    681, 798
Memoirs of Hadrian (Yourcenar), 389
Mencken, H. L., 862
  Prejudices, 395
"Men in the Making" (Wright), 147, 765
Mennen, Aubry, 409, 416
Merchant Marine, U.S.:
  Ellison's description of convoy's
    movement across sea, 118, 174–75
  Ellison's service in, 7, 111, 118–19, 165,
    167, 173–78, 191, 213, 252, 266, 702n,
    734–35, 797–98, 823, 829, 994, 995
Messenger, Miss, Ellison's March 7,
    1983, letter to, 789–90
Mexicans, cultural and economic
    conditions of black Americans
    compared to, 24, 106
Mexico:
  Ellison's views on travel to, 24, 105, 106
  Wright's sojourns in (1940–46), 130,
    131, 137
Mexico City:
  Cultural Freedom in the Western
    Hemisphere conference in (1956),
    277, 455, 456, 459, 460–61, 462,
    467, 468, 997
  Ellison's impressions of, 459, 461,
    467–68
Michelangelo, 385

Middlebury College (Vt.):
  Bread Loaf Writer's Conference at
    (1959), 547, 554, 557, 558
  Ellison's lecture at (1959), 546–47, 549
Middle Passage (Johnson), 1002
Mies van de Rohe, Ludwig, 511, 938
Milano, Paolo, 397
Miller, Charlie, 427, 989
Miller, Doren, 150
Miller, Eva Hamlin, 318
Miller, Henry, 554
Miller, Loren, 210–12
Milles, Karl, 392
Millford, Mary A., 785
Minnie (Ralph's aunt in Chicago), 42,
    56, 325
Minor, Robert, 169, 185
minstrelsy, 936–37
Minton, Bruce, 224
Minton's Playhouse (Harlem), Ellison's
    Esquire piece on, 529, 530, 536
Minus, Marian, 889
Mitchell, Cabbie, 687
Mitchell, Gwen, 627
Mitchell, Rudolph, 380
Mitgang, Herbert, 767, 768
Mizener, Arthur, 408
Moby-Dick (Melville), 290, 494, 561, 595,
    651, 681, 798
Modern Language Association (MLA),
    807, 812–13, 814
Monk, Thelonious, 531
Monster, The (Crane), 585
Montgomery, Ala., civil rights movement
    in, 480, 511–12, 544
  bus boycott (1956), 274, 417, 594
Moon, Bucklin, 181
Moon, Mary, 325
Moon, Molly, 251
Moore, Archie, 561
Moore, Audley, 133
Moore, Dick, 180
Moore, Gordon, 38, 60, 61
Moore, Julia ("Chubby" or "Chubbie"),
    34, 38, 41, 55, 61
Moravia, Alberto, 397, 436

Morisey, Alexander (Ralph's cousin),
215n, 314n, 315, 316n, 324, 801, 891
Ellison's letters to
June 9, 1946, 215
April 9, 1953 (and Juanita), 316–17
Morisey, Juanita, 315, 316n
Ellison's April 9, 1953, letter to Alex
and, 316–17
Morisey, Mamie (aunt), 215n, 314n, 315,
316, 324, 326
Morris, Linda, Ellison's letters to:
September 22, 1983, 805–6
December 12, 1983, 815
Morris, Willie, 756, 979n
Ellison's April 12, 1993, letter to,
979–80
Ellison's June 16, 1993, letter to, 980–82
Morris, Wright, 458, 473, 485
The Field of Vision, 458, 481
Love Among the Cannibals, 501
Morrison, Toni, 658, 705n
Morton, Jellyroll, 410, 648–49, 650, 960
Moscow, show trials and purges in
(1936–38), 106, 170, 185, 802
Moss, Carlton, 135, 137–38, 139, 142, 825,
828–29, 830
Moton, Allen, 72, 305, 832
Muhammad, Elijah, 594
Muhlhauser, Fred, 411
Ellison's July 28, 1955, letter to Lucille
Muhlhauser and, 381–83
mulattoes, 254–55, 287
Muldrow, Cheryl, Ellison's April 10,
1985, letter to, 851–52
Mumford, Lewis:
The Condition of Man, 165
The Culture of Cities, 420
The Golden Day, 817–18
Technics and Civilization, 420
Murphy, Frank, 181
Murphy, George, 167
Murray, Albert, 3, 7, 236, 312, 328, 329,
381–82, 546, 576, 607, 611, 642n,
643, 738, 870, 871, 965
in Army Air Corps (later Air Force),
266, 382, 516, 536, 633

asked to check on Herbert Ellison,
533, 536
in Casablanca, Morocco, 276, 382, 415,
417, 418, 422–23, 436, 516
Ellison's letter of recommendation for,
632–34
Ellison's letters to, 8–9, 265–67, 269,
277, 282, 283, 568–70, 576
January 24, 1950, 266, 286–88
March 22, 1950, 288–89
April 16, 1950, 289–91
May 14, 1951, 266, 291
June 6, 1951, 266–67, 292–95
January 8, 1952, 295–97
February 4, 1952, 297–301
March 18, 1953, 313
April 9, 1953, 317–23
July 24, 1953, 3, 268–69, 330–37
August 6, 1953, 337
September 22, 1953, 339–41
October 16, 1953, 341–42
October 23, 1953, 342–43
November 20, 1953, 345–46
February 1, 1954, 346–49
March 6, 1954, 353–54
April 12, 1954, 356–59
August 9, 1954, 364–66
August 19, 1954, 370
April 12, 1955, 273, 379–81
October 22, 1955, 272, 387–90
January 30, 1956, 394–97
March 16, 1956, 273–74, 415–19
April 1, 1956, 274–75, 421–23
April 12, 1956, 275, 431–32
April 24, 1956, 432–34
May 18, 1956, 440–42
May 22, 1956, 442–44
September 15, 1956, 276, 455–58
September 24, 1956, 460
November 7, 1956, 467–70
April 4, 1957, 277, 477–80
June 2, 1957, 280, 489–92
July 28, 1957, 280, 493–96
August 17, 1957, 280, 500–502
October 3, 1957, 511–13
February 6, 1958, 282, 517–20

September 28, 1958, 530–35
June 27, 1959, 551–56, 567
July 17, 1959, 557–62
April 2, 1960, 568–69, 583–87
Ellison's relationship with, 265–66, 286n
Ellisons' travels in Europe with (1956),
    418, 419, 436, 440–41, 443–44, 447,
    448–49, 457, 997
Ellison's visit to Tuskegee and (1954),
    345, 346–47, 349–50, 353
letters exchanged by Ellison and,
    collected in *Trading Twelves*, 8, 14,
    286n, 559–60
misinformation provided to Ellison's
    biographer by, 942–43
in Paris, 296
The Spyglass Tree, 297n
stereo sound system of, 645
Train Whistle Guitar, 297n, 334
writing his first novel ("Jack the
    Bear"), 266–67, 287, 293, 294–95,
    296, 297–300, 320
Murray, Gilbert, 279, 473
The Classical Tradition in Poetry, 410
Murray, Michele ("Mique"), 288n, 329,
    333, 353, 364, 443, 561–62, 585,
    609, 611, 613
Murray, Mozelle ("Mokie" or "Moque"),
    288n, 294, 328–611, 329, 333, 341,
    348, 353, 358, 364
Musician's Amplifier, 844
"My Kinsman, Major Molineux"
    (Hawthorne), 739
"Myth of the Flawed White Southerner,
    The" (Ellison), 884

NAACP, 131, 279, 441–42, 463, 473, 512,
    556
Nabokov, ex–Mrs., 311
Nabokov, Vladimir, *Lolita*, 527, 547
Nadar (Gaspard-Félix Tournachon), 684
Nadel, Alan, 11
    Ellison's letters to
        January 27, 1984, 816–22
        April 19, 1988, 944–45
    Invisible Criticism, 816–22, 944–45

Nation, 279, 453n, 999
Nation, Carrie, 932
national anthems, Ellison on, 834
National Book Awards, 481, 501, 518,
    546, 547, 548, 1002
    for *Invisible Man*, 267, 270, 321, 323,
        347–48, 407, 571, 586, 588, 995
    Roth acceptance speech for, 588
    won by Bellow, 276n, 347–48
National Council on the Arts, 805, 826,
    858, 877, 999
National Endowment for the Arts, 875
National Guard, 276, 457
National Institute for Arts and Letters, 520
National Institute of the Arts, 999
nationalism, 162, 204
    African, 370–71
National Medal of Arts ceremony (1985),
    857–58, 876–78, 1002
National Negro Congress (Washington,
    D.C.; 1940), 114, 134–36, 993
National Portrait Gallery (Washington,
    D.C.), 826, 1001
National Youth Administraton (NYA),
    125, 126
Native Son (Wright), 95, 98, 128, 146,
    181, 187, 197, 248, 249, 291n, 309n,
    667–76, 861, 993
    adapted for stage, 132–33, 137–38, 139,
        142–43
    Ellison's and Baldwin's references in
        print to, 668–72
    responses to, 114, 131–34, 135, 138, 140,
        143, 679
    chauvinism uncovered in, 133–34
    Ellison's interpretations of
        characters, 131–32
    in Harlem, 114, 129
    of MacLeish, 139
    of Marxists and CP members,
        129–30, 131–32, 135
    reviews of, 128, 129, 131, 135
    by Cohn in *Atlantic*, Wright's reply
        to, 139
    Life's 1970 review ("Native Son
        Strikes Home"), 658, 667–76

naturalism, 678

nature, Americans' ambivalence toward, 195–96

Nausea (Sartre), 789

necessity, consciousness of, 866–67

Neely, Alvin ("Capt."), 32, 34, 57, 59, 305, 327–28, 989, 990

"Negro artists" or "Negro American experience," use of terms, 676–79

Negro Caravan, The (eds. Brown, Davis, and Lee), 150

Negro Digest, 675

Negroes or Negro Americans, *see* African Americans

Negro Folk Symphony (Dawson), 966, 988

Negro Publication Society, 150

Negro Quarterly, 150, 152, 154, 159–61, 162–63, 822, 823, 993–94

"Negro question," 201, 224

Negro Story Magazine, 640

"Negro Writer in America, The" (Ellison and Hyman), 519–20, 521, 522

Neo-Platonism, 410

New Challenge, 6, 93, 95, 640, 991

New England poets, 683–84

New Essays on Invisible Man (ed. O'Meally), 753–54, 956, 958

New Leader, 637, 670–71

New Masses (*NM*), 93, 95, 134, 138, 140, 143, 161, 163, 164–65, 224, 249, 251, 802, 822, 824, 879, 917, 993

   Ellison's "A Congress Jim Crow Did Not Attend" in, 114, 135–36, 993

   Ellison's book reviews for, 187

   Ellison's refusal to continue writing for (1943), 161

   Negro writers and subjects in, 136–37, 150

"New Negro" concept, 323

New Orleans:

   Globetrotters' performance in, 358

   Mardi Gras in, 350, 351, 356

   as viciously Jim-Crowed city, 351, 356

   see also Dillard University

Newport Jazz Festival, 501, 531, 532, 537, 551, 576, 587

New Republic, 95, 167, 187, 189, 216, 919, 959

New School (New York), 203n, 204, 826, 917

Newspaper Publishers convention (1945), 185

Newsweek, 513

New World Writing, 341, 358–59, 406, 471

New York:

   considered center of world's cultural activities by Ellison, 397

   Ellisons' apartment at Beaumont (730 Riverside Drive), 13, 269, 312, 483, 611, 806–7, 888, 892–93, 905, 915, 995

   burglary at, 425, 432, 463

   move to larger apartment, 561, 998

   problems at, during Rome fellowship, 461–62, 463, 466, 467

   Ellison's brief stay in (1956), 461–66, 467, 468

   Ellison's early years in

      first letters written during (1936–37), 17, 21–23, 79–91

      fullest account of, 24, 25, 102–8

      living arrangements in 1940s, 152, 209–10, 229, 230, 248

      move from Oklahoma City (1936), 6, 20–21, 55, 56, 57, 58, 77, 103, 990–91

      observations on details of life around him, 22, 23, 89–90

      return after mother's death (1938), 6, 24, 96–97, 99–101, 104–5

   Ellison's living situations during his first year in the city (1936–37), 21, 83–84, 87, 88

   Esquire's commission for piece on, 570, 586

   first stage play seen by Ellison in, 803–4

   see also Harlem

New York Days (Morris), 979n, 980n

New Yorker, 201, 202–3, 306, 360, 473, 591, 658

   Anderson's profile of Ellison for, 11, 658, 729–30, 1001

New York Foundation, 635–36

New York Post, 138n, 219, 225, 510n, 994

New York Public Library, 718, 809

New York Review of Books, 751, 914–15

New York Times, 165, 256, 287, 340, 615, 767, 773, 834

New York Times Book Review, 314n, 546

New York Times Magazine, 537, 1002

New York University (NYU), 214, 306, 709

   Ellison's Albert Schweitzer Professorship at, 10, 11, 657, 704, 749, 826, 1000

   Ellison's lecture on western jazz at (1951), 288, 291, 301

   Ellison's letter of recommendation to, on behalf of Lewis, 770–71

   Ellison's retirement from, and title of Professor Emeritus, 10, 11, 662, 745, 749, 826, 856

Niebuhr, Reinhold, 698

Nieman Fellowship, 316

Nietzsche, Friedrich, 442, 861

"Night-Talk" (Ellison), 576–77, 662, 1000

Nina (assistant), 400, 461, 463, 464, 499

Nixon, Richard M., 478, 873–74, 876

Noble Savage, 550, 567, 582, 600, 604, 662

   "And Hickman Arrives" excerpt published in, 9, 267, 283, 556, 557, 567, 568, 577, 581, 583, 662, 998

No Chariot Let Down (eds. Johnson and Roark), 891

Norman, Dorothy, 217–18, 219, 763

North, Alex, 100

North, Joe, 143

North Canadian River, 812

North Carolina:

   Ellison's visit to (1953), 267–68, 314n, 316–20, 323–24

   see also Bennett College

Notes from Underground (Dostoevsky), 487, 680, 862, 863–64

Notes on a Horsethief (Faulkner), 297

novel, form of:

   American, experimental nature of, 871

   Ellison's essay "Society, Morality, and the Novel," 10, 277, 280, 477, 480, 481, 485, 522n, 584, 738, 884

   Harvard conference on (1953), 269, 334, 337, 338, 340, 357, 996

   Hyman's essay on folk tradition and, 486–88, 490–92, 519–20, 521

   literary culture as basis for, 486–87

   music as influence on, 546, 870–71

   national framework of experience and, 340, 506, 871

   "Novel as a Function of American Democracy, The" (Ellison), 884

O'Connor, Flannery, 707

O'Connor, Frank, 334, 337, 340

O'Connor, William Van, 261

Odets, Clifford, *Rocket to the Moon*, 98

Oklahoma:

   celebration of 60th anniversary of state (1966), 854, 930

   Ellison's second novel and, 267, 268–69, 271, 273, 302, 314, 315, 317, 321, 330–37, 339, 371–72, 996

   land rush of 1889 in, 271

   segregation in, 322, 332, 367, 537, 696, 805, 986

   statehood of, 932

Oklahoma City:

   burial sites of Ellison's relatives in, 342

   changes in, 367–68

   "dear folks" letters to old friends and relations from, 4, 19, 271

      [undated, probably written early in July 1937], 86

      October 17, 1937, 6, 92

      July 15, 1953, 330

   drill team on school grounds in, 558–59

   Ralph Ellison Library in, 11, 716–19, 729, 745, 806, 910, 1001

   Ellison's attachment to, 1, 111, 427–28, 658–59

   Ellison's birth and boyhood in, 3, 4, 12, 17, 143–46, 344–45, 695–97, 702, 805–6, 854–55, 942, 985–88, 996

   Ellison's dreams about, 427

Oklahoma City (*cont'd*):
  Ellison's letters full of memories about
    his past in, 273, 423–30, 537–38,
    558–59, 616–20, 685–91, 719–27,
    775–79, 842–45, 846–49, 881–82
  Ellison's letters to old friends from, 4,
    7, 10, 11, 271, 574–75, 659, 754–55
    see also specific recipients
  Ellison's poem about his return to
    ("Deep Second"), 269, 334–37
  Ellison's return to (1953), 267, 268–69,
    315, 326, 327–37, 373–74, 616, 658,
    996
  Ellison's trip to (1966), 999
  Ellison's trip to (1986), 909–10, 914–15
  Ferris wheel at carnival in, 575
  integration in, 400, 537
  key figures from Ellison's life in, 64n
  May Belle's death and funeral in
    (1953), 40n, 341, 342–44, 362, 996
  Negro births not registered or
    recorded in, 702n
  race relations in, 332, 367, 368, 400
  segregated library branch in, 805
  at time of statehood, 932
  urban renewal in, 659, 686, 697, 713,
    718, 846–48, 910
Oklahoma City Times, 717
Oklahoma Hall of Fame, 914
Oklahoma Territory, Hyman's essay on,
  931–32
Old Abbeville (Ware), 11–12, 967, 975,
  977–78
"Old Man" (Faulkner), 120
Oliver, Paul, 931
Ollie (Oklahoma City friend), 430, 631,
  848
Olson, Carl ("Bobo"), 396, 489
Omans, Stuart E., Ellison's September 14,
  1971, letter to, 694–95
O'Meally, Robert, 11, 753–54, 765, 870
  The Craft of Ralph Ellison, 753, 772, 939
  Ellison's letters to
    September 28, 1979, 743
    March 11, 1988, 753, 939–44
    April 17, 1989, 753–54, 956–58

inaccuracies and distortions ascribed
  to, 743, 753, 765, 939
New Essays on Invisible Man, 753–54,
  956, 958
quotations and information about
  Ellison queried by, 753, 939–44
"On Becoming a Writer" (Ellison), 635
"On Being the Target of Discrimination"
  (Ellison), 19, 1002
One More Day's Journey (Ballard),
  891–92
"On Initiation Rites and Power"
  (Ellison), 884
On Native Grounds (Kazin), 442
Opportunity, 62
Oram, Harold, 999
Orangeburg State College (S.C.), 805
Orchard Park School (Oklahoma City),
  344, 362, 696
Ortenberg, Neil, Ellison's October 19,
  1985, letter to, 878–79
Orwell, Mrs. George, 311
Ottley, Roi, 115, 197–98, 248, 310, 825,
  828
Our American Cousin, 728
Out of Africa (Dinesen), 381
"Out of the Hospital and Under the Bar"
  (Ellison), 611n, 640
Outsider, The (Wright), 113, 310, 313, 314,
  682, 761, 864
Overstreet, Harry A., 171, 214

Page, Inman, 662, 744–45, 884, 988
Page, Oran ("Hot Lips"), 402, 494, 671,
  861, 988
Painter's Eye, The (Grossner), 442
Pakistan:
  partition of India and, 508, 511
  PEN International event in (1957), 265,
    280, 504, 505, 506–7, 508, 511–12,
    997
Palm, Coran, Ellison's November 30,
  1956, letter to, 470–71
Panofsky, Erwin, *Meaning in the Visual
  Arts*, 442
papacy, Ellison's thoughts on, 274–75

Paris:
  conference on African culture in
    (1956), 453, 455
  as writing venue, 267
Paris Review, 451, 473, 478, 481, 485,
    640, 707
Park, Robert E., 206
Park East Magazine, 306
Parker, Charlie, 530–31, 552
Parker, Stephen, 376
Parks, Gordon, 248, 258, 262, 288, 461,
    463, 468
Partage des Eaux, Le, aka *The Last Steps*
    (Carpentier), 437–38, 444–45
Partisan Review, 251, 288, 301, 314, 383,
    447, 448, 481, 519, 583, 588, 634n,
    637, 998
  Ellison's piece on background of
    Negro writing for, 320–21
  prologue of *Invisible Man* published
    in, 296, 301, 995
  Wright's *Black Boy* reviewed in,
    185–86, 193
passing for white, Ellison's critique of
    Taylor's script and, 252–57
Passport Office, Los Angeles, Ellison's
    May 31, 1972, letter to, 701–2
Patriotic Gore (Wilson), 716, 919
Patterson, Dr. (Tuskegee), 74, 417, 831
Patterson, Mrs. (Tuskegee), 82, 417, 831
Patterson, William and Louise, 802–3
Payton, Benjamin, Ellison's May 9, 1988,
    letter to, 946–47
Peculiar Institution, The (Stampp), 472
Pell, Claiborne, 877
PEN International events:
  Ellison's decision to cut back on,
    585–86
  in Frankfurt (1959), 554, 557, 560,
    998
  in Japan (1957), 485, 490, 493–94, 497,
    499, 500, 504, 505, 506, 997
  in Karachi (1957), 265, 280, 504, 505,
    506–7, 508, 511–12, 997
  in London (1956), 447, 448, 452,
    455–56, 997

  in Mexico City (1956), 277, 455, 456,
    459, 460–61, 462, 467, 468, 997
Penn, Irving, 694
Pensacola, Fla., Ellison's trips to, 53, 57,
    58, 70, 71
Perrio, Armistead, 42
personality:
  integration of, 4, 5, 11, 269–70, 360
  Marxist-Leninist literature's failure to
    provide humanist treatment of, 114,
    129–30
  Mumford's *The Condition of Man* on
    development of, 165
"Perspective of Literature" (Ellison),
    746, 884
Peters, Ada, 300
"Peter Wheatstraw" (trickster figure),
    649, 940, 943–44, 956–57
Petrillo, J. Caesar, 805
Phenomenology of Mind (Hegel), 133
Philadelphia, southern Negroes settled
    in, 891–92
Philadelphia Orchestra, 43, 988
Phillips, William, 436, 521, 522, 528, 549
picaresque novels, 652–53
Picasso, Pablo, 391, 445, 909
Pierro, Babel, and family, 351, 354, 358
Pierson, Leroy, 753, 939–40
Pillar of Salt (Jackson), 226
Pious, Robert S., 82
Pittman, Fanny, 305, 356, 831
Pittsburgh Courier, 219
Pius XII, Pope, 274, 422, 424–25
Plainfield, Mass., Ellisons' summer home
    in, 662, 704–5, 744, 767, 774, 798,
    827, 833, 869, 875, 882–83, 884,
    885–86, 899, 918, 928, 934, 965,
    999–1000
  purchase of, 575
  ravaged by mysterious fire (November
    1967), 9–10, 571, 575–76, 641,
    642–43, 650, 657, 704, 709, 1000
  small cabin adapted as replacement in,
    709–10
  writing of second novel at, 575–76, 1000
Plimpton, Cal, 731

P.M., 681

Podhoretz, Norman, 635

Poe, Edgar Allan, 863–64
 Tales, 651

Poetics (Aristotle), 257, 261

Poetics of Music (Stravinsky), 458

Poetry and Criticism (Hyman), 595–96

Poindexter, Rose (Ralph's first wife), 6,
  24, 99–100, 102, 104–5, 111, 112, 121,
  125, 130, 131, 133, 178, 856, 981, 993,
  994, 995
 Ralph's July 19, 1940, letter to, 112,
  140–41

policy (illegal lottery), motive of 1369
  light bulbs and, 628, 787

polio research, 350

Polito, Ron, Ellison's November 22,
  1983, letter to, 810–11

Pondermaker, Hortense, *After Freedom*,
  103

Porgy and Bess, 907

Porkchopper (Davidson's racehorse),
  643–44, 661, 692

Porter, Arabel, 334, 341, 346, 381

Porter, Horace, 11
 Ellison's letters to
  December 22, 1976, 658, 731–34
  February 29, 1986, 751, 892–99

Porter, Katherine Anne, 334

Portrait of a Lady (James), 990

"Portrait of Inman Page, A" (Ellison), 884

Portrait of the Artist as a Young Man
  (Joyce), 83, 198, 200, 201, 602

Poston, Ted, 137, 138, 927

Pound, Ezra, 553, 556, 573, 652, 819, 861
 treason conviction and imprisonment
  of, 475–76

Powe, Ralph, 340

Powell, Adam, Jr., 792

Powers, Lyall H., 908

Prejudices (Mencken), 395

Présence Africaine, 115, 251, 252, 470

Presidential Medal of Freedom, 1000

Price, Bill, 722–24

Price, Leontyne, 646, 857, 876–77

Pride, Ella, 562, 563

Primer for White Folks (ed. Moon), 181

primitives and primitive art, 259, 260,
  435–36, 534, 678, 796
 Carpentier's *The Lost Steps* and,
  444–45

Princeton University, 447, 918, 921, 922
 Ellison's lecture at (1953), 265, 269,
  314, 317, 321, 326, 996
 Negroes in attendance at, 311
 Wilson's lectures on Civil War writing
  at, 311

Printers Row Book Fair (Chicago), 975,
  976

Prix de Rome fellowship:
 awarded to Ellison, 400, 439n, 544,
  586, 588, 996
 Ellison's financial situation and,
  376–79
 see also American Academy, Rome,
  Ellison's Prix de Rome fellowship
  at

Prokofiev, Sergei, 833

proletarian concept, 132, 159n, 308

Promises (Warren), 963

propaganda, fiction vs., for cause of
  Negro Americans, 594–95

prostitution, Bronx Slave Market and,
  128–29

*Protestant Ethic and the Spirit of
  Capitalism, The* (Weber), 420

Proust, Marcel, 293

Provincetown, Mass., Ellison's visit to
  (1953), 338, 340

Pruitt, Marmon, 430

Psychology of Dreams, The (Freud), 805

*Public Hearings on the Condition of the
  Urban Colored Population*, 128

Public Television, 826

Pudd'nhead Wilson (Twain), 958

Pulitzer Prize, 407, 522

Pushkin, Alexander, 862

Putnam, Jim, 485, 492

Queneau, Raymond, 302

Quogue, N.Y., letters written by Ellison
  from, 7, 111, 216–21

Rabb, Mike, 99, 103, 334, 346, 352, 990

race:
differences in experience and, 155
discord of sensibilities and, 207
Ellison's experience of, after reading Wright's *12 Million Black Voices*, 114–15, 143–46, 993
passing for white and, 252–57
popularity as professor or writer and, 622
rhetoric of, dismissed by Ellison, 398–99
stereotypes and, 323
Race and Caste, 455
"race," as loaded term, 204
race relations, 185, 978
drama of self-definition and, 960
Ellison's assumed exile in Rome and, 544–45
Ellison's critique of Taylor's script and, 252–57
Ellison's views on future of, 654
in European Theater of Operations during World War II, 734–35
Life's "white appeasement" charge and, 668
Negroes' distrust of whites during war years, 162–63
possibility of real change in, 316
potential for civil conflict and, 205–6
violence against Negroes and, 221; see also lynchings
see also civil rights movement; desegregation; integration; segregation
racial approaches to culture, 455, 661, 683–84
racial identity, 661
inescapability of, 683–84
not fundamental to problems as artist, 572, 622
racial injustice:
protesting as only one means of doing something about, 731–33
see also civil rights movement

racial prejudice, 399, 594, 622
ascribed to *Life* reviewer, 673–74
Radical Republicanism, 784
Radin, Paul, *The Trickster*, 448
Raglan, Lord, 447
The Hero, 407, 420
Rahv, Philip, 301, 436, 707
"rainbow" notion, 755, 825
Ralph Ellison (ed. Bloom), 916–17
Rampersad, Arnold, 9n, 114n, 116n, 129n, 133n, 138n, 168n, 203n, 279–80, 577, 667n, 702n, 879, 981n
Ellison's October 23, 1988, letter to, 953
Ramsey, Eugene, 905
Randolph, A. Philip, 802
Randolph, Iphegenia ("Cute"), 64n, 720, 846n, 847, 848, 854, 859
Randolph, James ("Jim"), 11, 64n, 430, 687, 702n, 742, 759, 760, 854, 859, 987
Ellison's letter after death of, 900–901
Ellison's letters to
September 18, 1953 (addressed to Jim and Madge), 338–39
March 1, 1974, 719–27
May 2, 1982, 773–75
Randolph, Jefferson Davis ("J. D.," or "Grandpa"), 64n, 430, 574, 846n, 848, 854
Randolph, Madeline, 727, 760, 773
Randolph, Madge, 720
Ellison's September 18, 1953, letter to Jim and, 338–39
Randolph, Saretta, 64n
Randolph, Taylor, 430, 721, 723, 858–59, 888, 941–42
Randolph, Thomas Jefferson ("Bud" or "T. J."), 44, 64n, 375, 428–29, 430, 719, 987
Hettie's story that Ellison was son of, 429
Randolph, Uretta, 574, 846n, 985
Random House, 151, 226, 290, 296, 411n, 1000, 1001
Ellison's first meeting with Faulkner at, 321–22

Random House (*cont'd*):
  Ellison's second novel and, 1000, 1001
  Forrest's *There Is a Tree More Ancient Than Eden* and, 658, 705n
  Invisible Man and, 225, 229, 230, 232, 258n, 291n, 302, 765, 766, 925, 995
rape, 880
  Himes's *A Case of Rape* and, 879–81
Raphael, Lenox, 999
"Ras," as term, 657
Ras Tafari sect, 657, 735
Ravello, Italy, Ellison's trip to (1956), 273–74, 275, 406–7, 408–9, 415–16, 425–26
Raymond, Allen, 316
readers:
  both skilled and unskilled important to Ellison, 867–69
  collaborative relationship of writer and, 893–94
Reagan, Nancy, 858, 877
Reagan, Ronald, 795, 857–58, 876–77, 1002
Reconstruction, 3, 604, 653, 704, 710, 715, 784, 851, 919, 931, 969, 977
Reddick, L. D., 129, 310
Redding, J. Saunders, 318
  Stranger and Alone, 287, 290
Reid (Tuskegee), 360
Reiger, Wallingford, 100, 930
Religion and the Rise of Capitalism (Tawney), 420
"Remembering Richard Wright" (Ellison), 791, 884
Reminiscences of Tolstoi, Chekhov and Andreyev (Gorky), 223
Remnick, David, 752
Renaissance, 272, 389, 395
"Renaissance Men," 805–6
Reporter, 287, 463, 995
Republicans, 307–8
Revels, Hiram Rhodes (Cayton's grandfather), 600–602, 604
Reynal and Hitchcock, 167, 169, 171, 214, 221, 225, 229, 230, 302, 765, 994–95
Reynolds, Paul R., & Son, 137, 139, 147

"Rhetoric of Hitler's Battle, The" (Burke), 116–17, 203n, 204, 917, 959
Rhone, Camille Randolph, 4, 64n, 271, 720, 846n, 854, 855, 887–88, 900, 901
  Ellison's letters to
    December 7, 1954 (addressed to Pat and Camille), 373–74
    March 18, 1985, 846–49
    October 22, 1985, 881–84
    December 2, 1985, 886–87
Rhone, Iphigenia, 64n, 846n, 854
Rhone, James, 630
Rhone, Mamie, 4
  Ellison's letters to
    April 30, 1985, 858–59
    December 3, 1985, 887–90
    June 22, 1986 (addressed to Mamie and Mitch), 900–901
Rhone, Mitchell, 854, 858, 859
  Ellison's June 22, 1986, letter (addressed to Mamie and Mitch), 900–901
Rhone, Mrs. Mitchell, 854, 855
Rhone, Pat, 271, 854, 881, 882
  Ellison's December 7, 1954, letter to Camille and, 373–74
Rhone, Pat ("Little Pat"), 373–74, 375
Rhone, Taylor, 858–59
"Richard Wright's Blues" (Ellison), 157n, 164, 186, 187, 189, 191–92, 201, 204, 206, 669, 886, 995
riots:
  in Harlem (1943), 138n
  in Tulsa, Okla. (1921), 986
  zoot suit (Los Angeles; 1943), 159–60
Ripley, Dillon, 911
Roark, James L., 891, 978
  Ellison's November 23, 1982, letter to, 782–85
Roberts, Laurence, 412, 451, 475, 510
Robeson, Lattrell, 704
Robeson, Paul, 132, 186, 194, 650
Robinson, Sugar Ray, 396, 489, 561, 919
Roche, John, Ellison's November 6, 1984, letter to, 832–35
Rockefeller Foundation, 588, 636n

Rocket to the Moon (Odets), 98
Rodgers, J. A., 180
Roethke, Ted, 434, 437, 446, 918, 919
Rogers, Bill, 407
Rolland, Romain, *Jean-Christophe*, 955
*Romare Bearden: Paintings and
    Projections* (Albany, 1968),
    Ellison's introduction in catalogue
    for, 676, 677–78, 1000
Rome:
    Ellison alleged to have expatriated to,
        539, 544–45
    Ellison's hunt for pickling spices in,
        275, 432
    Ellison's impressions of, 394, 435,
        539–40, 997
    see also American Academy, Rome,
        Ellison's Prix de Rome fellowship at
Roos, Mr. (Key West, Fla.), 926
Roosevelt, Franklin D., 102, 139, 160, 256
Roosevelt, Teddy, 713
Root, Grace and Edward, 553–54, 556
"Roscoe Dunjee and the American
    Language" (Ellison), 987
Rosenbaum, Ben, Ellison's May 20, 1985,
    letter to, 867–69
Rosenfeld, George, 598
Julius Rosenwald Fund, 203, 213–14, 586,
    588, 995
Roth, Philip, 588, 599
Rothschild, John and Connie, 312
Rouen, France, Ellison aboard ship
    docked in (1945), 111, 118–19,
    176–78, 196, 213, 252, 995
Rourke, Constance, 97
Rousseau, Jean-Jacques, 94
Roy, Claude, 224
Royal Way, The (Malraux), 395–96
Ruby (friend in Dayton, Ohio), 324–25
Ruggles of Redgap (1935 film), 279, 473
Rung That Broke Bercha, The (Thomas),
    911–13
Rushing, Jimmy, 272, 389, 531, 532, 538,
    616, 649, 671, 988, 998
Ruskin, John, *The King of the Golden
    River*, 651

Russell, Richard, Jr., 501, 512
Rutgers University (New Brunswick,
    N.J.), 569, 584, 637
    Ellison's honorary doctorate from, 999
    Ellison's visiting professorship at
        (1962–64), 621, 624, 634n, 636n,
        998
Ruzicka, Dolores A., Ellison's
    November 10, 1969, letter to, 573,
    652–53

Sag Harbor, N.Y., Ellison's visit to
    (1944), 168
Saint-Exupéry, Antoine de, 955
"Saint Louis Blues," 834
St. Louis Woman (Hughes), 98
St. Peter's Basilica, Ellison's visit to
    (1956), 274–75, 422, 424–25
Salzburg Seminar in American Studies,
    Ellison's 1954 lectures at, 347, 350,
    361, 363–64, 365, 367, 370, 375,
    377–78, 381n, 382, 386, 471, 769, 996
Salzman, 217, 218
Sancton, Tom, 209
Sandborn, Charlesetta, 121–25, 688
Sarser, Dave, 365, 383n, 461, 518, 627,
    844–45, 1002
    Ellison's letters to
        October 21, 1955, 383–84
        August 28, 1956, 451–52
Sartre, Jean-Paul, 183, 311, 320, 629, 789,
    790, 862
Saturday Review (previously *Saturday
    Review of Literature*), 219, 306,
    323, 529–30, 531, 996, 997
Saunders, Lorraine, 556, 778
Saunders, Silvia, Ellison's March 28,
    1982, letter to, 767–68
Savage, Augusta, 80, 743
Savoy (New York), 380
Savoy Ballroom (Harlem), 811
Eugene Saxton Fellowship, 67, 671
Scales, James Ralph, 775
Schaenen, Eve, Ellison's October 8,
    1986, letter to, 908–9
Scheider, Isadore, 171, 202

Schlamm, Willi, 180–81

Schomburg Collection, 225, 718

school integration, 8
  Brown v. Board of Education and, 4,
    269–70, 360
  at college level, 593
  in Little Rock, Ark. (1957), 508, 510,
    512, 569, 594
  and mob violence in Clinton, Tenn.
    (1956), 276, 457

Schwartz, Delmore, 919

Albert Schweitzer Chair in the
    Humanities (NYU), 10, 11, 657,
    704, 749, 826, 1000

Science and Society, 186–87, 204

Scientific American, 796–97, 845

Scott, Hazel, 182

Scott, Nathan A., Jr., 571n, 591, 607, 657,
    998
  Ellison's February 17, 1972, letter of
    recommendation for, 697–700
  Ellison's letters to
    November 23, 1964, 571, 638–39
    July 17, 1989, 962–64
  as insightful religious thinker, 698

Scott, Shirley, 644

Scottsboro Boys, 31n, 154n

Scruggs, John, 616, 649–50, 948–49

Seagrave, Gordon, 613, 626n, 631, 826

Sea Nymph, 995

second chances, America as land of,
    795–96

segregation, 19, 545, 958
  Brown v. Board of Education, 4,
    269–70, 360
  Ellison's artist heroes and, 861, 862
  in Oklahoma, 322, 332, 367, 537, 696,
    986
  in one's own mind, 675
  Short's background as contrast to, 693
  of U.S. armed forces during World
    War II, 7, 139, 735
  see also desegregation; integration

Segregation (Warren), 485

Seize the Day (Bellow), 280, 437, 481

Self-Analysis (Horney), 148

Seton Hall University (South Orange,
    N.J.), 915

Seven Gothic Tales (Dinesen), 381

Sewanee, 588

Shadow and Act (Ellison's first collection
    of essays), 9, 248n, 494n, 519n, 522,
    532, 549, 553, 574, 575, 584n, 630,
    634–35, 638, 672, 696, 738, 805,
    852, 872, 903, 990, 995, 998, 999
  reviews of, 571, 634–35

"Shadow and the Act, The" (Ellison), 995

Shaffer, Bertha, 524

Shah of Iran, 876

Shakespeare, William, 491, 872

Shaplen, Robert, *A Forest of Tigers*, 433,
    438–39

Shaw, Artie, 441

Shaw, George Bernard, 64n, 651–52, 732,
    861, 988

Shaw, Irwin, 528

Shawn, Ben, 407

Sheppard, Bernard (Shep), 536, 689,
    704, 906, 948–49, 950

Sherman, William T., 714, 716

Shippensburg, Pa., Ellison's visit to
    (1979), 740–41

Shirley, Don, 380

Short, Bobby, *Black and White Baby*,
    661, 692–94

Signet, 326

Sillen, Samuel, 140, 169, 187

Silone, Dorina, 250, 311, 407, 436, 833

Silver, Bob, 751

Silver, Horace, 531

Silvers, Robert, Ellison's January 28,
    1987, letter to, 914–16

Silvestri, Pat, 916

Simenon, Georges, 334, 337, 346, 880

Simms, Alberta, 186

Simms, Noble, 348

Simpson (Chicago), 598, 615

Single Pebble, A (Hersey), 437, 438, 439

Sjoman, Vilgot, 471

Slaughter, Edna Randolph, 34, 64n, 73,
    368, 574, 616, 618, 619, 689, 859,
    888

Ellison's letters to
    April 11, 1956, 273, 275, 423–30
    November 23, 1964, 630–32
Slaughter, Dr. Wyatt, 423n, 426, 619,
    840–41
Slaughter, Wyatt, Jr., 64n, 427, 858–59,
    985
Slaughter's Hall (Oklahoma City), 559,
    686, 718, 777, 988
slavery, 472, 678, 728, 818, 851, 936, 958
    emancipation and, 919, 931, 936
    free slaveholding caste of antebellum
        Negroes and, 782–83, 978
"Slick Gonna Learn" (Ellison), 993
Sloane, William, 334
Slochwer, Harry, 150
Smalls, Robert, 809
Smith, Bessie, 491, 931, 933
Smith, G. A., Ellison's March 20, 1977,
    letter to, 734–35
Smith, Samuel Francis, "America," 834
Smithsonian, 932–33
*Smithsonian Collection of Newspaper
    Comics* (eds. Williams and
    Blackbeard), 933
Sneed, Sherman, 779
Sneed, Walter, 76, 81
Snowden, Frank M., Jr., 390
social hierarchies, *Vogue*'s mystification
    of, 694
socialists, 802
"Society, Morality, and the Novel"
    (Ellison), 10, 277, 280, 477, 480,
    481, 485, 522n, 584, 738, 884
Solo (Whitmore), 422
"Song of Innocence, A" (Ellison), 1000
Sontag, Susan, 637
Soon, One Morning (ed. Hill), 611, 640
Sothern, Eva, 305
Souls of Black Folk, The (DuBois), 652
Sound and the Fury, The (Faulkner), 365,
    395, 585
sound systems, 287, 297, 341, 365, 501–2,
    844–45
    Ellison's "Living with Music" and,
    272, 391, 997

    installed at American Academy in
        Rome, 272, 384, 389, 392, 451, 469,
        501–2
    stereo conversion and, 564, 645, 761–62
    tape technology and, 468–69
South Carolina:
    Ellison family's past in, 710, 711–12,
        713–14, 782–84, 808–9, 851–52, 919,
        967–72, 977
    Ellison family's property in, 711,
        713–14, 784, 809
    free slaveholding caste of antebellum
        Negroes in, 782–83, 978
    Ralph's grandfather's role in politics
        in, 711–12, 784, 800, 968, 969
    see also Abbeville, S.C.
Southern Harvest, A, 477
Southern Historical Association, 738
Southern Manifesto of 1956, 7, 277
Southern Railroad, 712, 713
Southern University (Baton Rouge, La.),
    Ellison's visit and lecture at (1954),
    347, 354, 355–57, 361
Soviet Union, 132, 162, 222, 470
    Ellison's views on travel to, 24, 105, 106
    Moscow show trials of 1936–38 in, 106,
        170, 185, 802
Spalding, Albert, 930
Spanish America, Negroes' fascination
    with, 648
Spanish-American War, 611, 648, 713,
    799
Spanish Civil War, 87, 89, 103, 834, 955,
    991
Sparks, Garvis and Gladys, 951
Speaking for You (Benston), 780n, 792
Spears, Gladys, 687
Spence, Muriel Morisey, 741n, 891n
    Ellison's February 2, 1986, letter to,
        891–92
Spender, Stephen, 453, 507
Spenser, Elizabeth, 472, 474, 481
    The Voice at the Back Door, 481
Spiegel, Sydney, Ellison's December 13,
    1959, letter to, 562–63
Spingarn, Arthur and Mrs., 801

Sprague, Morteza, 8, 300, 304, 323, 328, 334, 346–47, 349, 350, 364, 380, 494, 553, 564, 607, 990
  Ellison's letters to
    May 19, 1954, 4, 269–70, *284–85*, 359–60
    July 17, 1959, 556–57
    June 7, 1963, 625
    student stories sent to Ellison by, 553, 557
Spyglass Tree, The (Murray), 297n
Stalin, Joseph, 422
  show trials and purges of (1936–38), 106, 170, 185, 802
Stampp, Kenneth M., *The Peculiar Institution*, 472
Stanley, Edward, Ellison's September 27, 1974, letter to, 727–28
Stargell, Willie, 812
State Department, U.S., 103, 196, 455, 714, 991
States, Mark, Ellison's August 24, 1983, letter to, 801–3
State Training School for Negro Boys (Boley, Okla.), 5, 29, 989
State University of New York (SUNY):
  at Albany, Bearden exhibition at (1968), 676, 677–78, 1000
  at Stony Brook, 636, 836–37
Stearns, Marshall, 291, 586
Steegmuller, Beatrice, 228n, 243, 244–45, 306n, 307, 474
  Ellison's August 23, 1947, letter to Francis and, 228–29
Steegmuller, Francis, 228n, 243, 244, 258, 288, 297, 307, 480, 490
  Ellison's August 23, 1947, letter to Beatrice and, 228–29
Steig, William, 170, 209
Stein, Edwin, 227, 229, 245, 247
Stein, Gerda, 227, 228, 229, 245, 306n
  Ellison's letters to
    October 15, 1947, 246–47
    May 11, 1952, 306–7
Stein, Gertrude, *The Making of Americans*, 223

Steinbeck, John, 488
  The Grapes of Wrath, 107, 151n, 153, 672, 675
Steloff, Frances, Ellison's September 19, 1969, letter to, 651–52
Stendhal, 395, 629
"Stepchild Fantasy" (Ellison), 219
"Stephen Crane and the Mainstream of American Fiction" (Ellison), 584, 998
Stepto, Robert, 733, 739, 762
Sterling, Dorothy, 640
Stern, Richard G., 7, 598, 599, 606, 609, 612, 613, 998
  Ellison's 1961 interview with, 669–70
  Ellison's May 23, 1960, letter to, 590–91
  Galk, 591
Stevenson, Adlai, 468, 470, 479, 512
Stevenson, Robert Louis, *Treasure Island*, 651
Steveson, Vivian, 5, 18, 20, 29, 32, 35–36, 38, 45, 51, 60, 64n, 69, 78, 537
  Ellison's June 1, 1935, letter to, 71–72
Stewart, Jimmy, 4, 11, 537, 630, 687, 717, 720, 729, 730
  Ellison's letters to
    October 8, 1979, 662, 744–45
    March 3, 1985, 840–42
Stillness at Appomattox, A (Catton), 270, 360, 472
Stokes, Lawyer, 889–90
Stokes, Marie, 889
Stokes, W. O., 324, 992
"Storm of Blizzard Proportions, A" (Ellison), 734n, 994
Storyville (New Orleans), 454
Stowe, Harriet Beecher, 728, 972
  Uncle Tom's Cabin, 291n, 360
Strange, John, 324, 325
Strange, Mrs. John, 325
Stranger, The (Camus), 407, 420
Stranger and Alone (Redding), 287, 290
Stravinsky, Igor, 445, 495
  Poetics of Music, 458
Strayhorn, Billy, 489
Styron, William, 408, 738

"Subjective Account of Something Very Old" (McPherson), 658, 706–7

Sue, Eugène, 132

Suez crisis (1956), 276, 457, 470, 478

Suitcase Theater, 98n, 99

Sullivan, Harry Stack, 21, 80–81, 86n, 103, 927, 991

Sumpter, Martha Ann, 354

Sun Also Rises, The (Hemingway), 457

Sundial, The (Jackson), 522–23

Sun-Yat-Sen, SS, 994

Supreme Court, U.S., 274, 417, 441–42, 512, 534, 595
> *Brown v. Board of Education*, 4, 269–70, 360

Surat, Dennis, 485, 492

Survey Graphic, 219

Suthern, Orrin, 215, 831

Sword from the Rock, The (Levy), 420

Sykes, Gerald, 437

Sylvia (Wading River), 312

symbolism, Ellison on, 820–21

Sypher, Wylie, 395

Szigeti, Joseph, 930

Tabor, Ida, 199

Taggart, John, Ellison's February 27, 1979, letter to, 740–41

Tale of Two Cities, A (Dickens), 651

Talladega College (Ala.), 44, 317

Tallchief, Maria, 854, 930

Tamiment summer camp (Bushkill, N.Y.), 363

Tar Baby (trickster figure), 956, 961, 981

Tar-baby's Dawn (Wright), 187

Tate, Allen, 390, 409, 415, 439n, 470, 963

Tate, Buddy, 380

Tatum, Goose, 358

Tawney, H. H., *Religion and the Rise of Capitalism*, 420

Taylor, Billy, 974

Taylor, Frank, 223, 225, 226, 229, 236, 244, 261, 323, 376, 553, 556, 765, 767
> break in Ellisons' friendship with, 924–29

Ellison's [July 1948] letter to, 252–58

Ellison's notes on script written by, 252–57

homosexuality of, 924–25, 926

Teat (Ralph's aunt), 315, 324, 343

Technics and Civilization (Mumford), 420

Teilhard de Chardin, Pierre, 638

television:
> in Europe vs. U.S., 394–95
> public, establishment of, 999

"Tell It Like It Is, Baby" (Ellison), 7, 10, 277–79, 453n, 455, 457, 471, 472–73, 477, 485, 659, 739, 884, 997, 999

Temperance, 932

"Ten Young Novelists in Search of Pity" (Kazin), 521–22

Terry, Clark, 644

Thailand, Ellison's trip to (1957), 497, 512, 514

"That I Had the Wings" (Ellison), 163, 994

"That Same Pain, That Same Pleasure" (Ellison), 696

Themis (Harrison), 419

There Is a Tree More Ancient Than Eden (Forrest), 658, 705–6, 736–37

These Low Grounds (Turpin), 95n

Thiebault, Claire, Ellison's June 7, 1989, letter to, 756, 961–62

Thomas, Bettye, Ellison's December 4, 1986, letter to, 911–14

Thomas, Dylan, 921–22

Thomas, Jessie O., 44–45

Thomas, Norman, 459, 460, 468

Thomasson, Reginald, 687, 805

Thompson, James, 999

Thoreau, Henry David, 194, 216, 728

Three Days Before the Shooting . . . (Ellison; eds. Callahan and Bradley), 9, 379n, 662

Time, 5, 10, 306, 314, 433–34, 501, 521, 539, 795, 1000
> Ellison's November 27, 1958, letter to the Editor of, 544–46

Tin Pan Alley, 728

Tivoli, N.Y., Bellow's house at, 282–83, 482, 524–30

    Ellison staying in (1958–59 and 1959–60), 282–83, 482n, 524–30, 533, 536, 539, 540, 541–43, 561, 577, 582, 597–99, 998

      work on his second novel and, 526, 533, 536, 538, 547, 548–49, 551, 554–56, 577–81

    offer made to Ellison to purchase home, 561

    Rufus the cat at, 525–27, 529, 542, 547–48, 598

Tobacco Road (Caldwell), 803–4

Today show, 632, 773

To Have and Have Not (Hemingway), 95, 675, 707–8

Tolson, Melvin B., 181–82

Tolstoi, Leo, 223

Tomorrow, 164, 640, 994

Tompkins, Ted, 513–14

Tom Sawyer (Twain), 651

Topping, Edgar, 772

Tourgee, Albion, *Congaree Sketches*, 651

Town, The (Faulkner), 480, 490, 494

Townsend, Alonzo, 121, 236

Townsend, Charles, 778

Townsend, Elvira, 778

Townsend, John A., 324, 367, 376, 690

Trading Twelves (Ellison and Murray), 8, 14, 286n, 559–60

"Tradition and Innovation" (Callahan), 796–98

Tragic Sense of Life, The (Unamuno), 419, 629, 790

Train Whistle Guitar (Murray), 297n, 334

Treasure Island (Stevenson), 651

Trial, The (Kafka), 680

Trickster, The (Radin), 448

trickster figures, 486

    in Negro American folklore, 649, 651, 943–44, 956–57

Trilling, Lionel, 477

Triumph of the Will, 209

Trotsky, Leon, 140

True, 381

Tucker, Booker, 779, 844–45, 906, 950, 951

Tucker, Charles Etta, 4

  Ellison's letters to

    May 9, 1982, 775–79

    April 22, 1985, 853–57

    September 7, 1986, 904–6

    May 21, 1988, 948–51

Tulsa, Okla., riot in (1921), 986

Tumin, Mel, 918

Turner, Nat, 165, 738

Turn of the Screw, A (James), 816

Turpin, Waters, *These Low Grounds*, 95n

Tuskegee Institute, now Tuskegee University (Ala.), 7–8, 24, 99, 197, 265, 266, 286n, 293, 300, 304–5, 321, 323, 390, 417, 493, 494, 552, 556, 575, 619, 625, 649, 731, 756, 800–801, 803, 805, 815, 833, 855–56, 861, 902, 940, 942, 946–47, 955, 989–91

  anniversary convocations at, 946

  bakery job held by Ellison at, 31, 33, 35, 38, 47, 50

  Carver myth and, 206

  Ellison honored as most distinguished alumnus of, 1002

  Ellison in band at, 19, 30, 34, 35, 36, 39, 40, 42, 44, 61–63, 70, 429

  Ellison's acceptance to, 988–89

  Ellison's daily routine at, 32–33, 38, 73

  Ellison's departure from, 20, 21, 58, 81, 925

  Ellison's dissatisfaction with, 21, 57–58, 59, 60, 70, 81

  Ellison's hoboing journey to, 18, 30, 31, 427n, 989

  Ellison's Honorary Doctorate degree from, 624

  Ellison's lecture at (1953), 327–29, 996

  Ellison's lecture at (1954), 269, 271–72, 345, 346–47, 349–51, 352–53, 354, 360, 361, 362–63

  Ellison's letters to former teachers and mentors at, *see* Dawson, William L.; Harrison, Hazel; Sprague, Morteza

Ellison's letters to old pals from, 24–25, 96–97, 99–101, 102–8
Ellison's library job at, 48, 51, 52, 59, 60, 64
Ellison's music studies at, 6, 19, 35, 36, 38–39, 40, 45, 46, 50, 52, 54, 55, 57, 64, 66, 67, 68, 69, 76, 100, 946, 966
fire in Chapel at, 480
Hughes's brief encounter with Ellison at, 21n
letters written by Ellison at, 4, 5–6, 17–20, 26–28, 30–78
money worries plaguing Ellison at, 18–19, 30, 32, 35, 36–37, 38–41, 42, 43, 45, 46–47, 49, 50–51, 52–53, 54, 55, 57–59, 61, 74, 77, 81
Murray and Ellison's first encounter at, 265, 286n
polio research at Carver Research Center of, 350
proposed cultural center at, 519
School of Education at, considered by Ellison, 39, 40
seminar in American literature at (1954), 350, 353, 356, 358, 359–60, 361, 363, 367
sexual favors sought by registrar and dean of men at, 19, 57
student stories from, sent to Ellison for review, 553, 557
young women encountered by Ellison at, 19–20, 24, 34, 38, 41, 96–97, 105
TV Guide, 948, 951
Twain, Mark, 410, 549, 584, 728, 736, 737, 793, 817, 819, 824, 861, 871, 913, 937, 1002
The Adventures of Huckleberry Finn, 32n, 369, 471, 473, 479, 651, 809, 819–20, 904, 907, 931, 932
Pudd'nhead Wilson, 958
Tom Sawyer, 651
12 Million Black Voices (Wright), 150
Ellison's personal response to, 114–15, 143–46, 993

"Men in the Making" section from, reprinted in *Negro Quarterly*, 147, 765
Twentieth Century Fiction (Beach), 420
"Twentieth-Century Fiction and the Black Mask of Humanity" (Ellison), 340, 996
Twice a Year, 202

UCLA, Ellison's lectures at (1964), 631
UCLA, Ewing Lectures at (1964), 631n, 999
Uffizi Gallerie, Florence, 389, 391
Ulysses (Joyce), 520
Unamuno, Miguel de, 790
The Tragic Sense of Life, 419, 629, 790
Uncle Remus stories (Harris), 708
Uncle Tom's Cabin (Stowe), 291n, 360
Uncle Tom's Children (Wright), 92n, 145n
Under the Volcano (Lowry), 420
UNESCO, 251
Union League, 800
unions, discrimination against Negroes by, 764
United States Information Service (USIS), 377
universalism, "felt experience" of being Negro American in relation to, 204–5
University of Alabama, 417
University of Chicago, 13, 560–61, 584, 621, 638n, 740
Ellison's letters to Fanny from, 573–74, 605–13
Ellison's professorship at (1961), 571n, 605n, 607, 608, 698, 998
Scott's professorship at, 571n, 698, 699
University of Chicago Press, 641
University of Iowa:
Ellison's refusal of offer to return to (1960), 588–89
Ellison's talk on Wright at (1971), 790–91, 792, 794
symposium on contemporary writing at (1959), 554, 561, 569, 581–82, 586, 588

University of Iowa Press, 816n
University of Iowa Writers' Workshop, 376n, 588
  story by student in, critiqued by Ellison, 751–52, 960–61
University of Michigan, 999
University of Oklahoma, 322, 332
University of Tennessee, 640
University of Texas, 13
University of Wisconsin, Ellison's February 17, 1972, letter supporting Nathan Scott for position at, 697–700
Unvanquished, The (Faulkner), 561
Unwritten War, The (Aaron), 657, 715–16
urban renewal, 659, 686, 697, 713, 718, 848–49, 910

Valentine, Charles, Ellison's December 8, 1967, letter to, 9–10, 575–76, 641
Valéry, Paul, 220, 629
  Variety, 420
Vanity Fair, 494
Van Vechten, Carl, 560, 801
Variety (Valéry), 420
Velasco, John, 197–98, 219, 828
Vermont:
  country life and dancing in, 194–95
  Ellison's descriptions of his surroundings in, 161, 190–91, 192–93, 194–96, 199, 233, 235–36, 246–47
  Ellison's pleas for help from, 188–89, 191, 199, 200–201
  Ellison's stay at Stein's cottage in (Winhall Station, 1947), 119–20, 226–48
  Ellison's stays at Bates' farm in (Waitsfield, 1943 and 1945), 7, 111, 160, 161–62, 184, 188–200, 764, 952, 994, 995
  impact of place on Ellison, 111, 161–62, 229, 230
  straight lines in architecture of, 194, 195–96

writing of *Invisible Man* in, 187n, 190, 192–93, 197, 228–29, 230, 232, 234, 239, 241, 247, 306–7, 952, 995
vernacular, 249n, 661, 728, 736, 750, 755–56, 787, 824, 838–39, 864, 871, 935, 937–38, 943, 957, 959, 972
  Afro-American, of Harold Washington, 975–76
  Afro-American, white Americans' lack of familiarity with, 956–57
  Berryman's uses of dialect and, 922–23
  conflict between "cultivated" style and, 972
  doggerel from advertisement, 937–38
  Ellison's book recommendations and, 972
  in Ellison's letters to Fanny, 118
  Ellison's Tuskegee friendships and, 990
  funky fashion of 1980s and, 935
  in James's wordpile, 755–56
  Joyce as master of, 756
  Kouwenhoven's shared interest in, 935–38
  power of, overlooked by proletarian writers, 308
  "3-6-9" in, 787–88
  Waller's incongruous juxtapositions and, 755
"Very Stern Discipline: An Interview with Ralph Ellison, A" (Thompson, Raphael, and Cannon), 884, 999
Vienna State Opera, 408
Viking, 477
Vintage, 407, 409, 419–20, 457–58
violence of American culture, 205–6, 207
Vogue, 694
Voice at the Back Door, The (Spenser), 481
Volkening, Henry, 201, 302
voting rights, 430
Voyages Mercure, 497, 504

Waddkins, Tom, 688
Wade (Oklahoma City friend), 430, 848
Wagner, Richard, 6, 861

Waitsfield, Vt., Ellison's sojourns in, *see* Vermont

Walcott, Alexander, 549, 556

Wales:
comparisons of New England and, 194, 195
Ellison's experiences as merchant marine in, 734–35, 994
Ellison's short story about seaman in ("In a Strange Country"), 164, 166, 640, 657, 734–35, 994

Walker, Margaret, 137, 181, 186
biography of Wright written by, 754, 954

Walker, Saunders ("Sandy"), 340, 347, 364, 625

Walker, Sticks, 721

Wallace, Henry A., 224, 251

Wallace, Ted, "Work House Blues," 931, 933

Waller, Fats, 755, 825, 838, 853, 938, 965

Walter, Eugene, 473, 478, 481, 485

Ward, Theodore ("Ted"), 25, 129, 135, 219–20
Big White Fog, 108, 187

Ware, Lowry P., 11–12, 756
Ellison's letters to
September 7, 1990, 11–12, 967–72
June 17, 1992, 975–78
Old Abbeville, 12, 967, 975, 977–78

Warren, Billie (formerly Willie Mae McConnell; Fanny's mother), 172, 200, 232, 400, 574, 606, 608, 609, 611, 612, 614–15, 623, 624

Warren, Eleanor, 472, 623, 962
Ellison's August 5, 1989, letter to, 964–65

Warren, George (Fanny's stepfather), 232, 606, 607, 608, 609–10, 612, 614–15

Warren, Robert Penn ("Red"), 3, 277, 439n, 446–47, 469, 472, 474, 481, 485, 518, 636n, 707, 962–64, 979
Ellison and Walter's interview of, for *Paris Review*, 478, 481, 485
Ellison's letters to
September 7, 1960, 592
June 1, 1963, 623

Ellison's relationship with, 478, 518, 997
Promises, 963
Scott's essay on, 962, 963
Segregation, 485
You Emperors, and Others, 592

Warren, Rosanna, 760n, 964

War Shipping Administration (WSA), 165, 191
see also Merchant Marine, U.S.

Washburn College (Ind.), Ellison's lecture at (1960), 584

Washington, Booker T., 51, 206, 300, 604, 728, 781, 855–56, 872, 905, 947

Washington, Harold, 975

Washington Post, 886, 960, 1002

Waste Land, The (Eliot), 158, 320, 990

Waters, Ethel, 98–99

Waters, Ruth, 608

Watkins, Allen (Ralph's uncle), 630, 644, 724–27

Watkins, Ellen (Ralph's aunt), 630, 724

Weary Blues, The (Hughes), 652

"Weary Blues, The" (Hughes), 231n, 652

Weaver, Ed, 125

Weber, Max, *The Protestant Ethic and the Spirit of Capitalism*, 420

Webern Anton, 495–96

Weeks, Edward, Ellison's February 17, 1969, letter to, 576, 645–46

Weinbaum, Bernie, 472, 474

Weinstock, Herbert, Ellison's letters to:
May 15, 1956, 437–38
June 21, 1956, 444–45

Weiscopf, Franz, 150

Welles, Orson, 137–38, 142n

Wertham, Frederick, 212–13, 216, 218, 248

Wesleyan University, 1001

West, Anthony, 337, 340

West, Dorothy, 6, 142, 991

West, Hollie, 743

West, Rebecca, 839

Weston, Jesse, *From Ritual to Romance*, 216

West Point, 704, 809

Wharton, Edith, 770

"What America Would Be Like Without Blacks" (Ellison), 10, 884, 1000

"What Happened to Ralph Ellison" (Podhoretz), 635n

"What These Children Are Like" (Ellison), 884

Wheatley, Phillis, 661, 682, 683–84

Wheeler, Jack, 524, 525, 527, 528, 547

Whitby, A. Baxter, 64n

Whitby, Leo, 30

Whitby, Malcolm, 30, 31, 34, 37, 39, 43, 44, 47, 51, 64n, 67, 951, 988

White (author of book about John H. Johnson), 253–54

White, Josh, 263

White, Stanford, 402

White House, National Medal of Arts ceremony at (1985), 857–58, 876–78, 1002

"white Negro":
  Mailer's notion of, 534, 569, 684
  writers, 682–84

whites, Negro attitudes and emotions toward, 660–61, 676

white skin:
  magic properties ascribed to, 254
  mulattoes and, 254–55
  passing for white and, 252–57

Whiting Foundation, Ellison's address to (1992), 660, 986, 1002

Whitmore, Stanford, *Solo*, 422

Whittaker, John C., 704, 809

Gertrude Clarke Whittall lecture series, 1001–2

Whose Names Were Unknown (Babb), 149–50, 151, 152–54

Wideman, John Edgar, 808

Wienstock, Clarence, 132

Wilberforce College (Ohio), 62, 63, 889

Wilbur, Charlee, 927–28

Wilbur, Richard, 3, 391–92, 643, 762, 1001
  Ellison's February 24, 1987, letter to, 10, 754, 923–29

Wiley, Dr. (Oklahoma City), 369, 430

Wilkerson, Doxey A., 194, 251

Wilkins, Roy, 192, 533

Will (Ralph's uncle in Chicago), 42, 62, 325, 535

William, Vanessa, 820

William & Mary College (Williamsburg, Va.), 704, 1001

Williams, Camilla, 355

Williams, Ceeley, 105

Williams, Cootie, 380

Williams, Ferris, 324

Williams, Joe, 479, 491, 504

Williams, John A., 640

Williams, Martin, Ellison's July 4, 1987, letter to, 932–33

Williams, Mary, 463, 464, 509, 513

Williams, Minnie, 305

Williams, Walter B., 20, 47–48, 52, 54, 59, 61, 64, 68, 69, 73, 75, 104, 304, 305, 357, 649, 990

Wilson, Edmund "Bunny," 202–3, 311, 360, 494, 918–20
  Axel's Castle, 419
  The Fifties, 918, 920
  Gauss Seminars, 202, 918, 919, 921
  Patriotic Gore, 716, 919

Wilson, Flip, 694, 761–62

Wilson, Hank, Ellison's May 18, 1971, letter to, 691

Wilson, John, 532

Wilson, Reuel, 920

Wilson, Teddy, 263, 317

Wingate, Henry T., 981

Winhall Station, Vt., Ellison's sojourn in, *see* Vermont

Winsten, Archer, 201

Winston-Salem, N.C., Ellison's visit to (1953), 316, 317, 318, 324, 808

Wolfe, Bernard, 534

Wolfe, Thomas, 488
  "You can't go home again" epigram of, 273, 427–28

women:
  Ellison on thought process of, 134
  Negro, reacting to Wright's *Native Son*, 133

Woodburn, John, 201, 312

Woods, William, 163n

Woodward, C. Vann, 783, 809

Woolcott, Alexander, 553

Woolf, Atwood, 226

"Work House Blues" (Wallace), 931, 933

Works Progress Administration (WPA), 6, 88, 89, 91, 139, 678, 809

  Federal Writers' Project, 24, 98, 101–2, 104, 121, 137n, 754, 823, 825, 855, 877, 902, 993

    Folklore section of, 260

  National Youth Administraton (NYA), 125, 126

"World and the Jug, The" (Ellison), 10, 998

"World of Difference, A" (Ellison), 537n

World War I, 610

  parade in Chicago for veterans from (1961), 610–11

World War II, 7, 125, 136, 138, 139–40, 160, 196, 219, 268n, 734

  atom bomb in, 115, 188, 189, 196, 424

  devastation in France and Britain during, 915

  Draft Board in, 154, 191

  Ellison as merchant marine during, 7, 111, 118–19, 165, 167, 173–78, 191, 213, 252, 266, 702n, 734–35, 797–98, 823, 829, 994, 995

  Murray and Ellison's chance meeting during, 265–66

  Pound's treason conviction and, 475–76

  segregation of U.S. armed forces during, 7, 139, 735

Wright, Ellen, 134–35, 138, 145, 168, 186, 267, 311, 685, 764, 954, 996

  Ellison's letters to

    September 23, 1946, 224–25

    March 26, 1952, 7, 301–2

  rumored to have separated from Richard, 221–22

Wright, John, 772

Wright, Julia, 311

Wright, Rachel, 302, 311

Wright, Richard, 3, 6, 7, 10, 25, 92n, 105–6, 108, 112, 150, 168, 189, 240,

293, 299, 300, 301, 302, 320, 650, 681, 756, 790, 823, 830, 880, 881, 889, 900, 917, 959, 991, 992, 993

  African culture and issues and, 455, 470

  Baldwin's relationship with, 761

  Black Power, 365, 370–71

  "Blueprint for Negro Writing," 129

  break with American Communists, 169–71, 207–8, 219, 865–66

  Canadian sojourn of, 114, 186, 188, 218–19, 221

  Cayton's planned biography of, 666–67

  "Claire Étoile du Matin," 115

  comparisons of Ellison to, 314

  conscious of writing technique, 669–70, 671–72

  Davis's piece on, 761

  Ellison's analysis of esthetic of, 206–7

  Ellison's essay "Remembering Richard Wright," 791, 884

  Ellison's lecture at University of Iowa on (1971), 790–91, 792, 794

  Ellison's letters to, 13, 112, 113–15

    October 27, 1937, 6, 17, 23–24, 92–94

    November 8, 1937, 24, 94–95

    April 14, 1940, 114, 128–30

    April 22, 1940, 114, 130–34

    May 11, 1940, 134–37

    May 15, 1940, 137–39

    May 26, 1940, 139–40

    July 29, 1940, 141

    September 23, 1940, 142

    April 12, 1941, 114–15, 142–43

    November 3, 1941, *122–24*, 143–46

    March 24, 1942, 147

    August 29, 1944, 169

    September 5, 1944, 169–71

    September 30, 1944, 171

    July 22, 1945, 115, 179–84

    August 5, 1945, 184–88

    August 18, 1945, 192–99

    April 4, 1946, 212–13

    June 24, 1946, 217–21

    August 24, 1946, 221–24

Wright, Richard (*cont'd*):
Ellison's letters to
February 1, 1948, 115, 247–52
October 17, 1949, 262
November 7, 1949, 262–63
January 21, 1953, 4, 309–13
Ellison's relationship with, 6, 112,
113–15, 187, 750
controversy over, related to Fabre's
manuscript, 752–53, 762–65,
954–55
O'Meally criticized for inaccuracies
related to, 753, 765, 939
Ellison's research efforts on behalf of,
128–29, 130–31, 133
Ellison's thoughts on conflicts in
radical Marxist politics shared
with, 169–71, 181–83, 184–85,
186–87, 188, 193–94, 197
Ellisons' visit in Paris with (1954), 996
"Ethics of Living Jim Crow," 181
expatriated to France, 113, 217, 219,
221–22, 225, 251–52, 310–11, 455,
483, 544n, 545, 996
Fabre as biographer of, 685, 752–53
first wife of (Dhimah Rose Meadman),
133, 134, 140, 141
The God That Failed, 865–66
Hyman's essay on (1970), 660–61, 676,
679–82
influence on Ellison ascribed to,
248–49, 661, 671, 680–82, 860–67
LaFargue Clinic and, 212–13, 218
Lawd Today!, 187
Life's 1970 review purportedly about,
658, 667–76
literary influences on, 862, 863
"The Man Who Lived Underground,"
487, 679–80, 681, 860, 862–67

"Men in the Making," 147, 765
Mexican sojourns of, 130, 131, 137
Negro self-acceptance and, 206
The Outsider, 113, 310, 313, 314, 682,
761, 864
political affiliations of, 802
rumored to be unhappy, 135
rumored to have separated from Ellen,
221–22
Tar-baby's Dawn, 187
12 Million Black Voices, 114–15, 143–47,
150, 765, 993
Uncle Tom's Children, 92n, 145n
Walker's biography of, 754, 954
see also *Black Boy*; *Native Son*
Wuthering Heights (Brontë), 861, 990
Wypher, Eylie, *Guines' Captive Mind*,
209

Yaddo, 224, 225, 228, 232
Yale University (New Haven, Conn.), 13,
278n, 679, 733, 770, 802
Ellison as visiting fellow in American
Studies at (1964–65), 636, 999
Ellison's talks at (1960 and 1961), 590,
598, 599
Yarde, Richard, 744, 810–11
Yeats, William Butler, 487, 750, 956
Yerby, Frank, 661, 682
Yergan, Max, 171, 194, 251
You Emperors, and Others (Warren), 592
Young, Lester ("Pres"), 494, 560
Youngblood, Mrs. Harry, 900
Art Young Memorial Prize, 164–65
Yourcenar, Marguerite, *Memoirs of
Hadrian*, 389

Zeller, Victor, 130, 140
zoot suits, 159–60, 751

About the Editors

JOHN F. CALLAHAN is Ralph Ellison's Literary Executor and Morgan S. Odell Professor Emeritus of Humanities at Lewis and Clark College. He is author of *The Illusions of a Nation: Myth and History in the Novels of F. Scott Fitzgerald* (1972) and *In the African American Grain: Call and Response in 20th Century Black Fiction* (2008, 2011). Callahan is the editor of several of Ellison's posthumous books, including *The Collected Essays of Ralph Ellison* (1995, 2003); *Flying Home and Other Stories* (1996, 2nd Vintage International Edition, 2012); *Juneteenth* (1999, 2001); and *Three Days Before the Shooting . . .* , edited by Callahan and Adam F. Bradley (2010, 2011). He is also author of the novel *A Man You Could Love* (2007, 2008).

MARC C. CONNER is the Jo M. and James M. Ballengee Professor of English and Provost at Washington and Lee University. He is the editor of *The Aesthetics of Toni Morrison: Speaking the Unspeakable* (2000) and *The Poetry of James Joyce Reconsidered* (2012), and co-editor of *Charles Johnson: The Novelist as Philosopher* (2007), *The New Territory: Ralph Ellison and the Twenty-First Century* (2016), and *Screening Modern Irish Fiction and Drama* (2016).

About the Type

This book was set in Bulmer, a typeface designed in the late eighteenth century by the London type cutter William Martin (1757–1830). The typeface was created especially for the Shakespeare Press, directed by William Bulmer (1757–1830)—hence the font's name. Bulmer is considered to be a transitional typeface, containing characteristics of old-style and modern designs. It is recognized for its elegantly proportioned letters, with their long ascenders and descenders.